Camping &
 caravanning
Europe

GW00697101

Published by RAC Publishing, RAC House,
PO Box 100, South Croydon CR2 6XW.
© RAC Motoring Services Limited 1996

ISBN 0 86211-367 9 (paperback)
ISBN 0 86211-377 6 (hardback)

A CIP catalogue record for this book is available from the British Library.

Written and compiled for RAC Publishing by Millrace Books

> Editorial Office
> PO Box 8
> Harleston
> Norfolk IP20 0EZ
> Tel: 01986 788 808
> Fax: 01986 788 195

Managing Editor:	Lawrie Hammond
Design:	Douglas Whitworth
Editorial:	Aardvark Editorial; Zibba George; Sandrine Thierry; Stephanie Wren
Display Advertising Sales:	West One Publishing Ltd Portland House 4 Great Portland Street London W1N 4AA Tel: 0171 580 6886
Cartography:	RAC Publishing.
Printed and bound in Spain by:	Grafo SA, Bilbao

CONTENTS

© 1996 RAC Motoring Services Ltd.

This book is sold subject to the conditions that it shall not, by way of trade,
or otherwise, be lent, re-sold, hired out or otherwise circulated without
the publisher's prior consent in any form of binding, or cover other
than that in which it is printed.

Published by RAC Publishing,
RAC House, Bartlett Street, South Croydon, CR2 6XW.

All rights reserved. No parts of this work may be reproduced, stored in a
retrieval system or transmitted by any means without permission. Whilst
every effort has been made to ensure that the information contained in this
publication is accurate and up to date, the publisher does not accept any
responsibility for any error, omission or misrepresentation. All liability for loss,
disappointment, negligence or other damage caused by reliance on the
information contained in this publication, or in the event of bankruptcy,
or liquidation, or cessation of trade of any company, individual or firm
mentioned is hereby excluded.

Created and typeset by West One (Trade) Publishing Ltd. for RAC Publishing
Cartography by RAC Publishing
Printed in Spain

ISBN 0-86211-360-1

INTRODUCTION

For 1997 *RAC Camping and Caravanning in Europe* is again fully revised and covers more than 3000 sites across mainland Europe. All countries, barring the former Yugoslavia, are included, with sites as far flung as Hungary, Poland, the Czech republic & Slovakia. Don't be daunted by distances, for there are delightful and different camp sites at every stage of your pan-European tour, as well as alternative ways of eating up the kilometres (see Getting There).

Please remember that details may change during the year, so it is always wise to check with the site beforehand and reserve when possible. The proliferation of the fax machine makes this easier and is a particular benefit where the member of staff who justifies the 'English Spoken' symbol is not available.

If you have any comments on the sites, *good* or *bad*, or indeed on other sites that you would like to see included, do

Map locations

These refer to the series of maps near the end of the book. The site may not be in the town itself, but nearby. The site entry gives the full address and precise location.

Key to symbols and abbreviations

5D	map location	**R**	reservations accepted
☎	public telephone on site		washing machine
ha	hectares (1 ha is 2.5 acres)		shop on site
elec	electricity hook-up		shop on site, restricted opening (usually out of season)
static	permanent or residential-type pitch	**☕**	snacks/take-away food
WC	toilet	**✕**	restaurant
CWP	chemical waste disposal unit		swimming pool
	site beside the sea		swimming pool (may be entrance charge)
	site beside lake		cabins for hire
	site beside river		caravans for hire
	can swim in water above		tents for hire
	cannot swim in water above		some facilities for disabled people
	open site, no shade		no dogs on site
	some trees, a little shade	PRICES	guide prices in local currency (see page 7)
	many trees, some shade	CC	credit cards
	heavily wooded, shady	km	kilometres (1 km is 0.62 miles)

if more than one type for hire, in this order (applies to cabins, caravans and tents for hire)

please write to our Editorial Office (address Page 2). Your letters are always most welcome.

This guide includes a wide range of sites, from the huge and highly organised, to the small and simple. They are arranged alphabetically, first by country, and then by the nearest town or resort within the country. Remember that in warmer countries, there may be a siesta period in the middle of the day, when shops and other facilities are closed. When planning your journey, reckon to arrive by 4 pm, especially if you have not booked ahead.

Insurance and International Camping Card

UK car insurance generally provides some cover in Europe, but usually just third party, the minimum legal requirement. For more comprehensive cover you should obtain an International Motor Insurance Certificate (Green Card) from your insurers. You should inform them if you intend to tow a caravan as an extra premium may be due. A Green Card is essential for all travel in certain countries – ask your insurer for details – in Turkey for example the Green Card must be valid for both European and Asian sectors. Rescue facilities are available as part of RAC European Motoring Assistance.

The Camping Card International (CCI) gives proof of identity, covers third party liability (personal, not car) and provides personal accident cover up to a stated sum, for the holder and family. A CCI is essential in certain countries, such as Denmark. Some sites offer reductions to holders. CCIs are obtainable from the RAC: call RAC Travel Services on 0800 550055.

Gas, open fires and electricity

Camping Gaz International is available throughout Europe. Calor Gas may not be, so take sufficient supplies with you. However, in some countries it may be possible to refill a Calor Gas cylinder because the connector screw threads fit those of other suppliers. For safety reasons, never put propane in a butane cylinder, and fill cylinders only to 80% capacity. Regulations govern carrying gas on ferries, hovercraft, planes and motorail services. So ask the operator beforehand, and be prepared to arrive early at the terminal so that your gas supplies, and the way that they are packed, can be checked as necessary.

Open fires and barbecues are forbidden in many European countries because of the danger of forest fires. It is advisable (compulsory in Greece, Turkey) to carry a fire extinguisher.

Out of season

Prices may be lower out of high season, but some amenities may be restricted or unavailable. It is wise to enquire in advance about which amenities will be available during your planned stay.

Most European sites have some electricity hook-ups. British users may require an adaptor, usually available from the camp shop, although more sites are fitting UK-type sockets. Most of Europe has 220-volts supply, as in the UK, though this still may drop to 110 volts in remote areas.

Pitches and shops

In many countries of southern Europe, the sun shines long and strong, and shade is vitally important. A caravan or tent can become impossibly hot. Choose a pitch that is shaded, especially around the hottest part of the day. The ground may be hard and rocky, so campers are advised to use steel pegs and a hammer.

Many sites have their own shops; weigh up the sometimes high prices against the undoubted convenience. In some areas, milk is sterilised rather than fresh, while bread is fresh rather than wrapped. Shopping in a local market may be interesting, but not necessarily cheaper than a supermarket.

Health

Medical expenses can be covered by the RAC Personal Travel Insurance (call RAC Travel Services on 0800 550055 for details) or under reciprocal agreements in EU countries; for information, contact your main Post Office (form E111). Carry a small collection of remedies for problems such as minor cuts, sunburn, insect bites, stomach upsets, headaches, toothache and so on. Be sure to take any prescription medicines you may need. Water supplies are safe in much of Europe now, though in the south it may be wise to drink bottled mineral water and avoid ice in drinks.

Rabies is present in much of Europe. Do not approach dogs, and warn children against patting or fondling them.

Prices and credit cards

Guide prices are in local currency, except where indicated. They include typical high-season prices for a family of two adults and two children with a touring caravan with electricity and a car, and two adults with a medium-sized tent. In winter sports areas, high season may be in winter. Currency exchange rates fluctuate daily, so check the rate in daily newspapers or at banks. Once on site, you may find that pitch prices vary depending on location and facilities. Credit cards are: Amex (American Express), Euro/Access (Eurocard/Access), Visa (Visa/Barclaycard).

Mountain passes

Some European mountain passes are unsuitable for caravans. If you plan to tow a caravan across the Alps or Pyrenees, consult the RAC Motoring in Europe.

THE WHOLE OF THE CONTINENT BECKONS

WHEN YOU SAIL WITH SALLY FERRIES

Cross from Ramsgate to either France or Belgium and, when you disembark, you'll find that all points, North, South, East and West in Europe are easily accessible.

Extensive motorway systems will get you quickly and directly to your destination.

And, as only Sally sail to Dunkirk and Ostend, there's little or no congestion leaving the ports. You're off and away.

For more information call Sally Ferries on 0990 59 55 22.

GETTING THERE

Getting across the English Channel is no longer the big deal it once was. For the short Dover–Calais crossing the Tunnel is increasingly popular, combining maximum speed and minimum fuss. But the Tunnel has prompted significant price-cutting from the ferry companies, and their high-standard ferries, offering restaurant facilities not found in many a high street, mean that the sea-crossing is still the preferred choice of many who consider the shipboard experience an enjoyable part of their holiday.

For more westerly destinations, more and more travellers are choosing to do more of their driving on this side of the water, making crossings like Plymouth–Roscoff increasingly busy. Others choose the overnight ferry option. For with good cabin facilities this can be a pleasant and economic alternative to the expense of the short crossing plus overnight accommodation in France. Or why not let the *Train Grand Vitesse* high speed trains take the strain out of the long haul south, to deliver you, your family *and* your car, daisy-fresh in, say, Avignon? Finally, the fly-drive option: by allowing you to fly out and *start* your holiday from a distant town, this can represent the best value in the long run, where time and/or driving stamina are in short supply. The fly-drive alternative opens up countless new possibilities for the British motorist with limited time at his or her disposal.

Talking of new possibilities for holiday destinations, the map on page 10 includes a number of ferry lines to the mythical, underpopulated countries of Scandinavia. If 'getting away from it all' is your priority, this could be for you... Scandinavian summer days are fine, warm, very clear and *very long!*

If you do decide to drive long distances, remember it can be a good idea to make your journey a part of the holiday. Far too often we opt to clock up the maximum number of kilometres on a motorway when we might do better to take a more leisurely route, allowing for a coffee stop in a pretty market square, or a picnic pause where the view compels a photo stop.

Whatever your chosen mode of *Getting there*, may we wish you *Bon voyage!*

FERRY PORTS AND ROUTES

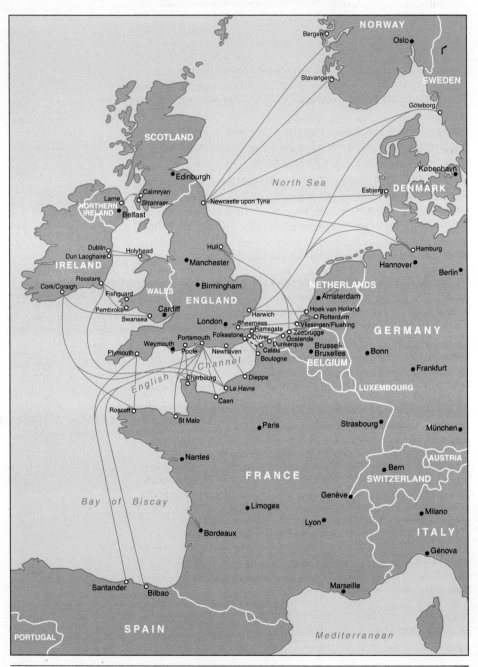

Belgium

Ramsgate-Oostende 4 hr *Sally Ferries (Ostend line)* – 6 per day.
Also Jetfoil (Passengers only) 100 mins *Sally Ferries* – 2-6 daily
Hull-Zeebrugge 14 hr *North Sea Ferries* – 1 per day
Dover-Zeebrugge *P & O Stena Line* – (contact ferry company for details)

Denmark

Harwich-Esbjerg 19½-20 hr *Scandinavian Seaways* – up
to 3 per week
Newcastle-upon-Tyne-Esbjerg 19½- 20 hr *Scandinavian Seaways*
– every 5 days

France

Dover-Calais 1½ hr *P & O Stena Line* (catamaran and ferry) – up to
22 per day
1½ hr *Sea France* (contact ferry company for details)
Dover-Calais 35-50 min *Hoverspeed* Hovercraft/Seacat – up to 14 per day
Folkestone-Boulogne 55mins *Hoverspeed* Seacat – up to 6 per day
Newhaven-Dieppe (catamaran and ferry) 2-3½ hr *P & O Stena Line* – up
to 4 per day each
Plymouth-Roscoff 6 hr *Brittany Ferries* – up to 3 per day (summer),
up to 3 per week (winter)
Poole-Cherbourg 4¼ hr *Brittany Ferries* 2 per day
Poole-St Malo 8 hr *Brittany Ferries* (May-Sept) – 4 per week
Portsmouth-Caen 6 hr *Brittany Ferries* – up to 3 per day
Portsmouth-Cherbourg (day) 5 hr, (night) 7-8¼ hr
P & O European Ferries – up to 4 per day
Portsmouth-Le Havre (day) 5½ hr, (night) 7½-8 hr
P & O European Ferries – up to 3 per day
Portsmouth-St Malo 9 hr *Brittany Ferries*
– 1 per day (up to 2 per week in winter)
Ramsgate-Dunkerque 2½ hr *Sally Ferries* – 5 per day (service will
cease Spring 1997)
Southampton-Cherbourg 5-9 hr *Stena Line* – up to 2 per day

Germany

Harwich-Hamburg 23 hr *Scandinavian Seaways* – 3-4 per week
Newcastle-upon-Tyne-Hamburg 23½ hr *Scandinavian Seaways*
– every 4 days
Oslo-Kiel 19 hr *Color Line* – daily

Netherlands

Harwich-Hoek van Holland (day) 6½ hr, (night) 10 hr *Stena Line*
– 2 per day
Hull-Rotterdam (Europoort) 14 hr *North Sea Ferries* – 1 per day
Newcastle-Amsterdam *Scandinavian Seaways* 15-17½ hr – up to
4 per week
Sheerness-Vlissingen (day) 7½ hr (night) 9½ hr *Eurolink Ferries*
– 2 per day (route under review in 1997)

Norway

Hirtshals-Oslo $8^{1/4}$ hr *Color Line* – daily (summer)
Kiel-Oslo 19 hr *Color Line* – daily
Hirtshals-Kristiansand $4^{1/4}$ hr (day) $6^{1/2}$ hr (night) *Color Line* – 3-4 per day
Newcastle upon Tyne-Bergen $19^{1/4}$-$25^{1/2}$ hr *Color Line*
– 3 per week (summer) 2 per week (winter)
Newcastle upon Tyne-Stavanger 17-$27^{1/2}$ hr *Color Line* – 3 per week (summer)
2 per week (winter)
Newcastle upon Tyne-Haugesund $19^{3/4}$-$25^{3/4}$ hr *Color Line* – up to 2 per week

Spain

Plymouth-Santander (from mid March) 23-24 hr *Brittany Ferries* – up to 2 per week
Portsmouth-Santander (winter only) 30-31 hr *Brittany Ferries* – 1 per week
Portsmouth-Bilbao 30-35 hr *P & O European Ferries* – 2 per week

Sweden

Harwich-Göteborg 23 hr *Scandinavian Seaways* – up to 3 per week
Newcastle-upon-Tyne-Göteborg 23-24 hr *Scandinavian Seaways* – 1 per week

FERRY COMPANIES

Brittany Ferries
Millbay Docks, Plymouth
PL1 3EW
☎ (01752) 221321
The Britanny Centre,
Wharf Road,
Portsmouth PO2 8RU
☎ (01705) 827701
Caen ☎ 02 31 96 88 80
Cherbourg ☎ 02 33 43 43 68
Cork ☎ (021) 277801
Roscoff ☎ 02 98 29 28 28
Santander ☎ 22 00 00
St Malo ☎ 02 99 40 64 41

Color Line
International Ferry Terminal,
Royal Quays, North Shields
NE29 6EE
☎ (0191)-296 1313

Eurolink Ferries
The Ferry Terminal,
Sheerness Dock, Sheerness
ME12 1AX
☎ (01795) 581000

Hoverspeed Ltd
International Hoverport,
Western Dock, Dover, Kent
CT17 9TG ☎ (01304) 240241
Boulogne ☎ 03 21 30 27 26
Calais ☎ 03 21 46 14 14

North Sea Ferries
King George Dock, Hedon
Road, Hull HU9 5QA
☎ (01482) 77177

P & O European Ferries
Channel House, Channel
View Road, Dover CT17 9TJ
☎ (01304) 203388
Calais ☎ 03 21 46 04 40
Cairnryan ☎ (01581) 200276
Le Havre ☎ 02 35 19 78 50
Cherbourg ☎ 02 33 88 65 70
Felixstowe ☎ (01394) 604040
Portsmouth ☎ (01705) 827677
Larne ☎ (01574) 274321
Bilbao ☎ (94) 423 4477

Sea France
106 East Camber Bdg, East
Docks, Dover CT16 1JA
☎ (01304) 212696

Sally Ferries
Sally Line Ltd, Argyle Centre,
York Street, Ramsgate, Kent
CT11 9DS
☎ (01843) 595522
☎ (0181)-858 1127
Dunkerque ☎ 03 28 21 43 44
Oostende ☎ 59 55 99 54

Scandinavian Seaways
Scandinavia House,
Parkeston Quay, Harwich,
Essex CO12 4QG
☎ (01255) 240240
Esbjerg ☎ 75 12 48 00
Göteborg ☎ (031) 65 06 00
Hamburg ☎ (040) 3 89 03 71

Stena Line
Charter House, Ashford,
Kent
☎ (01233) 647047
Calais ☎ 03 21 46 80 00
Cherbourg ☎ 02 33 20 43 38
Dieppe ☎ 02 35 06 39 00
Hoek van Holland
☎ 47 82 351

Sail away to the sites and delights of Denmark, Norway, Sweden and Holland.

Camping Holidays in Scandinavia and Holland are perfect for the outdoor life and great value when you sail away, in style, with Scandinavian Seaways.

One, all-inclusive price covers transportation for you, your family and your car aboard one of our sleek white liners plus camping vouchers to any one of a large selection of superb sites all over Sweden, Norway, Denmark or Holland. You get a lot more than you imagine, for a lot less than you think.

See your travel agent or call our 24-hour Brochure Line on 0990 333 666 (quote ref 97/PN1018) for the Motoring Holidays Brochure.

From £80 per person

SCANDINAVIAN SEAWAYS
A BETTER WAY OF TRAVELLING

ANDORRA

An autonomous principality for 1,100 years, the 179 square miles of Andorra constitute the largest of the small states of Europe (Monaco, San Marino and Liechtenstein). It lies high in the Pyrenees between France and Spain on one of the main routes through the Pyrenees, and this perhaps accounts for it being a popular stopping-off place, with the added attraction of duty-free status. Andorra has no currency of its own but maximises its tourist income by accepting and using both French francs and Spanish pesetas.

The chief town of Andorra La Vella is extremely busy, but quieter villages are not far away. Les Escaldes is a year-round resort with sulphur springs and a hydroelectric station. Andorra offers excellent skiing in winter and, in summer, the same resorts make wonderful bases for hill-walking with chair-lifts to help those willing to compromise. The valley-and-peak landscape has dramatic summits rising to 2500 m. Only a small fraction of Andorra's land is arable; fields of cereals and potatoes in the sheltered lower valleys, a few vineyards, and everywhere, little corners of land growing tobacco. In summer, sheep graze the higher pastures which they share with small groups of wild horses.

Emergency numbers

Police 17

Fire Brigade and Ambulance 18

Warning information

Green card compulsory

ANDORRA LA VELLA 9D

Camping Valira Andorra la Vella.
Tel 22384.
OPEN: all year. SIZE: 1.5 ha, 150 pitches (all with elec), 18 hot showers, 19 WCs, 1 CWP. ⊂ ᴔ

☒☐☒☐☒☐ ☒☒ ☐☐

Bungalows available.
PRICES: (1996) Caravan with family 3025, Tent with two adults 1960. CC: none.
On the outer road, close to sports complex.

ARINSAL 9D

Camp/Caravan La Xixerella Ercs-Erts.
Tel 836613, Fax 839113. English spoken.
OPEN: all year. SIZE: 6 ha, 220 pitches (200 with elec), 24 hot showers, 26 WCs, 2 CWPs. ⊂ ᴔ

☒☒☒☐☒☒☒☒☒☒

Mini-golf, ball games, pub.
PRICES: (1996) Caravan with family 2900, Tent with two adults 1700. CC: Amex, Visa.
Just south of Arinsal. From Andorra la Vella follow signs to La Massana. In La Massana follow directions towards Pal (Pistes de Pal) and Ercs-Erts is the first village. Turn left in the village and campsite is about 1 km.

CANILLO 9D

Camping Santa Creu Canillo, Andorra la Vella.
OPEN: 15/06–15/09. SIZE: 4 hot showers, 5 WCs.

☐☒☒☐☐☐☐☒☐

Shop at 0.1 km. Restaurant at 0.1 km. Swimming pool 200 m.
PRICES: (1996) Caravan with family 1350, Tent with two adults 1100. CC: none.
Follow signs from Canillo to campsite.

ST JULIA DE LORIA 9D

Camping Huguet St Julia de Loria, Andorra la Vella.
Tel 843718, Fax 843803. English spoken.
OPEN: all year. SIZE: 1.5 ha, 10 hot showers, 15 WCs, 1 French WC, 1 CWP. ⊂

☒☒☒☒☐☐☐☐☐☐

Shop at 0.1 km. Restaurant at 0.1 km.
PRICES: (1996) Caravan with family 2825, Tent with two adults 1900. CC: Amex, Euro/Access, Visa.
2.5 km from the Spanish border.

AUSTRIA

Two-thirds of this landlocked country of richly varied topography is accounted for by the eastern Alps which march in from the south-west across the borders of Switzerland, Italy and former Yugoslavia.

Historic Innsbruck, its old town ringed round with snow-capped peaks, is an obvious centre for exploring the high Alps, but with countless smaller alternatives, each Tyrolean village seemingly prettier than the last. The toll road up to the Rattenbach glacier is worth every *Schilling*... as is the Gaislachkopf cable-car ride, rising to over 3000 m... while from Obergurgl, the highest parish in Europe, the Hohe Mute chair-lift affords views over 21 glaciers.

Salzburg is one of Europe's most beautiful cities, as well as enjoying a great musical reputation as the birthplace of Mozart – the Salzburg Festival is in August.

Vienna, Austria's capital in the north east, stands at the foot of the Vienna Woods on the River Danube and has a rich musical and theatrical inheritance; this, combined with fine museums and parks, makes the home of the Vienna Boys' Choir and the world-famous Opera House a great tourist magnet. Linger if you can, in one of the many historic coffee houses; take a 'Donaubus' boat trip on the Danube; or for wonderful views over the city, choose between St Stephen's Cathedral and the giant fairground wheel in Prater Park.

Emergency numbers

Police 133

Fire Brigade 122

Ambulance 144

These numbers are used with a local prefix

Warning information

First aid kit compulsory

Warning triangle must be carried

Blood alcohol legal limit 80 mg

ABTENAU   19B/D

Oberwötzlhof Camp Reiter Erlfeld 37, 5441 Abtenau.
Tel 06243 2698, Fax 06243 269855.
OPEN: all year. SIZE: 2 ha, 50 pitches (all with elec, 20 statics), 4 hot showers (charge), 5 WCs, 1 CWP.

| | 🔥 | R | 🔲 | 🍴 | ☕ | | 🎣 | 🏥 | |

Restaurant at 1.5 km. Sauna, solarium.
PRICES: (1996) Caravan with family 302,
Tent with two adults 241.40. CC: none.
Heading south from Salzburg on autobahn exit Golling-Abtenau. After 14 km turn left to Erfeld-West and campsite is within 200 m.

ACHENKIRCH   19A

Camping Schwarzenau 6215 Achenkirch.
Tel 05246 6568, Fax 05246 6551. English spoken.
OPEN: 01/05–15/10. SIZE: 2 ha, 60 pitches (all with elec), 6 hot showers, 7 WCs, 1 CWP. 🛎

| ≈ | ⛵ | 🏕 | | 🔲 | 🍴 | ☕ | | | |

Restaurant at 2 km. Windsurfing school.
PRICES: (1996) Caravan with family 280,
Tent with two adults 190. CC: Euro/Access.
Campsite is right beside the lake, between the villages of Achenkirch and Maurach. Signposted.

ALLAND   19B

Camping Hirtenberg Marktgemeinde, 2552 Hirtenberg.
Tel 02256 81111.
OPEN: 01/06–15/09. SIZE: 3 ha, 40 pitches (all with elec), 2 hot showers, 9 WCs.

| | 🔥 | R | | | | | | 🐕 | |

Shop at 0.1 km. Restaurant at 0.4 km.
PRICES: Caravan with family 210,
Tent with two adults 130. CC: none.
From A1 motorway exit at Alland and go through Weisenbach-Berndorf to Hirtenberg.

ASCHACH   19B

Camping Kaiserhof 4082 Aschach.
Tel 07273 6221.
OPEN: all year. SIZE: 2.3 ha, 40 pitches (all with elec, 145 statics), 4 hot showers (charge), 12 WCs, 1 CWP. 🛎 ♿

| ≈ | ⛵ | 🚿 | R | 🔲 | | ☕ | ✗ | | |

Shop at 6 km. Very pretty site; boating, fishing.
PRICES: (1996) Caravan with family 215,
Tent with two adults 135. CC: none.
Site is beside the River Donau and well signposted.

ATTERSEE   19B

See-Camping Gruber Dorfstrasse 65,
4865 Nussdorf-Attersee.
Tel 07666 80450, Fax 07666 80456.
English spoken.
OPEN: 15/04–15/10. SIZE: 2.8 ha, 80 pitches
(all with elec, 80 statics), 14 hot showers, 25 WCs,
2 CWPs. ℓ ⅋

≈ ⚓ ⌖ R ⊙ ⍰ ⬤ ✗ ⸮

Facilities updated for 1997 including new, heated
pool. Sauna, solarium and gym.
PRICES: (1996) Caravan with family 367,
Tent with two adults 244. CC: none.
From Attersee go south to Nussdorf.
SEE ADVERTISEMENT

BAD AUSSEE   19B

Camping Bad Aussee Grundlsee Str 21,
8990 Bad Aussee.
Tel 03622 54565, Fax 03622 52427.
English spoken.
OPEN: all year. SIZE: 1 ha, 50 pitches (30 with elec,
2 statics), 4 hot showers (charge), 6 WCs, 1 CWP. ℓ

∼ ⚓ ⌖ R ⊙   ✗ ⸮ ⍰

Shop at 2 km. Children's playground.
PRICES: Caravan with family 230,
Tent with two adults 150. CC: none.

*From Bad Aussee go towards Grundlsee; campsite
is 2.5 km ahead on the left, beside the Gasthof.*

BAD ISCHL   19B

Camping Klausner-Höll Lahn 201,
4830 Hallstatt.
Tel 06134 8322, Fax 06134 8322. English spoken.
OPEN: 15/04–15/10. SIZE: 0.5 ha, 30 pitches
(all with elec), 7 hot showers, 8 WCs, 1 CWP. ℓ

≈ ⚓ ⌖ R ⊙ ⍰ ⬤ ✗ ⸮ ⍐

Children's playground.
PRICES: Caravan with family 275,
Tent with two adults 180. CC: none.
*From Bad Ischl follow signs to Bad Goisern then
Hallstatt. Site is well signposted.*

Campingplatz Schönblick Gschwendt 33,
5342 Strobl/Abersee.
Tel 06138 2471. English spoken.
OPEN: 01/05–15/10. SIZE: 1.4 ha, 80 pitches
(all with elec, 40 statics), 6 hot showers, 12 WCs,
1 CWP. ℓ

≈ ⚓ ⌖   ⊙ ⍰

Restaurant at 0.1 km.
PRICES: (1996) Caravan with family 255,
Tent with two adults 180. CC: none.
*From Bad Ischl go west on B158 towards
St Gilgen. Turn right at Km 36 marker for campsite.*

BLUDENZ   19C

Auhof Camping 6706 Bürs.
Tel 05552 67044, Fax 05552 31926. English spoken.
OPEN: all year. SIZE: 0.6 ha, 60 pitches (all with
elec, 20 statics), 6 hot showers, 5 WCs.

⚲ R ⊙ ⬤

Shop at 0.3 km. Restaurant at 0.3 km. Horse-
riding; swimming pool 1 km.
PRICES: (1996) Caravan with family 252,
Tent with two adults 154. CC: none.
*Just off the Bludenz-Bürs motorway, 300 m from
Interspar supermarket. Well signposted.*

Camping Sonnenberg 6714 Nüziders.
Tel 05552 64035, Fax 05552 33900. English spoken.
OPEN: 17/05–04/10. SIZE: 1.8 ha, 120 pitches
(all with elec), 8 hot showers, 12 WCs, 2 CWPs. ℓ

⚲ R ⊙ ⍰   ⍐ ✖

Restaurant at 0.3 km.
PRICES: (1996) Caravan with family 310,
Tent with two adults 240. CC: none.
*Exit Bludenz-West off A14/E60 (Feldkirch to
Bludenz).*

Camping Zelfen 6774 Tschagguns.
Tel 05556 72326. English spoken.
OPEN: all year. SIZE: 2 ha, 100 pitches (all
with elec), 6 hot showers (charge), 11 WCs,
1 CWP. ℓ ⅋

Austria *(vertical side text)*

Tennis, playground.
PRICES: Caravan with family 335,
Tent with two adults 209. CC: none.
Leave A14 at Bludenz-Ost and go south-east to Tschagguns on B188. Campsite is signposted.

BREGENZ 19C

See Camping Bodangasse 7, 6900 Bregenz am Bodensee.
Tel 05574 71895/96, Fax 05574 71895/96.
English spoken.
OPEN: 15/05–15/09. SIZE: 8 ha, 420 pitches (all with elec), 32 hot showers, 37 WCs, 2 CWPs. ♿ ⛟

Boats for hire; children's playground.
PRICES: Caravan with family 334,
Tent with two adults 274. CC: none.
On the road to Switzerland, turn right towards Lake Constance and Bregenz.

BRIXEN 19C

Camping Brixen im Thale
6364 Brixen im Thale.
Tel 05334 8113, Fax 05334 8469. English spoken.
OPEN: all year. SIZE: 3 ha, 30 pitches (all with elec), 33 WCs, 2 CWPs. ♿ ⛟

Swimming pool nearby.
PRICES: (1996) Caravan with family 265,
Tent with two adults 179. CC: none.
From the Kufstein to Innsbruck motorway take the Wörgl-Ost exit to Brixen.

BRUCK 19C

Sport Camp Woferlgut 5671 Bruck.
Tel 06545 73030, Fax 06545 73033.
English spoken.
OPEN: all year. SIZE: 2 ha, 170 pitches (all with elec, 20 statics), 16 hot showers (charge), 27 WCs, 3 CWPs. ♿

Exceptional site with excellent facilities and nearly all summer/winter sports.
PRICES: (1996) Caravan with family 356,
Tent with two adults 242. CC: none.
South-west of Bruck. Take Grossglockner exit from road 311 (Bruck by-pass) and follow signs to site.

DÖLLACH 19C

Camping Zirknitzer Döllach,
9843 Grosskirchheim.
Tel 04825 451. English spoken.
OPEN: 01/06–30/09. SIZE: 1 ha, 60 pitches (all with elec), 6 hot showers, 9 WCs, 1 CWP. ♿

Sauna.
PRICES: (1996) Caravan with family 243,
Tent with two adults 171.70. CC: none.
Take the Tauern autobahn from Spittal to Döllach.

DORNBIRN 19C

Camping Feurstein 6951 Lingenau.
Tel 05513 6114, Fax 05513 61144.
OPEN: all year. SIZE: 1 ha, 15 pitches (all with elec, 15 statics), 2 hot showers, 5 WCs, 1 CWP.

Shop at 2 km. Restaurant at 2 km.
PRICES: (1996) Caravan with family 270,
Tent with two adults 170. CC: none.
From Dornbirn go towards Bregenzerwald on the B200 as far as Muselbach then take B205 to Lingenau; in Lingenau turn right and campsite is 500 m.

EHRWALD 19C

Camping Dr-Ing E Lauth 6632 Ehrwald.
Tel 05673 2666, Fax 05673 26664. English spoken.
OPEN: all year. SIZE: 70 pitches (all with elec, 40 statics), 8 hot showers, 13 WCs, 1 CWP. ♿

Discount for stays of 7 days +.
PRICES: Caravan with family 357,
Tent with two adults 229. CC: none.
From the Fernpassbundesstrasse to Ehrwald go towards Zugspitzbahn and campsite is signposted after 1 km.

Feriencenter Biberhof Schmitte 8,
6633 Biberwier.
Tel 05673 2950, Fax 05673 295022. English spoken.
OPEN: all year. SIZE: 2 ha, 80 pitches (all with elec, 60 statics), 17 hot showers (charge), 20 WCs, 1 CWP. ♿

Restaurant at 1 km. Mountain-bike hire; children's playground with trampoline; swimming pool 3 km.
PRICES: (1996) Caravan with family 258,
Tent with two adults 171. CC: none.
Go from Kempten to Reutte and then to Lermoos. From Lermoos go to Biberwier and turn left after 500 m.

Happy Camp Garmischerstr 21, 6631 Lermoos.
Tel 05673 2980. English spoken.
OPEN: 01/06–30/10 & 15/12–30/04. SIZE: 1 ha, 74 pitches (all with elec, 20 statics), 4 hot showers, 11 WCs, 1 CWP. ♿

Shop at 0.1 km.
PRICES: (1996) Caravan with family 320,
Tent with two adults 218. CC: none.

From Ehrwald head towards Lermoos on the B187. The site is just 500 m before Lermoos.

FELDKIRCH 19C

Waldcamping Feldkirch Postfach 564, 6803 Feldkirch-Gisingen.
Tel 05522 74304. English spoken.
OPEN: all year. SIZE: 4 ha, 170 pitches (130 with elec, 30 statics), 24 hot showers, 22 WCs, 1 CWP. 🌣

Shop at 1 km. Restaurant at 1 km. Children's playground, tennis, football.
PRICES: (1996) Caravan with family 280, Tent with two adults 185. CC: none.
About 4 km from the town centre. Follow signs to Gisingen Stadium.

FERLACH 19D

Camping Rosenthal-Roz 9173 Gotschunchen.
Tel 04226 246, Fax 04226 24615. English spoken.
OPEN: 01/04−30/09. SIZE: 10 ha, 350 pitches (300 with elec), 40 hot showers, 50 WCs, 2 CWPs. 🌣 ♿

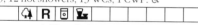

Children's playground.
PRICES: Caravan with family 295, Tent with two adults 203. CC: none.
West of Ferlach on route 85.

Naturist Camping Rosental Roz 9173 Gotschunchen.
Tel 04226 246, Fax 04226 24615. English spoken.
OPEN: 15/05−15/09. SIZE: 4 ha, 90 pitches (all with elec), 12 hot showers, 13 WCs, 1 CWP. ♿

Restaurant at 0.5 km. Swimming pool 0.5 km.
PRICES: (1996) Caravan with family 286, Tent with two adults 198. CC: none.
West of Ferlach on route 85.

FIEBERBRUNN 19C

Tirol Camp Lindau 20, 6391 Fieberbrunn.
Tel 05354 6666, Fax 05354 2516. English spoken.
OPEN: all year. SIZE: 5 ha, 320 pitches (all with elec, 86 statics), 20 hot showers, 36 WCs, 2 CWPs. 🌣

Bike hire, tennis.
PRICES: (1996) Caravan with family 351, Tent with two adults 315. CC: Amex, Euro/Access, Visa.
From Kufstein go to St Johann and then to Fieberbrunn.

FROHNLEITEN 19D

Camping Lanzmaierhof Ungersdorf, 8130 Frohnleiten.
Tel 03126 2360. English spoken.

OPEN: 01/04−15/10. SIZE: 0.5 ha, 30 pitches (all with elec), 2 hot showers (charge), 2 WCs, 1 CWP.

Shop at 2 km. Table tennis, playground.
PRICES: (1996) Caravan with family 184, Tent with two adults 120. CC: none.
Coming from the south, leave S35 north of Peggau in the village of Badl and then go 3 km north along L121 to Ungersdorf. Follow campsite directions from there.

FÜRSTENFELD 19D

Camping Jennersdorf 8380 Jennersdorf.
Tel 03329 46133, Fax 03329 626121. English spoken.
OPEN: 15/03−31/10. SIZE: 1 ha, 41 pitches (all with elec, 15 statics), 6 hot showers (charge), 8 WCs, 1 CWP. 🌣 ♿

Shop at 0.8 km. Restaurant at 1 km. Tennis and swimming pool nearby. (Charge for electricity.).
PRICES: (1996) Caravan with family 232, Tent with two adults 166. CC: none.
Leave A2 west of Graz at Fürstenfeld. East on the B65 to Eltendorf then south on B57 to Jennersdorf.

Campingclub Fürstenfeld 8280 Fürstenfeld.
Tel 03382 54940, Fax 03382 51671. English spoken.
OPEN: 15/04−15/10. SIZE: 3.5 ha, 80 pitches (all with elec, 30 statics), 4 hot showers, 10 WCs, 1 CWP. 🌣

Shop at 0.3 km. Restaurant at 0.2 km. Country's largest outdoor pool nearby.
PRICES: (1996) Caravan with family 175, Tent with two adults 130. CC: none.
Campsite is 2 km off B65 and is last campsite before reaching the borders.

FUSCH 19C

Camping Lampenhausl Glocknerstrasse 15, 5672 Fusch-Glocknerstrasse.
Tel 06546 215, Fax 06546 215302. English spoken.
OPEN: 01/05−31/10. SIZE: 1 ha, 60 pitches (30 with elec), 2 hot showers, 5 WCs. 🌣

PRICES: (1996) Caravan with family 200, Tent with two adults 140. CC: none.
In the centre of the village.

GLEINSTATTEN 19D

Camping Gleinstatten 8443 Gleinstatten.
Tel 03457 2215, Fax 03457 22156. English spoken.
OPEN: 25/03−31/10. SIZE: 0.7 ha, 60 pitches (all with elec, 5 statics), 6 hot showers (charge), 6 WCs, 1 CWP. 🌣 ♿

| ≈ | ⚓ | ⚙ | R | 🔲 | 🍺 | 🍴 | | 🔦 | | |

Shop at 0.1 km. Restaurant at 0.1 km.
PRICES: (1996) Caravan with family 185,
Tent with two adults 110. CC: none.
*From the Graz to Slovenia autobahn exit at
Leibnitz and go along B74 to Gleinstatten.*

GMÜND 19B

Campingplatz Assangteich 3950 Gmünd.
Tel 02852 51552, Fax 02852 54514. English spoken.
OPEN: 01/04–30/09. SIZE: 0.45 ha, 37 pitches
(all with elec), 8 hot showers, 8 WCs, 1 CWP. 🔦

| | ⚙ | R | 🔲 | 🍴 | 🍺 | | | | |

Restaurant at 0.1 km. Swimming pool 100 m, lake
200 m.
PRICES: Caravan with family 251,
Tent with two adults 181. CC: none.
*Campsite is towards Waldenstein off B41 near
Gmünd-Mitte junction. Well signposted.*

GRAZ 19D

Camping Central Matinhofstrasse 3,
8054 Graz-Strassgang.
Tel 0316 281831, Fax 0316 28183183.
English spoken.
OPEN: 01/04–31/10. SIZE: 4 ha. 🔦

| | ⚙ | R | 🔲 | 🍴 | | 🍴 | 🔦 | | | |

PRICES: (1996) Caravan with family 300,
Tent with two adults 210. CC: none.
On the outskirts of Graz and well signposted.

Camping Lieboch Radlstrasse 12,
8501 Graz-Lieboch.
Tel 03136 61797. English spoken.
OPEN: 01/05–31/10. SIZE: 0.3 ha, 30 pitches (all with
elec, 30 statics), 2 hot showers, 3 WCs, 1 CWP. 🔦

| | | ⚙ | R | 🔲 | 🍴 | • | | 🄷 | | |

Shop at 0.8 km. Restaurant at 0.1 km. Table tennis;
heated swimming pool 150 m.
PRICES: (1996) Caravan with family 280,
Tent with two adults 200. CC: none.
*The campsite is 7 km south-west of Graz at the
Lieboch junction of the A2 motorway.*

Strand Camping Turnersee 9123 St Primus.
Tel 04239 2350, Fax 04239 235032. English spoken.
OPEN: 27/04–05/10. SIZE: 6.5 ha, 400 pitches
(all with elec, 96 statics), 43 hot showers, 63 WCs,
5 CWPs. 🔦 &

| ≈ | ⚓ | ⚙ | R | 🔲 | 🍴 | 🍺 | 🍴 | | 🄷 | |

Good facilities for children; apartments also
available.
PRICES: (1996) Caravan with family 407,
Tent with two adults 293. CC: none.
*Leave the B70 (Klagenfurt-Graz) towards
Klopeinersee and drive through St Kanzian to the
west shore of the Turnersee.*

HALL IN TIROL 19C

Campingplatz Judenstein 6074 Rinn.
Tel 05223 8620, Fax 05223 887715. English spoken.
OPEN: 15/04–15/10. SIZE: 1 ha, 50 pitches (20 with
elec), 6 hot showers, 7 WCs, 1 CWP. 🔦

| | | ⚙ | R | 🔲 | | | 🍴 | | | |

Shop at 1 km.
PRICES: (1996) Caravan with family 232,
Tent with two adults 157. CC: none.
*From Innsbruck motorway, exit at Hall in Tirol
and go through Tulfes to Rinn.*

HALLEIN 19A

Camping Rif 5400 Hallein-bei-Salzburg.
Tel 06245 76114. English spoken.
OPEN: 01/04–31/10. SIZE: 0.6 ha, 50 pitches
(all with elec), 4 hot showers, 4 WCs, 1 CWP.

| ≈ | ⚓ | ⚙ | R | 🔲 | 🍴 | 🍺 | | | | |

Restaurant at 1.6 km. Barbecue facilities;
swimming pool 600 m.
PRICES: (1996) Caravan with family 304,
Tent with two adults 172. CC: none.
*From A10/E55 (München-Salzburg-Villach
motorway) take exit 8 on to B160, then B159 and
turn off after 2 km. Campsite is signposted.*

HERMAGOR 19C

Camping Schluga-Seecamping Hermagor-
Presseggersee, 9620 Hermagor.
Tel 04282 2051, Fax 04282 288120. English spoken.
OPEN: 20/05–20/09. SIZE: 7 ha, 400 pitches
(all with elec), 32 hot showers, 55 WCs, 6 CWPs. 🔦

| ≈ | ⚓ | ⚙ | R | 🔲 | 🍺 | 🍴 | 🍴 | | 🄷 | |

Children's playroom and games room, sauna;
children under 6 free of charge.
PRICES: Caravan with family 401,
Tent with two adults 315. CC: none.
*6 km from Hermagor going towards Villach, on
the left.*

Campingplatz Presseggersee 9620 Hermagor.
Tel 04282 2039, Fax 04282 3034. English spoken.
OPEN: 01/05–30/09. SIZE: 1 ha, 80 pitches (all with
elec), 6 hot showers, 14 WCs, 1 CWP. 🔦

| ≈ | ⚓ | ⚙ | R | 🔲 | 🍺 | 🍴 | 🍴 | | 🄷 | |

PRICES: (1996) Caravan with family 239,
Tent with two adults 160. CC: none.
The campsite is well signposted in Hermagor.

Schluga Camping 9620 Hermagor-Vellach.
Tel 04282 2051, Fax 04282 288120.
English spoken.
OPEN: all year. SIZE: 5 ha, 300 pitches (all with elec,
15 statics), 28 hot showers, 41 WCs, 6 CWPs. &

| | | ⚙ | R | 🔲 | 🍺 | 🍴 | 🍴 | 🔦 | 🄷 | |

Sauna; children under 6 free of charge.

PRICES: Caravan with family 401, Tent with two adults 315. CC: none.
2 km from Hermagor towards Villach, on the left.

IMST   19C

Camping Imst-West Langgasse 62, 6460 Imst.
Tel 05412 66293, Fax 05412 63364. English spoken.
OPEN: all year. SIZE: 1 ha, 70 pitches (all with elec),
4 hot showers, 9 WCs, 1 CWP.

Restaurant at 0.5 km. Playground, swimming pool
1.5 km.
PRICES: (1996) Caravan with family 294,
Tent with two adults 194. CC: none.
Follow signs to campsite on B171, west of Imst.

INNSBRUCK   19C

Camping Mils Bundesstrasse 7, 6068 Mils in Tyrol.
Tel 05223 6360, Fax 05223 636052. English spoken.
OPEN: all year. SIZE: 1 ha, 60 pitches (all with elec,
10 statics).

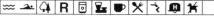

PRICES: (1996) Caravan with family 332, Tent with
two adults 222. CC: Amex, Euro/Access, Visa.
*From Innsbruck-Salzburg motorway take Hall in
Tirol exit. Go through Hall and turn right.
Campsite is 2 km ahead on the left.*

Camping Natterer See Natters bei Innsbruck,
6161 Natters.
Tel 0512 546732, Fax 0512 546695. English spoken.
OPEN: 01/01–30/09 & 15/12–31/12. SIZE: 7 ha,
200 pitches (all with elec), 16 hot showers,
2 CWPs. ℓ ら

Flume, bikes, tennis, horse-riding, table tennis;
rooms available.
PRICES: Caravan with family 491,
Tent with two adults 323. CC: none.
*From A13 motorway take exit 3
(Mutters/Natters/Innsbruck-Süd) and go through
village of Natters. Follow green signs to the
campsite (2.5 km from Natters).*

KLAGENFURT   19D

Camping Strandbad Metnitzstrand,
9020 Klagenfurt.
Tel 0463 21169, Fax 0463 2116993.
English spoken.
OPEN: 01/05–30/09. SIZE: 4 ha, 400 pitches (all
with elec), 24 hot showers, 48 WCs, 2 CWPs. ℓ ら

PRICES: (1996) Caravan with family 364,
Tent with two adults 204. CC: none.
*A2 from either Villach or Klagenfurt. Exit
Klagenfurt See, turn right and follow signs.*

KÖTSCHACH-MAUTHEN   19C

Alpen Camping Nr 284, 9640 Kötschach-Mauthen.
Tel 04715 429, Fax 04715 429. English spoken.
OPEN: 01/05–15/10. SIZE: 1.4 ha, 8 hot showers,
9 WCs, 1 CWP. ℓ ら

Large playground, indoor/outdoor pools.
PRICES: (1996) Caravan with family 311,
Tent with two adults 210. CC: none.
*Head south-east from the 100/110
towards Italian border (about 35 km). Signposted
from centre of Kötschach-Mauthen on B111.*

KREMS   19B

Camping Donau 3500 Krems an der Donau-Stein.
Tel 02732 84455. English spoken.
OPEN: 15/04–15/10. SIZE: 0.8 ha, 80 pitches, 8 hot
showers, 12 WCs. ℓ ら

Restaurant at 0.3 km.
PRICES: (1996) Caravan with family 271,
Tent with two adults 171. CC: none.
*Campsite is in the main street of Krems, near the
harbour.*

Camping Hochstubai 6167 Neustift.
Tel 05226 3484, Fax 05226 2610. English spoken.
OPEN: all year. SIZE: 50 pitches (all with elec,
60 statics), 10 hot showers, 18 WCs, 1 CWP. ℓ

Shop at 6 km.
PRICES: (1996) Caravan with family 274,
Tent with two adults 162. CC: none.
*East of Krems on route 3, and just north of the
River Donau.*

KUFSTEIN   19A

Camping Seespitz Seespitz 1, 6344 Walchsee.
Tel 05374 5359, Fax 05374 5845. English spoken.
OPEN: all year. SIZE: 2 ha, 150 pitches (all with elec,
80 statics), 12 hot showers, 26 WCs, 1 CWP. ℓ ら

PRICES: (1996) Caravan with family 340,
Tent with two adults 210. CC: none.
*From München take motorway towards Salzburg
and near Rosenheim take the exit to Innsbruck.
Then take the exit to Oberaudorf (the last one
before Kufstein) and follow signs to Walchsee.*

LANDECK   19C

Camping Riffler 6500 Landeck.
Tel 05442 624774, Fax 05442 624775.
English spoken.
OPEN: 01/01–01/05 & 01/06–31/12. SIZE: 2.5 ha,
48 pitches (all with elec, 30 statics), 6 hot showers,
7 WCs, 4 CWPs.

Austria

~ ✗ ⚄ R ⎕ ⛲ ⛟ ✗ ☐ ☐ ☐ ☐

Swimming pool 500 m.
PRICES: (1996) Caravan with family 320,
Tent with two adults 215. CC: Euro/Access.
*Coming from Innsbruck on motorway take
Landeck-West exit and Riffler is the second
campsite going towards Landeck town centre.*

LÄNGENFELD 19C

Comfort Camping Ötztal 6444 Längenfeld.
Tel 05253 5348, Fax 05253 5909. English spoken.
OPEN: all year. SIZE: 3 ha, 180 pitches (all with elec,
30 statics), 15 hot showers, 26 WCs, 3 CWPs. ⛾

☐ ⚄ R ⎕ ⛲ ⛟ ✗ ⚅ ⚆ ☐ ☐

Sauna, solarium, sports room, TV.
PRICES: (1996) Caravan with family 288,
Tent with two adults 198. CC: none.

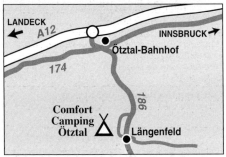

*Leave the A12 motorway at Ötztal (approx 50 km
west of Innsbruck) and go south to Längenfeld on
the 186 road. In Längenfeld turn right before the
bridge to the campsite.*

Sölden Camping Wohlfahrt 500,
6450 Sölden/Ötztal.
Tel 05254 2627, Fax 05254 26725. English spoken.
OPEN: 01/01–05/05 & 05/06–31/12. SIZE: 1.3 ha,
97 pitches (all with elec), 11 hot showers, 18 WCs,
1 CWP. ☎ ⛾

~ ✗ ☐ R ⎕ ☐ ✗ ☐ ☐ ☐

Shop at 0.2 km. Sauna, fitness centre, solarium.
PRICES: (1996) Caravan with family 406. CC: none.
*Sölden is south of Längenfeld on route 186. Site is
well signposted.*

Ötztaler Naturcamping Ötztaler, Sölden,
6444 Huben.
Tel 05253 5855/5538, Fax 05253 5538.
English spoken.
OPEN: all year. SIZE: 70 pitches (all with elec,
20 statics), 8 hot showers (charge), 10 WCs, 1 CWP. ☎

~ ✗ ⚄ R ⎕ ☐ ⛟ ☐ ☐ ☐

Shop at 0.5 km. Restaurant at 0.3 km.
PRICES: (1996) Caravan with family 298,
Tent with two adults 192. CC: none.

*Coming from Imst take the road to Ötztal, go
through the valley for about 25 km, over the
bridge and to the right in Huben.*

LANGENWANG 19D

Europa Camping Siglstrasse 5,
8665 Langenwang.
Tel 03854 2950. English spoken.
OPEN: all year. SIZE: 0.6 ha, 40 pitches (all with elec,
15 statics), 4 hot showers (charge), 5 WCs, 1 CWP.

~ ⚓ ⚄ R ⎕ ☐ ☐ ☐ ☐ ☐

Shop at 0.1 km. Restaurant at 0.1 km. Table tennis,
bicycles for hire.
PRICES: Caravan with family 235,
Tent with two adults 160. CC: none.
*From Wien on S6, exit at Langenwang just south
of Mürzzuschlag. Campsite is behind the Hotel
Kohlbacher.*

LECH 19C

Alpencamping 6754 Klösterle-Langen am Arlberg.
Tel 05582 269. English spoken.
OPEN: all year. SIZE: 1.5 ha, 105 pitches (all with
elec, 15 statics), 9 hot showers, 16 WCs, 1 CWP. ☎

~ ✗ ⚄ R ⎕ ⛲ ⛟ ✗ ⚐ ☐ ☐

Fitness centre, playground.
PRICES: (1996) Caravan with family 295,
Tent with two adults 180. CC: none.
*Turn off the St Anton to Bludenz road at Langen
and go north through Lech to Klösterle.*

LIENZ 19C

Camping Falken Eichholz 7, 9900 Leinz.
Tel 04852 64022, Fax 04852 640226. English spoken.
OPEN: 15/12–31/10. SIZE: 1.5 ha, 110 pitches
(all with elec), 16 hot showers (charge), 19 WCs,
2 CWPs. ☎ ⛾

⚄ R ⎕ ⛲ ⛟ ✗ ☐ ☐ ☐

Swimming pool 500 m.
PRICES: (1996) Caravan with family 329,
Tent with two adults 209. CC: none.
*From Lienz go towards Hallenbad and the
campsite is signposted.*

LIEZEN 19D

Camping Hohenberg Seeruhe 8943 Aigen im
Ennstal.
Tel 03682 8130.
OPEN: 01/04–31/10. SIZE: 2 ha, 10 hot showers
(charge), 14 WCs, 2 CWPs. ☎ ⛾

≈ ⚊ ⚄ R ⎕ ⛲ ☐ ☐ ⚐ ☐

Restaurant at 1 km. Playground; beautiful
location.
PRICES: (1996) Caravan with family 192,
Tent with two adults 116. CC: none.

Go south-west from Liezen on route 308. Turn south at Wörschach towards Aigen and then turn right after petrol station. Campsite is on the north shore of the lake and well signposted.

LINZ 19B

Campingplatz Linz Pichlingersee Wiener Strasse 937, 4030 Linz.
Tel 0732 305314, Fax 0732 3053144. English spoken.
OPEN: 01/03–30/11. SIZE: 2.4 ha, 130 pitches (all with elec, 40 statics), 10 hot showers, 16 WCs, 1 CWP.

Table tennis.
PRICES: (1996) Caravan with family 270,
Tent with two adults 206. CC: none.
Leave A1 at Asten-St-Florian exit towards Linz and campsite is signposted 3 km north.

LOFER 19C

Camping Steinplatte 6384 Waidring/Tirol.
Tel 05353 5345, Fax 05353 5406. English spoken.
OPEN: all year. SIZE: 4 ha, 330 pitches (all with elec, 150 statics), 24 WCs, 3 CWPs.

Sauna, solarium, massage.
PRICES: (1996) Caravan with family 304,
Tent with two adults 209. CC: none.
Waidring is west of Lofer via the B312.

Park Camping Grubhof 5092 St Martin bei Lofer.
Tel 06588 8237/8405, Fax 06588 8237/8405.
English spoken.
OPEN: 01/05–30/09. SIZE: 10 ha, 200 pitches (170 with elec, 10 statics), 10 hot showers, 28 WCs, 2 CWPs.

Motor caravan services.
PRICES: Caravan with family 301,
Tent with two adults 194. CC: none.
On the B311, 1 km south of Lofer towards Schloss-Grubhof on the left.
SEE ADVERTISEMENT

MALTA 19D

Terrassencamping Maltatal 9854 Malta.
Tel 04733 234, Fax 04733 358. English spoken.
OPEN: 01/04–31/10. SIZE: 3 ha, 230 pitches (all with elec), 30 hot showers, 32 WCs, 2 CWPs.

Playground, ball games.
PRICES: Caravan with family 330,
Tent with two adults 243. CC: none.
Take the Tauern autobahn to Gmünd and then go 5 km on to Malta.

MARIAZELL 19B

Campingplatz Am Erlaufsee Bundesstrasse 1, 8630 St Sebastien bei Mariazell.
Tel 03882 2148, Fax 03882 4268.
OPEN: 01/05–15/09. SIZE: 1 ha, 40 pitches (all with elec), 3 hot showers (charge), 6 WCs.

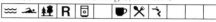

Shop at 3 km.
PRICES: Caravan with family 220,
Tent with two adults 170. CC: none.
From St Polten go to Mariazell and then to Erlaufsee.

MATREI 19C

Camping Edengarten 9971 Matrei.
Tel 04875 5111. English spoken.
OPEN: 01/05–30/10. SIZE: 1 ha, 80 pitches (all with elec), 10 hot showers, 12 WCs, 1 CWP.

PRICES: Caravan with family 274,
Tent with two adults 214. CC: none.
1 km south of Matrei on the Felssertauernstrasse and well signposted.

MAURACH 19C

Karwendel Camping 6212 Maurach.
Tel 05243 6116. English spoken.

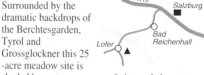

OPEN: all year. SIZE: 1.5 ha, 40 pitches (all with elec, 40 statics), 8 hot showers (charge), 10 WCs, 1 CWP.

Shop at 0.5 km. Children's playground.
PRICES: (1996) Caravan with family 295,
Tent with two adults 186. CC: none.
Leave the main road in Wiesing/Achenseestrasse and go to Maurach. Take the road to Pertisau and just before Pertisau turn into a small road on the left to campsite.

MELK 19B

Gasthof Stumpfer 3392 Schonbuhel 7.
Tel 02752 8510, Fax 02752 8510. English spoken.
OPEN: 01/04–31/10. SIZE: 1 ha, 60 pitches (all with elec, 10 statics), 4 hot showers (charge), 7 WCs, 1 CWP.

Shop at 5 km.
PRICES: Caravan with family 220,
Tent with two adults 155. CC: none.
From the A1, exit at Melk towards Melk-Nord, and go to Wachau. From there take route 33 to Schonbuhl (4 km).

MILLSTÄTT 19D

Camping Brunner am See 9873 Döbriach.
Tel 04246 7189/7386, Fax 04246 7837.
English spoken.
OPEN: all year. SIZE: 2.5 ha, 250 pitches (all with elec).

Shop at 0.5 km. Children's activities; organised entertainment. Special group discounts.
PRICES: (1996) Caravan with family 450,
Tent with two adults 340. CC: none.
From Tauernautobahn exit at Millstättersee and go to Döbriach.

Camping Neubauer Dellach 3, 9872 Millstätt.
Tel 04766 2530/2532, Fax 04766 2532.
OPEN: 09/04–30/10. SIZE: 1.5 ha, 100 pitches (all with elec), 10 hot showers, 15 WCs, 3 CWPs.

Shop at 0.2 km. Restaurant at 0.2 km. Excellent sports facilities on site and nearby.
PRICES: (1996) Caravan with family 296,
Tent with two adults 226. CC: none.
From A10 exit at Millstättersee and go towards Radenthein on the B98 for 8 km to Dellach.

Komfort Campingpark Burgstaller
Glanzerstrasse 54, 9873 Döbriach-Karnten.
Tel 04246 7774, Fax 04246 77744. English spoken.
OPEN: all year. SIZE: 7 ha, 420 pitches (all with elec, 30 statics), 28 hot showers, 59 WCs, 5 CWPs.

Good campervan facilities; disco.
PRICES: (1996) Caravan with family 497,
Tent with two adults 267. CC: none.
East of Millstätt on route 98 towards Döbriach am See.

MONDSEE 19A

Camping Fohlenhof Hof 17,
5310 Mondsee-Tiefgraben.
Tel 06232 2600. English spoken.
OPEN: 09/04–10/10. SIZE: 3 ha, 70 pitches (all with elec, 70 statics), 6 hot showers, 11 WCs, 1 CWP.

PRICES: (1996) Caravan with family 210,
Tent with two adults 134. CC: none.
Take A1 motorway west to Mondsee then turn left to Lake Irrsee. After about 2 km turn left, opposite a furniture factory. Go a further 1.5 km to the campsite.

NASSEREITH 19C

Romantik-Camping Schloss Fernsteinsee,
6465 Nassereith.
Tel 05265 5210/157, Fax 05265 52174.
English spoken.
OPEN: 01/05–31/10. SIZE: 8 ha, 100 pitches (36 with elec), 12 hot showers, 16 WCs, 3 French WCs, 1 CWP.

Shop at 4 km. Restaurant at 0.3 km. Playground, sauna, barbecue area.
PRICES: (1996) Caravan with family 291,
Tent with two adults 203. CC: none.
From Innsbruck or Imst via Nassereith, go 4 km beyond the village towards the Fernpass and campsite is on the left.

NENZING 19C

Camping Grosswalsertal 6741 Raggal-Plazera.
Tel 05553 209. English spoken.
OPEN: 01/05–30/09. SIZE: 0.8 ha, 60 pitches (50 with elec, 1 static), 4 hot showers, 7 WCs, 1 CWP.

Restaurant at 2 km.
PRICES: (1996) Caravan with family 230,
Tent with two adults 150. CC: none.
Leave A14 at Nenzing exit and follow signs to Ludesch and then Raggal-Plazera. Campsite is 2 km from Raggal.

NEULENGBACH 19B

Campingplatz Finsterhof Inprugg,
3040 St Pölten.
Tel 02772 52130, Fax 02772 52130. English spoken.

OPEN: all year. SIZE: 2 ha, 75 pitches (all with elec, 120 statics), 10 hot showers (charge), 9 WCs, 2 CWPs. ⚓ ♿

Restaurant at 0.2 km. Cycle track.
PRICES: (1996) Caravan with family 150, Tent with two adults 125. CC: Euro/Access.
Approaching from Vienna leave A1 at Altlengbach or from Salzburg at St Christophen.

NEUMARKT 19A/B

Seecamp Neumarkt Uferstr 3, 5202 Neumarkt.
Tel 06216 4400, Fax 06216 44004. English spoken.
OPEN: 01/05–31/10. SIZE: 3 ha, 170 pitches (all with elec, 70 statics), 10 hot showers, 20 WCs, 1 CWP. ⚓ ♿

Ball games, sailing, windsurfing.
PRICES: (1996) Caravan with family 320, Tent with two adults 225. CC: none.
20 km north of Salzburg; leave motorway at Wallersee. Campsite well signposted.

OBERWÖLZ 19D

Waldcamping Schloss Rothenfels
Schloss Rothenfels, 8832 Oberwölz.
Tel 03581 208, Fax 03581 2084. English spoken.
OPEN: 01/04–31/10. SIZE: 8 ha, 180 pitches (150 with elec, 20 statics), 20 hot showers, 20 WCs, 4 CWPs. ⚓

Shop at 1 km. Restaurant at 1 km. Solarium.
PRICES: Caravan with family 240, Tent with two adults 170. CC: none.
The campsite is well signposted.

PASSAU 19B

Camping Gasthof Weiss Puhret 5, 4143 Neustift.
Tel 07284 8104, Fax 07284 810460. English spoken.
OPEN: 01/04–31/10. SIZE: 1 ha, 25 pitches (18 with elec), 4 hot showers, 4 WCs.

Sauna, tennis, playground.
PRICES: (1996) Caravan with family 225, Tent with two adults 170. CC: none.
From the motorway take the Passau-Nord exit on to B388 and go through Obernzell - Untergriesbach - Gottsdorf - Grenzubergang - Neustift to Puhret.

RADSTADT 19D

Camping Radstadt Schloss Str 17, 5550 Radstadt.
Tel 06452 42150, Fax 06452 42154. English spoken.
OPEN: all year. SIZE: 1 ha, 100 pitches (all with elec), 6 hot showers, 15 WCs, 2 CWPs. ⚓

PRICES: (1996) Caravan with family 269, Tent with two adults 205. CC: none.
The campsite is just 300 m from the centre of Radstadt with access from either of the two town entrances and is clearly marked.

Camping Zirngast 8970 Schladming.
Tel 03687 23195, Fax 03687 23495. English spoken.
OPEN: all year. SIZE: 1.5 ha, 80 pitches (all with elec, 20 statics), 6 hot showers (charge), 10 WCs, 1 CWP. ⚓

Good summer/winter sports, sauna; pool 200 m.
PRICES: (1996) Caravan with family 330, Tent with two adults 200. CC: Amex, Euro/Access, Visa.
East of Radstadt on route 308. Site is well signposted.

Forellcamp Gaismairallee 51, 5550 Radstadt.
Tel 06452 7861, Fax 06452 5092. English spoken.
OPEN: all year. SIZE: 1 ha, 120 pitches (all with elec), 6 hot showers, 12 WCs. ⚓

Shop at 1 km. Swimming pool 1 km.
PRICES: Caravan with family 254, Tent with two adults 164. CC: none.
Follow directions to campsite in Radstadt.

RATTENBERG 19C

Seen Camping Stadlerhof, 6233 Kramsach.
Tel 05337 63371, Fax 05337 65311.
English spoken.
OPEN: all year. SIZE: 3 ha, 110 pitches (all with elec, 30 statics), 10 hot showers, 16 WCs, 1 CWP. ⚓

Sauna, solarium, playground, entertainment.
PRICES: (1996) Caravan with family 338, Tent with two adults 223. CC: none.
Turn off motorway between Arlberg and Worgl at Rattenburg, and Kramsach is just north-west. The campsite is well signposted.

RAURIS 19C

Nationalpark-Camping Andrelwirt
Goldbergweg 3, 5661 Wörth.
Tel 06544 7168, Fax 06544 7184. English spoken.
OPEN: all year. SIZE: 2 ha, 100 pitches (all with elec), 15 hot showers, 15 WCs, 1 CWP.

Shop at 0.2 km. Restaurant at 0.2 km. Sauna, swimming pool 4 km.
PRICES: (1996) Caravan with family 300, Tent with two adults 200. CC: none.
From Salzburg go to Bischofshofen then through Schwarzach/St Veit, Taxenbach and Rauris to Wörth.

Austria

RIED 19C

Camping Dreiländereck Oberinntal, 6531 Ried.
Tel 05472 6571, Fax 05472 62947. English spoken.
OPEN: all year. SIZE: 1 ha, 80 pitches (all with elec,
20 statics), 12 hot showers (charge), 12 WCs,
1 CWP. ☎

Restaurant at 0.2 km. Baby-sittng service,
children's playground.
PRICES: Caravan with family 285,
Tent with two adults 200. CC: none.
15 km south of Landeck on route 315 towards
Switzerland and Italy.

ST JOHANN IM PONGAU 19C

Camping Wieshof 5600 St Johann im Pongau.
Tel 06412 8519, Fax 06412 82929. English spoken.
OPEN: all year. SIZE: 1.2 ha, 130 pitches (all with
elec, 50 statics), 7 hot showers, 9 WCs, 2 French
WCs, 1 CWP.

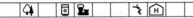

Shop at 0.4 km.
PRICES: (1996) Caravan with family 230,
Tent with two adults 180. CC: none.
Turn off the A10 south of Salzburg on the 311/S11
to St Johann im Pongau.

ST PÖLTEN 19B

Camping Kulmhof Kulmhof, 3160 Traisen.
Tel 02762 52900, Fax 02762 54391.
English spoken.
OPEN: all year. SIZE: 2 ha, 30 pitches (all with elec,
80 statics), 2 hot showers, 8 WCs, 1 CWP. ☎

Restaurant at 0.8 km.
PRICES: (1996) Caravan with family 220,
Tent with two adults 135. CC: none.
South from St Pölten on route 20, 15 km to
Traisen. Turn up hill by church.

Camping Kulmhof
near St Pölten
Camping-in-the-round on a green hill
that's NOT so far away!

Paradise Garden Höfnergraben 2, 2572 Kaumberg.
Tel 02765 388, Fax 02765 388. English spoken.
OPEN: 01/04–31/10. SIZE: 2 ha, 35 pitches (all with
elec, 65 statics), 4 hot showers (charge), 6 WCs,
2 CWPs. ☎

Shop at 3 km. Restaurant at 3 km.

PRICES: (1996) Caravan with family 180, Tent with
two adults 130. CC: none.
Take route 20 south for 15 km to Traisen and turn
left on to B18 towards Hainfeld. About 3 km east
of Kaumberg turn right and continue for 1 km to
campsite, which is signposted.

ST WOLFGANG 19B

Campingplatz Berau Schwarzenbach 16,
5360 St Wolfgang.
Tel 06138 2543, Fax 06138 254355. English spoken.
OPEN: all year. SIZE: 2 ha, 180 pitches (all with elec,
30 statics), 20 hot showers, 20 WCs, 2 CWPs. ☎ ♿

Restaurant at 0.5 km. Rooms and apartments
available.
PRICES: (1996) Caravan with family 403,
Tent with two adults 249. CC: none.
From Bad Ischl head towards Salzburg, turn right
in Strobl. Site is on left 2 km before St Wolfgang.

SALZBURG 19A

Camping Nord Sam Samstrasse 22A, 5023 Salzburg.
Tel 0662 660611. English spoken.
OPEN: 22/03–31/10. SIZE: 2 ha, 100 pitches
(all with elec), 8 hot showers, 9 WCs, 1 CWP.

PRICES: (1996) Caravan with family 298,
Tent with two adults 205. CC: none.
From Salzburg - Wien motorway, take the
Salzburg-Nord exit and follow the signs to
campsite (500 m).

Panorama Camping Stadblick
Rauchenbichlerstrasse 21, 5020 Salzburg.
Tel 0662 450652, Fax 0662 458018. English spoken.
OPEN: 20/03–15/11. SIZE: 1 ha, 70 pitches (all with
elec), 8 hot showers, 9 WCs, 1 CWP. ☎

PRICES: (1996) Caravan with family 250,
Tent with two adults 170. CC: none.

From A1 motorway (München-Wien) exit at
Salzburg Nord Zentrum. Turn towards the city

and turn right at the first lights, then follow signs to campsite.

Camping Schloss Aigen 5026 Salzburg-Aigen.
Tel 0662 622079. English spoken.
OPEN: 01/05–01/10. SIZE: 25 ha, 5 hot showers, 13 WCs, 1 CWP. ℓ

		⌖	R	⬛	🐌	☕	✕				

PRICES: (1996) Caravan with family 228,
Tent with two adults 155. CC: none.
From motorway take the Salzburg-Süd turning and go through Anif and Glasenbach to Salzburg-Aigen.

SCHARNITZ   19C

Camping Alm Innsbruckerstr 284, 6108 Scharnitz.
OPEN: 16/12–15/04 & 01/05–31/10. SIZE: 1 ha, 40 pitches (all with elec, 20 statics), 4 hot showers, 7 WCs, 1 CWP. ℓ

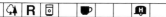

Shop at 0.5 km. Restaurant at 0.5 km. Children's activities.
PRICES: (1996) Caravan with family 214,
Tent with two adults 154. CC: none.
On the B177 between Innsbruck and Garmisch.

SCHWAZ   19C

Campingplatz Plankenhof
Pill 6, 6130 Pill bei Schwaz.
Tel 05242 641950, Fax 05242 72344. English spoken.
OPEN: 01/06–01/10. SIZE: 1 ha, 40 pitches (all with elec), 4 hot showers.

PRICES: (1996) Caravan with family 277, Tent with two adults 172. CC: Amex, Euro/Access, Visa.
Leave the main road at Schwaz and head towards Innsbruck. Pill is on the right 3 km beyond Schwaz and camp is signposted.

SEEBODEN   19D

Camping Ferienpark Lieseregg
Kras 27, 9871 Seeboden.
Tel 04762 2723, Fax 04762 33857. English spoken.
OPEN: 01/04–31/10. SIZE: 4 ha, 210 pitches (all with elec), 20 hot showers, 34 WCs, 2 CWPs. ℓ

PRICES: Caravan with family 403,
Tent with two adults 303. CC: none.
From the A10 Tauernautobahn, exit at Radenthein/Millstättersee. Turn right at the first lights and right again after 50 m. Follow signs from there.

SEEFELD   19C

Holiday Camping Reindlau 230 B, 6105 Leutasch.
Tel 05214 6570, Fax 05214 657030. English spoken.
OPEN: 07/05–05/11 & 07/12–20/04. SIZE: 3 ha, 120 pitches (all with elec), 17 hot showers, 20 WCs, 2 CWPs. ℓ ♿

∿	⛴	⌖	R	⬛	🐌	☕	✕	⤳	Ⓗ		

Heated indoor swimming pool; sauna.
PRICES: (1996) Caravan with family 400,
Tent with two adults 240. CC: none.
From Seefeld go north to Leutasch where the campsite is well signposted.

SPITAL AM PYHRN   19B

Air Campingplatz Pyhrn Priel
4582 Spital am Pyhrn.
Tel 07562 7066, Fax 07562 7192. English spoken.
OPEN: 01/04–31/10. SIZE: 1 ha, 35 pitches (58 with elec, 17 statics), 4 hot showers, 5 WCs, 1 CWP.

		⌖	R	⬛		☕					

Shop at 3 km. Restaurant at 3 km. 3 km from lake and swimming pool; on-site paragliding school.
PRICES: (1996) Caravan with family 310, Tent with two adults 175. CC: Euro/Access, Visa.
Follow signs to campsite in Spital.

SPITTAL   19D

Camping Waldbad 9772 Dellach im Drautal.
Tel 04714 288, Fax 04714 2343.
OPEN: 01/05–30/09. SIZE: 2 ha, 200 pitches (all with elec), 18 hot showers (charge), 25 WCs, 3 CWPs. ℓ ♿

		⌖		⬛	🐌	☕	✕	⤳			

Restaurant at 0.5 km. Children's playground, sports field.
PRICES: Caravan with family 330,
Tent with two adults 230. CC: none.
Take the A10 Tauernautobahn to Spittal and go 40 km towards Lienz and then to Dellach.

Draufluss Camping 9800 Spittal an der Drau.
Tel 04762 2466, Fax 04762 36299. English spoken.
OPEN: 01/04–31/10. SIZE: 1 ha, 100 pitches (all with elec), 6 hot showers, 11 WCs, 1 CWP. ♿

∿	⛴	⌖	R	⬛	🐌	☕	✕	⤳	Ⓗ		

Reduction for stay over 3 nights.
PRICES: Caravan with family 299,
Tent with two adults 179. CC: none.
The campsite is signposted in Spittal. From motorway, exit at Spittal-Ost.

TELFS   19C

Camping Eichenwald
Schiepstand weg 10, 6422 Stams.
Tel 05263 6159, Fax 05263 6159.
English spoken.
OPEN: 01/05–30/09. SIZE: 3 ha, 80 pitches (all with elec, 20 statics), 12 hot showers, 10 WCs, 1 CWP. ℓ ♿

☐ ⟨♨⟩ ⟨R⟩ ⟨🖬⟩ ⟨🛈⟩ ⟨🍳⟩ ⟨🏇⟩ ⟨H⟩ ☐ ☐

Walking trails and tennis nearby.
PRICES: (1996) Caravan with family 295.50,
Tent with two adults 189.10. CC: none.
*Take Stams/Mötz exit west of Telfs on A12.
Campsite is signposted after 1 km.*

UMHAUSEN 19C

Ötztal Arena Camp Krismer 6441 Umhausen.
Tel 05255 5390, Fax 05254 819633.
English spoken.
OPEN: all year. SIZE: 1 ha, 60 pitches (100 with
elec), 8 hot showers (charge), 16 WCs, 2 CWPs. ☎

☐ ⟨〜⟩ ⟨✈⟩ ⟨♀⟩ ⟨R⟩ ⟨🖬⟩ ☐ ⟨🛈⟩ ⟨🍳⟩ ☐ ☐

Shop at 0.2 km. Quiet; excellent children's
activities; skiing in winter.
PRICES: (1996) Caravan with family 300,
Tent with two adults 200. CC: none.
*(Highly recommended). Take the Ötztal Valley
exit from the Imst-Innsbruck motorway and
Umhausen is 13 km towards Solden. Well
signposted in the village.*

UNTERACH 19B

Insel Camping 4866 Unterach am Attersee.
Tel 07665 8311. English spoken.
OPEN: 15/05–15/09. SIZE: 1.8 ha, 100 pitches
(all with elec, 45 statics), 8 hot showers
(charge), 22 WCs.

☐ ⟨〜⟩ ⟨✈⟩ ⟨♨⟩ ☐ ⟨🖬⟩ ⟨🛥⟩ ☐ ☐ ☐

Shop at 0.02 km. Restaurant at 0.4 km.
PRICES: (1996) Caravan with family 242,
Tent with two adults 171. CC: none.
Follow directions to campsite in Unterach.

VELDEN 19D

Camping Weisses Rössl Auen 47,
9535 Auen-Schiefling.
Tel 04274 2898, Fax 04274 28984. English spoken.
OPEN: 01/05–30/09. SIZE: 3 ha, 150 pitches
(50 with elec), 10 hot showers, 18 WCs, 1 CWP. ☎

☐ ⟨〜⟩ ⟨✈⟩ ⟨♨⟩ ⟨R⟩ ⟨🖬⟩ ⟨🛥⟩ ☐ ⟨🍳⟩ ☐ ⟨H⟩ ☐

Golf 1 km.
PRICES: (1996) Caravan with family 362,
Tent with two adults 237. CC: none.
*From the motorway, exit at Velden-Wörthersee
and then go towards Maria Wörth for approx
6 km. From Klagenfurt, go towards Maria Wörth,
and then a further 6 km towards Velden.*

Campingplatz Bruckler-Sud
9074 Keutschach am See.
Tel 04273 2773, Fax 04273 27734. English spoken.
OPEN: 01/05–25/09. SIZE: 2 ha, 180 pitches
(all with elec, 40 statics), 8 hot showers (charge),
17 WCs, 2 CWPs. ☎

☐ ⟨〜⟩ ⟨🛥⟩ ⟨♨⟩ ☐ ⟨🖬⟩ ⟨🛥⟩ ⟨🛈⟩ ⟨🍳⟩ ☐ ☐

PRICES: (1996) Caravan with family 347,
Tent with two adults 227. CC: none.
*From Velden go to Keutschach Seental. By Gasthof
Brückler turn to the south side of the lake; campsite
is about 900 m ahead and well signposted.*

FKK Camping Mullerhof
Dobein 10, 9074 Keutschach am See.
Tel 04273 2517, Fax 04273 25175. English spoken.
OPEN: 01/05–30/09. SIZE: 6 ha, 300 pitches (all with
elec, 20 statics), 20 hot showers, 45 WCs, 2 CWPs. ☎

☐ ⟨〜⟩ ⟨🛥⟩ ⟨♨⟩ ⟨R⟩ ⟨🖬⟩ ⟨🛥⟩ ☐ ⟨🍳⟩ ☐ ⟨🏇⟩ ☐

Naturist site; sauna, massage; children's plaground.
PRICES: Caravan with family 390,
Tent with two adults 265. CC: none.
*From Velden/Wörthersee go through Schiefling
am See to Keutschach am See.*

VILLACH 19D

Camping Gerli St Georgenerstr 170, 9500 Villach.
Tel 04242 57402. English spoken.
OPEN: all year. SIZE: 2 ha, 80 pitches (all with elec),
7 hot showers, 25 WCs, 7 CWPs. ♿

☐ ☐ ⟨♨⟩ ⟨R⟩ ⟨🖬⟩ ⟨🛥⟩ ⟨🛈⟩ ⟨🍳⟩ ⟨🏇⟩ ⟨H⟩ ☐

Shop at 1 km. Mini-golf, children's playground;
musical entertainment.
PRICES: Caravan with family 302,
Tent with two adults 191. CC: none.
*From motorway, exit at Villach-West and go
towards Italy. The campsite is signposted.*

Camping Mittewald Fuchsbichlweg 9,
9580 Drobollach.
Tel 04242 37392, Fax 04242 373928. English spoken.
OPEN: all year. SIZE: 3 ha, 95 pitches (all with elec,
30 statics), 10 hot showers, 21 WCs, 1 CWP. ☎ ♿

☐ ⟨♨⟩ ⟨R⟩ ⟨🖬⟩ ⟨🛥⟩ ⟨🛈⟩ ⟨🍳⟩ ⟨🏇⟩ ⟨H⟩ ☐

PRICES: Caravan with family 297,
Tent with two adults 185. CC: none.
*From Halien motorway exit at Maria-Gail and go
to Drobollach and then Faaker See.*

Komfort-Camping Poglitsch 9583 Faak am See.
Tel 04254 2718, Fax 04254 4144. English spoken.
OPEN: 20/03–31/10. SIZE: 7 ha, 20 hot showers,
40 WCs, 32 French WCs, 3 CWPs. ☎ ♿

☐ ⟨〜⟩ ⟨🛥⟩ ⟨♨⟩ ⟨R⟩ ⟨🖬⟩ ⟨🛥⟩ ⟨🛈⟩ ⟨🍳⟩ ☐ ⟨H⟩ ☐ ⟨🏍⟩

Disco.
PRICES: (1996) Caravan with family 442,
Tent with two adults 286. CC: none.
*From Villach go to Lake Faak and campsite is
near the church in village of Faak am See.*

WEISSBRIACH 19C

Camping Knaller Techendorf 16, 9762 Weissensee.
Tel 04713 223450, Fax 04713 223411. English spoken.

OPEN: 01/05–31/10. SIZE: 1.5 ha, 180 pitches (all with elec, 5 statics), 8 hot showers, 50 WCs, 1 CWP.

PRICES: (1996) Caravan with family 310, Tent with two adults 210. CC: none.
From Weissbriach go north on route 87 towards Greifenburg. Take right turn to Weissensee and Techendorf, left over bridge and follow signs.

WERFEN   19C

Camping Vierthaler 5452 Werfen.
Tel 06468 657, Fax 06468 657/4. English spoken.
OPEN: 15/04–30/09. SIZE: 1 ha, 60 pitches (all with elec), 3 hot showers (charge), 6 WCs, 1 CWP. ⚓

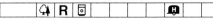

Swimming pool 2 km.
PRICES: Caravan with family 195,
Tent with two adults 140. CC: none.
Take Werfen exit from A10 and follow B159 south towards Bischofshofen for 2 km. Campsite is signposted to the left.

WIEN (VIENNA)   19B

Camping Krackingberg Kracking,
3443 Pressbaum.
Tel 02274 8344. English spoken.
OPEN: all year. SIZE: 2 ha, 40 pitches (all with elec, 20 statics), 5 hot showers, 8 WCs, 2 CWPs.

Shop at 2 km. Restaurant at 2 km. Playground.
PRICES: (1996) Caravan with family 240,
Tent with two adults 150. CC: none.
From the Westautobahn A1, exit at Pressbaum and go 1 km towards Wien, then turn left towards Sieghartskirchen. After going through Tierolersiedlung turn left and go 1 km to campsite.

Camping Wienerwald Stangau, Leopoldipasse 2, 2392 Sulz in Wienerwald.
Tel 02238 8448.
OPEN: 15/04–15/10. SIZE: 1 ha, 40 pitches (all with elec), 4 hot showers, 5 WCs, 1 CWP. ⚓

Shop at 0.7 km. Restaurant at 0.6 km.
PRICES: (1996) Caravan with family 215,
Tent with two adults 150. CC: none.
South of Wien on A21, exit Heiligen Kreuz, then follow signs to Sittendorf and on to Sulz.

WÖRGL   19C

Panorama Camping 6363 Westendorf.
Tel 05334 6166, Fax 05334 6843. English spoken.
OPEN: all year. SIZE: 2 ha, 145 pitches (all with elec, 145 statics), 18 hot showers, 20 WCs, 1 CWP. ⚓ ♿

Sauna, solarium, fitness room.

Swimming pool and paragliding nearby.
PRICES: (1996) Caravan with family 318,
Tent with two adults 230. CC: none.
From the München-Innsbruck motorway take the Wörgl-Ost exit and go towards Brixental (14 km). Drive through Hopfgarten, next village is Westendorf. Campsite is just before Westendorf village on the right.

Schlossberg Itter 140, 6361 Hopfgarten.
Tel 05335 2181, Fax 05335 2182. English spoken.
OPEN: all year. SIZE: 4 ha, 150 pitches (all with elec, 50 statics), 18 hot showers, 23 WCs, 2 CWPs. ⚓ ♿

Children's playground, large sports field.
PRICES: (1996) Caravan with family 349,
Tent with two adults 226. CC: none.
From München to Innsbruck motorway, exit at Wörgl-Ost and take B312 signposted Felbertauern for 4 km. Turn right at signpost to Brixental, then left for Hopfgarten. Site on left after 2 km.

ZELL AM SEE   19C

Seecamp Thumerbachstrasse 34, 5700 Zell am See.
Tel 06542 2115, Fax 06542 211515. English spoken.
OPEN: all year. SIZE: 3 ha, 126 pitches (all with elec, 10 statics), 24 hot showers, 32 WCs, 1 CWP. ⚓ ♿

PRICES: Caravan with family 360, Tent with two adults 250. CC: Amex, Euro/Access, Visa.
On the B311 from Lofer to Zell am See, turn towards Thumersbach.

ZELL AM ZILLER   19C

Camping Aufenfeld Distelberg 1,
6274 Aschau im Zillertal.
Tel 05282 2916, Fax 05282 291611. English spoken.
OPEN: 02/12–04/11. SIZE: 4 ha, 150 pitches (all with elec, 50 statics), 31 hot showers, 34 WCs, 2 CWPs. ⚓

Indoor pool, tennis, sauna and solarium, riding.
PRICES: (1996) Caravan with family 340,
Tent with two adults 221. CC: none.
Aschau im Zillertal is just north of Zell am Ziller on B169. Campsite is well signposted.

Camping Hofer Gerlosstr 33, 6280 Zell am Ziller.
Tel 05282 2248, Fax 05282 22488. English spoken.
OPEN: all year. SIZE: 1 ha, 100 pitches (all with elec), 8 hot showers, 11 WCs, 1 CWP. ⚓

Recently updated site; choice of organised activities to suit all tastes.
PRICES: (1996) Caravan with family 283,
Tent with two adults 186. CC: none.
From Schwaz going towards Inntal, turn off at Strass and go south to Zell am Ziller.

Austria

BELGIUM

Belgium consists of two quite distinct parts, geographically and culturally.

Flemish-speaking Flanders in the north is mostly very low-lying, protected from the North Sea by man-made sea defences and sand dunes. Its best known towns are Bruges, a city of canals whose medieval heart is best seen by boat, Ghent, centre of the famous Flemish wool trade in the 13th and 14th centuries and Antwerp, centre of the world diamond trade – as well as birthplace of Rubens and Van Dyck.

Southern Belgium is called Wallonia and here the main language is French. Compared with Flanders, Wallonia is mountainous, rising to some 694 m near the German border!

Centre-stage between Flanders and Wallonia, Brussels is home to the European Commission. The *Grand-Place*, lined with fine guild houses, and decorated by a daily flower market, is considered by many to be one of Europe's finest squares. Ample museums, cafés to dally in, everywhere little parks, and plenty of places to buy the excellent chocolates for which Belgium is so famous.

Emergency numbers

Police 101

Fire Brigade & Ambulance 100

Warning information

Warning triangle must be carried

Blood alcohol legal limit 50 mg

Every parent will agree that the one thing that can make – or break – a holiday, is the contented – or otherwise – child. The Belgians have accordingly set about enhancing the chances of family harmony by providing a very generous scattering of theme parks...Aqualibi and Walibi near Brussels, Bobbejaanland near Antwerp, and Bellewaerde near Ypres, to name a few.

ARLON 7D

Camp-Caravan de la Vallée de Rabais
rue du Bonlieu, 6760 Virton.
Tel 086 322717, Fax 086 322882. English spoken.
OPEN: all year. SIZE: 8 ha, 250 pitches (all with elec, 50 statics), 24 hot showers, 24 WCs, 1 CWP.

Shop at 2 km. Restaurant at 0.2 km. Playground.
PRICES: (1996) Caravan with family 680,
Tent with two adults 560. CC: none.
South-west of Arlon on route 82.

Camping Portail de la Forêt
6720 Habay-La-Neuve.
Tel 063 422312, Fax 063 422312. English spoken.
OPEN: 01/02–15/12. SIZE: 4 ha, 120 pitches (all with elec, 70 statics), 6 hot showers, 14 WCs, 2 CWPs.

PRICES: (1996) Caravan with family 550,
Tent with two adults 360. CC: none.
From Arlon take N40 to Habay-La-Neuve and follow signs.

Camping Sud 61 rue de la Libération, 6717 Attert.
Tel 063 223715, Fax 063 223715. English spoken.
OPEN: 01/04–01/11. SIZE: 2 ha, 80 pitches (60 with elec), 4 hot showers, 8 WCs, 2 CWPs.

PRICES: (1996) Caravan with family 735,
Tent with two adults 445. CC: none.
From Arlon take N4 to Attert. Follow signs to campsite.

BASTOGNE 7D

Pont de Berguème rue Berguème 9,
6970 Tenneville.
Tel 084 455443, Fax 084 456231. English spoken.
OPEN: all year. SIZE: 3 ha, 120 pitches (all with elec, 70 statics), 7 hot showers (charge), 24 WCs, 1 CWP.

Restaurant at 2 km.
PRICES: (1996) Caravan with family 490,
Tent with two adults 290. CC: Euro/Access, Visa.
From Bastogne take N4 north-west to Tenneville and follow signs to campsite.

BELOEIL 7A

Camping de l'Orangerie rue du Major 3,
7972 Beloeil.
Tel 069 689190, Fax 069 688782.
OPEN: 09/04–31/10. SIZE: 3 ha, 170 pitches

(150 with elec, 130 statics), 4 hot showers (charge), 18 WCs, 2 CWPs.

Shop at 1 km. Restaurant at 1 km.
PRICES: (1996) Caravan with family 500,
Tent with two adults 300. CC: none.
Follow signs in town centre.

BERTRIX 7D

Info-Camping Bertrix route de Mortehan,
6880 Bertrix.
Tel 061 412281, Fax 061 412588. English spoken.
OPEN: 25/03–12/11. SIZE: 14 ha, 500 pitches
(all with elec, 10 statics), 22 hot showers, 40 WCs,
5 CWPs. ℃ �&

Entertainment.
PRICES: Caravan with family 880,
Tent with two adults 880. CC: none.
Follow signs from Bertrix to campsite.

BLANKENBERGE 7A

Camping Dallas A Ruzettelaan 191,
8370 Blankenberge.
Tel 050 418157, Fax 050 429479. English spoken.
OPEN: 15/03–25/09. SIZE: 3 ha, 200 pitches
(all with elec, 60 statics), 14 hot showers (charge),
22 WCs, 7 French WCs, 1 CWP.

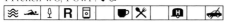

Restaurant at 0.7 km.
PRICES: (1996) Caravan with family 690. CC: none.
*Take coast road from Blankenberge to Zeebrugge
and follow signs to campsite which is on the
beach, 15 km from Brugge.*

Camping Jamboree BVBA Popelier, Polderlaan
52, 8370 Blankenberge.
Tel 050 414545, Fax 050 414545. English spoken.
OPEN: 15/03–15/11. SIZE: 5 ha, 40 pitches (all with
elec, 300 statics), 8 hot showers (charge), 35 WCs,
1 French WC, 1 CWP. ℃ ㅐ

Shop at 0.05 km. Playground, children's farm.
PRICES: (1996) Caravan with family 950,
Tent with two adults 560. CC: none.
*From railway station turn right, go past the
supermarket (on the right) and follow signs to
campsite from there.*

BRUGGE (BRUGES) 7A

Camping St Michiels Tillegemstraat,
8200 St-Michiels.
Tel 050 380819. English spoken.
OPEN: all year. SIZE: 6 ha, 300 pitches (200 with
elec, 60 statics), 30 hot showers, 30 WCs,
1 CWP. ㅐ

PRICES: (1996) Caravan with family 670,
Tent with two adults 540. CC: Euro/Access, Visa.
1.5 km from Brugge station, towards Loppem.

BRUXELLES (BRUSSELS) 7A

Camping Grimbergen Veldtkanstraat 64,
1850 Grimbergen.
Tel 0270 9597, Fax 0270 9597.
English spoken.
OPEN: 01/04–31/10. SIZE: 2 ha, 50 pitches (40 with
elec), 10 hot showers, 8 WCs, 1 CWP. ℃

Shop at 1 km. Restaurant at 0.05 km.
PRICES: (1996) Caravan with family 480,
Tent with two adults 350. CC: none.
*From ring road north of Bruxelles, take exit 7 for
Grimbergen town centre.*

Diepvennen 100 Autostrade A12,
1840 Londerzeel.
Tel 052 309492, Fax 052 305716.
English spoken.
OPEN: all year. SIZE: 11 ha, 190 pitches (all with
elec, 150 statics), 10 hot showers (charge),
20 WCs, 4 CWPs. ㅐ

Tennis, fishing, pétanque, playground.
PRICES: Caravan with family 850, Tent with two
adults 530. CC: Euro/Access, Visa.

From Bruxelles take A12 north to Londerzeel.

Kamping Provincial Domein Prov Domein 6,
1654 Huizingen.
Tel 023 830026, Fax 023 830026.
English spoken.
OPEN: 15/03–30/09. SIZE: 2 ha, 80 pitches (all with
elec), 4 hot showers, 22 WCs, 1 CWP. ℃

Shop at 0.5 km. Restaurant at 0.4 km.
PRICES: (1996) Caravan with family 220,
Tent with two adults 150. CC: none.
*From Bruxelles go south on E19. Take exit 15,
then go right, right again and left.*

Belgium

DIEST 7B

Camping Kasteel Meerlaer Verboekt 105,
Vorst Meerlaer, 2430 Laakdal.
Tel 013 661420, Fax 013 667512. English spoken.
OPEN: all year. SIZE: 8 ha, 25 pitches (all with elec,
148 statics), 8 hot showers (charge), 14 WCs,
1 CWP. ℓ

Shop at 1 km. Restaurant at 2 km. 10% discount for
RAC members.
PRICES: (1996) Caravan with family 405,
Tent with two adults 240. CC: none.
*From Diest go north on N127 towards Laakdal.
Turn right at roundabout on to the 141 as far as
Vorst Meerlaer church and then follow signs.*

DINANT 7D

Camping de Crève Coeur rue Cardinal Mercier,
Bouvignes Dinant, 5500 Bouvignes.
Tel 082 223586. English spoken.
OPEN: 01/05–30/09. SIZE: 1 ha, 26 pitches (all with
elec, 20 statics), 2 hot showers (charge), 4 WCs,
2 CWPs. ℓ

Shop at 0.5 km. Restaurant at 2.5 km.
PRICES: (1996) Caravan with family 350,
Tent with two adults 230. CC: none.
*From Dinant go north on N96 to Bouvignes. Turn
left towards Sommière. Campsite is 700 m on left.*

Camping du Bocq av de la Vallée, 5530 Yvoir.
Tel 082 612269. English spoken.
OPEN: 01/04–30/09. SIZE: 2 ha, 80 pitches (all with
elec), 4 hot showers (charge), 1 CWP.

Shop at 1.7 km.
PRICES: (1996) Caravan with family 610,
Tent with two adults 360. CC: none.
*Leave autoroute at exit 19 for Yvoir. Follow signs
for campsite in town.*

Camping Le Quesval chaussée de Dinant,
5530 Spontin.
Tel 083 699331. English spoken.
OPEN: 01/04–30/09. SIZE: 4 ha, 80 pitches (all with
elec, 40 statics), 2 hot showers (charge), 8 WCs,
3 CWPs.

Shop at 0.5 km.
PRICES: (1996) Caravan with family 400,
Tent with two adults 350. CC: none.
*From E411 take exit 19 towards Spontin. Follow
signs to campsite.*

EGHEZEE 7B

Camping du Manoir de Là-Bas route de
Gembloux 180, 5310 Aische-en-Refail.

Tel 081 655353. English spoken.
OPEN: 01/04–30/10. SIZE: 22 ha, 600 pitches
(all with elec), 14 hot showers (charge), 74 WCs,
3 CWPs.

Shop at 0.5 km. Tennis.
PRICES: (1996) Caravan with family 405,
Tent with two adults 225. CC: none.
*From E411 take exit no 12 towards Eghezée and
follow signs.*

EUPEN 7B

Camping Wesertal rue de l'Invasion 66-68,
4837 Membach.
Tel 087 555961, Fax 087 556555. English spoken.
OPEN: all year. SIZE: 55 pitches (all with elec,
10 statics), 6 hot showers, 8 WCs, 1 CWP. ℓ

Shop at 3 km. Restaurant at 0.3 km. Sauna, salt-
water pool, solarium.
PRICES: (1996) Caravan with family 470,
Tent with two adults 325. CC: none.
*From E40 (A3) take exit 38 for Eupen. Campsite
signposted from there.*

GENT 7A

Camping Blaarmeersen Zuiderlaan 12,
Watersportlaan, 9000 Gent.
Tel 092 215399, Fax 092 208228. English spoken.
OPEN: 01/03–15/10. SIZE: 7 ha, 224 pitches
(206 with elec), 33 hot showers, 50 WCs, 4 CWPs.
ℓ &

PRICES: (1996) Caravan with family 595,
Tent with two adults 435. CC: Euro/Access, Visa.
*From Gent town centre head towards Drongen
(E40 Ostend road) and follow signs to campsite.*

Camping Cante Claer 9630 Munkzwalm.
Tel 055 499688, Fax 055 499688. English spoken.
OPEN: all year. SIZE: 4 ha, 40 pitches (all with elec,
150 statics), 4 hot showers, 14 WCs, 1 CWP. ℓ

Shop at 0.6 km.
PRICES: (1996) Caravan with family 380,
Tent with two adults 260. CC: none.
*From Zeebrugge go to Gent then take R4 to
Merelbeke, Brakel and Zwalm. Follow directions
to campsite from Zwalm.*

Groeneveld 9800 Bachte-Maria-Leerne.
Tel 093 801014, Fax 093 801760. English spoken.
OPEN: 19/03–11/11. SIZE: 2 ha, 100 pitches
(all with elec, 25 statics), 2 hot showers, 6 WCs,
3 French WCs, 1 CWP. ℓ

Shop at 1 km. Restaurant at 1 km.

PRICES: (1996) Caravan with family 545, Tent with two adults 360. CC: none.
Take exit 13 from E40. Campsite is then 5 km and well signposted.

GERAARDSBERGEN 7A

VZW Prov Domein de Gavers Onkerzelestraat 280, 9500 Geraardsbergen.
Tel 054 416324, Fax 054 410388. English spoken.
OPEN: all year. SIZE: 10 ha, 367 pitches (290 statics), 36 hot showers (charge), 42 WCs, 4 CWPs.

Shop at 1 km.
PRICES: (1996) Caravan with family 470, Tent with two adults 470. CC: Visa.
From Geraardsbergen go towards Onkerzele and follow signs to campsite.

HOUTHALEN 7B

Camping Hengelhoef Tulpenstraat 1, 3530 Houthalen.
Tel 089 380166, Fax 089 386940. English spoken.
OPEN: 01/04–11/11. SIZE: 8 ha, 540 pitches (all with elec, 450 statics), 35 hot showers, 54 WCs, 24 French WCs, 5 CWPs.

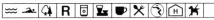

Sub-tropical pool (chargeable) as well as free outdoor pool.
PRICES: (1996) Caravan with family 785, Tent with two adults 725. CC: none.
From E314, take exit 30.

Vakantiecentrum de Lage Kempen
Kiefheelistraat 19, 3941 Eksel.
Tel 011 402243, Fax 011 348812. English spoken.
OPEN: 01/04–22/10. SIZE: 4 ha, 77 pitches (65 with elec, 5 statics), 4 hot showers (charge), 8 WCs, 3 French WCs.

Bicycle hire, volley ball, mini-golf, boules.
PRICES: (1996) Caravan with family 670, Tent with two adults 490. CC: none.
From Houthalen take N74/N715 beyond Hechtel-Eksel. Exit for Kerkhoven and campsite is signposted on left after 3.5 km.

HUY 7B/D

Camping l'Hirondelle 4210 Oteppe.
Tel 085 711131, Fax 085 711021. English spoken.
OPEN: 01/04–31/10. SIZE: 50 ha, 1100 pitches (all with elec, 700 statics), 24 hot showers, 120 WCs, 5 CWPs.

Tennis, trout fishing, barbecue, games, luna park.
PRICES: (1996) Caravan with family 800, Tent with two adults 520. CC: Visa.
Between E40 (exit 27/28) and E42 (exit 10).

KNOKKE-HEIST 7A

Camping du Vuurtoren Heistlaan 168, 8301 Knokke-Heist-aan-Zee.
Tel 050 511782. English spoken.
OPEN: 15/03–15/10. SIZE: 6 ha, 350 pitches (all with elec, 275 statics), 10 hot showers (charge), 21 WCs, 2 CWPs.

PRICES: (1996) Caravan with family 770, Tent with two adults 460. CC: none.
From Zeebrugge take N34 Heist-aan-Zee, then right on to N300. Campsite is 700 m from sea.

LEUVEN 7B

Ter Munck Kampingweg, 3001 Heverlee.
Tel 016 238668. English spoken.
OPEN: 12/06–10/09. SIZE: 3 ha, 50 pitches (all with elec), 2 hot showers (charge), 6 WCs, 1 CWP.

Shop at 1 km. Restaurant at 1 km.
PRICES: (1996) Caravan with family 430, Tent with two adults 360. CC: none.
Leave E40 at crossing with A2. Follow Leuven sign then left at first traffic lights (Terbank) and immediately (30 m) left again. Signposted.

LIEGE 7B

Camping les Murets chemin d'Enonck 57, 4130 Hony.
Tel 041 801987, Fax 041 801987.
English spoken.
OPEN: 01/04–01/11. SIZE: 1.6 ha, 92 pitches (40 with elec, 20 statics), 5 hot showers (charge), 10 WCs, 1 CWP.

Shop at 1 km. Restaurant at 1 km.
PRICES: (1996) Caravan with family 510, Tent with two adults 310. CC: none.
From Liège, following signs to Les Ardennes, go south on N633 to Hony. Pass the bridge and follow main road to the left.

MALMEDY 7D

Camping Familial rue des Bruyères 19, 4960 Arimont-Malmédy.
Tel 080 330862. English spoken.
OPEN: all year. SIZE: 2.2 ha, 102 pitches (all with elec, 70 statics), 6 hot showers (charge), 20 WCs, 2 CWPs.

PRICES: Caravan with family 535, Tent with two adults 325. CC: none.
From centre of Malmédy follow signs to St-Vith, then follow campsite signs.

Belgium

MARCHE-EN-FAMENNE   7D

Euro-Camping Paola rue de Panorama 10,
6900 Marche-en-Famenne.
Tel 084 311704. English spoken.
OPEN: all year. SIZE: 13 ha, 265 pitches (220 with
elec, 200 statics), 3 hot showers (charge), 21 WCs,
3 French WCs, 2 CWPs. ℓ

		♀	R			●				

Shop at 1 km. Restaurant at 1 km.
PRICES: Caravan with family 370,
Tent with two adults 330. CC: none.
From Marche-en-Famenne go north-east on N86
towards Hotton. At cemetery turn right and then
left. Well signposted.

MIDDELKERKE   7A

Camping Albatros Koninklijke Baan 160,
8434 Westende.
Tel 058 233963, Fax 058 232855.
English spoken.
OPEN: 01/04–30/09. SIZE: 8 ha, 335 pitches
(all with elec, 250 statics), 16 hot showers
(charge), 40 WCs, 1 French WC, 2 CWPs. ℓ

		♀		ō	♨	●	✕		⊞		⇛

Tennis; sea 30 m.
PRICES: (1996) Caravan with family 725,
Tent with two adults 525. CC: none.
Take N318 to Westende. Campsite is on left,
signposted.

Camping Westende Westendelaan 341,
8434 Westende.
Tel 058 233254, Fax 058 233254.
English spoken.
OPEN: 15/03–30/09. SIZE: 5 ha, 60 pitches
(all with elec, 300 statics), 9 hot showers,
20 WCs, 2 CWPs. ℓ ⅚

		♀		ō	♨		✕	⌇	⌂	

Sea 1 km.
PRICES: (1996) Caravan with family 760,
Tent with two adults 550. CC: none.
Take N318 to Westende. Campsite is 100 m before
church on the right. Signposted.

MONS   7A

Camping du Waux-Hall av St-Pierre,
7000 Mons.
Tel 065 337923, Fax 065 356336.
English spoken.
OPEN: all year. SIZE: 1.44 ha, 75 pitches (all with
elec), 6 hot showers (charge), 8 WCs, 1 CWP. ℓ

~	✖	♨♨	R		ō					

Shop at 0.5 km. Restaurant at 0.6 km. Direct access
to Waux-Hall park; swimming pool 500 m.
PRICES: Caravan with family 338,
Tent with two adults 251. CC: none.

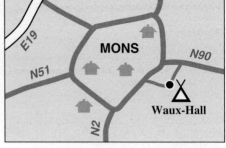

From Mons take inner ring road N90 towards
Binche. Campsite is well signposted just before
Waux-Hall public park.

NAMUR   7B/D

Camping les Trieux 5020 Malonne.
Tel 081 445583, Fax 081 308023.
OPEN: 01/04–31/10. SIZE: 2 ha, 64 pitches (all with
elec, 10 statics), 4 hot showers, 10 WCs, 1 CWP. ℓ

		♀	R	ō	ⓩ			⊞	

Shop at 0.3 km. Restaurant at 1 km.
PRICES: (1996) Caravan with family 550,
Tent with two adults 360. CC: none.

NEUFCHATEAU   7D

Camping du Lac route de Florenville,
6840 Neufchâteau.
Tel 061 277615. English spoken.
OPEN: all year. SIZE: 6 ha, 148 pitches (all with elec,
20 statics), 4 hot showers (charge), 4 WCs,
1 CWP. ℓ ⅚

≈	✖	♀	R	ō	♨	●		⌇	⊞	

Shop at 2 km. Restaurant at 1 km.
PRICES: (1996) Caravan with family 282,
Tent with two adults 186. CC: none.
From Neufchâteau take N85 towards Florenville
and follow signs to campsite.

NIEUWPOORT   7A

Camping de Lombarde Duinendorp
Elisabethlaan 4, 8434 Lombardsyde.
Tel 058 236839, Fax 058 239908. English spoken.
OPEN: 21/03–11/11. SIZE: 9 ha, 370 pitches (all
with elec), 21 hot showers, 30 WCs, 8 CWPs. ℓ ⅚

≈	✖	⚄	R	ō	♨	●	✕		⌂		⇛

PRICES: (1996) Caravan with family 695,
Tent with two adults 695. CC: none.
From Nieuwpoort take N34 towards Oostende for
1 km. Campsite on right, follow signs.

Camping Zomerzon Elizabethlaan 1,
8434 Lombardsyde.
Tel 058 237396. English spoken.

OPEN: 29/03–31/10. SIZE: 10 ha, 300 pitches
(all with elec, 70 statics), 30 hot showers, 30 WCs,
2 CWPs.

Shop at 0.2 km. Restaurant at 0.2 km.
PRICES: unavailable. CC: none.
*From Nieuwpoort take N318 to Lombardsyde and
follow signs to campsite.*

IC Camping Brugsesteenweg 49,
8620 Nieuwpoort.
Tel 058 236037, Fax 058 232682. English spoken.
OPEN: 28/03–12/11. SIZE: 24 ha, 887 pitches
(all with elec), 70 hot showers, 130 WCs,
6 CWPs. ⌖ &

Shop at 2 km. Restaurant at 2 km.
PRICES: (1996) Caravan with family 970. CC: none.
*From the centre of Nieuwpoort, head towards
Oostende/Brugge, bear right towards Oudenburg,
pass over several canals then sharp right towards
St-Joris. Site on left.*

OOSTENDE (OSTEND)　　　7A

Camping Thalassa Duinenstraat 108,
8450 Bredene.
Tel 059 323120, Fax 059 320594. English spoken.
OPEN: all year. SIZE: 4 ha, 60 pitches (all with elec,
100 statics), 6 hot showers, 8 WCs, 1 CWP. ⌖ &

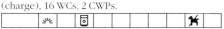

Shop at 0.5 km. Restaurant at 0.5 km.
PRICES: (1996) Caravan with family 550,
Tent with two adults 450. CC: none.
*Follow the main road between Bredene-Duinen
and Bredene-Dorp for 700 m.*

Camping Tropical Bredeweg 76a,
8420 De-Haan.
Tel 059 236341, Fax 059 236341.
English spoken.
OPEN: 01/04–30/09. SIZE: 3 ha, 150 pitches
(100 with elec, 50 statics), 10 hot showers
(charge), 16 WCs, 2 CWPs.

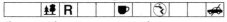

Shop at 0.2 km. Restaurant at 0.2 km.
PRICES: (1996) Caravan with family 720,
Tent with two adults 550. CC: none.
*From Oostende take N34 towards Blankenberge.
Follow signs to campsite.*

OUDENAARDE　　　7A

T Populierenhof Stationstraat 8, 9890 Gavère.
Tel 093 841429. English spoken.
OPEN: 01/04–30/09. SIZE: 1 ha, 40 pitches (all with
elec), 1 hot shower (charge), 8 WCs, 2 CWPs.

Shop at 0.3 km. Restaurant at 0.2 km.
PRICES: (1996) Caravan with family 340, Tent with
two adults 260. CC: none.
*From Oudenaarde go north on N60 and take exit
for Gavère.*

LA ROCHE-EN-ARDENNE　　　7D

Camping Lohan route de Houffalize 20a,
6980 La Roche-en-Ardenne.
Tel 084 411545. English spoken.
OPEN: 01/04–01/11. SIZE: 4 ha, 69 pitches
(180 with elec, 130 statics), 12 hot showers
(charge), 23 WCs, 23 French WCs, 2 CWPs. ⌖

Fishing, canoeing, playground.
PRICES: (1996) Caravan with family 550,
Tent with two adults 370. CC: none.
*From La Roche-en-Ardenne take N860 towards
Houffalize for 3 km.*

ROCHEFORT　　　7D

Camping Le Roptai rue Roptai 34,
5580 Ave et Auffe.
Tel 084 388319, Fax 084 387327.
English spoken.
OPEN: 01/02–31/12. SIZE: 10 ha, 330 pitches
(290 with elec, 220 statics), 11 hot showers
(charge), 35 WCs, 3 French WCs, 3 CWPs. ⌖

Entertainment in HS, table tennis, playground;
caves and Han-sur-Lesse 4 km.
PRICES: (1996) Caravan with family 585, Tent with
two adults 355. CC: Euro/Access, Visa.
*Take exit 23 from E411 and campsite is 2 km, on
the road to Han-sur-Lesse and well signposted.*

ST-NIKLAAS　　　7A

Camping Reinaert Lunterbergstraat 4,
9190 Stekene.
Tel 037 798525. English spoken.
OPEN: all year. SIZE: 135 pitches (all with elec),
4 hot showers, 14 WCs, 1 CWP.

Shop at 0.5 km. Restaurant at 4 km.
PRICES: (1996) Caravan with family 330,
Tent with two adults 270. CC: none.
*From St-Niklaas head towards Hulst on N60. After
10 km turn left to Stekene, then on towards
Moerbeke. Site on left.*

SPA　　　7B

Parc des Sources rue de la Sauvenière 141,
4900 Spa.
Tel 087 772311. English spoken.
OPEN: 01/04–31/10. SIZE: 3 ha, 110 pitches
(80 with elec, 70 statics), 8 hot showers, 18 WCs,
1 French WC, 1 CWP. ⌖

Belgium

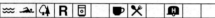

Shop at 1 km. Restaurant at 1 km.
PRICES: (1996) Caravan with family 610,
Tent with two adults 395. CC: none.
From Spa go south towards Malmédy for 1.5 km. Signposted.

TINTIGNY 7D

Camping Chênefleur 6730 Tintigny.
Tel 063 444078, Fax 063 444078. English spoken.
OPEN: 01/04–15/10. SIZE: 6 ha, 93 pitches (42 with elec, 60 statics), 12 hot showers, 20 WCs, 2 CWPs. ☏

Shop at 0.2 km. Restaurant at 0.2 km. Fishing, kayaking.
PRICES: (1996) Caravan with family 580,
Tent with two adults 370. CC: none.
From E411/E25 take exit 28B towards Habay-la-Neuve, Etalle and Tintigny. Follow signs in Tintigny.

TURNHOUT 7B

Baalse Hei 't Groene Caravanpark
Roodhuisstraat 10, 2300 Turnhout.
Tel 014 421931, Fax 014 420853. English spoken.
OPEN: all year. SIZE: 30 ha, 55 pitches (all with elec, 395 statics), 13 hot showers (charge), 11 WCs, 2 CWPs. ☏ ♿

Shop at 3 km. Surrounded by a nature reserve; cycling, walking; cabins for hire.
PRICES: Caravan with family 680,
Tent with two adults 650. CC: none.

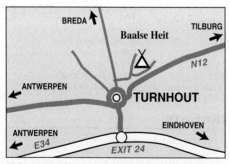

Take exit 24 (Turnhout centre) from E24. Head towards Breda/Baarle-Hertog, turn right at the end of the ringroad and then right again to campsite after 2.5 km.

Camping de Lilse Bergen Strandweg 6, 2275 Gierle.
Tel 014 557901, Fax 014 554454. English spoken.
OPEN: all year. SIZE: 17 ha, 495 pitches (all with elec, 260 statics), 38 hot showers, 43 WCs, 6 CWPs. ☏ ♿

PRICES: (1996) Caravan with family 580,
Tent with two adults 550. CC: none.
From A21 (Antwerpen to Eindhoven) turn north at exit 22 towards Beerse/Turnhout and Gierle.

Houtum Houtum 51, 2460 Kasterlee.
Tel 014 1853049, Fax 015 1853803.
English spoken.
OPEN: all year. SIZE: 9 ha, 75 pitches (all with elec, 141 statics), 10 hot showers (charge), 20 WCs, 1 CWP. ☏ ♿

Shop at 1 km. Indoor children's playroom.
PRICES: (1996) Caravan with family 540,
Tent with two adults 388. CC: Visa.
From Turnhout go south on N19 towards Geel and campsite is about 1 km past Kasterlee centre.

ZEEBRUGGE 7A

Camping International Zilvermeeuw 166 Heistlane, 8301 Knokke-Heist.
Tel 050 512726. English spoken.
OPEN: 01/03–15/11. SIZE: 7 ha, 475 pitches (all with elec, 435 statics), 16 hot showers, 45 WCs, 3 CWPs.

Restaurant at 0.1 km.
PRICES: (1996) Caravan with family 765,
Tent with two adults 575. CC: none.
From Zeebrugge take N34 towards Knokke-Heist then turn right on to N300 towards Ramskapelle. Campsite is 500 m from the sea. Well signposted.

CZECH REPUBLIC & SLOVAKIA

Since the Velvet Revolution of 1989 the Czech Republic & Slovakia have become very popular with British holidaymakers, intrigued by mighty castles, grand cathedrals, but especially by some of Europe's most spectacular landscapes.

Prague, the capital of the Czech Republic, is often called the most beautiful capital in Europe. The view from Charles Bridge up towards the castle and St Vitus' Cathedral is particularly fine. Behind, in the old town, are the famous astronomical clock and the Powder Tower, both dating from the 15th century.

Bohemia is well known for its spas and the most famous of these is Karlovy Vary; while Moravia, part of the Czech Republic since 1918, attracts visitors to its huge limestone caves, known as Moravsky Dras. Slovakia, an independent country since the division of Czechoslovakia, is a land of mountains rising towards the High Tatras on the Polish border. The drive east through Slovakia takes in spectacular castles, among them Oravsky Zamek and, perhaps most impressive of all, Spissky Hrad.

Emergency numbers

Police 158

Fire Brigade 150

Ambulance 155

Warning information

First aid kit compulsory

Warning triangle must be carried

Blood Alcohol Legal Limit 0 mg

* Please note: the limit shown above is correct ie any alcohol in the blood is illegal.

BANSKA BYSTRICA   22D

Autocamping Tajov 97634 Tajov, Slovakia.
Tel 088 97320. English spoken.
OPEN: all year. SIZE: 2 ha, 40 pitches (50 with elec), 6 hot showers, 10 WCs. ℄

| ⌗R | | 🛈 | | ✕ | | ⌂ | |

PRICES: (1996) Caravan with family 350,
Tent with two adults 230. CC: none.
Tajov is about 5 km west of Banska Bystrica.

BRNO   22C

Autocamping Obora, Brnenska Prehrada, 63500 Brno.
Tel 05 79 19 88, Fax 05 79 11 05. English spoken.
OPEN: 01/03–01/10. SIZE: 11 ha, 1000 pitches (all with elec, 3500 statics), 40 hot showers, 80 WCs.

| ≈⚓ | 🛉 R | | | ✕ ⭍ ⌂ |

PRICES: (1996) Caravan with family 310,
Tent with two adults 160. CC: none.
From Brno, drive 6 km on the D384 to Bystre Kurim. The campsite is on the left of the lake.

FRANTISKOVY LAZNE   22C

Autokempink Drenice 35099 Cheb, Czech Rep.
Tel 0166 31591. English spoken.
OPEN: 15/05–25/09. SIZE: 4 ha, 26 pitches (18 with elec), 13 hot showers, 16 WCs. ℄

| ≈ ⚓⌗ | | 🛈 ☕ ✕ | | ⌂ |

Tennis, fishing.
PRICES: (1996) Caravan with family 268,
Tent with two adults 192. CC: none.
From Frantiskovy Lezne go south to Cheb, take the E48 towards Sokolov and after 5 km turn on to route 21 towards Drenice. Follow signs to campsite.

HODONIN   22C

Autocamping Straznice 69662 Straznice, Czech Rep.
Tel 0631 332037, Fax 0631 332041.
English spoken.
OPEN: 01/05–30/10. SIZE: 2 ha, 360 pitches (120 with elec), 8 hot showers, 25 WCs. ℄

| ⌗ | | 🖥 🛈 ☕ ✕ ⌗ ⌂ |

Shop at 1 km.
PRICES: (1996) Caravan with family 309,
Tent with two adults 204. CC: none.
From Hodonin south-east on road 55 to Straznice.

HRANICE 22C

AMK Kemp Hranice Pod Hurkou 12,
75301 Hranice, Czech Rep.
Tel 0642 201633. English spoken.
OPEN: 15/05–15/09. SIZE: 2 ha, 30 pitches (24 with elec, 50 statics), 10 hot showers, 18 WCs, 2 CWPs. ✆

~	⚊	🏕	R	⊡		🍵			🄷	

Shop at 0.5 km. Restaurant at 1 km. Table tennis; swimming pool 1.5 km.
PRICES: (1996) Caravan with family 330,
Tent with two adults 240. CC: none.
Site is 1 km south-east of Hranice and well signposted.

Autokempink Fulnek 74245 Fulnek, Czech Rep.
Tel 0656 923316.
OPEN: 01/05–30/09. SIZE: 6 ha, 60 pitches (40 with elec, 35 statics), 16 hot showers, 24 WCs. ✆ ♿

		🏕		⊡		🍵		🄷		🚗

Shop at 0.5 km. Restaurant at 2 km. Table tennis, mini-golf.
PRICES: (1996) Caravan with family 260,
Tent with two adults 150. CC: none.
From Hranice take route 47 to Fulnek then go 2 km on road to Vitkov and site is signposted.

KARLOVY VARY 22C

Autokamp Sasanka Sadov, 36261 Karlovy Vary, Czech Rep.
Tel 017 3311130. English spoken.
OPEN: 01/04–31/10. SIZE: 3 ha, 150 pitches (all with elec), 3 hot showers, 9 WCs, 2 CWPs. ✆

	🄀	R		🛒	🍵		🄷	

Restaurant at 0.1 km.
PRICES: (1996) Caravan with family 360,
Tent with two adults 210. CC: none.
Highway from Karlovy Vary to Ostrov. Turn left in village of Bor. Campsite well signposted.

KRALOVICE 22C

Autokempink Jesenice 27033 Jesenice, Czech Rep.
Tel 0313 99279, Fax 0313 99279. English spoken.
OPEN: 01/04–30/10. SIZE: 3 ha, 100 pitches (48 with elec), 14 hot showers (charge), 18 WCs, 3 CWPs. ✆

≋	⚊	🄀	R	⊡	🛒	🍵	✕	🄷	

PRICES: (1996) Caravan with family 235,
Tent with two adults 160. CC: none.
Jesenice is a small town 82 km west of Praha. The campsite is 300 m south of the town, 200 m from the road.

LIBEREC 22C

Autokempink Pavlovice Liberec ul Letna,
46013 Liberec, Czech Rep.
Tel 048 5123468, Fax 048 5123468. English spoken.
OPEN: 01/05–30/09. SIZE: 4 ha, 80 pitches (all with elec, 50 statics). ✆

	🄀	R	⊡		🍵	✕	⚘	🄷	

Shop at 0.2 km. Lake 3 km.
PRICES: (1996) Caravan with family 310,
Tent with two adults 200. CC: none.
Campsite is in the north of Liberec, on route 35 towards Frydlant. Well signposted.

LITOMERICE 22C

Autokempink Litomerice Strelecky Ostrov,
41201 Litomerice, Czech Rep.
Tel 0416 6694. English spoken.
OPEN: 01/05–30/09. SIZE: 0.2 ha, 20 pitches (17 with elec), 5 hot showers, 8 WCs, 4 French WCs, 1 CWP. ✆

~	⚊	🄀	R		🛒	🍵	✕		🄷	

Swimming pool nearby.
PRICES: (1996) Caravan with family 375,
Tent with two adults 210. CC: none.
From Praha take E55 north towards Teplice for about 60 km. Turn right to Litomerice, go over the bridge and then turn left towards campsite.

MARTIN 22D

Autocamping Turiec 03608 Martin, Slovakia.
Tel 0842 284215. English spoken.
OPEN: all year. SIZE: 2 ha, 20 pitches (all with elec), 4 hot showers, 7 WCs, 1 CWP.

≋	⚊	🏕	R		🛒	🍵	✕		🄷	

Hiking, skiing, swimming pool nearby.
PRICES: (1996) Caravan with family 290,
Tent with two adults 170. CC: Euro/Access.
Approach Martin from Zilina on the E50. In Vrutky turn off towards Martinske Hole.

MOHELNICE 22C

Autocamp Morava 78985 Mohelnice.
Tel 0648 51001, Fax 0648 51011.
English spoken.
OPEN: all year. SIZE: 5 ha, 150 pitches (80 with elec), 16 hot showers, 16 WCs. ✆

≋	⚊	🄀	R	⊡	🛒	🍵	✕	⚘	🄷	

Shop at 1 km.
PRICES: (1996) Caravan with family 250,
Tent with two adults 180. CC: none.
Road 35 from Hradec Kralove to Olomouc.

NACHOD 22C

Camp Nachod-Beloves 54701 Nachod-Beloves, Czech Rep.
Tel 0441 23014.
OPEN: 14/05–15/09. SIZE: 12 ha, 15 pitches (all with elec, 97 statics), 6 hot showers (charge), 7 WCs. ♿

Czech Republic & Slovakia

Shop at 0.2 km.
PRICES: (1996) Caravan with family 260,
Tent with two adults 150. CC: none.
North-east of Praha 200 m from the E67. Signposted.

POPRAD   22D

Camping Stara Lesna Verejnetaborisko,
Stara Lesna, 05981 Dolny Smokovek, Slovakia.
Tel 0969 967493, Fax 0969 2754. English spoken.
OPEN: 01/06–30/09. SIZE: 10 ha, 150 pitches
(all with elec), 4 hot showers, 16 WCs.

Shop at 2 km. Mini-golf, tennis.
PRICES: (1996) Caravan with family 390,
Tent with two adults 260. CC: none.
*Stara Lesna is between Stary Smokovek and
Tatranska Lomnica, about 12 km north of Poprad.*

PRAHA (PRAGUE)   22C

Autokempink Visnova II U Krivoklatu,
27023 Krivoklat, Czech Rep.
Tel 0313 98184.
OPEN: 01/06–31/08. SIZE: 1 ha, 28 pitches (all with
elec), 4 hot showers, 12 WCs.

Shop at 0.1 km. Restaurant at 0.3 km.
PRICES: (1996) Caravan with family 340,
Tent with two adults 220. CC: none.
*From Praha take E48 to Jenec, turn left to Unhast
and go on to Krivoklat. Site is on route 201, about
3 km from Krivoklat. Follow signs.*

Camp Dzban Nad Lávkou 3, 16005 Praha 6,
Vokovice, Czech Rep.
Tel 0236 8551, Fax 0236 1365. English spoken.
OPEN: all year. SIZE: 4.5 ha, 120 pitches (96 with
elec, 400 statics), 20 hot showers, 15 WCs.

Shop at 0.5 km. Tennis, mini-golf. Swimming pool
nearby.
PRICES: (1996) Caravan with family 680,
Tent with two adults 400. CC: none.
*From the centre of Praha take the Evropska road
(route 7). Campsite is signposted.*

Camp Sokol Troja Trojska 171, 17100 Praha.
Tel 0285 42908, Fax 0268 81177. English spoken.
OPEN: all year. SIZE: 1 ha, 80 pitches (40 with elec,
10 statics), 7 hot showers, 17 WCs, 3 French WCs,
1 CWP.

PRICES: Caravan with family 600,
Tent with two adults 350. CC: none.
*From the centre of Praha take E55 to the north,
following signs to Praha Troja. Campsite is
signposted.*

Caravan Park/Yacht Club Cisarska Louka 599,
15000 Praha 5, Czech Rep.
Tel 0254 0925, Fax 0254 3305. English spoken.
OPEN: all year. SIZE: 15 ha, 70 pitches (all with elec,
40 statics), 22 hot showers (charge), 22 WCs,
1 CWP.

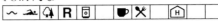

Shop at 0.2 km. Swimming pool 2 km.
PRICES: (1996) Caravan with family 550,
Tent with two adults 360. CC: none.
*At the end of motorway D5 follow signs to Praha
Smichov, then Zlichov and Cisarska Louka.*

Caravancamp Motol, Plzenska str 279,
15000 Praha 5, Czech Rep.
Tel 0252 4714, Fax 052 1632. English spoken.
OPEN: 01/04–31/10. SIZE: 3 ha, 150 pitches
(all with elec), 21 hot showers, 27 WCs, 2 CWPs.

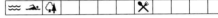

Shop at 0.5 km.
PRICES: unavailable. CC: none.
About 4 km from the centre of Praha.

Intercamp Kotva Branik U ledaren 55,
14700 Praha 4, Czech Rep.
Tel 0246 1397, Fax 0246 6110. English spoken.
OPEN: 01/04–30/10. SIZE: 9 ha, 60 pitches (all with
elec, 120 statics), 18 hot showers, 26 WCs.

Boat hire, tennis; swimming pool 2 km. Rooms
available year-round.
PRICES: (1996) Caravan with family 600,
Tent with two adults 370. CC: none.
*Near to motorways D1 and D5. Follow signs to
Praha Modrany or Praha Branik. Site is
signposted. (Open for caravans all year.)*

Penzion A Camping Eva 15500 Praha 5, Czech Rep.
Tel 0230 19213, Fax 0230 19213. English spoken.
OPEN: 01/03–31/10. SIZE: 50 pitches (all with elec,
1 static), 12 hot showers, 10 WCs, 1 CWP.

Shop at 0.05 km. Restaurant at 0.3 km. Swimming
pool 2 km.
PRICES: Caravan with family 560,
Tent with two adults 320. CC: none.
*Western side of Praha, between highway Praha to
Plzen to Nurnberk (D5) and main road Praha to
Karlovy Vary E6.*

Sportcamp Motol Str nad Hlinikem 1202,
15000 Praha, Czech Rep.
Tel 052 1802, Fax 052 1632. English spoken.
OPEN: 01/04–31/10. SIZE: 3 ha, 80 pitches (56 with
elec), 17 hot showers, 22 WCs.

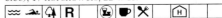

Shop at 1 km.
PRICES: unavailable. CC: none.
About 4 km from the centre of Praha; signposted.

Czech Republic & Slovakia

Czech Republic & Slovakia

Triocamp Obsluzna 043, Dolni Chabry, 18400 Praha 8, Czech Rep.
Tel 0268 81180, Fax 0268 81180. English spoken.
OPEN: all year. SIZE: 1 ha, 50 pitches (35 with elec), 6 hot showers, 6 WCs, 1 CWP. &

Shop at 1 km. Restaurant at 1.5 km.
PRICES: (1996) Caravan with family 720,
Tent with two adults 460. CC: Euro/Access.
From E55/D8 exit Zdiby. Campsite is then 2 km, on road 608 towards Way Dolni Chabry. Signposted.

ROZNOV POD RADHOSTEM 22D

Camping Roznov Roznov pod Radhostem, 75661 Czech Rep.
Tel 0651 55442, Fax 0651 55442. English spoken.
OPEN: 01/05–30/09. SIZE: 3 ha, 120 pitches (all with elec), 15 hot showers, 20 WCs. ℭ

Bike hire.
PRICES: (1996) Caravan with family 395,
Tent with two adults 230. CC: none.
On eastern edge of town on E442 towards Zilina.

SENEC 22C

Slnecne Jazera 90301 Senec, Slovakia.
Tel 07 923324, Fax 07 924718. English spoken.
OPEN: all year. SIZE: 80 ha, 1120 pitches (all with elec), 80 hot showers, 150 WCs, 6 CWPs. ℭ

PRICES: (1996) Caravan with family 329,
Tent with two adults 220. CC: none.
North-east of Bratislava on the E75 (25 km).

SUMPERK 22C

Camping Stity Sumperk 78991 Sumperk, Czech Rep.
Tel 0648 901292. English spoken.
OPEN: 01/06–30/09. SIZE: 6 ha, 100 pitches (24 with elec), 6 hot showers, 12 WCs.

Shop at 1 km. Restaurant at 1 km.
PRICES: (1996) Caravan with family 226,
Tent with two adults 156. CC: none.
West from Sumperk on road no 11 then left on to road no 43 to Stity. Turn right in town then 1.2 km.

SVITAVY 22C

Kemp Borova 56982 Borova u Policky, Czech Rep.
Tel 0463 93186, Fax 0463 93186. English spoken.
OPEN: 01/05–30/09. SIZE: 1 ha, 10 hot showers, 14 WCs, 2 CWPs. ℭ

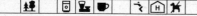

Restaurant at 0.2 km. Cinema.

PRICES: (1996) Caravan with family 365, Tent with two adults 250. CC: none.
Site is 10 km from Policky on route 34 Hlinsko to Svitavy road.

TREBIC 22C

Autocamping Pousov 67401 Trebic-Pousov, Czech Rep.
Tel 0618 850641, Fax 0618 850641. English spoken.
OPEN: 01/05–30/09. SIZE: 1 ha, 40 pitches (20 with elec), 6 hot showers, 20 WCs.

Mini-golf; swimming pool 500 m.
PRICES: Caravan with family 220,
Tent with two adults 130. CC: none.
Arriving in Trebic on route 23, campsite is 1 km.

TRSTENA 22D

Autocamping Oravice 02712 Liesek, Slovakia.
Tel 0847 94114, Fax 0847 94259. English spoken.
OPEN: all year. SIZE: 1 ha, 70 pitches (30 with elec, 2 statics), 6 hot showers, 12 WCs. ℭ

Thermal pool; paragliding and abseiling courses; winter sports, mountain bikes.
PRICES: Caravan with family 300,
Tent with two adults 200. CC: none.
Recommended campsite. From Trstena drive through Liesek, Cimhova, Vitanova and then turn right to Oravice. Campsite is signposted.

TURNOV 22C

Autocamping Jiskra 51246 Harrachov, Czech Rep.
Tel 0432 529332, Fax 0432 529456. English spoken.
OPEN: all year. SIZE: 3 ha, 50 pitches (all with elec), 8 hot showers, 20 WCs, 2 CWPs. ℭ

Shop at 0.3 km. Restaurant at 0.1 km. Tennis; swimming pool 1.5 km.
PRICES: (1996) Caravan with family 330,
Tent with two adults 190. CC: none.
Take E65 from Turnov to Harrachov.

ZVOLEN 22D

Autocamping Neresnica Zapotockeho 28, 96001 Zvolen, Slovakia.
Tel 0855 22651. English spoken.
OPEN: 15/04–15/10. SIZE: 2.5 ha, 70 pitches (30 with elec, 28 statics), 20 hot showers, 40 WCs.

Special discounts for groups.
PRICES: (1996) Caravan with family 340,
Tent with two adults 180. CC: none.
Zvolen is north of Budapest (E77). Campsite is 500 m from the centre of town.

DENMARK

Arriving at Esbjerg on the Danish west coast, resist the temptation to head straight for Billund and *Legoland*. Denmark is a country of green landscapes and pleasant towns, distributed through her many islands, all ringed around with countless miles of sandy beaches. Mainland Jutland is itself only joined to Germany by a narrow neck of land.

The capital, Copenhagen, though two islands on from Esbjerg, is only one ferry crossing away, the arm of sea between Jutland and Fyn (Denmark's second largest island) being crossed by bridge. Fyn, with more than its fair share of handsome manor houses and gardens, deserves its reputation as the Garden of Denmark and its main town of Odense, birthplace of Hans Christian Andersen, draws many visitors.

Andersen is also remembered in Copenhagen harbour by his Little Mermaid statue. To get the best out of a visit to Copenhagen you should abandon your car and invest in a Copenhagen Card for free entry to over fifty places of interest plus free travel on public transport around the city.

The Viking past is frequently recalled in Denmark: Ladby on Fyn has a ship burial site while Aarhus in Jutland has a museum in the basement of a bank! Ribe, on Jutland's west coast and said to be the country's oldest town, was a Viking trading centre that remained important throughout the Middle Ages: well-preserved houses and a 14th-century church tower to climb for a rewarding view over the surrounding countryside.

Emergency numbers

Police, Fire Brigade and Ambulance 112

Warning information

Warning triangle must be carried

Blood alcohol legal limit 80 mg

ÅBENRÅ 12C

Lundtoft Skov Camping Lundtoftvej 26, Kliplev, 6200 Åbenrå.
Tel 74 68 78 89. English spoken.
OPEN: 03/04–07/10. SIZE: 2 ha, 80 pitches (all with elec), 5 hot showers (charge), 12 WCs, 2 CWPs. ⚲

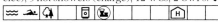

Restaurant at 4 km.
PRICES: (1996) Caravan with family 150, Tent with two adults 76. CC: none.
Campsite is on road 170 between Åbenrå and Kruså, near Lake Søgaard.

AERØSKØBING 12C

Aerøskøbing Camping og Feriecenter
Sygehusvej 40B, 5970 Aerøskøbing, Aerø Island.
Tel 62 52 18 54, Fax 62 52 14 36. English spoken.
OPEN: 01/05–30/09. SIZE: 4 ha, 236 pitches (60 with elec), 25 hot showers (charge), 25 WCs, 2 CWPs.

Restaurant at 0.05 km. Bicycle hire.
PRICES: unavailable. CC: Visa.
Aerø Island lies between Svendborg and Sønderborg. Site is at Aerøskøbing, a 16th-century town.

ÅLBAEK 12A

FDM Camping Ålbaek Strand, Jerupvej 2, 9982 Ålbaek.
Tel 98 48 82 61, Fax 98 48 89 34. English spoken.
OPEN: 15/04–15/09. SIZE: 11 ha, 350 pitches (270 with elec, 600 statics), 38 hot showers (charge), 52 WCs, 4 CWPs. ⚲ ♿

Shop at 1 km. Restaurant at 1 km. discounts for RAC members.
PRICES: (1996) Caravan with family 131, Tent with two adults 76. CC: none.
Ålbaek is south of Skagen. Campsite is beside the beach.

ÅLBORG 12A

Løgstor Camping Granlyvej 6, 9670 Løgstor.
Tel 98 67 10 51, Fax 98 67 10 51. English spoken.
OPEN: 01/05–01/09. SIZE: 3 ha, 125 pitches (110 with elec, 16 statics), 6 hot showers, 14 WCs, 1 CWP. ⚲ ♿

Restaurant at 0.5 km. Tennis.

Denmark

Denmark

PRICES: (1996) Caravan with family 153, Tent with two adults 90. CC: none.
Situated on outskirts of Løgstor. Go west from Ålborg on roads 187 and 567.

Strandparkens Camping Skydebanevej 20, 9000 Ålborg.
Tel 98 12 76 29, Fax 98 12 76 73. English spoken.
OPEN: 01/05–15/09. SIZE: 2 ha, 822 pitches, 8 hot showers, 16 WCs. ⚓ ⚐

Restaurant at 0.3 km.
PRICES: (1996) Caravan with family 150, Tent with two adults 86. CC: Euro/Access, Visa.
Follow Ålborg West signs and campsite is signposted.

ÅRHUS   12A

Camping Blommehaven Århus Orneredevej 35, 8270 Hojbjerg.
Tel 86 27 02 07, Fax 86 27 45 22. English spoken.
OPEN: 26/03–14/09. SIZE: 8 ha, 385 pitches (310 with elec, 395 statics), 18 hot showers, 29 WCs, 2 CWPs. ⚓ ⚐

PRICES: Caravan with family 202, Tent with two adults 126. CC: Euro/Access, Visa.
5 km outside Århus (Jylland's capital).

Holken Camping Toldvej 50, Holken, 8300 Odder.
Tel 86 55 63 06, Fax 86 55 65 60. English spoken.
OPEN: 01/02–30/11. SIZE: 3.3 ha, 125 pitches (all with elec, 75 statics), 8 hot showers (charge), 32 WCs, 1 CWP. ⚐

PRICES: Caravan with family 166, Tent with two adults 98. CC: Euro/Access, Visa.
From Århus, drive south to Odder, then go to Hov. Pass the windmill and turn left to Hølken.

ASÅ   12A

Aså Camping Vodbindervej 13, 9340 Asa.
Tel 98 85 13 40, Fax 98 85 13 40. English spoken.
OPEN: all year. SIZE: 5 ha, 400 pitches (200 with elec), 15 hot showers (charge), 23 WCs, 1 CWP. ⚐

Restaurant at 0.3 km.
PRICES: (1996) Caravan with family 135, Tent with two adults 80. CC: Euro/Access, Visa.

ASPERUP   12C

Båringskov Camping Kystvejen 4, 5466 Asperup.
Tel 64 48 10 53, Fax 64 48 10 45. English spoken.
OPEN: 01/04–01/10. SIZE: 2.5 ha, 100 pitches (all with elec), 4 hot showers (charge), 11 WCs, 1 CWP. ⚓

PRICES: (1996) Caravan with family 136, Tent with two adults 84. CC: none.
From E66 turn towards Båring, second exit (no 57) after the bridge. Continue straight ahead to campsite at Asperup/Båring.

ASSENS   12A

Camping Willemoes Naesvej 15, 5610 Assens.
Tel 64 71 15 43, Fax 64 71 15 83. English spoken.
OPEN: 04/04–08/09. SIZE: 7 ha, 200 pitches (150 with elec, 50 statics), 12 hot showers (charge), 33 WCs, 12 CWPs. ⚓ ⚐

Restaurant at 0.3 km.
PRICES: (1996) Caravan with family 187, Tent with two adults 88. CC: none.
Situated just beside Assens Marina.

BILLUND   12C

Billund Camping Ellehammers Alle 2, 7190 Billund.
Tel 75 33 15 21, Fax 75 35 37 36. English spoken.
OPEN: 10/01–31/12. SIZE: 14 ha, 650 pitches (450 with elec), 25 hot showers (charge), 50 WCs, 4 CWPs. ⚓ ⚐

Discounts for RAC members.
PRICES: Caravan with family 162, Tent with two adults 96. CC: Amex, Euro/Access, Visa.
At the crossroads of route 28 (east-west) and route 176 (north-south). In central Jylland.

BORNHOLM

RØNNE   12D

Gallokken Camping Strandvejen 4, 3700 Rønne, Bornholm Island.
Tel 56 95 23 20, Fax 56 95 37 66. English spoken.
OPEN: 15/05–31/08. SIZE: 2 ha, 120 pitches (60 with elec, 5 statics), 10 hot showers (charge), 20 WCs, 1 CWP. ⚓

Restaurant at 0.2 km.
PRICES: Caravan with family 148, Tent with two adults 88. CC: none.
1.5 km south of Rønne on coast road to Nekso. Well signposted.

Nordskoven Camping Antoinettevej 2, 3700 Rønne, Bornholm Island.
Tel 56 95 22 81, Fax 56 95 37 66. English spoken.
OPEN: 01/05–10/09. SIZE: 4 ha, 190 pitches (100 with elec, 10 statics), 10 hot showers (charge), 25 WCs, 1 CWP. ⚓ ⚐

Shop at 0.5 km.
PRICES: Caravan with family 148,
Tent with two adults 88. CC: none.
North of Rønne on road to Allinge. Well signposted.

SNOGEBAEK 12D

FDM-Camping Balka Strand Klynevej 6,
3730 Snogebaek, Bornholm Island.
Tel 56 48 80 74, Fax 56 48 80 75. English spoken.
OPEN: 19/04–14/09. SIZE: 3 ha, 160 pitches
(140 with elec, 15 statics), 10 hot showers
(charge), 25 WCs, 2 CWPs.

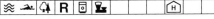

Discounts for RAC members.
PRICES: Caravan with family 162, Tent with two
adults 96. CC: Amex, Euro/Access, Visa.
*Go south from Nekso to Snogebaek and follow
signs.*

SVANEKE 12D

Camping Møllebakken 3740 Svaneke,
Bornholm Island.
Tel 56 49 64 62, Fax 56 49 64 62. English spoken.
OPEN: 15/05–15/09. SIZE: 2 ha, 100 pitches, 4 hot
showers (charge), 10 WCs, 1 CWP.

Restaurant at 0.5 km.
PRICES: (1996) Caravan with family 180,
Tent with two adults 100. CC: none.
*Signposted from the northern edge of town, near a
windmill and triangular water tower.*

END OF BORNHOLM RESORTS

BROAGER 12C

Spar-Es Camping Skeldebro, 6310 Broager.
Tel 74 44 14 18, Fax 74 44 14 18. English spoken.
OPEN: all year. SIZE: 2 ha, 65 pitches (all with elec,
60 statics), 9 hot showers (charge), 20 WCs,
1 CWP.

Restaurant at 5 km.
PRICES: (1996) Caravan with family 161,
Tent with two adults 92. CC: none.
*From Broager follow signs to Skelde/Dynt and
500 m after Dynt the campsite is signposted
on the left.*

CHRISTIANSFELD 12C

Taps Camping International Aastorpvej 91,
Taps, 6070 Christiansfeld.
Tel 75 57 30 21, Fax 75 57 30 21. English spoken.
OPEN: 15/05–15/09. SIZE: 2 ha, 90 pitches (60 with
elec), 5 hot showers (charge), 13 WCs, 1 CWP.

Playground, mini-golf, boules.
PRICES: (1996) Caravan with family 139,
Tent with two adults 84. CC: none.
*Coming from the south on E45, exit 66 at
Christiansfeld, follow 170 north to Taps. Turn
right and follow signs.*

EBELTOFT 12B

Camping Krakaer Gl Kaervej 18, 8400 Ebeltoft.
Tel 86 36 21 18, Fax 86 36 21 87. English spoken.
OPEN: 01/04–15/09. SIZE: 7 ha, 300 pitches (150 with
elec), 12 hot showers (charge), 20 WCs, 1 CWP.

Good playground; sea 3 km.
PRICES: (1996) Caravan with family 170,
Tent with two adults 96. CC: Visa.
*Follow route 21 from Århus to Ebeltoft. 10 km before
Ebeltoft turn right and follow signs to Krakaer.*

Solystgard Camping Dragsmurvej 15, Fuglso
Bay Ebeltoft, 8420 Knebel.
Tel 86 35 12 39. English spoken.
OPEN: 01/04–20/09. SIZE: 9 ha, 284 pitches (all with
elec), 10 hot showers (charge), 32 WCs, 1 CWP.

Restaurant at 2 km.
PRICES: Caravan with family 173,
Tent with two adults 102. CC: none.
*Århus to Rønde, turn off to Mols and look for a
sign to Fuglso or camping sign.*

Vibaek Camping Nordre Strandvej 23,
8400 Ebeltoft.
Tel 86 34 12 14, Fax 86 34 55 33. English spoken.
OPEN: all year. SIZE: 9 ha, 400 pitches (300 with
elec, 100 statics), 26 hot showers (charge),
40 WCs, 4 CWPs.

Restaurant at 1 km. Windsurfing.
PRICES: (1996) Caravan with family 147,
Tent with two adults 88. CC: none.
*North of the town approached from the Århus-
Grenå highway.*

ELSEGÅRDE 12B

Blushoj Camping 8400 Elsegårde.
Tel 86 34 12 38. English spoken.
OPEN: 01/04–15/09. SIZE: 230 pitches (200 with
elec, 5 statics), 12 hot showers (charge), 28 WCs,
1 CWP.

Restaurant at 5 km.
PRICES: (1996) Caravan with family 135,
Tent with two adults 88. CC: none.
*In Elsegårde turn left at the pond and campsite is
500 m ahead.*

Denmark

ESBJERG 12C

Houstrup Camping Houstrupvej 90,
6830 Norre Nebel.
Tel 75 28 83 40, Fax 75 28 75 88. English spoken.
OPEN: 15/04–15/09. SIZE: 6 ha, 170 pitches
(125 with elec, 45 statics), 8 hot showers (charge),
22 WCs, 1 CWP. ✆

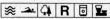

Restaurant at 0.2 km. Mini-golf, tennis.
PRICES: Caravan with family 180,
Tent with two adults 92. CC: none.
*From Esbjerg take route 12 to Varde then route
181 heading towards Nymindegab. Go through
Norre Nebel to Lonne (3 km). Turn south towards
Houstrup.*

FÅBORG 12C

Bøjden Strandcamping Bøjdenlandevej 12,
5600 Fåborg.
Tel 62 60 12 84, Fax 62 60 12 94. English spoken.
OPEN: 01/04–15/09. SIZE: 5 ha, 180 pitches
(all with elec, 100 statics), 14 hot showers
(charge), 35 WCs. ✆ ♿

Restaurant at 0.1 km. Lovely beach; year-round
accommodation available.
PRICES: (1996) Caravan with family 191,
Tent with two adults 108. CC: none.
On route 8 from Faaborg.

Camping Faldsled Strand Assensvei 461,
Faldsled, 5642 Fåborg.
Tel 62 68 10 95, Fax 62 61 74 61. English spoken.
OPEN: 28/04–04/09. SIZE: 3 ha, 130 pitches
(100 with elec, 10 statics), 10 hot showers
(charge), 14 WCs, 2 CWPs. ✆

Restaurant at 0.5 km. Family site. Good facilities
including bouncy castle.
PRICES: (1996) Caravan with family 179,
Tent with two adults 92. CC: Euro/Access, Visa.
*Faldsled is just off the main Assens to Fåborg road
and the campsite is well signposted.*

FALSTER

NYKØBING 12D

FDM-Camping Østersoparken Bøtøvej 243,
Bøtø, 4873 Vaeggerløse, Falster.
Tel 54 13 67 86, Fax 54 13 61 90. English spoken.
OPEN: 22/03–14/09. SIZE: 4.3 ha, 200 pitches
(125 with elec, 15 statics), 18 hot showers
(charge), 15 WCs, 1 CWP. ♿

Restaurant at 1 km. Reduction for RAC members.

PRICES: Caravan with family 162, Tent with two
adults 96. CC: Amex, Euro/Access, Visa.
Signposted in Bøtø.

END OF FALSTER RESORTS

FARSØ 12A

Ertebolle Camping Ertebollevej 42, 9640 Farsø.
Tel 98 63 63 75, Fax 98 63 64 34. English spoken.
OPEN: 01/04–30/09. SIZE: 4 ha, 140 pitches
(all with elec, 40 statics), 6 hot showers (charge),
16 WCs, 1 CWP. ✆

Restaurant at 5 km. Mini-golf, sauna; tropical
swimming centre 10 km.
PRICES: (1996) Caravan with family 161,
Tent with two adults 96. CC: Euro/Access, Visa.

FJELLERUP 12B

Dalgaard Camping Nordkystvesen 65,
Skovgaarde, 8961 Allingaabro.
Tel 86 31 70 13, Fax 86 31 70 13. English spoken.
OPEN: 27/03–15/09. SIZE: 5 ha, 110 pitches
(100 with elec, 60 statics), 5 hot showers (charge),
22 WCs, 3 CWPs. ✆

Restaurant at 3 km.
PRICES: (1996) Caravan with family 166,
Tent with two adults 96. CC: none.
Follow road 547 until 3 km west of Fjellerup.

FJERRITSLEV 12A

Klim Strand Camping Havvejen 167, Klim
Strand, 9690 Fjerritslev.
Tel 98 22 53 40, Fax 98 22 57 77. English spoken.
OPEN: 15/03–22/10. SIZE: 24 ha, 600 pitches (all
with elec), 48 hot showers, 57 WCs, 4 CWPs. ♿

PRICES: Caravan with family 238, Tent with two
adults 135. CC: Amex, Euro/Access, Visa.
On the coast, 10 km north-west of Fjerritslev.

FREDERICIA 12C

Sønderskov Camping Sønderskovvej 61,
7000 Fredericia.
Tel 75 94 21 47, Fax 75 94 21 47. English spoken.
OPEN: 01/04–01/10. SIZE: 2 ha, 70 pitches (50 with
elec), 6 hot showers (charge), 12 WCs, 1 CWP. ✆

Restaurant at 3 km.
PRICES: (1996) Caravan with family 156,
Tent with two adults 98. CC: none.
*Site is close to the 161 between Kolding and
Middelfart. Approx 2 km before you reach old bridge
across Little Belt, turn south via Sønderskovvej.*

FREDERIKSHAVN 12A/B

Nordstrand Camping Apholmenvej, 9900 Frederikshavn.
Tel 98 42 93 50, Fax 98 43 47 85. English spoken.
OPEN: 01/04–01/10. SIZE: 11 ha, 500 pitches (328 with elec, 55 statics), 32 hot showers (charge), 64 WCs, 3 CWPs. ᴜ ᴆ

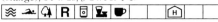

Restaurant at 3 km. Tennis, bike hire, solarium, mini-golf.
PRICES: (1996) Caravan with family 195, Tent with two adults 120. CC: Amex, Euro/Access, Visa.
3 km north of Frederikshavn towards Skagen.

GLAMSBJERG 12C

Hjemstavnsgaardens Camping Klaregade 15, 5620 Glamsbjerg.
Tel 64 72 33 63. English spoken.
OPEN: 01/05–15/09. SIZE: 1 ha, 50 pitches (30 with elec), 5 hot showers (charge), 5 WCs, 1 CWP. ᴆ

Shop at 0.3 km. Restaurant at 3 km. Swimming pool: 3 km, golf: 5 km; excellent area for biking.
PRICES: Caravan with family 114, Tent with two adults 68. CC: none.
2 km south of Glamsbjerg towards Hårdy.

GRÅSTEN 12C

Laerkelunden Camping Nederbyvej 17-25, Rinkenaes, 6300 Gråsten.
Tel 74 65 02 50, Fax 74 65 02 25. English spoken.
OPEN: 01/04–22/10. SIZE: 5 ha, 250 pitches (225 with elec, 50 statics), 20 hot showers (charge), 37 WCs, 2 CWPs. ᴜ ᴆ

Restaurant at 2 km.
PRICES: (1996) Caravan with family 151, Tent with two adults 90. CC: Euro/Access, Visa.
Drive from Kruså by road 8 towards Gråsten and Sønderborg, turn right at the church in Rinkenaes; campsite is approx 400 m.

GRENÅ 12B

FDM-Camping Hegedal Ravnsvej 3, 8585 Glesborg.
Tel 86 31 77 50, Fax 86 31 77 40. English spoken.
OPEN: 22/03–21/09. SIZE: 2 ha, 110 pitches (84 with elec, 60 statics), 8 hot showers (charge), 11 WCs, 1 CWP. ᴜ

Restaurant at 2 km. Discounts for RAC members.
PRICES: Caravan with family 162, Tent with two adults 96. CC: Amex, Euro/Access, Visa.
From Grenå go north to Fjellerup. 1 km west of Fjellerup turn by Ravnsbjergvej in the direction of the beach (follow the sign).

Fornaes Camping Stensmarkvej 36, 8500 Grenå.
Tel 86 33 23 30, Fax 86 33 24 23. English spoken.
OPEN: 01/04–30/09. SIZE: 9 ha, 14 hot showers (charge), 29 WCs, 1 CWP. ᴜ ᴆ

PRICES: (1996) Caravan with family 163, Tent with two adults 96. CC: Euro/Access, Visa.
Follow A15 or A16 to Grenaa ferry harbour, turn left towards 'Fornas' along Kattegatvej, turn on to Stensmarkvej and go for approx 4 km to campsite.

Polderrev Camping Fuglsangvej 58, 8500 Grenå.
Tel 86 32 17 18, Fax 86 30 95 55. English spoken.
OPEN: all year. SIZE: 22 ha, 470 pitches (all with elec, 15 statics), 49 hot showers (charge), 42 WCs, 18 French WCs, 2 CWPs. ᴆ

Solarium.
PRICES: Caravan with family 215.00, Tent with two adults 117.00. CC: Euro/Access, Visa.
Route 15 from Randers or route 16 from Århus. Campsite is 2 km from the harbour.

GRINDSTED 12C

Grindsted Aktiv Camping Sondre Boulevard 15, 7200 Grindsted.
Tel 75 32 17 51, Fax 75 32 45 75. English spoken.
OPEN: 01/04–30/10. SIZE: 1.6 ha, 90 pitches (65 with elec), 5 hot showers (charge), 7 WCs, 12 French WCs, 1 CWP. ᴜ ᴆ

PRICES: (1996) Caravan with family 159, Tent with two adults 90. CC: Visa.
In Grindsted go south on route 30 to Esbjerg. Follow signs to campsite.

HADERSLEV 12C

Årosund Camping V/Hanne og Bent, 6100 Haderslev.
Tel 74 58 42 97, Fax 74 58 42 99. English spoken.
OPEN: all year. SIZE: 8 ha, 350 pitches (all with elec), 10 hot showers (charge), 40 WCs, 2 CWPs. ᴜ ᴆ

Restaurant at 1 km. Children's playground.
PRICES: (1996) Caravan with family 149, Tent with two adults 96. CC: Euro/Access, Visa.
Drive from Haderslev via Osby towards Årosund.

HESSELAGER 12D

Lundeborg Strand Camping Gl Lundeborgvej 46, Lundeborg, 5874 Hesselager.
Tel 62 25 14 50, Fax 62 25 20 22. English spoken.
OPEN: 15/04–15/09. SIZE: 2 ha, 200 pitches (all with elec, 60 statics), 16 hot showers (charge), 20 WCs, 1 CWP. ᴜ ᴆ

Denmark

Restaurant at 0.5 km. Fishing, cycling.
PRICES: (1996) Caravan with family 195,
Tent with two adults 115. CC: Euro/Access, Visa.
South-east of Hesselager, on the coast.

HIRTSHALS 12A

Hirtshals Camping Kystvejen, 9850 Hirtshals.
Tel 98 94 25 35, Fax 98 94 33 43. English spoken.
OPEN: 03/05–14/09. SIZE: 3 ha, 170 pitches
(130 with elec, 10 statics), 8 hot showers (charge),
18 WCs, 2 CWPs.

Restaurant at 0.5 km. Bike hire.
PRICES: (1996) Caravan with family 154,
Tent with two adults 90. CC: none.
*On the west side of Hirtshals, between the
lighthouse and the sea.*

Skiveren Camping 9982 Skiveren.
Tel 98 93 22 00, Fax 98 93 21 60. English spoken.
OPEN: 01/04–01/10. SIZE: 18 ha, 600 pitches
(436 with elec, 80 statics), 51 hot showers
(charge), 68 WCs, 15 French WCs, 3 CWPs.

Tennis, solarium.
PRICES: (1996) Caravan with family 218,
Tent with two adults 116. CC: none.
*From Hirtshals, east to Tuen where campsite is
signposted.*

Tornby Strand Camping Strandvejen,
9850 Hirtshals.
Tel 98 97 78 77, Fax 98 97 78 81. English spoken.
OPEN: all year. SIZE: 10 ha, 400 pitches (250 with
elec), 16 hot showers (charge), 44 WCs.

Restaurant at 0.1 km.
PRICES: (1996) Caravan with family 167, Tent with
two adults 86. CC: Amex, Euro/Access, Visa.
*Hirtshals is right on the coast, north of Ålborg on
E39.*

HJØRRING 12A

Tannisby Camping Tversted Strand,
9881 Bindslev.
Tel 98 93 12 50, Fax 98 93 12 86. English spoken.
OPEN: 27/03–14/09. SIZE: 3 ha, 180 pitches
(170 with elec), 22 hot showers (charge), 22 WCs,
2 CWPs.

Shop at 0.2 km. Sauna, solarium, bistrot.
PRICES: (1996) Caravan with family 168,
Tent with two adults 105. CC: Euro/Access, Visa.
*From Hjørring go to Tversted then turn left to the
beach. The campsite is 1 km ahead, on the right-
hand side.*

HOBRO 12A

Hobro Camping Gattenborg Skivevej 35,
9500 Hobro.
Tel 98 52 32 88, Fax 98 52 56 61. English spoken.
OPEN: 30/03–30/09. SIZE: 5 ha, 150 pitches
(110 with elec, 6 statics), 9 hot showers (charge),
23 WCs, 1 CWP.

Restaurant at 1 km.
PRICES: (1996) Caravan with family 184.50,
Tent with two adults 96. CC: none.
*From E45 take exit 35 on to road 579. Hobro is
2.5 km and campsite is signposted.*

HOLBAEK 12A

FDM-Camping Holbaek Sofiesmindes Alle 1,
4300 Holbaek.
Tel 53 43 50 64, Fax 53 43 50 64. English spoken.
OPEN: 22/03–19/10. SIZE: 5.4 ha, 210 pitches
(175 with elec, 10 statics), 12 hot showers
(charge), 23 WCs, 1 CWP.

Restaurant at 2 km. Reduction for RAC members.
PRICES: Caravan with family 162, Tent with two
adults 96. CC: Amex, Euro/Access, Visa.
Campsite is near the golf course.

HVALPSUND 12A

Hvalpsund Camping Overgaden 24, 9640 Farsø.
Tel 98 63 81 23. English spoken.
OPEN: 01/04–30/09. SIZE: 5 ha, 100 pitches
(all with elec, 60 statics), 5 hot showers (charge),
11 WCs, 1 CWP.

Restaurant at 0.5 km.
PRICES: (1996) Caravan with family 161,
Tent with two adults 96. CC: none.
*Halfway between Viborg and Løgstøt turn to
Hvalpsund.*

HVIDBJERG 12A

Hvidbjerg Strand Camping Hvidbjerg Strandvej
27, 6857 Blavand.
Tel 75 27 90 40, Fax 75 27 80 28. English spoken.
OPEN: 10/03–22/10. SIZE: 12 ha, 565 pitches (all
with elec), 67 hot showers, 77 WCs, 4 CWPs.

PRICES: (1996) Caravan with family 235, Tent with
two adults 123. CC: Euro/Access, Visa.
*Turn left at first intersection in Hvidbjerg and
follow signs.*

Tambosund Camping Jegindovej 27,
7790 Thyholm.
Tel 97 87 17 72, Fax 97 87 17 72. English spoken.

OPEN: 15/04–15/09. SIZE: 3 ha, 150 pitches (120 with elec), 6 hot showers (charge), 16 WCs. ☎

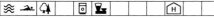

Restaurant at 0.5 km.
PRICES: (1996) Caravan with family 155, Tent with two adults 90. CC: none.
From main road A11 towards Hvidbjerg, then follow signs to Jegindo.

HVIDE SANDE 12A

FDM-Camping Holmsland Klit
6960 Hvide Sande.
Tel 97 31 13 09, Fax 97 31 35 20. English spoken.
OPEN: 22/03–14/09. SIZE: 5 ha, 200 pitches (114 with elec, 20 statics), 10 hot showers (charge), 15 WCs, 1 CWP. &

Reduced prices for RAC members.
PRICES: Caravan with family 162, Tent with two adults 96. CC: Amex, Euro/Access, Visa.
At Km 27.8 on Nymindegab to Søndervig road 181.

Fiskerogeriets Camping Bjerregård, 6960 Hvide Sande.
Tel 97 31 50 44, Fax 97 31 53 44. English spoken.
OPEN: 20/05–20/09. SIZE: 6 ha, 200 pitches (all with elec, 40 statics), 16 hot showers (charge), 21 WCs, 1 CWP. ☎

Shop at 0.5 km. Restaurant at 5 km.
PRICES: (1996) Caravan with family 146, Tent with two adults 90. CC: Euro/Access, Visa.
Situated on Ringkøbing Fjord, 1 km from the North Sea coast and 5 km north of Nymindegab.

JUELSMINDE 12C

Juelsminde Camping Rovsthoj Alle 1, 7130 Juelsminde.
Tel 75 69 32 10. English spoken.
OPEN: 01/04–25/09. SIZE: 7 ha, 275 pitches (240 with elec), 12 hot showers (charge), 38 WCs, 3 CWPs. &

PRICES: (1996) Caravan with family 142, Tent with two adults 84. CC: none.
The site is at the end of the main street by the beach and marina.

KARUP 12A

Hessellund So Camping Hessellundvej 12, 7470 Karup.
Tel 97 10 16 04, Fax 97 10 11 61. English spoken.
OPEN: 27/03–04/10. SIZE: 14 ha, 155 pitches (all with elec, 80 statics), 13 hot showers (charge), 26 WCs, 2 CWPs. ☎ &

Restaurant at 5 km.

PRICES: (1996) Caravan with family 144, Tent with two adults 84. CC: Euro/Access, Visa.
From road 13 towards Viborg, turn left towards Herning/Karup (no 12). Follow road through Karup and turn right about 50 m outside the town towards Hessellund and campsite (road 467).

KERTEMINDE 12D

Bøgebjerg Strand Camping Blaesenborgvej 200, 5380 Dalby.
Tel 65 34 10 52, Fax 65 34 11 52. English spoken.
OPEN: 21/03–14/09. SIZE: 7.7 ha, 215 pitches (200 with elec, 80 statics), 30 hot showers (charge), 34 WCs, 1 CWP. ☎ &

On the spot watersports and fishing.
PRICES: (1996) Caravan with family 161, Tent with two adults 92. CC: Euro/Access, Visa.
Campsite is 9 km from Kerteminde, via the small village of Måle. After passing through Måle, follow the sign on the right to Blaesenborgvej and to campsite.

Kerteminde Camping Hindsholmvej 80, 5300 Kerteminde.
Tel 65 32 19 71, Fax 65 32 23 27. English spoken.
OPEN: 25/03–08/09. SIZE: 5 ha, 200 pitches (125 with elec, 50 statics), 15 hot showers (charge), 25 WCs, 2 CWPs. ☎ &

PRICES: Caravan with family 160, Tent with two adults 98. CC: none.
1.5 km north of Kerteminde on road 315.

KOLDING 12C

Grønninghoved Strand Camping
6093 Grønninghoved Strand.
Tel 75 57 40 45, Fax 75 57 43 45. English spoken.
OPEN: 01/04–15/09. SIZE: 6 ha, 200 pitches (150 with elec, 140 statics), 17 hot showers (charge), 34 WCs, 9 CWPs. ☎ &

Restaurant at 4 km. Tennis, mini-golf, sauna, playground.
PRICES: (1996) Caravan with family 186, Tent with two adults 106. CC: Euro/Access, Visa.
Exit Kolding-South from E45. Drive south via Kolding Vonsild, Sjolund and Grønninghoved. Follow signs.

Vonsild Camping & Feriecenter Vonsildvej 19, 6000 Kolding.
Tel 75 52 13 88, Fax 75 52 45 29. English spoken.
OPEN: all year. SIZE: 6 ha, 225 pitches (135 with elec, 20 statics), 11 hot showers (charge), 23 WCs, 1 CWP. ☎ &

Restaurant at 0.2 km.

Denmark (side margin)

PRICES: (1996) Caravan with family 170, Tent with two adults 100. CC: none.
Leave motorway at exit Kolding-South (no 65) towards Kolding, turn right at the first traffic lights (road no 170) and site is 500 m.

KRUSÅ   12C

FDM-Camping Kollund Fjordvejen 29a, 6340 Kruså.
Tel 74 67 85 15, Fax 74 67 83 85. English spoken.
OPEN: 22/03–19/10. SIZE: 3.5 ha, 237 pitches (183 with elec, 30 statics), 17 hot showers (charge), 28 WCs, 1 CWP. ⚓ ♿

≋ ⚓ 🏕 R 🚽 🛍   🏠

Restaurant at 0.2 km. Discounts for RAC members.
PRICES: Caravan with family 162, Tent with two adults 96. CC: Amex, Euro/Access, Visa.
From Kruså, east towards Sønderborg on route 8. 1 km from junction in Kruså go right, drive through Kollund and campsite is on the left.

LANGELAND

RISTINGE   12D

Ristinge Camping Ristingevej 104, 5932 Humble, Langeland.
Tel 62 57 13 29, Fax 62 57 13 29. English spoken.
OPEN: 01/04–08/09. SIZE: 4 ha, 90 pitches, 19 hot showers (charge), 35 WCs, 1 CWP. ♿

≋ ⚓ 🛝 R 🚽 🛍 🍴 ✕   🏠

PRICES: unavailable. CC: Euro/Access, Visa.
Follow signs to Ristinge from Humble. Only campsite in Ristinge.

TRANEKAER   12D

Emmerbolle Strandcamping Emmerbollevej 24, 5953 Tranekaer, Langeland.
Tel 62 59 12 26, Fax 62 59 12 28. English spoken.
OPEN: 07/04–24/09. SIZE: 10 ha, 240 pitches (180 with elec, 20 statics), 14 hot showers (charge), 32 WCs, 2 CWPs. ⚓ ♿

Restaurant at 4 km. Trampoline; tame animals.
PRICES: (1996) Caravan with family 213, Tent with two adults 120. CC: none.
From Rudkøbing towards Lohals. Turn towards Lejbolle 5 km north of Tranekaer Castle.

END OF LANGELAND RESORTS

LØKKEN   12A

FDM-Camping Gl Klitgaard Nr Lyngbyvej 331, 9480 Løkken.
Tel 98 99 62 06, Fax 98 99 62 06. English spoken.
OPEN: 22/03–19/10. SIZE: 8 ha, 400 pitches

120 with elec, 20 statics), 20 hot showers (charge), 47 WCs, 1 CWP. ♿

≋ 🏊 🏕 R 🚽 🛍 🛍   🔌 🏠

Restaurant at 4 km. Discounts for RAC members.
PRICES: Caravan with family 162, Tent with two adults 96. CC: Amex, Euro/Access, Visa.
From Løkken go north to nr Lyngby and campsite is signposted.

LOLLAND

NAKSKOV   12D

Albuen Camping Vesternasvej 70, Ydo, 4900 Ydo, Lolland.
Tel 53 94 87 62. English spoken.
OPEN: 30/03–20/10. SIZE: 10 ha, 150 pitches (120 with elec, 30 statics), 8 hot showers (charge), 20 WCs, 1 CWP. ⚓ ♿

≋ ⚓ 🏕 R 🚽 🛍 🛍   🌐 🏠

Restaurant at 12 km.
PRICES: (1996) Caravan with family 167, Tent with two adults 84. CC: Visa.
From Nakskov by the harbour go over the new bridge (Nybro). Turn right towards Albuen Camping, Skandsen, Vestenskov and Langø for 10 km. Then turn left to the campsite.

END OF LOLLAND RESORTS

MARIAGER   12A

Mariager Camping 9550 Mariager.
Tel 98 54 13 42, Fax 98 54 25 80.
English spoken.
OPEN: 01/04–31/10. SIZE: 3 ha, 100 pitches (all with elec, 50 statics), 8 hot showers (charge), 16 WCs, 4 CWPs. ⚓ ♿

~ ⚓ 🚰 R 🚽 🛍   🏠

Restaurant at 0.5 km. Sailing, windsurfing, fishing.
PRICES: Caravan with family 165, Tent with two adults 100. CC: none.

MIDDELFART   12C

Rojle Klint Camping Rojleklintevej 29, 5500 Middelfart.
Tel 64 40 13 81, Fax 64 40 13 81. English spoken.
OPEN: 01/04–01/10. SIZE: 4 ha, 112 pitches (all with elec), 4 hot showers (charge), 10 WCs. ⚓ ♿

≋ ⚓ 🛝 R 🚽 🛍 🛍   🏠

Restaurant at 3 km.
PRICES: (1996) Caravan with family 160, Tent with two adults 88. CC: none.
From Middelfart, go over the bridge (gate nr 58) to Strib. Turn right by the church in Strib and then follow signs to campsite.

Ronaes Strand Camping Ronaesvej, 5580 Nr Aby.
Tel 64 42 17 63, Fax 64 42 17 73. English spoken.
OPEN: 30/03–15/09. SIZE: 4 ha, 130 pitches
(all with elec, 60 statics), 14 hot showers (charge),
31 WCs, 3 CWPs. &

Restaurant at 0.5 km.
PRICES: (1996) Caravan with family 172,
Tent with two adults 108. CC: none.
*From the Middelfart to Assens road (313) follow
signs Rolund/Udby, 12 km from Middelfart.
Follow the Margurite route from Middelfart.*

MØN

STEGE   12D

Ulvshale Camping Ulvshalevej 236,
4780 Stege, Møn.
Tel 55 81 53 25, Fax 55 81 55 23. English spoken.
OPEN: 01/04–30/09. SIZE: 2 ha, 50 pitches (all with
elec, 50 statics), 6 hot showers (charge), 14 WCs.

Restaurant at 0.9 km.
PRICES: unavailable. CC: none.
*From Stege go in direction of Ulvshale-Nyord for
6 km.*

END OF MØN RESORTS

MORS

NYKØBING   12A

Jesperhus Feriecenter Legindvej 30, Legind
Bjerge, 7900 Nykøbing, Mors.
Tel 97 72 37 01, Fax 97 71 02 55. English spoken.
OPEN: all year. SIZE: 11 ha, 570 pitches (all with
elec, 56 hot showers, 89 WCs, 20 French WCs,
3 CWPs. & &

Shop at 3 km.
PRICES: (1996) Caravan with family 228, Tent with
two adults 158. CC: Euro/Access, Visa.
*From Nykøbing go towards Skive and follow signs
for Jesperhus Blomsterpark. The campsite is 200 m
past this attraction.*

END OF MORS RESORTS

NORDBORG   12C

Augustenhof Camping Augustenhofvej 30,
6430 Nordborg.
Tel 74 45 03 04. English spoken.
OPEN: all year. SIZE: 6 ha, 100 pitches (60 with elec,
45 statics), 8 hot showers (charge), 16 WCs,
2 CWPs. &

Shop at 4 km. Restaurant at 4 km.
PRICES: (1996) Caravan with family 173.50,
Tent with two adults 94. CC: none.
*Follow the campsite signs through Nordborg
towards Købingsmark then turn left towards
Augustenhof.*

NØRRE SNEDE   12A

Hampen Sø Camping Hovedgaden 31b,
7362 Hampen.
Tel 75 77 52 55, Fax 75 77 52 66. English spoken.
OPEN: 01/05–01/09. SIZE: 10 ha, 250 pitches
(114 with elec), 12 hot showers, 23 WCs, 2 CWPs.
& &

Restaurant at 1.5 km. Within reach of Legoland.
PRICES: (1996) Caravan with family 187,
Tent with two adults 96. CC: none.
*10 km north of Nørre Snede on route 13. Turn
sharp left in Hovedgaden and drive 2 km.*

Rorbaek Sø Camping Rorbaekvej 52,
7361 Ejstrupholm.
Tel 75 73 61 61, Fax 75 73 62 61. English spoken.
OPEN: 01/04–23/10. SIZE: 5 ha, 120 pitches
(80 with elec), 8 hot showers (charge), 14 WCs,
2 French WCs, 1 CWP. &

Fishing.
PRICES: Caravan with family 169,
Tent with two adults 88. CC: none.
*In Nørre Snede on road 13 go towards Brande on
the 411 for 800 m, then turn left. Campsite is
signposted.*

NYBORG   12D

Gronnehave Strand Camping Resstrupvej 83,
5800 Nyborg.
Tel 65 36 15 50, Fax 65 36 15 50. English spoken.
OPEN: 03/04–13/09. SIZE: 7 ha, 120 pitches
(all with elec, 30 statics), 8 hot showers (charge),
20 WCs, 1 CWP. & &

Restaurant at 1.5 km.
PRICES: (1996) Caravan with family 168,
Tent with two adults 86. CC: none.
*Situated between Nyborg and Kerteminde, 4 km
north of Nyborg. On road E20, exit 46. Follow the
signs.*

NYMINDEGAB   12C

Nymindegab Økologisk Camping Lyngtoften,
Nymindegab, 6830 Nr Nebel.
Tel 75 28 91 83, Fax 75 28 94 30. English spoken.
OPEN: 07/04–01/10. SIZE: 8 ha, 318 pitches

(all with elec, 50 statics), 15 hot showers (charge), 37 WCs, 2 CWPs. ☎ &

Restaurant at 1 km. Camp shop specialises in organic produce.
PRICES: Caravan with family 174,
Tent with two adults 100. CC: none.
Follow sign to campsite from centre of village.

ODENSE 12C

Camp Blommenslyst Middelfartsvej 494, 5491 Blommenslyst.
Tel 65 96 76 41. English spoken.
OPEN: 01/05–15/09. SIZE: 2 ha, 60 pitches (20 with elec), 4 hot showers (charge), 7 WCs, 1 French WC, 1 CWP. ☎

Shop at 0.5 km. Restaurant at 0.5 km.
PRICES: (1996) Caravan with family 149,
Tent with two adults 76. CC: none.
6 km from Odense, going west, to Middelfartsvej.

OKSBØL 12C

Borsmose Strand Camping Borsmosevej 3, 6840 Oksbøl.
Tel 75 27 70 70, Fax 75 27 77 70. English spoken.
OPEN: 22/03–15/09. SIZE: 23 ha, 409 pitches (all with elec, 200 statics), 40 hot showers (charge), 65 WCs, 3 CWPs. ☎ &

Restaurant at 10 km.
PRICES: (1996) Caravan with family 188,
Tent with two adults 96. CC: none.
Turn left by the church in Oskbøl and drive 10 km westwards.

FDM-Camping Groerup Strand Groeruphavvej 4, Groerup, 6840 Oksbøl.
Tel 75 27 70 49, Fax 75 27 79 49. English spoken.
OPEN: 19/04–14/09. SIZE: 2.5 ha, 130 pitches (90 with elec, 20 statics), 6 hot showers (charge), 10 WCs, 1 CWP.

Restaurant at 10 km. Reduction for RAC members.
PRICES: Caravan with family 162, Tent with two adults 96. CC: Amex, Euro/Access, Visa.
3 km south-west of Oksbøl on road 431, take turning for Groerup and campsite is 7 km.

ØSLØS 12A

Bygholm Camping 7742 Øsløs.
Tel 97 99 31 39, Fax 97 99 38 02.
English spoken.
OPEN: all year. SIZE: 2.9 ha, 150 pitches (110 with elec, 30 statics), 10 hot showers (charge), 18 WCs, 2 French WCs, 2 CWPs. ☎ &

Shop at 0.5 km. Reservations essential in winter.
PRICES: (1996) Caravan with family 161,
Tent with two adults 84. CC: Euro/Access, Visa.
*Route A11 between Thisted and Fjerritslev.
Campsite is signposted at Øsløs.*

ØSTBIRK 12A/C

Camping Vestbirk 8752 Østbirk.
Tel 75 78 12 92, Fax 75 78 02 11. English spoken.
OPEN: 15/04–15/09. SIZE: 5 ha, 250 pitches (200 with elec, 50 statics), 11 hot showers (charge), 14 WCs, 1 CWP. ☎ &

Restaurant at 3 km. Sauna, spa/whirlpool, boats, deer park, fishing.
PRICES: (1996) Caravan with family 175,
Tent with two adults 100. CC: Euro/Access, Visa.
*From Østbirk follow the road towards Nim (409).
After passing Vestbirk follow signs to the right.*

RANDERS 12A

Fladbro Camping Hedevej 9, 8900 Randers.
Tel 86 42 93 61, Fax 86 42 93 61. English spoken.
OPEN: 28/03–10/10. SIZE: 9 ha, 100 pitches (all with elec, 50 statics), 10 hot showers (charge), 25 WCs, 1 CWP. ☎ &

Restaurant at 0.6 km.
PRICES: (1996) Caravan with family 131,
Tent with two adults 66. CC: none.
*From Randers go in direction of Viborg (A16).
Turn to the left towards Langå (525) for 3 km.*

RIBE 12C

Ribe Campingplads Farupvej, 6760 Ribe.
Tel 75 41 07 77, Fax 75 41 00 01. English spoken.
OPEN: 01/01–01/11. SIZE: 5.5 ha, 300 pitches (200 with elec), 15 hot showers (charge), 17 WCs, 2 CWPs. ☎ &

Restaurant at 1 km.
PRICES: (1996) Caravan with family 148,
Tent with two adults 90. CC: Euro/Access, Visa.
*Ribe is approx 30 km south of Esbjerg on route 11.
Campsite is 1.5 km to the north of Ribe and well signposted.*

RINGKØBING 12A

Aeblehavens Camping Herningvej 105, 6950 Ringkøbing.
Tel 97 32 04 20. English spoken.
OPEN: 01/03–31/10. SIZE: 9 ha, 90 pitches (104 with elec, 60 statics), 6 hot showers (charge), 18 WCs, 3 French WCs, 1 CWP. ☎ &

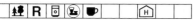

Shop at 4.5 km. Restaurant at 2 km. Roller-skating, riding, mini-golf.
PRICES: Caravan with family 178, Tent with two adults 88. CC: none.
Site is 5 km east of Ringkøbing on the main road 15.

RØNDE 12B

Kaløvig Camping Folle Strandvej 150, 8410 Rønde.
Tel 86 37 13 05. English spoken.
OPEN: all year. SIZE: 2 ha, 92 pitches (all with elec), 7 hot showers (charge), 17 WCs, 1 CWP.

PRICES: Caravan with family 150, Tent with two adults 88. CC: none.
Campsite is signposted from Rønde.

RY 12A

Birkhede Camping I/S Lyngvej 14, 8680 Ry.
Tel 86 89 13 55, Fax 86 89 03 13. English spoken.
OPEN: 01/05–15/09. SIZE: 10 ha, 225 pitches (all with elec, 11 statics), 18 hot showers (charge), 32 WCs, 3 CWPs. ⚓ ♿

Restaurant at 3 km.
PRICES: (1996) Caravan with family 190, Tent with two adults 121. CC: none.
Campsite is 1 km from Ry towards Laven and well signposted.

Holmens Camping Klostervej 148, 8680 Ry.
Tel 86 89 17 62, Fax 86 89 17 12. English spoken.
OPEN: 30/03–01/10. SIZE: 8 ha, 300 pitches (255 with elec), 24 hot showers (charge), 38 WCs, 2 CWPs. ⚓ ♿

Restaurant at 2 km.
PRICES: (1996) Caravan with family 178, Tent with two adults 99. CC: none.

SAEBY 12B

Hedebo Strand Camping 9300 Saeby.
Tel 98 46 14 49, Fax 98 40 13 13. English spoken.
OPEN: 01/04–05/09. SIZE: 12 ha, 550 pitches (450 with elec, 200 statics), 44 hot showers (charge), 53 WCs, 3 CWPs. ⚓ ♿

Shop at 2 km. Restaurant at 0.4 km. 10 minutes from the ferry connections to Norway and Sweden.
PRICES: (1996) Caravan with family 171, Tent with two adults 96. CC: none.
This highly recommended campsite is on route 180, 1.5 km north of Saeby. Approaching from Frederikshavn, take exit 12 and drive for 7 km.

SALTUM 12A

Jambo Vesterhav Camping Solvejen 58, 9493 Saltum.
Tel 98 88 16 66, Fax 98 88 18 08. English spoken.
OPEN: 01/05–01/09. SIZE: 13 ha, 450 pitches (400 with elec, 25 statics), 42 hot showers (charge), 47 WCs, 3 French WCs, 2 CWPs. ⚓ ♿

Large playground; Sea 2 km, sauna, solarium, tennis.
PRICES: (1996) Caravan with family 210, Tent with two adults 120. CC: Euro/Access, Visa.
Take road 55 along Saltum Strandvej for 2 km then turn left along Solvejen.

SEJS 12A

Sejs Bakker Camping Borgdalsvej 15, Sejs, 8600 Silkeborg.
Tel 86 84 63 83, Fax 86 84 63 82. English spoken.
OPEN: 01/04–15/09. SIZE: 3.4 ha, 170 pitches (90 with elec, 30 statics), 7 hot showers (charge), 19 WCs, 1 CWP. ⚓ ♿

Restaurant at 0.2 km.
PRICES: (1996) Caravan with family 143, Tent with two adults 88. CC: none.
From A15 follow signs to resort. From centre of Silkeborg follow signs to harbour and campsite.

SILKEBORG 12A

FDM-Camping Jyllandsringen Resenbro, Skelberuprej 38, 8600 Silkeborg.
Tel 86 85 31 76, Fax 86 85 31 84. English spoken.
OPEN: 22/03–19/10. SIZE: 10 ha, 500 pitches (200 with elec, 84 statics), 18 hot showers (charge), 27 WCs, 2 CWPs. ♿

Restaurant at 4 km. Discounts for RAC members.
PRICES: Caravan with family 162, Tent with two adults 96. CC: Euro/Access, Visa.
From Silkeborg head for Resenbro and the campsite is signposted from there.

SINDAL 12A

Sindal Camping route 35, Hjorringvej 125, 9870 Sindal.
Tel 98 93 65 30, Fax 98 93 69 30. English spoken.
OPEN: 01/04–01/10. SIZE: 6 ha, 108 pitches (95 with elec, 20 statics), 9 hot showers (charge), 18 WCs, 3 CWPs. ⚓ ♿

Restaurant at 1 km. Sauna and solarium.
PRICES: (1996) Caravan with family 160, Tent with two adults 100. CC: Euro/Access, Visa.
1 km west of Sindal.

Denmark

SJAELLAND

FAKSE LADEPLADS 12D

Vemmetofte Strand Camping Nystrandskov 1, 4640 Fakse, Sjaelland.
Tel 53 71 02 26, Fax 53 71 02 59. English spoken.
OPEN: all year. SIZE: 6 ha, 150 pitches (all with elec, 150 statics), 12 hot showers (charge), 32 WCs, 2 CWPs. ✆

Tame animals, sauna.
PRICES: (1996) Caravan with family 159,
Tent with two adults 94. CC: none.
From Rønnede drive to Fakse, then to Fakse Ladeplads. From there, turn left to Vemmetofte and just before the castle turn right to the campsite.

HELSINGØR 12B

Helsingør Camping Gronnehave Campingvej 1, 3000 Helsingør, Sjaelland.
Tel 49 21 58 56, Fax 49 21 58 56. English spoken.
OPEN: all year. SIZE: 100 ha, 90 pitches (all with elec), 4 hot showers (charge), 12 WCs, 1 French WC.

Trampoline.
PRICES: (1996) Caravan with family 144,
Tent with two adults 84. CC: none.
Next to the Hamlet Castle, Kronborg.

HILLERØD 12B

Undinegardens Camping Ganlose, 3660 Stenlose, Sjaelland.
Tel 48 18 30 32, Fax 48 18 47 32. English spoken.
OPEN: all year. SIZE: 4 ha, 65 pitches (58 with elec, 90 statics), 6 hot showers (charge), 10 WCs, 1 CWP. ✆

Restaurant at 2.5 km. Golf course 1 km.
PRICES: Caravan with family 160,
Tent with two adults 94. CC: none.
On route 233, 25 km north-west of Copenhagen.

HØRVE 12D

Sanddobberne's Camping Kalundborgvej 28, 4534 Hørve, Sjaelland.
Tel 59 65 35 35, Fax 59 65 50 35. English spoken.
OPEN: 01/04–15/09. SIZE: 3 ha, 240 pitches (220 with elec, 80 statics), 17 hot showers, 26 WCs, 2 French WCs, 1 CWP. ✆ ✆

Restaurant at 1 km. Direct access to a sandy family beach.
PRICES: (1996) Caravan with family 148,
Tent with two adults 90. CC: none.

Only an hours drive from København, site is off route 225, next door to Dragsholm castle.

ISHOJ HAVN 12D

FDM-Camping Tangloppen 2635 Ishoj Havn, Sjaelland.
Tel 43 54 07 67, Fax 43 54 07 64. English spoken.
OPEN: 19/04–14/09. SIZE: 2.5 ha, 105 pitches (25 with elec), 12 hot showers, 10 WCs, 1 CWP. ✆ ✆

Restaurant at 1 km. Sea 500 m. Discounts for RAC members.
PRICES: Caravan with family 162,
Tent with two adults 96. CC: Euro/Access, Visa.
E20/E47/E55 and 151 (Kogevejen) to Ishoj.

KALUNDBORG 12D

FDM-Camping Bjerge Strand Osvejen 30, 4480 Store Fuglede, Sjaelland.
Tel 53 49 78 03, Fax 53 49 78 03. English spoken.
OPEN: 22/03–19/10. SIZE: 3 ha, 140 pitches (102 with elec, 60 statics), 14 hot showers (charge), 15 WCs, 1 CWP. ✆ ✆

Restaurant at 5 km. Discounts for RAC members.
PRICES: Caravan with family 162, Tent with two adults 96. CC: Amex, Euro/Access, Visa.
On the E22 between Kalundborg and Slagelse. In Bjerge drive to Urhojvej and further on to Osvejen. From there, follow the signs.

Urhojgard Camping Urhojvej 14, 4480 St Fulglede, Sjaelland.
Tel 53 49 72 00, Fax 53 49 72 77. English spoken.
OPEN: 01/04–30/09. SIZE: 9 ha, 230 pitches (all with elec, 130 statics), 8 hot showers (charge), 30 WCs, 1 CWP. ✆

Table tennis, mini-golf.
PRICES: (1996) Caravan with family 150,
Tent with two adults 90. CC: none.
About 12 km from Kalundborg.

KORSØR 12D

Campinggaarden Boeslunde Rennebjergvej 110, 4242 Boeslunde, Sjaelland.
Tel 53 54 02 08, Fax 53 54 03 40. English spoken.
OPEN: all year. SIZE: 3 ha, 60 pitches (50 with elec, 20 statics), 7 hot showers (charge), 10 WCs, 1 CWP. ✆ ✆

Shop at 2 km. Restaurant at 2 km. Toddlers pool, table tennis, pony riding, trampoline.
PRICES: (1996) Caravan with family 175,
Tent with two adults 92. CC: none.
From Korsør go 8 km along road 265. Turn right

towards Rennebjergvej. Coming from Slagelse, take road 259 for 15 km and turn right towards Rennebjergvej.

NYKØBING 12A

FDM-Camping Nykobing Nordstrand
Nordstrandsvej 107, 4500 Nykøbing, Sjaelland.
Tel 53 41 16 42, Fax 53 41 16 42. English spoken.
OPEN: 22/03−21/09. SIZE: 5 ha, 210 pitches
(100 with elec, 80 statics), 14 hot showers
(charge), 30 WCs, 1 CWP. &

Restaurant at 1 km. Discounts for RAC members.
PRICES: Caravan with family 162, Tent with two
adults 96. CC: Amex, Euro/Access, Visa.
Access from village via Nordstrandvej.

Skaerby Camping 4500 Nykøbing, Sjaelland.
Tel 53 41 08 50, Fax 53 41 07 50. English spoken.
OPEN: 08/04−21/10. SIZE: 6 ha, 14 hot showers
(charge), 30 WCs, 2 CWPs. &

PRICES: (1996) Caravan with family 161, Tent with
two adults 82. CC: r one.
East of route 21.

RINGSTED 12D

Camping Skovly Nebs Mollevej 65, Ortved,
4100 Ringsted, Sjaelland.
Tel 53 62 82 61, Fax 53 62 86 25.
English spoken.
OPEN: 01/04−30/09. SIZE: 3 ha, 28 pitches (40 with
elec, 80 statics), 5 hot showers (charge), 13 WCs,
1 CWP. &

Restaurant at 1 km.
PRICES: (1996) Caravan with family 184146, Tent
with two adults 9488. CC: Euro/Access, Visa.
*On road 14, 7 km from Ringsted towards
Roskilde. Follow signs in Ortved.*

ROSKILDE 12D

Borrevejle Camping Hornsherredvej 3,
4060 Kr Saby, Sjaelland.
Tel 42 40 01 40, Fax 42 40 00 85.
English spoken.
OPEN: all year. SIZE: 2 ha, 130 pitches (all with
elec), 8 hot showers (charge), 10 WCs,
1 CWP. & &

Horses.
PRICES: (1996) Caravan with family 147, Tent with
two adults 88. CC: Amex, Euro/Access, Visa.
*From Roskilde go west along the Holboek
motorway (route 21/23). Turn off after approx
12 km and follow the Fredrikssund road.*

VORDINGBORG 12D

Ore Strand Camping Orevej 145,
4760 Vordingborg, Sjaelland.
Tel 53 77 06 03, Fax 53 77 06 03. English spoken.
OPEN: all year. SIZE: 3 ha, 200 pitches (all with elec,
23 statics), 10 hot showers (charge), 24 WCs,
2 CWPs. & &

PRICES: (1996) Caravan with family 165,
Tent with two adults 88. CC: Euro/Access, Visa.
From E47, just before Masnedsund bridge.

END OF SJAELLAND RESORTS

SKAGEN 12B

Grenen Camping Fyrvej 16, 9990 Skagen.
Tel 98 44 25 46, Fax 98 44 65 46. English spoken.
OPEN: 03/05−07/09. SIZE: 6 ha, 270 pitches
(190 with elec), 13 hot showers (charge), 23 WCs,
1 CWP. & &

Restaurant at 1.5 km.
PRICES: Caravan with family 179,
Tent with two adults 104. CC: none.
*Go through Skagen towards Grenen, and the
campsite is on the right.*

Poul Eegs Camping Batterivej 31, 9990 Skagen.
Tel 98 44 14 70, Fax 98 45 14 60. English spoken.
OPEN: 08/05−31/08. SIZE: 9 ha, 420 pitches
(300 with elec), 23 hot showers (charge), 35 WCs,
2 CWPs. & &

Restaurant at 1.5 km.
PRICES: (1996) Caravan with family 202,
Tent with two adults 104. CC: none.
Follow signs to campsite from resort.

Rabjerg Mile Camping Kandestedvej 55,
9990 Skagen.
Tel 98 48 75 00, Fax 98 48 75 88. English spoken.
OPEN: 01/04−15/09. SIZE: 9 ha, 350 pitches
(230 with elec), 17 hot showers (charge), 35 WCs,
1 CWP. & &

Restaurant at 1 km. Tennis courts.
PRICES: (1996) Caravan with family 161, Tent with
two adults 96. CC: Euro/Access, Visa.

SKANDERBORG 12A

Skanderborg So Camping Horsenvej 21,
8660 Skanderborg.
Tel 86 51 13 11, Fax 86 51 17 33. English spoken.
OPEN: 27/03−02/11. SIZE: 9 ha, 230 pitches
(200 with elec, 20 statics), 20 hot showers
(charge), 40 WCs, 3 CWPs. & &

Denmark

Restaurant at 2 km.
PRICES: (1996) Caravan with family 159,
Tent with two adults 100. CC: Euro/Access, Visa.
*From the E45 south of Skanderborg take exit 54
towards Ejer Baynerhoj then turn left towards
Tebstrup, left again towards Skanderborg and the
campsite is 5 km ahead on the right.*

SKIVE 12A

FDM-Camping Skive Marienlyst Strand 15,
7800 Skive.
Tel 97 51 44 55, Fax 97 51 44 55. English spoken.
OPEN: 22/03–19/10. SIZE: 2 ha, 210 pitches
(150 with elec, 10 statics), 10 hot showers
(charge), 18 WCs, 1 CWP. &

Restaurant at 5 km. Reduction for RAC members.
PRICES: Caravan with family 162, Tent with two
adults 96. CC: Amex, Euro/Access, Visa.
Follow signs to campsite in Skive.

SØNDERBORG 12C

Lysabildskov Feriecenter Skovforten 4,
6470 Sydals.
Tel 74 40 43 98, Fax 74 40 43 98. English spoken.
OPEN: 01/04–01/10. SIZE: 4.2 ha, 192 pitches
(170 with elec, 50 statics), 10 hot showers,
18 WCs, 1 CWP. ✆ &

Restaurant at 3 km. Whirlpool, solarium, sauna,
tennis.
PRICES: (1996) Caravan with family 140,
Tent with two adults 85. CC: none.
*From Sønderborg go east and then south-east
towards Skovby. Then follow signs to Lysabild.*

SØNDERVIG 12A

Søndervig Camping Solvej 2, Søndervig,
6950 Ringkøbing.
Tel 97 33 90 34, Fax 97 33 90 34. English spoken.
OPEN: 07/04–31/10. SIZE: 3 ha, 185 pitches
(173 with elec, 15 statics), 12 hot showers
(charge), 24 WCs, 2 CWPs. ✆

PRICES: (1996) Caravan with family 154,
Tent with two adults 90. CC: Visa.
*Søndervig is on main road 181, just north-west of
Ringkøbing.*

SPØTTRUP 12A

Limfjords Camping Albaek Strandvej 5, Lihme,
7860 Spøttrup.
Tel 97 56 02 50, Fax 97 56 06 54. English spoken.
OPEN: all year. SIZE: 12 ha, 180 pitches (300 with

elec, 150 statics), 14 hot showers (charge),
20 WCs, 2 CWPs. ✆ &

Restaurant at 5 km. Fitness centre.
PRICES: (1996) Caravan with family 183,
Tent with two adults 96. CC: none.
20 km west of Skive on the Limfjord.

STRUER 12A

Bremdal Camping Fjordvejen 12, 7600 Struer.
Tel 97 85 16 50, Fax 97 84 09 50. English spoken.
OPEN: 15/04–15/09. SIZE: 4 ha, 120 pitches
(all with elec, 70 statics), 9 hot showers (charge),
35 WCs, 1 CWP. ✆ &

Restaurant at 1 km.
PRICES: (1996) Caravan with family 153,
Tent with two adults 90. CC: none.
*Follow signs from the main road (A11) going
through Struer.*

SVENDBORG 12A

FDM-Camping Thurø Smormosevej 7, Thurø,
5700 Svendborg.
Tel 62 20 52 54, Fax 62 20 52 54. English spoken.
OPEN: 12/04–14/09. SIZE: 2 ha, 260 pitches
(168 with elec, 50 statics), 14 hot showers
(charge), 30 WCs, 1 CWP. &

Reduction for RAC members.
PRICES: Caravan with family 162, Tent with two
adults 96. CC: Amex, Euro/Access, Visa.
*From Svendborg cross the dyke to Thurø, turn left
to centre and campsite is 800 m ahead.*

Knarreborg Molle Camping Knarreborg
Mollevej 25, 5883 Oure.
Tel 62 28 10 56, Fax 62 28 18 61. English spoken.
OPEN: 01/04–30/09. SIZE: 5 ha, 160 pitches (all
with elec), 6 hot showers, 25 WCs, 1 CWP. ✆ &

PRICES: (1996) Caravan with family 154,
Tent with two adults 88. CC: Visa.
*From Svendborg go to Oure. By the church turn
right, go about 3 km and follow the signs.*

Åbyskov Strand Camping Skarupore Strandvej
74, Åbyskov, 5881 Skarup Fyn.
Tel 62 23 13 20, Fax 62 23 13 20. English spoken.
OPEN: 01/04–15/09. SIZE: 4.7 ha, 200 pitches
(152 with elec), 1 CWP. ✆

Restaurant at 6 km.
PRICES: (1996) Caravan with family 152,
Tent with two adults 80. CC: none.
*From Svendborg take road 163. Turn off in
Vejstrup and campsite is 4 km, well signposted*

THISTED 12A

Nordse Camping Klitmoller, 7700 Thisted.
Tel 97 97 50 71, Fax 97 97 50 71. English spoken.
OPEN: 30/03–23/10. SIZE: 2.9 ha, 100 pitches (all
with elec), 9 hot showers (charge), 10 WCs, 1 CWP. ⬤

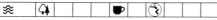

Restaurant at 0.5 km.
PRICES: (1996) Caravan with family 153,
Tent with two adults 92. CC: none.
Signposted in the town.

ULFBORG 12A

Vestjydsk Fritidscenter Sportsveg 1, 6990 Ulfborg.
Tel 97 49 17 56, Fax 97 49 26 96. English spoken.
OPEN: 11/06–15/08. SIZE: 15 hot showers, 2 WCs,
1 CWP. ⬤

Shop at 1 km. Restaurant at 1 km.
PRICES: (1996) Caravan with family 100,
Tent with two adults 50. CC: none.
Campsite well signposted.

VARDE 12C

Henneby Camping Hennebysvej 20,
6854 Henne.
Tel 75 25 51 63. English spoken.
OPEN: 30/03–01/11. SIZE: 3 ha, 150 pitches (100 with
elec), 14 hot showers (charge), 20 WCs, 1 CWP. ⬤ ⬤

Restaurant at 3 km. Close to local attractions;
riding.
PRICES: (1996) Caravan with family 172,
Tent with two adults 100. CC: none.
*From Varde drive towards Henne Strand, and
turn right after Henneby.*

Naturistcamping Lyngboparken
Strandfogedvej 15, 6854 Henne.
Tel 75 25 50 92. English spoken.
OPEN: 20/06–01/09. SIZE: 8 ha, 75 pitches (all with
elec, 20 statics), 4 hot showers, 9 WCs, 1 CWP.

Shop at 2 km. Restaurant at 2 km. Official naturist
beach nearby.
PRICES: (1996) Caravan with family 135,
Tent with two adults 90. CC: none.
*From Varde go north-west towards Henne Strand.
Campsite is about 2.5 km before Henne Strand.*

VEDERSØ KLIT 12A

Campinggarden Vederso 6990 Vedersø Klit.
Tel 97 49 51 60, Fax 97 49 51 60. English spoken.
OPEN: 01/03–02/01. SIZE: 2.7 ha, 117 pitches
(90 with elec), 7 hot showers (charge), 17 WCs,
1 CWP. ⬤ ⬤

Restaurant at 0.5 km.
PRICES: (1996) Caravan with family 150,
Tent with two adults 88. CC: none.
*Vedersø Klit is about 18 km north of Søndervig.
Campsite is well signposted.*

VEJEN 12C

Vejen Camping Vorupvaenget 2, 6600 Vejen.
Tel 75 36 20 99, Fax 75 36 20 99. English spoken.
OPEN: 19/04–28/09. SIZE: 3 ha, 95 pitches (34 with
elec, 10 statics), 4 hot showers (charge), 9 WCs,
1 CWP. ⬤

Shop at 0.5 km. Restaurant at 0.5 km.
PRICES: (1996) Caravan with family 135,
Tent with two adults 76. CC: none.
On road 66, 22 km west of Kolding.

VEJLE 12C

Vejle Camping Helligkildevej 5, 7100 Vejle.
Tel 75 82 33 35, Fax 75 82 33 35. English spoken.
OPEN: 02/04–15/09. SIZE: 3 ha, 155 pitches (100 with
elec), 12 hot showers (charge), 23 WCs, 1 CWP. ⬤

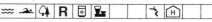

Restaurant at 1 km.
PRICES: (1996) Caravan with family 154,
Tent with two adults 90. CC: none.
*Pass the new bridge over Vejle bay, turn left to
Vejle and follow signs to campsite and football
stadium, north of the town.*

VIBORG 12A

Tjele Langso Camping
Hobro Landevej 79, 8830 Tjele.
Tel 86 65 23 12, Fax 86 65 23 39. English spoken.
OPEN: 27/03–14/09. SIZE: 6 ha, 120 pitches
(100 with elec, 50 statics), 6 hot showers (charge),
25 WCs, 8 French WCs, 2 CWPs. ⬤

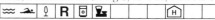

Restaurant at 1 km.
PRICES: (1996) Caravan with family 156,
Tent with two adults 92. CC: none.
*From Viborg take road 16 towards Randers. After
10 km turn left towards Hobro on the 517. 1 km
after passing Tjele Manor turn left at sign to site.*

Vammen Camping Vammen-Viborg, 8830 Tjele.
Tel 86 69 01 52, Fax 86 69 03 58. English spoken.
OPEN: 01/05–01/09. SIZE: 7 ha, 100 pitches (all with
elec), 6 hot showers (charge), 12 WCs, 2 CWPs. ⬤

Restaurant at 1.5 km. Musicians welcomed!
PRICES: (1996) Caravan with family 144,
Tent with two adults 88. CC: none.
A13 to 8 km north of Viborg, then right to Vammen.

Denmark (side margin)

FINLAND

Finland's landscapes are as impressive as its leisure facilities are outstanding. To avoid the long drive north through Sweden, consider a fly-drive holiday. Alternatively, you could shortcut across the Baltic to Helsinki from Stockholm in Sweden, or cross from Travemünde in northern Germany.

If time is limited in Helsinki, try to include the Temppeliaukio rock church, the sea fortress of Suomenlinna, the open-air museum in the Seurasaari park, and for a very agreeable sample of Finnish style and design, a stroll along the *Esplanade*, Helsinki's smartest thoroughfare.

The circuit from Helsinki north to Varkaus then back by Tampere to Turku (capital prior to 1819) is a popular introduction to Finland, passing through the Finnish lake district, where there are some 200 000 lakes. At Varkaus, the lure of Lapland may tempt your further north, but bear in mind that the distance between Rovaniemi, just inside the Arctic Circle, and Helsinki, is approximately 1200 km.

You are never far from water in Finland, and boats, whether sailing or motor, can be hired, as can bikes, canoes and angling equipment. Slightly less obvious is the Finns' enthusiasm for golf and tennis... until you remember that a Finnish summer day offers unusually long hours of sunshine; and the mid-continental climate means temperatures can remain high for quite a few hours.

Emergency numbers

Police 10022

Fire Brigade and Ambulance 112

Warning information

Carrying a warning triangle recommended

Blood Alcohol Legal Limit 50 mg

ÄMMÄNSAARI   10D

Kiantajarvi 89600 Ämmänsaari.
Tel 986 711209. English spoken.
OPEN: 01/06–30/09. SIZE: 4 ha, 200 pitches
(40 with elec), 8 hot showers, 12 WCs, 1 CWP. ℄

Shop at 4 km. Restaurant at 4 km.
PRICES: (1996) Caravan with family 72, Tent with two adults 55. CC: Amex, Euro/Access, Visa.
North-east of Ämmänsaari, near Suomussalmi.

ESPOO   11B

Oittaa Camping 02740 Espoo Kunnarlantie.
Tel 908 62585, Fax 907 13713.
English spoken.
OPEN: 17/05–25/08. SIZE: 6 ha, 170 pitches
(24 with elec), 10 hot showers, 19 WCs, 6 French WCs, 1 CWP. ℄ ❧

Restaurant at 5 km. Sauna, water chute.
PRICES: (1996) Caravan with family 103, Tent with two adults 85. CC: Euro/Access, Visa.
5 km from Espoo centre; signposted.

HANKO   11B

Camping Silversand
10960 Hanko Pohjoinen.
Tel 911 2485500, Fax 907 13773.
English spoken.
OPEN: 27/05–14/08. SIZE: 10 ha, 400 pitches
(80 with elec), 18 hot showers, 16 WCs, 2 CWPs. ℄

Shop at 1 km.
PRICES: (1996) Caravan with family 93, Tent with two adults 75. CC: Euro/Access, Visa.
Follow signs to campsite from Hanko.

HELSINKI   11B

Rastila Camping Vuosaari, Helsinki-Rastila, 00980 Helsinki.
Tel 358 0316551, Fax 358 03441578.
English spoken.
OPEN: 15/05–15/09. SIZE: 15 ha, 900 pitches
(300 with elec), 40 hot showers, 40 WCs, 2 CWPs. ❧

PRICES: (1996) Caravan with family 95, Tent with two adults 80. CC: none.
From city centre take road east to Vuosaari for 15 km. Site is well signposted.

IMATRA 11B

Imatra Camping 55720 Imatra.
Tel 954 24055, Fax 954 205339. English spoken.
OPEN: 09/06–13/08. SIZE: 10 ha, 8 hot showers,
12 WCs, 1 CWP. ↔ ☼

Shop at 1 km. Restaurant at 0.5 km.
PRICES: (1996) Caravan with family 88,
Tent with two adults 70. CC: Euro/Access, Visa.
Well signposted either from route 6 or from the town centre.

INARI 10B

Uruniemi Camping Uruniemi, 99870 Inari.
Tel 969 7671331, Fax 969 7671200.
English spoken.
OPEN: 01/03–15/05 & 01/06–20/09. SIZE: 4 ha,
40 pitches (20 with elec), 4 hot showers (charge),
10 WCs, 1 CWP. ↔

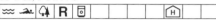

Shop at 2 km. Restaurant at 2 km.
PRICES: (1996) Caravan with family 75,
Tent with two adults 55. CC: Visa.
2 km south of Inari on E75.

JARVENPÄÄN 11B

Jarvenpään Camping Vanhankyl Anniemi,
04410 Jarvenpään.
Tel 02 87775, Fax 02 911441. English spoken.
OPEN: all year. SIZE: 6 ha, 400 pitches (150 with
elec), 12 hot showers, 13 WCs, 1 CWP. ↔ ☼

Shop at 1 km. Mini-golf.
PRICES: (1996) Caravan with family 75, Tent with
two adults 55. CC: Amex, Euro/Access, Visa.
3 km west of town, by Lake Tuusula and next door to the Health Centre.

JOENSUU 10D

Linnunlahti Camping 80110 Joensuu.
Tel 973 126272. English spoken.
OPEN: 31/05–18/08. SIZE: 6 ha, 70 pitches (56 with
elec), 11 hot showers, 18 WCs, 1 CWP. ☼

Shop at 0.3 km. Restaurant at 0.2 km.
PRICES: (1996) Caravan with family 90,
Tent with two adults 75. CC: none.
The campsite is in eastern Finland, 1.5 km from the centre of Joensuu. Access from Lansikatu road.

KALAJOKI 10D

Hiekkasarkat Camping 85100 Kalajoki.
Tel 983 4692400, Fax 983 4692211.
English spoken.

OPEN: all year. SIZE: 25 ha, 60 hot showers, 30 WCs,
2 CWPs. ↔ ☼

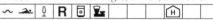

Tropical spa pool; children's amusement park
open June and July.
PRICES: (1996) Caravan with family 95, Tent with
two adults 75. CC: Amex, Euro/Access, Visa.
Situated in the resort, by highway 8.

KEMI 10D

Törmä Camping Rovaniementie 1298,
95315 Törmä.
Tel 969 8276210. English spoken.
OPEN: 01/06–15/09. SIZE: 3 ha, 100 pitches (20 with
elec), 5 hot showers (charge), 8 WCs, 1 CWP. ↔

Restaurant at 12 km. Salmon fishing.
PRICES: (1996) Caravan with family 75,
Tent with two adults 60. CC: none.
20 km north of Kemi on the road to Rovaniemi, on west bank of the Kemi river. Turn east off the R4, and the site is 4 km.

KEMIJARVI 10D

Hietaniemi Camping 98100 Kemijarvi.
Tel 969 2813640, Fax 969 2815005. English spoken.
OPEN: 01/03–30/09. SIZE: 2 ha, 50 pitches (40 with
elec), 6 hot showers, 6 WCs, 1 CWP. ↔ ☼

Shop at 0.2 km. Restaurant at 0.3 km. Sauna,
fishing lake.
PRICES: (1996) Caravan with family 90, Tent with
two adults 75. CC: Euro/Access, Visa.
1 km from railway station.

KOKKOLA 10D

Suntinsuu Camping 67100 Kokkola 10.
Tel 968 8314006, Fax 968 8310406. English spoken.
OPEN: all year. SIZE: 9 ha, 50 pitches (30 with elec,
50 statics), 10 hot showers, 10 WCs, 1 CWP. ↔

Shop at 1 km.
PRICES: (1996) Caravan with family 65,
Tent with two adults 50. CC: none.
North-east of Kokkola, 2 km from the town centre.

KOUVOLA 11B

Saaramaa Camping Finn-Camping Caravan Ky,
45670 Saaramaa.
Tel 053 32503, Fax 053 32553. English spoken.
OPEN: 10/05–15/09. SIZE: 3 ha, 80 pitches (all with
elec), 2 hot showers, 5 WCs, 1 CWP. ↔

Restaurant at 8 km. Canoes, sauna, mini-golf,
windsurfing, fishing.

Finland

PRICES: Caravan with family 80, Tent with two adults 65. CC: Euro/Access, Visa.
From the centre of Kouvola (which is 174 km north-east of Helsinki), go for 25 km on the Lappeenranta road and then turn right. Campsite at Saaramaa is 9 km ahead and well signposted.

KUOPIO 10D

Camping Atrain 71160 Kuopio.
Tel 971 723038. English spoken.
OPEN: 01/06–20/08. SIZE: 6 ha, 100 pitches (60 with elec), 6 hot showers, 11 WCs, 1 CWP. ⟨ ⟩

Shop at 3 km. Sauna.
PRICES: Caravan with family 85,
Tent with two adults 65. CC: none.
About 30 km from Kuopio on road 17, going towards Joensuu or, coming from Joensuu, the campsite is about 110 km north-west.

Kuopio Camping Rauhalahti Kiviniementie, 70700 Kuopio.
Tel 971 3612244, Fax 971 2624004. English spoken.
OPEN: 23/05–30/08. SIZE: 26 ha, 700 pitches (237 with elec), 20 hot showers, 37 WCs, 3 CWPs. ⟨ ⟩

Shop at 0.5 km. Sauna, water sports; canoes, water bikes, surf boards and bikes for hire.
PRICES: Caravan with family 105,
Tent with two adults 75. CC: Euro/Access, Visa.
1 km off route 5, 6.5 km south of town centre.

KUUSAMO 10D

Oulanka Camping Oulanka, 93600 Kuusamo.
Tel 989 863429. English spoken.
OPEN: 01/06–30/09. SIZE: 11 ha, 6 hot showers, 1 CWP. ⟨

Shop at 14 km. Restaurant at 30 km. Small shop on site. Boating and fishing.
PRICES: (1996) Caravan with family 70, Tent with two adults 55. CC: Euro/Access, Visa.
From Kuusamo take route 5 to Oulanka, then follow the signs for Oulanka National Park.

LAHTI 11B

Camping Mukkula 15240 Lahti.
Tel 188 8231500, Fax 188 8231522.
English spoken.
OPEN: all year. SIZE: 2 ha, 120 pitches (90 with elec, 300 statics), 15 hot showers, 15 WCs, 7 CWPs. ⟨ ⟩

Shop at 1 km. Tennis, mini-golf, surfing.
PRICES: Caravan with family 88, Tent with two adults 70. CC: Amex, Euro/Access, Visa.
Camspite is signposted to the north of town.

LAPPEENRANTA 11B

Huhmarkallio Camping Taipalsaarentie 1158, 54920 Taipalsaari.
Tel 353 4142134. English spoken.
OPEN: 20/05–22/08. SIZE: 3 ha, 60 pitches (30 with elec, 20 statics), 4 hot showers, 8 WCs, 1 CWP. ⟨

Restaurant at 0.7 km.
PRICES: (1996) Caravan with family 65,
Tent with two adults 50. CC: none.
Take route 408 north to Taipalsaari for about 15 km. Campsite is on the left beside Lake Saimaa.

Huhtiniemi Camping 53810 Lappeenranta.
Tel 534 531888, Fax 534 515558. English spoken.
OPEN: 01/02–15/12. SIZE: 12.6 ha, 325 pitches (45 with elec), 20 hot showers, 33 WCs, 1 CWP. ⟨ ⟩

Shop at 1 km.
PRICES: Caravan with family 93,
Tent with two adults 75. CC: Euro/Access, Visa.
Off route 6, campsite is on the lake and close to Lappeenranta centre.

NURMES 10D

Hyvarila Camping Lomatie, 75500 Nurmes.
Tel 976 481770, Fax 976 481775. English spoken.
OPEN: 15/05–15/09. SIZE: 10 ha, 300 pitches (60 with elec), 10 hot showers, 20 WCs, 1 CWP. ⟩

Shop at 0.3 km.
PRICES: (1996) Caravan with family 100, Tent with two adults 100. CC: Euro/Access, Visa.
From Nurmes town take route 73 towards Lieksa. After about 2 km turn right to Kohtavaara.

OULU 10D

Nallikari Camping 90500 Oulu.
Tel 981 5541541, Fax 981 377837. English spoken.
OPEN: 01/05–30/10. SIZE: 12 ha, 500 pitches (100 with elec), 16 hot showers, 24 WCs, 2 CWPs. ⟩

Shop at 2 km.
PRICES: (1996) Caravan with family 95,
Tent with two adults 75. CC: none.
3 km north-west of Oulu on the road to Kemi.

Seljänperän Leirintä Leiritie 50, 91140 Olhava.
Tel 08 8175257. English spoken.
OPEN: 20/05–31/08. SIZE: 7 ha, 80 pitches (40 with elec), 4 hot showers, 10 WCs, 4 French WCs, 2 CWPs. ⟨

Restaurant at 14 km. Sauna, boat hire.
PRICES: (1996) Caravan with family 90, Tent with two adults 70. CC: none.

Finland

The campsite is near the beach, 53 km to the north of Oulu, which is the nearest town.

PIETARSAARI   10D

Camping Joutsen Luodontie 50, 68600 Pietarsaari. Tel 967 7230660. English spoken. OPEN: 15/05–31/08. SIZE: 2 ha, 70 pitches (20 with elec), 14 hot showers (charge), 15 WCs, 1 CWP. &

Shop at 2 km. Restaurant at 2.5 km. PRICES: (1996) Caravan with family 80, Tent with two adults 60. CC: none. *About 4 km north of the town centre.*

PORI   11B

Yyteri Camping Yyteri, 28840 Pori. Tel 039 6383778, Fax 039 6335251. English spoken. OPEN: 24/05–25/08. SIZE: 10 ha, 10 hot showers, 8 WCs, 1 CWP. & &

Winter-equipped cottage for hire. PRICES: (1996) Caravan with family 109, Tent with two adults 80. CC: Euro/Access, Visa. *Halfway up the coast on the Gulf of Bothnia.*

PUTIKKO   11B

Kultakivi Camping Punkaharju, 58550 Putikko. Tel 957 645151, Fax 957 645110. English spoken. OPEN: 15/05–31/08. SIZE: 23 ha, 24 hot showers, 29 WCs, 1 CWP.

PRICES: (1996) Caravan with family 90, Tent with two adults 70. CC: Amex, Euro/Access, Visa. *Follow signs to Punkaharju from Putikko.*

PUUMALA   11B

Koskenselan Lomakyla Camping Koskenselka, 52200 Puumala. Tel 015 4681119, Fax 015 4681809. English spoken. OPEN: 15/05–15/09. SIZE: 12 ha, 120 pitches (20 with elec), 11 hot showers, 15 WCs, 1 CWP. &

Shop at 2 km. Restaurant at 2.5 km. Canoes, bike hire, rooms for rent. PRICES: (1996) Caravan with family 85, Tent with two adults 70. CC: Euro/Access, Visa. *In the middle of Lake Saimaa 2 km from Puumala village on the road 62 and about 70 km from Mikkeli.*

PYHÄJOKI   10B

Kielosarren Lomat 86100 Pyhäjoki. Tel 983 433212, Fax 983 4390271. English spoken. OPEN: all year. SIZE: 3 ha, 50 pitches (35 with elec), 7 hot showers, 6 WCs, 1 CWP. & &

Shop at 1 km. Restaurant at 1 km. Children's swimming pool. PRICES: (1996) Caravan with family 80, Tent with two adults 70. CC: none. *Between Oulu and Kokkola on the coast road.*

RAUMA   11B

Poroholma Camping 26100 Rauma. Tel 938 8224666, Fax 938 8228211. English spoken. OPEN: 15/05–31/08. SIZE: 4 ha, 260 pitches (38 with elec, 10 statics), 9 hot showers, 12 WCs, 2 CWPs. &

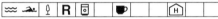

Rauma is famous for it's wooden houses. PRICES: (1996) Caravan with family 85, Tent with two adults 65. CC: Amex, Euro/Access, Visa. *Campsite is well signposted in town.*

ROVANIEMI   10D

Korvalan Rantapirtit Camping Korvala, 97540 Tiainen. Tel 016 737211, Fax 016 737211. English spoken. OPEN: all year. SIZE: 17.5 ha, 36 pitches (18 with elec), 4 hot showers, 8 WCs, 1 CWP.

Shop at 9 km. Restaurant at 56 km. Fishing, sauna, cross-country skiing, hiking paths. PRICES: (1996) Caravan with family 87.50, Tent with two adults 70. CC: none. *Korvala is 60 km north of Rovaniemi on the E75 to Sodankyla.*

Ounaskoski Camping Jaamerentie 1, 96200 Rovaniemi. Tel 949 692421, Fax 960 345304. English spoken. OPEN: 01/06–31/08. SIZE: 3 ha, 140 pitches (50 with elec), 10 hot showers, 17 WCs, 15 French WCs, 2 CWPs. & &

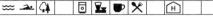

Restaurant at 0.4 km. PRICES: (1996) Caravan with family 100, Tent with two adults 80. CC: Euro/Access, Visa. *In the centre of Rovaniemi, on the bank of the Kemijoki river.*

SAVONLINNA   11B

Punkaharjun Lomakeskus Retretti Camping 58450 Punkaharju. Tel 015 739611, Fax 015 441784. English spoken. OPEN: all year. SIZE: 20 ha, 500 pitches (130 with elec), 26 hot showers, 39 WCs, 2 CWPs. &

Near Punkaharju ridge, forest, museum and caves.

Finland

PRICES: (1996) Caravan with family 105, Tent with two adults 85. CC: Euro/Access, Visa.
30 km south-east of Savonlinna on the R14 to Imatra.

SIMO 10D

Lapin Rinki Camping 95200 Simo.
Tel 698 266122. English spoken.
OPEN: 01/06–20/08. SIZE: 2 ha, 10 pitches (3 with elec), 4 hot showers, 4 WCs, 1 CWP. ℂ

Shop at 0.5 km. Restaurant at 0.5 km.
PRICES: (1996) Caravan with family 75, Tent with two adults 55. CC: none.
Simo is on the E75, 25 km south of Kemi and 80 km north of Oulu. Campsite is in the centre of Simo and well signposted.

TAMPERE 11B

Haapasaaren Lomakylä (Holiday Village) 34600 Ruovesi.
Tel 934 4861388, Fax 934 4861444. English spoken.
OPEN: 13/05–10/09. SIZE: 8 ha, 65 pitches (40 with elec), 6 hot showers, 10 WCs. ℂ

Shop at 1 km. Restaurant at 1 km.
PRICES: (1996) Caravan with family 95, Tent with two adults 75. CC: none.
From Tampere take the E80 for 40 km, then route 66 for another 40 km.

TORNIO 10D

Kukkolaforsen Pl 3446, 95391 Haparanda.
Tel 922 31000, Fax 922 31030. English spoken.
OPEN: all year. SIZE: 5 ha, 50 pitches (30 with elec), 10 hot showers, 12 WCs. ℂ &

Rafting, dip-net fishing, golf, sauna.
PRICES: (1996) Caravan with family 125, Tent with two adults 50. CC: Amex, Euro/Access, Visa.
14 km north of Tornio/Haparanda on route 400. Beside the River Torne.

TURKU 11B

Naantali Camping Kuparivuori, 21100 Naantali.
Tel 02 4350865, Fax 02 4360852. English spoken.
OPEN: all year. SIZE: 8 ha, 60 pitches (40 with elec), 20 hot showers, 20 WCs, 1 CWP. &

Shop at 0.5 km. Restaurant at 0.5 km. Reservations essential Sep to May.
PRICES: Caravan with family 95, Tent with two adults 75. CC: Euro/Access, Visa.
From Turku take the new Naantali road for about 15 km and then follow signs.

Finland

FRANCE

Whether beach, mountain or river holiday, wine drinking tour or gourmet binge, France has it all.

The longest beach in Europe stretches 250 km along the Atlantic Coast, from the mouth of the Gironde in the north to Biarritz, close to the Spanish border, in the south. The highest cable car station in Europe looks out over Mont Blanc in the French Alps, while the mountains of the Massif Central, formed by volcanic action, offer curiosities like hot springs at Chaudes-Aigues.

The great rivers of France, used until the last century as the main arteries of trade, today introduce visitors to the great châteaux of the Loire, the troglodyte cave dwellings of the Dordogne, or the wild and wonderful canoeing on the Ardèche.

In Provence, in the south – so called because it was once a province of the Roman empire – there are buildings in Arles, Orange and Nîmes still standing 1500 years after Barbarian invaders brought five centuries of Roman rule to an end.

But if Northern France is your choice for a mini-break... after Paris, discover historic Arras, or Rouen, where the old town is much as it was 500 years ago. Or walk the limestone tunnels beneath the Champagne city of Rheims.

Emergency numbers

Police 17

Fire Brigade 18

Ambulance Use number shown in call box or phone police

Warning information

Carrying a warning triangle recommended

Blood Alcohol Legal Limit 50 mg

ABBEVILLE Somme   2B

Camping Municipal Le Grand Pré Long, 80510 Lonpre-les-Corps-Saints.
Tel 03 22 31 84 27, Fax 03 22 31 82 39.
OPEN: 15/04–30/09. SIZE: 2 ha, 110 pitches (all with elec, 60 statics), 11 hot showers (charge), 10 WCs. **&**

≈	✈	♨	R					

Shop at 0.4 km. Restaurant at 0.4 km. Fishing in the nearby pond.
PRICES: (1996) Caravan with family 65.00, Tent with two adults 40.00. CC: none.
14 km from Abbeville and 30 km from Amiens. From Abbeville, go south east on the D901, then turn left on the D3 to Lonpré-les-Corps-Saints.

Camping Val de Trie Bouillancourt-sous-Miannay, 80870 Moyenneville.
Tel 03 22 24 42 68, Fax 03 22 31 35 33.
English spoken.
OPEN: 01/04–30/10. SIZE: 2.6 ha, 25 pitches (all with elec), 2 hot showers, 3 WCs, 1 CWP. **&**

~	✈	♨	R	▣	🍴	☕		🔥

Restaurant at 3 km. Fishing in a pond.
PRICES: Caravan with family 113.00, Tent with two adults 60.00. CC: none.
From Abbeville, take the D925 towards Le Tréport. In Miannay, turn left on the D86 towards Bouillancourt. Campsite is signposted.

LES ABRETS Isère   5B

Le Coin Tranquille 38490 Les Abrets.
Tel 04 76 32 13 48, Fax 04 76 37 40 67.
English spoken.
OPEN: 01/04–31/10. SIZE: 5 ha, 150 pitches (10 statics). **&**

	♨	R	▣	🍴		✗	🔥	

Shop at 2 km. Discounts in LS.
PRICES: (1996) Caravan with family 180.00, Tent with two adults 112.00. CC: Euro/Access, Visa.
From Les Abrets centre, towards Chambéry. Turn left 200 m before railway off national road, campsite 1 km.

ACCOUS Pyrénées-Atlan   4C

Camping Municipal 64490 Bedous.
Tel 05 59 34 70 45.
OPEN: 01/05–31/10. SIZE: 46 pitches (16 with elec), 6 hot showers, 6 WCs. **&**

~	✈	♨						

Shop at 0.5 km. Restaurant at 0.5 km.

France

PRICES: (1996) Caravan with family 75.00, Tent with two adults 49.00. CC: none.
North of Accous on N134, turn left on to D237 towards Osse-en-Aspe for campsite at Bedous.

AGDE Hérault   5C

Camping Les Sables d'Or rte de Rochelongue, 34300 Agde.
Tel 04 67 94 25 34, Fax 04 67 94 35 12. English spoken.
OPEN: 01/04–30/09. SIZE: 10 ha, 650 pitches (all with elec, 200 statics), 60 hot showers, 60 WCs, 4 CWPs. ✆ &

PRICES: (1996) Caravan with family 160.00, Tent with two adults 113.00. CC: none.
From Agde, drive towards Cap d'Agde then towards Rochelongue.

Camping Neptune route du Grau d'Agde, 34300 Agde.
Tel 04 67 94 23 94, Fax 04 67 94 48 77. English spoken.
OPEN: 09/04–30/09. SIZE: 2 ha, 50 pitches (all with elec, 24 statics), 19 hot showers, 17 WCs, 10 French WCs, 1 CWP. ✆ &

Restaurant at 1.5 km. Good sport facilities; sea 1.5 km; 1996 price winner for pretty gardens.
PRICES: (1996) Caravan with family 189.00, Tent with two adults 110.00. CC: Amex, Euro/Access, Visa.
From Agde take D32 towards Grau-d'Agde. Go right at first roundabout, right at second roundabout and follow signs to campsite.

La Canotte Le Grau d'Agde, 34300 Agde.
Tel 04 67 94 15 74. English spoken.
OPEN: 01/06–01/09. SIZE: 3 ha, 100 pitches (all with elec), 12 hot showers, 21 WCs. &

Restaurant at 0.5 km. sea 800 m.
PRICES: (1996) Caravan with family 114.00, Tent with two adults 57.00. CC: none.
3 km from Agde along the left bank of the River Hérault, on D32. The campsite is 800 m from the beach.

Les Champs Blancs route de Rochelongue, 34300 Agde.
Tel 04 67 94 23 42, Fax 04 67 21 36 75. English spoken.
OPEN: 01/04–30/09. SIZE: 4 ha, 103 pitches (all with elec), 40 hot showers, 35 WCs, 1 CWP. ✆ &

Shop at 1 km. Restaurant at 2 km. Playground, mini-golf, tennis, table tennis, boules, flume; sea 2 km.
PRICES: (1996) Caravan with family 200,00, Tent with two adults 180.00. CC: Euro/Access, Visa.
From the A9, exit at Agde/Pézénas turn-off. Follow road to Agde via Bessan. Once in Agde follow signs for the Mail-de-Rochelongue. Site on the road to Rochelongue.

Les Sabelettes Sarl chemin de Baluffe, 34300 Grau-d'Agde.
Tel 04 67 94 36 65. English spoken.
OPEN: 01/04–30/09. SIZE: 3 ha, 218 pitches (200 with elec, 40 statics), 15 hot showers, 15 WCs. ✆ &

Restaurant at 1 km.
PRICES: (1996) Caravan with family 181.00, Tent with two adults 109.00. CC: none.
South from Agde on D32E towards Grau-d'Agde. After 2 km look for left turn towards Notre-Dame.

AGON-COUTAINVILLE Manche   1B

Les Mouettes Les Passous, 50230 Agon-Coutainville.
Tel 02 33 45 38 63, Fax 02 33 45 75 66.
OPEN: 01/04–30/09. SIZE: 1.5 ha, 110 pitches (all with elec, 60 statics), 9 hot showers, 10 WCs, 1 CWP. ✆ &

Shop at 0.1 km. Restaurant at 0.05 km.
PRICES: (1996) Caravan with family 107.00, Tent with two adults 57.00. CC: none.
Go past Agon church and turn left 100 m before the sea.

AIGUES-MORTES Gard   5D

La Petite Camargue BP21, 30220 Aigues-Mortes.
Tel 04 66 53 84 77, Fax 04 66 53 83 48. English spoken.
OPEN: 26/04–20/09. SIZE: 13 ha, 611 pitches (306 with elec, 230 statics), 108 hot showers, 62 WCs, 4 CWPs. ✆ &

Equestrian centre. Mobile homes also available.
PRICES: Caravan with family 226.00, Tent with two adults 138.00. CC: Euro/Access, Visa.
From Aigues-Mortes take D62 towards La Grande-Motte. Campsite is about 2 km.

L'AIGUILLON-SUR-MER Vendée   4A

Bel-Air 85460 L'Aiguillon-sur-Mer.
Tel 02 51 56 44 05, Fax 02 51 97 15 58. English spoken.
OPEN: 01/05–15/09. SIZE: 6 ha, 250 pitches (all with elec, 75 statics), 37 hot showers, 36 WCs, 3 CWPs. ✆ &

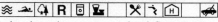

Indoor heated swimming pool with flume in LS.

PRICES: (1996) Caravan with family 159.00, Tent with two adults 100.00. CC: Amex, Euro/Access, Visa. *Well signposted in L'Aigullon-sur-Mer.*

AILLY-SUR-NOYE Somme   2B

Camping Municipal du Val de Noye
Berny-sur-Noye, 80250 Ailly-sur-Noye.
Tel 03 22 41 02 11.
OPEN: 01/04–30/09. SIZE: 20 ha, 76 pitches (all with elec, 30 statics), 8 hot showers, 8 WCs, 8 French WCs, 1 CWP. ♥ &

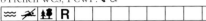

Shop at 1 km. Restaurant at 0.1 km. Mini-golf, pedal boats, fishing.
PRICES: (1996) Caravan with family 72.00, Tent with two adults 38.00. CC: none.

AIME Savoie   6A

Camping La Glière Villette, 73210 Aime.
Tel 04 79 09 77 61. English spoken.
OPEN: 01/06–15/09. SIZE: 1.5 ha, 30 pitches (all with elec), 7 hot showers, 9 WCs, 1 CWP. ♥ &

Restaurant at 0.5 km.
PRICES: (1996) Caravan with family 107.85, Tent with two adults 74.20. CC: none.
11 km from Moûtiers and 3 km before reaching Aime, on the N90.

Camping Les Lanchettes 73210 Peisey-Nancroix.
Tel 04 79 07 93 07, Fax 04 79 07 88 33.
English spoken.
OPEN: 01/11–26/04 & 24/05–20/09. SIZE: 2 ha, 90 pitches (all with elec), 14 hot showers, 9 WCs, 1 CWP. ♥

Shop at 0.5 km. Fishing, skiing, playground; tennis, archery and horse-riding nearby.
PRICES: Caravan with family 134.00, Tent with two adults 71.00. CC: Amex, Euro/Access, Visa.
From Aime, east on the N90 and then turn right onto D87. Campsite is signposted.

Camping Municipal de Montchavin
Montchavin T15, Bellentre, 73210 Aime.
Tel 04 79 07 83 23, Fax 04 79 07 80 18.
English spoken.
OPEN: all year. SIZE: 1 ha, 90 pitches (all with elec, 30 statics), 10 hot showers, 9 WCs, 6 French WCs, 1 CWP.

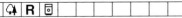

Shop at 0.3 km. Restaurant at 0.3 km.
PRICES: (1996) Caravan with family 91.00, Tent with two adults 54.00. CC: none.
From Aime, go east on D90 towards Bourg-St-Maurice. Turn right at sign to Bellentre and Montchavin, site well signed in village.

AIRVAULT Deux-Sèvres   2C

Camping de Courte Vallée Courte Vallée, 79600 Airvault.
Tel 05 49 64 70 65, Fax 05 49 70 84 58.
English spoken.
OPEN: 01/05–30/09. SIZE: 3.5 ha, 41 pitches (26 with elec, 1 static), 6 hot showers, 7 WCs, 1 CWP. ♥ &

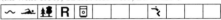

Restaurant at 1 km. Fishing, playground, ball games. Good sightseeing area.
PRICES: (1996) Caravan with family 118.00, Tent with two adults 69.00. CC: none.
From Airvault, drive towards Availles-Thouarsais and follow the signs.

AIX-EN-PROVENCE B-du-Rhône   5D

Arc-en-Ciel Pont des 3 Sautets, 13100 Aix-en-Provence.
Tel 04 42 26 14 28. English spoken.
OPEN: 15/03–31/10. SIZE: 3 ha, 65 pitches (all with elec), 12 hot showers, 20 WCs. ♥

Shop at 0.1 km. Restaurant at 0.1 km. Fishing, table tennis, canoeing, walking.
PRICES: (1996) Caravan with family 132.00, Tent with two adults 90.00. CC: none.
3 km south-east of the centre of Aix, towards Nice, exit autoroute at Aix-3 Sautets (junction A8/N7).

Camping de Ste-Victoire quartier le Paradore, 13100 Beaurecueil.
Tel 04 42 66 91 31, Fax 04 42 66 96 43.
English spoken.
OPEN: all year. SIZE: 2 ha, 80 pitches (3 statics), 6 hot showers, 8 WCs, 2 French WCs, 1 CWP. ♥

Restaurant at 3.5 km.
PRICES: (1996) Caravan with family 106.50, Tent with two adults 54.00. CC: none.
Take N7 east of Aix-en-Provence. Turn right at Pont-de-Bayeaux, turn left at crossroads and site is on the left (1 km).

AIX-LES-BAINS Savoie   6A

Camp Municipal Roger Milesy Gresy-sur-Aix, 73100 Aix-les-Bains.
Tel 04 79 88 28 21, Fax 04 79 34 82 40.
OPEN: 01/06–30/09. SIZE: 0.6 ha, 38 pitches (all with elec), 7 hot showers, 5 WCs, 1 CWP. ♥ &

Shop at 2 km. Restaurant at 2 km.
PRICES: (1996) Caravan with family 86.40, Tent with two adults 47.20. CC: none.
4 km from Aix-les-Bains towards Annecy.

France

Camping Alp'Aix 20 bd du Port-aux-Filles, 73100 Aix-les-Bains.
Tel 04 79 88 97 65. English spoken.
OPEN: 05/04–30/09. SIZE: 1.2 ha, 79 pitches (all with elec, 7 statics), 9 hot showers, 9 WCs, 1 CWP. &

Restaurant at 0.3 km.
PRICES: Caravan with family 109.00,
Tent with two adults 67.00. CC: none.
On the N201 at Aix-les-Bains, turn off towards the swimming pool and follow signs.

AIXE-SUR-VIENNE Haute-Vienne 4B

Camping Municipal Les Grèves av des Grèves, 87700 Aixe-sur-Vienne.
Tel 05 55 70 12 98. English spoken.
OPEN: 15/06–15/09. SIZE: 3 ha, 80 pitches (all with elec), 8 hot showers, 8 WCs, 3 French WCs, 1 CWP. & &

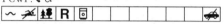

Shop at 0.3 km. Restaurant at 0.2 km. Climbing, canoeing, entertainment; swimming pool nearby.
PRICES: (1996) Caravan with family 71.00,
Tent with two adults 45.00. CC: none.
From Limoges westwards on the N21 for 10 km. No double-axle caravans.

AIZENAY Vendée 4A

Camp Municipal rue du Stade, 85220 La Chapelle-Hermier.
Tel 02 51 34 61 66, Fax 02 51 34 64 24.
OPEN: 15/06–15/09. SIZE: 1 ha.

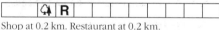

Shop at 0.2 km. Restaurant at 0.2 km.
PRICES: (1996) Caravan with family 60.00,
Tent with two adults 29.00. CC: none.
From Aizenay on D6 to Coëx (west), then D21 south to La Chapelle-Hermier. Turn off to the right near garage and campsite is on the left.

Camping Municipal La Forêt
85190 Aizenay.
Tel 02 51 34 78 12. English spoken.
OPEN: 01/06–30/09. SIZE: 2 ha, 90 pitches (all with elec, 10 statics), 6 hot showers, 10 WCs, 4 French WCs. &

Restaurant at 0.5 km. Tennis, golf, forest walks, archery.
PRICES: (1996) Caravan with family 52.00,
Tent with two adults 35.00. CC: none.
From La-Roche-sur-Yon take the D948 to Aizenay. The campsite is on the right just as you enter the town.

ALBAN Tarn 5C

Camping L'Amitié 81340 Trebas.
Tel 05 63 55 84 07, Fax 05 63 55 84 07.
English spoken.
OPEN: 01/05–15/09. SIZE: 0.8 ha, 60 pitches (all with elec), 5 hot showers, 6 WCs.

Shop at 0.2 km.
PRICES: (1996) Caravan with family 91.00,
Tent with two adults 53.00. CC: none.
From Alban, go north on the D 53 to Trebas.

Camping Municipal 81250 Villeneuve-sur-Tarn.
Tel 05 63 55 91 63. English spoken.
OPEN: 15/06–15/09. SIZE: 0.2 ha, 20 pitches (all with elec), 3 hot showers, 4 WCs. & &

Shop at 0.2 km. Restaurant at 0.2 km.
PRICES: (1996) Caravan with family 41.80,
Tent with two adults 21.00. CC: none.
From Alban, drive 10.5 km north on the D53 to Villeneuve-sur-Tarn.

ALBENS Savoie 6A

Camping Beausejour 73410 Albens.
Tel 04 79 54 15 20.
OPEN: 10/06–15/09. SIZE: 2 ha, 100 pitches (55 with elec), 6 hot showers, 12 WCs.

Shop at 0.5 km. Restaurant at 0.5 km.
PRICES: (1996) Caravan with family 62.50,
Tent with two adults 34.00. CC: none.
On N201, 10 km from Aix-les-Bains and 20 km from Annecy. From the church square in Albens, take the route de la Chambotte for 500m and then turn left.

ALBI Tarn 5C

Relais de l'Entre-Deux-Lacs 81120 Teillet.
Tel 05 63 55 74 45, Fax 05 63 55 75 65.
English spoken.
OPEN: all year. SIZE: 4 ha, 54 pitches (32 with elec), 7 hot showers, 9 WCs. &

Shop at 0.5 km.
PRICES: (1996) Caravan with family 117.00,
Tent with two adults 71.00. CC: Euro/Access.
From Albi bypass take the D81 south-east to Teillet (18 km). The campsite is on right at south end of the village.

ALENCON Orne 2C

Camping Municipal de Guéramé rue de Guéramé, 61000 Alençon.
Tel 02 33 26 34 95. English spoken.

OPEN: 01/05–30/09. SIZE: 1 ha, 60 pitches (all with elec), 9 hot showers, 12 WCs, 1 CWP. **t &**

Shop at 0.05 km. Tennis, table tennis, basket ball.
PRICES: (1996) Caravan with family 74.50, Tent with two adults 44.00. CC: none.

ALES Gard 5D

La Croix Clémentine 30480 Cendras.
Tel 04 66 86 52 69, Fax 04 66 86 54 84.
English spoken.
OPEN: 01/04–20/09. SIZE: 11 ha, 250 pitches (all with elec), 50 hot showers, 50 WCs, 10 French WCs, 5 CWPs. **t &**

Tennis, table tennis.
PRICES: Caravan with family 194.00, Tent with two adults 104.00. CC: Amex, Euro/Access, Visa.
The campsite is 5 km north-west of Alès, towards Mende.

ALLANCHE Cantal 5A

Pont-Vallat 15160 Allanche.
Tel 04 71 20 45 87.
OPEN: 15/06–15/09. SIZE: 3 ha, 90 pitches (54 with elec), 10 hot showers, 19 WCs.

Shop at 1 km. Restaurant at 0.2 km.
PRICES: (1996) Caravan with family 47.50, Tent with two adults 21.50. CC: none.
On the D679 south of Allanche.

AMBOISE Indre/Loire 2C

Le Jardin Botanique 9 rue de la Rivière, 37530 Limeray.
Tel 02 47 30 13 50, Fax 02 47 30 17 32.
English spoken.
OPEN: 27/03–31/10. SIZE: 2 ha, 74 pitches (54 with elec, 1 static), 6 hot showers, 7 WCs, 1 CWP. **t &**

PRICES: (1996) Caravan with family 127.00, Tent with two adults 79.00. CC: Amex, Euro/Access, Visa.
On N152 6 km east of Amboise and towards Blois.

AMIENS Somme 2B

Camping du Château 80260 Bertangles.
Tel 03 22 93 37 73, Fax 03 22 93 68 36.
OPEN: 26/04–07/09. SIZE: 1 ha, 33 pitches (all with elec), 4 hot showers, 6 WCs, 6 CWPs.

Shop at 0.3 km. Restaurant at 0.3 km.
PRICES: (1996) Caravan with family 94.00, Tent with two adults 53.00. CC: none.
Off N25, 8 km north of Amiens.

ANCENIS Loire-Atlan 1D

Camping Municipal de l'Ile Mouchet
44150 Ancenis.
Tel 02 40 83 08 43. English spoken.
OPEN: 01/04–30/09. SIZE: 3 ha, 150 pitches (all with elec), 20 hot showers, 25 WCs, 2 CWPs. **t &**

Restaurant at 1 km.
PRICES: (1996) Caravan with family 75.00, Tent with two adults 55.00. CC: none.
Ancenis is on the N23, beside the Loire.

ANDERNOS-LES-BAINS Gironde 4A

Camping de Fontaine Vieille 4 bd du Colonel Wurtz, 33510 Andernos-les-Bains.
Tel 05 56 82 01 67, Fax 05 56 82 09 81.
English spoken.
OPEN: 01/05–21/09. SIZE: 13 ha, 75 hot showers, 80 WCs. **&**

Shop at 1 km. Tennis, volley ball; mobile homes.
PRICES: Caravan with family 136.00, Tent with two adults 80.00. CC: Amex, Visa.
Approaching Andernos from the north on the D3, turn right into the town.
SEE ADVERTISEMENT

France

ANDUZE Gard   5D

Camping Caravaning Les Sources
30270 St-Jean-du-Gard.
Tel 04 66 85 38 03, Fax 04 66 85 16 09.
English spoken.
OPEN: 01/04–30/09. SIZE: 3 ha, 80 pitches (all with
elec), 8 hot showers, 8 WCs, 4 French WCs. ✆

Table tennis, playground, library.
PRICES: (1996) Caravan with family 113.00,
Tent with two adults 67.00. CC: Amex,
Euro/Access, Visa.
*Between Anduze and Florac. In St-Jean go
towards St-Etienne and Vallée-Française on the
D983. At the crossroads with D50, keep to the
right and go on D50 towards Mialet. After about
200 m, campsite entrance is on the right.*

Camping de l'Arche 30140 Anduze.
Tel 04 66 61 74 08, Fax 04 66 61 88 94.
English spoken.
OPEN: 01/04–30/09. SIZE: 10 ha, 250 pitches
(all with elec, 17 statics), 41 hot showers, 36 WCs,
20 CWPs. ✆ &

Archery, VTT; entertainment in high season.
PRICES: (1996) Caravan with family 119.50, Tent
with two adults 73.00. CC: none.
*In Anduze, going towards St-Jean-du-Gard, turn
right just before the hotel restaurant 'La Porte des
Cevennes'. The campsite is 500 m down the track.*

Camping Domaine de Gaujac
Boisset et Gaujac, 30140 Anduze.
Tel 04 66 61 80 65, Fax 04 66 60 53 90.
English spoken.
OPEN: 01/04–30/09. SIZE: 10 ha, 250 pitches
(all with elec), 34 hot showers, 32 WCs. ✆ &

Tennis, mini-golf, entertainment.
PRICES: (1996) Caravan with family 132.00,
Tent with two adults 79.00. CC: none.
*From Anduze follow the directions to Alès, and
then signs to campsite.*

Camping Les Fauvettes 30140 Anduze.
Tel 04 66 61 72 23, Fax 04 66 61 64 45.
English spoken.
OPEN: 28/04–24/09. SIZE: 3 ha, 120 pitches
(all with elec), 14 hot showers, 14 WCs,
1 CWP. ✆ &

Shop at 0.4 km. Restaurant at 0.1 km. Flume,
jacuzzi.
PRICES: (1996) Caravan with family 128.00,
Tent with two adults 80.00. CC: none.
*1.5 km From Anduze on D907 towards St-Jean-
du-Gard.*

ANGERS Maine/Loire   2C

Camping Le Lac de Maine 49000 Angers.
Tel 02 41 73 05 03, Fax 02 41 22 32 11.
English spoken.
OPEN: 10/02–20/12. SIZE: 4 ha, 162 pitches
(all with elec), 20 hot showers, 17 WCs,
3 CWPs. ✆ &

Shop at 2 km.
PRICES: Caravan with family 111.90, Tent with two
adults 72.00. CC: Amex, Euro/Access, Visa.

ANGERVILLE Loiret   2D

Domaine de la Joullière 45480 Andonville.
Tel 02 38 39 58 46, Fax 02 38 39 61 94.
English spoken.
OPEN: 01/02–31/12. SIZE: 10 ha, 216 pitches
(all with elec, 150 statics), 40 hot showers,
40 WCs, 3 CWPs. ✆

Good sports facilities; 2 swimming pools, fishing,
disco.
PRICES: (1996) Caravan with family 136.00,
Tent with two adults 96.00. CC: none.

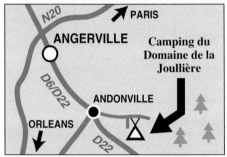

*From Angerville take D22 towards Pithiviers to
Andonville and campsite.*

ANGLET Pyrénées-Atlan   4C

Camping de Parme quartier Brindos,
64600 Anglet.
Tel 05 59 23 03 00. English spoken.
OPEN: all year. SIZE: 4 ha, 200 pitches (all with elec,
12 statics), 22 hot showers, 22 WCs, 1 CWP. &

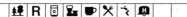

Tennis.
PRICES: (1996) Caravan with family 152.00, Tent with two adults 95.00. CC: Euro/Access, Visa.
From Bayonne go towards St-Jean-de-Luz on N10 and follow signposts to Anglet and site.

ANGOULEME Charente 4B

Camping des Graulges Crozes Loisirs
24340 Les Graulges.
Tel 05 53 60 74 73. English spoken.
OPEN: 01/03–30/10. SIZE: 8 ha, 50 pitches (16 with elec), 3 hot showers, 5 WCs, 2 CWPs. &

Fishing, boating, mini-golf.
PRICES: (1996) Caravan with family 98.00, Tent with two adults 56.00. CC: none.
D939 south-east of Angoulême. At Combiers (approx 35 km) turn left on to the D41 to Les Graulges.

ANNECY Haute-Savoie 6A

Auberge de la Caille 18 chemin de la Caille, 74330 La Balme-de-Sillingy.
Tel 04 50 68 85 21, Fax 04 50 68 74 56.
English spoken.
OPEN: 19/05–30/09. SIZE: 3 ha, 40 pitches (all with elec), 4 hot showers, 5 WCs, 2 French WCs, 3 CWPs.

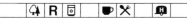

Shop at 2 km.
PRICES: (1996) Caravan with family 100.00, Tent with two adults 60.00.
CC: Euro/Access, Visa.
From Bellegarde to Frangy/Annecy on the N508. 12 km after Frangy turn left to Terre de la Caille.

Camping ACCCF Terrain de Sevrier, 74320 Sevrier.
Tel 04 50 52 40 14. English spoken.
OPEN: 01/04–31/10. SIZE: 99 pitches (all with elec, 40 statics), 11 hot showers, 12 WCs, 1 CWP. &

Shop at 0.5 km. Restaurant at 1 km.
PRICES: (1996) Caravan with family 148.00, Tent with two adults 81.00. CC: Euro/Access, Visa.
From Annecy, take the N508 towards Albertville and just after Sevrier turn left on the Route des Grands Prés.

Camping Europa 1444 route d'Albertville, 74410 St-Jorioz.
Tel 04 50 68 51 01, Fax 04 50 68 55 20.
English spoken.
OPEN: 15/05–20/09. SIZE: 3 ha, 210 pitches (200 with elec), 24 hot showers, 21 WCs, 2 CWPs. &

PRICES: (1996) Caravan with family 164.00, Tent with two adults 82.00. CC: none.
N508 south of Annecy towards Albertville. After the village of St-Jorioz, the site is signposted.

Lake Annecy = Nirvana, true!

Camping International du Lac Bleu
74210 Doussard.
Tel 04 50 44 30 18, Fax 04 50 44 84 35.
English spoken.
OPEN: 04/04–10/10. SIZE: 3.35 ha, 240 pitches (220 with elec), 28 hot showers, 32 WCs, 2 CWPs. &

Private beach.
PRICES: (1996) Caravan with family 122.00, Tent with two adults 89.00. CC: none.
16 km from Annecy going towards Albertville, at the southern end of the lake. Campsite is on the left, just after the village of Bout du Lac and well signposted.

Camping La Serraz
rue de la Poste, 74210 Doussard.
Tel 04 50 44 30 68, Fax 04 50 44 81 07.
English spoken.
OPEN: 15/05–30/09. SIZE: 3.5 ha, 184 pitches (all with elec), 25 hot showers, 25 WCs, 8 French WCs, 2 CWPs. &

PRICES: (1996) Caravan with family 169.00, Tent with two adults 104.00. CC: none.
From Annecy go towards Albertville on the N508 alongside Lake Annecy. Doussard is 1.5 km beyond the lake.

Camping Le Solitaire du Lac
route de Salles, 74410 St-Jorioz.
Tel 04 50 68 59 30.
English spoken.
OPEN: 01/04–30/09. SIZE: 2.5 ha, 200 pitches (all with elec), 25 hot showers, 24 WCs, 2 CWPs. &

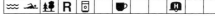

Shop at 1 km. Restaurant at 1 km.
PRICES: (1996) Caravan with family 123.00, Tent with two adults 75.00. CC: Amex, Euro/Access, Visa.
From Annecy, south on N508, west bank of lake to St-Jorioz. Campsite is beside lake.

France

Camping Le Crêtoux route d'Entredozon, 74410 St-Jorioz.
Tel 04 50 68 61 94. English spoken.
OPEN: 01/06–30/09. SIZE: 6 ha, 70 pitches (50 with elec, 3 statics), 8 hot showers, 12 WCs, 1 CWP. ✆ ⅋

Shop at 2 km. Restaurant at 1 km. Trout fishing; apartments for hire.
PRICES: (1996) Caravan with family 111.00, Tent with two adults 68.00. CC: none.
South from Annecy on N508 towards Albertville. In St-Jorioz, take the D10a (right at traffic lights) for 2 km. Follow signs.

Camping Le Crêtoux
near Annecy
In the trees, above the lake

ANSE Rhône   5B

Le Porte de Beaujolis 69480 Anse.
Tel 04 74 67 12 87, Fax 04 74 09 90 97.
English spoken.
OPEN: all year. SIZE: 7.5 ha, 171 pitches (96 with elec, 30 statics), 24 hot showers, 23 WCs, 6 French WCs, 3 CWPs. ✆ ⅋

New campsite which opened in 1995.
PRICES: Caravan with family 161.00, Tent with two adults 85.00. CC: Amex, Euro/Access, Visa.
1 km from town centre and 500 m from bridge over the River Azergues. Well signposted.

ANTIBES Alpes-Marit   6C

Camp du Pylône av du Pylône, La Brague, 06601 Antibes.
Tel 04 93 74 94 70, Fax 04 93 33 30 54.
English spoken.
OPEN: all year. SIZE: 10 ha, 600 pitches (all with elec, 300 statics), 120 hot showers, 120 WCs, 3 CWPs. ✆

Ball games, entertainments.
PRICES: Caravan with family 190.00, Tent with two adults 120.00. CC: none.
La Brague lies right on the coast, close to Biot and just north of Antibes.

Les Embruns route de Biot, La Brague, 06600 Antibes.
Tel 04 93 33 33 35, Fax 04 93 74 46 70.
English spoken.

OPEN: 01/05–30/09. SIZE: 1 ha, 30 pitches (all with elec), 8 hot showers, 12 WCs, 2 CWPs. ✆

Restaurant at 0.5 km.
PRICES: Caravan with family 170.00, Tent with two adults 90.00. CC: Amex, Visa.
From Antibes take the N7 towards Nice. Campsite is 2 km on left.

APT Vaucluse   5D

Les Chênes Blancs route de Gargas, 84490 St-Saturnin-d'Apt.
Tel 04 90 74 09 20, Fax 04 90 74 26 98.
English spoken.
OPEN: 15/03–31/10. SIZE: 3.2 ha, 190 pitches (125 with elec, 20 statics), 18 hot showers, 18 WCs, 1 CWP. ✆ ⅋

Restaurant at 4 km. Ball games, children's play area.
PRICES: (1996) Caravan with family 84.00, Tent with two adults 58.00. CC: Amex, Euro/Access, Visa.
From Apt take D101 to Gargas. Go through village then follow signs.

Le Lubéron route de Saignon, 84400 Apt.
Tel 04 90 04 85 40, Fax 04 90 74 12 19.
English spoken.
OPEN: 09/04–30/09. SIZE: 5 ha, 89 pitches (all with elec, 15 statics), 10 hot showers, 14 WCs, 2 CWPs. ✆ ⅋

Shop at 0.8 km. Award-winning campsite. Mini-golf, super walks, 2 pools.
PRICES: (1996) Caravan with family 110.00, Tent with two adults 58.00. CC: Visa.
From the centre of Apt, take the D48 to Saignon in the south-east. Site is 1.5 km from town.

ARBOIS Jura   3C

Camping des Vignes av Général Leclerc, 39600 Arbois.
Tel 03 84 66 14 12, Fax 03 84 66 25 50.
OPEN: 01/04–30/09. SIZE: 5 ha, 139 pitches (all with elec), 15 hot showers, 18 WCs, 1 CWP. ✆ ⅋

Shop at 0.8 km. Restaurant at 0.8 km. Boules, playground, library.
PRICES: (1996) Caravan with family 83.00, Tent with two adults 53.50. CC: none.
Follow signs in Arbois on the D469.

L'ARBRESLE Rhône   5B

Camping Les Cerisiers Le Blanc, route de Savigny, 69490 St-Romain-de-Popey.
Tel 04 74 05 80 48.

OPEN: all year. SIZE: 2 ha, 25 pitches (all with elec),
1 hot shower (charge), 3 WCs, 2 French WCs,
1 CWP.

Shop at 1 km. Restaurant at 1 km.
PRICES: (1996) Caravan with family 67.00,
Tent with two adults 37.00.
CC: none.
*North-west from L'Arbresle on the N7, turn left
after 7 km to St-Romain.*

ARCACHON Gironde   4A

Camping Club d'Arcachon
allée de la Galaxie, 33120 Arcachon.
Tel 05 56 83 24 15, Fax 05 57 52 28 51.
English spoken.
OPEN: all year. SIZE: 5.5 ha, 250 pitches (100 with
elec, 50 statics). ⬥ &

Beach 900 m; playground.
PRICES: (1996) Caravan with family 135.00,
Tent with two adults 100.00. CC: Amex,
Euro/Access, Visa.
*Follow signs from town centre. Campsite is 600 m
from the railway station.*

Camping Club d'Arcachon
at Arcachon
France's Wonderful Wild West

Camping de la Dune
route de Biscarosse, 33260 La Teste.
Tel 05 56 22 72 17, Fax 05 56 22 72 17.
English spoken.
OPEN: 01/05–30/09. SIZE: 6 ha, 150 pitches
(all with elec), 34 hot showers, 51 WCs. ⬥ &

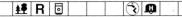

PRICES: (1996) Caravan with family 190.00,
Tent with two adults 110.00. CC: Visa.
From La Teste head towards Le Pyla-sur-Mer.

Ker Helen Le Teich, 33470 Gujan-Mestras.
Tel 05 56 66 03 79, Fax 05 56 66 51 59.
English spoken.
OPEN: all year. SIZE: 3 ha, 80 pitches (all with elec,
20 statics), 12 hot showers, 14 WCs, 1 CWP. ⬥ &

Mini-golf.
PRICES: (1996) Caravan with family 141.00,
Tent with two adults 85.00.
CC: none.
*From Arcachon go 10 km east via Gujan-Mestras
to campsite at Le Teich. Signposted.*

Le Petit Nice route de Biscarosse,
33115 Pyla-sur-Mer.
Tel 05 56 22 74 03, Fax 05 56 22 14 31.
English spoken.
OPEN: 01/04–15/10. SIZE: 5 ha, 225 pitches
(90 with elec, 15 statics), 24 hot showers, 24 WCs,
2 CWPs. ⬥ &

Heated pool, tennis; mobile homes for hire;
discounts in LS.
PRICES: (1996) Caravan with family 208.00,
Tent with two adults 126.00. CC: none.
*Take the coast road from Arcachon south towards
Biscarosse. Pass behind the Pyla dune and Le
Petit Nice is the 5th site along. Access direct to the
beach.*

ARCHIAC Charente-Marit   4B

Camping Municipal 17520 Archiac.
Tel 05 46 49 10 82, Fax 05 46 49 84 09.
English spoken.
OPEN: 01/06–15/09. SIZE: 1.5 ha, 44 pitches
(all with elec), 5 hot showers, 7 WCs.

Shop at 0.5 km. Restaurant at 0.5 km.
PRICES: (1996) Caravan with family 60.00,
Tent with two adults 29.00. CC: none.
*Coming from the north, Archiac is on the D731,
south of Cognac. Campsite is well signposted.*

ARCIS-SUR-AUBE Aube   3C

Camping de la Barbuise
10700 St-Rémy-sous-Barbuise.
Tel 03 25 37 50 95.
OPEN: all year. SIZE: 1 ha, 50 pitches (45 with elec),
4 hot showers, 6 WCs. ⬥ &

Shop at 0.5 km. Restaurant at 0.5 km. Flume, table
tennis, Subuteo; river 0.8 km; quiet site.
PRICES: (1996) Caravan with family 47.00,
Tent with two adults 25.00. CC: none.
*N77, 7 km south of Arcis-sur-Aube, near Voué.
Site is well signposted.*

ARDRES Pas-de-Calais   2B

Camping St-Louis rue Leulene, 62610 Autingues.
Tel 03 21 35 46 83. English spoken.
OPEN: 01/03–30/10. SIZE: 1.70 ha, 84 pitches
(all with elec, 50 statics), 5 hot showers,
7 WCs, 1 CWP. &

Restaurant at 1 km. Playroom, playground.
PRICES: (1996) Caravan with family 63.50, Tent
with two adults 40.00. CC: none.
*From Ardres, south-west on D224 for 1 km.
Follow signs.*

France

ARES Gironde 4A

Camping La Canadienne
rue du Général de Gaulle, 33740 Arès.
Tel 05 56 60 24 91, Fax 05 57 70 40 85.
English spoken.
OPEN: 01/04–20/10. SIZE: 2 ha, 100 pitches
(90 with elec), 12 hot showers, 16 WCs, 1 CWP.
ℂ ⅊

	⌗	R	⎗	⊛	⚍	✕	⚡	⌂		

Shop at 1 km. Cycling, water sports, horse-riding;
sea 1 km.
PRICES: Caravan with family 169.00, Tent with two
adults 105.00. CC: Amex, Euro/Access, Visa.
From Bordeaux take D106 towards Cap Ferret,
exit at Arès to D3, towards Lège.

Camping La Cigale
53 rue du Général de Gaulle, 33740 Arès.
Tel 05 56 60 22 59, Fax 05 57 70 41 66.
English spoken.
OPEN: 01/04–15/10. SIZE: 3 ha, 100 pitches
(10 statics), 12 hot showers, 10 WCs, 1 CWP. ℂ ⅊

	⌗	R	⎗		⚍	✕	⚡	⌂		

Shop at 0.5 km.
PRICES: (1996) Caravan with family 155.00,
Tent with two adults 95.00. CC: Amex, Visa.
From Bordeaux take D106 towards Cap Ferret.
Exit at Arès to D3, towards Lège. On arrival in
Arès, take the road to Lège and campsite is on the
left, 500 m from the church.

Camping Municipal Les Goelands 33740 Arès.
Tel 05 56 82 55 64, Fax 05 56 60 26 30.
English spoken.
OPEN: 01/04–30/09. SIZE: 10 ha, 175 pitches
(all with elec, 50 statics), 32 hot showers, 34 WCs,
5 CWPs. ℂ ⅊

	⌗	R	⎗	⊛		✕		⌂		

Shop at 1 km. Daily entertainment; sea 150m.
PRICES: (1996) Caravan with family 139.00, Tent
with two adults 88.00. CC: Euro/Access, Visa.
Campsite is off the D3 coastal road running north
to Arès. Well signposted.
SEE ADVERTISEMENT

ARGELES-GAZOST Htes-Pyrénées 4D

Camping de la Heche Arrens Marsous,
65400 Argelès-Gazost.
Tel 05 62 97 02 64. English spoken.
OPEN: all year. SIZE: 5 ha, 166 pitches (80 with
elec), 18 hot showers, 19 WCs, 1 CWP. ℂ ⅊

～	✕	⌗		⎗						

Shop at 0.2 km. Restaurant at 0.5 km.
PRICES: (1996) Caravan with family 74.00,
Tent with two adults 37.00. CC: none.
D918 south-west of Argelès-Gazost. The site is
500 m beyond Marsous, on the left.

Camping des 3 Vallées 65400 Argelès-Gazost.
Tel 05 62 90 35 47, Fax 05 62 97 53 64.
English spoken.
OPEN: 05/04–30/09. SIZE: 4 ha, 400 pitches, 40 hot
showers, 40 WCs, 2 CWPs. ⅊

	⌗	R	⎗				⚡		

Shop at 0.3 km. Restaurant at 0.3 km. Mini-golf, 2
flumes; river 0.3 m.
PRICES: (1996) Caravan with family 130.00,
Tent with two adults 69.00. CC: none.
13 km from Lourdes on N21. Campsite on the left
hand side at entrance of Argelès-Gazost.

Camping du Lac Arcizans Avant,
65400 Argelès-Gazost.
Tel 05 62 97 01 88, Fax 05 62 97 01 88. English spoken.
OPEN: 01/06–30/09. SIZE: 3 ha, 90 pitches (56 with
elec), 11 hot showers, 10 WCs, 1 CWP. ℂ

≈	✕	⌗	R	⎗	⚍	⚍	✕		

Exceptional location: lake, castle, mountains.
PRICES: (1996) Caravan with family 115.00,
Tent with two adults 60.00. CC: none.
On the road between Argelès and St-Savin.
(No motor caravans.)

Camping du Lavedan Lau-Balagnas,
65400 Argelès-Gazost.
Tel 05 62 97 18 84, Fax 05 62 97 55 56.
English spoken.

OPEN: 01/01–31/10. SIZE: 2 ha, 138 pitches (all with elec, 30 statics), 15 hot showers, 12 WCs, 2 CWPs. ☎ ♿

Shop at 2 km. Restaurant at 1 km. Covered pool.
PRICES: (1996) Caravan with family 123.50, Tent with two adults 90.00. CC: none.
From Argelès, 2 km south on N21 towards Cauterets.

Camping Le Viscos 65400 Beaucens-les-Bains.
Tel 05 62 97 05 45. English spoken.
OPEN: 15/05–30/09. SIZE: 2 ha, 110 pitches (60 with elec), 10 hot showers, 9 WCs, 1 CWP. ☎

Shop at 5 km.
PRICES: (1996) Caravan with family 88.00, Tent with two adults 45.00. CC: none.
From Argelès-Gazost follow directions to Beaucens-les-Bains (4 km). The campsite is 1 km from the village, signposted.

ARGELES-SUR-MER Pyrénées Orient 5C

Camping de Pujol route du Tamariguer, 66700 Argelès-sur-Mer.
Tel 04 68 81 00 25, Fax 04 68 81 21 21.
English spoken.
OPEN: 01/06–30/09. SIZE: 3 ha, 24 hot showers, 26 WCs, 5 CWPs. ♿

PRICES: (1996) Caravan with family 172.00, Tent with two adults 100.00. CC: none.
From Perpignan go south on N114 to Argelès. Come off at Taxo and turn left to Pujol.

Camping Europe route de la Plage, 66700 Argelès-sur-Mer.
Tel 04 68 81 08 10, Fax 04 68 95 71 84.
English spoken.
OPEN: 01/04–15/10. SIZE: 1 ha, 84 pitches (62 with elec), 10 hot showers, 12 WCs, 22 French WCs, 1 CWP. ☎ ♿

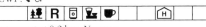

Restaurant at 0.2 km. Nursery.
PRICES: (1996) Caravan with family 145.00, Tent with two adults 90.00. CC: Amex, Euro/Access, Visa.
Centre Plage.

Camping La Massane quartier Pujol, 66702 Argelès-sur-Mer.
Tel 04 68 81 06 85, Fax 04 68 81 59 18.
English spoken.
OPEN: 15/03–15/10. SIZE: 2.7 ha, 175 pitches (all with elec, 9 statics), 17 hot showers, 21 WCs, 2 CWPs. ☎ ♿

Shop at 0.5 km. Restaurant at 0.1 km. Mini-golf.

PRICES: (1996) Caravan with family 160.00, Tent with two adults 100.00. CC: Euro/Access, Visa.
From central Argelès, head for the beach to find the site.

Camping La Roseraie 66700 Argelès-sur-Mer.
Tel 04 68 81 17 03, Fax 04 68 81 41 81.
English spoken.
OPEN: 01/04–30/10. SIZE: 7 ha, 100 pitches (60 with elec, 150 statics), 20 hot showers, 20 WCs. ☎ ♿

Tennis.
PRICES: (1996) Caravan with family 155.00, Tent with two adults 96.00. CC: none.
From Argelès take N114 north to Taxo crossroads. Campsite is 200 m on the right. Follow signs.

Camping Le Dauphin route de Taxo d'Avall, 66701 Argelès-sur-Mer.
Tel 04 68 81 17 54, Fax 04 68 95 82 60.
English spoken.
OPEN: 25/05–30/09. SIZE: 5.5 ha, 160 pitches (all with elec, 140 statics), 109 hot showers, 152 WCs. ☎ ♿

Tennis, playground.
PRICES: (1996) Tent with two adults 135.00.
CC: none.
N114 south from Elne. After Taxo-Plage Nord turn right towards Argelès. Exit 10. Cross the bridge and then follow sign 'Chemin de Taxo à la Mer'.

Camping Le Neptune Plage Nord, 66702 Argelès-sur-Mer.
Tel 04 68 81 02 98, Fax 04 68 81 00 41.
English spoken.
OPEN: 01/05–30/09. SIZE: 4.5 ha, 215 pitches (180 with elec), 28 hot showers, 52 WCs, 2 CWPs. ☎ ♿

Shop at 0.5 km. Flume, table tennis, pétanque.
PRICES: (1996) Caravan with family 240.00, Tent with two adults 140.00. CC: Amex, Euro/Access, Visa.
From centre of Argelès-sur-Mer, follow signs to Plage Nord.

Camping Les Cèdres route de Taxo Plage-Nord, 66701 Argelès-sur-Mer.
Tel 04 68 81 03 82.
OPEN: 01/06–30/09. SIZE: 3 ha, 170 pitches (50 with elec), 18 hot showers, 40 WCs, 2 CWPs. ☎ ♿

Shop at 1 km. Restaurant at 0.05 km.
PRICES: (1996) Caravan with family 143.40, Tent with two adults 82.20. CC: none.
From N114 go towards Taxo d'Avall Plage Nord.

France

Camping Les Galets route de Taxo d'Avall, 66700 Argelès-sur-Mer.
Tel 04 68 81 08 12, Fax 04 68 81 68 76.
English spoken.
OPEN: 22/03–01/11. SIZE: 5 ha, 100 pitches (all with elec, 100 statics), 20 hot showers, 16 WCs. &

Sea 1.5 km.
PRICES: Caravan with family 185.00, Tent with two adults 109.00. CC: none.
From N114, about 1 km before Argelès-sur-Mer village turn right at Taxo d'Avall crossroads. Campsite 1 km.

Camping Les Marsouins 66700 Argelès-sur-Mer.
Tel 04 68 81 14 81, Fax 04 68 95 93 58.
English spoken.
OPEN: 01/04–30/09. SIZE: 10 ha, 586 pitches (500 with elec, 87 statics), 60 hot showers, 74 WCs, 4 CWPs. & &

Mobile homes for hire.
PRICES: (1996) Caravan with family 166.00, Tent with two adults 102.00. CC: Visa.
Coming from Perpignan, take exit 10 (Argelès-sur-Mer) towards Pujols until the first roundabout. Turn left towards the sea, on chemin de Tamariguer.

Camping Municipal Roussillonnais 66700 Argelès-sur-Mer.
Tel 04 68 81 10 42, Fax 04 68 95 96 11.
English spoken.
OPEN: 15/04–15/10. SIZE: 10 ha, 730 pitches (700 with elec), 71 hot showers, 69 WCs, 32 French WCs, 5 CWPs. & &

PRICES: (1996) Caravan with family 168.00, Tent with two adults 100.00. CC: Euro/Access, Visa.
From Argelès follow directions towards Zone-Nord.

La Coste Rouge route de Collioure, 66700 Argelès-sur-Mer.
Tel 04 68 81 08 94, Fax 04 68 95 94 17. English spoken.
OPEN: 01/04–31/10. SIZE: 3 ha, 95 pitches (all with elec, 45 statics), 14 hot showers, 9 WCs, 6 French WCs, 4 CWPs. &

Shop at 2 km. Restaurant at 2 km. Mobile homes also available.
PRICES: (1996) Caravan with family 165.00, Tent with two adults 95.00. CC: Amex, Euro/Access, Visa.
South of Perpignan.

El Rancho Route de Sorède, 66700 Argelès-sur-Mer.
Tel 04 68 81 04 88, Fax 04 68 81 04 88.
English spoken.
OPEN: 01/04–30/09. SIZE: 4 ha, 60 pitches (all with elec, 23 statics), 16 hot showers, 24 WCs, 1 CWP. & &

Restaurant at 3.5 km. Mobile homes available.
PRICES: (1996) Caravan with family 130.00, Tent with two adults 70.00. CC: none.
From Argelès, drive 3 km towards Sorède. The campsite is on the left, 0.5 km after 'Le Bois Fleuri' campsite.

Le Front de Mer route du Racou, Argelès-Plage, 66700 Argelès-sur-Mer.
Tel 04 68 81 08 70, Fax 04 68 81 87 21.
English spoken.
OPEN: all year. SIZE: 7 ha, 588 pitches (400 with elec). & &

PRICES: (1996) Caravan with family 154.90, Tent with two adults 89.90. CC: Amex, Visa.
Signposted, 100 m towards Port Argelès on N114.

Le Romarin rte de Sorede, 66700 Argelès-sur-Mer.
Tel 04 68 81 02 63, Fax 04 68 56 62 33. English spoken.
OPEN: 01/06–30/09. SIZE: 2.5 ha, 150 pitches (100 with elec), 15 hot showers, 15 WCs. & &

Shop at 2 km.
PRICES: (1996) Caravan with family 140.00, Tent with two adults 85.00. CC: Euro/Access, Visa.
2 km from centre of Argelès-sur-Mer towards Sorède.

Le Soleil Plage-Nord, 66700 Argelès-sur-Mer.
Tel 04 68 81 14 48, Fax 04 68 81 44 34.
English spoken.
OPEN: 15/05–30/09. SIZE: 15 ha, 750 pitches (all with elec), 111 hot showers, 145 WCs, 145 French WCs. & &

Bar, disco.
PRICES: (1996) Caravan with family 227.00, Tent with two adults 149.00. CC: Visa.
Campsite is beside the sea, north of Argelès towards St-Cyprien.

ARGENTAN Orne   2C

Camp Municipal de la Noé rue de la Noé, 61200 Argentan.
Tel 02 33 36 05 69.
OPEN: 01/04–30/09. SIZE: 23 pitches (16 with elec), 6 hot showers, 6 WCs, 4 French WCs, 1 CWP. &

Shop at 0.4 km. Restaurant at 0.5 km. Fishing; swimming pool 0.4 km.
PRICES: (1996) Caravan with family 72.40, Tent with two adults 40.80. CC: none.
Campsite is well signposted.

France

Le Val de Baize 18 Mauvaisville, 61200 Argentan.
Tel 02 33 67 27 11. English spoken.
OPEN: all year. SIZE: 1 ha, 30 pitches (24 with elec),
3 hot showers, 5 WCs.

| ~ | 🏄 | 🏕 | R | | | | ✕ | | | | |

Shop at 1 km.
PRICES: (1996) Caravan with family 68.00, Tent
with two adults 42.00. CC: none.
*2 km south of Argentan on N158 (to Alençon).
Turn right in Mauvaisville.*

ARGENTAT Corrèze   5A

Camping Château du Gibanel 19400 Royan.
Tel 05 55 28 10 11, Fax 05 55 28 81 62.
English spoken.
OPEN: 01/06–15/09. SIZE: 8 ha, 250 pitches
(all with elec), 40 hot showers, 32 WCs, 45 French
WCs, 3 CWPs. ♿ &

| ≈ | 🏄 | 🏕 | R | 🔲 | 🏕 | 🍴 | ✕ | 🎣 | 🏨 | |

Shop at 4 km. Bar, table tennis.
PRICES: (1996) Caravan with family 151.50,
Tent with two adults 82.00. CC: Amex,
Euro/Access, Visa.
*From Tulle to Argentat on the N20 towards Centre
Ville, left on Route Egletons.*

Camping du Saulou Monceaux-sur-Dordogne,
19400 Argentat.
Tel 05 55 28 12 33, Fax 05 55 28 80 67.
English spoken.
OPEN: 01/04–30/09. SIZE: 7 ha, 150 pitches (all
with elec), 27 hot showers, 22 WCs, 1 CWP. ♿ &

| ~ | 🏄 | 🏕 | R | 🔲 | 🏕 | 🍴 | ✕ | 🎣 | 🏨 | |

Shop at 6 km. Boules, volley ball, playground,
table tennis, canoeing.
PRICES: (1996) Caravan with family 124.00, Tent
with two adults 72.00. CC: Euro/Access, Visa.
*Campsite is beside the River Dordogne, south-west
of Argentat on D12.*

Camping Le Chambon
Monceaux-sur-Dordogne, 19400 Argentat.
Tel 05 55 28 07 70, Fax 05 55 28 19 60.
English spoken.
OPEN: 01/04–31/10. SIZE: 4 ha, 9 hot showers,
10 WCs, 5 CWPs. ♿ &

| ~ | 🏄 | 🏕 | R | 🔲 | | | ✕ | | 🏨 | |

Shop at 1.5 km. Tennis, canoeing.
PRICES: (1996) Caravan with family 93.00,
Tent with two adults 50.00. CC: none.
*From Argentat drive south-west for about 1.5 km
on the D12. Well signposted.*

Le Vaurette Monceaux-sur-Dordogne,
19400 Argentat.
Tel 05 55 28 09 67, Fax 05 55 28 81 14.
English spoken.
OPEN: 01/05–01/10. SIZE: 5 ha, 120 pitches (100 with
elec), 20 hot showers, 14 WCs, 3 CWPs. ♿ &

| ~ | 🏄 | 🏕 | R | 🔲 | 🏕 | 🍴 | | 🎣 | | |

Restaurant at 9 km. Tennis, canoeing, boules,
volley ball, children's playground.
PRICES: Caravan with family 149.00, Tent with two
adults 82.00. CC: Amex, Euro/Access, Visa.
*The campsite is situated on D12, between
Argentat (9 km) and Beaulieu (14 km).*

ARGENTON-SUR-CREUSE Indre   4B

Camping Les Chambons
36200 Argenton-sur-Creuse.
Tel 02 54 24 15 26, Fax 02 54 27 46 20.
English spoken.
OPEN: 15/05–15/09. SIZE: 1.5 ha, 60 pitches
(30 with elec), 9 hot showers, 15 WCs, 1 CWP. ♿ &

| ~ | 🏄 | 🏕 | R | | 🏕 | | | | | |

Restaurant at 0.5 km.
PRICES: (1996) Caravan with family 89.50,
Tent with two adults 59.00. CC: none.
*Campsite is near the town centre and well
signposted.*

ARLES Bouches-du-Rhône   5D

Camping Municipal des Pins rue Michelet,
13990 Fontvieille.
Tel 04 90 54 78 69. English spoken.
OPEN: 01/04–15/10. SIZE: 3.5 ha, 57 pitches (all
with elec), 18 hot showers, 18 WCs, 4 CWPs. ♿ &

| | | 🏕 | R | 🔲 | | | | | | |

Shop at 2 km. Restaurant at 2 km. Table tennis,
children's play area.
PRICES: (1996) Caravan with family 114.00,
Tent with two adults 60.00. CC: none.
From Arles, D17 towards Les Baux-de-Provence.

Camping à la Ferme Mas Taraud les Roses,
route de Fourques, 30300 Beaucaire.
Tel 04 66 59 22 38.
OPEN: 01/03–31/10. SIZE: 0.5 ha, 10 pitches
(all with elec), 3 hot showers, 3 WCs, 3 French
WCs, 1 CWP. &

| ~ | 🏄 | 🏕 | R | 🔲 | | | | 🎣 | | |

Shop at 8 km. Restaurant at 8 km.
PRICES: (1996) Caravan with family 76.00,
Tent with two adults 54.00. CC: none.
*Leave the A9 at Fournés and go towards
Remoulin/Beaucaire/Fourques. After 8 km look
for the signpost to Camping à la Ferme.*

Crin-Blanc D37 Hameau de Saliers,
13123 Albaron.
Tel 04 66 87 48 78, Fax 04 66 87 18 66.
English spoken.
OPEN: 09/04–30/09. SIZE: 5 ha, 180 pitches, 24 hot
showers, 24 WCs, 24 French WCs, 2 CWPs. ♿ &

| | | 🏕 | R | 🔲 | 🏕 | 🍴 | ✕ | 🎣 | 🏨 | |

Tennis, volley ball, children's playground.

France

France

PRICES: (1996) Caravan with family 142.00, Tent with two adults 100.00. CC: Euro/Access.
From Arles take N572 towards St-Gilles-du-Gard for 13 km. Saliers is 3 km from St-Gilles-du-Gard towards Albaron and Stes-Maries-de-la-Mer.

ARLES-SUR-TECH Pyrénées Orient   5C

Camp Riuferrer Lieu-dit Mas d'en Ploume, 66150 Arles-sur-Tech.
Tel 04 68 39 11 06, Fax 04 68 39 12 09.
English spoken.
OPEN: all year. SIZE: 4 ha, 150 pitches (100 with elec, 18 statics), 17 hot showers, 21 WCs, 1 CWP. ☎ ও

Shop at 0.6 km. Restaurant at 0.6 km. Swimming pool next door to the campsite.
PRICES: Caravan with family 119.00,
Tent with two adults 63.00. CC: none.
Turn off the D115 between Prats de Mollo and Le Boulou at the exit for Arles-sur-Tech, then turn right.

ARNAY-LE-DUC Côte-d'Or   3C

Camping Municipal de Fouche
21230 Arnay-le-Duc.
Tel 03 80 90 02 23, Fax 03 80 90 11 91.
English spoken.
OPEN: all year. SIZE: 6 ha, 190 pitches (all with elec), 17 hot showers, 22 WCs, 4 CWPs. ☎ ও

Shop at 0.5 km. Restaurant at 0.5 km.
PRICES: (1996) Caravan with family 65.09,
Tent with two adults 33.02. CC: none.

ARRADON Morbihan   1D

Camping L'Allée l'Allée, 56610 Arradon.
Tel 02 97 44 01 98, Fax 02 97 44 73 74.
English spoken.
OPEN: 01/04–30/09. SIZE: 3 ha, 100 pitches (80 with elec), 12 hot showers, 12 WCs, 1 CWP. ☎ ও

Shop at 1.5 km. Restaurant at 1.5 km. Games room, table tennis; mini-golf and tennis nearby.
PRICES: (1996) Caravan with family 118.00,
Tent with two adults 67.00. CC: none.
Arradon is south-west of Vannes off D101. Stay on the Arradon bypass and turn right. Follow signs.

ARROMANCHES-LES-BAINS Calv   2A

Camping Quintefeuille 14960 Asnelles.
Tel 02 31 22 35 50. English spoken.
OPEN: 01/06–15/09. SIZE: 113 pitches (all with elec), 10 hot showers, 16 WCs, 14 French WCs, 1 CWP. ☎ ও

Shop at 0.5 km. Restaurant at 0.5 km. Tennis and sand yachting (with extra charge).
PRICES: (1996) Caravan with family 79.00,
Tent with two adults 47.00. CC: none.
From Arromanches-les-Bains, take the D65 towards Meuvaines and turn left to Asnelles.

ARUDY Pyrénées-Atlan   4D

Camping Le Rey route de Lourdes, 64260 Louvie-Juzon.
Tel 05 59 71 03 28, Fax 05 59 71 09 62.
English spoken.
OPEN: 15/06–15/09 & 01/12–30/05. SIZE: 4 ha, 52 pitches (40 with elec), 6 hot showers, 8 WCs. ☎ ও

Shop at 0.8 km. Restaurant at 0.8 km. Archery; organised sporting events.
PRICES: Caravan with family 85.00,
Tent with two adults 45.00. CC: none.
South of Arudy to Louvie-Juzon, turn left on to D35 towards Lourdes. Site 1 km on left.

ASPRES-SUR-BUECH Hautes-Alpes   6C

L'Adrech 05140 Aspres-sur-Büech.
Tel 04 92 58 60 45. English spoken.
OPEN: 01/01–31/10. SIZE: 7 ha, 160 pitches (100 with elec, 60 statics), 12 hot showers (charge), 15 WCs, 2 CWPs. ☎ ও

Restaurant at 1 km. Games, entertainment, swimming, hang-gliding nearby.
PRICES: (1996) Caravan with family 82.00,
Tent with two adults 52.00.
CC: Amex, Euro/Access, Visa.
100 km south of Grenoble on the N75.

ATHIS-DE-L'ORNE Orne   2A

La Ribardière 61430 Athis-de-l'Orne.
Tel 02 33 66 41 93. English spoken.
OPEN: 01/04–30/10. SIZE: 1 ha, 25 pitches (all with elec), 3 hot showers, 5 WCs.

Shop at 4 km. Restaurant at 4 km.
PRICES: Caravan with family 68.00,
Tent with two adults 35.00. CC: none.
North of Flers on D25 to Athis-de-l'Orne. Signposted.

AUBENAS Ardèche   5D

Camping Arle Blanc 07260 Rosières.
Tel 04 75 39 53 11, Fax 04 75 39 93 98.
English spoken.
OPEN: 01/04–30/10. SIZE: 7 ha. ☎ ও

PRICES: (1996) Caravan with family 129.00, Tent with two adults 95.00. CC: Euro/Access, Visa. *Rosières is 22 km south of Aubenas on the D104.*

Camping Arle Blanc

near Aubenas

On, in and by the Ardèche

Camping du Pont de Ville Aubenas Montélimar, 07200 St-Didier-sous-Aubenas.
Tel 04 75 35 25 80, Fax 04 75 93 04 79.
English spoken.
OPEN: all year. SIZE: 2 ha, 115 pitches (110 with elec, 12 statics), 10 hot showers, 20 WCs, 20 French WCs, 2 CWPs. ᴄ ᴅ

Trampoline.
PRICES: Caravan with family 123.00,
Tent with two adults 80.00. CC: Amex, Visa.

Leave Aubenas on N102 towards Montélimar. After 3 km and before the bridge in St-Didier, turn left.

Camping Le Ranc Davaine
St-Alban-Auriolles, 07120 Ruoms.
Tel 04 75 39 60 55, Fax 04 75 39 38 50.
English spoken.
OPEN: 22/03–15/09. SIZE: 7 ha, 298 pitches (all with elec, 54 statics), 54 hot showers, 52 WCs, 2 CWPs. ᴄ ᴅ

PRICES: Caravan with family 224.00,
Tent with two adults 138.00. CC: none.
From Aubenas take D104/D4 to Ruoms, then D208 to St-Alban-Auriolles. Follow signs.

Camping Les Roches 07200 Vogüé.
Tel 04 75 37 70 45. English spoken.
OPEN: 01/04–30/09. SIZE: 5 ha, 100 pitches, 11 hot showers, 13 WCs, 4 CWPs. ᴄ ᴅ

Tennis, entertainment.
PRICES: (1996) Tent with two adults 89.00.
CC: none.
Vogüé is south of Aubenas on the D579. By-pass Vogüé towards Vogüé Gare, site on left just beyond village.

Camping à la Ferme Marc Champanhet, 07200 St-Michel-de-Boulogne.
Tel 04 75 87 10 04. English spoken.
OPEN: 28/03–31/10. SIZE: 6 pitches (all with elec, 3 statics), 2 hot showers, 2 WCs. ᴄ

Restaurant at 15 km.
PRICES: (1996) Caravan with family 65.00,
Tent with two adults 31.00. CC: none.
From Aubenas, drive 10 north on the N104 then turn left on the D356 to St-Michel-de-Boulogne. The campsite is 3 km after the château de Boulogne.

Les Charmilles D258, 07170 Darbres.
Tel 04 75 94 25 22, Fax 04 75 94 25 22.
English spoken.
OPEN: 01/04–01/10. SIZE: 4 ha, 90 pitches (80 with elec), 11 hot showers, 11 WCs. ᴄ ᴅ

Children's playground, volley ball; mobile homes for hire.
PRICES: (1996) Caravan with family 164.00,
Tent with two adults 102.00. CC: none.
Follow the N102 east towards Montelimar. At Lavilledieu turn left (north) towards Lussas and Darbres (D224). After Darbres go towards Mirabel and Privas.

Les Chênes Verts Champredon, 07200 Vogüé.
Tel 04 75 37 71 54, Fax 04 75 37 71 54.
English spoken.
OPEN: 01/04–30/10. SIZE: 1.6 ha, 25 pitches (all with elec), 5 hot showers, 4 WCs, 2 French WCs. ᴄ ᴅ

Shop at 0.6 km. Canoeing; sightseeing tours.
PRICES: (1996) Caravan with family 115.00,
Tent with two adults 72.00. CC: none.
Vogüé is south of Aubenas on the D579.

Domaine du Cros d'Auzon
07200 St-Maurice-d'Ardèche.
Tel 04 75 37 75 86, Fax 04 75 37 01 02.
English spoken.
OPEN: 15/05–15/09. SIZE: 20 ha, 200 pitches (150 with elec, 8 statics), 40 hot showers, 20 WCs, 2 CWPs. ᴄ ᴅ

3 swimming pools, ponies, athletics track and playground.

France

PRICES: (1996) Caravan with family 152.00, Tent with two adults 92.00. CC: Amex, Euro/Access, Visa. *10 km south of Aubenas on road to Vallon-Pont d'Arc.*

AUBERIVE Haute-Marne 3C

Les Charbonnières 52160 Auberive.
Tel 03 25 84 21 13.
OPEN: 15/04–01/10. SIZE: 1 ha, 20 pitches (8 with elec), 8 hot showers, 3 WCs.

Shop at 0.5 km. Restaurant at 0.5 km. Children's playground; tennis nearby.
PRICES: (1996) Caravan with family 60.00, Tent with two adults 30.00. CC: none.
On the D428.

AUCH Gers 4D

Camp Le Talouch Roquelaure, 32810 Auch.
Tel 05 62 65 52 43, Fax 05 62 65 53 68.
English spoken.
OPEN: 01/04–30/09. SIZE: 3 ha, 90 pitches (all with elec, 6 statics), 10 hot showers, 10 WCs, 1 CWP.

PRICES: (1996) Caravan with family 141.00, Tent with two adults 80.00. CC: none.
Leave town centre towards Condom, then turn right towards Duran (D148). Follow signs from there to the campsite, approx 7 km.

AUMALE Seine Marit 2B

Camping Municipal Le Grand Mail
76390 Aumale.
Tel 02 35 93 40 50, Fax 02 35 93 86 79.
OPEN: 01/05–30/09. SIZE: 0.5 ha, 60 pitches (24 with elec), 10 hot showers (charge), 16 WCs.

Shop at 0.5 km. Restaurant at 0.5 km. Playground.
PRICES: (1996) Caravan with family 43.00, Tent with two adults 34.00. CC: none.
Off N29 to west of Aumale. Signposted.

AUNAC Charente 4B

Camping L'Angle 16460 Aunac.
Tel 05 45 22 24 38, Fax 05 45 22 23 17.
OPEN: 15/06–15/09. SIZE: 1 ha, 25 pitches, 2 hot showers, 2 WCs, 1 CWP.

Shop at 1 km. Restaurant at 1 km. Tennis, swimming pool and horse-riding nearby.
PRICES: (1996) Caravan with family 47.40, Tent with two adults 23.60. CC: none.
South of Ruffec on the N10. Follow signs to Les Maisons Rouges.

AUPS Var 6C

Camping Les Prés quartier les Faisses, 83630 Aups.
Tel 04 94 70 00 93, Fax 04 94 70 14 41.
English spoken.
OPEN: all year. SIZE: 2 ha, 121 pitches (all with elec, 15 statics), 9 hot showers, 11 WCs, 2 CWPs.

Shop at 0.2 km. Swimming pool 0.2 km.
PRICES: Caravan with family 101.00, Tent with two adults 53.00. CC: Amex, Euro/Access, Visa.

International Camping
route de Fox Amphoux, 83630 Aups.
Tel 04 94 70 06 80, Fax 04 94 70 10 51.
English spoken.
OPEN: 01/04–30/09. SIZE: 4 ha, 150 pitches (130 with elec, 30 statics), 18 hot showers, 24 WCs, 2 CWPs.

Shop at 0.5 km. Restaurant at 0.5 km.
PRICES: (1996) Caravan with family 114.50, Tent with two adults 58.00. CC: Euro/Access, Visa.
29 km north-west of Draguignan on D557. Turn left in centre of Aups on to D60, 500 m.

AURAY Morbihan 1C

Camping de Kergo Ploemel, 56400 Auray.
Tel 02 97 56 80 66. English spoken.
OPEN: 15/06–15/09. SIZE: 3 ha, 135 pitches (100 with elec), 14 hot showers, 15 WCs, 2 French WCs, 1 CWP.

Shop at 1.5 km. Restaurant at 2 km.
PRICES: (1996) Caravan with family 117.00, Tent with two adults 68.00. CC: Amex, Euro/Access, Visa.
N165 west from Vannes.

Camping Municipal 56400 Ste-Anne-d'Auray.
Tel 02 97 57 60 27, Fax 02 97 57 72 33.
English spoken.
OPEN: 01/06–30/09. SIZE: 1 ha, 115 pitches (68 with elec), 10 hot showers, 12 WCs.

Shop at 1 km. Restaurant at 2 km.
PRICES: (1996) Caravan with family 58.20, Tent with two adults 29.20. CC: none.
From Auray centre head east towards Vannes and turn off left (north) before leaving town, on D17 to Ste-Anne. As you arrive in the village, take the first left to Le Motten.

AURILLAC Cantal 5A

Camping Municipal 15800 Thiezac.
Tel 04 71 47 00 41, Fax 04 71 47 02 23.
English spoken.

France

OPEN: 01/06–15/09. SIZE: 2 ha, 116 pitches (96 with elec, 7 statics), 13 hot showers, 28 WCs. ✆ ♿

Shop at 0.5 km. Restaurant at 0.3 km.
PRICES: unavailable. CC: none.
25 km from Aurillac on the N122 towards Murat/Clermont-Ferrand.

AUTUN Saône/Loire 3C

Aire Naturelle Municipale
71540 Lucenay-l'Evêque.
Tel 03 85 82 65 41.
OPEN: 26/06–01/09. SIZE: 25 pitches (13 with elec), 6 hot showers, 3 WCs.

Shop at 0.5 km. Restaurant at 0.5 km.
PRICES: Caravan with family 60.00,
Tent with two adults 34.00. CC: none.
17 km from Autun, northwards on the D980 to Lucenay-l'Evêque.

AUXERRE Yonne 2D

Camping Municipal
8 route de Vaux, 89000 Auxerre.
Tel 03 86 52 11 15, Fax 03 86 52 18 34.
English spoken.
OPEN: 01/04–30/09. SIZE: 5 ha, 220 pitches (112 with elec), 24 hot showers, 17 WCs, 10 French WCs, 7 CWPs. ✆ ♿

Shop at 0.8 km. Restaurant at 1 km.
PRICES: (1996) Caravan with family 81.00, Tent with two adults 42.00. CC: Euro/Access, Visa.

AVALLON Yonne 3C

Camping Municipal Sous Roches 89200 Avallon.
Tel 03 86 34 10 39, Fax 03 86 34 46 25.
OPEN: 15/03–15/10. SIZE: 2 ha, 9 hot showers, 9 WCs, 1 CWP. ✆ ♿

Shop at 2 km. Restaurant at 2 km.
PRICES: (1996) Caravan with family 115.00, Tent with two adults 61.19. CC: none.
Well signposted.

AVIGNON Vaucluse 5D

Camping Bagatelle Ile de la Barthelasse, 84000 Avignon.
Tel 04 90 86 30 39, Fax 04 90 27 16 23.
English spoken.
OPEN: all year. SIZE: 4 ha, 100 pitches (all with elec), 36 hot showers, 30 WCs. ✆ ♿

Swimming pool nearby.

PRICES: (1996) Caravan with family 125.50, Tent with two adults 61.50. CC: Euro/Access, Visa.
800 m from the centre of Avignon, near the Daladier bridge.

Camping du Grand Bois La Tapy
14 chemin la Tapy, 84130 Le Pontet.
Tel 04 90 31 37 44. English spoken.
OPEN: 15/04–30/09. SIZE: 2 ha, 80 pitches (all with elec), 10 hot showers, 12 WCs, 12 French WCs, 1 CWP. ✆ ♿

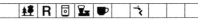

Restaurant at 0.1 km. Golf 1 km.
PRICES: Caravan with family 111.00, Tent with two adults 67.00. CC: none.
From motorway take Avignon-Nord exit to Le Pontet.

Camping Flory 84270 Vedène.
Tel 04 90 31 00 51. English spoken.
OPEN: 15/03–15/10. SIZE: 7 ha, 142 pitches (all with elec), 14 hot showers, 14 WCs, 2 CWPs. ✆ ♿

PRICES: (1996) Caravan with family 109.00, Tent with two adults 55.80. CC: none.
Vedène is north-east of Avignon, 4 km from the A7.

Le Jantou 84250 Le Thor.
Tel 04 90 33 90 07, Fax 04 90 33 79 84.
English spoken.
OPEN: 01/04–31/10. SIZE: 6 ha, 125 pitches (117 with elec, 25 statics), 17 hot showers, 13 WCs, 2 CWPs. ♿

Shop at 0.3 km. Restaurant at 0.5 km. 10% discount RAC members.
PRICES: (1996) Caravan with family 110.00, Tent with two adults 72.00. CC: Euro/Access, Visa.
Leave Avignon on N100 to Isle-sur-Sorgue and Apt. At the entrance to the village of Le Thor turn left just before the bridge and the supermarket. Follow signposts.

Camping Le Jantou
near Avignon
Provençal Perfection . . . You'll agree!

Camping Municipal St-Benezet
Ile de la Barthelasse, 84000 Avignon.
Tel 04 90 82 63 50, Fax 04 90 85 22 12.
English spoken.
OPEN: 01/03–30/10. SIZE: 9 ha, 130 pitches (all with elec), 44 hot showers, 36 WCs, 4 CWPs. ✆ ♿

France

France

Ball games.
PRICES: (1996) Caravan with family 102.00, Tent with two adults 48.00. CC: Euro/Access, Visa.
North of Avignon (Daladier Bridge). The site is on an island on the River Rhône, by the Pont d'Avignon.

AVRANCHES Manche   1D

Camp Municipal 50320 La Haye-Pesnel.
Tel 02 33 61 50 43, Fax 02 33 61 46 36.
OPEN: 01/06–15/09. SIZE: 0.4 ha, 17 pitches (13 with elec), 6 hot showers, 11 WCs. &

Shop at 0.2 km. Restaurant at 0.1 km.
PRICES: (1996) Caravan with family 60.00, Tent with two adults 30.00. CC: none.
From Avranches go north on D7 for 15 km. Turn right on to D165 at La Haye-Pesnel and campsite is 200 m.

Camping Les Coques d'Or
route de Bec d'Anbaine, 50530 Genêts.
Tel 02 33 70 82 57, Fax 02 33 70 86 83.
English spoken.
OPEN: 01/04–30/09. SIZE: 5 ha, 140 pitches (120 with elec, 7 statics), 22 hot showers, 11 WCs, 2 CWPs. ♥ &

Shop at 0.5 km. Restaurant at 0.5 km. Entertainment, bar, rifle shooting, volley ball, boules.
PRICES: (1996) Caravan with family 115.00, Tent with two adults 67.00. CC: Euro/Access, Visa.
From Avranches take the D911 towards Jullouville for 8 km to Genêts.

AX-LES-THERMES Ariège   5C

Camping Les Sapins 11340 Camurac.
Tel 04 68 20 38 11, Fax 04 68 20 74 75.
English spoken.
OPEN: all year. SIZE: 2 ha, 30 pitches (all with elec, 2 statics), 6 hot showers, 12 WCs, 2 French WCs, 1 CWP. ♥ &

Shop at 2 km. Playground, table tennis, volley ball; horse-riding nearby.
PRICES: (1996) Caravan with family 128.50, Tent with two adults 58.00. CC: none.
From Ax-les-Thermes take the D613. In Camurac turn right, and the site is 1.5 km on right.

AXAT Aude   5C

Camping Le Moulin du Pont d'Alies
Station des Pyrénées, St-Martin-Lys, 11140 Axat.
Tel 04 68 20 53 27, Fax 04 68 20 53 27.
English spoken.

OPEN: 01/04–15/11. SIZE: 2 ha, 104 pitches (all with elec), 10 hot showers, 1 CWP. ♥

Rafting and canoeing.
PRICES: (1996) Caravan with family 114.00, Tent with two adults 75.00. CC: Euro/Access, Visa.
At junction of D117 and D118, just north of Axat. Signposted.

AYDAT Puy-de-Dôme   5A

Camping Les Suquets La Garandie, 63970 Aydat.
Tel 04 73 79 31 00, Fax 04 73 79 31 00.
OPEN: 15/06–15/09. SIZE: 2 ha, 33 pitches (16 with elec), 2 hot showers, 3 WCs, 1 CWP.

Shop at 3 km. Restaurant at 3 km.
PRICES: Caravan with family 56.00, Tent with two adults 32.00. CC: none.
From Aydat take D788 towards La Garandie. The campsite is on the left before reaching La Garandie. Signposted.

BACCARAT Meurthe/Moselle   3D

Les Brimbelles rue du Moulin,
54120 Bertrichamps.
Tel 03 83 75 14 10, Fax 03 83 75 45 19.
OPEN: 01/05–30/09. SIZE: 1 ha, 50 pitches (32 with elec), 5 hot showers, 4 WCs, 1 CWP. &

Shop at 0.5 km. Restaurant at 1 km.
PRICES: (1996) Caravan with family 46.00, Tent with two adults 24.00. CC: none.
4 km from Baccarat on N59. Follow signs from Bertrichamps.

BAGNERES-DE-BIGORRE Htes-Pyr   4D

Camping Bigourdan Pouzac,
65200 Bagnères-de-Bigorre.
Tel 05 62 95 13 57.
OPEN: 01/04–30/09. SIZE: 0.6 ha, 33 pitches (all with elec), 4 hot showers, 10 WCs, 1 CWP. &

Shop at 0.1 km. Restaurant at 0.3 km. River 0.3 km, swimming pool 1.5 km.
PRICES: (1996) Caravan with family 102.00, Tent with two adults 54.50. CC: none.
On D935 Bagnères-de-Bigorre/Tarbes road, 1 km from the centre of Bagnères-de-Bigorre. Follow directions.

Les Fruitiers 91 route de Toulouse,
65200 Bagnères-de-Bigorre.
Tel 05 62 95 25 97. English spoken.
OPEN: 01/05–31/10. SIZE: 1 ha, 100 pitches (85 with elec), 9 hot showers, 15 WCs, 1 CWP.

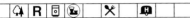

Shop at 0.5 km. Restaurant at 0.3 km.
PRICES: (1996) Caravan with family 98.00, Tent
with two adults 52.00. CC: none.
500 m from the town centre.

BAGNERES-DE-LUCHON Hte-Gar 4D

Camping La Lanette D 27, 31110 Luchon.
Tel 05 61 79 00 38. English spoken.
OPEN: all year. SIZE: 4 ha, 270 pitches (184 with
elec), 26 hot showers, 48 WCs, 27 French WCs,
6 CWPs.

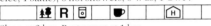

Shop at 2 km. Mobile homes for hire.
PRICES: (1996) Caravan with family 90.00,
Tent with two adults 78.00. CC: none.
*From N125 in Bagnères-de-Luchon, take D27 to
Montauban-de-Luchon and on to St-Mamet.
Some of the local signs may use 'Luchon' instead
of Bagnères-de-Luchon.*

BAGNOLES-DE-L'ORNE Orne 2C

Camping du Clos Normand
route de Bagnoles, 61410 Couterne.
Tel 02 33 37 92 43. English spoken.
OPEN: 01/04–30/09. SIZE: 1 ha, 65 pitches (30 with
elec, 1 static), 6 hot showers, 6 WCs, 1 CWP.

Shop at 2 km. Restaurant at 1 km.
PRICES: (1996) Caravan with family 74.50,
Tent with two adults 36.00. CC: none.
*From Bagnoles-de-l'Orne, south on the D916.
Site is north of Couterne.*

BAGNOLS-SUR-CEZE Gard 5D

Camping Les Cascades
30200 La Roque-sur-Cèze.
Tel 04 66 82 72 97, Fax 04 66 82 79 61.
English spoken.
OPEN: 01/04–30/09. SIZE: 5 ha, 90 pitches (60 with
elec), 12 hot showers, 18 WCs, 8 French WCs,
1 CWP.

Shop at 3 km. Lovely old village with Roman
bridge.
PRICES: (1996) Caravan with family 114.00, Tent
with two adults 70.00. CC: none.
*From Bagnols, north on N86 for about 1 km then
D980 west for approx 8 km. Turn left for La
Roque-sur-Cèze and campsite is signposted.*

Les Genets d'Or route de Carmignan,
30200 Bagnols-sur-Ceze.
Tel 04 66 89 58 67, Fax 04 66 89 58 67.
English spoken.
OPEN: 01/04–30/09. SIZE: 4 ha, 120 pitches

(all with elec, 15 statics), 18 hot showers, 17 WCs,
2 CWPs.

Shop at 2 km. Dogs allowed LS only.
PRICES: (1996) Tent with two adults 111.00.
CC: Amex, Euro/Access, Visa.
*Coming from the north on N86, turn left towards
Carmignan on D360, 500 m after entering
Bagnols-sur-Ceze.*

BAPAUME Pas-de-Calais 2B

Camping Verdure 62121 Sapignies.
Tel 03 21 07 15 47.
OPEN: all year. SIZE: 3 ha, 90 pitches (all with elec),
2 hot showers, 10 WCs, 1 CWP.

Shop at 2 km. Restaurant at 2 km.
PRICES: (1996) Caravan with family 74.00,
Tent with two adults 42.00. CC: none.
*Between Arras and Bapaume on N17.
Follow signs.*

BARCELONNETTE Alpes/Hte-Prov 6C

Camping Le Fontarache 04400 Les Thuiles.
Tel 04 92 81 90 42, Fax 04 92 81 90 42.
English spoken.
OPEN: 01/06–15/09. SIZE: 6 ha, 150 pitches
(all with elec), 17 hot showers, 13 WCs, 7 French
WCs, 1 CWP.

Shop at 0.4 km. Restaurant at 0.2 km. Ball games,
children's playground, tennis, water sports.
PRICES: Caravan with family 104.00,
Tent with two adults 56.00. CC: none.
*Les Thuiles is a few kilometres west of
Barcelonnette. Turn left to campsite as you enter
the village.*

BARFLEUR Manche 1B

La Blanche Nef rue des Ecoles, 50760 Barfleur.
Tel 02 33 23 15 40, Fax 02 33 23 95 14.
English spoken.
OPEN: all year. SIZE: 2.5 ha, 60 pitches (40 with
elec, 30 statics), 7 hot showers, 10 WCs, 1 CWP.

Restaurant at 0.5 km. Games room.
PRICES: (1996) Caravan with family 70.00,
Tent with two adults 40.00. CC: Visa.
*From Cherbourg into Barfleur, turn left into rue
Thomas Beckett. At the port bear left, and after
100 m turn left. Site is 300 m, facing the sea.*

Camping de la Hay 50760 Montfarville.
Tel 02 33 54 00 84. English spoken.
OPEN: 01/04–15/09. SIZE: 4 ha, 40 pitches (all with

France

elec), 7 hot showers, 17 WCs, 5 French WCs, 3 CWPs. ☍ ♿

≋ ♨ R ▭ ▭ ▭ ▭ ▭ �

Shop at 1 km. Restaurant at 1 km.
PRICES: (1996) Caravan with family 62.00, Tent with two adults 35.00. CC: none.
From Barfleur go towards St-Vaast-la-Hougue along the coast road. Turn right at Le Cap, 3 km from Barfleur. Signposted.

BARJAC Gard   5D

Camping Le Ran du Chabrier 30430 Barjac.
Tel 04 66 24 51 55. English spoken.
OPEN: 01/05–30/09. SIZE: 86 ha, 160 pitches (100 with elec), 13 hot showers, 15 WCs, 2 CWPs. ☍

~ ⛵ 🎣 R ▭ 🍺 ☕ ✗ ▭ ▭ ▭

Naturist site. Boating, fishing; beautiful surroundings.
PRICES: (1996) Caravan with family 106.00, Tent with two adults 54.00. CC: none.
South-east of Barjac on D901. Turn off through the hamlet of St-Privat-de-Champclos and on to the river. Well signposted.
SEE ADVERTISEMENT

Camping Universal Rochegude, 30430 Barjac.
Tel 04 66 24 41 26. English spoken.
OPEN: 01/06–15/09. SIZE: 4 ha, 90 pitches (72 with

elec), 9 hot showers, 15 WCs, 8 CWPs. ☍ ♿

~ ⛵ 🎣 R ▭ 🍺 ☕ ▭ ▭ ♨ ▭

Restaurant at 2 km.
PRICES: (1996) Caravan with family 118.00, Tent with two adults 66.00. CC: none.
In Barjac take D979 towards St-Jean-de-Maruéjols. The campsite site is 2 km after St-Jean-de-Maruéjols on the left.

La Genèse Méjannes-le-Clap, 30430 Barjac.
Tel 04 66 24 51 73, Fax 04 66 24 50 38.
English spoken.
OPEN: 01/04–15/10. SIZE: 26 ha, 392 pitches (319 with elec, 50 statics), 51 hot showers, 56 WCs, 3 CWPs. ♿

~ ⛵ 🎣 R ▭ 🍺 ☕ ✗ ♨ ⌂ ▭

PRICES: (1996) Caravan with family 143.00, Tent with two adults 90.00. CC: Euro/Access, Visa.
South of Barjac on D979 through St-Jean-de-Maruéjols, then turn right to Méjannes-le-Clap. The entrance to campsite is by the car park in village.

BARNEVILLE-CARTERET Manche   1B

Bel Sito Le Caumont de la rue, 50270 Baubigny.
Tel 02 33 04 32 74, Fax 02 33 04 02 69.
English spoken.
OPEN: 09/04–15/09. SIZE: 6 ha, 85 pitches (48 with elec), 10 hot showers, 10 WCs. ☍

≋ ⛵ ♨ R ▭ 🍺 ▭ ▭ ⌂ ▭

Restaurant at 0.9 km.
PRICES: (1996) Caravan with family 98.00, Tent with two adults 54.00. CC: none.
Take D904 north of Barneville-Carteret to Baubigny. Signposted.

Le Bocage rue du Bocage, 50270 Carteret.
Tel 02 33 53 86 91. English spoken.
OPEN: 09/04–30/09. SIZE: 4 ha, 200 pitches (all with elec), 30 hot showers, 26 WCs. ☍ ♿

≋ ⛵ ♨ R ▭ ▭ ▭ ▭ ▭ ▭

Shop at 0.5 km. Restaurant at 0.5 km.
PRICES: (1996) Caravan with family 86.00, Tent with two adults 52.00. CC: none.
D904 south of Cherbourg.

Camping l'Esperance 32 rte du Hameau des Gros, 50580 Denneville.
Tel 02 33 07 12 71, Fax 02 33 07 58 32.
English spoken.
OPEN: 01/04–30/09. SIZE: 3 ha, 49 pitches (all with elec, 55 statics), 6 hot showers, 6 WCs, 9 French WCs, 1 CWP.

≋ ⛵ ♨ R ▭ 🍺 ☕ ▭ ⌂ ▭

Restaurant at 0.5 km.
PRICES: (1996) Caravan with family 118.00, Tent with two adults 63.00. CC: Euro/Access, Visa.
From Barneville-Carteret take the D903. Fork

right on to the D650 and right again on to the D137; follow signs to Denneville-Plage.

Camping Les Carolins route de Lindberg, St-Lô-d'Ourville, 50580 Port-Bail.
Tel 02 33 04 84 85. English spoken.
OPEN: 15/03–15/11. SIZE: 3.5 ha, 75 pitches (64 with elec, 12 statics), 10 hot showers, 10 WCs.

Shop at 1 km. Restaurant at 1 km. Table tennis, volley ball; game room; mobile homes available.
PRICES: (1996) Caravan with family 79.00, Tent with two adults 48.00. CC: Amex, Euro/Access, Visa.
From Barneville-Carteret south on D903 to St-Lô-d'Ourville.

BAUD Morbihan 1C

Camping de Pont-Augan Pont-Augan, 56150 Baud.
Tel 02 97 51 04 74, Fax 02 97 39 07 22.
English spoken.
OPEN: 01/04–30/09. SIZE: 1 ha, 32 pitches (38 with elec), 8 hot showers, 16 WCs, 16 French WCs, 10 CWPs.

Shop at 4 km.
PRICES: (1996) Caravan with family 62.00, Tent with two adults 50.00. CC: none.
Take the D3 from Baud to Pont-Augan. Campsite is signposted. (No motor caravans.)

Camping Municipal de Camors 56330 Camors.
Tel 02 97 39 18 36, Fax 02 97 39 28 99.
English spoken.
OPEN: 15/06–15/09. SIZE: 1 ha, 30 pitches (all with elec).

Shop at 1 km. Restaurant at 1 km. Good sports/leisure facilities nearby.
PRICES: (1996) Caravan with family 56.00, Tent with two adults 28.00. CC: none.
From Baud go south on D768 to Camors. Turn right by the church towards Lambel and campsite is 1 km ahead, signposted.

LA BAULE Loire-Atlan 1D

Camping Tremondec rue du Château, Careil, 44350 La Baule.
Tel 02 40 60 00 07. English spoken.
OPEN: 15/04–30/09. SIZE: 3 ha, 100 pitches (40 with elec, 7 statics), 13 hot showers, 13 WCs, 2 CWPs.

Shop at 0.5 km. Restaurant at 0.5 km.
PRICES: Caravan with family 135.00, Tent with two adults 74.00. CC: Amex, Euro/Access, Visa.
D92 north of La Baule. Site is 1 km on the right.

La Govelle route de la Côte Sauvage, 44740 Batz-sur-Mer.
Tel 02 40 23 91 63. English spoken.
OPEN: 01/04–30/09. SIZE: 1 ha, 52 pitches (all with elec), 7 hot showers, 12 WCs, 2 CWPs.

Shop at 2 km.
PRICES: (1996) Caravan with family 200.00, Tent with two adults 155.00. CC: none.
D45 west of La Baule.

BAYEUX Calvados 2A

Bayeux Camping Municipal
bd Périphérique d'Eindhoven, 14400 Bayeux.
Tel 02 31 92 08 43, Fax 02 31 51 60 70.
English spoken.
OPEN: 15/03–15/11. SIZE: 4 ha, 150 pitches (all with elec), 26 hot showers, 17 WCs, 3 CWPs.

Shop at 0.1 km. Restaurant at 0.1 km. Organised sports July/August.
PRICES: (1996) Caravan with family 93.70, Tent with two adults 48.40. CC: none.
Campsite is in centre of Bayeux.

Camping Reine Mathilde route de Ste-Honorine, 14400 Etréham.
Tel 02 31 21 76 55. English spoken.
OPEN: 01/04–30/09. SIZE: 4 ha, 90 pitches (60 with elec, 25 statics), 9 hot showers, 9 WCs, 3 CWPs.

PRICES: (1996) Caravan with family 131.00, Tent with two adults 67.00. CC: none.
From Bayeux take N13, then D206 to Etréham. Follow signs.

Château de Martragny 14740 Martragny.
Tel 02 31 80 21 40, Fax 02 31 08 14 91.
English spoken.
OPEN: 01/05–15/09. SIZE: 8 ha, 160 pitches (150 with elec), 22 hot showers, 23 WCs, 7 French WCs, 2 CWPs.

Restaurant at 1 km. B&B available in Château (350FF per night) ; horse-riding nearby; sea 10 km.
PRICES: Caravan with family 192.00, Tent with two adults 113.00. CC: Euro/Access, Visa.
N13 south-east from Bayeux. Turn left on to D82 for Martragny after 7 km.

La Hague Le Grand Hameau, 14520 Ste-Honorine-des-Pertes.
Tel 02 31 21 77 24. English spoken.
OPEN: 15/06–10/09. SIZE: 1 ha, 66 pitches (52 with elec, 3 statics), 6 hot showers, 9 WCs, 1 CWP.

Shop at 0.5 km. Children's activity programme.

France

PRICES: Caravan with family 108.00, Tent with two adults 54.00. CC: none.
From Bayeux take D6 towards the sea. Turn left on to D514 to Ste-Honorine-des-Pertes and the campsite is signposted.

BAYONNE Landes 4C

Camping Caravaning Côte d'Argent
avenue de l'Océan, 40530 Labenne.
Tel 05 59 45 42 02, Fax 05 59 45 73 31.
English spoken.
OPEN: all year. SIZE: 4 ha, 215 pitches (all with elec, 80 statics), 21 hot showers, 16 WCs, 7 French WCs, 3 CWPs. ⬧ &

| ≋ | ⬥ | ⛺ | R | ⊟ | | ⬛ | ✕ | ⌁ | ⌂ | |

Shop at 0.1 km. Cycling.
PRICES: (1996) Caravan with family 161.00, Tent with two adults 97.00. CC: Euro/Access, Visa.
North of Bayonne on the N10. Turn right in Labenne on avenue de l'Océan. First site on the left, as you enter Labenne-Océan.

Camping Le Ruisseau
40390 St-André-de-Seignanx.
Tel 05 59 56 71 92. English spoken.
OPEN: all year. SIZE: 1 ha, 70 pitches (60 with elec, 4 statics), 6 hot showers, 11 WCs, 2 CWPs. ⬧

| | ⛺ | R | ⊟ | ⬛ | ⬛ | | ⌁ | ⌂ | |

Restaurant at 3 km.
PRICES: (1996) Caravan with family 104.00, Tent with two adults 60.00. CC: none.
N117 north of Bayonne, then left on to D154 to St-André-de-Seignanx.

La Chêneraie chemin de Cazenave, 64100 Bayonne.
Tel 05 59 55 01 31, Fax 05 59 55 11 17.
English spoken.
OPEN: 01/06–15/09. SIZE: 10 ha, 100 pitches (all with elec), 32 hot showers, 30 WCs, 2 CWPs. ⬧ &

| | ⬔ | R | ⊟ | ⬛ | ⬛ | ✕ | ⌁ | ⌂ | |

PRICES: Caravan with family 156.00, Tent with two adults 94.00. CC: none.
The site is 4 km north-east of Bayonne just off the main N117 road to Pau.

BEAULIEU-SUR-DORDOGNE Corrèze 5A

Camping des Iles Boulevard Saint Rodolphe, 19120 Beaulieu-sur-Dordogne.
Tel 05 55 91 02 65. English spoken.
OPEN: 01/05–30/09. SIZE: 4 ha, 76 pitches (all with elec), 18 hot showers, 19 WCs, 12 French WCs, 5 CWPs.

| ~ | ⬥ | ⛺ | R | ⊟ | | | | ⌂ | |

Shop at 0.1 km. Restaurant at 0.01 km.
PRICES: (1996) Caravan with family 97.00, Tent with two adults 62.00. CC: none.
Site is on an island in the River Dordogne, close to town centre.

BEAULIEU-SUR-LAYON Maine/Loire 1D

Camping à la Ferme Frogeroux
49750 Chanzeaux.
Tel 02 41 78 32 34. English spoken.
OPEN: 01/05–30/09. SIZE: 6 pitches (all with elec), 2 hot showers, 2 WCs, 1 CWP.

| ~ | ⬥ | ⛺ | R | ⊟ | | | ⌂ | | |

Shop at 0.7 km. Restaurant at 0.7 km.
PRICES: (1996) Caravan with family 72.00, Tent with two adults 40.00. CC: none.
From Angers take the N160 south-west towards Cholet. Pass through St-Lambert-du-Lattay, turn left at the first crossroads and follow signs.

BEAUMONT Dordogne 4B

Camping Les Remparts
24440 Beaumont-du-Périgord.
Tel 05 53 22 40 86. English spoken.
OPEN: 01/05–30/09. SIZE: 1.3 ha, 40 pitches (all with elec, 2 statics), 8 hot showers, 6 WCs, 1 CWP. ⬧ &

| | ⛺ | R | ⊟ | | ⬛ | | ⌁ | ⌂ | |

Shop at 0.5 km. Restaurant at 0.5 km. Tennis, football.
PRICES: (1996) Caravan with family 118.00, Tent with two adults 65.00. CC: none.
From the centre of Beaumont go south towards Villeréal for 0.5 km. Campsite is signposted.

Centre Naturiste de Vacances Le Couderc
Naussannes, 24440 Beaumont-du-Périgord.
Tel 05 53 22 40 40, Fax 05 53 23 90 98.
English spoken.
OPEN: 15/04–31/10. SIZE: 18 ha, 180 pitches (all with elec), 20 hot showers, 20 WCs, 10 CWPs. ⬧ &

| ~ | ⬥ | ⬔ | R | ⊟ | ⬛ | ⬛ | ✕ | ⌁ | ⌂ | |

Naturist campsite.
PRICES: (1996) Caravan with family 129.00, Tent with two adults 89.00. CC: Euro/Access.
From Beaumont take the D19 towards Bergerac, and after Naussannes the campsite is 3.5 km on the right.

BEAUNE Côte-d'Or 3C

Camping Les Bouleaux Vignolles, 21200 Beaune.
Tel 03 80 22 26 88.
OPEN: all year. SIZE: 1 ha, 40 pitches (all with elec), 2 hot showers, 6 WCs, 2 French WCs, 4 CWPs. ⬧

| ~ | ⬥ | ⛺ | R | | ⬛ | | | ⌂ | |  |

Restaurant at 2 km.
PRICES: Caravan with family 75.00, Tent with two adults 41.00. CC: none.
On east side of A6, 5 km from Beaune toll. Campsite is signposted.

France

Camping Municipal des Isles
21360 Bligny-sur-Ouche.
Tel 03 80 20 11 21, Fax 03 80 20 17 90.
OPEN: 15/05–15/09. SIZE: 1.29 ha, 70 pitches
(31 with elec), 8 hot showers (charge), 8 WCs. &

Shop at 0.5 km. Restaurant at 0.3 km. Tennis,
walking trails and touristic steam-powered train
0.1 km.
PRICES: (1996) Caravan with family 66.00,
Tent with two adults 31.00. CC: none.
From Beaune take D970 north-west towards
Pouilly. Campsite is 20 km further on at Bligny.

Camping Municipal Les Cent Vignes
10 rue Auguste-Dubois, 21200 Beaune.
Tel 03 80 22 03 91.
OPEN: 15/03–30/10. SIZE: 2 ha, 116 pitches
(79 with elec), 24 hot showers, 12 WCs. & &

PRICES: (1996) Caravan with family 109.00, Tent
with two adults 56.00. CC: Euro/Access, Visa.
1 km from the centre of Beaune, north-east
towards Dijon.

BEAUVAIS Oise   2B

Le Clos Norman 1 rue de l'Abbaye,
60650 St-Paul.
Tel 03 44 82 27 30.
OPEN: all year. SIZE: 2 ha, 66 pitches (all with elec,
20 statics), 4 hot showers, 8 WCs. & &

Shop at 4 km. Restaurant at 1 km.
PRICES: (1996) Caravan with family 69.00,
Tent with two adults 41.00. CC: none.
6 km west of Beauvais on the N31 towards Rouen.

BEDARIEUX Hérault   5C

Camping La Sieste 34260 Latour-sur-Orb.
Tel 04 67 23 72 96, Fax 04 67 23 72 96.
English spoken.
OPEN: 01/06–15/09. SIZE: 2 ha, 70 pitches (all with
elec), 8 hot showers, 10 WCs. &

PRICES: (1996) Caravan with family 82.00, Tent
with two adults 60.00. CC: Amex, Euro/Access, Visa.
10 km north of Bédarieux on the D35 towards
Lodève.

Camping La Sieste
near Bédarieux
Between the Med & the Mountains

BELLAC Haute-Vienne   4B

Camp Municipal Les Rochettes rue les
Rochettes, 87300 Bellac.
Tel 05 55 68 13 27, Fax 05 55 68 78 74.
OPEN: all year. SIZE: 1 ha, 100 pitches (56 with
elec), 12 hot showers, 14 WCs, 4 French WCs. &

Shop at 0.5 km. Restaurant at 0.5 km.
PRICES: (1996) Caravan with family 40.20,
Tent with two adults 22.20. CC: none.
Directions to campsite are given from the town
centre.

BELLEGARDE Loiret   2D

Caravaning de Nibelle
route de Boiscommun, 45340 Nibelle.
Tel 02 38 32 23 55, Fax 02 38 32 23 15.
English spoken.
OPEN: 01/03–30/11. SIZE: 6 ha, 60 pitches (all with
elec, 50 statics), 8 hot showers, 12 WCs, 1 CWP. &

Shop at 2 km. Restaurant at 0.2 km. Tennis, mini-
golf; excellent walking/hiking country.
PRICES: (1996) Caravan with family 190.00,
Tent with two adults 100.00. CC: none.
Nibelle is about 8 km north-west of Bellegarde.

BELLERIVE-SUR-ALLIER Allier   5A

Camping Les Acacias au Bord du Lac rue
Claude Decloitre, 03700 Bellerive.
Tel 04 70 32 36 22, Fax 04 70 32 58 48.
English spoken.
OPEN: 01/04–10/10. SIZE: 2 ha, 95 pitches
(all with elec, 12 statics), 13 hot showers,
55 WCs, 2 CWPs. &

Restaurant at 0.05 km. Boules, entertainment.
PRICES: (1996) Caravan with family 151.00, Tent
with two adults 84.00. CC: Euro/Access, Visa.
The campsite is on the left bank of the River Allier,
300 m upstream from bridge.

BELVES Dordogne   4B

Camping Caravaning Les Nauves
Bos Rouge, 24170 Belvès.
Tel 05 53 29 12 64. English spoken.
OPEN: 10/05–30/09. SIZE: 5 ha, 80 pitches (30 with
elec, 10 statics), 11 hot showers, 6 WCs, 12 French
WCs, 1 CWP. & &

Shop at 4 km. Restaurant at 2 km. Horse-riding,
tennis.
PRICES: Caravan with family 127.70,
Tent with two adults 73.10. CC: none.
At Belvès, take the road to Monpazier.

France

France

Les Hauts de Ratebout Belvès, 24170 Belvès.
Tel 05 53 29 02 10, Fax 05 53 29 08 28.
English spoken.
OPEN: 01/05–15/09. SIZE: 10 ha, 200 pitches
(180 with elec, 40 statics), 28 hot showers,
27 WCs, 4 CWPs. &

| 🄌 | R | 🄳 | 💺 | 🍺 | ✕ | 🔧 | 🄷 | 🦌 | | |

Peaceful site with covered pool, evening
entertainment and good LS discounts.
PRICES: (1996) Caravan with family 200.40, Tent
with two adults 115.20. CC: Euro/Access, Visa.
*Take D710 south of Belvès. Turn left on to D54
and the site is then 3 km.*

Le Moulin de la Pique 24170 Belvès.
Tel 05 53 29 01 15, Fax 05 53 28 29 09.
English spoken.
OPEN: 01/05–20/09. SIZE: 12 ha, 110 pitches
(all with elec, 10 statics), 17 hot showers, 17 WCs,
2 CWPs. ℄ &

| ≈ | ⚓ | 🏄 | R | 🄳 | 💺 | 🍺 | ✕ | 🔧 | 🄷 | | |

Tennis, fishing, boating, nursery.
PRICES: (1996) Caravan with family 189.80,
Tent with two adults 111.50. CC: Amex,
Euro/Access, Visa.
On D710, 2 km after Belvès heading towards Fumel.

BENODET Finistère 1C

Camping de la Pointe St-Gilles 29950 Bénodet.
Tel 02 98 57 05 37, Fax 02 98 57 27 52.
English spoken.
OPEN: 01/05–30/09. SIZE: 7 ha, 170 pitches
(all with elec, 250 statics), 48 hot showers,
75 WCs, 3 French WCs, 25 CWPs. &

| ≈ | ⚓ | 🏄 | | 🄳 | 💺 | | ✕ | 🔧 | | 🦌 | |

Sports complex with jacuzzi and flume, tennis.
PRICES: (1996) Caravan with family 183.00, Tent
with two adults 113.00. CC: none.
*Take the N165/D44 south of Quimper and
campsite is on the seafront.*

Camping de la Pointe St-Gilles
at Bénodet
Pools galore – for kids, what more

Camping de la Mer Blanche
route de Fouesnant, 29950 Bénodet.
Tel 02 98 57 00 75, Fax 02 98 57 25 04. English spoken.
OPEN: 01/04–01/11. SIZE: 6 ha, 200 pitches
(all with elec, 50 statics), 28 hot showers, 22 WCs,
2 CWPs. ℄ &

| 🏄 | R | 🄳 | 💺 | | ✕ | 🔧 | 🄷 | | |

Shop at 2 km. Gym.

PRICES: Caravan with family 140.00, Tent with two
adults 84.50. CC: Visa.
*Take the D34 south from Quimper to Bénodet and
from Bénodet, drive towards Fouesnant. Campsite
is signposted.*

Camping du Letty 29950 Bénodet.
Tel 02 98 57 04 69, Fax 02 98 66 22 56.
English spoken.
OPEN: 15/06–06/09. SIZE: 10 ha, 493 pitches
(all with elec). ℄ &

| ≈ | ⚓ | 🏄 | | 🄳 | 💺 | 🍺 | | | |

Restaurant at 0.3 km.
PRICES: (1996) Caravan with family 158.00,
Tent with two adults 97.00. CC: none.
Bénodet is on the D34 from Quimper.

Camping Le Helles 29120 Ste-Marine.
Tel 02 98 56 31 46.
OPEN: 01/06–30/09. SIZE: 3 ha, 160 pitches
(120 with elec), 10 hot showers, 14 WCs, 1 CWP. ℄

| 🄌 | R | 🄳 | | 🍺 | | | 🄋 | |

Shop at 1 km. Restaurant at 1 km. Sea and
river 1 km.
PRICES: Caravan with family 93.00,
Tent with two adults 52.00. CC: none.
*D34 north from Bénodet, then west on D44 via
Pont-de-Cornauaille.*

Camping Le Poulquer rue du Poulquer,
29950 Bénodet.
Tel 02 98 57 04 19, Fax 02 98 66 20 30.
English spoken.
OPEN: 15/05–30/09. SIZE: 3 ha, 240 pitches
(200 with elec). &

| ≈ | ⚓ | 🏄 | R | 🄳 | 💺 | 🍺 | | 🔧 | 🄷 | |

Restaurant at 0.2 km.
PRICES: (1996) Caravan with family 156.00,
Tent with two adults 89.00. CC: none.
D34 south of Quimper.

BERGERAC Dordogne 4B

Camping Caravanning de Lestaubire
24140 Pont-St-Mamet.
Tel 05 53 82 98 15, Fax 05 53 82 90 17.
English spoken.
OPEN: 15/05–07/09. SIZE: 5 ha, 66 pitches (all with
elec), 8 hot showers, 8 WCs, 1 CWP. ℄

| ≈ | ⚓ | 🏄 | R | 🄳 | 💺 | | | 🔧 | |

Restaurant at 0.5 km.
PRICES: (1996) Caravan with family 130.50, Tent
with two adults 71.00. CC: Euro/Access, Visa.
*Pont-Saint-Mamet is just west of the N21 between
Bergerac and Périgueux.*

Camping du Bourg 24140 Campsegret.
Tel 05 53 24 22 36.
OPEN: 01/06–30/09. SIZE: 1.3 ha, 50 pitches
(all with elec), 4 hot showers, 7 WCs. &

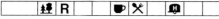

Shop at 0.1 km. Tennis nearby.
PRICES: (1996) Caravan with family 70.00,
Tent with two adults 36.00. CC: none.
From Bergerac go north on N21 towards
Périgueux to Campsegret.

Camping Municipal La Pelouse 8 bis rue J J
Rousseau, 24100 Bergerac.
Tel 05 53 57 06 67. English spoken.
OPEN: all year. SIZE: 1.5 ha, 70 pitches (all with
elec), 9 hot showers, 8 WCs, 1 French WC,
1 CWP.

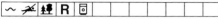

Shop at 0.2 km. Restaurant at 0.2 km.
PRICES: (1996) Caravan with family 71.00,
Tent with two adults 43.00. CC: none.
Bergerac is south of Périgueux on the N21.

BETHUNE Pas-de-Calais 2B

Camping Municipal rue Victor Duteriez,
62660 Beuvry.
Tel 03 21 65 08 00.
OPEN: 01/04–31/10. SIZE: 1 ha, 80 pitches (all with
elec), 3 hot showers (charge).

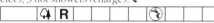

Shop at 0.5 km. Restaurant at 1 km.
PRICES: (1996) Caravan with family 75.10,
Tent with two adults 37.10. CC: none.
3 km from centre of Béthune, east on N43.
Signposted.

BEUZEVILLE Eure 2A

Camping du Domaine Catinière route
d'Honfleur, 27210 Fiquefleur-Equainville.
Tel 02 32 57 63 51, Fax 02 32 57 63 51.
English spoken.
OPEN: 01/04–30/10. SIZE: 2 ha, 83 pitches (all with
elec, 40 statics), 10 hot showers, 9 WCs, 1 CWP.

Shop at 4 km. Restaurant at 1 km. Mountain bike
hire.
PRICES: (1996) Caravan with family 150.00, Tent
with two adults 80.00. CC: none.
From A13, take exit 28 to Beuzeville then D22 to
Fiquefleur-Equainville. Signposted.

BEZIERS Hérault 5C

Camping Les Peupliers chemin de la Roussille,
34440 Colombier.
Tel 04 67 37 05 26, Fax 04 67 37 67 87.
English spoken.
OPEN: all year. SIZE: 2 ha, 50 pitches (32 with elec,
10 statics), 7 hot showers, 7 WCs.

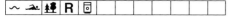

Shop at 0.5 km. Restaurant at 0.5 km.

PRICES: (1996) Caravan with family 88.00, Tent
with two adults 60.00. CC: none.
On A9, take the Béziers-Ouest exit to Colombier.
Signposted.

La Gabinelle 34410 Sauvian.
Tel 04 67 39 50 87. English spoken.
OPEN: 15/06–15/09. SIZE: 3 ha, 192 pitches
(140 with elec, 5 statics), 18 hot showers, 15 WCs.

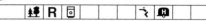

Shop at 0.1 km. Restaurant at 0.1 km. Tennis
0.1 km.
PRICES: (1996) Caravan with family 119.70,
Tent with two adults 90.00. CC: none.
D19 south of Béziers.

Le Rebau Montblanc, 34290 Servian.
Tel 04 67 98 50 78, Fax 04 67 98 68 63.
English spoken.
OPEN: 01/03–30/10. SIZE: 3 ha, 161 pitches
(100 with elec), 19 hot showers, 18 WCs,
2 CWPs.

Shop at 0.8 km. Restaurant at 0.8 km.
PRICES: (1996) Caravan with family 107.00,
Tent with two adults 80.00. CC: none.
Approaching from the N113, take D18 between
Béziers and Pézenas towards Montblanc.
Campsite is well signposted.

BIARRITZ Pyrénées-Atlan 4C

Biarritz Camping 28 rue d'Harcet,
64200 Biarritz.
Tel 05 59 23 00 12, Fax 05 59 43 74 67.
English spoken.
OPEN: 01/05–27/09. SIZE: 3 ha, 196 pitches (80 with
elec), 31 hot showers, 25 WCs, 1 CWP.

Table tennis, boules; mobile homes for hire.
PRICES: (1996) Caravan with family 163.40, Tent
with two adults 102.20. CC: Euro/Access, Visa.
From the centre of Biarritz take the beach road.
Follow signs.

Camping Erreka 64210 Bidart.
Tel 05 59 54 93 64, Fax 05 59 47 70 46.
English spoken.
OPEN: 01/06–15/09. SIZE: 6 ha, 100 pitches
(all with elec, 30 statics), 40 hot showers,
40 WCs, 1 CWP.

Restaurant at 0.1 km. 0.8 km from the beach and
the village.
PRICES: (1996) Caravan with family 128.00, Tent
with two adults 72.00. CC: Euro/Access, Visa.
Biarritz/Bidart exit from A63/E5 towards Spain.
Campsite is signposted to the left just before
crossroads.

France

Camping Résidence des Pins Airotel, N10b, 64210 Bidart.
Tel 05 59 23 00 29, Fax 05 59 41 24 59.
English spoken.
OPEN: 25/05–30/09. SIZE: 7 ha, 318 pitches (all with elec, 15 statics), 62 hot showers, 51 WCs. 🌊 ♿

| ≋ | ⛵ | 🏕️ | R | 🔲 | 🛒 | ☕ | ✕ | 🔱 | | 🔋 | |

PRICES: (1996) Caravan with family 170.00, Tent with two adults 105.00. CC: Amex, Euro/Access, Visa.
From A63, take exit 4. Continue for 1 km and follow signs.

Pavillon Royal av du Prince-de-Galles, 64210 Bidart.
Tel 05 59 23 00 54, Fax 05 59 23 44 47.
English spoken.
OPEN: 15/05–25/09. SIZE: 5 ha, 300 pitches (all with elec), 80 hot showers, 75 WCs. 🌊 ♿

| ≋ | ⛵ | ⛲ | R | 🔲 | 🛒 | ☕ | ✕ | 🔱 | | 🦌 | |

PRICES: (1996) Caravan with family 229.00, Tent with two adults 189.00. CC: Euro/Access, Visa.
From the A63 (Biarritz/Bidart exit) take the N10 towards Bidart, after approx 1 km look for signs and turn right.

BIESHEIM Haut-Rhin 3D

Camping Intercomm Ile du Rhin
68600 Biesheim.
Tel 03 89 72 57 95. English spoken.
OPEN: all year. SIZE: 3 ha, 255 pitches (all with elec, 193 statics), 36 hot showers, 36 WCs, 6 CWPs.

| ~ | ⛵ | 🏕️ | R | 🔲 | 🛒 | ☕ | | | | | |

Restaurant at 1 km. Swimming pool 0.5 km.
PRICES: (1996) Caravan with family 102.20, Tent with two adults 53.00. CC: none.
From Colmar, take N415 east towards Freiburg-im-Breisgau (Germany). Turn left just before customs point on German border.

BINIC Côtes-du-Nord 1D

Camping Le Panoramic rue Gasselin, 22520 Binic.
Tel 02 96 73 60 43. English spoken.
OPEN: 01/04–30/10. SIZE: 5 ha, 180 pitches (160 with elec, 2 statics), 26 hot showers, 19 WCs. 🌊

| | | 🏕️ | R | 🔲 | | ☕ | | 🔱 | 🔋 | |

Shop at 0.5 km. Restaurant at 0.5 km. Sandy beach 500 m.
PRICES: (1996) Caravan with family 130.00, Tent with two adults 77.00. CC: none.
On south side of Binic, off the D786.

Camping Les Etangs 22410 Lantic.
Tel 02 96 71 95 47. English spoken.
OPEN: 01/05–30/09. SIZE: 1.5 ha, 90 pitches (65 with elec), 8 hot showers, 9 WCs, 1 CWP. 🌊

| | ⛲ | R | 🔲 | | ☕ | | 🔱 | 🔋 | | | |

Shop at 3 km. Restaurant at 3 km.
PRICES: (1996) Caravan with family 88.00, Tent with two adults 47.00. CC: Euro/Access, Visa.
Leaving Binic from St-Brieuc, turn left towards Lantic and take the D4 to site.

BISCARROSSE Landes 4C

Campotel La Reserve Gastes, 40160 Parentis-en-Born.
Tel 05 58 09 75 96, Fax 05 58 09 76 13. English spoken.
OPEN: 15/05–17/09. SIZE: 35 ha, 830 pitches (459 with elec, 20 statics). 🌊 ♿

| ≋ | 🏊 | 🏕️ | R | 🔲 | 🛒 | ☕ | ✕ | 🔱 | 🔋 | | |

Mobile homes for hire; entertainments, good sport facilities, 3 swimming pools.
PRICES: (1996) Caravan with family 212.00, Tent with two adults 135.00. CC: Visa.
From Biscarrosse take the road to Parentis-en-Born, then south around the lake to Gastes. Drive through the village, site is on the right. Signposted.

BLAIN Loire-Atlan 1D

Camping du Château Le Gravier, route de St-Nazaire, 44130 Blain.
Tel 02 40 79 11 00.
OPEN: 01/05–30/09. SIZE: 5 hot showers, 7 French WCs, 1 CWP. 🌊 ♿

| ~ | ⛵ | ⛲ | R | | | | | | | | |

Shop at 1 km. Restaurant at 0.2 km.
PRICES: (1996) Caravan with family 39.00, Tent with two adults 26.00. CC: none.
Just south of Blain towards St-Nazaire. In the grounds of a château.

LE BLANC Indre 2C

Camping Avant 36300 Le Blanc.
Tel 02 54 37 88 22. English spoken.
OPEN: 01/05–15/09. SIZE: 2 ha, 81 pitches (64 with elec), 12 hot showers, 16 WCs, 1 CWP. 🌊 ♿

| ~ | ⛵ | 🏕️ | R | | | ☕ | | 🎿 | | | |

Shop at 1 km. Restaurant at 0.5 km.
PRICES: (1996) Caravan with family 55.00, Tent with two adults 33.00. CC: Euro/Access.

Camping Municipal Les Coteaux
Angles-sur-l'Anglin, 86260 St-Pierre-de-Maille.
Tel 05 49 48 86 87. English spoken.
OPEN: 01/04–31/10. SIZE: 3 hot showers, 3 WCs.

| ~ | ⛵ | 🏕️ | | | | | | | | | |

Shop at 0.5 km. Restaurant at 0.5 km.
PRICES: (1996) Caravan with family 43.00, Tent with two adults 23.00. CC: none.
From Le Blanc head north-west on D950 to Tournon. Left over the river on the D6 to Angles.

BLOIS Loir-et-Cher 2D

Camping du Cosson 1 rue de la Forêt,
41120 Chailles.
Tel 02 54 79 41 35.
OPEN: 15/06–16/09. SIZE: 0.6 ha, 26 pitches (all with
elec), 3 hot showers, 2 WCs, 3 French WCs. ↻

Shop at 0.2 km. Restaurant at 0.5 km.
PRICES: (1996) Caravan with family 88.00,
Tent with two adults 44.00. CC: none.
Take the D751 south of Blois, towards
Montrichard.

Camping La Grande Tortue route de Pontlevoy,
41120 Cande-sur-Beuvron.
Tel 02 54 44 15 20. English spoken.
OPEN: 15/04–30/09. SIZE: 6 ha, 208 pitches (100 with
elec), 19 hot showers, 21 WCs, 3 CWPs. ↻ ᕦ

Tennis, volley ball, children's playground.
PRICES: (1996) Caravan with family 141.00,
Tent with two adults 80.00. CC: none.
Near the Loire on the D751 between Blois and
Amboise.

Camping Municipal
av du Général de Gaulle, 41150 Onzain.
Tel 02 54 20 85 15, Fax 02 54 20 74 34.
OPEN: 19/05–05/09. SIZE: 1 ha, 40 pitches (all with
elec), 4 hot showers, 6 WCs, 1 French WC,
1 CWP. ᕦ

Shop at 1 km. Restaurant at 0.5 km.
PRICES: (1996) Caravan with family 52.00,
Tent with two adults 34.00. CC: none.
From Blois on N152 towards Onzain, 150 m after
Pont du Chaumont crossroad. Entrance to
campsite is on the right.

Le Château de la Grenouillère Suevres,
41500 Mer.
Tel 02 54 87 80 37, Fax 02 54 87 84 21.
English spoken.
OPEN: 15/05–15/09. SIZE: 11 ha, 250 pitches
(all with elec), 33 hot showers, 36 WCs,
3 CWPs. ᕦ

Sauna/solarium, ball games; Paris excursions.
PRICES: (1996) Caravan with family 200.00, Tent
with two adults 120.00. CC: Euro/Access, Visa.
From A10, take exit 7 for Mer. Campsite is
signposted.

Le Parc du Val de Loire 41150 Mesland.
Tel 02 54 70 27 18, Fax 02 54 70 21 71.
English spoken.
OPEN: 01/05–15/09. SIZE: 15 ha, 300 pitches
(all with elec, 35 statics), 39 hot showers,
35 WCs. ᕦ

Tennis, mini-golf, flume.
PRICES: (1996) Caravan with family 230.00, Tent
with two adults 130.00. CC: Amex, Visa.
From Blois take N152 towards Tours. After approx
16 km turn right towards Onzain. From Onzain
follow the signs to Mesland.

𝕷𝖊 𝕻𝖆𝖗𝖈 𝖉𝖚 𝖁𝖆𝖑 𝖉𝖊 𝕷𝖔𝖎𝖗𝖊

near Blois

The Loire Valley at its best

Les Saules 41700 Cheverny.
Tel 02 54 79 90 01, Fax 02 54 79 28 34.
English spoken.
OPEN: 01/04–30/09. SIZE: 10 ha, 160 pitches
(114 with elec), 25 hot showers, 25 WCs,
2 CWPs. ↻ ᕦ

Fishing, mini-golf, table tennis, puppets theatre.
PRICES: (1996) Caravan with family 154.00, Tent
with two adults 90.00. CC: Euro/Access, Visa.
From Blois take the road towards Vierzon and
Romorantin. Cheverny is 15 km on, and campsite
is 2 km after Château, towards Contres and
signposted.

BOIRY-NOTRE-DAME Pas-de-Calais 2B

Camping Flandres-Artois 1 rue Verte,
62156 Boiry-Notre-Dame.
Tel 03 21 48 15 40, Fax 03 21 22 07 24.
English spoken.
OPEN: 15/03–31/10. SIZE: 3 ha, 25 pitches (all with
elec, 80 statics), 8 hot showers, 8 WCs, 3 French
WCs, 2 CWPs. ↻ ᕦ

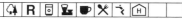

Shop at 0.3 km. Restaurant at 8 km. Tennis, mini-
golf, billiards, fishing; pizza bar.
PRICES: (1996) Caravan with family 99.00,
Tent with two adults 68.00. CC: none.
From A26 take A1. Leave at exit 15 (Cambrai, Les
Panneaux) ; campsite is 4 km and well
signposted.

Camping Flandres-Artois

at Boiry-Notre-Dame

On your holiday route

BOISSON Gard   5D

Castel Camping Château de Boisson
Boisson-les-Fumades, 30500 Allègre.
Tel 04 66 24 82 21, Fax 04 66 24 80 14.
English spoken.
OPEN: 01/04–31/10. SIZE: 7 ha, 147 pitches
(all with elec, 20 statics), 16 hot showers, 16 WCs,
2 CWPs. ₺ ᴠ

| | | ⌂ | R | ▣ | ᴇ | | ✗ | � ? | ⍟ | ✻ | |

Tennis, art school, cookery class, bridge; rooms
and mobile homes available.
PRICES: (1996) Caravan with family 197.00,
Tent with two adults 146.00. CC: none.
*From Bagnols-sur-Cèze take D6 towards Alès.
After 35 km take D7 towards Fumades and
Boisson is 10 km ahead on the right.*

Château de Boisson

at Boisson

Cultivated Camping in the Cévennes

BOLLENE Vaucluse   5D

Camping de la Simioune quartier Guffiage,
84500 Bollène.
Tel 04 90 30 44 62. English spoken.
OPEN: all year. SIZE: 1.5 ha, 70 pitches (all with
elec, 2 statics), 9 hot showers, 10 WCs. ₺ ᴠ

| | | ⍟ | R | ▣ | ᴇ | ⍟ | ✗ | ? | ⍟ | | |

Table tennis, boules, horse-riding.
PRICES: (1996) Caravan with family 115.00, Tent
with two adults 60.00. CC: none.
*From the motorway exit (A7) take the third turn
off roundabout, left at third crossroads, then
follow the signposts.*

Le Barry Lieu dit St-Pierre, 84500 Bollène.
Tel 04 90 30 13 20, Fax 04 90 40 48 64.
English spoken.
OPEN: all year. SIZE: 3 ha, 120 pitches (all with
elec), 15 hot showers, 21 WCs, 2 CWPs. ₺ ᴠ

| | | ⍟ | R | ▣ | ᴇ | ⍟ | ✗ | ? | ⍟ | | |

Boules, disco, mountain bikes.
PRICES: (1996) Caravan with family 140.00, Tent
with two adults 81.00. CC: Euro/Access, Visa.
*St-Pierre is 1.5 km north of Bollène. From Bollène,
follow the 'Site troglodyte' signs.*

BORDEAUX Gironde   4B

Les Gravières chemin de Macau,
33140 Villenave-d'Ornon.
Tel 05 56 87 00 36, Fax 05 56 87 24 60.
English spoken.

OPEN: all year. SIZE: 3 ha, 150 pitches (75 with
elec), 14 hot showers, 14 WCs, 1 CWP. ₺ ᴠ

| ≈ | ⬟ | ⍟ | R | ▣ | ᴇ | ⍟ | | | ⍟ |

Restaurant at 0.5 km.
PRICES: (1996) Caravan with family 121.50,
Tent with two adults 66.00. CC: none.
*From Bordeaux go south via Bègles and take
exit 20.*

BORMES-LES-MIMOSAS Var   6C

Camp du Domaine La Favière,
83230 Bormes-les-Mimosas.
Tel 04 94 71 03 12, Fax 04 94 15 18 67.
English spoken.
OPEN: 15/03–31/10. SIZE: 38 ha, 1200 pitches
(844 with elec), 123 hot showers, 147 WCs,
19 CWPs. ₺ ᴠ

| ≋ | ⬟ | ⍟ | R | ▣ | ᴇ | ⍟ | ✗ | | |

Children's playground, ball games, tennis, mini-
golf, water sports; mobile home.
PRICES: Caravan with family 171.00, Tent with two
adults 96.00. CC: Euro/Access, Visa.
*From Bormes-les-Mimosas, drive towards Le
Lavandou and at the roundabout, turn off N559
towards Favière/Bénat. After 2 km, turn left and
follow signs to campsite.*

Camping Clau Mar Jo chemin de Bénat,
83230 Bormes-les-Mimosas.
Tel 04 94 71 53 39. English spoken.
OPEN: 01/04–30/09. SIZE: 1 ha, 50 pitches
(all with elec, 10 statics), 11 hot showers, 10 WCs,
3 CWPs. ₺ ᴠ

| | | ⍟ | R | ▣ | | | | | ⍟ |

Shop at 0.5 km. Restaurant at 1.5 km.
PRICES: (1996) Caravan with family 146.00,
Tent with two adults 101.00. CC: none.
*From Bormes take road to Port-de-Bormes, then
first right to the campsite.*

Camping Manjastre 1789 route de Martegasse,
83230 Bormes-les-Mimosas.
Tel 04 94 71 03 28, Fax 04 94 71 63 62.
English spoken.
OPEN: all year. SIZE: 4 ha, 120 pitches (all with elec,
8 statics), 12 hot showers, 15 WCs, 1 CWP. ᴠ

| | | ⍟ | R | ▣ | ᴇ | ⍟ | | ? | ⍟ | ✻ | ⬟ |

Restaurant at 1 km.
PRICES: (1996) Caravan with family 169.00,
Tent with two adults 95.00. CC: Visa.
On the N98 halfway between Hyères and Cogolin.

BOULOGNE-SUR-MER Pas-de-Calais 2B

Camping Le Bois Groult Le Plouy, Heneveux,
62142 Colembert.
Tel 03 21 33 32 16. English spoken.
OPEN: all year. SIZE: 6 pitches (all with elec), 1 hot
shower (charge), 1 WC, 1 CWP.

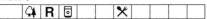

Shop at 2 km. Restaurant at 2 km.
PRICES: Caravan with family 52.00, Tent with two
adults 26.00. CC: none.
*From Boulogne-sur-Mer, N42 towards St-Omer for
15 km then turn right in Le Plouy. Go 1 km to Le
Bois Groult and campsite.*

Camping les Sapins 62360 La Capelle.
Tel 03 21 83 16 61. English spoken.
OPEN: all year. SIZE: 1 ha, 30 pitches (all with elec,
16 statics), 3 hot showers, 3 WCs, 2 French WCs,
8 CWPs.

Shop at 3 km.
PRICES: (1996) Caravan with family 73.00,
Tent with two adults 38.00. CC: none.
*From Boulogne-sur-Mer take the N42 to La Capelle-
les-Boulogne. The campsite is in centre of village.*

Olympic Camping rue de Camping,
62930 Wimereux.
Tel 03 21 32 45 63.
OPEN: 15/03–27/10. SIZE: 3 ha, 45 pitches (27 with
elec, 75 statics), 10 hot showers, 10 WCs, 1 CWP.

Shop at 0.5 km. Restaurant at 0.5 km. Sea 400m.
PRICES: (1996) Caravan with family 113.00,
Tent with two adults 56.00. CC: none.
*From D940 coast road or N1 exit at Wimereux-
Sud; campsite is signposted on entering the town.*

LE BOULOU Pyrénées Orient   5C

Les Bruyères route de Céret,
Maureillas Las Illas, 66400 Céret.
Tel 04 68 83 26 64, Fax 04 68 83 51 31.
English spoken.
OPEN: 01/05–15/10. SIZE: 4 ha, 80 pitches (all with
elec, 1 static), 16 hot showers, 8 WCs, 12 French
WCs, 3 CWPs.

Restaurant at 2 km.
PRICES: (1996) Caravan with family 170.00,
Tent with two adults 99.00. CC: none.
*From Le Boulou take N9 towards Spain. Turn
right onto D618 to Maureillas and campsite is
1 km the other side of the village on the left.*

Camp Sant Cristau 66740 Montesquieu.
Tel 04 68 89 71 01, Fax 04 68 89 71 01.
English spoken.
OPEN: all year. SIZE: 1.8 ha, 90 pitches (45 with
elec), 8 hot showers, 12 WCs, 1 CWP.

Shop at 4 km. Restaurant at 4 km. Pony-trekking
nearby.
PRICES: Caravan with family 87.00, Tent with two
adults 46.00. CC: none.

*From Le Boulou head east towards Argelès. Turn
right on to the D61 after 4 km to Montesquieu.*

Camping l'Olivette Les Thermes du Boulou,
66160 Le Boulou.
Tel 04 68 89 48 08. English spoken.
OPEN: 01/04–31/10. SIZE: 9 ha, 158 pitches
(all with elec), 13 hot showers, 18 WCs.

PRICES: (1996) Caravan with family 93.00,
Tent with two adults 59.00. CC: Amex,
Euro/Access, Visa.
*Les Thermes du Boulou is 1 km from Le Boulou on
the N9 towards Le Perthus.*

Camping Mas-Llinas 66160 Le Boulou.
Tel 04 68 83 25 46. English spoken.
OPEN: all year. SIZE: 3 ha, 100 pitches (70 with elec,
10 statics), 9 hot showers, 9 WCs.

Restaurant at 4 km.
PRICES: (1996) Caravan with family 105.00,
Tent with two adults 64.00. CC: none.
N9 south of Perpignan.

Camping Val Roma Park Les Thermes du
Boulou, 66480 Maureillas.
Tel 04 68 83 19 72, Fax 04 68 83 19 72.
English spoken.
OPEN: all year. SIZE: 3 ha, 100 pitches (75 with elec,
12 statics), 12 hot showers, 12 WCs, 1 CWP.

Tennis, table tennis, entertainment.
PRICES: (1996) Caravan with family 112.00,
Tent with two adults 72.00. CC: Amex,
Euro/Access, Visa.
*South of Le Boulou, just off the N11. Site is close to
and just south of Les Thermes, going towards
Perthus.*

BOURBON-L'ARCHAMBAULT Allier 2D

Parc Municipal de Bignon
03160 Bourbon-l'Archambault.
Tel 04 70 67 08 83.
OPEN: 01/03–01/11. SIZE: 3 ha, 157 pitches (all
with elec), 18 hot showers, 21 WCs, 6 CWPs.

Shop at 0.2 km. Restaurant at 0.6 km. Swimming
pool 0.3 km.
PRICES: (1996) Caravan with family 64.30,
Tent with two adults 37.00. CC: none.
*Site is south of Bourbon-l'Archambault on the
D953.*

BOURBON-LANCY Saône/Loire   5A

Camping du Plan d'Eau rue des Euriments,
71140 Bourbon-Lancy.
Tel 03 85 89 34 27. English spoken.

OPEN: 01/05–15/10. SIZE: 2 ha, 64 pitches (all with elec), 7 hot showers, 4 WCs, 2 French WCs, 1 CWP. ☎ ☐

Shop at 0.5 km. Restaurant at 0.5 km. Canoes, kayaks, fishing, horse-riding.
PRICES: (1996) Caravan with family 79.00, Tent with two adults 41.00. CC: none.
Well signposted in Bourbon-Lancy.

BOURBONNE-LES-BAINS Hte-Marne 3C

Le Montmorency rue du Stade, 52400 Bourbonne-les-Bains.
Tel 03 25 90 08 64. English spoken.
OPEN: 01/04–15/10. SIZE: 2 ha, 70 pitches (all with elec), 10 hot showers, 10 WCs, 3 French WCs, 3 CWPs. ☎

Restaurant at 1 km. Car-wash service.
PRICES: (1996) Caravan with family 83.45, Tent with two adults 42.35. CC: none.
In Bourbonne, near the swimming pool.

LA BOURBOULE Puy-de-Dôme 5A

Camping La Poutié 63150 La Bourboule.
Tel 04 73 81 04 54. English spoken.
OPEN: all year. SIZE: 3 ha, 165 pitches (all with elec, 20 statics), 20 hot showers, 20 WCs, 5 French WCs, 5 CWPs. ☎ ☐

Restaurant at 0.3 km. Good entertainment facilities, swimming pool nearby.
PRICES: Caravan with family 122.00, Tent with two adults 65.00. CC: Euro/Access, Visa.
In La Bourboule go to the SNCF station, keep left, go over railway bridge and campsite is 400 m ahead, well signposted.

BOURCEFRANC-LE-CHAPUS 4A

Camp Municipal La Giroflée route de Bonnemort, 17560 Bourcefranc-le-Chapus.
Tel 05 46 85 06 43.
OPEN: 01/06–15/09. SIZE: 3 ha, 160 pitches (80 with elec), 16 hot showers (charge), 18 WCs. ☎ ☐

Shop at 1.5 km. Restaurant at 0.5 km.
PRICES: (1996) Caravan with family 58.50, Tent with two adults 34.50. CC: none.
North-west of Marennes, fork right off the Oléron road before the bridge.

LE BOURG-D'OISANS Isère 5B

Camping Le Vernis 38520 Le Bourg-d'Oisans.
Tel 04 76 80 02 68.
OPEN: 01/12–01/05 & 01/06–15/09. SIZE: 1 ha,

54 pitches (60 with elec), 6 hot showers, 31 WCs, 3 CWPs. ☎

Shop at 1.5 km. Restaurant at 2 km. Mini-golf.
PRICES: (1996) Caravan with family 114.00, Tent with two adults 70.00. CC: none.
From Le Bourg-d'Oisans go towards Briançon. (No motor caravans July/August.)

La Cascade 38520 Le Bourg-d'Oisans.
Tel 04 76 80 02 42, Fax 04 76 80 22 63.
English spoken.
OPEN: 15/12–30/09. SIZE: 3 ha, 130 pitches (all with elec, 15 statics), 20 hot showers, 18 WCs, 2 CWPs. ☎

Shop at 0.5 km. Restaurant at 0.05 km. Climbing, hiking, skiing in winter.
PRICES: (1996) Caravan with family 144.00, Tent with two adults 116.00. CC: none.
From Le Bourg-d'Oisans drive towards l'Alpe-d'Huez, the site is at the foot of the hill.

Le Champ du Moulin Bourg-d'Arud, 38520 Venosc.
Tel 04 76 80 07 38, Fax 04 76 80 24 44.
English spoken.
OPEN: 15/05–15/09 & 15/12–30/04. SIZE: 1.5 ha, 51 pitches (all with elec), 9 hot showers, 9 WCs, 2 CWPs. ☎ ☐

Shop at 12 km. Flume; skiing, fishing and kayaking nearby.
PRICES: (1996) Caravan with family 157.00, Tent with two adults 97.00. CC: Euro/Access, Visa.
From Le Bourg-d'Oisans take road to Briançon, then turn right on to the D213 to Venosc/Le Bourg-d'Arud. In Venosc, the campsite is 200 m from the cable car on the right.

A la Rencontre du Soleil 38520 Le Bourg-d'Oisans.
Tel 04 76 80 00 33, Fax 04 76 80 26 37.
English spoken.
OPEN: 24/05–14/09. SIZE: 1.6 ha, 73 pitches (all with elec), 11 hot showers, 10 WCs, 2 French WCs, 1 CWP. ☎

Shop at 1 km. Tennis.
PRICES: Caravan with family 184.00, Tent with two adults 122.00. CC: Amex, Visa.
From the N91 in Le Bourg-d'Oisans take the D211 towards l'Alpe-d'Huez. The campsite is on the left.

BOURG-EN-BRESSE Ain 5B

Camping Municipal de Journans 01250 Journans.
Tel 04 74 51 64 45.
OPEN: 01/04–31/10. SIZE: 2 ha, 20 pitches (16 with

France

elec, 12 statics), 3 hot showers, 5 WCs, 3 French WCs. ᴥ

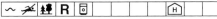

Shop at 2 km. Restaurant at 0.5 km.
PRICES: (1996) Caravan with family 72.00,
Tent with two adults 35.00. CC: none.
*From A42 take the Bourg-en-Bresse Sud exit, travel
for 1 km towards Pont-d'Ain, and then turn left.*

BOURG-MADAME Pyrénées Orient 5C

Camping de la Gare Ur, 66760 Bourg-Madame.
Tel 04 68 04 80 95.
OPEN: 01/01–30/09 & 01/11–31/12. SIZE: 1 ha,
69 pitches (59 with elec), 6 hot showers, 14 WCs,
3 CWPs. ᴥ ᴦ

Shop at 0.7 km. Restaurant at 0.6 km.
PRICES: (1996) Caravan with family 91.00, Tent
with two adults 46.50. CC: Euro/Access, Visa.
*On the N20 between Ur and Bourg-Madame,
3 km from the Spanish border.*

Camping Mas Piques 66760 Bourg-Madame.
Tel 04 68 04 62 11, Fax 04 68 04 68 32.
English spoken.
OPEN: all year. SIZE: 1.5 ha, 103 pitches (all with
elec), 10 hot showers, 10 WCs, 1 CWP. ᴦ

Shop at 0.2 km. Restaurant at 0.2 km.
PRICES: (1996) Caravan with family 118.00,
Tent with two adults 65.00. CC: none.
Well signposted in Bourg-Madame.

BOURG-ST-ANDEOL Ardèche 5D

Camping du Lion chemin de Chenevier,
07700 Bourg-St-Andéol.
Tel 04 75 54 53 20. English spoken.
OPEN: 01/04–15/09. SIZE: 8 ha, 140 pitches
(all with elec), 14 hot showers, 18 WCs, 6 French
WCs, 4 CWPs. ᴥ

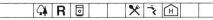

Football, boules, volley ball.
PRICES: (1996) Caravan with family 130.00,
Tent with two adults 82.00. CC: none.
Near centre of town. Follow signs.

Camping-Caravaning la Résidence
07700 St-Remèze.
Tel 04 75 04 26 87, Fax 04 75 04 35 90. English spoken.
OPEN: 28/03–31/12 & 27/10–31/12. SIZE: 1.8 ha,
60 pitches (all with elec), 11 hot showers, 11 WCs,
1 CWP. ᴦ

Shop at 0.1 km. Restaurant at 0.6 km.
PRICES: (1996) Caravan with family 137.00,
Tent with two adults 70.00. CC: none.
*St-Remèze is 16 km west of Bourg-St-Andéol on
the D4.*

Les Truffières route de St-Remèze,
07700 St-Marcel-d'Ardèche.
Tel 04 75 04 68 35, Fax 04 75 98 75 86.
English spoken.
OPEN: all year. SIZE: 5 ha, 35 pitches (all with elec,
10 statics), 8 hot showers, 8 WCs, 1 CWP. ᴥ

Shop at 2 km. Restaurant at 2 km. Canoeing.
PRICES: Caravan with family 111.00, Tent with two
adults 57.00. CC: none.
*From Bourg-St-Andéol, take N86 south for 7 km.
Turn right to St-Marcel- d'Ardèche, right in the
main square on to D201 and site is 4.5 km ahead.*

Vacanciel Domaine d'Imbours 07220 Larnas.
Tel 04 75 28 85 85, Fax 04 75 04 39 20.
English spoken.
OPEN: 15/06–05/09. SIZE: 10 ha, 360 pitches
(115 with elec, 20 statics), 43 hot showers,
43 WCs. ᴦ

Entertainment, tennis, mini-golf, volley ball, disco.
PRICES: (1996) Caravan with family 186.00, Tent
with two adults 92.00. CC: Visa.
*Take D4 to St-Remèze, and then D262 north to the
village of Larnas.*

BOURG-ST-MAURICE Savoie 6A

Le Reclus 73700 Séez.
Tel 04 79 41 01 05. English spoken.
OPEN: all year. SIZE: 1.8 ha, 108 pitches (all with
elec), 15 hot showers, 12 WCs, 2 CWPs. ᴥ ᴦ

Shop at 0.5 km. Restaurant at 0.5 km.
PRICES: (1996) Caravan with family 109.00, Tent
with two adults 56.00. CC: none.
*Campsite is just as you enter Séez, on the N90,
3 km east of Bourg-St-Maurice towards Val d'Isère.*

BOURGES Cher 2D

Camping Municipal 26 bd de l'Industrie,
18000 Bourges.
Tel 02 48 20 16 85. English spoken.
OPEN: 15/03–15/11. SIZE: 2.2 ha, 75 pitches (all
with elec), 17 hot showers, 23 WCs, 10 CWPs. ᴥ ᴦ

Shop at 0.8 km. Restaurant at 0.8 km. Table tennis,
mini-golf.
PRICES: (1996) Caravan with family 96.00, Tent
with two adults 46.00. CC: none.
Situated near the centre of Bourges.

Camping Municipal des Murailles
18380 La Chapelle-d'Angillon.
Tel 02 48 73 40 12, Fax 02 48 73 40 12.
OPEN: 01/05–30/09. SIZE: 2 ha, 35 pitches (all with
elec), 6 hot showers (charge), 10 WCs. ᴥ ᴦ

France

Shop at 1 km. Restaurant at 1 km.
PRICES: (1996) Caravan with family 54.90,
Tent with two adults 27.20. CC: none.
On the A71 south of Orléans.

LE BOURGET-DU-LAC Savoie   5B

L'Ile aux Cygnes 73370 Le Bourget-du-Lac.
Tel 04 79 25 01 76. English spoken.
OPEN: 01/05–30/09. SIZE: 4.5 ha, 192 pitches
(all with elec), 32 hot showers, 30 WCs. &

Shop at 0.6 km. Restaurant at 0.8 km.
PRICES: (1996) Caravan with family 120.40,
Tent with two adults 77.20. CC: none.
*From N504 at Le Bourget-du-Lac. Follow signs to
the lake.*

BRANTOME Dordogne   4B

Camping du Bas Meygnaud Valeuil,
24310 Brantôme.
Tel 05 53 05 58 44. English spoken.
OPEN: 01/04–30/09. SIZE: 1.7 ha, 50 pitches
(all with elec), 4 hot showers, 6 WCs, 3 French
WCs, 1 CWP. & &

Shop at 5 km. Restaurant at 3 km.
Playground/sports field; canoeing, horse-riding
nearby.
PRICES: (1996) Caravan with family 102.00,
Tent with two adults 62.00. CC: none.
*From Brantôme south on D939 towards
Périgueux for 5 km. Turn right at Lassere and
then follow signs to campsite.*

Camping Municipal avenue André-Maurois,
24310 Brantôme.
Tel 05 53 05 75 24, Fax 05 53 35 45 18.
English spoken.
OPEN: 01/05–30/09. SIZE: 4.9 ha, 170 pitches
(100 with elec), 15 hot showers, 14 WCs,
1 CWP. &

Shop at 1 km. Restaurant at 1 km.
PRICES: (1996) Caravan with family 77.00, Tent
with two adults 41.00. CC: none.
*From Brantôme take the D78 towards Thiviers.
Just after the tennis courts turn to the right.*

BRASSAC Tarn   5C

Camping Le Manoir route de Lacabarede,
81260 Brassac.
Tel 05 63 70 96 06, Fax 05 63 70 96 06.
English spoken.
OPEN: 09/04–30/10. SIZE: 3 ha, 160 pitches (all
with elec), 30 hot showers, 23 WCs, 1 CWP. & &

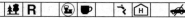

Shop at 0.5 km. Boating, sailing, fishing, disco.
PRICES: (1996) Caravan with family 155.00, Tent
with two adults 115.00. CC: none.
*From Béziers, north-west on N112 to St-Pons. Go
for 7 km on D907 north of St-Pons and then turn
left on to D68 to Angles.*

Camping Le Plo du Bez 81260 Le Bez.
Tel 05 63 74 00 82.
OPEN: 15/06–30/09. SIZE: 2.5 ha, 30 pitches
(all with elec), 7 hot showers, 8 WCs. & &

Shop at 0.2 km. Restaurant at 4 km. Children's
playground, volley ball, table tennis.
PRICES: Caravan with family 66.00,
Tent with two adults 35.00. CC: none.
From Brassac, take the D53 to Le Bez.

BRAY-DUNES Nord   2B

Club Camping Perroquet 59123 Bray-Dunes.
Tel 05 28 58 37 37, Fax 05 28 58 37 01.
English spoken.
OPEN: 01/04–05/10. SIZE: 28 ha, 856 pitches
(all with elec, 700 statics), 65 hot showers,
95 WCs, 5 CWPs. &

Free entertainment.

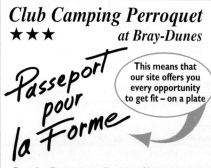

PRICES: (1996) Caravan with family 152.00, Tent with two adults 76.00. CC: none.
From town centre follow camp signs towards De Panne. Just before border, turn seawards.
SEE ADVERTISEMENT

BRECEY Manche 1D

Camp Municipal du Pont Roulland
50370 Brécey.
Tel 02 33 48 60 60, Fax 02 33 89 21 09.
English spoken.
OPEN: 01/06–30/09. SIZE: 1 ha, 52 pitches (all with elec), 6 hot showers.

Shop at 1.5 km. Restaurant at 1.5 km.
PRICES: (1996) Caravan with family 82.00, Tent with two adults 42.00. CC: none.
Well signposted in Brécey.

LA BRESSE Vosges 3D

Camping Belle Hutte 88250 La Bresse.
Tel 03 29 25 49 75, Fax 03 29 25 52 63.
English spoken.
OPEN: all year. SIZE: 3 ha, 100 pitches (all with elec, 30 statics), 17 hot showers, 20 WCs, 1 CWP.

Restaurant at 0.5 km. New toilet/shower block with baby facilities.
PRICES: (1996) Caravan with family 99.00, Tent with two adults 51.00. CC: Amex, Euro/Access, Visa.
9 km from La Bresse on the road to Col de la Schlucht (D34). At the foot of the biggest downhill ski-station in the Vosges.

BRETENOUX Lot 5A

Camp La Bourgnatelle 46130 Bretenoux.
Tel 05 65 38 44 07. English spoken.
OPEN: 01/05–15/09. SIZE: 6 ha, 135 pitches (all with elec), 14 hot showers, 16 WCs, 2 CWPs.

Shop at 0.1 km. Restaurant at 0.1 km. Tennis, bookshop, entertainment.
PRICES: (1996) Caravan with family 90.50, Tent with two adults 58.00. CC: Visa.

Camping La Sole 46130 Bretenoux.
Tel 05 65 10 93 33, Fax 05 65 10 93 34.
English spoken.
OPEN: 01/04–30/09. SIZE: 3 ha, 66 pitches (all with elec), 12 hot showers, 13 WCs, 1 CWP.

2 swimming pools.
PRICES: (1996) Caravan with family 105.00, Tent with two adults 61.00. CC: Euro/Access, Visa.
From Bretenoux take D703 to Puybrun. Follow signs.

BRETIGNOLLES-SUR-MER Vendée 1D

Camp des Dunes 85470 Bretignolles-sur-Mer.
Tel 02 51 90 55 32, Fax 02 51 90 54 85.
English spoken.
OPEN: 01/04–31/10. SIZE: 12 ha, 760 pitches, 18 WCs.

Indoor and outdoor pools.
PRICES: Caravan with family 222.00, Tent with two adults 172.00. CC: Euro/Access, Visa.
From Bretignolles-sur-Mer take the road towards Les Sables-d'Olonne. Campsite is signposted.

Camping La Motine 4 rue des Morinières, 85470 Bretignolles-sur-Mer.
Tel 05 51 90 04 42, Fax 05 51 33 80 52.
English spoken.
OPEN: 01/04–30/09. SIZE: 1.8 ha, 89 pitches (all with elec, 10 statics), 12 hot showers, 13 WCs, 2 CWPs.

Shop at 0.3 km. Quiet and friendly family site.
PRICES: (1996) Caravan with family 148.00, Tent with two adults 95.00. CC: none.
From the roundabout in Bretignolles, take the road to Plage-de-la-Parée; the campsite is 400 m along on the right.

Camping Pong rue du Stade, 85220 Landevielle.
Tel 02 51 22 92 63. English spoken.
OPEN: 01/04–30/09. SIZE: 3 ha, 162 pitches (120 with elec, 9 statics), 14 hot showers, 15 WCs, 2 CWPs.

Shop at 0.7 km. Restaurant at 0.3 km. Tennis, sailing, golf, flume.
PRICES: (1996) Caravan with family 130.00, Tent with two adults 85.00. CC: none.
Halfway between St-Gilles-Croix-de-Vie and Les Sables-d'Olonne, close to Brétignolles-sur-Mer

BRIANCON Hautes-Alpes 6A

Camping de l'Iscle de Prelles 05120 Prelles.
Tel 04 92 20 28 66, Fax 04 92 20 28 66.
English spoken.
OPEN: 01/06–15/09. SIZE: 4 ha, 150 pitches (all with elec), 19 hot showers, 19 WCs, 8 French WCs, 5 CWPs.

Shop at 1 km. Restaurant at 2 km. Exercise/fitness room, entertainment.
PRICES: (1996) Caravan with family 113.70, Tent with two adults 69.20. CC: none.
N94, 6 km from Briançon.

Camping Municipal Le Courounba
05120 Les Vigneaux.
Tel 04 92 23 02 09, Fax 04 92 23 07 26.
English spoken.

France

OPEN: 01/05–30/09. SIZE: 12 ha, 180 pitches (all with elec), 30 hot showers, 46 WCs, 2 CWPs. ✆ &

Shop at 0.5 km. Tennis, fishing, entertainments. PRICES: (1996) Caravan with family 140.00, Tent with two adults 70.00. CC: Euro/Access, Visa. *From Briançon take N94 south towards L'Argentière-la-Bessée. Turn right onto N994 towards Les Vigneaux for 5 km and follow signs to campsite.*

BRIENNE-LE-CHATEAU Aube 3C

Camping du Tertre route de Radonoilliers, 10500 Dienville.
Tel 03 25 92 26 50, Fax 03 25 92 26 50.
English spoken.
OPEN: 15/03–15/10. SIZE: 3.5 ha, 143 pitches (102 with elec, 30 statics), 16 hot showers, 16 WCs, 4 CWPs. ✆ &

Restaurant at 0.2 km. Entertainment in July/August.
PRICES: (1996) Caravan with family 99.00, Tent with two adults 57.00. CC: Euro/Access, Visa. *From Brienne go south on the D443 towards Vendeuvre.*

BRIVE-LA-GAILLARDE Corrèze 4B

Camping à l'Etape de la Ferme 19600 Noailles.
Tel 05 55 85 81 33. English spoken.
OPEN: all year. SIZE: 6 pitches (all with elec), 2 hot showers, 2 WCs, 2 CWPs. &

Shop at 0.2 km. Restaurant at 3 km. Children's playground.
PRICES: (1996) Caravan with family 63.00, Tent with two adults 29.00. CC: none. *9 km south of Brive on D920 or on A20 take Noailles exit 52.*

BROU Eure-et-Loir 2D

Camping du Parc de Loisirs de Brou Base de Plein Aire, routes des Moulins, 28160 Brou.
Tel 02 37 47 02 17, Fax 02 37 47 07 85.
OPEN: 16/02–15/12. SIZE: 4 ha, 250 pitches (all with elec), 24 hot showers, 64 WCs, 4 CWPs. ✆ &

Shop at 1.5 km.
PRICES: (1996) Caravan with family 125.00, Tent with two adults 65.00. CC: none. *South of Chartres on A11, exit D955 to Brou.*

BRULON Sarthe 2C

Camping Brûlon Le Lac 72350 Brûlon.
Tel 02 43 95 68 96, Fax 02 43 92 60 36.
English spoken.

OPEN: 01/04–30/10. SIZE: 3 ha. ✆ &

Shop at 1 km. Tennis, archery, pétanque, canoeing, mini-golf.
PRICES: (1996) Caravan with family 70.00, Tent with two adults 40.00. CC: none. *Well signposted in Brûlon.*

BRUYERES Vosges 3D

Les Pinasses 88600 La Chapelle-devant-Bruyères.
Tel 03 29 58 51 10, Fax 03 29 58 54 21.
OPEN: 01/04–10/09. SIZE: 3 ha, 140 pitches (all with elec), 30 hot showers, 18 WCs, 4 CWPs. ✆ &

Restaurant at 5 km.
PRICES: Caravan with family 143.00, Tent with two adults 78.00. CC: Euro/Access, Visa. *D423 south of Bruyères, then the D60 towards Corcieux.*

LE BUGUE Dordogne 4B

Camping Brin d'Amour St-Cirq, 24260 Le Bugue.
Tel 05 53 07 23 73, Fax 05 53 54 18 06.
English spoken.
OPEN: all year. SIZE: 4 ha, 50 pitches (all with elec, 4 statics), 6 hot showers, 6 WCs, 1 CWP. ✆ &

Restaurant at 5 km. Tennis.
PRICES: (1996) Caravan with family 101.00, Tent with two adults 54.00. CC: Euro/Access. *D703 south of Le Bugue towards Les Eyzies and St-Cirq.*

Camping La Forêt Pézuls, 24510 St-Alvère.
Tel 05 53 22 71 69, Fax 05 53 23 77 79.
English spoken.
OPEN: 01/04–01/10. SIZE: 8 ha, 70 pitches (all with elec, 4 statics), 9 hot showers, 12 WCs, 2 CWPs. ✆ &

Shop at 4 km. Restaurant at 4 km.
PRICES: (1996) Caravan with family 121.40, Tent with two adults 73.00. CC: none. *Take the D703 from Le Bugue towards Lalinde/Pézuls. The campsite is on the north side of the river.*

Camping Le Clou Le Coux et Bigaroque, 24220 Meynard.
Tel 05 53 31 63 32, Fax 05 53 31 69 33.
English spoken.
OPEN: 09/04–01/10. SIZE: 3 ha, 100 pitches (all with elec, 11 statics), 16 hot showers, 14 WCs, 1 CWP. ✆ &

Golf 7 km.
PRICES: (1996) Caravan with family 150.00, Tent with two adults 83.00. CC: none. *Between Le Bugue and Belvès on D703.*

Camping St-Avit Loisirs Le Bugue,
24260 St-Avit-de-Vialard.
Tel 05 53 02 64 00, Fax 05 53 02 64 39.
English spoken.
OPEN: 02/04–30/09. SIZE: 42 ha, 199 pitches
(all with elec), 23 hot showers, 4 CWPs. ⚓ ⚹

BMX, ball games, flume, mini-golf.
PRICES: (1996) Caravan with family 193.40, Tent
with two adults 112.80. CC: Euro/Access, Visa.
*5 km north-west of Le Bugue on the D710
Périgueux road. Before reaching Le Bugue turn
left on to D201, signposted St-Avit-de-Vialard.
Follow signs to the site.*

La Faval Le Coux et Bigaroque, 24220 Le Coux.
Tel 05 53 31 60 44.
OPEN: 01/04–15/10. SIZE: 3 ha, 100 pitches
(80 with elec), 10 hot showers, 10 WCs, 6 French
WCs, 2 CWPs. ⚓ ⚹

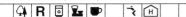

Shop at 0.8 km. Restaurant at 0.5 km.
PRICES: (1996) Caravan with family 156.00,
Tent with two adults 89.00. CC: none.
*At the D710/D703 crossroads, 300 m north of the
River Dordogne.*

LE BUISSON Dordogne   4B

Camping La Grande Veyière 24480 Molières.
Tel 05 53 63 25 84. English spoken.
OPEN: 01/04–15/11. SIZE: 5 ha, 64 pitches (50 with
elec), 8 hot showers, 8 WCs, 1 CWP. ⚓ ⚹

Restaurant at 3 km.
PRICES: (1996) Caravan with family 130.50, Tent
with two adults 73.00. CC: Euro/Access, Visa.
*From Le Buisson take D25 to Cadouin. Carry on
for 3 km and then turn right on to D27 to
Molières. Campsite is signposted from there.*

Camping Le Port de Limeuil
24480 Alles-sur-Dordogne.
Tel 05 53 63 29 76, Fax 05 53 63 04 19.
English spoken.
OPEN: 01/05–30/09. SIZE: 7 ha, 90 pitches
(all with elec, 2 statics), 15 hot showers, 13 WCs,
2 CWPs. ⚓ ⚹

Restaurant at 0.5 km. Bicycle and canoe hire.
PRICES: (1996) Caravan with family 160.00, Tent
with two adults 97.00. CC: Amex, Euro/Access, Visa.
*Off the D2, just west of Le Buisson. Campsite is
signposted.*

CADENET Vaucluse   5D

Camping Val de Durance 84160 Cadenet.
Tel 04 90 68 37 75, Fax 04 42 95 03 63. English spoken.

OPEN: 29/03–12/10. SIZE: 7 ha, 190 pitches
(150 with elec), 10 hot showers, 22 WCs, 2 French
WCs, 3 CWPs. ⚓ ⚹

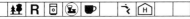

Shop at 2.5 km. Restaurant at 2.5 km. Mobile
homes for hire.
PRICES: (1996) Caravan with family 165.00, Tent
with two adults 93.00. CC: Euro/Access, Visa.
*Arriving in Cadenet village take the D59, go past
the wine co-operative, then take first left.*

CAEN Calvados   2A

Camping Municipal rte de Louvigny (D212),
14000 Caen.
Tel 02 31 73 60 92, Fax 02 31 30 73 32.
English spoken.
OPEN: 01/05–30/09. SIZE: 2.2 ha, 8 hot showers,
10 WCs, 1 CWP. ⚓ ⚹

Shop at 1.5 km. Restaurant at 1.5 km.
PRICES: (1996) Caravan with family 96.00,
Tent with two adults 47.00. CC: none.
On the D212 and well signposted.

CAGNES-SUR-MER Alpes-Marit   6C

Camping La Rivière chemin des Salles,
Val-de-Cagnes, 06800 Cagnes-sur-Mer.
Tel 04 93 20 62 27, Fax 04 93 20 62 27.
English spoken.
OPEN: all year. SIZE: 1.2 ha, 90 pitches (all with
elec), 7 hot showers, 13 WCs, 1 CWP. ⚓ ⚹

Entertainment, video games, boules.
PRICES: Caravan with family 128.50, Tent with two
adults 84.00. CC: Euro/Access, Visa.
*From the centre of Cagnes-sur-Mer take the road
to Haut-de-Cagnes, then Val-de-Cagnes.*

CAHORS Lot   4D

Camping Base Nautique Floiras
46140 Anglars-Juillac.
Tel 05 65 36 27 39, Fax 05 65 21 41 00.
English spoken.
OPEN: 14/04–15/10. SIZE: 1 ha, 25 pitches (all with
elec), 5 hot showers, 5 WCs, 1 French WC, 2 CWPs. ⚹

Restaurant at 1 km.
PRICES: (1996) Caravan with family 105.00, Tent
with two adults 59.00. CC: Euro/Access, Visa.
*D911 north-west of Cahors. Turn left in
Castelfranc (25 km) then right onto the D8. Site is
3.5 km on the right.*

Camping de la Plage St-Cirq-Lapopie,
46330 Cabrerets.
Tel 05 65 30 29 51, Fax 05 65 30 26 48. English spoken.

France

OPEN: all year. SIZE: 3 ha, 120 pitches (60 with elec, 10 statics), 18 hot showers, 18 WCs, 3 CWPs. ⛿ ♿

| ~ | ♨ | ♿ | R | 🗑 | 🦢 | 🍴 | ✕ | | 🏠 | | |

Water sports, horse-riding, bike hire, entertainment.
PRICES: (1996) Caravan with family 135.00, Tent with two adults 60.00. CC: Euro/Access, Visa.
From Cahors take D653 to St-Cirq-Lapopie.

Camping La Truffière 46330 St-Cirq-Lapopie.
Tel 05 65 30 20 22. English spoken.
OPEN: 01/05–30/09. SIZE: 4 ha, 50 pitches (20 with elec), 11 hot showers, 12 WCs, 1 CWP. ⛿ ♿

| | ♨ | R | 🗑 | 🦢 | 🍴 | ✕ | ⁊ | 🏠 | |

Children's games; nice quiet site.
PRICES: (1996) Caravan with family 131.00, Tent with two adults 58.00. CC: Euro/Access, Visa.
From Cahors take D911 to Arcambal and then D8 to St-Cirq-Lapopie. Campsite is signposted.

Camping Les Graves 46090 St-Pierre-Lafeuille.
Tel 05 65 36 83 12. English spoken.
OPEN: 01/04–15/10. SIZE: 0.5 ha, 20 pitches (16 with elec), 2 hot showers, 3 WCs, 1 CWP. ⛿ ♿

| | ⚲ | R | | | | ⁊ | 🍺 | |

Shop at 0.3 km. Restaurant at 0.6 km. Children's pool, boules; 20% discount in LS.
PRICES: Caravan with family 115.00, Tent with two adults 65.00. CC: none.
10 km north of Cahors on the N20.

Camping Pompit 46090 Esclauzels.
Tel 05 65 31 53 40. English spoken.
OPEN: 15/03–01/10. SIZE: 4 ha, 25 pitches (all with elec, 7 statics), 4 hot showers, 6 WCs, 2 CWPs.

| | ♨ | R | 🗑 | 🦢 | 🍵 | 🍷 | | ⁊ | 🍺 | |

Restaurant at 6 km. Pony rides.
PRICES: (1996) Caravan with family 113.50, Tent with two adults 60.00. CC: none.
From Cahors head towards Rodez. In the village of Arcambal follow signs towards St-Cirq-Lapopie and Esclauzels is off this road.

Quercy-Vacances Mas de la Combe, 46090 St-Pierre-Lafeuille.
Tel 05 65 36 87 90. English spoken.
OPEN: 15/05–15/09. SIZE: 3 ha, 80 pitches (all with elec, 6 statics), 18 hot showers, 18 WCs, 1 CWP. ⛿ ♿

| | ♨ | R | 🗑 | | | ✕ | ⁊ | | |

Shop at 0.5 km. Games room, billiards, bar, disco.
PRICES: (1996) Caravan with family 150.00, Tent with two adults 90.00. CC: none.
From Cahors take the N20 north to St-Pierre (12 km).

CAJARC Lot   5C

Camping du Ruisseau de Treil 46160 Larnagol.
Tel 05 65 31 23 39. English spoken.
OPEN: 01/03–30/09. SIZE: 4 ha, 50 pitches (all with

elec, 8 statics), 9 hot showers, 11 WCs, 2 CWPs. ⛿ ♿

| | ⚲ | R | 🗑 | 🦢 | 🍷 | ✕ | ⁊ | 🍺 | |

Archery, tennis, playroom; river 0.2 km. 20 to 30% discount in LS.
PRICES: (1996) Caravan with family 179.00, Tent with two adults 102.00. CC: none.
8 km west of Cajarc on the D662.

CALAIS Pas-de-Calais   2B

Bal Parc Camping 500 rue du Vieux Château, 62890 Tournehem-sur-la-Hem.
Tel 03 21 35 65 90, Fax 03 21 35 18 57.
English spoken.
OPEN: all year. SIZE: 2 ha, 63 pitches (all with elec, 10 statics), 18 hot showers, 10 WCs. ⛿ ♿

| ~ | ⚷ | ⚲ | R | 🗑 | 🦢 | | ✕ | | 🍺 | |

Within easy reach of sea and lake; mobile homes available.
PRICES: (1996) Caravan with family 120.00, Tent with two adults 68.00. CC: Visa.
From Calais south on A26. Take exit 2 Ardres-Licques-Audruicq and go right on to D217/218. Follow camping signs.
SEE ADVERTISEMENT

Camping Caravaning Le Village Fréthun, 62185 Calais.
Tel 03 21 85 25 42. English spoken.

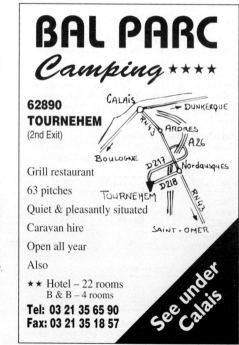
France

OPEN: all year. SIZE: 3 ha, 73 pitches (40 with elec, 2 statics), 4 hot showers (charge), 7 WCs, 2 CWPs.

Shop at 1 km. Restaurant at 1 km. Sea 4 km.
PRICES: (1996) Caravan with family 101.80,
Tent with two adults 59.80. CC: none.
Not far from the Channel Tunnel and close to TGV Fréthun station.

Camping Le Fremont 62910 Serques.
Tel 03 21 93 01 15. English spoken.
OPEN: 01/04–01/10. SIZE: 2 ha, 50 pitches (all with elec), 2 hot showers (charge), 5 WCs, 2 French WCs, 1 CWP.

Restaurant at 2 km.
PRICES: (1996) Caravan with family 70.00,
Tent with two adults 38.00. CC: none.
35 km from Calais and 12 km north of St-Omer. Take N43 south from Calais towards St-Omer, turn left to D214 and follow signs.

CAMARET-SUR-MER Finistère   1C

Camping Lambezen 29570 Camaret-sur-Mer.
Tel 02 98 27 91 41, Fax 02 98 27 93 72.
English spoken.
OPEN: 01/04–30/09. SIZE: 3 ha, 123 pitches (all with elec, 8 statics), 18 hot showers, 21 WCs, 2 CWPs.

Restaurant at 2.5 km. Mini-golf, tennis, flume.
PRICES: Caravan with family 177.00, Tent with two adults 107.00. CC: Amex, Euro/Access, Visa.
At the roundabout entering Camaret, turn right on to D355 towards La Pointe des Espagnols, then follow the first road on the right for 2 km.

Camping Plage de Trez-Rouz Trez Rouz,
29570 Camaret-sur-Mer.
Tel 02 98 27 93 96, Fax 02 98 27 84 54.
English spoken.
OPEN: 01/04–30/09. SIZE: 1 ha, 9 hot showers, 9 WCs, 1 CWP.

Shop at 3 km. Restaurant at 3 km.
PRICES: (1996) Caravan with family 126.00, Tent with two adults 70.00. CC: none.
From Camaret take D355 towards Pointe des Espagnols. Campsite is well signposted.

CANCALE Ille/Vilaine   1D

Camp Municipal 35114 St-Benoît-des-Ondes.
Tel 02 99 58 65 21, Fax 02 99 58 77 06.
English spoken.
OPEN: 17/06–15/09. SIZE: 1.5 ha, 121 pitches (all with elec), 9 hot showers, 14 WCs.

Shop at 0.1 km.
PRICES: (1996) Caravan with family 83.00,
Tent with two adults 45.00. CC: none.
D76 south from Cancale then turn left on to D155 to St-Benoît-des-Ondes. Site is signposted.

CANCON Lot/Garonne   4D

Camping des Bastides Monflanquin, 47150 Salles.
Tel 05 53 40 83 09, Fax 05 53 40 81 76.
English spoken.
OPEN: 15/05–15/09. SIZE: 6 ha, 80 pitches (all with elec), 12 hot showers, 9 WCs.

Flume.
PRICES: (1996) Caravan with family 154.00,
Tent with two adults 96.00. CC: Euro/Access.
From Cancon go through Monflanquin to Salles on the D150. The campsite is 1 km beyond Salles on the D150/D162 crossroads.

CANET-EN-ROUSSILLON Pyr Orient 5C

Camping Brasilia 66140 Canet.
Tel 04 68 80 23 82, Fax 04 68 73 32 97.
English spoken.
OPEN: 06/04–05/10. SIZE: 15 ha, 826 pitches (all with elec), 139 hot showers, 120 WCs, 8 CWPs.

PRICES: (1996) Caravan with family 198.00, Tent with two adults 130.00. CC: Euro/Access, Visa.
From Canet go to Canet-Nord and follow signs to Zone Technique du Port.

Camping La Pergola 21 avenue Fréderic Mistral, 66470 Ste-Marie.
Tel 04 68 73 03 07, Fax 04 68 73 04 67.
English spoken.
OPEN: 15/05–15/09. SIZE: 3 ha, 181 pitches (all with elec), 26 hot showers, 23 WCs, 2 CWPs.

Shop at 0.3 km.
PRICES: (1996) Caravan with family 174.00, Tent with two adults 100.00. CC: Euro/Access, Visa.
North on D81 from Canet towards Ste-Marie Plage.

Camping Les Peupliers Canet-Plage, 66140 Canet.
Tel 04 68 80 35 87, Fax 04 68 73 38 75.
English spoken.
OPEN: 01/06–30/09. SIZE: 4 ha, 145 pitches (all with elec, 92 statics), 23 hot showers, 35 WCs, 2 CWPs.

PRICES: (1996) Caravan with family 174.00, Tent with two adults 110.00. CC: Amex, Euro/Access, Visa.
From Perpignan on D617 towards coast to Canet-Plage, port access north.

France

Ma Prairie route de St-Nazaire, 66140 Canet.
Tel 04 68 73 26 17, Fax 04 68 73 28 82.
English spoken.
OPEN: 01/05–30/09. SIZE: 4 ha, 260 pitches
(210 with elec, 12 statics), 44 hot showers,
32 WCs, 3 CWPs. ᴄ ᴇ

Tennis, nursery, entertainment; 2 km from beach.
PRICES: (1996) Caravan with family 194.00, Tent
with two adults 116.00. CC: Euro/Access, Visa.
*From Canet take the D617 for about 300 m
following signs to Camping Village, then turn
right on to D11.*

CANNES Alpes-Marit   6C

Camping Les Pruniers bd de la Mer,
06210 Mandelieu-la-Napoule.
Tel 04 93 49 99 23, Fax 04 93 49 37 45.
English spoken.
OPEN: 01/04–15/10. SIZE: 0.5 ha, 36 pitches
(all with elec), 6 hot showers, 7 WCs, 1 CWP. ᴄ

Shop at 1 km. Restaurant at 0.5 km.
PRICES: (1996) Caravan with family 160.00,
Tent with two adults 120.00. CC: none.
*The campsite is near the Cannes Marina in
Mandelieu.*

Camping Panoramic quartier St-Jean, bd de la
République, 06550 La Roquette-sur-Siagne.
Tel 04 92 19 07 77, Fax 04 92 19 07 77.
English spoken.
OPEN: all year. SIZE: 1 ha, 40 pitches (all with elec),
13 hot showers, 18 WCs, 2 CWPs. ᴄ

Solarium, studio apartments also available.
PRICES: (1996) Caravan with family 151.00,
Tent with two adults 89.00. CC: none.
*From Cannes take D9 towards Grasse via La
Bocca. Turn right towards La Roquette-sur-Siagne
and follow signs to campsite.*

Camping Pré de Fanton 06580 Pégomas.
Tel 04 93 42 29 41.
OPEN: 15/05–15/09. SIZE: 1.3 ha, 35 pitches, 8 hot
showers, 12 WCs, 8 French WCs, 1 CWP. ᴄ

Shop at 1 km. Restaurant at 1 km.
PRICES: (1996) Caravan with family 112.00,
Tent with two adults 60.00. CC: none.
From Cannes, Pégomas lies to the north-west.

Le Ranch chemin St-Joseph, l'Aubarède,
06110 Le Cannet.
Tel 04 93 46 00 11, Fax 04 93 46 44 30.
English spoken.
OPEN: 01/04–30/10. SIZE: 2 ha, 130 pitches (all
with elec), 22 hot showers, 15 WCs, 1 CWP. ᴄ ᴇ

Restaurant at 1 km.
PRICES: (1996) Caravan with family 155.00, Tent
with two adults 100.00. CC: Euro/Access, Visa.
*5 km from Cannes; follow directions to
L'Aubarède and campsite is signposted.*

Les Cigales 505 av de la Mer, quartier d'Etang,
06210 Mandelieu.
Tel 04 93 49 23 53, Fax 04 93 49 30 45.
English spoken.
OPEN: all year. SIZE: 2 ha, 110 pitches (90 with
elec), 15 hot showers, 15 WCs, 23 French WCs,
1 CWP.

Shop at 0.3 km. Sea: 0.8 km.
PRICES: Caravan with family 215.00,
Tent with two adults 150.00. CC: none.
From Cannes go 6 km on the N98 to Mandelieu.

Les Mimosas 421 chemin de Cabrol,
06580 Pegomas.
Tel 04 93 42 36 11. English spoken.
OPEN: 01/04–01/10. SIZE: 2 ha, 135 pitches
(all with elec, 50 statics), 18 hot showers, 18 WCs,
2 CWPs. ᴄ ᴇ

Restaurant at 1 km. Mini-golf.
PRICES: (1996) Caravan with family 114.00,
Tent with two adults 90.00. CC: none.
*From Cannes take the N7 to Mandelieu, then the
D109 to Pegomas.*

CAP-FERRET Gironde   4A

Camping du Truc Vert route Forestière BP15,
33970 Cap-Ferret-Océan.
Tel 05 56 60 89 55, Fax 05 56 60 99 47.
English spoken.
OPEN: 15/05–30/09. SIZE: 11 ha, 430 pitches
(300 with elec), 73 hot showers. ᴄ ᴇ

PRICES: (1996) Caravan with family 160.40,
Tent with two adults 97.20. CC: none.
*Leave Bordeaux following signs to Cap-Ferret. At
Les Jacquets, turn right to Le Truc Vert. The
campsite is about 3 km along the forest road on
the left.*

CAPBRETON Landes   4C

Camping de la Pointe av Jean Lartigau,
40130 Capbreton.
Tel 05 58 72 14 98. English spoken.
OPEN: 01/06–30/09. SIZE: 4 ha, 32 hot showers,
32 WCs, 2 CWPs. ᴄ

PRICES: (1996) Caravan with family 133.00, Tent
with two adults 74.00. CC: none.

Exit 7 from A63 to Capbreton. Site is on the south side, D652 towards Bayonne.

CAPTIEUX Gironde 4D

Aire Naturelle de Camping Le Château,
40120 Bourriot-Bergonce.
Tel 05 58 93 36 22. English spoken.
OPEN: all year. SIZE: 1 ha, 20 pitches (4 with elec,
5 statics), 1 hot shower, 3 WCs, 1 CWP.

Shop at 2 km. Restaurant at 9 km.
PRICES: (1996) Caravan with family 64.00,
Tent with two adults 37.00. CC: none.
*14 km after Captieux on D932 turn left on to D24
(minor road), towards Bourriot/Losse/Gabaret
then drive 10 km to Bergonce. The campsite is at
the end of the village.*

CARANTEC Finistère 1C

Camping Les Mouettes 29660 Carantec.
Tel 02 98 67 02 46, Fax 02 98 78 31 46.
English spoken.
OPEN: 29/04–25/09. SIZE: 7 ha, 273 pitches (all
with elec, 23 statics), 21 hot showers, 20 WCs.

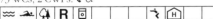

Restaurant at 1.8 km. Giant flume, billiards; fishing
nearby.
PRICES: (1996) Caravan with family 206.00, Tent
with two adults 132.00. CC: Euro/Access, Visa.
*The campsite is signposted on entering the village
of Carantec.*

CARCANS Gironde 4A

Camping de Maubuisson 33121 Carcans.
Tel 05 56 03 30 12, Fax 05 56 03 47 93. English spoken.
OPEN: 01/03–31/10. SIZE: 12.5 ha, 450 pitches
(200 with elec, 45 statics), 90 hot showers,
73 WCs, 2 CWPs.

Shop at 0.1 km. Restaurant at 0.1 km.
PRICES: (1996) Caravan with family 160.00, Tent
with two adults 100.00. CC: Amex, Euro/Access, Visa.
*From Carcans, take the D207 towards
Maubuisson and Carcans-Plage. The campsite is
in the centre of Maubuisson.*

Camping du Pin Franc
route de Maubuisson, 33121 Carcans.
Tel 05 56 03 33 57. English spoken.
OPEN: 15/06–30/09. SIZE: 7 ha, 39 pitches
(all with elec, 6 statics), 9 hot showers, 9 WCs.

Restaurant at 2 km.
PRICES: (1996) Caravan with family 92.00,
Tent with two adults 56.00. CC: none.
On the D207.

CARCASSONNE Aude 5C

Airotel Grand Sud Camping Lac du Breil d'Aude,
route de Limoux, 11250 Preixan.
Tel 04 68 26 88 18, Fax 04 68 26 85 07.
OPEN: 01/03–31/10. SIZE: 11 ha, 100 pitches
(70 with elec, 10 statics), 10 hot showers, 18 WCs,
2 French WCs, 1 CWP.

Restaurant at 6 km. Tennis, fishing, sauna, jacuzzi,
volley ball, table tennis, TV.
PRICES: Caravan with family 142.00, Tent with two
adults 85.00. CC: Visa.
*From Carcassonne head south on the D118 along
the west bank of the Aube towards Limoux.
Preixan is 7 km.*

Camp Municipal
chemin de la Lande, 11800 Trèbes.
Tel 04 68 78 61 75. English spoken.
OPEN: 01/06–10/10. SIZE: 2 ha, 85 pitches (48 with
elec, 62 statics), 14 hot showers, 17 WCs, 8 French
WCs, 2 CWPs.

Shop at 0.5 km.
PRICES: Caravan with family 88.00,
Tent with two adults 55.00. CC: none.
*Trèbes is due east of Carcassonne and there are
directions to the campsite in the village.*

Camping Au Pin d'Arnauteille
Domaine d'Arnauteille, 11250 Montclar.
Tel 04 68 26 84 53, Fax 04 68 26 91 10.
English spoken.
OPEN: 01/04–01/10. SIZE: 115 ha, 100 pitches
(80 with elec, 20 statics), 12 hot showers, 13 WCs,
1 CWP.

Shop at 3 km. Wonderful views; horse-riding,
walking; fishing nearby.
PRICES: (1996) Caravan with family 138.00,
Tent with two adults 80.00. CC: Euro/Access.
*Take D118 south of Carcassonne. After Rouffiac
turn right on to D43 and follow signs.*

Camping Au Pin d'Arnauteille

near Carcassonne
The medieval city beckons . . .

Les Campeoles Camping de la Cité,
11000 Carcassonne.
Tel 04 68 25 11 77, Fax 04 68 47 33 13.
English spoken.
OPEN: 01/03–10/10. SIZE: 7 ha, 200 pitches
(115 with elec).

France

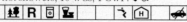

Tennis.
PRICES: (1996) Caravan with family 154.00, Tent
with two adults 85.00. CC: Euro/Access, Visa.
Well signposted in town.

Camping Das Pinhiers chemin du Pont-Neuf,
11620 Villemoustaussou.
Tel 04 68 47 81 90, Fax 04 68 71 43 49.
OPEN: 01/04–30/09. SIZE: 2 ha, 49 pitches (42 with
elec), 9 hot showers, 10 WCs, 1 CWP. ☎ ♿

Restaurant at 1.5 km. Mini-golf, bar, playground.
PRICES: Caravan with family 113.00, Tent with two
adults 58.00. CC: none.
*From Carcassonne go north towards Mazamet on
D118. Campsite is well signposted.*

Camping Les Lavandières
11610 Pennautier.
Tel 04 68 25 41 66.
OPEN: 01/04–31/10. SIZE: 1 ha, 36 pitches (all with
elec), 6 hot showers, 8 WCs, 4 CWPs. ☎

Shop at 0.4 km. Restaurant at 4 km.
PRICES: (1996) Caravan with family 111.00,
Tent with two adults 58.00. CC: none.
*From A61 go west on N113 towards Toulouse.
Turn off on D203 to Pennautier.*

La Commanderie 11800 Rustiques.
Tel 04 68 78 61 07.
English spoken.
OPEN: 01/06–30/10. SIZE: 3 ha, 50 pitches (40 with
elec), 6 hot showers, 9 WCs, 1 CWP. ☎ ♿

Shop at 1 km. Tennis, table tennis, pétanque,
volley ball.
PRICES: (1996) Caravan with family 100.00,
Tent with two adults 50.00. CC: none.
*From east or west on N113 follow signs into
Trèbes. Go over river and canal bridges. Take
immediate left and right and follow signs for
Intermarché. At Intermarché roundabout take
D206 towards Rustiques. Campsite is signposted
after approx 1 km.*

Le Martinet Rouge 11390 Brousses-et-Villaret.
Tel 04 68 26 51 98.
English spoken.
OPEN: 01/04–31/10. SIZE: 3 ha, 50 pitches (30 with
elec), 5 hot showers, 8 WCs, 1 CWP. ☎ ♿

Restaurant at 0.05 km.
PRICES: (1996) Caravan with family 109.00,
Tent with two adults 58.00. CC: none.
*From Carcassonne, west on N113. Turn right on
to D48 just after Pezens and continue for 8 km.
Campsite is signposted.*

CARENTAN Manche   1B

Le Haut Dick chemin du Grand-Bas Pays,
50500 Carentan.
Tel 02 33 42 16 89. English spoken.
OPEN: all year. SIZE: 2.5 ha, 120 pitches (84 with
elec), 14 hot showers, 14 WCs, 2 CWPs. ☎ ♿

Shop at 0.5 km. Restaurant at 0.1 km. Swimming
pool 0.05 km.
PRICES: (1996) Caravan with family 86.00,
Tent with two adults 47.00. CC: none.
*From N13 take Carentan exit and follow signs to
town centre and campsite.*

CARHAIX-PLOUGER Finistère   1C

Le Moulin Vert 29270 Cleden-Poher.
Tel 02 98 93 82 05.
OPEN: 01/06–19/09. SIZE: 3 ha, 45 pitches, 8 hot
showers, 12 WCs, 1 CWP. ☎ ♿

PRICES: (1996) Caravan with family 67.90,
Tent with two adults 39.30. CC: none.
*Take the N164 south-west of Carbaix for 7 km
and then turn left to Cleden-Poher.*

CARNAC Morbihan   1C

Les Bruyères Kerogile, 56340 Carnac.
Tel 02 97 52 30 57, Fax 02 97 52 30 57.
English spoken.
OPEN: 07/04–20/10. SIZE: 2 ha, 112 pitches
(80 with elec, 12 statics), 11 hot showers,
11 WCs, 1 CWP. ☎

Shop at 2 km. Restaurant at 2 km.
PRICES: (1996) Caravan with family 105.50, Tent
with two adults 63.00. CC: Euro/Access, Visa.
*From Carnac go north on the D4, and then take
the D768, signposted.*

Camping de l'Etang Kerlann, 56340 Carnac.
Tel 02 97 52 14 06. English spoken.
OPEN: 01/04–01/11. SIZE: 3 ha, 165 pitches
(100 with elec), 18 hot showers, 18 WCs. ☎ ♿

Restaurant at 1 km.
PRICES: (1996) Caravan with family 126.50,
Tent with two adults 75.00. CC: none.
From Carnac, north on D119. Follow signs.

Camping des Menhirs Carnac Plage,
56340 Carnac.
Tel 02 97 52 94 67, Fax 02 97 52 25 38.
English spoken.
OPEN: 01/05–30/09. SIZE: 6 ha, 150 pitches
(160 with elec, 160 statics), 40 hot showers,
40 WCs. ☎ ♿

France

PRICES: (1996) Caravan with family 306.00, Tent with two adults 221.00. CC: Amex, Euro/Access, Visa. *From the tourist office in town, go towards Carnac Plage.*

Camping des Sept Saints 56410 Erdeven. Tel 02 97 55 52 65, Fax 02 97 55 22 67. English spoken. OPEN: 15/05–15/09. SIZE: 7 ha, 200 pitches (160 with elec, 31 statics), 28 hot showers, 25 WCs, 2 CWPs. ⚡ ♿

Restaurant at 1 km. Ball games. PRICES: (1996) Caravan with family 166.00, Tent with two adults 104.00. CC: Amex, Euro/Access, Visa. *From Carnac take D781 to Erdeven and follow signs.*

Camping du Lac Le Lac, 56340 Carnac. Tel 02 97 55 78 78, Fax 02 97 55 86 03. English spoken. OPEN: 01/04–20/09. SIZE: 2.5 ha, 140 pitches (100 with elec, 6 statics), 16 hot showers, 19 WCs, 23 French WCs, 2 CWPs. ⚡ ♿

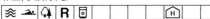

Restaurant at 3 km. Fishing, games, hairdresser. PRICES: Caravan with family 135.00, Tent with two adults 79.00. CC: Amex, Euro/Access, Visa. *From Carnac take D186 towards La Trinité-sur-Mer. Follow signs.*

Camping Le Dolmen Beaumer, 56340 Carnac. Tel 02 97 52 12 35, Fax 02 97 52 12 35. English spoken. OPEN: 15/06–05/09. SIZE: 2 ha, 130 pitches (85 with elec), 13 hot showers, 26 WCs, 06 French WCs, 1 CWP. ♿

Shop at 0.5 km. Restaurant at 0.2 km. PRICES: (1996) Tent with two adults 90.00. CC: Euro/Access, Visa. *From Carnac take the D781 towards La Trinité; the campsite is signposted on the right 1 km from town.*

Camping Le Men Du Beaumer, 56340 Carnac-Plage. Tel 02 97 52 04 23. English spoken. OPEN: 01/04–30/09. SIZE: 1.5 ha, 84 pitches (all with elec, 17 statics), 13 hot showers, 10 WCs, 1 CWP. ⚡

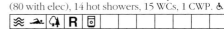

Shop at 0.5 km. Restaurant at 0.2 km. PRICES: (1996) Caravan with family 102.00, Tent with two adults 75.00. CC: none. *From Carnac continue on D119 to Carnac-Plage then D186 to La Trinité-sur-Mer in avenue des Druides. Signposted.*

Camping Le Moustoir route du Moustoir, 56340 Carnac. Tel 02 97 52 16 18, Fax 02 97 52 88 37. English spoken. OPEN: 01/04–30/09. SIZE: 5 ha, 165 pitches (all with elec), 20 hot showers, 16 WCs, 3 CWPs. ⚡

Restaurant at 0.2 km. PRICES: Caravan with family 131.00, Tent with two adults 89.00. CC: Amex, Euro/Access, Visa. *From Carnac, take D186 east and follow signs. If coming from Auray, D768 then D186.*

Camping Le Moustoir***
at Carnac
Everything on site but near the beaches too.

Camping Les Druides 55 chemin de Beaumer, 56343 Carnac. Tel 02 97 52 08 18, Fax 02 97 52 96 13. English spoken. OPEN: 30/04–09/09. SIZE: 2.5 ha, 110 pitches (80 with elec), 14 hot showers, 15 WCs, 1 CWP. ♿

Shop at 0.3 km. Restaurant at 0.4 km. PRICES: (1996) Caravan with family 161.50, Tent with two adults 125.00. CC: Euro/Access. *From Carnac, take the D781 towards Canac-Plage and turn right towards Beaumer.*

Camping Les Goelands Kergonan, 56340 Plouharnel. Tel 02 97 52 31 92. OPEN: 01/06–15/09. SIZE: 2 ha, 80 pitches (60 with elec), 6 hot showers, 9 WCs.

Shop at 1.5 km. Restaurant at 1.5 km. Pétanque, volley ball. PRICES: (1996) Caravan with family 67.00, Tent with two adults 36.50. CC: none. *From Carnac take the D119 to Plouharnel and then second turning right.*

Camping Les Saules route de Rosnual, 56340 Carnac. Tel 02 97 52 14 98. English spoken. OPEN: 01/04–30/09. SIZE: 2.5 ha, 120 pitches (100 with elec, 30 statics), 12 hot showers, 10 WCs. ⚡ ♿

Shop at 1.5 km. Restaurant at 0.3 km. PRICES: Caravan with family 132.00, Tent with two adults 84.00. CC: Euro/Access, Visa. *From Carnac, 1 km north on D119.*

France

Camping Moulin de Kermaux 56340 Carnac.
Tel 02 97 52 15 90, Fax 02 97 52 83 85.
English spoken.
OPEN: 08/04–16/09. SIZE: 3 ha, 100 pitches (all with elec, 10 statics), 15 hot showers, 16 WCs, 1 CWP. ℓ

≋ ⚓ 🏠 | R | 🗑 | 🍺 | 🍴 | | ⚡ | ℍ |

Restaurant at 0.3 km. Jacuzzi, sauna, mini-golf.
PRICES: (1996) Caravan with family 150.00, Tent with two adults 100.00. CC: Euro/Access, Visa.
Follow signs from Carnac on D119 then D196.

La Grande Metairie 56340 Carnac.
Tel 02 97 52 24 01, Fax 02 97 52 83 58.
English spoken.
OPEN: 22/09–13/09. SIZE: 15 ha, 575 pitches (all with elec, 211 statics), 44 hot showers, 40 WCs, 3 CWPs. ℓ ♿

≋ 🏊 🏠 | R | 🗑 | 🍺 | 🍴 | ✖ | ⚡ | ℍ |

Shop at 3 km. Restaurant at 1 km. Tennis, pony-riding, boating, mini-golf; bikes for hire.
PRICES: Caravan with family 248.00, Tent with two adults 174.00. CC: Amex, Euro/Access, Visa.
Campsite is well signposted in Carnac. (Limited services 22/03-23/05; discounts in LS.)

Les Ombrages Kerlann, 56340 Carnac.
Tel 02 97 52 16 52. English spoken.
OPEN: 15/05–15/09. SIZE: 1 ha, 70 pitches (all with elec), 8 hot showers, 8 WCs. ♿

≋ ⚓ 🛗 | R | 🗑 | 🍺 | | | 🎱 |

Restaurant at 0.3 km.
PRICES: (1996) Caravan with family 106.50, Tent with two adults 60.00. CC: none.
Turn right just before reaching Carnac on the D119 (by the Shell petrol station).

CARPENTRAS Vaucluse 5D

Camping La Roubine Loriol du Comtat,
84870 Carpentras.
Tel 04 90 65 72 87. English spoken.
OPEN: 15/05–30/09. SIZE: 4 ha, 116 pitches (all with elec), 14 hot showers, 14 WCs, 10 CWPs. ℓ ♿

🛗 | R | 🗑 | 🍺 | 🍴 | | ⚡ |

Restaurant at 1 km. Tennis, volley ball.
PRICES: (1996) Caravan with family 129.00, Tent with two adults 69.00. CC: none.
On the D950, approx 18 km from Orange.

Camping Municipal Les Queirades
84190 Vacqueyras.
Tel 04 90 65 84 24.
OPEN: 01/04–31/08. SIZE: 1 ha, 40 pitches (16 with elec), 6 hot showers, 10 WCs, 1 CWP. ℓ

| | 🏠 | R | | | | | |

Shop at 0.5 km. Restaurant at 0.5 km. Swimming pool 5 km.
PRICES: (1996) Caravan with family 60.00, Tent with two adults 28.00. CC: none.

North of Carpentras on the D7, through the village of Vacqueyras, and the site is on the left.

Domaine Naturiste de Bélézy 84410 Bédoin.
Tel 04 90 65 60 18, Fax 04 90 65 94 45.
English spoken.
OPEN: 13/03–17/10. SIZE: 25 ha, 200 pitches (all with elec), 40 hot showers, 44 WCs, 5 CWPs. ℓ ♿

| 🛗 | R | 🗑 | 🍺 | ⚡ | ✖ | | ℍ | 🎯 | 🚗 |

Naturist site with a wealth of activities and excellent facilities.
PRICES: (1996) Caravan with family 257.00, Tent with two adults 142.50. CC: Euro/Access, Visa.

VAISON-LA-ROMAINE

Malaucène ●

D938 D19 ● Bédoin

D974

○ CARPENTRAS Domaine Naturiste de Bélézy

Highly recommended. Orange exit from A7 then D950 to Carpentras. From Carpentras take D974 (Bédoin/Mt-Ventoux). Turn left under aqueduct to Bédoin, pass through and turn right to Mt-Ventoux. Follow signs to Bélézy from there.

Les Verguettes route de Carpentras,
84570 Villes-sur-Auzon.
Tel 04 90 61 88 18, Fax 04 90 61 97 87.
English spoken.
OPEN: 15/05–30/09. SIZE: 2 ha, 80 pitches (all with elec), 12 hot showers, 9 WCs, 1 CWP. ℓ ♿

| 🛗 | R | 🗑 | | | ✖ | ⚡ | |

Shop at 0.3 km. Tennis, mini-golf.
PRICES: (1996) Caravan with family 148.00, Tent with two adults 85.00. CC: none.
From Carpentras approx 17 km east on D942 towards Sault.

CARQUEIRANNE Var 6C

Camping Le Beau Veze 83320 Carqueiranne.
Tel 04 94 57 65 30, Fax 04 94 57 65 30.
English spoken.
OPEN: 01/06–20/09. SIZE: 7 ha, 90 pitches (all with elec), 40 hot showers, 40 WCs, 2 CWPs. ℓ

| 🛗 | R | 🗑 | 🍺 | ⚡ | ✖ | | ℍ |

Shop at 1 km. Tennis; windsurfing centre and sea/beaches close by.
PRICES: (1996) Caravan with family 208.00, Tent with two adults 124.00. CC: none.
From Toulon take Le Pradet exit from motorway and carry on to Carqueiranne.

France

CASTELJALOUX Lot/Garonne 4D

Camp Municipal de la Piscine
route de Marmande, 47700 Casteljaloux.
Tel 05 53 93 54 68.
OPEN: 25/03–30/10. SIZE: 1 ha, 50 pitches (all with elec), 10 hot showers, 8 WCs, 6 French WCs, 1 CWP. &

Shop at 0.1 km. Restaurant at 0.1 km.
PRICES: (1996) Caravan with family 65.50, Tent with two adults 29.50. CC: none.
Casteljaloux is on the D933, south of Marmande.

Moulin de Campech
47160 Villefranche-du-Queyran.
Tel 05 53 88 72 43, Fax 05 53 88 06 52.
English spoken.
OPEN: 01/04–30/10. SIZE: 5 ha, 60 pitches (all with elec, 4 statics), 9 hot showers, 10 WCs, 1 CWP. &

Free river trout fishing.
PRICES: (1996) Caravan with family 104.00, Tent with two adults 60.00. CC: Amex, Euro/Access, Visa.
From motorway A62 Bordeaux/Toulouse leave at exit 6. Turn left, signposted Mont-de-Monson. After approx 4 km at Cap du Bosc, turn right towards Casteljaloux. The site is 4 km on the right.

CASTELLANE Alpes/Hte-Prov 6C

Camp des Gorges du Verdon Domaine de la Salaou, 04120 Castellane.
Tel 04 92 83 61 29, Fax 04 92 83 69 37.
English spoken.
OPEN: 15/05–15/09. SIZE: 13 ha, 300 pitches (150 with elec, 50 statics), 79 hot showers, 72 WCs, 5 CWPs. & &

Archery, volley ball, football, entertainment, library, disco, fishing.
PRICES: (1996) Caravan with family 193.00, Tent with two adults 163.00. CC: none.
1.2 km west of Castellane towards Draguignan and Les Gorges du Verdon.

Camping Le Haut Chandelalar Briançonnet, 06850 St-Auban.
Tel 04 93 60 40 09, Fax 04 93 60 49 64.
English spoken.
OPEN: 01/06–15/09. SIZE: 10 ha, 36 pitches (30 with elec), 8 hot showers, 9 WCs, 1 CWP. &

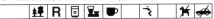

Restaurant at 2 km.
PRICES: (1996) Caravan with family 150.00, Tent with two adults 82.00. CC: none.
Take N85 east from Castellane and then D2211 north at Le Logis-du-Pin towards St-Auban. Briançonnet is signposted north of St-Auban.

Camping Les Lavendes rte des Gorges du Verdon, 04120 Castellane.
Tel 04 92 83 68 78, Fax 04 92 83 68 78.
English spoken.
OPEN: 01/04–30/09. SIZE: 6 ha, 60 pitches (all with elec, 9 statics), 5 hot showers, 6 WCs, 3 CWPs. & &

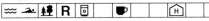

Shop at 0.3 km. Restaurant at 0.3 km. Swimming pool 300 m.
PRICES: (1996) Caravan with family 75.00, Tent with two adults 54.00. CC: Amex, Euro/Access, Visa.
From Castellane go towards Les Gorges du Verdon and campsite is about 300 m.

Camping Notre Dame route des Gorges du Verdon, 04120 Castellane.
Tel 04 92 83 63 02. English spoken.
OPEN: 01/04–20/10. SIZE: 0.6 ha, 44 pitches (35 with elec, 2 statics), 5 hot showers, 8 WCs, 2 CWPs. & &

Restaurant at 0.5 km.
PRICES: (1996) Caravan with family 113.00, Tent with two adults 79.00. CC: none.
Leave Castellane on D952 (Les Gorges du Verdon road) ; campsite is 600 m on the right.

Camping Provençal route de Digne, 04120 Castellane.
Tel 04 92 83 65 50. English spoken.
OPEN: 01/04–20/09. SIZE: 0.88 ha, 45 pitches (30 with elec), 8 hot showers, 7 WCs, 2 French WCs, 1 CWP. & &

Shop at 1 km. Restaurant at 1 km. Table tennis, playground, volley ball, boules.
PRICES: (1996) Caravan with family 108.00, Tent with two adults 55.00. CC: Euro/Access, Visa.
1.5 km from Castellane on the N85 towards Digne.

Clavet Loisirs 04120 Castellane.
Tel 04 92 83 68 96, Fax 04 92 83 75 40.
English spoken.
OPEN: 15/05–15/09. SIZE: 7 ha, 195 pitches (130 with elec, 3 statics), 32 hot showers, 32 WCs. & &

Tennis, riding.
PRICES: (1996) Caravan with family 184.00, Tent with two adults 98.00. CC: none.
On the N85 towards Grasse.

Domaine de Chasteuil-Provence
04120 Castellane.
Tel 04 92 83 61 21, Fax 04 92 83 75 62.
English spoken.
OPEN: 25/04–20/09. SIZE: 7 ha, 210 pitches (180 with elec), 27 hot showers, 21 WCs, 14 French WCs, 1 CWP. & &

Shop at 8 km.
PRICES: (1996) Caravan with family 140.00,
Tent with two adults 103.00. CC: none.
From Castellane take the road to Moustiers and
Les Gorges du Verdon for 8 km.

CASTETS Landes   4C

Camping Municipal Le Grandjean
40260 Linxe.
Tel 05 58 42 90 00, Fax 05 58 42 94 67.
English spoken.
OPEN: 24/06−03/09. SIZE: 3 ha, 54 pitches (all with
elec, 1 static), 12 hot showers, 12 WCs. ℄ ♿

Shop at 1 km.
PRICES: (1996) Caravan with family 90.00,
Tent with two adults 48.00. CC: none.
Take D42 westwards from Castets. Campsite is
signposted after Linxe on the road to Mixe.

CASTRES Tarn   5C

Camping Le Pessac 81570 Vielmur-sur-Agout.
Tel 05 63 74 30 24, Fax 05 63 74 30 24.
OPEN: all year. SIZE: 1 ha, 35 pitches (all with elec),
5 hot showers, 5 WCs. ℄ ♿

Shop at 0.2 km. Restaurant at 0.2 km.
PRICES: (1996) Caravan with family 93.00,
Tent with two adults 48.00. CC: none.
From Castres, drive 13 km west on the D112
towards St-Paul-Cap-de-Joux and then turn left to
Vielmur-sur-Agout.

CAUDEBEC-EN-CAUX Seine Marit   2A

Camping Municipal de Barre y Va route de
Villequier, 76490 Caudebec-en-Caux.
Tel 02 35 96 26 38.
OPEN: 01/04−30/09. SIZE: 1 ha, 61 pitches, 5 hot
showers, 7 WCs. ℄ ♿

Shop at 2 km. Restaurant at 2 km.
PRICES: (1996) Caravan with family 72.00,
Tent with two adults 39.50. CC: none.
Leave Caudebec-en-Caux and go straight ahead
to Villequier. Campsite is on the right-hand side.

CAUNES-MINERVOIS Aude   5C

Camping Vert du Clocher Les Barrys,
11160 Lespinassière.
Tel 04 68 78 03 72. English spoken.
OPEN: 01/04−30/09. SIZE: 1 ha, 4 hot showers, 4 WCs.

Shop at 0.5 km.

PRICES: Caravan with family 107.00, Tent with two
adults 57.00. CC: none.
From Caunes-Minervois go north on D620 until
you reach Lespinassière.

CAUTERETS Htes-Pyrénées   4D

Camping Le Cabaliros Pont de Secours,
65110 Cauterets.
Tel 05 62 92 55 36, Fax 05 62 92 55 36.
English spoken.
OPEN: 01/06−30/09. SIZE: 2 ha, 100 pitches
(60 with elec), 6 hot showers, 8 WCs, 1 CWP. ℄ ♿

Shop at 1.5 km. Library, TV.
PRICES: (1996) Caravan with family 92.00, Tent
with two adults 48.00. CC: Visa.
Only 1.5 km from Cauterets. Well signposted.

Le Mamelon Vert 32 av du Mamelon Vert,
65110 Cauterets.
Tel 05 62 92 51 56, Fax 05 62 92 51 56.
English spoken.
OPEN: 11/11−30/09. SIZE: 2 ha, 100 pitches
(65 with elec, 20 statics), 10 hot showers, 12 WCs,
1 CWP.

Shop at 0.3 km. Restaurant at 0.3 km.
PRICES: (1996) Caravan with family 103.00, Tent
with two adults 71.00. CC: Euro/Access, Visa.
Follow signs to campsite from centre of Cauterets.

CAVAILLON Vaucluse   5D

Camping Municipal de Maubec Les Royères du
Prieure, La Combe-St-Pierre, 84660 Maubec.
Tel 04 90 76 50 34.
OPEN: 01/04−30/09. SIZE: 1 ha, 75 pitches (all with
elec), 8 hot showers, 9 WCs, 4 French WCs, 2 CWPs. ℄

Shop at 0.1 km. Restaurant at 0.5 km.
PRICES: (1996) Caravan with family 60.50, Tent
with two adults 29.50. CC: none.
From Cavaillon take the road towards Apt. 100 m
after Robion turn right and then follow signs to La
Combe-St-Pierre and campsite.

CAVALAIRE-SUR-MER Var   6C

Camping Caravaning Cros de Mouton
83240 Cavalaire-sur-Mer.
Tel 04 94 64 10 87, Fax 04 94 05 46 38.
English spoken.
OPEN: 15/03−31/10. SIZE: 5 ha, 60 pitches (all with
elec, 38 statics), 20 hot showers, 22 WCs, 2 CWPs. ℄ ♿

PRICES: Caravan with family 160.00, Tent with two
adults 100.00. CC: Amex, Euro/Access, Visa.
Well signposted from the town.

Camping de la Baie bvd Pasteur,
83240 Cavalaire-sur-Mer.
Tel 04 94 64 08 15, Fax 04 94 64 66 10.
English spoken.
OPEN: 15/03–15/10. SIZE: 7 ha, 300 pitches
(all with elec, 60 statics). ☾ ᕤ

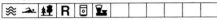

Shop at 0.2 km. Restaurant at 0.2 km. Sea: 0.4 km.
PRICES: (1996) Caravan with family 200.00, Tent
with two adults 140.00. CC: Euro/Access, Visa.
In town centre, well signposted.

Camping La Pinède chemin des Mannes,
83240 Cavalaire-sur-Mer.
Tel 04 94 64 11 14, Fax 04 94 64 19 25.
English spoken.
OPEN: 15/03–15/10. SIZE: 2 ha, 120 pitches (95 with
elec), 30 hot showers, 24 WCs, 2 CWPs. ☾ ᕤ

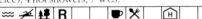

Restaurant at 0.5 km.
PRICES: (1996) Caravan with family 167.00, Tent
with two adults 100.00. CC: none.
*From the beach road through Cavalaire turn off
beside the Champion supermarket.*

CAVIGNAC Gironde 4B

Le Lac Vert Laruscade, 33620 Cavignac.
Tel 05 57 68 64 43. English spoken.
OPEN: 01/05–30/09. SIZE: 1.5 ha, 20 pitches (8 with
elec), 4 hot showers, 7 WCs.

Shop at 2 km. Mini-golf; fishing; forest nearby.
PRICES: (1996) Caravan with family 73.00, Tent
with two adults 36.00. CC: Euro/Access, Visa.
*From Cavignac, follow signs to the campsite in
Laruscade.*

CAZERES Haute-Garonne 4D

Le Moulin 31220 Martres-Tolosane.
Tel 05 61 98 86 40, Fax 05 61 98 66 90.
English spoken.
OPEN: 15/03–15/10. SIZE: 16 ha, 50 pitches (all with
elec, 12 statics), 5 hot showers, 8 WCs, 1 CWP. ☾

Shop at 1.5 km. Tennis, pétanque, entertainment.
PRICES: (1996) Caravan with family 115.00,
Tent with two adults 68.00. CC: none.
*Martres-Tolosane is 6 km west of Cazères.
Follow the signs in the village centre.*

CEAUCE Orne 2C

Camp Municipal Les Chauvières Le Bourg,
61350 St-Fraimbault.
Tel 02 33 38 32 22, Fax 02 33 38 02 47.
OPEN: 21/03–31/10. SIZE: 33 pitches (22 with elec),
8 hot showers, 9 WCs.

Shop at 0.2 km.
PRICES: (1996) Caravan with family 50.00,
Tent with two adults 21.00. CC: none.
*On the D24 between Ceaucé and Passais. [Village
well known for its flowers and the Fleuri 4 Fleurs
award.]*

CERNAY Haut-Rhin 3D

Camping Les Sources routes des Crêtes,
68700 Wattwiller.
Tel 03 89 75 44 94, Fax 03 89 75 71 98.
English spoken.
OPEN: 01/04–15/10. SIZE: 8 ha, 240 pitches
(265 with elec, 50 statics), 36 hot showers,
38 WCs, 3 CWPs. ☾ ᕤ

Mobile homes for hire.
PRICES: (1996) Caravan with family 163.00,
Tent with two adults 95.00. CC: Amex,
Euro/Access, Visa.
2.5 km north of Cernay.

CEZY Yonne 2D

Camping Municipal 6 rue de la Contemine,
89410 Cézy-St-Aubin.
Tel 03 86 63 17 87, Fax 03 86 63 02 84.
OPEN: 01/05–30/09. SIZE: 1 ha, 70 pitches (55 with
elec), 4 hot showers (charge), 8 WCs, 1 CWP. ☾ ᕤ

Shop at 0.5 km. Restaurant at 0.5 km. Fishing.
PRICES: Caravan with family 48.00, Tent with two
adults 25.00. CC: none.
*Cézy is 1 km from the N6 between Sens and
Joigny.*

CHABEUIL Drôme 5B

Camping Le Grand Lierne 26120 Chabeuil.
Tel 04 75 59 83 14, Fax 04 75 59 87 95.
English spoken.
OPEN: 05/04–25/09. SIZE: 4 ha, 110 pitches
(all with elec, 15 statics), 18 hot showers, 13 WCs,
3 CWPs. ☾ ᕤ

Indoor/outdoor pools; flume, trampoline;
mini-club, entertainment.
PRICES: (1996) Caravan with family 192.00, Tent
with two adults 132.00. CC: Euro/Access, Visa.
*Take Valence-Sud exit from A7 to Chabeuil and
follow signs to campsite from the town.*

CHAGNY Saône-et-Loire 3C

Camp Municipal des Sources av des Sources,
21590 Santenay-les-Bains.
Tel 03 80 20 66 55, Fax 03 80 21 65 74. English spoken.

France (sidebar)

OPEN: 01/04–31/10. SIZE: 2.3 ha, 130 pitches, 16 hot showers, 15 WCs, 2 CWPs. ⚓ ♿

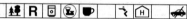

Mini-golf, ball games, boules, table tennis, playground, skittles.
PRICES: (1996) Caravan with family 139.50, Tent with two adults 78.00. CC: Amex, Euro/Access, Visa.
Santenay is about 4 km due east of Chagny on the D974.

CHALLANS Vendée   1D

Camping du Bois Joli 85710 Bois-de-Cene.
Tel 02 51 68 20 05, Fax 02 51 68 46 40.
English spoken.
OPEN: 01/04–15/09. SIZE: 3 ha, 49 pitches (63 with elec, 23 statics), 11 hot showers, 10 WCs, 1 CWP. ⚓ ♿

Shop at 0.2 km. Restaurant at 6 km. Tennis; fishing lake nearby.
PRICES: (1996) Caravan with family 122.00, Tent with two adults 68.00. CC: none.
From Challans take D58 (north of the town) for 9 km. The campsite is situated on entering Bois-de-Cene and well signposted.

CHALONS-EN-CHAMPAGNE Marne 3A

Camping Municipal rue de Plaisance, 51000 Châlons-en-Champagne.
Tel 03 26 68 38 00.
OPEN: 01/03–30/11. SIZE: 7 ha, 81 pitches (all with elec), 20 hot showers, 16 WCs. ⚓ ♿

Shop at 0.3 km. Restaurant at 3 km.
PRICES: (1996) Caravan with family 144.00, Tent with two adults 81.00. CC: none.
Châlons is south of Reims, just off the motorway. Take Châlons-Centre exit.

CHAMBERY Savoie   5B

Camping Les Charmilles Lac d'Aiguebelette, 73470 Novalaise-Lac.
Tel 04 79 36 04 67, Fax 04 79 36 04 67.
English spoken.
OPEN: 25/06–15/09. SIZE: 2.3 ha, 100 pitches (83 with elec), 12 hot showers, 15 WCs, 1 CWP. ⚓ ♿

Shop at 3 km. Restaurant at 0.3 km. Mini-golf, cycle hire, private jetty; boating, mountain walking, playground.
PRICES: (1996) Caravan with family 130.00, Tent with two adults 94.00. CC: none.
From Chambéry on A43 through the tunnel then take Lac d'Aiguebelette exit. 1 km on D921 towards St-Alban-de-Montbel.

LA CHAMBRE Savoie   6A

Le Bois Joli St-Martin-sur-la Chambre, 73130 La Chambre.
Tel 04 79 56 21 28, Fax 04 79 56 21 28.
English spoken.
OPEN: 01/04–30/09. SIZE: 4 ha, 88 pitches (all with elec, 9 statics), 14 hot showers, 14 WCs, 2 CWPs. ⚓ ♿

Shop at 2 km. Quiet site in picturesque surroundings.
PRICES: (1996) Caravan with family 120.00, Tent with two adults 65.00. CC: none.
In La Chambre turn north at crossroads and campsite is 2 km on D213.

CHAMONIX-MONT-BLANC   6A

Camping du Bourgeat 74310 Les Houches.
Tel 04 50 54 42 14.
OPEN: 15/06–15/09. SIZE: 1 ha, 35 pitches (all with elec), 8 hot showers, 8 WCs, 1 CWP. ⚓

Shop at 0.1 km. Restaurant at 0.4 km.
PRICES: Caravan with family 133.00, Tent with two adults 98.00. CC: none.
West of Chamonix on N506, turn left to Les Houches, then 300 m further to the site.

Camping du Glacier Argentière Les Chosalets, Argentière, 74400 Chamonix-Mont-Blanc.
Tel 04 50 54 17 36, Fax 04 50 54 03 73.
English spoken.
OPEN: 01/06–30/09. SIZE: 1 ha, 80 pitches (72 with elec), 7 hot showers, 9 WCs, 1 CWP. ♿

Shop at 0.5 km. Restaurant at 0.5 km. Breakfast available.
PRICES: (1996) Caravan with family 120.00, Tent with two adults 61.00. CC: none.
Take 506 towards Argentière and 1 km before reaching it turn right to campsite at Les Chosalets, which is well signposted.

Camping Iles des Barrats 185 ch de l'Ile des Barrats, 74400 Chamonix-Mont-Blanc.
Tel 04 50 53 51 44. English spoken.
OPEN: 01/05–30/09. SIZE: 1 ha, 50 pitches (all with elec), 6 hot showers, 6 WCs, 1 CWP. ♿

Shop at 0.6 km. Restaurant at 0.3 km.
PRICES: (1996) Caravan with family 146.00, Tent with two adults 86.00. CC: none.

Camping Les Drus Les Bois, 74400 Chamonix-Mont-Blanc.
Tel 04 50 53 49 20. English spoken.
OPEN: 15/03–15/10. SIZE: 70 pitches (all with elec), 5 hot showers, 8 WCs, 1 CWP. ⚓

France

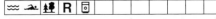

PRICES: (1996) Caravan with family 106.00, Tent with two adults 54.00. CC: none. *3 km from Chamonix-Mont-Blanc towards Argentière.*

La Mer de Glace chemin de la Bagna, 74400 Chamonix-Mont-Blanc.
Tel 04 50 53 44 03, Fax 04 50 53 60 83.
English spoken.
OPEN: 26/04–30/09. SIZE: 2 ha, 150 pitches (78 with elec), 17 hot showers, 14 WCs, 1 CWP. ✆ ♿

Shop at 0.6 km. Restaurant at 0.7 km. Golf, tennis, horse-riding 1 km.
PRICES: (1996) Caravan with family 169.00, Tent with two adults 95.00. CC: none.
Leave Chamonix-Mont-Blanc towards Argentière and Swiss border. The entrance to campsite is 1.5 km through the forest on the right.

Les Rosières 121 Clos des Rosières, 74400 Chamonix.
Tel 04 50 53 10 42, Fax 04 50 53 29 55.
English spoken.
OPEN: 15/12–12/10. SIZE: 2 ha, 60 pitches (all with elec), 17 hot showers, 19 WCs, 1 CWP. ✆ ♿

Restaurant at 0.8 km.
PRICES: (1996) Caravan with family 126.00, Tent with two adults 65.00. CC: none.
From Chamonix-Mont-Blanc go north. At roundabout follow signs to Mont-Blanc car park and town centre then turn right at crossroads towards Les Praz. Campsite is 1.2 km ahead.

CHAMPDOR Ain   5B

Le Vieux Moulin 01110 Champdor.
Tel 04 74 36 01 72. English spoken.
OPEN: all year. SIZE: 2 ha, 60 pitches (20 with elec, 5 statics), 10 hot showers, 10 WCs. ♿

Shop at 0.2 km. Restaurant at 0.2 km.
PRICES: Caravan with family 70.00, Tent with two adults 41.00. CC: none.
Take D21 north to Hauteville-Lompnes. On south-east side of village of Champdor, follow signs.

CHANTILLY Oise   2B

Camping Caravaning Campix
St-Leu-d'Esserent, 60340 St-Leu.
Tel 03 44 56 08 48, Fax 03 44 56 28 75. English spoken.
OPEN: 15/03–30/11. SIZE: 6 ha, 150 pitches (all with elec), 22 hot showers, 22 WCs, 1 CWP. ✆ ♿

Shop at 1 km. Restaurant at 1 km. Swimming pool 0.5 km, climbing wall.

PRICES: (1996) Caravan with family 125.00, Tent with two adults 75.00. CC: Euro/Access, Visa.
From Chantilly north-west on D44 to St-Leu-d'Esserent. 5 km from Chantilly, 20 km from Parc Asterix. Signposted from centre of St-Leu village.

CHAROLLES Saône/Loire   5B

Camping Municipal route de Viry, 71120 Charolles.
Tel 03 85 24 04 90.
OPEN: 15/03–15/10. SIZE: 1 ha, 45 pitches (all with elec), 5 hot showers, 10 WCs. ✆

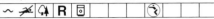

Shop at 1 km. Restaurant at 1 km.
PRICES: (1996) Caravan with family 66.00, Tent with two adults 39.00. CC: none.
From centre of Charolles, follow signs.

LA CHARTRE-SUR-LE-LOIR Sarthe   2C

Camping Municipal Le Vieux Moulin
72340 La-Chartre-sur-le-Loir.
Tel 02 43 44 41 18/0, Fax 02 43 44 27 40.
OPEN: 14/04–31/10. SIZE: 1.5 ha, 140 pitches (all with elec), 13 hot showers, 13 WCs, 1 CWP. ♿

Shop at 0.5 km. Restaurant at 0.5 km.
Children's playground.
PRICES: (1996) Tent with two adults 48.00. CC: none.
La-Chartre-sur-le-Loir is to the east of Château-du-Loir and site is well signposted in the village.

CHARTRES Eure-et-Loir   2D

Camp Municipal des Bords de L'Eure
rue de Launay, 28000 Chartres.
Tel 02 37 28 79 43, Fax 02 37 23 41 99.
English spoken.
OPEN: 22/04–02/09. SIZE: 3 ha, 96 pitches (48 with elec), 10 hot showers, 10 WCs, 1 CWP. ✆ ♿

Shop at 0.5 km. Restaurant at 1.5 km.
PRICES: (1996) Caravan with family 70.00, Tent with two adults 47.00. CC: none.
South of Chartres centre look for 3 Points Supermarché and follow signs to campsite from there.

CHATEAU-CHINON Nièvre   3C

Manoir de Bezolle St-Péreuse-en-Morvan, 58110 St-Péreuse.
Tel 03 86 84 42 55, Fax 03 86 84 43 77.
English spoken.
OPEN: 15/03–15/10. SIZE: 8 ha, 100 pitches (all with elec), 20 hot showers, 22 WCs, 3 CWPs. ✆ ♿

Horse-riding.

France

PRICES: (1996) Caravan with family 178.00, Tent with two adults 102.00. CC: Euro/Access, Visa. *From Château-Chinon go west on D978 for 10 km and then follow signs.*

CHATEAUBRIANT Loire-Atlan 1D

Camping Municipal L'Hermitage
36 av du Paradis, 44290 Guéméné-Penfao.
Tel 02 40 79 23 48, Fax 02 40 51 11 87.
English spoken.
OPEN: 01/04–30/10. SIZE: 2.5 ha, 110 pitches (100 with elec), 11 hot showers, 7 WCs, 16 French WCs, 1 CWP. ✆ ₥

	⚑	R	◙	☏			⸙	₥		🚙

Shop at 1.2 km. Restaurant at 1.2 km.
PRICES: (1996) Caravan with family 87.00, Tent with two adults 46.00. CC: Amex, Visa.
From Châteaubriant, go west on D775 to Guéméné-Penfao via Derval. Campsite is signposted.

CHATEAUDUN Eure-et-Loir 2D

Parc de Loisirs route de Montigny, 28220 Cloyes-sur-le-Loir.
Tel 02 37 98 50 53, Fax 02 37 98 33 84.
English spoken.
OPEN: 15/05–15/11. SIZE: 6 ha, 200 pitches (all with elec, 100 statics), 18 hot showers, 20 WCs, 1 CWP. ✆ ₥

~	⚓	⚒	R	◙	₤		✕	⸙	₥

Large playground, water sports, fishing.
PRICES: (1996) Caravan with family 130.00, Tent with two adults 80.00. CC: Visa.
On the N10, between Châteaudun and Vendôme.

CHATEAULIN Finistère 1C

Camping de l'Iroise Plage de Pors-ar-Vag, 29550 Plomodiern.
Tel 02 98 81 52 72, Fax 02 98 81 26 10.
English spoken.
OPEN: 01/04–30/09. SIZE: 3 ha, 119 pitches (all with elec, 16 statics), 14 hot showers, 14 WCs, 2 CWPs. ✆ ₥

≋	⚓	⚒	R	◙	₤	☕	✕	⸙	₥

Flume, mini-golf, tennis, playgroung, play room.
PRICES: (1996) Caravan with family 129.00, Tent with two adults 83.00. CC: Amex, Euro/Access, Visa.
From Plomodiern take road to Pors-ar-Vag beach.

Camping Ker-Ys Pentrez-Plage, 29550 St-Nic.
Tel 02 98 26 53 95. English spoken.
OPEN: 01/05–15/09. SIZE: 2 ha, 190 pitches (all with elec, 14 statics), 19 hot showers, 33 WCs, 1 CWP. ✆ ₥

≋	⚓	⚒	R	◙	₤			₥

Restaurant at 0.2 km. Tennis, volleyball, basketball, badminton.

PRICES: (1996) Caravan with family 106.50, Tent with two adults 60.00. CC: Visa.
D887 west of Châteaulin.

CHATEAUROUX Indre 2D

Camping Les Grands Pins
route de Les Maisons Neuves, 36330 Velles.
Tel 02 54 36 61 93, Fax 02 47 92 48 84.
English spoken.
OPEN: all year. SIZE: 5 ha, 50 pitches (all with elec, 10 statics), 5 hot showers, 8 WCs, 5 CWPs. ✆ ₥

	⚑	R	◙			✕	⸙	₥

Shop at 7 km.
PRICES: (1996) Caravan with family 107.00, Tent with two adults 56.00. CC: none.
7 km south of Châteauroux, on the N20 towards Les Maisons Neuves. (Check with site if wanting space for camper.)

CHATELAILLON-PLAGE Char-Marit 4A

Clos des Rivages 17340 Châtelaillon-Plage.
Tel 05 46 56 26 09. English spoken.
OPEN: 15/06–10/09. SIZE: 2.5 ha, 150 pitches (all with elec), 19 hot showers, 27 WCs, 4 CWPs. ✆

≋		⚒	R	◙	₤				

Restaurant at 0.5 km.
PRICES: (1996) Caravan with family 138.00, Tent with two adults 88.00. CC: none.
800 m from the centre of Châtelaillon-Plage.

LE CHATELARD Savoie 6A

Les Cyclamens 73630 Le Châtelard.
Tel 04 79 54 80 19.
OPEN: 15/05–15/09. SIZE: 1 ha, 33 pitches (all with elec), 5 hot showers, 5 WCs, 1 CWP.

	⚑	R	◙				₥

Shop at 0.5 km. Restaurant at 0.5 km. Table tennis, boules, barbecues.
PRICES: Caravan with family 84.00, Tent with two adults 53.00. CC: none.
From Aix-les-Bains take the D911 east to Le Châtelard. Site near the town centre, about 1 km from river.

CHATELLERAULT Vienne 2C

Camping Bec des Deux Eaux Port-de-Piles, 86220 Dange-St-Romain.
Tel 02 47 65 02 71. English spoken.
OPEN: 01/03–15/11. SIZE: 3.5 ha, 90 pitches (60 with elec, 20 statics), 10 hot showers, 8 WCs, 4 French WCs, 1 CWP. ✆ ₥

≋	⚓	⚒	R	◙	₤	☕		⸙	₥

Restaurant at 1 km. Library, entertainment, volley ball, boules, table tennis.
PRICES: (1996) Caravan with family 108.00,

Tent with two adults 65.00. CC: none.
Dange-St-Romain is north-east of Châtellerault towards Tours. Campsite at Port-de-Piles is well signposted.

Camping Le Petit Trianon
86220 Ingrandes-sur-Vienne.
Tel 05 49 02 61 47, Fax 05 49 02 68 81.
English spoken.
OPEN: 15/05–30/09. SIZE: 7 ha, 95 pitches (75 with elec), 19 hot showers, 14 WCs, 3 CWPs. ☎ ♿

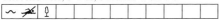

Restaurant at 0.1 km.
PRICES: (1996) Caravan with family 167.00, Tent with two adults 110.00. CC: Euro/Access, Visa.
North of Châtellerault on the N10, 4 km to Ingrandes. Turn right over rail bridge, then first left to St-Ustre. Site signed to the right.

Camping Municipal Chillou-d'Auzon
86100 Châtellerault.
Tel 05 49 21 94 02.
OPEN: 01/05–30/09. SIZE: 63 pitches (all with elec), 4 hot showers, 6 WCs, 6 French WCs. ☎ ♿

Shop at 1 km. Restaurant at 1 km. 20 minutes' drive from the Futuroscope.
PRICES: (1996) Caravan with family 63.00, Tent with two adults 34.00. CC: none.
From Châtellerault, go south on the N749 towards Chauvigny.

Parc de Loisirs de St-Cyr 86130 St-Cyr.
Tel 05 49 62 57 22, Fax 05 49 60 28 58.
English spoken.
OPEN: 01/04–30/09. SIZE: 2 ha, 198 pitches (all with elec, 5 statics), 15 hot showers, 15 WCs, 2 CWPs. ☎ ♿

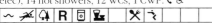

Tennis, archery, beach club.
PRICES: (1996) Caravan with family 160.00, Tent with two adults 110.00. CC: Euro/Access, Visa.
About 15 km from Châtellerault on N10. About 20 km from Poitiers on N10.

Le Relais du Miel route d'Antran,
86100 Châtellerault.
Tel 05 49 02 06 27, Fax 05 49 93 25 76.
English spoken.
OPEN: 01/05–30/09. SIZE: 4 ha, 80 pitches (all with elec), 14 hot showers, 12 WCs, 1 CWP. ☎ ♿

Fishing, boules, walking, playground.
PRICES: (1996) Caravan with family 170.00, Tent with two adults 130.00. CC: Euro/Access, Visa.
From the A10 motorway, take exit No 26 (Châtellerault-Nord) ; coming from N10, north of Châtellerault, drive towards the motorway A10 entrance (péage).
SEE ADVERTISEMENT

CHATILLON-EN-BAZOIS Nièvre   3C

Camping Municipal place Pierre Saury,
58110 Châtillon-en-Bazois.
Tel 03 86 84 14 76, Fax 03 86 84 11 43.
OPEN: 01/04–31/10. SIZE: 1 ha, 30 pitches (all with elec, 30 statics), 2 hot showers (charge), 3 WCs, 3 French WCs, 1 CWP. ♿

Shop at 0.1 km. Restaurant at 0.2 km. Tennis.
PRICES: (1996) Caravan with family 49.00, Tent with two adults 21.00. CC: none.
On outskirts of town.

CHATILLON-SUR-SEINE Côte-d'Or   3C

Camping Municipal
esplanade St-Vorles, 21400 Châtillon.
Tel 03 80 91 03 05. English spoken.
OPEN: 01/04–15/10. SIZE: 1 ha, 66 pitches (48 with elec), 8 hot showers, 7 WCs, 2 French WCs, 1 CWP. ☎ ♿

Shop at 0.7 km. Restaurant at 0.2 km.
PRICES: (1996) Caravan with family 84.00, Tent with two adults 45.00. CC: none.
North on N71 (from Paris/Troyes) into Châtillon-sur-Seine and the place Marmont roundabout.

France

Le Relais du Miel
★★★★

☆ Easy to reach (halfway between Paris and Bordeaux just off the A10, exit 26)

☆ Close to Futuroscope (14 minutes)

☆ Heated pool

☆ Beside the River Vienne

☆ In a park

~ A honey of a place ~

**Le Relais du Miel
route d'Antran
86100 Châtellerault**

See under Châtellerault

Left into rue de Seine, cross bridge into chemin Fontaine des Ducs, then right into esplanade St-Vorles. Site is on left.

LA CHATRE Indre   2D

Camping Château Solange-Sand
Montgivray, 36400 La Châtre.
Tel 02 54 48 37 83.
OPEN: 15/03–15/11. SIZE: 1 ha, 72 pitches (46 with elec), 6 hot showers, 10 WCs, 2 CWPs. &

PRICES: (1996) Caravan with family 64.35,
Tent with two adults 35.20. CC: none.
North of La Châtre off D943.

CHAUDES-AIGUES Cantal   5A

Camping Municipal Le Couffour
15110 Chaudes-Aigues.
Tel 04 71 23 57 08.
OPEN: 01/05–20/10. SIZE: 3 ha, 144 pitches (all with elec), 12 hot showers, 24 WCs, 2 CWPs. & &

Shop at 2 km. Restaurant at 2 km. Tennis, ball sports, boules, TV.
PRICES: (1996) Caravan with family 56.00,
Tent with two adults 32.00. CC: none.
The site is 2 km south of village on D921, going towards Rodez.

CHENONCEAUX Indre/Loire   2C

Le Moulin Fort 37150 Francueil.
Tel 02 47 23 86 22, Fax 02 47 23 80 93.
English spoken.
OPEN: 01/05–15/09. SIZE: 3 ha, 130 pitches (80 with elec), 16 hot showers, 16 WCs, 2 CWPs. & &

Mini-golf; canoe hire.
PRICES: (1996) Caravan with family 153.00,
Tent with two adults 88.00. CC: none.
From Chenonceaux follow signs to Chisseaux. Turn left after the bridge and follow signs to Francueil.

CHERBOURG Manche   1B

Camp L'Anse du Brick
Maupertus-sur-Mer, 50840 Fermanville.
Tel 02 33 54 33 57, Fax 02 33 54 49 66.
English spoken.
OPEN: 15/04–15/09. SIZE: 7 ha, 180 pitches (110 with elec, 60 statics), 13 hot showers, 13 WCs, 2 CWPs. & &

Flume, tennis.
PRICES: Caravan with family 144.00, Tent with two adults 88.00. CC: Euro/Access, Visa.

10 km east of Cherbourg along the coast on the D116. Site is well signposted.

Les Pins 50470 Tollevast.
Tel 02 33 43 00 78.
English spoken.
OPEN: all year. SIZE: 6 ha, 200 pitches (all with elec), 12 hot showers, 16 WCs, 3 CWPs. & &

Restaurant at 0.2 km. Forest walks and shopping mall nearby. Mobile homes available.
PRICES: (1997) Caravan with family 66.00,
Tent with two adults 50.00. CC: none.
From Cherbourg take N13 south. After 5 km, near the Auchan hypermarket, get into left-hand lane and then follow signs to campsite.

Les Pins

near Cherbourg (N13)

Handy for the ferry – open 24 hrs

CHOISY-LE-ROI Val-de-Marne   2D

Camping Paris Sud
125 Av de Villeneuve-St-George, (D38),
94600 Choisy-le-Roi.
Tel 01 48 90 92 30, Fax 01 48 84 27 30.
English spoken.
OPEN: all year. SIZE: 10 ha, 335 pitches (75 with elec), 3 CWPs. & &

Bar, disco.
PRICES: (1996) Caravan with family 170.00,
Tent with two adults 78.00. CC: Visa.
Take motorways A6/A86 to Choisy-le-Roi which is 10km south of Paris. Campsite is on the D38.

CHORGES Hautes-Alpes   6C

Camping La Viste
Serre-Ponçon, 05190 Rousset.
Tel 04 92 54 43 39, Fax 04 92 54 42 45.
OPEN: 15/05–30/09. SIZE: 5 ha, 200 pitches (80 with elec), 20 hot showers, 15 WCs, 1 CWP. & &

Water sports, hiking, white-water rafting nearby.
PRICES: (1996) Caravan with family 144.00,
Tent with two adults 84.00. CC: Amex, Euro/Access, Visa.
From Chorges on N94 or Espinasses on D900b, follow D3 towards Le Barrage-de-Serre-Ponçon and campsite is well signposted. Overlooks the largest man-made lake in Europe.

LA CIOTAT Bouches-du-Rhône 5D

Camping Santa Gusta Fontsainte,
13600 La Ciotat.
Tel 04 42 83 14 17, Fax 04 42 08 90 93.
English spoken.
OPEN: all year. SIZE: 2 ha, 186 pitches (167 with
elec, 100 statics), 20 hot showers, 18 WCs,
2 French WCs, 1 CWP. ⚓ ⛟

Shop at 0.2 km.
PRICES: (1996) Caravan with family 126.00,
Tent with two adults 87.00. CC: none.
*From the A50, exit at La Ciotat and go towards
Toulon. After crossing six roundabouts and going
under a bridge, the campsite is 200 m past the
traffic lights on the right.*

Camping St-Jean
30 avenue de St-Jean, St-Jean, 13600 La Ciotat.
Tel 04 42 83 13 01, Fax 04 42 71 46 41.
English spoken.
OPEN: 30/03–01/10. SIZE: 0.9 ha, 70 pitches
(all with elec), 15 hot showers, 12 WCs, 1 CWP. ⛟

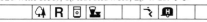

Studios available.
PRICES: (1996) Caravan with family 166.00,
Tent with two adults 120.00. CC: Amex,
Euro/Access, Visa.

CLAIRVAUX-LES-LACS Jura 5B

Camping Beauregard 39130 Mesnois.
Tel 03 84 48 32 51. English spoken.
OPEN: 15/04–30/08. SIZE: 2.5 ha, 140 pitches
(120 with elec), 13 hot showers, 23 WCs. ⚓ ⛟

Restaurant at 1 km. Mobile homes available.
PRICES: Caravan with family 128.00, Tent with two
adults 72.00. CC: none.
On N78 follow signs to Mesnois.

Camping La Pergola 39130 Marigny.
Tel 03 84 25 70 03, Fax 03 84 25 75 96. English spoken.
OPEN: 01/05–30/09. SIZE: 10 ha, 350 pitches
(all with elec), 57 hot showers, 3 CWPs. ⚓ ⛟

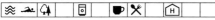

Entertainment.
PRICES: (1996) Caravan with family 257.00, Tent
with two adults 207.50. CC: Euro/Access, Visa.
*A short distance north-west of Clairvaux-les-Lacs,
take the road going north-east to Doucier and
then follow signs to the right to Lac de Chalain
and campsite.*

La Pergola Marigny, 39120 Clairvaux-les-Lacs.
Tel 03 84 25 70 03, Fax 03 84 25 75 96.
English spoken.
OPEN: 01/05–30/09. SIZE: 10 ha, 150 pitches
(all with elec, 40 statics). ⛟

PRICES: (1996) Caravan with family 160.00, Tent
with two adults 80.00. CC: Euro/Access, Visa.
*17 km north of Clairvaux-les-Lacs on the D27.
Campsite is beside the lake.*

Le Val d'Eté 39130 Etival.
Tel 03 84 44 87 31. English spoken.
OPEN: all year. SIZE: 1 ha, 42 pitches (20 with elec,
4 statics), 4 hot showers, 4 WCs, 4 French WCs,
4 CWPs.

Shop at 8 km. Restaurant at 5 km. Guided walks,
playground; lake 1 km.
PRICES: (1996) Caravan with family 70.00,
Tent with two adults 36.00. CC: none.
*From Clairvaux-les-Lacs take D118 through Châtel-
de-Joux and on to Etival. Signposted from Clairvaux.*

CLAMECY Nièvre 2D

Camping Municipal Les Fontaines
Brèves, 58530 Dornecy.
Tel 03 86 24 25 26. English spoken.
OPEN: 15/06–15/09. SIZE: 1.8 ha, 66 pitches
(32 with elec), 4 hot showers, 8 WCs. ⛟

Shop at 2 km. Restaurant at 2 km.
PRICES: (1996) Caravan with family 70.00,
Tent with two adults 41.50. CC: none.
*South-east of Clamecy, via Dornecy on D985.
Signposted.*

Terrain de Camping du Pont-Picot
58500 Clamecy.
Tel 03 86 27 05 97.
OPEN: 01/05–30/09. SIZE: 1.20 ha, 50 pitches
(all with elec), 8 hot showers, 11 WCs.

Shop at 1 km. Restaurant at 1 km.
PRICES: (1996) Caravan with family 78.00,
Tent with two adults 48.00. CC: none.
*Clamecy is due south of Auxerre. From bd Misset
in Clamecy turn left after the hospital, left again,
straight over junction and then first left.*

CLELLES Isère 5B

Camping Municipal La Chabannerie
38930 St-Martin-de-Clelles.
Tel 04 76 34 00 38, Fax 04 76 34 00 38. English spoken.
OPEN: all year. SIZE: 2.5 ha, 30 pitches (all with
elec), 4 hot showers, 5 WCs, 1 CWP. ⚓

Shop at 5 km. Volley ball, table tennis.
PRICES: (1996) Caravan with family 118.00,
Tent with two adults 56.00. CC: none.
*From Clelles take N75 towards Grenoble then
D262 to St-Martin-de-Clelles. Signposted.*

France

CLERMONT-FERRAND Puy-de-D   5A

Camping de l'Etang de Fléchat
Fléchat, 63210 Orcival.
Tel 04 73 65 82 96. English spoken.
OPEN: 15/05–15/09. SIZE: 3 ha, 83 pitches (42 with
elec, 10 statics), 12 hot showers, 9 WCs, 3 French
WCs, 2 CWPs.

≈	♨	🛱	R	◨			✕		Ⓗ		

Shop at 3 km.
PRICES: (1996) Caravan with family 129.00,
Tent with two adults 72.00. CC: none.
The site is located just outside Rochefort-
Montagne (between Rochefort and Orcival).

Camping des Dômes 63210 Nebouzat.
Tel 04 73 87 14 06, Fax 04 73 87 18 81.
English spoken.
OPEN: 15/05–15/09. SIZE: 1 ha, 65 pitches (all with
elec), 9 hot showers, 9 WCs, 1 CWP. ⚓

		🛱	R	◨	🝙	⬤	✕	⋏	Ⓗ	

Covered pool; river 100 m.
PRICES: (1996) Caravan with family 143.50,
Tent with two adults 69.50. CC: none.
From Clermont-Ferrand go south on N89 through
Ceyrat, swing west towards Ussel. At the 4 routes
crossroads at Nebouzat turn left on D216 towards
Orcival, site 100 m. Avoid the twisty D914a.

CLUNY Saône/Loire   5B

Camp Municipal St Vital
rue des Griottons, 71250 Cluny.
Tel 03 85 59 08 39. English spoken.
OPEN: 08/05–30/09. SIZE: 174 pitches (all with
elec), 20 hot showers, 12 WCs, 7 French WCs,
2 CWPs. ⚓ ⅍

		🛱	R	◨	⬤					

Shop at 1 km. Restaurant at 0.8 km. Swimming
pool next door.
PRICES: (1996) Caravan with family 92.00,
Tent with two adults 47.00. CC: none.
Cluny is north-west of Maçon on the N79/D980.

CLUSES Haute-Savoie   6A

Le Relais des Stations
138 rue des Grottes de Balme, 74300 Magland.
Tel 04 50 34 71 80.
OPEN: 01/07–15/09. SIZE: 1 ha, 50 pitches (all with
elec, 3 statics), 6 hot showers, 6 WCs, 4 French
WCs, 1 CWP. ⅍

		🛱								

Shop at 3 km. Restaurant at 0.2 km.
PRICES: (1996) Caravan with family 109.50,
Tent with two adults 69.00. CC: none.
A40, exit Cluses Centre, south on N205 towards
Magland. Campsite is 200 m from crossroads on
Araches-les-Carroz to Flaine road.

COGNAC Charente   4B

Camping de Cognac bd de Chatenay,
route de Ste-Sévère, 16100 Cognac.
Tel 05 45 32 13 32, Fax 05 45 36 55 29.
English spoken.
OPEN: 01/05–15/10. SIZE: 2 ha, 160 pitches
(all with elec), 20 hot showers, 20 WCs. ⚓ ⅍

～	✖	🛱	R	◨	🝙	⬤		⋏		

Restaurant at 0.1 km. Bike hire, boules, volley ball.
Boat trips, horse-riding and tennis nearby.
PRICES: (1996) Caravan with family 90.00,
Tent with two adults 70.00. CC: none.
Site is beside the river near the town centre.
Well signposted.

Camping de Cognac
at Cognac
Drink in the Charente as well!

LA COLLE-SUR-LOUP Alpes-Marit   6C

Camping Les Pinèdes route de Pont-de-Pierre,
06480 La Colle-sur-Loup.
Tel 04 93 32 98 94, Fax 04 93 32 50 20.
English spoken.
OPEN: 01/03–01/11. SIZE: 3.8 ha, 150 pitches
(120 with elec), 18 hot showers, 20 WCs, 3 CWPs. ⚓

～	♨	🛱	R	◨	🝙			✕	⋏	Ⓗ

Fishing, archery, library. Camper van service.
PRICES: Caravan with family 165.00, Tent with two
adults 84.00. CC: Amex, Euro/Access, Visa.
From motorway exit Cagnes-sur-Mer take the D6
towards La Colle-sur-Loup. The campsite is 50 m
from Le Loup river.

COLMAR Haut-Rhin   3D

Camping Municipal de l'Ile
68180 Horbourg-Wihr.
Tel 03 89 41 15 94. English spoken.
OPEN: 01/02–30/11. SIZE: 2 ha, 200 pitches (150 with
elec), 22 hot showers, 24 WCs, 4 CWPs. ⅍

～	♨	🛱			◨	🝙	⬤	✕		

PRICES: (1996) Caravan with family 85.50,
Tent with two adults 44.00. CC: none.
From Colmar on N415 follow signs to Horbourg
and Wihr.

Camping Municipal des Trois Châteaux 10
rue du Bassin, 68420 Eguisheim.
Tel 03 89 23 19 39, Fax 03 89 23 19 39.
English spoken.
OPEN: 01/04–30/09. SIZE: 2 ha, 108 pitches (all
with elec), 14 hot showers, 12 WCs, 1 CWP. ⚓ ⅍

France

Shop at 0.2 km. Restaurant at 0.1 km.
PRICES: (1996) Caravan with family 95.00,
Tent with two adults 48.00. CC: none.
*South from Colmar on N83. Turn right to
Eguisheim after 5 km. Drive right through village
to the site.*

Camping Municipal les Cigognes
quai de la Gare, 68230 Turckheim.
Tel 03 89 27 02 00.
OPEN: 10/03–31/10. SIZE: 2 ha, 150 pitches, 19 hot
showers, 23 WCs, 1 CWP. ⓛ ⓖ

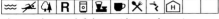

Shop at 1 km. Restaurant at 1 km.
PRICES: (1996) Caravan with family 111.00,
Tent with two adults 57.50. CC: Amex,
Euro/Access, Visa.
*Campsite is 300 m from railway station. Well
signposted. Turckheim is north-west of Colmar.*

COMBEAUFONTAINE Haute-Saône   3C

Camping du Lac 70120 Preigney.
Tel 03 84 68 54 68, Fax 03 84 68 55 59.
OPEN: 01/05–15/09. SIZE: 1 ha, 50 pitches (40 with
elec, 7 statics), 3 hot showers, 4 WCs, 2 CWPs. ⓛ ⓖ

Shop at 1.5 km. Fishing.
PRICES: Caravan with family 70.00,
Tent with two adults 41.00. CC: none.
*Just north of the N19 halfway between Fayl-la-
Forêt and Combeaufontaine.*

COMBOURG Ille/Vilaine   1D

Camping Le Bois Coudrais
Cuguen, 35270 Combourg.
Tel 02 99 73 27 45, Fax 02 99 73 27 45.
English spoken.
OPEN: 01/04–30/09. SIZE: 1 ha, 25 pitches (6 with
elec), 3 hot showers, 3 WCs, 1 CWP. ⓖ

Shop at 1 km.
PRICES: (1996) Caravan with family 71.00,
Tent with two adults 49.00. CC: none.
*D796 from Combourg to Tremebeuc, then D83 to
Cuguen. Site is 1 km on the left.*

Château de la Chapelle aux Filtzmeens
35190 St-Domineuc.
Tel 02 99 45 21 55, Fax 02 99 45 27 00.
English spoken.
OPEN: all year. SIZE: 5 ha, 200 pitches (125 with
elec, 5 statics), 34 hot showers, 24 WCs. ⓛ ⓖ

Close to the canal; fishing, riding and tennis
nearby.
PRICES: (1996) Caravan with family 170.00,

Tent with two adults 105.00. CC: none.
*On the D13 6 km south-west of Combourg. The
campsite is just after La Chapelle aux Filtzmeens.*

COMPIEGNE Oise   2B

Camping Municipal Attichy,
60350 Cuise-la-Motte.
Tel 03 44 42 15 97.
OPEN: all year. SIZE: 1.5 ha, 60 pitches (all with
elec, 30 statics), 5 hot showers, 6 WCs, 3 French
WCs, 12 CWPs. ⓖ

Shop at 0.5 km. Restaurant at 0.5 km.
PRICES: (1996) Caravan with family 55.50,
Tent with two adults 28.50. CC: Euro/Access.
Off the N31 between Soissons and Compiègne.

CONCARNEAU Finistère   1C

Camping Caravanning International Le
Pendruc Roz Penanguer, 29910 Trégunc.
Tel 02 98 97 66 28, Fax 02 98 97 65 11.
English spoken.
OPEN: 01/04–30/09. SIZE: 3.6 ha, 170 pitches
(all with elec), 18 hot showers, 20 WCs, 20 French
WCs, 3 CWPs. ⓛ ⓖ

Restaurant at 2 km. Sauna.
PRICES: (1996) Caravan with family 137.00,
Tent with two adults 79.00. CC: Amex,
Euro/Access, Visa.
*Leave N165/E60 at Kerampaou on to D122. Turn
left after a few km to Trégunc, carry on towards
Lambel and campsite is signposted.*

Camping de Kerandon 29110 Concarneau.
Tel 02 98 97 15 77. English spoken.
OPEN: 15/06–15/09. SIZE: 100 pitches (all with elec),
10 hot showers (charge), 10 WCs, 5 French WCs.

Shop at 0.1 km. Restaurant at 0.05 km. Tennis.
PRICES: Caravan with family 95.00, Tent with two
adults 65.00. CC: Euro/Access.
Well signposted in town.

Camping des Etangs de Trévignon
29910 Trégunc.
Tel 02 98 50 00 41, Fax 02 98 50 00 41.
English spoken.
OPEN: 01/06–15/09. SIZE: 3 ha, 172 pitches
(5 statics), 18 hot showers, 1 CWP. ⓛ ⓖ

Restaurant at 2 km. Mini-golf, billiards, flume.
PRICES: (1996) Caravan with family 148.00, Tent
with two adults 84.00. CC: Euro/Access, Visa.
*From Concarneau, take the N783 towards
Trégunc. In Trégunc, take the D1 towards Pointe
de Trévignon for 6 km then follow the signs 'Les
Etangs'.*

France

Camping La Pommeraie St-Philibert, 29910 Trégunc.
Tel 02 98 50 02 73, Fax 02 98 50 07 91.
English spoken.
OPEN: 01/04–30/09. SIZE: 5 ha, 180 pitches (150 with elec, 44 statics), 15 hot showers, 15 WCs, 15 French WCs, 2 CWPs. ⚬ &

Mini-golf, bar, playroom, entertainment; sea 1 km.
PRICES: (1996) Caravan with family 136.00, Tent with two adults 80.00. CC: Euro/Access, Visa.
Take the Kerampaou exit from E60 towards Trégunc and Trévignon for 6 km to St-Philibert; campsite is at crossroads.

Camping le Dorlett avenue du Dorlett, Les Sables Blancs, 29900 Concarneau.
Tel 02 98 97 16 44. English spoken.
OPEN: 01/06–01/10. SIZE: 3 ha, 12 hot showers, 15 WCs.

Shop at 0.1 km.
PRICES: (1996) Caravan with family 92.50, Tent with two adults 56.50. CC: none.
Leave Concarneau along the coast road with the sea on left to Les Sables-Blancs.

Les Prés Verts Kernovs, 29900 Concarneau.
Tel 02 98 97 09 74, Fax 02 98 50 72 34.
English spoken.
OPEN: 01/05–10/09. SIZE: 3 ha, 100 pitches (all with elec), 16 hot showers, 24 WCs, 2 CWPs. ⚬

Shop at 3 km. Restaurant at 3 km. Table tennis, bar.
PRICES: (1996) Caravan with family 214.00, Tent with two adults 116.00. CC: Euro/Access, Visa.
Follow the Concarneau to La Forêt-Fouesnant coast road and then the VC No 6 signs.

CONDOM Gers 4D

Le Camp de Florence 32480 La Romieu.
Tel 05 62 28 15 58, Fax 05 62 28 20 04.
English spoken.
OPEN: all year. SIZE: 6 ha, 100 pitches (90 with elec, 25 statics), 15 hot showers, 15 WCs, 2 CWPs. &

Shop at 0.2 km.
PRICES: (1996) Caravan with family 186.00, Tent with two adults 100.00. CC: Amex, Euro/Access, Visa.
Agen road to Condom on D931. Before Condom, take D41 to campsite.

Camping Municipal de Gauge 32100 Condom.
Tel 05 62 28 17 32, Fax 05 62 28 45 86.
OPEN: 01/04–30/09. SIZE: 1.6 ha, 75 pitches (49 with elec), 8 hot showers, 8 WCs, 1 CWP. ⚬ &

Shop at 1 km. Swimming pool 200 m.
PRICES: (1996) Caravan with family 104.00, Tent with two adults 50.00. CC: none.
Condom is on the D931 Agen road.

CONDRIEU Rhône 5B

Camping Belle Rive 69420 Condrieu.
Tel 04 74 59 51 08, Fax 04 74 59 51 08.
English spoken.
OPEN: 01/04–30/09. SIZE: 5 ha, 200 pitches (all with elec, 100 statics), 18 hot showers, 24 WCs, 3 CWPs. &

PRICES: (1996) Caravan with family 109.00, Tent with two adults 64.00. CC: none.
On N86 from Vienne, well-signposted right turn just before village of Condrieu.

Camping-Caravanning Le Daxia route du Pèage, 38370 St-Clair-du-Rhône.
Tel 04 74 56 39 20, Fax 04 74 56 39 20.
OPEN: 01/04–30/09. SIZE: 7.5 ha, 80 pitches (all with elec, 80 statics), 9 hot showers, 9 WCs, 1 CWP. ⚬ &

Shop at 2 km.
PRICES: (1996) Caravan with family 100.00, Tent with two adults 62.00. CC: Amex, Euro/Access.
Cross the Rhône, through Les Roches and follow the D4 south. The site is 2 km south of St-Clair-du-Rhône.

CONQUES Aveyron 5C

Camping Beau Rivage 12320 Conques.
Tel 05 65 69 82 23. English spoken.
OPEN: 01/04–30/09. SIZE: 1 ha, 60 pitches (all with elec), 7 hot showers, 8 WCs, 1 CWP. &

Site updated for 1997.
PRICES: (1996) Caravan with family 108.00, Tent with two adults 60.00. CC: none.
Campsite is 350 m from Conques and well signposted.

Camping de Coursavy Coursavy, 15340 Cassaniouze.
Tel 04 71 49 97 70, Fax 04 71 49 97 70.
English spoken.
OPEN: 20/04–30/09. SIZE: 2 ha, 40 pitches (all with elec), 4 hot showers, 6 WCs, 1 CWP. ⚬ &

Shop at 2 km. Restaurant at 1 km.
PRICES: Caravan with family 92.00, Tent with two adults 50.00. CC: none.
From Conques go north on D901 for about 7 km, cross the River Lot and turn right. Campsite is 1.8 km ahead on the right.

France

LE CONQUET Finistère 1C

Camping Municipal Le Theven
29217 Le Conquet.
Tel 02 98 89 06 90, Fax 02 98 89 12 17.
English spoken.
OPEN: 01/04–15/10. SIZE: 13 ha, 450 pitches (350 with elec), 30 hot showers, 50 WCs, 1 CWP. ✆ ⅋

Restaurant at 1.5 km.
PRICES: (1996) Caravan with family 91.50,
Tent with two adults 47.30. CC: none.
In Le Conquet, follow signs to station and campsite is signposted.

CORSE (CORSICA)

AJACCIO Corse-du-Sud 6D

Camping Benista Pisciatello,
20166 Ajaccio, Corse.
Tel 04 95 23 19 30, Fax 04 95 25 93 70.
English spoken.
OPEN: 01/04–30/10. SIZE: 4.5 ha, 165 pitches
(all with elec), 40 hot showers, 48 WCs, 56 French
WCs, 5 CWPs. ✆

PRICES: (1996) Caravan with family 178.00,
Tent with two adults 95.00. CC: none.
12 km east of Ajaccio and well signposted.

U Sommalu route de Casaglione,
20111 Tiuccia, Corse.
Tel 04 95 52 24 21. English spoken.
OPEN: 01/05–30/09. SIZE: 5 ha, 20 hot showers,
20 WCs. ✆

Mountain bikes, horse-riding, climbing wall.
PRICES: (1996) Caravan with family 138.00,
Tent with two adults 86.00. CC: none.
North on D81 for 28 km. Turn right after Tiuccia towards Casaglione. Signposted.

BONIFACIO Corse-du-Sud 6D

Camping U Farniente 20169 Bonifacio, Corse.
Tel 04 95 73 05 47, Fax 04 95 73 11 42.
English spoken.
OPEN: 01/04–15/10. ✆

Tennis, disco, children's games.
PRICES: (1996) Caravan with family 210.00,
Tent with two adults 122.00. CC: none.
On N198, 4 km north of Bonifacio.

CALVI Hte-Corse 6D

Camping Paduella 20260 Calvi, Corse.
Tel 04 95 65 06 16, Fax 04 95 65 17 50. English spoken.

OPEN: 01/05–30/10. SIZE: 4 ha, 36 hot showers,
45 WCs, 2 CWPs. ✆ ⅋

PRICES: Caravan with family 129.00, Tent with two
adults 77.00. CC: Amex, Euro/Access, Visa.
*Campsite is 1.5 km from the town centre on the
N197 towards Iles Rousses on the right.*

CARGESE Corse-du-Sud 6D

Camping Torraccia 20130 Cargèse, Corse.
Tel 04 95 26 42 39, Fax 04 95 20 40 21.
English spoken.
OPEN: 15/05–30/09. SIZE: 4 ha, 12 pitches (all with
elec), 20 hot showers, 14 WCs, 1 CWP. ✆

Shop at 4 km. Restaurant at 4 km.
PRICES: (1996) Caravan with family 169.00, Tent
with two adults 90.00. CC: Euro/Access, Visa.
*4 km north of Cargèse on D81. From Ajaccio, a
daily bus stops in front of site.*

FIGARI Corse-du-Sud 6D

Camping U Moru 20114 Figari, Corse.
Tel 04 95 71 23 40. English spoken.
OPEN: 01/03–31/10. SIZE: 6 ha, 20 pitches (all with
elec), 10 hot showers, 10 WCs, 2 CWPs. ✆ ⅋

PRICES: (1996) Caravan with family 152.00, Tent
with two adults 75.00. CC: Amex, Visa.
On D859 between Sotta and Figari.

GHISONACCIA Hte-Corse 6D

Camping Caravan Arinella Bianca
20240 Ghisonaccia, Corse.
Tel 04 95 56 04 78, Fax 04 95 56 12 54.
English spoken.
OPEN: 09/04–15/10. SIZE: 9 ha, 300 pitches, 50 hot
showers, 42 WCs, 10 French WCs, 2 CWPs. ✆ ⅋

PRICES: Caravan with family 221.00,
Tent with two adults 116.00. CC: Amex,
Euro/Access, Visa.
*N198 south from Aléria. On reaching
Ghisonaccia turn left between A Terrazza and Le
Caiman bars, then turn right opposite sign for
Arinella Bianca, and the campsite is 300 m.*

L'ILE-ROUSSE Hte-Corse 6D

Le Clos de Chênes Lozari,
20226 Belgodère, Corse.
Tel 04 95 60 15 13, Fax 04 95 60 21 16.
English spoken.
OPEN: 01/04–15/10. SIZE: 5.5 ha, 75 pitches
(all with elec, 29 statics), 21 hot showers, 21 WCs,
3 CWPs. ✆ ⅋

France (vertical sidebar text)

CORSE (CORSICA) RESORTS CONTINUED

≋ ⟿ 🏕 R ◻ 🍴 🐷 ✕ ʿ 🏠

Flume.
PRICES: (1996) Caravan with family 171.00, Tent
with two adults 90.00. CC: Euro/Access, Visa.
*East of L'Ile Rousse on the N197 coast road to
Lozari. Signposted.*

PORTO-VECCHIO Corse-du-Sud   6D

Club la Chiappa 20137 Porto-Vecchio, Corse.
Tel 04 95 70 00 31, Fax 04 95 70 07 70.
English spoken.
OPEN: 15/05–15/10. SIZE: 65 ha, 220 pitches
(150 with elec). ⟍

≋ ⟿ 🏕 R ◻ 🍴 🐷 ✕ ʿ 🏠 🍴

Naturist site; entertainment, sauna, fitness room,
water skiing, windsurfing.
PRICES: (1996) Caravan with family 160.00,
Tent with two adults 150.00. CC: Amex,
Euro/Access, Visa.
15 km from Porto-Vecchio.

La Baie des Voiles La Trinité,
20137 Port-Vecchio, Corse.
Tel 04 95 70 01 23. English spoken.
OPEN: 01/05–30/09. SIZE: 3 ha, 100 pitches (all
with elec), 22 hot showers, 30 WCs, 2 CWPs. ⟍ ﹠

≋ ⟿ 🏕 ◻ 🍴 ✕

Children's playground; swimming pool 100m.
PRICES: (1996) Caravan with family 146.00,
Tent with two adults 74.00. CC: none.
*5 km north of Port-Vecchio, turn first left, drive
1 km and then turn right.*

La Vetta La Trinité, 20137 Porto-Vecchio, Corse.
Tel 04 95 70 09 86, Fax 04 95 70 43 21.
English spoken.
OPEN: 01/06–01/10. SIZE: 6 ha, 100 pitches
(94 with elec), 18 hot showers, 23 WCs, 1 CWP. ⟍

🏕 R ◻ 🍴 ✕ ʿ 🏠

Shop at 1 km.
PRICES: (1996) Caravan with family 176.00,
Tent with two adults 92.00. CC: none.
*5 km north of Porto-Vecchio on the N198. Site is
first on the right.*

ST-FLORENT Hte-Corse   6D

Camping Kalliste 20217 St-Florent, Corse.
Tel 04 95 37 03 08, Fax 04 95 37 19 77.
English spoken.
OPEN: 01/04–30/10. SIZE: 3.5 ha, 50 pitches
(30 with elec, 28 statics), 35 hot showers. ⟍ ﹠

≋ 🏊 🏕 R ◻ 🍴 🐷 ✕ 🏠

Apartments also available.
PRICES: (1996) Caravan with family 140.00,
Tent with two adults 78.00. CC: none.

*From St-Florent follow the river Aliso. Go towards
the beach and turn right at the iron bridge to
campsite (200 m).*

END OF CORSE (CORSICA) RESORTS

CORDES Tarn   5C

Camp Moulin de Julien 81170 Cordes.
Tel 05 63 56 01 42.
OPEN: 01/04–30/09. SIZE: 9 ha, 60 pitches (all with
elec), 17 hot showers, 2 WCs, 2 CWPs. ⟍ ﹠

≋ ⟿ 🏕 R ◻ 🍴 ʿ 🏠 🚗

Shop at 1 km. Restaurant at 1.5 km.
PRICES: (1996) Caravan with family 128.00,
Tent with two adults 78.00. CC: none.
*On road from Cordes to Toulouse.
Well signposted.*

Camping Camp-Redon Livers-Cazelles,
81170 Cordes.
Tel 05 63 56 14 64. English spoken.
OPEN: 01/04–01/11. SIZE: 2 ha, 30 pitches (all with
elec, 5 statics), 4 hot showers, 5 WCs. ⟍ ﹠

🍴 R ◻ 🐷 ʿ 🍺 🚗

Shop at 5 km. Restaurant at 1.5 km. Table tennis.
PRICES: (1996) Caravan with family 100.00,
Tent with two adults 60.00. CC: none.
*Livers-Cazelles and the campsite is well
signposted.*

CORMEILLES Eure   2A

Camping Aire Naturelle
27260 St-Sylvestre-de-Cormeilles.
Tel 02 32 42 29 69. English spoken.
OPEN: all year. SIZE: 1 ha, 25 pitches (all with elec),
3 hot showers, 3 WCs, 1 CWP.

🍴 R 🍺

Shop at 4 km. Restaurant at 4 km.
PRICES: (1996) Caravan with family 70.00,
Tent with two adults 39.00. CC: none.
*From Cormeilles take D810 south-west. Turn left
towards Epaignes. After 1 km turn left and follow
signs to campsite (1 km on right).*

COSTAROS Haute-Loire   5A

Camping au Bord de l'Eau 43150 Goudet.
Tel 04 71 57 16 82. English spoken.
OPEN: 15/06–15/09. SIZE: 5 ha, 100 pitches
(all with elec, 8 statics), 10 hot showers, 10 WCs,
4 CWPs. ⟍ ﹠

⟿ 🍴 R ◻ 🍴 🐷 ✕ ʿ 🍺

Old château in grounds; children's playground,
entertainment.
PRICES: (1996) Caravan with family 124.00,
Tent with two adults 63.00. CC: none.
From Costaros on N88 take D49 to Goudet.

COUHE Vienne   4B

Camping Les Peupliers 86700 Couhé.
Tel 05 49 59 21 16, Fax 05 49 37 92 09.
English spoken.
OPEN: 01/05–30/09. SIZE: 8 ha, 120 pitches (all
with elec), 17 hot showers, 16 WCs, 2 CWPs. ✆ ♿

Mini-golf, 42 m flume, boating. 20% discounts
available LS.
PRICES: Caravan with family 166.00, Tent with two
adults 95.00. CC: Euro/Access, Visa.
*Coming from Poitiers on the N10, campsite is
signposted at the entrance of Couhé.*
SEE ADVERTISEMENT

COURNON-D'AUVERGNE Puy-de-D 5A

Camping Municipal
63800 Cournon-d'Auvergne.
Tel 04 73 84 81 30. English spoken.
OPEN: all year. SIZE: 4 ha, 200 pitches (160 with
elec), 21 hot showers, 16 WCs, 2 CWPs. ♿

Shop at 1.5 km. Restaurant at 1 km.
PRICES: (1996) Caravan with family 104.00,
Tent with two adults 55.00. CC: Amex,
Euro/Access, Visa.
Follow signs from Cournon-d'Auvergne.

Camping Municipal

at Cournon d'Auvergne

Volcanoes on the Doorstep!

COUTANCES Manche   1B

Camping Municipal 50490 St-Sauveur-Lendelin.
Tel 02 33 07 60 21.
OPEN: 01/07–31/08. SIZE: 38 pitches (all with elec),
3 hot showers, 4 WCs. ♿

Shop at 0.2 km.
PRICES: (1996) Caravan with family 78.50,
Tent with two adults 41.50. CC: none.
North of Coutances on D971 and well signposted.

Camping Municipal Les Vignettes
route de St-Malo, 50200 Coutances.
Tel 02 33 45 43 13, Fax 02 33 47 12 45.
English spoken.
OPEN: all year. SIZE: 1 ha, 80 pitches (50 with elec),
8 hot showers, 14 WCs, 8 French WCs, 2 CWPs. ✆ ♿

Shop at 0.5 km. Restaurant at 0.1 km.

Camping Caravanning
Les Peupliers ★ ★ ★ ★
86700 Couhé

On the N10 35 km south of Poitiers and
Futuroscope. Leafy 3 acre site beside the river.
Modern toilet/shower facilities. Shady pitches.
Entertainments in season.

*Shop, bar, restaurant, take-aways, TV &
games room. 2 floodlit heated pools,
42m-flume, paddling pool.
Volleyball. Mini-golf.
Children's play area.*

*Pedalo hire.
Private fishing lake.*

See under Couhé

France

PRICES: (1996) Caravan with family 69.00,
Tent with two adults 43.00. CC: none.
*From Coutances turn on to D44. Campsite is near
swimming pool on the left and well signposted.*

COZES Charente-Marit   4A

Camping Fleurs des Champs Le Coudinier,
Arces-sur-Gironde, 17120 Cozes.
Tel 05 46 90 40 11. English spoken.
OPEN: 01/06–30/09. SIZE: 1.40 ha, 33 pitches
(32 with elec), 2 hot showers, 5 WCs,
4 French WCs.

Shop at 6 km. Restaurant at 2 km. Archery and
mini-golf.
PRICES: (1996) Caravan with family 74.00,
Tent with two adults 45.00. CC: none.
*From Cozes take the D144 towards the coast to
Arces-sur-Gironde, 3 km.*

CRAC'H Morbihan   1C

Le Fort Espagnol 56950 Crac'h.
Tel 02 97 55 14 88, Fax 02 97 30 01 04.
English spoken.
OPEN: 01/04–30/09. SIZE: 4 ha, 140 pitches
(all with elec, 50 statics), 19 hot showers, 30 WCs,
26 French WCs, 2 CWPs. ✆ ♿

⌗ | 🎣 | R | 🔲 | 🦞 | 🍺 | | 🎣 | 🏠 |

Shop at 0.6 km. Restaurant at 0.8 km.
PRICES: (1996) Caravan with family 154.00, Tent
with two adults 91.00. CC: Euro/Access, Visa.
*Arriving in Crac'h on D28 from Auray, turn left at
second traffic lights and follow road for approx
600 m. Campsite is on the right, well signposted.*

Lodka route du Fort Pointe Espagnol,
56950 Crac'h.
Tel 02 97 55 03 97. English spoken.
OPEN: all year. SIZE: 2 ha, 25 pitches (all with elec,
6 statics), 3 hot showers, 5 WCs, 1 CWP. ♿ ⚓

〰 ✈ ⛲ R 🔲 🦞 🍺 🎣 🏠

Restaurant at 1 km. Book-stall, playground,
table tennis, boules.
PRICES: Caravan with family 165.00,
Tent with two adults 115.00. CC: none.
*1 km east of Crac'h on road to Fort Espagnol,
second campsite on the right.*

CRAON Mayenne 2C

La Grande Cantière (à la ferme)
53230 Cossé-le-Vivien.
Tel 02 43 98 88 86. English spoken.
OPEN: all year. SIZE: 1.5 ha, 6 pitches (all with elec,
1 static), 1 hot shower (charge), 1 WC, 1 French
WC, 2 CWPs.

〰 ✈ ⛲ R | | | | 🏠

Shop at 3 km. Restaurant at 3 km.
PRICES: (1996) Caravan with family 60.00,
Tent with two adults 40.00. CC: none.
*N171 north from Craon to Cossé-le-Vivien, then D4
west towards Méral. After 3 km turn right on C3
towards Montjean, then left on to C114 after 0.5 km.
Site is at the first farm you come to, signposted.*

CRECHES-SUR-SAONE Saône/Loire 5B

Camping Municipal Le Port d'Arciat,
71680 Crêches-sur-Saône.
Tel 03 85 37 11 83, Fax 03 85 37 48 48.
English spoken.
OPEN: 01/05–30/09. SIZE: 5 ha, 160 pitches
(all with elec, 60 statics), 16 hot showers, 20 WCs,
15 French WCs, 3 CWPs. ♿ ⚓

〰 🏊 ⌗ R 🔲 🦞 🍺 ✕ 🏠

Sailing, canoeing, pedal boats.
PRICES: (1996) Caravan with family 91.00, Tent
with two adults 45.00. CC: Euro/Access, Visa.
*On A6 take Mâcon-Sud exit then south on N6 to
Crêches-sur-Saône. Signposted.*

CREON Gironde 4B

Camping-Caravaning Bel-Air D671,
Lorient-Sadirac, 33670 Créon.
Tel 05 56 23 01 90, Fax 05 56 23 08 38. English spoken.

OPEN: all year. SIZE: 2 ha, 92 pitches (60 with elec),
9 hot showers, 7 WCs, 2 CWPs. ♿ ⚓

| ⛲ | R | | 🦞 | 🍺 | | 🎣 | 🏠 |

Shop at 2 km. Restaurant at 2 km. Playground.
PRICES: Caravan with family 113.00, Tent with two
adults 65.00. CC: Euro/Access, Visa.
*North-west of Créon off D671 or, coming from
Bordeaux, go east on D936 towards Bergerac
then fork right on D671 towards Créon after
11 km.*

LE CROISIC Loire-Atlan 1D

Camping Le Paradis
chemin du Turballo, 44490 Le Croisic.
Tel 02 40 23 07 89. English spoken.
OPEN: 15/05–15/09. SIZE: 1 ha, 110 pitches
(80 with elec), 8 hot showers, 20 WCs, 1 CWP. ♿

≋ ⚓ ♀ R | | 🍺 | | |

Shop at 0.2 km. Restaurant at 1 km.
PRICES: Caravan with family 110.00,
Tent with two adults 60.00. CC: none.
*The campsite is 1 km south-west of Le Croisic.
Follow signs.*

CROZANT Creuse 5A

Camping Municipal Font Bonne
23160 Crozant.
Tel 05 55 89 80 12.
OPEN: 01/04–30/09. SIZE: 0.4 ha, 33 pitches
(10 with elec), 7 hot showers, 7 WCs. ♿

〰 ✈ ⛲ R | | | | |

Shop at 0.2 km. Restaurant at 0.2 km.
Children's games.
PRICES: (1996) Caravan with family 70.00,
Tent with two adults 37.00. CC: none.

CROZON Finistère 1C

Camping de l'Aber
Tal-ar-Groas, 29160 Crozon.
Tel 02 98 27 02 96. English spoken.
OPEN: 15/03–30/10. SIZE: 2 ha, 80 pitches (all with
elec), 10 hot showers, 10 WCs, 6 French WCs,
2 CWPs.

| ⛲ | R | | | 🍺 | | 🏠 |

Shop at 1 km. Restaurant at 1 km. Mini-golf,
table tennis; sea 1 km.
PRICES: (1996) Caravan with family 95.00, Tent
with two adults 52.00. CC: Euro/Access, Visa.
*4 km east of Crozon. From roundabout in Tal-ar-
Groas, follow the sign Plage de l'Aber for 1 km.*

Camping du Bouis Morgat
Morgat, 29160 Crozon.
Tel 02 98 26 12 53. English spoken.
OPEN: 01/04–30/09. SIZE: 3 ha, 50 pitches (all with
elec), 16 hot showers, 16 WCs.

France

Restaurant at 1 km.
PRICES: (1996) Caravan with family 89.00,
Tent with two adults 57.00. CC: Euro/Access.
From Crozon go to Morgat, then follow directions
to Cap-de-la-Chèvre. Turn right where indicated.

Camping Les Pins route de la Pointe de Dinan,
29160 Crozon-Morgat.
Tel 02 98 27 21 95. English spoken.
OPEN: 06/06–20/09. SIZE: 3 ha, 130 pitches
(60 with elec, 3 statics), 16 hot showers, 14 WCs,
1 CWP. &

Shop at 0.7 km. Restaurant at 2 km.
PRICES: (1996) Caravan with family 120.50,
Tent with two adults 66.00. CC: none.
2 km from Crozon on the D308.

Camping Pen Ar Menez 29160 Crozon.
Tel 02 98 27 12 36. English spoken.
OPEN: 01/04–30/09. SIZE: 2.5 ha, 150 pitches
(40 with elec), 16 hot showers, 18 WCs, 2 CWPs.

Shop at 0.2 km. Restaurant at 0.1 km. Mobile
homes available.
PRICES: (1996) Caravan with family 96.00,
Tent with two adults 52.00. CC: none.
Leave Crozon and travel towards Camaret.

Les Pieds dans L'Eau St-Fiacre, 29160 Crozon.
Tel 02 98 27 62 43. English spoken.
OPEN: 15/06–15/09. SIZE: 1.8 ha, 70 pitches
(40 with elec), 10 hot showers, 9 WCs, 1 French
WC, 1 CWP. &

Shop at 1.2 km. Restaurant at 1.2 km. Mini-golf.
Tel in LS: 02 35 46 26 12.
PRICES: (1996) Caravan with family 104.00,
Tent with two adults 58.00. CC: none.
From Crozon go 6 km north-west and take D355
and D55 towards Ile Longue. Take first left after
200 m and campsite is signposted.

DAX Landes 4C

Airotel Saint Martin Moliets Plage,
40660 Moliets.
Tel 05 58 48 52 30, Fax 05 58 48 50 73.
English spoken.
OPEN: 09/04–15/10. SIZE: 18 ha, 660 pitches
(425 with elec), 76 hot showers, 93 WCs. &

Shop at 2 km. Archery, chess; mobile homes also
available.
PRICES: (1996) Caravan with family 154.00,
Tent with two adults 105.00. CC: Visa.
D16 north-west of Dax to Magescq, then Léon.
D652 to Moliets, then D117 to Moliets-Plage.

Camping Bertranborde 40180 Rivière.
Tel 05 58 97 58 39. English spoken.
OPEN: all year. SIZE: 0.5 ha, 12 pitches (all with
elec), 2 hot showers, 2 WCs, 1 CWP. &

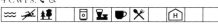

Table tennis, boules.
PRICES: (1996) Caravan with family 65.00,
Tent with two adults 33.00. CC: none.
From Dax, head east on the N124. After 11 km
turn left on the D113. Site is then 2 km.

Camping du Bois de Boulogne Bois de
Boulogne, 40100 Dax.
Tel 05 58 90 05 53, Fax 05 58 56 18 77.
English spoken.
OPEN: 01/04–01/11. SIZE: 5 ha, 250 pitches
(all with elec), 32 hot showers, 43 WCs,
4 CWPs. & &

PRICES: (1996) Caravan with family 113.00, Tent
with two adults 77.00. CC: Euro/Access, Visa.
In Dax go towards the centre of the town and then
follow the directions to the Bois de Boulogne.

Camping L'Etang d'Ardy route de Bayonne,
40990 St-Paul-les-Dax.
Tel 05 58 97 57 74. English spoken.
OPEN: 01/04–15/10. SIZE: 4 ha, 80 pitches (all with
elec), 53 hot showers, 55 WCs, 1 CWP. & &

Shop at 4 km. Restaurant at 2 km.
PRICES: (1996) Caravan with family 115.50,
Tent with two adults 65.00. CC: Euro/Access, Visa.
On the N124 towards Bayonne.

Camping Municipal d'Azur 40140 Azur.
Tel 05 58 48 30 72. English spoken.
OPEN: 15/06–15/09. SIZE: 6 ha, 130 pitches
(all with elec), 20 hot showers, 21 WCs,
2 CWPs. & &

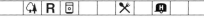

Playground, sailing, entertainment.
PRICES: (1996) Caravan with family 105.60,
Tent with two adults 60.30. CC: none.
D16 north-west of Dax to Magescq. Then take
D150 west to Azur.

Camping St-Vincent-de-Paul 40990 St-Vincent-
de-Paul.
Tel 05 58 89 99 60. English spoken.
OPEN: 01/04–31/10. SIZE: 2 ha, 97 pitches (57 with
elec, 18 statics), 8 hot showers, 8 WCs. &

Shop at 3 km.
PRICES: (1996) Caravan with family 85.00, Tent
with two adults 46.00. CC: none.
From Dax take N124 north-east towards Mont de
Marsan. St-Vincent-de-Paul is on the right and
campsite is in village.

France

Parc de Couchoy 40260 Lesperon.
Tel 05 58 89 60 15, Fax 05 58 89 60 15. English spoken.
OPEN: 01/05–30/09. SIZE: 1.3 ha, 72 pitches (all
with elec), 7 hot showers, 10 WCs, 1 French WC.

Shop at 3 km. Restaurant at 3 km. Mobile homes
available.
PRICES: Caravan with family 111.00, Tent with two
adults 72.00. CC: Euro/Access, Visa.
*D947 north from Dax to Castets. Then the N10
north before turning left on D140 to Lesperon.*

Le Toy 40990 Herm.
Tel 05 58 91 55 16. English spoken.
OPEN: 01/04–30/11. SIZE: 2 ha, 30 pitches (15 with
elec, 1 static), 4 hot showers, 6 WCs, 1 CWP.

Shop at 1 km. Restaurant at 1 km.
PRICES: (1996) Caravan with family 72.00,
Tent with two adults 40.00. CC: Euro/Access.
*From Dax take D947 towards Castets. Turn left on
to D150 to Herm.*

DEAUVILLE Calvados 2A

Camping de la Vallée
route de Beaumont, St-Arnoult, 14800 Deauville.
Tel 02 31 88 58 17, Fax 02 31 88 11 57. English spoken.
OPEN: 01/04–31/10. SIZE: 5 ha, 267 pitches (190 with
elec), 36 hot showers, 36 WCs, 3 CWPs.

Play areas, playroom, bar, fishing.
PRICES: (1996) Caravan with family 181.80,
Tent with two adults 92.30. CC: Euro/Access, Visa.

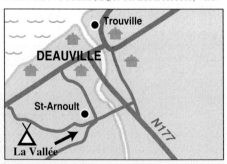

*From Deauville take the N177 towards St-Arnoult.
Follow signs to campsite.*

Camping Les Haras chemin de Calvaire,
Touques, 14800 Deauville.
Tel 02 31 88 44 84, Fax 02 31 88 97 08. English spoken.
OPEN: all year. SIZE: 4 ha, 100 pitches (all with
elec), 32 hot showers, 20 WCs, 2 CWPs.

Restaurant at 1 km.
PRICES: (1996) Caravan with family 174.00,

Tent with two adults 91.00. CC: Visa.
Touques is 2 km inland towards Pont-l'Evêque.

DIE Drôme 5B

Les Acacias Les Tours, 26340 Vercheny.
Tel 04 75 21 72 51, Fax 04 75 21 73 98.
English spoken.
OPEN: 01/04–30/09. SIZE: 3 ha, 100 pitches (90 with
elec), 11 hot showers, 11 WCs, 3 CWPs.

Restaurant at 1 km. Canoes for hire; swimming
pool in 1997.
PRICES: (1996) Caravan with family 104.00,
Tent with two adults 60.00. CC: none.
Vercheny is halfway between Die and Crest on D93.

Camping du Gap 26340 Vercheny.
Tel 04 75 21 72 62, Fax 04 75 21 76 40.
English spoken.
OPEN: 01/05–30/09. SIZE: 5 ha, 90 pitches (all with
elec), 10 hot showers, 10 WCs, 1 CWP.

Shop at 1 km. Restaurant at 6 km. Fishing, tennis,
entertainment; boating, hang-gliding and rock
climbing nearby.
PRICES: (1996) Caravan with family 117.00,
Tent with two adults 62.00. CC: none.
From Die, take the D93 west to Vercheny.

Camping La Pinède
quartier du Pont Neuf, 26150 Die.
Tel 04 75 22 17 77, Fax 04 75 22 22 73.
English spoken.
OPEN: 01/05–15/09. SIZE: 5 ha, 110 pitches (80 with
elec, 12 statics), 13 hot showers, 14 WCs, 2 CWPs.

Tennis, mini-golf, archery.
PRICES: Caravan with family 158.00,
Tent with two adults 78.00. CC: none.
Campsite is well signposted in Die.

Camping S I route de Romeyer, 26150 Die.
Tel 04 75 22 21 31.
OPEN: 15/04–30/09. SIZE: 90 pitches (44 with elec),
6 hot showers, 7 WCs, 3 French WCs.

Shop at 0.5 km. Restaurant at 0.5 km. Children's
playground.
PRICES: (1996) Caravan with family 83.00,
Tent with two adults 43.00. CC: none.
*Take D93 south from Die for 1 km then turn left
on to D742 and site is signposted.*

Le Glandasse
quartier de la Maladrerie, 26150 Die.
Tel 04 75 22 02 50, Fax 04 75 22 04 91.
English spoken.
OPEN: 01/04–15/09. SIZE: 3 ha, 90 pitches (all with
elec), 14 hot showers (charge), 4 CWPs.

France

PRICES: (1996) Caravan with family 130.00,
Tent with two adults 72.00. CC: none.
*Leave Die on D93 towards Gap and site is on the
right just after major junction.*

DIEPPE Seine Marit 2A

Camp du Colombier
453 rue Loucheur, 76550 Offranville.
Tel 02 35 85 21 14, Fax 02 35 04 24 54.
English spoken.
OPEN: 01/04–15/10. SIZE: 3 ha, 98 pitches (all with
elec, 50 statics), 18 hot showers, 18 WCs, 3 CWPs. ℓ ᕃ

Shop at 0.4 km.
PRICES: (1996) Caravan with family 86.50,
Tent with two adults 57.50. CC: none.
*From Dieppe take N27 towards Rouen then D54 to
Offranville (8 km). Signposted.*

Camping La Source Hautot-sur-Mer,
76550 Offranville.
Tel 02 35 84 27 04. English spoken.
OPEN: 15/03–15/10. SIZE: 3 ha, 85 pitches
(all with elec, 48 statics), 12 hot showers, 10 WCs,
2 CWPs. ℓ ᕃ

Shop at 1 km. Restaurant at 2.7 km. Fitness room;
open for late arrivals.
PRICES: (1996) Caravan with family 96.00,
Tent with two adults 57.00. CC: none.
*From Dieppe take N27/D925 towards St-Valéry,
then D153 to St-Aubin-sur-Scie. Campsite is
signposted.*

Camping Municipal de Martigny
76880 Martigny.
Tel 02 35 85 60 82, Fax 02 35 85 95 16.
OPEN: 01/04–15/10. SIZE: 6 ha, 15 hot showers,
11 WCs, 2 CWPs. ℓ ᕃ

Restaurant at 2 km.
PRICES: (1996) Caravan with family 85.60,
Tent with two adults 45.20. CC: none.
*From Dieppe take the D154 to Arques-la-Bataille.
The campsite is 2 km beyond Arques-la-Bataille.*

DIGNE-LES-BAINS Alpes/Hte-Prov 6C

Camping du Bourg Route de la Javie, 04000 Digne.
Tel 04 92 31 04 87, Fax 04 92 33 50 49.
English spoken.
OPEN: 01/04–30/10. SIZE: 3 ha, 120 pitches
(all with elec). ℓ ᕃ

Shop at 0.5 km. Restaurant at 0.5 km. Mobile
homes for hire.

PRICES: Caravan with family 107.00,
Tent with two adults 63.00. CC: none.

Societe Camping Les Eaux Chaudes
route des Thermes, 04000 Digne.
Tel 04 92 32 31 04, Fax 04 92 33 50 49.
English spoken.
OPEN: 01/04–30/10. SIZE: 3 ha, 153 pitches (all
with elec), 18 hot showers, 21 WCs, 2 CWPs. ℓ ᕃ

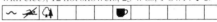

Shop at 0.5 km. Restaurant at 0.5 km. Mobile
homes for hire.
PRICES: Caravan with family 123.00,
Tent with two adults 73.00. CC: none.
*N85 northwards to Digne-les-Bains. Campsite is
well signposted.*

DIJON Côte-d'Or 3C

Camping du Lac 3 bd Chanoine Kir, 21000 Dijon.
Tel 03 80 43 54 72, Fax 03 80 43 54 72.
English spoken.
OPEN: 01/04–15/10. SIZE: 2.5 ha, 121 pitches (all
with elec), 12 hot showers, 23 WCs, 1 CWP. ℓ ᕃ

Shop at 1 km. Restaurant at 2 km.
PRICES: (1996) Caravan with family 67.90,
Tent with two adults 31.40. CC: none.
On west side of Dijon, look for signs to Lac Kir.

DINAN Côtes-du-Nord 1D

Camping International de la Hallerais
Taden, 22100 Dinan.
Tel 02 96 39 15 93, Fax 02 96 39 94 64.
English spoken.
OPEN: 15/03–31/10. SIZE: 10 ha, 190 pitches
(220 with elec, 30 statics), 51 hot showers,
32 WCs, 3 CWPs. ℓ ᕃ

Shop at 3 km. Restaurant at 2 km. Tennis, mini-
golf, playground, heated pool; 10% discount LS.
PRICES: (1996) Caravan with family 153.00, Tent
with two adults 94.00. CC: Euro/Access, Visa.

*Taden is near estuary, north-east of Dinan off
D12. Campsite is well signposted from Dinan.*

France (side tab)

DINARD Ille/Vilaine   1D

Camp de Longchamp
boulevard de St-Cast, 35800 St-Lunaire.
Tel 02 99 46 33 98, Fax 02 99 46 02 71.
English spoken.
OPEN: 15/05–10/09. SIZE: 5 ha, 300 pitches
(180 with elec), 30 hot showers, 30 WCs, 3 CWPs. ⚊

Tennis, mini-golf, mountain-bike hire.
PRICES: (1996) Caravan with family 146.00, Tent
with two adults 84.00. CC: Euro/Access, Visa.
*In Dinard take the road to St-Lunaire, then D786
towards St-Briac. The campsite is well signposted.*

Camping Municipal des Mielles
rue Jules Jeunet, 22770 Lancieux.
Tel 02 96 86 22 98, Fax 02 96 86 28 20.
English spoken.
OPEN: 01/04–30/09. SIZE: 2.5 ha, 170 pitches
(160 with elec), 24 hot showers, 24 WCs,
2 CWPs. ⅋

Shop at 0.2 km. Restaurant at 0.2 km.
PRICES: (1996) Caravan with family 92.50,
Tent with two adults 48.00. CC: none.
*Campsite is at the end of the road opposite the
town hall.*

DIVONNE-LES-BAINS Ain   6A

Campasun Divonne
quartier Vilard, 01220 Divonne-les-Bains.
Tel 04 50 20 01 95, Fax 04 50 20 34 39.
English spoken.
OPEN: 29/03–02/11. SIZE: 8 ha, 253 pitches
(180 with elec, 10 statics), 31 hot showers,
47 WCs, 5 CWPs. ⚊ ⅋

Shop at 2 km. Restaurant at 2 km. Mobile homes
also available.
PRICES: (1996) Caravan with family 165.00,
Tent with two adults 93.00.
CC: Euro/Access, Visa.

DOL-DE-BRETAGNE Ille/Vilaine   1D

Camping Castel des Ormes
35120 Dol-de-Bretagne.
Tel 02 99 73 49 59, Fax 02 99 73 49 55.
English spoken.
OPEN: 20/05–10/09. SIZE: 35 ha, 500 pitches. ⚊ ⅋

Playground, flume, tennis, canoeing, fishing,
entertainment, horse-riding.
PRICES: Caravan with family 219.00,
Tent with two adults 145.00. CC: none.
*From Dol go towards Combourg and Rennes.
Campsite is on the left after 10 km (D795).*

Camping des Tenguieres
rue de Dinan, 35120 Dol-de-Bretagne.
Tel 02 99 48 14 68, Fax 02 99 48 19 63.
English spoken.
OPEN: 15/05–15/09. SIZE: 2 ha, 95 pitches (21 with
elec), 10 hot showers, 16 WCs. ⅋

Shop at 0.3 km. Restaurant at 0.5 km.
PRICES: (1996) Caravan with family 80.00,
Tent with two adults 37.00. CC: none.
*From centre of Dol-de-Bretagne, 0.4 km on D676
to Dinan.*

Le Vieux Chêne
Baguer-Pican, 35120 Dol-de-Bretagne.
Tel 02 99 48 09 55, Fax 02 99 48 13 37.
English spoken.
OPEN: 15/04–20/09. SIZE: 5 ha, 160 pitches
(120 with elec), 29 hot showers, 28 WCs,
3 CWPs. ⚊ ⅋

Tennis, mini-golf, fishing, play areas, flume.
PRICES: Caravan with family 174.00,
Tent with two adults 115.00. CC: none.
*From Dol-de-Bretagne the campsite is reached via
the D576 towards Baguer-Pican. (Traditional
swimwear must be worn in the pool - not
shorts/bermudas).*

DOLE Jura   3C

Des Bords de Loue Parcey, 39100 Dôle.
Tel 03 84 71 03 82, Fax 03 84 81 72 21.
English spoken.
OPEN: 15/04–15/09. SIZE: 200 pitches
(all with elec), 29 hot showers, 20 WCs, 10 French
WCs. ⚊ ⅋

Shop at 1 km. Restaurant at 1 km. Tennis and
golf 1 km.
PRICES: Caravan with family 128.00,
Tent with two adults 83.00. CC: none.
*N5 towards Genève. Campsite is 5 km from Dôle
and well signposted. (Don't go into the town.)*

Des Bords de Loue Camping
near delightful old town of Dôle
... birthplace of Louis Pasteur

Le Pasquier 18 chemin Thevenot, 39100 Dôle.
Tel 03 84 72 02 61, Fax 03 84 79 23 44.
English spoken.
OPEN: 15/03–15/10. SIZE: 2 ha, 120 pitches
(all with elec), 12 hot showers, 12 WCs,
3 CWPs. ⅋

Restaurant at 0.5 km.
PRICES: (1996) Caravan with family 109.00, Tent with two adults 60.00. CC: Euro/Access, Visa.
From the town centre follow signs to stadium.

La Plage-Blanche 39380 Ounans.
Tel 03 84 37 69 63, Fax 03 84 37 60 21.
English spoken.
OPEN: 15/03–31/10. SIZE: 5 ha, 200 pitches (150 with elec), 21 hot showers, 17 WCs, 2 CWPs. ⚓ ﴾

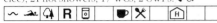

Shop at 1 km. Canoeing; swimming pool 1 km.
PRICES: (1996) Caravan with family 108.00,
Tent with two adults 70.00. CC: Amex,
Euro/Access, Visa.
From Dôle go towards Pontarlier/Genève on the
N5 to Mont-Sous-Vaudrey and then take the D472
for 5 km. Follow the signs to campsite.

DOUARNENEZ Finistère 1C

Camping de Kerleyou rue de Préfet,
29100 Douarnenez.
Tel 02 98 74 13 03. English spoken.
OPEN: 01/04–30/09. SIZE: 4 ha, 100 pitches
(80 with elec, 10 statics), 9 hot showers, 9 WCs,
3 CWPs. ⚓ ﴾

Shop at 0.5 km. Restaurant at 1 km. Table tennis.
PRICES: (1996) Caravan with family 98.00,
Tent with two adults 54.00. CC: none.
Follow the camping signs from town.

Camping International de Kervel
29550 Plonévez-Porzay.
Tel 02 98 92 51 54, Fax 02 98 92 54 96.
English spoken.
OPEN: 10/05–15/09. SIZE: 7 ha, 330 pitches (all with
elec, 50 statics), 34 hot showers, 25 WCs. ⚓ ﴾

Tennis, mini-golf, flume.
PRICES: Caravan with family 171.00, Tent with two
adults 115.00. CC: Euro/Access, Visa.
From Douarnenez go towards Châteaulin on
D107 and 2 km before Plonévez-Porzay, turn left
to campsite.

Le Pil Koad route de Douarnenez,
29100 Poullan-sur-Mer.
Tel 02 98 74 26 39, Fax 02 98 74 55 97.
English spoken.
OPEN: 06/04–15/09. SIZE: 4 ha, 110 pitches
(all with elec, 14 statics), 24 hot showers,
30 WCs, 4 CWPs. ⚓ ﴾

Shop at 0.5 km. Restaurant at 0.2 km. Tennis, mini-
golf, playground, mobile homes and chalets also
available.

PRICES: (1996) Caravan with family 204.00, Tent
with two adults 126.00. CC: Euro/Access, Visa.
D7 west of Douarnenez. Site is on the left, just
before the village of Poullan-sur-Mer.

DOULLENS Somme 2B

Le Val d'Authie 62760 Amplier.
Tel 03 21 48 57 07, Fax 03 21 58 08 60. English spoken.
OPEN: all year. SIZE: 3 ha, 75 pitches (70 with elec,
10 statics), 9 hot showers, 10 WCs, 1 CWP. ⚓

Mini-golf, fishing.
PRICES: (1996) Caravan with family 92.00, Tent
with two adults 50.00. CC: Euro/Access, Visa.
From Doullens take the N25 towards Arras. Turn
right after 2 km.

DOUSSARD Haute-Savoie 6A

Camping Caravaning Le Verger Fleuri
Lathuille, 74210 Faverges.
Tel 04 50 44 31 82. English spoken.
OPEN: 15/05–30/09. SIZE: 1.5 ha, 100 pitches
(60 with elec), 7 hot showers, 11 WCs, 8 French
WCs, 2 CWPs. ⚓ ﴾

Shop at 0.05 km. Restaurant at 0.05 km. Playground.
PRICES: (1996) Caravan with family 94.00,
Tent with two adults 58.00. CC: Amex.
North of Doussard along the west side of Lake
Annecy. Turn left to Lathuille.

Camping Le Verger Fleuri★★
near Doussard
Tucked away in the mountains, near the
cleanest lake in Europe

DRAGUIGNAN Var 6C

Camping Les Pins 83630 Les Salles-sur-Verdon.
Tel 04 94 70 20 80, Fax 04 94 84 23 27.
English spoken.
OPEN: 01/04–31/10. SIZE: 2 ha, 55 pitches (all with
elec), 12 hot showers, 12 WCs, 4 CWPs. ⚓ ﴾

Shop at 0.2 km. Restaurant at 0.2 km.
PRICES: (1996) Caravan with family 148.00, Tent
with two adults 74.00. CC: Euro/Access, Visa.
From Draguignan, head towards Aups then take
D957 to Les Salles-sur-Verdon.

Le Château Rouge av du Pont d'Aups,
83300 Draguignan.
Tel 04 94 68 50 67, Fax 04 94 68 50 67.
English spoken.

France

OPEN: 01/04−15/10. SIZE: 3 ha, 140 pitches (90 with elec), 14 hot showers, 14 WCs, 1 CWP. **𝄞 &**

| ~ | ⚓ | ⌂ | R | ▦ | 🍺 | ◐ | ✕ | ⚲ | ⒣ | | |

Playground; ornamental birds/small animal park; apartments for rent.
PRICES: Caravan with family 109.00,
Tent with two adults 70.00. CC: none.
The campsite is 1.9 km from the centre of Draguignan. Follow signs to Château Rouge.

DREUX Eure-et-Loir   2D

Camp Municipal 28500 Vernouillet.
Tel 02 37 46 69 57, Fax 02 37 42 92 90.
OPEN: 01/06−15/10. SIZE: 0.43 ha, 19 pitches (all with elec), 3 hot showers (charge), 8 WCs, 2 French WCs. &

| ~ | ⚓ | ⌂ | R | | | | | | | | 🏍 |

Shop at 1.5 km. Restaurant at 0.05 km.
PRICES: (1996) Caravan with family 76.00,
Tent with two adults 37.00. CC: none.
Vernouillet is just south of Dreux. Campsite is near the church.

Les Etangs Marsalin
28500 Vert-en-Drouais.
Tel 02 37 82 92 23, Fax 02 37 82 85 47.
English spoken.
OPEN: all year. SIZE: 2 ha, 65 pitches (all with elec), 8 hot showers, 6 WCs, 4 CWPs. **𝄞 &**

| ~ | ⚓ | ⛹ | R | | | ✕ | | | | | |

Shop at 3 km.
PRICES: (1996) Caravan with family 86.00,
Tent with two adults 43.50. CC: none.
Go west on N12 from Dreux towards Nonancourt then turn right to Vert-en-Drouais.

DUCEY Manche   1D

Camping St-Michel Courtils, 50220 Ducey.
Tel 02 33 70 96 90. English spoken.
OPEN: 01/04−30/09. SIZE: 3 ha, 60 pitches (50 with elec, 12 statics), 11 hot showers, 17 WCs, 1 French WC, 1 CWP. **𝄞 &**

| ≋ | ⚓ | ⌂ | R | ▦ | 🍺 | ☕ | | | ⚲ | ⒣ | |

Shop at 0.2 km. Restaurant at 0.2 km.
PRICES: (1996) Caravan with family 94.00,
Tent with two adults 54.00. CC: Visa.
From Ducey take the road to Courtils, turn left after passing through the village.

Camping St-Michel

near Ducey
Just a spin from The Mont

DUN-SUR-MEUSE Meuse   3A

Camping Le Brouzel 26 rue du Moulin, 55110 Sivry-sur-Meuse.
Tel 03 29 85 86 45.
OPEN: 01/04−01/10. SIZE: 1.5 ha, 50 pitches (all with elec), 3 hot showers, 2 WCs, 8 French WCs, 1 CWP. &

| ~ | ⚓ | ⚲ | | | | | ✕ | | | | |

Shop at 0.5 km.
PRICES: (1996) Caravan with family 74.00,
Tent with two adults 38.00. CC: none.
South-east of Dun-sur-Meuse on D964. Signposted in Sivry-sur-Meuse.

Camping Nantrise Romagne-sur-Montfaucon, 55110 Dun-sur-Meuse.
Tel 03 29 85 12 63.
OPEN: 09/04−30/09. SIZE: 0.4 ha, 25 pitches (15 with elec), 2 hot showers (charge), 6 WCs, 3 French WCs, 1 CWP.

| | | ⛹ | R | | | | | | | | |

Shop at 10 km. Restaurant at 0.5 km.
PRICES: (1996) Caravan with family 100.00,
Tent with two adults 50.00. CC: none.
From Dun take the D998 east to Romagne.

DURTAL Maine/Loire   2C

Camping International
9 rue du Camping, 49430 Durtal.
Tel 02 41 76 31 80. English spoken.
OPEN: 09/04−30/09. SIZE: 3 ha, 130 pitches (all with elec), 14 hot showers, 17 WCs, 3 CWPs. **𝄞 &**

| ~ | ⚓ | ⛹ | R | ▦ | | | | ⒣ | | | |

Shop at 0.5 km. Restaurant at 1 km. Swimming pool 50 m.
PRICES: Caravan with family 74.00,
Tent with two adults 46.00. CC: none.
Signposted from motorway A11-E501. Between Angers and Le Mans on N23. Campsite is beside the River Loir.

EBREUIL Allier   5A

Camping de la Filature 03450 Ebreuil.
Tel 04 70 90 72 01, Fax 04 70 90 79 48.
English spoken.
OPEN: 01/04−30/09. SIZE: 4 ha, 50 pitches (all with elec, 5 statics), 9 hot showers, 13 WCs, 1 CWP. **𝄞 &**

| ~ | ⚓ | ⛹ | R | ▦ | 🍺 | ◐ | | | ⒣ | | |

Shop at 1 km. Restaurant at 1 km. Canoes, bikes, riding, video, library, mini-golf, table tennis, bar.
PRICES: (1996) Caravan with family 114.00, Tent with two adults 75.00. CC: Euro/Access, Visa.
Campsite is signposted from exit 12 of A71 (5 km away). Clearly signposted on arrival in Ebreuil (1 km from Ebreuil on D915 towards Gorges-de-la-Sioule).

EGLETONS Corrèze 5A

Camping Le Lac 19300 Egletons.
Tel 05 55 93 14 75, Fax 05 55 93 14 75.
English spoken.
OPEN: all year. SIZE: 9 ha, 75 pitches (68 with elec),
8 hot showers, 10 WCs, 2 CWPs. **✆**

Shop at 2 km. Swimming pool 0.1 km, lake
0.5 km.
PRICES: (1996) Caravan with family 112.00,
Tent with two adults 64.00. CC: none.
*Campsite is 2 km past Egletons on the N89
towards Ussel.*

ELLIANT Finistère 1C

Camping Municipal de Keryanic 29370 Elliant.
Tel 02 98 94 16 19, Fax 02 98 94 12 22.
English spoken.
OPEN: 01/07–31/08. SIZE: 1 ha, 10 pitches (all with
elec), 7 hot showers, 10 WCs.

Shop at 0.8 km. Restaurant at 1.5 km. Swimming
pool 1 km.
PRICES: (1996) Caravan with family 62.90,
Tent with two adults 37.10. CC: none.
On D150.

EMBRUN Hautes-Alpes 6A

Camping Les Cariamas
05380 Châteauroux-les-Alpes.
Tel 04 92 73 22 63. English spoken.
OPEN: 01/07–24/08. SIZE: 10 ha, 150 pitches
(75 with elec), 21 hot showers, 21 WCs.

Shop at 1 km. Restaurant at 2 km.
PRICES: (1996) Caravan with family 148.00,
Tent with two adults 80.00. CC: none.
Between Gap and Briançon, just north of Embrun.

Les Pins 05380 Châteauroux-les-Alpes.
Tel 04 92 43 22 64.
OPEN: 01/05–30/09. SIZE: 3 ha, 80 pitches (all with
elec), 9 hot showers, 12 WCs, 2 CWPs. &

Shop at 0.5 km. Restaurant at 0.5 km. Excellent
base for canoeing, hiking, fishing, etc.
PRICES: (1996) Caravan with family 86.00,
Tent with two adults 44.00. CC: none.
*North from Embrun on the N94 to Châteauroux.
Turn left out of the central square. Well
signposted.*

ENTRAIGUES Isère 5B

Camping Municipal Les Vigneaux
38740 Entraigues.
Tel 04 76 30 22 21.

OPEN: 15/05–15/09. SIZE: 31 pitches (all with elec),
5 hot showers, 5 WCs, 1 CWP. **✆** &

Shop at 0.5 km. Restaurant at 0.4 km.
PRICES: (1996) Caravan with family 66.00,
Tent with two adults 32.00. CC: none.
*From Grenoble, south on E712 then left on D526
to Entraigues.*

EPERNAY Marne 3A

Camping Municipal allées de Cumières,
51200 Epernay.
Tel 03 26 55 32 14. English spoken.
OPEN: 01/04–30/09. SIZE: 2 ha, 130 pitches
(100 with elec), 13 hot showers, 32 WCs. **✆**

Shop at 1 km. Restaurant at 1 km.
PRICES: (1996) Caravan with family 66.50,
Tent with two adults 41.00. CC: none.
*From Epernay centre heading towards Reims on
the D301, the campsite is near the stadium and
well signposted.*

EPINAL Vosges 3D

Camping du Lac de Bouzey
19 rue du Lac, 88390 Sanchey.
Tel 03 29 82 49 41, Fax 03 29 64 28 03. English spoken.
OPEN: all year. SIZE: 2.5 ha, 162 pitches (all with
elec, 25 statics), 24 hot showers, 25 WCs. **✆** &

PRICES: (1996) Caravan with family 165.00, Tent
with two adults 95.00. CC: Amex, Euro/Access, Visa.
*From Epinal, take the D460 towards Darney.
Campsite is 300 m from intersection of D460 and
D41 at Sanchey.*

ERNEE Mayenne 1D

Camping Caravaning à la Ferme
La Lande, La Croixville, 53380 Juvigné.
Tel 02 43 68 57 00. English spoken.
OPEN: 01/04–01/11. SIZE: 0.7 ha, 6 pitches (all with
elec), 1 hot shower, 2 WCs, 1 CWP.

Shop at 4 km. Restaurant at 4 km.
PRICES: (1996) Caravan with family 49.00,
Tent with two adults 25.00. CC: none.
*From Ernée take D29 to Juvigné and from there
turn left to Le Bourgneuf.*

ERQUY Côtes-du-Nord 1D

Camping Les Roches Caroual Village, 22430 Erquy.
Tel 02 96 72 32 90, Fax 02 96 72 32 90.
English spoken.
OPEN: 01/04–01/10. SIZE: 2.8 ha, 140 pitches (100 with
elec), 13 hot showers, 15 WCs, 1 CWP. **✆** &

France

⌘   🏊   ♀   R   ⊡   🍴   ☕ | Ⓗ

Restaurant at 2.5 km. Mini-golf, table tennis, volley ball, boules.
PRICES: Caravan with family 96.00, Tent with two adults 54.00. CC: none.
From Erquy go towards Lamballe-St-Brieuc and the campsite is 2 km ahead on the right.

Camping Bellevue 22430 Erquy.
Tel 02 96 72 33 04. English spoken.
OPEN: 09/04–30/09. SIZE: 2 ha, 140 pitches (all with elec, 6 statics), 15 hot showers, 15 WCs, 2 CWPs. ☀ ♿

🏕   R   ⊡   🍴   ☕   ✕   ⌁   Ⓗ

Heated pool; 20% discount March to June and September.
PRICES: (1996) Caravan with family 127.00, Tent with two adults 69.00. CC: Euro/Access, Visa.
Between Erquy and Pléneuf-Val-André.

Camping Bellevue ★★★

at Erquy

Beautiful Brittany beckons

Le Vieux Moulin rue des Moulins, 22430 Erquy.
Tel 02 96 72 34 23, Fax 02 96 72 36 63.
English spoken.
OPEN: 01/04–25/09. SIZE: 4 ha, 173 pitches (120 with elec), 23 hot showers, 23 WCs, 3 CWPs. ☀ ♿

⌘   🏊   🏕   R   ⊡   🍴   ✕   ⌁   Ⓗ

Shop at 2 km.
PRICES: (1996) Caravan with family 184.00, Tent with two adults 110.00. CC: none.
Erquy is on D786 and campsite is well signposted.

ETABLES-SUR-MER Côtes-du-Nord   1D

L'Abri Cotier 22680 Etables-sur-Mer.
Tel 02 96 70 61 57, Fax 02 96 70 65 23.
English spoken.
OPEN: 06/05–20/09. SIZE: 2 ha, 140 pitches (all with elec, 4 statics), 14 hot showers, 15 WCs, 3 CWPs. ☀ ♿

⌘   🏊   🟢   R   ⊡   🍴   ☕ | ⌁   Ⓗ

Restaurant at 0.5 km. Sea 0.5 km.
PRICES: Caravan with family 174.00, Tent with two adults 98.00. CC: Euro/Access, Visa.
Take D786 from N12 after St-Brieuc. Site is well signposted.

ETAMPES Essonne   2D

Le Bois de la Justice 91930 Monnerville.
Tel 01 64 95 05 34, Fax 01 64 95 17 31. English spoken.

OPEN: 01/03–30/11. SIZE: 5.6 ha, 50 pitches (40 with elec, 100 statics), 20 hot showers, 20 WCs, 1 CWP. ♿

🟢   R   ⊡ | ⌁

Shop at 1.8 km. Restaurant at 5 km.
PRICES: (1996) Caravan with family 180.00, Tent with two adults 90.00. CC: none.
Monnerville is 50 km north of Orléans and 10 km south of Etampes.

Camping Le Bois de la Justice

near Etampes

Woodland camping in reach of Paris

Caravaning Le Vauvert
Ormoy-la-Rivière, 91150 Etampes.
Tel 01 64 94 21 39, Fax 01 69 92 72 59.
OPEN: 15/01–15/12. SIZE: 11 ha, 30 pitches (25 with elec, 258 statics), 36 hot showers, 36 WCs. ☀ ♿

~   🏊   🟢

Shop at 2 km. Restaurant at 2 km. Ball games, playground, tennis, boules; fishing nearby.
PRICES: (1996) Caravan with family 100.00, Tent with two adults 60.00. CC: none.
On D49 from Etampes. Campsite is signposted from N20 and is near the River Juine. (No motor caravans.)

ETEL Morbihan   1C

Camp Municipal de la Falaise rue de la Barre, 56410 Etel.
Tel 02 97 55 33 79, Fax 02 97 55 34 14.
English spoken.
OPEN: 01/06–15/09. SIZE: 220 pitches (180 with elec), 20 hot showers, 22 WCs, 5 CWPs.

⌘   🏊   🟢   R   ⊡

Shop at 0.3 km. Restaurant at 0.5 km.
PRICES: (1996) Caravan with family 101.00, Tent with two adults 48.50. CC: none.
Etel is 12 km north of Carnac.

Camping des Mégalithes Kerfélicité, 56410 Erdeven.
Tel 02 97 55 68 76.
OPEN: 01/04–30/09. SIZE: 5 ha, 100 pitches (60 with elec), 11 hot showers, 19 WCs, 1 CWP. ☀ ♿

🟢   R   ⊡   🍴   ☕ | Ⓗ

Shop at 1.5 km. Restaurant at 1.5 km.
PRICES: (1996) Caravan with family 125.00, Tent with two adults 72.00. CC: Euro/Access.
From Etel, south on the Carnac road (D781). In Erdeven, follow signs.

France

Camping Le Moteno
route du Magouer, 56680 Plouhinec.
Tel 02 97 36 76 63, Fax 02 97 85 81 84.
English spoken.
OPEN: 01/04–30/09. SIZE: 4 ha, 120 pitches
(all with elec). ℓ ᴧ

Shop at 3 km. Billiards, table tennis, games room;
mobile homes for hire.
PRICES: (1996) Caravan with family 147.00,
Tent with two adults 91.00. CC: none.
From Etel, take the D781 towards Port-Louis and
turn left before Plouhinec towards Magouer.

ETRETAT Seine Marit   2A

Camping Le Grand Hameau
76280 St-Jouin-Bauneval.
Tel 02 35 20 70 86. English spoken.
OPEN: 01/03–30/10. SIZE: 1.2 ha, 75 pitches
(63 with elec, 5 statics), 4 hot showers (charge),
5 WCs, 1 CWP. ℓ ᴧ

Shop at 3 km. Restaurant at 1 km.
PRICES: (1996) Caravan with family 80.00,
Tent with two adults 45.00. CC: none.
From Le Havre, take D940 towards Etretat. Turn
left 7 km before Etretat on to D111 and follow signs.

EVAUX-LES-BAINS Creuse   5A

Camping Municipal 23110 Evaux-les-Bains.
Tel 05 55 65 55 82.
OPEN: 01/04–01/11. SIZE: 1 ha, 50 pitches (40 with
elec), 6 hot showers, 7 WCs. ℓ ᴧ

Shop at 0.2 km. Restaurant at 0.4 km. Swimming
pool 0.2 km.
PRICES: (1996) Caravan with family 55.60,
Tent with two adults 27.00. CC: none.
South-west of Montluçon via D993.

EVIAN-LES-BAINS Haute-Savoie   6A

Camping Clos Savoyard Maxilly-sur-Léman,
74500 Evian-les-Bains.
Tel 04 50 75 45 94.
OPEN: 01/04–30/09. SIZE: 2 ha, 100 pitches
(all with elec), 11 hot showers, 16 WCs, 5 CWPs. ℓ

Restaurant at 1 km. Lake 1.5 km.
PRICES: (1996) Caravan with family 95.00,
Tent with two adults 50.00. CC: none.
Take D24 from Evian to Maxilly-sur-Léman.

Camping Le Rys 74500 Lugrin.
Tel 04 50 76 05 75. English spoken.
OPEN: 01/04–31/10. SIZE: 2 ha, 75 pitches (all with
elec), 8 hot showers, 12 WCs, 2 CWPs. ℓ ᴧ

Shop at 0.6 km. Restaurant at 0.6 km. Beautiful
lake and mountain views.
PRICES: (1996) Caravan with family 93.00,
Tent with two adults 52.00. CC: Euro/Access.
From Evian-les-Bains go east on N5 to Lugrin.
Campsite is signposted from the village.

Camping Vieille Eglise 74500 Lugrin.
Tel 04 50 76 01 95, Fax 04 50 76 13 12.
English spoken.
OPEN: 01/04–31/10. SIZE: 1 ha, 100 pitches (70 with
elec), 11 hot showers, 11 WCs, 2 CWPs. ℓ ᴧ

Restaurant at 0.8 km.
PRICES: (1996) Caravan with family 128.00,
Tent with two adults 73.00. CC: none.
Take N5 along Lac Léman; the campsite is 3 km
from Evian-les-Bains and 0.8 km from the lake.

De Grande Rive 74500 Evian-les-Bains.
Tel 04 50 75 42 19.
OPEN: 01/05–30/09. SIZE: 1 ha, 50 pitches (all with
elec), 6 hot showers (charge), 10 WCs, 14 French
WCs, 1 CWP.

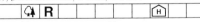

PRICES: unavailable. CC: Euro/Access.
300 m from marina, Port de Plaisance.

LES EYZIES-DE-TAYAC Dordogne   4B

Camping Le Mas
Sireuil, 24620 Les Eyzies-de-Tayac.
Tel 05 53 29 68 06, Fax 05 53 31 12 73.
English spoken.
OPEN: 15/04–30/09. SIZE: 5 ha, 130 pitches (100 with
elec, 5 statics), 20 hot showers, 20 WCs. ℓ ᴧ

PRICES: (1996) Caravan with family 144.00, Tent
with two adults 89.00. CC: Amex, Euro/Access, Visa.
Sireuil is next to Les Eyzies.

Camping à la Ferme
Le Queylou, 24620 Les Eyzies-de-Tayac.
Tel 05 53 06 94 71. English spoken.
OPEN: 01/04–01/11. SIZE: 2 ha, 8 pitches (all with
elec), 3 hot showers, 4 WCs, 1 CWP.

Shop at 4 km. Restaurant at 4 km.
PRICES: (1996) Caravan with family 74.00, Tent
with two adults 42.00. CC: none.
From Les Eyzies go south-west on D706 for 2 km.
Turn left and campsite is well signposted 1 km
ahead.

Camping à la Ferme du Poulou
Tursac, 24620 Les Eyzies-de-Tayac.
Tel 05 53 06 98 17.
OPEN: 15/03–15/11. SIZE: 3 ha, 33 pitches (all with

France

elec, 4 statics), 4 hot showers, 6 WCs, 1 CWP. ⚓ &

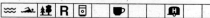

Shop at 3 km. Restaurant at 3 km. Way-marked
walks.
PRICES: (1996) Caravan with family 89.00,
Tent with two adults 45.00. CC: none.
*D706 to Les Eyzies, route de Montignac Lascaux.
The site is on right after leaving the town.*

Roc de Lavandre
24260 St-Félix-de-Reilhac.
Tel 05 53 03 23 47. English spoken.
OPEN: 01/05–30/09. SIZE: 4 ha, 40 pitches (32 with
elec, 5 statics), 3 hot showers, 4 WCs.

Shop at 10 km. Restaurant at 2 km. Fishing.
PRICES: (1996) Caravan with family 98.00,
Tent with two adults 46.00. CC: none.
On D47, 12 km north of Les Eyzies.

LE FAOU Finistère   1C

Camping Kerliver
Kerliver, 29460 Hanvec.
Tel 02 98 20 03 14.
OPEN: 15/06–15/09. SIZE: 1.25 ha, 75 pitches (25 with
elec), 6 hot showers, 6 WCs, 1 French WC. ⚓

Shop at 3 km. Restaurant at 3 km.
PRICES: (1996) Caravan with family 65.20,
Tent with two adults 31.60. CC: none.
*From Le Faou go north-east to Hanvec then
turn left towards Hôpital-Camfrout. Site is 4 km
on the left.*

Camping Le Seillou 29580 Le Faou.
Tel 02 98 81 92 14. English spoken.
OPEN: 01/04–30/09. SIZE: 3 ha, 120 pitches
(80 with elec, 20 statics), 7 hot showers, 14 WCs,
2 CWPs.

Restaurant at 0.3 km.
PRICES: (1996) Caravan with family 67.00,
Tent with two adults 36.00. CC: none.
5 km from Le Faou on the D791, towards Crozon.

LE FAOUET Morbihan   1C

Camping Municipal Beg er Roch
route de Lorient, 56320 Le Faouet.
Tel 02 97 23 15 11. English spoken.
OPEN: 09/03–15/09. SIZE: 3 ha, 85 pitches (70 with
elec), 7 hot showers, 10 WCs, 2 CWPs. ⚓ &

Shop at 2 km. Restaurant at 2 km.
PRICES: Caravan with family 122.00,
Tent with two adults 70.00. CC: none.
From Le Faouet go south on D769. Site on left.

FAVERGES Haute-Savoie   6A

Camping Champ Tillet
Marlens, 74910 Faverges.
Tel 04 50 44 40 07, Fax 04 50 44 40 07. English spoken.
OPEN: all year. SIZE: 3 ha, 120 pitches (80 with
elec), 12 hot showers, 12 WCs. &

Shop at 4 km.
PRICES: (1996) Caravan with family 135.00,
Tent with two adults 70.00. CC: Amex, Visa.
*Faverges is south of Lake Annecy and there are
signs to the campsite in the village.*

FERRETTE Haut-Rhin   3D

Camp des Hêtres Oberg, 68480 Bendorf.
Tel 03 89 40 34 72.
OPEN: 01/05–01/10. SIZE: 4 ha, 20 pitches (50 with
elec, 100 statics), 12 hot showers, 12 WCs,
2 CWPs. ⚓ &

Shop at 5 km. Restaurant at 5 km.
PRICES: (1996) Caravan with family 89.00,
Tent with two adults 55.00. CC: none.
*From Ferrette, take the D41 south. After 1.5 km
turn right to Bendorf.*

FEURS Loire   5B

Camping de la Route Bleue 42510 Balbigny.
Tel 04 77 27 24 97, Fax 04 77 28 18 05.
English spoken.
OPEN: 01/04–31/10. SIZE: 2.5 ha, 100 pitches
(60 with elec, 6 statics), 8 hot showers, 8 WCs,
8 French WCs, 3 CWPs. ⚓ &

Motorvan services; fishing, boating, windsurfing
nearby.
PRICES: (1996) Caravan with family 106.00,
Tent with two adults 60.00. CC: Amex,
Euro/Access, Visa.
*From Feurs north on N82. Campsite is in the
north of Balbigny, 2 km from N82.*

FIGEAC Lot   5C

Camp Municipal les Rives du Célé
Domaine du Surgié, 46100 Figeac.
Tel 05 65 34 59 00, Fax 05 65 34 59 00.
English spoken.
OPEN: 01/04–30/09. SIZE: 4 ha, 103 pitches
(all with elec), 15 hot showers, 21 WCs. ⚓ &

Shop at 2 km. Restaurant at 0.5 km. Large leisure
complex with excellent facilities nearby.
PRICES: (1996) Caravan with family 130.00, Tent
with two adults 95.00. CC: Euro/Access, Visa.
Campsite is 1.6 km from town centre.

France

LA FLECHE Sarthe-   2C

Camping La Chabotière 72800 Luché Pringé.
Tel 02 43 45 10 00, Fax 02 43 45 10 00.
English spoken.
OPEN: 01/04–15/10. SIZE: 1.7 ha, 75 pitches
(all with elec), 9 hot showers, 7 WCs, 4 French
WCs, 1 CWP. ☕ ♿

Restaurant at 0.1 km. Entertainment in HS;
mini-golf and tennis nearby.
PRICES: (1996) Caravan with family 82.50,
Tent with two adults 43.00. CC: none.
East of La Flèche on the D13.

FLORAC Lozère   5C

Camping Municipal La Malene
Florac, 48210 La Malene.
Tel 04 66 48 58 55, Fax 04 66 48 58 51.
OPEN: 01/04–15/10. SIZE: 1.5 ha, 100 pitches
(56 with elec), 5 hot showers, 9 WCs, 1 CWP. ☕

Shop at 0.5 km.
PRICES: (1996) Caravan with family 107.00,
Tent with two adults 50.00. CC: none.
On the N106 north of Florac.

FLUMET Savoie   6A

Camping de Vieux Moulin
Sous La Cour, 73590 Flumet.
Tel 04 79 31 70 06. English spoken.
OPEN: all year. SIZE: 2 ha, 120 pitches (86 with
elec), 10 hot showers, 13 WCs, 1 CWP. ♿

Shop at 1 km. Restaurant at 0.01 km. Ski-pass
reduction.
PRICES: (1996) Caravan with family 105.00,
Tent with two adults 53.00. CC: none.
*From Flumet go beyond the village on the road to
Megève; turn right after the tunnel and take the
middle road leading down to the ski-lift, 50 m.*

FOIX Ariège   5C

Camping Municipal Pré-Lombard
route d'Ussat, 09400 Tarascon-sur-Ariege.
Tel 05 61 05 61 94, Fax 05 61 05 78 93. English spoken.
OPEN: 01/02–01/11. SIZE: 4 ha, 180 pitches (all
with elec), 20 hot showers, 10 WCs, 3 CWPs. ☕ ♿

Shop at 0.4 km. Entertainments in summer;
motorvan services.
PRICES: Caravan with family 137.00,
Tent with two adults 78.00. CC: Amex, Visa.
*South from Foix on the N20. Turn off into Tarascon,
over the river bridge and follow signs south towards
Ussat (D23). Site is 1 km from centre beside the river.*

La Roucateille 15 rue de Pradal,
09330 Montgaillard.
Tel 05 61 65 22 50.
OPEN: 01/04–30/09. SIZE: 1 ha, 30 pitches (all with
elec), 5 hot showers (charge), 7 WCs, 1 CWP. ☕ ♿

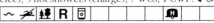

Shop at 2 km. Restaurant at 1 km. Swimming pool
nearby.
PRICES: (1996) Caravan with family 97.00,
Tent with two adults 42.00. CC: none.
*On the N20, 4 km south of Foix towards Andorra.
Campsite is signposted from the roundabout
leading to Montgaillard.*

FONT-ROMEU Pyrénées Orient   5C

Las Closas 66800 Err.
Tel 04 68 04 71 42, Fax 04 68 04 07 20.
English spoken.
OPEN: all year. SIZE: 2 ha, 111 pitches (all with elec,
50 statics), 14 hot showers, 25 WCs, 1 CWP. ☕ ♿

Shop at 0.05 km. Restaurant at 1 km.
PRICES: (1996) Caravan with family 122.00,
Tent with two adults 62.00. CC: Visa.
*Err is south of Font-Romeu on the D116 between
Saillagouse and the Spanish border.*

FONTAINEBLEAU Seine/Marne   2D

Camping Municipal Les Prés
chemin des Prés, 77880 Grez-sur-Loing.
Tel 01 64 45 72 75.
OPEN: 15/03–15/11. SIZE: 6 ha, 200 pitches
(100 with elec, 100 statics), 9 hot showers,
22 WCs, 1 CWP. ☕ ♿

Shop at 0.3 km. Restaurant at 0.3 km. Fishing, tennis.
PRICES: (1996) Caravan with family 83.00,
Tent with two adults 43.00. CC: none.
*Grez-sur-Loing is on N7 between Fontainebleau
and Nemours. After Bourron Marlotte, turn on the
left towards Moncourt. Turn right after Le Loing
river.*

Camping les Prés
at Fontainebleau
Pause here for Paris

Camping Les Canalous
Port de Plaisance, 77670 St-Mammes.
Tel 01 64 69 23 45, Fax 01 64 23 00 14. English spoken.
OPEN: all year. SIZE: 5 ha, 90 pitches (60 with elec,
15 statics), 12 hot showers, 10 WCs, 1 CWP. ☕ ♿

France

France

Shop at 0.8 km. Restaurant at 0.8 km.
PRICES: (1996) Caravan with family 90.00,
Tent with two adults 50.00. CC: none.
10 km east of Fontainebleau on the N6. Turn left through St-Moret. The campsite is 800 m from the railway station and signposted.

FONTENAY-LE-COMTE Vendée 4A

Camping La Joletière 85200 Mervent.
Tel 02 51 00 26 87, Fax 02 51 00 27 55.
OPEN: all year. SIZE: 39 ha, 73 pitches (all with elec), 6 hot showers, 12 WCs. ⚓ ♿

Shop at 0.8 km.
PRICES: (1996) Caravan with family 105.00, Tent with two adults 56.00. CC: Amex, Euro/Access.
From Fontenay-le-Comte go towards La Châtaigneraie; turn right to the lake and Mervent.

Camping Les Petits Prés
85770 Le Poire-sur-Velluire.
Tel 02 51 52 37 77.
OPEN: 01/04–31/10. SIZE: 3 ha, 50 pitches (40 with elec), 4 hot showers, 5 WCs, 1 CWP. ♿

Shop at 0.2 km. Restaurant at 0.5 km.
PRICES: (1996) Caravan with family 68.00, Tent with two adults 36.00. CC: none.
Take D938 from Fontenay-le-Comte to La Rochelle. Velluire is 7 km down this road and off to the right. Well signposted.

FORCALQUIER Alpes/Hte-Prov 6C

Camping La Rivière Lieu-dit Les Côtes,
St-Maime, 04300 Forcalquier.
Tel 04 92 79 54 66, Fax 04 92 79 54 66.
English spoken.
OPEN: all year. SIZE: 3.5 ha, 100 pitches, 10 hot showers, 10 WCs. ⚓ ♿

Restaurant at 5 km. Children's pool.
PRICES: Caravan with family 108.00,
Tent with two adults 61.00. CC: none.
From Folcalquier, drive south on the N100, then turn left on the D13 to St-Maime and the campsite is 1 km south-east of the village.

Camping Lac du Moulin de Ventre
04300 Niozelles.
Tel 04 92 78 63 31, Fax 04 92 79 86 92. English spoken.
OPEN: 01/04–25/09. SIZE: 28 ha, 100 pitches (79 with elec, 4 statics), 17 hot showers, 20 WCs, 3 CWPs. ⚓ ♿

Children's entertainment; meal for campers on Tuesdays.

PRICES: (1996) Caravan with family 185.00, Tent with two adults 105.00. CC: Euro/Access.
N100 east from Forcalquier. Site is on the right, between Niozelles and La Brillanne.

LA FORET-FOUESNANT Finistère 1C

Camping Club du St-Laurent Kerleven,
29940 La Forêt-Fouesnant.
Tel 02 98 56 97 65, Fax 02 98 56 92 51.
English spoken.
OPEN: 01/04–15/09. SIZE: 5 ha. ♿

Shop at 2 km. Restaurant at 2 km.
PRICES: (1996) Caravan with family 185.00,
Tent with two adults 135.00. CC: none.
In La Forêt-Fouesnant turn right towards Kerleven and follow signs to campsite.

Le Camping de Kerleven route de Port-la-Forêt,
29940 La Forêt-Fouesnant.
Tel 02 98 56 98 83, Fax 02 98 56 82 22.
English spoken.
OPEN: 20/05–30/09. SIZE: 4 ha, 185 pitches (160 with elec, 10 statics), 19 hot showers, 18 WCs, 2 CWPs. ⚓ ♿

Sailing, golf, tennis, children's playground.
PRICES: Caravan with family 165.00, Tent with two adults 98.00. CC: none.
From Fouesnant, 5 km west to La Forêt-Fouesnant, then turn right to Kerleven beach. At the beach turn right towards port. Site is 100 m on the right.

Camping de la Plage 29940 La Forêt-Fouesnant.
Tel 02 98 56 96 25. English spoken.
OPEN: all year. SIZE: 1 ha, 65 pitches (all with elec), 6 hot showers, 8 WCs, 2 CWPs. ⚓ ♿

Shop at 0.2 km. Restaurant at 0.2 km.
PRICES: (1996) Caravan with family 128.00,
Tent with two adults 75.00. CC: none.
From Fouesnant go east to La Forêt. Turn right after estuary to Port-la-Forêt and campsite is on the right as you enter Kerleven.

Manoir de Pen ar Steir
29940 La Forêt-Fouesnant.
Tel 02 98 56 97 75, Fax 02 98 51 40 34. English spoken.
OPEN: all year. SIZE: 3 ha, 105 pitches (all with elec, 24 statics), 18 hot showers, 19 WCs, 30 French WCs, 2 CWPs. ⚓ ♿

Shop at 0.1 km. Restaurant at 0.1 km. Tennis, mini-golf.
PRICES: (1996) Caravan with family 156.00,
Tent with two adults 93.00. CC: none.
On the D783 south of Quimper. The campsite is in the village.

FORGES-LES-EAUX Seine Marit 2B

Camping Municipal La Minière
bd Nicolas Thiessé, 76440 Forges-les-Eaux.
Tel 02 35 90 53 91.
OPEN: 01/04–30/09. SIZE: 2 ha, 125 pitches
(all with elec, 50 statics), 4 hot showers, 6 WCs,
4 French WCs. ℄

Shop at 0.6 km. Restaurant at 0.6 km. Playground,
table tennis, boules.
PRICES: (1996) Caravan with family 83.00,
Tent with two adults 42.00. CC: none.
The campsite is well signposted in Forges-les-Eaux.

FOUESNANT Finistère 1C

Le Camp du Vorlen Beg-Meil, 29170 Fouesnant.
Tel 02 98 94 97 36, Fax 02 98 94 97 23.
English spoken.
OPEN: 01/05–20/09. SIZE: 10 ha, 500 pitches (all
with elec, 50 statics), 70 hot showers, 65 WCs. ℄ &

Shop at 1 km. Restaurant at 1 km. Sea 200 m.
PRICES: Caravan with family 158.00, Tent with two
adults 98.00. CC: Euro/Access, Visa.
5 km south from Fouesnant to Beg-Meil.

Camping La Piscine Kerleya, 29170 Beg-Meil.
Tel 02 98 56 56 06, Fax 02 98 56 57 64.
English spoken.
OPEN: 15/05–15/09. SIZE: 4 ha, 160 pitches
(all with elec), 18 hot showers, 20 WCs, 4 French
WCs, 3 CWPs. ℄ &

Restaurant at 2.5 km. Flume, sauna, solarium.
PRICES: (1996) Caravan with family 148.50,
Tent with two adults 90.00. CC: Amex,
Euro/Access, Visa.
*From Fouesnant take D45 to Beg-Meil and follow
signs to campsite.*

La Roche Perlée Beg-Meil, 29170 Fouesnant.
Tel 02 98 94 94 15, Fax 02 98 94 48 05.
English spoken.
OPEN: 28/03–28/09. SIZE: 2 ha, 123 pitches
(all with elec, 48 statics), 17 hot showers, 24 WCs,
3 CWPs. ℄

Mobile homes for hire.
PRICES: Caravan with family 179.00, Tent with two
adults 115.00. CC: Euro/Access, Visa.
*From Fouesnant take the road to Beg-Meil (D45).
Campsite 1 km on left before entering Beg-Meil.*

FOUGERES Ille/Vilaine 1D

Camping Municipal de Paron 35300 Fougères.
Tel 02 99 99 40 81, Fax 02 99 94 88 17.
English spoken.

OPEN: all year. SIZE: 2.5 ha, 40 pitches (all with
elec), 15 hot showers, 15 WCs, 1 CWP. ℄ &

Shop at 0.3 km.
PRICES: (1996) Caravan with family 86.50, Tent
with two adults 46.60. CC: none.
*Leave town centre in Paris direction and then
take road towards La Chapelle-Janson.*

FOURAS Charente-Marit 4A

Camping Les Charmilles
St-Laurent-de-la-Pré, 17450 Fouras.
Tel 05 46 84 00 05, Fax 02 51 33 94 07.
English spoken.
OPEN: 01/04–15/09. SIZE: 3 ha, 150 pitches
(100 with elec, 10 statics), 30 hot showers,
30 WCs, 2 CWPs. ℄ &

Restaurant at 1.5 km. Flume, mini-golf.
PRICES: (1996) Caravan with family 198.00,
Tent with two adults 120.00. CC: Amex,
Euro/Access, Visa.
On the N137 in Fouras.

FRANGY Haute-Savoie 5B

Camping Municipal du Nant Matraz
15 route de Genève, 74910 Seyssel.
Tel 04 50 59 03 68. English spoken.
OPEN: 14/04–30/09. SIZE: 1 ha, 75 pitches (all with
elec, 3 statics), 8 hot showers, 10 WCs, 2 French
WCs, 2 CWPs. ℄ &

Shop at 0.1 km. Restaurant at 0.5 km. Water sports
and swimming pool 1 km.
PRICES: (1996) Caravan with family 89.00,
Tent with two adults 48.00. CC: none.
From Frangy take the D992 south to Seyssel.

FREJUS Var 6C

La Bastiane chemin des Suvières,
83480 Puget-sur-Argens.
Tel 04 94 45 51 31, Fax 04 94 81 50 55.
English spoken.
OPEN: 15/02–15/11. SIZE: 4 ha, 184 pitches
(all with elec, 37 statics), 22 hot showers, 24 WCs,
3 CWPs. ℄ &

Tennis, mini-golf, entertainment.
PRICES: Caravan with family 202.00,
Tent with two adults 95.00. CC: none.
*4 km inland from Fréjus, off the N7. From A8, take
Puget-sur-Argens exit. Turn left at the first lights.*

Camping de Fréjus
route de Bagnols, 83600 Fréjus.
Tel 04 94 40 88 03, Fax 04 94 40 87 68. English spoken.

France

OPEN: all year. SIZE: 6 ha, 230 pitches (120 with elec, 30 statics), 24 hot showers, 20 WCs, 3 CWPs. ☎

Shop at 1 km. Restaurant at 1.5 km. Flume. PRICES: (1996) Caravan with family 172.00, Tent with two adults 93.00. CC: Euro/Access, Visa. *North of Fréjus on the route de Bagnols-en-Forêt. The site is 3 km from the traffic lights.*

Camping Caravaning des Aubrèdes
83480 Puget-sur-Argens.
Tel 04 94 45 51 46, Fax 04 94 45 28 92. English spoken.
OPEN: 01/04–30/09. SIZE: 3.8 ha, 200 pitches (120 with elec, 20 statics), 25 hot showers, 28 WCs, 10 French WCs, 3 CWPs. ☎

Shop at 1 km. Playground, tennis, entertainment; family atmosphere.
PRICES: Caravan with family 170.00, Tent with two adults 102.00. CC: Euro/Access, Visa.

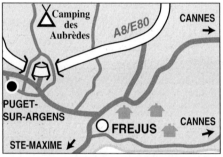

Just off the N7, 4 km inland from Fréjus. Leave motorway A8 at exit for Puget-sur-Argens. Well signposted.

Camping des Philippons
Les Adrets-de-l'Esterel, 83600 Fréjus.
Tel 04 94 40 90 67, Fax 04 94 19 35 92.
OPEN: 01/04–30/10. SIZE: 5 ha, 60 pitches (all with elec), 8 hot showers, 15 WCs. ☎

Shop at 3 km. Restaurant at 0.5 km. Table tennis, boules. Fishing nearby.
PRICES: (1996) Caravan with family 137.00, Tent with two adults 72.00. CC: Euro/Access, Visa.
4 km from the A8 on the D237, between Fréjus and Cannes.

Camping L'Etoile d'Argens 83370 St-Aygulf.
Tel 04 94 81 01 41, Fax 04 94 81 21 45.
English spoken.
OPEN: 01/04–30/09. SIZE: 11 ha, 420 pitches (all with elec, 120 statics), 84 hot showers, 84 WCs, 3 CWPs. ☎ ♿

Mini-golf, tennis; boating; sea 2km.

PRICES: (1996) Caravan with family 244.00. CC: none.
From Fréjus travel to St-Aygulf on N98.

Camping Le Dattier
route de Bagnols-en-Forêt, 83600 Fréjus.
Tel 04 94 40 88 93, Fax 04 94 40 89 01.
English spoken.
OPEN: 01/04–30/09. SIZE: 4 ha, 28 hot showers, 35 WCs. ☎ ♿

Shop at 1 km. Tennis, disco, boules, volley ball, table tennis; sea/water sports 3.5 km.
PRICES: (1996) Caravan with family 213.00, Tent with two adults 126.00. CC: none.
Recommended site. North of Fréjus, campsite is on the route de Bagnols-en-Forêt after approx 2 km. Well signposted.

Camping Le Dattier
at Fréjus
For sun babies of all ages

Camping Les Lauriers Roses
route de Roquebrune (D7), 83370 St-Aygulf.
Tel 04 94 81 24 46, Fax 04 94 81 79 63.
English spoken.
OPEN: 01/04–30/09. SIZE: 2 ha, 65 pitches (all with elec, 8 statics), 16 hot showers, 11 WCs, 1 CWP. ☎ ♿

Shop at 0.5 km. Restaurant at 2 km. Table tennis, basket and volley ball, children's playground, TV; sea 3km.
PRICES: (1996) Caravan with family 205.00, Tent with two adults 102.00. CC: none.
From the A8 exit Puget-sur-Argens towards Fréjus (N7), then take D8 towards St-Aygulf to D7, route de Roquebrune. Campsite is well signposted.

Camping Les Pins Parasols route des Bagnols, 83600 Fréjus.
Tel 04 94 40 88 43. English spoken.
OPEN: all year. SIZE: 4 ha, 189 pitches (all with elec, 20 statics), 30 hot showers, 24 WCs, 3 CWPs. ☎

48 pitches have private sanitary facilities; flume; tennis; sea 6 km.
PRICES: Caravan with family 191.00, Tent with two adults 125.00. CC: none.

Camping Montourey route de Bagnols-en-Forêt, chemin du Reyran, 83600 Fréjus.
Tel 04 94 53 26 41, Fax 04 94 53 26 75.
English spoken.
OPEN: 01/04–30/09. SIZE: 5 ha, 199 pitches (134 with elec, 40 statics), 36 hot showers, 36 WCs, 2 CWPs. ☎ ♿

France

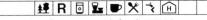

Shop at 1 km.
PRICES: (1996) Caravan with family 165.00,
Tent with two adults 95.00. CC: Amex,
Euro/Access, Visa.
*From central Fréjus go west on Aix road N7.
Turn right by Renault garage towards Bagnols/
Feyance, then right again into chemin du Reyran.*

Holiday Green route de Bagnols-en-Forêt,
quartier de la Lègue (D4), 83600 Fréjus.
Tel 04 94 40 88 20, Fax 04 94 40 78 59. English spoken.
OPEN: 22/03–24/10. SIZE: 15 ha, 120 pitches
(all with elec, 160 statics), 16 hot showers,
23 WCs. ⚲ ♿

PRICES: (1996) Caravan with family 257.00,
Tent with two adults 136.00. CC: Visa.
*Leaving Fréjus on the N7, at the first traffic lights
take the D4 on the right and drive 7 km towards
Bagnols-en-Forêt. Arriving by motorway take
Fréjus exit for 2 km.*
SEE ADVERTISEMENT

FRESNAY-SUR-SARTHE Sarthe   2C

Le Sans Souci rue de Haut-Ary,
72130 Fresnay-sur-Sarthe.
Tel 02 43 97 32 87. English spoken.

OPEN: 01/04–30/09. SIZE: 2 ha, 90 pitches (all with
elec), 10 hot showers, 9 WCs, 2 CWPs. ♿

Restaurant at 1 km. Canoes and kayaks, mini-golf.
PRICES: (1996) Caravan with family 57.50,
Tent with two adults 29.30. CC: none.
Follow signs to campsite in Fresnay-sur-Sarthe.

FRONCLES Haute-Marne   3C

Camp Municipal Les Deux Ponts
52320 Froncles-Buxières.
Tel 03 25 02 33 50.
OPEN: 15/03–15/10. SIZE: 1 ha, 22 pitches (all with
elec), 2 hot showers, 3 WCs, 1 CWP. ⚲

Shop at 0.2 km. Restaurant at 0.5 km.
PRICES: (1996) Caravan with family 38.70,
Tent with two adults 21.20. CC: none.
*Froncles is 4.5 km off the N67 and the campsite is
in the village centre, next to the town hall.*

FRONTIGNAN Hérault   5C

Camping Les Tamaris av d'Ingril,
34110 Frontignan.
Tel 04 67 43 44 77, Fax 04 67 51 20 29.
English spoken.
OPEN: 24/05–14/09. SIZE: 5 ha, 222 pitches
(all with elec, 38 statics), 34 hot showers, 27 WCs,
4 CWPs. ⚲ ♿

PRICES: Caravan with family 235.00, Tent with two
adults 155.00. CC: Euro/Access, Visa.
*From A9 take Sète exit towards Frontignan and
Les Plages. Follow signs to campsite.*

FUMEL Lot/Garonne   4D

Camping de Condat chemin de la Moute,
route de Cahors, 47500 Condat-Fumel.
Tel 05 53 71 45 72. English spoken.
OPEN: all year. SIZE: 2 ha, 70 pitches (all with elec),
6 hot showers, 10 WCs. ⚲ ♿

Restaurant at 3 km. Open for reserved pitches
only LS.
PRICES: (1996) Caravan with family 84.00,
Tent with two adults 46.00. CC: none.
On D911 east of Fumel. Well signposted.

Camping à la Ferme Valenty 46700 Soturac.
Tel 05 65 36 55 24. English spoken.
OPEN: all year. SIZE: 2 ha, 25 pitches (20 with elec,
2 statics), 4 hot showers, 4 WCs, 1 CWP. ⚲

Restaurant at 0.5 km. Mini-golf, mobil homes for
hire, 20% discount in LS.

France

PRICES: (1996) Caravan with family 114.00, Tent with two adults 52.00. CC: none.
From Fumel go east on D911 towards Cahors. Follow signs from Soturac.

Club de Vacances Duravel Le Port de Vire, 46700 Duravel.
Tel 05 65 24 65 06, Fax 05 65 24 64 96.
English spoken.
OPEN: 27/04–01/10. SIZE: 7.6 ha, 220 pitches (all with elec), 34 hot showers, 38 WCs, 4 CWPs. ℂ ♿

Tennis, fishing, canoeing, entertainment.
PRICES: (1996) Caravan with family 197.00, Tent with two adults 118.00. CC: Euro/Access, Visa.
From Fumel head east on D911 for 11 km to Duravel. Turn right in village on to D58 towards Vire.

GACE Orne   2C

Le Pressoir impasse Tahiti, 61230 Gace.
Tel 02 33 35 50 24, Fax 02 33 35 92 82.
English spoken.
OPEN: 01/06–06/09. SIZE: 1 ha, 22 pitches (16 with elec), 4 hot showers, 4 WCs.

Shop at 0.2 km. Restaurant at 0.2 km. Heated swimming pool and tennis 1 km.
PRICES: (1996) Caravan with family 43.00, Tent with two adults 24.00. CC: none.
24 km north of Sées on the N138.

GANNAT Allier   5A

Camping Municipal Rue du Stade 03800 Gannat.
Tel 04 70 90 12 16, Fax 04 70 90 15 22.
English spoken.
OPEN: 01/05–30/09. SIZE: 2 ha, 66 pitches (all with elec), 4 hot showers, 6 WCs, 5 French WCs, 1 CWP. ℂ

Shop at 1 km. Restaurant at 0.5 km. Very quiet site.
PRICES: (1996) Caravan with family 65.00, Tent with two adults 32.00. CC: none.
From Gannat, drive towards Clermont-Ferrand and turn right at the roundabout.

GAP Hautes-Alpes   6C

Alpes-Dauphiné route Napoléon, 05000 Gap.
Tel 04 92 51 29 95, Fax 04 92 53 58 42. English spoken.

OPEN: all year. SIZE: 5 ha, 180 pitches (all with elec, 40 statics), 27 hot showers, 17 WCs, 6 French WCs, 2 CWPs. ℂ ♿

PRICES: Caravan with family 149.00, Tent with two adults 82.00. CC: Euro/Access, Visa.
On N85. From Gap take the road to Grenoble. Campsite is 2 km on right.

Parc des Serigons La Roche-des-Arnauds, 05400 Veynes.
Tel 04 92 57 81 77. English spoken.
OPEN: 01/01–20/09. SIZE: 40 ha, 100 pitches (80 with elec), 19 hot showers, 15 WCs. ℂ ♿

Tennis.
PRICES: (1996) Caravan with family 109.00, Tent with two adults 61.00. CC: none.
From Gap take D994 towards Veynes. Follow signs from La Roche-des-Arnauds.

GENNES Maine/Loire   2C

Camping L'Européen 49320 Coutures.
Tel 02 41 57 91 63, Fax 02 41 57 91 63.
English spoken.
OPEN: 28/03–30/09. SIZE: 10 ha, 159 pitches (all with elec, 47 statics), 16 hot showers, 25 WCs, 2 CWPs. ℂ ♿

Restaurant at 4 km. Mobile homes for hire.
PRICES: (1996) Caravan with family 132.00, Tent with two adults 95.00. CC: Euro/Access, Visa.
10 km west of Gennes on N751. Well signposted.

GERARDMER Vosges   3D

Camp de Noirrupt 88530 Le Tholy.
Tel 03 29 61 81 27, Fax 03 29 61 83 05.
English spoken.
OPEN: 15/04–15/10. SIZE: 3 ha, 75 pitches (all with elec), 11 hot showers, 16 WCs, 1 CWP. ♿

Restaurant at 1 km. Free tennis.
PRICES: (1996) Tent with two adults 96.50. CC: none.
Follow D417 west of Gérardmer. Signposted from Le Tholy.

Camp Les Jonquilles 88400 Xonrupt-Longemer.
Tel 03 29 63 34 01. English spoken.
OPEN: 01/04–15/10. SIZE: 3 ha, 17 hot showers, 24 WCs, 1 CWP. ℂ ♿

Restaurant at 2 km.
PRICES: (1996) Caravan with family 91.00, Tent with two adults 50.00. CC: none.
From Gérardmer go east to Xonrupt. In front of the church, go towards the lake on the D67a.

France

Camping Belle Rive 2493 route du Lac, 88400 Xonrupt-Longemer.
Tel 03 29 63 31 12.
OPEN: 15/05–15/09. SIZE: 1 ha, 100 pitches (30 with elec), 6 hot showers (charge), 11 WCs, 1 CWP. ℓ

Restaurant at 2 km.
PRICES: (1996) Caravan with family 61.20, Tent with two adults 33.20. CC: none.
From Gérardmer head east on D417. Turn right in Xonrupt along west bank of Lake Longemer. Site is at southern end.

Camping de la Fôret
2 place du Centre, 88400 Liézey.
Tel 03 29 60 07 20, Fax 03 29 60 07 20.
OPEN: 01/04–15/10. SIZE: 1 ha, 35 pitches (25 with elec, 5 statics), 3 hot showers (charge), 5 WCs, 1 CWP. ℓ

Restaurant at 0.8 km.
PRICES: (1996) Caravan with family 65.00, Tent with two adults 33.00. CC: none.
From Gérardmer take the road to Le Tholy. Turn right 4 km after the Lac de Gérardmer to Liézey. The campsite is in the village opposite the church.

Camping Les Acacias
rue L de Vinci, 88650 Anould.
Tel 03 29 57 11 06. English spoken.
OPEN: all year. SIZE: 2.5 ha, 60 pitches (all with elec, 10 statics), 7 hot showers, 7 WCs, 1 French WC, 2 CWPs. ℓ &

Trampolining, bowling. Chalets for hire.
PRICES: Caravan with family 106.00, Tent with two adults 56.00. CC: none.
17 km north of Gérardmer on the D8 and N15 St-Die/Colmar.

GEX Ain 6A

Camping de Gex
400 av des Alpes, 01170 Gex.
Tel 04 50 41 61 46, Fax 04 50 41 68 77.
English spoken.
OPEN: 01/06–30/09. SIZE: 3.2 ha, 110 pitches (100 with elec), 9 hot showers, 9 WCs, 6 French WCs, 3 CWPs. ℓ &

Shop at 0.5 km. Restaurant at 0.5 km. Volley ball, table tennis, pétanque, swimming pool 200 m.
PRICES: (1996) Caravan with family 96.00, Tent with two adults 54.00. CC: none.
From Gex take D984 to Divonne-les-Bains. Campsite is near town centre, past railway station and on the right.

GIGNAC Hérault 5C

Camping Moulin de Siau 34150 Aniane.
Tel 04 67 57 51 08. English spoken.
OPEN: 15/06–15/09. SIZE: 3 ha, 115 pitches (56 with elec), 12 hot showers, 20 WCs, 2 CWPs. ℓ

Restaurant at 2 km. Fishing.
PRICES: (1996) Caravan with family 99.00, Tent with two adults 54.00. CC: none.
Located halfway between Gignac and Aniane on the D32.

GILETTE Alpes-Marit 6C

Camping du Moulin Nou
route de Carros, 06830 Gilette.
Tel 04 93 08 92 40, Fax 04 93 08 44 77.
English spoken.
OPEN: 01/04–30/09. SIZE: 5 ha, 125 pitches (all with elec), 20 hot showers, 24 WCs, 3 CWPs. ℓ &

Tennis, volley/basket ball.
PRICES: (1996) Caravan with family 171.00, Tent with two adults 95.50. CC: Euro/Access, Visa.
Go north for 25 km on the N202 from Nice, then cross the Pont Charles Albert and turn left. Campsite is 1 km further on.

GIVRY-EN-ARGONNE Marne 3A

Camping Municipal du Val d'Ante
51330 Givry-en-Argonne.
Tel 03 26 60 04 15.
OPEN: 28/03–15/09. SIZE: 1 ha, 34 pitches (24 with elec), 4 hot showers, 1 WC, 4 French WCs, 1 CWP. ℓ

Shop at 0.5 km. Restaurant at 0.5 km.
PRICES: Caravan with family 51.20, Tent with two adults 27.90. CC: none.
The campsite is east of Givry-en-Argonne. Well signposted.

GONCELIN Isère 6A

Camping Les 7 Laux Theys, 38570 Goncelin.
Tel 04 76 71 02 69, Fax 04 76 71 08 85.
OPEN: 15/06–15/09. SIZE: 2 ha, 70 pitches (60 with elec), 10 hot showers, 7 WCs. ℓ &

Restaurant at 4 km.
PRICES: (1996) Caravan with family 149.50, Tent with two adults 74.00. CC: none.
From Goncelin, go south on the D29 and D30.

GOURDON Lot 4B

Camp Municipal 46340 Salviac.
Tel 05 65 41 55 98. English spoken.

France

France

OPEN: 01/05–15/09. SIZE: 2 ha, 50 pitches (35 with elec), 7 hot showers, 7 WCs, 13 French WCs, 1 CWP. &

Shop at 0.5 km.
PRICES: (1996) Caravan with family 93.00, Tent with two adults 50.00. CC: none.
From Gourdon, 14 km south-west to Salviac on D673. Campsite is signposted.

Camping Le Rêve Revers, 46300 Le Vigan.
Tel 05 65 41 25 20, Fax 05 65 41 68 52.
English spoken.
OPEN: 23/04–23/09. SIZE: 3 ha, 52 pitches (all with elec), 6 hot showers, 7 WCs, 1 CWP. & &

Restaurant at 2 km. 25% discount in LS.
PRICES: (1996) Caravan with family 121.00, Tent with two adults 67.00. CC: none.
From Gourdon take D673 east. Follow signs to campsite.

GRAMAT Lot 5A

Les Chênes 46500 Padirac.
Tel 05 65 33 65 54, Fax 05 65 33 71 55.
English spoken.
OPEN: 01/05–15/09. SIZE: 4 ha, 120 pitches (all with elec), 19 hot showers, 16 WCs, 2 CWPs. & &

PRICES: (1996) Caravan with family 155.00, Tent with two adults 90.00. CC: Euro/Access, Visa.
From Gramat take D677 towards St-Céré. At Le Boutel turn left on to D673 to Padirac.

Le Teulières l'Hôpital Beaulieu Issendolus, 46500 Gramat.
Tel 05 65 40 86 71, Fax 05 65 33 40 89.
English spoken.
OPEN: all year. SIZE: 3 ha, 33 pitches (all with elec, 4 statics), 9 hot showers, 7 WCs, 2 French WCs. & &

Tennis, volley ball, playroom.
PRICES: Caravan with family 63.00, Tent with two adults 39.00. CC: none.
On N140, 6 km south-west of Gramat.

LA GRANDE-MOTTE Hérault 5D

Lous Pibols allée des Campings, 34280 La Grand-Motte.
Tel 04 67 56 50 08, Fax 04 67 56 23 13. English spoken.
OPEN: 15/03–15/10. SIZE: 3 ha, 200 pitches (all with elec), 30 hot showers, 30 WCs, 3 CWPs.

Restaurant at 0.1 km.
PRICES: (1996) Caravan with family 198.00, Tent with two adults 170.00. CC: none.
South-east of Montpellier.

GRANDPRE Ardennes 3A

Camping Municipal 08250 Grandpré.
Tel 03 24 30 50 71. English spoken.
OPEN: 01/04–30/09. SIZE: 2.5 ha, 100 pitches (all with elec, 50 statics), 10 hot showers, 10 WCs. & &

Shop at 0.3 km. Restaurant at 0.3 km.
PRICES: (1996) Caravan with family 45.70, Tent with two adults 20.50. CC: none.
200 m from the town centre, on D6.

GRANVILLE Manche 1B

Camping de l'Ecutot 50380 St-Pair-sur-Mer.
Tel 02 33 50 26 29, Fax 02 33 50 64 94.
English spoken.
OPEN: 01/04–30/09. SIZE: 3 ha, 176 pitches (all with elec, 50 statics), 36 hot showers, 36 WCs, 1 CWP.

Each pitch has its own bathroom.
PRICES: unavailable. CC: none.
2 km south of Granville towards Avranches.

Camping de l'Ecutot

near Granville

3★ camping within easy reach of Cherbourg

Camping Les Eaux St-Aubin-des-Préaux, 50380 St-Pair-sur-Mer.
Tel 02 33 51 66 09, Fax 02 33 51 92 02.
English spoken.
OPEN: 01/04–15/09. SIZE: 11 ha, 192 pitches (all with elec, 40 statics), 20 hot showers, 20 WCs, 3 CWPs. & &

Restaurant at 2 km. Flume, children's playground; beautiful surroundings.
PRICES: (1996) Caravan with family 213.00, Tent with two adults 110.00. CC: Euro/Access, Visa.
From Granville take the D973 south to St-Pair-sur-Mer.

GRASSE Alpes-Marit 6C

Camp Caravaning Les Gorges du Loup chemin des Vergers, 06620 Le Bar-sur-Loup.
Tel 04 93 42 45 06, Fax 04 93 42 45 06.
English spoken.
OPEN: 01/04–01/10. SIZE: 2 ha, 32 pitches (all with elec), 12 hot showers, 13 WCs, 1 CWP. &

Shop at 1 km. Site is situated in an olive grove.
PRICES: (1996) Caravan with family 177.00,

Tent with two adults 95.00. CC: none.
D2085 from Grasse towards Châteauneuf. At Pré-du-Lac turn on to D2210.

Camping Les Floralies 83440 Montauroux.
Tel 04 94 76 44 03.
OPEN: 01/04–30/10. SIZE: 1 ha, 65 pitches (all with elec, 12 statics), 8 hot showers, 10 WCs, 1 CWP. ☎

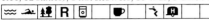

Shop at 1.5 km. Restaurant at 1 km.
PRICES: (1996) Caravan with family 112.50,
Tent with two adults 63.00. CC: none.
Autoroute A8 Aix-en-Provence to Nice; exit Les Adrets towards Fayence/Montauroux after 11 km.

Caravan Inn 18 rte de Cannes, 06650 Opio.
Tel 04 93 77 32 00, Fax 04 93 77 71 89.
English spoken.
OPEN: 30/03–15/09. SIZE: 5 ha, 43 pitches (all with elec, 70 statics), 18 hot showers, 15 WCs, 2 CWPs. ☎

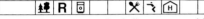

Shop at 1 km. Tennis, volley ball, pétanque, table tennis, basketball.
PRICES: (1996) Caravan with family 193.80.
CC: none.
Situated 6 km from Grasse, and 14 km from the A8. (No tents.)

Parc des Arboins 06460 St-Vallier-de-Thiey.
Tel 04 93 42 63 89, Fax 04 93 09 61 54.
English spoken.
OPEN: all year. SIZE: 4 ha, 100 pitches (all with elec), 25 hot showers, 25 WCs, 2 CWPs. ☎ ⅃

PRICES: (1996) Caravan with family 121.00,
Tent with two adults 74.00. CC: none.
From Grasse take N85 to St-Vallier-de-Thiey and follow signs to campsite. Autoroute A8 exit Grasse.

LE GRAU-DU-ROI Gard 5D

Camping Abri de Camargue
route du Phare de l'Espiguette, Port Camargue,
30240 Le Grau-du-Roi.
Tel 04 66 51 54 83, Fax 04 66 51 76 42.
English spoken.
OPEN: 29/03–19/10. SIZE: 4 ha, 42 hot showers,
36 WCs. ☎

Indoor swimming pool, boules, volley ball, playground; sea 900m.
PRICES: Caravan with family 217.00, Tent with two adults 205.00. CC: Euro/Access, Visa.
Before reaching Le Grau-du-Roi, turn towards left bank. After the bridge, follow signs to l'Espiguette. The campsite is immediately on the right.

Elysée Résidence route de l'Espiguette,
30240 Le Grau-du-Roi.
Tel 04 66 53 54 00, Fax 04 66 51 85 12. English spoken.

OPEN: 22/03–01/10. SIZE: 35 ha, 1000 pitches (all with elec, 400 statics), 248 hot showers, 240 WCs. ☎ ⅃

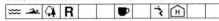

Tennis, archery, fitness room, children's club, dancing evenings, shows.
PRICES: Caravan with family 230.00, Tent with two adults 150.00. CC: Amex, Euro/Access, Visa.
Leave the autoroute at Gallargues and take the route des Plages towards Le Grau-du-Roi. In Le Grau-du-Roi take route de l'Espiguette, where campsite is signposted.

Les Jardins de Tivoli route de l'Espiguette,
30240 Le Grau-du-Roi.
Tel 04 66 51 82 96, Fax 04 66 51 09 81. English spoken.
OPEN: 01/04–30/09. SIZE: 7 ha, 200 pitches (all with elec), 200 hot showers, 200 WCs.

All pitches are fully serviced.
PRICES: (1996) Caravan with family 270.00. CC: none.
From Le Grau-du-Roi on D62 follow signs.

GRAULHET Tarn 5C

Camping Nabeillou 81300 Graulhet.
Tel 05 63 34 60 04.
OPEN: 01/05–30/09. SIZE: 2 ha, 25 pitches (all with elec, 6 statics), 2 hot showers, 4 WCs, 2 CWPs. ☎ ⅃

Shop at 1 km. Restaurant at 1 km. Hiking, mountain-biking.
PRICES: Tent with two adults 55.00. CC: none.

LA GRAVE Hautes-Alpes 6A

Le Grand Clot 05320 La Grave.
Tel 04 76 79 93 88. English spoken.
OPEN: 20/12–30/09. SIZE: 3 ha, 50 pitches (all with elec), 7 hot showers, 7 WCs, 2 CWPs. ☎

Shop at 3 km. Restaurant at 1 km.
PRICES: (1996) Caravan with family 112.00,
Tent with two adults 64.00. CC: none.
La Grave is on N91, north-west of Briançon.

GRAVELINES Nord 2B

Camping de la Plage Camping Municipal, de Grande-Fort-Philippe, 59153 Grand-Fort-Philippe.
Tel 03 28 65 31 95, Fax 03 28 65 47 40. English spoken.
OPEN: 01/04–31/10. SIZE: 2 ha, 84 pitches (60 with elec), 11 hot showers, 9 WCs, 6 French WCs, 2 CWPs. ☎ ⅃

Shop at 1 km. Restaurant at 0.5 km.
PRICES: (1996) Caravan with family 105.50,
Tent with two adults 64.50. CC: none.
From Gravelines take the D11 seawards to Grand-Fort-Philippe.

France

Camping Municipal des 3 Fermes
rue des 3 Fermes, 59820 Gravelines.
Tel 03 28 23 29 10, Fax 03 28 65 35 99. English spoken.
OPEN: 01/04–01/11. SIZE: 4.4 ha, 122 pitches
(all with elec), 6 hot showers, 6 WCs, 1 CWP. ℂ ⅆ

Shop at 0.6 km. Restaurant at 0.6 km. Boules,
volley ball, entertainment in HS, playground.
PRICES: (1996) Caravan with family 120.69, Tent
with two adults 78.60. CC: none.
*From the centre of Gravelines, take the road
towards Dunkerque, turn left at crossroads and
then follow the signs.*

GRAY Haute-Saône   3C

Camping Municipal Longue Rive
rue de la Plage, 70100 Gray.
Tel 03 84 64 90 44, Fax 03 84 65 22 29. English spoken.
OPEN: 01/04–30/09. SIZE: 4 ha, 120 pitches
(20 with elec), 14 hot showers, 14 WCs, 12 French
WCs, 2 CWPs. ℂ ⅆ

Shop at 1 km. Swimming pool 50 m.
PRICES: (1996) Caravan with family 65.40,
Tent with two adults 43.30. CC: none.
Follow signs in the town to campsite.

GRENOBLE Isère   6A

Camping de Luiset St-Martin-d'Uriage,
38410 Uriage.
Tel 04 76 89 77 98.
OPEN: 01/05–30/09. SIZE: 1 ha, 60 pitches (all with
elec, 20 statics), 4 hot showers, 6 WCs, 1 CWP. ⅆ

Shop at 0.2 km. Restaurant at 0.2 km. Swimming
pool nearby.
PRICES: (1996) Caravan with family 79.00,
Tent with two adults 42.00. CC: none.
East of Grenoble towards Chamrousse.

GRIMAUD Var   6C

Camping de la Plage Grimaud, 83310 Cogolin.
Tel 04 94 56 31 15, Fax 04 94 56 49 61.
English spoken.
OPEN: 01/04–04/10. SIZE: 18 ha, 450 pitches (all
with elec), 70 hot showers, 70 WCs, 8 CWPs. ℂ ⅆ

PRICES: (1996) Tent with two adults 100.00. CC: none.
*On the main coast road (N98), about 6 km south-
west of Ste-Maxime.*

La Pinède 83360 Grimaud.
Tel 04 94 56 04 36, Fax 04 94 56 30 86. English spoken.
OPEN: 01/04–31/10. SIZE: 4 ha, 200 pitches
(150 with elec, 12 statics), 18 hot showers,
20 WCs, 2 CWPs. ℂ ⅆ

Mini-golf, children's playground; mobile homes
available.
PRICES: (1996) Caravan with family 154.00,
Tent with two adults 92.00. CC: Visa.
*Between Grimaud and Pons-les-Mûres on D14.
Follow signs.*

GRISOLLES Tarn/Garonne   4D

Aquitaine Camping 82170 Grisolles.
Tel 05 63 67 33 22. English spoken.
OPEN: 15/04–30/10. SIZE: 3 ha, 30 pitches (all with
elec, 14 statics), 10 hot showers, 10 WCs, 5 French
WCs, 4 CWPs. ℂ ⅆ

Shop at 1 km. Restaurant at 0.5 km.
PRICES: Caravan with family 120.00,
Tent with two adults 72.00. CC: none.
On N20 1 km north-west of Grisolles. Signposted.

ILE-DE-GROIX Morbihan   1C

Camping les Sables Rouges
56590 Groix, Ile-de-Groix.
Tel 02 97 86 81 32, Fax 02 97 86 59 17.
English spoken.
OPEN: 29/05–10/09. SIZE: 2.5 ha, 120 pitches (80 with
elec), 13 hot showers, 15 WCs, 1 CWP. ℂ ⅆ

Shop at 1 km. Restaurant at 0.5 km.
PRICES: (1996) Caravan with family 154.50, Tent
with two adults 87.50. CC: Amex, Euro/Access, Visa.
*From Groix, drive towards Locmaria then
towards La Pointe-des-Chats and follow the signs.*

GUÉRANDE Loire-Atlan   1D

Camping Bréhadour rte de Cremeur,
44350 Guérande.
Tel 02 40 24 93 12, Fax 02 40 62 10 47.
English spoken.
OPEN: 29/03–28/09. SIZE: 7 ha, 271 pitches (100 with
elec), 28 hot showers, 5 WCs, 6 CWPs. ℂ ⅆ

Shop at 1 km. Restaurant at 1 km. Tennis,
mountain-bike track; mobile homes for hire.
PRICES: (1996) Caravan with family 165.00, Tent
with two adults 93.00. CC: Euro/Access, Visa.
*Drive south on D92 from Guérande towards La
Baule. Site is on the left.*

Camping de l'Etang 47 rue des Chênes,
Sandun, 44350 Guérande.
Tel 02 40 61 93 51, Fax 02 40 61 96 21. English spoken.
OPEN: 01/06–15/09. SIZE: 2 ha, 109 pitches (all with
elec, 7 statics), 9 hot showers, 12 WCs, 2 CWPs. ℂ ⅆ

Shop at 2 km. Restaurant at 7 km.

PRICES: (1996) Caravan with family 137.00, Tent with two adults 79.00. CC: Visa.
The campsite lies to the east of Guérande at Sandun.

Camping La Fontaine Kersavary, 44350 Guérande.
Tel 02 40 24 96 19.
OPEN: 01/05–30/09. SIZE: 2 ha, 100 pitches (44 with elec), 6 hot showers, 15 WCs. ℓ ♿

Shop at 2.5 km. Restaurant at 2.5 km.
PRICES: (1996) Caravan with family 85.90, Tent with two adults 48.00. CC: none.
From Guérande take the D774 towards Herbignac and immediately turn left on to the D233 towards St-Molf.

Le Château du Petit Bois 44420 Mesquer.
Tel 02 40 42 68 77, Fax 02 40 42 65 58.
English spoken.
OPEN: 01/04–31/10. SIZE: 10 ha, 200 pitches (180 with elec, 20 statics), 25 hot showers, 21 WCs, 3 French WCs, 2 CWPs. ♿

Shop at 1 km.
PRICES: Caravan with family 165.00, Tent with two adults 85.00. CC: Euro/Access, Visa.
From Guérande go north on the D774. Take left turn to Mesquer/Piriac (D48). The site is on the right (D52) after approx 3 km.

Le Château du Petit Bois

near La Baule-Escoublac

In woodland 5 minutes from the beach

Le Pré du Château Careil, 44350 Guérande.
Tel 02 40 60 22 99, Fax 02 40 60 22 99.
English spoken.
OPEN: 01/04–25/09. SIZE: 2 ha, 50 pitches (all with elec, 2 statics), 10 hot showers, 9 WCs, 1 CWP. ℓ ♿

Shop at 1 km. Restaurant at 0.5 km. Sauna; sea 2 km.
PRICES: Caravan with family 160.00, Tent with two adults 120.00. CC: none.
On the Guérande to La Baule road, at the end of Careil village.

GUICHEN Ille/Vilaine   1D

Camping Municipal La Courbe 11 rue du Camping, 35890 Bourg-des-Comptes.
Tel 02 99 05 62 62, Fax 02 99 05 62 69.
OPEN: 09/04–30/10. SIZE: 60 pitches (all with elec), 4 hot showers (charge), 5 WCs. ♿

Shop at 1 km. Restaurant at 1 km.
PRICES: (1996) Caravan with family 49.50, Tent with two adults 25.00. CC: none.
From Guichen go south on D84. Just after St-Marc turn left on to D38, cross the River Vilaine, and follow signs to the campsite.

GUIDEL-PLAGES Morbihan   1C

Camping de Kergal 56520 Guidel-Plages.
Tel 02 97 05 98 18. English spoken.
OPEN: 01/04–30/09. SIZE: 5 ha, 132 pitches (all with elec, 20 statics), 18 hot showers, 12 WCs, 1 CWP. ℓ ♿

Shop at 2 km. Restaurant at 1.5 km. Tennis, volley ball, mini-golf, boules.
PRICES: (1996) Caravan with family 89.00, Tent with two adults 32.00. CC: Euro/Access.
From Guidel go south-west on D306. Follow signs.

GUILVINEC Finistère   1C

Grand Camping de la Plage 29730 Guilvinec.
Tel 02 98 58 61 90, Fax 02 98 58 23 89.
English spoken.
OPEN: 01/05–15/09. SIZE: 14 ha, 410 pitches (350 with elec), 46 hot showers, 40 WCs. ♿

PRICES: Caravan with family 176.00, Tent with two adults 110.00. CC: Euro/Access, Visa.
South-west of Quimper.

GUINES Pas-de-Calais   2B

La Bien-Assise 62340 Guînes.
Tel 03 21 35 20 77, Fax 03 21 36 79 20.
English spoken.
OPEN: 20/04–25/09. SIZE: 12 ha, 180 pitches (130 with elec, 8 statics), 28 hot showers, 27 WCs, 3 CWPs. ℓ ♿

Shop at 1 km. Flume, billiards, padling-pool, mini-golf, TV.
PRICES: Caravan with family 143.00, Tent with two adults 100.00. CC: Amex, Euro/Access, Visa.
10 km south-west of Calais and 5 km from Eurotunnel area and TGV station. On D231, signposted in Guînes.

La Bien-Assise

at Guînes

Whether by chunnel or funnel, it's right on England's doorstep!

France

France

GUISE Aisne 2B

Camp de Vallée de l'Oise 02120 Guise.
Tel 03 23 61 14 86. English spoken.
OPEN: 01/04–31/10. SIZE: 3.5 ha, 80 pitches
(75 with elec, 20 statics), 11 hot showers, 10 WCs,
1 CWP. &

Shop at 0.3 km. Restaurant at 0.8 km. Tennis
0.1 km.
PRICES: (1996) Caravan with family 58.10,
Tent with two adults 31.10. CC: none.
*East of St-Quentin on N29. Arriving in Guise,
turn right down the hill towards Vervins at first
lights and then take second left.*

Camping de Bovalon 02120 Vadencourt.
Tel 03 23 61 07 03.
OPEN: 01/04–30/09. SIZE: 1.2 ha, 42 pitches
(22 with elec), 1 hot shower (charge), 3 WCs.

Shop at 0.2 km. Restaurant at 7 km.
PRICES: Caravan with family 39.00,
Tent with two adults 17.50. CC: none.
*From Guise take D960 towards Bohain then D69
right to Vadencourt.*

HAGUENAU Bas-Rhin 3B

Camp Municipal Eichelgarten Oberbronn
Zinswiller, 67110 Niederbronn-les-Bains.
Tel 03 88 09 71 96. English spoken.
OPEN: all year. SIZE: 3 ha, 139 pitches (all with elec,
50 statics), 16 hot showers, 16 WCs, 6 French WCs,
2 CWPs. & &

Restaurant at 2 km. Tennis, mini-golf, playground.
PRICES: (1996) Caravan with family 87.00,
Tent with two adults 47.00. CC: none.
*Travel north-west from Haguenau on N62 for
approx 20 km. Near Niederbronn turn left onto D68
for Oberbronn-Zinswiller. Campsite is signposted.*

HASPARREN Pyrénées-Atlan 4C

Camping Chapital route de Cambo,
64240 Hasparren.
Tel 05 59 29 62 94, Fax 05 59 29 69 71.
English spoken.
OPEN: 09/04–15/10. SIZE: 2.5 ha, 138 pitches
(70 with elec), 19 hot showers, 19 WCs, 10 French
WCs, 3 CWPs. & &

Restaurant at 0.5 km. Discount at pool 50 m away.
PRICES: (1996) Caravan with family 90.00, Tent
with two adults 49.00. CC: Euro/Access.
*From the A63 just south of Bayonne, take the
Cambo-les-Bains exit and at Cambo-les-Bains
take the D10 to Hasparren (about 10 km).*

HAUTEFORT Dordogne 4B

Le Moulin des Loisirs Nailhac, 24390 Hautefort.
Tel 05 53 50 46 55, Fax 05 53 50 46 55.
English spoken.
OPEN: 15/04–30/09. SIZE: 5 ha, 48 pitches (all with
elec, 12 statics), 7 hot showers, 8 WCs. & &

PRICES: (1996) Caravan with family 121.00, Tent
with two adults 71.00. CC: Amex, Euro/Access, Visa.
*Near the étang du Coucou, on the D71 between
St-Agnan and Badefols.*

Le Moulin des Loisirs
at Nailhac
*In the shadow of the most beautiful
château in Périgord*

LE HAVRE Seine Marit 2A

Camping Municipal Forêt de Montgeon,
76600 Le Havre.
Tel 02 35 46 52 39, Fax 02 35 19 60 07.
English spoken.
OPEN: 01/04–30/09. SIZE: 3.8 ha, 70 pitches.

PRICES: (1996) Caravan with family 81.00,
Tent with two adults 50.00. CC: none.
*Go north from Le Havre via Jenner Tunnel (D32)
to campsite at Forêt de Montgeon.*

LA HAYE-DU-PUITS Manche 1B

Camping L'Etang des Haizes St-Symphorien-le-
Valois, 50250 La Haye-du-Puits.
Tel 02 33 46 01 16, Fax 02 33 47 23 80.
English spoken.
OPEN: 15/04–30/10. SIZE: 3 ha, 100 pitches (80 with
elec, 25 statics), 16 hot showers, 17 WCs, 2 CWPs. & &

Shop at 0.8 km. Restaurant at 0.8 km. Flume,
fishing, archery.
PRICES: (1996) Caravan with family 176.00, Tent
with two adults 100.00. CC: none.
*Just north of La Haye-du-Puits on D900, turn
right on to D136, 100 m.*

Camping L'Etang des Haizes
near La Haye-du-Puits
For your first night in France

LES HERBIERS Vendée 1D

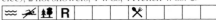

Camping Aire Naturelle La Norissonnière, St-Mars-la-Reorthe, 85590 Les-Epesses.
Tel 02 51 57 45 58.
OPEN: 01/05–31/10. SIZE: 4 ha, 25 pitches (10 with elec), 2 hot showers, 4 WCs, 4 French WCs. &

Shop at 2 km.
PRICES: (1996) Caravan with family 70.00, Tent with two adults 36.00. CC: Amex.
East from Les Herbiers on D752, then north on D79 to St-Mars-la-Reorthe. Campsite is signposted.

HIRSON Aisne 3A

Camping de la Cascade Blangy-Loisirs, 02500 Hirson.
Tel 03 23 58 18 97, Fax 03 23 58 25 39.
English spoken.
OPEN: 20/04–22/09. SIZE: 1.6 ha, 100 pitches (80 with elec), 6 hot showers (charge), 10 WCs, 1 CWP. (&

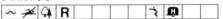

Shop at 2 km. Restaurant at 1.5 km.
PRICES: (1996) Caravan with family 53.70, Tent with two adults 26.00. CC: none.
18 km north-east of Vervins on D963.

HOSSEGOR Landes 4C

La Pomme de Pin 40230 Saubion.
Tel 05 58 77 00 71. English spoken.
OPEN: 01/04–31/10. SIZE: 3 ha, 120 pitches (80 with elec), 12 hot showers, 16 WCs. (

PRICES: (1996) Caravan with family 98.00, Tent with two adults 55.00. CC: none.
From Hossegor take D652 north to Seignosse, then D337 east to Saubion. Campsite is well signposted.

HOULGATE Calvados 2A

Camping de la Vallée 88 rue de la Vallée, 14519 Houlgate.
Tel 02 31 24 40 69, Fax 02 31 28 08 29.
English spoken.
OPEN: 01/04–30/09. SIZE: 11 ha, 170 pitches (all with elec, 90 statics), 32 hot showers, 20 WCs, 3 CWPs. (&

Camping de la Vallée

at Houlgate

Not far from the ferries – but a world apart

HOUPLINES Nord 2B

Camping L'Image 140 rue Brune, 59116 Houplines.
Tel 03 20 35 69 42. English spoken.
OPEN: all year. SIZE: 3 ha, 100 pitches (all with elec, 60 statics), 6 hot showers (charge), 10 WCs, 1 CWP.

Shop at 2 km. Restaurant at 2 km. Tennis, fishing; snacks available w/e.
PRICES: (1996) Caravan with family 55.00, Tent with two adults 35.00. CC: none.
From the A25 west of Lille, take exit 8 to Houplines. Turn first right after the traffic lights.

HOURTIN Gironde 4A

Camping Caravaning de la Côte d'Argent 33990 Hourtin-Plage.
Tel 05 56 09 10 25, Fax 05 56 09 24 96.
English spoken.
OPEN: 15/05–15/09. SIZE: 20 ha, 350 pitches (all with elec, 50 statics), 100 hot showers, 85 WCs, 5 CWPs. (&

Bike hire.
PRICES: (1996) Caravan with family 179.00, Tent with two adults 95.00. CC: Amex, Visa.
From Hourtin take D101/D101e to Hourtin-Plage. Well signposted.

Camping Caravaning La Mariflaude route de Pauillac, 33990 Hourtin.
Tel 05 56 09 11 97, Fax 05 56 09 24 01.
English spoken.
OPEN: 01/05–15/09. SIZE: 8 ha, 250 pitches (all with elec, 30 statics), 45 hot showers, 40 WCs. (&

Tennis, crazy golf, archery.
PRICES: Caravan with family 155.00, Tent with two adults 95.00. CC: none.
From the centre of Hourtin follow directions to Pauillac; the campsite entrance is 800 m along on the right-hand side.

HUANNE-MONTMARTIN Doubs 3D

Camping aux Etangs du Bois de Reveuge 25680 Huanne-Montmartin.
Tel 03 81 84 12 42, Fax 03 81 84 44 04. English spoken.
OPEN: 01/05–30/09. SIZE: 20 ha, 199 pitches (all with elec), 16 hot showers, 22 WCs. (&

France

France

All sports facilities free of charge.
PRICES: Caravan with family 220.00. CC: Amex, Visa.
A36, Baume-les-Dames exit towards Rougemont.
Approx 7 km.

HUELGOAT Finistère 1C

La Rivière d'Argent La Coudraie,
29690 Huelgoat.
Tel 02 98 99 72 50. English spoken.
OPEN: 01/05–10/09. SIZE: 2 ha, 84 pitches (all with
elec, 6 statics), 8 hot showers, 10 WCs, 1 CWP. ⚓ ⚐

Shop at 3 km. Restaurant at 0.5 km. Mobile homes
available.
PRICES: (1996) Caravan with family 92.00,
Tent with two adults 49.00. CC: none.
From Huelgoat head towards Carhaix and
Poullaouen via the tourist route through the forest.

HUNINGUE Haut-Rhin 3D

Camping au Petit Port
8 allee des Marronniers, 68330 Huningue.
Tel 03 89 69 05 25.
OPEN: 01/05–30/09. SIZE: 0.6 ha, 30 pitches
(all with elec, 10 statics), 4 hot showers, 4 WCs,
2 French WCs, 1 CWP. ⚐

Shop at 0.2 km. Restaurant at 0.2 km. Close to the
Swiss and Dutch borders.
PRICES: (1996) Caravan with family 90.00,
Tent with two adults 50.00. CC: none.
Between Huningue and St-Louis, off the N66. Site
is not clearly signposted but easy to find.

HYERES Var 6C

Camping Le Méditerranée
quartier du Pousset, 83400 Giens.
Tel 04 94 58 21 06. English spoken.
OPEN: 09/04–18/10. SIZE: 2 ha, 15 pitches (all with
elec, 3 statics), 28 hot showers, 18 WCs.

Restaurant at 0.3 km.
PRICES: (1996) Caravan with family 158.00,
Tent with two adults 100.00. CC: none.
From Hyères head towards Presqu'île-de-
Giens/Tour-Fondue. After about 9 km turn left
immediately after the riding school and the
campsite is third on the right, just before the beach.

Camping Presqu'île de Giens
153 route de la Madrague, 83400 Hyères.
Tel 04 94 58 22 86, Fax 04 94 58 11 63. English spoken.
OPEN: 01/04–15/10. SIZE: 7 ha, 460 pitches
(200 with elec, 80 statics), 80 hot showers,
80 WCs, 4 CWPs. ⚓

PRICES: (1996) Caravan with family 164.00,
Tent with two adults 92.00. CC: none.
From Hyères south on D97 to campsite,
signposted.

Domaine du Ceinturon III
83400 Hyères.
Tel 04 94 66 32 65, Fax 04 94 66 48 43.
English spoken.
OPEN: 01/04–30/09. SIZE: 3 ha, 34 hot showers,
24 WCs, 2 CWPs. ⚐

Tennis.
PRICES: Caravan with family 143.50,
Tent with two adults 81.00. CC: none.
Leave Toulon on motorway towards Hyères, take
ring road until fifth set of traffic lights and then
turn towards Ayguade. Campsite is about 1.6 km
ahead on the right.

IS-SUR-TILLE Côte-d'Or 3C

Camping des Capucins rue des Capucins,
21120 Is-sur-Tille.
Tel 03 80 95 02 08, Fax 03 80 95 08 33.
OPEN: 01/06–15/09. SIZE: 1 ha, 39 pitches (36 with
elec), 4 hot showers, 4 WCs.

Shop at 1 km. Restaurant at 1 km. Children's
playground.
PRICES: (1996) Caravan with family 67.50,
Tent with two adults 28.00. CC: none.
Go north from Dijon on N74 towards Langres. At
Til-Châtel, turn left on to the road to Is-sur-Tille.

L'ISLE-JOURDAIN Gers 4D

Camp du Lac de Thoux-St-Cricq
32430 Cologne.
Tel 05 62 65 71 29, Fax 05 62 65 74 81.
English spoken.
OPEN: 01/03–31/10. SIZE: 4 ha, 10 hot showers,
9 WCs, 1 CWP. ⚓

Archery, horse-riding.
PRICES: (1996) Caravan with family 104.00,
Tent with two adults 46.00. CC: none.
From L'Isle Jourdain, take the D654 north-west for
8 km. Campsite is on right, follow signs.

L'ISLE-SUR-LA-SORGUE Vaucluse 5D

Municipal Camping La Sorguette
84800 L'Isle-sur-la-Sorgue.
Tel 04 90 38 05 71, Fax 04 90 20 84 61.
English spoken.
OPEN: 15/03–23/10. SIZE: 3 ha, 164 pitches (all
with elec), 15 hot showers, 18 WCs, 3 CWPs. ⚓ ⚐

Shop at 3 km. Boats, fishing, biking, swimming nearby (2 km).
PRICES: (1996) Caravan with family 134.00, Tent with two adults 69.00. CC: Euro/Access, Visa.
Leave the A7 at exit Avignon-Sud. Follow signs into L'Isle-sur-la-Sorgue, then drive out of L'Isle on the N100 towards Apt.

Municipal Camping La Sorguette ★★★
at L'Isle-sur-la-Sorgue
Riverside haven, deep in Provence

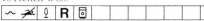

ISSOIRE Puy-de-Dôme 5A

Camping du Mas 63500 Issoire.
Tel 04 73 89 03 59, Fax 04 73 89 41 05.
OPEN: 01/04–31/10. SIZE: 3 ha, 140 pitches (69 with elec, 8 statics), 18 hot showers, 8 WCs, 10 French WCs.

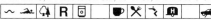

Shop at 1 km. Restaurant at 0.6 km.
PRICES: (1996) Caravan with family 64.10, Tent with two adults 33.00. CC: none.
From N9 or A75 take Orbeil exit to Issoire.

Château Camping La Grange Fort
63500 Les Pradeaux.
Tel 04 73 71 05 93, Fax 04 73 71 07 69.
English spoken.
OPEN: 01/03–31/10. SIZE: 22 ha, 80 pitches (all with elec), 14 hot showers, 17 WCs, 2 CWPs.

Shop at 1 km.
PRICES: (1996) Caravan with family 120.50, Tent with two adults 71.00. CC: none.
From A75 take exit 13 to Parentignat, D999 towards St-Germain-L'Herm, then first right on to D34. Follow the signs.

Real Château camping
LA GRANGE FORT
near Issoire
Ideal base for Parc du Livradois and Parc des Volcans

JARD-SUR-MER Vendée 4A

Camping La Bolée d'Air Le Bouil,
St-Vincent-sur-Jard, 85520 Jard-sur-Mer.
Tel 02 51 90 36 05, Fax 02 51 33 94 04.
English spoken.

OPEN: 15/04–30/09. SIZE: 6 ha, 150 pitches (all with elec, 20 statics), 45 hot showers, 60 WCs.
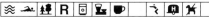
Restaurant at 0.4 km.
PRICES: (1996) Caravan with family 198.00, Tent with two adults 120.00. CC: Euro/Access, Visa.
St-Vincent is just south of Jard-sur-Mer on the coast road.

Camping Municipal La Ventouse
85520 Jard-sur-Mer.
Tel 02 51 33 58 65, Fax 02 51 33 91 00.
English spoken.
OPEN: 01/04–30/09. SIZE: 6 ha, 160 pitches (100 with elec), 18 hot showers, 17 WCs, 11 CWPs.

Shop at 0.5 km. Restaurant at 0.05 km.
PRICES: (1996) Caravan with family 109.00, Tent with two adults 55.00. CC: none.
300 m from the port at Jard-sur-Mer and well signposted.

Camping-Caravanning Les Ecureuils
route des Goffineaux, 85520 Jard-sur-Mer.
Tel 02 51 33 42 74, Fax 02 51 33 91 14/1.
English spoken.
OPEN: 18/05–09/09. SIZE: 4 ha, 140 pitches (all with elec), 30 hot showers, 28 WCs.

Restaurant at 0.3 km.
PRICES: Caravan with family 188.00, Tent with two adults 119.00. CC: none.
Signposted from Moutiers (D19).

Camping Les Ecureuils
at Jard-sur-Mer
Peacefully set in the midst of a forest

L'Océano d'Or rue G Clemenceau,
85520 Jard-sur-Mer.
Tel 02 51 33 65 08, Fax 02 51 33 94 04.
English spoken.
OPEN: 01/04–30/09. SIZE: 7 ha, 350 pitches (250 with elec, 40 statics), 50 hot showers, 50 WCs, 3 CWPs.

Restaurant at 0.5 km. Flume, tennis, mini-golf.
PRICES: (1996) Caravan with family 198.00, Tent with two adults 120.00. CC: Euro/Access, Visa.
From Talmont take D21 to Jard-sur-Mer. Campsite is at the end of the village on the right.

La Pomme de Pin rue Vincent Auriol,
85520 Jard-sur-Mer.
Tel 02 51 33 43 85, Fax 02 51 33 94 04. English spoken.

France

OPEN: 01/04–30/09. SIZE: 2 ha, 150 pitches (all with elec, 20 statics), 30 hot showers, 30 WCs, 2 CWPs. ♿ ㋐

Restaurant at 0.3 km.
PRICES: (1996) Caravan with family 198.00, Tent with two adults 120.00. CC: Euro/Access, Visa.
From Talmont take D21 to Jard-sur-Mer. Go through town centre towards Plage de Boivinet and the campsite is signposted.

JARGEAU Loiret   2D

Camping de l'Isle aux Moulins 45150 Jargeau.
Tel 02 38 59 70 04, Fax 02 38 59 92 62.
English spoken.
OPEN: 01/03–30/11. SIZE: 7 ha, 250 pitches (all with elec), 18 hot showers, 20 WCs. ♿ ㋐

Shop at 0.3 km. Restaurant at 0.3 km. Mountain bikes and canoes for hire.
PRICES: (1996) Caravan with family 79.50, Tent with two adults 40.50. CC: Euro/Access, Visa.
18 km east of Orléans. Follow signs from Jargeau.

JONZAC Charente-Marit   4B

Camping Megisseries BP 43, 17502 Jonzac.
Tel 05 46 48 51 20, Fax 05 46 48 51 07.
OPEN: 01/04–31/10. SIZE: 28 pitches (all with elec), 18 hot showers, 6 WCs.

PRICES: (1996) Caravan with family 69.00, Tent with two adults 42.00. CC: none.
Campsite is in centre of town.

JOSSELIN-GUEGON Morbihan   1D

Camping Bas de la Lande
56120 Guégon.
Tel 02 97 22 22 20, Fax 02 97 73 93 85.
English spoken.
OPEN: 01/05–30/09. SIZE: 2 ha, 60 pitches (58 with elec), 10 hot showers, 11 WCs. ♿ ㋐

Shop at 1 km. Restaurant at 1 km.
PRICES: Caravan with family 120.00, Tent with two adults 70.00. CC: none.
From Josselin take D126 to Guégon. Follow signs to campsite.

JUMIEGES Seine Marit   2A

Camping de la Base de Plein Air
rte du Mesnil, 76480 Jumièges.
Tel 02 35 37 93 84, Fax 02 35 37 99 97.
OPEN: 01/04–31/10. SIZE: 100 pitches (all with elec), 12 hot showers, 11 WCs, 1 French WC, 1 CWP. ♿ ㋐

Shop at 3 km. Restaurant at 3 km. Tennis, sailing, archery, mini-golf nearby.
PRICES: (1996) Caravan with family 75.60, Tent with two adults 45.50. CC: none.
From Jumièges, take the D65 towards Le Mesnil-sous-Jumièges and follow the signs 'Base de Plein Air'.

Camping Municipal de la Forêt Rue Mainberthe, 76480 Jumièges.
Tel 02 35 37 93 43, Fax 02 35 37 76 48.
English spoken.
OPEN: 15/03–15/11. SIZE: 2 ha, 85 pitches (all with elec, 4 statics), 15 hot showers, 11 WCs, 4 French WCs, 2 CWPs. ♿ ㋐

Shop at 0.6 km. Restaurant at 0.6 km. Video games, TV; archery, golf, tennis and lake nearby.
PRICES: Caravan with family 114.00, Tent with two adults 67.00. CC: none.

Camping de la Forêt
at Jumièges
For your holiday in the Val de Seine

KAYSERBERG Haut-Rhin   3D

Camping Municipal rue des Acacias, 68240 Kaysersberg.
Tel 03 89 47 14 47, Fax 03 89 78 11 12.
OPEN: 01/04–30/09. SIZE: 1.5 ha, 120 pitches (80 with elec), 12 hot showers, 14 WCs, 2 CWPs. ♿

Shop at 0.5 km. Restaurant at 0.2 km. Swimming pool 500 m.
PRICES: (1996) Caravan with family 128.00, Tent with two adults 60.00. CC: none.
200 m from the N415 and well signposted.

LACANAU Gironde   4A

Camping de Talaris route de l'Océan, 33680 Lacanau.
Tel 05 56 03 04 15, Fax 05 56 26 21 56.
English spoken.
OPEN: 15/06–15/09. SIZE: 6 ha, 200 pitches (all with elec, 9 statics), 39 hot showers, 42 WCs, 38 French WCs, 6 CWPs. ♿ ㋐

Restaurant at 0.5 km. Tennis, mini-golf; 'doggy-loo'.
PRICES: (1996) Caravan with family 195.00, Tent with two adults 120.00. CC: none.

Between Lacanau and Lacanau-Océan (4 km) on the D6. Campsite is signposted on the right.

Camping du Tedey
route de Longarisse, 33680 Lacanau.
Tel 05 56 03 00 15, Fax 05 56 03 01 90.
English spoken.
OPEN: 26/04–21/09. SIZE: 14 ha, 64 hot showers, 72 WCs, 3 CWPs. ☎ ♿

Restaurant at 2 km. Sailing, windsurfing, fishing, cycling. Mobile homes for hire.
PRICES: Caravan with family 147.00, Tent with two adults 98.00. CC: Euro/Access, Visa.
Turn off D6 at Lacanau and continue along narrow track through forest for 0.9 km.

SEE ADVERTISEMENT.

Camping Le Lac Le Moutchic, 33680 Lacanau.
Tel 05 56 03 00 26. English spoken.
OPEN: 01/04–15/10. SIZE: 1 ha, 40 pitches (all with elec), 8 hot showers, 10 WCs, 2 CWPs. ☎ ♿

Restaurant at 0.1 km.
PRICES: (1996) Caravan with family 105.00, Tent with two adults 90.00. CC: none.
Le Moutchic is 7.5 km from Lacanau on the D6 towards Lacanau-Ocean. Well signposted.

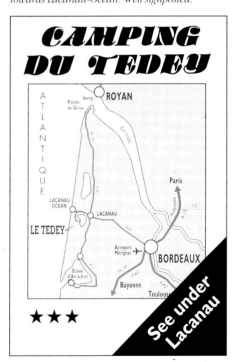

★ ★ ★

LAISSAC Aveyron 5C

La Grange de Monteillac 12310 Séverac-l'Église.
Tel 05 65 70 21 00, Fax 05 65 70 21 01.
English spoken.
OPEN: 01/07–30/09. SIZE: 4.5 ha, 60 pitches (40 with elec), 7 hot showers, 5 WCs, 2 French WCs. ☎ ♿

Restaurant at 3 km. Sporting activities and entertainment supervised by professionals.
PRICES: (1996) Caravan with family 127.00, Tent with two adults 93.00. CC: Euro/Access, Visa.
3 km east of Laissac on the N88.

LAMOTTE-BEUVRON Loir-et-Cher 2D

Camping La Grande Sologne Nouan-le-Fuzelier, 41600 Lamotte-Beuvron.
Tel 02 54 88 70 22. English spoken.
OPEN: 01/04–15/10. SIZE: 10 ha, 180 pitches (150 with elec, 40 statics), 20 hot showers, 20 WCs, 3 CWPs. ☎ ♿

Restaurant at 0.5 km.
PRICES: Caravan with family 91.00, Tent with two adults 45.00. CC: none.
South of Lamotte-Beuvron on N20.

Sologne Parc des Alicourts Les Alicourts, 41300 Pierrefitte-sur-Sauldre.
Tel 02 54 88 63 34, Fax 02 54 88 58 40.
English spoken.
OPEN: 01/05–15/09. SIZE: 25 ha, 230 pitches (200 with elec, 10 statics), 38 hot showers, 40 WCs, 4 CWPs. ☎ ♿

2 swimming pools with flume; large site with every facility.
PRICES: (1996) Caravan with family 177.00, Tent with two adults 108.00. CC: none.
Head east from Lamotte-Beuvron on D923. Turn right after 14 km on to D241 to Les Alicourts.

LANGRES Haute-Marne 3C

Camping La Croix d'Arles 52200 Bourg.
Tel 03 25 88 24 02, Fax 03 25 88 24 02.
English spoken.
OPEN: 01/04–31/10. SIZE: 3 ha, 66 pitches (all with elec), 5 hot showers, 7 WCs, 1 CWP. ☎ ♿

Children's games.
PRICES: Caravan with family 91.00, Tent with two adults 60.00. CC: Visa.
Leave motorway A31 at exit 6 Langres-Sud. Take D428 towards Langres. At junction with N74 turn right towards Dijon. Campsite is 1 km on the right. From Langres take N74 towards Dijon and camp is 5 km on right.

France

LANNEMEZAN Htes-Pyrénées   4D

Camping Les Craoues 65130 Capvern.
Tel 05 62 39 02 54. English spoken.
OPEN: 10/05−15/10. SIZE: 2 ha, 78 pitches (all with elec), 10 hot showers, 11 WCs, 10 French WCs, 1 CWP. ☎ ᘿ

Shop at 0.6 km. Restaurant at 0.4 km.
PRICES: (1996) Caravan with family 107.00,
Tent with two adults 56.00. CC: none.
Leave the A64 at exit 13 - Capvern or Lannemezan follow signs to Capvern and campsite is well signposted.

LANNILIS Finistère   1C

Camping des Abers
Dunes de Ste-Marguérite, 29214 Landeda.
Tel 02 98 04 93 35, Fax 02 98 04 84 35. English spoken.
OPEN: 01/05−30/09. SIZE: 4.5 ha, 180 pitches (all with elec, 4 statics), 20 hot showers (charge), 25 WCs, 3 CWPs. ☎ ᘿ

Shop at 0.5 km. Restaurant at 0.1 km. Lots of games for children, table tennis, volley ball; 20% discount LS.
PRICES: (1996) Caravan with family 105.00,
Tent with two adults 62.00. CC: none.
5 km east of Lannilis on the D128.

LAPALISSE Allier   5A

Camp Municipal 03120 Lapalisse.
Tel 04 70 99 26 31, Fax 04 70 99 34 73. English spoken.
OPEN: 30/04−15/09. SIZE: 1 ha, 66 pitches (60 with elec, 2 statics), 6 hot showers, 6 WCs. ☎ ᘿ

Shop at 0.3 km. Restaurant at 0.3 km. Swimming pool 0.8 km.
PRICES: (1996) Caravan with family 59.00,
Tent with two adults 38.00. CC: none.
Take the Lapalisse-Sud exit from the N7 coming from the Roanne/Lyon direction.

Camping Municipal 03130 Bert.
Tel 04 70 99 61 92.
OPEN: 15/06−15/09. SIZE: 0.6 ha, 16 pitches (all with elec), 2 hot showers, 2 WCs.

Shop at 0.2 km.
PRICES: (1996) Caravan with family 66.00,
Tent with two adults 36.00. CC: none.
Leave the N7 at Lapalisse and take D124 north-east to Bert for 12 km.

LARCHE Corrèze   4B

Camping Caravaning La Prairie Causse Correzien, Lissac-sur-Couze, 19600 Larche.
English spoken.

OPEN: 01/06−14/09. SIZE: 117 pitches (90 with elec, 10 statics), 20 hot showers, 32 WCs. ☎ ᘿ

Shop at 3 km. Restaurant at 4 km. Swimming pool: 0.3 km.
PRICES: (1996) Caravan with family 67.00,
Tent with two adults 52.00. CC: none.
From Larche, south on the D19.

LARRAU Pyrénées-Atlan   4C

Camping Ixtila Larrau, 64560 Licq-Athérey.
Tel 05 59 28 63 09.
OPEN: 15/03−11/11. SIZE: 1.4 ha, 34 pitches (25 with elec, 7 statics), 3 hot showers, 4 WCs, 1 French WC. ☎

Shop at 0.2 km. Restaurant at 0.2 km.
PRICES: (1996) Caravan with family 47.50,
Tent with two adults 27.50. CC: none.
Larrau is close to the Spanish border on D26 and campsite is signposted.

LARUNS Pyrénées-Atlan   4D

Camping d'Iscoo Eaux-Bonnes, 64440 Laruns.
Tel 05 59 05 36 81.
OPEN: 01/06−30/09. SIZE: 1 ha, 35 pitches (26 with elec), 3 hot showers (charge), 1 CWP. ☎

Shop at 1 km. Restaurant at 1 km.
PRICES: (1996) Caravan with family 80.00,
Tent with two adults 44.00. CC: none.
From Laruns take D918. Campsite is 1 km after Eaux-Bonnes towards Col d'Aubisque.

Camping des Gaves 64440 Laruns.
Tel 05 59 05 32 37, Fax 05 59 05 47 14.
English spoken.
OPEN: all year. SIZE: 2 ha, 96 pitches (87 with elec, 39 statics), 12 hot showers, 8 WCs, 3 French WCs, 1 CWP. ☎

Shop at 0.8 km. Restaurant at 0.8 km. Table tennis, fishing, boules, playground; swimming pool 0.8 km.
PRICES: (1996) Caravan with family 142.00,
Tent with two adults 95.00. CC: none.
On the D934 south of Pau. From Laruns D198 toward Eaux-Bonnes. 200 m after Esso station take left turn, continue for 500 m to campsite.

Camping du Valentin 64440 Laruns.
Tel 05 59 05 39 33. English spoken.
OPEN: 01/05−15/10. SIZE: 1.5 ha, 130 pitches (100 with elec), 9 hot showers (charge), 14 WCs, 1 CWP. ᘿ

Shop at 1 km. Restaurant at 0.3 km.

PRICES: (1996) Caravan with family 108.00,
Tent with two adults 65.00. CC: none.
*Take D918 east to Laruns towards Col
d'Aubisque. Well signposted.*

LAUTERBOURG Bas-Rhin 3B

Camping Municipal des Mouettes
67630 Lauterbourg.
Tel 03 88 54 68 60, Fax 03 88 54 61 11.
English spoken.
OPEN: 01/03–10/12. SIZE: 3 ha, 135 pitches
(all with elec, 50 statics), 14 hot showers, 17 WCs,
2 CWPs. ℓ &

Shop at 0.8 km. Restaurant at 1.2 km.
PRICES: Caravan with family 110.00,
Tent with two adults 65.00. CC: none.
D3 east of Wissembourg.

LAVAL Mayenne 1D

Camping Municipal Base de Coupeau,
53940 St-Berthevin.
Tel 02 43 69 38 37, Fax 02 43 69 20 88.
OPEN: 01/06–30/09. SIZE: 1 ha, 25 pitches (all with
elec), 2 hot showers (charge), 2 WCs.

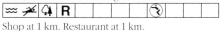

Shop at 1 km. Restaurant at 1 km.
PRICES: (1996) Caravan with family 83.50,
Tent with two adults 42.50. CC: none.
*Heading west from centre of Laval, turn left at
main traffic lights, go past the church, turn right,
left and then straight ahead for St-Berthevin.
Campsite is well signposted.*

LAVAUR Tarn 5C

Le Plan d'Eau St-Charles C rte B. Belin,
81220 Damiatte.
Tel 05 63 70 66 07, Fax 05 63 70 52 14.
OPEN: 15/04–15/10. SIZE: 6 ha, 67 pitches (50 with
elec, 17 statics), 9 hot showers, 10 WCs, 1 CWP. ℓ &

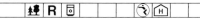

Restaurant at 2 km. Flume.
PRICES: (1996) Caravan with family 111.00,
Tent with two adults 69.00. CC: none.
*Turn left in Damiatte just before the railway
crossing.*

LAVELANET Ariège 5C

Camp Municipal Fount de Sicre
09300 Montferrier.
Tel 05 61 01 20 97.
OPEN: all year. SIZE: 20 pitches (all with elec,
2 statics), 4 hot showers, 4 WCs, 2 French WCs.

Shop at 0.1 km.

PRICES: (1996) Caravan with family 60.00,
Tent with two adults 30.00. CC: none.
*South from Lavelanet towards Foix, turn left after
1 km on the D109 towards Montségur;
Montferrier is 4 km on.*

Camping Municipal rue Jacquard,
09300 Lavelanet.
Tel 05 61 01 22 20, Fax 05 61 03 06 39.
English spoken.
OPEN: 15/04–30/09. SIZE: 2 ha, 100 pitches
(all with elec), 12 hot showers, 7 WCs, 3 French
WCs, 4 CWPs. &

Shop at 0.5 km. Restaurant at 2 km. Library.
PRICES: (1996) Caravan with family 130.00,
Tent with two adults 69.00. CC: none.
On the D117 east of Foix.

LEGE-CAP-FERRET Gironde 4A

Airotel Les Viviers Claouey,
33950 Lège-Cap-Ferret.
Tel 05 56 60 70 04, Fax 05 56 60 76 14.
English spoken.
OPEN: 01/05–30/09. SIZE: 33 ha, 400 pitches
(all with elec, 200 statics), 120 hot showers,
140 WCs, 10 CWPs. ℓ &

Shop at 1 km. Restaurant at 1 km.
PRICES: (1996) Caravan with family 209.00.
CC: Euro/Access, Visa.
Take D106 south of Lège-Cap-Ferret for Claouey.

LEMPDES Haute-Loire 5A

Camping Municipal 43410 Lempdes.
Tel 04 71 76 59 69, Fax 04 71 76 52 82.
English spoken.
OPEN: 01/06–15/09. SIZE: 2 ha, 80 pitches (all with
elec), 13 hot showers, 23 WCs. ℓ &

Restaurant at 0.5 km. Tennis, mini-golf; swimming
pool 0.1 km.
PRICES: (1996) Caravan with family 92.00,
Tent with two adults 70.00. CC: none.
*Take exit 19 or 20 from A75 and follow signs to
campsite.*

LESPARRE-MEDOC Gironde 4A

Camping L'Orée du Bois route d'Aquitaine,
33990 Hourtin.
Tel 05 56 09 15 88. English spoken.
OPEN: 15/06–15/09. SIZE: 2 ha, 100 pitches
(70 with elec), 10 hot showers, 10 WCs.

PRICES: (1996) Caravan with family 52.00. CC: none.
D3 south-west of Lesparre-Médoc.

France

Camping Les Ourmes avenue du Lac,
33990 Hourtin.
Tel 05 56 09 12 76, Fax 05 56 09 23 90.
English spoken.
OPEN: 01/04–30/09. SIZE: 6 ha, 270 pitches
(all with elec, 10 statics), 31 hot showers, 34 WCs,
4 French WCs, 3 CWPs. ℓ

≋ ⚊ ⚹ R ⊡ ⚌ ⚏ ✗ ⟑ ⌂

Shop at 1 km.
PRICES: (1996) Caravan with family 144.00,
Tent with two adults 90.00.
CC: none.
D3 south-west of Lesparre-Médoc.

LESSAY Manche 1B

Camping Plage aux Grands Espaces
St-Germain-sur-Ay, 50430 Lessay.
Tel 02 33 07 10 14, Fax 02 33 07 22 59.
English spoken.
OPEN: 15/05–15/09. SIZE: 15 ha, 200 pitches
(100 with elec, 350 statics), 30 hot showers,
40 WCs, 2 CWPs. ℓ

≋ ⚊ ⚹ R ⊡ ⚌ ⚏ ⟑ ⌂

Shop at 0.5 km. Restaurant at 0.5 km.
PRICES: (1996) Caravan with family 126.00,
Tent with two adults 67.00.
CC: none.
*From Lessay 9 km northwards along the coast to
St-Germain-sur-Ay on the D650.*

LEZIGNAN-CORBIERES Aude 5C

Camping La Pinède
11200 Lézignan-Corbières.
Tel 04 68 27 05 08, Fax 04 68 27 21 63.
English spoken.
OPEN: 01/04–15/10. SIZE: 3 ha, 90 pitches (all with
elec), 18 hot showers, 12 WCs, 3 CWPs. ℓ

⚹ R ⊡ ⚌ ⚏ ✗ ⟑ ⌂

PRICES: (1996) Caravan with family 106.00,
Tent with two adults 70.00. CC: none.
*From N13 at Lézignan-Corbières, make your way
to Le Patio swimming pool and campsite is
nearby.*

Le Pinada Villerouge-la-Crémade,
11200 Lézignan-Corbières.
Tel 04 68 47 67 88, Fax 04 68 43 68 61.
English spoken.
OPEN: 15/05–30/09. SIZE: 5 ha, 70 pitches (all with
elec), 17 hot showers, 3 WCs, 1 CWP. ℓ

⚹ R ⊡ ⟑ ⌂

Shop at 8 km. Restaurant at 5 km.
PRICES: (1996) Caravan with family 105.00,
Tent with two adults 80.00. CC: none.
*Leave A61 at Lézignan-Corbières in the direction
of Ferrals. Villerouge-la-Crémade is 5 km after
Ferrals on the D106.*

LIBOURNE Gironde 4B

Camping du Vieux Château 33420 Rauzan.
Tel 05 57 84 15 38, Fax 05 57 84 15 38.
English spoken.
OPEN: 01/04–01/11. SIZE: 2 ha, 35 pitches (28 with
elec), 3 hot showers, 3 WCs, 1 CWP. ℓ

⚹ R ⊡ ⚌ ⟑ ⌂

Restaurant at 0.5 km.
PRICES: (1996) Caravan with family 101.00,
Tent with two adults 55.00. CC: none.
*From Libourne, travel south on D670 (Bayonne-
bis route) towards Rauzan. The site is 200 m
north of Rauzan on D123, about 1.5 km off D670.*

LIGNIERES Cher 2D

Camping de l'Ange Blanc
rue de l'Ange Blanc, 18160 Lignières.
Tel 02 48 60 00 18.
OPEN: 01/04–30/09. SIZE: 1 ha, 30 pitches (all with
elec), 2 hot showers, 5 WCs, 3 CWPs. ⅗

⚊ ⚹ ⌂

Shop at 0.3 km. Restaurant at 0.8 km.
PRICES: (1996) Caravan with family 83.00,
Tent with two adults 39.00. CC: none.
Follow campsite signs in Lignières.

LIGUEIL Indre/Loire 2C

Moulin de la Touche Camping à la Ferme,
37240 Ligueil.
Tel 02 47 92 06 84, Fax 02 47 92 06 84.
English spoken.
OPEN: 01/03–31/10. SIZE: 1 ha, 6 pitches (all with
elec), 2 hot showers, 4 WCs.

⚊ ⚹ ⚑ R ⚏ ✗ ⌂

Shop at 2 km. Fishing.
PRICES: (1996) Caravan with family 79.00,
Tent with two adults 45.00. CC: Euro/Access, Visa.
*From Ligueil take the D31 towards Loches and the
campsite is 2 km ahead on the right.*

LIMOGES Haute-Vienne 4B

Camping du Château de Leychoisier
87270 Bonnac-la-Côte.
Tel 05 55 39 93 43, Fax 05 55 39 93 43.
English spoken.
OPEN: 01/04–20/09. SIZE: 2 ha, 80 pitches (50 with
elec, 6 statics), 10 hot showers, 9 WCs, 12 French
WCs, 1 CWP. ⅗

≋ ⚊ ⚹ R ⊡ ⚋ ⚏ ✗ ⟑ ⌂

Shop at 1 km. Tennis; free lake fishing; lovely
walks.
PRICES: (1996) Caravan with family 174.00,
Tent with two adults 98.00. CC: none.
*A20 Orléans-Châteauroux-Limoges. 7 km before
Limoges take exit for Bonnac-la-Côte.*

Les Rousilles St-Sylvestre-la-Crouzille, 87240 Ambazac.
Tel 05 55 71 04 62, Fax 05 55 71 04 62.
English spoken.
OPEN: all year. SIZE: 5 ha, 65 pitches (60 with elec, 12 statics), 15 hot showers, 15 WCs, 1 CWP. ⚓ &

PRICES: (1996) Caravan with family 92.50, Tent with two adults 50.00. CC: Euro/Access.
Take A20 north out of Limoges, leave at exit 26 towards La Crouzille and then follow signs to campsite.

LIMOGNE-EN-QUERCY Lot 5C

Bel Air 46260 Limogne-en-Quercy.
Tel 05 65 24 32 75. English spoken.
OPEN: 01/04–01/10. SIZE: 2 ha, 50 pitches (all with elec), 5 hot showers, 5 WCs. ⚓ &

Shop at 0.4 km. Restaurant at 0.4 km. Tennis nearby.
PRICES: (1996) Caravan with family 74.00, Tent with two adults 48.00. CC: none.
From Cahors take D911 east to Limogne-en-Quercy.

LIMOUX Aude 5C

Camping Val d'Aleth chemin de la Paoulette, 11580 Alet-les-Bains.
Tel 04 68 69 90 40, Fax 04 68 69 90 40.
English spoken.
OPEN: all year. SIZE: 37 pitches (all with elec), 6 hot showers, 6 WCs. ⚓

Restaurant at 0.2 km. English owners; Mineral water swimming pool 0.5 km, Kayak and rafting 0.4 km.
PRICES: (1996) Caravan with family 85.00, Tent with two adults 49.00. CC: none.
South of Limoux on D118, cross over River Aude into Alet-les-Bains, bear right and campsite is about 300 m ahead on the right. Large sign on house at entrance.

LISIEUX Calvados 2A

Château Camping Le Colombier 14590 Moyaux.
Tel 02 31 63 63 08, Fax 02 31 63 15 97.
English spoken.
OPEN: 01/05–15/09. SIZE: 6 ha, 200 pitches, 31 hot showers, 25 WCs, 3 CWPs. ⚓ &

Tennis, fishing, mini-golf.
PRICES: Caravan with family 213.00, Tent with two adults 132.00. CC: Euro/Access, Visa.
Moyaux in on D143 from Lisieux and campsite is well signposted.

LA LONDE-LES-MAURES Var 6C

Camping Caravaning Val Rose 83250 La Londe-les-Maures.
Tel 04 94 66 81 36, Fax 04 94 66 52 67.
English spoken.
OPEN: 15/02–30/10. SIZE: 2.5 ha, 45 pitches (all with elec, 120 statics), 14 hot showers, 10 WCs, 1 CWP. &

PRICES: (1996) Caravan with family 153.00, Tent with two adults 84.00. CC: Amex, Euro/Access, Visa.
From La Londe centre go towards Lavandou. Keep on old road (left at fork junction). Campsite is 3 km ahead, right-hand side.

LONS-LE-SAUNIER Jura 3C

Camping de la Marjorie 640 bd de l'Europe, 39000 Lons-le-Saunier.
Tel 03 84 24 26 94, Fax 03 84 24 08 40.
English spoken.
OPEN: 01/04–15/10. SIZE: 7 ha, 123 pitches (all with elec), 25 hot showers, 22 WCs, 2 CWPs. ⚓ &

Shop at 0.5 km. Restaurant at 0.5 km. Swimming pool 0.2 km.
PRICES: (1996) Caravan with family 97.00, Tent with two adults 60.00. CC: Amex, Euro/Access, Visa.
Between Besançon and Lyon. Follow signs from Lons-le-Saunier.

Camping de la Toupe
Baume-les-Messieurs, 39210 Voiteur.
Tel 03 84 44 63 57.
OPEN: 01/04–30/09. SIZE: 53 pitches (24 with elec), 4 hot showers, 6 WCs. &

Shop at 6 km. Restaurant at 1 km.
PRICES: (1996) Caravan with family 82.00, Tent with two adults 40.00. CC: none.
Baume-les-Messieurs is north-east of Lons-le-Saunier. Campsite is in the centre of the village and well signposted.

Camping de Surchauffant Pont-de-la-Pyle, 39270 La Tour-du-Meix.
Tel 03 84 25 41 08, Fax 03 84 35 56 88.
English spoken.
OPEN: 01/05–15/09. SIZE: 2.5 ha, 180 pitches (155 with elec), 24 hot showers, 22 WCs, 3 CWPs. ⚓ &

Lakeside beach.
PRICES: (1996) Caravan with family 117.50, Tent with two adults 69.00. CC: Euro/Access, Visa.
South-east of Lons-le-Saunier, on the D52 between Orgelet and Moirans-en-Montagne. Signposted.

France

Domaine de Chalain 39130 Doucier.
Tel 03 84 24 29 00, Fax 03 84 24 94 07.
English spoken.
OPEN: 02/05–17/09. SIZE: 30 ha, 800 pitches
(560 with elec, 130 statics), 130 hot showers,
110 WCs, 8 CWPs. ☎ &

Shop at 2 km.
PRICES: (1996) Caravan with family 142.00, Tent
with two adults 109.00. CC: Euro/Access, Visa.
From Lons-le-Saunier take the D471 towards
Champagnole. Turn right on the D27 to Doucier.

La Grisière et Europes Vacances
39130 Clairvaux-les-Lacs.
Tel 03 84 25 82 70, Fax 03 84 25 26 24.
English spoken.
OPEN: 01/05–30/09. SIZE: 11 ha, 655 pitches
(400 with elec), 30 hot showers, 50 WCs. ☎ &

Restaurant at 0.8 km. Mobile homes for hire.
PRICES: (1996) Caravan with family 103.00,
Tent with two adults 58.00. CC: none.
From Lons-le-Saunier take N78 to
Clairvaux-les-Lacs.

LORIOL-SUR-DROME Drôme 5B

Camping La Poche Mirmande, 26270 Loriol.
Tel 05 45 63 02 88. English spoken.
OPEN: 01/04–31/10. SIZE: 4 ha, 80 pitches (all with
elec, 20 statics), 6 hot showers, 9 WCs. ☎

Shop at 0.3 km.
PRICES: (1996) Caravan with family 98.00,
Tent with two adults 55.00. CC: none.
N7 south from Loriol. Left turn on to D57 to site.

LOURDES Htes-Pyrénées 4D

Arrouach 9 rue de Archauges,
65100 Lourdes.
Tel 05 62 94 25 75, Fax 05 62 42 05 27.
English spoken.
OPEN: all year. SIZE: 13 ha, 67 pitches, 8 hot
showers, 16 WCs. ☎

Shop at 1 km. Restaurant at 0.5 km. Lake nearby.
Rooms available.
PRICES: (1996) Caravan with family 86.00,
Tent with two adults 54.00. CC: none.
On outskirts of Lourdes. Access from D940 and
D937. Follow signs to campsite.

Camp Domec route de Julos, 65100 Lourdes.
Tel 05 62 94 08 79. English spoken.
OPEN: 09/04–01/10. SIZE: 2 ha, 100 pitches
(all with elec), 6 hot showers, 12 WCs, 18 French
WCs, 1 CWP. ☎ &

Restaurant at 0.5 km. Swimming pool 0.3 km.
PRICES: (1996) Caravan with family 72.00, Tent
with two adults 37.00. CC: none.
From Lourdes, take the road to Argelès. Campsite
on left and well signposted.

Les Deux Pics du Fer 16 rue Gallieui,
65100 Lourdes.
Tel 05 62 94 20 94. English spoken.
OPEN: 15/05–15/11. SIZE: 1 ha, 30 pitches (20 with
elec), 5 hot showers (charge), 15 WCs, 4 French
WCs. ☎

Shop at 0.1 km. Restaurant at 0.5 km.
PRICES: (1996) Caravan with family 62.00,
Tent with two adults 30.00. CC: none.
In city centre on N21 towards Argelès. (No motor
caravans.)

Le Moulin du Monge
av Jean Moulin, RN 21, 65100 Lourdes.
Tel 05 62 94 28 15, Fax 05 62 42 20 54.
English spoken.
OPEN: all year. SIZE: 1 ha, 67 pitches (all with elec,
5 statics), 8 hot showers, 12 WCs, 1 CWP. ☎

Restaurant at 0.5 km. Sauna.
PRICES: (1996) Caravan with family 119.50, Tent
with two adults 64.50. CC: Euro/Access, Visa.
North of Lourdes on N21 and avenue Jean Moulin.

LOUVIERS Eure 2A

Le Bel Air St-Lubin, 27400 Louviers.
Tel 02 32 40 10 77. English spoken.
OPEN: 01/03–31/10. SIZE: 2.5 ha, 92 pitches
(all with elec, 70 statics), 8 hot showers, 8 WCs,
1 French WC, 1 CWP. ☎

Restaurant at 3 km.
PRICES: (1996) Caravan with family 128.00,
Tent with two adults 69.50. CC: none.
From Louviers take D81 west towards La Haye-
Malherbe. Campsite at St-Lubin is signposted.

Caravaning Château-Gaillard
Bernières-sur-Seine, 27700 Les Andelys.
Tel 02 32 54 18 20, Fax 02 32 54 32 66.
English spoken.
OPEN: 01/02–31/12. SIZE: 24 ha, 185 pitches, 16 hot
showers, 19 WCs. ☎

Restaurant at 2 km. Archery, water sports.
PRICES: (1996) Caravan with family 120.00,
Tent with two adults 73.00. CC: Visa.
Take the D135 between Les Andelys and Louviers
and about 3 km from Les Andelys, turn towards
Bernières. Signposted.

France

LUCON Vendée   4A

Camping Municipal 1er rue Pierre Mendès-France, 85450 Champagne-les-Marais.
Tel 02 51 56 61 10, Fax 02 51 56 50 19.
English spoken.
OPEN: 15/06–15/09. SIZE: 1 ha, 70 pitches (18 with elec), 10 hot showers, 12 WCs, 3 CWPs. ⌕

	⌂	R							

Shop at 0.1 km. Restaurant at 0.1 km.
PRICES: (1996) Caravan with family 53.00,
Tent with two adults 31.00. CC: none.
From Luçon, south on D746 to Triaize. Left to Champagne-les-Marais.

LUNEL Hérault   5D

Les Amandiers chemin de Cafoulin,
30660 Gallargues-le-Montueux.
Tel 04 66 35 28 02, Fax 04 66 35 28 02.
English spoken.
OPEN: 08/05–07/09. SIZE: 3 ha, 150 pitches (all with elec, 14 statics), 15 hot showers, 15 WCs, 1 CWP. ⌕ &

	⌂	R	▣	☕			⌕	Ⓗ

Restaurant at 0.3 km. Tennis, volley ball, entertainment; river 0.8 km.
PRICES: Caravan with family 131.00, Tent with two adults 68.00. CC: Euro/Access, Visa.
From N113, turn right 20 km after Nîmes. From motorway, exit A9 at Gallargues-les-Plages and turn immediately right into village. The campsite is well signposted.

Camping Bon Port 34400 Lunel.
Tel 04 67 71 15 65, Fax 04 67 83 60 27.
English spoken.
OPEN: 01/03–31/10. SIZE: 5 ha, 300 pitches (220 with elec, 30 statics), 32 hot showers, 36 WCs, 3 CWPs. ⌕ &

	🏕	R	▣	☕	☕	✕	⌕	Ⓗ

Shop at 3 km. Mini-golf; river 1 km, sea 10 km.
PRICES: (1996) Caravan with family 125.00, Tent with two adults 73.00. CC: Euro/Access, Visa.
From Lunel exit off motorway, take D61 towards La Grande-Motte for 3 km.

LURE Haute-Saône   3D

Camping à la Ferme Aire Naturelle La Bergereine route des Vosges, 70270 Melisey.
Tel 03 84 20 00 90.
OPEN: 01/04–31/10. SIZE: 1.1 ha, 25 pitches (all with elec, 10 statics), 1 hot shower (charge), 4 WCs. ⌕

~	⚓	🏕	R				Ⓗ	

Shop at 5 km. Restaurant at 0.1 km.
PRICES: (1996) Caravan with family 48.00, Tent with two adults 26.00. CC: none.
10 km north of Lure on D486.

LUSIGNAN Vienne   4B

Camp Municipal de Vauchiron 86600 Lusignan.
Tel 05 49 43 30 08, Fax 05 49 43 61 19.
English spoken.
OPEN: 15/04–31/10. SIZE: 4 ha, 90 pitches (64 with elec), 9 hot showers, 9 WCs. ⌕ &

~	⚓	🏕						

Shop at 0.5 km. Restaurant at 0.5 km. Mini-golf, canoes/kayaks.
PRICES: (1996) Caravan with family 47.50, Tent with two adults 24.50. CC: none.
Approx 25 km south-west of Poitiers on N11. Site is well signposted in Lusignan.

LUSSAC Gironde   4B

Camping Le Pressoir Petit-Palais, 33570 Lussac.
Tel 05 57 69 73 25, Fax 05 57 69 77 36.
English spoken.
OPEN: 01/05–30/09. SIZE: 3 ha, 100 pitches (all with elec), 14 hot showers, 14 WCs, 2 CWPs. ⌕ &

	⌂	R	▣		☕	✕	⌕	⚠

Shop at 2 km.
PRICES: (1996) Caravan with family 150.00, Tent with two adults 80.00. CC: Euro/Access, Visa.
From A10 exit Poitiers-Sud, follow signs to Angoulême and green signs 'Route Bis Bayonne/Toulouse' to St-Médard-de-Guizières. Campsite is signposted from there.

LUYNES Indre/Loire   2C

Camping Municipal Les Granges
37230 Luynes.
Tel 02 47 55 60 85. English spoken.
OPEN: 08/05–17/09. SIZE: 8 ha, 63 pitches (53 with elec), 8 hot showers, 6 WCs, 3 CWPs. ⌕ &

	⌂	R	▣				Ⓗ	

Shop at 0.2 km. Restaurant at 0.3 km. Table tennis, playground; river 0.1 km.
PRICES: (1996) Caravan with family 68.80, Tent with two adults 30.90. CC: none.
Luynes is 12 km from Tours on the N152 going towards Saumur.

LUZ-ST-SAUVEUR Htes-Pyrénées   4D

Le Bergons Esterre, 65120 Luz-St-Sauveur.
Tel 05 62 92 90 77. English spoken.
OPEN: 15/12–20/10. SIZE: 1 ha, 77 pitches, 8 hot showers, 12 WCs, 2 French WCs, 1 CWP. &

~	⚓	⌂	R	▣			Ⓗ	

Shop at 0.5 km. Restaurant at 0.5 km.
PRICES: (1996) Caravan with family 90.50, Tent with two adults 49.00. CC: none.
From Luz-St-Sauveur take the D918 east towards Barèges. As you come in to the village of Esterre, the campsite is on the right.

France

Camping International 65120 Luz-St-Sauveur.
Tel 05 62 92 82 02, Fax 05 62 92 96 87.
English spoken.
OPEN: 01/06–30/09 & 15/12–30/04. SIZE: 4 ha,
133 pitches (120 with elec), 20 hot showers,
18 WCs, 1 CWP. ✆ ♿

Half-court tennis.
PRICES: (1996) Caravan with family 129.50, Tent
with two adults 86.00. CC: Euro/Access, Visa.
*Luz-St-Sauveur is well signposted and the
campsite is on the left about 800 m before
reaching Luz Centre sign.*

Camping La Ribère Barèges,
65120 Luz-St-Sauveur.
Tel 05 62 92 69 01, Fax 05 62 92 69 92.
English spoken.
OPEN: 20/12–01/05 & 15/05–15/10. SIZE: 2 ha,
70 pitches (all with elec, 10 statics), 11 hot
showers, 8 WCs, 1 CWP. ♿

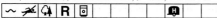

Shop at 0.6 km. Restaurant at 0.3 km.
PRICES: Caravan with family 108.00, Tent with two
adults 55.00. CC: Euro/Access, Visa.
*From Luz-St-Sauveur, eastwards on the D918 to
Barèges (8 km), going towards Col du Tourmalet.*

Le Honta Sassis, 65120 Luz-St-Sauveur.
Tel 05 62 92 95 90. English spoken.
OPEN: 23/12–15/10. SIZE: 2 ha, 70 pitches (50 with
elec, 10 statics), 6 hot showers, 9 WCs, 1 CWP. ♿

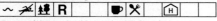

Shop at 1 km. Restaurant at 1 km.
PRICES: (1996) Caravan with family 95.00,
Tent with two adults 49.00. CC: none.
*From Luz-St-Sauveur take road to Sassis and
campsite is signposted.*

Le Relais d'Espagne 65120 Gèdre.
Tel 05 62 92 47 70.
OPEN: all year. SIZE: 2 ha, 50 pitches (all with elec),
6 hot showers (charge), 10 WCs. ✆

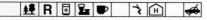

Shop at 1 km. Swimming pool 1 km.
PRICES: (1996) Caravan with family 63.00,
Tent with two adults 32.00. CC: none.
12 km north of Luz-St-Sauveur.

LUZECH Lot 4D

La Tuque Naturiste Belaye, 46140 Luzech.
Tel 05 65 21 34 34, Fax 05 65 21 39 89.
English spoken.
OPEN: 15/04–30/09. SIZE: 10 ha, 100 pitches
(all with elec, 12 statics), 11 hot showers, 13 WCs,
8 CWPs. ✆ ♿

Restaurant at 12 km. Naturist site with good sports

facilities and entertainment programme.
PRICES: Caravan with family 160.00, Tent with two
adults 90.00. CC: none.
Well signposted from town, close to the River Lot.

LUZY Nièvre 3C

Camping du Lac Marnant
route de Decize, 58250 La Nocle-Maulaix.
Tel 03 86 30 81 28.
OPEN: 01/05–30/09. SIZE: 1 ha, 17 pitches
(all with elec), 2 hot showers, 2 WCs, 1 CWP. ✆

Shop at 0.3 km. Restaurant at 0.3 km.
PRICES: (1996) Caravan with family 59.50,
Tent with two adults 45.00. CC: none.
*West from Luzy on N81. After 15 km turn left to La
Nocle. Site on right 300 m before the church.*

Camping Municipal de la Bedure
route d'Autun, 58170 Luzy.
Tel 03 86 30 02 34.
OPEN: 01/06–15/09. SIZE: 2 ha, 30 pitches
(all with elec), 10 WCs, 2 CWPs.

Shop at 0.7 km. Restaurant at 0.7 km.
PRICES: (1996) Caravan with family 81.00,
Tent with two adults 41.00. CC: none.
*The site is 0.7 km from town centre in the
direction of Autun, and near the
swimming pool.*

Château de Chigy Tazilly, 58170 Luzy.
Tel 03 86 30 10 80, Fax 03 86 30 09 22.
English spoken.
OPEN: 01/04–30/09. SIZE: 35 ha, 250 pitches
(170 with elec), 34 hot showers, 30 WCs,
4 CWPs. ♿

Shop at 4.5 km. Mini-golf.
PRICES: (1996) Caravan with family 158.00,
Tent with two adults 87.00.
CC: Euro/Access, Visa.
*In Luzy take the D973 towards Moulins.
Campsite is 4 km ahead on the left.*

MACON Saône/Loire 5B

Camping du Lac St-Point, 71630 Tramayes.
Tel 03 85 50 52 31, Fax 03 85 50 54 84.
English spoken.
OPEN: 01/04–01/10. SIZE: 3 ha.

Shop at 0.2 km.
PRICES: (1996) Caravan with family 75.00,
Tent with two adults 59.00. CC: none.
*N79 west from Mâcon, then left turn on to the D22
at La Valouze. The site is 200 m from the village
of St-Point.*

MAISONS-LAFFITTE Yvelines 2B

Camping Caravaning International
1 rue Johnson, 78600 Maisons-Laffitte.
Tel 01 39 12 21 91, Fax 01 34 93 02 60.
English spoken.
OPEN: all year. SIZE: 7 ha, 200 pitches (180 with
elec, 40 statics), 1 CWP. ℓ &

Shop at 0.5 km. Swimming pool 2 km; 1 hour from
Disneyland Paris by train.
PRICES: Caravan with family 190.00, Tent with two
adults 120.00. CC: Euro/Access, Visa.
*The campsite is 10 minutes' walk from the railway
station in Maisons-Laffitte.*

MALBUISSON Doubs 3D

Les Fuvettes 25160 Malbuisson.
Tel 03 81 69 31 50, Fax 03 81 69 70 46.
English spoken.
OPEN: 01/04–15/10. SIZE: 6 ha, 320 pitches
(220 with elec, 50 statics), 37 hot showers,
30 WCs. ℓ &

Restaurant at 1 km. Swimming pool nearby,
boating.
PRICES: (1996) Caravan with family 133.00,
Tent with two adults 79.00. CC: Amex,
Euro/Access, Visa.
*From Pontarlier take the N57 south. The site is on
the right-hand side of St-Point lake.*

MALESHERBES Loiret 2D

Camping Ile de Boulancourt
77760 Boulancourt.
Tel 01 64 24 13 38, Fax 01 64 24 10 43.
English spoken.
OPEN: all year. SIZE: 5 ha, 100 pitches (all with elec,
60 statics), 6 hot showers, 12 WCs, 1 CWP. ℓ &

Shop at 0.1 km. Restaurant at 0.1 km. Fishing;
swimming, boating, golf, climbing and tennis
nearby.
PRICES: (1996) Caravan with family 72.00,
Tent with two adults 48.00. CC: none.
*On D410, 4 km south of Malesherbes. Campsite is
signposted to the right.*

MALLEMORT Bouches-du-Rhône 5D

Camping Durance Lubéron
Domaine du Vergon, 13370 Mallemort.
Tel 04 90 59 13 36, Fax 04 42 95 03 63.
English spoken.
OPEN: 01/05–15/09. SIZE: 4 ha, 110 pitches
(all with elec), 12 hot showers, 14 WCs, 6 French
WCs, 2 CWPs. ℓ

Shop at 2 km. Restaurant at 0.5 km. Tennis; horse-
riding 0.1 km.
PRICES: (1996) Caravan with family 165.00, Tent
with two adults 93.00. CC: Euro/Access, Visa.
*Take D561 near the Pont-Royal golf course and
turn left after bus stop to campsite.*

MANDELIEU Alpes-Marit 6C

Azur Vacances bd du Bon Puits,
06210 Mandelieu-la-Napoule.
Tel 04 93 49 91 12. English spoken.
OPEN: 01/04–30/09. SIZE: 12 ha, 540 pitches, 15 hot
showers (charge), 40 WCs, 1 CWP. ℓ

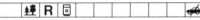

Golf nearby.
PRICES: (1996) Caravan with family 145.00,
Tent with two adults 87.00. CC: none.

MANOSQUE Alpes/Hte-Prov 5D

Camp Municipal Le Chaffère
route de Corbière, 04220 Ste-Tulle.
Tel 04 92 78 22 75, Fax 04 92 78 31 57.
OPEN: 01/06–30/09. SIZE: 1 ha, 54 pitches (all with
elec), 6 hot showers, 6 WCs, 3 French WCs. &

Shop at 0.1 km. Restaurant at 0.2 km. Swimming
pool 300 m.
PRICES: (1996) Caravan with family 65.60,
Tent with two adults 35.40. CC: none.
*N96 autoroute towards Aix-en-Provence and
Manosque.*

LE MANS Sarthe 2C

Camping La Châtaigneraie
72530 Yvre-l'Evêque-Le Mans.
Tel 02 43 89 60 68, Fax 02 43 89 60 68.
English spoken.
OPEN: 01/04–30/09. SIZE: 1.2 ha, 55 pitches
(all with elec, 4 statics), 6 hot showers, 6 WCs,
10 French WCs, 1 CWP. ℓ

Shop at 0.8 km. Restaurant at 0.8 km. Games
room, table tennis, basketball.
PRICES: (1996) Caravan with family 95.00,
Tent with two adults 55.00. CC: none.
*Just east of Le Mans, 5 minutes from the town
centre. A11 exit Le Mans-Est on to N23 towards
Paris. Well signposted.*

Castel Camping Château de Chanteloup
Sille le Philippe, 72460 Savigné-l'Evêque.
Tel 02 43 27 51 07, Fax 02 43 89 05 05.
English spoken.
OPEN: 01/06–03/09. SIZE: 24 ha, 100 pitches (80 with
elec), 16 hot showers, 11 WCs, 1 CWP. ℓ &

France

� **R** ⊡ **L** ✕ ⁀

Good sports facilities/fishing nearby.
PRICES: (1996) Caravan with family 183.00,
Tent with two adults 107.00. CC: none.
*From motorway take exit for Le Mans-Est, then
follow signs for Yvre-l'Evêque and Savigné-
l'Evêque. Go through village on D301 towards
Chanteloup and follow signs to campsite.*

MAREUIL Dordogne   4B

L'Etang Bleu Périgord Vert, 24340 Vieux-Mareuil.
Tel 05 53 60 92 70, Fax 05 53 60 92 70.
English spoken.
OPEN: 01/04–31/10. SIZE: 5 ha, 142 pitches (96 with
elec), 20 hot showers, 22 WCs, 3 French WCs. ↻ &

≈ ⊸ 🛉 **R** ⊡ **L** ▯ ✕ ⁀ ⓗ

PRICES: (1996) Caravan with family 115.00,
Tent with two adults 75.00. CC: Amex,
Euro/Access, Visa.
South of Mareuil on D939. Follow signs.

MARQUISE Pas-de-Calais   2B

Camping Les Primevères 62250 Leubringhen.
Tel 03 21 87 13 33. English spoken.
OPEN: 01/04–31/10. SIZE: 1 ha, 63 pitches (42 with
elec, 20 statics), 4 hot showers, 7 WCs, 1 CWP. &

⊕ **R** | **L** | ⊞

Restaurant at 2 km.
PRICES: (1996) Caravan with family 76.00,
Tent with two adults 38.00. CC: none.
*A16 north of Marquise. Past St-Inglevert
(Canadian cemetery) and turn left after
motorway. First village you come to.*

L'Escale Wacquinghen, 62250 Marquise.
Tel 03 21 32 00 69. English spoken.
OPEN: 01/03–15/11. SIZE: 11 ha, 68 pitches (all with
elec, 130 statics), 24 hot showers, 15 WCs. ↻ &

⊕ | **L** ▯ | ⓗ

Restaurant at 4 km.
PRICES: (1996) Caravan with family 84.50, Tent
with two adults 47.00. CC: Euro/Access, Visa.
From Calais, take the A16 to Marquise.

MARSEILLAN Hérault   5C

Camping La Plage 69 chemin du Pairollet,
34340 Marseillan-Plage.
Tel 04 67 21 92 54, Fax 04 67 01 63 57.
English spoken.
OPEN: 20/03–20/10. SIZE: 1.3 ha, 105 pitches
(all with elec), 14 hot showers, 9 WCs, 5 French
WCs, 3 CWPs. ↻ &

≋ ⊸ 🛉 **R** ⊡ | ▯ ✕

Shop at 0.1 km. Playground.
PRICES: (1996) Caravan with family 184.00,

Tent with two adults 140.00. CC: none.
The campsite is by the sea and well signposted.

La Jasse-sur-Mer Chemin du Pairolet,
34340 Marseillan-Plage.
Tel 04 67 21 92 47, Fax 04 67 98 38 13.
OPEN: 01/04–30/09. SIZE: 2 ha, 180 pitches
(all with elec), 26 hot showers, 16 WCs. ↻

≋ ⊸ ⊕ **R** ⊡

Shop at 0.3 km. Restaurant at 0.3 km.
PRICES: (1996) Caravan with family 141.90,
Tent with two adults 114.20. CC: none.
*From Agde go towards Sète on the N112 and at
the first set of lights turn right. Campsite is 500 m
on the left.*

La Nouvelle Floride
34340 Marseillan-Plage.
Tel 04 67 21 94 49, Fax 04 67 21 81 05.
English spoken.
OPEN: 01/05–01/10. SIZE: 6.5 ha, 400 pitches
(all with elec, 100 statics). ↻ &

≋ ⊸ 🛉 **R** ⊡ **L** ▯ ✕ ⁀ ⓗ

Disco, playground, entertainment.
PRICES: (1996) Caravan with family 235.00,
Tent with two adults 200.00. CC: none.
Marseillan-Plage is 6 km south of Marseillan.

MARTEL Lot   5A

Camping Le Port 46600 Creysse.
Tel 05 65 32 20 40, Fax 05 65 38 78 21.
English spoken.
OPEN: 01/05–30/09. SIZE: 4 ha, 100 pitches
(52 with elec), 10 hot showers, 10 WCs,
2 CWPs. ↻

∼ ⊸ ⊕ **R** | **L** | ⁀

Restaurant at 0.1 km. Fishing, canoeing,
mountain-biking.
PRICES: (1996) Caravan with family 97.00,
Tent with two adults 51.00. CC: Amex,
Euro/Access, Visa.
*From Martel take D23 to Creysse, and the
campsite is signposted.*

MASEVAUX Haut-Rhin   3D

Camping Municipal
rue du Stade, 68290 Masevaux.
Tel 03 89 82 42 29. English spoken.
OPEN: 01/04–30/09. SIZE: 4 ha, 150 pitches
(134 with elec, 30 statics), 24 hot showers,
22 WCs, 1 CWP. ↻ &

∼ ⚓ 🛉 **R** ⊡ | | ⊗

Shop at 0.4 km. Restaurant at 0.5 km. Nursery.
PRICES: (1996) Caravan with family 92.80,
Tent with two adults 46.40. CC: none.
*Masevaux is on the D466 and the campsite is
signposted.*

MASSIAC Cantal 5A

Camping Municipal de l'Allagnon
av de Courcelles, 15500 Massiac.
Tel 04 71 23 03 93. English spoken.
OPEN: 01/05–30/09. SIZE: 2.5 ha, 90 pitches (all
with elec), 10 hot showers, 6 WCs, 1 CWP. ⚓ ♿

Shop at 0.5 km. Restaurant at 0.1 km.
PRICES: (1996) Caravan with family 56.00,
Tent with two adults 34.00. CC: none.
Massiac is on the A75.

LES MATHES Charente-Marit 4A

Bonne Anse Plage La Palmyre, 17570 Les Mathes.
Tel 05 46 22 40 90, Fax 05 46 22 42 30.
English spoken.
OPEN: 25/05–08/09. SIZE: 18 ha, 600 pitches
(all with elec), 121 hot showers, 100 WCs,
45 French WCs, 8 CWPs. ⚓ ♿

3 flumes; up to 40% discount 25/5-06/7 & 18/8-
08/9 if reserved in advance.
PRICES: (1996) Caravan with family 214.00, Tent
with two adults 128.00. CC: Euro/Access, Visa.
*D141 south of La Tremblade, towards Phare de la
Coubre.*

Camping Caravaning La Pinède 17570 Les Mathes.
Tel 05 46 22 45 13, Fax 05 46 22 50 21. English spoken.
OPEN: 01/04–30/09. SIZE: 5 ha, 200 pitches (all
with elec), 35 hot showers, 35 WCs, 2 CWPs. ⚓ ♿

Free use of aquatic fun park.
PRICES: (1996) Caravan with family 185.00.
CC: Euro/Access, Visa.
*From Les Mathes north on D141, 2.5 km to
La Fouasse and site.*

La Pinède ★★★★
at Les Mathes
Big on big flumes – big with kids

Camping Caravaning Palmyre Loisirs
La Grande Ligne, 17570 Les Mathes.
Tel 05 46 23 67 66, Fax 05 46 22 48 81.
English spoken.
OPEN: all year. SIZE: 13 ha, 300 pitches (all with
elec, 100 statics), 70 hot showers, 70 WCs. ⚓ ♿

Flume.
PRICES: (1996) Caravan with family 203.00,
Tent with two adults 150.00. CC: none.

*On D141 south of La Tremblade. The campsite is
near the racecourse.*

Camping L'Orée du Bois La Fouasse,
17570 Les Mathes.
Tel 05 46 22 42 43, Fax 05 46 22 54 76.
English spoken.
OPEN: 11/05–15/09. SIZE: 6 ha, 40 pitches (all with
elec). ⚓ ♿

Tennis, flume, entertainment in HS, children's club.
PRICES: (1996) Caravan with family 194.00,
Tent with two adults 150.00. CC: none.
4 km from sea.

Les Charmettes av de la Palmyre, 17570 Les Mathes.
Tel 05 46 22 50 96, Fax 05 46 23 69 70.
English spoken.
OPEN: 22/03–03/10. SIZE: 24 ha, 40 pitches (14 with
elec, 260 statics), 10 hot showers, 8 WCs, 2 CWPs. ⚓ ♿

Tennis, archery, flume; clubs for children and
teenagers.
PRICES: (1996) Caravan with family 195.00,
Tent with two adults 185.00. CC: Visa.
*From La Palmyre follow signs to Les Mathes. Take
first exit at roundabout and campsite is on the
left. Well signposted.*

SEE ADVERTISEMENT

France

MAULEON-LICHARRE Pyr-Atlan 4C

Camping Pont d'Abense
Alos Sibas Abense, 64470 Tardets.
Tel 05 59 28 58 76.
OPEN: 01/05−31/10. SIZE: 1.5 ha, 75 pitches (40 with elec, 5 statics), 6 hot showers, 10 WCs, 1 CWP. ℓ

Shop at 0.5 km. Restaurant at 0.5 km.
PRICES: Caravan with family 105.50,
Tent with two adults 60.00. CC: none.
South of Mauleon-Licharre on the D918.

Camping Uhaitza Le saison
route de Libarrenx, 64130 Mauléon-Licharre.
Tel 05 59 28 18 79, Fax 05 59 28 00 78.
English spoken.
OPEN: 09/04−30/09. SIZE: 1.13 ha, 50 pitches (45 with elec), 5 hot showers, 5 WCs, 2 CWPs. ℓ も

Restaurant at 1 km. Trout fishing, canoes and kayaks.
PRICES: (1996) Caravan with family 109.00,
Tent with two adults 65.50. CC: none.
On the D918. The campsite is well signposted.

MAURS Cantal 5A

Camping Moulin de Chaules
route de Calvinet, 15600 St-Constant.
Tel 04 71 49 11 02, Fax 04 71 49 13 63.
English spoken.
OPEN: 20/04−20/10. SIZE: 3 ha, 56 pitches (40 with elec, 3 statics), 7 hot showers, 8 WCs, 2 CWPs. ℓ

PRICES: (1996) Caravan with family 125.00,
Tent with two adults 79.50. CC: none.
From Maurs, take D663 east to St-Constant then follow D28 east for 2 km.

MAUZE-SUR-LE-MIGNON 4B

Camping Municipal Le Gue de la Rivière,
79210 Mauze-sur-le-Mignon.
Tel 05 49 26 76 28.
OPEN: 01/06−15/09. SIZE: 1.4 ha, 74 pitches (6 statics), 9 hot showers (charge).

Shop at 1 km. Restaurant at 2 km.
PRICES: (1996) Caravan with family 43.30,
Tent with two adults 21.30. CC: none.
North from Mauze-sur-le-Mignon on N11 via D101 towards St-Hilaire-la-Palud. Signposted.

MEGEVE Haute-Savoie 6A

Camp Bornand 74120 Megève.
Tel 04 50 93 00 86, Fax 04 50 93 02 48.
English spoken.

OPEN: 01/06−01/09. SIZE: 1 ha, 50 pitches (all with elec), 9 hot showers, 9 WCs, 1 CWP. も

Shop at 1 km. Restaurant at 0.2 km.
PRICES: (1996) Caravan with family 98.00,
Tent with two adults 55.00. CC: none.
On the N212, on the the northern outskirts of Megève. Signposted.

MELUN Seine/Marne 2D

La Belle Etoile Quai Joffre,
77000 Melun-la-Rochette.
Tel 01 64 39 48 12, Fax 01 64 37 25 55.
English spoken.
OPEN: 01/04−01/11. SIZE: 3.5 ha, 190 pitches (150 with elec), 20 hot showers, 19 WCs, 3 CWPs. ℓ

Shop at 1 km. Restaurant at 0.4 km. Children's playground.
PRICES: Caravan with family 124.50,
Tent with two adults 65.00. CC: none.
Only 1 km from town centre. Follow signs.

MENAT Puy-de-Dôme 5A

Camp Municipal 63390 St-Gervais-d'Auvergne.
Tel 04 73 85 84 74, Fax 04 73 85 85 26.
English spoken.
OPEN: 15/04−30/09. SIZE: 1.5 ha, 130 pitches (all with elec), 15 hot showers, 14 WCs, 5 French WCs, 2 CWPs. ℓ も

Shop at 0.7 km. Restaurant at 0.7 km.
PRICES: (1996) Caravan with family 57.00. CC: none.
South-west of Menat and the N144. Well signposted.

MENDE Lozère 5C

Camping Tivoli av des Gorges du Tarn,
48000 Mende.
Tel 04 66 65 00 38. English spoken.
OPEN: all year. SIZE: 2 ha, 100 pitches (50 with elec, 4 statics), 9 hot showers, 10 WCs, 2 CWPs. ℓ も

Shop at 1 km. Restaurant at 1 km.
PRICES: (1996) Caravan with family 123.00,
Tent with two adults 67.00. CC: none.
Take N88 towards Millau and Rodez. After Citroën garage/supermarket, turn right and follow signs.

MENTON Alpes-Marit 6C

Camping Fleur de Mai
67 route de Gorbio, 06500 Menton.
Tel 04 93 57 22 36. English spoken.
OPEN: 01/04−30/09. SIZE: 1 ha, 10 pitches (all

France

with elec), 10 hot showers, 11 WCs, 2 CWPs. &

Shop at 1.5 km. Restaurant at 1.5 km. Beach, swimming pool, tennis nearby.
PRICES: Caravan with family 173.00, Tent with two adults 100.00. CC: none.
Menton is easily accessed from the N7 and motorway.

MER Loir-et-Cher   2D

Château des Marais 41500 Muides-sur-Loire.
Tel 02 54 87 05 42, Fax 02 54 87 05 43.
English spoken.
OPEN: 15/05–20/09. SIZE: 11 ha, 200 pitches (all with elec), 36 hot showers, 28 WCs, 2 CWPs. ℃ &

PRICES: (1996) Caravan with family 195.00, Tent with two adults 115.00. CC: Euro/Access, Visa.
From Mer, head south over the Loire to Muides. Follow signs to campsite.

MERDRIGNAC Côtes-du-Nord   1D

Le Val de Landrouet 22230 Merdrignac.
Tel 02 96 28 47 98, Fax 02 96 26 55 44.
English spoken.
OPEN: 01/06–15/09. SIZE: 2 ha, 58 pitches (50 with elec), 10 hot showers, 10 WCs. ℃ &

Shop at 0.5 km. Restaurant at 0.5 km. Fishing, tennis, bike hire; swimming pool: 2 km.
PRICES: Caravan with family 89.00,
Tent with two adults 47.00. CC: none.
Signposted from Merdrignac centre, towards Brieuc on D6, then right at the water tower.

MEYRUEIS Lozère   5C

Camping de Capelan 48150 Meyrueis.
Tel 04 66 45 60 50, Fax 04 66 45 60 50.
English spoken.
OPEN: 30/04–20/09. SIZE: 2 ha, 120 pitches (100 with elec, 34 statics), 16 hot showers, 26 WCs, 14 French WCs, 1 CWP. ℃ &

Restaurant at 1 km.
PRICES: (1996) Caravan with family 122.00, Tent with two adults 74.00. CC: Euro/Access, Visa.
On the D996 to Millau, Gorges de la Jonte, on river bank. Well signposted.

Camping Le Terondel 30750 Camprieu.
Tel 04 67 82 61 89. English spoken.
OPEN: 01/06–30/09. SIZE: 2 ha, 80 pitches (60 with elec, 5 statics), 10 hot showers, 8 WCs. ℃ &

Shop at 1 km. Restaurant at 1 km. Mobile homes

available; good outdoor sports facilities nearby.
PRICES: (1996) Caravan with family 108.00, Tent with two adults 55.00. CC: none.
From Meyrueis, south on D986 to Camprieu. Campsite is on the right, 100 m after the Pont du Moulin and well signposted.

Domaine de Pradines 30750 Lanuejols.
Tel 04 67 82 73 85. English spoken.
OPEN: 01/03–15/10. SIZE: 30 ha, 40 pitches (all with elec), 10 hot showers, 10 WCs. &

Tennis, horse-riding. Discount for long stays.
PRICES: (1996) Caravan with family 155.00, Tent with two adults 70.00. CC: Euro/Access, Visa.
On the D28, 15 km south-west of Meyrueis. Site is well signposted.

Domaine de Pradines
near Meyrueis
Far from the maddening crowds

France

Le Champ d'Ayres
route de la Brêze, 48150 Meyrueis.
Tel 04 66 45 60 51, Fax 04 66 45 60 51.
English spoken.
OPEN: 01/04–20/09. SIZE: 1.5 ha, 85 pitches (60 with elec), 10 hot showers, 8 WCs, 1 CWP. ℃ &

Shop at 0.3 km. Restaurant at 0.4 km. Children's plyground.
PRICES: (1996) Caravan with family 116.00, Tent with two adults 72.00. CC: none.
The campsite is 300 m from station going towards Château-d'Ayres.

Le Pré de Charlet route de Florac, 48150 Meyrueis.
Tel 04 66 45 63 65. English spoken.
OPEN: 01/05–01/10. SIZE: 2 ha, 40 pitches (all with elec), 8 hot showers, 12 WCs. ℃ &

Restaurant at 1 km. River safe for children; fishing.
PRICES: Caravan with family 100.00, Tent with two adults 58.00. CC: none.
In Meyrueis on D986.

MILLAU Aveyron   5C

Camp Municipal Millau-Plage 12100 Millau.
Tel 05 65 60 10 97. English spoken.
OPEN: 01/04–30/09. SIZE: 5 ha, 250 pitches (all with elec), 36 hot showers, 34 WCs, 4 CWPs. ℃ &

Shop at 2 km.

PRICES: (1996) Caravan with family 132.00, Tent with two adults 76.00. CC: Visa. *Follow camp signs from Millau.*

Camping Peyrelade 12640 Rivière-sur-Tarn. Tel 05 65 62 62 54, Fax 05 65 61 33 59. English spoken.
OPEN: 01/06 – 15/09. SIZE: 4 ha, 190 pitches (165 with elec, 13 statics), 30 hot showers, 25 WCs, 2 CWPs. ᴸ ᶜ

| ~ | ⚓ | 🏕 | R | 🚽 | 🛒 | | ✕ | ⚲ | Ⓗ | | |

Stunning scenery; canoeing, riding, mountain-biking, organised hikes/climbing.
PRICES: (1996) Caravan with family 166.00, Tent with two adults 105.00. CC: none. *From Millau take the route des Gorges-du-Tarn via Aguessac. Campsite is well signposted.*

Camping Peyrelade
near Millau
In the Gorges du Tarn . . . nature in its pure state

Castel Val de Cantobre 12230 Nant. Tel 05 65 62 25 48, Fax 05 65 62 10 36. English spoken.
OPEN: 15/05 – 15/09. SIZE: 6.5 ha, 200 pitches (all with elec, 20 statics), 42 hot showers, 30 WCs, 2 CWPs. ᴸ ᶜ

| ~ | ⚓ | 🏕 | R | 🚽 | 🛒 | 🛍 | ✕ | ⚲ | Ⓗ | | |

PRICES: (1996) Caravan with family 200.00, Tent with two adults 140.00. CC: Euro/Access, Visa. *On D991, 27 km east of Millau.*

International Camping des Gorges du Tarn Mostuejouls, 12720 Peyreleau. Tel 05 65 62 62 94. English spoken.
OPEN: 01/05 – 15/09. SIZE: 2 ha, 110 pitches (all with elec), 15 hot showers, 12 WCs, 1 CWP. ᶜ

| ~ | ⚓ | 🚶 | R | 🚽 | 🛒 | 🛍 | | Ⓗ | | | |

PRICES: (1996) Caravan with family 119.00, Tent with two adults 70.00. CC: Visa.

MILLY-LA-FORET Essonne   2D

La Musardière route des Grandes Vallées 27, 91490 Milly-la-Forêt. Tel 01 64 98 91 91, Fax 01 64 98 91 91. English spoken.
OPEN: 15/02 – 15/12. SIZE: 12 ha, 200 pitches (all with elec, 160 statics), 20 hot showers, 20 WCs, 33 French WCs, 4 CWPs. ᴸ ᶜ

| | | 🏕 | R | | | | | | | | |

Shop at 4 km. Restaurant at 2 km.
PRICES: (1996) Caravan with family 140.00,

Tent with two adults 76.00. CC: none. *From A6 take exit for Milly-la-Forêt, D837. Follow signs to campsite.*

MIMIZAN Landes   4C

Camping de la Route des Lacs route des Lacs, 40200 Aureilhan. Tel 05 58 09 01 42. English spoken.
OPEN: 01/04 – 31/10. SIZE: 4 ha, 100 pitches (85 with elec), 14 hot showers, 16 WCs. ᴸ

| | | 🚶 | R | 🚽 | 🛒 | 🛍 | | | Ⓗ | | |

Restaurant at 0.5 km. Quiet site 1.5 km from a lake.
PRICES: (1996) Caravan with family 83.00, Tent with two adults 48.00. CC: none. *From Mimizan take D626 towards Bordeaux. After 2 km pass through village of Aureilhan. Turn left before cycling path. Campsite 100 m on left. Signposted.*

Camping Le Talucat 40200 St-Paul-en-Born. Tel 05 58 07 44 16. English spoken.
OPEN: 15/04 – 30/09. SIZE: 3.3 ha, 150 pitches (65 with elec, 17 statics), 12 hot showers, 14 WCs, 2 CWPs. ᴸ ᶜ

| ~ | ⚓ | 🚶 | R | 🚽 | | 🛍 | | | Ⓗ | | |

Shop at 0.8 km. Restaurant at 0.8 km. Mini-golf, volley ball, entertainment, evening dances.
PRICES: (1996) Caravan with family 118.00, Tent with two adults 68.00. CC: none. *N10/E5 to Labouheyre then D626 towards Mimizan. St-Paul-en-Born is east of Mimizan.*

Camping Les Bruyères chemin Laffont, Ste-Eulalie-en-Born, 40200 Mimizan. Tel 05 58 09 73 36, Fax 05 58 09 75 58. English spoken.
OPEN: 15/04 – 30/09. SIZE: 3 ha, 135 pitches (all with elec, 10 statics), 10 hot showers, 10 WCs, 17 French WCs, 3 CWPs. ᴸ ᶜ

| | | 🏕 | R | 🚽 | 🛒 | 🛍 | ✕ | ⚲ | Ⓗ | | |

Sea 12 km, lake and river nearby. Superior pitches also available.
PRICES: Caravan with family 130.30, Tent with two adults 97.20. CC: Amex, Euro/Access, Visa. *North of Mimizan via D87/D652. Site is well signposted.*

Camping Les Bruyères
near Mimizan
Peace and quiet . . . a game of tennis . . . a splash in the pool . . .

Camping Municipal Le Lac 40200 Aureilhan. Tel 05 58 09 10 88, Fax 05 58 09 38 23. English spoken.

OPEN: 25/05–22/09. SIZE: 8 ha, 440 pitches (400 with elec), 36 hot showers, 30 WCs, 10 French WCs, 1 CWP. ☎ &

Restaurant at 1 km.
PRICES: (1996) Caravan with family 80.00, Tent with two adults 42.00. CC: Euro/Access, Visa.
From Mimizan take D626 to Aureilhan. Turn left at signs for camping and the lake.

Parcmontana-Eurolac promenade de l'Etang, 40200 Aureilhan.
Tel 05 58 09 02 87, Fax 05 58 09 41 89.
English spoken.
OPEN: 01/05–30/09. SIZE: 13 ha, 275 pitches, 52 hot showers, 54 WCs, 8 CWPs. ☎ &

Tennis, volley ball; chalets for hire.
PRICES: (1996) Caravan with family 180.00, Tent with two adults 110.00. CC: Euro/Access, Visa.
D626 east from Mimizan to Lake Aureilhan.

Le Tatiou route de Lespecier, 40170 Bias.
Tel 05 58 09 04 76, Fax 05 58 82 44 36.
English spoken.
OPEN: 28/03–30/10. SIZE: 10 ha, 505 pitches (300 with elec), 34 hot showers, 47 WCs, 1 CWP. ☎ &

Mini-golf, tennis, entertainment.
PRICES: (1996) Caravan with family 113.00, Tent with two adults 63.00. CC: Amex, Euro/Access.
South from Mimizan on D652, turn right in Bias.

MIRAMONT-DE-GUYENNE Lot/Gar 4D

Lac du Saut du Loup 47800 Miramont-de-Guyenne.
Tel 05 53 93 22 35, Fax 05 53 93 55 33.
English spoken.
OPEN: 15/03–15/11. SIZE: 5 ha, 150 pitches (all with elec), 20 hot showers, 44 WCs, 3 CWPs. ☎ &

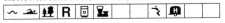

Shop at 2 km.
PRICES: (1996) Caravan with family 142.00, Tent with two adults 75.00. CC: none.
Off D1 and well signposted. (No motor caravans.)

MIRANDOL-BOURGNOUNAC Tarn 5C

Les Clots 81190 Mirandol-Bourgnounac.
Tel 05 63 76 92 78, Fax 05 63 76 92 78.
English spoken.
OPEN: 07/04–01/10. SIZE: 3 ha, 44 pitches (39 with elec), 8 hot showers, 11 WCs, 1 CWP. ☎

Restaurant at 5 km.
PRICES: (1996) Caravan with family 127.00, Tent with two adults 90.00. CC: none.
18 km north of Carmaux on the D905. Campsite is 5 km north of Mirandol-Bourgnounac.

MOELAN-SUR-MER Finistère 1C

Camping de l'Ile Percée Plage de Trenez, 29116 Moëlan-sur-Mer.
Tel 02 98 71 16 25. English spoken.
OPEN: 01/05–15/10. SIZE: 0.85 ha, 65 pitches (all with elec, 2 statics), 8 hot showers, 6 WCs, 1 CWP. ☎

Shop at 4 km. Restaurant at 4 km. Table tennis, volley ball, boules, children's playground.
PRICES: (1996) Caravan with family 100.00, Tent with two adults 66.00. CC: none.
Campsite is near the beach.

Camping de la Grande Lande Kergroës, 29350 Moëlan-sur-Mer.
Tel 02 98 71 00 39. English spoken.
OPEN: 01/04–30/09. SIZE: 3 ha, 100 pitches (92 with elec, 20 statics), 11 hot showers, 5 WCs, 8 French WCs, 1 CWP. &

Shop at 0.5 km. Restaurant at 0.5 km.
PRICES: (1996) Caravan with family 127.00, Tent with two adults 74.00.
CC: none.
From Quimperlé centre follow signs to Moëlan-sur-Mer; the campsite in Kergroës is 5 km after Moëlan-sur-Mer on the road to Kerfany.

MOISSAC Tarn/Garonne 4D

Camping Municipal Ile de Bidounet 82200 Moissac.
Tel 05 63 32 52 52. English spoken.
OPEN: 01/04–30/09. SIZE: 6 ha, 140 pitches (all with elec), 16 hot showers, 14 WCs, 2 CWPs. ☎ &

Shop at 1 km. Restaurant at 0.8 km. Updated in 1994 and new swimming pool in 1995.
PRICES: (1996) Caravan with family 103.00, Tent with two adults 49.00. CC: none.
Leave A62 at Castelsarasin and take N113 to Moissac. Campsite is near the River Tarn and well signposted.

MONDOUBLEAU Loir-et-Cher 2C

Camping Municipal
rue des Loisirs, 41170 Souday.
Tel 02 54 80 74 81, Fax 02 54 80 78 50.
OPEN: 01/04–31/10. SIZE: 1 ha, 15 pitches (10 with elec), 4 hot showers, 4 WCs.

Shop at 0.2 km. Fishing.
PRICES: (1996) Caravan with family 42.00, Tent with two adults 22.00. CC: none.
D117 north of Mondoubleau.

France

MONESTIER-DE-CLERMONT Isère 6A

Camping Les 4 Saisons
38650 Gresse-en-Vercors.
Tel 04 76 34 30 27, Fax 04 76 34 30 27.
English spoken.
OPEN: 15/02–16/03 & 01/06–08/09. SIZE: 1.4 ha,
100 pitches (all with elec), 10 hot showers,
13 WCs, 2 CWPs. ⛧ ⅙

Shop at 1 km. Restaurant at 1 km.
PRICES: (1996) Caravan with family 120.00,
Tent with two adults 65.00. CC: Euro/Access, Visa.
South-west of Monestier-de-Clermont, to the west of N75 and well signposted.

MONPAZIER Dordogne 4B

Le Moulin de David Gaugeac,
24540 Monpazier.
Tel 05 53 22 65 25, Fax 05 53 23 99 76.
English spoken.
OPEN: 01/06–15/09. SIZE: 14 ha, 100 pitches
(all with elec, 20 statics), 20 hot showers, 16 WCs,
2 CWPs. ⛧ ⅙

Tennis, entertainment, archery, trampoline.
PRICES: (1996) Caravan with family 174.00,
Tent with two adults 109.00. CC: none.
From Monpazier, take the D2 to Villeréal. Site is 3 km on the left.

Le Moulinal 24540 Biron.
Tel 05 53 40 84 60, Fax 05 53 40 81 49.
English spoken.
OPEN: 30/04–13/09. SIZE: 11 ha, 250 pitches
(all with elec, 41 statics), 1 CWP. ⛧ ⅙

Tennis.
PRICES: Caravan with family 231.00, Tent with two
adults 135.00. CC: Euro/Access, Visa.
From Monpazier follow signs towards Lacapelle-Biron and campsite is signposted.

LE MONT-DORE Puy-de-Dôme 5A

Camping Municipal L'Esquiladou
route des Cascades, 63240 Le Mont-Dore.
Tel 04 73 65 23 74, Fax 04 73 65 25 66.
English spoken.
OPEN: 15/05–15/10. SIZE: 2 ha, 100 pitches
(all with elec, 6 statics), 20 hot showers, 16 WCs,
3 CWPs. ⛧ ⅙

Shop at 0.2 km. Restaurant at 0.2 km.
PRICES: Caravan with family 75.00, Tent with two
adults 45.00. CC: Euro/Access, Visa.
From Mont-Dore, take D996 for La Bourboule. Follow signs from Le Queureuilh.

MONT-LOUIS Pyrénées Orient 5C

Camping Le Cerdan 66800 Saillagouse.
Tel 04 68 04 70 46, Fax 04 68 04 05 26.
OPEN: 01/11–30/09. SIZE: 0.8 ha, 50 pitches
(all with elec), 6 hot showers, 7 WCs,
1 CWP. ⛧ ⅙

Shop at 0.3 km. Restaurant at 0.3 km. Mobile
homes for hire.
PRICES: (1996) Caravan with family 113.00,
Tent with two adults 62.00. CC: none.
Take N116 south-west from Mont-Louis towards the Spanish border. Saillagouse is approx 10 km and campsite is signposted.

LE MONT-ST-MICHEL Manche 1D

Camping Caravaning du Mont-St-Michel
rte du Mont-St-Michel, BP 8,
50116 Mont-St-Michel.
Tel 02 33 60 09 33, Fax 02 33 68 22 09.
English spoken.
OPEN: 08/02–01/11. SIZE: 300 pitches (150 with
elec), 50 hot showers, 50 WCs. ⅙

PRICES: (1996) Caravan with family 89.00, Tent
with two adults 54.00. CC: Euro/Access, Visa.
On D976. Signposted.

Camping Le Gué de Beauvoir
Château de Beauvoir, 50170 Pontorson.
Tel 02 33 60 09 23. English spoken.
OPEN: 01/04–30/09. SIZE: 0.8 ha, 3 hot showers,
5 WCs. ⛧

Shop at 0.01 km. Restaurant at 0.01 km.
PRICES: (1996) Caravan with family 91.00, Tent
with two adults 46.00. CC: Euro/Access, Visa.
On the D976 towards Pontorson. Turn left in Beauvoir.

Camping Sous Les Pommiers
28 route du Mont-St-Michel, 50170 Beauvoir.
Tel 02 33 60 11 36, Fax 02 33 60 11 36.
English spoken.
OPEN: 01/04–20/10. SIZE: 2 ha, 70 pitches (all with
elec, 20 statics), 10 hot showers, 14 WCs, 1 CWP. ⛧

Fishing; tennis 0.9 km; horse-riding 2 km; mobile
home hire.
PRICES: (1996) Caravan with family 100.50, Tent
with two adults 53.00. CC: Euro/Access, Visa.
4 km south of Mont-St-Michel on D976.

MONTBAZON Indre/Loire 2C

Camping de la Grange Rouge
37250 Montbazon.
Tel 02 47 26 06 43. English spoken.

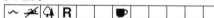

OPEN: 01/05–15/09. SIZE: 2 ha, 108 pitches (84 with elec), 14 hot showers, 13 WCs, 2 CWPs. &

Fishing.
PRICES: (1996) Caravan with family 96.00, Tent with two adults 48.00. CC: Visa.
10 km to the south of Tours. Coming from Tours, arriving at Montbazon, the campsite is on the right at the first traffic lights.

MONTBRON   Charente   4B

Camping Gorges du Chambon
Le Chambon, 16220 Montbron.
Tel 05 45 70 71 70, Fax 05 45 70 80 02.
English spoken.
OPEN: 15/05–10/09. SIZE: 7 ha, 100 pitches (all with elec), 16 hot showers, 14 WCs. &

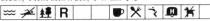

PRICES: (1996) Caravan with family 178.00, Tent with two adults 104.00. CC: Euro/Access, Visa.
From Montbron take D6, signposted Piegut Pluviers. After 5 km turn left at La Tricherie and follow signs to the campsite, approx 2.5 km.

MONTCABRIER   Lot   4D

Camping Le Carbet Le Lac, 46700 Cassagnes.
Tel 05 65 36 61 79. English spoken.
OPEN: 01/04–30/09. SIZE: 2 ha, 25 pitches (all with elec), 4 hot showers, 4 WCs. &

Table tennis, fishing.
PRICES: (1996) Caravan with family 118.00, Tent with two adults 68.00. CC: none.
From Montcabrier, take the D673 towards Frayssinet-le-Gélat.

Camping Moulin de Laborde 46700 Montcabrier.
Tel 05 65 24 62 06, Fax 05 65 36 51 33.
English spoken.
OPEN: 01/05–15/09. SIZE: 10 ha, 90 pitches (86 with elec), 12 hot showers, 8 WCs, 1 CWP. &

Paddling pool, bike hire, climbing; organized activities Jul/Aug; discounts LS.
PRICES: (1996) Caravan with family 169.00, Tent with two adults 95.00. CC: none.
Heading towards Gourdon, Montcabrier is on D673, 12 km from Fumel in the Thèze valley.

Camping Moulin de Laborde
at Montcabrier
A friendly site in the beautiful LOT region

MONTDIDIER   Somme   2B

Camp Le Pré Fleuri 46 rue d'Ailly-sur-Noye, 80500 Montdidier.
Tel 03 22 78 93 22.
OPEN: 01/04–30/10. SIZE: 1 ha, 40 pitches (all with elec, 6 statics), 6 hot showers, 5 WCs, 2 CWPs. & &

Shop at 1 km. Restaurant at 1 km. Tennis, boules; riding and fishing nearby; mobile homes available.
PRICES: (1996) Caravan with family 90.00, Tent with two adults 45.00. CC: none.
From Montdidier on D930 take D26 and follow signs to Ailly-sur-Noye.

MONTELIMAR   Drôme   5D

Floral Camping La Coucorde Derbières, 26740 Montélimar.
Tel 04 75 90 06 69. English spoken.
OPEN: all year. SIZE: 1 ha, 30 pitches (20 with elec, 4 statics), 2 hot showers, 6 WCs, 1 CWP. &

Rooms available for rent.
PRICES: (1996) Caravan with family 95.00, Tent with two adults 50.00. CC: none.
Exit autoroute A7 Montélimar-Nord, access N7 towards Montélimar (3 km). At the end of La Coucourde, turn left.

International Deux Saisons chemin des Aléxis, 26200 Montélimar.
Tel 04 75 01 88 99. English spoken.
OPEN: 01/03–30/11. SIZE: 2 ha, 90 pitches (40 with elec), 9 hot showers, 15 WCs, 5 French WCs. &

Shop at 0.3 km.
PRICES: (1996) Caravan with family 125.00, Tent with two adults 68.00. CC: none.
From Montélimar town centre, travel towards Dieulefit. Site is second on right after crossing the bridge and well signposted.

MONTFLANQUIN   Lot/Garonne   4D

Camp Naturiste Laborde 47150 Monflanquin.
Tel 05 53 63 14 88, Fax 05 53 61 60 23.
English spoken.
OPEN: 01/05–01/10. SIZE: 20 ha, 120 pitches (all with elec), 18 hot showers, 14 WCs, 3 CWPs. & &

Naturist site; subtropical indoor pool.
PRICES: (1996) Caravan with family 150.00, Tent with two adults 90.00. CC: none.
From Montflanquin take D272 towards Monpazier and follow signs marked 'Laborde' FFN to campsite.

France

MONTIGNAC Dordogne   4B

Camp La Fage La Chapelle-Aubareil,
24290 Montignac.
Tel 05 53 50 76 50, Fax 05 53 50 79 19.
English spoken.
OPEN: 15/05–25/09. SIZE: 5 ha, 60 pitches (70 with
elec, 20 statics), 15 hot showers, 15 WCs. & &

Entertainment.
PRICES: (1996) Caravan with family 176.00, Tent
with two adults 101.00. CC: Euro/Access, Visa.
*La Chapelle-Aubareil is 7 km from Montignac, off
the D704.*

Camping Cantegrel Domaine Touvent,
24580 Rouffignac.
Tel 05 53 05 48 30, Fax 05 53 05 40 67. English spoken.
OPEN: 01/04–31/10. SIZE: 50 ha, 130 pitches (all
with elec), 16 hot showers, 16 WCs, 3 CWPs. & &

Tennis, horse-riding, mountain biking,
entertainment.
PRICES: Caravan with family 117.00, Tent with two
adults 105.00. CC: Euro/Access, Visa.
*From Montignac go south on D706 to Moustier,
then turn right on to D6 to Rouffignac. Turn right
in the village and the campsite is approx 200 m
on the right.*

Camping La Castillanderie Thonac,
24290 Montignac.
Tel 05 53 50 76 79, Fax 05 53 51 59 13.
English spoken.
OPEN: 01/04–31/10. SIZE: 15 ha, 65 pitches
(36 with elec), 8 hot showers, 10 WCs, 2 CWPs. &

Shop at 2 km.
PRICES: Caravan with family 155.00,
Tent with two adults 84.00. CC: none.
*From Montignac, take the road to Les Eyzies.
Follow the road to Thonac, then turn right at
crossroads and follow signs.*

MONTMEDY Meuse   3A

Camp Municipal La Citadelle Tivoli,
55600 Montmédy.
Tel 03 29 80 10 40, Fax 03 29 80 12 98.
OPEN: 01/05–30/09. SIZE: 1 ha, 30 pitches (18 with
elec), 2 hot showers, 4 WCs.

Shop at 1 km. Restaurant at 1 km.
PRICES: (1996) Caravan with family 57.50,
Tent with two adults 27.50. CC: none.
Signposted from the centre of Montmédy.

Camping Loisirs de l'Othai 55600 Marville.
Tel 03 29 88 15 15, Fax 03 29 88 14 60.
English spoken.

OPEN: 01/04–31/10. SIZE: 1 ha, 92 pitches (70 with
elec, 20 statics), 0 hot showers, 8 WCs, 2 French
WCs, 1 CWP. & &

Shop at 1 km. Restaurant at 1 km.
PRICES: (1996) Caravan with family 58.00,
Tent with two adults 36.00. CC: Amex, Visa.
12 km south-east of Montmédy on N43.

MONTMIRAIL Marne   2B

Camping Municipal Les Chataigniers
rue du Petit St-Lazare, 51210 Montmirail.
Tel 03 26 81 11 46, Fax 03 26 81 14 27.
OPEN: 01/04–31/10. SIZE: 2 ha, 50 pitches, 4 hot
showers, 6 WCs. &

Shop at 0.5 km. Restaurant at 0.5 km.
PRICES: (1996) Caravan with family 40.00,
Tent with two adults 14.60. CC: none.
*Near the police station and stadium, on entering
Montmirail.*

MONTMORILLON Vienne   4B

Camping Municipal de l'Allochon
31 av F Tribot, 86500 Montmorillon.
Tel 05 49 91 02 33, Fax 05 49 91 58 26.
OPEN: all year. SIZE: 1 ha, 80 pitches (all with elec).

Shop at 0.5 km. Restaurant at 0.3 km. Swimming
pool nearby.
PRICES: (1996) Caravan with family 27.80,
Tent with two adults 18.40. CC: none.
*Follow signs for town centre and Lathus. Campsite
is 300 m from town centre. (No motor caravans.)*

MONTPELLIER Hérault   5D

Camping Domaine de Cantagrils
Viols-le-Fort, 34380 Cantagrils.
Tel 04 67 55 01 88, Fax 04 67 55 70 77.
English spoken.
OPEN: 09/04–15/10. SIZE: 4 ha, 100 pitches (all with
elec, 2 statics), 8 hot showers, 14 WCs, 1 CWP.

PRICES: (1996) Caravan with family 117.00,
Tent with two adults 68.00. CC: none.
*From Montpellier on D986 towards Ganges, left
on to D32 to Viols-le-Fort, then D127 to
Cantagrils.*

Camping Le Fou du Roi 34130 Lansargues.
Tel 04 67 86 78 08. English spoken.
OPEN: 01/04–20/09. SIZE: 3 ha, 82 pitches (all with
elec), 10 hot showers, 10 WCs. &

Canoeing, horse-riding, mountain bikes, tennis.

PRICES: (1996) Caravan with family 122.80, Tent with two adults 64.20. CC: Euro/Access, Visa. *Lansargues is just off N113, 8 km from Montpellier towards Lunel.*

Le Lac des Rêves rte de Pérole, 34970 Lattes. Tel 04 67 50 26 00, Fax 04 67 50 33 26. English spoken.
OPEN: 22/03–26/09. SIZE: 33 ha, 20 pitches (all with elec, 300 statics), 10 hot showers, 10 WCs. ✆ �

Tennis, archery, flume; clubs for children.
PRICES: (1996) Caravan with family 185.00, Tent with two adults 185.00. CC: Euro/Access, Visa.
From A9 take Montpellier-Sud exit. Follow signs for Palavas then Lattes. After the bridge, continue straight on until roundabout then head towards Pérole on D132. Campsite is about 2 km and well signposted.

SEE ADVERTISEMENT

Le Parc 34970 Lattes.
Tel 04 67 65 85 67, Fax 04 67 20 20 58. English spoken.
OPEN: 01/06–25/09. SIZE: 1.6 ha, 50 pitches (all with elec, 10 statics), 12 hot showers, 15 WCs, 1 CWP. ✆

Restaurant at 0.8 km. Lots of flowers; barbecue.

LE LAC DES REVES
★★★★
MontpelliER

PRICES: (1996) Caravan with family 150.00, Tent with two adults 95.00. CC: none.
From Montpellier, motorway A9, exit Montpellier-Est. From the D21 turn right on to the D172 to Lattes. Campsite is signposted.

Le Plein Air des Chênes Clapiers, 34170 Castellnau-le-Lez.
Tel 04 67 02 02 53, Fax 04 67 59 42 19. English spoken.
OPEN: all year. SIZE: 8 ha, 280 pitches (all with elec, 30 statics), 64 hot showers, 74 WCs, 5 CWPs. ✆ �

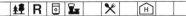

Shop at 0.3 km. Tennis, ball games.
PRICES: Caravan with family 190.00, Tent with two adults 190.00. CC: none.
N113 from Nîmes, through Castellnau, then D65 to Clapiers. Just north of Montpellier.

MONTPON-MENESTEROL Dordogne 4B

Caravaning La Tuilière
24700 St-Rémy-sur-Lidoire.
Tel 05 53 82 47 29. English spoken.
OPEN: 15/04–15/09. SIZE: 8 ha, 66 pitches (48 with elec, 16 statics), 10 hot showers, 6 WCs, 1 CWP. �

Fishing, mini-golf.
PRICES: Caravan with family 106.00, Tent with two adults 60.00. CC: Euro/Access, Visa.
From Montpon take the D708 towards Ste-Foy-la-Grande. The site is 3 km ahead on the right.

MONTREDON-LABESSONNIE Tarn 5C

Camping La Forêt 81330 St-Pierre-de-Trivisy.
Tel 05 63 50 48 69, Fax 05 63 74 58 85.
OPEN: 15/06–15/09. SIZE: 2 ha, 48 pitches (all with elec, 10 statics), 5 hot showers, 7 WCs, 2 French WCs, 1 CWP. ✆ �

Shop at 0.2 km. Restaurant at 0.3 km.
PRICES: (1996) Caravan with family 60.00, Tent with two adults 36.00. CC: none.
From Montredon, drive 11 km east on the D89. After La Glevade, turn left on the D53 to St-Pierre-de-Trivisy.

MONTREJEAU Haute-Garonne 4D

Camping Es Pibous
31510 St-Bertrand-de-Comminges.
Tel 05 61 88 31 42, Fax 05 61 88 31 42. English spoken.
OPEN: 01/03–01/10. SIZE: 2 ha, 80 pitches (all with elec), 8 hot showers, 10 WCs. �

PRICES: (1996) Caravan with family 80.00, Tent with two adults 41.00. CC: none.
From Montrejeau take the D125 towards

Bagnères-de-Luchon. At Labroquère turn right to St-Bertrand-de-Comminges.

MONTREVEL-EN-BRESSE Ain   5B

Camp Municipal La Plaine Tonique
Base de Plein Air, 01340 Montrevel-en-Bresse.
Tel 04 74 30 80 52, Fax 04 74 30 80 77.
English spoken.
OPEN: 01/05–30/09. SIZE: 15 ha, 600 pitches
(all with elec, 100 statics), 87 hot showers,
12 WCs, 2 CWPs. ℂ ♿

| ≋ | ⚓ | 🏕 | R | 🔲 | 🅿 | 🛒 | ✗ | | | 🅗 | | |

Water sports, mountain biking, tennis, mini-golf.
PRICES: Caravan with family 143.00, Tent with two
adults 99.00. CC: Euro/Access, Visa.
9 km north of Bourg-en-Bresse on the D975.
SEE ADVERTISEMENT

Camping à la Ferme Malafretz,
01340 Montrevel-en-Bresse.
Tel 04 74 30 81 19.
OPEN: all year. SIZE: 6 pitches, 1 hot shower,
1 WC, 1 CWP.

| ∼ | 🏊 | 🏕 | R | | | ✗ | | |

Shop at 2 km. Horse-riding; fishing nearby.
PRICES: (1996) Caravan with family 77.00,
Tent with two adults 44.00. CC: none.
North of Bourg-en-Bresse on the D975.

MONTRICHARD Loir-et-Cher   2D

Camping Touraine Vacances
Faverolles-sur-Cher, 41400 Montrichard.
Tel 02 54 32 06 08, Fax 02 54 32 06 08.
English spoken.
OPEN: 16/03–31/10. SIZE: 3.5 ha, 100 pitches
(70 with elec, 2 statics), 10 hot showers, 21 WCs,
2 CWPs. ♿

| 🏕 | R | 🔲 | | 🛒 | ✗ | ⟡ | 🅗 | | 🚗 |

Shop at 0.2 km. Good shopping and leisure facilities;
mobile homes available, 20% discount in LS.
PRICES: (1996) Caravan with family 134.00, Tent
with two adults 80.00. CC: Euro/Access, Visa.
*Faverolles-sur-Cher is on D764, just south of
Montrichard.*

MONTSAUCHE-LES-SETTONS   3C

Camping Les Mésanges
58230 Montsauche-les-Settons.
Tel 03 86 84 55 77. English spoken.
OPEN: 01/05–15/09. SIZE: 5 ha, 100 pitches
(all with elec), 9 hot showers, 9 WCs, 1 CWP. ℂ ♿

| ≋ | ⚓ | 🅖 | R | 🔲 | 🅿 | 🛒 | | | | |

Shop at 1 km. Restaurant at 1 km. Water-skiing,
fishing.
PRICES: (1996) Caravan with family 131.00,
Tent with two adults 71.00. CC: none.

*On the left bank of the lake at Les Settons, just
south of Montsauche-les-Settons.*

Camping Les Settons Plage du Midi
rive droite du Lac, 58230 Montsauche-les-Settons.
Tel 03 86 84 51 97, Fax 03 86 84 57 31.
English spoken.
OPEN: 05/04–30/09. SIZE: 4 ha, 160 pitches (all with
elec), 18 hot showers, 14 WCs, 14 French WCs. ✆ &

Restaurant at 0.2 km. Water-skiing, fishing.
PRICES: Caravan with family 140.00, Tent with two
adults 74.00. CC: Amex, Euro/Access, Visa.
*On the banks of the lake, 200 m from the D193 at
Les Settons, just south of Montsauche-les-Settons.*

L'Hermitage de Chevigny
58230 Montsauche-les-Settons.
Tel 03 86 84 50 97. English spoken.
OPEN: 01/04–30/09. SIZE: 2.2 ha, 120 pitches
(90 with elec), 12 hot showers, 12 WCs, 6 French
WCs, 1 CWP. ✆ &

Restaurant at 3 km. Lakeside beach 0.1 km, table
tennis; B&B available.
PRICES: Caravan with family 132.00,
Tent with two adults 71.00. CC: none.
*From Montsauche-les-Settons take road on left bank
of Lac des Settons and follow signs to campsite.*

MORET-SUR-LOING Seine/Marne   2D

**Camping-Caravanning Int Les Courtilles de
Lido** 77250 Veneux-les-Sablons.
Tel 01 60 70 46 05, Fax 01 64 70 62 65.
OPEN: 15/04–30/09. SIZE: 2.5 ha, 60 pitches (all with
elec), 7 hot showers (charge), 8 WCs, 1 CWP. ✆

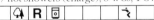

Shop at 1 km. Restaurant at 1 km. Mini-golf,
boules, table tennis, children's playground, tennis.
PRICES: (1996) Caravan with family 124.50,
Tent with two adults 66.00. CC: none.
*From Fontainebleau take N6 towards Sens, exit
Veneux-les-Sablons then follow signs to Moret-sur-
Loing.*

Camping Les Courtilles du Lido
near Moret-sur-Loing
5 mins from Fontainebleau on N6

MOREZ Jura   5B

Camp Municipal La Bugle Morbier, 39400 Morez.
Tel 03 84 33 37 17. English spoken.
OPEN: 05/06–20/09. SIZE: 1.5 ha, 16 pitches

(all with elec), 6 hot showers, 6 WCs, 7 French
WCs, 4 CWPs.

Shop at 0.3 km.
PRICES: Caravan with family 86.00,
Tent with two adults 52.00. CC: none.
*From Morez, north on N5 to Morbier. Continue on
this road and turn right after small bridge.*

Camping Caravaning de Baptaillard
Longchaumois, 39400 Morez.
Tel 03 84 60 62 34. English spoken.
OPEN: all year. SIZE: 4 ha, 130 pitches (100 with
elec), 13 hot showers, 14 WCs, 2 CWPs.

Shop at 3 km. Restaurant at 3 km. Mini-golf, volley
ball; cross-country skiing in winter.
PRICES: (1996) Caravan with family 82.00,
Tent with two adults 47.00. CC: none.
*From Morez take the road to Saint Claude on the
D69, through the village of La Mouille on to
Baptaillard, then follow signs to campsite.*

MORLAIX Finistère   1C

Camping du Trégor Kerjean, 29630 Plougasnou.
Tel 02 98 67 37 64.
OPEN: all year. SIZE: 1 ha, 60 pitches (40 with elec),
4 hot showers, 9 WCs. ✆

Shop at 1 km. Restaurant at 1 km.
PRICES: (1996) Caravan with family 67.00,
Tent with two adults 34.00. CC: none.
*From Morlaix take D46 north to Plougasnou and
the campsite is signposted.*

MORTAGNE-SUR-SEVRE Vendée   1D

Camp Municipal Le Poupet
St-Malo-du-Bois, 85590 Les Epesses.
Tel 02 51 92 33 32, Fax 02 51 92 38 65.
English spoken.
OPEN: 01/05–30/09. SIZE: 2 ha, 115 pitches
(94 with elec, 15 statics), 10 hot showers, 10 WCs,
1 CWP. ✆ &

Shop at 3 km.
PRICES: (1996) Caravan with family 75.00,
Tent with two adults 40.00. CC: none.
*N149 from Mortagne-sur-Sèvre towards Poitiers.
At St-Laurent-sur-Sèvre turn south to St-Malo du
Bois and campsite is well signposted.*

MORTEAU Doubs   3D

Camping Le Lava 25650 Gilley.
Tel 03 81 43 30 88. English spoken.
OPEN: all year. SIZE: 1 ha, 40 pitches (all with elec),
2 hot showers, 1 WC, 5 French WCs. &

France (side margin)

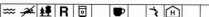

Restaurant at 1 km. Boules, BMX, hiking, children's playground.
PRICES: (1996) Caravan with family 81.00, Tent with two adults 42.00. CC: none.
On the D48 west of Morteau.

LA MOTHE-ACHARD Vendée 1D

Camp du Lac de Jaunay La Servantière, Landevieille, 85220 Coex.
Tel 02 51 22 91 61, Fax 02 51 22 90 41. English spoken.
OPEN: 01/05–30/09. SIZE: 4.7 ha, 128 pitches (all with elec, 13 statics), 16 hot showers, 13 WCs, 1 CWP. (&

Shop at 4 km. Restaurant at 8 km.
PRICES: (1996) Caravan with family 172.00, Tent with two adults 100.00. CC: Euro/Access, Visa.
2 km north-east of La Mothe-Achard on D12. Near Lac du Jaunay.

Camping L'Evasion Landevieille, 85220 Coex.
Tel 02 51 22 90 14. English spoken.
OPEN: 01/06–15/09. SIZE: 2.2 ha, 100 pitches (50 with elec), 6 hot showers, 8 WCs, 10 French WCs. (

Shop at 0.8 km. Restaurant at 0.4 km. Sea, lake and river within 5 km.
PRICES: Caravan with family 104.00, Tent with two adults 65.00. CC: none.
From La Mothe-Achard take the D12 west towards the coast and Landevieille, (13 km).

Camping le Pavillon rue des Sables, 85150 La Mothe-Achard.
Tel 02 51 05 63 46. English spoken.
OPEN: 28/03–30/09. SIZE: 4 ha, 57 pitches (90 with elec, 33 statics), 17 hot showers, 15 WCs, 1 CWP. (&

Shop at 0.8 km. Restaurant at 0.6 km. Fishing in the nearby pond.
PRICES: (1996) Caravan with family 112.00, Tent with two adults 62.00. CC: Amex, Euro/Access, Visa.
Coming from La Roche-sur-Yon, the campsite is 0.5 km after the constabulary, on the left.

La Garangeoire 85150 St-Julien-des-Landes.
Tel 02 51 46 65 39, Fax 02 51 46 60 82. English spoken.
OPEN: 15/05–15/09. SIZE: 15 ha, 300 pitches (280 with elec, 60 statics), 48 hot showers, 40 WCs, 6 CWPs. &

2 heated swimming pools, flume, fishing.
PRICES: (1996) Caravan with family 186.00, Tent

with two adults 135.00. CC: Euro/Access, Visa.
From La Mothe-Achard go north-west on D12 to St-Julien. Turn right on D21, site 2 km.

MOUSTIERS-STE-MARIE 6C

Camping St-Jean 04360 Moustiers-Ste-Marie.
Tel 04 92 74 66 85. English spoken.
OPEN: 12/04–22/09. SIZE: 2 ha, 100 pitches (all with elec), 14 hot showers, 11 WCs, 4 French WCs, 3 CWPs. (&

Restaurant at 1 km. Mini-golf, volley ball, playground, table tennis.
PRICES: Caravan with family 110.00, Tent with two adults 59.00. CC: none.
Campsite is to the west of the town, on the D952 towards Riez.

MULHOUSE Haut-Rhin 3D

Camp Municipal des Lupins
rue de l'Ancienne Gare, 68580 Seppois-le-Bas.
Tel 03 89 25 65 37, Fax 03 89 07 63 34. English spoken.
OPEN: 01/04–31/10. SIZE: 4 ha, 160 pitches (all with elec, 90 statics), 19 hot showers, 24 WCs, 2 CWPs. &

Shop at 0.5 km. Restaurant at 0.1 km. Mini-golf, tennis.
PRICES: (1996) Caravan with family 108.00, Tent with two adults 60.00. CC: Euro/Access, Visa.
Leave A36 at Burnhaupt (between Belfort and Mulhouse) and take D103 to Dannemarie, then D7 bis to Seppois.

MUNSTER Haut-Rhin 3D

Camp Municipal du Parc de la Fecht
route de Gunsbach, 68140 Munster.
Tel 03 89 77 31 08, Fax 03 89 77 04 55. English spoken.
OPEN: 05/04–30/09. SIZE: 4 ha, 260 pitches (132 with elec), 32 hot showers, 32 WCs.

Restaurant at 0.3 km.
PRICES: (1996) Caravan with family 92.40, Tent with two adults 47.80. CC: Euro/Access, Visa.
From Colmar via Turckheim on the D10.

Camping Beau Rivage 8 rue des Champs, Gunsbach, 68140 Munster.
Tel 03 89 77 44 62, Fax 03 89 77 44 62.
OPEN: all year. SIZE: 2 ha, 125 pitches (120 with elec, 30 statics), 8 hot showers, 13 WCs, 1 CWP. (

Restaurant at 0.5 km. Children's playground, bar.
PRICES: (1996) Caravan with family 78.00, Tent with two adults 38.00. CC: Euro/Access, Visa.
Gunsbach is east of Munster.

France

Camping Municipal Langenwasen
68380 Mittlach.
Tel 03 89 77 63 77, Fax 03 89 77 74 36.
English spoken.
OPEN: 01/05–30/09. SIZE: 3 ha, 75 pitches (63 with elec), 8 hot showers, 16 WCs, 1 CWP. **℄**

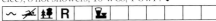

Restaurant at 3 km.
PRICES: (1996) Caravan with family 87.20, Tent with two adults 44.00. CC: none.
From Munster take D10 south to Mittlach. Signposted.

Les Amis de la Nature rue du Château, 68140 Luttenbach.
Tel 03 89 77 38 60, Fax 03 89 77 25 72.
English spoken.
OPEN: 10/02–15/11. SIZE: 7 ha, 400 pitches (380 with elec, 200 statics), 40 hot showers, 40 WCs, 6 CWPs. **℄ &**

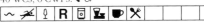

Mini-golf, volley ball, table tennis; sauna, tennis, horse-riding nearby.
PRICES: (1996) Caravan with family 91.50, Tent with two adults 45.50. CC: Amex, Euro/Access, Visa.
2 km outside Munster on the D10.

MUR-DE-BRETAGNE Côtes-du-Nord 1C

Camping Nautic International
route de Beau Rivage, 22530 Caurel.
Tel 02 96 28 57 94, Fax 02 96 26 02 00.
English spoken.
OPEN: 28/03–25/09. SIZE: 3.5 ha, 120 pitches (all with elec), 13 hot showers, 11 WCs, 2 CWPs. **℄ &**

Restaurant at 0.2 km. Tennis, sauna.
PRICES: (1996) Caravan with family 162.00, Tent with two adults 95.00. CC: Euro/Access, Visa.
Caurel is on the N164 bis just north of Mur-de-Bretagne. From Caurel head towards Beau-Rivage (2 km) and campsite is first turning on the left.

LA MURE Isère 5B

Camping Belvedere de l'Oubiou Les Egats, St-Laurent-en-Beaumont, 38350 La Mure-d'Isère.
Tel 04 76 30 40 80. English spoken.
OPEN: 01/05–30/09. SIZE: 1 ha, 50 pitches (all with elec), 5 hot showers (charge), 7 WCs, 2 CWPs. **℄ &**

Shop at 9 km. Restaurant at 4 km.
PRICES: (1996) Caravan with family 106.00, Tent with two adults 55.00. CC: none.
South of La Mure on the N85.

Les Mouettes Les Thénaux-St-Théoffrey, 38119 Pierre-Châtel.
Tel 04 76 83 02 49.
OPEN: 01/07–31/08. SIZE: 1.5 ha, 60 pitches (40 with elec), 4 hot showers (charge), 5 WCs, 1 CWP. **&**

Shop at 3 km. Restaurant at 3 km. Ball games; lakeside beach.
PRICES: (1996) Caravan with family 63.00, Tent with two adults 39.00. CC: none.
St-Théoffrey is 10 km north of La Mure on N85. Campsite is on the right, between Lac de Pierre-Chatel and Lac de Petichet.

MUROL Puy-de-Dôme 5A

Le Repos du Baladin 63790 Murol.
Tel 04 73 88 61 93, Fax 04 73 88 66 41.
English spoken.
OPEN: 01/05–15/09. SIZE: 1.6 ha, 45 pitches (all with elec), 6 hot showers, 6 WCs, 6 French WCs, 1 CWP. **℄ &**

Shop at 1 km.
PRICES: (1996) Caravan with family 116.00, Tent with two adults 65.00. CC: none.
Arriving in Murol, go towards the Tourist Office and follow signs to campsite from there.

LE MUY Var 6C

Parc Camping Les Cigales
Les Valettes, 83490 Le Muy.
Tel 04 94 45 12 08, Fax 04 94 45 92 80.
English spoken.
OPEN: 01/04–15/09. SIZE: 10 ha, 180 pitches (150 with elec), 32 hot showers, 26 WCs, 1 CWP. **℄ &**

Tennis, table tennis.
PRICES: (1996) Caravan with family 168.00, Tent with two adults 93.00. CC: Euro/Access, Visa.
Take the A8 exit at Le Muy and the campsite is 300 m.

MUZILLAC Morbihan 1D

Camping Le Moulin de Cadillac
56190 Noyal-Muzillac.
Tel 02 97 67 03 47, Fax 02 97 67 00 02.
English spoken.
OPEN: 01/05–30/09. SIZE: 2 ha, 70 pitches (45 with elec), 10 hot showers, 10 WCs. **℄ &**

Restaurant at 10 km. Tennis, table tennis, fishing.
PRICES: (1996) Caravan with family 97.00, Tent with two adults 54.00. CC: none.
5 km north of Muzillac on the D5.

France

Camping Municipal Lann-Floren 56450 Surzur.
Tel 02 97 42 10 74, Fax 02 97 42 03 54.
OPEN: 15/06–15/09. SIZE: 1 ha, 85 pitches (56 with elec), 7 hot showers, 6 WCs.

Shop at 0.8 km. Restaurant at 0.8 km.
PRICES: (1996) Caravan with family 63.00,
Tent with two adults 31.00. CC: none.
From Muzillac head west on the D20, 11 km to Surzur. Then follow the signs Camping Municipal or Camping Lann Floren.

Camping Relais de l'Océan Ambon,
56190 Muzillac.
Tel 02 97 41 66 48. English spoken.
OPEN: 01/04–30/09. SIZE: 2 ha, 90 pitches (all with elec, 5 statics), 12 hot showers, 17 WCs, 4 CWPs.

Restaurant at 1 km. Tennis, playground, TV, entertainments.
PRICES: Caravan with family 110.00,
Tent with two adults 64.00. CC: none.
From Muzillac take road to Ambon. Campsite is 300 m from first roundabout.

Camping Ty Breiz 15 Grande Rue, Kervoyal,
56750 Damgan.
Tel 02 97 41 13 47. English spoken.
OPEN: 01/05–01/10. SIZE: 1 ha, 58 pitches (all with elec), 6 hot showers, 10 WCs, 2 CWPs.

Shop at 0.02 km. Restaurant at 0.03 km. Mobile homes also available.
PRICES: (1996) Caravan with family 104.00,
Tent with two adults 72.50. CC: none.
D153 south of Muzillac to Damgan. Kervoyal is on the left.

NAILLOUX Haute-Garonne   5C

Camping Le Parc de la Thesauque
31560 Nailloux.
Tel 05 61 81 34 67, Fax 05 61 81 34 67.
English spoken.
OPEN: 01/03–31/10. SIZE: 2 ha, 30 pitches (all with elec), 9 hot showers, 9 WCs, 3 CWPs. ⚓ &

Restaurant at 0.2 km. Tennis, mini-golf.
PRICES: (1996) Caravan with family 90.00,
Tent with two adults 80.00. CC: none.
South-east of Toulouse.

NANCY Meurthe/Moselle   3D

Camping Le Grand Vanne 54210 Tonnoy.
Tel 03 83 26 62 36.
OPEN: 01/06–31/08. SIZE: 7 ha, 200 pitches (all with elec, 150 statics), 23 hot showers, 24 WCs. & &

Shop at 0.5 km. Also open w/e only Apr/May/Sep/Oct.
PRICES: (1996) Caravan with family 73.80,
Tent with two adults 40.00. CC: none.
From Nancy go south on A330; take Flavigny exit and then N57 and D74 to Tonnoy.

NANS-LES-PINS Var   6C

Camping International de la Ste-Baume
83860 Nans-les-Pins.
Tel 04 94 78 92 68, Fax 04 94 78 67 37.
English spoken.
OPEN: 01/04–30/09. SIZE: 5 ha, 24 hot showers, 2 CWPs. &

Shop at 0.5 km. Tennis, table tennis, entertainment.
PRICES: (1996) Caravan with family 223.00,
Tent with two adults 130.00. CC: none.
From A8 exit or from N7 at St-Maximin, then take N560 followed by D80.

NANTES Loire-Atlan   1D

Camping du Chêne
44450 St-Julien-de-Concelles.
Tel 02 40 54 12 00, Fax 02 40 36 54 79.
English spoken.
OPEN: 01/04–31/10. SIZE: 2 ha, 100 pitches (90 with elec), 9 hot showers, 10 WCs. & &

Shop at 0.8 km. Restaurant at 0.8 km. Fishing, tennis, boating, mini-golf, pedal boat, cellar visits.
PRICES: (1996) Caravan with family 91.00,
Tent with two adults 49.00. CC: none.
Leave Nantes north on N23. After 11 km turn right on to D37 to Thouaré. Cross the river and continue for approximately 3 km.

Camping La Pindière La Denais, 44810 Héric.
Tel 02 40 57 65 41, Fax 02 40 57 65 41.
English spoken.
OPEN: all year. SIZE: 2 ha, 56 pitches (all with elec), 7 hot showers, 10 WCs, 8 CWPs. & &

Shop at 0.5 km. Lake 3 km.
PRICES: (1996) Caravan with family 91.00, Tent with two adults 53.00. CC: Visa.
From Nantes go north on N137 to Héric. Turn left on to D16 and campsite is 1 km ahead.

Camping Municipal Les Grenettes La Varenne,
49270 St-Laurent-des-Autels.
Tel 02 40 98 58 92.
OPEN: 01/06–15/09. SIZE: 1 ha, 35 pitches (16 with elec, 2 statics), 2 hot showers, 6 WCs, 1 CWP. &

Shop at 0.3 km. Restaurant at 0.5 km.

PRICES: (1996) Caravan with family 66.00, Tent with two adults 28.00. CC: none.
Head east from Nantes, but on the south bank of the Loire (D751) for 17 km towards Champtoceaux. Site is on the banks of the Loire and well signed in La Varenne.

NARBONNE Aude 5C

Camping Côte des Roses
11100 Narbonne-Plage.
Tel 04 68 49 83 65. English spoken.
OPEN: 01/04–30/09. SIZE: 16 ha, 408 pitches (all with elec), 85 hot showers, 94 WCs, 5 CWPs. (&

Boules, tennis, basketball, volleyball, playground.
PRICES: (1996) Caravan with family 135.00, Tent with two adults 71.00. CC: Euro/Access, Visa.
Follow signs to Narbonne-les-Plages. Campsite is between road and beach, on the road towards Gruissan.

Camping Les Roches Grises
11100 Narbonne.
Tel 04 68 41 75 41, Fax 04 68 41 75 41.
English spoken.
OPEN: all year. SIZE: 3 ha, 130 pitches (100 with elec), 6 hot showers, 13 WCs, 24 French WCs, 1 CWP. (&

LE RELAIS DE LA NAUTIQUE

The site stands close to the 'Etang de Bages' lake, ideal for sailing and windsurfing, but also offering the extensive sport and leisure facilities that you expect from quality sites in the south of France.

All pitches now have their own private sanitary block.

Reservations are strongly advised .....which tells its own story.

**Le Relais de la Nautique
La Nautique
11100 Narbonne
Tel: 04 68 90 48 19
Fax: 04 68 90 73 39**

See under Narbonne

Shop at 2 km. Casino and supermarket nearby.
PRICES: (1996) Caravan with family 111.00, Tent with two adults 63.00. CC: none.
Leave A61 at exit for Narbonne-Sud. Follow road to Perpignan N9 for 4 km. Signposted.

Le Relais de la Nautique La Nautique, 11100 Narbonne.
Tel 04 68 90 48 19, Fax 04 68 90 73 39.
English spoken.
OPEN: 01/03–30/10. SIZE: 16 ha, 390 pitches (all with elec, 40 statics), 390 hot showers, 390 WCs. (&

Shop at 2 km. Restaurant at 1 km.
PRICES: (1996) Caravan with family 150.00, Tent with two adults 125.00. CC: Euro/Access, Visa.
From Narbonne take Narbonne-Sud exit off motorway and follow signs to campsite. Campsite is 2.5 km on the right.
SEE ADVERTISEMENT

NAUCELLE Aveyron 5C

Camping du Lac de Bonnefon 12800 Naucelle.
Tel 05 65 47 00 67. English spoken.
OPEN: 01/06–25/09. SIZE: 3 ha, 90 pitches (60 with elec), 10 hot showers, 6 WCs, 12 French WCs, 1 CWP. (&

Shop at 1 km. Mini-golf.
PRICES: (1996) Caravan with family 112.00, Tent with two adults 58.00. CC: none.
Naucelle is on the N88 between Rodez and Albi.

NEUFCHATEAU Vosges 3C

Camping Municipal place Pitet, 88300 Neufchâteau.
Tel 03 29 94 19 03. English spoken.
OPEN: 15/04–15/10. SIZE: 0.7 ha, 50 pitches (40 with elec), 5 hot showers, 8 WCs, 1 CWP. &

Shop at 1 km. Restaurant at 1 km. Swimming pool next door.
PRICES: (1996) Caravan with family 97.60, Tent with two adults 54.00. CC: none.
Campsite is near the sports stadium and well signposted.

NEUVILLE-SUR-SARTHE Sarthe 2C

Camping du Vieux Moulin
72190 Neuville-sur-Sarthe.
Tel 02 43 25 31 82, Fax 02 43 25 38 11. English spoken.
OPEN: 15/04–15/10. SIZE: 1 ha, 100 pitches (all with elec, 9 statics), 10 hot showers, 9 WCs, 2 French WCs, 2 CWPs. (

France

[~ ✗ ⊕ R 🔲 ⛺ ☕ | ⚲ 🅗 | |]

Restaurant at 0.5 km. Tennis, mini-golf, playground; fishing nearby.
PRICES: Caravan with family 115.00, Tent with two adults 64.00. CC: Euro/Access, Visa.
Highly recommended campsite. From the A10/11, leave at Le Mans-Nord towards Alençon and follow signs from there on.

NEVEZ Finistère 1C

Airotel International Le Raguenès Plage
19 rue des Iles, Raguenès, 29920 Névez.
Tel 02 98 06 80 69, Fax 02 98 06 89 05.
English spoken.
OPEN: 15/04–30/09. SIZE: 5 ha, 287 pitches (all with elec), 41 hot showers, 50 WCs. ⚲ ♿

[≋ ⚓ ⊕ R 🔲 ⛺ ☕ ✗ ⚲ 🅗 |]

Near Pont-Aven and beach; sauna.
PRICES: (1996) Caravan with family 185.00, Tent with two adults 114.00. CC: none.
From Névez go south towards Raguenès beach and site is 3 km.

Camp St-Nicolas Port-Manech, 29920 Névez.
Tel 02 98 06 89 75, Fax 02 98 06 74 61.
English spoken.
OPEN: 01/05–30/09. SIZE: 3 ha, 120 pitches (all with elec), 18 hot showers, 22 WCs, 12 CWPs. ⚲ ♿

[≋ ⚓ ⊕ R 🔲 | | ✗ | 🅗 |]

Shop at 0.3 km. Restaurant at 0.3 km. Good sports facilities nearby.
PRICES: (1996) Caravan with family 125.50, Tent with two adults 72.50. CC: none.
From Pont-Aven take D783 west for about 2 km. Turn left on to D77, go through Névez and on to Port-Manech.

Camping de l'Océan
Ker Oren, Raguenès, 29920 Névez.
Tel 02 98 06 87 13, Fax 02 98 06 78 26.
English spoken.
OPEN: 15/05–15/09. SIZE: 2.5 ha, 150 pitches (all with elec), 16 hot showers, 26 WCs, 19 French WCs, 2 CWPs. ♿

[≋ ⚓ ⊕ R 🔲 | | ✗ | |]

Shop at 3 km. Restaurant at 0.06 km.
PRICES: Caravan with family 131.50, Tent with two adults 75.00. CC: none.
Campsite is 3 km south of Nevez, near the beach.

NIMES Gard 5D

Camping Domaine de la Bastide route de Générac, 30900 Nîmes.
Tel 04 66 38 09 21. English spoken.
OPEN: all year. SIZE: 5 ha, 132 pitches (all with elec, 20 statics), 24 hot showers, 24 WCs, 3 CWPs. ⚲ ♿

[| ⊕ R 🔲 ⛺ ☕ ✗ | 🅗 |]

Swimming pool 100 m.
PRICES: (1996) Caravan with family 110.00, Tent with two adults 57.50. CC: Euro/Access, Visa.
Motorway exit Nîmes-West. First right in direction of Avignon and then turn right at traffic lights, signposted Générac. Site is 3 km ahead on the right.

Les Cypres rue de la Bastide, Bezouce, 30320 Marguerittes.
Tel 04 66 75 24 30.
OPEN: all year. SIZE: 33 pitches (20 with elec), 5 hot showers, 6 WCs, 3 French WCs, 1 CWP. ⚲

[| 🏕 R 🔲 | ☕ ✗ ⚲ 🅗 |]

Shop at 0.5 km.
PRICES: (1996) Caravan with family 100.00, Tent with two adults 53.00. CC: Euro/Access, Visa.
Bezouce is 12 km from Nîmes on the N86 towards Remoulins/Avignon. At the traffic lights in Bezouce, turn second left.

NONTRON Dordogne 4B

Camping Municipal Masvicontreaux, 24300 Nontron.
Tel 05 53 56 02 04, Fax 05 53 56 19 55.
OPEN: 01/06–15/09. SIZE: 2 ha, 70 pitches (all with elec), 9 hot showers.

[~ ✗ 🏕 R | | ☕ | 🎣 |]

Shop at 1 km. Restaurant at 1 km.
PRICES: (1996) Caravan with family 51.50, Tent with two adults 26.50. CC: none.
Nontron lies on D675 north of Périgueux.

NORT-SUR-ERDRE Loire-Atlan 1D

Camping Municipal du Port Mulon
44390 Nort-sur-Erdre.
Tel 02 40 72 23 57, Fax 02 40 72 16 09.
OPEN: 01/03–30/10. SIZE: 1.95 ha, 70 pitches (32 with elec), 4 hot showers.

[~ ✗ 🏕 R 🔲 | | | |]

Shop at 1 km. Restaurant at 1 km.
PRICES: (1996) Caravan with family 59.30, Tent with two adults 39.50. CC: none.
North of Nantes. (No motor caravans.)

NOTRE-DAME-DE-MONTS Vendée 1D

Le Grand Jardin route de la Barre de Monts, 85690 Notre-Dame-de-Monts.
Tel 02 51 58 87 76. English spoken.
OPEN: 01/05–30/09. SIZE: 2 ha, 90 pitches (70 with elec), 12 hot showers, 13 WCs, 3 CWPs. ⚲

[≋ ⚓ 🏕 R 🔲 ⛺ ☕ | | 🄷 ✗]

Shop at 0.6 km. Restaurant at 0.6 km. Sports field, playground, table tennis.

PRICES: (1996) Caravan with family 90.00,
Tent with two adults 65.00. CC: none.
7 km north of St-Jean-de-Monts on D38.

NOZAY Loire-Atlan 1D

Camping du S I route de Rennes,
44170 Nozay.
Tel 02 40 79 31 64. English spoken.
OPEN: 15/05–15/09. SIZE: 1 ha, 21 pitches (all with
elec), 3 hot showers, 4 WCs. &

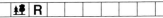

Shop at 0.5 km. Restaurant at 0.5 km. Swimming
pool nearby.
PRICES: (1996) Caravan with family 68.00,
Tent with two adults 38.00. CC: none.
*On Nozay to Rennes road (N137), just outside
Nozay.*

NYONS Drôme 5D

Camping Le Sagittaire Pont-de-Mirabel,
Vinsobres, 26110 Nyons.
Tel 04 75 27 00 00, Fax 04 75 27 00 39.
English spoken.
OPEN: all year. SIZE: 14 ha, 270 pitches (all with
elec, 25 statics), 24 hot showers, 36 WCs, 2 French
WCs, 3 CWPs. ℂ &

Lakeside flume, tennis, mini-golf; horse-riding and
bike hire nearby.
PRICES: (1996) Caravan with family 125.00,
Tent with two adults 88.00. CC: Amex,
Euro/Access, Visa.
*On A7, take Bollène exit, east on D94. Campsite is
5 km south-west of Nyons.*

Le Clos Camping 26110 Nyons.
Tel 04 75 26 29 90, Fax 04 75 26 29 90.
OPEN: all year. SIZE: 2 ha, 150 pitches (all with
elec). ℂ &

Shop at 1 km. Restaurant at 1 km.
PRICES: (1996) Caravan with family 80.00,
Tent with two adults 70.00. CC: none.
*Nyons is on the D94 heading towards Gap. Site is
well signposted.*

OLERON

LE CHATEAU-D'OLERON Char-Marit 4A

Airotel d'Oléron Domaine de Montrabail,
17480 Château-d'Oléron.
Tel 05 46 47 61 82, Fax 05 46 47 79 67.
English spoken.
OPEN: 01/03–31/10. SIZE: 4 ha, 120 pitches
(100 with elec, 80 statics), 35 hot showers,
30 WCs. ℂ &

Golf, naturist beaches and boating nearby; mobile
homes also available.
PRICES: (1996) Caravan with family 171.00,
Tent with two adults 114.00. CC: Amex,
Euro/Access, Visa.
*1 km from town centre. D733 from Rochefort to
St-Agnant, right onto D123, then right again onto
D728/734 over the water to Château-d'Oléron.*

Camping La Brande 17480 Château-d'Oléron.
Tel 05 46 47 62 37, Fax 05 46 47 71 70.
English spoken.
OPEN: 15/03–15/11. SIZE: 4 ha, 200 pitches
(150 with elec, 20 statics), 33 hot showers,
21 WCs, 2 CWPs. ℂ &

Shop at 2 km. Ball games, flume, evening
entertainment HS.
PRICES: (1996) Caravan with family 194.00, Tent
with two adults 110.00. CC: Euro/Access, Visa.
*2.5 km north of Le Château, along the route des
Huîtres.*

ST-DENIS-D'OLERON Charente-Marit 4A

Camping Phare-Ouest
17650 St-Denis-D'Oléron.
Tel 05 46 47 90 00. English spoken.
OPEN: 01/04–30/09. SIZE: 4 ha, 175 pitches
(all with elec), 36 hot showers, 40 WCs.

PRICES: (1996) Caravan with family 89.00,
Tent with two adults 58.00. CC: none.
*St-Denis-d'Oléron is 12 km north of St-Pierre-
d'Oléron on the D734.*

ST-PIERRE-D'OLERON Char-Marit 4A

Camping La Pierrière route de St-Georges,
17310 St-Pierre-d'Oléron.
Tel 05 46 47 08 29, Fax 05 46 75 12 82.
English spoken.
OPEN: 01/04–30/09. SIZE: 3 ha, 140 pitches
(all with elec), 18 hot showers, 18 WCs,
2 CWPs. ℂ &

Shop at 0.3 km. Table tennis, pétanque, billiards.
PRICES: (1996) Caravan with family 168.00, Tent
with two adults 119.00. CC: none.
*Arriving in St-Pierre, turn right at the third set of
traffic lights and left at the next set.*

Rex Domino Domino,
17190 St-Georges d'Oléron.
Tel 05 46 76 55 97, Fax 05 46 76 67 88.
English spoken.
OPEN: 01/05–15/09. SIZE: 10 ha, 450 pitches
(all with elec). ℂ &

France

OLERON RESORTS CONTINUED

Shop at 0.5 km. Restaurant at 0.5 km. Tennis, mini-golf, sauna, table tennis, playground.
PRICES: (1996) Caravan with family 195.00, Tent with two adults 105.00. CC: Amex, Euro/Access, Visa.
From St-Pierre-d'Oléron, drive 5 km north on the D734 to Chéray, then turn left towards Domino. In Domino, follow the signs 'Grande Plage' or 'Petite Plage'.

END OF OLERON RESORTS

LES OLLIERES-SUR-EYRIEUX   5B

Camping Municipal
07360 St-Fortunat-sur-Eyrieux.
Tel 04 75 65 22 80. English spoken.
OPEN: 01/04–01/10. SIZE: 40 pitches (all with elec), 8 hot showers, 8 WCs. **⌣** &

Shop at 0.5 km. Restaurant at 0.5 km. Mountain bikes for hire.
PRICES: (1996) Caravan with family 63.00, Tent with two adults 39.00. CC: none.
From Les Ollières, east on D120 following the river. Site is well signposted.

OLONNE-SUR-MER   Vendée   4A

Camping de Sauveterre 3 rte des Amies de la Nature, 85340 Olonne-sur-Mer.
Tel 02 51 33 10 58. English spoken.
OPEN: 01/05–15/09. SIZE: 2 ha, 170 pitches (150 with elec), 18 hot showers, 22 WCs, 2 CWPs. **⌣** &

Shop at 2 km.
PRICES: (1996) Caravan with family 98.00, Tent with two adults 56.00. CC: none.
3 km from Olonne-sur-Mer on D80 and 6 km to north of Les Sables-d'Olonne.

Camping Le Havre de la Gachère Les Granges, 85340 Olonne-sur-Mer.
Tel 02 51 90 59 85, Fax 02 51 20 11 92. English spoken.
OPEN: 30/03–30/09. SIZE: 5 ha, 200 pitches (all with elec, 22 statics), 18 hot showers, 32 WCs, 24 French WCs, 2 CWPs. **⌣** &

Restaurant at 0.5 km. Mini-golf.
PRICES: (1996) Caravan with family 127.00, Tent with two adults 68.00. CC: Euro/Access, Visa.
Campsite is well signposted.

Camping Le Moulin de la Salle
85340 Olonne-sur-Mer.
Tel 02 51 95 99 10, Fax 02 51 96 96 13. English spoken.

OPEN: 01/06–01/10. SIZE: 5 ha, 200 pitches (all with elec, 20 statics), 14 hot showers, 25 WCs, 5 CWPs. **⌣** &

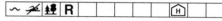

Shop at 2 km.
PRICES: (1996) Caravan with family 110.00, Tent with two adults 95.00. CC: none.
Campsite is just beside the D122, off the D80.

Camping Les Ormeaux 85340 Olonne-sur-Mer. Tel 02 51 95 65 98. English spoken.
OPEN: 15/06–15/09. SIZE: 4 ha, 110 pitches (all with elec), 21 hot showers, 23 WCs. **⌣** &

Restaurant at 3.5 km. Children's playground.
PRICES: (1996) Caravan with family 103.50, Tent with two adults 59.50. CC: none.
Take N160 into Olonne-sur-Mer and follow directions towards St-Gilles-Croix-de-Vie. Turn left after 1 km at railway bridge and campsite is signposted.

OLONZAC   Hérault   5C

Le Mas de Lignières Montcélèbre, 34210 Cesseras.
Tel 04 68 91 24 86, Fax 04 68 91 24 86.
English spoken.
OPEN: all year. SIZE: 7 ha, 26 pitches (all with elec, 26 statics), 6 hot showers, 6 WCs, 1 CWP. **⌣** &

Shop at 3 km. Restaurant at 1.5 km. Naturist site.
PRICES: (1996) Caravan with family 160.00, Tent with two adults 88.00. CC: Euro/Access, Visa.
D182 North of Olonzac to Cesseras.

OLORON-STE-MARIE   Pyrénées-Atlan 4C

Camping Le Vieux Moulin Feas, 64570 Aramits.
Tel 04 59 39 81 18. English spoken.
OPEN: all year. SIZE: 1.5 ha, 50 pitches (40 with elec, 20 statics), 4 hot showers, 4 WCs.

Shop at 3 km. Restaurant at 0.1 km.
PRICES: (1996) Caravan with family 52.30, Tent with two adults 30.35. CC: none.
From Oloron-Ste-Marie, south-west on the D919 to Aramits.

Camping Municipal de Lauzart 64490 Lescun.
Tel 05 59 34 51 77, Fax 05 59 34 51 77.
OPEN: 15/04–30/09. SIZE: 2 ha, 25 pitches (all with elec), 5 hot showers, 6 WCs, 1 CWP. **⌣**

Shop at 2 km. Restaurant at 2 km.
PRICES: Caravan with family 74.50, Tent with two adults 48.50. CC: none.
N134 south from Oloron in the direction of Somport. After Accous, follow the signs to Lescun on the D239.

ORANGE Vaucluse   5D

Camping Beauregard Route d'Uchaux,
84550 Mornas.
Tel 03 90 37 02 08, Fax 03 90 37 07 23.
English spoken.
OPEN: all year. SIZE: 11 ha, 251 pitches (200 with elec,
150 statics), 25 hot showers, 30 WCs, 1 CWP. ℓ ♿

Tennis, mini-golf; 30 mobile homes and 3 chalets
for hire.
PRICES: (1996) Caravan with family 127.00, Tent
with two adults 70.00. CC: Euro/Access, Visa.
*From Orange go north. Campsite in Mornas is on
the road to Uchaux and well signposted.*

Camping du Moulin 84350 Courthezon.
Tel 03 90 70 26 65, Fax 03 90 70 26 65. English spoken.
OPEN: 01/04–31/10. SIZE: 1 ha, 20 pitches (all with
elec, 4 statics), 4 hot showers, 4 WCs, 14 CWPs. ℓ

Restaurant at 0.3 km. Games/TV room; boules;
bikes for hire.
PRICES: (1996) Caravan with family 106.00,
Tent with two adults 60.00. CC: Visa.
*From Orange take N7 for 8 km towards Avignon.
Campsite is signposted in Courthezon.*

Camping Le Jonquier rue Alexis Carrel,
84100 Orange.
Tel 03 90 34 19 83, Fax 03 90 34 86 54. English spoken.
OPEN: 01/04–30/10. SIZE: 5 ha, 120 pitches
(66 with elec, 15 statics), 14 hot showers, 15 WCs,
6 French WCs. ♿

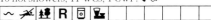

Restaurant at 0.5 km.
PRICES: (1996) Caravan with family 165.00, Tent
with two adults 90.00. CC: Amex, Euro/Access, Visa.
*1.5 km from the centre of Orange near the Arc de
Triomphe.*

ORLEANS Loiret   2D

Camp Municipal d'Olivet rue de Pont Bouchet,
45160 Olivet.
Tel 02 38 63 53 94. English spoken.
OPEN: 01/04–15/10. SIZE: 40 pitches (all with elec),
10 hot showers, 11 WCs, 1 CWP. ℓ ♿

Restaurant at 3 km.
PRICES: (1996) Caravan with family 93.90,
Tent with two adults 43.40. CC: none.
*From the town centre, take the N20 towards
Vierzon/Bourges. After crossing the river Loire,
continue for about 3.5 km. Just after the Auchan
supermarket (on your right), cross the small river
Loiret and turn first right immediately after the
bridge. Turn left at the roundabout and follow the
signs to the campsite.*

ORTHEZ Pyrénées-Atlan   4C

Camping de la Source 64300 Orthez.
Tel 04 59 67 04 81, Fax 04 59 69 12 00.
OPEN: 01/04–15/10. SIZE: 2 ha, 29 pitches (all with
elec), 4 hot showers, 6 WCs, 4 French WCs,
1 CWP. ℓ ♿

Shop at 1.5 km. Restaurant at 1.5 km. Children's
playground.
PRICES: unavailable. CC: none.
*From the town centre, drive 1 km towards Pau,
then turn left towards Mont-de-Marsan, drive on
the Boulevard Charles de Gaulle and then turn
first right.*

OUCQUES Loir-et-Cher   2D

Camp Municipal rue de Châteaudun,
41290 Oucques.
Tel 02 54 23 11 00, Fax 02 54 23 11 04.
OPEN: 09/04–01/11. SIZE: 1 ha, 33 pitches (all with
elec), 3 hot showers, 4 WCs. ℓ

Shop at 0.3 km. Equestrian centre; golf 4 km.
PRICES: (1996) Caravan with family 60.00,
Tent with two adults 34.00. CC: none.
*Leave Oucques along Châteaudun road.
Campsite is signposted.*

OUISTREHAM Calvados   2A

Camping des Capucines 14860 Ranville.
Tel 02 31 78 69 82, Fax 02 31 78 16 94.
English spoken.
OPEN: all year. SIZE: 4 ha, 160 pitches (100 with
elec, 14 statics), 16 hot showers, 20 WCs,
8 CWPs. ℓ ♿

Restaurant at 1 km. Sea 5 km.
PRICES: (1996) Caravan with family 110.00,
Tent with two adults 58.00. CC: Amex,
Euro/Access, Visa.

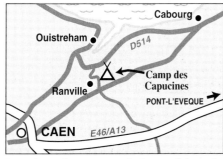

*From Ouistreham go towards Caen and then take
D514 to Ranville.*

France

PARAY-LE-MONIAL Saône/Loire 5B

Camping de Mambre route du Gué Léger, 71600 Paray-le-Monial.
Tel 03 85 88 89 20, Fax 03 85 88 87 81.
English spoken.
OPEN: 15/03–15/10. SIZE: 4 ha, 198 pitches (60 with elec), 21 hot showers, 21 WCs, 3 CWPs. &

Restaurant at 1 km. Bicycles.
PRICES: Caravan with family 117.00,
Tent with two adults 74.00. CC: Visa.
Paray-le-Monial is 10 km east of Digoin (N79).

PARIS Paris 2B

Camping du Bois de Boulogne
allée du Bord de l'Eau, 75016 Paris.
Tel 01 45 24 30 00, Fax 01 42 24 42 95.
English spoken.
OPEN: all year. SIZE: 7 ha, 220 pitches (all with elec, 59 statics). &

PRICES: (1996) Caravan with family 110.00,
Tent with two adults 75.00. CC: Visa.
Well signposted from Porte-Maillot.

PAU Pyrénées-Atlan 4D

Camping Hôtel des Sapins route de Tarbes, Ousse, 64320 Bizanos.
Tel 04 59 81 74 21. English spoken.
OPEN: 01/05–15/10. SIZE: 0.7 ha, 35 pitches (22 with elec), 4 hot showers, 5 WCs, 2 French WCs, 1 CWP.

Shop at 0.6 km. Restaurant at 0.1 km. Rooms also available.
PRICES: (1996) Caravan with family 98.00,
Tent with two adults 54.00. CC: none.
On N117, 5 km south of Pau and well signposted.

Camping Le Terrier 64230 Lescar.
Tel 04 59 81 01 82, Fax 04 59 81 26 83.
English spoken.
OPEN: all year. SIZE: 5 ha, 110 pitches (80 with elec, 15 statics), 10 hot showers, 11 WCs, 5 French WCs, 3 CWPs. &

Tennis, boules, volley ball.
PRICES: Caravan with family 114.00, Tent with two adults 74.00. CC: Euro/Access, Visa.
From Pau, N117 to Lescar. Turn left at cross-roads towards Monnein and campsite is 1 km ahead, just before the river.

PAYRAC Lot 4B

Camping à la Ferme Le Treil-Loupiac, 46350 Payrac.
Tel 05 65 37 64 87. English spoken.

OPEN: 01/05–30/10. SIZE: 1 ha, 20 pitches (all with elec), 4 hot showers, 4 WCs, 3 CWPs. &

Shop at 4 km. Restaurant at 1 km.
PRICES: (1996) Caravan with family 78.00, with two adults 48.00. CC: none.
Coming from Souillac go 12 km south along N20 to Payrac. Campsite is on the right, 500 m from the main road.

Caravaning Les Hirondelles
Loupiac, 46350 Payrac.
Tel 05 65 37 66 25, Fax 05 65 41 91 58.
English spoken.
OPEN: 09/04–30/10. SIZE: 3 ha, 47 pitches (all with elec, 23 statics), 7 hot showers, 8 WCs, 1 French WC, 1 CWP. & &

Nursery, TV, entertainment.
PRICES: (1996) Caravan with family 118.00,
Tent with two adults 78.00. CC: Amex, Euro/Access, Visa.
Just west of N20, approximately 5 km north of Payrac.

Les Cigales 46500 Rocamadour.
Tel 05 65 33 64 44, Fax 05 65 33 69 60.
English spoken.
OPEN: 22/06–05/09. SIZE: 3 ha, 100 pitches (68 with elec), 13 hot showers, 10 WCs, 1 CWP. &

Mini-golf.
PRICES: (1996) Caravan with family 130.00,
Tent with two adults 80.00. CC: Visa.
From Payrac east on D673 to Rocamadour.

Le Panoramic route de Loupiac, 46350 Payrac.
Tel 05 65 37 98 45. English spoken.
OPEN: all year. SIZE: 1.5 ha, 55 pitches (24 with elec, 12 statics), 4 hot showers, 5 WCs. & &

PRICES: Caravan with family 82.00, Tent with two adults 44.00. CC: Amex, Euro/Access, Visa.
On N20, just north of Payrac, turn right towards Loupiac. Follow signs.

Les Pins 46350 Payrac.
Tel 05 65 37 96 32, Fax 05 65 37 91 08.
English spoken.
OPEN: 05/04–15/09. SIZE: 4 ha, 125 pitches (all with elec), 17 hot showers, 17 WCs, 1 CWP. & &

Recreation park free; flume, mobile homes for hire; 50% discount in LS.
PRICES: (1996) Caravan with family 192.00,
Tent with two adults 112.00. CC: Visa.
On N20, 15 km south of Souillac. Follow signs.
(Bookings and further information from UK telephone number: 01722 322 583.)

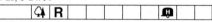

Relais du Campeur 46500 Rocamadour.
Tel 05 65 33 63 28, Fax 05 65 33 69 60.
English spoken.
OPEN: 28/03–30/09. SIZE: 1.7 ha, 100 pitches
(40 with elec), 8 hot showers, 9 WCs, 1 CWP.

PRICES: (1996) Caravan with family 98.00,
Tent with two adults 60.00. CC: Visa.
From Payrac, east on D673 to Rocamadour.

PENESTIN Morbihan 1D

Camping Les Iles La Pointe du Bile,
56760 Pénestin-sur-Mer.
Tel 02 99 90 30 24, Fax 02 99 90 44 55.
English spoken.
OPEN: 12/04–30/09. SIZE: 4 ha, 150 pitches
(all with elec, 30 statics), 30 hot showers, 19 WCs,
2 CWPs. ૯ ੬

Tennis, sports field.
PRICES: (1996) Caravan with family 198.00,
Tent with two adults 128.00. CC: Amex,
Euro/Access, Visa.
4 km south of Pénestin on D201.

Camping Les Parcs
route de la Roche-Bernard, 56760 Pénestin.
Tel 02 99 90 30 59, Fax 02 99 90 30 59.
English spoken.
OPEN: 01/04–30/09. SIZE: 2 ha, 75 pitches (60 with
elec, 6 statics), 13 hot showers, 6 WCs, 11 French
WCs, 2 CWPs. ૯ ੬

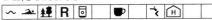

Shop at 0.3 km. Restaurant at 0.3 km.
PRICES: Caravan with family 118.00, Tent with two
adults 67.00. CC: Amex, Euro/Access, Visa.
On D34 300 m east of Pénestin.

PERIGUEUX Dordogne 4B

Camping Barnabe 80 rue des Bains, Boulazac,
24750 Périgueux.
Tel 05 53 53 41 45. English spoken.
OPEN: all year. SIZE: 1.5 ha, 80 pitches (all with
elec), 7 hot showers, 8 CWPs. ૯ ੬

Shop at 1 km. Restaurant at 0.8 km.
PRICES: (1996) Caravan with family 87.00,
Tent with two adults 54.00. CC: Visa.
*From centre of Périgueux take N89 Clermont-
Ferrand/Tulle road. Turn left just outside the town.*

Camping de l'Isle route de Brive,
24750 Périgueux-Boulazac.
Tel 05 53 53 57 75. English spoken.
OPEN: 15/05–25/09. SIZE: 100 ha, 100 pitches
(85 with elec), 9 hot showers, 10 WCs, 10 French
WCs, 1 CWP. ૯

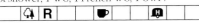

Shop at 0.5 km. Restaurant at 0.2 km.
PRICES: (1996) Caravan with family 112.50,
Tent with two adults 63.50. CC: none.
*Campsite at Boulazac is 3 km from Périgueux, on
E70 towards Brive.*

PERONNE Somme 2B

Camping à la Ferme Plaquet 22 rue Basse,
80240 Vraignes-en-Vermandois.
Tel 03 22 85 64 68, Fax 03 22 85 63 20.
English spoken.
OPEN: all year. SIZE: 0.5 ha, 6 pitches (all with elec),
1 hot shower, 1 WC, 1 French WC, 1 CWP.

Shop at 5 km.
PRICES: (1996) Caravan with family 66.00,
Tent with two adults 44.00. CC: none.
*From Péronne south-east on D44 towards St-
Quentin. Then D15 to Vraignes-en-Vermandois.*

PERPIGNAN Pyrénées Orient 5C

Camping Caravaning La Garenne
66170 Néfiach.
Tel 04 68 57 15 76.
OPEN: all year. SIZE: 2 ha, 73 pitches (50 with elec),
8 hot showers, 8 WCs, 6 French WCs, 2 CWPs. ੬

Shop at 0.5 km. Restaurant at 3 km.
PRICES: (1996) Caravan with family 99.00,
Tent with two adults 52.00. CC: none.
*From Perpignan take N116 west towards Prades
for 20 km to Néfiach.*

Camping Les Rives du Lac
66180 Villeneuve de la Raho.
Tel 04 68 55 83 51, Fax 04 68 55 80 98.
English spoken.
OPEN: 01/03–30/11. SIZE: 2.5 ha, 112 pitches
(all with elec, 5 statics), 18 hot showers, 17 WCs,
6 CWPs. ૯ ੬

Shop at 1.5 km. Restaurant at 1.5 km.
Entertainment in season; mobile homes available.
PRICES: (1996) Caravan with family 119.00,
Tent with two adults 50.00. CC: none.
*From motorway A9 exit Perpignan Sud and turn
right after the department store 'Auchan'.
Campsite is signposted.*

PERROS-GUIREC Côtes-du-Nord 1A

Camping Claire Fontaine Toul ar Lann,
22700 Perros-Guirec.
Tel 02 96 23 03 55, Fax 02 96 49 06 19.
English spoken.
OPEN: 01/05–30/09. SIZE: 3 ha, 180 pitches

France

(90 with elec), 25 hot showers, 25 WCs, 2 CWPs.

Shop at 0.25 km. Restaurant at 0.7 km. Bar in beautiful old building.
PRICES: (1996) Caravan with family 150.00, Tent with two adults 78.00. CC: none.
Entering Perros on D788 from Lannion, turn left after roundabout. Follow signs.

Camping Municipal Renan Louannec, 22700 Perros-Guirec.
Tel 02 96 23 11 78, Fax 02 96 23 35 42.
English spoken.
OPEN: 01/06–30/09. SIZE: 5 ha, 265 pitches (185 with elec, 4 statics), 29 hot showers, 27 WCs, 6 French WCs, 1 CWP.

PRICES: (1996) Caravan with family 97.50, Tent with two adults 54.50. CC: none.
From Perros-Guirec, drive 1 km east on the D6 towards Louannec.

Castel Camping Le Ranolien 22700 Ploumanac'h.
Tel 02 96 91 43 58, Fax 02 96 91 41 90.
English spoken.
OPEN: all year. SIZE: 16 ha, 350 pitches (all with elec, 150 statics), 54 hot showers, 50 WCs, 13 French WCs, 6 CWPs.

Shop at 1 km. Mini-golf, tennis, disco, indoor swimming pool and slides.
PRICES: (1996) Caravan with family 240.00, Tent with two adults 130.00. CC: Euro/Access, Visa.
Take the D786 from Perros-Guirec towards Trégastel. Campsite is 4.5 km ahead, on the outskirts of Ploumanac'h.

PEYRELEAU Aveyron 5C

Camping Beldoire 48210 Les Vignes.
Tel 04 66 48 82 79. English spoken.
OPEN: 01/04–01/10. SIZE: 6 ha, 100 pitches (all with elec), 21 hot showers, 25 WCs, 8 French WCs, 2 CWPs.

Restaurant at 0.5 km. Canoeing, fishing.
PRICES: (1996) Caravan with family 116.00, Tent with two adults 65.00. CC: Visa.
From Peyreleau drive north up the D907 (Gorges du Tarn) to Les Vignes. Site 600 m north of village.

PEZENAS Hérault 5C

Camp Municipal 34290 Servian.
Tel 04 67 39 12 07, Fax 04 67 39 25 87.
OPEN: 15/03–15/10. SIZE: 2 ha, 40 pitches (all with elec), 7 hot showers, 6 WCs.

Shop at 0.2 km. Restaurant at 0.5 km. Boules, tennis nearby.
PRICES: (1996) Caravan with family 83.30, Tent with two adults 40.75. CC: Euro/Access.
Leave N9 south-west of Pézenas and take D18 north-east at La Roque for campsite at Servian.

Camping Borepo Domaine St-Raymond, 34560 Villeveyrac.
Tel 04 67 78 07 27, Fax 04 67 78 05 55.
English spoken.
OPEN: 01/04–30/10. SIZE: 5 ha, 65 pitches (all with elec, 30 statics), 18 hot showers, 10 WCs, 1 CWP.

PRICES: (1996) Caravan with family 102.50, Tent with two adults 66.50. CC: Amex, Euro/Access, Visa.
From Pézenas, go to Montagnac, then take D5 towards Villeveyrac.

Camping Les Cigales Conas, 34120 Pézenas.
Tel 04 67 98 97 99.
OPEN: 01/06–30/09. SIZE: 45 pitches (all with elec, 4 statics), 3 hot showers, 6 WCs, 6 French WCs.

Shop at 1 km. Restaurant at 0.2 km. River 0.6 km.
PRICES: (1996) Caravan with family 97.00, Tent with two adults 66.00. CC: none.
1 km from Pézénas on road to Agde.

Camping St. Christol route de Nizas, 34120 Pezenas.
Tel 04 67 98 09 00, Fax 04 67 98 85 07.
English spoken.
OPEN: 15/06–07/09. SIZE: 1.5 ha, 93 pitches (all with elec), 10 hot showers, 10 WCs, 2 CWPs.

Restaurant at 1 km. Barbecues available.
PRICES: (1996) Caravan with family 103.90, Tent with two adults 67.70. CC: none.
N113 from Montpellier; at Montagnac turn left onto D161 to Pezenas. No motor caravans.

PIERREFORT Aveyron 5A

Camping Caravaning La Source Laussac, 12600 Therondels.
Tel 05 65 66 05 62, Fax 05 65 66 21 00.
English spoken.
OPEN: 01/07–31/08. SIZE: 4.5 ha, 85 pitches (all with elec), 13 hot showers, 19 WCs, 1 CWP.

PRICES: (1996) Caravan with family 170.00, Tent with two adults 130.00. CC: Euro/Access, Visa.
From Pierrefort take D990/D34 south-west to Paulienc and then Laussac. Site is well signposted.

LES PIEUX Manche 1B

Le Grand Large Anse de Sciotot, 50340 Les Pieux.
Tel 02 33 52 40 75, Fax 02 33 52 58 20.
English spoken.
OPEN: 05/04 – 14/09. SIZE: 4 ha, 220 pitches
(all with elec, 50 statics), 20 hot showers,
18 WCs, 2 CWPs. ⚓ ⚐

Tennis.
PRICES: Tent with two adults 95.00. CC: Visa.
*Les Pieux is 20 km west of Cherbourg on the
D904. From Les Pieux take the D117.*

LA PLAINE-SUR-MER Loire-Atlan 1D

Camping La Renaudière
44770 La Plaine-sur-Mer.
Tel 02 40 21 50 03, Fax 02 40 21 09 41.
English spoken.
OPEN: 01/04 – 30/09. SIZE: 2.8 ha, 82 pitches
(49 with elec, 4 statics), 15 hot showers, 14 WCs,
1 CWP. ⚓ ⚐

Shop at 0.8 km. Playroom, sports ground,
entertainment in English.
PRICES: (1996) Caravan with family 151.00, Tent
with two adults 91.00. CC: Euro/Access, Visa.
*From Pornic take the D13 to La-Plaine-sur-Mer
and follow signs to campsite.*

Camping Le Ranch Le Cormier,
44770 La Plaine-sur-Mer.
Tel 02 40 21 52 62. English spoken.
OPEN: 01/03 – 20/10. SIZE: 3 ha, 136 pitches
(115 with elec), 12 hot showers, 10 WCs,
4 CWPs. ⚐

Restaurant at 1 km. Horse-riding.
PRICES: (1996) Caravan with family 139.50,
Tent with two adults 82.00. CC: Visa.
On D13 from Pornic.

La Tabardière 44770 La Plaine-sur-Mer.
Tel 02 40 21 58 83, Fax 02 40 21 02 68.
English spoken.
OPEN: 01/04 – 15/10. SIZE: 4 ha, 180 pitches
(150 with elec, 20 statics), 22 hot showers,
34 WCs, 2 CWPs. ⚓ ⚐

Shop at 3 km. Restaurant at 1 km. Tennis,
mini-golf.
PRICES: (1996) Caravan with family 132.00, Tent
with two adults 78.00. CC: Euro/Access, Visa.
6 km from Pornic, on the D13.

PLENEUF-VAL-ANDRE Côtes-du-N 1D

Camping du Minihy 22370 Pleneuf-Val-André.
Tel 02 96 72 22 95. English spoken.

OPEN: 01/06 – 15/09. SIZE: 2 ha, 70 pitches (all with
elec), 8 hot showers, 8 WCs, 2 CWPs.

Shop at 1 km. Restaurant at 0.2 km.
PRICES: (1996) Caravan with family 100.00, Tent
with two adults 60.00. CC: Euro/Access, Visa.

PLEUBIAN Côtes-du-Nord 1A

Camping de Port la Chaine 22610 Pleubian.
Tel 02 96 22 92 38, Fax 02 96 22 87 92.
English spoken.
OPEN: 01/06 – 10/09. SIZE: 5 ha, 200 pitches (184 with
elec), 20 hot showers, 20 WCs, 2 CWPs. ⚓

Shop at 1.5 km. Restaurant at 1.5 km.
PRICES: Caravan with family 136.00,
Tent with two adults 78.00. CC: none.
*From Pleubian, north on N20 to coast. Well
signposted.*

PLOERMEL Morbihan 1D

Camping du Lac Les Belles Rives
56800 Ploërmel.
Tel 02 97 74 01 22. English spoken.
OPEN: 01/04 – 30/09. SIZE: 3 ha, 135 pitches (all
with elec), 12 hot showers, 25 WCs, 3 CWPs. ⚓ ⚐

Restaurant at 2 km. Mobile homes for hire; various
water sports.
PRICES: (1996) Caravan with family 92.00,
Tent with two adults 49.00. CC: none.
To the north of Ploërmel by the lake.

La Vallée du Ninian Le Rocher, 56800 Taupont.
Tel 02 97 93 53 01, Fax 02 97 93 57 27.
English spoken.
OPEN: 01/05 – 30/09. SIZE: 2.7 ha, 48 pitches
(all with elec), 7 hot showers, 7 WCs, 1 CWP. ⚓ ⚐

Restaurant at 3 km. Mobile homes for hire.
PRICES: (1996) Caravan with family 88.00,
Tent with two adults 60.00. CC: none.
West of Ploërmel. First road on left after Taupont.

PLOUBAZLANEC Côtes-du-Nord 1A

Camping Le Rohou L'Arcouest,
22620 Ploubazlanec.
Tel 02 96 55 87 22. English spoken.
OPEN: all year. SIZE: 1.5 ha, 70 pitches (all with elec),
7 hot showers, 7 WCs, 5 French WCs, 1 CWP. ⚓ ⚐

Shop at 0.2 km. Restaurant at 0.5 km. Boat trips.
PRICES: (1996) Caravan with family 95.00,
Tent with two adults 61.00. CC: none.
*2.5 km north of Ploubazlanec on D789 from
Paimpol. Follow signs to the right.*

France

PLOUEZEC Côtes-du-Nord 1A

Camping Le Cap Horn Port Lazo, 22470 Plouézec.
Tel 02 96 20 64 28, Fax 02 96 20 63 88.
English spoken.
OPEN: 01/04–15/10. SIZE: 5 ha, 150 pitches
(86 with elec), 16 hot showers, 18 WCs, 3 CWPs.

Restaurant at 1 km.
PRICES: (1996) Caravan with family 154.00,
Tent with two adults 89.00. CC: none.
3 km north-east of Port Lazo on D77.

PLOUEZOCH Finistère 1C

Camping Baie de Terenez 29252 Plouézoch.
Tel 02 98 67 26 80. English spoken.
OPEN: 09/04–30/09. SIZE: 3 ha, 140 pitches
(90 with elec), 18 hot showers, 2 CWPs.

Shop at 3 km. Mini-golf.
PRICES: (1996) Caravan with family 137.00, Tent
with two adults 78.00. CC: Euro/Access, Visa.
*After leaving N12 at Morlaix, go to port and take
D76 along the river to Plouézoch village. Continue
through village towards Terénez for 3 km.*

PLOUGASNOU Finistère 1C

Camp Municipal de la Pointe Primel-Trégastel,
29630 Plougasnou.
Tel 02 98 72 37 06. English spoken.
OPEN: 15/06–15/09. SIZE: 60 pitches, 7 hot showers
(charge), 7 WCs, 3 French WCs.

Shop at 0.5 km. Restaurant at 0.5 km. Children's
playground; swimming pool 1 km.
PRICES: (1996) Caravan with family 109.00,
Tent with two adults 75.00. CC: none.
Take the D46 from Plougasnou to Primel-Trégastel.

PLOUGASTEL-DAOULAS Finistère 1C

Camping St-Jean 29470 Plougastel-Daoulas.
Tel 02 98 40 32 90, Fax 02 98 04 23 11. English spoken.
OPEN: all year. SIZE: 2 ha, 100 pitches (85 with
elec), 8 hot showers, 20 WCs, 1 CWP.

Shop at 2 km. Restaurant at 2 km.
PRICES: Caravan with family 99.00,
Tent with two adults 55.00. CC: none.
*From Plougastel-Daoulas take the D29 to
Landerneau and follow the arrows to the campsite.*

PLOUGUERNEAU Finistère 1C

Camping de la Grève Blanche
29880 Plouguerneau.
Tel 02 98 04 70 35. English spoken.

OPEN: 01/06–15/09. SIZE: 2 ha, 100 pitches
(all with elec), 8 hot showers (charge), 9 WCs,
3 French WCs, 3 CWPs.

Restaurant at 1 km. Children's games.
PRICES: (1996) Caravan with family 70.00,
Tent with two adults 36.00. CC: none.
The campsite is signposted from Plouguerneau.

PLOUHARNEL Morbihan 1C

Camping Les Bruyères 56340 Plouharnel.
Tel 02 97 52 30 57, Fax 02 97 52 30 57.
English spoken.
OPEN: 03/04–20/10. SIZE: 2 ha, 112 pitches (80 with
elec, 12 statics), 11 hot showers, 11 WCs, 1 CWP.

Shop at 2 km. Restaurant at 2 km.
PRICES: (1996) Caravan with family 105.50, Tent
with two adults 63.00. CC: Euro/Access, Visa.
*Auray to Quiberon on D768, then D4, 2 km from
Plouharnel.*

PLOZEVET Finistère 1C

Camping de Cornouaille
route de Pont-l'Abbé, 29710 Plozévet.
Tel 02 98 91 30 81. English spoken.
OPEN: 25/06–10/09. SIZE: 2 ha, 80 pitches (36 with
elec), 5 hot showers, 9 WCs, 1 CWP.

Shop at 2 km.-Restaurant at 2 km. Indoor/outdoor
play areas for children.
PRICES: Caravan with family 93.00,
Tent with two adults 50.00. CC: none.
*From Quimper take D784 towards Audierne.
From centre of Plozévet turn left towards Pont-
l'Abbé. Campsite is 2 km on right.*

La Corniche route de la Corniche,
29710 Plozévet.
Tel 02 98 91 33 91, Fax 02 98 91 41 53.
English spoken.
OPEN: 01/05–20/09. SIZE: 1.5 ha, 80 pitches (all with
elec, 5 statics), 9 hot showers, 8 WCs, 2 CWPs.

Shop at 0.5 km. Restaurant at 0.5 km. Volley ball,
boules, table tennis, playground.
PRICES: (1996) Caravan with family 129.00,
Tent with two adults 86.00. CC: Amex,
Euro/Access, Visa.
*On the D784, 25 km west of Quimper. Follow
signs from centre of Plozévet.*

PONCIN Ain 5B

Camping Municipal
allée des Terres d'Ain, 01450 Poncin.
Tel 04 74 37 20 78. English spoken.

OPEN: 01/04–15/10. SIZE: 1.5 ha, 100 pitches (al with elec, 70 statics), 12 hot showers, 10 WCs. ♨

Shop at 0.4 km. Restaurant at 0.4 km.
PRICES: (1996) Caravan with family 70.00, Tent with two adults 35.00. CC: none.
From Poncin take N84 south or from A40 take exit for Pont-d'Ain and follow signs.

PONS Charente-Marit 4B

Camping Chardon 17800 Pons.
Tel 05 46 94 04 96. English spoken.
OPEN: 01/04–30/09. SIZE: 1 ha, 21 pitches (15 with elec), 2 hot showers, 2 WCs. ♨

Shop at 1 km. Restaurant at 2 km.
PRICES: Caravan with family 79.00, Tent with two adults 40.00. CC: none.
On A10 take exit 36 towards Pons and then the second road on right. Well signposted.

Camping Chardon
at Pons
Good stopover for west coast travellers

PONT-AVEN Finistère 1C

Domaine de Kerlann Land Rosted, 29930 Pont-Aven.
Tel 02 98 06 01 77, Fax 02 98 06 18 50.
English spoken.
OPEN: 02/05–26/09. SIZE: 17 ha, 232 pitches (136 with elec, 118 statics), 46 hot showers, 50 WCs, 4 CWPs. ♿

Mini-golf, tennis, flume, children's games and club.
PRICES: (1996) Caravan with family 132.00, Tent with two adults 91.00. CC: Euro/Access, Visa.
From Pont-Aven take road towards Concarneau and then turn left on to D77 towards Névez. Campsite is 1 km ahead on the right and well signposted.

SEE ADVERTISEMENT

PONT-DE-BEAUVOISIN Savoie 5B

Camping les Trois Lacs Les Chaudonnes, 73330 Belmont-Tramonet.
Tel 04 76 37 04 03, Fax 04 76 37 37 60.
English spoken.
OPEN: 01/04–15/09. SIZE: 5 ha, 90 pitches (all with elec), 12 hot showers, 12 WCs, 1 CWP. ♨ ♿

Shop at 3 km. Swimming pool, on-site entertainment, canoeing, bike hire, tennis.
PRICES: (1996) Caravan with family 159.00, Tent with two adults 92.00. CC: none.
2 km from the A43 and 3 km north of Pont-de-Beauvoisin (towards St-Genix-sur-Guiers). Follow signs in Belmont-Tramonet.

Camping les Trois Lacs ★★★★
near Pont-de-Beauvoisin
Savoie flair beside 2 rivers

PONT-DE-SALARS Aveyron 5C

Camping du Lac 12290 Pont-de-Salars.
Tel 05 65 46 84 86, Fax 05 65 74 33 10.
English spoken.
OPEN: 15/06–07/09. SIZE: 5 ha, 200 pitches (all with elec), 35 hot showers, 48 WCs, 2 CWPs. ♨ ♿

Shop at 1 km. Restaurant at 1 km.
PRICES: (1996) Caravan with family 127.00, Tent with two adults 76.00. CC: none.

DOMAINE DE KERLANN
★★★★
PONT AVEN

With spacious, secluded pitches measuring at least 120m^2 in wooded parkland, Domaine de Kerlann is an ideal base from which to explore southern Brittany.
Children will have a great time too, with our free Tiger Club for 4-12 year olds.
Facilities include: Swimming pool complex, waterslide, tennis, volleyball, bar, restaurant, takeaway, Tiger Tots crèche for 2-4 year olds.
Open 2nd May – 26th September.
Ferry inclusive packages available.
To obtain a brochure
call 0990 143 285
quoting FMA02.

France

Le Caussanel 12290 Canet-de-Salars.
Tel 05 65 46 85 19, Fax 05 65 46 89 85. English spoken.
OPEN: 01/04–30/10. SIZE: 10 ha, 235 pitches (all with elec), 30 hot showers, 25 WCs, 5 CWPs. ✆ &

Shop at 3 km.
PRICES: Caravan with family 152.00, Tent with two adults 90.00. CC: none.
From Pont-de-Salars take D993 for approx 3 km. Fork right to Canet-de-Salars.

PONT-DE-VAUX Ain   5B

Les Peupliers Le Port, 01190 Pont-de-Vaux.
Tel 03 85 30 33 65, Fax 03 85 30 33 65.
English spoken.
OPEN: 28/03–30/09. SIZE: 7 ha, 160 pitches (all with elec, 40 statics), 22 hot showers, 14 WCs, 13 French WCs, 1 CWP. ✆ &

Boating, evening entertainment.
PRICES: Caravan with family 84.00, Tent with two adults 51.00. CC: Amex, Euro/Access, Visa.
From A6, take Tournus exit and go south on N6 to Fleurville then take D933 towards Pont-de-Vaux for 1 km.

PONT-L'ABBE Finistère   1C

Camping Kerlaz 29720 Tréguennec.
Tel 02 98 87 76 79. English spoken.
OPEN: 01/04–30/10. SIZE: 1.3 ha, 66 pitches (all with elec, 13 statics), 6 hot showers, 10 WCs, 9 French WCs, 3 CWPs. &

Shop at 0.5 km. Restaurant at 0.5 km. Playground, ball games. Water sports, horse-riding, tennis and archery nearby.
PRICES: (1996) Caravan with family 119.00, Tent with two adults 70.00. CC: none.
From Pont-l'Abbé, go north-west to Ploneour-Lanvern. Then take the D156 to Tréguennec and site is well signposted.

Camping Kerlaz
near Pont l'Abbé
A haven on dramatic Brittany coast

Camping de Kergall 29750 Loctudy.
Tel 02 98 87 45 93.
OPEN: 01/04–30/09. SIZE: 1.3 ha, 100 pitches (80 with elec), 7 hot showers, 13 WCs, 19 French WCs.

Shop at 0.8 km. Restaurant at 1 km.

PRICES: (1996) Caravan with family 93.00, Tent with two adults 53.00. CC: none.
From Pont-l'Abbé, south along the coast on the D2 to Loctudy. (No motor caravans.)

Camping Menez Lanveur 29120 Combrit.
Tel 02 98 56 47 62. English spoken.
OPEN: 15/03–15/10. SIZE: 2 ha, 80 pitches (64 with elec), 7 hot showers, 9 WCs. ✆ &

Shop at 0.1 km. Restaurant at 0.1 km. Mobile homes available.
PRICES: (1996) Caravan with family 79.00, Tent with two adults 52.50. CC: none.
D44 north-east of Pont-l'Abbé.

Manoir de Kerlut 29740 Plobannalec.
Tel 02 98 82 23 89, Fax 02 98 82 26 49.
English spoken.
OPEN: 15/05–18/09. SIZE: 12 ha, 240 pitches (all with elec), 36 hot showers, 26 WCs. ✆ &

Restaurant at 1.5 km. Sauna, solarium; ball games; bike hire; entertainment HS.
PRICES: Caravan with family 170.00, Tent with two adults 110.00.
CC: Amex, Euro/Access, Visa.
D102 south from Pont-l'Abbé to Lesconil. Site is well signposted to the left just after Plobannalec.

PONT-L'EVEQUE Calvados   2A

Camping Le Brèvedent Le Brèvedent, 14130 Pont-l'Evêque.
Tel 02 31 64 72 88, Fax 02 31 64 33 41.
English spoken.
OPEN: 15/05–15/09. SIZE: 2.5 ha, 138 pitches (all with elec), 18 hot showers, 1 CWP. ✆

PRICES: (1996) Caravan with family 170.00, Tent with two adults 96.00. CC: none.

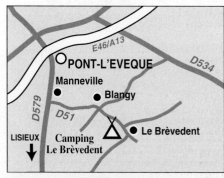

From Pont l'Evêque, take the D579 south towards Lisieux. Turn off left to Blangy on D51. Site is 2km past Blangy almost in Le Brèvedent.

Camping Domaine du Lac
14130 Blangy-le-Château.
Tel 02 31 64 62 00. English spoken.
OPEN: 01/04–30/10. SIZE: 7 ha, 70 pitches (60 with elec, 30 statics), 12 hot showers, 8 WCs, 1 CWP. **ㄴ**

PRICES: (1996) Caravan with family 110.00, Tent with two adults 65.00. CC: Euro/Access, Visa.
Travel south on D579 from Pont-l'Evêque towards Lisieux. Turn left on D51 to Blangy.

PONT-ST-ESPRIT Gard 5D

Camping Carrefour de l'Ardèche St-Remèze, 07700 Bourg-St-Andéol.
Tel 04 75 04 15 75, Fax 04 78 02 40 39.
English spoken.
OPEN: 01/06–15/09. SIZE: 3 ha, 90 pitches (70 with elec), 10 hot showers, 1 CWP. **ㄴ �**

PRICES: (1996) Caravan with family 120.00, Tent with two adults 69.00. CC: Amex, Visa.
From Pont-St-Esprit, north on the N86 to Bourg-St-Andéol and then D4 to St-Remèze.

PONTARLIER Doubs 3D

Camping de la Fôret route de Septfontaine, 25270 Levier.
Tel 03 81 89 53 46. English spoken.
OPEN: 01/06–15/09. SIZE: 1.8 ha, 70 pitches (40 with elec), 10 hot showers, 10 WCs, 1 CWP. **ㄴ ㄑ**

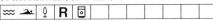

Shop at 0.5 km. Restaurant at 1 km.
PRICES: (1996) Caravan with family 106.00, Tent with two adults 60.00. CC: Visa.
From Pontarlier, 20 km east on D72. 1 km before Levier turn right on to D41 towards Septfontaine and campsite is signposted.

Camping Municipal de St-Point-Lac
25160 St-Point-Lac.
Tel 03 81 69 61 64. English spoken.
OPEN: 01/05–30/09. SIZE: 74 pitches (60 with elec), 10 hot showers, 10 WCs. **ㄴ**

Shop at 0.5 km. Restaurant at 0.5 km. Playground.
PRICES: (1996) Caravan with family 95.00, Tent with two adults 55.00. CC: Euro/Access, Visa.
From Pontarlier go south then turn west on to D437. After Oye-et-Pallet, take the D129 and follow signs to campsite.

PONTAUBAULT Manche 1D

Camping Vallée de la Selune 7 rue Mal Leclerc, 50220 Pontaubault.
Tel 02 33 60 39 00. English spoken.
OPEN: 01/04–20/10. SIZE: 1.25 ha, 100 pitches

(75 with elec, 4 statics), 6 hot showers, 9 WCs, 1 CWP. **ㄴ ㄑ**

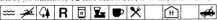

Restaurant at 0.5 km. Children's playground.
PRICES: (1996) Caravan with family 81.00, Tent with two adults 50.00. CC: none.
From the Avranche bypass travelling south, take turn-off for Cromel on D43, E2 then follow signs for Pontaubault.

PONTAUMUR Puy-de-Dôme 5A

Camping Plage de Confolant Confolant, 63380 Miremont.
Tel 04 73 79 92 76. English spoken.
OPEN: 01/05–15/09. SIZE: 2.5 ha, 11 hot showers, 9 WCs, 1 CWP. **ㄴ ㄑ**

PRICES: (1996) Caravan with family 101.00, Tent with two adults 54.00. CC: none.
From Portaumur, north on D987 to Grégottier then D19 and D19e to Miremont.

PONTCHATEAU Loire-Atlan 1D

Camping du Bois de Beaumard
44160 Pontchâteau.
Tel 02 40 88 03 36. English spoken.
OPEN: 01/03–31/10. SIZE: 1 ha, 25 pitches (all with elec), 3 hot showers, 5 WCs, 1 CWP. **ㄴ ㄑ**

Shop at 2 km. Restaurant at 1 km. Archery, table tennis; bike hire.
PRICES: Caravan with family 105.00, Tent with two adults 55.00. CC: none.
Beaumard is north-west of Pontchâteau, just off the N165. From Pontchâteau-Centre follow signs for Le Flêchage.

Camping Municipal Les Platanes
Les Chênes Verts, 44780 Missillac.
Tel 02 40 88 38 88, Fax 02 40 19 32 02.
English spoken.
OPEN: 01/07–31/08. SIZE: 2 ha, 60 pitches (40 with elec), 5 hot showers, 8 WCs, 3 French WCs. **ㄴ ㄑ**

Shop at 1 km. Restaurant at 1 km. Fishing; tennis and golf nearby.
PRICES: (1996) Caravan with family 76.00, Tent with two adults 37.00. CC: none.
Site is next to N165, north-west of Pontchâteau, on the way to Vannes from Nantes.

Castel Campingfay Château du Deffay, Ste-Reine de Bretagne, 44160 Pontchâteau.
Tel 02 40 88 00 57, Fax 02 40 01 66 55.
English spoken.
OPEN: 04/05–06/09. SIZE: 8 ha, 100 pitches (90 with elec), 22 hot showers, 19 WCs, 2 CWPs. **ㄴ ㄑ**

Pedal-boats, fishing, tennis.
PRICES: (1996) Caravan with family 153.00,
Tent with two adults 96.00. CC: none.
*From the N165, take the D33 west of Pontchâteau,
then go towards Ste-Reine-de-Bretagne. The
campsite is 1.5 km after the Calvaire, on the right-
hand side.*

PONTGIBAUD Puy-de-Dôme 5A

Camping Municipal route de Rochefort-
Montagne, 63230 Pontgibaud.
Tel 04 73 88 70 42, Fax 04 73 88 77 77.
English spoken.
OPEN: 15/04–15/10. SIZE: 4 ha, 100 pitches
(76 with elec), 7 hot showers, 7 WCs, 8 French
WCs, 4 CWPs. ⛄ ♿

Shop at 0.4 km. Restaurant at 0.1 km.
PRICES: (1996) Caravan with family 59.00,
Tent with two adults 37.00. CC: none.
*Situated on the Rochefort-Montagne road, D941.
400 m on the left after bridge over river.*

PONTOISE Val-d'Oise 2B

Parc de Séjour de l'Etang 10 chemin des Belles
Vues, Val d'Oise, 95690 Nesles-la-Vallée.
Tel 05 34 70 62 89. English spoken.
OPEN: 01/03–31/10. SIZE: 6 ha, 160 pitches
(140 with elec, 100 statics), 22 hot showers,
21 WCs, 13 French WCs, 10 CWPs. ⛄ ♿

Shop at 0.8 km.
PRICES: (1996) Caravan with family 138.00,
Tent with two adults 72.00. CC: none.
*From Pontoise take D927 to Hérouville then D79
to Nesles-la-Vallée. Signposted.*

PONTRIEUX Côtes-du-Nord 1C

Camping de Traou Meledern Traou Meledern,
22260 Pontrieux.
Tel 02 96 95 69 27. English spoken.
OPEN: all year. SIZE: 1 ha, 25 pitches, 3 hot
showers, 5 WCs, 1 CWP. ⛄ ♿

Shop at 0.2 km. Restaurant at 0.5 km.
PRICES: (1996) Caravan with family 60.00,
Tent with two adults 36.00. CC: none.
Signposted from Pontrieux, near the church.

PORNIC Loire-Atlan 1D

Camping International Le Patisseau
Le Pâtisseau, 44210 Pornic.
Tel 02 40 82 10 39, Fax 02 40 82 22 81.
English spoken.

OPEN: 01/05–13/09. SIZE: 4 ha, 232 pitches (220 with
elec), 25 hot showers, 26 WCs, 2 CWPs. ⛄ ♿

Sea 2.5 km.
PRICES: (1996) Caravan with family 171.00, Tent
with two adults 10500. CC: Euro/Access, Visa.
*Campsite is just off the roundabout junction of the
D751/D213, south-east of Pornic.*

LE PORTEL Pas-de-Calais 2B

Camping du Phare
quai de la Violette, 62480 Le Portel.
Tel 03 21 31 69 20. English spoken.
OPEN: 01/04–15/09. SIZE: 7 ha, 150 pitches
(all with elec, 250 statics), 30 hot showers,
46 WCs. ⛄

Restaurant at 0.5 km. Entertainment in HS.
PRICES: (1996) Caravan with family 122.00,
Tent with two adults 70.00. CC: none.
*South of Boulogne, cross the bridges towards Le
Portel. Follow the coast road to the cliff-top
campsite.*

POUANCE Maine/Loire 1D

Camp Municipal La Roche Martin
28 rue des Etangs, 49420 Pouancé.
Tel 02 41 92 43 97, Fax 02 41 92 62 30.
English spoken.
OPEN: 01/05–30/09. SIZE: 1.2 ha, 41 pitches
(40 with elec), 4 hot showers, 6 WCs. ⛄

Shop at 1 km.
PRICES: (1996) Caravan with family 57.00,
Tent with two adults 32.00. CC: none.
*Leave Pouancé towards La Guerche on D72. Site
is on the left bordering Etang de St-Aubin. Well
signposted.*

POUILLY-SOUS-CHARLIEU Loire 5B

Camp Municipal Les Ilots
42720 Pouilly-sous-Charlieu.
Tel 04 77 60 80 67, Fax 04 77 69 96 15.
OPEN: 01/05–30/09. SIZE: 2 ha, 6 hot showers, 6 WCs.

Shop at 0.5 km. Restaurant at 0.5 km. Good sports
facilities on site/nearby.
PRICES: (1996) Caravan with family 59.00,
Tent with two adults 30.00. CC: none.
Pouilly-sous-Charlieu is just west of Charlieu.

LE POULDU Finistère 1C

Les Embruns rue du Philosophe Alain,
29360 Le Pouldu.
Tel 02 98 39 91 07, Fax 02 98 39 97 87. English spoken.

France

OPEN: 10/04–20/09. SIZE: 4 ha, 180 pitches (150 with elec, 30 statics), 17 hot showers, 22 WCs, 2 CWPs. ✆ ᷁

Restaurant at 0.1 km. Mini-golf, ball games, billiards, table tennis.
PRICES: (1996) Caravan with family 134.00, Tent with two adults 75.50.
CC: Euro/Access, Visa.
Campsite is well signposted in Le Pouldu.

PRADES Pyrénées Orient 5C

Camping Bellevue 8 rue Bellevue, 66500 Ria-Sirach.
Tel 04 68 96 48 96.
OPEN: 01/04–30/09. SIZE: 2.2 ha, 94 pitches (60 with elec), 11 hot showers, 15 WCs. ✆ ᷁

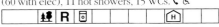

Shop at 0.5 km. Restaurant at 1 km. Table tennis.
PRICES: Caravan with family 94.00, Tent with two adults 50.00. CC: Visa.
Leave the N116 at Prades and take the D26a to Ria-Sirach. (No motor caravans.)

Camping Les Sauterelles Col de Millères, Fillols, 66820 Vernet-les-Bains.
Tel 04 68 05 63 72. English spoken.
OPEN: 01/06–30/09. SIZE: 3 ha, 75 pitches (15 with elec), 9 hot showers, 10 WCs, 2 French WCs. ✆ ᷁

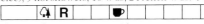

Shop at 5 km. Restaurant at 2 km.
PRICES: Caravan with family 95.00, Tent with two adults 51.00. CC: none.
From Prades, take D22/D27 leading to abbey of St-Michel-de-Cuxa. Follow the road signs for Fillols for about 6 km after the abbey. 2 km before Fillols turn left on the forest trail. An old cannon marks the campsite entrance.

PRAT-BONREPAUX Ariège 4D

Les Orpailleurs 09160 Prat-Bonrepaux.
Tel 05 61 96 61 62. English spoken.
OPEN: 01/05–31/10. SIZE: 1 ha, 20 pitches (all with elec), 2 hot showers, 4 WCs, 1 CWP.

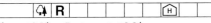

Shop at 0.3 km. Restaurant at 0.3 km.
PRICES: (1996) Caravan with family 60.00, Tent with two adults 35.00. CC: none.
On D117 between St-Girons and Salies-du-Salat.

PRAUTHOY Haute-Marne 3C

Camping du Lac Commune de Villegusien, 52190 Villegusien-le-Lac.
Tel 03 25 88 47 25. English spoken.
OPEN: 15/04–30/09. SIZE: 1 ha, 60 pitches (40 with elec), 4 hot showers, 6 WCs, 1 CWP. ✆ ᷁

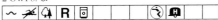

Shop at 1.5 km. Restaurant at 2.5 km.
PRICES: (1996) Caravan with family 71.00, Tent with two adults 35.00. CC: none.
From Prauthoy north on the N74 to Villegusien.

PRECY-SOUS-THIL Côte-d'Or 3C

Camp Municipal rue de l'Hotel de Ville, 21390 Precy-sous-Thil.
Tel 03 80 64 57 18, Fax 03 80 64 43 37.
English spoken.
OPEN: 01/04–31/10. SIZE: 1 ha, 40 pitches, 10 hot showers. ᷁

Shop at 0.3 km. Restaurant at 0.3 km.
PRICES: (1996) Caravan with family 77.00, Tent with two adults 35.00. CC: none.
Precy-sous-Thil is north-east of Saulieu on the D980.

PRIVAS Ardèche 5B

Camping Municipal Espace Ouvèze bd de Paste, route de Montélimar, 07000 Privas.
Tel 04 75 64 05 80, Fax 04 75 64 83 34.
English spoken.
OPEN: 30/03–15/10. SIZE: 5 ha, 166 pitches (84 with elec), 17 hot showers, 17 WCs, 2 CWPs. ᷁

Shop at 0.1 km. Restaurant at 1.5 km.
PRICES: (1996) Caravan with family 92.00, Tent with two adults 50.00. CC: Euro/Access, Visa.
On D2 at edge of Privas town, on the road to Montélimar going south-east. Signposted.

Camping Municipal Les Civelles d'Au St-Lager-Bressac, 07210 Chomérac.
Tel 04 75 65 01 86.
OPEN: 01/05–15/09. SIZE: 1.5 ha, 40 pitches (38 with elec), 4 hot showers, 4 WCs. ✆ ᷁

Shop at 2 km. Restaurant at 2 km.
PRICES: (1996) Caravan with family 72.00, Tent with two adults 31.00. CC: none.
From Privas take D22 to Chomérac, then turn right to St-Lager. Follow signs to campsite.

LE PUY-EN-VELAY Haute-Loire 5A/B

Camping Gérance Libre La Rochelambert, 43350 St-Paulien.
Tel 04 71 00 44 43, Fax 04 71 00 52 00.
OPEN: 01/04–30/09. SIZE: 3 ha, 100 pitches (all with elec, 18 statics), 10 hot showers, 15 WCs, 4 French WCs, 1 CWP. ✆ ᷁

New swimming pool built in 1995.

France

PRICES: (1996) Caravan with family 79.00,
Tent with two adults 52.00. CC: none.
*From Puy-en-Velay north on N102/906 for 14 km
to St-Paulien then east on the D13/D25 to La
Rochelambert and campsite.*

Municipal Camp Bouthezard BP 317,
43011 Le Puy.
Tel 04 71 09 55 09, Fax 04 71 02 62 08.
English spoken.
OPEN: 09/04–15/10. SIZE: 8 pitches (all with elec),
11 hot showers, 13 WCs. &

~	≠	🛉	R					

Shop at 0.5 km. Restaurant at 0.5 km.
PRICES: (1996) Caravan with family 73.00,
Tent with two adults 43.00. CC: none.
*Coming from St-Etienne, go towards Clermont
Ferrand or coming from Clermont, drive towards
St-Etienne.*

PUY-L'EVEQUE Lot   4D

Camping Le Ch'Timi Touzac, 46700 Puy-l'Evêque.
Tel 05 65 36 52 36, Fax 05 65 36 52 36.
English spoken.
OPEN: 15/05–30/09. SIZE: 3 ha, 70 pitches (all with
elec, 10 statics), 8 hot showers, 8 WCs, 2 CWPs. ℃

~	⚓	🛝	R	🔥	🍺	🍴	🏕	🏛

Shop at 1 km. Restaurant at 1 km. 25% discount in
LS and discounts for RAC members.
PRICES: Caravan with family 135.00,
Tent with two adults 76.00. CC: none.
*On the D911 between Fumel and Puy-l'Evêque.
Turn south on D8 following signposts. Both
Touzac and Camping Le Ch'Timi are signposted
from the D911.*

PYLA-SUR-MER Gironde   4C

Camping la Foret Oceane Route de Biscarosse
Plage, 33115 Pyla-sur-Mer.
Tel 05 56 22 73 28, Fax 05 56 22 70 50.
English spoken.
OPEN: 01/03–31/10. SIZE: 12 ha, 6 CWPs. ℃ &

≋	⚓	🛉	R	🔥	🍺	🍺	🍴	🏕	🏛	

Tennis, bikes available, volley ball, children club,
evening entertainment.
PRICES: (1996) Caravan with family 190.00,
Tent with two adults 110.00. CC: Amex, Visa.
*From Pyla-sur-Mer, go south towards La Dune du
Pyla and campsite is signposted.*

Camping Panorama 33115 Pyla-sur-Mer.
Tel 05 56 22 10 44, Fax 05 56 22 10 12.
English spoken.
OPEN: 01/05–30/09. SIZE: 15 ha, 300 pitches
(all with elec, 7 statics), 60 hot showers, 60 WCs,
7 CWPs. ℃ &

≋	⚓	🛉	R	🔥	🍺	🍺	🍴	🏕	🏛	

Tennis, mini-golf, sauna.

PRICES: (1996) Caravan with family 185.00, Tent
with two adults 141.00. CC: none.
Well signposted in the town.

Pyla Camping 33115 Pyla-sur-Mer.
Tel 05 56 22 74 56, Fax 05 56 22 10 31.
English spoken.
OPEN: 01/05–30/09. SIZE: 8 ha, 200 pitches
(120 with elec), 40 hot showers, 40 WCs,
5 CWPs. &

≋	⚓	🛉	R	🔥	🍺		🍴	🏕	🏛

PRICES: (1996) Caravan with family 171.00, Tent
with two adults 99.00. CC: Euro/Access, Visa.
*South from Pyla-sur-Mer towards Biscarrosse.
Third campsite on the right.*

QUETTEHOU Manche   1B

Le Rivage 50630 Quettehou.
Tel 02 33 54 13 76.
OPEN: 01/04–30/09. SIZE: 2 ha, 50 pitches (all with
elec, 45 statics), 6 hot showers, 12 WCs, 8 French
WCs, 3 CWPs. ℃

		🥤	R	🔥		☕			

Shop at 1.5 km. Restaurant at 0.5 km. Sea 0.4 km.
PRICES: (1996) Caravan with family 80.00,
Tent with two adults 42.00. CC: none.
*From Quettehou south on D14. Follow signs from
Morsalines.*

QUIBERON Morbihan   1C

Camping Bois d'Amour rue St-Clément,
56170 Quiberon.
Tel 02 97 50 13 52, Fax 02 97 50 42 56.
English spoken.
OPEN: 29/03–28/09. SIZE: 4.5 ha, 244 pitches
(all with elec, 46 statics), 33 hot showers, 54 WCs,
3 CWPs. ℃ &

≋	⚓	☀	R	🔥	🥤	☕		🏕	

Shop at 2 km. Restaurant at 2 km. Mobile homes
for hire.
PRICES: (1996) Caravan with family 216.00, Tent
with two adults 131.00. CC: Euro/Access, Visa.

Camping Municipal Penthièvre
56510 St-Pierre-Quiberon.
Tel 02 97 30 92 00, Fax 02 97 30 87 20.
OPEN: 01/04–31/10. SIZE: 20 ha, 665 pitches (502 with
elec), 81 hot showers, 70 WCs, 10 CWPs. ℃ &

≋		🥤		🔥	🥤	☕			

Shop at 0.1 km. Restaurant at 0.1 km. Boules.
PRICES: (1996) Caravan with family 117.00, Tent
with two adults 70.00. CC: none.
*Penthièvre is off the D768, approx 8 km north of
Quiberon on the peninsular.*

Les Joncs du Roch rue de l'Aérodrome,
56170 Quiberon.
Tel 02 97 50 24 37. English spoken.

OPEN: 30/03–30/09. SIZE: 2 ha, 163 pitches (148 with elec), 18 hot showers, 17 WCs, 2 CWPs. ☎ ♿

Shop at 0.8 km. Restaurant at 0.6 km. Sea 0.5 km.
PRICES: (1996) Caravan with family 164.00, Tent with two adults 94.00. CC: Euro/Access, Visa.
In Quiberon, go past the church on the left, take second right and then follow aerodrome and campsite signs.

Park-er-Lann 56510 St-Pierre-Quiberon.
Tel 02 97 50 24 93.
OPEN: 14/04–15/09. SIZE: 3 ha, 135 pitches (all with elec), 12 hot showers, 16 WCs, 1 CWP. ☎

Shop at 0.3 km.
PRICES: (1996) Caravan with family 152.00, Tent with two adults 88.00. CC: none.
From Auray over the causeway on the D768, just after St-Pierre the campsite is on the right.

QUILLAN Aude   5C

Camping Eden II Domaine de Carbonas, 11230 Villefort.
Tel 04 68 69 26 33, Fax 04 68 69 29 95. English spoken.
OPEN: 15/04–01/10. SIZE: 8 ha, 75 pitches (all with elec, 75 statics), 29 hot showers, 17 WCs, 2 French WCs, 1 CWP. ☎ ♿

Tennis, entertainments in HS; water sports nearby.
PRICES: (1996) Caravan with family 121.00, Tent with two adults 65.00. CC: Euro/Access, Visa.
From Quillan, D117 east to Puivert, D16 north to Chalabre, then turn left 1.5 km before Villefort.

QUIMPER Finistère   1C

Castel Camping L'Orangerie de Lanniron
29000 Quimper.
Tel 02 98 90 62 02, Fax 02 98 52 15 56. English spoken.
OPEN: 15/05–15/09. SIZE: 17 ha, 199 pitches (180 with elec, 20 statics), 24 hot showers, 32 WCs, 3 CWPs. ☎ ♿

Tennis, mini-golf, canoeing, archery, children's games; mountain bikes for hire.
PRICES: Caravan with family 192.00, Tent with two adults 118.00. CC: Euro/Access, Visa.
From the centre of Quimper follow signs for Quimper-Sud and Bénodet, then camping symbols. L'Orangerie de Lanniron is well signposted.

QUIMPERLE Finistère   1C

Bois des Ecureuils 29300 Guilligomarc'h.
Tel 02 98 71 70 98. English spoken.
OPEN: 01/04–31/10. SIZE: 1.5 ha, 40 pitches (20 with elec), 4 hot showers, 8 WCs, 2 CWPs. ☎

Restaurant at 3 km. Fishing, canoeing, walking, bicycles for hire.
PRICES: Caravan with family 85.00, Tent with two adults 47.00. CC: none.
From Quimperlé, east on D2. Just beyond Arzano turn left on to D222 to Guilligomarc'h.

Camping du Quinquis Le Pouldu, 29360 Clohars-Carnoët.
Tel 02 98 39 92 40, Fax 02 98 39 96 56. English spoken.
OPEN: 30/04–30/09. SIZE: 7 ha, 162 pitches (100 with elec, 40 statics), 13 hot showers, 20 WCs. ♿

Shop at 2 km. Restaurant at 1 km.
PRICES: Caravan with family 144.00, Tent with two adults 84.00. CC: none.
N165 from Quimperlé, exit Guidel. At La Guidel take D162 towards Clohars-Carnoët, continue over bridge Pont St-Maurice then turn left at crossroads onto D49 for Le Pouldu. Campsite is signposted 2 km on right.

Le Ty-Nadan route d'Arzano, 29310 Locunolé.
Tel 02 98 71 75 47, Fax 02 98 71 77 31. English spoken.
OPEN: 24/05–05/09. SIZE: 12 ha, 140 pitches (80 with elec), 34 hot showers, 34 WCs, 2 French WCs, 3 CWPs. ☎ ♿

Boating, canoeing, fishing, sauna, tennis.
PRICES: Caravan with family 177.00, Tent with two adults 107.00. CC: Euro/Access, Visa.
From Quimperlé go to Arzano on D22 and then follow signs to Locunolé.

RAMBOUILLET Yvelines   2D

Camping Municipal de l'Etang d'Or
rue du Château d'Eau, 78120 Rambouillet.
Tel 01 30 41 07 34, Fax 01 34 83 15 36. English spoken.
OPEN: all year. SIZE: 5 ha, 220 pitches (180 with elec, 80 statics), 20 hot showers, 22 WCs, 4 CWPs. ☎ ♿

Shop at 1.5 km. Restaurant at 1.5 km.
PRICES: (1996) Caravan with family 108.00, Tent with two adults 61.50. CC: none.
Rambouillet is on the N10, north-east of Chartres.

Camping Municipal de l'Etang d'Or

in forest-encircled Rambouillet

Visit the sumptuous château and unique model museum

France

RAON-L'ETAPE Vosges   3D

Camp Beaulieu sur l'Eau rue de Trieuche,
88480 Etival-Clairefontaine.
Tel 03 29 41 53 51, Fax 03 29 41 53 51.
English spoken.
OPEN: all year. SIZE: 1.7 ha, 66 pitches (58 with elec, 17 statics), 4 hot showers, 6 WCs, 4 French WCs, 1 CWP. ✆ ⅋

Restaurant at 2 km.
PRICES: (1996) Caravan with family 84.00, Tent with two adults 48.00. CC: none.
South of Raon-l'Etape on the N59, exit Etival-Clairefontaine and follow signs to campsite.

ILE DE RE

ARS Charente-Marit   4A

Camping du Soleil 17590 Ars, Ile de Ré.
Tel 05 46 29 40 62, Fax 05 46 29 41 74.
OPEN: all year. SIZE: 2 ha, 18 hot showers, 22 WCs. ✆ ⅋

PRICES: (1996) Caravan with family 170.25, Tent with two adults 119.00. CC: Amex.
Ars is 24 km from the causeway crossing to the island, next to La Rochelle.

LE BOIS-PLAGE Charente-Marit   4A

Camping Interlude Plage de Gros Jonc, 17580 Le Bois-Plage, Ile de Ré.
Tel 05 46 09 18 22, Fax 05 46 09 23 38.
English spoken.
OPEN: 06/04–30/09. SIZE: 7 ha, 300 pitches (255 with elec, 45 statics), 39 hot showers, 27 WCs, 4 CWPs. ⅋

Sauna, fitness centre.
PRICES: (1996) Caravan with family 238.00, Tent with two adults 184.00. CC: Euro/Access, Visa.
From La Rochelle go over the Pont de l'Ile; the campsite is 15 km from the centre of the island on the Atlantic coast.

LA FLOTTE Charente-Marit   4A

Camping Les Peupliers 17630 La Flotte-en-Ré.
Tel 05 46 09 62 35, Fax 05 46 09 59 76.
English spoken.
OPEN: 01/05–15/09. SIZE: 4 ha, 200 pitches (160 with elec, 20 statics), 19 hot showers, 30 WCs, 6 French WCs, 2 CWPs. ✆ ⅋

Shop at 1 km. Restaurant at 1 km.
PRICES: Caravan with family 215.00,

Tent with two adults 165.00. CC: Euro/Access, Visa.
From the bridge take D735 towards La Flotte-en-Ré. Campsite is before the village, on the left.

Ile Blanche Deviation de la Flotte,
17630 La Flotte, Ile de Ré.
Tel 05 46 09 52 43, Fax 05 46 09 36 94.
English spoken.
OPEN: 01/04–11/11. SIZE: 4 ha, 90 pitches (all with elec, 80 statics), 18 hot showers, 18 WCs, 3 CWPs. ⅋

Shop at 0.5 km. Restaurant at 1 km. Indoor swimming pool, tennis.
PRICES: (1996) Caravan with family 211.00, Tent with two adults 142.00. CC: Euro/Access, Visa.
From the bridge, go north towards St-Martin. Follow the diversion at La Flotte (do not enter village) and the campsite is signposted along that road.

ST-MARTIN-DE-RE Charente-Marit   4A

Camping de l'Océan La Passe,
17670 La Couarde sur Mer, Ile de Ré.
Tel 05 46 29 87 70, Fax 05 46 29 92 13.
English spoken.
OPEN: 01/04–30/09. SIZE: 7 ha, 330 pitches (all with elec), 36 hot showers, 37 WCs, 3 CWPs. ✆ ⅋

Shop at 2.5 km.
PRICES: Caravan with family 164.00, Tent with two adults 81.00. CC: Visa.
From St-Martin-de-Ré take D735 beyond La Couarde-sur-Mer towards Ars-en-Ré. Signposted.

END OF ILE DE RE RESORTS

REDON Ille-et-Vilaine   1D

Camp Municipal La Digue
St-Martin-sur-Oust, 56200 La Gacilly.
Tel 02 99 91 55 76.
OPEN: 01/05–30/09. SIZE: 1 ha, 78 pitches (all with elec, 28 statics), 6 hot showers, 9 WCs, 2 French WCs. ✆ ⅋

Shop at 0.3 km. Restaurant at 0.3 km. Children's playground.
PRICES: (1996) Caravan with family 46.00, Tent with two adults 21.00. CC: none.
From Redon, north on D773 to La Gacilly then west on D777 to St-Martin-sur-Oust. Campsite is near the canal and well signposted.

REIMS Marne   3A

Camp Municipal Val de Vesle
51360 Val-de-Vesle.
Tel 03 26 03 91 79.
OPEN: 01/04–15/10. SIZE: 1.2 ha, 50 pitches

France

(38 with elec, 20 statics), 4 hot showers, 4 WCs, 2 French WCs, 2 CWPs.

PRICES: (1996) Caravan with family 48.80, Tent with two adults 24.90. CC: none.
16 km south-east of Reims. N44 towards Chalons-en-Champagne then turn left on the D34 to Val-de-Vesle.

REMOULINS Gard 5D

Camping Municipal La Sousta
av du Pont du Gard, 30210 Remoulins.
Tel 04 66 37 12 80, Fax 04 66 37 23 69.
English spoken.
OPEN: all year. SIZE: 14 ha, 200 pitches (all with elec), 50 hot showers, 50 WCs, 5 CWPs. &

Shop at 2 km. 6-hole golf, canoes, tennis.
PRICES: (1996) Caravan with family 123.00, Tent with two adults 75.00. CC: Visa.
Take the A9, exit Remoulins, Pont-du-Gard.
Follow signs to campsite.

International les Gorges du Gardon
Vers Pont du Gard, 30210 Remoulins.
Tel 04 66 22 81 81, Fax 04 66 22 90 12.
English spoken.
OPEN: 15/03–15/10. SIZE: 4.8 ha, 190 pitches (160 with elec), 20 hot showers, 28 WCs, 9 French WCs, 2 CWPs. &

PRICES: (1996) Caravan with family 112.50, Tent with two adults 63.00. CC: none.
From Remoulins, take the D981 towards Uzès and after the Pont-du-Gard junction, drive 1 km and then turn left.

RENNES Ille/Vilaine 1D

Camping La Rivière chemin du Halage, Pont-Réan, 35580 Guichen.
Tel 02 99 42 21 91.
OPEN: 15/04–15/09. SIZE: 1 ha, 60 pitches (40 with elec), 4 hot showers (charge), 16 WCs, 2 CWPs.

Shop at 0.2 km. Restaurant at 0.2 km.
PRICES: (1996) Caravan with family 76.00, Tent with two adults 42.00. CC: none.
Take D177 out of Rennes south-west towards Redon.
Take Pont-Bruz exit and continue on to Guichen.

RETHEL Ardennes 3A

Camping Municipal L'Abbaye
08460 Signy-L'Abbaye.
Tel 03 24 52 87 73.
OPEN: 01/05–30/09. SIZE: 1.25 ha, 44 pitches (all with elec), 12 hot showers, 11 WCs. &

Shop at 0.3 km. Restaurant at 0.5 km.
PRICES: (1996) Caravan with family 58.00, Tent with two adults 27.00. CC: none.
23 km north of Rethel on the D985. Follow signs from town centre.

REVIN Ardennes 3A

Les Bateaux Quai Edgar Quinet, 08500 Revin.
Tel 03 24 40 15 65, Fax 03 24 41 20 98.
English spoken.
OPEN: 09/04–30/09. SIZE: 1 ha, 85 pitches, 5 hot showers, 4 CWPs.

Shop at 0.5 km. Restaurant at 0.5 km.
PRICES: (1996) Caravan with family 73.60, Tent with two adults 38.80. CC: none.
North of Charleville-Mézières.

RIBEAUVILLE Haut-Rhin 3D

Base Pierre de Coubertin
23 rue de Landau, 68150 Ribeauvillé.
Tel 03 89 73 66 71.
OPEN: 01/03–01/11. SIZE: 4 ha, 260 pitches (all with elec), 27 hot showers, 30 WCs, 2 CWPs.

Shop at 1 km. Restaurant at 1 km.
PRICES: (1996) Caravan with family 120.00, Tent with two adults 65.00. CC: Euro/Access, Visa.

Camping Les Reflets du Val d'Argent route d'Echery, 68160 Ste-Marie-aux-Mines.
Tel 03 89 58 64 83. English spoken.
OPEN: all year. SIZE: 3 ha, 120 pitches (60 with elec, 10 statics), 11 hot showers, 12 WCs, 1 CWP. &

Restaurant at 1 km.
PRICES: Caravan with family 131.00, Tent with two adults 68.00. CC: Amex, Euro/Access, Visa.
From Ribeauville, go north-west on D416 to Ste-Marie-aux-Mines and then follow signs to campsite.

RIBERAC Dordogne 4B

Camping du Grand Etang 24410 La Jemaye.
Tel 05 53 90 18 51.
OPEN: 01/07–31/08. SIZE: 3 ha, 33 pitches (24 with elec), 2 hot showers, 3 WCs.

Shop at 0.3 km.
PRICES: (1996) Caravan with family 52.50, Tent with two adults 31.00. CC: none.
12 km south-west of Ribérac on D708.

Camping Municipal de la Dronne route d'Angoulême, 24600 Ribérac.
Tel 05 53 90 50 08, Fax 05 53 91 35 13.

France (vertical, right margin)

OPEN: 15/06–15/09. SIZE: 2 ha, 100 pitches (92 with elec), 8 hot showers, 16 WCs. ✆ &

Shop at 0.5 km. Restaurant at 0.5 km. Canoes and kayaks, mountain-bike tracks.
PRICES: (1996) Caravan with family 57.50, Tent with two adults 30.00. CC: none.
On the D708 towards Angoulême.

RIEZ Alpes/Hte-Prov   6C

Camping Ferme de Vauvenières
Vauvenières, 04410 St-Jurs.
Tel 04 92 74 72 24, Fax 04 92 74 44 18.
English spoken.
OPEN: 01/04–01/10. SIZE: 3 ha, 25 pitches (all with elec), 3 hot showers, 3 WCs, 3 CWPs. ✆ &

Shop at 1 km. Restaurant at 1 km. Children's playground, volley ball, boules.
PRICES: (1996) Caravan with family 78.00, Tent with two adults 39.00. CC: none.
From Riez head north to Puimoisson. After 1 km turn right to St-Jurs which is 5 km ahead on D108.

Centre Naturiste, Domaine d'Enriou
04500 St-Laurent-du-Verdon.
Tel 04 92 74 41 02, Fax 04 92 74 01 20.
English spoken.
OPEN: 15/05–15/09. SIZE: 150 ha, 100 pitches (45 with elec), 14 hot showers, 12 WCs, 1 CWP. ✆

Shop at 4 km. Restaurant at 4 km. Canoeing, archery, guided tours in the Gorges du Verdon.
PRICES: (1996) Caravan with family 196.00, Tent with two adults 88.00. CC: none.
East of D11. 3 km from Quinson on the Riez to Quinson road, turn left. Campsite is 2 km from St-Laurent-du-Verdon and well signposted.

Côteau de la Marine 04730 Montpézat-Montagnac.
Tel 04 92 77 53 33, Fax 04 42 29 03 22.
English spoken.
OPEN: 01/05–15/09. SIZE: 10 ha, 200 pitches (all with elec, 4 statics), 34 hot showers, 30 WCs, 3 CWPs. ✆ &

Shop at 15 km. Tennis, canoeing, table tennis, basketball.
PRICES: (1996) Caravan with family 160.00, Tent with two adults 130.00. CC: Euro/Access, Visa.
South of Riez on D11, then left on to D211 to Montpézat.

RIOM Puy-de-Dôme   5A

Camping Clos de Balanède route de la Piscine, 63140 Châtel-Guyon.
Tel 04 73 86 02 47, Fax 04 73 86 18 46. English spoken.

OPEN: 10/04–05/10. SIZE: 4 ha, 285 pitches (250 with elec, 4 statics), 29 hot showers, 31 WCs, 48 French WCs, 8 CWPs. ✆ &

Shop at 1.5 km. 30% discount in LS.
PRICES: (1996) Caravan with family 110.00, Tent with two adults 60.00. CC: Euro/Access, Visa.
On A71 take Riom exit towards Châtel-Guyon (D685).

Camping Clos de Balanède

near Riom

Tranquillity in the Volcanic Park!

Camping Le Colombier Aubiat, 63260 Aigueperse.
Tel 04 73 97 21 16. English spoken.
OPEN: 15/05–15/09. SIZE: 1 ha, 50 pitches (24 with elec), 4 hot showers, 8 WCs, 1 CWP. &

PRICES: (1996) Caravan with family 79.00. CC: none.
Aubiat is just off the N9, north of Riom. Site is signposted.

RIVES Isère   5B

Camping Municipal Le Verdon
185 av de la Piscine, 38140 Renage.
Tel 04 76 91 48 02. English spoken.
OPEN: 01/04–15/10. SIZE: 2 ha, 75 pitches (all with elec, 12 statics), 6 hot showers, 8 WCs, 8 CWPs. ✆

Shop at 0.8 km. Restaurant at 0.5 km. Swimming pool nearby.
PRICES: Caravan with family 90.00, Tent with two adults 48.00. CC: none.
From Rives cross N85 on to D45 to Renage.

ROANNE Loire   5B

La Belle Etoile St-Alban-les-Eaux, 42370 Renaison.
Tel 04 77 65 84 07.
OPEN: 01/05–30/09. SIZE: 0.6 ha, 30 pitches (all with elec, 3 statics), 2 hot showers (charge), 4 WCs, 1 CWP.

Shop at 1.5 km. Restaurant at 1.5 km.
PRICES: (1996) Caravan with family 78.00, Tent with two adults 42.00. CC: none.
From Roanne westwards on the D9 towards Vichy.

LA ROCHE-DERRIEN Côtes-du-Nord 1A

Les Prajou 22450 La Roche-Derrien.
Tel 02 96 91 36 31, Fax 02 96 91 39 03.

OPEN: 15/06–15/09. SIZE: 33 pitches (28 with elec), 2 hot showers, 6 WCs, 4 CWPs. ℂ ௬

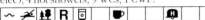

Shop at 0.8 km. Restaurant at 0.5 km. Canoeing nearby.
PRICES: (1996) Caravan with family 56.50, Tent with two adults 30.90. CC: none.
From the city centre, take the road opposite the 'Credit Agricole' and follow the signs.

ROCHEFORT-EN-TERRE Morbihan 1D

Camping du Moulin-Neuf
56220 Rochefort-en-Terre.
Tel 02 97 43 37 52, Fax 02 97 43 35 45.
English spoken.
OPEN: 01/04–30/09. SIZE: 2.5 ha, 60 pitches (44 with elec), 13 hot showers, 10 WCs, 1 CWP. ℂ ௬

Restaurant at 0.5 km. Tennis, basketball, table tennis, playground.
PRICES: (1996) Caravan with family 133.00, Tent with two adults 80.00. CC: none.
From Rochefort-en-Terre, go south on the D774. Campsite is on the right-hand side.

ROCHEFORT-MONTAGNE Puy-de-D 5A

Camping de la Haute Sioule St-Bonnet-Près-Orcival, 63210 Rochefort-Montagne.
Tel 04 73 65 83 32, Fax 04 73 65 85 19.
English spoken.
OPEN: 01/04–30/10. SIZE: 3 ha, 70 pitches (60 with elec), 4 hot showers, 9 WCs, 1 CWP.

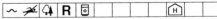

Shop at 0.1 km. Restaurant at 0.1 km. Mini-golf, table tennis.
PRICES: (1996) Caravan with family 81.00, Tent with two adults 80.00. CC: none.
From Rochefort-Montagne, north-east on D216. Signposted in St-Bonnet.

LA ROCHELLE Charente-Marit 4A

Camping du Port 17170 La Ronde.
Tel 05 46 27 82 78. English spoken.
OPEN: 01/04–30/09. SIZE: 1 ha, 25 pitches (all with elec), 5 hot showers, 5 WCs, 1 CWP. ௬

Shop at 0.2 km.
PRICES: Caravan with family 79.00, Tent with two adults 41.00. CC: none.
From La Rochelle take N11 towards Niort. Turn left on to D116 to La Ronde.

Camping-Village La Taillée
3 rue du Bois-Gaillard, 17290 Aigrefeuille-d'Aunis.
Tel 05 46 35 50 88.
OPEN: 01/06–15/09. SIZE: 1.6 ha, 59 pitches (all with elec), 9 hot showers, 12 WCs, 1 CWP. ℂ ௬

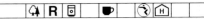

Shop at 0.4 km. Restaurant at 0.4 km. 18-hole mini-golf, children's playground.
PRICES: (1996) Caravan with family 107.50, Tent with two adults 56.00. CC: Euro/Access, Visa.
South-east of La Rochelle to the north of the D939.

Les Sables chemin du Pontreau, 17440 Aytré.
Tel 05 46 45 40 30, Fax 05 46 44 19 33.
English spoken.
OPEN: 01/06–15/09. SIZE: 5 ha, 250 pitches (all with elec), 30 hot showers, 30 WCs, 3 CWPs. ℂ ௬

Shop at 1.5 km. Flume.
PRICES: (1996) Caravan with family 137.00, Tent with two adults 110.00. CC: none.
Aytré is to the south of La Rochelle on D937.

Camping Les Sables
with pool ★ ★ ★
near La Rochelle
On Aytré beach

France

Le Trepied du Plomb 17137 L'Houmeau.
Tel 05 46 50 90 82. English spoken.
OPEN: 20/05–26/09. SIZE: 2 ha, 132 pitches (70 with elec), 16 hot showers, 18 WCs, 20 French WCs, 2 CWPs.

Shop at 0.3 km. Restaurant at 0.3 km.
PRICES: (1996) Caravan with family 106.00, Tent with two adults 62.00. CC: none.
From La Rochelle on N237 towards Ile-de-Ré, take exit for Lagord and follow signs.

RODEZ Aveyron 5C

Camping de Layoule 12000 Rodez.
Tel 05 65 67 09 52.
OPEN: 01/06–30/09. SIZE: 3 ha, 80 pitches (all with elec), 16 hot showers, 9 WCs, 2 CWPs. ℂ ௬

Shop at 0.8 km. Restaurant at 1 km.
PRICES: (1996) Caravan with family 78.00, Tent with two adults 46.00. CC: none.
Follow signs to 'zone industrielle' from Rodez.

Terrasses du Lac route du Vibal,
12290 Pont-de-Salars.
Tel 05 65 46 88 18, Fax 05 65 46 85 38. English spoken.
OPEN: 15/06–15/09. SIZE: 6 ha, 180 pitches (160 with elec, 30 statics), 33 hot showers, 40 WCs, 4 CWPs. ℂ ௬

Fishing, water sports, entertainment.

PRICES: Caravan with family 153.00, Tent with two adults 95.00. CC: Euro/Access, Visa.
N88 south from Rodez to La Primaube, then D911 to Pont-de-Salars.

ROMANS-SUR-ISERE Drôme 5B

Camping Municipal de Romans Les Chasses, 26100 Romans-sur-Isère.
Tel 04 75 72 35 27. English spoken.
OPEN: 01/05–30/09. SIZE: 1 ha, 40 pitches (all with elec), 4 hot showers, 6 WCs, 4 French WCs, 4 CWPs. &

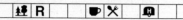

Shop at 1 km.
PRICES: (1996) Caravan with family 70.30, Tent with two adults 38.10. CC: none.
North-east of Romans-sur-Isere on the N92 to St-Paul-les-Romans. The site is on the left.

LA ROQUE-D'ANTHERON 5D

Camping Caravan Domaine des Iscles 13640 La Roque-d'Anthéron.
Tel 04 42 50 44 25, Fax 04 42 50 56 29.
English spoken.
OPEN: 01/03–15/10. SIZE: 10 ha, 270 pitches (all with elec, 20 statics), 30 hot showers, 30 WCs, 3 CWPs. & &

PRICES: (1996) Caravan with family 166.00, Tent with two adults 114.00. CC: Amex, Euro/Access, Visa.
From Sénas, take the N7 south-east towards Aix-en-Provence. At Pont-Royal turn right on the D561 to La Roque-d'Anthéron.

Camping Silvacane en Provence Silvacane en Provence, 13640 La Roque-d'Anthéron.
Tel 04 42 50 40 54, Fax 04 42 50 43 75.
English spoken.
OPEN: all year. SIZE: 3.5 ha, 130 pitches (all with elec), 18 hot showers, 26 WCs, 2 CWPs. & &

Restaurant at 0.3 km. River 1 km.
PRICES: Caravan with family 166.00, Tent with two adults 114.00. CC: Amex, Euro/Access, Visa.
Go north-east of Lambesc on D67a to La Roque-d'Anthéron and then follow signs to campsite.

ROQUEBRUNE-SUR-ARGENS Var 6C

Camping de Vaudois D7, 83520 Roquebrune-sur-Argens.
Tel 04 94 81 37 70. English spoken.
OPEN: 15/05–30/09. SIZE: 3 ha, 50 pitches, 6 hot showers (charge), 12 WCs, 1 CWP. &

Restaurant at 1 km. Mini-golf; fishing.

PRICES: (1996) Caravan with family 115.00, Tent with two adults 70.00. CC: none.
From motorway, take exit for Roquebrune-sur-Argens and St-Aygulf.

Camping des Pêcheurs
83520 Roquebrune-sur-Argens.
Tel 04 94 45 71 25, Fax 04 94 81 65 13.
English spoken.
OPEN: 01/05–30/09. SIZE: 3 ha, 150 pitches (all with elec), 32 hot showers, 30 WCs, 2 CWPs. & &

Kayaks, mini-club and water-skiing.
PRICES: (1996) Caravan with family 193.00, Tent with two adults 135.00. CC: none.
Leave motorway at Le Muy and take the D7 to Roquebrune-sur-Argens. Campsite is on the lake near the village.

Camping Lei Suves
83520 Roquebrune-sur-Agens.
Tel 04 94 45 43 95, Fax 04 94 81 63 13.
English spoken.
OPEN: 15/03–15/10. SIZE: 8 ha, 310 pitches (all with elec, 20 statics), 21 hot showers, 25 WCs, 2 CWPs. & &

Tennis, entertainment.
PRICES: Caravan with family 212.50, Tent with two adults 147.00. CC: Euro/Access, Visa.
Leave the A8 at Le Muy and take the N7 towards Fréjus. Campsite is signposted after 5 km with a left turn at the crossroads.

Moulin des Iscles
83520 Roquebrune-sur-Agens.
Tel 04 94 45 70 74, Fax 04 94 45 46 09.
English spoken.
OPEN: 01/04–30/09. SIZE: 2 ha, 90 pitches (all with elec, 5 statics), 13 hot showers, 14 WCs, 6 CWPs. & & '

PRICES: (1996) Tent with two adults 100.00. CC: none.
Coming from the motorway into Roquebrune, cross over a small bridge, turn left and the campsite is signposted from there.

ROQUEFORT Landes 4D

Camping Le Pin route de Roquefort, 40240 St-Justin.
Tel 05 58 44 88 91, Fax 05 58 44 88 91.
English spoken.
OPEN: 01/03–30/11. SIZE: 3 ha, 50 pitches (all with elec), 9 hot showers, 10 WCs, 2 CWPs. & &

PRICES: (1996) Caravan with family 144.00, Tent with two adults 80.00. CC: none.

On the left 2 km north of St-Justin towards Roquefort (D626).

ROSCOFF Finistère 1C

Camping Manoir de Kerestat
Kerestat, 29680 Roscoff.
Tel 02 98 69 71 92, Fax 02 98 69 71 92.
English spoken.
OPEN: 01/07–15/09. SIZE: 2 ha, 45 pitches (16 with elec), 8 hot showers, 5 WCs, 5 CWPs. ⌕

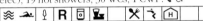

Shop at 0.8 km. Restaurant at 1 km. Free tennis; sea 500m.
PRICES: Caravan with family 142.00, Tent with two adults 102.00. CC: none.
The site is less than 2 km from ferry terminal at Roscoff (Brittany Ferries). Head towards Morlaix and take the first minor road after the roundabout.

Camping Village de Roguennic
29233 Cléder.
Tel 02 98 69 63 88, Fax 02 98 69 63 88.
English spoken.
OPEN: 01/04–01/10. SIZE: 8 ha, 300 pitches (250 with elec), 19 hot showers, 30 WCs, 1 CWP. ⌕ &

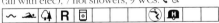

PRICES: Caravan with family 97.20, Tent with two adults 56.20. CC: Euro/Access, Visa.
From Roscoff go to St-Pol-de-Léon, then to Cléder and follow the signs.

ROSTRENEN Côtes-du-Nord 1C

Camping Tost Aven
Le Bout du Pont, 22570 Gouarec.
Tel 02 96 24 85 42. English spoken.
OPEN: 01/04–31/12. SIZE: 2.5 ha, 100 pitches (all with elec), 7 hot showers, 9 WCs. ⌕ &

Shop at 0.5 km. Restaurant at 0.5 km. Table tennis, boules, children's playground.
PRICES: (1996) Caravan with family 72.00, Tent with two adults 42.00. CC: none.
East of Rostrenen on N164. Campsite is well signposted.

Fleur de Bretagne Kerandouaron,
22110 Rostrenen.
Tel 02 96 29 16 45. English spoken.
OPEN: 01/04–31/10. SIZE: 6 ha, 100 pitches (30 with elec), 10 hot showers, 10 WCs, 1 CWP. &

Shop at 1.5 km. Fishing.
PRICES: (1996) Caravan with family 90.00, Tent with two adults 59.00. CC: none.
From Rostrenen take the D764 south-east towards

Pontivy, the campsite is situated approximately 1.5 km along this road on the left (signposted).

ROUEN Seine Marit 2A

Camping de l'Aubette 23 rue Vert Buisson,
76160 St-Léger-du-Bourg-Denis.
Tel 02 35 08 47 69. English spoken.
OPEN: all year. SIZE: 0.8 ha, 56 pitches (36 with elec), 4 hot showers, 8 WCs, 4 French WCs, 2 CWPs. ⌕ &

Restaurant at 0.2 km.
PRICES: (1996) Caravan with family 75.00, Tent with two adults 36.00. CC: none.
Take N31 Beauvais road east from Rouen and St-Léger is just south of Darnetal.

Le Clos Normand 235 route de Pont-Audemer,
27310 Bourg-Achard.
Tel 02 32 56 34 84. English spoken.
OPEN: 01/04–30/09. SIZE: 1 ha, 85 pitches (56 with elec), 10 hot showers, 6 French WCs. ⌕ &

Shop at 0.5 km. Mini-golf, tennis, table tennis, children's playground.
PRICES: (1996) Caravan with family 106.00, Tent with two adults 57.00. CC: none.
Bourg-Achard is 1 km from the A13, south-west of Rouen.

ROUSSILLON Isère 5B

Camping du Temps Libre
38150 Bougé-Chambalud.
Tel 04 74 84 04 09, Fax 04 74 84 15 71.
English spoken.
OPEN: 30/03–31/10. SIZE: 6 ha, 160 pitches (all with elec, 80 statics), 38 hot showers, 25 WCs, 2 CWPs. ⌕ &

Shop at 0.8 km. Restaurant at 0.8 km. Tennis, flume, mini-golf, trampolines.
PRICES: Caravan with family 175.00, Tent with two adults 95.00. CC: none.
South-bound on A7 from Roussillon, exit at Chanas and go towards Grenoble. Bougé-Chambalud is 6 km ahead on the D519.

ROYAN Charente-Marit 4A

Camping Côte de Beauté Plage de Suzac,
17132 Meschers-sur-Gironde.
Tel 05 46 06 02 29. English spoken.
OPEN: 01/04–30/09. SIZE: 4 ha.

PRICES: (1996) Caravan with family 146.00, Tent with two adults 100.00. CC: none.
From Royan south along the coast on the D25 to Meschers-sur-Gironde.

France

Camping Clairefontaine
allée des Peupliers, Pontaillac, 17200 Royan.
Tel 05 46 39 08 11, Fax 05 46 38 13 79.
English spoken.
OPEN: 27/05–10/09. SIZE: 4 ha, 33 hot showers, 3 CWPs. ℂ ♿

Restaurant at 0.3 km. Children's pool.
PRICES: (1996) Caravan with family 169.00,
Tent with two adults 129.00. CC: Amex,
Euro/Access, Visa.
Situated 300 m from the beach Royan Pontaillac.

Camping Clairefontaine
in Royan
. . . 300 m from Pontaillac beach!

Camping Ideal No 1 av de Suzac,
17110 St-Georges-de-Didonne.
Tel 05 46 05 29 04, Fax 05 46 06 32 36. English spoken.
OPEN: 01/05–15/09. SIZE: 8 ha. ℂ ♿

Playground, games room.
PRICES: (1996) Caravan with family 113.00,
Tent with two adults 92.00. CC: none.
*From Royan take road to St-Georges-de-Didonne.
Campsite is 2 km south of the town on the coast.*

Camping L'Escale 100 route de Semussac,
17132 Meschers-sur-Gironde.
Tel 05 46 02 71 53, Fax 05 46 02 58 30. English spoken.
OPEN: 01/04–31/10. SIZE: 6 ha, 300 pitches
(230 with elec, 140 statics), 24 hot showers. ℂ ♿

Restaurant at 1 km. Tennis, mini-golf; sea 1.2 km.
PRICES: (1996) Caravan with family 115.00,
Tent with two adults 75.00. CC: Amex,
Euro/Access, Visa.
*From Royan south to Meschers-sur-Gironde along
the coast. Site is well signposted.*

Camping La Ferme de Chez Filleux
Bardecille, 17120 Cozes.
Tel 05 46 90 84 33, Fax 05 46 06 92 84. English spoken.
OPEN: 01/05–15/09. SIZE: 2 ha, 150 pitches (5 with
elec), 12 hot showers, 15 WCs, 1 CWP. ℂ ♿

Shop at 3 km. Restaurant at 3 km. Tennis,
mini-golf; sea 3 km.
PRICES: (1996) Caravan with family 92.00,
Tent with two adults 58.00. CC: Amex,
Euro/Access, Visa.
*From A10 take exit 26 towards Royan. At Cozes go
towards Arces, then Semussac on D244.*

Camping Le Relax Taupignac, 17920 Breuillet.
Tel 05 46 22 75 11. English spoken.
OPEN: 01/05–15/09. SIZE: 1.9 ha, 86 pitches (80 with
elec, 14 statics), 13 hot showers, 2 CWPs. ℂ ♿

Shop at 2 km. Restaurant at 0.5 km. Games room,
table tennis, entertainment.
PRICES: (1996) Caravan with family 112.50,
Tent with two adults 62.50. CC: none.
*From Royan, north on D141/D140 towards
Breuillet for about 3 km.*

Camping Les Chênes
La Verdonnerie, 17600 Médis.
Tel 05 46 06 72 46, Fax 05 46 06 74 32.
English spoken.
OPEN: 09/04–01/10. SIZE: 6 ha, 150 pitches
(all with elec, 150 statics), 25 hot showers,
25 WCs, 10 French WCs. ℂ ♿

PRICES: (1996) Caravan with family 110.00,
Tent with two adults 64.00. CC: none.
*From Royan, first village on the main road Royan
to Saintes. At the end of the village, campsite is on
the right and signposted.*

Camping Les Coquelicots
rue des Coquelicots, 17200 Royan.
Tel 05 46 38 23 21. English spoken.
OPEN: 01/04–30/09. SIZE: 3 ha, 200 pitches
(171 with elec, 14 statics), 22 hot showers,
29 WCs, 2 CWPs. ℂ ♿

Restaurant at 2 km. Table tennis, boules, sports field.
PRICES: (1996) Caravan with family 92.00,
Tent with two adults 58.00. CC: none.
*From Royan take D733 Rochefort road. After
crossing D141 turn left along rue des Cendrilles.
Turn left at crossroads into rue des Coquelicots.*

Camping Park Hotel Bois Soleil
2 av de Suzac, 17116 St-Georges-de-Didonne.
Tel 05 46 05 05 94, Fax 05 46 06 27 43.
English spoken.
OPEN: 01/04–30/09. SIZE: 8.5 ha, 419 pitches
(all with elec, 190 statics), 74 hot showers,
49 WCs, 11 CWPs. ℂ ♿

Children's pool.
PRICES: (1996) Caravan with family 155.00, Tent
with two adults 110.00. CC: Euro/Access, Visa.
On the coast, just south of Royan.

Camping à La Source 58 rue de Royan,
17640 Vaux-sur-Mer.
Tel 05 46 39 10 51.
OPEN: all year. SIZE: 3.5 ha. ℂ

Restaurant at 2 km.

France

PRICES: (1996) Caravan with family 123.00, Tent with two adults 88.00. CC: Amex, Visa.
From Royan, drive towards La Palmyre. Vaux-sur-Mer is 2 km from the town centre.

Chantaco 21 av de Courlay, 17640 Vaux-sur-Mer.
Tel 05 46 39 12 08, Fax 05 46 39 46 21.
English spoken.
OPEN: 01/04–30/09. SIZE: 2 ha, 100 pitches
(all with elec, 20 statics), 12 hot showers, 25 WCs, 5 CWPs. &

≈ ⚓ 🛁 R 🖻 🅿 🛒 ✕ ⟲ 🏠

PRICES: (1996) Caravan with family 103.00, Tent with two adults 75.00. CC: Amex, Euro/Access, Visa.
From Royan take coast road towards St-Palais/La-Palmyre until reaching Vaux. Follow signs.

Le Clos Fleuri 17600 Médis.
Tel 05 46 05 62 17, Fax 05 46 06 75 61.
English spoken.
OPEN: 01/06–15/09. SIZE: 3.50 ha, 140 pitches

(110 with elec), 24 hot showers, 12 WCs, 6 French WCs, 2 CWPs. 📞 &

⚓ R 🖻 🛁 🅿 ✕ ⟲ 🏠

Sauna, mini-golf, archery, football.
PRICES: Caravan with family 181.00,
Tent with two adults 109.00. CC: none.
On N150 from Royan. Turn right to campsite on entering Médis.

SEE ADVERTISEMENT

Les Vignes 3 rue des Ardillers,
17570 St-Augustin-sur-Mer.
Tel 05 46 23 23 51. English spoken.
OPEN: 01/06–30/09. SIZE: 4 ha, 125 pitches
(50 with elec, 8 statics), 9 hot showers, 12 WCs, 4 CWPs. &

≈ ⚓ R ✕ ⟲ 🏠 🚗

Shop at 0.3 km. Fishing nearby.
PRICES: (1996) Caravan with family 81.00,
Tent with two adults 47.00. CC: none.
From Royan take the D141. Turn right on the D145 to St-Augustin.

RUOMS Ardèche 5D

Camping International Pradons, 07120 Ruoms.
Tel 04 75 39 66 07, Fax 04 75 39 79 08.
English spoken.
OPEN: 01/04–30/09. SIZE: 3 ha, 45 pitches
(5 statics), 9 hot showers, 12 WCs, 1 CWP. 📞 &

〜 ⚓ 🏨 R 🖻 🅿 ✕ ⟲ 🏠 🚗

Shop at 0.5 km. Canoeing.
PRICES: (1996) Tent with two adults 105.00.
CC: Amex, Euro/Access, Visa.
Just north of Ruoms on D579. Signposted.

Camping La Digue 07120 Ruoms.
Tel 04 75 39 63 57, Fax 04 75 39 75 17.
English spoken.
OPEN: 20/03–30/09. SIZE: 2 ha, 100 pitches
(all with elec, 10 statics), 9 hot showers, 9 WCs, 6 CWPs. 📞 &

〜 ⚓ 🏨 R 🖻 🛁 🅿 ⟲ 🏠

Restaurant at 0.8 km.
PRICES: (1996) Caravan with family 142.00, Tent with two adults 83.00. CC: Euro/Access, Visa.
Coming from Vallon-Pont-d'Arc on D579, site is just after Ruoms on the left.

Camping Laborie Pradons, 07120 Ruoms.
Tel 04 75 39 72 26.
OPEN: 01/05–30/09. SIZE: 3 ha, 100 pitches
(80 with elec), 12 hot showers, 10 WCs. 📞 &

〜 ⚓ 🏨 R 🖻 🛁 🅗

Restaurant at 0.6 km.
PRICES: Caravan with family 107.00, Tent with two adults 65.00. CC: none.
On D579, north of Ruoms. Campsite is signposted.

France

SABLE-SUR-SARTHE Sarthe 2C

Camp Municipal de l'Hippodrome Prairie du Château, All Quebec, 72300 Sablé-sur-Sarthe. Tel 02 43 95 42 61. English spoken. OPEN: 01/04–30/09. SIZE: 3 ha, 120 pitches (all with elec), 12 hot showers, 12 WCs, 4 CWPs.

Restaurant at 0.4 km. PRICES: Caravan with family 62.50, Tent with two adults 49.80. CC: none. *Well signposted in town.*

LES SABLES-D'OLONNE Vendée 4A

Camping du Bel Air Le Château-d'Olonne, 85100 Les Sables-d'Olonne. Tel 02 51 22 09 67, Fax 02 51 22 16 47. English spoken. OPEN: all year. SIZE: 5 ha, 250 pitches (200 with elec, 30 statics), 22 hot showers, 26 WCs, 1 CWP.

Restaurant at 2 km. Mobile homes for hire; heated pool. PRICES: (1996) Caravan with family 120.00, Tent with two adults 72.00. CC: Amex, Euro/Access, Visa. *Campsite is to the south of Les Sables-d'Olonne on the N160.*

Camping La Dune des Sables route de l'Aubraie, La Chaume, 85100 Les Sables-d'Olonne. Tel 02 51 32 31 21, Fax 02 51 33 94 04. English spoken. OPEN: 01/04–15/09. SIZE: 7 ha, 200 pitches (all with elec, 20 statics), 36 hot showers, 72 WCs, 27 French WCs, 2 CWPs.

Tennis; golf nearby. PRICES: (1996) Caravan with family 198.00, Tent with two adults 120.00. CC: Amex, Euro/Access, Visa. *Take D32 north from Les Sables-d'Olonne, then D80. Follow signs.*

Camping La Vertonne La Petite Jariette, 85440 Grosbreuil. Tel 02 51 22 65 74. English spoken. OPEN: 01/04–30/09. SIZE: 2.5 ha, 85 pitches (51 with elec, 11 statics), 11 hot showers, 11 WCs, 2 CWPs.

Shop at 1 km. Restaurant at 10 km. PRICES: (1996) Caravan with family 111.00, Tent with two adults 62.00. CC: Amex, Euro/Access, Visa. *From Les Sables-d'Olonne, take the Château d'Olonne road (D36) to Grosbreuil.*

Camping Le Brandais 85470 Brem-sur-Mer. Tel 02 51 90 55 87, Fax 02 51 20 12 74. OPEN: 01/04–30/10. SIZE: 2 ha, 100 pitches (all with elec), 21 hot showers, 21 WCs.

Shop at 0.8 km. Restaurant at 0.3 km. PRICES: (1996) Caravan with family 96.00, Tent with two adults 83.00. CC: none. *From Les Sables-d'Olonne, north on the D32, D80. Signposted from Brem-sur-Mer.*

Camping Le Chaponnet rue du Chaponnet, 85470 Brem-sur-Mer. Tel 02 51 90 55 56, Fax 02 51 90 91 67. English spoken. OPEN: 01/05–15/09. SIZE: 6 ha, 340 pitches (330 with elec, 55 statics), 51 hot showers, 60 WCs, 42 French WCs, 6 CWPs.

Shop at 0.2 km. Restaurant at 1 km. PRICES: (1996) Caravan with family 170.50, Tent with two adults 132.00. CC: Amex, Euro/Access, Visa. *From Les Sables-d'Olonne, take D32 north to Vaire; from Vaire take D54 to Brem-sur-Mer.*

Les Pirons rue des Marchais la Pironnière, Le Château d'Olonne, 85100 Les Sables-d'Olonne. Tel 02 51 95 26 75, Fax 02 51 23 93 17. English spoken. OPEN: 01/04–30/09. SIZE: 6 ha, 435 pitches (300 with elec, 80 statics), 50 hot showers, 48 WCs, 5 French WCs, 5 CWPs.

Shop at 0.2 km. Restaurant at 0.3 km. Tennis, dancing, entertainment, flume. PRICES: Caravan with family 136.00, Tent with two adults 100.00. CC: Euro/Access, Visa. *From Les Sables-d'Olonne head south to coast road D32B. 300 m from sea, follow signs.*

ST-AMANS-DES-COTS Aveyron 5A

Camping Les Tours 12460 St-Amans-des-Cots. Tel 05 65 44 88 10, Fax 05 65 44 83 07. English spoken. OPEN: 20/05–15/09. SIZE: 15 ha, 200 pitches (all with elec, 60 statics), 30 hot showers, 32 WCs, 4 French WCs, 4 CWPs.

Tennis; 20% discount in LS. PRICES: (1996) Caravan with family 187.00, Tent with two adults 124.00. CC: Amex, Euro/Access, Visa. *From St-Amans take D97 south-west to Colombiès, then D599 to the campsite.*

ST-AMANS-SOULT Tarn 5C

Camping La Vallée du Thoré 81240 St-Amans-Soult. Tel 05 63 98 87 31. OPEN: 01/05–30/09. SIZE: 1 ha, 45 pitches (all with elec), 3 hot showers, 8 WCs, 6 French WCs.

France

Shop at 0.3 km. Restaurant at 0.3 km.
PRICES: (1996) Caravan with family 54.00,
Tent with two adults 35.00. CC: none.
From Mazamet take N112 east towards
St-Amans-Soult.

ST-ANDRE-DE-CUBZAC Gironde   4B

Camping Le Port Neuf
33240 St-André-de-Cubzac.
Tel 05 57 43 16 44, Fax 05 57 43 16 44.
English spoken.
OPEN: 15/03–30/09 & 31/10–31/12. SIZE: 2.5 ha,
60 pitches (40 with elec), 9 hot showers, 8 WCs,
3 French WCs, 1 CWP.

Shop at 2 km.
PRICES: (1996) Caravan with family 93.00,
Tent with two adults 50.00. CC: none.
Signposted from St-André-de-Cubzac on D669,
going towards Bourg.

ST-ANTONIN-NOBLE-VAL Tarn/Gar   5C

Camping Les Trois Cantons Vivens,
82140 St-Antonin-Noble-Val.
Tel 05 63 31 98 57, Fax 05 63 31 25 93.
English spoken.
OPEN: 15/04–30/09. SIZE: 5 ha, 80 pitches (all with
elec), 8 hot showers, 10 WCs, 2 CWPs.

Restaurant at 3 km. Tennis, volley ball,
entertainment; mountain bike hire; mobile homes
for hire.
PRICES: (1996) Caravan with family 151.00, Tent
with two adults 87.00. CC: Amex, Euro/Access, Visa.
On D926 between Caussade and Caylus.

ST-AUBIN-SUR-MER Seine Marit   2A

Camping Municipal Les Garennes
Bourg Dun, 76740 Fontaine-le-Dun.
Tel 02 35 83 03 39, Fax 02 35 83 03 39.
OPEN: 01/04–30/09. SIZE: 1.5 ha, 90 pitches
(all with elec), 8 hot showers, 10 WCs,
13 French WCs.

Shop at 0.3 km. Sea 3 km.
PRICES: (1996) Caravan with family 62.50,
Tent with two adults 29.50. CC: none.
From St-Aubin, south on D237. Campsite is
signposted at Bourg Dun.

ST-AYGULF Var   6C

Camping au Paradis des Campeurs
La Gaillarde-Plage, 83380 Les Issambres.
Tel 04 94 96 93 55. English spoken.

OPEN: 25/03–01/10. SIZE: 1.50 ha, 125 pitches (all
with elec), 30 hot showers, 27 WCs, 2 CWPs.

50% LS discount.
PRICES: (1996) Caravan with family 166.00,
Tent with two adults 118.00. CC: none.
From St-Aygulf take N98 towards Les Issambres.

ST-BREVIN-LES-PINS Loire-Atlan   1D

Camping Le Fief 57 chemin du Fief,
44250 St-Brévin-les-Pins.
Tel 02 40 27 23 86, Fax 02 40 64 46 19.
English spoken.
OPEN: all year. SIZE: 7 ha, 400 pitches (all with elec,
80 statics), 44 hot showers.

Fitness activities, tennis.
PRICES: (1996) Caravan with family 172.00, Tent
with two adults 100.00. CC: Euro/Access, Visa.
From St-Brévin-les-Pins travel towards St-Brévin-
l'Océan.

ST-BRIEUC Côtes-du-Nord   1D

Camping Bellevue Lermot,
Pointe des Guettes, 22120 Hillion.
Tel 02 96 32 20 39, Fax 02 96 32 20 39.
English spoken.
OPEN: 01/04–30/09. SIZE: 1 ha, 55 pitches (all with
elec), 4 hot showers, 6 WCs, 1 CWP.

Shop at 2 km. Restaurant at 2 km. Fishing,
walking.
PRICES: (1996) Caravan with family 75.00,
Tent with two adults 39.00. CC: none.
From St-Brieuc, go east on N12 through Yffiniac
then turn left to Hillion. Site is at Lermot, on north
side of Hillion. Well signposted.

ST-CAST-LE-GUILDO Côtes-du-Nord 1D

Camping Le Châtelet
rue des Nouettes, 22380 St-Cast-le-Guildo.
Tel 02 96 41 96 33, Fax 02 96 41 97 99.
English spoken.
OPEN: 06/04–15/09. SIZE: 7 ha, 195 pitches
(190 with elec, 40 statics), 34 hot showers,
44 WCs, 5 CWPs.

Restaurant at 0.4 km. Lovely views; good facilities.
PRICES: (1996) Caravan with family 208.00, Tent
with two adults 136.00. CC: Amex, Euro/Access, Visa.
Between St-Malo and Cap Fréhel.

ST-CERE Lot   5A

Camping Le Soulhol 46400 St-Céré.
Tel 05 65 38 12 37, Fax 05 65 38 12 37. English spoken.

France

France

OPEN: 01/04–30/09. SIZE: 150 pitches (100 with elec), 18 hot showers, 28 WCs, 3 CWPs. &

Shop at 0.2 km. Restaurant at 0.2 km. River swimming, cycling, playground; swimming pool nearby.
PRICES: (1996) Caravan with family 91.00, Tent with two adults 59.00. CC: Amex, Euro/Access, Visa.
Well signposted in St-Céré.

Les Trois Sources Calviac, 46190 Sousceyrac.
Tel 05 65 33 03 01, Fax 05 65 33 06 45.
English spoken.
OPEN: 15/05–01/10. SIZE: 7.5 ha, 150 pitches (all with elec). ‹

PRICES: (1996) Caravan with family 146.00, Tent with two adults 86.00. CC: none.
From St-Céré take D673 east to Sousceyrac, D653 north, then D25 to Calviac. Campsite is signposted.

ST-CHERON Essonne 2D

Parc des Roches La Petite Beauce, 91530 St-Chéron.
Tel 01 64 56 65 50, Fax 01 64 56 54 50.
English spoken.
OPEN: 01/03–15/12. SIZE: 23 ha, 380 pitches (all with elec, 330 statics), 39 hot showers, 45 WCs, 4 CWPs. ‹ &

Tennis, table tennis, video games, playground; evening entertainment.
PRICES: (1996) Caravan with family 160.00, Tent with two adults 98.00. CC: none.
From St-Chéron take D132 south-east for 3 km towards Souzy. Campsite is convenient for St-Chéron railway station and well signposted.

Parc des Roches
near St-Chéron
Paris on the doorstep

ST-CIERS-SUR-GIRONDE Gironde 4B

Camping Chez Gendron
2 Chez Gendron, 33820 St-Palais-de-Blaye.
Tel 05 57 32 96 47, Fax 05 57 32 96 47.
English spoken.
OPEN: all year. SIZE: 1.5 ha, 50 pitches (all with elec, 6 statics), 4 hot showers, 6 WCs. &

Shop at 3 km.

PRICES: (1996) Caravan with family 99.00, Tent with two adults 60.00. CC: none.
St-Palais-de-Blaye is 2.5 km north-west of St-Ciers-sur-Gironde.

ST-CLAUDE Jura 5B

Camping Municipal du Martinet
39200 St-Claude.
Tel 03 84 45 00 40. English spoken.
OPEN: 01/05–30/09. SIZE: 3 ha, 90 pitches (all with elec), 18 hot showers. ‹ &

PRICES: (1996) Caravan with family 105.00, Tent with two adults 57.00. CC: none.
North-west of Genève.

ST-CYR-SUR-MER Var 6C

Clos Ste-Therese route de Bandol, 83270 St-Cyr-sur-Mer.
Tel 04 94 32 12 21, Fax 04 94 32 12 21. English spoken.
OPEN: 01/04–30/09. SIZE: 3 ha, 64 pitches (all with elec), 14 hot showers, 15 WCs, 1 CWP. ‹

Shop at 1 km. Golf, tennis and horse-riding 200 m; sea 3 km.
PRICES: (1996) Caravan with family 130.00, Tent with two adults 76.00. CC: none.
From Bandol D559 to St-Cyr-sur-Mer for 3 km. Signposted.

ST-DIE Vosges 3D

Camping de la Vanne de Pierre
La Vanne de Pierre, 88100 St-Dié-des-Vosges.
Tel 03 29 56 23 56, Fax 03 29 56 72 30.
English spoken.
OPEN: all year. SIZE: 3 ha, 118 pitches (all with elec), 11 hot showers, 9 WCs. &

Restaurant at 1 km.
PRICES: (1996) Caravan with family 104.00, Tent with two adults 52.00. CC: none.

ST-EMILION Gironde 4B

Camping La Barbanne 33330 St-Emilion.
Tel 05 57 24 75 80, Fax 05 57 24 75 80.
English spoken.
OPEN: 05/04–30/09. SIZE: 5 ha, 160 pitches (all with elec), 20 hot showers, 20 WCs, 2 French WCs, 3 CWPs. ‹ &

Restaurant at 3 km. Tennis, mini-golf, flume.
PRICES: (1996) Caravan with family 128.40, Tent with two adults 69.20. CC: Amex, Euro/Access, Visa.
In St-Emilion take the D122 towards Montagne. The campsite is 3 km ahead.

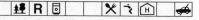

ST-FLORENTIN Yonne 3C

Terrain de Camping de l'Armancon
89600 St-Florentin.
Tel 03 86 35 08 13.
OPEN: 15/04–30/09. SIZE: 3.5 ha, 160 pitches
(all with elec), 18 hot showers, 14 WCs. &

Restaurant at 0.5 km. Mini-golf.
PRICES: (1996) Caravan with family 67.00,
Tent with two adults 53.00. CC: none.
Near the river, off N77, just south of St-Florentin.
Site is signposted.

ST-FLOUR Cantal 5A

Camping Hotel Le Belvédère 15260 Lanau.
Tel 04 71 23 50 50, Fax 04 71 23 58 93.
English spoken.
OPEN: 22/05–06/09. SIZE: 3.5 ha, 80 pitches
(all with elec, 6 statics), 18 hot showers, 17 WCs,
2 CWPs. & &

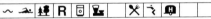

Excellent facilities on site/nearby; hotel
accommodation available; lake 0.5 km.
PRICES: (1996) Caravan with family 120.00,
Tent with two adults 105.00. CC: Amex, Visa.
From A75 take exit 28 (St-Flour-Nord) then
D921 St-Flour/Rodez. Lanau is 20 km south
of St-Flour, 5 km north of Chaudes-Aignes.

Camping Intl La Roche Murat
15100 St-Flour.
Tel 04 71 60 43 63. English spoken.
OPEN: 01/04–01/11. SIZE: 130 pitches (all with
elec), 12 hot showers, 12 WCs, 2 CWPs. &

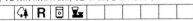

Restaurant at 1.5 km.
PRICES: (1996) Caravan with family 72.45,
Tent with two adults 39.00. CC: none.
Leave A75 at exit 28.

ST-GALMIER Loire 5B

Camping Val de Coise Les Campéoles,
42330 St-Galmier.
Tel 04 77 54 14 82, Fax 04 77 54 02 45.
English spoken.
OPEN: 01/04–30/09. SIZE: 3 ha, 100 pitches
(all with elec, 60 statics), 6 hot showers, 5 WCs,
1 CWP. &

Shop at 2 km. Restaurant at 2 km. Mini-golf, volley
ball, basketball.
PRICES: (1996) Caravan with family 130.00,
Tent with two adults 80.00. CC: none.
From St-Etienne take the A72 north towards
Roanne. After 5 km take the D12 to St-Galmier
and the campsite is clearly signposted.

ST-GENIEZ-D'OLT Aveyron 5C

Camping Marmotel 12130 St-Geniez-d'Olt.
Tel 05 65 70 42 20, Fax 05 65 47 41 38.
English spoken.
OPEN: 01/06–15/09. SIZE: 4 ha, 140 pitches (all
with elec), 30 hot showers, 30 WCs, 6 CWPs. & &

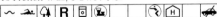

Shop at 0.4 km. Nursery; archery, boating, horse-
riding nearby.
PRICES: (1996) Caravan with family 150.00,
Tent with two adults 110.00.
CC: Euro/Access, Visa.
West of La Canourgue, on D988.

ST-GEORGES-SUR-LOIRE Maine/Loire 1D

Camping Municipal du Layon
St-Aubin-de-Luigne, 49190 Rochefort-sur-Loire.
Tel 02 41 78 33 28, Fax 02 41 78 68 55.
OPEN: 01/05–30/09. SIZE: 35 pitches (30 with elec),
6 hot showers, 3 WCs, 2 CWPs. & &

Shop at 0.1 km. Restaurant at 0.1 km.
PRICES: (1996) Caravan with family 37.00,
Tent with two adults 19.00. CC: none.
Cross river to Chalonnes-sur-Loire on D961, then
go east along river on D751 and follow signs to
campsite at St-Aubin-de-Luigne.

Camping St-Offrange route de Savennières,
St-Offrange, 49190 Rochefort-sur-Loire.
Tel 02 41 78 82 11. English spoken.
OPEN: 01/05–01/10. SIZE: 5 ha, 110 pitches
(all with elec, 6 statics), 12 hot showers, 16 WCs,
10 French WCs, 1 CWP. & &

Shop at 0.3 km. Restaurant at 0.2 km.
PRICES: Caravan with family 60.00,
Tent with two adults 47.00. CC: none.
St-Georges-sur-Loire is west of Angers on N23.
From St-Georges, head south over the Loire on
D961. Turn left (east) along south bank
(Angevine) to Rochefort.

ST-GERMAIN-DU-BEL-AIR Lot 4D

Camping Moulin des Donnes
46310 Concorès.
Tel 05 65 31 03 90, Fax 05 65 24 51 45.
English spoken.
OPEN: 01/04–30/09. SIZE: 66 pitches
(all with elec), 1 CWP. &

Shop at 0.4 km. Restaurant at 4 km. Boules,
fishing, volley ball, entertainment, hiking.
PRICES: (1996) Caravan with family 129.00, Tent
with two adults 83.00. CC: Amex, Euro/Access, Visa.
3.5 km west of St-Germain-du-Bel-Air on the D2.

France

ST-GILLES Gard 5D

Camping La Chicanette
rue de la Chicanette, 30800 St-Gilles.
Tel 04 66 87 28 32, Fax 04 66 87 46 14.
English spoken.
OPEN: 01/04–31/10. SIZE: 1.5 ha, 45 pitches
(all with elec, 20 statics), 14 hot showers, 16 WCs,
5 French WCs, 2 CWPs. ⚓ ♿

Shop at 0.1 km. Restaurant at 0.1 km.
PRICES: (1996) Caravan with family 123.00,
Tent with two adults 72.00.
CC: Euro/Access, Visa.
*St-Gilles is on the N572 between Arles and
Vauvert. Site is signposted from centre of St-Gilles.*

ST-GILLES-CROIX-DE-VIE Vendée 4A

Camping Bellevue 15 rue du Centre, Le
Feneuiller, 85800 St-Gilles-Croix-de-Vie.
Tel 02 51 55 11 35. English spoken.
OPEN: 15/06–15/09. SIZE: 7.5 ha, 11 hot showers,
15 WCs.

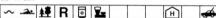

Restaurant at 0.4 km. Games room.
PRICES: (1996) Caravan with family 78.00,
Tent with two adults 65.00. CC: none.
*From St-Gilles-Croix-de-Vie take D754 to Le
Fenouiller.*

Camping Les Alouettes
route de St-Gilles, 85220 La Chaize-Giraud.
Tel 02 51 22 96 21.
OPEN: 09/04–15/09. SIZE: 3 ha, 96 pitches (70 with
elec, 10 statics), 10 hot showers, 9 WCs, 6 French
WCs, 1 CWP. ⚓ ♿

Shop at 2 km. Restaurant at 2 km. Sea 4.5 km.
PRICES: (1996) Caravan with family 114.00, Tent
with two adults 66.00. CC: none.
D12 to La Chaize-Giraud.

Domaine de Beaulieu route des Sables,
Givrand, 85800 St-Gilles-Croix-de-Vie.
Tel 02 51 55 59 46, Fax 02 51 33 94 04.
English spoken.
OPEN: 15/04–30/09. SIZE: 6 ha, 300 pitches
(all with elec, 30 statics), 50 hot showers, 50 WCs,
2 CWPs. ⚓ ♿

Flume, mini-golf, tennis.
PRICES: (1996) Caravan with family 198.00,
Tent with two adults 120.00. CC: Amex,
Euro/Access, Visa.
*From Nantes, take D937 to La Roche-sur-Yon and
D948 to Aizenay. From Aizenay D6 towards the
coast to St-Gilles-Croix-de-Vie. At St-Gilles (in the
direction of Bretignolles) 2 km on left.*

Domaine Le Pas Opton 85800 Le Fenouiller.
Tel 02 51 55 11 98, Fax 02 51 55 44 94.
English spoken.
OPEN: 15/05–10/09. SIZE: 6 ha, 200 pitches
(170 with elec, 6 statics), 25 hot showers, 25 WCs,
1 CWP. ⚓ ♿

Restaurant at 0.35 km. Flume, entertainment; river
fishing nearby.
PRICES: (1996) Caravan with family 160.00,
Tent with two adults 91.00. CC: Amex,
Euro/Access, Visa.
At the junction of D32 and D754, south of Challans.

ST-GIRONS Haute-Garonne 4D

Camp Municipal 31260 Salies-du-Salat.
Tel 05 61 90 39 93, Fax 05 61 90 47 43.
English spoken.
OPEN: 01/06–30/09. SIZE: 1 ha, 50 pitches (all with
elec), 5 hot showers, 8 WCs, 3 French WCs,
2 CWPs. ⚓ ♿

Shop at 0.2 km. Restaurant at 0.2 km.
PRICES: (1996) Caravan with family 70.00,
Tent with two adults 25.00. CC: none.
*From St-Girons, Salies-du-Salat is to the north-
west on the D117. The campsite is near the spa.*

Camp Municipal La Justale Mane,
31260 St-Girons.
Tel 05 61 90 68 18.
OPEN: 01/05–01/10. SIZE: 3 ha, 23 pitches (all with
elec), 5 hot showers, 3 WCs, 5 French WCs,
1 CWP. ⚓ ♿

Shop at 0.3 km. Restaurant at 0.3 km.
PRICES: (1996) Caravan with family 79.00,
Tent with two adults 45.00. CC: none.
*From St-Girons north-west on D117 towards
Salies-du-Salat. Campsite at Mane is well
signposted.*

Camping Le Haut Salat 09140 Seix.
Tel 05 61 66 81 78. English spoken.
OPEN: 03/01–15/09 & 15/10–20/12. SIZE: 2.5 ha,
90 pitches (80 with elec, 40 statics), 14 hot
showers, 5 WCs, 9 French WCs, 1 CWP. ⚓

Shop at 0.6 km. Restaurant at 0.6 km.
PRICES: (1996) Caravan with family 115.00, Tent
with two adults 60.00. CC: Euro/Access, Visa.
18 km south of St-Girons on D3. Well signposted.

ST-HILAIRE-DE-RIEZ Vendée 4A

Camping Les Biches route de Notre-Dame-de-
Riez, 85270 St-Hilaire-de-Riez.
Tel 05 51 54 38 82, Fax 05 51 54 30 74. English spoken.

France

OPEN: 20/05–15/09. SIZE: 13 ha, 400 pitches (380 with elec), 35 hot showers, 64 WCs, 2 CWPs. ℭ ⴕ

≋ ⟿ 🎣 R ⬚ 🍴 ☕ ✗ ⟲ ⟨H⟩

Tennis, fishing, mini-golf, flume, jacuzzi.
PRICES: (1996) Caravan with family 205.00.
CC: none.
From St-Gilles-Croix-de-Vie go north on D38 towards Notre-Dame-de-Riez.

Camping Riez de la Vie 9 av Parée Preneau, 85270 St-Hilaire-de-Riez.
Tel 05 51 54 30 49, Fax 05 51 55 86 58.
English spoken.
OPEN: 01/05–15/09. SIZE: 3 ha, 189 pitches (all with elec, 70 statics), 30 hot showers, 40 WCs, 4 CWPs. ℭ ⴕ

≋ ⟿ ⟨⟩ R ⬚ ⟨🍺⟩ ☕ ⟲ ⟨H⟩

Shop at 1 km. Restaurant at 1 km.
PRICES: (1996) Caravan with family 126.00, Tent with two adults 79.00. CC: Euro/Access, Visa.
From St-Hilaire-de-Riez, go towards St-Jean-de-Monts and look for signs.

Camping Sol-a-Gogo 61 av de la Pège, 85270 St-Hilaire-de-Riez.
Tel 05 51 54 29 00, Fax 05 51 54 88 74.
English spoken.
OPEN: 15/05–20/09. SIZE: 4 ha, 196 pitches (all with elec, 12 statics), 28 hot showers, 28 WCs, 2 CWPs. ℭ ⴕ

≋ ⟿ ⚲ R ⬚ 🍺 ☕ ✗ ⟲ ⟨H⟩

Flume, jacuzzi, private beach.
PRICES: (1996) Caravan with family 189.00, Tent with two adults 165.00. CC: none.
Follow the signs from the BP station in centre of St-Hilaire-de-Riez.

Le Chateau Vieux rue du Château, 85270 St-Hilaire-de-Riez.
Tel 02 51 54 35 88, Fax 02 51 60 05 34.
English spoken.
OPEN: 15/05–15/09. SIZE: 7 ha, 340 pitches (all with elec, 140 statics), 30 hot showers, 40 WCs. ℭ ⴕ

≋ ⟨⟩ R ⬚ 🍺 ☕ ✗ ⟲ ⟨H⟩

Indoor pool, jacuzzi, flume.
PRICES: Caravan with family 185.00.
CC: Euro/Access, Visa.
Between St-Jean-de-Monts and Les Sables-d'Olonne, 800 m from St-Hilaire-de-Riez.

Les Ecureuils 100 av de la Pège, 85270 St-Hilaire-de-Riez.
Tel 02 51 54 33 71, Fax 02 51 55 69 08.
English spoken.
OPEN: 15/05–15/09. SIZE: 4 ha, 174 pitches (all with elec, 56 statics), 38 hot showers, 29 WCs, 2 CWPs. ⴕ

≋ ⟿ ⟨⟩ R ⬚ 🍺 ✗ ⟲

Tennis, boules, table tennis, games room.

PRICES: (1996) Caravan with family 188.00, Tent with two adults 135.00. CC: none.
In St-Hilaire-de-Riez on D59, just north of St-Gilles-Croix-de-Vie.

La Parée des Joncs Sion-sur-l'Océan, 219 av de la Forêt, 85270 St-Hilaire-de-Riez.
Tel 02 51 54 32 92, Fax 02 51 54 47 85.
English spoken.
OPEN: 01/04–30/09. SIZE: 1.8 ha, 150 pitches (all with elec). ⴕ

≋ ⟿ ⟨⟩ ⬚ ⟨H⟩

Shop at 0.1 km. Restaurant at 0.5 km.
PRICES: (1996) Caravan with family 121.10, Tent with two adults 85.00. CC: none.
West of St-Hilaire-de-Riez, on the coast. Signposted.

La Petite Martinière (Aire Naturelle) 85270 St-Hilaire-de-Riez.
Tel 02 51 54 42 08.
OPEN: 15/06–15/09. SIZE: 1 ha, 25 pitches (24 with elec), 3 hot showers, 2 WCs, 3 French WCs. ℭ

≋ ⟿ 🎣 R ⟨H⟩

Shop at 2 km. Restaurant at 2 km.
PRICES: (1996) Caravan with family 62.50, Tent with two adults 32.00. CC: none.
Follow signs from the centre of St-Hilaire-de-Riez.

La Puerta del Sol Les Borderies, 85270 St-Hilaire-de-Riez.
Tel 02 51 49 10 10, Fax 02 51 49 84 84.
English spoken.
OPEN: 15/05–19/09. SIZE: 4 ha, 180 pitches (all with elec, 37 statics), 39 hot showers, 27 WCs, 3 CWPs. ℭ ⴕ

⟨⟩ R ⬚ 🍺 ☕ ✗ ⟲ ⟨H⟩

Tennis, entertainment, bicycles; chalets available.
PRICES: Caravan with family 198.00, Tent with two adults 165.00. CC: Amex, Euro/Access, Visa.
From Challans take the road to St-Gilles-Croix-de-Vie (D69). 5 km after Soullans the campsite is signposted on the right.

Riez à la Vie 85270 St-Hilaire-de-Riez.
Tel 02 51 54 30 49, Fax 02 51 55 86 58.
English spoken.
OPEN: 15/04–15/09. SIZE: 3 ha, 150 pitches (all with elec, 80 statics), 30 hot showers, 30 WCs, 4 CWPs. ℭ ⴕ

≋ ⟿ ⟨⟩ R ⬚ ⟨🍺⟩ ☕ ⟲ ⟨H⟩

Shop at 2 km. Restaurant at 2 km.
PRICES: (1996) Caravan with family 129.00, Tent with two adults 79.00. CC: Euro/Access, Visa.
From St-Hilaire go towards the coast in the direction of Sion for 3 km. Follow signposts.

ST-JEAN-D'ANGELY Charente-Marit 4B

Le Lizot St-Mandé-sur-Bredoire, 17470 Aulnay.
Tel 05 46 33 12 93, Fax 05 46 33 13 53. English spoken.

France

OPEN: 01/04–15/10. SIZE: 12 ha, 100 pitches (30 with elec), 11 hot showers, 11 WCs, 7 French WCs, 1 CWP. ℃ 占

| | | 🏕 | R | 🗇 | 🍺 | 👕 | ✕ | ⌦ | 🕀 | | |

Shop at 7 km. Naturist campsite.
PRICES: (1996) Caravan with family 125.00, Tent with two adults 85.00. CC: none.
From St-Jean-d'Angély to Aulnay-de-Saintonge on the D950. From Aulnay along the D129 to St-Mandé-sur-Bredoire. Campsite is signposted 1 km from St-Mandé on the left.

ST-JEAN-DE-LUZ Pyrénées-Atlan   4C

Camp Maya 64500 St-Jean-de-Luz.
Tel 05 59 26 54 91. English spoken.
OPEN: 15/06–15/09. SIZE: 1.5 ha, 50 pitches (40 with elec), 11 hot showers, 10 WCs. 占

| ≋ | | 🏕 | | 🗇 | | | | 🕀 | | |

Shop at 0.3 km. Restaurant at 0.2 km.
PRICES: (1996) Caravan with family 162.00, Tent with two adults 76.00. CC: none.
A63 south of Bayonne, 2 km after Guethary take the road on your right to quartier Acotz.

Camping Alegera 64250 Souraide.
Tel 05 59 93 91 80.
OPEN: all year. SIZE: 3 ha, 222 pitches (all with elec), 24 hot showers, 28 WCs, 2 CWPs. ℃ 占

| ∼ | ✕ | 🏕 | | 🗇 | 🍺 | 👕 | | ⌦ | 🕀 | |

Restaurant at 0.2 km. Mobile homes available.
PRICES: (1996) Caravan with family 104.00, Tent with two adults 56.00. CC: none.
Leave St-Jean-de-Luz on D918 towards Espelette. Souraide is just before Espelette.

Camping d'Iratzia chemin d'Erromardie, 64500 St-Jean-de-Luz.
Tel 05 59 26 14 89. English spoken.
OPEN: 15/03–30/09. SIZE: 4 ha, 280 pitches (252 with elec, 5 statics), 40 hot showers, 40 WCs, 25 French WCs, 5 CWPs. ℃ 占

| ≋ | ⚓ | 🏕 | R | 🗇 | 🍺 | 👕 | | | 🕀 | |

Restaurant at 1.5 km. Children's games, table tennis.
PRICES: (1996) Caravan with family 150.40, Tent with two adults 86.20. CC: Euro/Access, Visa.
From the centre of St-Jean-de-Luz, go over the railway bridge towards Plage d'Erromardie.

Camping de la Ferme Erromardie, 64500 St-Jean-de-Luz.
Tel 05 59 26 34 26. English spoken.
OPEN: 15/03–15/10. SIZE: 2 ha, 176 pitches (all with elec), 25 hot showers, 3 CWPs. ℃ 占

| ≋ | ⚓ | ⚑ | R | 🗇 | 🍺 | | ✕ | | | |

Shop at 1 km.
PRICES: (1996) Caravan with family 153.00, Tent with two adults 90.00. CC: Visa.

Take the St-Jean-de-Luz-Nord exit from A63 then go south on N10. The campsite is well signposted and on the beach.

Camping du Col d'Ibardin 64122 Urrugne.
Tel 05 59 54 31 21, Fax 05 59 54 62 28.
English spoken.
OPEN: 15/05–30/09. SIZE: 5 ha, 190 pitches (150 with elec), 26 hot showers, 22 WCs, 2 CWPs. 占

| | ⚑ | R | 🗇 | 🍺 | 👕 | | ⌦ | 🕀 | |

Restaurant at 0.8 km. Tennis.
PRICES: (1996) Caravan with family 156.00, Tent with two adults 96.00. CC: Euro/Access.

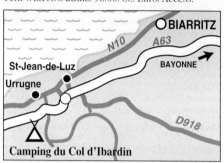

Camping du Col d'Ibardin

South on the A63. Take St-Jean-de-Luz-Sud/Urrugne exit. From Urrugne take D4 towards Col d'Ibardin for 3.5 km.

Camping International d'Erromardie
Plage d'Erromardie, 64500 St-Jean-de-Luz.
Tel 05 59 26 07 74. English spoken.
OPEN: 15/05–30/09. SIZE: 4 ha, 200 pitches (all with elec), 25 hot showers, 33 WCs, 4 CWPs. ℃

| ≋ | ⚓ | ⚑ | R | 🗇 | 🍺 | 👕 | ✕ | ⌦ | 🕀 | |

Shop at 1 km. Direct access to the beach; playground, boules; mobile homes for hire.
PRICES: (1996) Caravan with family 185.00, Tent with two adults 135.00. CC: Euro/Access, Visa.
1 km north of St-Jean-de-Luz. Follow camping signs from the N10.

Camping Merko-Lacarra
quartier Acotz, 64500 St-Jean-de-Luz.
Tel 05 59 26 56 76. English spoken.
OPEN: 01/04–31/10. SIZE: 2 ha, 11 hot showers, 18 WCs. ℃ 占

| ≋ | ⚓ | ⚑ | R | 🗇 | | 👕 | | | |

Shop at 0.05 km. Restaurant at 0.02 km.
PRICES: (1996) Caravan with family 127.50, Tent with two adults 68.00. CC: Visa.
From motorway take exit for St-Jean-de-Luz-Nord and follow N10 towards Bayonne. First left and follow signs.

Camping Playa Acotz, 64500 St-Jean-de-Luz.
Tel 05 59 26 55 85, Fax 05 59 47 75 21.
English spoken.

France

OPEN: 01/04–30/10. SIZE: 2 ha, 100 pitches (75 with elec, 15 statics), 10 hot showers, 110 WCs, 1 CWP. ✆ ♿

Shop at 1 km. Good LS reduction; mobile homes also available.
PRICES: (1996) Caravan with family 210.00, Tent with two adults 125.00. CC: Amex, Euro/Access, Visa.
From the motorway take St-Jean-de-Luz-Nord exit and follow the road to Bayonne. Take first left towards the beach.

Luz Europ quartier Acotz, 64500 St-Jean-de-Luz.
Tel 05 59 26 51 90. English spoken.
OPEN: 09/04–30/09. SIZE: 2 ha, 24 hot showers, 19 WCs, 3 CWPs.

PRICES: (1996) Caravan with family 132.00, Tent with two adults 74.00. CC: none.
Leave the A63 at St-Jean-de-Luz-Nord. Turn right and the site is 1.5 km on the left.

Les Tamaris Plage Acotz, 64500 St-Jean-de-Luz.
Tel 05 59 26 55 90, Fax 05 59 47 70 15.
English spoken.
OPEN: 01/04–30/09. SIZE: 1 ha, 30 pitches (all with elec), 14 hot showers, 9 WCs, 3 French WCs, 2 CWPs. ✆ ♿

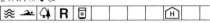

Shop at 0.1 km. Restaurant at 0.1 km.
PRICES: (1996) Caravan with family 225.00, Tent with two adults 130.00. CC: Visa.
Leave at St-Jean-de-Luz-Nord on the motorway towards Bayonne. After 500 m turn right to Acotz.

ST-JEAN-DE-MONTS Vendée 4A

Le Bois Masson rue Sables d'Olonne, 85160 St-Jean-de-Monts.
Tel 02 51 58 62 62, Fax 02 51 58 29 97. English spoken.
OPEN: 28/03–30/09. SIZE: 7.5 ha, 250 pitches (all with elec, 245 statics). ✆ ♿

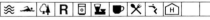

PRICES: (1996) Caravan with family 209.00, Tent with two adults 162.00. CC: Amex, Euro/Access, Visa.
From St-Jean-de-Monts, take D38 towards Les Sables d'Olonne. Campsite is 2 km from town centre.

Camping Plein Sud 85160 St-Jean-De-Monts.
Tel 05 51 59 10 40, Fax 05 51 58 92 29.
English spoken.
OPEN: 15/06–15/09. SIZE: 2 ha, 110 pitches (100 with elec, 20 statics), 20 hot showers, 20 WCs, 2 CWPs. ✆ ♿

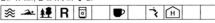

Shop at 0.3 km. Restaurant at 0.5 km. Tennis, entertainment, bar, TV.

PRICES: (1996) Caravan with family 142.00.
CC: Amex, Visa.
4 km from town centre towards Ile de Noirmoutier.

Camping Acapulco av des Epines, 85160 St-Jean-de-Monts.
Tel 02 51 59 20 64, Fax 02 51 59 53 12.
English spoken.
OPEN: 15/05–15/09. SIZE: 7.5 ha, 35 hot showers, 40 WCs, 5 CWPs. ✆ ♿

PRICES: Caravan with family 185.00, Tent with two adults 160.00. CC: Euro/Access, Visa.
Off the D38 heading for Les Sables d'Olonne. Turn towards the beach at Orouet and campsite is 300 m after Les Genêts. Well signposted.

Camping aux Coeurs Vendéens 251 rte de Notre-Dame-de-Monts, 85160 St-Jean-de-Monts.
Tel 02 51 58 84 91, Fax 02 51 68 56 61.
English spoken.
OPEN: 01/05–15/09. SIZE: 2 ha, 117 pitches (all with elec, 26 statics), 22 hot showers, 16 WCs, 2 CWPs. ✆ ♿

Mountain-biking.
PRICES: (1996) Caravan with family 163.00, Tent with two adults 153. CC: Euro/Access, Visa.
From St-Jean-de-Monts take D38 towards Notre-Dame-de-Monts for 4 km. Site is signposted to the left.

Camping Caravaning La Yole chemin des Bosses, Orouet, 85160 St-Jean-de-Monts.
Tel 02 51 58 67 17, Fax 02 51 59 05 35.
English spoken.
OPEN: 15/05–15/09. SIZE: 7 ha, 278 pitches (all with elec, 10 statics), 44 hot showers, 41 WCs, 2 CWPs. ✆ ♿

Tennis, sports field, indoor pool, flume, jacuzzi.
PRICES: (1996) Caravan with family 185.00, Tent with two adults 131.00. CC: Euro/Access, Visa.
From St-Jean-de-Monts go south on D38 to St-Gilles-Croix-de-Vie and then follow signs to Orouet and campsite.

Camping L'Abri des Pins route de Notre-Dame-de-Monts, 85160 St-Jean-de-Monts.
Tel 02 51 58 83 86, Fax 02 51 59 30 47. English spoken.
OPEN: 15/05–15/09. SIZE: 3 ha, 100 pitches (200 with elec, 80 statics). ✆ ♿

Restaurant at 0.2 km. Flume, fitness room, mini-golf, dancing, games room, tennis, volley ball.
PRICES: (1996) Caravan with family 178.00, Tent with two adults 141.00. CC: none.
Campsite is 3 km out of St-Jean-de-Monts, off the D38 towards Noirmoutier. 600 m from the sea and near the forest.

Camping le Bois Dormant
85160 St-Jean-de-Monts.
Tel 05 51 58 62 62, Fax 05 51 58 29 97.
English spoken.
OPEN: 15/05–15/09. SIZE: 10 ha, 350 pitches
(all with elec, 150 statics). **℄ ⅋**

Shop at 0.2 km. Restaurant at 0.2 km.
PRICES: (1996) Caravan with family 209.00,
Tent with two adults 162.00. CC: Amex,
Euro/Access, Visa.
From St-Jean-de-Monts, take the D38 towards Les Sables d'Olonne. Campsite is 2 km from town centre.

Camping Le Bois Joly 85160 St-Jean-de-Monts.
Tel 02 51 59 11 63, Fax 02 51 59 11 06.
English spoken.
OPEN: 05/04–30/09. SIZE: 5.2 ha, 291 pitches
(234 with elec, 30 statics), 48 hot showers,
39 WCs, 3 CWPs. **℄ ⅋**

Shop at 1 km. Entertainment in HS.
PRICES: (1996) Caravan with family 152.00, Tent
with two adults 95.00. CC: Euro/Access, Visa.
Campsite is first on the right, just north of St-Jean-de-Monts on the D38.

Camping Le Clarys Plage
85160 St-Jean-de-Monts.
Tel 02 51 58 10 24, Fax 02 51 59 51 96.
English spoken.
OPEN: 15/05–20/09. SIZE: 5.3 ha, 304 pitches
(all with elec, 10 statics), 30 hot showers, 32 WCs,
2 CWPs. **℄ ⅋**

Flume, jacuzzi. 20% LS reduction.
PRICES: (1996) Caravan with family 193.00,
Tent with two adults 141.00. CC: none.
Well signposted in the town.

Camping Les Genêts
av des Epines, Orouet, 85160 St-Jean-de-Monts.
Tel 02 51 58 93 94, Fax 02 51 59 53 12.
English spoken.
OPEN: 01/05–15/09. SIZE: 7.5 ha, 250 pitches
(all with elec, 150 statics), 40 hot showers,
60 WCs, 5 CWPs. **℄ ⅋**

Indoor and outdoor swimming pools; jacuzzi,
tennis, disco.
PRICES: (1996) Caravan with family 188.00,
Tent with two adults 160.00. CC: none.
South of St-Jean on the D38 towards St-Gilles.

Camping Les Jardins de l'Atlantique 100 rue
de la Caillauderie, 85160 St-Jean-de-Monts.
Tel 02 51 58 05 74. English spoken.
OPEN: 01/04–31/10. SIZE: 5 ha, 310 pitches (200 with
elec, 6 statics), 20 hot showers, 40 WCs, 1 CWP. **⅋**

PRICES: (1996) Caravan with family 130.00,
Tent with two adults 70.00. CC: none.
From St-Jean-de-Monts take D38 towards Plage des Demoiselles.

Camping les Pins 166 av Valentin,
85160 St-Jean-de-Monts.
Tel 02 51 58 17 42. English spoken.
OPEN: 12/06–12/09. SIZE: 1 ha, 128 pitches
(all with elec), 18 hot showers, 2 CWPs. **℄**

Restaurant at 1 km. Chalets available.
PRICES: (1996) Caravan with family 121.00. CC: none.
Go towards Noirmoutier for 3 km from St-Jean-de-Monts.

Camping Municipal de la Maison Blanche
Le Perrier, 85300 Challans.
Tel 02 51 49 39 23. English spoken.
OPEN: 15/06–15/09. SIZE: 2.2 ha, 240 pitches
(200 with elec), 22 hot showers, 28 WCs,
22 French WCs. **⅋**

Shop at 0.15 km. Restaurant at 2 km.
PRICES: (1996) Tent with two adults 45.00.
CC: none.
6 km from St-Jean-de-Monts on the road to Challans. Campsite near centre of Le Perrier.

ST-JEAN-PIED-DE-PORT Pyr-Atlan   4C

Camping Inxauseta 64120 Bunus.
Tel 02 59 37 81 49.
OPEN: 01/07–31/08. SIZE: 1 ha, 40 pitches (20 with
elec), 4 hot showers, 6 WCs, 4 French WCs.

Shop at 1 km. Restaurant at 4 km. Meeting room.
PRICES: (1996) Caravan with family 97.00,
Tent with two adults 51.00. CC: none.
From St-Jean go east on D933 for 16 km, then turn right to Bunus on the D918. Campsite is on the left just before the village.

Camping Municipal Mairie,
64430 St-Etienne-de-Baigorry.
Tel 02 59 37 40 80, Fax 02 59 37 48 20.
OPEN: all year. SIZE: 25 pitches, 12 hot showers,
12 WCs. **℄ ⅋**

Shop at 0.05 km. Restaurant at 0.2 km.
PRICES: (1996) Caravan with family 82.00,
Tent with two adults 41.00. CC: none.
Due west from St-Jean on the D15.

Camping Narbaitz route de Bayonne-Ascarat,
64220 St-Jean-Pied-de-Port.
Tel 05 59 37 10 13. English spoken.
OPEN: 01/04–31/10. SIZE: 2.4 ha, 133 pitches

France

(all with elec), 12 hot showers, 22 WCs, 12 French WCs, 1 CWP. **� ☕**

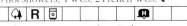

Shop at 2 km. Restaurant at 0.5 km. Fishing, pétanque.
PRICES: (1996) Caravan with family 112.00, Tent with two adults 64.00. CC: none.
D918 from Bayonne at Ascarat. The campsite is 2 km from St-Jean-Pied-de-Port.

Europ' Camping 64220 Ascarat.
Tel 02 59 37 12 78, Fax 02 59 37 29 82.
English spoken.
OPEN: 30/03–15/10. SIZE: 2 ha, 93 pitches (all with elec), 16 hot showers, 22 WCs, 4 French WCs, 2 CWPs. ☕ ☕

PRICES: (1996) Caravan with family 197.00, Tent with two adults 110.00. CC: none.
From St-Jean-Pied-de-Port take D918 north towards Bayonne. Site is just off the road on the left before you reach Ascarat.

ST-JULIEN-EN-BORN Landes   4C

Camping Municipal La Lette Fleurie
40170 St-Julien-en-Born.
Tel 05 58 42 74 09, Fax 05 58 42 41 51.
English spoken.
OPEN: 01/04–01/10. SIZE: 8.5 ha, 180 pitches (all with elec, 35 statics), 30 hot showers, 36 WCs, 10 CWPs. ☕

Canoeing, fishing, horse-riding nearby.
PRICES: (1996) Caravan with family 92.30, Tent with two adults 50.50. CC: Amex, Euro/Access, Visa.
From the N10, exit D41 west to St-Julien-en-Born.

Les Cigales quartier Orvignac,
40170 St-Julien-en-Born.
Tel 05 58 42 86 27.
OPEN: 24/06–05/09. SIZE: 2 ha, 25 pitches (16 with elec), 5 hot showers, 4 WCs, 2 French WCs. ☕

Shop at 3 km. Restaurant at 3 km. Barbecues available, boules, mini-golf, volley ball.
PRICES: (1996) Caravan with family 74.00, Tent with two adults 37.00. CC: none.
Between Bias and St-Julien-en-Born on the D652.

ST-LARY Htes-Pyrénées   4D

Camping Le Rioumajou Bourisp, 65170 St-Lary.
Tel 05 62 39 48 32, Fax 05 62 39 48 32.
English spoken.
OPEN: all year. SIZE: 5 ha, 117 pitches (all with elec, 25 statics). ☕ ☕

Restaurant at 1 km. Sauna, jacuzzi.

PRICES: (1996) Caravan with family 154.50, Tent with two adults 76.00. CC: none.
Follow signs from St-Lary-Soulan.

ST-LAURENT-DU-PONT Isère   6A

Camping de Martinière route du Col de Porte, 38380 St-Pierre-de-Chartreuse.
Tel 04 76 88 60 36, Fax 04 76 88 60 36.
English spoken.
OPEN: 08/05–20/09. SIZE: 2 ha, 100 pitches (all with elec, 20 statics), 10 hot showers, 10 WCs, 1 CWP. ☕

Shop at 3 km. Tennis, mini-golf, table tennis, hiking.
PRICES: (1996) Caravan with family 113.70, Tent with two adults 69.00. CC: none.
From St-Laurent-du-Pont take D520b to St-Pierre-de-Chartreuse.

ST-MALO Ille/Vilaine   1D

Camping Bel Event St-Père, 35430 Châteauneuf.
Tel 02 99 58 83 79, Fax 02 99 58 83 79.
English spoken.
OPEN: 01/03–30/11. SIZE: 2 ha, 96 pitches (78 with elec, 7 statics), 12 hot showers, 11 WCs, 11 French WCs, 3 CWPs. ☕ ☕

Restaurant at 2 km.
PRICES: Caravan with family 110.00, Tent with two adults 66.00. CC: none.
From St-Malo head towards Rennes on N137. Turn off for Châteauneuf and follow the directions to Cancale. The campsite is about 1.5 km on the left before St-Père turning.

Camping La Ville Huchet
route de la Passagère, 35400 St-Malo.
Tel 02 99 81 11 83, Fax 02 99 56 07 08.
English spoken.
OPEN: 05/04–30/09. SIZE: 6 ha, 85 pitches (all with elec, 3 statics), 15 hot showers, 22 WCs, 3 CWPs. ☕ ☕

Restaurant at 2 km. Children's playground.
PRICES: (1996) Caravan with family 104.00, Tent with two adults 58.00. CC: none.
In St-Malo, take the N137 towards Rennes and then turn right to La Passagère.

France *(side margin)*

Camping La Ville Huchet
at St-Malo
Lounge on the lawns of a château

Camping Le P'tit Bois
35430 St-Jouan-des-Guérêts.
Tel 02 99 21 14 30, Fax 02 99 81 74 14.
English spoken.
OPEN: 01/05–15/09. SIZE: 6 ha, 200 pitches
(all with elec, 20 statics), 34 hot showers, 30 WCs,
3 CWPs. ✆ ❧

| | 🞉 | R | ⬚ | ⚓ | 🖰 | ✕ | ⚲ | | ⚠ | | |

Tennis, mini-golf, flume, entertainment, ball
sports area; mobile home available.
PRICES: (1996) Caravan with family 197.00, Tent
with two adults 127.00. CC: Euro/Access, Visa.
*2 km south of St-Malo on the N137, take
St-Jouan/Quelmer exit.*

Camping Le P'tit Bois★★★★
near St-Malo
*Quiet, well-landscaped site
in a rural setting*

ST-MATHIEU Haute-Vienne   4B

Camping du Lac
Centre Touristique, 87440 St-Mathieu.
Tel 05 55 00 34 30, Fax 05 55 48 80 62.
English spoken.
OPEN: 01/05–30/09. SIZE: 33 pitches (all with elec),
7 hot showers, 10 WCs, 1 CWP.

| ≋ | ⚓ | 🖰 | R | | | ✕ | | | |

Shop at 2 km.
PRICES: (1996) Caravan with family 70.0064,
Tent with two adults 3835.00. CC: none.
On the D675. Signposted.

ST-MAURICE-SUR-MOSELLE Vosges 3D

Les Deux Ballons 17 rue du Stade,
88560 St-Maurice-sur-Moselle.
Tel 03 29 25 17 14. English spoken.
OPEN: 15/02–03/11 & 20/12–02/01. SIZE: 3 ha,
160 pitches (all with elec, 20 statics), 15 hot
showers, 14 WCs, 3 CWPs. ✆ ❧

| ～ | ⚓ | R | ⬚ | 🖰 | | | ⚲ | Ⓗ | | |

Restaurant at 0.5 km. Tennis, flume; nice quiet site.
PRICES: (1996) Caravan with family 125.00,
Tent with two adults 63.00. CC: none.
*This recommended campsite is at the entrance to
the village, west side. Well signposted.*

ST-MAXIMIN Var   6C

Camping Caravaning Provençal chemin de
Mazaugues, 83470 St-Maximin-la-Ste-Beaume.
Tel 04 94 78 16 97, Fax 04 94 78 16 97.
English spoken.

OPEN: 01/04–30/09. SIZE: 5 ha, 100 pitches
(10 statics). ✆

| | ⚲ | R | ⬚ | 🖰 | | ✕ | ⚲ | ⬚ | | |

PRICES: Caravan with family 130.00,
Tent with two adults 70.00. CC: none.
*From St-Maximin, take the D560 and turn left on
the D64 towards Mazaugues.*

ST-NECTAIRE Puy-de-Dôme   5A

Camping L'Oasis Route Granges,
63710 St-Nectaire-le-Bas.
Tel 04 73 88 52 68.
OPEN: 15/04–30/09. SIZE: 2 ha, 170 pitches
(99 with elec), 11 hot showers, 17 WCs.

| ～ | ✖ | 🛠 | R | ⬚ | | | | Ⓗ | |

Shop at 0.5 km. Restaurant at 0.6 km. Swimming
pool 8 km.
PRICES: (1996) Caravan with family 104.50,
Tent with two adults 56.50. CC: none.
*On the route des Granges. The campsite is well
signposted.*

Camping Municipal Le Vignet
63710 St-Nectaire.
Tel 04 73 88 53 30, Fax 04 73 88 53 80.
English spoken.
OPEN: 01/06–30/09. SIZE: 4 ha, 77 pitches (50 with
elec), 10 hot showers, 11 WCs, 1 CWP. ✆ ❧

| | ⚓ | R | ⬚ | | ☕ | | | Ⓗ | | 🚗 |

Shop at 0.5 km. Restaurant at 0.5 km.
PRICES: (1996) Caravan with family 99.00,
Tent with two adults 54.00. CC: none.
St-Nectaire is just off the D996.

La Hutte des Dômes Saillant, 63710 St-Nectaire.
Tel 04 73 88 50 22.
OPEN: 01/04–30/09. SIZE: 0.7 ha, 46 pitches
(16 with elec), 4 hot showers, 6 WCs. ✆

| | ⚓ | R | ⬚ | | | | | | |

Shop at 2 km. Restaurant at 2 km.
PRICES: (1996) Caravan with family 89.00,
Tent with two adults 47.00. CC: none.
2 km from St-Nectaire on the D996.

ST-OMER Pas-de-Calais   2B

Camping Château de Gandspette
62910 Eperlecques.
Tel 03 21 93 43 93, Fax 03 21 95 74 98.
English spoken.
OPEN: 01/04–30/09. SIZE: 8 ha, 127 pitches
(all with elec, 60 statics), 12 hot showers, 12 WCs,
1 CWP. ✆

| | ⚓ | R | ⬚ | | ☕ | ✕ | ⚲ | | | |

Shop at 1 km. Tennis; wooded parkland.
PRICES: (1996) Caravan with family 165.00,
Tent with two adults 95.00. CC: Visa.

France

North from St-Omer towards Calais. Fork right after Tilques towards Dunkerque and then turn left to Eperlecques. Campsite is signposted.

Camping de l'Yser
9 route de St-Omer, 59470 Broxeele.
Tel 03 28 62 40 19. English spoken.
OPEN: all year. SIZE: 1 ha, 40 pitches (all with elec), 2 hot showers (charge), 4 WCs, 4 French WCs.

Shop at 2 km.
PRICES: (1996) Caravan with family 63.80,
Tent with two adults 38.00. CC: none.
12 km north-east of St-Omer on D928.

Camping du Clairmarais
Clairmarais, 62500 St-Omer.
Tel 03 21 98 62 98, Fax 03 21 98 37 05.
OPEN: 15/03–15/10. SIZE: 30 pitches (all with elec, 149 statics), 22 hot showers, 26 WCs, 1 CWP. ✆ ♿

Shop at 2 km. Restaurant at 1 km.
PRICES: (1996) Caravan with family 121.50,
Tent with two adults 58.00. CC: none.
From St-Omer, drive towards the railway station, then towards Clairmarais. In Clairmarais, turn left at the church.

ST-PALAIS-SUR-MER Charente-Marit 4A

Camp du Logis
22 rue des Palombes, 17420 St-Palais-sur-Mer.
Tel 05 46 93 20 23, Fax 05 46 23 10 61.
English spoken.
OPEN: 01/04–30/09. SIZE: 20 ha, 400 pitches (all with elec, 40 statics), 120 hot showers, 80 WCs, 10 CWPs. ✆ ♿

Restaurant at 0.6 km. Tennis, volley ball, basketball, entertainment; mobile homes and bikes for hire.
PRICES: (1996) Caravan with family 145.00,
Tent with two adults 95.00. CC: Amex,
Euro/Access, Visa.
On north edge of St-Palais, turn off N25 in north-east direction. 200 m from the sea.

Camping de la Grande Côte
17420 St-Palais-sur-Mer.
Tel 05 46 23 20 18, Fax 05 46 23 47 10.
English spoken.
OPEN: 09/04–30/09. SIZE: 1 ha, 73 pitches (all with elec), 7 hot showers, 7 WCs, 4 French WCs, 1 CWP. ♿

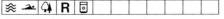

Shop at 0.2 km. Restaurant at 0.1 km.
PRICES: Caravan with family 112.00, Tent with two adults 78.00. CC: Euro/Access, Visa.
10 km north of Royan and 2 km north of St-Palais centre.

ST-PAUL-DE-VARAX Ain 5B

Base de Plein Air
Etang du Moulin, 01240 St-Paul-de-Varax.
Tel 04 74 42 53 30, Fax 04 74 42 56 13.
English spoken.
OPEN: 01/05–15/09. SIZE: 34 ha, 200 pitches (all with elec, 20 statics). ✆ ♿

Shop at 3 km.
PRICES: (1996) Caravan with family 134.40,
Tent with two adults 91.40. CC: none.
14 km south of Bourg-en-Bresse. The Etang du Moulin lakes lie to the east of the village.

ST-PAUL-DE-VENCE Alpes-Marit 6C

Camping Caravaning St-Paul
637 chemin-du-Malvan, 06570 St-Paul-de-Vence.
Tel 04 93 32 93 71, Fax 04 93 32 01 97.
English spoken.
OPEN: 01/04–30/10. SIZE: 1.5 ha, 96 pitches (all with elec), 15 hot showers, 12 WCs, 5 CWPs. ✆ ♿

Shop at 0.5 km.
PRICES: (1996) Caravan with family 145.00,
Tent with two adults 95.00. CC: Amex,
Euro/Access, Visa.
*From Vence proceed southerly on D36 to St-Paul.
Follow signs.*

ST-PEE-SUR-NIVELLE Pyr-Atlan 4C

Camping d'Ibarron
64310 St-Pée-sur-Nivelle.
Tel 05 59 54 10 43. English spoken.
OPEN: 15/05–20/09. SIZE: 3 ha, 194 pitches (130 with elec), 19 hot showers, 25 WCs, 2 CWPs. ✆ ♿

Restaurant at 0.5 km. Tennis, walking.
PRICES: (1996) Caravan with family 108.20,
Tent with two adults 59.60. CC: Euro/Access.
From A63 take St-Jean-de-Luz-Nord exit. Site is 2 km before St-Pée-sur-Nivelle.

Camping Goyetchea 64310 St-Pée-sur-Nivelle.
Tel 05 59 54 19 59. English spoken.
OPEN: 01/06–20/09. SIZE: 3.50 ha, 130 pitches (105 with elec, 2 statics), 14 hot showers, 22 WCs, 2 CWPs. ✆ ♿

Restaurant at 0.8 km. Mobile homes for hire.
PRICES: (1996) Caravan with family 130.00,
Tent with two adults 76.00. CC: none.
From St-Jean-de-Luz take D918 south towards St-Pée-sur-Nivelle. At Ibarron, turn left in front of Hôtel Bonnet towards Ahetze. Follow signs, 800 m.

France

ST-POURÇAIN-SUR-SIOULE Allier 5A

Camping Deneuvre Les Graves,
03500 Châtel-de-Neuvre.
Tel 04 70 42 04 51. English spoken.
OPEN: 01/04–01/10. SIZE: 1.2 ha, 85 pitches
(40 with elec), 9 hot showers, 11 WCs, 1 CWP. ℓ ⅋

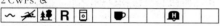

PRICES: (1996) Caravan with family 90.00, Tent
with two adults 54.00. CC: none.
*Go north from St-Pourçain on N9 towards
Moulins. After Châtel-de-Neuvre campsite is
200 m on the right.*

Camping La Courtine 03500 Châtel-de-Neuvre.
Tel 04 70 42 06 21. English spoken.
OPEN: 15/04–30/09. SIZE: 2 ha, 40 pitches (30 with
elec), 6 hot showers, 3 WCs, 12 French WCs,
2 CWPs. ⅋

Shop at 0.3 km. Restaurant at 0.3 km. Fishing,
ball games.
PRICES: (1996) Caravan with family 77.00,
Tent with two adults 52.00. CC: none.
*South of Moulins on N7 towards Roanne and
Lyon. Campsite is on right after Bessais and
well signposted.*

ST-QUENTIN Aisne 2B

Camping Le Vivier aux Carpes
02790 Seraucourt-le-Grand.
Tel 03 23 60 50 10, Fax 03 23 60 51 69.
English spoken.
OPEN: 02/01–22/12. SIZE: 3 ha, 60 pitches
(all with elec, 16 statics), 6 hot showers, 6 WCs,
2 CWPs. ℓ ⅋

Shop at 0.2 km. Restaurant at 4 km. Fishing; golf,
swimming, tennis and horse-riding nearby.
PRICES: (1996) Caravan with family 105.00,
Tent with two adults 70.00. CC: none.
*Exit 11 from A26, then D1 to Essigny-le-Grand
and D72 to Seraucourt-le-Grand. Site is well
signposted. (English speaking phone number
23 60 51 02.)*

ST-RAPHAEL Var 6C

Camping Douce Quiétude
3435 bd Jacques Baudino, 83700 St-Raphaël.
Tel 04 94 44 30 00, Fax 04 94 44 30 30.
English spoken.
OPEN: 15/04–30/09. SIZE: 10 ha. ℓ ⅋

PRICES: (1996) Caravan with family 232.00. CC: Visa.
*From St-Raphaël train station take the avenue du
Valescure then turn right into bd Jacques
Baudino.*

Camping International du Dramont
Le Dramont par Agay, 83700 St-Raphaël.
Tel 04 94 82 07 68, Fax 04 94 82 75 30.
English spoken.
OPEN: 01/04–15/10. SIZE: 7 ha, 200 pitches
(all with elec), 55 hot showers, 52 WCs,
3 CWPs. ⅋

PRICES: (1996) Caravan with family 228.00,
Tent with two adults 145.00. CC: Visa.
*7 km from St-Raphaël, following the coast road
east. Le Dramont is on the coast just before Agay.*

Camping Vallée du Paradis 83700 St-Raphaël.
Tel 04 94 82 16 00, Fax 04 94 82 72 21.
English spoken.
OPEN: 15/03–15/10. SIZE: 3 ha, 213 pitches (200 with
elec), 39 hot showers, 36 WCs, 3 CWPs. ℓ ⅋

Boating; sea 0.5 km.
PRICES: (1996) Caravan with family 151.00,
Tent with two adults 94.00. CC: none.
*From St-Raphaël take N98 as far as Agay. Turn
left into avenue du Gratadis and site is 500 m.*

Esterel Caravaning
route de Valescure, Agay, 83700 St-Raphaël.
Tel 04 94 82 03 28, Fax 04 94 82 87 37.
English spoken.
OPEN: 01/04–30/09. SIZE: 12 ha, 255 pitches
(all with elec, 240 statics), 71 hot showers,
80 WCs, 3 CWPs. ℓ ⅋

Golf, horse-riding, squash, tennis.
PRICES: (1996) Caravan with family 200.00.
CC: none.
*From St-Raphaël take the road to Agay and from
there the road to Valescure where the campsite is
located. (No tents.)*

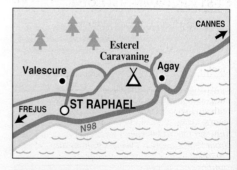

ST-SAUVEUR-DE-MONTAGUT 5B

Camping L'Ardechois Le Chambon, Gluiras,
07190 St-Sauveur-de-Montagut.
Tel 04 75 66 61 87, Fax 04 75 66 63 67.
English spoken.

France

OPEN: 29/03–25/09. SIZE: 5 ha, 95 pitches (all with elec, 21 statics), 14 hot showers, 14 WCs, 2 CWPs. ✆ &

PRICES: Caravan with family 156.00, Tent with two adults 98.00. CC: none.
From St-Sauveur-de-Montagut take the D102 towards Albon. Campsite is 8 km ahead.

ST-SAVINIEN Charente-Marit 4A

Camping du Roy 17350 Crazannes.
Tel 05 46 90 18 54. English spoken.
OPEN: 01/04–30/09. SIZE: 2 ha, 30 pitches (20 with elec), 2 hot showers, 4 WCs, 4 CWPs.

Shop at 0.5 km. Restaurant at 0.5 km. Swimming pool 2 km.
PRICES: (1996) Caravan with family 61.00,
Tent with two adults 32.00. CC: none.
From St-Savinien go south on D119 to Crazannes. Campsite is at entrance to village.

ST-SYMPHORIEN Gironde 4D

Camping de la Hure
route de Sore, 33113 St-Symphorien.
Tel 05 56 25 79 54, Fax 05 56 25 79 54.
English spoken.
OPEN: all year. SIZE: 4 ha, 70 pitches (all with elec), 15 hot showers, 15 WCs, 1 CWP. ✆ &

Shop at 0.8 km. Fishing.
PRICES: Caravan with family 93.00,
Tent with two adults 55.00. CC: none.
St-Symphorien is on the D3 and the campsite is well signposted.

ST-SYMPHORIEN-SUR-COISE 5B

Camping Municipal du Chatelard
69440 Ste-Catherine.
Tel 04 78 81 80 60.
OPEN: 01/03–30/11. SIZE: 4 ha, 61 pitches (all with elec), 10 hot showers, 9 WCs. ✆ &

Shop at 1.5 km. Restaurant at 1.5 km. Quiet site with superb views and wonderful walks.
PRICES: (1996) Caravan with family 66.00,
Tent with two adults 33.50. CC: none.
From St-Symphorien-sur-Croise go south-east on D97/D63 to Ste-Catherine. Campsite is well signposted.

ST-THEOFFREY Isère 5B

Camping Ser Sirant
Petichet, St-Théoffrey, 38119 Vizille.
Tel 04 76 83 91 97.

OPEN: 02/07–19/08. SIZE: 2 ha, 100 pitches (all with elec), 20 hot showers, 7 WCs, 1 CWP. ✆

Shop at 5 km. Restaurant at 0.3 km.
PRICES: Caravan with family 139.00,
Tent with two adults 74.00. CC: none.
On the N85 south of Vizille and just north of St-Théoffrey. The campsite is beside the lake.

ST-TROPEZ Var 6C

Selection Camping 83420 La Croix-Valmer.
Tel 04 94 79 61 97, Fax 04 94 54 25 14.
English spoken.
OPEN: 15/03–15/10. SIZE: 4 ha, 215 pitches (all with elec, 25 statics), 60 hot showers, 42 WCs, 10 CWPs. ✆ &

Mini-golf, table tennis, children's playground.
PRICES: (1996) Caravan with family 180.00,
Tent with two adults 125.00. CC: Amex, Euro/Access, Visa.
Exit motorway at Muy. Take D25 to Ste-Maxime, N98 towards St-Tropez and then D559 to La Croix-Valmer.

ST-YORRE Allier 5A

La Gravière Centre Omnisports, 03270 St-Yorre.
Tel 04 70 59 21 00, Fax 04 70 59 27 37.
OPEN: 22/04–30/09. SIZE: 2 ha, 82 pitches (all with elec), 10 hot showers, 8 WCs, 2 CWPs. &

Shop at 0.5 km. Restaurant at 0.5 km.
PRICES: (1996) Caravan with family 75.20,
Tent with two adults 39.50. CC: none.

STE-ENIMIE Lozère 5C

Camp Couderc
route de Millau, 48210 Ste-Enimie.
Tel 04 66 48 50 53, Fax 04 66 48 58 59.
English spoken.
OPEN: 01/04–30/09. SIZE: 1 ha, 80 pitches (50 with elec), 2 CWPs. ✆ &

Restaurant at 1.5 km. Canoes and kayaks.
PRICES: (1996) Caravan with family 104.00,
Tent with two adults 72.00. CC: none.
Take D907 bis towards Millau and follow signs.

STE-GENEVIEVE-DES-BOIS Essonne 2D

Le Village Voie des Prés,
91700 Villiers-sur-Orge.
Tel 01 60 16 17 86, Fax 01 60 16 31 46.
English spoken.
OPEN: all year. SIZE: 2.5 ha, 100 pitches (all with elec, 50 statics), 12 hot showers, 11 WCs, 4 CWPs. ✆

France

~ ✈ 🏕 R 🚽 | 🍵 | 🏥

Shop at 0.4 km. Restaurant at 0.5 km. 20 minutes from Paris by train; RER line C.
PRICES: (1996) Caravan with family 123.00, Tent with two adults 67.00. CC: none.
From A6, take Savigny/Orge exit, then D25 towards Montlhéry. From N20, take Villiers/Orge exit, then D35 towards Ste-Geneviève-des-Bois.

STE-MAURE-DE-TOURAINE   2C

Camp Municipal La Croix de la Motte, Nouâtre Marcilly, 37800 Ste-Maure-de-Touraine.
Tel 02 47 65 20 38. English spoken.
OPEN: 15/06–15/09. SIZE: 1.5 ha, 61 pitches (all with elec, 4 statics), 6 hot showers, 8 WCs, 1 CWP. ⛄ ♿

~ ⚓ 🚶 R | 🥾 | 🏥

Restaurant at 1 km.
PRICES: (1996) Caravan with family 79.00, Tent with two adults 40.00. CC: none.
From Ste-Maure-de-Touraine, drive 6.5 km south on the N10, then turn right on the D91 towards Maillé and Nouâtre

Camping Municipal Le Reveillon Draché, 37800 Ste-Maure-de-Touraine.
Tel 02 47 65 02 13, Fax 02 47 65 02 13.
OPEN: 15/06–30/08. SIZE: 0.8 ha, 16 pitches (12 with elec), 1 hot shower, 2 WCs. ⛄

| | | 🚶 | | | | | |

Shop at 0.1 km. Restaurant at 0.5 km. Children's playground.
PRICES: (1996) Caravan with family 42.20, Tent with two adults 25.40. CC: none.
From Ste-Maure-de-Touraine, drive 6.5 km south on the N10 then turn left to Draché.

STE-MAXIME   Var   6C

Camping La Baumette
Quartier de la Baumette, 83120 Sainte-Maxime.
OPEN: 28/03–30/09. SIZE: 1.05 ha, 60 pitches, 9 hot showers, 12 WCs, 1 CWP. ⛄ ♿

~ ✈ 🚶 R 🚽

Shop at 0.03 km. Restaurant at 1.5 km. Barbecues.
PRICES: (1996) Caravan with family 125.00, Tent with two adults 64.00. CC: none.
On the D25 towards Le Muy.

Camping Les Mures 83360 Grimaud.
Tel 04 94 56 16 97, Fax 04 94 56 37 91. English spoken.
OPEN: 20/03–30/09. SIZE: 7 ha, 700 pitches (600 with elec, 40 statics), 71 hot showers, 78 WCs, 6 CWPs. ⛄ ♿

≈ 🏊 🚶 | 🚽 🥾 | ✂ | 🏥

PRICES: (1996) Caravan with family 182.00, Tent with two adults 106.00. CC: none.
From St-Maxime go on N98 towards St-Tropez for 5 km.

STE-MERE-EGLISE   Manche   1B

Le Cormoran 50480 Ravénoville.
Tel 02 33 41 33 94, Fax 02 33 95 16 08.
English spoken.
OPEN: 04/04–28/09. SIZE: 6 ha, 110 pitches (all with elec, 120 statics), 11 hot showers, 17 WCs, 2 CWPs. ⛄ ♿

≈ 🏊 🏕 R 🚽 🥾 🍵 ✂ 🎣 🏥

Tennis, go-karts, bike hire, shrimping; entertainment in Jul/Aug.
PRICES: Caravan with family 147.00, Tent with two adults 78.00. CC: Amex, Euro/Access, Visa.
From Ste-Mère-Eglise go to Ravénoville-Plage. Turn right towards Utah Beach and campsite is 400 m.

Camping Le Cormoran
near Ste-Mère-Eglise
A frisbee fling from the beach

SAIGNES   Cantal   5A

Camping à la Ferme La Vigne, 15240 Saignes.
Tel 04 71 40 61 02. English spoken.
OPEN: all year. SIZE: 30 ha, 15 pitches. ♿

| | | 🏕 R 🚽 | | 🍵 ✂ 🎣 🏥 | |

Shop at 0.5 km.
PRICES: (1996) Caravan with family 70.00, Tent with two adults 36.00. CC: Amex, Euro/Access, Visa.
From Saignes take D30 towards Trizac and La Vigne is 300 m to the left.

SAINTES   Charente-Marit   4B

Camping au Fil de l'Eau
6 rue de Courbiac, 17100 Saintes.
Tel 05 46 93 08 00. English spoken.
OPEN: 15/05–15/09. SIZE: 6 ha, 214 pitches (126 with elec), 22 hot showers, 37 WCs, 24 French WCs, 2 CWPs. ⛄ ♿

~ 🏊 🚶 R 🚽 🥾 🍵 ✂ 🎣 🏥

PRICES: (1996) Caravan with family 99.00, Tent with two adults 61.00. CC: Euro/Access, Visa.
From the town centre, go to Quai de l'Yser. Follow the quay until rue de Courbiac.

Camping à la Ferme La Roulerie, Le Douhet, 17100 Saintes.
Tel 05 46 97 74 83, Fax 05 46 95 01 06.
English spoken.
OPEN: 01/03–30/10. SIZE: 0.9 ha, 25 pitches (20 with elec), 2 hot showers, 4 WCs. ⛄

♨	R						

Shop at 5 km. Restaurant at 1.4 km.
PRICES: Caravan with family 76.00,
Tent with two adults 45.00. CC: none.
North from Saintes on the N150 towards St-Jean-d'Angely. Campsite is on the left after about 7 km.

La Garenne av Bernard Chambenoit,
17250 Pont-l'Abbé-d'Arnoult.
Tel 05 46 97 01 46, Fax 05 46 97 12 31.
English spoken.
OPEN: 15/06–15/09. SIZE: 3 ha, 106 pitches
(all with elec), 10 hot showers, 10 WCs, 5 French
WCs, 1 CWP. ⛽ ♿

♨	R	⊙				⊞	

Shop at 0.3 km. Restaurant at 0.3 km. Swimming
pool 0.05 km.
PRICES: (1996) Caravan with family 95.00,
Tent with two adults 48.00. CC: none.
*From Saintes take N137 to Rochefort and then
turn right on to D18 to Pont-l'Abbé-d'Arnoult.*

SALLES-CURAN Aveyron 5C

Camping Beau Rivage Lac de Pareloup,
12410 Salles-Curan.
Tel 05 65 46 33 32, Fax 05 65 46 01 64.
English spoken.
OPEN: 01/06–30/09. SIZE: 2 ha, 81 pitches
(all with elec, 1 static), 18 hot showers, 18 WCs,
1 CWP. ⛽ ♿

Restaurant at 2 km. Water sports, disco,
entertainment.
PRICES: (1996) Caravan with family 140.00,
Tent with two adults 100.00. CC: none.
*Lac de Pareloup is north of Salles-Curan.
Campsite is on the eastern shores of the lake and
well signposted.*

Camping Les Genêts 12410 Salles-Curan.
Tel 05 65 46 35 34, Fax 05 65 78 00 72.
English spoken.
OPEN: 01/06–15/09. SIZE: 3 ha, 100 pitches
(all with elec, 30 statics), 16 hot showers, 16 WCs,
1 CWP. ⛽ ♿

≈	⚓	⚑	R	⊙	⛽	☕	✗	⟿	⊞

PRICES: Caravan with family 160.00,
Tent with two adults 95.00. CC: Visa.
*Situated near the Lac de Pareloup. Take the D577
to Salles-Curan.*

SANARY-SUR-MER Var 6C

Campasun Mas de Pierredon
chemin du Pierredon, 83110 Sanary-sur-Mer.
Tel 04 94 74 25 02, Fax 04 94 74 03 65.
English spoken.
OPEN: 01/04–15/10. SIZE: 4 ha, 130 pitches (all
with elec), 30 hot showers, 30 WCs, 1 CWP. ⛽ ♿

♨	R	⊙	ⓣ	☕	✗	⟿	⊞	

Restaurant at 1 km. Tennis, mini-golf, volley ball,
boules.
PRICES: (1996) Caravan with family 160.00, Tent
with two adults 95.00. CC: Amex, Euro/Access, Visa.
*Campsite is 2 km from the sea and well
signposted.*

Camping Les Girelles chemin de Beaucours,
83110 Sanary-sur-Mer.
Tel 04 94 74 13 18.
OPEN: 04/04–28/09. SIZE: 2 ha, 100 pitches
(all with elec), 24 hot showers, 32 WCs, 2 CWPs.

10% discount in LS for stays over 15 days.
PRICES: (1996) Caravan with family 175.50,
Tent with two adults 102.00. CC: none.

SARLAT Dordogne 4B

Aqua Viva Carsac, 24200 Sarlat.
Tel 05 53 31 46 00, Fax 05 53 29 36 37.
English spoken.
OPEN: 28/03–15/10. SIZE: 10 ha, 186 pitches (160 with
elec), 26 hot showers, 22 WCs, 3 CWPs. ⛽ ♿

≈	⚓	⚑	R	⊙	⛽	☕	✗	⟿	⊞

Mini-golf, volley ball, badminton, table tennis,
boules, entertainment.
PRICES: Caravan with family 181.00,
Tent with two adults 107.00. CC: none.
*From Sarlat, drive 3 km south towards
Cahors/Souillac then turn left on the D704
towards Souillac, drive 3 km again and the
campsite is on the right-hand side.*

Camping Le Beau Rivage
Gaillardou, 24250 La Roque-Gageac.
Tel 05 53 28 32 05, Fax 05 53 29 63 56.
English spoken.
OPEN: 15/01–15/12. SIZE: 6 ha, 199 pitches
(all with elec), 36 hot showers, 46 WCs,
2 CWPs. ⛽ ♿

∼	⚓	⚑	R	⊙	⛽	☕	✗	⟿	⊞

Restaurant at 0.02 km.
PRICES: (1996) Caravan with family 157.00, Tent
with two adults 90.00. CC: Euro/Access, Visa.
*Gaillardou 'lieu-dit' is a small village about 7 km
south of Sarlat on D703, towards La Roque-Gageac.*

Les Granges Groléjac, 24250 Domme.
Tel 05 53 28 11 15, Fax 05 53 28 57 13.
English spoken.
OPEN: 01/05–25/09. SIZE: 6 ha, 139 pitches
(133 with elec, 23 statics), 31 hot showers,
19 WCs, 2 CWPs. ⛽ ♿

Playground, Flume, mini-golf; boating and fishing
nearby.

France

PRICES: (1996) Caravan with family 185.00,
Tent with two adults 107.00. CC: none.
Groléjac is 12 km south-east of Sarlat on D704.
Site is signposted in Groléjac.

Le Plein Air des Bories
au bord de la Dordogne, Carsac, 24200 Sarlat.
Tel 05 53 28 15 67, Fax 05 53 28 15 67.
English spoken.
OPEN: 01/06–20/09. SIZE: 3 ha, 90 pitches (70 with
elec), 16 hot showers, 14 WCs, 1 CWP. ⛄ ♿

| ~ | ♨ | 🏕 | R | ō | | ● | | ⟡ | | 🐎 | |

Shop at 0.6 km. Restaurant at 1 km. Canoes for
hire, playground; tennis nearby.
PRICES: (1996) Caravan with family 141.00,
Tent with two adults 80.00. CC: none.
From Sarlat, take the D704 to Carsac.

SAUMUR Maine/Loire   2C

Camping Ile d'Offard Ile d'Offard, 49400 Saumur.
Tel 02 41 40 30 00, Fax 02 41 67 37 81.
English spoken.
OPEN: 15/01–15/12. SIZE: 4.5 ha, 258 pitches
(162 with elec), 37 hot showers, 3 CWPs. ⛄ ♿

| ~ | ♨ | 🏕 | R | ō | ♨ | ● | ✕ | ⟡ | | | |

Tennis, mini-golf, volley ball, entertainment in HS,
bike hire.
PRICES: (1996) Caravan with family 172.50,
Tent with two adults 100.00. CC: Amex,
Euro/Access, Visa.
On the River Loire and well signposted in Saumur.

Camping L'Etang de la Brèche
49730 Varennes-sur-Loire.
Tel 02 41 51 22 92, Fax 02 41 51 27 24.
English spoken.
OPEN: 15/05–14/09. SIZE: 8 ha, 160 pitches
(150 with elec, 30 statics), 29 hot showers,
30 WCs, 3 CWPs. ⛄ ♿

| ≈ | ♨ | 🏕 | R | ō | ♨ | ● | ✕ | ⟡ | | | |

Flume, tennis, sports ground.
PRICES: Caravan with family 186.00, Tent with two
adults 130.00. CC: Euro/Access, Visa.
From Saumur, go towards Tours on N152 for
6 km. Campsite is on the left.

SCIEZ Haute-Savoie   6A

Camping Le Grand Foc
Le Port, 74140 Sciez-Léman.
Tel 04 50 72 62 70.
OPEN: 25/03–30/09. SIZE: 1.4 ha, 65 pitches
(all with elec, 15 statics), 10 hot showers, 7 WCs,
2 CWPs. ⛄ ♿

| ≈ | ♨ | 🏕 | R | ō | ♨ | ● | ✕ | | | | |

Shop at 2 km.
PRICES: (1996) Caravan with family 85.00, Tent
with two adults 50.00. CC: Amex, Euro/Access, Visa.

From Genève, head towards Thonon-les-Bains.
Go through Sciez and then fork left to Bonnatrait
towards the lake.

SERIGNAN Hérault   5C

La Camargue 34410 Sérignan.
Tel 04 67 32 19 64, Fax 04 67 39 78 20.
English spoken.
OPEN: 01/04–15/10. SIZE: 4 ha, 250 pitches
(all with elec), 30 hot showers, 21 WCs,
3 CWPs. ⛄ ♿

| ≈ | ♨ | 🏕 | R | ō | ♨ | ● | ✕ | ⟡ | ℍ | | |

PRICES: (1996) Caravan with family 145.00,
Tent with two adults 115.00. CC: none.
Take D37 from Sérignan to the beach.

Le Clos Virgile 34410 Sérignan-Plage.
Tel 04 67 32 20 64, Fax 04 67 32 05 42.
English spoken.
OPEN: 01/05–30/09. SIZE: 5 ha, 300 pitches (250 with
elec), 46 hot showers, 31 WCs, 2 CWPs. ⛄ ♿

| ≈ | ♨ | 🏕 | R | ō | ♨ | ● | ✕ | ⟡ | ℍ | | |

PRICES: (1996) Caravan with family 190.00,
Tent with two adults 120.00. CC: Visa.
Leaving autoroute at Béziers Est go towards
Sérignan and then Sérignan-Plage. Site is well
signposted.

SERRES Hautes-Alpes   6C

Camping des 2 Soleils 05700 Serres.
Tel 04 92 67 01 33, Fax 04 92 67 08 02.
English spoken.
OPEN: 01/05–30/09. SIZE: 26 ha, 100 pitches (90 with
elec), 25 hot showers, 29 WCs, 25 CWPs. ⛄ ♿

| | ♨ | R | ō | ♨ | ● | ✕ | ⟡ | ℍ | | | |

Games room, archery, flume; river and lake
swimming/fishing nearby, bikes.
PRICES: (1996) Tent with two adults 121.00.
CC: Amex, Euro/Access.
Take second turning left when travelling
southwards towards Sisteron on N75. Campsite is
signposted.

SETE Hérault   5C

Camping Le Castellas RN 112, 34200 Sète.
Tel 04 67 51 63 00, Fax 04 67 51 63 01.
English spoken.
OPEN: 08/05–20/09. SIZE: 20 ha, 128 hot showers,
174 WCs, 9 CWPs. ⛄ ♿

| ≈ | ♨ | 🏕 | R | ō | ♨ | ● | ✕ | ⟡ | ℍ | | |

Restaurant at 3 km. Entertainment, volley ball,
mini-golf, horse-riding, playground.
PRICES: (1996) Caravan with family 189.00,
Tent with two adults 127.00.
CC: Euro/Access, Visa.
On the N112 in Sète.

SEZANNE Marne 3C

Camping Municipal route de Launat, 51120 Sézanne.
Tel 03 26 80 57 00.
OPEN: 09/04–05/10. SIZE: 100 ha, 78 pitches (68 with elec, 20 statics), 6 hot showers, 6 WCs, 4 French WCs, 1 CWP. &

Shop at 1 km. Restaurant at 1 km.
PRICES: (1996) Caravan with family 70.00, Tent with two adults 35.00. CC: none.
Signposted from Sézanne, towards Paris. 1 km east of D373/N4 junction.

Camping Municipal Parc du Château 51230 Connantre.
Tel 03 26 81 08 76, Fax 03 26 80 11 73.
English spoken.
OPEN: 01/04–31/10. SIZE: 1.95 ha, 98 pitches (all with elec), 6 hot showers, 7 WCs, 1 CWP. &

Restaurant at 0.5 km.
PRICES: (1996) Caravan with family 74.00, Tent with two adults 42.00. CC: none.
From Sézanne, take N4 east to Connantre. Follow signs to campsite.

SIGNES Var 6C

Camping Caravaning des Promenades 83870 Signes.
Tel 04 94 90 88 12, Fax 04 94 90 82 68.
English spoken.
OPEN: all year. SIZE: 2 ha, 91 pitches (all with elec, 50 statics), 15 hot showers, 11 WCs, 5 CWPs. & &

Shop at 0.1 km. Restaurant at 0.1 km. Recently updated facilities; entertainment in HS.
PRICES: (1996) Caravan with family 92.00, Tent with two adults 56.00. CC: none.
At the end of town, towards Méounes-les-Montrieux (D2). Behind the Avia petrol station.

SISTERON Alpes-de-Htes-Provence 6C

Camping des Princes d'Orange 05700 Orpierre.
Tel 04 92 66 22 53, Fax 04 92 66 31 08.
English spoken.
OPEN: 01/04–15/11. SIZE: 3 ha, 120 pitches (all with elec), 26 hot showers, 24 WCs, 5 CWPs. & &

Shop at 0.3 km. Restaurant at 0.3 km. Flume.
PRICES: Caravan with family 141.00, Tent with two adults 100.00. CC: none.
North from Sisteron on the N75 through Laragne-Montéglin. Turn left in Eyguians on the D30 to Orpierre, and left again just before the square.

Camping Le Clot du Jay 04250 Clamensane.
Tel 04 92 68 32 29, Fax 04 92 68 38 73.
English spoken.
OPEN: 15/05–30/09. SIZE: 4 ha, 40 pitches (all with elec, 4 statics), 7 hot showers, 8 WCs. & &

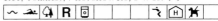

Shop at 0.8 km. Restaurant at 0.8 km. Boating lake; mobile homes for hire; many activities nearby.
PRICES: (1996) Caravan with family 127.00, Tent with two adults 60.00. CC: none.
From Sisteron take the D951 north towards La Motte-du-Caire, then the D1 to Clamensane. Signposted.

SOSPEL Alpes-Marit 6C

Camping des Merveilles quartier Vasta, route Moulinet, 06380 Sospel.
Tel 04 93 04 04 66. English spoken.
OPEN: 25/06–25/09. SIZE: 1 ha, 30 pitches (all with elec, 2 statics), 2 hot showers, 4 WCs, 6 French WCs. &

Shop at 2 km. Restaurant at 2 km.
PRICES: (1996) Caravan with family 105.00, Tent with two adults 62.00. CC: none.
2 km from Sospel towards Moulinet. Follow campsite signs.

Domaine Ste-Madeleine route de Moulinet, 06380 Sospel.
Tel 04 93 04 10 48. English spoken.
OPEN: 01/04–30/10. SIZE: 4 ha, 50 pitches (all with elec), 9 hot showers (charge), 11 WCs, 1 CWP. & &

Shop at 4 km. Restaurant at 4 km.
PRICES: (1996) Caravan with family 117.00, Tent with two adults 75.00. CC: none.
4 km from Sospel, north on the road to Moulinet.

SOUILLAC Lot 4B

Camping La Draille La Draille, 46200 Souillac.
Tel 05 53 28 90 31, Fax 05 65 37 06 20.
English spoken.
OPEN: 09/04–01/10. SIZE: 27 ha, 100 pitches (90 with elec). & &

Shop at 6 km.
PRICES: (1996) Caravan with family 141.00, Tent with two adults 93.00. CC: Visa.
From Souillac head north-west towards Saugnac on D15. Site is 5 km out of town at La Draille.

Camping Le Pit Mayrac/Souillac, 46200 Mayrac.
Tel 05 65 32 25 04. English spoken.
OPEN: 15/05–30/09. SIZE: 4 ha, 50 pitches (48 with elec), 7 hot showers, 5 WCs, 1 CWP.

France

PRICES: Caravan with family 155.00, Tent with two adults 105.00. CC: Euro/Access, Visa.
From Souillac take D703 towards Martel. At Baladou turn right on to D33 to Mayrac and the campsite is signposted.

Domaine de la Paille Basse 46200 Souillac.
Tel 05 65 37 85 48, Fax 05 65 37 09 58.
English spoken.
OPEN: 15/05–15/09. SIZE: 80 ha, 254 pitches (all with elec, 15 statics), 29 hot showers, 2 CWPs. ॐ &

PRICES: (1996) Caravan with family 199.00, Tent with two adults 116.00. CC: Euro/Access, Visa.
From N20 at Souillac, take D15 towards Salignac for about 6.5 km, then turn right for 2 km.

SOULAC-SUR-MER Gironde 4A

Camping de l'Océan Passe de la Négade-l'Amélie, 33780 Soulac-sur-Mer.
Tel 05 56 09 76 10. English spoken.
OPEN: 01/06–15/09. SIZE: 6 ha, 300 pitches (248 with elec), 30 hot showers, 33 WCs, 6 CWPs. ॐ &

Restaurant at 0.2 km. Tennis; sea 0.3 km.
PRICES: (1996) Caravan with family 129.00, Tent with two adults 80.00. CC: none.
From Soulac-sur-Mer take road to l'Amélie and follow signs to campsite.

Camping des Sables d'Argent
boulevard de l'Amélie, 33780 Soulac-sur-Mer.
Tel 05 56 09 82 87. English spoken.
OPEN: 09/04–30/09. SIZE: 3 ha, 150 pitches (120 with elec), 17 hot showers, 21 WCs, 1 CWP. ॐ &

PRICES: (1996) Caravan with family 136.00, Tent with two adults 82.00. CC: Amex, Euro/Access, Visa.

Camping Le Vieux Moulin 33590 Vensac.
Tel 05 56 09 45 98. English spoken.
OPEN: 01/06–30/09. SIZE: 5 ha, 100 pitches (all with elec), 14 hot showers, 20 WCs, 2 CWPs. ॐ &

Shop at 0.5 km. Restaurant at 0.5 km. Sea 8 km.
PRICES: (1996) Caravan with family 70.00, Tent with two adults 55.50. CC: none.
South-east of Soulac on N215 towards Lesparre-Médoc. Campsite is signposted.

Camping Les Genêts
L'Amélie, 33780 Soulac-sur-Mer.
Tel 05 56 09 85 79, Fax 05 56 09 93 09.
English spoken.
OPEN: 01/04–30/09. SIZE: 4 ha, 150 pitches (all with elec, 17 statics), 25 hot showers, 25 WCs, 2 CWPs. ॐ &

Restaurant at 2 km.
PRICES: (1996) Caravan with family 126.00, Tent with two adults 78.00. CC: none.
Well signposted.

LA SOUTERRAINE Creuse 4B

Camping Municipal Les Tilleuls
Arnac la Poste, 87160 St-Sulpice-les-Feuilles.
Tel 05 55 76 81 30, Fax 05 55 76 81 30.
English spoken.
OPEN: 22/06–08/09. SIZE: 0.4 ha, 25 pitches (all with elec), 6 hot showers, 4 WCs. ॐ &

Shop at 0.3 km. Restaurant at 1 km.
PRICES: (1996) Caravan with family 48.00, Tent with two adults 23.00. CC: none.
From La Souterraine, drive about 8 km on the D912 towards St-Sulpice-les-Feuilles and then turn left towards Arnac-la-Poste.

STENAY Meuse 3A

Camping Les Paquis 55700 Stenay.
Tel 03 29 80 64 56.
OPEN: all year. SIZE: 4 ha, 150 pitches (all with elec), 6 hot showers, 20 WCs, 1 CWP. ॐ &

Restaurant at 1.5 km.
PRICES: (1996) Caravan with family 63.00, Tent with two adults 35.00. CC: none.
At the crossroads of the D964 and D947.

STRASBOURG Bas-Rhin 3D

Camping Montagne Verte
rue Robert Forrer, 67000 Strasbourg.
Tel 03 88 30 25 46. English spoken.
OPEN: 01/03–31/10. SIZE: 3.25 ha, 190 pitches (150 with elec), 28 hot showers, 27 WCs, 5 CWPs. &

Shop at 1 km. Restaurant at 1 km.
PRICES: (1996) Caravan with family 81.00, Tent with two adults 56.00. CC: Euro/Access.
From A34 or A35 take Montagne Verte exit. Campsite is signposted.

SULLY-SUR-LOIRE Loiret 2D

Camping de Sully chemin de la Salle Verte, 45600 Sully-sur-Loire.
Tel 02 38 36 23 93.
OPEN: 22/03–31/10. SIZE: 3.4 ha, 205 pitches (138 with elec), 17 hot showers, 17 WCs. ॐ &

Shop at 0.3 km. Restaurant at 0.3 km. Swimming pool, fishing, tennis and riding nearby.

France

PRICES: (1996) Caravan with family 65.70, Tent with two adults 34.40. CC: none.
42 km east of Orléans, near the Château de Sully-sur-Loire and 300 m from the town centre.

Caravaning St-Père-sur-Loire
route d'Orléans, 45600 St-Père-sur-Loire.
Tel 02 38 36 35 94.
OPEN: 01/04–31/10. SIZE: 2.7 ha, 80 pitches (all with elec), 13 hot showers, 17 WCs. ♦ &

Shop at 1 km. Restaurant at 0.7 km. Tennis, fishing and horse-riding nearby.
PRICES: (1996) Caravan with family 76.30, Tent with two adults 42.70. CC: none.
1 km north of Sully-sur-Loire towards Orléans, on the D60.

TAIN-L'HERMITAGE Drôme 5B

Camp Municipal Les Lucs 24 avenue Président Roosevelt, 26600 Tain-l'Hermitage.
Tel 04 75 08 32 82, Fax 04 75 07 16 31.
English spoken.
OPEN: 15/03–31/10. SIZE: 2 ha, 10 hot showers, 10 WCs, 2 CWPs. ♦ &

Shop at 0.1 km.
PRICES: (1996) Caravan with family 115.00, Tent with two adults 40.00. CC: none.
Take N7 from Tain-l'Hermitage towards Valence.

TALMONT-ST-HILAIRE Vendée 4A

Camping Le Littoral
Le Porteau, 85440 Talmont-St-Hilaire.
Tel 02 51 22 04 64, Fax 02 51 22 05 37.
English spoken.
OPEN: 01/04–30/09. SIZE: 9 ha, 300 pitches (all with elec, 150 statics), 44 hot showers, 40 WCs, 40 French WCs, 5 CWPs. ♦ &

Entertainment, sauna.
PRICES: (1996) Caravan with family 205.00, Tent with two adults 161.00. CC: Euro/Access, Visa.
From Talmont-St-Hilaire take road to Port-Bourgenay and the coast road towards Les Sables-d'Olonne. Campsite is signposted.

TARASCON Bouches-du-Rhône 5D

Camping St-Gabriel 13150 Tarascon.
Tel 04 90 91 19 83.
OPEN: 01/04–31/10. SIZE: 1 ha, 75 pitches (48 with elec), 8 hot showers, 9 WCs, 2 CWPs.

Restaurant at 0.1 km.
PRICES: (1996) Caravan with family 102.00, Tent with two adults 54.00. CC: none.

Take N570 from Tarascon towards Arles. Turn left at crossroads on to D33 towards Fontvieille and then turn right after 50 m.

Lou Vincen 30300 Vallabrègues.
Tel 04 66 59 21 29, Fax 04 66 59 07 41.
English spoken.
OPEN: 01/03–31/10. SIZE: 1.4 ha, 80 pitches (all with elec), 6 hot showers, 9 WCs, 1 CWP. ♦

Tennis, fishing, playground.
PRICES: (1996) Caravan with family 118.00, Tent with two adults 63.00. CC: Visa.
From Tarascon head north on D81a, then D183 to Vallabrègues.

TARBES Htes-Pyrénées 4D

Camping Municipal de l'Echez
65700 Maubourguet.
Tel 05 62 96 37 44. English spoken.
OPEN: 01/07–30/09. SIZE: 1 ha, 30 pitches (all with elec, 10 statics), 3 hot showers, 5 WCs, 3 French WCs. ♦

Shop at 0.3 km. Restaurant at 0.5 km. Entertainment; swimming pool 0.5 km; fishing lake nearby.
PRICES: (1996) Caravan with family 90.00, Tent with two adults 43.00. CC: none.
Maubourget is north of Tarbes on the D935. Campsite is near the River Echez. Follow signs.

TELGRUC-SUR-MER Finistère 1C

Camping de Pen-Bellec
Plage de Trez-Bellec, 29560 Telgruc-sur-Mer.
Tel 02 98 37 31 87, Fax 02 98 27 71 95.
OPEN: 01/05–30/09. SIZE: 1 ha, 45 pitches (40 with elec), 6 hot showers (charge), 9 WCs. &

Restaurant at 2 km. Shrimping, sailing, kite-flying.
PRICES: (1996) Caravan with family 79.50, Tent with two adults 42.30. CC: none.
Highly recommended. Campsite is beside the beach at Trez-Bellec.

THANN Haut-Rhin 3D

Camp de la Mine d'Argent 68690 Moosch.
Tel 03 89 82 30 66. English spoken.
OPEN: 01/05–30/09. SIZE: 2 ha, 70 pitches (all with elec, 45 statics), 5 hot showers, 8 WCs, 1 CWP. ♦

Shop at 1.5 km. Restaurant at 1.5 km.
PRICES: (1996) Caravan with family 76.00, Tent with two adults 37.00. CC: none.
On the N66 7 km north of Thann and 2 km south of St-Amarin. Campsite is 1.5 km from the town of Moosch. Well signposted.

France

THENON Dordogne 4B

Camping Jarry Carrey 24210 Thenon.
Tel 05 53 05 20 78, Fax 04 77 27 03 45.
English spoken.
OPEN: 01/04–30/09. SIZE: 11 ha, 66 pitches
(5 statics), 6 hot showers, 7 WCs. ⌕

Shop at 3 km. Restaurant at 3 km.
PRICES: (1996) Caravan with family 79.00,
Tent with two adults 47.00. CC: none.
*From Thenon take the D67 to Montignac. The
campsite is 3 km ahead on the right.*

LE THILLOT Vosges 3D

Camping Aire Naturelle des Pommiers
88360 Ferdrupt.
Tel 03 29 25 98 35.
OPEN: 01/05–30/08. SIZE: 1.20 ha, 25 pitches
(20 with elec), 3 hot showers, 4 WCs.

Shop at 1 km. Restaurant at 2 km. Swimming pool
3 km.
PRICES: (1996) Caravan with family 60.00,
Tent with two adults 34.00. CC: none.
*From Thillot head north-west for Remiremont on
the N66. Look for signs.*

THIONVILLE Moselle 3B

Camping Municipal 6 rue de Parc,
57100 Thionville.
Tel 03 82 53 83 75. English spoken.
OPEN: 01/04–01/10. SIZE: 2 ha, 33 pitches (all with
elec), 7 hot showers, 7 WCs, 4 French WCs. ⌕ ⌖

Shop at 0.5 km. Restaurant at 0.5 km.
PRICES: (1996) Caravan with family 47.00,
Tent with two adults 20.00. CC: none.
*Exit A31 at Brettete-de-Yutz and go towards the
centre of Thionville, cross the bridge over the river
Moselle and follow signs.*

THONES Haute-Savoie 6A

Camping Caravaning L'Escale
74450 Le Grand-Bornand.
Tel 04 50 02 20 69, Fax 04 50 02 36 04. English spoken.
OPEN: 01/06–30/09 & 15/12–30/04. SIZE: 2.6 ha,
110 pitches (all with elec), 13 hot showers,
17 WCs, 2 CWPs. ⌕

Shop at 0.25 km. Restaurant at 0.25 km.
Playground; excellent sporting facilities nearby.
PRICES: (1996) Tent with two adults 65.00. CC: none.
*North-east of Thônes. Arriving in Le Grand-
Bornand, take first right before bridge, carry on
and campsite is signposted to the right.*

Camping Le Lachat La Cour, 74230 Thônes.
Tel 04 50 02 96 65.
OPEN: 01/04–15/10. SIZE: 1 ha, 70 pitches (40 with
elec), 4 hot showers, 11 WCs, 11 French WCs,
1 CWP. ⌕ ⌖

Shop at 0.8 km. Restaurant at 0.8 km.
PRICES: (1996) Caravan with family 83.00,
Tent with two adults 46.00. CC: none.
1 km from Thônes.

THOUARS Deux-Sèvres 2C

Camping Municipal de Crevant 79100 Thouars.
Tel 05 49 66 17 99, Fax 05 49 66 16 09.
OPEN: 03/06–15/09. SIZE: 4 ha. ⌖

Shop at 1.4 km. Restaurant at 1.4 km.
PRICES: (1996) Caravan with family 66.00,
Tent with two adults 33.00. CC: none.
*Follow the signs from the station towards 'Place
Lavault' and tourist office.*

THUEYTS Ardèche 5B

Camping du Pont de Mercier 07330 Thueyts.
Tel 04 75 36 46 08.
OPEN: 01/05–30/09. SIZE: 3 ha, 60 pitches (30 with
elec, 3 statics), 8 hot showers. ⌕ ⌖

Restaurant at 1.5 km. Fishing.
PRICES: (1996) Caravan with family 109.00,
Tent with two adults 66.00. CC: Euro/Access.
*From Thueyts take N102 towards Aubenas, and
the site is approximately 800 m ahead.*

THURY-HARCOURT Calvados 2A

Camping du Traspy rue du Pont Benoit,
14220 Thury-Harcourt.
Tel 02 31 79 61 80, Fax 02 31 84 76 19.
English spoken.
OPEN: 12/06–15/09. SIZE: 90 pitches (all with elec). ⌕

Restaurant at 0.4 km. Super wooded site; aquatic
centre 250 m; boating and horse-riding nearby.
PRICES: (1996) Caravan with family 133.00, Tent
with two adults 69.00. CC: none.
*Arriving in Thury-Harcourt from the north, turn
left 20 m after the aquatic centre and then first
left. Campsite is well signposted.*

TINTENIAC Ille/Vilaine 1D

Camping des Peupliers La Besnelais,
35190 Tinténiac.
Tel 02 99 45 49 75. English spoken.
OPEN: 01/03–30/10. SIZE: 4 ha, 60 pitches (50 with
elec, 30 statics), 11 hot showers, 15 WCs. ⌕ ⌖

Shop at 1.8 km. Restaurant at 0.8 km.
PRICES: (1996) Caravan with family 109.50,
Tent with two adults 56.50. CC: none.
From Tinténiac go south towards Hédé.
Follow signs.

TOUL Meurthe/Moselle   3C

L'Orée de la Forêt La Reine route de la Forêt,
54470 Mandres-aux-Quatre-Tours.
Tel 03 83 23 17 31, Fax 03 83 23 13 85.
OPEN: 01/04–31/10. SIZE: 4 ha, 40 pitches (20 with
elec), 6 hot showers (charge), 4 WCs. **L**

Shop at 10 km. Restaurant at 4 km. Tennis,
mini-golf; fishing nearby.
PRICES: (1996) Caravan with family 40.50,
Tent with two adults 19.00. CC: none.
From Toul go north on D904 for 22 km. Left at
Bernécourt and left again into Mandres.

TOULOUSE Haute-Garonne   5D

Camp de Rupe 21 chemin du Pont de Rupe,
31200 Toulouse.
Tel 05 61 70 07 35, Fax 05 62 11 10 09.
English spoken.
OPEN: all year. SIZE: 3.5 ha, 173 pitches, 26 WCs,
25 French WCs. &

PRICES: (1996) Caravan with family 106.50,
Tent with two adults 62.00. CC: none.
5 km north of Toulouse centre.

LE TOUQUET-PARIS-PLAGE   2B

Caravaning de Stoneham av François Godin,
62520 Le Touqet-Paris-Plage.
Tel 03 21 05 16 55.
OPEN: 15/02–30/11. SIZE: 4.50 ha, 217 pitches (all
with elec, 190 statics), 12 hot showers, 15 WCs. **L**

Shop at 1 km. Restaurant at 1 km.
PRICES: (1996) Caravan with family 133.00. CC: none.
Well signposted. (No tents.)

TOURNON-SUR-RHONE Ardèche   5B

Camping L'Iserand 07610 Vion.
Tel 04 75 08 01 73. English spoken.
OPEN: 15/03–15/10. SIZE: 2 ha, 60 pitches (all with
elec, 30 statics), 8 hot showers, 10 WCs, 1 CWP. **L** &

Restaurant at 1 km. Mini-golf, volley ball, boules,
games room, table tennis, children's playground.
PRICES: (1996) Caravan with family 120.00, Tent
with two adults 66.00. CC: none.

Take N86 north from Tournon and site is just
beyond Vion on left. Or, take N7 after Chanas to
St-Vallier, cross the Rhône to Sarras on N86 and
go south for 7 km.

Municipal Camping Site 1 Promenade Roche de
France, 07300 Tournon-sur-Rhône.
Tel 04 75 08 05 28. English spoken.
OPEN: 15/03–31/10. SIZE: 1 ha, 85 pitches (all with
elec), 10 hot showers, 10 WCs, 1 CWP.

Shop at 0.2 km. Restaurant at 0.2 km.
PRICES: (1996) Caravan with family 94.00,
Tent with two adults 56.00. CC: none.
The campsite is near a large car park in the
centre of town, on the banks of the Rivers Rhône
and Doux.

TOURNUS Saône/Loire   5B

Camping Château de l'Epervière
Gigny-sur-Saône, 71240 Sennecey-le-Grand.
Tel 03 85 44 83 23, Fax 03 85 44 74 20.
English spoken.
OPEN: 15/04–30/09. SIZE: 10 ha, 100 pitches
(all with elec, 2 statics), 20 hot showers, 12 WCs,
2 CWPs. **L** &

Tennis, fishing, volley ball; apartments available.
PRICES: (1996) Caravan with family 129.00, Tent
with two adults 105.00. CC: Euro/Access, Visa.
Leave A6 in Tournus and go north to Sennecey-le-
Grand.

TOURS Indre/Loire   2C

Camping La Mignardière
37510 Ballan-Miré.
Tel 02 47 73 31 00, Fax 02 47 73 31 01.
English spoken.
OPEN: 23/04–20/09. SIZE: 3 ha, 167 pitches
(all with elec, 10 statics), 21 hot showers,
21 WCs, 4 CWPs. &

Tennis, mini-golf.
PRICES: Caravan with family 164.00, Tent with two
adults 100.00. CC: Euro/Access, Visa.
From Tours go south-west towards Chinon on
D751. Turn right 2 km before Ballan-Miré at the
traffic lights near the Hôtel Campanile.

Camping La Mignardière
near Tours
8 km south-west of Tours in the
idyllic Loire Valley

France

Camping Municipal des Rives du Cher
37550 Saint Avertin.
Tel 02 47 27 27 60.
OPEN: 01/04–15/10. SIZE: 3 ha, 150 pitches
(all with elec), 16 hot showers, 6 WCs, 2 French
WCs, 2 CWPs. ✆ &

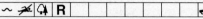

Shop at 0.5 km. Restaurant at 0.1 km. Swimming
pool 0.5 km.
PRICES: (1996) Caravan with family 81.50,
Tent with two adults 44.50. CC: none.
N76 towards Vierzon. (No motor caravans.)

Camping Municipal Les Peupliers
37270 Montlouis-sur-Loire.
Tel 02 47 50 81 90, Fax 02 47 45 15 74.
English spoken.
OPEN: 15/03–15/10. SIZE: 6 ha, 253 pitches, 26 hot
showers, 55 WCs. ✆ &

PRICES: (1996) Caravan with family 85.00,
Tent with two adults 40.00. CC: none.
East of Tours on the D751.

Parc de Fierbois
37800 Ste-Cathérine-de-Fierbois.
Tel 02 47 65 43 35, Fax 02 47 65 53 75.
English spoken.
OPEN: 15/05–15/09. SIZE: 30 ha. ✆ &

PRICES: (1996) Caravan with family 191.00, Tent
with two adults 135.00. CC: Euro/Access, Visa.
*South of Tours on the N10. From motorway A10,
take exit for St-Mauré.*

LA TRANCHE-SUR-MER Vendée   4A

Camping Bel rue de Bottereau,
85360 La Tranche-sur-Mer.
Tel 02 51 30 47 39, Fax 02 51 27 72 81. English spoken.
OPEN: 25/05–15/09. SIZE: 3.5 ha, 200 pitches (all
with elec), 40 hot showers, 27 WCs, 2 CWPs. ✆ &

Restaurant at 0.2 km. Gymnasium, basket ball;
tennis nearby.
PRICES: (1996) Caravan with family 172.00,
Tent with two adults 106.00. CC: none.
Close to the the town centre.

Camping du Jard
123 route de la Faute, 85360 La Tranche-sur-Mer.
Tel 02 51 27 43 79, Fax 02 51 27 42 92.
English spoken.
OPEN: 25/05–15/09. SIZE: 6 ha, 350 pitches (300 with
elec), 44 hot showers, 36 WCs, 3 CWPs. &

PRICES: (1996) Caravan with family 184.00,
Tent with two adults 115.00. CC: Amex,
Euro/Access, Visa.

Camping La Savinière route des Sables-
d'Olonne, 85360 La Tranche-sur-Mer.
Tel 02 51 27 42 70, Fax 02 51 27 40 48.
English spoken.
OPEN: 10/04–30/09. SIZE: 3 ha, 65 pitches
(10 statics), 16 hot showers, 14 WCs. ✆ &

Shop at 1 km. Restaurant at 1 km.
PRICES: (1996) Caravan with family 142.00,
Tent with two adults 92.00. CC: none.
*On D105b north-west of La Tranche centre; the
site is 1.5 km on the left.*

Le Cottage Fleuri
La Grière-Plage, 85360 La Tranche-sur-Mer.
Tel 02 51 30 34 57, Fax 02 51 27 74 77.
English spoken.
OPEN: 01/04–30/09. SIZE: 5 ha, 280 pitches
(207 with elec, 83 statics), 50 hot showers,
28 WCs, 2 CWPs. ✆ &

PRICES: (1996) Caravan with family 172.00, Tent
with two adults 105.00. CC: Euro/Access, Visa.
*From Tranche-sur-Mer south on the D46 coast
road towards La Faute-sur-Mer.*

Le Sable d'Or La Terrière,
85360 La Tranche-sur-Mer.
Tel 02 51 27 46 74, Fax 02 51 30 17 14.
English spoken.
OPEN: 15/05–15/09. SIZE: 4 ha, 198 pitches
(all with elec, 30 statics), 26 hot showers, 26 WCs,
26 French WCs, 3 CWPs. &

Giant flume.
PRICES: (1996) Caravan with family 152.00,
Tent with two adults 115.00. CC: Amex,
Euro/Access, Visa.
*From La Tranche take the D105 towards Les
Sables-d'Olonne and site is on the left.*

TREBEURDEN Côtes-du-Nord   1A

Armor Loisirs 22560 Trébeurden.
Tel 02 96 23 52 31. English spoken.
OPEN: 24/05–06/09. SIZE: 2.2 ha, 122 pitches
(68 with elec, 2 statics), 12 hot showers, 9 WCs,
1 CWP. ✆ &

Shop at 0.5 km. Games rooms.
PRICES: (1996) Caravan with family 121.00,
Tent with two adults 68.00. CC: none.
Follow signs to camping and Porsmabo.

Camping de l'Esperance Penvern,
22560 Trébeurden.
Tel 02 96 91 95 05. English spoken.
OPEN: 01/04–30/09. SIZE: 1 ha, 55 pitches
(all with elec), 9 hot showers, 10 WCs,
1 CWP. ✆ &

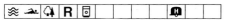

Shop at 0.5 km. Restaurant at 0.5 km.
PRICES: (1996) Caravan with family 126.00,
Tent with two adults 74.00. CC: none.
*Between Trébeurden and Trégastel-Plage on the
coast road. Follow signs.*

TREGASTEL-PLAGE Côtes-du-Nord 1A

Camping du Port
Landrellec, 22560 Pleumeur-Bodou.
Tel 02 96 23 87 79, Fax 02 96 47 30 40.
English spoken.
OPEN: 01/04–30/09. SIZE: 2 ha, 83 pitches (60 with
elec), 12 hot showers, 24 WCs, 1 CWP.

Shop at 0.2 km. Restaurant at 3 km.
PRICES: (1996) Caravan with family 146.00, Tent
with two adults 82.00. CC: Euro/Access, Visa.
*From D788 south of Trégastel-Plage, turn on to
D21.*

TREGUIER Côtes-du-Nord 1A

Camp Le Varlen
route de Pors Hir, 22820 Plougrescant.
Tel 02 96 92 52 15, Fax 02 96 92 50 34.
English spoken.
OPEN: 01/02–30/11. SIZE: 10 ha, 65 pitches
(all with elec, 13 statics), 8 hot showers, 8 WCs,
2 CWPs.

Shop at 2 km. Restaurant at 3 km. Apartments
available.
PRICES: Caravan with family 105.00,
Tent with two adults 60.00. CC: Visa.
*From Tréguier, north towards coast on the D8 to
Plougrescant; follow signs to campsite.*

TREIGNAC Corrèze 5A

Camping de la Plage
Lac des Barriousses, 19260 Treignac.
Tel 05 55 98 08 54. English spoken.
OPEN: 01/04–30/09. SIZE: 4 ha, 130 pitches
(90 with elec, 16 statics), 25 hot showers, 32 WCs,
3 CWPs.

Restaurant at 4 km.
PRICES: (1996) Caravan with family 90.00,
Tent with two adults 45.00. CC: none.
4 km north of Treignac on D940.

TRELEVERN Côtes-du-Nord 1A

Camping de Port L'Epine
Venelle de Pors Garo, 22660 Trélévern.
Tel 02 96 23 71 94, Fax 02 96 23 77 83.
English spoken.

OPEN: 02/04–16/10. SIZE: 3 ha, 150 pitches
(120 with elec, 4 statics), 13 hot showers, 14 WCs,
4 CWPs.

Shop at 1 km. Fishing.
PRICES: (1996) Caravan with family 130.00,
Tent with two adults 75.00.
CC: Euro/Access, Visa.
*On reaching the centre of Trélévern go direct to
Port l'Epine beach. The site is on the left, near the
beach and close to the Camping Municipal.*

Camping Le Mat 38 rue de Trestel,
22660 Trévou-Tréguignec.
Tel 02 96 23 71 52.
OPEN: 15/06–15/09. SIZE: 1.6 ha, 100 pitches
(80 with elec), 10 hot showers, 12 WCs, 5 French
WCs, 5 CWPs.

Shop at 0.2 km. Restaurant at 0.2 km. Children's
playground.
PRICES: (1996) Caravan with family 134.00,
Tent with two adults 78.00. CC: none.
*From Trélévern take the D38 to Trévou-
Tréguignec.*

LE TREPORT Seine Marit 2B

Parc International du Golf
route de Dieppe, 76470 Le Tréport.
Tel 02 35 86 33 80, Fax 02 35 50 33 54.
English spoken.
OPEN: 01/04–15/09. SIZE: 5 ha, 200 pitches
(130 with elec), 38 hot showers, 77 WCs,
18 CWPs.

Shop at 0.5 km. Restaurant at 0.5 km.
PRICES: (1996) Caravan with family 144.00,
Tent with two adults 71.00. CC: Amex,
Euro/Access, Visa.
*From Le Tréport take the D940 towards Dieppe
for a short distance and the campsite is on
your right.*

TREPT Isère 5B

Les 3 Lacs 38460 Trept.
Tel 04 74 92 92 06, Fax 04 74 92 93 35.
English spoken.
OPEN: 15/04–15/09. SIZE: 3 ha, 160 pitches
(140 with elec, 15 statics), 27 hot showers,
24 WCs, 30 French WCs, 2 CWPs.

Shop at 2 km. Restaurant at 1 km. Fishing, roller
skating, tennis, mini-golf, games room,
entertainment.
PRICES: Caravan with family 150.00,
Tent with two adults 85.00. CC: Visa.
On D517 between Crémieu and Morestel.

France

TREVIERES Calvados 1B

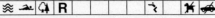

Le Picard 14330 Tournières.
Tel 02 31 22 82 44. English spoken.
OPEN: all year. SIZE: 1.95 ha, 11 pitches (all with elec, 3 statics), 2 hot showers, 2 WCs, 1 CWP.

Shop at 0.5 km. Restaurant at 4 km. Quiet site, ideal for families.
PRICES: (1996) Caravan with family 100.00, Tent with two adults 60.00. CC: none.
South of Trévières and west of Bayeux on D15. Well signposted.

LA TRINITE-SUR-MER Morbihan 1C

Camping and Caravaning La Baie
Plage de Kervillen, 56470 La Trinité-sur-Mer.
Tel 02 97 55 73 42, Fax 02 97 55 88 81.
English spoken.
OPEN: 15/05–15/09. SIZE: 2 ha, 160 pitches (all with elec, 6 statics), 25 hot showers, 24 WCs, 2 CWPs. &

Flume.
PRICES: (1996) Caravan with family 217.00, Tent with two adults 159.00. CC: none.
From Auray, take the exit for La Trinité-sur-Mer (D28). Go through the port of La Trinité and turn left at the first traffic lights, signposted Plage de Kervillen.

Camping & Caravaning La Baie ★★★★
at La Trinité-sur-Mer
Wedged between two fine sandy beaches

Camping de la Plage Plage de Kervillen, 56470 La Trinité-sur-Mer.
Tel 02 97 55 73 28, Fax 02 97 55 88 31.
English spoken.
OPEN: 08/05–17/09. SIZE: 3 ha, 176 pitches (all with elec, 24 statics), 25 hot showers, 30 WCs, 2 CWPs. & &

Tennis, mini-golf.
PRICES: (1996) Caravan with family 192.00, Tent with two adults 145.00. CC: Euro/Access, Visa.
From La Trinité-sur-Mer, D186 towards Carnac-Plage. Follow signs to left for Plage de Kervillen.

Camping Park Plijadur 94 route de Carnac, Le Quéric, 56470 La Trinité-sur-Mer.
Tel 02 97 55 72 05. English spoken.
OPEN: 01/06–30/09. SIZE: 5 ha, 198 pitches (148 with elec), 23 hot showers, 31 WCs, 1 CWP. & &

Shop at 1 km. Restaurant at 1 km. Mini-golf.
PRICES: (1996) Caravan with family 148.50, Tent with two adults 90.00. CC: Euro/Access, Visa.
From La Trinité-sur-Mer go towards Carnac, take first road on right and follow signs to campsite.

TROYES Aube 3C

Camping Municipal 7 rue Roger Salengro, Pont-Ste-Marie, 10150 Troyes.
Tel 03 25 81 02 64, Fax 03 25 81 02 64.
OPEN: 01/04–15/10. SIZE: 3.5 ha, 100 pitches (all with elec), 15 hot showers, 13 WCs. & &

Restaurant at 0.5 km. TV, children's playground.
PRICES: (1996) Caravan with family 140.00, Tent with two adults 75.00. CC: none.
Leave Troyes centre on the N77. Pont-Ste-Marie is just over the Seine and is well signposted.

TULLE Corrèze 5A

L'Etang de Miel 19190 Beynat.
Tel 05 55 85 50 66. English spoken.
OPEN: 28/03–30/09. SIZE: 9 ha, 180 pitches (150 with elec), 24 hot showers, 26 WCs, 1 CWP. & &

Restaurant at 0.2 km. Fishing, ponies, pedal boats.
PRICES: (1996) Caravan with family 106.00, Tent with two adults 56.00. CC: none.
From Tulle go south on D940/N121 to Beynat.

Le Pré du Moulin 19150 Laguenne.
Tel 05 55 20 18 60, Fax 05 55 20 18 60. English spoken.
OPEN: 15/05–30/09. SIZE: 1 ha, 28 pitches (20 with elec), 3 hot showers, 4 WCs, 1 CWP. & &

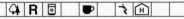

Shop at 1 km. Restaurant at 1 km.
PRICES: (1996) Caravan with family 118.00, Tent with two adults 64.00. CC: none.
South of Limoges on the N20. Campsite is through Tulle on N120, signposted.

LA TURBALLE Loire-Atlan 1D

Camping Amor-Heol route de Guérande, 44420 Piriac-sur-Mer.
Tel 02 40 23 57 80, Fax 02 40 23 59 42. English spoken.
OPEN: 15/04–15/09. SIZE: 4.5 ha, 160 pitches (100 with elec, 40 statics), 18 hot showers, 18 WCs, 2 CWPs. & &

Shop at 1 km. Restaurant at 1 km. Tennis, flumes, children's club.
PRICES: Caravan with family 160.00, Tent with two adults 92.00. CC: Amex, Euro/Access, Visa.
Go north from La Turballe on D333 to Piriac-sur-Mer.

Camping Le Pouldroit 44420 Piriac-sur-Mer.
Tel 02 40 23 50 91, Fax 02 40 23 69 12.
English spoken.
OPEN: 01/04–15/09. SIZE: 12 ha, 258 pitches
(150 with elec, 19 statics), 31 hot showers,
32 WCs, 53 French WCs, 3 CWPs. 🌣 ⅋

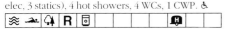

Restaurant at 0.6 km. Volley ball, tennis, children's
playground, table tennis.
PRICES: (1996) Caravan with family 164.00,
Tent with two adults 93.00. CC: none.
The campsite is 18 km from La Baule on the D52.

Camping Le Praderoi allée des Barges,
Quimiac, 44420 Mesquer.
Tel 02 40 42 66 72. English spoken.
OPEN: 13/05–30/09. SIZE: 1 ha, 30 pitches (all with
elec, 3 statics), 4 hot showers, 4 WCs, 1 CWP. ⅋

Shop at 0.3 km. Restaurant at 0.3 km.
PRICES: (1996) Caravan with family 129.00,
Tent with two adults 79.00. CC: none.
From La Turballe go to Mesquer and then
Quimiac. From the central square in Quimiac
take the road to Piriac and turn right.

Parc St-Brigitte Trescalan, 44420 La Turballe.
Tel 02 40 24 88 91, Fax 02 40 23 30 42.
English spoken.
OPEN: 01/04–30/09. SIZE: 10 ha, 96 pitches (all
with elec), 30 hot showers, 28 WCs, 2 CWPs. 🌣 ⅋

Shop at 3 km. Restaurant at 2 km. Fishing, table
tennis.
PRICES: (1996) Caravan with family 170.50,
Tent with two adults 90.00. CC: none.
On D99 between Guérande and La Turballe.
400 m before Clis, and signposted to the left.

UZES Gard   5D

Camping du Mas de Rey 30700 Arpaillargues.
Tel 04 66 22 18 27, Fax 04 66 22 18 27.
English spoken.
OPEN: 01/04–15/10. SIZE: 5 ha, 60 pitches (all with
elec, 5 statics), 8 hot showers, 8 WCs, 1 CWP. 🌣 ⅋

Tennis, table tennis, boules, volley ball,
playground.
PRICES: (1996) Caravan with family 121.00, Tent
with two adults 74.00. CC: Euro/Access, Visa.
On the D982, south-west of Uzès on the road to
Anduze.

Camping Le Moulin Neuf
St-Quentin-la-Poterie, 30700 Uzès.
Tel 04 66 22 17 21, Fax 04 66 22 91 82.
English spoken.
OPEN: 09/04–15/09. SIZE: 5 ha, 130 pitches
(110 with elec), 2 CWPs. 🌣 ⅋

PRICES: (1996) Caravan with family 117.00,
Tent with two adults 83.00. CC: Visa.
St-Quentin-la-Poterie is 4 km north of Uzès (east
of D979.)

VAISON-LA-ROMAINE Vaucluse   5D

Camping du Bon Crouzet 84340 Entrechaux.
Tel 04 90 46 01 62.
OPEN: 01/04–30/09. SIZE: 1.2 ha, 45 pitches (all with
elec, 1 static), 5 hot showers, 7 WCs, 1 CWP. 🌣 ⅋

Restaurant at 3 km.
PRICES: (1996) Caravan with family 100.00,
Tent with two adults 51.00. CC: none.
In Vaison-la-Romaine, take the D938 towards
Malaucène. After 1 km, go towards St-Marcellin
and then follow signs to campsite.

VALENCAY Indre   2D

Camping Municipal Les Chênes route de Lucay
de Male, 36600 Valençay.
Tel 02 54 00 03 92, Fax 02 54 00 32 39.
English spoken.
OPEN: all year. SIZE: 5 ha, 45 pitches (all with elec),
6 hot showers, 6 WCs, 1 CWP. ⅋

Shop at 0.8 km. Restaurant at 0.8 km.
PRICES: (1996) Caravan with family 85.00, Tent
with two adults 46.00. CC: none.

VALENCE Drôme   5B

Camping Municipal de l'Epervière chemin de
l'Epervière, 26000 Valence.
Tel 04 75 42 32 00, Fax 04 75 56 20 67.
English spoken.
OPEN: all year. SIZE: 3.5 ha, 140 pitches (110 with
elec, 30 statics), 14 hot showers, 15 WCs, 2 CWPs.
🌣 ⅋

Shop at 1 km. Mini-golf. Pool open summer only.
PRICES: Caravan with family 118.00, Tent with two
adults 72.00. CC: Euro/Access, Visa.
2 km from A7, exit Valence-Sud and follow
Epervière signs.

VALENCIENNES Nord   2B

Camping Les Pommiers
rue de la Haute Ville, 59970 Odomez.
Tel 03 27 34 10 45.
OPEN: 15/03–31/10. SIZE: 1 ha, 45 pitches (all with
elec), 3 hot showers, 4 WCs.

Shop at 1.5 km. Restaurant at 2 km.

France (side margin)

PRICES: (1996) Caravan with family 67.50, Tent with two adults 38.00. CC: none.
North of Valenciennes on the Condé road. Turn left in Condé towards Odomez and St-Amand-les-Eaux.

VALLON-PONT-D'ARC Ardèche   5D

Camping Beau Rivage
Les Mazes, 07150 Vallon-Pont-d'Arc.
Tel 04 75 88 03 54, Fax 04 75 88 03 54.
OPEN: 01/05–15/09. SIZE: 2 ha, 100 pitches, 16 hot showers, 16 WCs, 1 CWP. ⚑ ♿

~	⚓	⛱	R	🚿	🍽	☕				

Restaurant at 2 km.
PRICES: (1996) Tent with two adults 90.00.
CC: none.
D579 north-west of Vallon. Site is 2 km on the left.

Camping L'Ardèchois route Touristique des Gorges, 07150 Vallon-Pont-d'Arc.
Tel 04 75 88 06 63, Fax 04 75 37 14 97.
English spoken.
OPEN: 28/03–20/09. SIZE: 5 ha, 244 pitches (all with elec, 12 statics), 36 hot showers, 34 WCs, 3 CWPs. ⚑ ♿

~	⚓	⛱	R	🚿	⛱		🍽	🎣	Ⓗ	

Canoes for hire.

PRICES: Caravan with family 223.00, Tent with two adults 136.00. CC: Euro/Access, Visa.
From Vallon-Pont-d'Arc, take D290 for 500 m. Site is on right. Signposted.
SEE ADVERTISEMENT

Camping de la Bastide Bastide, 07120 Sampzon.
Tel 04 75 39 64 72, Fax 04 75 39 73 28.
English spoken.
OPEN: 23/03–15/09. SIZE: 6 ha, 300 pitches (all with elec, 50 statics), 33 hot showers, 16 WCs, 20 French WCs, 1 CWP. ⚑ ♿

~	⚓	⛱	R	🚿	🛒		🍽	🎣		Ⓗ	

Shop at 2 km. Restaurant at 1 km. Tennis, volley ball, fitness room, sauna.
PRICES: (1996) Caravan with family 210.00, Tent with two adults 130.00. CC: none.
On D111, 7 km from Vallon.

La Plage Fleurie Les Mazes, 07150 Vallon-Pont-d'Arc.
Tel 04 75 88 01 15, Fax 04 75 88 11 31.
English spoken.
OPEN: 01/04–01/10. SIZE: 12 ha, 300 pitches (all with elec), 32 hot showers, 30 WCs, 2 CWPs. ⚑ ♿

~	⚓	⛱	R	🚿	⛱	☕				🚗

Restaurant at 3 km. Mobile homes available.
PRICES: Caravan with family 149.00, Tent with two adults 89.00. CC: none.

Take the D579 north of Vallon-Pont-d'Arc to Ruoms. Turn left to Les Mazes after 3 km.

SEE ADVERTISEMENT

Camping Le Casque Roi
Salavas, 07150 Vallon-Pont-d'Arc.
Tel 04 75 88 04 23, Fax 04 75 37 18 64. English spoken.
OPEN: 01/03–15/11. SIZE: 0.4 ha, 29 pitches
(20 with elec, 14 statics), 7 hot showers, 8 WCs,
4 French WCs, 1 CWP. &

Shop at 0.1 km. Music in the evenings.
PRICES: Caravan with family 158.00,
Tent with two adults 100.00. CC: Amex, Visa.
*From Vallon-Pont-d'Arc go south on D579
towards Barjac. The campsite is 800 m from the
entrance to Salavas.*

Mondial Camping route des Gorges,
07150 Vallon-Pont-d'Arc.
Tel 04 75 88 00 44, Fax 04 75 37 13 73.
English spoken.
OPEN: 15/03–30/09. SIZE: 4.2 ha, 240 pitches
(all with elec), 48 hot showers, 30 WCs, 3 CWPs. &

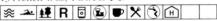

Good sports facilities on site/nearby.
PRICES: (1996) Caravan with family 212.00,
Tent with two adults 129.00. CC: none.
Follow signs to campsite in Vallon-Pont-d'Arc.

VALRAS-PLAGE Hérault   5C

Camping Blue Bayou
Vendres-Plage-Ouest, 34350 Valras-Plage.
Tel 04 67 37 41 97, Fax 04 67 37 53 00.
English spoken.
OPEN: 01/05–15/09. SIZE: 6 ha, 335 pitches
(all with elec, 40 statics), 39 hot showers, 35 WCs,
13 French WCs, 4 CWPs. & &

Shop at 1 km. Excellent swimming facilities.
PRICES: (1996) Caravan with family 210.00, Tent
with two adults 140.00. CC: none.

*From motorway La Languedocienne A9, exit
Béziers-Ouest. Follow signs towards Valras-Plage
and then Vendres-Plage-Ouest and campsite is
beside the beach.*

Camping L'Occitanie 34350 Valras-Plage.
Tel 04 67 39 59 06, Fax 04 67 32 58 20.
English spoken.
OPEN: 17/05–13/09. SIZE: 6 ha, 415 pitches
(all with elec, 51 statics), 60 hot showers, 65 WCs,
5 CWPs. & &

PRICES: Caravan with family 145.00, Tent with two
adults 115.00. CC: Euro/Access, Visa.
*From A9, exit at Béziers-Est towards Valras-Plage.
Campsite is 12 km, just on entering Valras-Plage-
Est.*

Camping Les Foulegues
Grau-de-Vendres, 34350 Valras-Plage.
Tel 04 67 37 33 65, Fax 04 67 37 54 75. English spoken.
OPEN: 01/06–30/09. SIZE: 5.5 ha, 340 pitches
(all with elec, 110 statics), 60 hot showers,
55 WCs, 3 CWPs. &

Tennis, mini-golf, volley ball, archery.
PRICES: (1996) Caravan with family 184.00,
Tent with two adults 140.00. CC: Amex,
Euro/Access, Visa.
From the A9 take Béziers exit then D19 to Valras.

Domaine de la Yole 34350 Valras-Plage.
Tel 04 67 37 33 87, Fax 04 67 37 44 89.
English spoken.
OPEN: 03/05–20/09. SIZE: 20 ha, 990 pitches
(all with elec, 80 statics), 112 hot showers,
112 WCs, 3 French WCs. &

Amusement park, entertainment.
PRICES: (1996) Caravan with family 190.00, Tent
with two adults 156.00. CC: Euro/Access, Visa.
*From A9 take Béziers-Ouest exit and Valras-Plage
is 10 km on D19.*
SEE ADVERTISEMENT

France

VANNES Morbihan 1D

Camp Municipal de Conleau
188 av du Maréchal Juin, 56000 Vannes.
Tel 02 97 63 13 88, Fax 02 97 40 38 82. English spoken.
OPEN: 01/04–30/09. SIZE: 5 ha, 275 pitches
(145 with elec), 21 hot showers, 21 WCs,
15 French WCs, 3 CWPs. ⚭ ⚭

≋		🄰	R	⊡	🄻	🍵				

Restaurant at 3 km. Children's playground;
swimming pool 0.3 km; 20% discount in LS.
PRICES: (1996) Caravan with family 151.00,
Tent with two adults 89.00. CC: Amex,
Euro/Access, Visa.
*In Vannes follow signs to Parc du Golf, then
Conleau. Campsite is well signposted.*

Camping Mane Guernehue 56870 Baden.
Tel 02 97 57 02 06, Fax 02 97 57 15 43.
English spoken.
OPEN: 10/04–30/09. SIZE: 5 ha, 200 pitches (all with
elec, 20 statics), 29 hot showers, 21 WCs, 2 CWPs. ⚭ ⚭

		🄰	R	⊡	🄻	🍵		⤳	🄷	

Restaurant at 1 km. Children's playground, flume,
archery, fitness, sauna, billiards.
PRICES: (1996) Caravan with family 179.00,
Tent with two adults 116.00. CC: Amex,
Euro/Access, Visa.
On D101 Auray to Vannes road. Follow signs.

Camping Penboch 56610 Arradon.
Tel 02 97 44 71 29, Fax 02 97 44 79 10.
English spoken.
OPEN: 05/04–20/09. SIZE: 4 ha, 175 pitches (all with
elec), 24 hot showers, 20 WCs, 1 CWP. ⚭ ⚭

≋	⤳	🄰	R	⊡	🄽	🍵		⤳	🄷	

Restaurant at 2 km. Flume.
PRICES: (1996) Caravan with family 176.00, Tent
with two adults 116.00. CC: Euro/Access, Visa.
*Turn off N165 west of Vannes to Arradon. Site
signposted.*

La Peupleraie Le Marais, 56450 Theix.
Tel 02 97 43 09 46.
OPEN: 15/04–15/10. SIZE: 3 ha, 100 pitches
(60 with elec), 6 hot showers, 10 WCs, 1 CWP. ⚭

		🌳	R	⊡					🄷	

Shop at 2.5 km. Restaurant at 2.5 km. Boules,
children's playground; small lake.
PRICES: (1996) Caravan with family 83.50,
Tent with two adults 43.50. CC: Euro/Access.
*From Vannes, take N165 towards Nantes, turn off
at Theix on to D104 towards Tréfféan. Campsite
is about 2.5 km further along and signposted.*

VARENNES-EN-ARGONNE Meuse 3A

Le Paquis rue Saint-Jean,
55270 Varennes-en-Argonne.
Tel 03 29 80 71 01.

OPEN: 06/04–29/09. SIZE: 1.50 ha, 150 pitches
(all with elec), 9 hot showers, 9 WCs, 3 French
WCs, 1 CWP. ⚭ ⚭

~	✈	🄰	R						🄷	

Shop at 0.3 km. Restaurant at 0.2 km.
PRICES: (1996) Caravan with family 59.90,
Tent with two adults 27.70. CC: none.
*Campsite in centre of village of Varennes-en-
Argonne.*

VARENNES-SUR-ALLIER Allier 5A

Camp du Château de Chazeuil
03150 Varennes-sur-Allier.
Tel 04 70 45 00 10.
OPEN: 15/04–15/10. SIZE: 2 ha, 60 pitches (50 with
elec), 19 hot showers, 10 WCs, 1 CWP. ⚭ ⚭

		🄰	R	⊡			⤳		

Shop at 1.5 km. Restaurant at 2 km.
PRICES: (1996) Caravan with family 181.00,
Tent with two adults 111.00. CC: Visa.
2.5 km north of Varennes-sur-Allier on N7.

Camping Les Plans d'Eau Chazeuil,
03150 Varennes-sur-Allier.
Tel 04 70 45 01 55. English spoken.
OPEN: 15/05–15/09. SIZE: 4 ha, 80 pitches (64 with
elec), 8 hot showers, 8 WCs. ⚭

≈	⤳	🄰	R			🍵		⤳	

Shop at 1 km. Restaurant at 2 km. Tennis,
children's playground.
PRICES: Caravan with family 133.00,
Tent with two adults 74.00. CC: none.
*D46 north of Varennes. The site is just before the
bridge, 1 km from the traffic lights.*

VARZY Nièvre 2D

Camp Municipal du Moulin Naudin 58210 Varzy.
Tel 03 86 29 43 12.
OPEN: 01/05–30/09. SIZE: 1.5 ha, 50 pitches
(40 with elec), 4 hot showers, 13 WCs. ⚭ ⚭

≈	⤳	🛉	R	⊡			✗		

Shop at 1.5 km.
PRICES: (1996) Caravan with family 80.00,
Tent with two adults 42.00. CC: none.
On N151 (Bourges to Auxerre). Signposted at Varzy.

VATAN Indre 2D

Camping Municipal
rue Ferdinand de Lesseps, 36150 Vatan.
Tel 02 54 49 76 31, Fax 02 54 49 81 67.
English spoken.
OPEN: / –31/12. SIZE: 2 ha, 25 pitches (all with
elec), 4 hot showers, 4 WCs, 1 CWP. ⚭ ⚭

~	⤳	🄰	R				🄭	🄷	

Shop at 0.2 km. Restaurant at 0.2 km. Tennis 200m.

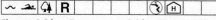

PRICES: unavailable. CC: none.
From town centre go west towards Guilly on D34, the follow signs to campsite on the left.

VAUVERT Gard 5D

Camping Caravaning des Mourgues
Gallician, 30600 Vauvert.
Tel 04 66 73 30 88. English spoken.
OPEN: 01/04–15/09. SIZE: 2 ha, 80 pitches (42 with elec), 6 hot showers, 11 WCs, 1 CWP. ⚓ ⚭

Shop at 1 km. Restaurant at 1 km. Table tennis, barbecue, boules, swings for children.
PRICES: (1996) Caravan with family 116.00, Tent with two adults 63.00. CC: none.
6 km from Vauvert on the N572 towards St-Gilles. Site is at junction of road to Gallician.

VAYRAC Lot 5A

Camping Les Granges 46110 Vayrac.
Tel 05 65 32 46 58, Fax 05 65 32 57 94.
OPEN: 15/05–15/09. SIZE: 5 ha, 100 pitches (all with elec, 20 statics), 21 hot showers, 18 WCs, 18 French WCs, 1 CWP. ⚓

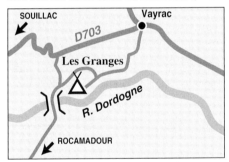

Shop at 3 km. Restaurant at 3 km. Boating, VTT, pot-holing and climbing, fishing, boating; entertainment.
PRICES: (1996) Caravan with family 115.00, Tent with two adults 68.00. CC: Euro/Access, Visa.

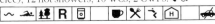

From Vayrac on D703. Well signposted.

VEIGNE Indre/Loire 2C

Camping de la Plage 37250 Veigné.
Tel 02 47 26 23 00, Fax 02 47 26 94 31.
English spoken.
OPEN: 01/05–10/09. SIZE: 3 ha, 121 pitches (100 with elec), 12 hot showers, 10 WCs, 2 CWPs. ⚓ ⚭

Shop at 0.2 km. Canoes, kayaks, fishing.
PRICES: (1996) Caravan with family 104.00, Tent with two adults 56.00. CC: Euro/Access, Visa.

From Tours take N10 towards Poitiers, then D50 to Veigné (13 km south of Tours).

VENCE Alpes-Marit 6C

Caravaning Les Rives du Loup
route de la Colle, 06140 Tourrettes-sur-Loup.
Tel 04 93 24 15 65, Fax 04 93 24 15 65.
English spoken.
OPEN: 27/03–15/10. SIZE: 2 ha, 10 pitches (all with elec, 40 statics), 6 hot showers, 6 WCs, 1 CWP. ⚓ ⚭

20 mins from the coast.
PRICES: (1996) Caravan with family 152.50, Tent with two adults 78.00. CC: Euro/Access, Visa.
From Vence take road to Tourrettes-sur-Loup (3 km), then to Pont-du-Loup from where the campsite is signposted.

Domaine de la Bergerie
route de la Sine, 06140 Vence.
Tel 04 93 58 09 36. English spoken.
OPEN: 25/03–15/10. SIZE: 13 ha, 450 pitches (257 with elec), 46 hot showers, 47 WCs, 5 CWPs. ⚓ ⚭

Tennis; swimming pool nearby.
PRICES: (1996) Caravan with family 121.00, Tent with two adults 82.50. CC: Amex, Euro/Access, Visa.
From Vence, drive towards Grasse. At the roundabout, turn left towards La Sine.

VENDAYS-MONTALIVET Gironde 4A

Camping Les Peupliers
33930 Vendays-Montalivet.
Tel 05 56 41 70 44.
OPEN: 01/06–30/09. SIZE: 2 ha, 93 pitches (84 with elec, 10 statics), 14 hot showers, 12 WCs, 1 CWP. ⚓ ⚭

Restaurant at 0.15 km.
PRICES: (1996) Caravan with family 89.00, Tent with two adults 51.00. CC: none.
On the D101 coast road, signposted.

VENDEUVRE-SUR-BARSE Aube 3C

Camping de Voie Colette
route du Lac, 10140 Mesnil-St-Père.
Tel 03 25 41 27 15. English spoken.
OPEN: 01/04–15/10. SIZE: 4 ha, 300 pitches (200 with elec), 18 hot showers, 27 WCs. ⚭

Shop at 2 km. Restaurant at 0.1 km. Volley ball, playground.
PRICES: (1996) Caravan with family 85.50, Tent with two adults 46.50. CC: Euro/Access, Visa.
From Vendeuvre, west on E54/N19 for 3 km and then turn right to Mesnil.

France

France

VENDOME Loir-et-Cher 2C

Camping Municipal de la Bonne Aventure
41100 Thoré-la-Rochette.
Tel 02 54 72 00 59, Fax 02 54 72 73 38.
English spoken.
OPEN: 01/05–01/10. SIZE: 2 ha, 52 pitches (all with elec), 10 hot showers, 10 WCs, 2 CWPs. &

Shop at 1 km. Restaurant at 1 km.
PRICES: Caravan with family 62.00,
Tent with two adults 37.00. CC: none.
From Vendôme go west towards Montoire (D917) and after approximately 5 km turn right on to D82 to Thoré, by the bridge.

Camping Municipal Les Ilots 41100 Pezou.
Tel 02 54 23 40 69, Fax 02 54 23 62 40.
English spoken.
OPEN: 07/05–15/09. SIZE: 1 ha, 33 pitches (12 with elec), 2 hot showers, 3 WCs, 1 French WC, 1 CWP. &

Shop at 0.5 km. Restaurant at 0.5 km. Tennis nearby.
PRICES: (1996) Caravan with family 57.00,
Tent with two adults 28.00. CC: none.
From Vendôme, take N10 north to Pezou (8 km). Signposted. (No motor caravans).

VERMENTON Yonne 3C

Camping Municipal des Coullemières
89270 Vermenton.
Tel 03 86 81 53 02, Fax 03 86 81 63 95.
English spoken.
OPEN: 10/04–10/10. SIZE: 1 ha, 50 pitches (40 with elec), 6 hot showers, 6 WCs, 1 CWP. & &

Restaurant at 0.5 km. Good sports facilities nearby.
PRICES: Caravan with family 82.00, Tent with two adults 50.00. CC: none.
Vermenton is on N6 between Auxerre and Avallon. Follow signs to campsite.

VERTEILLAC Dordogne 4B

Camping Petit Vos Nanteuil de Bourzac, 24320 Verteillac.
Tel 05 53 91 00 05. English spoken.
OPEN: 01/03–01/11. SIZE: 1 ha, 8 pitches (all with elec, 3 statics), 1 hot shower (charge), 2 WCs, 1 CWP.

Shop at 5 km.
PRICES: (1996) Caravan with family 59.00,
Tent with two adults 31.00. CC: none.
From Verteillac take D1 north-west to Nanteuil-de-Bourzac, then the D202 to Vendoire at the top of the hill. Follow signs to campsite from there.

VIAS Hérault 5C

Le Bourricot 34450 Vias-Plage.
Tel 04 67 21 64 27. English spoken.
OPEN: 20/05–20/09. SIZE: 2 ha, 152 pitches (140 with elec), 27 hot showers, 16 WCs, 2 CWPs. &

PRICES: (1996) Caravan with family 161.00,
Tent with two adults 115.00. CC: none.
In Vias-Plage, drive towards the sea. The campsite is 150 m ahead, on the right-hand side.

Camping Californie Plage 34450 Vias-sur-Mer.
Tel 04 67 21 64 69, Fax 04 67 21 70 66.
English spoken.
OPEN: 01/04–31/10. SIZE: 5 ha, 290 pitches (all with elec, 40 statics). & &

Entertainment in HS.
PRICES: (1996) Caravan with family 185.00,
Tent with two adults 130.00. CC: none.
In Vias, go towards Vias-Plage and 'Côte Ouest'.

Camping Club International Le Napoléon
34450 Vias-Plage.
Tel 04 67 21 64 37, Fax 04 67 21 75 30.
English spoken.
OPEN: 01/04–30/09. SIZE: 3 ha, 200 pitches (180 with elec, 10 statics), 36 hot showers, 26 WCs, 2 CWPs. & &

Volley ball, fitness room; organised entertainment.
PRICES: (1996) Caravan with family 194.00,
Tent with two adults 120.00. CC: none.
From Vias go towards the sea. The campsite is 100 m before the beach on the right-hand side.

Camping Gai Soleil 34450 Vias-Plage.
Tel 04 67 21 64 77, Fax 04 67 21 70 66.
English spoken.
OPEN: all year. SIZE: 5 ha, 288 pitches (50 with elec, 50 statics), 3 CWPs. & &

Sea 0.6 km.
PRICES: (1996) Caravan with family 144.00,
Tent with two adults 95.00. CC: none.
To the west of Vias-Plage and well signposted.

Camping L'Air Marin 34450 Vias-Plage.
Tel 04 67 94 21 89, Fax 04 67 21 26 73.
English spoken.
OPEN: 15/06–30/09. SIZE: 7 ha, 2 CWPs. & &

Archery, boating, ball games, table tennis, children's club.
PRICES: (1996) Tent with two adults 128.00. CC: none.
From Vias, drive towards Vias-Plage, just after the bridge turn right and turn right again. Campsite is well signposted.

Camping Les Mimosas Port-Cassafières,
34420 Portiragnes-Plage.
Tel 04 67 90 92 92, Fax 04 67 90 85 39.
English spoken.
OPEN: 01/05–30/09. SIZE: 7 ha, 400 pitches
(51 statics), 4 CWPs. ☎ &

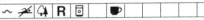

2 flumes, children's pool.
PRICES: Caravan with family 180.00,
Tent with two adults 125.00. CC: Visa.
*From Vias, go west on the N112 towards Béziers
and turn left on the D37 to Portiragnes and Port-
Cassafières.*

VIC-SUR-CERE Cantal   5A

Camping Municipal allée des Tilleuls,
15800 Vic-sur-Cère.
Tel 04 71 47 51 04, Fax 04 71 47 50 59.
English spoken.
OPEN: 01/04–30/09. SIZE: 2 ha, 250 pitches
(all with elec), 25 hot showers, 41 WCs.

Shop at 0.5 km. Restaurant at 0.5 km.
PRICES: (1996) Caravan with family 73.50,
Tent with two adults 38.00. CC: none.
North-east of Aurillac on N122. Signposted.

VICHY Allier   5A

Beau Rivage rue Claude Decloitre,
03700 Bellerive-sur-Allier.
Tel 04 70 32 26 85, Fax 04 70 32 03 94.
English spoken.
OPEN: 01/05–30/09. SIZE: 2 ha, 80 pitches (all with
elec, 5 statics), 12 hot showers, 12 WCs, 1 CWP. ☎ &

Canoeing, aqua-toboggans, archery.
PRICES: Caravan with family 165.00, Tent with two
adults 90.00. CC: Euro/Access, Visa.
Bellerive is on the western side of Vichy.

Camping La Croix Gognat
03250 Châtel-Montagne.
Tel 04 70 59 31 38. English spoken.
OPEN: 01/04–01/11. SIZE: 1 ha, 33 pitches (all with
elec), 4 hot showers, 5 WCs, 1 CWP. ☎ &

Mobile homes available; river 0.3 km.
PRICES: (1996) Caravan with family 81.00,
Tent with two adults 42.00. CC: none.
*From Vichy east to Cusset, then D25 to Châtel-
Montagne for 20 km. Well signposted.*

VIDAUBAN Var   6C

Les Ombrages Hameau de Ramatuelle,
83550 Vidauban.
Tel 04 94 73 06 95. English spoken.

OPEN: 01/03–30/10. SIZE: 4 ha, 140 pitches
(100 with elec), 8 hot showers, 10 WCs, 10 French
WCs, 1 CWP.

PRICES: (1996) Caravan with family 101.00,
Tent with two adults 53.00. CC: none.
*Located halfway between Vidauban and Le Luc,
on N7.*

VIELLE-ST-GIRONS Landes   4C

Camping Eurosol route de la Plage,
40560 Vielle-St-Girons.
Tel 05 58 47 90 14, Fax 05 58 47 76 74.
English spoken.
OPEN: 01/06–15/09. SIZE: 18 ha, 672 pitches
(350 with elec, 42 statics), 88 hot showers,
88 WCs, 6 CWPs. ☎ &

Tennis, mini-golf, horse-riding; bikes for hire.
PRICES: (1996) Caravan with family 180.00, Tent
with two adults 105.00. CC: Euro/Access, Visa.
*From St-Girons village take the beach road.
Eurosol is the first site on the left.*

Camping Le Col Vert Léon,
40560 Vielle-St-Girons.
Tel 05 58 42 94 06, Fax 05 58 42 91 88.
English spoken.
OPEN: 28/03–30/10. SIZE: 24 ha, 370 pitches
(all with elec, 61 statics), 97 hot showers, 64 WCs,
8 CWPs. ☎ &

Covered pool, sauna, tennis, windsurfing, horse-
riding.
PRICES: (1996) Caravan with family 219.00, Tent
with two adults 116.00. CC: Euro/Access, Visa.
*Take N10 from Bordeaux to Castets and then D42
to St-Girons.*

Centre Naturiste Arnaoutchot,
40560 Vielle-St-Girons.
Tel 05 58 49 11 11, Fax 05 58 48 57 12.
English spoken.
OPEN: 01/04–30/09. SIZE: 45 ha, 250 pitches
(all with elec, 120 statics), 85 hot showers,
55 WCs, 8 CWPs. ☎ &

PRICES: (1996) Caravan with family 223.00, Tent
with two adults 148.00. CC: Euro/Access, Visa.
*N10 Bordeaux/Biarrtz, exit at Castets towards St-
Girons (D42). At Linxe take road to Vielle. From
Vielle take D328 towards Moliets, then follow signs.*

VIENNE Isère   5B

Camping des Nations N7,
38550 Auberives-sur-Varèze.
Tel 04 74 84 95 13, Fax 04 74 86 34 40.

France

France

OPEN: 01/03–31/10. SIZE: 1.5 ha, 40 pitches (all with elec), 9 hot showers, 9 WCs, 1 CWP. ℂ ℷ

Shop at 2 km.
PRICES: Caravan with family 135.00, Tent with two adults 75.00. CC: Euro/Access, Visa.
South from Vienne on N7 for 13 km, look for sign 2 km after Auberives-sur-Varèze.

Hôtel de Plein Air du Bontemps 38150 Vernioz.
Tel 04 74 57 83 52, Fax 04 74 57 83 70. English spoken.
OPEN: 01/04–30/09. SIZE: 6 ha, 100 pitches (all with elec, 50 statics), 14 hot showers, 18 WCs, 3 CWPs. ℂ ℷ

Fishing, archery, mini-golf, horse-riding, tennis.
PRICES: (1996) Caravan with family 135.00, Tent with two adults 80.00. CC: none.
From Vienne take N7 south and just outside town turn left on to D131e. Follow signs from Vernioz.

VIERZON Cher 2D

Camping Municipal Les Saules 18120 Quincy.
Tel 02 48 51 34 19.
OPEN: 15/05–30/09. SIZE: 1 ha, 35 pitches, 1 hot shower (charge), 3 WCs.

Shop at 0.5 km. Restaurant at 1 km.
PRICES: (1996) Caravan with family 30.50, Tent with two adults 13.50. CC: none.
From Vierzon go south-east towards Bourges. 15 km from Vierzon turn right at Mehun-sur-Yèvre to Quincy (5 km).

VIEUX-BOUCAU-LES-BAINS Landes 4C

Camping de Moisan
route de la Plage, 40660 Messanges.
Tel 05 58 48 92 06. English spoken.
OPEN: 15/05–30/09. SIZE: 5 ha, 220 pitches (150 with elec), 25 hot showers, 22 WCs, 6 CWPs. ℂ

Restaurant at 1 km.
PRICES: (1996) Caravan with family 122.00, Tent with two adults 69.00. CC: none.
From Vieux-Boucau take D652 north to Messanges. The campsite is signposted, towards the beach.

Camping Municipal Les Sablères
bd du Marensin, 40480 Vieux-Boucau.
Tel 05 58 48 12 29. English spoken.
OPEN: 01/04–15/10. SIZE: 13 ha, 46 hot showers, 45 WCs, 11 CWPs. ℂ ℷ

Shop at 0.8 km. Restaurant at 0.6 km.
PRICES: (1996) Caravan with family 118.80, Tent with two adults 81.40. CC: Euro/Access, Visa.
From Vieux-Boucau on D652, approaching the

roundabout follow the signs north to the beach (about 700 m).

LE VIGAN Gard 5C

Le Val de l'Arre 30120 Le Vigan.
Tel 04 67 81 02 77, Fax 04 67 81 71 23. English spoken.
OPEN: 01/04–30/09. SIZE: 4 ha, 180 pitches (130 with elec), 18 hot showers, 19 WCs, 1 CWP. ℂ ℷ

Shop at 2 km. Restaurant at 2 km.
PRICES: (1996) Caravan with family 118.00, Tent with two adults 74.00. CC: Amex, Euro/Access, Visa.
On the Millau to Nîmes road. From Le Vigan drive 2 km towards Nîmes/Ganges and turn right over river. Please note this is a difficult turn if towing and there is an alternative route via back roads; campsite will send a map on request.

Le Val de l'Arre
at Le Vigan
*In the Cévennes, by a river.
Sounds OK to me.*

VILLARD-DE-LANS Isère 5B

Camping Primé L'Oursière
38250 Villard-de-Lans.
Tel 04 76 95 14 77, Fax 04 76 95 11 58.
English spoken.
OPEN: 01/01–30/09 & 22/10–31/12. SIZE: 4.5 ha, 200 pitches (185 with elec, 50 statics), 24 hot showers, 32 WCs, 6 CWPs. ℂ ℷ

Restaurant at 0.7 km. Skiing and climbing close by.
PRICES: (1996) Caravan with family 101.00, Tent with two adults 72.00. CC: Amex, Visa.
From Grenoble take D106 then left onto D531 to Villard-de-Lans.

VILLENEUVE-LOUBET Alpes-Marit 6C

Camping Parc des Maurettes 730 avenue du Doct Léfèvre, 06270 Villeneuve-Loubet.
Tel 04 93 20 91 91. English spoken.
OPEN: 10/01–15/11. SIZE: 2 ha, 100 pitches (all with elec), 23 hot showers, 29 WCs. ℂ ℷ

Motor caravan services.
PRICES: (1996) Caravan with family 181.00, Tent with two adults 110.00. CC: Euro/Access, Visa.
From Villeneuve-Loubet, drive 800m towards Antibes and turn right to campsite

Le Sourire/Parc Montana route de Grasse,
06270 Villeneuve-Loubet.
Tel 04 93 20 96 11, Fax 04 93 22 07 52. English spoken.
OPEN: 01/01–15/11 & 15/12–31/12. SIZE: 8 ha,
250 pitches (all with elec, 150 statics), 55 hot
showers, 47 WCs, 1 CWP. ✆ ら

Sauna, mini-golf; mobile homes for hire;
tennis nearby.
PRICES: (1996) Caravan with family 182.00, Tent
with two adults 122.00. CC: Euro/Access, Visa.
*From Villeneuve-Loubet take the D2085 towards
Grasse. The campsite is 2 km from the village.
Follow signs for La Vanade.*

La Vieille Ferme bd des Groules,
06270 Villeneuve-Loubet.
Tel 04 93 33 41 44, Fax 04 93 33 37 28. English spoken.
OPEN: all year. SIZE: 3 ha, 102 pitches (all with
elec), 20 hot showers, 16 WCs. ✆ ら

Shop at 1 km. Restaurant at 1 km. Free covered
pool all year.
PRICES: Caravan with family 187.00, Tent with two
adults 100.00. CC: Amex, Euro/Access, Visa.
*Leave motorway at Antibes and staying on N7
follow signs towards Nice for about 10 km.
Campsite is 1 km on the left after Marineland.*

SEE ADVERTISEMENT

VILLENEUVE-SUR-LOT Lot-et-Gar 4D

Camping du Clos Bouyssac 46700 Touzac.
Tel 05 65 63 52 21, Fax 05 65 24 68 51. English spoken.
OPEN: 05/05–30/09. SIZE: 1.5 ha, 85 pitches
(all with elec, 3 statics), 14 hot showers, 10 WCs,
5 French WCs, 4 CWPs. ✆ ら

Restaurant at 0.5 km. 4 mobile homes for hire.
PRICES: (1996) Caravan with family 133.00, Tent
with two adults 72.00. CC: Visa.
*From Villeneuve D911 to Fumel, Soturac, then
right on to D8 Touzac.*

Camping Le Moulin Lassalle, 47290 Monbahus.
Tel 05 53 01 68 87. English spoken.
OPEN: all year. SIZE: 2 ha, 10 pitches (5 with elec),
1 hot shower, 3 WCs, 1 CWP.

Shop at 3 km.
PRICES: (1996) Caravan with family 85.00. CC: none.
*North on N21 from Villeneuve-sur-Lot to Cancon,
then west on D124. The campsite is 3 km on the
right after Monbahus.*

VILLEREAL Lot/Garonne 4D

Camping du Château de Fonrives
Rives, 47210 Villeréal.
Tel 05 53 36 63 38, Fax 05 53 36 09 98. English spoken.
OPEN: 15/05–20/09. SIZE: 20 ha, 150 pitches (all
with elec, 50 statics), 40 hot showers, 30 WCs. ✆ ら

Mini-golf, table tennis; boating and golf nearby.
PRICES: (1996) Caravan with family 175.00, Tent
with two adults 101.00. CC: Euro/Access, Visa.
*On D207 just north of Villeréal heading towards
Bergerac.*

Camping les Ormes Fauquie-Haut,
47210 St-Etienne-de-Villeréal.
Tel 05 53 36 60 26, Fax 05 53 36 69 90. English spoken.
OPEN: 01/04–30/09. SIZE: 20 ha, 140 pitches (110 with
elec), 21 hot showers, 22 WCs, 1 CWP. ✆ ら

Horse-riding, Romany wagons for hire, tennis,
volley ball.
PRICES: (1996) Caravan with family 151.00,
Tent with two adults 86.00. CC: none.
*From Villeréal take D255 south to St-Etienne-de-
Villeréal. Follow signs.*

VILLERS-COTTERETS Aisne 2B

Castel des Biches Parc du château A. Dumas,
02600 Villers-Hélon.
Tel 03 23 96 04 99, Fax 03 23 72 93 33.
English spoken.
OPEN: all year. SIZE: 7 ha, 120 pitches (all with
elec), 16 hot showers, 21 WCs, 2 CWPs. ✆ ら

France (side margin)

Shop at 4 km. Restaurant at 4 km. Tennis, horse-riding, boules, fishing, table tennis, playground, mini-golf.
PRICES: (1996) Caravan with family 135.00., Tent with two adults 70.00. CC: none.
From Villers-Cotterêts take the N2 towards Soissons. After 7 km, turn right to Longpont and then follow signs for 3.5 km to campsite which is set in the grounds of the Alexandre Dumas 16th-century moated château.

VILLERS-FARLAY Jura   3C

La Halte Jurassienne Quartier Bel Air, 39330 Mouchard.
Tel 03 84 37 83 92.
OPEN: 15/04–15/10. SIZE: 1 ha, 10 pitches (all with elec), 2 hot showers (charge), 3 WCs, 3 French WCs.

Restaurant at 0.9 km.
PRICES: (1996) Caravan with family 86.50, Tent with two adults 51.10. CC: none.
D472 south-east of Villers-Farlay towards Salins-les-Bains.

VINEUIL Loir-et-Cher   2D

Airotel Lac de Loire Lac de Loire, 41350 Vineuil.
Tel 02 54 78 82 05, Fax 02 54 78 62 03. English spoken.
OPEN: 01/04–15/10. SIZE: 190 pitches (all with elec, 13 statics). ✆ &

Shop at 4 km. Water-skiing, sailing, tennis, mini-golf.
PRICES: (1996) Caravan with family 106.00.
CC: Euro/Access, Visa.
On the D951 exit Blois towards Chambord.

SEE ADVERTISEMENT

Camp des Châteaux Lac de Loire, 41350 Vineuil.
Tel 02 54 78 82 05, Fax 02 54 78 62 03.
English spoken.
OPEN: 01/04–15/10. SIZE: 8 ha, 187 pitches (37 with elec). ✆ &

Shop at 4 km. Water-skiing, sailing, tennis, mini-golf.
PRICES: (1996) Caravan with family 115.00, Tent with two adults 56.00. CC: Euro/Access, Visa.
On the D951, just outside Blois going towards Chambord.

VIZILLE Isère   5B

Camp Municipal Les Grandes Sagnes
Laffrey, 38220 Vizille.
Tel 04 76 73 11 37. English spoken.
OPEN: 15/06–15/09. SIZE: 2 ha. &

Restaurant at 0.2 km.
PRICES: (1996) Caravan with family 33.00. CC: none.
Go south from Vizille on N85 to Laffrey.

Camping Municipal Le Bois de Cornage
38220 Vizille.
Tel 04 76 68 12 39. English spoken.
OPEN: 01/05–15/10. SIZE: 2.5 ha, 128 pitches (all with elec), 12 hot showers, 16 WCs, 2 CWPs. ✆ &

Restaurant at 1 km. Montain bikes for hire.
PRICES: (1996) Caravan with family 86.00, Tent with two adults 46.00. CC: none.
Well signposted in Vizille.

VOIRON Isère   5B

Camping 3 Etoiles
Porte de la Chartreuse, 38500 Voiron.
Tel 04 76 05 14 20. English spoken.
OPEN: 15/01–30/11. SIZE: 1.5 ha, 52 pitches (all with elec), 7 hot showers, 12 WCs, 2 CWPs. ✆ &

Shop at 0.5 km. Restaurant at 0.5 km. 10% discount to RAC Members.
PRICES: (1996) Caravan with family 110.00, Tent with two adults 64.00. CC: none.
1.5 km from centre of Voiron, Bourg-en-Bresse road.

VOLONNE Alpes/Hte-Prov   6C

Camping des Salettes 04160 Château-Arnoux.
Tel 04 92 64 02 40, Fax 04 92 64 25 06.
English spoken.
OPEN: all year. SIZE: 4 ha, 300 pitches (250 with elec, 70 statics), 36 hot showers, 48 WCs, 56 French WCs, 5 CWPs. ✆ &

Shop at 0.5 km. Archery, mini-golf.
PRICES: (1996) Caravan with family 118.50, Tent with two adults 63.00. CC: Euro/Access, Visa.
Cross the River Durance from Volonne to Château-Arnoux and campsite is on road towards Sisteron.

L'Hippocampe 04290 Volonne.
Tel 04 92 33 50 00, Fax 04 92 33 50 49.
English spoken.
OPEN: 01/04–30/09. SIZE: 8 ha, 447 pitches (350 with elec, 64 statics), 53 hot showers, 41 WCs, 3 CWPs. ✆ &

Shop at 0.6 km. Entertainment in high season.
PRICES: (1996) Caravan with family 176.00, Tent with two adults 115.00. CC: Euro/Access, Visa.
Volonne is 12 km south of Sistéron. Campsite is well signposted.

VOREY Haute-Loire   5B

Camping Les Moulettes chemin de Félines, 43800 Vorey-sur-Arzon.
Tel 04 71 03 70 48. English spoken.
OPEN: 01/05–20/09. SIZE: 2 ha, 43 pitches (all with elec, 8 statics), 4 hot showers, 6 WCs, 1 CWP. &

Shop at 0.2 km. Restaurant at 0.2 km. Playground; swimming pool 0.1 km.
PRICES: (1996) Caravan with family 98.00, Tent with two adults 58.00. CC: Euro/Access.
In the centre of Vorey, signposted.

VOUILLE Vienne   4B

Camp Municipal chemin de la Piscine, 86190 Vouillé.
Tel 05 49 51 90 10, Fax 05 49 51 14 47.
OPEN: 01/05–14/09. SIZE: 1 ha, 43 pitches (36 with elec), 5 hot showers, 7 WCs, 6 French WCs, 1 CWP. &

Shop at 0.5 km. Restaurant at 0.1 km. Tennis, volley ball, pétanque.
PRICES: (1996) Caravan with family 62.70, Tent with two adults 32.00. CC: none.
15 km from Poitiers on N149 towards Poitiers/Nantes, via Partenay. Go to the centre of Vouillé and the campsite is by the river.

LA VOULTE-SUR-RHONE Ardèche   5B

Camping La Garenne 07800 St-Laurent-du-Pape.
Tel 04 75 62 24 62. English spoken.
OPEN: 01/03–01/10. SIZE: 4 ha, 120 pitches (all with elec, 5 statics), 19 hot showers, 20 WCs, 2 CWPs. ✆ &

Tennis.
PRICES: (1996) Caravan with family 176.00, Tent with two adults 105.00. CC: none.
From La Voulte-sur-Rhône, follow signs north to St-Laurent-du-Pape.

Camping Les Voiliers 07800 Beauchastel.
Tel 04 75 62 24 04, Fax 04 75 62 42 32.
English spoken.
OPEN: all year. SIZE: 1.5 ha, 120 pitches (all with elec, 4 statics), 10 hot showers, 12 WCs. ✆

Shop at 1 km. Restaurant at 1 km.
PRICES: (1996) Caravan with family 104.00, Tent with two adults 56.00. CC: none.
North of La Voulte-sur-Rhône on N86. Campsite is well signposted.

VOUVRAY Indre/Loire   2C

Camping du Bec de Cisse 37210 Vouvray.
Tel 02 47 52 68 81, Fax 02 47 52 67 76.
English spoken.
OPEN: 01/05–30/09. SIZE: 2 ha, 35 pitches (28 with elec), 10 hot showers, 5 WCs, 1 CWP. ✆ &

Shop at 0.2 km. Restaurant at 0.2 km. Swimming pool 0.3 km.
PRICES: (1996) Caravan with family 98.00, Tent with two adults 53.00. CC: none.
Take exit 21 from A10. Campsite is 200 m from centre of Vouvray village and well signposted.

YENNE Savoie   5B

Camping du Flon av du Rhône, 73170 Yenne.
Tel 04 79 36 82 70, Fax 04 79 36 77 18.
English spoken.
OPEN: 01/07–31/08. SIZE: 6 hot showers, 6 WCs. ✆ &

Shop at 0.5 km. Restaurant at 0.5 km.
PRICES: (1996) Caravan with family 74.00, Tent with two adults 42.00. CC: none.
From Chambéry/Aix-les-Bains on N504 head for Yenne town centre. Look for signs to the campsite on the right.

France

GERMANY

Standing at the very heart of Europe, and sharing its borders with nine other countries, recently united Germany has traditionally been best known to the tourist for the Black Forest – or *Schwarzwald* – and the River Rhine.

The *Schwarzwald* lies close to the French and Swiss borders and is counted the most visited upland area of Europe. The Rhine runs from Basle in Switzerland north through Germany, then on into the Netherlands, to enter the North Sea at Rotterdam.

The Rhine's commercial traffic is as important as the *Rheindampfer* tourist cruisers with on-board orchestras, that steam daily up and down this important waterway. South of Koblenz, the river passes the famous *Loreleifelsen,* where legend has it the siren Lorelei lures ships on to the rock.

In the East, the Elbe flows from the Czech Republic through Dresden and Magdeburg (formerly in East Germany) on to the North Sea at the great port of Hamburg. Here, one of Germany's two stretches of coastline runs from the Netherlands in the west, north to the Danish border; while the second stretch of German coast borders the Baltic.

Munich is southern Germany's largest city, lying between the Danube and the Alps near the Austrian border. It is a city of 36 museums, abundant baroque and rococo architecture and a passion for beer.

Emergency numbers

Police 110

Fire Brigade 112

Ambulance 110 (115 in former East German states)

Warning information

Warning triangle must be carried

Blood alcohol legal limit 80 mg

AACHEN   16A

Campingplatz der Stadt Aachen Pass Str 79, 52070 Aachen.
Tel 0241 158502, Fax 0241 158502. English spoken.
OPEN: 15/04–15/10. SIZE: 1 ha, 60 pitches (36 with elec), 4 hot showers (charge), 9 WCs, 1 CWP.

	🔩	R	🗊	🍺	💌			

Restaurant at 0.5 km. Quiet location.
PRICES: (1996) Caravan with family 33.00,
Tent with two adults 21.00. CC: none.
In the centre of Aachen. From the motorway junction (Aachener Kreuz A4/A44), take the A4 and then the A544 to Europaplatz. Then follow the signs.

ACHERN   16C

Campingplatz Grasselmuhle Blumberg 1, Obersasbach, 77880 Obersasbach.
Tel 07841 4147. English spoken.
OPEN: 01/05–30/09. SIZE: 2 ha, 10 pitches (all with elec, 50 statics), 6 hot showers (charge), 6 WCs, 2 CWPs.

	♀	R	🗊					🍴

Restaurant at 0.8 km. Minimum stay 3 nights.
PRICES: (1996) Caravan with family 32.00,
Tent with two adults 20.00. CC: none.

AITRACH   16D

Campingplatz Iller Illerstrasse 57, 88319 Aitrach.
Tel 07565 5415, Fax 07565 5222. English spoken.
OPEN: 01/05–30/09. SIZE: 3 ha, 70 pitches (all with elec, 150 statics), 14 hot showers (charge), 20 WCs, 1 CWP. 📞 ♿

〰	✖	♀	R	🗊	🅿	💌		⛵	🏣	

Shop at 1 km. Restaurant at 1 km. Fitness room.
PRICES: (1996) Caravan with family 30.50,
Tent with two adults 22.00. CC: none.
Leave motorway from Memmingen at Aitrach and go for 3 km to campsite.

AITRANG   16D

Camping Elbsee Familie Martin, Am Elbsee 3, 8955 Aitrang.
Tel 08343 248, Fax 08343 1406. English spoken.
OPEN: 01/01–02/11 & 12/12–31/12. SIZE: 3.5 ha, 120 pitches (all with elec, 180 statics), 24 hot showers, 33 WCs, 4 CWPs.

〜	⚓	♀	R	🗊	🍺	☕	💌		🏣	

Restaurant at 0.2 km.
PRICES: Caravan with family 35.00,
Tent with two adults 29.00. CC: none.

From Kempten, take B12 towards Marktoberdorf and turn left to Aitrang.

ALPIRSBACH 16D

Campingplatz-Wolpert 72275 Alpirsbach.
Tel 07444 6313. English spoken.
OPEN: 20/05–20/09. SIZE: 1 ha, 40 pitches (all with elec), 4 hot showers, 10 WCs, 1 CWP.

Restaurant at 0.3 km. Tennis.
PRICES: (1996) Caravan with family 27.60,
Tent with two adults 20.60. CC: none.
Follow the signs to the campsite from Alpirsbach centre.

ALTENAU 14D

Campingplatz Okertalsperre Kornhardtweg 2,
38707 Altenau/Oberharz.
Tel 05328 702, Fax 05328 702.
OPEN: all year. SIZE: 3 ha, 80 pitches (all with elec, 50 statics), 9 hot showers, 17 WCs, 1 CWP.

PRICES: (1996) Caravan with family 40.40,
Tent with two adults 28.00. CC: none.
Follow signposts in Altenau.

ALTENBERG 15D

Camping Kleiner Galgenteich 08242 Altenberg.
Tel 035056 31995, Fax 035056 31995.
OPEN: all year. SIZE: 8 ha, 100 pitches (all with elec), 8 hot showers (charge), 24 WCs, 1 CWP.

Sauna.
PRICES: (1996) Caravan with family 26.00,
Tent with two adults 17.00. CC: none.
From Dresden south on E55 to Altenberg and follow signs.

ALTENBURG 15C

Campingplatz im Erholungspark Pahna
04617 Pahna bei Altenburg.
Tel 034343 51914, Fax 034343 51912.
English spoken.
OPEN: all year. SIZE: 20 ha, 50 pitches (25 with elec, 500 statics), 14 hot showers (charge), 50 WCs.

PRICES: (1996) Caravan with family 23.00,
Tent with two adults 16.00. CC: none.
From Altenburg, B93 towards Borna. In Treben, turn right at garage to Pahna.

ALTENKIRCHEN 16A

Camping Hofgut Schönerlen 56244 Steinen.
Tel 02666 207, Fax 02666 8429. English spoken.

OPEN: 01/12–30/10. SIZE: 15 ha, 80 pitches (all with elec, 220 statics), 24 hot showers, 25 WCs, 2 CWPs.

Restaurant at 1 km. Voted best county campsite in 1995.
PRICES: (1996) Caravan with family 38.00,
Tent with two adults 26.00. CC: none.
From Altenkirchen, go south-east towards Limburg on B8 and the campsite at Steinen is signposted.

ALTENSTEIG 16D

Schwarzwald Camping Im Oberen Tal 3,
7272 Altensteig.
Tel 07453 8415. English spoken.
OPEN: all year. SIZE: 30 ha, 100 pitches (all with elec, 100 statics), 10 hot showers, 16 WCs, 2 CWPs.

PRICES: Caravan with family 32.50,
Tent with two adults 22.50. CC: Euro/Access.
On B28, campsite well signposted from Altensteig.

ANDERNACH 16A

Camping am Laacher See 56653 Wassenach.
Tel 02636 2485. English spoken.
OPEN: 01/04–30/09. SIZE: 7 ha, 100 pitches (all with elec, 100 statics), 6 hot showers (charge), 35 WCs, 1 CWP.

PRICES: (1996) Caravan with family 46.50,
Tent with two adults 33.00. CC: none.
10 km west of Andernach, campsite is on west shore of lake near A61.

AUGSBURG 17C

Lech Camping 86444 Mühlhausen bei Augsburg.
Tel 08207 2200, Fax 08207 2202. English spoken.
OPEN: 01/03–31/10. SIZE: 5 ha, 190 pitches (all with elec, 150 statics), 10 hot showers, 18 WCs, 3 CWPs.

PRICES: (1996) Caravan with family 43.00,
Tent with two adults 22.00. CC: Amex,
Euro/Access, Visa.
Leave the motorway A8 at Augsburg-Ost towards Neuburg. Site on the right after 4 km.

Lech Camping near Augsburg
A warm welcome awaits

Germany

BACHARACH 16A

Campingplatz Sonnenstrand
55422 Bacharach-am-Rhein.
Tel 06743 1752, Fax 06743 3192. English spoken.
OPEN: 01/04–31/10. SIZE: 1.2 ha, 55 pitches (65 with elec, 20 statics), 4 hot showers, 8 WCs, 1 CWP.

| ~ | ⚓ | 🅖 | R | 🔟 | | 🍵 | ✕ | | |

Shop at 0.5 km.
PRICES: (1996) Caravan with family 35.50,
Tent with two adults 24.00. CC: Euro/Access.
From A61, take Rheinböllen exit. Campsite is south of Bacharach on the bank of the Rhein.

Campingplatz Sonnenstrand
at Bacharach
Romantic and fine, the Mittelrhein

BACKNANG 16D

Campingplatz Waldsee 7157 Murrhardt-Fornsbach.
Tel 07192 6436, Fax 07192 5283.
OPEN: all year. SIZE: 2 ha, 120 pitches (all with elec, 65 statics), 16 hot showers (charge), 18 WCs, 1 CWP.

| ≈ | ⚓ | 🅖 | | 🔟 | 🍴 | 🍵 | ✕ | | 🅗 | |

Boating, playground, mini-golf, fishing.
PRICES: (1996) Caravan with family 36.00,
Tent with two adults 22.00. CC: none.
From Backnang, north-east on B14 then turn right towards Gaildorf. Campsite at Murrhardt is well signposted.

BAD BRAMSTEDT 14B

Naturcamping Weisser Brunnen Seestr 12, 23829 Wittenborn.
Tel 04554 1413, Fax 04554 4833. English spoken.
OPEN: 01/04–31/10. SIZE: 6 ha, 100 pitches (all with elec, 300 statics), 30 hot showers, 60 WCs, 4 CWPs.

| ≈ | ⚓ | ♀ | R | 🔟 | 🅑 | 🍵 | ✕ | | 🅗 | |

PRICES: (1996) Caravan with family 38.00,
Tent with two adults 21.00. CC: Euro/Access.
From A7, take Bad Bramstedt/Bad Segeberg exit and then B206 towards Segeberg. Campsite is signposted in Wittenborn.

BAD DOBERAN 15A

Ferien-Camp Börgerende Deichstrasse, 18211 Börgerende.
Tel 038203 81126, Fax 038203 81284. English spoken.

OPEN: 01/04–31/10. SIZE: 10 ha, 350 pitches (300 with elec, 80 statics), 20 hot showers (charge), 50 WCs, 1 CWP.

| ≈ | ⚓ | ⚡ | R | 🔟 | 🅑 | 🍵 | ✕ |

Entertainment.
PRICES: (1996) Caravan with family 32.00,
Tent with two adults 19.00. CC: none.
From Bad Doberan, go north and turn left to Börgerende.

BAD DÜRRHEIM 16D

Kurcamping Sunthauser See 78073 Bad Dürrheim.
Tel 07706 712.
OPEN: 01/04–30/09. SIZE: 10 ha, 150 pitches (all with elec, 150 statics), 31 hot showers (charge), 55 WCs, 1 CWP.

| ≈ | ⚓ | 🅖 | | 🔟 | | | | | 🅗 | |

Shop at 0.5 km. Restaurant at 0.5 km.
PRICES: (1996) Caravan with family 43.00,
Tent with two adults 27.00. CC: none.
From A81, exit at Tuningen and beyond Tuningen turn left to Bad Dürrheim and Sonthausen.

BAD EMS 16A

Campingplatz Bad Ems Lahnstrasse 4, 5427 Bad Ems.
Tel 02603 4679, Fax 02603 4487. English spoken.
OPEN: 15/03–31/10. SIZE: 2.2 ha, 80 pitches (all with elec, 60 statics), 10 hot showers, 12 WCs, 2 CWPs.

| ~ | ⚓ | 🅖 | R | 🔟 | 🅑 | 🍵 | ✕ | ⚓ | 🅗 | |

Very good on-site facilities; lots to do and see nearby.
PRICES: (1996) Caravan with family 34.00,
Tent with two adults 23.80. CC: none.
Site is well signposted in Bad Ems.

BADEN-BADEN 16C

Frezeitcenter Oberrhein 7587 Rheinmunster.
Tel 07227 2500, Fax 07227 2400.
English spoken.
OPEN: all year. SIZE: 36 ha, 250 pitches (all with elec, 460 statics), 81 hot showers, 99 WCs, 8 CWPs.

| ≈ | ⚓ | ♀ | R | 🔟 | 🅑 | 🍵 | ✕ | | 🅗 | |

Tennis, surfing. (Charge for electricity.).
PRICES: (1996) Caravan with family 56.50,
Tent with two adults 38.50. CC: Amex, Euro/Access, Visa.
Highly recommended site (August 1996). Take Rheintal motorway (from Karlsruhe to Basel) and exit at Baden-Baden or Bühl and go on to Rheinmunster/Stollhofen (17 km).

BAD FÜSSING 17D

Kurcamping MAX Blumenstr 5,
94072 Bad Füssing.
Tel 08537 356, Fax 08537 356. English spoken.
OPEN: all year. SIZE: 3 ha, 140 pitches (all with elec,
10 statics), 10 hot showers (charge), 25 WCs,
2 CWPs. ♥ ⅋

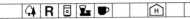

Restaurant at 0.3 km. Massage facilities.
PRICES: (1996) Caravan with family 36.80,
Tent with two adults 25.80. CC: none.
Coming from München, east on B12 to Bad Füssing.

BAD GANDERSHEIM 14D

DCC Kurcamping Park an der B64,
37581 Bad Gandersheim.
Tel 05382 1595, Fax 05382 1599. English spoken.
OPEN: all year. SIZE: 9 ha, 290 pitches (all with elec,
150 statics), 40 hot showers (charge), 46 WCs,
2 CWPs. ♥

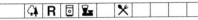

Swimming pool 1 km.
PRICES: (1996) Caravan with family 42.75,
Tent with two adults 31.50. CC: Euro/Access.
*From the A7, exit at Seesen (B64) and go 8 km to
Bad Gandersheim.*

BAD HONNEF 16A

Camping Auf dem Salmenfang
53619 Rheinbreitbach.
Tel 02224 71103.
OPEN: 01/05–15/10. ♥

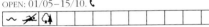

Small site for tents only. Swimming pool 1 km.
PRICES: Tent with two adults 25.00. CC: none.
On B42 between Bad-Honnef and Unkel.

Camping Jillieshof Ginterbergweg 6,
Aegidienberg, 53604 Bad Honnef.
Tel 02224 972066, Fax 02224 972067.
English spoken.
OPEN: all year. SIZE: 4 ha, 25 pitches (all with elec,
215 statics), 14 hot showers, 28 WCs, 2 CWPs. ⅋

PRICES: (1996) Caravan with family 33.80,
Tent with two adults 23.00. CC: none.
Off the A3, south-east of Bonn.

BAD KISSINGEN 16B

Camping Park Euerdorferstr 1,
97688 Bad Kissingen.
Tel 0971 5211, Fax 0971 5211. English spoken.
OPEN: 01/04–15/10. SIZE: 2 ha, 100 pitches
(all with elec), 8 hot showers (charge), 16 WCs,
1 CWP. ♥ ⅋

PRICES: Caravan with family 48.00,
Tent with two adults 33.00. CC: none.
*From the Kassel/Würzburg road take Bad
Kissingen exit and follow signs to campsite.*

BAD KREUZNACH 16A

Camping Guldental 6531 Guldental.
Tel 06707 633, Fax 06707 8468. English spoken.
OPEN: all year. SIZE: 7 ha, 50 pitches (270 statics),
4 hot showers (charge), 15 WCs, 7 CWPs. ♥

Swimming pool 3 km.
PRICES: (1996) Caravan with family 28.00,
Tent with two adults 21.00. CC: none.
*From motorway A61 Koblenz-Bingen exit
Waldlaubersheim-Windesheim (Autobahn-
Kirche). Site is well signposted.*

Kur-Campingplatz Salinental, Marga Oberst,
6550 Bad Kreuznach.
Tel 0671 27304. English spoken.
OPEN: 01/03–30/11. SIZE: 1 ha, 66 pitches
(110 with elec, 40 statics), 9 hot showers (charge),
11 WCs, 2 CWPs.

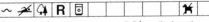

Shop at 2 km. Swimming pool 100 m.
PRICES: (1996) Caravan with family 90.00.
CC: Euro/Access.
*From Bad Kreuznach go on B48 towards Salinen.
Go through Tal, Schwimmbad, Bad Münster and
Ebernburg. Before the Salinen bridge, turn left.*

BAD NEUENAHR 16A

Campingplatz Ahrweiler Kalvarienbergstr 1,
5483 Ahrweiler.
Tel 02641 36250.
OPEN: 01/04–31/10. SIZE: 1 ha, 28 pitches (all with
elec, 11 statics), 4 hot showers, 6 WCs.

Shop at 0.3 km. Restaurant at 0.2 km. Swimming
pool nearby.
PRICES: (1996) Caravan with family 24.00,
Tent with two adults 20.00. CC: none.
*Bad Neuenahr/Ahrweiler exit from A61
Köln/Koblenz. Follow directions to Ahrweiler. At
traffic light opposite Aral petrol station turn right.
After 1 km turn left just before city gate, drive
another 1 km along city wall to next gate on your
right, fork left, over bridge, campsite on right
beside river.*

Campingplatz Zur Burgwiese
53508 Mayschoss/Ahr.
Tel 02643 7652.
OPEN: 01/04–31/10. SIZE: 2 ha, 30 pitches
(110 with elec, 80 statics), 4 hot showers (charge),
15 WCs, 2 CWPs.

Germany

🜨		🔲				🔧		

Shop at 0.3 km. Restaurant at 0.3 km.
PRICES: (1996) Caravan with family 36.00,
Tent with two adults 25.00. CC: none.
From Bonn go to Bad Neuenahr and from there to Mayschoss/Ahr.

BAD PYRMONT 14D

Camping Im Schellental
31812 Bad Pyrmont-Friedensthal.
Tel 05281 8772. English spoken.
OPEN: all year. SIZE: 6 ha, 150 pitches (all with elec, 80 statics), 6 hot showers, 10 WCs, 2 CWPs. ℄

		🏕	R	🔲	🍺	☕	✕		

PRICES: (1996) Caravan with family 34.00,
Tent with two adults 25.00. CC: none.
From Hameln south on B83. Follow signs to campsite from 'Thal'.

BAD REICHENHALL 17C

Kuracamping Staufeneck 83435 Bad Reichenhall.
Tel 08651 2134. English spoken.
OPEN: 01/04–20/10. SIZE: 2.7 ha, 100 pitches (all with elec, 30 statics), 6 hot showers (charge), 12 WCs, 1 CWP. ℄

~	✈	🜨	R	🔲	🍺				

Restaurant at 0.3 km.
PRICES: Caravan with family 36.00,
Tent with two adults 24.00. CC: none.
1.5 km from the centre of Bad Reichenhall and well signposted.

BAD SCHWALBACH 16A

Wisper Park Camping
6208 Bad Schwalbach/Wispertal.
Tel 06124 9297, Fax 06120 978554.
English spoken.
OPEN: all year. SIZE: 15 pitches (all with elec, 65 statics), 2 hot showers, 7 WCs, 1 CWP.

		⚲	R	🔲	🍺	🍺	✕		

PRICES: (1996) Caravan with family 30.00,
Tent with two adults 17.00. CC: none.
South of Bad Schwalbach, turn left for 5 km towards Ramschied and follow signs.

BAD TÖLZ 17C

Waldcamping Königsdorf 82549 Königsdorf.
Tel 08171 81580, Fax 08171 81165. English spoken.
OPEN: all year. SIZE: 8.6 ha, 400 pitches (all with elec, 250 statics), 22 hot showers, 43 WCs, 2 CWPs. ℄

≈	⚲	⚲	R	🔲	🍺	🍺	✕		

PRICES: (1996) Caravan with family 33.50,
Tent with two adults 24.00. CC: none.

Königsdorf is north-west of Bad Tölz. In Königsdorf, take the B11 towards Wolfratshausen and turn left after 3 km. Campsite is well signposted.

BAD URACH 16D

Camping Pfahlhof 7432 Bad Urach.
Tel 07125 8098, Fax 07125 8091.
English spoken.
OPEN: all year. SIZE: 4 ha, 50 pitches (all with elec, 180 statics), 7 hot showers, 14 WCs, 1 CWP. ℄

~	✈	🏕	R	🔲	🍺		✕		Ⓗ

PRICES: (1996) Caravan with family 35.50,
Tent with two adults 20.75. CC: none.
Follow the signs to the campsite in Bad Urach.

BAD WILDUNGEN 16B

Campingplatz Kellerwald 34632 Jesberg.
Tel 06695 7213, Fax 06695 96010.
English spoken.
OPEN: all year. SIZE: 5 ha, 40 pitches (180 with elec, 140 statics), 6 hot showers (charge), 24 WCs, 1 CWP. ℄ ♿

~	✈	🜨	R	🔲			✕	🏹	

Shop at 1 km. Tennis, mini-golf, children's playground, table tennis.
PRICES: (1996) Caravan with family 28.00,
Tent with two adults 16.00. CC: none.
From Kassel, south on A49, exit Borken, then B3 towards Marburg. Follow signs from Jesberg.

BAMBERG 17A

Campingplatz Insel Am Campingplatz 1,
96049 Bamberg.
Tel 09515 6320. English spoken.
OPEN: all year. SIZE: 5 ha, 250 pitches (all with elec), 17 hot showers, 21 WCs, 3 CWPs. ♿

~	⚓	🜨	R	🔲	🍺	🍺		🏹	

PRICES: (1996) Caravan with family 39.00,
Tent with two adults 25.00. CC: none.
From Nürnberg-Würzburg motorway, exit at Bamberg and take B505 for about 20 km to Pettstadt/Stegaurach and the campsite is signposted from there.

BERCHTESGADEN 17D

Allweglehen 8240 Berchtesgaden.
Tel 08652 2396, Fax 08652 63503.
OPEN: all year. SIZE: 2 ha, 120 pitches (all with elec), 14 hot showers, 14 WCs, 2 CWPs. ℄

		⚲	R	🔲	🍺		✕	🏹	🏹

Beautiful scenery; ski-lift.
PRICES: (1996) Caravan with family 35.80,
Tent with two adults 24.00. CC: Euro/Access.
2 km east of Berchtesgaden.

BERNE 14B

Campingplatz Juliusplatz 27804 Berne.
Tel 04406 6881, Fax 04406 1666. English spoken.
OPEN: 15/04–30/09. SIZE: 4 ha, 40 pitches (all with
elec, 170 statics), 6 hot showers, 17 WCs.

PRICES: (1996) Caravan with family 22.00,
Tent with two adults 17.00. CC: none.
*North of Delmenhorst on the B212, towards
Nordenham. Follow campsite signs in Berne.*

BERNKASTEL-KUES 16A

Camping Schenk Hauptstr 165,
54470 Bernkastel-Wehlen.
Tel 06531 8176, Fax 06531 7681. English spoken.
OPEN: 15/04–31/10. SIZE: 1 ha, 50 pitches (all with
elec, 50 statics), 6 hot showers, 9 WCs, 1 CWP.

Shop at 0.6 km. Restaurant at 0.1 km. Small pool
on site; large pool 2 km.
PRICES: (1996) Caravan with family 36.00,
Tent with two adults 24.00. CC: none.
From Wittlich go to Bernkastel and then Wehlen.

Kueser Werth Camping Platz Am Hafen 2,
54470 Bernkastel-Kues.
Tel 06531 8200. English spoken.
OPEN: 01/04–30/10. SIZE: 2 ha, 200 pitches
(180 with elec, 50 statics), 8 hot showers (charge),
20 WCs, 1 CWP.

PRICES: (1996) Caravan with family 37.00,
Tent with two adults 24.00. CC: none.
*Leave A48 at Wittlich (coming from Koblenz) and
follow B50 to Bernkastel-Kues. Campsite is
signposted from the bridge.*

BETZENSTEIN 17A

Campingplatz Betzenstein Hauptstr 69,
8571 Betzenstein.
Tel 09244 7305, Fax 09244 18152.
OPEN: all year. SIZE: 60 pitches (all with elec,
90 statics), 25 hot showers, 25 WCs, 2 CWPs.

Sauna and solarium; swimming pool 1 km.
PRICES: Caravan with family 40.00,
Tent with two adults 30.00. CC: none.
*From Nürnberg to Berlin motorway exit at Plech,
and go to Betzenstein.*

BEVERUNGEN 14D

Camping Axelsee Wurgassen am Axelsee,
37688 Beverungen an der Weser.
Tel 05273 88818. English spoken.
OPEN: all year. SIZE: 6 ha, 200 pitches (all with elec,
160 statics), 1 CWP.

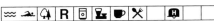

PRICES: (1996) Caravan with family 27.00,
Tent with two adults 21.00. CC: none.
*From Beverungen, at junction of B64/B241,
follow signs to Wurgassen-am-See and campsite.*

BIELEFELD 14D

Campingplatz am Furlbach Anne Auster, Am
Furlbach 33, 33758 Schloss Holte-Stukenbrock.
Tel 05257 3373. English spoken.
OPEN: 01/04–01/11. SIZE: 9 ha, 50 pitches (all with
elec, 210 statics), 12 hot showers, 23 WCs,
2 CWPs.

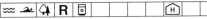

Restaurant at 1.5 km. Playground.
PRICES: (1996) Caravan with family 36.50,
Tent with two adults 24.50. CC: none.
*From A33 (Paderborn to Osnabruck), exit at
Stukenbrock-Senne and go 2 km towards
Stukenbrock.*

BIRKENFELD 16A

Campingpark Waldwiesen 55765 Birkenfeld.
Tel 06782 5215, Fax 06782 5219. English spoken.
OPEN: 15/04–15/10. SIZE: 4.5 ha, 90 pitches
(all with elec, 10 statics), 10 hot showers, 9 WCs,
2 CWPs.

Shop at 0.6 km. Restaurant at 0.8 km. Children's
playground; swimming pool 1.5 km.
PRICES: Caravan with family 46.00,
Tent with two adults 28.00. CC: none.
*Exit A62 (Landstuhl to Trier) at Birkenfeld, then
5 km on B41 to Birkenfeld. The site is situated on
the east side of town and well signposted.*

BISPINGEN 14B

Camping Brunantal 296116 Bispingen-
Behringen.
Tel 05194 840. English spoken.
OPEN: all year. SIZE: 2.7 ha, 80 pitches (70 with
elec, 30 statics), 7 hot showers, 10 WCs, 1 CWP.

Restaurant at 0.2 km.
PRICES: (1996) Caravan with family 33.00,
Tent with two adults 24.00. CC: none.
*Leave A7 at Bispingen exit and follow signs
towards Behringen and campsite.*

BLANKENHEIM 16A

Campinganlage Stahlhütte 53533 Dorsel/Ahr.
Tel 02693 438, Fax 02693 511. English spoken.
OPEN: all year. SIZE: 5 ha, 100 pitches (60 with elec,
160 statics), 15 hot showers (charge), 19 WCs,
1 CWP.

PRICES: (1996) Caravan with family 38.00,
Tent with two adults 28.00. CC: none.
*On B258 (Aachen to Koblenz) about 16 km
south-east of Blankenheim.*

Campingplatz Freilinger-See 5378 Freilingen.
Tel 02697 282, Fax 02697 292. English spoken.
OPEN: all year. SIZE: 8 ha, 80 pitches (all with elec,
260 statics), 18 hot showers, 24 WCs, 2 CWPs.

PRICES: (1996) Caravan with family 28.50,
Tent with two adults 22.00. CC: Euro/Access.
*From Blankenheim, south-east on B258 towards
Koblenz for about 3 km. Campsite is signposted.*

Campingplatz Jakobs-Muhle 5378 Ahrdorf.
Tel 02697 425, Fax 02697 1451.
English spoken.
OPEN: all year. SIZE: 3 ha, 80 pitches (all with elec,
120 statics), 12 hot showers (charge), 11 WCs,
2 CWPs.

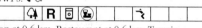

Swimming pool 6 km.
PRICES: (1996) Caravan with family 26.00,
Tent with two adults 18.00. CC: none.
*From Blankenheim take B258 towards
Nürburgring and the campsite is well signposted.*

BLECKEDE 15A

ADAC-Ferienplatz Alt Garge
21354 Bleckede-Alt Garge.
Tel 05854 311, Fax 05854 1640.
OPEN: all year. SIZE: 6.6 ha, 50 pitches (all with
elec, 250 statics), 27 hot showers, 48 WCs,
3 CWPs.

Shop at 0.6 km. Restaurant at 0.6 km. Tennis,
sauna.
PRICES: (1996) Caravan with family 27.00,
Tent with two adults 16. CC: none.
*Bleckede is east of Lüneburg. From Bleckede go to
Alt Garge and campsite is well signposted.*

BLEIALF 16A

Eifellux-Ferienpark Bleialf Am Hallenbad,
54608 Bleialf.
Tel 06555 1059, Fax 06555 294.
English spoken.
OPEN: all year. SIZE: 3 ha, 166 pitches (all with elec,
70 statics), 11 hot showers, 24 WCs, 1 CWP.

Shop at 1 km.
PRICES: (1996) Caravan with family 47.00,
Tent with two adults 28.80. CC: none.
*From the A60 Trier-Bitburg, exit Bleialf and
follow signs.*

BOPPARD 16A

Camping Park Sonneneck 56154 Boppard.
Tel 06742 2121, Fax 06742 2076. English spoken.
OPEN: 01/05–31/10. SIZE: 8 ha, 150 pitches (all
with elec), 12 hot showers, 23 WCs, 1 CWP.

Tennis, mini-golf, billiards, volley ball,
badminton.
PRICES: (1996) Caravan with family 48.00,
Tent with two adults 30.60. CC: none.
*On B9, 14 km from Koblenz and 4 km outside
Boppard on the banks of the Rhein.*

BRAUNLAGE 15C

Campingplatz am Barenbache
38700 Hohegeiss.
Tel 05583 323 1306, Fax 05583 323 1300.
English spoken.
OPEN: all year. SIZE: 2 ha, 95 pitches (all with elec,
35 statics), 12 hot showers, 18 WCs, 1 CWP.

Shop at 1 km.
PRICES: (1996) Caravan with family 30.00,
Tent with two adults 22.00. CC: none.
*Hohegeiss is just south of Braunlage and campsite
is well signposted.*

Erikabrucke An de B27, Swischen, Bad
Lauterberg/Braunlage, 37444 St Andreasberg.
Tel 05582 1431, Fax 05582 1431.
OPEN: all year. SIZE: 9 ha, 250 pitches (all with elec,
250 statics), 11 hot showers, 20 WCs, 2 CWPs.

PRICES: (1996) Caravan with family 29.50, Tent
with two adults 21.50. CC: Amex, Euro/Access.
*On B27 between Braunlage and Bad Lauterberg.
Well signposted.*

BREMEN 14B

Camping Freie Hansestadt Bremen
Am Stadtwaldsee 1, 28359 Bremen.
Tel 0421 212002, Fax 0421 219857.
English spoken.
OPEN: 14/03–03/11. SIZE: 5.8 ha, 100 pitches (all
with elec), 12 hot showers, 19 WCs, 1 CWP.

Sea 700 m.
PRICES: Caravan with family 37.50,
Tent with two adults 28.50. CC: none.
*Follow 'Universität' and then camping signs from
Bremen.*

Campingplatz Eikhofe 27367 Sottrum-
Everinghausen.
Tel 04205 430. English spoken.
OPEN: all year. SIZE: 3 ha, 30 pitches (all with elec,
100 statics), 1 CWP.

Germany

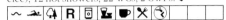

Shop at 5 km. Restaurant at 4 km. Playground.
PRICES: (1996) Caravan with family 30.00,
Tent with two adults 18.50. CC: none.
B75 east to Sottrum. Follow signs to
Everingbausen and then to campsite.

BULLAY
16A

Baren-Camp Am Moselufer 1, 56859 Bullay.
Tel 06542 900097, Fax 06542 900098.
English spoken.
OPEN: 01/04–05/11. SIZE: 2 ha, 10 pitches (all with
elec), 12 hot showers, 22 WCs, 2 CWPs. ℓ

PRICES: (1996) Caravan with family 31.50,
Tent with two adults 23.50. CC: none.
Follow the signposts in Bullay to the campsite.

CALW
16D

Campingplatz Bad Liebenzell 75378 Bad
Liebenzell/Schwarzwald.
Tel 07052 40460, Fax 07052 40475.
English spoken.
OPEN: all year. SIZE: 2 ha, 240 pitches (all with
elec), 13 hot showers, 2 CWPs. ℓ ♿

PRICES: (1996) Caravan with family 41.50,
Tent with two adults 30.50. CC: none.
North of Calw and 20 km south of Pforzheim.
Well signposted.

CHEMNITZ
15C

Camping Naherholungszentrum
Oberrabenstein 9033 Chemnitz.
Tel 03718 50608.
OPEN: 01/04–31/10. SIZE: 3 ha, 60 pitches (all with
elec, 80 statics), 6 hot showers, 8 WCs, 1 CWP. ♿

PRICES: (1996) Caravan with family 25.00,
Tent with two adults 14.00. CC: Euro/Access.
Take A72 to Chemnitz-Süd towards Oberlungwitz.

CHIEMING
17C

Campingplatz Kupferschmiede
Trostbergerstr 4, 83339 Arlaching.
Tel 08667 446, Fax 08667 16198. English spoken.
OPEN: 01/04–30/09. SIZE: 2 ha, 80 pitches (all with
elec, 150 statics), 17 hot showers (charge),
25 WCs, 2 CWPs. ℓ ♿

PRICES: Caravan with family 44.60,
Tent with two adults 30.70. CC: none.
To the north of Chieming and Chiemsee (the lake)
and towards Seebruck.

Campingplatz Sport-Ecke 83339 Chieming.
Tel 08664 500, Fax 08664 500. English spoken.
OPEN: 01/05–30/08. SIZE: 1.1 ha, 90 pitches
(80 with elec, 30 statics), 8 hot showers, 17 WCs,
1 CWP. ℓ

Restaurant at 2 km.
PRICES: (1996) Caravan with family 42.00,
Tent with two adults 29.00. CC: none.
Take München to Salzburg motorway, exit at
Grabenstätt and go towards Chieming (6 km).
Campsite first on left.

CLAUSTHAL-ZELLERFELD
14D

Camping Prahljust An den langen Bruchen 4,
38678 Clausthal-Zellerfeld.
Tel 05323 1300, Fax 05523 78393.
English spoken.
OPEN: all year. SIZE: 12 ha, 400 pitches (all with
elec, 400 statics), 50 hot showers, 60 WCs,
16 CWPs. ℓ ♿

Sauna and solarium.
PRICES: (1996) Caravan with family 37.80. CC: none.
The campsite is 5 km from Clausthal-Zellerfeld.
Go towards Braunlage/St Andreasberg (B242),
turn right after 2 km and there is a farmhouse
right in front of the drive.

COBURG
17A

Camping Ruckert-Klause
96190 Untermerzbach.
Tel 09533 288. English spoken.
OPEN: 01/04–31/10. SIZE: 1.0 ha, 30 pitches
(all with elec, 30 statics), 6 hot showers (charge),
10 WCs, 1 CWP.

Shop at 3 km. Restaurant at 4 km. Children's
playground.
PRICES: Caravan with family 29.40,
Tent with two adults 17.00. CC: none.
From Coburg, south on B4. Follow signs from
Untermerzbach.

COCHEM
16A

Am Alten Forsthaus Hauptstr 2,
56814 Landkern.
Tel 02671 8701. English spoken.
OPEN: all year. SIZE: 6 ha, 100 pitches (80 with
elec, 150 statics), 8 hot showers (charge),
25 WCs, 1 CWP.

PRICES: Caravan with family 31.00, Tent with two
adults 22.00. CC: Euro/Access.
From Cochem go to Landkern where campsite is
signposted.

Germany

Camping Burgen 56332 Burgen/Mosel.
Tel 02605 2396, Fax 02605 4919.
OPEN: 01/04–20/10. SIZE: 4 ha, 180 pitches
(all with elec, 60 statics), 9 hot showers,
27 WCs, 1 CWP.

Restaurant at 0.3 km.
PRICES: (1996) Caravan with family 33.00,
Tent with two adults 23.00. CC: none.
*Highly recommended. From Cochem B49 towards
Koblenz. At Burgen turn east and follow signs for
the campsite.*

Camping Schausten Endertstr 124, 5590 Cochem.
Tel 02671 7528. English spoken.
OPEN: 01/04–31/10. SIZE: 1 ha, 70 pitches (60 with
elec, 20 statics), 6 hot showers (charge), 10 WCs,
1 CWP.

Shop at 0.5 km. Restaurant at 0.5 km. Lively site;
table tennis; swimming pool 2 km.
PRICES: (1996) Caravan with family 40.00,
Tent with two adults 29.00. CC: none.
*Recommended site, 0.8 km from Cochem towards
Mayen.*

Camping zur Winnenburg Endertstr 141,
5590 Cochem.
Tel 02671 4527, Fax 02671 4523. English spoken.
OPEN: 01/04–30/11. SIZE: 1 ha, 50 pitches
(10 statics), 5 hot showers, 8 WCs, 1 CWP.

PRICES: (1996) Caravan with family 33.00,
Tent with two adults 24.00. CC: Amex,
Euro/Access, Visa.
On the L98 in Cochem.

Campingplatz Nehren/Mosel
56820 Nehren/Mosel.
Tel 02673 4612. English spoken.
OPEN: 01/04–12/10. SIZE: 5 ha, 300 pitches
(all with elec, 250 statics), 16 hot showers,
26 WCs, 1 CWP.

PRICES: (1996) Caravan with family 31.50,
Tent with two adults 24.00. CC: none.
From Cochem take B49 towards Trier (17 km).

Camplatz Mosel-Islands Mosel Boating Center,
Forststrasse 51, 56253 Treis-Karden.
Tel 02672 2613. English spoken.
OPEN: 01/04–31/10. SIZE: 4 ha, 300 pitches
(220 with elec, 98 statics), 28 hot showers
(charge), 26 WCs.

Shop at 0.3 km. Restaurant at 0.2 km.
PRICES: (1996) Caravan with family 32.00,
Tent with two adults 21.50. CC: none.
From Cochem go east to Treis.

Ferienland Senheim 56820 Senheim-Mosel.
Tel 02673 4660/4100, Fax 02673 4100.
English spoken.
OPEN: 15/04–15/10. SIZE: 3.5 ha, 150 pitches
(80 with elec, 50 statics), 16 hot showers, 24 WCs,
1 CWP.

Tennis, yacht marina.
PRICES: (1996) Caravan with family 35.00,
Tent with two adults 23.00. CC: none.
*Take B48 from Cochem towards Zell. In Senheim
go over a bridge to Senheim.*

DAGEBÜLL   14B

Campingplatz Nuewarft 25899 Dagebüll.
Tel 04667 325, Fax 04667 325. English spoken.
OPEN: 01/04–31/10. SIZE: 60 ha, 35 pitches
(all with elec, 25 statics), 10 hot showers (charge),
10 WCs, 1 CWP.

PRICES: (1996) Caravan with family 30.00,
Tent with two adults 19.50. CC: none.
*From Flensburg go to Leck, Niebüll and then
Dagebüll. Campsite is well signposted.*

DAHME   15A

Familiencamp Stieglitz 2435 Dahme.
Tel 04364 1435, Fax 04364 9610. English spoken.
OPEN: 01/04–31/10. SIZE: 12 ha, 200 pitches
(all with elec, 270 statics), 31 hot showers
(charge), 1 CWP.

PRICES: (1996) Caravan with family 42.00,
Tent with two adults 30.00. CC: none.
*Leaving motorway at Lensahn go to Cismar and
then to Dahme.*

DIETFURT   17C

Jura-Camping Markt Breitenbrunn, Martplatz 13,
92363 Breitenbrunn.
Tel 09495 337, Fax 09495 1431. English spoken.
OPEN: all year. SIZE: 10 ha, 90 pitches (all with elec,
78 statics), 10 hot showers, 8 WCs, 2 CWPs.

Shop at 0.5 km. Restaurant at 0.2 km.
PRICES: (1996) Caravan with family 30.50,
Tent with two adults 19.50. CC: none.
*Going north from Dietfurt to Breitenbrunn, you
will see campsite on the left side of the road.*

DIEZ/LAHN   16A

Camping Oranienstein Strandbadweg, 6252 Diez.
Tel 06432 2122, Fax 06432 2122. English spoken.
OPEN: 01/04–30/10. SIZE: 7 ha, 150 pitches
(120 with elec), 13 hot showers (charge), 1 CWP.

PRICES: Caravan with family 26.00,
Tent with two adults 21.00. CC: none.
Next to the town; follow the blue camping signs.

DINKELSBÜHL 16D

DCC Campingpark Romantische-Strasse,
91550 Dinkelsbühl.
Tel 09851 7817, Fax 09851 7817.
OPEN: all year. SIZE: 9 ha, 333 pitches (all with elec,
142 statics), 2 CWPs.

PRICES: (1996) Caravan with family 42.75,
Tent with two adults 41.50. CC: none.
Signposted in Dinkelsbühl.

DONAUWÖRTH 17C

Donau-Lech Camping Campingweg 1,
86698 Eggelstetten, Donauwörth.
Tel 09002 4044, Fax 09002 4046. English spoken.
OPEN: all year. SIZE: 5 ha, 89 pitches (all with elec,
30 statics), 8 hot showers (charge), 10 WCs,
1 CWP. ₵

Restaurant at 0.8 km. Sauna, playground,
barbecue area.
PRICES: Caravan with family 43.10,
Tent with two adults 27.70. CC: none.
To the east of the A2, just south of Donauwörth.
Campsite is signposted.

DORTMUND 14C

Camping Hohensyburg
44265 Dortmund-Hohensyburg.
Tel 0231 774374, Fax 0231 774332.
English spoken.
OPEN: all year. SIZE: 40 ha, 150 pitches (100 with
elec, 350 statics), 24 hot showers (charge),
30 WCs, 2 CWPs. ₵ ₺

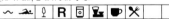

PRICES: (1996) Caravan with family 42.00,
Tent with two adults 28.00. CC: none.
From A1 take Hagen-Nord exit and go towards
Hohensyburg or from A45 take Dortmund-Süd
exit towards Hohensyburg and campsite is
signposted.

DREIECH-OFFENTHAL 16B

Camping Dreiech-Offenthal Bahnhofstrasse 77,
63303 Dreiech-Offenthal.
Tel 06074 5629, Fax 06074 5629.
English spoken.
OPEN: 01/03–31/10. SIZE: 3 ha, 200 pitches
(all with elec, 160 statics), 9 hot showers, 18 WCs,
2 CWPs. ₵

Restaurant at 0.3 km. Playground.
PRICES: (1996) Caravan with family 28.00,
Tent with two adults 18.00. CC: none.
North-east of Offenthal on the road to
Dietzenbach, 0.5 km out of town.

DRESDEN 15D

Camp Bad Sonnenland Dresdner Str 115,
01468 Reichenberg.
Tel 0351 4727788, Fax 0351 4727787.
English spoken.
OPEN: 01/04–31/10. SIZE: 18 ha, 200 pitches
(all with elec, 200 statics), 24 hot showers
(charge), 35 WCs, 2 CWPs. ₵

PRICES: Caravan with family 32.00, Tent with two
adults 17.50. CC: Euro/Access, Visa.
From A4 Chemnitz to Dresden motorway, take the
Dresden-Nord exit and go north-west to Boxdorf
(about 6 km).

Camping am Waldstrandbad Jonsdorfer Str,
02779 Grossschönau.
Tel 035841 2493, Fax 035841 2553.
OPEN: 01/04–31/10. SIZE: 5 ha, 50 pitches (all with
elec), 6 hot showers, 24 WCs, 1 CWP.

PRICES: (1996) Caravan with family 20.00,
Tent with two adults 12.00. CC: none.
Leave Dresden on A4 motorway going east and at
Bautzen take the turning to Zittau and campsite
is well signposted.

DÜSSELDORF 14C

Campingplatz Unterbacher See Kleiner
Torfbruch 31, 4000 Düsseldorf.
Tel 0211 8992038, Fax 0211 89929132.
English spoken.
OPEN: 09/04–31/08. SIZE: 5 ha, 100 pitches
(80 with elec, 230 statics), 14 hot showers
(charge), 38 WCs, 3 CWPs. ₺

Shop at 1 km. Watersports, mini-golf, billiards,
playground, table tennis, fishing.
PRICES: (1996) Caravan with family 35.50,
Tent with two adults 21.00. CC: none.
From A46 take exit Düsseldorf-Erkath. At the
traffic lights turn left to Unterbach. Go straight
along Rothenbergstrasse for 1.5 km.

EHRENFRIEDERSDORF 17B

Erholungsgebiet Greifenbachstauweiher
Postfach 10, O-9373 Ehrenfriedersdorf.
Tel Amt Geyer 1454, Fax Amt Geyer 1218.
OPEN: 01/05–30/09. SIZE: 20 ha, 100 pitches

Germany

(50 with elec, 200 statics), 8 hot showers (charge), 20 WCs, 1 CWP. &

PRICES: (1996) Caravan with family 30.50, Tent with two adults 18.00. CC: none.
Campsite is signposted from the town.

ELBINGERODE 15C

Camping am Brocken Schützenring 6, 38875 Elbingerode.
Tel 039454 42589, Fax 039454 42589.
OPEN: all year. SIZE: 2.5 ha, 170 pitches (all with elec, 15 statics), 14 hot showers (charge), 20 WCs, 1 CWP. & &

Restaurant at 0.05 km.
PRICES: (1996) Caravan with family 35.00, Tent with two adults 25.00. CC: none.
From Bad Harzburg, go through Wernigerode to Elbingerode.

ENGEN 16D

Campingplatz Sonnental 78234 Engen.
Tel 7733 7529, Fax 7733 2666. English spoken.
OPEN: all year. SIZE: 4 ha, 80 pitches (all with elec, 70 statics), 8 hot showers, 19 WCs, 2 CWPs. & &

Basketball, playground, bike hire; swimming pool 150 m.
PRICES: (1996) Caravan with family 38.30, Tent with two adults 24.00. CC: Euro/Access, Visa.
1 km to the west of Engen and well signposted.

ERLANGEN 17A

Campingplatz Rangau Campinstr 44, 91056 Erlangen.
Tel 09135 8866, Fax 09135 8866.
English spoken.
OPEN: 01/04−30/09. SIZE: 2 ha, 105 pitches (90 with elec, 60 statics), 10 hot showers, 16 WCs, 1 CWP. &

Shop at 1 km.
PRICES: (1996) Caravan with family 34.50, Tent with two adults 21.00. CC: none.
From Erlangen-West go approximately 3 km to Dechsendorf.

ESSEN 14C

DCC Stadtcamping Essen-Werden
Im Löwental 67, 45239 Essen.
Tel 0201 492978, Fax 0201 492978.
OPEN: all year. SIZE: 4 ha, 100 pitches (all with elec, 200 statics), 14 hot showers (charge), 36 WCs, 3 CWPs.

Shop at 1 km. Restaurant at 1 km.
PRICES: (1996) Caravan with family 40.50, Tent with two adults 40.00. CC: none.
Take road nos 52/430/44 then B224.

ETZELWANG 17A

Frankenalb-Camping 92268 Etzelwang.
Tel 09663 815.
OPEN: all year. SIZE: 2 ha, 50 pitches (all with elec, 100 statics), 2 CWPs. &

Shop at 0.2 km. Restaurant at 0.2 km.
PRICES: (1996) Caravan with family 30.00, Tent with two adults 20.00. CC: none.
East from Nürnberg through Hersbruck. At Weigendorf turn north for 4.5 km to Etzelwang.

EUTIN 15A

Natur-Camping Prinzenholz 23701 Eutin.
Tel 04521 5281, Fax 04521 3610. English spoken.
OPEN: 01/04−31/10. SIZE: 2.1 ha, 110 pitches (all with elec, 40 statics), 12 hot showers, 16 WCs, 1 CWP. & &

Restaurant at 0.4 km.
PRICES: (1996) Caravan with family 40.50, Tent with two adults 27.00. CC: none.
From Eutin take road to Matente. After 0.5 km, follow signs.

EXTERTAL 14D

Camping Eimke im Extertal Eimke 4, 4923 Extertal.
Tel 05262 3307. English spoken.
OPEN: all year. SIZE: 5 ha, 30 pitches (all with elec, 300 statics), 25 hot showers, 30 WCs, 3 CWPs. &

Restaurant at 0.5 km.
PRICES: (1996) Caravan with family 29.50, Tent with two adults 20.00. CC: none.
Leave the A2 at Bad Eilsen/Rinteln and go towards Barntrup.

EYSTRUP 14D

Campingplatz Gut Hamelsee Heemson, 3071 Eystrup.
Tel 04254 92123, Fax 04254 92125. English spoken.
OPEN: 01/04−30/09. SIZE: 24 ha, 50 pitches (all with elec, 500 statics), 18 hot showers, 50 WCs, 3 CWPs. &

Shop at 3 km. Restaurant at 2 km. Table tennis, volley ball,

PRICES: Caravan with family 43.00, Tent with two adults 30.00. CC: none.
Go east from Eystrup towards Rethem and turn right in Hamelhausen to campsite.

FEHMARN

BURG   15A

Camping Ostsee Katherinenhof, 2448 Katharinenhof, Fehmarn.
Tel 04371 9032, Fax 04371 9032. English spoken.
OPEN: 01/04–15/10. SIZE: 7 ha, 180 pitches (all with elec, 150 statics), 28 hot showers, 40 WCs, 2 CWPs. ⚓ ♿

PRICES: Caravan with family 41.00, Tent with two adults 30.00. CC: none.
From Burg, on the island of Fehmarn, go towards Katharinenhof and turn left to the campsite which is well signposted.

FEHMARNSUND   15A

Campingplatz Miramar-Fehmarnsund
23769 Fehmarnsund, Fehmarn.
Tel 04371 3220/2221, Fax 04371 6907.
English spoken.
OPEN: all year. SIZE: 12 ha, 310 pitches (all with elec, 290 statics), 40 hot showers (charge), 80 WCs, 3 CWPs. ♿

Tennis, mini-golf.
PRICES: (1996) Caravan with family 48.00, Tent with two adults 35.00. CC: none.
Take E47 (Hamburg-Puttgarden) to Fehmarn Island and then first turning right to Avendorf and Fehmarnsund.

LANDKIRCHEN   15A

Strand-Camping Wallnau 23769 Westfehmarn.
Tel 04372 456, Fax 04372 1829. English spoken.
OPEN: 27/03–19/10. SIZE: 27 ha, 850 pitches (all with elec, 400 statics), 65 hot showers, 125 WCs, 7 CWPs. ⚓ ♿

Sauna and solarium.
PRICES: Caravan with family 61.60, Tent with two adults 38.80. CC: none.
From the Lubeck to Puttgarden road, exit at Landkirchen to Petersdorf, Bojendorf and then Wallnau. Follow signs.

WULFEN   15A

Campingplatz Wulfener Hals
2448 Wulfen, Fehmarn.
Tel 04371 86280, Fax 04371 3723. English spoken.

OPEN: all year. SIZE: 34 ha, 370 pitches (all with elec, 380 statics), 66 hot showers (charge), 90 WCs, 8 CWPs. ⚓ ♿

PRICES: (1996) Caravan with family 56.30, Tent with two adults 39.40. CC: Euro/Access.
Wulfen is on the south coast of Fehmarn island. Campsite is well signposted.

END OF FEHMARN RESORTS

FICHTELBERG   17A

Camping Fichtelsee 8591 Fichtelberg.
Tel 09272 801. English spoken.
OPEN: 15/12–06/11. SIZE: 2.6 ha, 130 pitches (all with elec, 25 statics), 12 hot showers, 17 WCs, 3 French WCs, 2 CWPs. ♿

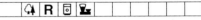

Shop at 0.5 km. Restaurant at 0.3 km. New facilities for 1997.
PRICES: Caravan with family 40.00, Tent with two adults 26.50. CC: none.
Well signposted in town.

FRANKFURT AM MAIN   16B

Campingplatz Huberkushof
Bezirkstrasse 2, 65817 Eppstein.
Tel 0177 456 7000, Fax 06198 7000.
English spoken.
OPEN: all year. SIZE: 3 ha, 50 pitches (all with elec, 120 statics), 9 hot showers (charge), 19 WCs, 3 CWPs. ⚓

Restaurant at 1 km.
PRICES: (1996) Caravan with family 41.00, Tent with two adults 27.00. CC: none.
From Frankfurt am Main, leave A3 towards Köln at Wiesbaden-Niedernhausen exit. Take B455 for Eppstein/Niederjosbach and campsite is signposted.

FREIBURG   16C

Camping Platz Kirchzarten 79199 Kirchzarten.
Tel 07661 39375, Fax 07661 61624.
English spoken.
OPEN: all year. SIZE: 6 ha, 410 pitches (all with elec, 80 statics), 70 WCs, 3 CWPs. ⚓ ♿

Horse-riding, sports stadium, golf, gliding.
PRICES: (1996) Caravan with family 51.00, Tent with two adults 35.00. CC: Euro/Access, Visa.
Take motorway Karlsruhe to Basel, A5/E35, and leave it at Freiburg-Mitte. Then take B31 towards Donaueschingen as far as Kirchzarten (about 10 km from Freiburg). From B31 turn right and follow signs to campsite.

Germany

Camping Steingrubenhof 79271 St Peter.
Tel 07660 210, Fax 07660 1604. English spoken.
OPEN: all year. SIZE: 1.5 ha, 50 pitches (all with elec, 100 statics), 8 hot showers, 11 WCs, 1 CWP. &

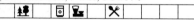

Shop at 1 km. Swimming pool 1 km.
PRICES: (1996) Caravan with family 32.00,
Tent with two adults 21.50. CC: none.
Take A5 motorway to Freiburg-Nord then B294 to Denzlingen, Glottertal and then St Peter.

Ferein und Kurbad Camping Waldseestr 77, 79117 Freiburg.
Tel 0761 72938, Fax 0761 77578. English spoken.
OPEN: 20/03–20/10. SIZE: 7 ha, 80 pitches (40 with elec), 6 hot showers, 7 WCs, 1 CWP. ℓ

Sauna.
PRICES: (1996) Caravan with family 38.00,
Tent with two adults 25.00. CC: none.
From Freiburg go 3 km towards Titisee. Right at town hall.

FREUDENSTADT   16D

Camping Platz Lagenwald 7290 Freudenstadt.
Tel 07441 2862, Fax 07441 2893. English spoken.
OPEN: 15/04–15/10. SIZE: 1.5 ha, 90 pitches (all with elec, 10 statics), 10 hot showers, 20 WCs, 2 CWPs. ℓ &

Swimming pool 2 km.
PRICES: Caravan with family 37.00,
Tent with two adults 28.00. CC: Euro/Access.
3 km west of Freudenstadt on the B28. Site is on the left and signposted.

Hohencamping Konigkanzel
7295 Dornstetten-Hallwangen.
Tel 07443 6730, Fax 07443 4574. English spoken.
OPEN: all year. SIZE: 9 ha, 50 pitches (all with elec, 50 statics), 16 hot showers, 20 WCs, 1 CWP. ℓ &

Restaurant at 0.5 km.
PRICES: Caravan with family 38.00,
Tent with two adults 29.00. CC: none.
8 km from Freudenstadt towards Stuttgart on B28.

FRIESENHEIM   16C

Campingplatz Baggersee Schuttern
77948 Friesenheim.
Tel 07808 2847, Fax 07821 633759.
OPEN: 01/04–30/09. SIZE: 40 ha, 150 pitches (all with elec, 290 statics), 10 hot showers, 21 WCs, 2 CWPs. ℓ &

Fishing, rowing, windsurfing.

PRICES: Caravan with family 28.00, Tent with two adults 22.00. CC: none.
From A5 Karlsruhe to Basel, exit at Offenburg or Lahr and take B3 to Friesenheim. Follow signs to campsite.

FULDA   16B

Campingplatz Kreuzberg
8789 Oberwildflecken.
Tel 09745 2294. English spoken.
OPEN: all year. SIZE: 2 ha, 20 pitches (all with elec, 60 statics), 4 hot showers, 8 WCs, 2 CWPs. ℓ

Shop at 0.2 km. Restaurant at 0.2 km.
PRICES: (1996) Caravan with family 25.00,
Tent with two adults 17.00. CC: none.
From A7 take Bad Brückenau/Wildflecken exit, go for 2 km towards Wildfleken and then turn right to Oberwildflecken. Site is well signposted.

Campingplatz Rothemann
Maulkuppenstr 17, 6405 Rothemann.
Tel 06659 2285.
OPEN: 01/04–31/10. SIZE: 1 ha, 50 pitches (26 with elec), 4 hot showers (charge), 4 WCs, 1 CWP.

Restaurant at 0.3 km.
PRICES: (1996) Caravan with family 26.80,
Tent with two adults 20.00. CC: none.
From Fulda go south on B27 towards Bad Brückenau for 10 km. Campsite is signposted.

FÜRTH   16B

Campingplatz Tierfertswinkel Krumbacherstr, 64658 Fürth in Odenwald.
Tel 06253 5804. English spoken.
OPEN: 01/02–01/12. SIZE: 4 ha, 30 pitches (all with elec, 100 statics), 10 hot showers, 14 WCs, 4 CWPs. ℓ

Shop at 0.2 km. Restaurant at 0.1 km. Playground.
PRICES: (1996) Caravan with family 33.20, Tent with two adults 18.20. CC: none.
From A5 motorway between Dormstadt and Heidelberg, take the exit at Heppenheim on to B460 to Fürth, where the campsite is signposted.

FÜSSEN   17C

Camping Waritska 87669 Rieden-Rosshaupten.
Tel 08367 406, Fax 08367 1256. English spoken.
OPEN: all year. SIZE: 3 ha, 10 hot showers, 23 WCs. ℓ

Playground; water sports/boating nearby.
PRICES: (1996) Caravan with family 43.00,
Tent with two adults 27.00. CC: none.

From Füssen go 10 km north, towards Marktoberdorf. Turn right to the campsite 1 km from Rosshaupten.

Campingplatz Hopfensee 87629 Füssen.
Tel 08362 917710. English spoken.
OPEN: 17/12–02/11. SIZE: 7 ha, 375 pitches (all with elec, 10 statics), 32 hot showers, 40 WCs, 3 CWPs. ℂ ☉

Sauna and solarium, nursery, cinema, children's playground.
PRICES: Caravan with family 79.70. CC: none.
From Füssen go to Hopferou where campsite is signposted.

Ferienplatz Brunnen Seestr 81, 87645 Brunnen.
Tel 08362 8273, Fax 08362 81738. English spoken.
OPEN: 20/12–08/11. SIZE: 2 ha, 280 pitches (all with elec), 18 hot showers, 43 WCs, 3 CWPs. ℂ ☉

Restaurant at 0.1 km.
PRICES: Caravan with family 45.00,
Tent with two adults 28.00. CC: none.
Coming from Kempten, turn left in Schwangau.

GARMISCH-PARTENKIRCHEN   17C

Alpen-Caravanpark Tennsee
82493 Klais-Krün/Obb.
Tel 08825 170, Fax 08825 17236. English spoken.
OPEN: 14/12–16/11. SIZE: 52 ha, 35 pitches (all with elec, 250 statics), 65 hot showers, 67 WCs, 1 CWP. ℂ ☉

PRICES: Caravan with family 67.80,
Tent with two adults 40.00. CC: none.
From Garmisch follow signs east towards Mittenwald. Drive through Klais (15 km) and site is 2 km ahead on the right and well signposted.

Camping Platz Zugspitze
8104 Garmisch-Partenkirchen.
Tel 08821 3180, Fax 089 55255666.
English spoken.
OPEN: all year. SIZE: 3.5 ha, 180 pitches (200 with elec, 40 statics), 20 hot showers (charge), 20 WCs, 2 CWPs. ℂ

PRICES: (1996) Caravan with family 31.40, Tent with two adults 26.10. CC: none.
Near the River Loisach, 1 km out of Garmisch heading towards Griessen and the Austrian border.

GEMÜNDEN   16B

Ferien-Campingplatz Schönrain Schönrainstr 12-14, 97737 Gemünden-Hofstetten.
Tel 09351 8645, Fax 09351 8721. English spoken.

OPEN: 01/04–30/09. SIZE: 7 ha, 80 pitches (all with elec), 6 hot showers, 12 WCs, 1 CWP. ℂ

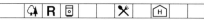

Chldren's playgroung; bikes for hire.
PRICES: (1996) Caravan with family 34.00,
Tent with two adults 23.00. CC: none.
From the Frankfurt-Würzburg autobahn, take the Weibersbrunn-Lohr exit and then B26 to Gemünden. Turn right over the bridge to Hofstetten. Campsite is well signposted.

GERSFELD   16B

Camping Hoch Rhon Schachen,
36129 Gersfeld.
Tel 06654 7836, Fax 06654 7413.
English spoken.
OPEN: all year. SIZE: 4 ha, 100 pitches (all with elec, 100 statics), 8 hot showers (charge), 16 WCs, 4 CWPs.

Shop at 1 km. Restaurant at 0.3 km.
PRICES: (1996) Caravan with family 28.00,
Tent with two adults 20.00. CC: none.
From A7 motorway (Kassel to Fulda) take the last Fulda exit and then on to Gersfeld. From A7 motorway (Würzbürg to Fulda) take the Wildfleckin exit and then on to Gersfeld.

GILLENFELD   16A

Campingplatz Pulvermaar
54558 Gillenfeld/Eifel.
Tel 06573 311, Fax 06573 715.
OPEN: 01/04–31/10. SIZE: 1.5 ha, 150 pitches (82 with elec, 60 statics), 8 hot showers, 13 WCs, 1 CWP.

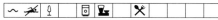

Shop at 1.5 km. Restaurant at 2 km.
PRICES: (1996) Caravan with family 29.00,
Tent with two adults 21.00. CC: none.
From Koblenz, south-east on A48, exit Daun, then 3 km to Gillenfeld.

GIROD BEI MONTABAUR   16A

Campingplatz Eisenbachtal
56412 Girod bei Montabaur.
Tel 06485 766, Fax 06485 4938.
OPEN: all year. SIZE: 3 ha, 30 pitches (all with elec, 130 statics), 10 hot showers (charge), 15 WCs, 1 CWP. ℂ ☉

Sports field; walking and rambling.
PRICES: (1996) Caravan with family 43.00,
Tent with two adults 26.00. CC: none.
From Köln-Frankfurt motorway (A3) take exit 40 at Montabaur and go towards Limburg. After 6 km turn right to campsite.

Germany

GOSLAR 14D

Campingplatz Am Krähenberg Wolfshagen im Harz, 38685 Langelsheim.
Tel 05326 4089, Fax 05326 7014.
OPEN: all year. SIZE: 100 pitches (all with elec, 310 statics), 18 hot showers, 56 WCs. ⚓

PRICES: (1996) Caravan with family 35.20. CC: none.
From Goslar take the B82 towards Langelsheim. Before entering the town turn left to Wolfshagen im Harz and the campsite is well signposted.

GREDING 17C

Bauer-Keller Kraftsbucher Str 1, 91171 Greding.
Tel 08463 203/64000, Fax 08463 640033.
English spoken.
OPEN: 01/05–30/09. SIZE: 1 ha, 100 pitches, 2 hot showers (charge), 6 WCs.

Shop at 1 km.
PRICES: Caravan with family 20.00,
Tent with two adults 13.00. CC: none.
From A9 motorway to Greding; campsite is well signposted.

GUNZENHAUSEN 17C

See-Camping Langlau Seestr 30,
8821 Pfofeld-Langlau.
Tel 09834 96969, Fax 09834 96968. English spoken.
OPEN: 01/03–15/11. SIZE: 12 ha, 330 pitches (all with elec, 90 statics), 36 hot showers, 46 WCs, 4 French WCs, 2 CWPs. ⚓

Water sports, fishing.
PRICES: (1996) Caravan with family 40.50,
Tent with two adults 28.00. CC: none.
From Gunzenhausen go 10 km towards Pleinfeld. Campsite is well signposted.

HAHNENKLEE 14D

Campingplatz Am Kreuzeck 38644 Goslar.
Tel 05325 2570. English spoken.
OPEN: all year. SIZE: 5 ha, 200 pitches (all with elec, 80 statics), 10 hot showers, 20 WCs, 2 CWPs. ⚓

Sauna, solarium, playground.
PRICES: Caravan with family 39.90,
Tent with two adults 29.10. CC: Euro/Access.
Coming from Goslar to Hahnenklee branch right for 50 m to campsite.

HAMBURG 14B

Campingplatz Schnelsen Nord
Wunderbrunner 2, 2000 Hamburg.
Tel 040 5591225, Fax 040 5507334. English spoken.

OPEN: 01/04–31/10. SIZE: 3 ha, 100 pitches (all with elec), 12 hot showers, 18 WCs, 1 CWP. &

Restaurant at 1 km.
PRICES: (1996) Caravan with family 44.00,
Tent with two adults 29.00. CC: none.
From Hamburg, take the motorway A7 north towards Flensburg and exit Schnelsen Nord, then follow signs to campsite.

HASLACH 16C

Campingplatz Kinzigtal
77790 Steinach/Kinzigtal.
Tel 07832 8122, Fax 07832 6619. English spoken.
OPEN: 15/03–15/10. SIZE: 150 pitches (all with elec, 100 statics). &

PRICES: (1996) Caravan with family 41.50,
Tent with two adults 27.00. CC: none.
From A5 Karlsruhe to Basel, exit Offenburg. On B33 follow signs to Villingen-Schweningen and take Steinach exit.

HATTEN-KIRCHHATTEN 14B

Campingplatz Hatten Freizeitzentrum,
2904 Hatten-Kirchhatten.
Tel 04482 677, Fax 04482 922239. English spoken.
OPEN: all year. SIZE: 12 ha, 250 pitches (all with elec, 200 statics), 32 hot showers, 32 WCs, 2 CWPs. ⚓ &

Children's playground, tennis, crazy golf, large pool complex.
PRICES: (1996) Caravan with family 34.00,
Tent with two adults 23.00. CC: none.
From A1 exit at Wildeshausen-Nord, drive north to Hatten-Kirchhatten.

HEIDELBERG 16B

Camping Haide Kleingemünd,
69151 Neckargemünd.
Tel 06223 2111, Fax 06223 71959. English spoken.
OPEN: 01/04–31/10. SIZE: 4 ha, 180 pitches (80 with elec), 23 hot showers (charge), 32 WCs, 2 CWPs. ⚓ &

Swimming pool 3 km.
PRICES: Caravan with family 36.00, Tent with two adults 24.00. CC: Euro/Access, Visa.
Coming from the Rhine Valley or the motorway drive through Heidelberg-Ziegelhausen and on for about another 2 km towards Kleingemünd.

Erholungsanluge St Leoner See 68789 St Leon-Rot.
Tel 06227 59009, Fax 06227 880988. English spoken.
OPEN: all year. SIZE: 80 ha, 370 pitches (180 with elec,

650 statics), 28 hot showers, 120 WCs, 4 CWPs. ☎ ♿

Watersports, fishing, walking and rambling.
PRICES: (1996) Caravan with family 41.00, Tent
with two adults 22.00. CC: Euro/Access, Visa.
*From A5 exit at Wiesloch/Walldorf go to Reilingen
and then St Leon.*

HEIDENAU 14B

Ferienzentrum Heidenau 2111 Heidenau.
Tel 04182 4272, Fax 040 6069100.
OPEN: all year. SIZE: 30 ha, 50 pitches (all with elec,
400 statics), 12 hot showers, 24 WCs, 4 CWPs. ☎

Mini-golf, sauna, tennis.
PRICES: (1996) Caravan with family 43.00,
Tent with two adults 35.00. CC: none.
Campsite signposted from motorway at Heidenau.

HEILBRONN 16D

Camping Cimbria Rolf Fuchs K6,
74865 Neckarzimmern.
Tel 06261 2562, Fax 06261 35716. English spoken.
OPEN: 01/04–31/10. SIZE: 3 ha, 90 pitches (50 with
elec, 80 statics), 10 hot showers (charge), 17 WCs,
1 CWP. ☎

Shop at 0.4 km. Slipway for boats, playground,
table tennis.
PRICES: Caravan with family 35.00,
Tent with two adults 24.00. CC: none.
*From Heilbronn take B27 towards Mosbach for
about 25 km. Turn left after Neckarzimmern and
follow signs to campsite.*

HEIMBACH 16A

Campingplatz Rurthal Burg Bleus Hausener
Strasse, 52396 Heimbach.
Tel 02446 3377, Fax 02446 1095. English spoken.
OPEN: all year. SIZE: 7 ha, 40 pitches (all with elec,
360 statics), 18 hot showers (charge), 38 WCs,
1 CWP. ☎ ♿

Restaurant at 0.5 km. Playground.
PRICES: (1996) Caravan with family 34.40,
Tent with two adults 22.20. CC: none.
*From Köln to Zülpich, Wollersheim, Heimbach
and then Hausen. In Hausen turn right at the
lights and campsite is 300 m.*

HELLENTHAL 16A

Camping Hellenthal 53940 Hellenthal-Eifel.
Tel 02482 1500, Fax 02482 2171. English spoken.
OPEN: all year. SIZE: 6 ha, 140 pitches (all with elec,
300 statics), 15 hot showers, 4 CWPs. ☎

Shop at 1.4 km.
PRICES: (1996) Caravan with family 38.00,
Tent with two adults 27.00. CC: Euro/Access.
*On B265 going towards Trier, at the southern end
of town.*

HELMSTEDT 15C

Camping und Erholungspark Nord-Elm
Rabke, 38373 Supplingen.
Tel 05355 8352. English spoken.
OPEN: all year. SIZE: 65 pitches (all with elec,
252 statics), 20 hot showers, 21 WCs, 2 CWPs. ☎ ♿

Shop at 1 km. Minigolf, barbecue.
PRICES: Caravan with family 36.50,
Tent with two adults 21.50. CC: none.
*Leave A2/E30 at Helmstedt and take B1 west to
Supplingen. Follow signs to Rabke and campsite.*

HERBOLZHEIM 16C

Camping Platz Oase 77955 Ettenheim.
Tel 07822 9881. English spoken.
OPEN: 25/03–05/10. SIZE: 6 ha, 220 pitches
(all with elec, 80 statics), 22 hot showers (charge),
31 WCs, 2 CWPs. ☎ ♿

Children's playground, mini-golf; tennis nearby.
PRICES: Caravan with family 43.00, Tent with two
adults 28.00. CC: none.
*North of Herbolzheim. Take Ettenheim exit off A5
and campsite is signposted after about 4 km.*

Terrassencampingplatz Herbolzheim Im Lave
1, 7834 Herbolzheim.
Tel 07643 1460, Fax 07643 1460. English spoken.
OPEN: 22/03–15/10. SIZE: 2 ha, 50 pitches (all with
elec, 40 statics), 8 hot showers, 17 WCs. ☎

PRICES: (1996) Caravan with family 35.00,
Tent with two adults 25.00. CC: none.
*From A5 north of Freiburg, go to Herbolzheim
and follow signs to campsite.*

HERINGEN 16B

Werracamping Postfach 1241,
36266 Heringen (Werra).
Tel 06624 9330, Fax 06624 933100.
OPEN: all year. SIZE: 40 pitches (all with elec,
40 statics), 4 hot showers, 7 WCs, 1 CWP. ☎

Shop at 0.5 km.
PRICES: Caravan with family 26.00,
Tent with two adults 19.00. CC: none.
*Take Friedewald exit off A4/E40 for Heringen and
follow signs to the campsite.*

HERSBRUCK 17A

Pegnitz Camping Eschenbacher Weg 4,
91224 Hohenstadt bei Hersbruck.
Tel 09154 1500. English spoken.
OPEN: 15/03–15/11. SIZE: 60 pitches (all with elec,
40 statics), 5 hot showers, 10 WCs, 3 CWPs.

Shop at 0.8 km.
PRICES: (1996) Caravan with family 31.00,
Tent with two adults 22.00. CC: none.
*Exit A9 towards Hersbruck then take B14 and exit
at Hohenstadt. Follow signs to campsite from there.*

HILDESHEIM 14D

Seecamp Derneburg 31188 Holle.
Tel 05062 565, Fax 05062 8785.
English spoken.
OPEN: 01/04–15/09. SIZE: 8 ha, 100 pitches
(60 with elec, 240 statics), 10 hot showers
(charge), 23 WCs, 2 CWPs.

PRICES: (1996) Caravan with family 36.50,
Tent with two adults 22.50. CC: none.
*Take B6 south-east from Hildesheim to Goslar
and, 300 m before motorway 7, turn right.
Campsite well signposted.*

HOF 17A

Campingplatz Auensee Am Auensee,
95189 Joditz/Köditz.
Tel 09295 381, Fax 09281 706666.
OPEN: all year. SIZE: 4 ha, 50 pitches (all with elec,
150 statics), 8 hot showers (charge), 16 WCs,
1 CWP.

Shop at 0.5 km. Boating.
PRICES: Caravan with family 24.80,
Tent with two adults 13.00. CC: none.
*8 km from Hof in Ortsteil Joditz, north of
Nürnberg (A9) and south of Plauen (A72).*

HOFGEISMAR 14D

Camping am Parkschwimmbad
Schöneberger Str 16, 3520 Hofgeismar.
Tel 05671 1215. English spoken.
OPEN: all year. SIZE: 1.5 ha, 50 pitches (40 with
elec, 60 statics), 8 hot showers (charge), 12 WCs,
1 CWP.

Shop at 1 km. Restaurant at 1 km. Children's
playground.
PRICES: (1996) Caravan with family 24.00,
Tent with two adults 15.00. CC: Euro/Access.
*From Kassel, take B83 to Hofgeismar and follow
directions to campsite.*

HOLZMINDEN 14D

Weserbergland-Campingplatz Holzminden
Am Freibad, 37603 Holzminden 1.
Tel 05531 3588. English spoken.
OPEN: 01/04–30/09. SIZE: 1 ha, 90 pitches (all with
elec, 30 statics), 6 hot showers, 8 WCs, 1 CWP.

Shop at 0.1 km. Restaurant at 0.5 km.
PRICES: Caravan with family 23.00,
Tent with two adults 15.00. CC: none.
*From Hameln on B83 to Holzminden. Campsite is
in front of the bridge over the Weser, on the right.*

HORB 16D

Hohencamping Schuttehof Schutteberg 7,
7240 Horb am Neckar.
Tel 07451 3951, Fax 07451 1348. English spoken.
OPEN: all year. SIZE: 6 ha, 50 pitches (all with elec,
250 statics), 12 hot showers (charge), 27 WCs,
1 CWP.

Adventure playground.
PRICES: (1996) Caravan with family 45.50,
Tent with two adults 28.50. CC: none.
*Outside Horb, follow the signs to Freudenstadt
and the campsite is well signposted.*
*(a) RESORT:*Horn 14D

Campingplatz Eggewald Kempenerstr 33,
4934 Horn-Bad Meinberg.
Tel 05255 236, Fax 05255 1375. English spoken.
OPEN: all year. SIZE: 2 ha, 20 pitches (all with elec,
40 statics), 10 WCs, 1 CWP.

Tractor museum nearby.
PRICES: (1996) Caravan with family 25.00,
Tent with two adults 20.00. CC: none.
*From the Hannover to Dortmund motorway, exit
at Herford on to B239 and go to Horn, then B1
towards Paderborn. At the restaurant
'Waldschossen', take turning to Attenbeken and
campsite is 8 km.*

HUSUM 14B

Campingplatz Nordsee 25813 Husum.
Tel 04841 61911, Fax 04841 4402.
English spoken.
OPEN: 23/03–27/10. SIZE: 2 ha, 130 pitches
(120 with elec, 40 statics), 12 hot showers
(charge), 16 WCs, 1 CWP.

Bikes for hire; swimming pool 4 km.
PRICES: (1996) Caravan with family 36.50,
Tent with two adults 22.50. CC: none.
*3 km north-west of Husum on the coast. Well
signposted.*

Germany

IDAR-OBERSTEIN 16A

Campingplatz Harfenmuhle
55758 Asbacherhutte.
Tel 06786 7076, Fax 06786 7570. English spoken.
OPEN: all year. SIZE: 6 ha, 90 pitches (80 with elec, 70 statics), 10 hot showers (charge), 14 WCs, 2 CWPs. &

Tennis, sauna, solarium, table tennis, playground.
PRICES: Caravan with family 34.50,
Tent with two adults 25.00. CC: none.
From Idar-Oberstein on B41 to Fischbach, and then on to route 160 to Herstein. A further 5 km from Herstein, campsite on the right.

IRREL 16A

Camping Nimseck 54666 Irrel.
Tel 06525 314, Fax 06525 1299. English spoken.
OPEN: 18/03–04/11. SIZE: 8 ha, 150 pitches (all with elec, 150 statics), 15 hot showers, 27 WCs, 2 CWPs. &

PRICES: (1996) Caravan with family 50.00,
Tent with two adults 31.50. CC: none.
From Bitburg go 14 km south-west to Irrel, which is on Luxembourg border.

ISNY 16D

Camping Waldbad 88316 Isny.
Tel 07562 2389, Fax 07562 5654.
OPEN: 15/12–30/10. SIZE: 2.5 ha, 30 pitches (50 with elec, 6 statics), 4 hot showers, 9 WCs, 1 CWP. & &

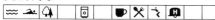

Shop at 1.5 km. Tennis, playground and barbecue 100 m.
PRICES: (1996) Caravan with family 36.40,
Tent with two adults 24.60. CC: Euro/Access.
On the B12/E54. Site is well signposted.

Campingplatz am Badsee 88316 Isny-Beuren.
Tel 07567 1026, Fax 07567 1026.
OPEN: 15/04–15/10. SIZE: 4 ha, 80 pitches (all with elec, 200 statics), 16 hot showers (charge), 30 WCs, 1 CWP. & &

Shop at 2.5 km.
PRICES: (1996) Caravan with family 35.00,
Tent with two adults 23.00. CC: none.
Motorway Memmingen to Lindau, exit Leutkirch to Isny, Beuren and then the campsite.

JENA 15C

Campingplatz Rabeninsel 07778 Porstendorf.
Tel 036427 22256, Fax 036427 22256.
English spoken.

OPEN: 01/05–31/10. SIZE: 3 ha, 100 pitches (all with elec, 25 statics), 20 hot showers, 20 WCs. &

Shop at 0.2 km. Restaurant at 0.5 km.
PRICES: (1996) Caravan with family 28.00,
Tent with two adults 22.00. CC: none.
Leave A4 at Jena-Lobeda exit and take B88 towards Naumberg. In Porstendorf go right at railway and carry on to campsite.

KAISERSLAUTERN 16A

Azur Camping am Königsberg
67752 Wolfstein/Pfalz.
Tel 06304 7543. English spoken.
OPEN: all year. SIZE: 1.5 ha, 100 pitches (all with elec, 50 statics), 14 hot showers, 14 WCs, 1 CWP. &

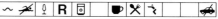

PRICES: (1996) Caravan with family 41.90,
Tent with two adults 26.70. CC: none.
B270 towards Wolfstein and campsite is about 300 m before reaching the village. Well signposted.

KALKAR-WISSEL 14C

Wisseler See 4192 Kalkar-Wissel.
Tel 02824 6613, Fax 02824 6493. English spoken.
OPEN: all year. SIZE: 22 ha, 100 pitches (60 with elec, 520 statics), 3 CWPs. &

PRICES: (1996) Caravan with family 41.00,
Tent with two adults 30.00. CC: Euro/Access.
The campsite is situated between Kalkar and Kleve.

KASSEL 14D

Campingplatz Hofgeismar am Parkschwimmbad 3510 Hofgeismar.
Tel 05671 1215. English spoken.
OPEN: all year. SIZE: 1.5 ha, 50 pitches (110 with elec, 60 statics), 9 hot showers (charge), 14 WCs, 1 CWP. &

Shop at 0.5 km. Restaurant at 1 km.
PRICES: (1996) Caravan with family 24.00,
Tent with two adults 15.00. CC: none.
From Kassel go north on the B83 to Hofgeismar and follow directions from there.

KEMPTEN 16D

Camping Oschlesee 87477 Sulzberg.
Tel 08376 93040, Fax 08376 93041.
English spoken.
OPEN: all year. SIZE: 4.0 ha, 200 pitches (all with elec, 100 statics), 20 hot showers, 28 WCs, 2 CWPs. & &

Restaurant at 0.4 km. New sanitary block opening June 1997.
PRICES: (1996) Caravan with family 41.00, Tent with two adults 28.00. CC: none.
Take motorway A7, Kreuz Allgäu, then A980 towards Durach/Sulzberg and exit Sulzberg.

Campingplatz Sonnenbuckl 88167 Riedholz.
Tel 08383 383, Fax 08383 9355. English spoken.
OPEN: all year. SIZE: 1.5 ha, 30 pitches (all with elec, 25 statics), 7 hot showers, 6 WCs, 1 CWP. ℄

Shop at 1.5 km.
PRICES: Caravan with family 35.50, Tent with two adults 23.00. CC: none.
From Kempten go to Grossholzleute and then Maierhofen and from there to Riedholz where there are signs to the campsite.

KIEL 14B

Campingplatz Kiel-Falckenstein
Palisadenweg 171, 24159 Kiel.
Tel 0431 392078, Fax 0431 392078.
English spoken.
OPEN: 01/04–31/10. SIZE: 100 pitches (all with elec, 260 statics), 28 hot showers, 40 WCs, 3 CWPs. ℄ 占

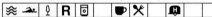

Shop at 3 km.
PRICES: (1996) Caravan with family 34.00, Tent with two adults 21.50. CC: none.
Coming from Kiel drive towards Olympia Zentrum. Turn right at windmill and follow the signs.

KINDING 17C

Campingplatz Kratsmuehle 8079 Kinding.
Tel 08461 525, Fax 08461 9535. English spoken.
OPEN: all year. SIZE: 12 ha, 165 pitches (all with elec, 270 statics), 30 hot showers, 38 WCs, 3 CWPs. 占

PRICES: (1996) Caravan with family 38.00, Tent with two adults 26.00. CC: none.
From the Nürnberg-München motorway, exit at Kinding/Altmüntal, and campsite is 5 km.

KIRTORF 16B

Camping Heimertshausen 6322 Kirtorf 1.
Tel 06635 206, Fax 06635 206. English spoken.
OPEN: 01/04–30/09. SIZE: 4 ha, 80 pitches (all with elec, 120 statics), 10 hot showers, 20 WCs, 2 CWPs.

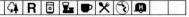

Table tennis, playground.

PRICES: Caravan with family 27.50, Tent with two adults 20.00. CC: none.
From A48 (Kassel to Frankfurt) exit at Alsfeld-West and go to Romrod, Zell and then Heimertshausen where campsite is well signposted.

KITZINGEN 16B

Campingplatz Schiefer Turm
Marktbreiter Str, Hohenfeld, 97318 Kitzingen.
Tel 09321 33125, Fax 09321 34158.
English spoken.
OPEN: 01/04–31/10. SIZE: 3 ha, 70 pitches (150 with elec, 90 statics), 16 hot showers, 24 WCs, 1 CWP. 占

PRICES: (1996) Caravan with family 39.50, Tent with two adults 26.00. CC: none.
Outside Kitzingen, near indoor and outdoor swimming pools.

KNITTLINGEN 16D

Stromberg Camping Diefenbacher Str 70, 7134 Knittlingen 2.
Tel 07043 2160, Fax 07043 40405.
English spoken.
OPEN: all year. SIZE: 8.5 ha, 50 pitches (all with elec, 550 statics), 26 hot showers, 32 WCs, 4 CWPs. ℄ 占

(Extra charge for electricity). Mini-golf, playground, pony rides, skittles.
PRICES: (1996) Caravan with family 43.00, Tent with two adults 29.00. CC: none.
From Knittlingen (east of Bretten) go to Freudenstein and follow signs to Stromberg Camping.

KOBLENZ 16A

Boots and Camping Centre Laguna
5401 Burgen/Koblenz.
Tel 02605 2511. English spoken.
OPEN: 15/04–15/10. SIZE: 4 ha, 60 pitches (all with elec, 60 statics), 8 hot showers (charge), 14 WCs, 1 CWP. 占

PRICES: (1996) Caravan with family 33.00, Tent with two adults 23.00. CC: none.
From motorway south of Koblenz, exit at Dieblich and go on B49 past Burgen to the campsite (on the banks of the Mosel).

Camping Insel Ziehfurt 56333 Winningen.
Tel 02606 357, Fax 02606 2752. English spoken.
OPEN: 01/05–30/09. SIZE: 7 ha, 200 pitches (all with elec, 200 statics), 10 hot showers, 30 WCs, 1 CWP. ℄

Water sports, river cruises.
PRICES: Caravan with family 35.00,
Tent with two adults 24.00. CC: none.
On A61 from Köln to Ludwigshafen take the
Winningen exit. In Winningen on B416 drive
400 m towards Cochem and take a left turn at the
swimming pool (10 km from Koblenz).

Camping Platz Burg Lahneck Oberlahn,
56112 Lahnstein/Rhein.
Tel 02621 2765. English spoken.
OPEN: 01/04–31/10. SIZE: 1.8 ha, 115 pitches
(all with elec, 10 statics), 10 hot showers (charge),
13 WCs, 1 CWP.

Swimming pool adjacent, spa centre 2 km.
PRICES: (1996) Caravan with family 44.50,
Tent with two adults 32.00. CC: none.
From the B42 by pass, take Oberlahnstein exit
and follow signs for Burg Lahneck (the castle).

Freizeitpark Moselbogen Am Gülser
Moselbogen 20, 56072 Koblenz-Güls.
Tel 0261 44474, Fax 0261 44494. English spoken.
OPEN: all year. SIZE: 7 ha, 80 pitches (all with elec,
70 statics), 9 hot showers, 15 WCs, 1 CWP.

Shop at 1 km. Restaurant at 0.5 km.
PRICES: Caravan with family 40,
Tent with two adults 27. CC: none.
From motorway A61 exit Koblenz, drive towards
Güls. Campsite is signposted.

KOCHEL   17C

Campingplatz Kesselberg 8113 Kochel.
Tel 08851 464. English spoken.
OPEN: 01/04–25/09. SIZE: 1 ha, 70 pitches
(30 statics), 8 hot showers, 10 WCs, 1 CWP.

Shop at 0.05 km.
PRICES: (1996) Caravan with family 36.80,
Tent with two adults 24.00. CC: none.
Campsite is well signposted in Kochel.

Campingplatz Renken Mittenwalder Str,
82431 Kochel am See.
Tel 08851 5776. English spoken.
OPEN: 01/04–30/09. SIZE: 0.9 ha, 70 pitches
(all with elec, 10 statics), 6 hot showers (charge),
13 WCs, 1 CWP.

Restaurant at 0.4 km.
PRICES: (1996) Caravan with family 39.70,
Tent with two adults 25.50. CC: none.
From München on A95, exit Murnau/Kochel. In
Kochel turn right towards Mittenwald, travelling
south. Campsite is on right.

KÖLN (COLOGNE)   14C

Camping Platz Berger Uferstrasse 71,
50996 Köln.
Tel 0221 392211, Fax 0221 3955246.
English spoken.
OPEN: all year. SIZE: 6 ha, 125 pitches (all with elec,
125 statics), 13 hot showers, 29 WCs, 2 CWPs.

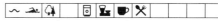

Playground.
PRICES: (1996) Caravan with family 35.00,
Tent with two adults 22.00. CC: none.
Leave motorway at Köln-Bayenthal towards
Rodenkirchen and follow signs to the campsite.

Campingplatz der Stadt Köln
Weidenweg 46, 5000 Köln.
Tel 0221 831966. English spoken.
OPEN: 01/05–30/09. SIZE: 2 ha, 100 pitches
(80 with elec), 10 hot showers (charge), 9 WCs,
1 CWP.

PRICES: (1996) Caravan with family 33.00,
Tent with two adults 20.00. CC: none.
On A4 motorway take Köln/Poll exit.

Freies Ortskartell Peter Baum Weg, 5 Waldbad,
51069 Köln-Dünnwald.
Tel 0221 603315. English spoken.
OPEN: all year. SIZE: 32 pitches (30 with elec,
50 statics), 10 hot showers, 10 WCs, 1 CWP.

PRICES: (1996) Caravan with family 28.00,
Tent with two adults 14.00. CC: none.
Leave the A3 at Köln-Leverkusen exit; take the
ring road to Berlinerstr and follow signs.

KONSTANZ   16D

Camping Sandseele 78479 Insel Reichenau.
Tel 07534 7384, Fax 07534 98976. English spoken.
OPEN: 01/04–30/09. SIZE: 3 ha, 120 pitches
(all with elec, 100 statics), 12 hot showers,
22 WCs, 1 CWP.

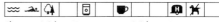

Windsurfing school, playground.
PRICES: (1996) Caravan with family 34.90,
Tent with two adults 27.30. CC: none.
From Konstanz take causeway to Reichenau and
campsite is well signposted on the western shore.

Campingplatz Klausenhorn
78465 Konstanz-Dingelsdorf.
Tel 07533 6372, Fax 07533 7541. English spoken.
OPEN: 01/04–30/09. SIZE: 4 ha, 200 pitches
(all with elec, 50 statics), 20 hot showers (charge),
34 WCs, 2 CWPs.

Shop at 1.2 km. Restaurant at 1.2 km.

Germany

PRICES: (1996) Caravan with family 45.50, Tent with two adults 35.50. CC: none.
Take the B33 to Allensbach. Take road to Dettingen, then on to Wallhausen and campsite is on the way to Dingelsdorf.

KRANICHFELD 15C

Camping am Stausee 05301 Hohenfelden.
Tel 036450 42081, Fax 036450 42081. English spoken.
OPEN: all year. SIZE: 22.5 ha, 60 pitches (all with elec, 280 statics), 15 hot showers (charge), 20 WCs, 1 CWP. ℂ ⅙

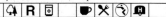

PRICES: Caravan with family 36.00, Tent with two adults 22.50. CC: Amex, Euro/Access, Visa.
From A4 exit at Erfurt-Ost towards Kranichfeld where campsite is signposted.

LAHN 16B

Camping Park Braunfels Am Weiherstieg, 35619 Braunfels.
Tel 06442 4366, Fax 06442 6895. English spoken.
OPEN: all year. SIZE: 5 ha, 70 pitches (140 statics).

Shop at 0.5 km. Restaurant at 0.2 km.
PRICES: (1996) Caravan with family 31.50, Tent with two adults 21.00. CC: none.
From Lahn, north-east of Meppen, go to Braunfels where campsite is signposted.

LAHNSTEIN 16A

Burg Lahneck Campsite 5420 Lahnstein.
Tel 02621 2765, Fax 02621 18290. English spoken.
OPEN: 01/04–31/10. SIZE: 1.8 ha, 115 pitches (all with elec, 10 statics), 10 hot showers (charge), 13 WCs, 1 CWP. ℂ

Panoramic views. Spa centre 2 km.
PRICES: (1996) Caravan with family 37.50, Tent with two adults 30.50. CC: none.
Leave B42 at Oberlahnstein then follow signs to campsite.
SEE ADVERTISEMENT

LAHNTAL-KERNBACH 16B

Camping Kernbach 3551 Lahntal-Kernbach.
Tel 06420 7496. English spoken.
OPEN: all year. SIZE: 2.6 ha, 60 pitches (all with elec, 60 statics), 4 hot showers, 8 WCs, 1 CWP. ℂ

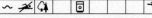

Shop at 1 km. Restaurant at 1 km.
PRICES: (1996) Caravan with family 36.00, Tent with two adults 22.00. CC: none.
Campsite signposted in Lahntal.

LAHR 16C

Ferienparadies Schwarzwälder Hof
77960 Seelbach bei Lahr.
Tel 07823 2777, Fax 07823 2120. English spoken.
OPEN: 01/04–31/10. SIZE: 2.5 ha, 100 pitches (70 with elec, 30 statics), 11 hot showers, 22 WCs, 2 CWPs. ℂ ⅙

Restaurant at 0.5 km.
PRICES: (1996) Caravan with family 38.00, Tent with two adults 23.00. CC: Euro/Access, Visa.
Heading south on A5 take Lahr exit onto B415. Go through Lahr to Lahr-Reichenbach and then turn right to Seelbach. Campsite is signposted.

LAICHINGEN 16D

Heidehof Campinggesellschaft
Blaubeurer Str 50, 89150 Laichingen 3.
Tel 07333 6408, Fax 07333 21463. English spoken.
OPEN: all year. SIZE: 25 ha, 150 pitches (all with elec, 800 statics), 40 hot showers (charge), 75 WCs, 6 CWPs. ℂ ⅙

Sauna, whirlpool. Children's playground.
PRICES: (1996) Caravan with family 35.00, Tent with two adults 24.00. CC: none.
From Stuttgart-Ulm motorway, exit at Merklingen and go towards Blaubeuren (5 km).

LAM 17B/D

Campingplatz am Fusse des Osser
Ginglmuhlerweg 1, Lam, 93462 Bayer Wald.
Tel 09943 1386.
OPEN: all year. SIZE: 1 ha, 40 pitches (30 with elec),
4 hot showers, 6 WCs, 1 CWP.

~	✈	♀		🗗					

Shop at 0.1 km. Restaurant at 0.1 km. Swimming
pool 400m.
PRICES: (1996) Caravan with family 32.60,
Tent with two adults 21.60. CC: none.
*Lam is east of Kotzting; campsite is well signposted
in Lam.*

LANDAU 16A

Campingplatz Klingbachtal
76831 Billigheim-Ingenheim.
Tel 06349 6278.
OPEN: 01/04–31/10. SIZE: 2.5 ha, 180 pitches
(140 statics), 4 hot showers, 12 WCs.

	♀		🗗			✕	⊙		

Shop at 0.5 km.
PRICES: (1996) Caravan with family 32.00,
Tent with two adults 20.00. CC: none.
*A65 exit Landau-Sud, towards Bad Bergzabern
(B38). From Landau-Sud to Impflingen and then
Billigheim-Ingenheim.*

LANDSBERG-AM-LECH 17C

DCC Campingpark Romantik am Lech
Am Possinger Wald, 86899 Landsberg-am-Lech.
Tel 08191 47505, Fax 08191 21406.
English spoken.
OPEN: all year. SIZE: 6 ha, 130 pitches.

✖	R	⊙	🗲						

Restaurant at 2 km. Swimming pool 4 km.
PRICES: (1996) Caravan with family 42.00,
Tent with two adults 32.00.
CC: Euro/Access, Visa.

*Leave the motorway at Landsberg-Ost and go
towards Landsberg where campsite is well
signposted.*

LENZKIRCH 16C

Kur-Campingplatz Kreuzhof 7825 Lenzkirch.
Tel 07653 700, Fax 07653 6623. English spoken.
OPEN: all year. SIZE: 1 ha, 100 pitches (all with elec,
30 statics), 18 hot showers, 22 WCs, 1 CWP.

≈	✈	♀	R	⊙	🗲	🗗	✕	⊰	

Sauna, games room, basketball, children's
playground.
PRICES: (1996) Caravan with family 45.80,
Tent with two adults 30.80. CC: Visa.
*From Freiburg motorway head east towards
Donaueschingen, turning right to Lenzkirch.
Campsite is on the eastern edge of Lenzkirch.*

LICHTENFELS 17A

Maincamping Krosswehrstrasse 52,
96215 Lichtenfels.
Tel 09571 71729.
OPEN: 01/04–15/10. SIZE: 2 ha, 68 pitches (85 with
elec, 68 statics), 8 hot showers, 16 WCs, 1 CWP.

≈	⚓	♀	R	⊙					

Shop at 1 km. Restaurant at 0.3 km. Swimming
pool 1.5 km.
PRICES: (1996) Caravan with family 28.50,
Tent with two adults 19.00. CC: none.
*From Berlin-Munchen A9 motorway, exit at
Bayreuth or Kulmbach and take either B289 or
B173 and go to Lichtenfels-Ost where the campsite
is signposted.*

LINDAU 16D

Camping Gohren 7993 Kressbronn.
Tel 07543 8656. English spoken.
OPEN: 10/04–20/10. SIZE: 38 ha, 500 pitches
(all with elec, 1500 statics).

≈	⚓	♀		⊙	🗲		✕		

Diving, water sports, biking.
PRICES: (1996) Caravan with family 37.00,
Tent with two adults 26.00. CC: none.
*The campsite is situated between Lindau and
Friedrichshafen. Follow the signposts Camping
Gohren from the B31.*

Campingplatz Lindau-Zech
Fraunhoferstr 20, 8990 Lindau.
Tel 08382 72236.
English spoken.
OPEN: 01/04–15/10. SIZE: 5 ha, 298 pitches
(all with elec, 73 statics), 20 hot showers,
46 WCs, 1 CWP.

≈	⚓	🛉		⊙	🗲	🗗	✕		🐾

PRICES: (1996) Caravan with family 39.00,
Tent with two adults 27.00. CC: none.
*Take B31 towards Bregenz and exit just before the
border. Turn right by the Hotel Zum Zecher, and
campsite is 150 m.*

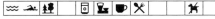

Germany

Campingpark Gitzenweiler Hof
88131 Lindau-Oberreitnau.
Tel 08382 5475, Fax 0931 6369. English spoken.
OPEN: all year. SIZE: 14 ha, 350 pitches (all with elec, 350 statics), 40 hot showers, 60 WCs, 2 CWPs. ⌯

| ⌂ | R | 🗑 | 🧺 | | ✕ | ⸮ | | | |

Adventure playground, club; lake 4 km.
PRICES: (1996) Caravan with family 39.00, Tent with two adults 27.00. CC: none.
Take Sigmarszell exit from Ulm to Lindau autobahn then carry on for 3 km to Lindau-Oberreitnau. Campsite is well signposted.
SEE ADVERTISEMENT

LINDENFELS   16B

Terrassencamping Schlierbach Am Zentbuckel 11, 6145 Lindenfels.
Tel 06255 630, Fax 06255 3526.
OPEN: 01/04–31/10. SIZE: 4 ha, 35 pitches (all with elec, 120 statics), 8 hot showers, 17 WCs, 1 CWP. ⌯

| ⌂ | R | 🗑 | 🧺 | | | 🎣 | | | |

Restaurant at 0.3 km.
PRICES: (1996) Caravan with family 35.30, Tent with two adults 23.30. CC: none.
The campsite is situated on the road south from Lindenfels to Fürth.

Campingpark Gitzenweiler Hof

GERMANY
●Konstanz
Lake Constance
●Lindau
SWITZERLAND

High on a meadow just 4km from Lake Constance

Swimming pool, table tennis, mini-golf, carp fishing, children's zoo and entertainments.

Plus direct access to 220 km cycle circuit round Lake Constance and close to the fairytale castles of Neuschwanstein and Hohenschwangau.

Campingpark Gitzenweiler Hof
88131 Lindau-Oberreitnau

Tel: 08382 5475
Fax: 08382 6369

See under Lindau

LOHMEN   15A

Campingplatz am Garder See 18276 Lohmen.
Tel 038458 20722, Fax 038458 20722.
OPEN: 01/04–31/10. SIZE: 6 ha, 95 pitches (all with elec, 250 statics), 6 hot showers (charge), 24 WCs, 1 CWP. ⌯ ⌖

| ≈ | ⚓ | ♀ | R | 🗑 | 🧺 | 🍺 | ✕ | | Ⓗ | |

Boats and bikes for hire.
PRICES: (1996) Caravan with family 27.00, Tent with two adults 14.50. CC: Euro/Access, Visa.
South of route 104 and well signposted near the Garder See.

LÖRRACH   16C

Camping Wiesengrund Hilda Lederer uber der Brucke1, 7863 Zell.
Tel 07625 7600.
OPEN: 15/03–10/10. SIZE: 1 ha, 2 hot showers, 6 WCs, 1 CWP. ⌯

| ～ | ⚓ | ⌂ | R | 🗑 | | 🍺 | | 🎣 | |

Shop at 0.5 km. Restaurant at 0.5 km.
PRICES: (1996) Caravan with family 32.00, Tent with two adults 21.00. CC: none.
North from Basel on B317 to Lörrach then on through Schopfheim, Zell and Mannbach.

Campingplatz im Grutt Gruttweg 8, 7850 Lörrach.
Tel 07621 82588, Fax 07621 165034. English spoken.
OPEN: 15/03–31/10. SIZE: 2.6 ha, 125 pitches (all with elec, 40 statics), 11 hot showers (charge), 15 WCs, 1 CWP. ⌯ ⌖

| ～ | ⚓ | ⌂ | R | 🗑 | | | ✕ | | | |

Shop at 0.3 km. (Charge for electricity). Tennis, swimming pool 0.5 km.
PRICES: (1996) Caravan with family 33.00, Tent with two adults 21.00. CC: none.
From Basel to Karlsruhe motorway, exit at Lörrach (B317) where the campsite is well signposted.

LOSHEIM   16A

Campingplatz Losheim 6646 Losheim.
Tel 06872 4770, Fax 06872 7768. English spoken.
OPEN: all year. SIZE: 8 ha, 120 pitches (all with elec, 300 statics), 44 hot showers, 52 WCs, 4 CWPs. ⌖

| ≈ | ⚓ | ⌂ | R | 🗑 | ⊙ | 🍺 | ✕ | 🎣 | ⚠ | |

PRICES: (1996) Caravan with family 41.00, Tent with two adults 20.00. CC: none.
Losheim is 40 km south of Trier and the campsite is well signposted in the town.

LÜBECK   15A

Campingplatz Lübeck-Schonbocken
Steinrader Damm 12, 23556 Lübeck-Schonbocken.
Tel 0451 893090. English spoken.

Germany

OPEN: 01/04–31/10. SIZE: 70 pitches (50 with elec), 8 hot showers (charge), 10 WCs, 1 CWP.

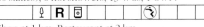

Restaurant at 1 km. 20 min drive to beach. PRICES: (1996) Caravan with family 34.00, Tent with two adults 22.00. CC: none. *About 1.5 km from the A1 exit Lübeck - Moisling, towards Schonbocken.*

LÜNEBURG 14B

Campingplatz Ebstorf 29574 Ebstorf. Tel 05822 3251, Fax 05822 3251. OPEN: all year. SIZE: 30 pitches (all with elec, 60 statics), 6 hot showers, 13 WCs, 1 CWP.

Shop at 1 km. Restaurant at 2 km. PRICES: (1996) Caravan with family 32.00, Tent with two adults 20.00. CC: none. *From Lüneburg, due south for approx 25 km to Ebstorf which is west of the B4.*

MAINZ 16B

Camping Mainz-Wiesbaden Maarau 6502 Kostheim. Tel 06134 4383. OPEN: 15/03–31/10. SIZE: 2 ha, 45 pitches (all with elec), 18 hot showers, 15 WCs, 2 CWPs.

PRICES: (1996) Caravan with family 33.50, Tent with two adults 22.50. CC: none. *Cross the bridge from Mainz to island of Maarau and follow signs to campsite via Kostheim.*

MANNHEIM 16B

Camping Strandbad Strandbadweg 1, 68199 Mannheim. Tel 0621 856240, Fax 0621 826721. English spoken. OPEN: 01/04–30/09. SIZE: 1 ha, 20 pitches (all with elec, 40 statics), 8 hot showers, 15 WCs, 1 CWP.

Shop at 2.5 km. PRICES: (1996) Caravan with family 39.00, Tent with two adults 23.50. CC: none. *From Mannheim go to Vorort Neckarau and from there to Rhein-Strandbad where campsite is well signposted.*

MARBURG 14D

Camping Platz-Lahnaue 3550 Marburg an de Lahn. Tel 06421 21331, Fax 06421 21331. English spoken. OPEN: 15/03–15/11. SIZE: 10 ha, 75 pitches (60 with elec, 12 statics), 6 hot showers (charge), 10 WCs, 1 CWP.

Shop at 2 km. Restaurant at 2 km. Mini-golf, swimming pool 0.5 km. PRICES: (1996) Caravan with family 28.00, Tent with two adults 19.00. CC: none. *From motorway, take exit Marburg Mitte and follow signs to campsite.*

MARKDORF 16D

Camping Wirthshof Steibensteg, 7778 Markdorf. Tel 07544 2325, Fax 07544 3982. English spoken. OPEN: 15/03–30/10. SIZE: 6.5 ha, 300 pitches (all with elec, 90 statics), 35 hot showers, 56 WCs, 3 CWPs.

Restaurant at 0.1 km. PRICES: Caravan with family 48.00, Tent with two adults 33.00. CC: none. *Take B33 from Ravensberg to Meersberg. Follow signs to campsite in Markdorf.*

MARKTHEIDENFELD 16B

Camping Main-Spessart-Park Spessantstrasse 30, 97855 Triefenstein. Tel 09395 1079, Fax 09395 8295. English spoken. OPEN: all year. SIZE: 10 ha, 140 pitches (all with elec, 200 statics), 15 hot showers, 31 WCs, 2 CWPs.

Sports ground. PRICES: (1996) Caravan with family 36.50, Tent with two adults 22.50. CC: none. *From Marktheidenfeld go to Triefenstein-Lengfurt, where the campsite is well signposted.*

MEERSBURG 16D

Camping Platz Seeperle Seefelden Haus Nr 6, 88690 Uhldingen-Mühlhofen. Tel 07556 5454, Fax 07556 5454. English spoken. OPEN: 01/04–03/10. SIZE: 0.7 ha, 36 pitches (all with elec, 40 statics), 6 hot showers (charge), 11 WCs, 1 CWP.

Shop at 1 km. Restaurant at 1 km. PRICES: (1996) Caravan with family 54.10, Tent with two adults 37.00. CC: none. *From Meersburg, follow lake north-west on B31. Take Uhldingen exit and go towards Seefelden.*

Camping Seeblick 88709 Hagnau am Bodensee. Tel 07532 6313. OPEN: 01/04–10/10. SIZE: 0.3 ha, 10 pitches (10 statics), 4 hot showers (charge), 11 WCs, 2 CWPs.

PRICES: (1996) Caravan with family 40.00, Tent with two adults 28.00. CC: none. *Just to the east of Hagnau and well signposted.*

Germany

MEISSEN 15D

Campingplatz Rehbocktal Batzdorf Nr 14, 01665 Scharfenberg.
Tel 0352 1452680.
OPEN: 01/04–30/10. SIZE: 1 ha, 40 pitches (30 with elec), 6 hot showers, 20 WCs, 1 CWP.

PRICES: (1996) Caravan with family 31.00,
Tent with two adults 19.50. CC: none.
From Meissen go 3 km south on B6 to Scharfenberg.

MONSCHAU 16A

Campingplatz Perlenau 52156 Monschau.
Tel 02472 4136, Fax 02472 4493. English spoken.
OPEN: 15/03–31/10. SIZE: 2 ha, 75 pitches (all with elec, 25 statics), 8 hot showers, 13 WCs, 2 CWPs.

Family bathrooms.
PRICES: (1996) Caravan with family 34.50,
Tent with two adults 25.50. CC: none.
Highly recommended campsite. Well signposted from town.

Campingplatz zum Jone Bur Gruenentalstrasse 34-36, 52156 Monschau.
Tel 02472 3931, Fax 02472 4694. English spoken.
OPEN: 15/12–01/11. SIZE: 3 ha, 40 pitches (all with elec, 150 statics), 16 hot showers, 21 WCs, 2 CWPs.

Shop at 0.4 km. Low season and long stay discounts.
PRICES: (1996) Caravan with family 40.00,
Tent with two adults 26.00. CC: none.
From Monschau go north on the road to Imgenbroich and Roetgen. Take the road to Rurtal on the southern edge of Imgenbroich and the campsite is 0.4 km ahead.

MÜHLHAUSEN 14D

Camping Luttergrund 37359 Grossbartloff.
Tel 036075 4687. English spoken.
OPEN: 01/05–31/10. SIZE: 5 ha, 50 pitches (all with elec, 150 statics), 8 hot showers (charge), 7 WCs, 12 French WCs.

Swimming pool nearby. Guest house accommodation available.
PRICES: Caravan with family 27.50,
Tent with two adults 16.00. CC: none.
From Mühlhausen head west. Turn right to Grossbartloff. Site is east side of village.

MÜNCHEN (MUNICH) 17C

München-Obermenzing Lochausener Str 59, 81247 München.
Tel 08981 12235, Fax 08981 44807. English spoken.

OPEN: 15/03–31/10. SIZE: 5 ha, 200 pitches (150 with elec), 12 hot showers, 30 WCs, 19 CWPs.

Restaurant at 1 km.
PRICES: (1996) Caravan with family 34.00,
Tent with two adults 26.00. CC: none.
At the beginning of motorway to Stuttgart, west of the city.

MURNAU 17C

Camping Brugger am Riegsee Dorfstrasse 5, 82418 Hofheim am Riegsee.
Tel 08847 728, Fax 08847 728. English spoken.
OPEN: 01/12–30/10. SIZE: 90 pitches (all with elec, 300 statics), 10 hot showers (charge), 27 WCs, 1 CWP.

PRICES: (1996) Caravan with family 34.00,
Tent with two adults 27.00. CC: none.
From A95 München to Garmisch, exit at Sindelsdorf and go left to Murnau. After Habach go 6 km to Hofheim. Follow Campingplatz Brugger and Restaurant Brugger Hutte sign in Hofheim.

NAUMBURG 15C

Camping im Blutengrund 04800 Naumburg.
Tel 0202711.
OPEN: all year. SIZE: 6 ha, 100 pitches (all with elec, 200 statics), 2 CWPs.

Shop at 4 km. Restaurant at 1 km.
PRICES: (1996) Caravan with family 29.00,
Tent with two adults 18.00. CC: Euro/Access.
From A9, exit Naumburg. From main railway station take B180 over railway crossing, go first right and campsite is about 2 km ahead, well signposted.

NECKARGEMÜND 16B

Campingplatz am der Friedenbrücke Falltorstr 4, 69151 Heidelberg-Neckargemünd.
Tel 06223 2178. English spoken.
OPEN: 01/04–30/09. SIZE: 3 ha, 150 pitches (all with elec, 40 statics), 12 hot showers, 16 WCs, 1 CWP.

PRICES: (1996) Caravan with family 29.50,
Tent with two adults 19.50. CC: none.
From Heidelberg continue on B37 along left bank of River Neckar. Signposted.

NECKARSULM 16D

Camping Reisachmühle 74172 Neckarsulm.
Tel 07132 2169. English spoken.

OPEN: all year. SIZE: 2.3 ha, 50 pitches (all with elec), 6 hot showers, 11 WCs, 1 CWP. ℓ

Restaurant at 0.5 km.
PRICES: (1996) Caravan with family 35.00,
Tent with two adults 22.00. CC: none.
Take Heilbronn/Neckarsulm exit off Stuttgart to Würzburg autobahn and follow signs to Neckarsulm and campsite.

NESSELWANG 16D

International Gruntensee Camping
Postfach 47, 8965 Wertach/Allgau.
Tel 08365 375, Fax 08365 1221. English spoken.
OPEN: 05/12–05/11. SIZE: 5 ha, 150 pitches (all with elec, 120 statics), 25 hot showers, 25 WCs.

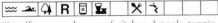

Shop at 2 km. Good sports/health facilities.
PRICES: (1996) Caravan with family 51.00,
Tent with two adults 29.00. CC: none.
Approaching from Kempten, turn right on entering Nesselwang and follow signs to the campsite.

NEUENBÜRG 16C

Gugel-Dreilander Camping u Freizeitpark
Oberer Wald 3, 79395 Neuenbürg.
Tel 07631 7719, Fax 07635 3393. English spoken.
OPEN: all year. SIZE: 13 ha, 220 pitches (180 with elec, 230 statics), 16 hot showers, 33 WCs, 3 CWPs. ℓ ᵫ

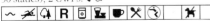

Site offers a good range of pitches. 3 pools, tennis, mini-golf, bike hire.
PRICES: (1996) Caravan with family 42.50,
Tent with two adults 30.00. CC: none.
From A5 take Neuenbürg exit; turn towards Neuenbürg-West at traffic lights and follow signs for 2 km.

NEUERBURG 16A

Campingplatz Neuerberg 54673 Neuerburg.
Tel 06564 2660, Fax 06564 2979. English spoken.
OPEN: all year. SIZE: 150 pitches (all with elec, 50 statics), 2 CWPs. ℓ ᵫ

PRICES: Caravan with family 24.00, Tent with two adults 18.00. CC: Euro/Access, Visa.
Campsite is well signposted.

NEUMARKT 17A

Campingplatz Olkuchenmuhle
92369 Sengenthal bei Neumarkt.
Tel 09181 6545.
OPEN: all year. SIZE: 2 ha, 30 pitches (20 with elec), 2 hot showers, 12 WCs, 1 CWP.

Restaurant at 1.5 km.
PRICES: (1996) Caravan with family 17.00,
Tent with two adults 11.00. CC: none.
From Nürnberg-Regensburg motorway, exit Neumarkt. Take B299 towards Landshut. Turn right near Sengenthal and follow signs.

NEUSTADT AM MAIN 16B

Main-Spessort Camping International
97845 Neustadt am Main.
Tel 09393 639, Fax 09393 1607. English spoken.
OPEN: 01/04–30/09. SIZE: 5.6 ha, 90 pitches (all with elec, 160 statics), 12 hot showers, 26 WCs, 2 CWPs. ℓ

Restaurant at 2.5 km. Children's playground, ball games, table tennis.
PRICES: (1996) Caravan with family 34.50,
Tent with two adults 24.50. CC: none.
Neustadt is on the west bank of the river.

NEUSTADT AM RÜBENBERGE 14D

Camping Mardorf-Seelord Erlenweg,
3057 Neustadt am Rübenberge.
Tel 05036 529, Fax 05036 1393. English spoken.
OPEN: all year. SIZE: 2 ha, 50 pitches (all with elec, 80 statics), 12 hot showers (charge), 18 WCs, 1 CWP. ℓ

PRICES: (1996) Caravan with family 37.50,
Tent with two adults 27.00. CC: none.
Neustadt is north-west of Hannover on route 6. Just after Neustadt turn left for Schneeren, Mardorf and Steinhuder Lake.

NEUSTADT IM HOLSTEIN 15A

Camping Lotsenhaus Sandberger Weg,
23730 Neustadt im Holstein.
Tel 04561 2557, Fax 04561 16582. English spoken.
OPEN: 01/04–30/09. SIZE: 6 ha, 60 pitches (40 with elec, 230 statics), 16 hot showers (charge), 28 WCs, 2 CWPs. ℓ

Playground.
PRICES: (1996) Caravan with family 37.00,
Tent with two adults 25.00. CC: none.
Go south from Neustadt towards Puttgarden until the harbour, then go over the bridge and after 500 m the campsite is signposted.

Camping Seeblick Pelzerhakener str 55-59,
23730 Neustadt.
Tel 04561 7428, Fax 04561 7947. English spoken.
OPEN: 01/04–30/09. SIZE: 3 ha, 80 pitches (all with elec, 150 statics), 16 hot showers (charge), 32 WCs, 1 CWP. ℓ ᵫ

Germany

Shop at 1 km. Restaurant at 1 km. Solarium.
PRICES: (1996) Caravan with family 37.00,
Tent with two adults 25.00. CC: none.
*Turn off motorway A1 at Neustadt-Süd and take
road to Pelzerhaken. Seeblick is fourth site on the
right by the sea.*

Campingplatz am Strande Pelzerhakener Str,
23730 Neustadt im Holstein.
Tel 04561 4188, Fax 04361 7125. English spoken.
OPEN: 01/04–30/09. SIZE: 4 ha, 200 pitches
(all with elec, 200 statics), 20 hot showers
(charge), 60 WCs, 3 CWPs.

Bicycle hire.
PRICES: (1996) Caravan with family 36.00,
Tent with two adults 24.00. CC: Euro/Access.
*From Neustadt im Holstein follow the road
towards Pelzerhaken-Ostsee and the campsite is
on the outskirts of the town on the right.*

NIDEGGEN 16A

Campingplatz Hetzingen 52385 Nideggen-Brück.
Tel 02427 508, Fax 02427 1294. English spoken.
OPEN: all year. SIZE: 3 ha, 120 pitches (all with elec,
300 statics), 20 hot showers (charge), 28 WCs,
3 CWPs. ✆

Sauna.
PRICES: (1996) Caravan with family 30.00,
Tent with two adults 18.00. CC: none.
*From A4 turn off south through Dürea, on to
Niederau and Nideggen. Campsite is just south of
Nideggen at Brück. Signposted in Nideggen.*
SEE ADVERTISEMENT

NIEWISCH 15D

**Camp am nordlichen Ostufer des
Schwielochsees** 15848 Niewisch.
Tel 03367 65186, Fax 03367 65186.
OPEN: 15/04–15/10. SIZE: 3.2 ha, 65 pitches
(185 with elec, 120 statics), 10 hot showers
(charge), 25 WCs, 1 CWP. ✆ ♿

Shop at 0.3 km.
PRICES: (1996) Caravan with family 36.00,
Tent with two adults 20.00. CC: none.
*From Beeskow to Friedland on N168 then go to
Niewisch and follow signs.*

NOHFELDEN 16A

Freizeitzentrum Bostalsee 6697 Nohfelden-Bosen.
Tel 06852 1620, Fax 06852 1690.
OPEN: all year. SIZE: 14 ha, 445 pitches (all with
elec, 175 statics), 30 hot showers (charge),
60 WCs, 3 CWPs. ✆ ♿

PRICES: (1996) Caravan with family 26.00,
Tent with two adults 14.00. CC: none.
*From A62, exit Türkismühle towards Bosen and
follow signs.*

NORDERNEY

NORDERNEY 14A

Campingplatz Booken 2982 Norderney.
Tel 04932 448. English spoken.
OPEN: all year. SIZE: 100 pitches (all with elec,
50 statics), 14 hot showers, 28 WCs, 1 CWP. ✆ ♿

Shop at 0.3 km. Sea 0.35 km.
PRICES: (1996) Caravan with family 50.00,
Tent with two adults 30.00. CC: none.
*Norderney is 45 minutes from the mainland by
ferry. Site is on western tip of island, signposted.*

END OF NORDERNEY RESORTS

NORDEN 14A

Nordsee Camp Deichstrasse 21, Norddeich,
26506 Norden.
Tel 04931 8073, Fax 04931 8074. English spoken.

OPEN: 15/03–30/10. SIZE: 20 ha, 600 pitches (all with elec, 150 statics), 80 hot showers, 60 WCs, 10 CWPs. ☎ �&

PRICES: (1996) Caravan with family 54.50, Tent with two adults 37.50. CC: Amex, Euro/Access, Visa.
From Norden go to Norden-Norddeich by the sea.

NORTHEIM 14D

Camping Sultmer Berg Sultmer Berg 3, 37154 Northeim.
Tel 05551 51559, Fax 05551 5656. English spoken.
OPEN: 15/03–31/12. SIZE: 5 ha, 150 pitches (all with elec, 50 statics), 12 hot showers, 18 WCs.

Children's pool; large pool 2 km.
PRICES: (1996) Caravan with family 35.00, Tent with two adults 23.00. CC: none.
From A7 Hannover to Kassel motorway, exit at Northeim-Nord and the campsite is 2 km and well signposted.

NÜRBURG 16A

Camping am Nürburgring
53520 Müllenbach/Eifel.
Tel 02692 224, Fax 02692 1020. English spoken.
OPEN: all year. SIZE: 30 ha, 1020 pitches (800 with elec, 200 statics), 52 hot showers, 108 WCs, 1 CWP. &

PRICES: (1996) Caravan with family 42.00, Tent with two adults 30.00. CC: Euro/Access.
On B258 Mayen to Blankenheim. At Nürburgring stadium turn left towards Müllenbach. Site on right behind car parks.

NÜRNBERG 17A

Camping im Volkspark Dutzendteich
Hans Kalb Str 56, 90471 Nürnberg.
Tel 09118 11122. English spoken.
OPEN: 01/05–30/09. SIZE: 3 ha, 200 pitches (130 with elec), 16 hot showers, 26 WCs, 4 CWPs. ☎ &

Restaurant at 1 km.
PRICES: (1996) Caravan with family 35.00, Tent with two adults 26.00. CC: none.
Well signposted.

OBERSTAUFEN 16D

Camping Aach Aach, 87534 Oberstaufen.
Tel 08386 363/7777, Fax 08325 1261. English spoken.
OPEN: all year. SIZE: 20 ha, 40 pitches (all with elec, 80 statics), 8 hot showers, 16 WCs, 3 CWPs.

Indoor swimming pool.
PRICES: (1996) Caravan with family 37.40, Tent with two adults 24.00. CC: none.
Aach is just south of Oberstaufen. Campsite is signposted.

OBERWESEL 16A

Camping am Mühlenteich 56291 Lingerhahn.
Tel 06746 533, Fax 06746 1566. English spoken.
OPEN: all year. SIZE: 15 ha, 100 pitches (all with elec, 300 statics), 22 hot showers (charge), 41 WCs, 3 CWPs. ☎

PRICES: (1996) Caravan with family 39.00, Tent with two adults 26.00. CC: none.
South of Oberwesel. Take Laudert exit off A61 and follow signs to Lingerhahn and campsite.
SEE ADVERTISEMENT

Germany

OBERWÖSSEN 17C

Campingplatz Litzelau 83246 Oberwössen.
Tel 08640 8704, Fax 08640 5265. English spoken.
OPEN: all year. SIZE: 4 ha, 140 pitches (100 with
elec, 80 statics), 20 hot showers (charge), 32 WCs,
1 CWP. ✆ ♿

| ≈ | ⚓ | ♀ | R | 🎍 | 🍺 | 🛒 | ✗ | | H | |

Swimming pool 1 km, sauna, solarium, table
tennis, skittles, playground.
PRICES: (1996) Caravan with family 40.00,
Tent with two adults 25.00. CC: none.
*Autobahn A8, exit Bernau towards Reit im
Winkel. Between Unterwössen and Reit im
Winkel.*

OLCHING 17C

Camping Ampersee 82140 Olching.
Tel 08142 12786, Fax 08142 45114.
English spoken.
OPEN: 01/05–01/10. SIZE: 18 ha, 120 pitches
(all with elec), 5 hot showers, 9 WCs, 1 CWP. ✆

| ≈ | ⚓ | ♀ | | 🎍 | 🍺 | 🛒 | ✗ | | H | |

Shop at 3 km. Playground.
PRICES: (1996) Caravan with family 40.00,
Tent with two adults 27.00. CC: none.
*From A8, take Fürstenfeldbruck exit and then
follow camping signs.*

OLDENBURG 15A

Campingplatz Triangel 23758 Weissenhaus.
Tel 04361 2868, Fax 04361 3164.
English spoken.
OPEN: 01/04–30/09. SIZE: 12 ha, 150 pitches
(all with elec, 550 statics), 51 hot showers
(charge), 90 WCs, 4 CWPs. ✆ ♿

| ≋ | ⚓ | ♀ | R | 🎍 | 🍺 | 🛒 | ✗ | | | |

PRICES: (1996) Caravan with family 46.50,
Tent with two adults 29.00. CC: Visa.
*Take Oldenburg-Mitte exit from A1 and turn right
after 5 km for Weissenhäuser Strand.*

OLPE 14C

Biggesee-Sondern Am Sonderner Kopf 1,
5960 Olpe-Sondern.
Tel 02761 944111, Fax 02761 944122.
English spoken.
OPEN: all year. SIZE: 5.7 ha, 255 pitches (all with
elec, 45 statics), 24 hot showers, 36 WCs,
2 CWPs. ✆ ♿

| ≈ | ⚓ | ♿ | R | 🎍 | 🍺 | | | | | |

Restaurant at 0.2 km.
PRICES: (1996) Caravan with family 45.50,
Tent with two adults 37.50. CC: none.
*From motorway A45/E41, exit at Olpe towards
Attendorn and then to Sondern-Biggesee.*

Campinganlage Gut Kalberschnacke
57489 Drolshagen.
Tel 02763 7501, Fax 02763 7879. English spoken.
OPEN: all year. SIZE: 10 ha, 130 pitches (all with
elec, 370 statics), 35 hot showers, 61 WCs,
4 CWPs. ♿

| ≈ | ⚓ | ♿ | R | 🎍 | 🍺 | | ✗ | | | |

Playground, tennis, sauna, solarium, football.
PRICES: (1996) Caravan with family 42.00,
Tent with two adults 28.00. CC: none.
*From A45/E41, take Wegeringhausen/Drolshagen
exit 17. Turn left and head for Biggesee for 5 km.*

Erholungsanlage Biggesee-Kessenhammer
Kessenhammer, 57462 Olpe-Kessenhammer.
Tel 02761 94420, Fax 02761 944299.
English spoken.
OPEN: all year. SIZE: 5 ha, 120 pitches (all with elec,
120 statics), 28 hot showers, 40 WCs, 3 CWPs. ✆

| ≈ | ⚓ | ♿ | R | 🎍 | 🍺 | | | | | |

Restaurant at 0.2 km.
PRICES: (1996) Caravan with family 44.00,
Tent with two adults 30.00. CC: none.
*From A45/E41, exit at Olpe towards Lennestadt,
then take Rhode exit for campsite.*

OSNABRÜCK 14D

Campingplatz Niedersachsenhof Nordstr 109,
49084 Osnabrück.
Tel 05417 7226, Fax 05417 0627. English spoken.
OPEN: all year. SIZE: 3 ha, 60 pitches (all with elec,
80 statics), 6 hot showers, 15 WCs, 2 CWPs. ✆

| | | ♿ | R | 🎍 | | | ✗ | | | |

Shop at 2 km.
PRICES: (1996) Caravan with family 32.00,
Tent with two adults 21.00. CC: none.
Via motorway A33 or B51.

OSTERODE 14D

Camping im Waldwinkel 3421 Zorge.
Tel 05586 1048, Fax 05586 1048. English spoken.
OPEN: all year. SIZE: 1.2 ha, 120 pitches
(all with elec, 20 statics), 12 hot showers, 16 WCs,
2 CWPs. ✆ ♿

| | | ♀ | R | 🎍 | 🍺 | 🛒 | ✗ | ☺ | H | |

PRICES: Caravan with family 30.00,
Tent with two adults 22.00. CC: none.
*From Osterode, south to Bad Sachsa and Zorge
and follow signs to campsite.*

Campingplatz am Sosestausee Osterode am
Harz, 37520 Osterode.
Tel 05522 3319, Fax 05522 72378. English spoken.
OPEN: all year. SIZE: 5 ha, 150 pitches (100 with
elec, 50 statics), 8 hot showers, 20 WCs, 2 CWPs. ✆

| ≈ | ⚓ | ♿ | R | 🎍 | 🍺 | 🛒 | | | | |

Restaurant at 0.5 km. Children's playground.

PRICES: (1996) Caravan with family 32.00, Tent with two adults 21.00. CC: none.
From B243 Seesen to Herzberg exit at Osterode-Süd. Drive south in the direction of Sosetals then take B498 to the campsite which is well signposted.

OTTERNDORF 14B

Campingplatz See Achtern Diek
Deichstrasse 14, 21762 Otterndorf.
Tel 04751 2933, Fax 04751 919103.
English spoken.
OPEN: 01/04–31/10. SIZE: 13 ha, 500 pitches (all with elec, 300 statics), 50 hot showers, 50 WCs, 2 French WCs, 1 CWP. ℂ ㄜ

≋	⚄	⌂	R	⬛	⟈	☕	✕	⚓		

PRICES: (1996) Caravan with family 34.00, Tent with two adults 23.00. CC: none.
On the banks of a lake near the dyke on the B73 from Cuxhaven.

OY-MITTELBERG 16D

Wertacher Hof Haslach am Gruntensee, 87466 Oy-Mittelberg 5.
Tel 08361 770, Fax 08361 770. English spoken.
OPEN: all year. SIZE: 3.5 ha, 100 pitches (all with elec, 150 statics), 21 hot showers, 21 WCs, 2 CWPs. ℂ

≋	⚄	⌂	R	⬛	⟈		✕		

PRICES: (1996) Caravan with family 38.00, Tent with two adults 27.00. CC: none.
On A7 motorway, exit at Oy-Mittelberg and go towards Wertach. After about 3 km turn off to Haslach.

PASSAU 17D

Drei-Flüsse-Camping 94113 Passau-Irring.
Tel 08546 633, Fax 08546 2686. English spoken.
OPEN: 01/04–31/10. SIZE: 4 ha, 150 pitches (all with elec), 25 hot showers, 25 WCs, 1 CWP. ℂ ㄜ

~	⚄	⌂	R	⬛	⟈	☕	✕	⊗	⌂	

Shop at 10 km. Restaurant at 10 km. Indoor swimming pool.
PRICES: (1996) Caravan with family 41.80, Tent with two adults 24.50. CC: Euro/Access.
Recommended site. Exit motorway A3 at Passau-Nord. From Passau centre follow signs to Drei-Flüsse campsite.

Drei-Flüsse Camping
near Passau
Passing Passau? Pop in!

PERL 16A

Camping Sonnenrödchen
6643 Perl-Oberleuken.
Tel 06865 93391, Fax 06865 93392.
OPEN: all year. SIZE: 3 ha, 55 pitches (45 with elec, 55 statics), 4 hot showers, 9 WCs, 2 CWPs. ℂ

	⌂	R	⬛	⟈	☕		

Restaurant at 2.5 km.
PRICES: (1996) Caravan with family 33.00, Tent with two adults 20.00. CC: none.
From Luxembourg to Remich and Nennig, then 6 km towards Saarbrücken to major junction. Straight on towards Mettlach, and 1.5 km after Oberleuken turn right at campsite sign.

PFARRKIRCHEN 17C

Kur Camping Arterhof Haupstr 3 - Lengham, 84364 Bad Birnbach.
Tel 08563 93130, Fax 08563 961343.
English spoken.
OPEN: all year. SIZE: 4 ha, 170 pitches (all with elec, 20 statics), 20 hot showers, 17 WCs, 1 CWP. ℂ ㄜ

~	⚄	⌂	R	⬛	⟈	☕	✕	⚓	⊞	

Solarium, massage/beauty salon.
PRICES: (1996) Caravan with family 44.00, Tent with two adults 22.00. CC: none.
On B388 about 14 km east from Pfarrkirchen, turn left to Lengham/Bad Birnbach.

Kur-und Feriencamping Singham 28a, 94086 Bad Griesbach.
Tel 08532 96130, Fax 08532 961350.
English spoken.
OPEN: all year. SIZE: 2 ha, 125 pitches (all with elec, 20 statics), 15 hot showers, 22 WCs, 1 CWP. ℂ ㄜ

	⌂	R	⬛	⟈	☕	✕		⌂	

PRICES: (1996) Caravan with family 38.50, Tent with two adults 24.00. CC: none.
Bad Griesbach is east of Pfarrkirchen and the campsite is signposted.

PFORZHEIM 16D

Camping Quellgrund 75339 Hofen ad Enz.
Tel 07081 6984.
OPEN: all year. SIZE: 36 ha, 60 pitches (all with elec, 150 statics), 6 hot showers (charge), 12 WCs, 3 CWPs. ℂ

~	⚄	⌂	R	⬛	⟈			

Shop at 0.2 km. Restaurant at 0.1 km.
PRICES: (1996) Caravan with family 29.50, Tent with two adults 20.50. CC: none.
From Pforzheim, go south on B294 towards Freudenstadt. Campsite is well signposted.

Campingplatz Kleinenzhof 75323 Bad Wildbad.
Tel 07081 3435/3556, Fax 07081 3770.
English spoken.

Germany

OPEN: all year. SIZE: 6 ha, 65 pitches (all with elec, 260 statics), 22 hot showers, 31 WCs, 4 CWPs. ⚊ ⚊

Sauna, playground; rooms also available.
PRICES: (1996) Caravan with family 33.20,
Tent with two adults 23.60. CC: none.
From Pforzheim on B294 to Bad Wildbad and Calmbach. Campsite is 5 km after Calmbach.

Hohen-Camping Langenbrand
75328 Schömberg 3-Langenbrand.
Tel 07084 6131, Fax 07084 6131. English spoken.
OPEN: all year. SIZE: 1.6 ha, 35 pitches (all with elec, 65 statics), 10 hot showers, 14 WCs, 2 CWPs.

PRICES: Caravan with family 36.50,
Tent with two adults 26.00. CC: none.
Take Pforzheim-West exit from A8 and go south towards Schömberg, via Büchenbronn and Salmbach, to campsite in Langenbrand.

International Camping Schwarzwald
Schellbronn, 75242 Neuhausen.
Tel 07234 6517, Fax 07234 5180. English spoken.
OPEN: all year. SIZE: 5 ha, 80 pitches (all with elec, 260 statics), 9 hot showers (charge), 29 WCs, 2 CWPs. ⚊ ⚊

Health and fitness studio.
PRICES: (1996) Caravan with family 33.00,
Tent with two adults 22.00. CC: none.
From Pforzheim go south towards Calw (463) but turn left off this road as soon as possible onto the smaller road that runs through Huchenfeld, Hohenwart, and then Schellbronn. Turn right (west) in the village to the campsite (about 16 km from Pforzheim-West motorway exit).

PIRMASENS 16A

Campingpatz Buttelwoog Jm Buttelwoog,
66994 Dahn/Pfalz.
Tel 06391 5622, Fax 06391 5326. English spoken.
OPEN: all year. SIZE: 6 ha, 100 pitches (all with elec, 90 statics), 12 hot showers, 26 WCs, 4 CWPs. ⚊ ⚊

Mini-golf, playground.
PRICES: (1996) Caravan with family 41.00,
Tent with two adults 28.00. CC: none.
From Trier to Pirmasens motorway take the Dahn exit.

PLAUEN 17A

Campingplatz Möschwitz Gunzenburg
Gunzenburg, 08543 Pöhl-Ot Möschwitz.
Tel 03743 96201, Fax 03743 96813. English spoken.
OPEN: 15/04–30/10. SIZE: 5 ha, 90 pitches (all with elec, 10 statics), 22 hot showers, 28 WCs, 1 French WC, 1 CWP. ⚊ ⚊

PRICES: (1996) Caravan with family 27.00, Tent with two adults 21.00. CC: Euro/Access.
From A9 take B282 to Plauen, then B173 and exit/follow signs for Talsperre Pöhl.

PLÖN 14B

Camping Ruhleben 24306 Plön.
Tel 04522 8347, Fax 04522 6348.
English spoken.
OPEN: 01/04–30/09. SIZE: 12 ha, 150 pitches (all with elec, 200 statics), 23 hot showers (charge), 47 WCs. ⚊ ⚊

Restaurant at 2 km. Water sports.
PRICES: (1996) Caravan with family 36.00,
Tent with two adults 27.00. CC: none.
Off the B76, on the east side of the lake and well signposted.

Camping Spitzenort Aschberger Str 76,
24306 Plön.
Tel 04522 2769, Fax 04522 4574.
English spoken.
OPEN: 01/04–15/10. SIZE: 4 ha, 180 pitches (all with elec, 30 statics), 21 hot showers, 32 WCs, 2 CWPs. ⚊

PRICES: (1996) Caravan with family 42.00, Tent with two adults 27.00. CC: none.
Coming from Plön take the road to Neuminster (B430). After 2 km turn left.

POTSDAM 15C

Campingplatz Riegelspitze
14542 Werder-Havel.
Tel 03327 42397, Fax 03327 42397.
English spoken.
OPEN: 01/04–25/10. SIZE: 2.5 ha, 130 pitches (120 with elec, 115 statics), 18 hot showers (charge), 26 WCs, 1 CWP. ⚊ ⚊

PRICES: (1996) Caravan with family 33.80,
Tent with two adults 20.00. CC: none.
Werder is a short distance south-west of Potsdam. Campsite is signposted.

Campingplatz Sanssouci-Gaisberg A d
Pirschheide/Templiner See, 14471 Potsdam.
Tel 03327 55680, Fax 03327 55680.
English spoken.
OPEN: 01/04–31/10. SIZE: 6 ha, 190 pitches (all with elec, 70 statics), 18 hot showers, 42 WCs, 4 CWPs. ⚊ ⚊

Shop at 2 km.
PRICES: (1996) Caravan with family 35.60,

Germany

Tent with two adults 31.80. CC: none.
In Potsdam town follow signs to Bunderstrasse,
towards Brandenburg.

RANGSDORF 15D

Camping am Rangsdorfer See Seebadallee 63,
15834 Rangsdorf.
Tel 033708 20428, Fax 033708 20428.
English spoken.
OPEN: 15/04–15/10. SIZE: 4 ha, 40 pitches
(all with elec, 160 statics), 8 hot showers (charge),
40 WCs.

PRICES: (1996) Caravan with family 21.00,
Tent with two adults 8.00. CC: none.
Rangsdorf is on B96, just south of Berlin.
Well signposted.

RASTATT 16C

Camping Rastatter Freizeitparadies
Im Teilergrund 1, 76437 Rastatt.
Tel 07222 10150, Fax 07222 101530.
English spoken.
OPEN: all year. SIZE: 40 ha, 100 pitches (120 with
elec, 300 statics), 20 hot showers (charge),
30 WCs, 2 CWPs.

Mini-golf, keep-fit, tennis, diving, windsurfing.
PRICES: (1996) Caravan with family 45.50,
Tent with two adults 31.50. CC: Amex,
Euro/Access, Visa.
From A5 exit Rastatt. Right at first traffic lights
and carry straight on to Mercedes Benz factory.
Turn right in front of factory to Plittersdorf and
from there follow signs to campsite.

RECHLIN 15A

Campingplatz Bolter Ufer 17248 Rechlin.
Tel 0398 2321261.
OPEN: 01/04–31/10. SIZE: 10 ha, 150 pitches
(all with elec, 80 statics), 16 hot showers, 24 WCs,
1 CWP.

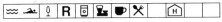

Restaurant at 2 km.
PRICES: unavailable. CC: none.
South of Lake Moritz near Rechlin.

REGEN 17D

Camping Waldhof Nebelberg 26,
94264 Langdorf.
Tel 09922 1024. English spoken.
OPEN: all year. SIZE: 1 ha, 40 pitches (26 with elec,
10 statics), 2 hot showers, 7 WCs, 1 CWP.

Apartments available.

PRICES: (1996) Caravan with family 30.00,
Tent with two adults 22.00. CC: none.
From Regen, go north to Langdorf and then follow
signs to Nebelberg and campsite (about 3 km).

REGENSBURG 17C

Pielenhofen-Naabtal 93188 Regensburg.
Tel 09409 373, Fax 09409 723.
English spoken.
OPEN: all year. SIZE: 6 ha, 130 pitches (all with elec,
200 statics), 19 hot showers, 29 WCs, 2 CWPs.

Tennis, sauna, solarium, playground, table tennis.
PRICES: (1996) Caravan with family 37.20, Tent
with two adults 25.20. CC: none.
Coming south from Nürnberg on the E56/A3, take
the Nittendorf exit and go on B8 towards
Regensberg. Just after Etterhausen, by the petrol
station, turn left and go towards Amberg
(6 km to Pielenhofen).

REMAGEN 16A

Camping Platz Rheineck
53498 Bad-Breisig.
Tel 02633 95645, Fax 02633 97182.
English spoken.
OPEN: all year. SIZE: 50 pitches (30 with elec,
200 statics), 6 hot showers, 16 WCs, 3 CWPs.

Restaurant at 0.5 km.
PRICES: Caravan with family 41.00,
Tent with two adults 25.00. CC: none.
From A61, exit Niederzissen/Bad Breisig,
towards Bad Breisig on the B9, south of Breisig
follow signs.

Campingplatz Goldene Meile
Simrockweg 8-13, 53424 Remagen.
Tel 02642 22222, Fax 02642 1555.
English spoken.
OPEN: all year. SIZE: 11 ha, 300 pitches (all with
elec, 280 statics), 17 hot showers (charge),
52 WCs, 2 CWPs.

PRICES: (1996) Caravan with family 42.00,
Tent with two adults 21.00. CC: none.
Just off B9 between Koblenz and Bonn to
Remagen where campsite is on banks
of the Rhein.

Campingplatz Goldene Meile
at Remagen
Holiday haven by the enchanted Rhein

Germany

REMICH 16A

Camping Mosella am Rothaus
66706 Perl-Nennig.
Tel 06866 510, Fax 06866 1486. English spoken.
OPEN: 15/03–15/10. SIZE: 2 ha, 100 pitches
(all with elec), 10 hot showers, 10 WCs, 1 CWP. ⚓

≋ ⚓ ⌂ R ☓ ✕ ↯ ⒣

Shop at 0.5 km.
PRICES: (1996) Caravan with family 35.00,
Tent with two adults 25.00. CC: none.
*Cross the bridge in Remich towards Saarbrücken
and campsite is immediately on the left.*

Camping Mosella am

Rothaus

opposite Remich
On the Moselle River

REUTLINGEN 16D

Azur Rosencamping Schwäbische Alb
72820 Sonnenbühl-Erpfingen.
Tel 07128 466, Fax 07128 30137. English spoken.
OPEN: all year. SIZE: 9 ha, 250 pitches (200 with
elec, 430 statics), 18 hot showers, 30 WCs,
2 CWPs. ⚐

⚑ R ☓ ⚑ ⚑ ↯

Restaurant at 1 km. Most sports, including skiing,
nearby.
PRICES: (1996) Caravan with family 41.20,
Tent with two adults 28.30. CC: Euro/Access.
*From Reutlingen, go south on B313 to Erpfingen
where campsite is signposted.*

RINTELN 14D

Doktor-See 3260 Rinteln 1.
Tel 05751 2611, Fax 05751 41956. English spoken.
OPEN: all year. SIZE: 152 ha, 500 pitches (all with
elec, 1020 statics), 64 hot showers, 220 WCs,
8 CWPs. ⚓ ⚐

≋ ⚓ ⚑ R ☓ ☓ ⚑ ✕ ↯ ⒣

Mini-golf, skittles, playground, disco, table tennis,
boating, tennis.
PRICES: Caravan with family 38.00,
Tent with two adults 26.00. CC: none.
*From the A2/E30, take the Rinteln exit and drive
for about 4 km.*

ROSENBERG 16D

Waldcamping Hüttenhof Hüttenhof 1,
73494 Rosenberg.
Tel 07963 203. English spoken.

OPEN: all year. SIZE: 4 ha, 50 pitches (all with elec,
100 statics), 8 hot showers (charge), 23 WCs,
2 CWPs. ⚓ ⚐

≋ ⚓ ⌂ R ☓ ⚑

Shop at 4 km. Restaurant at 4 km. Bike hire,
fishing, large sports hall.
PRICES: Caravan with family 26.00,
Tent with two adults 19.00. CC: none.
*Leave A7 (Würzburg-Ulm) at Ellwangen and go
towards Schwäbisch-Hall. Campsite is signposted
in Rosenberg.*

ROSENHEIM 17C

Campingplatz Erlensee Rosenheimer Str 61,
bei Rosenheim, 8201 Schechen.
Tel 08039 1695. English spoken.
OPEN: all year. SIZE: 5 ha, 75 pitches (50 with elec,
124 statics), 1 CWP. ⚓ ⚐

≋ ⚓ ⚑ R ☓ ⚑ ✕

Shop at 5 km.
PRICES: (1996) Caravan with family 37.00,
Tent with two adults 23.50. CC: none.
*From Rosenheim, take the B15 towards Landshut
for about 15 km to Schechen.*

Campingplatz Hofbauer 8210 Prien/Chiemsee.
Tel 08051 4136, Fax 08051 62657.
OPEN: 01/04–30/10. SIZE: 1 ha, 100 pitches (90 with
elec), 6 hot showers (charge), 10 WCs, 2 CWPs. ⚓

⚑ R ☓ ⚑

Shop at 0.8 km. Restaurant at 1.5 km.
PRICES: (1996) Caravan with family 39.30,
Tent with two adults 27.40. CC: none.
*From A8 München to Salzburg, exit Bernau
towards Prien (3 km).*

ROSTOCK 15A

Ostseecamp-Rostoker Heide Seeheilbad Graal-
Müritz, 18181 Graal-Müritz.
Tel 03820 6580, Fax 03820 6580. English spoken.
OPEN: 01/04–30/09. SIZE: 30 ha, 500 pitches
(175 with elec, 600 statics), 36 hot showers
(charge), 1 CWP. ⚓ ⚐

≋ ⚓ ⚑ R ☓ ⚑ ⚑ ✕

Restaurant at 1 km. Cycling, surf school.
PRICES: (1996) Caravan with family 33.00,
Tent with two adults 20.00. CC: none.
*From Rostock, go north-east to Rövershagen then
turn off to Graal-Müritz (25 km).*

ROTHENBURG 16B

Camping Tauber Idyll
91541 Rothenburg ob der Tauber.
Tel 09861 3177, Fax 09861 92848. English spoken.
OPEN: 22/03–31/10. SIZE: 1 ha, 40 pitches (all with
elec), 4 hot showers, 8 WCs, 1 CWP.

Restaurant at 0.2 km.
PRICES: (1996) Caravan with family 34.00,
Tent with two adults 21.00. CC: none.
From Rothenburg, go towards Bad Mergentheim.
Turn left to Detwang and the campsite is next to
the church.

Camping Tauberromantik Detwang 39,
91541 Rothenburg.
Tel 09861 6191. English spoken.
OPEN: 01/04–04/11. SIZE: 1 ha, 120 pitches (100 with
elec), 11 hot showers, 15 WCs, 2 CWPs. ✆ ♿

PRICES: (1996) Caravan with family 38.50, Tent
with two adults 23.00. CC: Amex, Euro/Access, Visa.
From Rothenburg, head towards Bad
Mergentheim. About 1 km out of Rothenburg drive
to Detwang. Turn right to campsite immediately
on entering the village.

Campingplatz Frankenhöhe
91583 Schillingsfürst.
Tel 09868 5111, Fax 09868 5111. English spoken.
OPEN: all year. SIZE: 1.5 ha, 110 pitches (all with elec,
50 statics), 7 hot showers, 15 WCs, 1 CWP. ✆ ♿

PRICES: (1996) Caravan with family 28.50, Tent
with two adults 20.50. CC: Euro/Access.
Take A7 south of Rothenburg, exit towards
Schillingsfürst. Turn off after 300 m and campsite
is 1.5 km ahead.

Campingplatz Frankenhöhe
near Rothenburg
Simple Sylvan Serenity

RÜDESHEIM   16A

Campingplatz am Rhein 65385 Rüdesheim.
Tel 06722 2528/2582, Fax 06722 2528/2582.
English spoken.
OPEN: 01/05–03/10. SIZE: 3 ha, 210 pitches (182 with
elec), 12 hot showers, 22 WCs, 1 CWP. ✆ ♿

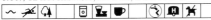

Restaurant at 0.6 km.
PRICES: (1996) Caravan with family 39.10,
Tent with two adults 27.30. CC: none.
Turn off B42 towards the banks of the Rhein
(signposted).

Suleika Camping PO Box 80/R, 65382 Rüdesheim.
Tel 06726 9464. English spoken.
OPEN: 15/03–15/11. SIZE: 3 ha, 120 pitches
(all with elec), 7 hot showers, 14 WCs.

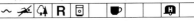

River 0.5 km, swimming pool 5 km.
PRICES: (1996) Caravan with family 33.90,
Tent with two adults 21.50. CC: none.
Well signposted, halfway between Rüdesheim and
Lorch, close to the Rhein.

RUHPOLDING   17C

Camping Ortnerhof Ort 5, 83324 Ruhpolding.
Tel 08663 1764, Fax 08663 5073. English spoken.
OPEN: all year. SIZE: 2.4 ha, 135 pitches (all with
elec, 85 statics), 14 hot showers, 25 WCs, 2 CWPs. ✆

Shop at 1 km. Children's playground, bowling;
swimming pool 3 km.
PRICES: (1996) Caravan with family 38.50,
Tent with two adults 25.00. CC: none.
From the München/Salzburg motorway, exit at
Siegsdorf/Ruhpolding and follow campsite signs.

SAARBURG   16A

Camping Leukbachtal 54439 Saarburg.
Tel 06581 2228, Fax 06581 5008.
OPEN: 09/04–15/10. SIZE: 3 ha, 120 pitches (all with
elec, 30 statics), 8 hot showers, 20 WCs, 1 CWP.

Shop at 1 km. Restaurant at 1 km. Swimming pool
0.8 km.
PRICES: (1996) Caravan with family 41.50,
Tent with two adults 29.00. CC: none.
From Saarburg, head towards Saarbrocken and
follow signs to campsite.

Camping Walfrieden Jm Fichtenhain 4,
54439 Saarburg.
Tel 06581 2255, Fax 06581 5908. English spoken.
OPEN: 01/03–31/10. SIZE: 1 ha, 90 pitches (65 with
elec, 25 statics), 8 hot showers, 10 WCs, 1 CWP.
✆ ♿

Shop at 1.5 km. Restaurant at 0.5 km. Tennis;
swimming pool 1.5 km.
PRICES: (1996) Caravan with family 28.00,
Tent with two adults 17.00. CC: none.
South of Saarburg leave the B407 and follow the
route 132 towards Nennig and Luxembourg.

Landal Greenparks
54439 Saarburg/Trierer Land.
Tel 06581 91460, Fax 06581 2514. English spoken.
OPEN: 21/03–03/11. SIZE: 10 ha, 430 pitches
(all with elec), 30 hot showers, 44 WCs, 3 CWPs.
✆ ♿

Sports ground, tennis, mini-golf, table tennis; free
cable car.
PRICES: (1996) Caravan with family 50.50,

Germany

Tent with two adults 29.50. CC: none.
Going south-west from Trier through Konz follow the sign to Saarburg. After the village of Ayl follow the sign Niederleuken (left). In Saarburg follow sign to campsite.

SAARLOUIS 16A

Gemeindecampingplatz Siersburg Platzwart Josef Becker, 66780 Rehlingen-Siersburg.
Tel 06835 2100, Fax 06835 508119.
OPEN: 01/04–31/10. SIZE: 5 ha, 150 pitches (all with elec, 150 statics), 24 hot showers, 32 WCs, 2 French WCs, 1 CWP. ℓ

Shop at 0.5 km.
PRICES: (1996) Caravan with family 31.50,
Tent with two adults 17.50. CC: none.
Go north from Saarlouis on A620 and take Rehlingen exit on to 170. Turn left to Siersburg and follow camping signs.

ST GOAR 16A

Friedenau Gruendelbach 103,
56329 St Goar/Rhein.
Tel 06741 368, Fax 06741 368. English spoken.
OPEN: 01/04–30/11. SIZE: 1 ha, 45 pitches (all with elec), 10 hot showers, 8 WCs, 2 CWPs. &

Swimming pool 1 km.
PRICES: (1996) Caravan with family 31.00,
Tent with two adults 21.00. CC: none.
From A61, exit at Emmelshaus and go to St Goar heading towards Loreley.

ST GOARSHAUSEN 16A

Campingplatz Loreleystad
56346 St Goarshausen.
Tel 06771 2592, Fax 02137 2637. English spoken.
OPEN: 20/03–31/10. SIZE: 2 ha, 90 pitches (70 with elec, 90 statics), 7 hot showers (charge), 10 WCs, 2 CWPs. &

Shop at 0.3 km. Restaurant at 0.2 km. Swimming pool 5 km. 20% discount for stays of 12 nights plus.
PRICES: (1996) Caravan with family 32.00,
Tent with two adults 23.00. CC: none.
35 km from Koblenz on the B42, campsite is on the banks of the Rhein and clearly signposted.

SCHILTACH 16D

Campingplatz Schiltach Bahnhofstrasse 6,
77761 Schiltach.
Tel 07836 7289. English spoken.
OPEN: 01/05–04/10. SIZE: 4 ha, 40 pitches (all with elec), 4 hot showers (charge), 7 WCs, 1 CWP.

Shop at 0.4 km. Restaurant at 0.3 km. Swimming pool 1.5 km.
PRICES: Caravan with family 27.50,
Tent with two adults 20.50. CC: Euro/Access.
From A5 motorway, take Offenburg exit and go towards Donaueschingen-Villingen (B33). Turn left at Hausach, on the B294 towards Freudenstadt.

SCHLEIDEN 16A

Campingplatz and Pension Weiermühle
Weiermühle 5, 53937 Schleiden.
Tel 02445 7235. English spoken.
OPEN: all year. SIZE: 2 ha, 40 pitches (all with elec, 50 statics), 4 hot showers (charge), 15 WCs, 3 CWPs. ℓ

Highly recommended campsite.
PRICES: (1996) Caravan with family 25.50,
Tent with two adults 16.50. CC: none.
2 km from Schleiden on the B258. Campsite is on the left and well signposted.

Campingplatz Schleiden Im Wiesengrund 39,
53937 Schleiden.
Tel 02445 7030. English spoken.
OPEN: all year. SIZE: 5 ha, 35 pitches (all with elec, 180 statics). ℓ &

Small playground; swimming pool 400 m.
PRICES: (1996) Caravan with family 34.00,
Tent with two adults 23.00. CC: Euro/Access.
1 km from Schleiden on road to Monschau.

SCHLESWIG 14B

Haithabu-Haddeby 24866 Busdorf.
Tel 04621 32450, Fax 04621 33122. English spoken.
OPEN: 01/03–30/10. SIZE: 4 ha, 200 pitches (all with elec, 40 statics), 8 hot showers, 20 WCs.

PRICES: (1996) Caravan with family 50.00,
Tent with two adults 27.00. CC: none.
From A7 motorway, take Jagel exit, follow the road until just before Schleswig and then go towards Kiel. Campsite is on the left.

SCHÖNBERG 14B

Campingpark California Deichweg 46-47,
24217 Ostseebad Kalifornien.
Tel 04344 9591, Fax 04344 4817. English spoken.
OPEN: 01/04–30/09. SIZE: 8 ha, 25 pitches (all with elec, 450 statics), 44 hot showers (charge), 66 WCs, 2 CWPs. ℓ &

Mini-golf, boat hire.

PRICES: (1996) Caravan with family 41.00, Tent with two adults 27.00. CC: none. *Off the B502, north of Schönberg on the coast. Site is well signposted.*

Campingplatz Heidkoppel 24217 Wisch.
Tel 04344 9098, Fax 04344 4257.
OPEN: 01/05–15/09. SIZE: 12 ha, 70 pitches (all with elec, 630 statics), 42 hot showers (charge), 2 CWPs. ⚬ ⚬

Shop at 0.3 km. Restaurant at 0.5 km.
PRICES: (1996) Caravan with family 38.50, Tent with two adults 30.00. CC: none. *Wisch is off the B502, north of Schönberg towards Heidkate. Site is well signposted.*

SCHONGAU 17C

DCC-Ferien-Freizeitzentrum Stadt Essen
86983 Lechbruck.
Tel 08862 8426, Fax 08862 7570.
OPEN: all year. SIZE: 15 ha, 620 pitches (all with elec, 260 statics). ⚬ ⚬

Superb indoor pool; watersports, tennis, mini-golf; winter sports.
PRICES: (1996) Caravan with family 45.00, Tent with two adults 35.00. CC: Euro/Access, Visa.

From Schongau, drive 16 km south on route 17, then turn right to Lechbruck. Campsite is right beside the lake and well signposted.
SEE ADVERTISEMENT

Terrassencamping am Richterbichl
82401 Rottenbuch.
Tel 08867 1500, Fax 08867 8300. English spoken.
OPEN: all year. SIZE: 1 ha, 70 pitches (all with elec, 40 statics), 6 hot showers, 11 WCs, 1 CWP. ⚬

Restaurant at 1 km. Children's playground; bike hire.
PRICES: (1996) Caravan with family 36.00, Tent with two adults 26.00. CC: none.
From Schongau, south on the B23 to Rottenbuch. Well signposted.

SCHWÄBISH HALL 16D

Camping Am Steinbacher See
74523 Schwäbish Hall.
Tel 0791 2984. English spoken.
OPEN: 01/04–30/10. SIZE: 1 ha, 100 pitches (all with elec, 50 statics), 8 hot showers (charge), 10 WCs, 1 CWP. ⚬

Shop at 0.8 km. Restaurant at 0.3 km. Swimming pool 2 km.

Germany

PRICES: (1996) Caravan with family 37.00, Tent with two adults 23.00. CC: none.
Campsite is signposted from Schwäbish Hall.

SCHWEICH 16A

Campingplatz zum Fahrturm 54338 Schweich.
Tel 06502 91300, Fax 06502 913050.
English spoken.
OPEN: 01/04–30/10. SIZE: 3 ha, 150 pitches (all with elec, 150 statics), 11 hot showers (charge), 19 WCs, 2 CWPs. ☏

Shop at 0.1 km.
PRICES: (1996) Caravan with family 32.00, Tent with two adults 19.50. CC: none.
The campsite is in Schweich 500 m from town centre.

Landal Greenparks Sonnenberg, 54340 Leiwen/Mosel.
Tel 06507 93690, Fax 06507 936936.
English spoken.
OPEN: 07/02–03/11. SIZE: 23 ha, 148 pitches (all with elec), 12 hot showers, 23 WCs, 2 CWPs. ☏ ♿

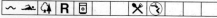

Mini-golf, sports ground, indoor pool, sauna, solarium, tennis. Very lively site.
PRICES: Caravan with family 56.00, Tent with two adults 39.00. CC: none.
From Köln, take A1 to Trier, exit at Schweich and take road to Leiwen. In Leiwen follow the sign to the campsite.

SEEFELD 17C

Camping Strandbad Pilsensee 82229 Seefeld.
Tel 08152 7232, Fax 08152 78473.
OPEN: all year. SIZE: 10 ha, 50 pitches (all with elec, 400 statics), 12 hot showers, 52 WCs, 3 CWPs. ☏

Boat hire, windsurfing school.
PRICES: (1996) Caravan with family 41.00, Tent with two adults 28.00. CC: none.
From München to Lindau motorway, take the Oberpfaffenhofen and Herrsching exit and go towards Herrsching. After about 800 m, turn to Seefeld (the campsite is signposted).

SIGMARINGEN 16D

Campingplatz Kreisstadt Sigmaringen
Geory-Zimmererstraße 6, 72488 Sigmaringen.
Tel 07571 50411, Fax 07571 50412.
OPEN: all year. SIZE: 1.5 ha, 110 pitches (65 with elec, 10 statics), 8 hot showers (charge), 10 WCs, 1 CWP. ☏ ♿

Shop at 0.2 km. Mini-golf.

PRICES: Caravan with family 36.00, Tent with two adults 21.00. CC: none.
In the south of Sigmaringen, behind the 'Stadthalle' and near the river.

Campingplatz Wagenburg
88631 Hausen im Tal.
Tel 07579 559, Fax 07466 1525. English spoken.
OPEN: 15/04–15/10. SIZE: 1.2 ha, 100 pitches (70 with elec, 25 statics), 6 hot showers (charge), 10 WCs, 1 CWP.

Restaurant at 0.2 km.
PRICES: (1996) Caravan with family 34.00, Tent with two adults 21.00. CC: none.
Hausen im Tal is approx 20 km west of Sigmaringen towards Tuttlingen. Campsite is well signposted.

SOLINGEN 14C

Waldcamping Gluder Inh Olaf Wieden, 42659 Solingen.
Tel 0212 242120. English spoken.
OPEN: all year. SIZE: 2 ha, 20 pitches (all with elec, 100 statics), 4 hot showers, 9 WCs, 1 CWP. ☏

Shop at 3 km. Restaurant at 2 km. Children's playground; swimming pool 2 km.
PRICES: Caravan with family 35.00, Tent with two adults 21.00. CC: none.
From A3 motorway, exit at Solingen-Langenfeld and take B229 to Solingen, then go towards Witzhelden. Campsite is signposted.

SONTHOFEN 16D

Campingplatz an der Iller Arnikaweg 55, 87527 Sonthofen.
Tel 08321 2350, Fax 08321 71561.
OPEN: 21/12–31/10. SIZE: 2 ha, 130 pitches (all with elec, 40 statics), 10 hot showers, 16 WCs, 2 CWPs. ☏ ♿

Restaurant at 1 km.
PRICES: (1996) Caravan with family 35.00, Tent with two adults 35.00. CC: none.
Take A96 to Kempten then B19 to Sonthofen where campsite is signposted.

SPIEGELAU 17D

Camping Am Nationalpark
94518 Spiegelau/Klingenbrunn.
Tel 08553 727, Fax 08553 6930. English spoken.
OPEN: all year. SIZE: 4 ha, 100 pitches (all with elec), 14 hot showers, 11 WCs, 1 CWP.

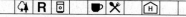

Shop at 1 km. Restaurant at 1 km.

PRICES: Caravan with family 32.00, Tent with two adults 23.00. CC: none.
Follow signs to campsite from Spiegelau.

Camping am Nationalpark
near Spiegelau
Tucked away in a clearing in the woods

STADTKYLL 16A

Landal Greenparks 54589 Stadtkyll/Eifel.
Tel 06597 92920, Fax 06597 929250. English spoken.
OPEN: all year. SIZE: 6 ha, 160 pitches (all with elec, 110 statics), 16 hot showers, 27 WCs, 3 CWPs.

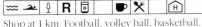

Sauna, solarium, sports ground, tennis, table tennis, bowling, indoor pool.
PRICES: (1996) Caravan with family 51.50, Tent with two adults 33.50. CC: none.
A1 from Köln to Trier, exit 114 towards Blankenheim and then 23 km to Stadtkyll where the campsite is signposted.

STAUFEN 16C

Campingplatz Belchenblick
Münstertälerstrasse 43, 79219 Staufen.
Tel 07633 7045, Fax 07633 7908. English spoken.
OPEN: all year. SIZE: 2 ha, 180 pitches (all with elec, 30 statics), 33 hot showers, 32 WCs, 3 CWPs.

Restaurant at 0.5 km. Very friendly site; indoor swimming pool.
PRICES: (1996) Caravan with family 58.40, Tent with two adults 37.50. CC: none.
Highly recommended campsite. From A5/E35 (Karlsruhe to Basel), exit at Bad Krozingen and Staufen, then continue south-east.

STORKOW 15D

Camping Waldsee 15518 Kolpin.
Tel 033631 5037, Fax 033631 5037. English spoken.
OPEN: all year. SIZE: 3 ha, 80 pitches (all with elec, 80 statics), 12 hot showers (charge), 19 WCs, 1 CWP.

Shop at 1 km. Football, volley ball, basketball.
PRICES: (1996) Caravan with family 32.50, Tent with two adults 19.00. CC: none.
From A12 motorway Berlin/Frankfurt, exit to Storkow. At Storkow turn left to Fürstenwalde. Drive through Kolpin and then right into a small forest. Campsite is 1 km and well signposted.

SYLT

TINNUM 14B

Campingplatz Sudhorn Jensen-Dau OHG, 25980 Tinnum.
Tel 04651 3607, Fax 04651 3619.
OPEN: all year. SIZE: 2 ha, 150 pitches (all with elec, 40 statics), 19 hot showers, 28 WCs, 2 CWPs.

PRICES: (1996) Caravan with family 53.00, Tent with two adults 28.00. CC: none.
Arriving on Sylt Island, turn to the right and follow sign to campsite.

WESTERLAND 14B

Dünen-Camping Sylt Rantumer Str, 25980 Westerland/Sylt.
Tel 04651 994499, Fax 04651 994321.
English spoken.
OPEN: 01/04–31/10. SIZE: 7.5 ha, 207 pitches (all with elec, 135 statics), 27 hot showers (charge), 60 WCs.

PRICES: (1996) Caravan with family 57.00, Tent with two adults 31.00. CC: none.
On the west coast of the island. Campsite is well signposted.

END OF SYLT RESORTS

TARMSTEDT 14B

Camping Rethbergsee 2733 Tarmstedt.
Tel 04283 422, Fax 04283 980139. English spoken.
OPEN: all year. SIZE: 10 ha, 40 pitches (all with elec, 40 statics), 16 hot showers, 23 WCs, 2 CWPs.

Restaurant at 1.5 km.
PRICES: (1996) Caravan with family 32.50, Tent with two adults 21.00. CC: none.
Leave motorway at Bremen University, drive to Lilienthal and then carry on to Tarmstedt (towards Zeven).

TETTNANG 16D

Gutshof-Camping Badhutten, 7992 Tettnang.
Tel 07543 9633-0, Fax 07543 9633-15.
English spoken.
OPEN: 27/03–31/10. SIZE: 10 ha, 500 pitches (all with elec, 230 statics), 43 hot showers (charge), 70 WCs, 2 CWPs.

Very good sports facilities.
PRICES: Caravan with family 40.50, Tent with two adults 29.00. CC: none.
Follow signs to campsite in Tettnang.

Germany

TITISEE 16C

Camping Bankenhof Bruderhalde 3,
7820 Titisee.
Tel 07652 1351, Fax 07652 5907. English spoken.
OPEN: all year. SIZE: 3 ha, 150 pitches (all with elec,
30 statics), 16 hot showers, 25 WCs, 4 CWPs. ℄ ↟

Swimming pool 2.5 km.
PRICES: (1996) Caravan with family 36.00,
Tent with two adults 28.00. CC: Euro/Access.
*From the centre of Titisee go towards Bruderhalde
and Bankenhof is the third campsite from the
town.*

Camping Wutachschlucht
79879 Wutach-Ewattingen.
Tel 07709 1378. English spoken.
OPEN: 01/04–30/10 & 23/12–06/01. SIZE: 1 ha,
30 pitches (all with elec, 20 statics), 7 hot showers,
6 WCs, 1 CWP. ℄

Shop at 0.1 km. Restaurant at 0.1 km.
PRICES: (1996) Caravan with family 29.00,
Tent with two adults 22.00. CC: Euro/Access.
*From Titisee, south on B315 to Bonndorf then left
to Wutach-Ewattingen.*

Terrassencamping Sandbank 79822 Titisee.
Tel 07651 8243, Fax 07651 8286. English spoken.
OPEN: 01/04–20/10. SIZE: 3 ha, 200 pitches
(all with elec, 10 statics), 16 hot showers (charge),
26 WCs, 2 CWPs. ℄ ↟

PRICES: (1996) Caravan with family 43.10,
Tent with two adults 30.60. CC: none.
*From Freiburg, take B31 to Titisee. From the
centre follow the signs to the campsite.*

TODTNAU 16C

Camping Hochschwarzwald
79674 Todtnau-Muggenbrunn.
Tel 07671 1288.
OPEN: all year. SIZE: 2.5 ha, 80 pitches (all with
elec, 30 statics), 5 hot showers, 11 WCs, 1 CWP. ℄

Swimming pool 5 km; playground.
PRICES: (1996) Caravan with family 32.90,
Tent with two adults 24.90. CC: none.
*Go 25 km south-east of Freiburg to Todtnau where
campsite is signposted.*

TRAVEMÜNDE 15A

Camping Ivendorf Frankenrogweg 2-4,
23570 Lübeck-Ivendorf.
Tel 04502 4865, Fax 04502 75516. English spoken.
OPEN: 01/03–31/10. SIZE: 3.5 ha, 120 pitches
(all with elec, 30 statics). ↟

PRICES: Caravan with family 39.00, Tent with two
adults 20.00. CC: none.
*From the A1, exit Travemünde-Skandinavia Kai,
onto B75. Follow signs.*

TRENDELBURG 14D

Campingplatz Trendelburg 3526 Trendelburg.
Tel 05675 301, Fax 05675 5888. English spoken.
OPEN: all year. SIZE: 45 pitches (all with elec,
45 statics), 4 hot showers, 11 WCs, 1 CWP.

Tennis.
PRICES: (1996) Caravan with family 25.80,
Tent with two adults 17.40. CC: none.
*From Kassel, take B83 to Trendelburg; cross the
bridge then turn left along the riverbank.*

TRIER 16A

Camping Trier City 5500 Trier.
Tel 06518 6921, Fax 0651 83079. English spoken.
OPEN: 01/04–31/10. SIZE: 1.5 ha, 150 pitches
(90 with elec, 10 statics), 18 hot showers, 20 WCs,
1 CWP. ℄ ↟

Panoramic terrace, playground.
PRICES: (1996) Caravan with family 37.50,
Tent with two adults 24.00. CC: none.
*In the east of Trier, on the south bank of the Mosel
between Römerbrücke and Konrad-Adenauer
bridges. Well signposted.*

TÜBINGEN 16D

Campingplatzwesen Rappenberghalde 42,
72070 Tübingen.
Tel 07071 43145. English spoken.
OPEN: 05/04–31/10. SIZE: 1.5 ha, 100 pitches
(all with elec), 8 hot showers, 12 WCs, 1 CWP. ↟

Swimming pool 1.5 km.
PRICES: (1996) Caravan with family 40.00,
Tent with two adults 25.50. CC: none.
On B27 south of Stuttgart.

ÜBERLINGEN 16D

Campingpark West Bahnhofstr 57,
88662 Überlingen.
Tel 07551 64583, Fax 07551 64583. English spoken.
OPEN: 01/04–05/10. SIZE: 3 ha, 160 pitches
(100 with elec, 50 statics), 18 hot showers
(charge), 30 WCs, 2 CWPs. ℄ ↟

PRICES: (1996) Caravan with family 48.00, Tent
with two adults 36.00. CC: none.

From Stockach go towards Überlingen, then at Goldbach exit, turn right and follow road to the lakeside.

Campingplatz Nell 88662 Überlingen Nussdorf. Tel 07551 4254. English spoken. OPEN: 01/04–15/10. SIZE: 1 ha, 17 pitches (all with elec, 33 statics), 4 hot showers, 7 WCs, 1 CWP.

Shop at 0.3 km. Restaurant at 0.3 km. PRICES: (1996) Caravan with family 40.00, Tent with two adults 29.00. CC: none. *From the B31 motorway, exit at Nussdorf (not Überlingen). Drive through the old town of Überlingen and site is on right.*

UETZE 14D

Camping Irenensee Dahrenhorst 2a, 31311 Uetze. Tel 05173 7583, Fax 05173 24387. English spoken. OPEN: all year. SIZE: 120 ha, 150 pitches (all with elec, 450 statics), 32 hot showers, 40 WCs, 6 CWPs. ♿ &

PRICES: (1996) Caravan with family 45.00, Tent with two adults 30.00. CC: none. *Campsite in Uetze on the Hannover/Gifborn road (B188) and well signposted. SEE ADVERTISEMENT.*

Family campsite near historical Celle.

Adults and children's entertainments, lakeside pitches and caravans for hire.

See under Uetze

USLAR 14D

Camp Bergsee Bergseestrasse 1, Delliehausen, 37170 Uslar. Tel 05573 1217, Fax 05573 1631. English spoken. OPEN: all year. SIZE: 1 ha, 50 pitches (all with elec), 8 hot showers, 8 WCs, 2 CWPs.

Shop at 0.5 km. Restaurant at 0.5 km. Bathroom for children; swimming pool 2 km; table tennis. PRICES: (1996) Caravan with family 37.40, Tent with two adults 26.80. CC: none. *From the Dortmund-Kassel motorway, drive towards Warburg (B241) until Volpriehausen. Branch off to the left towards Delliehausen; in the middle of the village branch off again to the left.*

VLOTHO 14D

Familienfreizeitplatz Borlefzen GmbH Borlefzen 2, 32602 Vlotho. Tel 05733 80008. English spoken. OPEN: 01/04–31/10. SIZE: 36 ha, 80 pitches (all with elec, 820 statics), 50 hot showers, 60 WCs, 6 CWPs. &

Mini-golf, boating, sports room. PRICES: (1996) Caravan with family 42.00, Tent with two adults 28.00. CC: none. *Take Exter or Bad Oeynhausen exit from A2 to Vlotho and campsite is signposted in the town.*

Sonnenwiese in Borlefzen Friedrich Schulte, Borlefzen 1, 32602 Vlotho. Tel 05733 8217, Fax 05733 80289. English spoken. OPEN: all year. SIZE: 10 ha, 100 pitches (all with elec, 400 statics), 8 hot showers (charge), 33 WCs, 2 CWPs. ♿ &

Private bathroom; sauna, solarium, keep-fit, boating, play area, entertainment. PRICES: Caravan with family 41.00, Tent with two adults 29.00. CC: none. *Vlotho is south-west of Hannover off the A2, towards Köln. In Vlotho, follow the signs to campsite.*

VOLKACH 16B

Camping Katzenkopf 97334 Sommerach/Main. Tel 09381 9215, Fax 09381 6028. English spoken. OPEN: 01/04–20/10. SIZE: 4 ha, 132 pitches (all with elec, 108 statics), 19 hot showers, 30 WCs, 2 CWPs. ♿ &

PRICES: (1996) Caravan with family 40.50, Tent with two adults 27.00. CC: none. *From the Würzburg to Nürnberg motorway (A3), exit for Kitzingen, Schwarzach, Volkach, head for Volkach via Münsterschwarzach and the campsite is signposted after about 7 km.*

Germany

VOLLRATHSRUHE 15A

Camping Dahmen O-2051 Dahmen.
Tel Vollrath 70379, Fax 039933 70379.
English spoken.
OPEN: all year. SIZE: 3 ha, 120 pitches (100 with elec, 10 statics), 6 hot showers, 19 WCs.

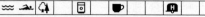

Shop at 0.3 km. Restaurant at 0.5 km.
PRICES: (1996) Caravan with family 35.50,
Tent with two adults 21.00. CC: none.
*From Teterow head towards Vollrathsruhe, turn
left to Malchin. Site 6 km ahead at Dahmen.*

WAGING AM SEE 17C

Camping Gut Horn
83329 Tettenhausen-Gut-Horn.
Tel 08681 227, Fax 08681 4282. English spoken.
OPEN: 01/03–30/11. SIZE: 5 ha, 250 pitches
(all with elec), 18 hot showers (charge), 50 WCs,
2 CWPs. ✆ ⅋

Restaurant at 1.5 km. Apartments.
PRICES: Caravan with family 36.00,
Tent with two adults 26.00. CC: none.
*Just north of Waging am See. Well signposted in
Tettenhausen-Gut-Horn.*

Strandcamping Gmbh 83329 Waging am See.
Tel 08681 552, Fax 08681 45010. English spoken.
OPEN: 01/04–30/09. SIZE: 15 ha, 500 pitches
(all with elec, 500 statics), 107 hot showers,
134 WCs, 5 CWPs. ✆ ⅋

PRICES: (1996) Caravan with family 42.60, Tent
with two adults 31.60. CC: none.
*Leave the München to Salzburg autobahn at
Traunstein and Waging am See is 15 km north-east.*

WALDKIRCH 16C

Camping Elztablick
79183 Waldkirch/Siensbach.
Tel 07681 7433. English spoken.
OPEN: 01/03–15/11. SIZE: 1.5 ha, 50 pitches (all with
elec, 25 statics), 6 hot showers, 7 WCs, 1 CWP. ⅋

PRICES: Caravan with family 33.50, Tent with two
adults 23.00. CC: none.
*From Waldkirch, go through the tunnel and take
Waldkirch Ost exit. Campsite is in Siensbach,
3 km ahead.*

WALDMÜNCHEN 17A

Campingplatz am Perlsee Alte Ziegelhutte,
93449 Waldmünchen.
Tel 09972 1469, Fax 09972 3782. English spoken.

OPEN: 21/03–15/10 & 16/12–15/02. SIZE: 5 ha,
165 pitches (all with elec, 80 statics), 22 hot
showers, 23 WCs, 3 CWPs. ✆ ⅋

PRICES: (1996) Caravan with family 29.95, Tent
with two adults 21.15. CC: none.
*Turn off the B22 (Weiden to Cham) in Schönthal;
go to Waldmünchen where the site is signposted.*

WALDSHUT 16C

Rhein Camping Waldshut
79761 Waldshut-Tiengen.
Tel 07751 3152, Fax 07751 3252. English spoken.
OPEN: all year. SIZE: 2 ha, 100 pitches (all with elec,
30 statics), 10 hot showers (charge), 19 WCs,
1 CWP. ✆

Shop at 1 km. Rooms for hire.
PRICES: (1996) Caravan with family 37.00, Tent
with two adults 24.00. CC: Euro/Access, Visa.
*Between Basel and Schaffhausen on the B34 or
E54. After Waldshut, go right in the village.
Campsite by the river.*

WALTENHOFEN 16D

Insel-Camping 87448 Waltenhofen.
Tel 08379 881, Fax 08379 7308.
OPEN: all year. SIZE: 1.5 ha, 70 pitches (all with
elec, 50 statics), 8 hot showers, 14 WCs, 1 CWP.
✆ ⅋

Restaurant at 1 km. Boating, fishing, tennis, table
tennis, playground, bowls.
PRICES: (1996) Caravan with family 36.00,
Tent with two adults 23.00. CC: none.
*From the A7, take A98 towards Lindau. Left on to
B19 towards Oberstdorf, and take right fork at
Kuhnen. Follow road to Membölz and the
campsite is signposted.*

WALTERSHAUSEN 17A

Campingplatz Paulfeld 14 Hauptstr 05,
99887 Catterfeld/Thür.
Tel 036253 25171, Fax 036253 25165.
English spoken.
OPEN: all year. SIZE: 7 ha, 280 pitches (256 with
elec, 100 statics), 10 hot showers (charge),
25 WCs, 1 CWP. ✆ ⅋

Sauna and solarium.
PRICES: (1996) Caravan with family 35.00,
Tent with two adults 20.00. CC: none.
*Take motorway from Eisenach to Waltershausen
and then take B88 to Friedrichroda and
Georgenthal to Catterfeld.*

WARNITZ 15B

Camping Oberuckersee/Ostufer
17291 Warnitz.
Tel 039863 459, Fax 039863 459. English spoken.
OPEN: 01/04–05/10. SIZE: 8 ha, 50 pitches (all with elec, 100 statics), 16 hot showers, 12 WCs. ♿ ♿

Shop at 0.5 km. Restaurant at 0.2 km. Biking, boating and canoeing.
PRICES: (1996) Caravan with family 29.00, Tent with two adults 19.00. CC: none.
Campsite is near the Oberuckersee, just west of the A11. Take Warnitz exit.

WAXWEILER 16A

Ferienpark Waxweiler GmbH
Schwimmbad str. 7, 54649 Waxweiler.
Tel 06554 92000, Fax 06554 1280. English spoken.
OPEN: all year. SIZE: 1 ha, 100 pitches (all with elec), 8 hot showers, 17 WCs, 2 CWPs. ♿

Tennis, mini-golf.
PRICES: (1996) Caravan with family 46.00, Tent with two adults 29.00. CC: none.

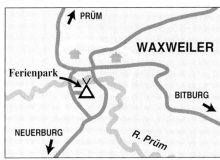

South-west of Waxweiler and well signposted.

WEILBURG 16B

Camping Odersbach
35781 Weilburg-Odersbach.
Tel 06471 7620, Fax 06471 7620.
OPEN: 01/04–30/10. SIZE: 5 ha, 75 pitches (all with elec, 235 statics), 20 hot showers, 35 WCs, 2 CWPs. ♿ ♿

Campingplatz Odersbach
near Weilburg
Super spot beside the Lahn

Restaurant at 0.05 km.
PRICES: Caravan with family 25.50, Tent with two adults 18.00. CC: none.
From Weilburg going north-west, turn left to Odersbach before reaching the B49. Site is signposted.

WEILHEIM 17C

Campingplatz St Alban
86911 Diessen-Ammersee.
Tel 08807 7305, Fax 08807 1057.
OPEN: 01/04–30/09. SIZE: 48 pitches (all with elec, 4 statics), 4 hot showers, 2 French WCs, 2 CWPs. ♿

PRICES: (1996) Caravan with family 40.50, Tent with two adults 27.50. CC: none.
A96 Lindau-München motorway, exit Greifenberg, main road to Diessen and turn first left.

WEISSENSEE 15C

Camping am Terrassenbad 5237 Weissensee.
Tel 036374 20369, Fax 036374 20369.
English spoken.
OPEN: 01/04–31/10. SIZE: 5 ha, 70 pitches (all with elec, 70 statics), 10 hot showers (charge), 18 WCs, 1 CWP. ♿

PRICES: (1996) Caravan with family 30.00, Tent with two adults 17.50. CC: none.
35 km north of Erfurt on the B4, then take the B86 to Weissensee.

WEISSWASSER 15D

Camping am Halbendorfer See
02953 Halbendorf.
Tel 035773 413.
OPEN: 01/04–15/10. SIZE: 2 ha, 80 pitches (all with elec, 40 statics), 21 hot showers (charge). ♿ ♿

Shop at 3 km.
PRICES: (1996) Caravan with family 27.50, Tent with two adults 17.00. CC: none.
From Weisswasser take road to Spremberg for 7 km. Campsite signed from village of Halbendorf.

WERTHEIM 16B

Campingpark Wertheim-Bettingen
Geiselbrunnweg 31,
97877 Wertheim-Bettingen.
Tel 09342 7077. English spoken.
OPEN: 01/04–31/10. SIZE: 7 ha, 100 pitches (all with elec, 120 statics), 8 hot showers, 16 WCs, 1 CWP. ♿

Germany

PRICES: Caravan with family 32.50, Tent with two adults 20.00. CC: none.
From the A3 (Frankfurt to Nürnberg), take the Wertheim/Lengfurt exit and then 2 km to campsite.

Forelle im Taubertal Forellenhofzum Ottersberg 14, 97877 Wertheim-Reicholzheim.
Tel 09342 4435, Fax 09342 6151.
OPEN: 01/04–01/10. SIZE: 4 ha, 150 pitches (120 with elec, 50 statics), 4 hot showers (charge), 11 WCs, 2 CWPs. **(**

Playground.
PRICES: (1996) Caravan with family 29.50, Tent with two adults 23.50. CC: none.
From Frankfurt, go to Marktheidenfeld, turn right to Wertheim and carry on to Reicholzheim im Taubertal.

WIETZENDORF 14D

Südsee-Camp Soltau-Süd, 29647 Wietzendorf.
Tel 05196 98016, Fax 05196 98099.
English spoken.
OPEN: all year. SIZE: 55 ha, 380 pitches (all with elec, 380 statics), 140 hot showers (charge), 241 WCs, 9 CWPs. **(** &

Disco, tropical pool complex.
PRICES: (1996) Caravan with family 68.40, Tent with two adults 59.40. CC: none.
From Soltau-Süd, take A7/E45 (Hannover to Hamburg) then on to B3 through Bergen and Colle and a further 4 km to Wietzendorf.

WILLSTÄTT-SAND 16C

Europa Camping Waldstrasse 32, 77731 Willstätt-Sand.
Tel 07852 2311, Fax 07852 2311. English spoken.
OPEN: all year. SIZE: 1 ha, 60 pitches (all with elec, 20 statics), 4 hot showers (charge), 10 WCs, 1 CWP. **(**

Shop at 0.5 km. Swimming pool 5 km.
PRICES: (1996) Caravan with family 27.00, Tent with two adults 22.00. CC: none.
From highway A5, take exit to Strasbourg and after 1 km follow the camping signs.

WINTERBERG 14D

Camping an der Vossmecke Niedersfeld, 59955 Winterberg.
Tel 02985 8418, Fax 02985 553. English spoken.
OPEN: all year. SIZE: 4 ha, 30 pitches (all with elec, 220 statics), 13 hot showers (charge), 33 WCs, 3 CWPs. **(** &

Table tennis, skiing/ski-lifts, playground.
PRICES: (1996) Caravan with family 32.60, Tent with two adults 22.60. CC: none.
Coming from Olsberg to Winterberg on the N480, follow signs to Niedersfeld and the campsite.

WISMAR 15A

Campingpark Kuhlungsborn Waldstrasse, 18225 Kuhlungsborn.
Tel 038293 7195, Fax 038293 7192. English spoken.
OPEN: 01/04–31/10. SIZE: 10 ha, 350 pitches (300 with elec, 80 statics), 20 hot showers (charge), 50 WCs, 1 CWP. **(**

PRICES: (1996) Caravan with family 32.00, Tent with two adults 19.00. CC: none.
From Wismar to Rostock on B105, turn left at Neubukow, Kuhlungsborn, then take first left and left again.

Ostsee Campingplatz Zierow Am Strand, 2401 Zierow.
Tel 03841 642377, Fax 03841 642377.
English spoken.
OPEN: all year. SIZE: 13 ha, 300 pitches (150 with elec, 60 statics), 18 hot showers (charge), 36 WCs, 1 CWP. **(** &

Windsurfing school nearby.
PRICES: (1996) Caravan with family 35.00, Tent with two adults 22.00. CC: Euro/Access.
From the Lübeck to Wismar road (B105) turn left 3 km before Wismar to Zierow and go to Ostsee Strand.

WITZENHAUSEN 14D

Campingplatz Werratal Am Sande 11, 37213 Witzenhausen.
Tel 05542 1465, Fax 05542 72418. English spoken.
OPEN: all year. SIZE: 3 ha, 60 pitches (all with elec, 60 statics), 14 hot showers, 19 WCs, 2 CWPs.

Restaurant at 0.3 km. New sanitary block in 1996; bikes for hire, boating.
PRICES: (1996) Caravan with family 27.50, Tent with two adults 19.00. CC: none.
From Göttingen to Kassel highway take Friedland exit and then B27 to Witzenhausen. From Kassel to Göttingen highway, take Werratal exit and then B80 to Witzenhausen.

WORMS 16B

Camping Platz Nibelungenbrucke
Motorsportbluc,
68623 Worms/Rhein/Rosengarten.

Tel 06241 24355, Fax 06241 24410. English spoken. OPEN: 01/04–30/09. SIZE: 150 pitches (80 with elec, 120 statics), 6 hot showers (charge), 12 WCs, 1 CWP.

Swimming pool 3 km.
PRICES: (1996) Caravan with family 34.50, Tent with two adults 24.00. CC: none.
From Worms, cross the Rhein towards Bürstadt then turn right towards Lampertheim and follow signs to campsite.

WÜRZBURG 16B

Camping Platz Kalte Quelle
Winterhausenstrasse 160, 97084 Wuerzburg. Tel 0931 65598, Fax 0931 612611. English spoken. OPEN: 17/03–26/11. SIZE: 4 ha, 60 pitches (50 with elec, 130 statics), 6 hot showers (charge), 13 WCs, 1 CWP. ☎

Swimming pool 5 km.
PRICES: (1996) Caravan with family 29.80, Tent with two adults 16.50. CC: Visa.
From A3, take Würzburg/Heidingsfeld exit. Go towards Heidingsfeld and Winterhausen for about 8 km and campsite is on the left of the River Main.

Campingplatz Estenfeld Maidbronner Str 38, 97230 Estenfeld.
Tel 09305 228, Fax 09305 8006. English spoken. OPEN: 01/03–23/12. SIZE: 1 ha, 50 pitches (42 with elec), 4 hot showers, 9 WCs, 1 CWP.

Children's playground; cooking and baby facilities.
PRICES: Caravan with family 34.00, Tent with two adults 20.00. CC: none.

From A7 (Kassel to Würzburg), exit at Würzburg-Estenfeld and go towards Würzburg on B19 for 1 km. Then exit at Estenfeld and follow sign to campsite.

ZWEIBRUCKEN 16A

Campingplatz Hengstbachermuhle
66482 Zweibrucken-Mittelbach.
Tel 06332 18128, Fax 06332 904001.
English spoken.
OPEN: 01/04–31/10. SIZE: 20 pitches (all with elec, 30 statics), 2 hot showers (charge), 5 WCs, 1 CWP.

Shop at 2 km. Restaurant at 7 km.
PRICES: Caravan with family 24.00, Tent with two adults 14.00. CC: none.
From the A8, exit Zweibrucken/Ixheim. Go towards Mittelbach for 3 km and campsite is on left.

Germany

GREECE

Many British holidaymakers choose to fly to one of the Greek islands for their annual fix of Mediterranean sunshine, but exploring the mainland, from the Turkish border in the north-east to Cape Ta'naron at the foot of the Mani peninsula, is an exciting alternative.

Salonica, in the north, is the country's second largest city and to its east lies the part of Greece where you are least likely to find tourists in large numbers. You will meet more if you drive south towards Athens. The road follows the coast passing between the sea and Mount Olympus, Greece's highest mountain and the mythical home of the gods. Athens is crowded in summertime, but you may still feel a visit to the Acropolis is an essential part of your holiday.

West of Athens, the road crosses the Corinth canal on its way to the hand-shaped Peloponnese, the most southern region of the Greek mainland. Snatch a look as you cross the bridge, for this is the best view you will have of the amazing canal. Built between 1882 and 1893 it is only 23 m wide but cuts through rock which is sometimes as much as 80 m deep, Originally on the drawing board in the first century AD, this project took some 1800 years to come to fruition. In the Peloponnese, the two outstanding ancient sites are Mycenae, with its famous lion gate, and Olympia, home of the ancient games for over a thousand years.

Emergency numbers

For emergency numbers see the local directory

Warning information

Warning Triangle must be carried

Blood Alcohol Legal Limit 50 mg

Fire extinguisher essential

First aid kit compulsory

AIYION   24C

Camping Eleon Beach Eleonas, 25003 Diacofto. Tel 0691 42111, Fax 0691 42112. English spoken. OPEN: 15/04–15/10. SIZE: 7 ha, 100 pitches (all with elec), 16 hot showers, 16 WCs, 16 French WCs, 1 CWP. ✆

Shop at 1 km. Good water sports facilities; caves nearby.
PRICES: (1996) Caravan with family 5000, Tent with two adults 3500. CC: Euro/Access, Visa.
From Aiyion, go east on E65 and Eleonas is about 1.5 km before reaching Diacofto.

AKRATAS   24C

Camping Krioneri 25006 Akratas. Tel 0696 31405. English spoken. OPEN: 01/04–31/10. SIZE: 60 pitches (all with elec), 6 hot showers, 10 WCs.

20% LS discount and for long stayers.
PRICES: (1996) Caravan with family 5700, Tent with two adults 3740. CC: none.
On the E65 midway between Patras and Korinthos, beside a small marina.

ALEXANDROUPOLIS   24A

Municipal Camping 68100 Alexandroupolis. Tel 0551 28735, Fax 0551 28735. English spoken. OPEN: all year. SIZE: 70 ha, 50 hot showers, 50 WCs, 50 French WCs. ✆

Restaurant at 1 km. Campsite had Blue Flag awarded in 1994, 1995 and 1996.
PRICES: (1996) Caravan with family 4850, Tent with two adults 3230. CC: none.
Campsite is on the national road, just as you enter Alexandroupolis.

ARGALASTI   24A

Camping Olizon Milina, Volos, Milina. Tel 0423 65236, Fax 0423 65600. English spoken. OPEN: 01/05–01/10. SIZE: 10 ha, 60 pitches (36 with elec), 9 hot showers, 9 WCs, 1 CWP.

PRICES: (1996) Caravan with family 5000, Tent with two adults 3100. CC: Euro/Access.
A few km south of Argalasti on the coast. As you leave Milina, campsite is signposted to the left.

ATHINA (ATHENS) 24C

Camping Athens 198-200 Leoforos Athinon, Peristeri, 12136 Athina.
Tel 0158 14113/4, Fax 0158 20353. English spoken.
OPEN: all year. SIZE: 1.4 ha, 66 pitches (all with elec), 10 hot showers, 14 WCs, 2 CWPs. ✆ ♿

〔♨ R ⊡ ▯ ☕ ✕〕

PRICES: Caravan with family 7100, Tent with two adults 4100. CC: none.
On the Athina-Korinthos main road, 7 km from the centre of Athina and 10 km from Piraeus.

Camping Dionissotis 14564 Nea Kifissia.
Tel 0620 4848. English spoken.
OPEN: all year. SIZE: 122 pitches (all with elec), 12 hot showers, 12 WCs, 1 CWP. ✆

〔♨ R ▯ ☕ ✕ ↯〕

PRICES: (1996) Caravan with family 5900, Tent with two adults 3800. CC: none.
18 km from Athina on the Athina to Lamia national road.

DELFI (DELPHI) 24A

Camping Apollon 33054 Delfi.
Tel 0265 82762, Fax 0265 82639. English spoken.
OPEN: all year. SIZE: 1.6 ha, 130 pitches (33 with elec), 21 hot showers, 20 WCs, 1 CWP. ♿

〔⌂ R ⊡ ▯ ☕ ✕ ↯ ▯〕

Volley ball, table tennis.
PRICES: (1996) Caravan with family 4400, Tent with two adults 3000. CC: none.
1.5 km from the town of Delfi. Well signposted.

Camping Delfi Chrisso, 33055 Delfi.
Tel 0265 82745, Fax 0265 82363. English spoken.
OPEN: 01/03–30/10. SIZE: 2.2 ha, 80 pitches (all with elec), 20 hot showers, 20 WCs, 20 French WCs, 2 CWPs. ✆

〔～ ✈ ♨ R ⊡ ▯ ☕ ✕ ↯ ⚠〕

PRICES: (1996) Caravan with family 6050, Tent with two adults 3900. CC: Visa.
3.5 km from Delfi on the road to Itea.

Chrissa Camping Chrisso, 33055 Delfi.
Tel 0265 82050, Fax 0265 83148. English spoken.
OPEN: all year. SIZE: 2 ha, 95 pitches (60 with elec), 10 hot showers, 20 WCs, 1 CWP. ✆

〔≈ ⚓ ♨ R ⊡ ▯ ☕ ✕ ↯〕

PRICES: (1996) Caravan with family 4500, Tent with two adults 3500. CC: none.
7 km along the Delfi to Itea main road. Campsite is signposted.

EPANOMI 24A

EOT Camping Epanomis Thessaloniki, 57500 Epanomi.

Tel 0392 41378, Fax 0392 41660. English spoken.
OPEN: 01/04–31/10. SIZE: 5.5 ha, 630 pitches (all with elec), 66 hot showers, 84 WCs, 1 CWP. ✆ ♿

〔≈ ⚓ ♨ R ▯ ☕ ✕〕

Tennis, football, volley ball.
PRICES: (1996) Caravan with family 5870, Tent with two adults 3920. CC: none.
From Thessaloniki go south past the airport and continue for approx 32 km. The site is about 3 km south of Epanomi.

ERATINI 24C

Doric Camping Agios Nikolaos, 33058 Eratini.
Tel 0266 31722, Fax 0266 31196. English spoken.
OPEN: 01/05–30/09. SIZE: 2 ha, 75 pitches (35 with elec), 12 hot showers, 22 WCs, 2 CWPs. ✆ ♿

〔≈ ⚓ ⌂ R ▯ ✕ ↯ Ⓗ〕

Children's playground, beach; ideal location.
PRICES: (1996) Caravan with family 4700, Tent with two adults 3000. CC: Euro/Access, Visa.
37 km east of Naffpaktos on the coastal road and 11 km from Eghion which is linked via ferry.

GITHIO (GYTHION) 24C

Camping Gythion Bay 23200 Githio.
Tel 733 22522/23441, Fax 733 23523.
English spoken.
OPEN: all year. SIZE: 4 ha, 200 pitches (100 with elec), 27 hot showers, 34 French WCs, 1 CWP. ✆ ♿

〔≈ ⚓ ♨ R ⊡ ▯ ☕ ✕ ⚠〕

Shop at 0.1 km.
PRICES: (1996) Caravan with family 6200, Tent with two adults 3900. CC: none.
4 km from Githio towards Areópoli.

IGOUMENITSA 24A

Camping Nautilos Plataria-Thesprotias, 46100 Igoumenitsa.
Tel 6657 1416/7, Fax 6512 9921. English spoken.
OPEN: 01/06–30/09. SIZE: 150 pitches (212 statics), 55 hot showers, 55 WCs. ✆

〔≈ ⚓ ♨ R ⊡ ☕ ✕ ↯ ⚠〕

Own beach.
PRICES: (1996) Caravan with family 5470, Tent with two adults 2850. CC: none.
Recommended campsite. 15 km south of Igoumenitsa on the Parga road and well signposted.

IOANNINA 24A

Camping Limnopoula 45500 Ioannina.
Tel 0651 25265, Fax 0651 38060. English spoken.
OPEN: all year. SIZE: 16 hot showers, 12 WCs. ✆

Greece

≋ ⚓ ⛺ R　⛾ ☕ ✗　ⓗ ✶

PRICES: (1996) Caravan with family 5400, Tent with two adults 3300. CC: none.
Campsite is 1 km from the town, on the lake shore.

ITEA　24A

Camping Kaparelis Kirra-Itea-Fokidos, 33200 Kirra.
Tel 0265 32989, Fax 0265 32977.
English spoken.
OPEN: all year. SIZE: 12 pitches (all with elec, 10 statics), 20 hot showers, 10 WCs, 2 CWPs.

≋ ⚓ ⛺ R ⏣ ⛾ ☕ ✗　ⓗ

PRICES: (1996) Caravan with family 3500, Tent with two adults 2150. CC: Amex, Euro/Access, Visa.
Go east from Itea (just south of Delfi) to Kirra. Campsite is the second you come to, 100 m above the sea and with beautiful views. Well signposted.

KALAMATA　24C

Camping Maria (Sea and Sun) Verga, 24100 Kalamata.
Tel 0721 41060. English spoken.
OPEN: all year. SIZE: 11 ha, 40 pitches (all with elec, 105 statics), 12 hot showers, 26 French WCs, 1 CWP. ℓ ⚅

≋ ⚓ ⛺ R ⏣ ⛾ ☕ ✗　ⓗ

PRICES: (1996) Caravan with family 5850, Tent with two adults 3740. CC: none.
Going towards Arepoli, turn right in Verga at the chapel Agia Jion. Campsite is 150 m ahead.

Camping Petalidi Beach 24005 Petalidi.
Tel 0722 31154. English spoken.
OPEN: 01/04–30/09. SIZE: 14 hot showers, 18 WCs. ℓ

≋ ⚓ ⛺ R ⏣ ⛾　✗　ⓗ

Boating, children's playground.
PRICES: (1996) Caravan with family 5360, Tent with two adults 3320. CC: Euro/Access.
From Kalamata, take coast road west for about 28 km to Petalidi.

KALAMBAKA　24A

Camping Theopetra Theopetra, 42200 Kalambaka.
Tel 0432 81406. English spoken.
OPEN: 01/04–31/10. SIZE: 2.2 ha, 67 pitches (all with elec), 10 hot showers, 20 WCs, 20 French WCs.

⛺ R　　　✗ ⚘

Shop at 5 km.
PRICES: Caravan with family 3000, Tent with two adults 2300. CC: none.
On E92 north of Trikala and 5 km south of Kalambaka.

KAMENA VOURLA　24A

Camping Venezuela Agios Serafim, 35009 Molos.
Tel 0235 41691/2, Fax 01 6548224. English spoken.
OPEN: 01/05–31/10. SIZE: 90 pitches (all with elec), 12 hot showers, 24 WCs, 1 CWP.

≋ ⚓ ⛺ R　ⓢ ☕ ✗

PRICES: (1996) Caravan with family 5400, Tent with two adults 3500. CC: none.
Turn to the right at Km 185 of the Athina-Lamia national road, 6 km north of Kamena Vourla. Follow the road to Agios Serafim and then follow signs to the beach.

KARDAMYLI　24C

Camping Melitsina 24022 Kardamyli.
Tel 0721 73461, Fax 0721 73334. English spoken.
OPEN: 01/05–30/09. SIZE: 1.5 ha, 20 pitches (40 with elec, 50 statics), 14 hot showers, 28 WCs, 1 CWP. ⚅

≋ ⚓ ⚘　⏣ ⓢ ☕ ✗

Shop at 1.5 km.
PRICES: (1996) Caravan with family 5590, Tent with two adults 3350. CC: none.
Kardamyli is about 35 km south of Kalamata. Campsite is well signposted in Kardamyli.

KAVALA　24A

Akti Camping Batis, EOT Batis, 65500 Kavala.
Tel 0512 43051, Fax 0512 45690. English spoken.
OPEN: all year. SIZE: 150 pitches (all with elec), 14 hot showers, 20 French WCs, 1 CWP. ℓ

≋ ⚓ ⛺ R ⏣ ⛾ ☕ ✗

PRICES: (1996) Caravan with family 5133, Tent with two adults 3370. CC: none.
Kavala is on the E90, and the campsite is very well signposted.

Camping Irini Terma Perigiali, 65001 Kavala.
Tel 0512 29785, Fax 0512 29748. English spoken.
OPEN: all year. SIZE: 2.5 ha, 180 pitches (all with elec), 16 hot showers, 24 WCs, 20 French WCs. ℓ

≋ ⚓ ⛺ R ⏣ ⛾ ☕ ✗　ⓗ

Tennis, volley and basket ball.
PRICES: (1996) Caravan with family 5000, Tent with two adults 3300. CC: none.
4 km east of the town centre, the campsite is on the right of the national road E90 (Thessaloniki to Turkey), just after the BP petrol station.

KEFALLINIA

ARGOSTOLI　24C

Camping Argostoli Beach Phanari, 28100 Argostoli, Kefalonia.
Tel 0671 23487, Fax 0671 24525. English spoken.

Greece

OPEN: 01/05–01/10. SIZE: 15 pitches (all with elec, 160 statics), 30 hot showers, 30 WCs, 8 French WCs, 2 CWPs. ☏

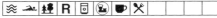

Shop at 1 km.
PRICES: (1996) Caravan with family 6500,
Tent with two adults 4000. CC: none.
1.5 km from Argostoli towards the lighthouse.

SAMI   24C

Camping Karavomilos Beach Sami,
28080 Kefallinia.
Tel 0674 22480, Fax 0674 22932. English spoken.
OPEN: 01/05–30/09. SIZE: 4 ha, 243 pitches
(100 with elec), 28 hot showers, 27 WCs,
10 French WCs, 1 CWP. ☏

Shop at 1 km.
PRICES: (1996) Caravan with family 6780,
Tent with two adults 4250. CC: none.
Approx 1 km from Sami village on the road to St Efimia. Well signposted.

END OF KEFALLINIA RESORTS

KERKIRA (CORFU)

IPSOS   24A

Camping Corfu Ipsos Ipsos, 49083 Kerkira.
Tel 0661 93246/93579, Fax 0661 93741.
English spoken.
OPEN: 01/05–31/10. SIZE: 1.4 ha, 40 pitches
(all with elec), 25 hot showers, 20 WCs. ☏ &

PRICES: (1996) Caravan with family 5950, Tent with
two adults 3400. CC: none.
Ipsos is 12 km north of Kerkira Town. In Ipsos, take the coast road and campsite is on the left.

KAVADADES   24A

San George Camping Karoussades, Kavadades,
49081 Kerkira.
Tel 0663 51194, Fax 0663 51759. English spoken.
OPEN: 15/05–30/09. SIZE: 1.3 ha, 5 pitches (10 with
elec), 8 hot showers, 20 WCs. ☏

Shop at 0.5 km. Windsurfing.
PRICES: (1996) Caravan with family 5400,
Tent with two adults 3200. CC: Visa.
On the north-west coast of Kerkira.

KERKIRA TOWN   24A

Camping Dionysos Dassia, 49100 Kerkira.
Tel 0661 91417, Fax 0661 91760. English spoken.

OPEN: 20/04–30/10. SIZE: 2.3 ha, 107 pitches
(15 with elec, 6 statics), 20 hot showers, 20 WCs. ☏

Volley ball, table tennis, badminton, basketball;
bus service.
PRICES: (1996) Caravan with family 4545,
Tent with two adults 3285. CC: none.
From Kerkira town follow coast road north for 8 km. Turn right at Tzavros and campsite is 1 km on right.

Karda Beach Camping Dassia, 49100 Kerkira.
Tel 0661 93595, Fax 0661 93595. English spoken.
OPEN: 15/04–15/10. SIZE: 3 ha, 127 pitches
(all with elec), 32 hot showers, 34 WCs, 16 French
WCs, 1 CWP. ☏

Boat hire, paragliding, water-skiing, windsurfing.
PRICES: (1996) Caravan with family 6570, Tent with
two adults 3900. CC: none.
On the main road from Kerkira town going north towards Kassiopi, 12 km on the right-hand side. Site is well signposted.

Karda Beach Camping
near Kerkira Town
100m from Dassia Beach

RODA   24A

Roda Beach Camping 49081 Roda, Kerkira.
Tel 0663 63120/209, Fax 0663 63081.
English spoken.
OPEN: 20/04–20/10. SIZE: 100 pitches (38 with elec,
83 statics), 20 hot showers, 29 French WCs. ☏

Watersports, paragliding; mini-cruises.
PRICES: (1996) Caravan with family 5200,
Tent with two adults 3400. CC: none.
Follow signs for Roda and just before the crossroads and village turn left down a small lane. Campsite is 200 m and well signposted.

END OF KERKIRA RESORTS

KOMOTINI   24A

EOT Fanari Campsite 67063 Fanari.
Tel 0535 31217, Fax 0535 31270. English spoken.
OPEN: 01/04–31/10. SIZE: 5.8 ha, 250 pitches (150 with
elec), 20 hot showers, 38 French WCs, 1 CWP. ☏

PRICES: (1996) Caravan with family 6070, Tent with
two adults 4570. CC: none.

Greece (side margin)

Greece

Just south of the Bulgarian border. On the main road, east of Kavala and 250 km east of Thessaloniki.

KORINTHOS (CORINTH) 24C

Blue Dolphin Camping Lecheon, 20011 Korinthos.
Tel 0741 25766, Fax 0741 72561. English spoken.
OPEN: 01/04–15/10. SIZE: 5 ha, 90 pitches (60 with elec, 20 statics), 22 hot showers, 22 WCs, 1 CWP.

Water sports.
PRICES: (1996) Caravan with family 6000,
Tent with two adults 3400. CC: none.
From Patras, go east on the E65 to Korinthos. Look for the sign 'Ancient Korinthos' and then follow camping signs to Lecheon village, by the sea.

KORONI 24C

Camping Memi Beach 24004 Koroni.
Tel 0725 22130. English spoken.
OPEN: 01/06–30/09. SIZE: 1 ha, 88 pitches (40 with elec, 48 statics), 16 hot showers, 16 WCs.

PRICES: (1996) Caravan with family 5170, Tent with two adults 3320. CC: none.
Turn left off the Kalamata to Pylos road at Rizomilos, go through Petalidi towards Koroni and 2 km before Koroni turn right towards Vasilitsi. Campsite is beside the beach.

KOS

KOS TOWN 24D

Kos Camping Psalidi, 85300 Kos.
Tel 0242 23910. English spoken.
OPEN: 15/04–05/10. SIZE: 1 ha, 144 pitches (26 with elec), 31 hot showers, 16 French WCs.

Car and bike hire, volley ball, disco; buses to Kos town; island tours.
PRICES: (1996) Caravan with family 5200,
Tent with two adults 3800. CC: none.
The campsite is 3 km east of the town of Kos, right beside the sea.

END OF KOS RESORTS

KRITI (CRETE)

AGIOS NIKOLAOS 24C

Gournia Moon Camping 72200 Ierapetra, Kriti.
Tel 0842 93243. English spoken.
OPEN: 01/04–30/10. SIZE: 1 ha, 55 pitches (50 with

elec), 12 hot showers, 20 WCs, 1 CWP.

PRICES: (1996) Caravan with family 5500,
Tent with two adults 3100. CC: none.
15 km east of Agios Nikolaos, on the E75 towards Sitia.

IRAKLION (CANDIA) 24C

Camping Creta Gouves, 71500 Iraklion, Kriti.
Tel 0897 41400, Fax 0897 41792. English spoken.
OPEN: 01/04–30/10. SIZE: 2.2 ha, 50 pitches (all with elec, 92 statics), 18 hot showers, 22 WCs, 2 CWPs.

10% discount for RAC members.
PRICES: (1996) Caravan with family 6500,
Tent with two adults 3800. CC: none.
About 20 km from Iraklion towards Malia. Site is signposted.

Camping Karavan 70014 Hersonissos, Kriti.
Tel 0897 22025, Fax 0813 41808.
English spoken.
OPEN: 01/04–30/09. SIZE: 0.7 ha, 20 pitches (all with elec, 70 statics), 8 hot showers, 10 WCs.

PRICES: (1996) Caravan with family 5100,
Tent with two adults 3450. CC: none.
About 30 km east of Iraklion, near the beach.

END OF KRITI (CRETE) RESORTS

LEFKAS 24A

Camping Episkopos Beach Katouna, 31100 Lefkas.
Tel 0645 71388, Fax 0645 71388.
English spoken.
OPEN: all year. SIZE: 20 pitches (all with elec), 12 hot showers, 14 WCs.

PRICES: (1996) Caravan with family 5200,
Tent with two adults 3500. CC: none.
Campsite is well signposted.

Camping Poros Beach Poros, 31100 Lefkas.
Tel 0645 95452/23203, Fax 0645 95152.
English spoken.
OPEN: 01/05–30/09. SIZE: 50 pitches (all with elec), 10 hot showers, 10 WCs, 5 French WCs, 1 CWP.

PRICES: (1996) Caravan with family 5000,
Tent with two adults 3000. CC: none.
Lefkas is connected to the mainland by road. On arrival, head south towards Basilliki and campsite at Poros is signposted.

LESVOS

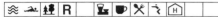

VATERA   24B

Camping Dionysos Vatera, 81300 Lesvos.
Tel 0252 61151/3/4, Fax 0252 61155.
English spoken.
OPEN: 15/05–15/09. SIZE: 20 pitches (all with elec,
15 statics), 20 hot showers, 25 WCs, 20 CWPs. ✆

≋ ⚓ 🏍 Ⓡ ▯ 🍺 🍴 ⚡ 🏠 ▯

PRICES: (1996) Caravan with family 7000,
Tent with two adults 5000. CC: Visa.
In the centre of the village and well signposted.

END OF LESVOS RESORTS

LITOCHORON   24A

Camping Olympos Beach 60200 Plaka.
Tel 0352 22112, Fax 0352 22300. English spoken.
OPEN: 01/05–30/09. SIZE: 2.7 ha, 109 pitches
(all with elec, 52 statics), 28 hot showers, 28 WCs,
14 French WCs, 4 CWPs. ⚓

≋ ⚓ 🏍 Ⓡ ▣ 🍺 🍴 ⚡ 🏠 ▯

PRICES: (1996) Caravan with family 5500,
Tent with two adults 3700. CC: none.
*Litochoron is about 20 km south of Katerini on
the E75. Campsite at Plaka is on the beach and
well signposted.*

LYGIA   24C

Camping Apartments Ionion Beach Glifa
Bartholomio, 27050 Ilias.
Tel 0623 96395, Fax 0623 96425.
English spoken.
OPEN: all year. SIZE: 4 ha, 230 pitches (210 with
elec), 34 hot showers, 38 WCs. ✆ ⚓

≋ ⚓ 🏍 Ⓡ ▣ 🍺 🍴 ⚡ 🏠 ▯

PRICES: Caravan with family 4550, Tent with two
adults 3050. CC: Amex, Euro/Access.
*From the Patras to Pyrgos national road, turn off
for Gastouni and Bartholomio. When you reach
Lygia, turn off for Glifa and the campsite is
signposted.*

MEGARA   24C

Camping Poseidon Alepochori, 19100 Mégara.
Tel 0296 51489/92, Fax 0193 30154.
English spoken.
OPEN: 01/06–30/09. SIZE: 100 pitches (60 with elec,
40 statics), 20 hot showers, 20 WCs, 1 CWP. ✆

≋ ⚓ 🏍 Ⓡ ▣ 🍺 🍴 ⚡ 🚐 ▯

Basketball, playground.
PRICES: (1996) Caravan with family 5800,
Tent with two adults 3750. CC: none.
A 1-hour drive west from Athens.

METHONI   24A

Camping Agiannis Pierias, 60066 Methoni.
Tel 0353 41386. English spoken.
OPEN: 01/05–20/10. SIZE: 70 pitches (all with elec,
100 statics), 17 hot showers, 17 WCs.

≋ ⚓ 🏍 Ⓡ ▯ 🍺 🍴 ⚡ ▯

Shop at 1 km.
PRICES: (1996) Caravan with family 4800,
Tent with two adults 2800. CC: none.
*Heading south, turn right when you see the sign
for Methoni and follow signs to campsite. About
2 km from Methoni centre.*

MOUDANIA   24A

Camping Ouzouni Beach 63200 Halkidiki.
Tel 0373 42100/4, Fax 0373 42105.
English spoken.
OPEN: 01/05–30/09. SIZE: 1.7 ha, 170 pitches
(all with elec), 16 hot showers (charge), 16 WCs,
1 CWP. ✆ ⚓

≋ ⚓ 🏍 Ⓡ ▣ 🍺 🍴 ⚡ 🏠

Water sports, cooking facilities.
PRICES: (1996) Caravan with family 7350,
Tent with two adults 5200. CC: none.
Between the villages of Moudania and Potidea.

MYCENAE   24C

Camping Mykines 21200 Mycenae.
Tel 0751 76121, Fax 0751 76247. English spoken.
OPEN: all year. SIZE: 10 pitches (all with elec,
18 statics), 8 hot showers, 8 WCs, 8 French WCs,
1 CWP. ✆

🏍 Ⓡ ▣ 🍺 🍴 ⚡ ⚠ ▯

PRICES: (1996) Caravan with family 5100, Tent with
two adults 3320. CC: none.
*Mycenae is north of Argos and well signposted.
Campsite is just 100 m from the centre of the
village on the right.*

NAFPLION   24B

Camping Bekas Beach 21059 Palea Epidavros.
Tel 0753 41524/41714, Fax 0753 41394.
English spoken.
OPEN: 01/03–30/10. SIZE: 3.1 ha, 350 pitches
(150 with elec), 60 hot showers, 48 WCs,
20 French WCs, 2 CWPs. ⚓

≋ ⚓ 🏍 Ⓡ ▣ 🍺 🍴 ⚡ 🏠

PRICES: (1996) Caravan with family 5200, Tent with
two adults 3300. CC: Euro/Access.
*From Nafplion go east towards coast and Palea
Epidavros. Campsite is on the beach.*

Camping Sunset Tolon, 21056 Nafplion.
Tel 0752 59566, Fax 0752 59195. English spoken.
OPEN: 01/04–31/10. SIZE: 80 pitches (70 with elec,

Greece (side tab)

150 statics), 20 hot showers, 23 WCs, 4 CWPs.

≋ ☂ 🏕 R 🔥 ☕ 🍴 ✕ | (H)

PRICES: Caravan with family 5000, Tent with two adults 3500. CC: Euro/Access, Visa.
From Nafplion head towards Tolon. Turn right immediately after Asine and then right again at the intersection and continue for about 800 m. Campsite is on the right, just as you enter Tolon.

Poseidon Iria, Nafplion, 21100 Argolida.
Tel 0752 94341. English spoken.
OPEN: 01/04–30/10. SIZE: 200 pitches (100 with elec), 12 hot showers, 14 WCs, 1 CWP. ☎

≋ ☂ 🏕 R 🔥 ☕ 🍴 ✕

10% discount for stays of 7 days plus.
PRICES: (1996) Caravan with family 5900, Tent with two adults 3700. CC: none.
Go to the village of Drepano, which is 12 km from Navplion and follow signs from there.

NAVPAKTOS 24A

Camping Platanitis Beach 30300 Navpaktos.
Tel 0634 32555/31200, Fax 0634 31075.
English spoken.
OPEN: 15/05–30/09. SIZE: 3 ha, 105 pitches (all with elec), 20 hot showers, 20 WCs, 18 CWPs. ☂

≋ ☂ 🏕 R | ☕ 🍴 ✕ | (H)

Restaurant at 0.1 km.
PRICES: (1996) Caravan with family 5800, Tent with two adults 3300. CC: Euro/Access, Visa.
Navpaktos is on the E65 coastal road. The campsite is 5 km from Navpaktos near the beach.

NAXOS

AGIA ANNA 24C

Camping Maragas Agia Anna, 84300 Naxos.
Tel 0285 24552, Fax 0285 24552. English spoken.
OPEN: 01/05–15/10. SIZE: 2.5 ha, 100 pitches (60 with elec, 600 statics), 40 hot showers, 14 WCs, 30 French WCs. ☎ ☂

≋ ☂ 🏕 R | ☕ 🍴 ✕ | ⚠

PRICES: Caravan with family 4800, Tent with two adults 2600. CC: Euro/Access, Visa.
One of the Cyclades islands which can be reached by ferry from Pireaus, coming from the north, or from Kriti coming from the south. Campsite is well signposted in Agia Anna.

END OF NAXOS RESORTS

NEOS MARMARAS 24A

Camping Areti 63081 Neos Marmaras, Chalkidiki.
Tel 0375 71573/71430, Fax 0375 71573.
English spoken.

OPEN: 01/05–15/10. SIZE: 20 ha, 60 pitches (130 with elec, 130 statics), 26 hot showers, 24 WCs, 1 CWP. ☎ ☂

≋ ☂ ⛲ R 🔥 ☕ 🍴 ✕ | (H)

Tennis, water sports, ball games; discounts in LS.
PRICES: (1996) Caravan with family 6600, Tent with two adults 4400. CC: Euro/Access, Visa.
Site is 12 km east of Neos Marmaras.

Camping Kastello 63081 Neos Marmaras, Chalkidiki.
Tel 375 71095, Fax 375 72003. English spoken.
OPEN: 25/05–10/09. SIZE: 196 pitches (all with elec), 24 hot showers, 24 WCs, 1 CWP. ☎ ☂

≋ ☂ 🏕 R 🔥 ☕ 🍴 ✕

PRICES: (1996) Caravan with family 6700, Tent with two adults 4200. CC: Visa.
Campsite is 3.5 km from Neos Marmaras.

Camping Marmara 63081 Neos Marmaras, Chalkidiki.
Tel 0375 710901. English spoken.
OPEN: 01/05–10/10. SIZE: 3 ha, 150 pitches (all with elec), 30 hot showers, 30 WCs. ☎

≋ ☂ 🏕 R 🔥 ☕ 🍴 ✕ | ⚠

Private beach.
PRICES: (1996) Caravan with family 6000, Tent with two adults 3800. CC: none.
On the western coastal road in the Sithonia region. At the crossroads in Neos Marmaras turn right for campsite. Signposted.

Camping Sithon 63078 Metamorfosi, Chalkidiki.
Tel 0375 22414, Fax 0375 61384. English spoken.
OPEN: 01/05–30/09. SIZE: 5 ha, 120 pitches (all with elec), 40 hot showers, 35 WCs, 10 French WCs, 1 CWP. ☎

≋ ☂ 🏕 R | ☕ 🍴 ✕ | (H)

Water sports.
PRICES: Caravan with family 5000, Tent with two adults 3400. CC: Visa.
Metamorfosi is north of Neos Marmaras. Follow the signs to Vatopedi, turn right and the campsite is about 3 km.

OLYMPIA 24C

Camping Diana 27065 Olympia.
Tel 0624 22314, Fax 0624 22425. English spoken.
OPEN: all year. SIZE: 0.5 ha, 50 pitches (all with elec, 150 statics), 10 hot showers, 12 WCs, 3 French WCs, 2 CWPs. ☎

～ ✈ 🏕 R | ☕ 🍴 ✕ ↷

PRICES: (1996) Caravan with family 6200, Tent with two adults 3900. CC: none.
Coming from Pyrgos, turn right in the centre of Olympia and the campsite is 200 m ahead and well signposted.

Greece (side tab)

PALIOURI 24A

Camping Xenia Paliouri 63085 Paliouri, Chalkidiki.
Tel 0374 92206, Fax 0374 92254. English spoken.
OPEN: 01/05–30/09. SIZE: 50 pitches (200 with elec, 20 statics), 18 hot showers, 40 WCs. ℓ

Shop at 2 km. Restaurant at 0.5 km.
PRICES: (1996) Caravan with family 6962,
Tent with two adults 5200. CC: none.
South east of Kassandra.

PATRAI (PATRAS) 24C

Camping Rion Pan-Paraskevopoulos, 26500 Rion-Patras.
Tel 0619 91585. English spoken.
OPEN: all year. SIZE: 4.8 ha, 44 pitches (25 with elec), 9 hot showers, 9 WCs. ℓ

Shop at 0.7 km.
PRICES: (1996) Caravan with family 6600,
Tent with two adults 4100. CC: none.
From Patras, go north on coast road for 8 km to Rion, then follow signs to campsite.

Kato Alissos Camping Kato Alissos, 25002 Patras.
Tel 0693 71249, Fax 0693 71150. English spoken.
OPEN: 01/04–15/10. SIZE: 1.2 ha, 60 pitches (all with elec), 13 hot showers, 16 WCs, 1 CWP. ℓ

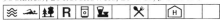

PRICES: (1996) Caravan with family 4216, Tent with two adults 2632. CC: Amex, Euro/Access, Visa.
21 km west of Patras and 500 m from the old national road, Patras-Olympia. Campsite is well signposted, on the beach, and a landmark is the huge, ancient olive tree growing in taverna garden.

PILOS 24C

Camping Navarino Beach
Gialova, Messinias, 24001 Pilos.
Tel 0723 22761, Fax 0723 23512. English spoken.
OPEN: all year. SIZE: 110 pitches (all with elec, 90 statics), 20 hot showers, 20 WCs, 3 CWPs. ℓ

PRICES: (1996) Caravan with family 6300,
Tent with two adults 4100. CC: none.
Just north of Pilos on the main Pilos-Kyparissia road.

RODOS (RHODES)

FALIRAKI 24D

Faliraki Camping Kalithies, 85105 Faliraki.
Tel 0241 85358. English spoken.

OPEN: 01/05–10/10. SIZE: 2 ha, 25 pitches (125 with elec, 125 statics), 22 hot showers, 22 WCs, 22 French WCs. ℓ

Cars and motorbikes for hire.
PRICES: (1996) Caravan with family 5850,
Tent with two adults 2750. CC: none.
The campsite is 2 km from Faliraki centre, and 16 km from the town of Rodos.

END OF RODOS (RHODES) RESORTS

SERIFOS

SERIFOS 24C

Camping Korali 84005 Serifos.
Tel 281 51500, Fax 281 51073. English spoken.
OPEN: 01/05–15/10. SIZE: 2.5 ha, 10 pitches, 12 hot showers, 15 WCs, 1 CWP. ℓ �

A mini-bus takes campers from the port to the campsite.
PRICES: (1996) Caravan with family 7450, Tent with two adults 3600. CC: Amex, Euro/Access, Visa.
One of the Cyclades islands, Serifos is served by ferry from Piraeus on the mainland and from the island of Kriti.

END OF SERIFOS RESORTS

SKALA 24C

Camping Lykourgos Lakonia, 23055 Glykovrissi.
Tel 0735 91580/91581, Fax 0735 91582. English spoken.
OPEN: all year. SIZE: 4 ha, 233 pitches (all with elec), 36 hot showers, 52 WCs, 2 CWPs. ℓ

PRICES: (1996) Caravan with family 6100, Tent with two adults 3900. CC: none.
From Skala, take Monemvasia to Blaxhioti road, then road to Glykovrissi. The campsite is 3.5 km outside the village, near the sea and on road to Elea.

SOFIKON 24C

Camping Biarritz Almiri Corinthias, 20100 Korinthos.
Tel 0741 33441. English spoken.
OPEN: all year. SIZE: 1 ha, 40 pitches (30 with elec), 8 hot showers, 12 WCs.

PRICES: (1996) Caravan with family 4700, Tent with two adults 2900. CC: none.
Just north towards coast to Kato Almiri.

Greece

SPARTI (SPARTA) 24C

Camping Castle View Mistras, 23100 Sparti.
Tel 0731 83303, Fax 0731 20028. English spoken.
OPEN: 01/04–20/10. SIZE: 1 ha, 100 pitches
(40 with elec), 30 hot showers, 30 WCs, 2 CWPs.

PRICES: (1996) Caravan with family 5900, Tent with
two adults 3600. CC: none.
5 km from Sparti, heading west on the main road.

Camping Mistras Paleologio Mistras, 23100 Sparti.
Tel 0731 22724, Fax 0731 25256. English spoken.
OPEN: all year. SIZE: 80 pitches (40 with elec),
16 hot showers, 22 WCs.

PRICES: (1996) Caravan with family 4100, Tent with
two adults 3100. CC: none.
*The campsite is located between Sparti and
Mistras, 2.5 km from Sparti.*

STILIS 24A

Interstation Camping 35300 Stylida.
Tel 0238 23827. English spoken.
OPEN: all year. SIZE: 140 pitches (all with elec),
24 hot showers, 24 WCs.

PRICES: (1996) Caravan with family 4600, Tent with
two adults 3000. CC: Euro/Access.
*Between Athens and Thessaloniki on the coast,
3 km from Stilis.*

THASOS

THASOS 24A

Camping Daedalos 64004 Sotiras, Thasos.
Tel 0593 71365. English spoken.
OPEN: 25/05–30/09. SIZE: 30 ha, 100 pitches
(all with elec, 200 statics), 26 hot showers,
26 WCs, 26 French WCs, 10 CWPs.

Right on the beach; water sports, disco, children's
playground.
PRICES: (1996) Caravan with family 4800,
Tent with two adults 3450. CC: none.
Sotiras is on the west coast of the island.

END OF THASOS RESORTS

THESSALONIKI (THESSALONICA) 24A

Camping EOT Akti Thermaikou
54007 Agia Triada.
Tel 0392 51352, Fax 0392 51265. English spoken.
OPEN: all year. SIZE: 12 ha, 5 pitches (220 with elec,
220 statics), 60 hot showers, 60 WCs, 60 French
WCs.

PRICES: (1996) Caravan with family 6796, Tent with
two adults 4483. CC: none.
*On the way to the airport, about 12 km from
Thessaloniki.*

VARKIZA 24C

Varkiza Beach 16672 Varkiza.
Tel 0897 3614, Fax 0897 0012. English spoken.
OPEN: 01/05–30/09. SIZE: 3.5 ha, 150 pitches
(all with elec, 20 statics), 25 hot showers, 24 WCs,
2 CWPs.

Shop at 1 km. Volley ball.
PRICES: (1996) Caravan with family 7050,
Tent with two adults 4100. CC: none.
*27 km from Athina, on the coastal road to Cape
Sounion, by the sea.*

VOLOS 24A

Camping Marina Kato Gatzea, 38500 Volos.
Tel 0423 22167/22277. English spoken.
OPEN: 01/05–10/10. SIZE: 4 ha, 70 pitches (all with
elec, 50 statics), 14 hot showers, 24 WCs, 1 CWP.

PRICES: (1996) Caravan with family 4700, Tent with
two adults 3000. CC: none.
*From Volos, take the coast road towards Agria
and Kato Gatzea.*

Sikia-Fig Tree Kato Gatzea, 38500 Volos.
Tel 0423 22279, Fax 0423 22720. English spoken.
OPEN: 15/03–31/10. SIZE: 3 ha, 200 pitches
(all with elec, 22 statics), 30 hot showers, 30 WCs,
1 CWP.

PRICES: (1996) Caravan with family 4450, Tent with
two adults 2600. CC: none.
*Head south-east from Volos towards Tsangarada.
Go through Kato Gatzea and site is just beyond.*

VOURVOUROU 24A

Camping Lacara Akti Koutloumoussi,
63088 Vourvourou, Chalkidiki.
Tel 0375 91444, Fax 0375 91456. English spoken.
OPEN: 01/05–30/09. SIZE: 8 ha, 250 pitches
(all with elec), 43 hot showers, 40 WCs, 5 French
WCs, 1 CWP.

PRICES: (1996) Caravan with family 7301, Tent with
two adults 4136. CC: Visa.
*On the east side of Sithonia, 18 km from Nikitas
towards Sarti.*

Greece

HUNGARY

Budapest, the capital of Hungary, is known as the 'Pearl of the Danube' and lies astride the river, with Buda rising to the west, overlooking Pest sprawled out below on the opposite bank. For a first impression, go to Castle Hill in Buda and look out from the decorative Fisherman's Bastion across the Danube to the bustling streets of Pest. Visit the richly decorated Mátyás church, the Royal Palace and the Gellért Turkish Baths, all in Buda; and, having crossed the river, see the neo-Gothic parliament building and the Opera House.

To the west lies Lake Balaton, the largest area of fresh water in Central Europe – for a comprehensive view, go to Csúcs Hill on the Tihany peninsula, which became Hungary's first National Park in 1952. From here, a car ferry crosses the lake, to take visitors south to delightful Pécs, lying beneath the vine-covered slopes of the Mecsek Hills.

To try Hungary's most famous wines, you need to visit the hilly region south of the Slovakian border, where the principal wine-producing towns are Eger and Tokaj. Eger, which is also famous for its mosqueless minaret, produces Egri Bikavér, the strong red wine which we know as Bull's Blood.

Finally, there is the great plain to the south with the Hortobágy National Park at its centre. This is described as a living heritage museum and is Hungary's answer to the Wild West. It is at its liveliest during the International Horse Show in July and during the Bridge Fair in August.

Emergency numbers

Police 007, Fire Brigade 005, and Ambulance 004.

If phoning from Budapest, drop one of the 0s

Warning information

Warning triangle must be carried

Blood alcohol legal limit 0 mg

BAJA   23C

Sugovica Camping Petofi Sziget, 6500 Baja.
Tel 79 321 755, Fax 79 323 155. English spoken.
OPEN: 01/05–30/09. SIZE: 3 ha, 200 pitches
(181 with elec), 16 hot showers, 16 WCs, 1 CWP.

Shop at 0.5 km.
PRICES: (1996) Caravan with family 1200,
Tent with two adults 800. CC: Amex, Visa.
The campsite is on a small island, just 500 m from the town centre.

BALATONAKARATTYA   23C

FKK-Camping Piroska Aligai 15,
8172 Balatonakarattya.
Tel 88 381 084, Fax 88 426 874. English spoken.
OPEN: 11/05–08/09. SIZE: 3.5 ha, 200 pitches
(all with elec, 182 statics), 16 hot showers,
25 WCs, 2 CWPs.

Restaurant at 1 km. Naturist site.
PRICES: (1996) Caravan with family 33.00,
Tent with two adults 21.30. CC: none.
On the E71, on the north-east bank of Lake Balaton. (Prices in DM.)

BALATONALMADI   23C

Kristof-Camping 8220 Balatonalmadi.
Tel 88 338902, Fax 88 426874.
English spoken.
OPEN: 04/04–13/10. SIZE: 1 ha, 33 pitches (all with
elec, 33 statics), 6 hot showers, 6 WCs, 1 CWP.

Shop at 0.5 km. Restaurant at 0.5 km. Tennis;
500 m to nearest beach.
PRICES: (1996) Caravan with family 33.90. CC: none.
North tip of Lake Balaton on E71. (Prices in DM.)

Yacht-Camping Jozsef Attila u 16,
8220 Balatonalmadi.
Tel 88 338506, Fax 88 426874.
English spoken.
OPEN: 21/05–15/09. SIZE: 3.5 ha, 250 pitches
(all with elec, 132 statics), 12 hot showers,
20 WCs, 2 CWPs.

Shop at 0.4 km. Restaurant at 0.3 km.
PRICES: (1996) Caravan with family 35.50,
Tent with two adults 20.20. CC: none.
Just off E71 on edge of Lake Balaton, across the railway line. (Prices in DM.)

Hungary

BALATONFÜRED 23C

Camping Füred 8230 Balatonfüred.
Tel 86 343823, Fax 86 342341. English spoken.
OPEN: 01/04–13/10. SIZE: 24 ha, 1000 pitches
(all with elec, 1172 statics), 108 hot showers,
216 WCs, 5 CWPs. ☎ &

≈ ⚓ 🏕 R 🍴 🐟 ☕ ✕ | ℍ 🎯

Sailing, water-skiing, windsurfing, tennis,
mini-golf, private beach.
PRICES: (1996) Caravan with family 33.50.
CC: Amex, Visa.
*Well signposted from E71, just west of town on
edge of Lake Balaton. (Prices in DM.)*

Diana Camping Aszofo, Veszprem,
Balatontourist, 8241 Aszofo.
Tel 87 445013, Fax 87 445013. English spoken.
OPEN: 26/04–28/09. SIZE: 8 ha, 150 pitches (all with
elec, 10 statics), 16 hot showers, 65 WCs, 1 CWP. ☎

≈ ⚓ 🏕 R 🍴 🐟 | ✕ | | |

PRICES: Caravan with family 14.00, Tent with two
adults 7.90. CC: none.
*Drive south-west along lake road to Aszofo.
Campsite is just north of town and well
signposted. Prices in DM.*

BALATONKENESE 23C

Balaton Camping Badacsonyors
8257 Badacsonyors.
Tel 87 471253, Fax 87 471253. English spoken.
OPEN: 25/05–01/09. SIZE: 6 ha, 300 pitches (all with
elec, 180 statics), 16 hot showers, 31 WCs, 1 CWP. ☎

≈ ⚓ 🍴 R 🍴 🐟 ☕ ✕

Windsurfing.
PRICES: (1996) Caravan with family 25.00,
Tent with two adults 14.60. CC: none.
Next to Lake Balaton, off E71. (Prices in DM.)

BALATONSZEPEZD 23C

Venus Camping 8252 Balatonszepezd.
Tel 87 468048, Fax 87 468048. English spoken.
OPEN: 18/05–04/09. SIZE: 2.8 ha, 240 pitches
(all with elec, 138 statics), 16 hot showers,
24 WCs, 2 CWPs. &

≈ ⚓ 🏕 R 🍴 🐟 ☕ | | 🎯

Restaurant at 1 km. Table tennis, fishing.
PRICES: (1996) Caravan with family 30.00,
Tent with two adults 17.40. CC: none.
*Next to Lake Balaton, own beach on the north
bank. Main road E71. (Prices in DM).*

BUDAPEST 23A

Camping Hars-Hegy Hars-Hegy ut 7,
1021 Budapest.
Tel 1 200 8803, Fax 1 176 1921. English spoken.

OPEN: 01/04–20/10. SIZE: 3 ha, 100 pitches
(all with elec), 34 hot showers, 48 WCs, 1 CWP. ☎

🏕 R 🍴 🐟 ☕ ✕ | ℍ

PRICES: Caravan with family 3000, Tent with two
adults 2500. CC: Amex, Visa.
*From Budapest centre or from highway M1/M7
via Budakeszi.*

Camping Romai Furdo Szentendrei 189,
1031 Budapest.
Tel 11 686 260, Fax 12 500 426. English spoken.
OPEN: all year. SIZE: 6 ha, 100 pitches (500 with
elec, 50 statics), 80 hot showers, 72 WCs,
4 CWPs. ☎

~ ⚓ 🏕 R 🍴 🐟 ☕ ✕ ⚓ ℍ

PRICES: (1996) Caravan with family 3500, Tent with
two adults 2800. CC: none.
*On banks of Danube, 10 km north of the centre,
campsite on the right.*
SEE ADVERTISEMENT

Camping Urom Urom, 2096 Budapest.
Tel 26 350 300.
OPEN: 15/03–15/10. SIZE: 1 ha, 70 pitches (50 with
elec), 9 hot showers, 9 WCs.

🍴 R 🍴 🐟 ☕ | | ℍ

Restaurant at 1 km.
PRICES: unavailable. CC: none.
Campsite is to the north of Budapest.

Hungary

Fortuna Camping 2045 Torokbalint.
Tel 23 335 364, Fax 23 339 697. English spoken.
OPEN: all year. SIZE: 2.5 ha, 120 pitches (all with
elec), 20 hot showers, 20 WCs, 1 CWP.

PRICES: Caravan with family 29.00, Tent with two
adults 20.00. CC: none.
*14 km south-west of Budapest on the M7 towards
Baladon. (Prices in DM.)*

Gobe Kemping Farkashegy, 2092 Budakeszi.
Tel 60 344 600, Fax 23 450 694.
English spoken.
OPEN: 15/05–01/10. SIZE: 1 ha, 50 pitches (16 with
elec), 14 hot showers, 13 WCs. ℃

Shop at 2 km. Restaurant at 2 km. Children's pool;
panoramic pleasure flights.
PRICES: (1996) Caravan with family 1790,
Tent with two adults 1230. CC: none.
*Motorway M1/M7, exit Torokbalint-Budakeszi,
towards Budakeszi (4 km).*

Tunderhegyi/Feeberg Camping 1121 Budapest.
Tel 60 336 256, Fax 13 222 836.
English spoken.
OPEN: all year. SIZE: 1 ha, 15 pitches (all with elec,
32 statics), 6 hot showers, 7 WCs, 1 CWP. ℃

Shop at 0.5 km. Restaurant at 0.5 km.
PRICES: (1996) Caravan with family 2400,
Tent with two adults 1760. CC: none.
*From M1/M7 autoroute go to Moszkva Square,
take Szilagyi E street and then follow signs to
campsite.*

Zugligeti Niche Camping
Zugligeti u 101, 1121 Budapest.
Tel 1 200 83 46, Fax 1 200 83 46.
English spoken.
OPEN: 01/03–30/11. SIZE: 2 ha, 100 pitches
(all with elec), 18 hot showers, 22 WCs,
2 CWPs. &

Shop at 0.5 km.
PRICES: (1996) Caravan with family 3900,
Tent with two adults 2100. CC: none.
*From M1/M7 junction drive direct through the
north-west of the city via Moszkva Square. Follow
signposts with squirrel logo to campsite.*

Zugligeti "Niche"
in Budapest
Nearest campsite to city centre

DEBRECEN 23B

Dorkas Center & Camping Vekeri To,
Erdospuszta, 4002 Debrecen.
Tel 52 441 119, Fax 52 441 119. English spoken.
OPEN: 01/05–30/09. SIZE: 7 ha, 50 pitches (all with
elec, 1 static), 36 hot showers, 40 WCs, 3 CWPs. ℃

Horse-riding, goulash parties.
PRICES: (1996) Caravan with family 2200, Tent with
two adults 1200. CC: Euro/Access, Visa.
*Follow road 47 and then follow signposts to
campsite.*

Kerekstelepi Strand Camping
Szavay Gyula Str, 4030 Debrecen.
Tel 52 321299.
OPEN: 15/01–01/09. SIZE: 4.5 ha, 8 hot showers,
16 WCs. ℃

Shop at 1 km. Spa nearby.
PRICES: Caravan with family 2100,
Tent with two adults 1150. CC: none.
2 km from Debrecen Airport (now unused).

DÖMÖS 23A

Dömös-Camping Dunapart, 2027 Dömös.
Tel 33 371 163, Fax 33 314 800. English spoken.
OPEN: 01/05–15/09. SIZE: 3 ha, 80 pitches (all with
elec), 18 hot showers, 18 French WCs, 1 CWP. ℃ &

Shop at 0.3 km. Restaurant at 0.3 km.
PRICES: (1996) Caravan with family 2410,
Tent with two adults 1625. CC: none.
*Turn off towards the Danube at Km 48.8 on route
11 (Budapest to Esztergom). Site approx 200 m.*

EGER 23B

Autos Camping Rakoczi ut 79, 3300 Eger.
Tel 36 410 558, Fax 36 411 768. English spoken.
OPEN: 15/04–15/10. SIZE: 16 ha, 350 pitches
(200 with elec, 222 statics), 30 hot showers,
65 WCs, 65 French WCs. ℃ &

Tennis, bowling, wine bar, cooking facilities.
PRICES: (1996) Caravan with family 1820, Tent with
two adults 1080. CC: Amex, Euro/Access, Visa.
*E71 (M3) then turn left on to road
no 25 to Eger. Campsite is in the north of Eger,
behind the Shell petrol station.*

ERD 23A

Blue Flamingo Camping Furdo Str 4, 2030 Erd.
Tel 23 375 328.
OPEN: all year. SIZE: 1 ha, 100 pitches (70 with
elec), 6 hot showers, 14 WCs.

Hungary

≈ ✈ 🏕 R ⬚ | ☕ ✕ 🔥 Ⓗ

Shop at 0.1 km.
PRICES: (1996) Caravan with family 1551,
Tent with two adults 990. CC: none.
*17 km from Budapest on M7/70 towards Balaton.
Well signposted.*

KAPUVAR 23A

Hansag Camping 9330 Kapuvár.
Tel 962 41524.
OPEN: 01/05–15/09. SIZE: 1 ha, 100 pitches
(all with elec), 12 hot showers, 12 WCs, 1 CWP.

⚲ R ⬚ | | | ⚠

Shop at 0.3 km. Restaurant at 0.1 km. Thermal
baths and swimming pool nearby.
PRICES: (1996) Caravan with family 25.00,
Tent with two adults 13.00. CC: none.
*From Sopron, east on road no 85 (40 km). Follow
signs to campsite which is to the east side of the
town. (Prices in DM.)*

KESZTHELY 23C

Caravan Camping Madach u 43,
8315 Gyenesdias.
Tel 83 316 020, Fax 83 316 382. English spoken.
OPEN: 01/04–31/10. SIZE: 2 ha, 150 pitches
(120 with elec), 10 hot showers, 16 WCs, 1 CWP. ☎

≈ ✈ ⟨ᴴ⟩ R ⬚ 🍴 ☕ ✕ 🔥 Ⓔ

Shop at 0.1 km. Restaurant at 0.1 km.
PRICES: (1996) Caravan with family 2500,
Tent with two adults 1800. CC: none.
On the western tip of Lake Balaton.

Naturistacamping 8649 Balatonbereny.
Tel 85 377 715. English spoken.
OPEN: 15/05–15/09. SIZE: 6 ha, 250 pitches
(120 with elec), 20 hot showers, 18 WCs, 2 CWPs.

≈ ⟨ᴴ⟩ R ⬚ 🍴 ☕ ✕

Shop at 0.05 km.
PRICES: (1996) Caravan with family 35.10, Tent
with two adults 23.70. CC: Euro/Access.
*From Keszthely, 12 km on B71 to Balatonbereny.
(Prices in DM.)*
*(a) RESORT:*Kiskunmajsa 23D

Jonathermal Motel-Camping
6120 Kiskunmajsa.
Tel 77 381855, Fax 77 381013. English spoken.
OPEN: all year. SIZE: 5 ha, 120 pitches (100 with
elec, 50 statics), 8 hot showers, 12 WCs,
5 CWPs. ♿

≈ ⟨ᴴ⟩ R ⬚ 🍴 ☕ ✕ ⊗ Ⓗ

Thermal baths, fishing; riding nearby.
PRICES: (1996) Caravan with family 1200,
Tent with two adults 600. CC: Amex, Visa.
*Kiskunmajsa is approx 26 km south-west of
Kiskunfelegyhaza. Well signposted.*

KISTELEK 23D

Vandormarasztalo Tanya 570, 6760 Kistelek.
Tel 03 30 436 351. English spoken.
OPEN: 15/04–31/10. SIZE: 1 ha, 360 pitches
(60 with elec), 6 hot showers, 8 WCs, 6 French
WCs, 2 CWPs. ♿

🏕 R 🍴 ☕ | Ⓗ

Restaurant at 3 km.
PRICES: (1996) Caravan with family 1380,
Tent with two adults 750. CC: none.
*On the right side of the road E75 from Budapest to
Szeged. 4 km before Kistelek.*

KOTCSE 23C

Stop-Camping Kultelekh, 8627 Kotcse.
Tel 84 367 552. English spoken.
OPEN: 01/05–15/09. SIZE: 3 ha, 50 pitches (all with
elec), 6 hot showers, 8 WCs, 1 CWP. ♿

≈ ⟨ᴴ⟩ ⚲ | ⬚ 🍴 ☕ ✕ 🔥 Ⓗ

Shop at 1 km. Restaurant at 0.3 km. Horse-riding.
PRICES: (1996) Caravan with family 1900, Tent with
two adults 1400. CC: Euro/Access, Visa.
About 9 km from Balatonszarszo. Signposted.

PALOZNAK 23C

Camping Nyarfa 8229 Paloznak.
Tel 86 446806, Fax 86 446806.
English spoken.
OPEN: 11/05–08/09. SIZE: 5 ha, 500 pitches
(330 with elec), 28 hot showers, 30 WCs, 2 CWPs.

≈ ⟨ᴴ⟩ 🏕 R ⬚ ⊛ ☕ ✕

Lakeside swimming, watersports, tennis, beach-
volley.
PRICES: (1996) Caravan with family 33.50,
Tent with two adults 20.60. CC: none.
*Near Balatonfüred on north-east bank of Lake
Balaton. Access is via E71 at Km 31.7.
(Prices in DM.)*

PANNONHALMA 23A

Panorama Camping 9090 Pannonhalma.
Tel 96 471 240.
OPEN: 01/04–31/10. SIZE: 1.2 ha, 70 pitches
(all with elec), 10 hot showers, 12 WCs. ☎

≈ ⟨ᴴ⟩ R ⬚ 🍴 ☕ ✕ 🔥 Ⓗ

1000-year-old abbey close by.
PRICES: Caravan with family 1690,
Tent with two adults 1190. CC: none.
*20 km south of Györ, road no 82. Turn left at
Pannonhalma and follow signs to campsite.*

PECS 23C

Orfu Camping Dollar ut 1, 7677 Orfu.
Tel 72 378 501, Fax 72 378 434. English spoken.

OPEN: 15/05–15/10. SIZE: 20 ha, 500 pitches (400 with elec, 120 statics), 27 hot showers, 42 WCs. &

Thermal baths, sporting facilities.
PRICES: (1996) Caravan with family 3200, Tent with two adults 2200. CC: Amex, Euro/Access, Visa.
16 km north of Pecs.

SIOFOK   23C

Strand Camping Szent Laszlo utca, 8600 Siófok.
Tel 84 353 700, Fax 3222 836. English spoken.
OPEN: 20/05–30/09. SIZE: 3 ha, 250 pitches (100 with elec), 17 hot showers, 19 WCs, 1 CWP.

Separate naturist area.
PRICES: (1996) Caravan with family 2400, Tent with two adults 1400. CC: none.
Siofok is on the south bank of Lake Balaton. Well signposted.

SOPRON   23A

Ozon Camping Erdi Malom Koz 3, 9400 Sopron.
Tel 99 331 144, Fax 99 331 145.
OPEN: 15/04–15/10. SIZE: 1 ha, 60 pitches (all with elec), 14 hot showers, 14 WCs, 1 CWP.

Shop at 0.4 km. Sauna.
PRICES: Caravan with family 33.00,
Tent with two adults 21.00. CC: none.
4 km from Sopron towards Brennberg. (Prices in DM.)

Termal Camping Nyarta 14, 9437 Hegyko.
Tel 99 376818.
OPEN: 01/05–30/09. SIZE: 1 ha, 100 pitches (40 with elec), 6 hot showers, 5 WCs, 1 CWP.

Shop at 0.2 km. Swimming pool 50 m.
PRICES: (1996) Caravan with family 1800,
Tent with two adults 950. CC: Visa.
From Sopron take road 85 towards Györ; after about 20 km turn left (north) to Hegyko.

TISZAFÜRED   23B

Termal Kemping 5350 Tiszafüred 2.
Tel 593 52911, Fax 593 51228. English spoken.
OPEN: 01/04–31/10. SIZE: 5.2 ha, 200 pitches (all with elec, 116 statics), 8 hot showers, 24 WCs, 1 CWP.

Shop at 0.5 km. Restaurant at 0.2 km. Water sports, fishing, tennis.
PRICES: (1996) Caravan with family 1730, Tent with two adults 1070. CC: Amex, Euro/Access, Visa.
East of Budapest on the bank of Tisza river.

VELENCE   23A

Panorama Kemping 2481 Velence, Budapest.
Tel 22 472 043, Fax 22 472 964. English spoken.
OPEN: 15/04–15/10. SIZE: 9 ha, 580 pitches (all with elec), 56 hot showers, 56 WCs, 4 CWPs.

PRICES: (1996) Caravan with family 24.00, Tent with two adults 19.60. CC: Euro/Access.
Leave motorway M7/E71 (Budapest to Balaton) at Km 44.5, at an AFOR garage. Site 2 km towards lake. (Prices in DM.)

Hungary

ITALY

Italy is a land of contrasts, not the least of which is the affluence of the north and the poverty of the south, but other strong cultural, as well as geographic, distinctions exist between its twenty regions – Italy did not achieve unified nation status until 1861.

From Piemonte region in the Alps to Calabria region in the south, the country can be loosely divided into three areas: the north with the Alps and the wonderful Italian lakes nestling at their southern edge; second, the valley of the River Po, whose broad plain cuts right across the country from west to east and embraces most of Italy's industrial heartland; third the long, boot-shaped part of the country – Tuscany, Umbria, Lazio, Marche, Abruzzi, Molisse, Puglia and Basilicata – with the Apennines running down the centre of the 'leg' and Calabria forming the toe of the boot.

It need hardly be said that the great magnets are Rome, Florence and Venice. But these can be crowded, hot and tiring in summer, and are much more enjoyable to visit out of season. Getting to know Italy on a motoring holiday is a delightful experience, from the rugged terrain and fierce independence of Abruzzi facing the Adriatic due east of Rome, to the mountains of the Dolomites; from Roman Pompeii to Renaissance Florence, from the smart streets of Milan to the quiet attraction of a small village in the Apennines. The Italian people combine with the Italian countryside to make this one of Europe's most vivacious holiday destinations.

Emergency numbers

Police 113, Fire Brigade 115, and Ambulance 118

Warning information

Warning triangle must be carried

Green Card recommended

Blood alcohol legal limit 80 mg

ACCIAROLI   21B

Camping Ondina 84041 Acciaroli.
Tel 0974 904040. English spoken.
OPEN: 01/04–31/10. SIZE: 100 pitches (all with elec, 10 statics), 7 hot showers, 21 WCs. ✆

Restaurant at 2 km.
PRICES: (1996) Caravan with family 63,500, Tent with two adults 64,000. CC: Euro/Access.

ALBENGA   20C

Camping Delfino Albenga.
Tel 0182 55085, Fax 0182 51998. English spoken.
OPEN: 01/04–30/09. SIZE: 120 pitches (all with elec), 10 hot showers (charge), 24 WCs, 4 CWPs. ✆ &

PRICES: (1996) Caravan with family 58,000, Tent with two adults 38,000. CC: none.
From Albenga follow Alassio/Imperia signs and campsite is second left after the tunnel.

Camping Lungomare Albenga, Savona.
Tel 0182 51449, Fax 0182 58525. English spoken.
OPEN: all year. SIZE: 1.4 ha, 120 pitches (all with elec, 50 statics), 25 hot showers, 33 WCs. ✆

Shop at 0.5 km.
PRICES: (1996) Caravan with family 60,000, Tent with two adults 48,000. CC: none.
On the south side of the river, 300 m from railway and 500 m from main road.

ALBINIA   21A

Camping Hawaii via Aurelia Km 154,5, 58010 Orbetello.
Tel 0564 870164. English spoken.
OPEN: 01/05–30/09. SIZE: 4 ha, 12 hot showers (charge), 40 WCs, 8 CWPs. ✆

Table tennis, games room.
PRICES: (1996) Caravan with family 45,000, Tent with two adults 32,000. CC: Euro/Access.
Campsite is 4 km from village.

ALLEGHE   20A

Camping Alleghe Masare, 32022 Alleghe.
Tel 0437 723737. English spoken.
OPEN: 01/12–30/04 & 15/06–30/09. SIZE: 2 ha, 120 pitches (all with elec, 70 statics), 26 hot showers (charge), 26 WCs, 1 CWP. ✆

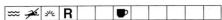

Shop at 0.5 km. Restaurant at 0.1 km.
PRICES: (1996) Caravan with family 46,000,
Tent with two adults 23,000. CC: none.

ANGERA 20A

Camping Citta di Angera via Bruschera 99,
21021 Angera.
Tel 0331 930736, Fax 0331 960367.
English spoken.
OPEN: 01/02–31/12. SIZE: 8 ha, 540 pitches
(all with elec, 490 statics), 45 hot showers,
84 WCs, 42 French WCs, 8 CWPs. ℭ

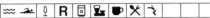

PRICES: (1996) Caravan with family 61,000, Tent
with two adults 39,000. CC: Euro/Access, Visa.
From Angera, 3 km to campsite.

AOSTA 20C

Camping Arvier 11010 Aosta.
Tel 0165 99088. English spoken.
OPEN: 20/06–31/08. SIZE: 10 ha, 84 pitches
(all with elec), 14 hot showers (charge), 18 WCs,
1 CWP. ℭ

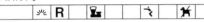

Restaurant at 0.1 km.
PRICES: (1996) Caravan with family 36,800,
Tent with two adults 25,000. CC: Visa.
Signposted in the town.

Camping Val di Rhêmes 11010 Aosta.
Tel 0165 907648.
OPEN: 01/06–10/09. SIZE: 120 pitches (all with
elec), 8 hot showers, 15 WCs, 2 CWPs. ℭ

Restaurant at 4 km.
PRICES: (1996) Caravan with family 36,000,
Tent with two adults 22,200. CC: none.
*From Aosta, take the road to Villeneuve then
south to Rhêmes-St-George. Follow signs.*

Camping Ville d'Aoste via Grand S Bernard 37,
11100 Aosta.
Tel 0165 361360. English spoken.
OPEN: 01/06–30/09. SIZE: 10 ha, 50 pitches
(all with elec), 4 hot showers, 8 WCs, 2 French
WCs, 1 CWP. ℭ

Restaurant at 1 km.
PRICES: (1996) Caravan with family 36,000,
Tent with two adults 21,500. CC: none.
On the road to Gran San Bernardo.

ARCIDOSSO 21A

Camping Lucherino 58047 Monticello Amiata.
Tel 0564 992975. English spoken.

OPEN: 15/06–15/09. SIZE: 2 ha, 53 pitches (all with
elec, 10 statics), 8 hot showers, 10 WCs, 4 French
WCs. ℭ

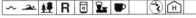

Shop at 0.2 km. Tennis, children's playground.
PRICES: (1996) Caravan with family 45,000,
Tent with two adults 24,000. CC: none.
*From Siena take S223 towards Grosseto. Take
Monte Amiata exit at Paganico, keep going, turn
right to Monticello Amiaco and campsite is 5
minutes' drive ahead.*

ARCO 20B

Campeggio Arco Arco.
Tel 0464 517491, Fax 0464 517491.
English spoken.
OPEN: 01/03–30/11. SIZE: 4 ha, 192 pitches
(all with elec, 20 statics), 25 hot showers, 36 WCs,
4 CWPs. ℭ &

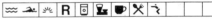

Restaurant at 0.8 km. Tennis, volley ball.
PRICES: (1996) Caravan with family 47,000,
Tent with two adults 32,000. CC: none.
Well signposted from Arco.

ARONA 20A

Camping Lago Azzurro via E Fermi 2,
28040 Dormelletto.
Tel 0322 497197, Fax 0322 497197.
English spoken.
OPEN: all year. SIZE: 2.5 ha, 210 pitches (46 with
elec, 105 statics), 18 hot showers (charge),
34 WCs, 3 CWPs. ℭ &

PRICES: (1996) Caravan with family 36,000,
Tent with two adults 24,500. CC: Euro/Access.
*Turn off S33 to Dormelletto just before reaching
Arona. Site is well signposted.*

Camping Lago Maggiore via L da Vinci 7,
28040 Dormelletto.
Tel 0322 497193, Fax 0322 497193.
English spoken.
OPEN: 01/04–30/09. SIZE: 5 ha, 280 pitches
(all with elec), 34 hot showers (charge), 54 WCs,
5 CWPs. ℭ

PRICES: (1996) Caravan with family 50,000,
Tent with two adults 32,000. CC: none.
*North of Milan on the S33 to Lake Maggiore. Turn
towards the site at Dormelletto just before Arona.*

ASIAGO 20C

Camping Ekar-Asiago Localita Ekar,
36012 Asiago.
Tel 0424 455157, Fax 0424 455457. English spoken.

Italy

OPEN: 01/06–30/09 & 15/11–14/04. SIZE: 3.5 ha, 282 pitches (all with elec, 150 statics), 23 hot showers, 28 WCs, 28 French WCs, 2 CWPs. ⚓

PRICES: (1996) Caravan with family 40,000, Tent with two adults 31,000. CC: none.
From Trento on S349.

ASSISI 20C

Campeggio Fontemaggio via Eremo delle Carceri 9, 06081 Assisi.
Tel 075 813636, Fax 075 813749. English spoken.
OPEN: all year. SIZE: 10 ha, 30 hot showers, 40 WCs, 3 CWPs. ⚓ &

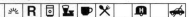

PRICES: (1996) Caravan with family 30,000, Tent with two adults 23,000. CC: none.

Camping Internazionale Assisi via S Giovanni/Campiggione 110, 06081 Assisi.
Tel 0758 16816, Fax 0758 12335. English spoken.
OPEN: 28/03–31/10. SIZE: 3 ha, 200 pitches (all with elec, 11 statics), 31 hot showers, 41 WCs, 7 French WCs, 2 CWPs. ⚓ &

PRICES: (1996) Caravan with family 40,000, Tent with two adults 26,000. CC: Amex, Euro/Access, Visa.
From Assisi, on S147 for 2 km.

BAIA DOMIZIA 21B

Camping Baia Domizia 81030 Baia Domizia.
Tel 0823 930164, Fax 0823 930375.
English spoken.
OPEN: 01/05–30/09. SIZE: 30 ha, 1200 pitches (all with elec, 200 statics), 174 hot showers, 157 WCs, 25 French WCs, 6 CWPs. &

PRICES: (1996) Caravan with family 73,000, Tent with two adults 47,800. CC: none.
North of Naples on coast road S07. Turn off at Km 6 and go 3 km towards sea where campsite is signposted.

BARDOLINO 20B

Camping Cisano 37010 Cisano di Bardolino.
Tel 045 622 9098, Fax 045 622 9059. English spoken.
OPEN: 15/03–30/09. SIZE: 14 ha, 800 pitches (all with elec), 80 hot showers, 77 WCs, 43 French WCs, 1 CWP. ⚓ &

PRICES: (1996) Caravan with family 56,000, Tent with two adults 38,000. CC: none.
Leave motorway at Affi/Lago di Garda Sud exit and follow signs for Bardolino. Campsite is signposted.

Camping Europa via S Cristina, 37011 Bardolino.
Tel 0457 211089, Fax 0457 210073. English spoken.
OPEN: 01/04–30/09. SIZE: 1 ha, 109 pitches (20 statics), 16 hot showers, 16 WCs, 1 CWP. ⚓ &

PRICES: (1996) Caravan with family 40,000, Tent with two adults 31,000. CC: none.
From Brescia, on S11 east.

Camping San Vito via Prelesi, 37010 Cisano di Bardolino.
Tel 045 6229026, Fax 045 7210049. English spoken.
OPEN: 15/03–30/09. SIZE: 6 ha, 200 pitches (all with elec), 15 hot showers, 36 WCs. ⚓ &

PRICES: (1996) Caravan with family 56,000, Tent with two adults 38,000. CC: none.
Motorway exit Affi/Lago di Garda Sud, towards Bardolino. Follow signs to campsite.

La Rocca Camp Loc. San Pietro, 37011 Bardolino.
Tel 045 7211111, Fax 045 7211300. English spoken.
OPEN: 01/05–30/09. SIZE: 8 ha, 531 pitches (all with elec, 21 statics), 57 hot showers, 84 WCs, 4 CWPs. ⚓

PRICES: (1996) Caravan with family 52,000, Tent with two adults 35,000. CC: none.

BATTIPAGLIA 21B

Camping Lido Mediterraneo via Litoranea SP 175, 84091 Battipaglia.
Tel 0828 624097, Fax 0828 624097. English spoken.
OPEN: 15/04–30/09. SIZE: 1 ha, 80 pitches (all with elec, 12 statics), 12 hot showers (charge), 28 WCs, 16 French WCs, 2 CWPs. ⚓ &

Restaurant at 0.2 km. Private beach.
PRICES: (1996) Caravan with family 65,000, Tent with two adults 40,000. CC: none.
From Battipaglia, take the road directly to the coast at Spineto Nuova. Turn left (south) along coast road 175.

BAVENO 20A

Campeggio Diverio via Gramsci 31, 28042 Baveno, Lago Maggiore.
Tel 0323 923593, Fax 0323 923593.
English spoken.
OPEN: 15/03–31/10. SIZE: 4 ha, 42 pitches (all with elec, 10 statics), 4 hot showers (charge), 15 WCs, 10 French WCs, 2 CWPs. ⚓ &

PRICES: Caravan with family 31,000, Tent with two adults 21,000. CC: Euro/Access, Visa.
In the middle of Baveno town near the church, turn right after the bridge.

Italy

Camping Parisi via Piave 50, 28042 Baveno, Lago Maggiore.
Tel 0323 923156. English spoken.
OPEN: 01/04–30/09. SIZE: 6 ha, 66 pitches (all with elec), 8 hot showers, 12 WCs, 6 French WCs, 2 CWPs.

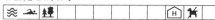

PRICES: (1996) Caravan with family 46,000,
Tent with two adults 30,000. CC: Euro/Access.
From Milano take S33 or A26. Arriving in Baveno take via Garibaldi or Piave and follow signs to campsite.

BELLARIA 20C

Camping Green via A Vespucci 8, San Mauro Mare, 47030 Forli.
Tel 0541 346929, Fax 0541 346929. English spoken.
OPEN: 01/04–30/11. SIZE: 12 ha, 120 pitches (96 with elec), 30 hot showers, 30 WCs, 30 French WCs, 2 CWPs.

Shop at 0.1 km. Restaurant at 0.1 km.
PRICES: (1996) Caravan with family 42,500,
Tent with two adults 26,000. CC: none.
From Bellaria, north on coast road.

Delle Rose via Adriatica 29, 47043 Gatteo al Mare.
Tel 0547 86213, Fax 0547 87583. English spoken.
OPEN: 01/05–30/09. SIZE: 5 ha, 400 pitches (350 with elec, 25 statics), 26 hot showers, 72 WCs, 14 French WCs, 4 CWPs. & &

Mini-golf.
PRICES: (1996) Caravan with family 57,200,
Tent with two adults 35,200. CC: none.
From Bellaria, take coast road towards Cesenatico.

BELLUNO 20C

Camping al Lago via Campagna 14, 32030 Arsie.
Tel 0439 58471, Fax 0439 58471. English spoken.
OPEN: 01/04–30/10. SIZE: 1 ha, 50 pitches (all with elec, 20 statics), 6 hot showers, 14 WCs.

PRICES: (1996) Caravan with family 33,500, Tent with two adults 22,500. CC: Euro/Access, Visa.
From Belluno, go west on the S50 for about 50 km. Arsie is on the right, before the junction with the S47 and the tunnel.

BERCETO 20C

Camping I Pianelli via Nazionale 109, 43042 Berceto.
Tel 0525 64521. English spoken.
OPEN: all year. SIZE: 12 ha, 180 pitches (all with elec, 120 statics), 28 hot showers, 30 WCs, 2 CWPs.

Shop at 1 km.
PRICES: Caravan with family 48,000,
Tent with two adults 28,000. CC: none.
Leave the A15 (Parma to La Spezia) at Berceto exit, site is then 6 km via steep gravel road.

BOGLIASCO 20C

Genova Est via Marconi, Localita Cassa, 16031 Bogliasco.
Tel 0103 472053, Fax 0103 472053. English spoken.
OPEN: 01/02–30/11. SIZE: 12 ha, 20 pitches (all with elec, 4 statics), 10 hot showers (charge), 14 WCs, 8 French WCs, 2 CWPs.

PRICES: (1996) Caravan with family 46,000, Tent with two adults 27,000. CC: Euro/Access, Visa.
From Genova, 8 km east on S1.

BOLSENA 21A

Lido Camping Village 01023 Bolsena.
Tel 0761 799258, Fax 0761 799258. English spoken.
OPEN: 08/04–30/09. SIZE: 10 ha, 600 pitches (all with elec, 50 statics), 75 hot showers (charge), 75 WCs, 6 CWPs.

Sailing, windsurfing, tennis, bowling.
PRICES: Caravan with family 60,500,
Tent with two adults 34,500. CC: none.
Situated on lakeside on the outskirts of Bolsena. Well signposted.

BOLZANO 20A

Moosbauer via S Maurizio 83, 39100 Bolzano.
Tel 0471 918492, Fax 0471 204894. English spoken.
OPEN: all year. SIZE: 1 ha, 80 pitches (all with elec), 10 hot showers, 15 WCs, 11 French WCs, 1 CWP. & &

PRICES: (1996) Caravan with family 52,000, Tent with two adults 36,000. CC: Euro/Access, Visa.
Take Bolzano Sud exit from motorway and go for approx 5 km towards Merano.

BRACCIANO 21A

Camping Roma Flash Sporting 00062 Bracciano.
Tel 0902 3669, Fax 0902 2270. English spoken.
OPEN: 01/04–30/09. SIZE: 6 ha, 200 pitches (all with elec, 40 statics), 10 hot showers (charge), 30 WCs, 7 French WCs, 1 CWP. & &

Shop at 3 km. Restaurant at 2 km. 10% discount with RAC guide book.
PRICES: (1996) Caravan with family 40,500, Tent with two adults 22,000. CC: none.
Follow signs to site.

Italy

BRESCIA 20C

Camping Fornella via Fornella 1,
25010 San Felice del Benaco.
Tel 0365 62294/62200, Fax 0365 559418.
English spoken.
OPEN: 01/05–20/09. SIZE: 7 ha, 305 pitches
(all with elec, 5 statics), 42 hot showers, 63 WCs,
3 French WCs, 7 CWPs. ✆ ♿

Tennis, children's playground.
PRICES: (1996) Caravan with family 56,000,
Tent with two adults 38,000. CC: none.
From Brescia to Desenzano on S11, exit on to
S572 towards Salo. Turn right towards San Felice
del Benaco, straight over at crossroads, go for
2 km and take next right.

Camping La Rocca
via Cavalle 22, 25080 Manerba.
Tel 0365 551738, Fax 0365 552045. English spoken.
OPEN: 01/04–30/09. SIZE: 5 ha, 200 pitches
(all with elec, 40 statics), 31 hot showers, 40 WCs,
20 French WCs, 4 CWPs. ✆ ♿

Restaurant at 0.3 km.
PRICES: (1996) Caravan with family 51,500,
Tent with two adults 35,000. CC: none.
From Brescia on A4, exit Desenzano-Salo, follow
S572 to campsite.

Camping Venus via Trento 90, 25074 Idro.
Tel 0365 83190, Fax 0365 83190. English spoken.
OPEN: 31/03–30/09. SIZE: 2 ha, 120 pitches (all with
elec, 25 statics), 10 hot showers, 20 WCs, 3 CWPs. ✆

Watersports; lovely location.
PRICES: (1996) Caravan with family 41,500,
Tent with two adults 28,500. CC: none.
From Brescia, take main road S237 to
Caffaro, Km 44.

Camping Zocco via del Zocco, Localita Zocco,
25080 Manerba del Garda.
Tel 0365 551605, Fax 0365 552053. English spoken.
OPEN: 10/04–27/09. SIZE: 5 ha, 240 pitches (all with
elec, 30 statics), 27 hot showers, 48 WCs, 5 CWPs. ✆ ♿

Restaurant at 1 km. Tennis, table tennis, boating.
PRICES: (1996) Caravan with family 47,700, Tent
with two adults 33,100. CC: Euro/Access, Visa.
From Brescia on S11 east, exit S572, take road
from Desenzano to Salo. (Minimum stay 7 days
LS, 14 days HS if reservation made in advance.)

BRINDISI 21B

Pineta al Mare Lido Specchiolla,
72012 Specchiolla di Carovigno.
Tel 0831 987821, Fax 0831 987826. English spoken.

OPEN: 01/03–30/10. SIZE: 6 ha, 220 pitches
(all with elec, 100 statics), 27 hot showers,
33 WCs, 2 CWPs. ✆ ♿

Last campsite before Greece!
PRICES: (1996) Caravan with family 59,000, Tent
with two adults 37,000. CC: Amex, Euro/Access, Visa.
From Brindisi, take S379 north towards Bari,
leave S379 at exit for Specchiolla.

BRUNICO 20A

Camping Corones Rasen, 39030 Brunico.
Tel 0474 496490, Fax 0474 498250. English spoken.
OPEN: all year. SIZE: 2.5 ha, 125 pitches (all with
elec), 18 hot showers, 14 WCs, 2 CWPs. ✆

Tennis, sauna, solarium, heated pool.
PRICES: unavailable. CC: none.
Rasen is just east of Brunico.

Camping Gisser St Sigmundo, via Vel Pusterie
26, 39030 Kiens.
Tel 0474 569605, Fax 0474 569657. English spoken.
OPEN: 10/05–10/10. SIZE: 2 ha, 130 pitches
(all with elec), 8 hot showers, 20 WCs, 1 CWP. ✆

PRICES: (1996) Caravan with family 38,500,
Tent with two adults 25,500. CC: none.
On the S49, 17 km east of A22 exit heading
towards Brunico. Site is well signposted.

BUSSOLENO 20C

Camping Pro Bussoleno
via del Campeggio, 10053 Bussoleno.
English spoken.
OPEN: 01/06–30/09. SIZE: 7 ha, 50 pitches (all with
elec, 20 statics), 4 hot showers, 10 WCs, 2 French
WCs, 1 CWP. ✆ ♿

Shop at 0.1 km. Restaurant at 0.1 km.
PRICES: Caravan with family 25,000,
Tent with two adults 16,000. CC: none.
Due west of Turin to Susa, signed to Bussoleno.

CALCERANICA 20C

Al Pescatore via Pescatore, 38000 Calceranica.
Tel 0461 723062, Fax 0461 724212.
English spoken.
OPEN: 01/06–15/09. SIZE: 3.8 ha, 250 pitches
(all with elec, 40 statics), 20 hot showers, 30 WCs,
20 French WCs, 6 CWPs. ✆ ♿

Shop at 1 km.
PRICES: (1996) Caravan with family 44,000.
CC: none.

Camping Belvedere via Venezia 6, Lago di Caldonazzo, 38050 Calceranica al Lago. Tel 0461 723239, Fax 0461 723239. English spoken. OPEN: 01/05–30/09. SIZE: 1 ha, 69 pitches (all with elec), 6 hot showers (charge), 12 WCs, 2 CWPs. ℂ

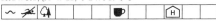

Restaurant at 0.05 km.
PRICES: (1996) Caravan with family 41,200, Tent with two adults 27,200. CC: Euro/Access.

CANAZEI   20A

Campeggio Catinaccio Rosengarten via Avisio 15, 38036 Pozza di Fassa. Tel 0462 763305, Fax 0462 763501. English spoken. OPEN: 01/06–30/09 & 01/11–30/04. SIZE: 2.5 ha, 208 pitches (all with elec, 45 statics), 20 hot showers, 35 WCs, 4 CWPs. ℂ &

Shop at 0.02 km. Restaurant at 0.02 km. Entertainment; skiing and sports centre nearby. PRICES: (1996) Caravan with family 60,000, Tent with two adults 38,000. CC: Euro/Access, Visa. *From SS48 (Cavalese to Predazzo), turn off in Pozza. Site on right.*

Camping Vidor via Valle San Nicolo, 38036 Pozza di Fassa. Tel 0462 763247, Fax 0462 764780. English spoken. OPEN: 01/06–31/12. SIZE: 2 ha, 92 pitches (all with elec, 30 statics), 8 hot showers, 14 WCs, 2 CWPs. ℂ

PRICES: (1996) Caravan with family 43,000, Tent with two adults 27,000. CC: Euro/Access, Visa. *South of Canazei towards Bolzano on S48. In the centre of Pozza, turn left over the bridge and drive for 2 km.*

CANNOBIO   20A

Camping Campagna 28052 Cannobio. Tel 0323 70100, Fax 0323 72398. English spoken. OPEN: 15/03–15/10. SIZE: 1 ha, 100 pitches (all with elec), 16 hot showers, 20 WCs, 15 French WCs, 2 CWPs. ℂ &

Water sports.
PRICES: (1996) Caravan with family 50,000, Tent with two adults 34,000. CC: none. *Campsite is 3 km from the Swiss border and 10 km from Ascona-Locarno.*

Camping International Paradis 28052 Cannobio. Tel 0323 71227, Fax 0323 72591. English spoken. OPEN: 01/04–31/10. SIZE: 1.2 ha, 114 pitches (all with elec), 13 hot showers, 23 WCs, 3 CWPs. ℂ &

Restaurant at 0.1 km.

PRICES: (1996) Caravan with family 55,500, Tent with two adults 43,500. CC: none. *Cannobio is south of Locarno on the S34 and about 4 km from the Swiss border. Campsite is well signposted.*

Camping Riviera via Darbedo, 28052 Cannobio. Tel 0323 71360, Fax 0323 71360. English spoken. OPEN: 15/03–19/10. SIZE: 3.5 ha, 280 pitches (230 with elec, 28 statics), 35 hot showers, 40 WCs, 8 CWPs. ℂ &

Water sports.
PRICES: (1996) Caravan with family 53,500, Tent with two adults 34,000. CC: none. *South of Locarno on S34.*

Valle Romantica via Valle Cannobina, 28052 Cannobio. Tel 0323 71249, Fax 0323 71360. English spoken. OPEN: 15/03–30/09. SIZE: 5 ha, 150 pitches (all with elec, 8 statics), 16 hot showers, 26 French WCs, 4 CWPs. ℂ

PRICES: (1996) Caravan with family 57,500, Tent with two adults 40,000. CC: none. *From Locarno south on S34.*

CAORLE   20D

Camping Pra delle Torri via Altanea, Porto S Margherita, 30020 Caorle. Tel 0421 299063. English spoken. OPEN: 30/04–25/09. SIZE: 53 ha, 834 pitches (all with elec, 2 statics), 108 hot showers, 160 WCs, 12 CWPs.

PRICES: (1996) Caravan with family 45,000, Tent with two adults 35,000. CC: Euro/Access, Visa. *From Caorle, 6 km to campsite.*

CASSINO   21B

Camping Terme Varroniane 03043 Cassino, Frosinone. Tel 0776 22144/22339. English spoken. OPEN: all year. SIZE: 3 ha, 200 pitches (100 with elec), 5 hot showers (charge), 28 WCs. &

Shop at 0.5 km. Restaurant at 0.5 km. PRICES: (1996) Caravan with family 34,500, Tent with two adults 23,500. CC: none. *Leave motorway at Cassino Centre exit and campsite is 3 km.*

CASTAGNETO CARDUCCI   20C

Le Pianacce via Bolgherese, 57022 Castagneto Carducci. Tel 0565 763667, Fax 0565 763667. English spoken.

OPEN: 01/03–31/10. SIZE: 8.5 ha, 120 pitches (all with elec), 38 hot showers, 29 WCs, 4 CWPs. ✆ &

Bungalows for hire; mini-club.
PRICES: (1996) Caravan with family 47,000,
Tent with two adults 33,000. CC: none.
Turn off the S1 at the Km 264 post, (Donoratico), and head for Castagneto Carducci and Sasseta. After 3 km turn left towards Bolgheri.

CASTEL DEL PIANO 21A

Camping Amiata via Roma 15,
Localita Montoto, 58033 Castel del Piano.
Tel 0564 955107, Fax 0564 955107. English spoken.
OPEN: all year. SIZE: 4.2 ha, 220 pitches (all with elec), 27 hot showers, 35 WCs, 4 French WCs, 2 CWPs. ✆ &

PRICES: (1996) Caravan with family 49,500,
Tent with two adults 29,400. CC: none.
On outskirts of Castel del Piano on S323, towards Arcidosso.

CASTELVECCHIO 21B

Camping Il Collaccio Frazione Castelvecchio, 06047 Castelvecchio do Preci.
Tel 0743 939005, Fax 0743 939094. English spoken.
OPEN: 01/04–15/10. SIZE: 10 ha, 100 pitches (all with elec, 10 statics), 29 hot showers, 38 WCs, 4 CWPs. ✆

Shop at 2 km.
PRICES: (1996) Caravan with family 37,000,
Tent with two adults 27,000. CC: Amex.
From the main road, S209 Valerina, follow the yellow signs to Preci and Castelvecchio.

CASTIGLIONE DEL LAGO 20C

Camping Badiaccia
Loc Badiaccia Borghetto, 06061 Borghetto.
Tel 075 9659097/98, Fax 075 9659019.
English spoken.
OPEN: 01/04–30/09. SIZE: 5 ha, 180 pitches (51 with elec, 20 statics), 38 hot showers, 40 WCs, 6 CWPs. ✆ &

Tennis, mini-golf, boating, cycling.
PRICES: Caravan with family 51,000, Tent with two adults 31,000. CC: Euro/Access, Visa.
From Perugia on S75 to Castiglione del Lago.

CASTIGLIONE DELLA PESCAIA 21A

Camping Maremma Sans Souci Localita Casamora, 58043 Castiglione della Pescaia.
Tel 0564 933765, Fax 0564 935759. English spoken.

OPEN: 01/04–30/10. SIZE: 10 ha, 400 pitches (all with elec), 62 hot showers (charge), 80 WCs, 3 CWPs. ✆ &

Shop at 2.5 km. 40% discount in LS.
PRICES: (1996) Caravan with family 66,000,
Tent with two adults 42,000. CC: none.
2.5 km north from Castiglione della Pescaia.

CASTIGLIONE DELLA PESCAIA 21A

Camping Santapomata Strada delle Rocchette, Castiglione della Pescaia.
Tel 0564 941037, Fax 0564 941221. English spoken.
OPEN: 01/04–20/10. SIZE: 5 ha, 344 pitches (all with elec, 42 statics), 36 hot showers, 44 WCs, 23 French WCs, 2 CWPs. ✆

PRICES: (1996) Caravan with family 66,000,
Tent with two adults 42,000. CC: none.
From Castiglione della Pescaia, north towards Roccette (5 km). Campsite is first on the left.

CASTIGLIONE DELLA PESCAIA 21A

Puntala Camping 58043 Castiglione della Pescaia.
Tel 0564 922294. English spoken.
OPEN: 01/04–30/10. SIZE: 27 ha, 680 pitches (all with elec), 150 hot showers, 250 French WCs, 10 CWPs. ✆ &

PRICES: (1996) Caravan with family 78,000,
Tent with two adults 44,000. CC: none.
Campsite is just to the north of Castiglione della Pescaia.

CATANZARO 21D

Camping Internazioale dello Ionio via Nazionale, Localita S Giorgio, 88060 Guardavalle.
Tel 0967 86002, Fax 0967 86271. English spoken.
OPEN: 01/06–10/09. SIZE: 5 ha, 300 pitches (all with elec, 30 statics), 24 hot showers, 40 WCs, 20 French WCs, 3 CWPs. ✆ &

PRICES: (1996) Caravan with family 41,200, Tent with two adults 26,200. CC: Amex, Euro/Access, Visa.
From Catanzaro, approx 40 km south on S106.

CAVALLINO 20C

Camping al Boschetto via delle Batterie 18, Ca'Savio, 30010 Treporti, Venezia.
Tel 0419 66145, Fax 0415 301191. English spoken.
OPEN: 15/05–30/09. SIZE: 7 ha, 330 pitches (all with elec, 70 statics), 42 hot showers, 48 WCs, 4 CWPs. ✆ &

Tennis.

PRICES: (1996) Caravan with family 46,000, Tent with two adults 30,000. CC: none.
From Cavallino south to Punta Sabbioni.

Camping Cavallino via delle Batterie 164, 30013 Cavallino, Venezia.
Tel 0413 966133, Fax 0415 300827. English spoken. OPEN: 01/05–30/09. SIZE: 8 ha, 450 pitches (all with elec, 60 statics), 58 hot showers, 68 WCs. ⟨ &

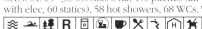

Shop at 2 km. Mini-golf, table tennis, playground, entertainment.
PRICES: (1996) Caravan with family 64,000, Tent with two adults 44,400. CC: Visa.
Campsite is well signposted.

Camping Europa 30013 Cavallino, Venezia.
Tel 0419 68069, Fax 0415 370150. English spoken. OPEN: 01/04–30/09. SIZE: 11 ha, 556 pitches (all with elec), 72 hot showers, 72 WCs, 36 French WCs, 3 CWPs.

PRICES: (1996) Caravan with family 51,800, Tent with two adults 35,800. CC: none.
Campsite is well signposted.

Camping Garden Paradiso via F Baracca 55, 30013 Cavallino, Venezia.
Tel 0419 68075, Fax 0415 370382. English spoken. OPEN: 01/05–30/09. SIZE: 13 ha, 835 pitches (all with elec, 69 statics), 107 hot showers, 116 WCs, 10 French WCs, 5 CWPs. ⟨ &

Tennis, mini-golf, windsurfing.
PRICES: (1996) Caravan with family 73,500, Tent with two adults 45,500. CC: Euro/Access, Visa.
Campite is well signposted.

Camping Italy via Fausta 272, 30013 Cavallino, Venezia.
Tel 0419 68090, Fax 0415 370355. English spoken. OPEN: 28/03–21/09. SIZE: 3.9 ha, 303 pitches (all with elec, 40 statics), 44 hot showers, 44 WCs, 2 CWPs. ⟨ &

Children's club, entertainment.
PRICES: (1996) Caravan with family 61,000, Tent with two adults 42,000. CC: Euro/Access, Visa.
From Cavallino, south towards Punta Sabbioni.

Camping Mediterraneo Ca'Savio, 30010 Treporti, Venezia.
Tel 0966 721/2, Fax 0966 944. English spoken. OPEN: 01/05–30/09. SIZE: 17 ha, 750 pitches (all with elec, 118 statics), 108 hot showers, 120 WCs, 150 French WCs, 5 CWPs. ⟨ &

Discounts in LS.
PRICES: (1996) Caravan with family 72,200, Tent with two adults 43,100. CC: Amex, Euro/Access, Visa.

From Cavallino, south to Punta Sabbioni.
Campsite is signposted.

Camping Scarpiland via Poerio 14, 30010 Treporti, Venezia.
Tel 0419 66488, Fax 0419 66488. English spoken. OPEN: 01/05–30/09. SIZE: 3 ha, 230 pitches (all with elec, 80 statics), 25 hot showers, 28 WCs, 11 French WCs, 1 CWP. ⟨

Flats and apartments also available.
PRICES: Caravan with family 55,000, Tent with two adults 37,400. CC: none.
From Cavallino go south to Punta Sabbioni.

Camping Silva via F Baracca 53, 30013 Cavallino, Venezia.
Tel 0419 68087, Fax 0419 68087. English spoken. OPEN: 15/05–15/09. SIZE: 3 ha, 276 pitches (all with elec), 36 hot showers, 38 WCs, 4 French WCs, 2 CWPs. ⟨

PRICES: (1996) Caravan with family 51,000, Tent with two adults 33,000. CC: none.
Campite is well signposted in Cavallino.

Camping Union Lido via Fausta 258, 30013 Cavallino, Venezia.
Tel 041 968080, Fax 041 5370355. English spoken. OPEN: 01/05–30/09. SIZE: 60 ha, 2270 pitches (all with elec, 150 statics), 322 hot showers, 418 WCs, 21 CWPs. ⟨ &

Excellent sports facilities; aqua park; hotel accommodation also available.
PRICES: (1996) Caravan with family 72,500, Tent with two adults 47,000. CC: Euro/Access, Visa.
2.5 km south of Cavallino.

Vela Blu Camping Village Via Radaelli 10, 30013 Cavallino, Venezia.
Tel 041 968068, Fax 041 5371003. English spoken. OPEN: 27/04–21/09. SIZE: 3.3 ha, 271 pitches (all with elec, 32 statics), 26 hot showers, 39 WCs, 2 CWPs. ⟨ &

TV room.
PRICES: (1997) Caravan with family 56,500, Tent with two adults 37,500. CC: none.
Campsite is well signposted in Cavallino.

Vela Blu Camping Village ★★
at Cavallino
Sit on the beach – watch Venice float past

Camping Villa al Mare via del Faro 12,
30013 Cavallino, Venezia.
Tel 0419 68066, Fax 0415 370576. English spoken.
OPEN: 30/04–25/09. SIZE: 2 ha, 176 pitches
(all with elec), 22 hot showers, 30 WCs, 6 French
WCs, 2 CWPs.

≋ ⚓ 🏕 R 🗑 🛒 💷 ✕ 🏠 🏃

Cycling, fishing.
PRICES: (1996) Caravan with family 58,000, Tent
with two adults 40,000. CC: Euro/Access, Visa.
*In Cavallino, turn right on bridge, go next left
and follow sign.*

CECINA 20C

Camping L'Esperidi via del Cavalleggeri Nord
25, Marina di Bibbona, 57020 Bibbona.
Tel 0586 600196, Fax 0586 681985.
English spoken.
OPEN: 09/04–30/09. SIZE: 10 ha, 500 pitches
(all with elec), 48 hot showers (charge), 98 WCs,
3 CWPs.

≋ ⚓ 🏕 🛒 💷 ✕ 🏃 🚗

PRICES: (1996) Caravan with family 63,000,
Tent with two adults 39,000. CC: none.
*South from Cecina to Marina di Bibbona. Turn
right at crossroads. Site last on left, on the beach.*

Camping Montescudaio via del Poppetto Km 2,
56040 Montescudaio.
Tel 0586 683477, Fax 0586 630932.
English spoken.
OPEN: 10/05–28/09. SIZE: 25 ha, 470 pitches
(all with elec, 170 statics), 94 hot showers,
94 WCs, 4 CWPs.

≋ 🏕 R 🗑 💷 ✕ 🏠 🏃

PRICES: (1996) Caravan with family 60,000,
Tent with two adults 41,000. CC: none.
*From new Livorno to Grosseto motorway, take
Cecina/Guardistallo/Montescudaio exit. Follow
signs to Guardistallo, ignoring signs to
Montescudaio. Campsite is on the Cecina to
Guardistallo road, 2 km from Cecina and well
signposted. http://www vol it camping
montescudaio or Email: mocamp @ /op multinet it.*

Camping Valla Gaia via Cecinese,
56040 Casale Marittimo.
Tel 0586 681236, Fax 0586 683551.
English spoken.
OPEN: 22/03–18/10. SIZE: 4 ha, 150 pitches
(all with elec), 45 hot showers, 42 WCs, 40 French
WCs, 4 CWPs.

🏕 R 🗑 🛒 💷 ✕ 🏠

Tennis, 2 pool complexes, entertainment,
excursions; sea 9 km; LS discounts.
PRICES: Caravan with family 60,700,
Tent with two adults 40,300. CC: none.
Following the autostrada/superstrada south from

*Livorno, take the second exit for Cecina/Casale
Marittimo. Immediately after exit, campsite is
signposted and is on road to Casale Marittimo.*

CERVIA 20C

Camping Adriatico via Pinarella 90,
48015 Cervia.
Tel 0544 71537, Fax 0544 988463. English spoken.
OPEN: 11/05–15/09. SIZE: 3 ha, 280 pitches
(all with elec, 80 statics), 24 hot showers, 23 WCs,
30 French WCs, 5 CWPs.

≋ ⚓ 🏕 R 🗑 🛒 💷 ✕ 🌐

5% discount for RAC members.
PRICES: (1996) Caravan with family 44,500, Tent
with two adults 29,500. CC: Amex, Euro/Access, Visa.
From Cervia, follow signs on S16, about 1 km.

Nuovo International Camping via Meldola 1,
48020 Lido di Savio.
Tel 0544 949014, Fax 0544 949085. English spoken.
OPEN: 04/05–10/09. SIZE: 5 ha, 469 pitches
(all with elec), 31 hot showers, 69 WCs, 59 French
WCs, 6 CWPs.

≋ ⚓ 🏕 🛒 💷 ✕ 🏃

PRICES: (1996) Caravan with family 45,500,
Tent with two adults 28,500. CC: Euro/Access.
From Lido di Savio, 100 m to campsite.

CHIOGGIA 20C

Atlanta via Barbarigo 302, 30019 Sottomarina.
Tel 041 4965333, Fax 041 4967198. English spoken.
OPEN: 15/05–15/09. SIZE: 4 ha, 250 pitches
(all with elec, 50 statics), 40 hot showers, 40 WCs,
40 French WCs, 2 CWPs.

≋ ⚓ 🏕 💷 🏃

Restaurant at 1 km.
PRICES: (1996) Caravan with family 55,000,
Tent with two adults 41,000. CC: none.
*From centre of Chioggia, 1 km to Little Venice,
and then 0.25 km to campsite.*

Camping Adriatico
Lungomare Adriatico, 30019 Sottomarina.
Tel 0414 92907, Fax 0414 92907. English spoken.
OPEN: 01/04–30/09. SIZE: 15 ha, 150 pitches
(all with elec, 40 statics), 32 hot showers, 28 WCs,
6 French WCs, 2 CWPs.

≋ ⚓ 🏕 R 🗑 🛒 💷 ✕ 🏃

PRICES: (1996) Caravan with family 51,000,
Tent with two adults 33,000. CC: none.
S309 from Padova or Venezia and Ravenna.

Camping La Margherita via Foci Adige 10,
Rosalina Mare, 45010 Rovigo.
Tel 0426 68212, Fax 0426 68212. English spoken.
OPEN: 01/05–30/09. SIZE: 6 ha, 270 pitches
(all with elec), 37 hot showers, 45 WCs,
4 CWPs.

PRICES: (1996) Caravan with family 58,500, Tent with two adults 35,000. CC: Euro/Access, Visa. *Rosalina Mare is south of Chioggia on the coast. Follow signs.*

Camping Oasi 30019 Chioggia Sottomarina.
Tel 041 490801, Fax 041 490801.
English spoken.
OPEN: 01/04–20/09. SIZE: 2.5 ha, 200 pitches
(all with elec, 12 statics), 50 hot showers, 30 WCs,
30 French WCs, 2 CWPs. &

Shop at 1 km. Football ground, tennis, basketball, volley ball, entertainment.
PRICES: (1996) Caravan with family 54,000,
Tent with two adults 35,000. CC: none.
On the via A Barbarigo. Well signposted in town.

Camping Rosapineta
45010 Rosolina Mare, Rovigo.
Tel 0426 68033, Fax 0426 68105.
English spoken.
OPEN: 10/05–21/09. SIZE: 40 ha, 750 pitches
(all with elec, 100 statics), 165 hot showers,
164 WCs, 4 CWPs. &

PRICES: (1996) Caravan with family 38,800,
Tent with two adults 26,500. CC: Visa.
Follow signs from Chioggia to Rosolina Mare and site is signposted.

Villaggio Turistico Isamar
Isola Verde, 30010 Chioggia.
Tel 0414 98100, Fax 0414 90440. English spoken.
OPEN: 09/05–27/09. SIZE: 30 ha, 750 pitches
(all with elec, 176 statics), 80 hot showers,
89 WCs, 3 CWPs. &

Shop at 1 km. Horse-riding, tennis, gym, archery, indoor driving range, disco.
PRICES: Caravan with family 89,000, Tent with two adults 41,000. CC: Euro/Access, Visa.
Isola Verde is on the coast, just south of Chioggia and campsite is signposted.

CIRO   21D

Camping Torrenova via Torrenova,
88072 Ciro Marina.
Tel 0962 31482. English spoken.
OPEN: 01/05–30/09. SIZE: 1 ha, 75 pitches (all with elec, 40 statics), 14 hot showers, 30 WCs, 8 French WCs, 3 CWPs. &

Shop at 1 km.
PRICES: (1996) Caravan with family 48,000,
Tent with two adults 36,000. CC: none.
South of Ciro Marina.

CITTA DI CASTELLO   20C

Camping la Montesca La Montesca,
06012 Citta di Castello.
Tel 075 8558566, Fax 075 8558566. English spoken.
OPEN: 01/04–30/09. SIZE: 4 ha, 100 pitches (all with elec, 55 statics), 10 hot showers, 15 WCs. &

Shop at 3 km.
PRICES: (1996) Caravan with family 36,500,
Tent with two adults 22,500. CC: none.
Campsite is 3 km from Citta di Castello at Collina.

COLICO   20A

Camping au Lac de Como
via C Battisti, 22010 Sorico, Lago Como.
Tel 0344 84035, Fax 0344 84802. English spoken.
OPEN: all year. SIZE: 2 ha, 120 pitches (all with elec), 9 hot showers, 20 WCs. &

Private beach; watersports; hunting, fishing & hang-gliding nearby.
PRICES: (1996) Caravan with family 49,000,
Tent with two adults 35,000. CC: none.
From Colico drive west around Lake Como towards Gravedona. In Sorico turn towards the lake at the Total garage.

COMACCHIO   20C

International Camping Mare e Pineta
via delle Acacie, 44024 Lido Degli Estensi.
Tel 0533 330110, Fax 0533 330052. English spoken.
OPEN: 24/04–22/09. SIZE: 16 ha, 1326 pitches
(all with elec, 30 statics), 213 hot showers,
284 WCs, 40 French WCs, 20 CWPs. &

Camp surfing school, canoeing, aerobics.
PRICES: Caravan with family 63,200, Tent with two adults 39,100. CC: Euro/Access, Visa.
From Ferrara on S225 to the coast.

International Camping Tre Moschettieri via Capanno di Garibaldi 22, 44020 Lido di Pomposa.
Tel 0533 380376, Fax 0533 380377. English spoken.
OPEN: 01/05–21/09. SIZE: 11 ha, 600 pitches
(all with elec, 100 statics), 110 hot showers,
130 WCs, 2 CWPs. &

PRICES: (1996) Caravan with family 48,000,
Tent with two adults 26,000. CC: none.
From Comacchio, 9 km north on S309.

Spina Camping via del Campeggio 99,
44024 Lido di Spina, Ferrara.
Tel 0533 330179, Fax 0533 333566. English spoken.
OPEN: 01/04–20/09. SIZE: 24 ha, 1000 pitches
(all with elec), 180 hot showers, 250 WCs,
10 CWPs. &

Italy

| ≈ | ⚓ | ⚐ | R | ⎁ | ⚑ | ⛾ | ✕ | ⟨ | ⟨H⟩ | | |

Tennis, basketball, volley ball; sauna, massage.
PRICES: (1996) Caravan with family 42,800,
Tent with two adults 27,900. CC: none.
From Ferrara, take motorway to coast, exit Lido Spina.

COMO   20A

International Camping via Cecilio, 22100 Como.
Tel 0315 21435, Fax 0315 21435. English spoken.
OPEN: 15/04–15/10. SIZE: 2 ha, 80 pitches (all with elec), 3 CWPs. ✆

| ≈ | ⚓ | ⚐ | R | ⎁ | ⚑ | ⛾ | ✕ | ⟨ | ⟨H⟩ | | |

PRICES: (1996) Caravan with family 24,700,
Tent with two adults 16,500. CC: none.
A9 Milano-Como-Chiasso, exit Como South.

CORIGLIANO CALABRO   21D

Camping Thurium 87064 Corigliano Calabro.
Tel 0983 851092/955, Fax 0981 953367.
English spoken.
OPEN: 01/06–15/09. SIZE: 16 ha, 600 pitches
(all with elec, 30 statics), 40 hot showers (charge), 95 WCs, 3 CWPs. ✆ ♿

| ≈ | ⚓ | ⚐ | R | ⎁ | ⚑ | ⛾ | ✕ | | ⟨H⟩ | | |

Separate campervan facilities. Discounts in July.
PRICES: (1996) Caravan with family 63,500,
Tent with two adults 40,500. CC: Amex, Visa.
From Corigliano on the S106 towards Rossano.

CORTINA D'AMPEZZO   20A

Camping Cortina via Campo 2, 32043 Cortina d'Ampezzo.
Tel 0436 867575, Fax 0436 867917. English spoken.
OPEN: all year. SIZE: 4 ha, 360 pitches (all with elec, 200 statics), 39 hot showers, 50 WCs, 2 CWPs. ✆ ♿

| ~ | ⚓ | ⚐ | | ⎁ | ⚑ | ⛾ | ✕ | ⟨ | | | |

PRICES: (1996) Caravan with family 41,000, Tent with two adults 31,000. CC: Amex, Euro/Access, Visa.
1.5 km from town centre near river.

Camping Palafavera Palafavera, 32010 Zoldo Alto.
Tel 0437 788506. English spoken.
OPEN: 01/12–30/04 & 01/06–20/09. SIZE: 5 ha, 200 pitches (all with elec, 80 statics), 18 hot showers, 22 WCs, 1 CWP. ✆ ♿

| ~ | ⚓ | ⚙ | R | | ⎁ | ⚑ | ✕ | | ✗ | | |

Shop at 2 km. Playground.
PRICES: (1996) Caravan with family 42,000,
Tent with two adults 21,000. CC: none.
35 km south of Cortina d'Ampezzo.

International Camping Olympia Fiammes, 32043 Cortina d'Ampezzo.
Tel 0436 5057, Fax 0436 5057. English spoken.
OPEN: all year. SIZE: 4 ha, 314 pitches (all with elec,

115 statics), 28 hot showers (charge), 44 WCs, 2 CWPs. ✆

| ~ | ⚓ | ⚐ | R | | ⎁ | ⚑ | ✕ | | ⟨H⟩ | | |

PRICES: (1996) Caravan with family 41,000,
Tent with two adults 31,000. CC: Euro/Access.
From Cortina, north on S51 for 4 km.

Internationl Camping Dolomiti
32043 Cortina D'Ampezzo.
Tel 0436 2485, Fax 0436 2485. English spoken.
OPEN: 15/05–20/09. SIZE: 5.4 ha, 390 pitches
(all with elec), 35 hot showers, 27 WCs, 8 French WCs, 1 CWP. ✆ ♿

| ~ | ⚓ | ⚙ | | | ⎁ | ⚑ | | ⟨ | | | |

Restaurant at 3 km.
PRICES: (1996) Caravan with family 69,000,
Tent with two adults 43,000. CC: none.
Campsite is signposted in the town.

CREMONA   20C

Camping Parco Al Po via Lungo Po Europa 12, 26100 Cremona.
Tel 0372 21268, Fax 0372 27137.
English spoken.
OPEN: 01/04–30/09. SIZE: 1 ha, 109 pitches
(36 statics), 8 hot showers (charge), 18 WCs. ✆ ♿

| ~ | ⚓ | ⚐ | R | ⎁ | | ⚑ | ✕ | | ⟨H⟩ | | |

Shop at 0.5 km.
PRICES: (1996) Caravan with family 36,500, Tent with two adults 21,500. CC: Euro/Access, Visa.
Recommended campsite.22/7/95

CUNEO   20C

Campeggio Turistico Communale Cuneo.
Tel 0171 491334.
OPEN: all year. SIZE: 3.7 ha, 200 pitches (all with elec, 100 statics), 16 hot showers, 33 WCs, 8 French WCs, 4 CWPs. ✆ ♿

| | | ⚙ | R | ⎁ | | ⚑ | | ⟨ | | | |

Restaurant at 0.5 km.
PRICES: (1996) Caravan with family 25,500,
Tent with two adults 17,500. CC: none.
Campsite is well signposted in Cuneo.

Camping Acti Lago Pontechianale, Cuneo.
Tel 011 5175321, Fax 011 5613118.
OPEN: 15/06–30/09. SIZE: 1.2 ha, 105 pitches
(all with elec), 8 hot showers, 18 WCs, 2 CWPs.

| ≈ | ⚓ | ⚐ | R | | | | | | | | |

Shop at 0.2 km. Restaurant at 0.2 km.
PRICES: (1996) Caravan with family 30,500,
Tent with two adults 19,000. CC: none.

Campo Base Fr Chiappera, 12021 Acceglio.
Tel 0171 99068.
OPEN: 01/05–30/10. SIZE: 1 ha, 27 pitches (all with elec), 6 hot showers (charge), 9 WCs, 1 CWP. ✆ ♿

PRICES: (1996) Caravan with family 28,800, Tent with two adults 14,400. CC: none.
From Cuneo, take S22 west to Acceglio.

DEIVA MARINA   20C

Camping Costabella Localita Ghiare,
19013 Deiva Marina.
Tel 0187 825343, Fax 0187 816433. English spoken.
OPEN: 01/04–15/10. SIZE: 2 ha, 100 pitches
(all with elec, 80 statics), 20 hot showers, 36 WCs,
10 French WCs. ☎ &

Shop at 1 km. Restaurant at 1 km.
PRICES: (1996) Caravan with family 56,500,
Tent with two adults 33,000. CC: none.

Villaggio Turistico Camping Arenella
19013 Deiva Marina.
Tel 0187 825259, Fax 0187 816861. English spoken.
OPEN: all year. SIZE: 16.9 ha, 120 pitches (all with
elec, 80 statics), 20 hot showers, 28 WCs,
2 CWPs. ☎ &

Sea 2.5 km.
PRICES: (1996) Caravan with family 55,500,
Tent with two adults 31,500. CC: none.
*Leave the motorway at Deiva Marina exit and
campsite is signposted.*

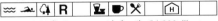

**Villaggio
Turistico**
at Deiva Marina
Ligurian Lido!

DESENZANO   20B

Camping La Ca via S Cassiano, 25080 Padenghe.
Tel 0309 907006, Fax 0309 907693. English spoken.
OPEN: all year. SIZE: 20 ha, 134 pitches (all with
elec), 29 hot showers, 35 WCs, 2 CWPs. ☎

PRICES: (1996) Caravan with family 54,200, Tent
with two adults 36,200. CC: none.
*Leave Lake Garda road (SS572) 1.5 km north of
Padenghe, turn sharply towards lake and
campsite is 150 m ahead on the left.*

DIANO MARINA   20C

Camping Edy via Diano Calderina,
18013 Diano Marina.
Tel 0183 497040, Fax 0183 498288. English spoken.
OPEN: all year. SIZE: 130 pitches (all with elec,

70 statics), 26 hot showers, 28 WCs, 4 CWPs. ☎

PRICES: (1996) Caravan with family 70,000, Tent
with two adults 42,000. CC: Amex, Euro/Access, Visa.
From Alassio, south on S1 or A10.

Camping Marino via S Novaro,
18013 Diano Marina.
Tel 0183 498288, Fax 0183 498288. English spoken.
OPEN: all year. SIZE: 124 pitches (all with elec,
60 statics), 24 hot showers, 28 WCs, 4 CWPs. ☎

PRICES: (1996) Caravan with family 70,000, Tent
with two adults 42,000. CC: Amex, Euro/Access, Visa.
From Alassio, south on S1 or A10.

Camping Ulivi via Costa Frazione Pairola,
18016 San Bartolomeo al Mare.
Tel 0183 400961. English spoken.
OPEN: 01/04–30/09. SIZE: 1 ha, 10 pitches (all with
elec, 45 statics), 2 hot showers (charge), 16 WCs. ☎

PRICES: (1996) Caravan with family 49,000,
Tent with two adults 26,000. CC: none.
*From Diano Marina take A10, exit at San
Bartolomeo al Mare, on to Pairola then 30 m to
site.*

DOMASO   20A

Camping Gardenia via case Sparse 138,
22013 Domaso.
Tel 0344 96262, Fax 0344 83381.
OPEN: 01/04–30/09. SIZE: 2 ha, 158 pitches
(all with elec), 10 hot showers (charge), 25 WCs,
2 CWPs. ☎

Restaurant at 0.01 km.
PRICES: (1996) Caravan with family 35,500,
Tent with two adults 22,100. CC: none.
On west bank of Lake Como.

EDOLO   20A

Adamello 25048 Edolo.
Tel 0364 71694.
OPEN: all year. SIZE: 12 ha, 60 pitches (all with elec,
10 statics), 10 hot showers, 10 WCs, 1 CWP. ☎

Restaurant at 1 km. Swimming pool 1 km.
PRICES: (1996) Caravan with family 40,100,
Tent with two adults 22,000. CC: none.
From Edolo, take the road up hill for 1 km.

Camping Villaggio Aprica via Nazionale 507,
25040 Corteno Golgi.
Tel 0342 710001, Fax 0342 710001. English spoken.
OPEN: all year. SIZE: 2.4 ha, 106 pitches (all with
elec, 60 statics), 12 hot showers, 21 WCs, 2 CWPs. ☎

Italy

Swimming pool 1 km.
PRICES: (1996) Caravan with family 49,000,
Tent with two adults 27,000. CC: none.
*West from Edolo on route 39 to Corteno Golgi and
campsite at Aprica.*

ELBA

CAPOLIVERI 21B

Camping le Calanchiole Localita Calanchiole,
57031 Capoliveri, Elba.
Tel 0565 933488, Fax 0565 940001. English spoken.
OPEN: 01/04–15/10. SIZE: 4 ha, 200 pitches
(all with elec, 10 statics), 47 hot showers, 60 WCs,
2 CWPs. ❤ ♿

PRICES: (1996) Caravan with family 83,300,
Tent with two adults 52,800. CC: none.
Between Portoferraio and Porto Azzurro.

PORTOFERRAIO 21A

Camping Acquaviva 57037 Portoferraio, Elba.
Tel 0565 930674, Fax 0565 915592. English spoken.
OPEN: 01/05–31/10. SIZE: 1.7 ha, 50 pitches
(all with elec, 5 statics). ❤

Restaurant at 1 km. Flats also available.
PRICES: Caravan with family 65,200, Tent with two
adults 39,000. CC: Euro/Access, Visa.
Campsite is 3 km from Portoferraio.

Camping Enfola Enfola,
57037 Portoferraio, Elba.
Tel 0565 939001, Fax 0565 918613.
English spoken.
OPEN: 01/04–30/09. SIZE: 1 ha, 27 pitches (all with
elec, 15 statics), 6 hot showers (charge), 16 WCs,
4 French WCs. ❤

Shop at 6 km.
PRICES: (1996) Caravan with family 74,000,
Tent with two adults 44,500. CC: Euro/Access.
From Portoferraio towards Enfola for 6.5 km.

Camping Tallinucci Localita Locano,
57037 Portoferraio, Elba.
Tel 0565 964069, Fax 0565 964333.
English spoken.
OPEN: 01/04–31/10. SIZE: 1 ha, 100 pitches
(all with elec), 24 hot showers, 25 WCs,
1 CWP. ❤ ♿

PRICES: (1996) Caravan with family 90,500,
Tent with two adults 52,000. CC: none.
On road between Portoferraio and Lacona.

RIO NELL 21A

Camping Sole e Mare Loc Nisporto,
57039 Nisporto, Elba.
Tel 0565 934907, Fax 0565 961180. English spoken.
OPEN: 01/04–10/10. SIZE: 1 ha, 100 pitches
(all with elec), 30 hot showers, 30 WCs, 15 French
WCs, 1 CWP. ❤

Entertainment.
PRICES: (1996) Caravan with family 68,000,
Tent with two adults 44,000. CC: none.
Between Portoferraio and Rio Marina.

END OF ELBA RESORTS

FANO 20D

Camping Gabbiano via Faa di Bruno 95,
61035 Marotta.
Tel 0721 96691, Fax 0721 96691. English spoken.
OPEN: 01/05–30/09. SIZE: 2 ha, 220 pitches
(51 with elec, 130 statics), 26 hot showers
(charge), 40 WCs. ❤ ♿

LS reduction for minimum stay of 3 days.
PRICES: (1996) Caravan with family 50,000,
Tent with two adults 36,000. CC: none.
From Pesaro on S16 south to Fano.

FERRARA 20C

Campeggio Estense via Gramicia, 44100 Ferrara.
Tel 0532 752396, Fax 0532 240555.
English spoken.
OPEN: 01/03–30/09. SIZE: 3.5 ha, 50 pitches
(all with elec), 8 hot showers, 8 WCs, 4 French
WCs, 1 CWP. ❤ ♿

Shop at 1 km. Restaurant at 1 km. Children under
8 free of charge.
PRICES: (1996) Caravan with family 30,000,
Tent with two adults 20,000. CC: Amex.

FIESOLE 20C

Camping Panoramico Fiésole via Peramonda
1, 50014 Firenze.
Tel 0555 99069, Fax 0555 9186.
English spoken.
OPEN: all year. SIZE: 5 ha, 200 pitches (all with
elec), 18 hot showers, 26 WCs, 1 CWP. ❤ ♿

Shop at 1.5 km. Motor bikes for hire.
PRICES: (1996) Caravan with family 55,000,
Tent with two adults 41,000. CC: Amex,
Euro/Access, Visa.
*Exit Firenze-Sud from A1 and follow signs
towards Fiesole. Campsite is signposted.*

FINALE LIGURE 20C

Camping San Martino Le Manie, 17029 Varigotti.
Tel 0196 98250, Fax 0196 98698. English spoken.
OPEN: all year. SIZE: 15 ha, 157 pitches (all with elec, 80 statics), 22 hot showers (charge), 80 WCs, 4 CWPs. ℂ

PRICES: (1996) Caravan with family 51,000, Tent with two adults 31,000. CC: none.
From Finale Ligure, drive north along the coast road to Varigotti. Turn up hill to Le Manie area and campsite is 300 m above sea level and well signposted.

FIRENZE (FLORENCE) 20C

Camping Autosole via Vittorio Emanuelle 11, 50041 Calenzano, Firenze.
Tel 0558 825526, Fax 0558 825576. English spoken.
OPEN: all year. SIZE: 2 ha, 71 pitches (all with elec, 30 statics), 12 hot showers (charge), 26 WCs, 2 CWPs. ℂ &

PRICES: (1996) Caravan with family 44,500, Tent with two adults 31,500. CC: none.
From A1, take exit 19 (Calenzano-Sesto Florentino) and campsite is well signposted.

Camping Barco Reale via dei Nardini 11-13, Lamporecchio, 51030 San Baronto.
Tel 0573 88332, Fax 0573 88332. English spoken.
OPEN: 01/04–30/09. SIZE: 8.5 ha, 163 pitches (150 with elec, 3 statics), 24 hot showers, 28 WCs, 10 French WCs, 2 CWPs. ℂ &

Ball games, skating, chess.
PRICES: (1996) Caravan with family 53,200, Tent with two adults 30,700. CC: none.
From Firenze, on A11 towards Mare, exit at Pistoia and then follow road signs to Lamporecchio/Vinci/San Baronto.

Camping Internazionale Firenze Bottai 50029 Firenze.
Tel 0552 374704, Fax 0552 373412. English spoken.
OPEN: 01/04–15/10. SIZE: 6 ha, 300 pitches (all with elec), 27 hot showers (charge), 38 WCs, 1 CWP. ℂ &

Bike and motorcycle hire.
PRICES: (1996) Caravan with family 54,000, Tent with two adults 40,000. CC: Amex, Euro/Access, Visa.
5 km south of centre of Firenze and well signposted.

Firenze Parco di Campeggio Michelangelo viale Michelangelo 80, 50125 Firenze.
Tel 055 6811977, Fax 055 689348. English spoken.
OPEN: 01/04–03/11. SIZE: 4 ha, 180 pitches (all with elec), 38 hot showers, 48 WCs, 1 CWP. ℂ &

Restaurant at 1 km.
PRICES: (1996) Caravan with family 52,000, Tent with two adults 34,000. CC: none.
From Firenze centre follow signs to "Piazzale Michelangelo" and the campsite.

FORTE DEI MARMI 20C

Camping Internazionale della Versilia via Vittoria Apuana Coerceta, Lucca, Forte dei Marmi.
Tel 0584 880764, Fax 0584 752118. English spoken.
OPEN: 01/04–30/09. SIZE: 4 ha, 294 pitches (all with elec), 30 hot showers (charge), 3 CWPs.

PRICES: (1996) Caravan with family 31,800, Tent with two adults 26,000. CC: none.
From A12 Sestri Levante to Livorno motorway, take Versilia exit towards Forte dei Marmi.

GARDA 20B

Camping San Zeno via A Vespucci 91, Castelletto sur Garda, 37010 Verona.
Tel 0457 430231. English spoken.
OPEN: 01/05–30/09. SIZE: 1.3 ha, 116 pitches (all with elec, 40 statics), 8 hot showers, 22 WCs, 10 French WCs. ℂ

Shop at 1 km. Restaurant at 1 km.
PRICES: Caravan with family 45,000, Tent with two adults 29,000. CC: none.
From Garda, north towards Malcesine for 10 km. Campsite is well signposted.

GRADO 20D

Campeggio Tenuta Primero Localita Primero, 34073 Grado.
Tel 0431 81523/371, Fax 0431 85940. English spoken.
OPEN: 07/05–15/09. SIZE: 20 ha, 890 pitches (all with elec, 200 statics), 196 hot showers, 230 WCs, 52 French WCs, 10 CWPs. ℂ &

No charge for children in LS; excellent sport facilities.
PRICES: (1996) Caravan with family 67,000, Tent with two adults 49,000. CC: Amex, Euro/Access, Visa.
West of Trieste on S14 coast road.

GROSSETO 21A

Camping Rosmarina via delle Colonie 37, 58046 Marina di Grosseto.
Tel 0564 36319, Fax 0564 34758. English spoken.

Italy

OPEN: 10/05–21/09. SIZE: 1 ha, 70 pitches (all with elec), 20 hot showers (charge), 35 WCs, 1 CWP. ✆ ⚥

PRICES: Caravan with family 65,000, Tent with two adults 34,000. CC: none.
From Grosseto on S322 to Marina di Grosseto.

IMPERIA 20C

Camping Eden Park via Cesare Battisti 2, 18016 San Bartolomeo al Mare.
Tel 0183 400995. English spoken.
OPEN: 01/05–30/09. SIZE: 1 ha, 30 pitches (all with elec, 90 statics), 8 hot showers, 26 WCs. ✆

PRICES: (1996) Caravan with family 54,000, Tent with two adults 46,000. CC: none.
Motorway exit San Bartolomeo al Mare. Drive towards sea for 350 m and campsite is on right.

Camping Il Persiano via Civezza 135, 18017 San Lorenzo al Mare.
Tel 0183 91994, Fax 0183 91994. English spoken.
OPEN: all year. SIZE: 10 pitches (all with elec, 30 statics), 9 hot showers (charge), 11 WCs, 8 French WCs, 2 CWPs. ✆

Shop at 0.6 km.
PRICES: (1996) Caravan with family 43,000, Tent with two adults 28,000. CC: none.
From the motorway (A10), take the Imperia-Ovest exit towards San Remo.

Camping Lino via N Sauro 4, 18010 Cervo.
Tel 0183 400087, Fax 0183 400089. English spoken.
OPEN: 26/03–15/10. SIZE: 1 ha, 102 pitches (all with elec, 11 statics), 23 hot showers, 29 WCs, 14 French WCs, 1 CWP. ✆ ⚥

Restaurant at 0.1 km. Mountain bikes, private beach.
PRICES: (1996) Caravan with family 53,000, Tent with two adults 47,000. CC: none.
Via Aurelia, go towards Alassio in Cervo, then straight on for via N Sauro, campsite on right.

ISEO 20C

Camping Punta d'Oro via I Antonioli 51/53, 25049 Iseo.
Tel 0309 80084, Fax 0309 80084. English spoken.
OPEN: 01/04–15/10. SIZE: 2 ha, 61 pitches (all with elec, 20 statics), 7 hot showers, 9 WCs, 1 CWP. ✆ ⚥

Restaurant at 0.5 km.
PRICES: (1996) Caravan with family 41,000, Tent with two adults 30,000. CC: none.
From Brescia, north-west on S510.

Camping Quai via I Antoniola 73, 25049 Iseo.
Tel 0309 821610, Fax 0309 81161. English spoken.
OPEN: 01/04–30/09. SIZE: 1 ha, 110 pitches (all with elec, 20 statics), 12 hot showers, 20 WCs, 10 French WCs, 2 CWPs. ✆

Shop at 0.8 km. Restaurant at 1 km. Slipway.
PRICES: (1996) Caravan with family 40,000, Tent with two adults 29,000. CC: none.
800 m from Iseo centre, close to lake, between national road Brescia to Edolo and city hospital.

Caravan Camping Sassabanek via Colombera 2, 25049 Iseo.
Tel 0309 80300, Fax 0309 821360. English spoken.
OPEN: 01/04–31/10. SIZE: 250 pitches (all with elec, 150 statics), 34 hot showers, 44 WCs, 4 CWPs. ⚥

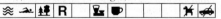

PRICES: (1996) Caravan with family 52,600, Tent with two adults 30,600. CC: Amex, Euro/Access, Visa.
From Brescia, north-west on S11 and S510.

ISOLA D'ISCHIA

BARANO D'ISCHIA 21B

Camping Mirage Lido dei Maronti, 80070 Barano d'Ischia.
Tel 0819 90551, Fax 0819 90551. English spoken.
OPEN: all year. SIZE: 1 ha, 60 pitches (all with elec), 5 hot showers (charge), 12 WCs, 1 CWP. ✆

Shop at 2 km. Water sports.
PRICES: (1996) Caravan with family 77,500, Tent with two adults 39,000. CC: Euro/Access.
Well signposted.

END OF ISOLA D'ISCHIA RESORTS

ISOLA DI CAPO RIZZUTO 21D

Maneuso CP 58, 88076 Isola di Capo Rizzuto.
Tel 0962 799190. English spoken.
OPEN: all year. SIZE: 30 ha, 300 pitches (all with elec), 6 hot showers (charge), 20 WCs. ✆ ⚥

Restaurant at 0.05 km. 10% discount offered to English tourists.
PRICES: (1996) Caravan with family 46,000, Tent with two adults 27,000. CC: none.
At Capo Rizzuto, south of Isola.

JESOLO 20C

Camping Ca'Savio Lido 30010 Treporti, Venezia.
Tel 0419 66017, Fax 0415 300707. English spoken.
OPEN: 01/05–30/09. SIZE: 28 ha, 1500 pitches (1000 with elec, 102 statics), 174 hot showers, 172 WCs, 2 CWPs. ✆

PRICES: (1996) Caravan with family 60,000, Tent with two adults 41,000. CC: Euro/Access, Visa. *From Cavallino, follow signs to Ca'Ballarin and Ca'Pasquali. At Ca'Savio junction, turn left at traffic lights towards beach and campsite is at end of road, well signposted.*

Camping dei Fiori Ca'Savio, 30010 Treporti, Venezia.
Tel 0419 66448, Fax 0419 66724. English spoken.
OPEN: 01/05–30/09. SIZE: 10 ha, 444 pitches (all with elec), 77 hot showers, 85 WCs, 2 CWPs. ✆ ♿

Fitness centre, whirlpool, watersports and boating close by.
PRICES: (1996) Caravan with family 80,600, Tent with two adults 48,400. CC: Euro/Access, Visa. *From the Venezia to Trieste motorway, exit at Jesolo-Cavallino, then head towards Cavallino for about 15 km.*

LANZO TORINESE 20C

Camping Luigi Bergera Strada Valli di Lanzo, Lanzo Torinese.
Tel 0123 29400.
OPEN: all year. SIZE: 1.7 ha, 130 pitches (all with elec, 90 statics), 10 hot showers (charge), 20 WCs, 2 CWPs. ✆ ♿

PRICES: (1996) Caravan with family 33,500, Tent with two adults 20,000. CC: none.

LAZISE 20B

Camping du Parc Loc Sentieri, 37017 Lazise.
Tel 0457 580127, Fax 0456 470150. English spoken.
OPEN: 10/03–31/10. SIZE: 4 ha, 300 pitches (all with elec, 30 statics), 30 hot showers, 40 WCs, 50 French WCs, 3 CWPs. ✆ ♿

PRICES: (1996) Caravan with family 53,500, Tent with two adults 36,500. CC: none.
From Verona, take S11 east. Campsite is 500 m from town centre.

Camping Fossalta Localita Fossalta, 37017 Lazise, Verona.
Tel 0457 590231, Fax 0457 520999.
English spoken.
OPEN: 09/04–30/09. SIZE: 6 ha, 120 pitches (51 with elec), 26 hot showers, 42 WCs, 4 French WCs, 2 CWPs. ✆ ♿

Restaurant at 0.5 km. Tennis.
PRICES: (1996) Caravan with family 47,000, Tent with two adults 34,000. CC: none.
From Lazise, south for 3 km.

LECCO 20A

Campeggio Riviera di Garlate
via Statale 122, 22050 Garlate.
Tel 0341 680346, Fax 0341 680346. English spoken.
OPEN: 15/06–30/09. SIZE: 1 ha, 90 pitches (all with elec, 80 statics), 6 hot showers (charge), 14 WCs, 12 French WCs, 2 CWPs. ✆ ♿

Shop at 0.5 km. Restaurant at 0.2 km. Open at weekends year-round; children's pool.
PRICES: (1996) Caravan with family 51,000, Tent with two adults 33,000. CC: none.
From Lecco, west on coast road S36 for about 3 km.

Camping 2 Laghi 22040 Isella di Civate.
Tel 0341 550101, Fax 0341 550101. English spoken.
OPEN: 01/04–30/09 & 01/10–30/03.
SIZE: 60 pitches (all with elec, 100 statics), 11 hot showers, 22 WCs, 4 French WCs, 3 CWPs. ✆

PRICES: (1996) Caravan with family 41,000, Tent with two adults 27,000. CC: none.
From the S36, Milano to Lecco road, exit at Isella and follow the signs to the campsite.

LIDO DI OSTIA 21A

Campeggio Intl di Castelfusano
00056 Lido Di Roma.
Tel 0656 23304, Fax 0656 70260. English spoken.
OPEN: 15/03–30/10. SIZE: 4.2 ha, 101 pitches (all with elec), 18 hot showers, 36 WCs, 2 CWPs. ✆ ♿

Table tennis, volley ball.
PRICES: (1996) Caravan with family 54,500, Tent with two adults 32,000. CC: Euro/Access, Visa.
From the centre of Ostia, south for 6 km along the beach road.

LIVORNO 20C

International Camping Etruria
Marina di Castagneto Carducci, 57024 Livorno.
Tel 0565 744254, Fax 0565 744494. English spoken.
OPEN: 01/04–30/09. SIZE: 10 ha, 650 pitches (all with elec), 50 hot showers, 153 WCs, 7 CWPs.

PRICES: Caravan with family 68,000, Tent with two adults 44,000. CC: none.
From the Livorno to Grosseto freeway take Donoratico exit.

LUINO 20A

Camping Lido via G Pietraperzia 13, 21010 Maccagno.
Tel 0332 560250. English spoken.
OPEN: 01/04–02/10. SIZE: 7.5 ha, 80 pitches (40 with elec), 8 hot showers, 15 WCs, 2 CWPs.

Italy

Shop at 0.5 km. Restaurant at 0.3 km.
PRICES: (1996) Caravan with family 39,000,
Tent with two adults 26,000. CC: none.
North of Luino on the S394.

MAGIONE 20C

Camping Il Villaggio Italgest via Martiri di
Cefalonia, 06060 San Arcangelo di Magione.
Tel 075 848238, Fax 075 848085. English spoken.
OPEN: 01/04–30/09. SIZE: 3.5 ha, 200 pitches
(all with elec, 40 statics), 36 hot showers, 32 WCs,
5 CWPs.

Excellent sports facilities.
PRICES: Caravan with family 51,500, Tent with two
adults 31,500. CC: Amex, Euro/Access, Visa.
From Perugia on S75 west, exit at Magione.

MALCESINE 20B

Camping Le Maior
37010 Castelletto di Brenzone.
Tel 0457 430333, Fax 0456 200180. English spoken.
OPEN: 09/04–30/09. SIZE: 1 ha, 80 pitches (all with
elec, 10 statics), 12 hot showers, 16 WCs, 3 French
WCs.

Restaurant at 0.8 km.
PRICES: (1996) Caravan with family 51,000,
Tent with two adults 32,000. CC: none.
South of Malcesine on the lake road.

Camping Primavera via Benaco 5,
37010 Brenzone.
Tel 0457 420421. English spoken.
OPEN: 01/04–30/09. SIZE: 1 ha, 75 pitches (all with
elec), 10 hot showers, 13 WCs, 1 CWP.

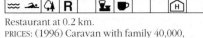

Restaurant at 0.2 km.
PRICES: (1996) Caravan with family 40,000,
Tent with two adults 26,000. CC: none.
On east bank of Lake Garda, south of Malcesine.

MALE 20A

Camping Dolomiti di Brenta 38025 Dimaro.
Tel 0463 974332, Fax 0463 973200. English spoken.
OPEN: 01/06–30/09 & 19/12–30/04. SIZE: 3 ha,
193 pitches (all with elec), 20 hot showers,
36 WCs, 4 French WCs, 4 CWPs.

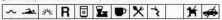

Canoeing, tennis.
PRICES: Caravan with family 56,000, Tent with two
adults 32,000. CC: Euro/Access, Visa.
*From Brennero motorway, take San Michele
all'Adige exit towards Passo Tonale to Dimaro
(35 km).*

MALGA CIAPELA 20A

Camping Malga Ciapela Marmolada Loc Malga
Ciapela 116, 32020 Malga Ciapela, Rocca Pietore.
Tel 0437 722064. English spoken.
OPEN: 01/12–25/04 & 01/06–22/09. SIZE: 3 ha,
180 pitches (150 with elec, 90 statics), 21 hot
showers, 21 WCs.

Restaurant at 0.8 km.
PRICES: (1996) Caravan with family 42,000,
Tent with two adults 22,000. CC: none.
800 m west of Malga Ciapela.

MANERBA DEL GARDA 20B

Camping Il Faro 25080 Pieve di Manerba.
Tel 0365 651704, Fax 0356 552437. English spoken.
OPEN: 15/04–15/09. SIZE: 1 ha, 92 pitches (all with
elec), 16 hot showers, 24 WCs, 1 CWP.

Shop at 0.1 km.
PRICES: (1996) Caravan with family 43,000,
Tent with two adults 29,000. CC: none.
*From the A4, exit at Desenzano, take the S572 to
Manerba del Garda and follow signs.*

MARCELLI DI NUMANA 20D

Camping Conero Azzurro via Litoranea,
60026 Marcelli di Numana.
Tel 0717 390507, Fax 0717 390986.
OPEN: 01/05–15/09. SIZE: 5 ha, 100 pitches
(all with elec), 64 hot showers, 96 WCs,
8 CWPs.

PRICES: (1996) Caravan with family 64,000,
Tent with two adults 40,000. CC: none.

MARINA DI BIBBONA 20C

Camping del Forte via dei Platani 58,
57020 Marina di Bibbona.
Tel 0586 600155, Fax 0586 600123. English spoken.
OPEN: 01/04–20/09. SIZE: 8 ha, 200 pitches
(all with elec, 100 statics), 80 hot showers,
70 WCs.

PRICES: (1996) Caravan with family 58,200,
Tent with two adults 38,000. CC: none.

Camping Free Beach 57020 Marina di Bibbona.
Tel 0586 600388, Fax 0586 600388. English spoken.
OPEN: 01/04–30/09. SIZE: 9 ha, 500 pitches
(all with elec, 250 statics), 108 hot showers,
128 WCs, 10 French WCs, 6 CWPs.

PRICES: (1996) Caravan with family 55,000, Tent
with two adults 30,000. CC: Euro/Access, Visa.

Italy

On the Livorno to Grosseto road, turn off to Marina di Bibbona and follow signs to campsite.

Camping Le Capanne via Aurelia, Km 273, 57020 Marina di Bibbona.
Tel 0586 600064, Fax 0586 600198. English spoken.
OPEN: 01/05–15/09. SIZE: 6 ha, 319 pitches (all with elec), 40 hot showers, 56 WCs, 28 French WCs, 3 CWPs. ✆

PRICES: (1996) Caravan with family 52,200, Tent with two adults 32,600. CC: Visa.
From Cecina drive south (away from Livorno), just after village of La California, site on left.

MARINA DI CAMEROTA 21B

Happy Camping 84059 Marina di Camerota.
Tel 0974 932326, Fax 0974 932769. English spoken.
OPEN: 25/05–28/09. SIZE: 12 ha, 400 pitches (all with elec), 45 hot showers, 60 WCs, 2 CWPs. ✆

Canoeing, horse-riding, scuba-diving.
PRICES: (1996) Caravan with family 120,000, Tent with two adults 72,000. CC: none.
Battipaglia exit from Salerno-Reggio Calabria motorway, then to Paestum, and on to Agropoli, Vallo Scalo, Palinuro and Marina di Camerota.

MARINA DI MASSA 20C

International Touring Camping via Baracchini 119, Loc Partaccia, 54037 Marina di Massa.
Tel 0585 780021, Fax 0585 780622. English spoken.
OPEN: 09/04–20/09. SIZE: 3 ha, 210 pitches (all with elec, 130 statics), 20 hot showers (charge), 40 WCs. ✆

Shop at 0.1 km. Restaurant at 0.3 km. Table tennis, soccer, billiards.
PRICES: (1996) Caravan with family 58,000, Tent with two adults 48,000. CC: Euro/Access, Visa.
Close to station and motorway exit.

MAROTTA 20D

Camping Club Cesano via Ugo Foscola 22, 61035 Marotta.
Tel 0721 960730, Fax 0721 960730.
English spoken.
OPEN: 01/05–30/09. SIZE: 1 ha, 139 pitches (all with elec, 40 statics), 12 hot showers, 28 WCs. ✆

Shop at 1 km.
PRICES: (1996) Caravan with family 56,700, Tent with two adults 36,100. CC: none.
Take Senigallia exit from A14 (Bologna to Ancona) then go north on S16 to Km 267 post. Turn seawards after bridge over River Cesano.

MASSA 20C

Camping Giardino via delle Pinete 136, 54037 Marina di Massa.
Tel 0585 869291, Fax 0585 240781. English spoken.
OPEN: 01/04–30/09. SIZE: 128 pitches (all with elec, 100 statics), 24 hot showers (charge), 54 WCs, 20 French WCs, 4 CWPs. ✆ ♿

PRICES: (1996) Caravan with family 54,000, Tent with two adults 40,000. CC: Euro/Access, Visa.

MATTINATA 21B

Camping Funni 71030 Mattinata.
Tel 0884 550736, Fax 0884 550736. English spoken.
OPEN: all year. SIZE: 1.2 ha, 70 pitches (all with elec, 4 statics), 8 hot showers (charge), 20 WCs, 8 French WCs, 1 CWP. ✆

Archery, trekking, volley ball, table tennis.
PRICES: (1996) Caravan with family 42,000, Tent with two adults 20,400. CC: none.
From Foggia, north on S89.

Centro Turistico Archita cda Liberatore, 71030 Mattinata.
Tel 0884 49021.
OPEN: all year. SIZE: 1 ha, 30 pitches (all with elec), 4 hot showers (charge), 12 WCs, 12 French WCs, 1 CWP. ✆

PRICES: (1996) Caravan with family 51,000, Tent with two adults 30,000. CC: none.
On the northern coast just above 'the foot', north-east of Foggia.

MERANO 20A

Camping Latsch and Etsch Reichsstrasse 4, 39021 Latsch.
Tel 0473 623217, Fax 0473 623217. English spoken.
OPEN: all year. SIZE: 1.5 ha, 100 pitches (all with elec), 11 hot showers, 14 WCs, 2 French WCs, 2 CWPs. ✆

Bowling.
PRICES: (1996) Caravan with family 37,600, Tent with two adults 26,500. CC: Amex, Euro/Access, Visa.
North-west from Merano on route 40 towards the Reschenpass. Latsch is on the left, on the banks of the River Adige.

METAPONTO 21B

Camel Camping Club 75010 Lido di Metaponto.
Tel 0835 330298, Fax 0835 335041. English spoken.
OPEN: 01/06–30/09. SIZE: 400 pitches (all with elec), 10 hot showers (charge), 40 WCs. ✆

PRICES: (1996) Caravan with family 47,000, Tent with two adults 27,000. CC: none.
South west of Taranto on the SS 106.

Camping California strada Turistica-Archeologica, Santa Palagina, 75010 Metaponto. Tel 0835 741842, Fax 0835 741782. English spoken. OPEN: all year. SIZE: 3 ha, 200 pitches (all with elec, 30 statics), 8 hot showers (charge), 24 WCs, 4 CWPs. ✆

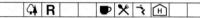

PRICES: (1996) Caravan with family 29,500, Tent with two adults 22,000. CC: Euro/Access, Visa.
Metaponto lies on the coast, west of Taranto.

MODENA 20C

Camping La Chiocciola
41050 Maserno do Montese, Modena. Tel 0599 80005, Fax 0599 80025. English spoken. OPEN: all year. SIZE: 2 ha, 80 pitches (all with elec, 40 statics), 8 hot showers (charge), 14 WCs, 1 French WC, 1 CWP. ✆ ♿

Shop at 0.2 km.
PRICES: (1996) Caravan with family 55,000, Tent with two adults 35,000. CC: none.
From Modena take road south to Vignola then Maserno.

International Camping Modena via Cave Ramo 111, Localita Bruciata, 41100 Modena. Tel 0593 32252, Fax 0593 32252. English spoken. OPEN: 01/04–30/09. SIZE: 1 ha, 40 pitches (all with elec), 5 hot showers, 8 WCs, 8 French WCs.

PRICES: (1996) Caravan with family 47,000, Tent with two adults 30,000. CC: none.
Exit motorway Modena-Nord.

MONIGA 20B

Camping Sereno via San Sivino 72, 25080 Moniga del Garda. Tel 0365 502080, Fax 0365 502378. English spoken. OPEN: 01/04–30/09. SIZE: 4 ha, 150 pitches (all with elec, 100 statics), 20 hot showers, 50 WCs, 10 CWPs. ✆

PRICES: (1996) Caravan with family 50,000, Tent with two adults 35,000. CC: none.
Site is signposted.

Trevisago via Prato Negro 10, 25080 Moniga del Garda. Tel 0365 502355, Fax 0365 502252. English spoken. OPEN: all year. SIZE: 2 ha, 65 pitches (all with elec, 65 statics), 10 hot showers (charge), 18 WCs, 2 French WCs, 2 CWPs. ✆

Shop at 0.8 km. 2 swimming pools.
PRICES: (1996) Caravan with family 35,000, Tent with two adults 24,000. CC: none.
North from Desenzano around west side of Lake Garda to Moniga del Garda.

MONTE SANT'ANGELO 21B

Camping Baia del Monaco
Localita Varcaro, 71030 Macchia. Tel 0884 530280. English spoken. OPEN: 01/06–31/08. SIZE: 5 ha, 220 pitches (all with elec), 16 hot showers (charge), 40 WCs, 2 CWPs. ✆

PRICES: (1996) Caravan with family 44,000, Tent with two adults 27,000. CC: none.
From Foggia, S89 to Mattinata.

MONTECATINI TERME 20C

Camping Belsito via delle Vigne 1a, Localita Vico, 51016 Montecatini Terme. Tel 0572 67373, Fax 0572 67373. English spoken. OPEN: all year. SIZE: 4 ha, 64 pitches (all with elec, 4 statics), 64 hot showers, 64 WCs. ✆

PRICES: (1996) Caravan with family 56,000, Tent with two adults 24,000. CC: none.
From Montecatini Terme, campsite is on the hill towards Montecatini Alto.

MONTEGROTTO TERME 20C

Camping Termale Sporting Centre via Roma 123, 35036 Montegrotto. Tel 0497 93400, Fax 0498 911551. English spoken. OPEN: 05/03–10/11. SIZE: 6 ha, 185 pitches (all with elec), 45 hot showers, 45 WCs, 10 French WCs, 2 CWPs.

Shop at 1 km.
PRICES: (1996) Caravan with family 47,000, Tent with two adults 32,000. CC: none.
From Padova, south on S16 and exit at Montegrotto Terme.

MONTERIGGIONI 20C

Camping Luxor Trasqua, 53011 Castellina in Chianti. Tel 0577 743047, Fax 0577 743047. English spoken. OPEN: 05/06–06/09. SIZE: 3 ha, 4 hot showers, 14 WCs, 12 French WCs. ✆

Italy

PRICES: (1996) Caravan with family 38,100, Tent with two adults 26,400. CC: none.

Between Siena and Poggibonsi. Well signposted.

NICOTERA 21D

Camping Sabbia d'Oro contrada de Rinazzi, 88033 Nicotera Marina.
Tel 0963 886345, Fax 0966 653312. English spoken.
OPEN: 01/06–30/09. SIZE: 2 ha, 100 pitches (all with elec), 12 hot showers (charge), 24 WCs.

Shop at 1 km.
PRICES: (1996) Caravan with family 34,000, Tent with two adults 24,000. CC: none.

ORBETELLO 21A

Camping Acapulco Km 155 via Aurelia, 58010 Fonteblanda, Orbetello.
Tel 0564 870165, Fax 0564 870165. English spoken.
OPEN: 15/05–15/09. SIZE: 2 ha, 119 pitches (all with elec), 15 hot showers, 25 WCs, 1 CWP. ⚓ ㄜ

PRICES: (1996) Caravan with family 49,000, Tent with two adults 32,000. CC: none.
From the Grosseto to Roma road, take Km 155 exit and follow signs.

Camping Il Gabbiano 58010 Albinia.
Tel 0564 870202, Fax 0564 863335. English spoken.
OPEN: 01/04–30/09. SIZE: 3 ha, 180 pitches (all with elec), 16 hot showers, 38 WCs. ㄜ

Archery, water sports.
PRICES: (1996) Caravan with family 75,000, Tent with two adults 45,000. CC: none.
On the coast, just north of Albinia.

International Camping Argentario
58010 Albinia, Grosseto.
Tel 0564 870302, Fax 0564 871380. English spoken.
OPEN: 01/04–30/09. SIZE: 470 pitches (all with elec), 42 hot showers, 94 WCs, 3 CWPs. ⚓ ㄜ

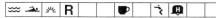

PRICES: (1996) Caravan with family 75,000, Tent with two adults 45,000. CC: none.
Well signposted in town.

ORTA 20A

Camping Cusio Lyons Edda via G Bosco 5, 28016 Orta San Giulio.
Tel 0322 902290, Fax 0322 911892. English spoken.
OPEN: 01/04–30/11. SIZE: 2 ha, 80 pitches (all with elec), 12 hot showers (charge), 19 WCs, 12 French WCs, 3 CWPs.

Shop at 0.7 km. Restaurant at 0.7 km. Tennis. Picturesque surroundings.
PRICES: (1996) Caravan with family 43,500, Tent with two adults 25,000. CC: Euro/Access.
Coming from the north, turn left at the traffic lights in Orta and then follow signs to campsite.

Camping La Punta di Crabbia via Crabbia, 28028 Pettenasco.
Tel 0323 89117. English spoken.
OPEN: 01/04–31/10. SIZE: 110 pitches (all with elec, 80 statics), 8 hot showers (charge), 22 WCs, 17 French WCs. ⚓

Restaurant at 1 km.
PRICES: (1996) Caravan with family 40,500, Tent with two adults 22,500. CC: none.
South of Omegna to the east of Lago d'Orta on S229.

PALINURO 21B

Camping Marbella Club Localita Piana Mingardo, 84064 Palinuro.
Tel 0974 931003, Fax 0974 938364. English spoken.
OPEN: 22/06–15/09. SIZE: 5 ha, 300 pitches (all with elec), 26 hot showers, 55 WCs, 1 CWP. ⚓

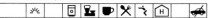

PRICES: (1996) Caravan with family 75,000, Tent with two adults 30,000. CC: none.
From Palinuro south, turn off S562 towards sea.

PARMA 20C

Camping Arizona via Tabiano 40, 43030 Salsomaggiore.
Tel 0524 565648, Fax 0524 565648. English spoken.
OPEN: 01/04–15/10. SIZE: 11 ha, 300 pitches (all with elec, 50 statics), 30 hot showers, 30 WCs, 37 French WCs, 8 CWPs. ⚓ ㄜ

Tennis, flume, hydro-massage.
PRICES: (1996) Caravan with family 54,500, Tent with two adults 28,000. CC: none.
From Parma towards Fidenza and Tabiano on S9, exit at Tabiano, 500 m to campsite.

Italy

PAVIA 20C

Camping Ticino Pavia.
Tel 0382 527039. English spoken.
OPEN: 15/03–10/10. SIZE: 80 pitches (all with elec, 50 statics), 10 hot showers (charge), 15 WCs, 2 CWPs.

Shop at 0.2 km. Restaurant at 0.1 km. Public pool next door (50% disc).
PRICES: (1996) Caravan with family 33,500, Tent with two adults 21,500. CC: none.
From Milano to Genova motorway (A7), exit at Bereguarda, west towards Pavia. Campsite by river.

PEGLI 20C

Campeggio Villa Doria via Al Campeggio Villa Doria 1, 16156 Pegli, Genova.
Tel 0106 969600, Fax 0106 969600. English spoken.
OPEN: all year. SIZE: 1 ha, 50 pitches (all with elec), 10 hot showers, 12 WCs, 8 French WCs, 1 CWP.

Restaurant at 1 km. Solarium.
PRICES: (1996) Caravan with family 37,000, Tent with two adults 30,000. CC: Amex, Euro/Access, Visa.
Pegli is 10 km from centre of Genova.

PEJO 20A

Camping Cevedale 38026 Fucine di Ossana.
Tel 0463 751630, Fax 0463 751630. English spoken.
OPEN: all year. SIZE: 211 pitches (all with elec, 10 statics), 18 hot showers, 26 WCs, 2 CWPs.

Restaurant at 0.3 km. Barbecue; tennis, rafting, archery, skiing nearby.
PRICES: unavailable. CC: none.
Fucine di Ossana is between Pellizzano and Passo Tonale on the route 42.

PERGINE 20A

Camping Punta Indiani Lago di Caldonazzo, 38057 Pergine.
Tel 0461 548062. English spoken.
OPEN: 10/05–30/09. SIZE: 1.5 ha, 115 pitches (all with elec), 12 hot showers, 22 WCs, 2 CWPs.

PRICES: (1996) Caravan with family 44.000, Tent with two adults 28,000. CC: none.

PERUGIA 20C

Camping Europa San Donato, 06065 Passignano sul Trasimeno.
Tel 0758 27405, Fax 0758 28200. English spoken.
OPEN: 01/04–10/10. SIZE: 3 ha, 110 pitches (all with elec, 10 statics), 15 hot showers, 25 WCs, 5 CWPs.

Water sports, horse-riding, tennis. 10% discount LS to RAC members.
PRICES: (1996) Caravan with family 41,500, Tent with two adults 25,000. CC: none.
From Perugia on S75 or from Firenze, exit Passignano east. Campsite directly on lakeside.

Camping Kursaal Lago Trasimeno, viale Europa 41, 06065 Passignano.
Tel 0758 28085, Fax 0758 27182. English spoken.
OPEN: 01/04–10/10. SIZE: 3 ha, 170 pitches (all with elec), 20 hot showers, 20 WCs, 5 French WCs, 10 CWPs.

Boating; lovely surroundings.
PRICES: (1996) Caravan with family 53,000, Tent with two adults 32,000. CC: Euro/Access, Visa.
From Perugia on S75 take Passignano Est exit.

Camping Punta Navaccia 06069 Tuoro sul Trasimeno.
Tel 075 826357, Fax 075 826357. English spoken.
OPEN: 15/03–31/10. SIZE: 6.5 ha, 170 pitches (all with elec, 230 statics), 33 hot showers, 41 WCs, 8 French WCs, 3 CWPs.

Excellent free sports/leisure facilities.
PRICES: Caravan with family 50,000, Tent with two adults 30,000. CC: none.
From Perugia on S75 exit Tuoro.

PESARO 20D

Camping Panorama strada Panoramica S Bartolo, 61010 Fiorenzuola di Focara, Pesaro.
Tel 0721 208145, Fax 0721 208145. English spoken.
OPEN: 01/05–30/09. SIZE: 2 ha, 150 pitches (all with elec), 17 hot showers, 31 WCs, 2 CWPs.

Shop at 3 km.
PRICES: (1996) Caravan with family 60,000, Tent with two adults 36,500. CC: Euro/Access.
Campsite is well signposted from Pesaro.

PESCARA 21B

Camping Europe Garden via Belvedere 11, 64028 Marina di Silvi.
Tel 085 330137, Fax 085 932845. English spoken.
OPEN: 01/05–30/09. SIZE: 5 ha, 150 pitches (all with elec, 40 statics), 20 hot showers, 68 WCs, 20 French WCs, 4 CWPs.

PRICES: (1996) Caravan with family 57,500, Tent with two adults 37,000. CC: none.
From Pescara, north on S16 for approx 5 km to Silvi.

Camping Lake Placid 64029 Silvi Marina.
Tel 0859 32567. English spoken.
OPEN: all year. SIZE: 3.5 ha, 100 pitches (all with elec), 12 hot showers. ☎

Shop at 0.3 km.
PRICES: (1996) Caravan with family 48,000,
Tent with two adults 28,000. CC: Euro/Access.
Follow signs to site.

PESCHICI 21B

Baia San Nicola Loc San Nicola, 71010 Peschici.
Tel 0884 964231, Fax 0884 964231. English spoken.
OPEN: 10/05–30/09. SIZE: 1 ha, 25 pitches (all with elec), 15 hot showers, 18 WCs, 1 CWP. ☎

Restaurant at 0.3 km. Watersports. Swimming pool 0.2 km.
PRICES: (1996) Caravan with family 41,400,
Tent with two adults 28,200. CC: Euro/Access.
The campsite is 3 km south of Peschici. Well signposted.

Camp Internz Manacore Del Gargano
via Cavour 27, 71010 Peschici.
Tel 0884 911020, Fax 0884 911049. English spoken.
OPEN: 01/04–15/10. SIZE: 15 ha, 600 pitches (all with elec), 71 hot showers, 55 WCs, 8 French WCs, 4 CWPs. ☎ ㅎ

PRICES: (1996) Caravan with family 49,000,
Tent with two adults 29,000. CC: Euro/Access.
From Peschici follow coast road S159 for 10 km towards Vieste.

Centro Turistico San Nicola Localita San Nicola, 71010 Peschici.
Tel 0884 964024, Fax 0884 964025. English spoken.
OPEN: 01/04–15/10. SIZE: 13 ha, 700 pitches (all with elec), 80 hot showers, 80 WCs, 100 French WCs, 3 CWPs. ☎ ㅎ

Watersports.
PRICES: (1996) Caravan with family 73,500,
Tent with two adults 50,500. CC: Euro/Access.
From Peschici towards Vieste.

PESCHIERA 20B

Camping del Garda 37019 Peschiera del Garda.
Tel 0457 550540, Fax 0456 400711. English spoken.
OPEN: 01/04–30/09. SIZE: 270 ha, 960 pitches (all with elec), 101 hot showers, 117 WCs, 5 CWPs. ☎ ㅎ

PRICES: (1996) Caravan with family 55,000,
Tent with two adults 37,000. CC: none.
1 km north of the centre of Peschiera del Garda and well signposted.

Camping Wien Localita Fornaci,
37010 Peschiera del Garda.
Tel 0457 55039. English spoken.
OPEN: 09/04–30/09. SIZE: 4 ha, 150 pitches (all with elec), 22 hot showers, 30 WCs, 20 French WCs. ☎

PRICES: (1996) Caravan with family 37,500,
Tent with two adults 27,500. CC: none.
On S11 between Brescia and Verona.

PIEVEPELAGO 20C

Campo Fra' Dolcino 41027 Roccapelago.
Tel 0536 71229. English spoken.
OPEN: all year. SIZE: 3.7 ha, 80 pitches (all with elec, 45 statics), 8 hot showers, 10 WCs, 8 French WCs, 1 CWP. ☎ ㅎ

Restaurant at 1.5 km.
PRICES: (1996) Caravan with family 42,000,
Tent with two adults 23,000. CC: none.
2 km north of Pievepelago towards Roccapelago.

PINETO 21B

Camping Heliopolis 64025 Pineto.
Tel 0859 492720, Fax 0859 492171.
English spoken.
OPEN: 01/04–30/09. SIZE: 1.2 ha, 110 pitches (all with elec, 12 statics), 82 hot showers, 82 WCs, 3 CWPs. ☎ ㅎ

PRICES: (1996) Caravan with family 68,000, Tent with two adults 32,000. CC: Euro/Access, Visa.
Leave Adriatica highway, A14, at Km 354, take Atri-Pineto exit and then follow signs to campsite. (Discounts given to those showing RAC Camping guide.)

International Camping C de Torre Cerrano,
64025 Pineto.
Tel 0859 30639, Fax 0859 30639. English spoken.
OPEN: 01/05–30/09. SIZE: 2 ha, 140 pitches (all with elec, 15 statics), 12 hot showers (charge), 40 WCs, 1 CWP. ☎ ㅎ

PRICES: (1996) Caravan with family 61,500, Tent with two adults 40,000. CC: none.
15 km north of Pescara, beside the beach.

PIOMBINO 21A

Camping Communale Sant'Albinia
Populonia, 57025 Piombino.
Tel 0565 29389, Fax 0565 221310.
English spoken.
OPEN: 01/05–15/09. SIZE: 3 ha, 100 pitches (all with elec, 7 statics), 36 hot showers, 36 WCs, 1 CWP. ☎

Italy (side margin)

Shop at 2 km.
PRICES: (1996) Caravan with family 55,200,
Tent with two adults 32,600. CC: none.
From Piombino towards Livorno for 10 km.

Pappasole Localita Carbonifera,
57020 Vignale Riotorto.
Tel 0565 20414, Fax 0565 20346. English spoken.
OPEN: 22/03–11/10. SIZE: 13 ha, 431 pitches
(all with elec), 500 hot showers, 500 WCs,
500 French WCs, 3 CWPs. ☏ &

Private bathroom on each pitch.
PRICES: Caravan with family 61,000, Tent with two
adults 43,000. CC: Amex, Euro/Access, Visa.
Well signposted.

PISA 20C

Camp Torre Pendente
via delle Cascine 86, 56100 Pisa.
Tel 050 561704, Fax 050 561734. English spoken.
OPEN: 01/04–15/10. SIZE: 2.5 ha, 220 pitches (all
with elec), 24 hot showers, 36 WCs, 2 CWPs. ☏ &

PRICES: Caravan with family 51,000,
Tent with two adults 31,000. CC: none.
*300 m from via Aurelia. 800 m from Leaning
Tower.*

PIZZO 21D

Camping Dolomiti sur Mere
S522 per Tropea, 88031 Briatico.
Tel 0963 391948, Fax 0963 393009. English spoken.
OPEN: 01/04–30/09. SIZE: 5 ha, 250 pitches
(all with elec, 9 statics), 43 hot showers, 60 WCs,
40 French WCs, 1 CWP. ☏ &

Pedalos, canoes, windsurfing. 20% discount to
RAC members.
PRICES: (1996) Caravan with family 64,000,
Tent with two adults 37,500. CC: none.
*Briatico is on the coast road between Pizzo and
Tropea. Site is well signposted.*

POGGIBONSI 20C

Camping Semifonte Barberina Val d'Esla,
Poggibonsi, 50021 Firenze.
Tel 055 8075454, Fax 055 8075454. English spoken.
OPEN: 15/03–05/11. SIZE: 1.7 ha, 50 pitches
(all with elec), 10 hot showers, 12 WCs, 2 French
WCs, 2 CWPs.

Shop at 0.2 km. Restaurant at 0.2 km. Children's
pool.

PRICES: (1996) Tent with two adults 25,500. CC: none.
*North of Poggibonsi to Tavarnelle Val di Pesa and
follow signs.*

Il Boschetto di Piemma Localita Santa Lucia,
53037 San Gimignano.
Tel 0577 940352, Fax 0577 941982. English spoken.
OPEN: 01/04–15/10. SIZE: 2 ha, 10 hot showers,
10 WCs. ☏ &

Restaurant at 1 km.
PRICES: (1996) Caravan with family 28,000,
Tent with two adults 19,500. CC: none.
*West from Poggibonsi to San Gimignano, then
towards Volterra. Turn left, campsite 1.5 km.*

POMPEII 21B

Camping Spartacus via Plinio 127,
80045 Pompeii.
Tel 0815 369519, Fax 0818 637749.
English spoken.
OPEN: all year. SIZE: 11 ha, 100 pitches (all with
elec), 10 hot showers, 20 WCs, 6 French WCs,
3 CWPs. ☏ &

Sea 3 km.
PRICES: (1996) Caravan with family 32,000,
Tent with two adults 20,000. CC: Amex.
*50 m from ruins of Pompei and a few hundred
metres from the Napoli to Salerno motorway, exit
Pompei.*

PONTECAGNANO 21B

Fior d'Arancio via Pompei 36, Falano,
84093 Pontecagnano.
Tel 0892 01176, Fax 0892 01176. English spoken.
OPEN: all year. SIZE: 1 ha, 100 pitches (all with elec,
30 statics), 4 hot showers (charge), 11 WCs,
2 CWPs. ☏ &

PRICES: (1996) Caravan with family 45,000, Tent
with two adults 34,000. CC: Euro/Access.
From Pontecagnano exit on A3.

PORTO SAN GIORGIO 20D

Johnny Camping Santa Maria a Mare,
63010 Marina Palmense.
Tel 0734 53457, Fax 0734 53734. English spoken.
OPEN: 01/06–10/09. SIZE: 1.3 ha, 70 pitches
(all with elec), 17 hot showers, 19 WCs. ☏ &

Solarium, table tennis, volley ball.
PRICES: (1996) Caravan with family 45,000,
Tent with two adults 32,000. CC: none.
*From S14, exit 277 to Porto San Giorgio/Fermo.
Campsite is signposted.*

PORTO SANT'ELPIDIO 20D

Camping La Risacca via Gabbie 38,
63018 Porto Sant'Elpidio.
Tel 0734 991423, Fax 0734 997276.
English spoken.
OPEN: 01/05–30/09. SIZE: 8 ha, 460 pitches
(all with elec, 20 statics), 68 hot showers, 99 WCs,
2 CWPs. ✆ ♿

PRICES: (1996) Caravan with family 57,400,
Tent with two adults 36,800. CC: none.
From Ancona exit A14 Civitanova Marche on to
S16. Go south for 3 km then take underpass at
crossroads towards sea. Well signposted.

POZZUOLI 21B

Camping Averno via Domiziana Km 55,
80078 Pozzuoli.
Tel 0818 042666, Fax 0818 042570.
English spoken.
OPEN: all year. SIZE: 5 ha, 40 pitches (all with elec,
20 statics), 6 hot showers, 10 WCs, 2 CWPs. ✆

Tennis, basketball, disco, mini-golf, gym, sauna.
PRICES: (1996) Caravan with family 55,000,
Tent with two adults 35,000. CC: Visa.
From Pozzuoli, take S7 north along coast to Lago
di Averno.

Camping Vulcano Solfatara
via Solfatara 161, 80078 Pozzuoli.
Tel 0815 267413, Fax 0815 263482. English spoken.
OPEN: 01/04–31/10. SIZE: 8 ha, 150 pitches
(90 with elec, 5 statics), 20 hot showers, 35 WCs,
4 French WCs, 2 CWPs. ✆ ♿

Excursions; volcanic crater nearby.
PRICES: (1996) Caravan with family 58,000, Tent
with two adults 41,000. CC: Euro/Access, Visa.
From Pozzuoli, follow signs for Solfatara. From
A2/A3, turn off along Tangenziale, Agnano exit
towards Pozzuoli.

RAVENNA 20C

Camping Adriano Punta Marina,
48100 Ravenna.
Tel 0544 437230, Fax 0544 438510. English spoken.
OPEN: 20/04–22/09. SIZE: 14 ha, 900 pitches
(all with elec), 52 hot showers, 132 WCs,
35 French WCs, 20 CWPs. ✆ ♿

PRICES: (1996) Caravan with family 54,000, Tent
with two adults 28,000. CC: Euro/Access, Visa.
From centre of Ravenna, travel north-east
towards coast. Campsite is signposted in Punta
Marina.

Camping Co-op 3 via dei Campeggi 8,
48020 Punta Marina.
Tel 0544 437353, Fax 0544 438144. English spoken.
OPEN: 25/04–15/09. SIZE: 7 ha, 690 pitches
(all with elec, 12 statics), 68 hot showers,
100 WCs, 10 CWPs. ✆ ♿

PRICES: (1996) Caravan with family 50,400,
Tent with two adults 28,900. CC: Visa.
From Ravenna to the coast.

Camping Internazionale Piomboni
Lungomare 421, 48023 Marina di Ravenna.
Tel 0544 530230, Fax 0544 538618. English spoken.
OPEN: 01/05–20/09. SIZE: 5 ha, 400 pitches (all
with elec), 32 hot showers, 80 WCs, 8 CWPs. ✆ ♿

Games room, disco, bikes and tandems.
PRICES: (1996) Caravan with family 45,000,
Tent with two adults 28,000. CC: Euro/Access.
From Ravenna, north on S67.

RICCIONE 20C

Camping Alberello via Torino 80,
47036 Riccione.
Tel 0541 615402. English spoken.
OPEN: 01/05–20/09. SIZE: 4 ha, 333 pitches
(all with elec, 100 statics), 27 hot showers,
53 WCs, 5 CWPs. ✆ ♿

Shop at 0.1 km.
PRICES: (1996) Caravan with family 56,200,
Tent with two adults 34,800. CC: none.
From Riccione town centre go to sea-front and
campsite.

RIMINI 20C

Camping Misano Adriatico
via Litoranea Sud 60, 47046 Misano Adriatico.
Tel 0541 614330, Fax 0541 613502.
English spoken.
OPEN: 14/04–30/09. SIZE: 7 ha, 640 pitches
(all with elec, 10 statics), 48 hot showers,
128 WCs, 42 French WCs, 8 CWPs. ✆ ♿

Free private beach, entertainment.
PRICES: (1996) Caravan with family 26,500,
Tent with two adults 21,000. CC: none.
South of Rimini on coast road to Misano
Adriatico. From centre turn towards the sea.

RIVA DEL GARDA 20B

Camping Nanzel 25010 Limone sul Garda.
Tel 0365 954155, Fax 0365 954468. English spoken.
OPEN: 01/03–31/10. SIZE: 0.7 ha, 12 pitches, 6 hot
showers (charge), 11 WCs, 1 CWP. ✆

Italy

Restaurant at 0.7 km. Private beach; children under 4 free.
PRICES: (1996) Caravan with family 37,500, Tent with two adults 27,500. CC: Euro/Access, Visa.
From Riva del Garda, travel south along lakeside road, through Limone sul Garda and campsite is 1.5 km outside town.

Monte Brione Camping via Brione 32, 38066 Riva del Garda.
Tel 0464 520885, Fax 0464 553178. English spoken.
OPEN: 28/03–01/10. SIZE: 3 ha, 116 pitches (100 with elec), 30 hot showers, 28 WCs, 4 CWPs. ✆ ♿

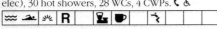

Restaurant at 0.3 km. Mountain bikes, mini-golf, disco.
PRICES: Caravan with family 55,000, Tent with two adults 39,000. CC: Amex, Euro/Access, Visa.
Turn off the road SS240 east of the village. Campsite is signposted.

RODI GARGANICO   21B

Camping Adria Lido del Sole, 71012 Rodi Garganico.
Tel 0884 97179, Fax 0884 97644. English spoken.
OPEN: 01/04–30/09. SIZE: 1.5 ha, 70 pitches (all with elec), 10 hot showers, 30 WCs, 10 French WCs, 2 CWPs. ✆ ♿

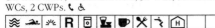

Tennis, children's playground.
PRICES: Caravan with family 67,000, Tent with two adults 42,000. CC: Amex, Euro/Access, Visa.
Lido del Sole is 4 km from Rodi Garganico and campsite is well signposted.

Camping Ripa via Ripa, 71012 Rodi Garganico.
Tel 0884 965367, Fax 0884 965695. English spoken.
OPEN: 01/06–30/09. SIZE: 6 ha, 60 pitches (all with elec, 20 statics), 29 hot showers, 30 WCs. ✆

Water sports, tennis, bowls, football, entertainment.
PRICES: (1996) Caravan with family 51,000, Tent with two adults 30,000. CC: none.
Just north of Rodi Garganico town centre.

ROMA (ROME)   21A

Camping Fabulous viale Cristoforo Colombo, Acilia, 00125 Roma.
Tel 06 5259354. English spoken.
OPEN: all year. SIZE: 30 ha, 300 pitches (all with elec, 700 statics), 28 hot showers (charge), 129 WCs, 4 CWPs. ✆ ♿

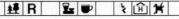

PRICES: (1996) Caravan with family 55,000, Tent with two adults 32,000. CC: Amex.

From Rome 18 km south-east on via Cristoforo Colombo.

Camping Seven Hills via Cassia 1216, 00189 Roma.
Tel 0630 310826, Fax 0630 310039. English spoken.
OPEN: all year. SIZE: 5.5 ha, 300 pitches (all with elec), 40 hot showers, 80 WCs, 1 CWP. ✆

Horse-riding; lots of birds and animals.
PRICES: (1996) Caravan with family 60,000, Tent with two adults 36,000. CC: none.
To the north-west of the city, towards Viterbo and 2.5 km north-east of the outer ring road. Well signposted.

Camping Tiber via Tiberina Km 1,4, 00188 Prima Porta, Roma.
Tel 0633 612314, Fax 0633 612314. English spoken.
OPEN: 01/03–30/11. SIZE: 5 ha, 300 pitches (all with elec), 25 hot showers, 36 WCs, 1 CWP. ✆

PRICES: (1996) Caravan with family 45,600, Tent with two adults 29,400. CC: none.
From all directions take the GRA (ring road) to Roma North and exit at via Flaminia-Prima Porta, No 6. Then follow campsite signs.

SEE ADVERTISEMENT

Italy

ROSARNO 21D

Camping Mimosa Localita Mortelleto, 88033 Nicotera. Tel 0963 81397/81933, Fax 0963 81397/81933. English spoken. OPEN: 15/06–10/09. SIZE: 4 ha, 200 pitches (all with elec, 7 statics), 12 hot showers (charge), 25 WCs, 1 CWP. ☎

Children club; discount for groups, elderly people and long stays. PRICES: (1996) Caravan with family 38,500, Tent with two adults 16,500. CC: none. *From Rosarno towards Nicotera for 8 km.*

ROSETO DEGLI ABRUZZI 21B

Camping Gilda via Makarska, 64026 Roseto degli Abruzzi. Tel 0858 941023. English spoken. OPEN: 01/06–31/08. SIZE: 1.5 ha, 120 pitches (all with elec), 8 hot showers, 20 WCs, 1 CWP. ☎ &

Swimming pool 200 m. PRICES: (1996) Caravan with family 47,500, Tent with two adults 33,500. CC: none. *From Pescara, north on S16.*

Eurcamping Roseto Lungomare Trieste 90, 64026 Roseto degli Abruzzi. Tel 085 8993179, Fax 085 8941463. English spoken. OPEN: all year. SIZE: 6 ha, 500 pitches (all with elec, 30 statics), 37 hot showers, 50 WCs, 3 CWPs. ☎ &

PRICES: (1996) Caravan with family 50,500, Tent with two adults 34,100. CC: none.

ROSSANO 21D

Camping Village Marina di Rossano Club Cda Leuca, 87068 Rossano. Tel 0983 516054, Fax 0983 312069. English spoken. OPEN: 01/04–30/09. SIZE: 70 ha, 250 pitches (all with elec, 50 statics), 44 hot showers, 56 WCs, 4 French WCs, 1 CWP. ☎ &

Updated in 1996. Watersports, tennis, children's playground/club, entertainment. PRICES: Caravan with family 56,000, Tent with two adults 42,000. CC: Amex, Euro/Access, Visa. *Campsite is well signposted.*

SALERNO 21B

Camping La Risacca via delle Barche 11, 84059 Marina di Camerota. Tel 0974 932415, Fax 0974 932035. English spoken. OPEN: 20/05–15/09. SIZE: 2 ha, 130 pitches (all with elec), 10 hot showers, 30 WCs, 2 CWPs. ☎

Shop at 1 km. PRICES: (1996) Caravan with family 76,000, Tent with two adults 49,000. CC: none.

SAN BENEDETTO DEL TRONTO 20D

Camping Duca Amedeo Lungomare Europa 158, 64014 Martinsicuro. Tel 0861 797376, Fax 0861 797264. English spoken. OPEN: 01/05–25/09. SIZE: 1.2 ha, 121 pitches (all with elec, 30 statics), 10 hot showers (charge), 28 WCs, 2 CWPs. ☎ &

Shop at 0.2 km. Restaurant at 0.2 km. PRICES: (1996) Caravan with family 44,000, Tent with two adults 31,000. CC: Euro/Access. *Turn off the A14 (Ancona to Pescara) at San Benedetto del Tronto on to S16, cross railway line to Martinsicuro. Site 500 m from centre.*

International Camping Don Diego Lungo Mare de Gasperi 124, 63013 Grottammare. Tel 0735 583266, Fax 0735 583166. English spoken. OPEN: 01/06–15/09. SIZE: 2 ha, 280 pitches (all with elec), 20 hot showers, 25 WCs, 2 CWPs. ☎ &

Private beach. PRICES: (1996) Caravan with family 48,600, Tent with two adults 33,000. CC: none. *From San Benedetto, 900 m on road to Grottammare.*

SAN FELICE DEL BENACO 20B

Camping Villa Portesina via Magnolia 2, 25010 San Felice del Benaco. Tel 0365 41454, Fax 0365 41454. English spoken. OPEN: 01/04–30/09. SIZE: 10 ha, 20 pitches (all with elec, 10 statics), 5 hot showers (charge), 12 WCs, 12 French WCs.

PRICES: (1996) Caravan with family 51,000, Tent with two adults 35,000. CC: none. *From Salo south 4 km.*

Camping Weekend via Vallone della Selva 10, San Felice del Benaco, 25010 Brescia. Tel 0365 43712, Fax 0365 42196. English spoken. OPEN: 01/05–26/09. SIZE: 9 ha, 202 pitches (all with elec, 20 statics), 16 hot showers, 34 WCs, 11 French WCs, 4 CWPs. ☎ &

Water sports, playground, entertainment; tennis and golf nearby. PRICES: Caravan with family 58,000, Tent with two adults 42,000. CC: none. *From Desenzano towards Salo on S572, right at Cunnetone roundabout and right at fork to Salo. Follow this road and campsite is on left.*

Italy

SAN MARINO   20C

Centro Turistico San Marino Str San Michele 50, Cailungo, 47031 San Marino.
Tel 0549 903964, Fax 0549 907120. English spoken.
OPEN: all year. SIZE: 10 ha, 150 pitches (all with elec, 10 statics), 22 hot showers, 22 WCs, 3 CWPs. ✆ ⅊

Good range of sporting activities; sea 12 km, lake 8 km.
PRICES: (1996) Caravan with family 49,000, Tent with two adults 32,500. CC: Visa.
From A14, exit Rimini-Sud towards San Marino. Turn to Cailungo after the village of Serravalle. Site is well signposted.

SAN MARTINO DI CASTROZZA   20A

Camping Sass Maor via Laghetto 48, 38058 San Martino di Castrozza.
Tel 0439 68347, Fax 0439 68347. English spoken.
OPEN: all year. SIZE: 2 ha, 168 pitches (all with elec), 12 hot showers, 26 WCs, 22 French WCs, 2 CWPs. ✆

PRICES: (1996) Caravan with family 70,000, Tent with two adults 45,000. CC: none.
Turn off downhill from S50 (Predazzo to Fonzaso) at San Martino and continue for 800 m but it is easier to come from Fiera di Primiero since you do not have to drive through Passo Rolle (2000 m high).

SAN PIERO IN BAGNO   20C

Altosavio Camping S P 43, 37c, 47026 San Piero in Bagno.
Tel 0543 917670. English spoken.
OPEN: 24/04–30/09. SIZE: 1.3 ha, 74 pitches (all with elec, 20 statics), 10 hot showers, 16 WCs, 4 French WCs. ✆

Shop at 2 km. Restaurant at 2 km.
PRICES: (1996) Caravan with family 39,500, Tent with two adults 24,000. CC: none.
From San Piero in Bagno, take road 43 towards Alfero for 2 km.

SAN VINCENZO   21A

Camping Park Albatross 57027 San Vincenzo.
Tel 0565 701018, Fax 0565 703589. English spoken.
OPEN: 29/03–07/09. SIZE: 11 ha, 678 pitches (all with elec, 30 statics), 109 hot showers, 115 WCs, 2 CWPs. ✆

Bike hire; tennis, horse-riding and disco nearby.
PRICES: Caravan with family 60,900, Tent with two adults 38,700. CC: Amex, Euro/Access, Visa.

From Livorno, leave S1 at San Vincenzo-Nord exit, go south along coast road for 7 km, then turn left.

SANTA MARIA DI CASTELLABATE   21B

Camping Trezene
84072 Santa Maria di Castellabate.
Tel 0974 965013. English spoken.
OPEN: 01/04–31/10. SIZE: 2.5 ha, 200 pitches (all with elec, 60 statics), 12 hot showers (charge), 38 WCs, 2 CWPs. ⅊

PRICES: (1996) Caravan with family 58,000, Tent with two adults 42,000. CC: none.
Campsite is on the coast, just off route 267.

SANTHIA   20C

Fraz Comuna 45 13040 Viverone.
Tel 0161 98169.
OPEN: 01/04–30/09. SIZE: 3 ha, 220 pitches (all with elec, 210 statics), 10 hot showers (charge), 44 WCs, 3 CWPs. ✆

Restaurant at 1 km. Water sports.
PRICES: (1996) Caravan with family 39,000, Tent with two adults 27,000. CC: none.
Exit the A4 (Turin/Milan) at Santhia, head north on 143 and then take S228 towards Ivrea. In Viverone turn left by the petrol station.

SARDEGNA (SARDINIA)

AGLIENTU   21A

Camping Baia Blu La Tortuga Loc Vignola Mare, 07020 Aglientu, Sardegna.
Tel 0796 02060, Fax 0796 02040. English spoken.
OPEN: 19/04–04/10. SIZE: 17 ha, 700 pitches (all with elec), 179 hot showers (charge), 187 WCs, 133 French WCs, 24 CWPs. ✆ ⅊

Windsurfing, tennis, excursions.
PRICES: (1996) Caravan with family 72,500, Tent with two adults 43,500. CC: none.
From Porto Torres, take road to Castelsardo, Valledoria then Vignola (92 km).

ALES   21A

Camping Sennisceddu 09090 Pau, Sardegna.
Tel 0783 939281, Fax 0783 52255.
English spoken.
OPEN: all year. SIZE: 4 ha, 38 pitches (all with elec), 16 hot showers (charge), 20 WCs. ✆ ⅊

Shop at 2 km.
PRICES: (1996) Caravan with family 36,500, Tent

with two adults 21,000. CC: Euro/Access, Visa.
*From Ales, take the 442 north-east towards Laconi
and follow signs to Pau.*

BUDONI 21A

Camping Malamuri Marina di Ottiolu,
08020 Budoni, Sardegna.
Tel 0784 846007, Fax 0784 846275. English spoken.
OPEN: 15/05–30/09. SIZE: 3 ha, 200 pitches
(all with elec), 13 hot showers (charge), 10 WCs,
25 French WCs.

PRICES: (1996) Caravan with family 54,200,
Tent with two adults 30,400. CC: none.
*30 km south of Olbia on S125. Head for Marina
di Ottiolu and follow signs to campsite.*

DORGALI 21A

Camping Cala Gonone via Collodi 1,
08020 Cala Gonone, Sardegna.
Tel 0784 93165, Fax 0784 93256. English spoken.
OPEN: 01/04–10/10. SIZE: 5 ha, 50 hot showers,
80 WCs, 10 French WCs, 4 CWPs.

Tennis.
PRICES: (1996) Caravan with family 71,600,
Tent with two adults 43,800. CC: none.
*Turn off the S125 approx 2 km south of Dorgali,
go through tunnel, then 7 km of winding road to
sea and site.*

MILIS 21A

Camping Nurapolis 09026 Narbolia, Sardegna.
Tel 0783 52283, Fax 0783 52255.
English spoken.
OPEN: all year. SIZE: 12 ha, 275 pitches (all with
elec, 70 statics), 27 hot showers, 55 WCs,
10 CWPs. &

PRICES: (1996) Caravan with family 41,500, Tent
with two adults 25,500. CC: Amex, Euro/Access, Visa.
From Milis, follow signs to Narbolia and campsite.

MURAVERA 21C

Camping Torre Salinas Torre Salinas,
09043 Muravera, Sardegna.
Tel 070 999032, Fax 070 999001.
English spoken.
OPEN: 01/04–15/10. SIZE: 1 ha, 100 pitches
(all with elec), 15 hot showers, 21 WCs, 4 French
WCs. & &

PRICES: (1996) Caravan with family 49,500, Tent
with two adults 31,500. CC: none.
8 km south of Muravera.

OLBIA 21A

Camping Villaggio Isuledda
07020 Cannigione di Arzachena, Sard.
Tel 0789 86012, Fax 0789 86089. English spoken.
OPEN: 01/04–15/10. SIZE: 15 ha, 650 pitches (all
with elec), 157 hot showers, 198 WCs, 1 CWP. &

PRICES: (1996) Caravan with family 84,000, Tent
with two adults 58,000. CC: Amex, Euro/Access, Visa.
*From Olbia port north on 125, turn right just
before Arzachena to Cannigione.*

ORISTANO 21A

Camping Is Arenas Narbolia,
09070 Oristano, Sardegna.
Tel 0783 52284, Fax 0783 52284. English spoken.
OPEN: 01/04–30/09. SIZE: 6 ha, 150 pitches
(20 statics), 12 hot showers, 40 French WCs. & &

PRICES: (1996) Caravan with family 53,700,
Tent with two adults 35,500. CC: Visa.
*Leave the S131 (the main road on the island) at
Oristano and drive north on S292 to Riola Sardo
then follow signs to site (8 km).*

SANT'ANTIOCO 21C

Camping Tonnara Localita Calasapone,
09017 Sant'Antioco, Sardegna.
Tel 0781 809058, Fax 0781 809036. English spoken.
OPEN: 01/04–31/10. SIZE: 7 ha, 130 pitches
(all with elec), 48 hot showers, 48 WCs, 3 CWPs. &

Tennis, beach volley.
PRICES: (1996) Caravan with family 61,500, Tent
with two adults 34,000. CC: Amex, Euro/Access, Visa.
*On a small island just off the south coast of
Sardegna. 12 km from town on Calasapone beach.*

SASSARI 21A

Camping International Valledoria
07039 Valledoria, Sardegna.
Tel 0795 84070, Fax 0795 84058. English spoken.
OPEN: 01/06–30/09. SIZE: 10 ha, 300 pitches
(all with elec, 25 statics), 24 hot showers,
80 WCs, 4 CWPs. &

PRICES: (1996) Caravan with family 64,000,
Tent with two adults 32,500. CC: Visa.
Site is well signposted in Valledoria.

SINISCOLA 21A

Selema Camping Tiria Soliana, Santa Lucia,
08029 Siniscola, Sardegna.
Tel 0784 819068, Fax 0784 819068. English spoken.

Italy

OPEN: 15/05–15/10. SIZE: 7.5 ha, 150 pitches (all with elec, 30 statics), 26 hot showers, 26 WCs, 4 CWPs. ✆

≋ ⚞ 🏍 R ⬛ 🍺 ☕ ✗ ▢ ⬛ 🚙

PRICES: (1996) Caravan with family 68,000, Tent with two adults 35,000. CC: none.
From Olbia south on S125. Campsite is 8 km south of Siniscola.

SORSO 21A

Camping International Cristina Localita Platamona, 07037 Sorso, Sardegna.
Tel 0793 10230, Fax 0793 10589. English spoken.
OPEN: 01/06–30/09. SIZE: 10 ha, 500 pitches (250 with elec), 26 hot showers, 88 WCs. ✆ ♿

≋ 🏍 R ⓢ ☕ ✗ ⤳ ⬛

PRICES: (1996) Caravan with family 59,000, Tent with two adults 31,500. CC: none.
From Porto Torres, 7 km east on S200.

VALLEDORIA 21A

Camping La Foce 07039 Valledoria, Sardegna.
Tel 0795 82109, Fax 0795 82191. English spoken.
OPEN: 15/05–30/09. SIZE: 25 ha, 34 hot showers, 120 WCs. ✆

≋ ⚞ ⚲ R ⬛ 🍺 ☕ ✗ ⤳ 🏠 🚙

Tennis, watersports, boat trips.
PRICES: (1996) Caravan with family 61,000, Tent with two adults 30,500. CC: Euro/Access, Visa.
Follow signs to campsite in Valledoria.

END OF SARDEGNA (SARDINIA) RESORTS

SARZANA 20C

Senato Park Senato di Lerici, 19032 Lerici.
Tel 0187 988396, Fax 0187 988396. English spoken.
OPEN: 01/06–30/09. SIZE: 3 ha, 100 pitches (all with elec, 30 statics), 37 hot showers, 27 WCs, 1 CWP. ✆ ♿

~ ⚲ R ⬛ 🍺 ☕ ✗ ⤳ 🏠

PRICES: (1996) Caravan with family 48,800, Tent with two adults 27,900. CC: none.
Lerici is just south of Sarzana; campsite at Senato di Lerici is well signposted.

SAVONA 20C

Camping Letimbro via Cima Valle 125d, 17040 Santuario, Savona.
Tel 0198 79031. English spoken.
OPEN: 15/05–15/09. SIZE: 1 ha, 80 pitches (all with elec), 4 hot showers (charge), 18 WCs, 18 French WCs, 1 CWP. ♿

~ ⚞ 🏍 R ▢ 🍺 ☕ ✗ ⤳ ⬛

PRICES: (1996) Caravan with family 42,000, Tent

---

with two adults 24,000. CC: Euro/Access.
From Savona, north for 7 km. Follow signs.

Camping Stella via Rio Basco 62, 17040 Stella San Giovanni.
Tel 0197 03269, Fax 0194 87590. English spoken.
OPEN: 01/04–30/09. SIZE: 1 ha, 80 pitches (all with elec, 25 statics), 8 hot showers (charge), 21 WCs, 2 CWPs. ✆

~ ⚞ ⚴ R ▢ ☕ ⤳

Shop at 2 km. Restaurant at 1.5 km. Sea 5.5 km.
PRICES: (1996) Caravan with family 54,000, Tent with two adults 30,000. CC: none.
Leaving the A10 at Albissola, take the S334 towards Sassello for 5 km. Campsite is well signposted in Stella San Giovanni.

SESTO CALENDE 20A

Camping Italia Lido via Cicegnola 88, 28053 Castelletto Ticino.
Tel 0331 923032, Fax 0331 923032. English spoken.
OPEN: 01/03–30/10. SIZE: 2 ha, 200 pitches (all with elec, 140 statics), 12 hot showers, 28 WCs, 20 French WCs, 1 CWP. ✆

≋ ⚞ 🏍 R ▢ 🍺 ☕ ✗ ⬛

PRICES: (1996) Caravan with family 39,000, Tent with two adults 22,000. CC: Visa.
2 km west of Sesto Calende on S33. A8 from Milano. A26 from Torino-Genova.

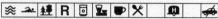

Camping Italia Lido

near Sesto Calende

On the shore.....of Lake Maggiore

Camping La Sfinge via Angera 1, 21018 Sesto Calende.
Tel 0331 924531, Fax 0331 924531. English spoken.
OPEN: 01/03–30/10. SIZE: 6 ha, 165 pitches (all with elec, 135 statics), 8 hot showers, 32 WCs, 28 French WCs, 4 CWPs. ✆ ♿

≋ ⚞ 🏍 R ⬛ 🍺 ☕ ✗ ⤳ ⬛

PRICES: Caravan with family 50,000, Tent with two adults 34,000. CC: none.
1 km from Sesto Calende.

SICILIA (SICILY)

AGRIGENTO 21D

Camping Internationale San Leone, Agrigento, Sicily.
Tel 0922 416121, Fax 0922 416121. English spoken.

OPEN: all year. SIZE: 120 pitches (all with elec, 10 statics), 5 hot showers, 40 WCs, 2 French WCs. ℓ

PRICES: (1996) Caravan with family 47,500, Tent with two adults 30,500. CC: none.
San Leone is 3 km south of Agrigento on the coast.

AUGUSTA 21D

Camping Baia del Silenzio Brucoli, 96010 Augusta, Sicilia.
Tel 0931 981881. English spoken.
OPEN: all year. SIZE: 1.5 ha, 140 pitches (all with elec), 10 hot showers, 50 WCs, 1 CWP. ℓ &

PRICES: (1996) Caravan with family 43,000, Tent with two adults 26,000. CC: none.
From Augusta go north for about 5 km to Brucoli; turn right after railway station in Brucoli and campsite is 3 km.

AVOLA 21D

Camping Pantanello Lungomare, Avola (Siracusa), Sicilia.
Tel 0931 823275.
OPEN: all year. SIZE: 0.7 ha, 30 pitches, 2 hot showers (charge), 10 WCs, 2 French WCs, 1 CWP.

Shop at 0.1 km. Restaurant at 0.1 km.
PRICES: (1996) Caravan with family 34,000, Tent with two adults 22,000. CC: none.

CAPO D'ORLANDO 21D

Camping Santarosa via Trazzera Marina, 98071 Capo d'Orlando, Sicilia.
Tel 0941 901723, Fax 0941 912384. English spoken.
OPEN: 15/06–15/09. SIZE: 2.8 ha, 124 pitches (89 with elec, 10 statics), 21 hot showers, 33 WCs, 7 French WCs, 1 CWP. ℓ

Shop at 0.5 km.
PRICES: (1996) Caravan with family 42,500, Tent with two adults 22,500. CC: none.
From A20, take Brolo or Rocca di Caprileone exits and follow signs to campsite.

CATANIA 21D

Camp Villagio Turistica Europeo
via Kennedy 91, 95100 Catania, Sicilia.
Tel 0955 91026, Fax 0591 911. English spoken.
OPEN: 01/06–30/09. SIZE: 6 ha, 80 pitches (all with elec), 15 hot showers (charge), 32 WCs. ℓ

PRICES: (1996) Caravan with family 43,800, Tent with two adults 24,000. CC: Amex, Visa.
Site is 7 km south of Catania towards Siracusa.

ISOLA DELLE FEMMINE 21D

Camping La Playa via Marino 55, 90040 Isola delle Femmine, Sicilia.
Tel 0918 677001, Fax 0918 677001. English spoken.
OPEN: 01/04–31/10. SIZE: 2.2 ha, 80 pitches (all with elec, 10 statics), 6 hot showers (charge), 20 WCs, 2 CWPs. ℓ

Playground, ball games, table tennis, boules.
PRICES: (1996) Caravan with family 34,000, Tent with two adults 23,000. CC: Amex, Euro/Access, Visa.
From Palermo, drive south towards Trapani on A29 and take Isola exit.

MARINA DI RAGUSA 21D

Camping Baia del Sol 97010 Marina di Ragusa.
Tel 0932 230344, Fax 0932 239844. English spoken.
OPEN: all year. SIZE: 40 hot showers, 40 WCs. ℓ &

PRICES: (1996) Caravan with family 48,000, Tent with two adults 28,000. CC: none.
Well signposted.

Camping Rocca dei Tramonti
Punta Braccetto, 97019 Vittoria, Sicily.
Tel 0932 918054, Fax 0932 918054. English spoken.
OPEN: 05/04–15/10. SIZE: 3 ha, 200 pitches (all with elec), 8 hot showers (charge), 80 WCs, 1 CWP. ℓ

PRICES: Caravan with family 42,500, Tent with two adults 26,000. CC: Visa.
10 km north west of Marina di Ragusa.

MESSINA 21D

Camping Lo Scoglio
98079 Castel di Tusa, Sicilia.
Tel 0921 34345. English spoken.
OPEN: 15/06–15/09. SIZE: 1 ha, 100 pitches (all with elec, 4 statics), 8 hot showers, 20 WCs, 4 French WCs, 2 CWPs. ℓ

PRICES: (1996) Caravan with family 50,000, Tent with two adults 28,000. CC: none.

Camping Villaggio Turistico Marinello
via del Sole 17, 98060 Oliveri, Sicilia.
Tel 0941 313000, Fax 0941 313702. English spoken.
OPEN: 01/04–30/10. SIZE: 3 ha, 250 pitches (all with elec), 20 hot showers, 68 WCs, 30 French WCs, 3 CWPs. ℓ &

Tennis, basket ball, table tennis.
PRICES: (1996) Caravan with family 57,000, Tent with two adults 36,000. CC: Amex, Euro/Access, Visa.

Italy (side margin)

SICILIA (SICILY) RESORTS CONTINUED

PORTOPALO DI CAPO PASSERO 21D

Camping Capo Passero
96010 Portopalo do Capo Passero.
Tel 0931 842333.
OPEN: 01/03–15/10. SIZE: 0.3 ha, 100 pitches
(50 with elec, 20 statics), 4 hot showers, 40 WCs,
10 French WCs.

Restaurant at 1 km.
PRICES: (1996) Caravan with family 47,000,
Tent with two adults 26,000. CC: Euro/Access.
Portopalo is on the southernmost tip of the island.

SELINUNTE 21C

Camping Il Maggiolino S115 Dir A,
91022 Castelvetrano, Sicilia.
Tel 0924 46044. English spoken.
OPEN: 01/03–30/10. SIZE: 0.7 ha, 30 pitches
(15 with elec), 4 hot showers, 7 WCs, 3 CWPs.

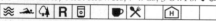

Shop at 1.5 km.
PRICES: (1996) Caravan with family 34,500,
Tent with two adults 20,000.
CC: Euro/Access, Visa.
From Castelvetrano 10 km south.

SFERRACAVALLO 21D

Camping degli Ulivi via Pegaso 25,
Sferracavallo, 90148 Palermo, Sicilia.
Tel 091 533021, Fax 091 530265.
English spoken.
OPEN: all year. SIZE: 5 ha, 30 pitches (50 with elec),
3 hot showers, 10 WCs, 1 CWP.

PRICES: Caravan with family 39,000, Tent with two
adults 18,000. CC: none.
From Palermo on A29 coast road.

SIRACUSA 21D

Villagio Agrituristico/Camping La Torre
contrada Torre Judica, via Primosole,
96010 Palazzolo Acreide, Sicilia.
Tel 0931 882171, Fax 0931 881522.
English spoken.
OPEN: all year. SIZE: 30 ha, 90 pitches,
12 hot showers, 12 WCs.

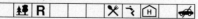

Shop at 1 km. Tennis; good archaeological area
and within reach of Europe's largest necropolis.
PRICES: Caravan with family 32,000,
Tent with two adults 22,000. CC: none.
From Siracusa on S124 to Palazzolo Acreide.

TAORMINA 21D

Camping Internazionale Almoetia via San
Marco 19, 95011 Calatabiano, Sicilia.
Tel 0956 41936, Fax 0956 41936. English spoken.
OPEN: all year. SIZE: 2 ha, 10 hot showers (charge),
36 WCs, 10 French WCs, 1 CWP.

Excursions arranged.
PRICES: (1996) Caravan with family 45,000,
Tent with two adults 25,000. CC: none.
*Approx 8 km south of Taormina, turn seawards
from S114. Signposted.*

La Focetta Sicula via Torrente Agro,
98030 Sant Alessio Siculo, Sicilia.
Tel 0942 751657, Fax 0954 92277. English spoken.
OPEN: all year. SIZE: 1 ha, 120 pitches (all with elec,
6 statics), 4 hot showers (charge), 20 WCs,
10 French WCs.

PRICES: (1996) Caravan with family 45,000,
Tent with two adults 31,000. CC: none.
*From Taormina north on S114 then follow
campsite signs. (10% discount with RAC guide.)*

TRAPANI 21C

Camping Egad 91023 Favignana, Sicilia.
Tel 0923 921555, Fax 0923 539370.
English spoken.
OPEN: 01/03–31/10. SIZE: 2 ha, 50 pitches (all with
elec), 12 hot showers (charge), 36 WCs, 25 French
WCs, 2 CWPs.

Bicycle hire, diving centre, sports field, organised
day trips.
PRICES: (1996) Caravan with family 51,000,
Tent with two adults 29,000. CC: none.
*1 hour from Trapani by ferry, or 20 minutes by
hydrofoil. Well signposted on island (Isole
Favignana).*

END OF SICILIA (SICILY) RESORTS

SIENA 20C

Siena Colleverde Camping strada di
Scacciapensieri 47, 53100 Siena.
Tel 0577 280044, Fax 0577 281041.
English spoken.
OPEN: 21/03–10/11. SIZE: 4 ha, 110 pitches
(all with elec), 30 hot showers, 51 WCs, 16 French
WCs, 2 CWPs.

PRICES: (1996) Caravan with family 63,500,
Tent with two adults 26,000. CC: none.
*Coming from Firenze or Grosseto exit Siena Nord
and campsite is 3 km, well signposted.*

Italy

SORRENTO 21B

Camping Santa Fortunata Campogaio
via Capo 39, 80060 Sorrento.
Tel 081 8073574, Fax 081 8073590.
English spoken.
OPEN: 01/04–30/09. SIZE: 50 ha, 800 pitches
(all with elec, 50 statics), 35 hot showers,
105 WCs, 30 French WCs, 8 CWPs.

PRICES: (1996) Caravan with family 65,000,
Tent with two adults 31,000. CC: Euro/Access.
1 km from Sorrento.

International Camping 80067 Sorrento.
Tel 081 8781344, Fax 081 8073450. English spoken.
OPEN: all year. SIZE: 15 ha, 70 pitches (all with elec,
10 statics), 12 hot showers, 34 WCs, 1 CWP.

PRICES: (1996) Caravan with family 58,000,
Tent with two adults 35,000. CC: Amex.
*Campsite is 300 m from Sorrento going towards
Capo di Sorrento and well signposted.*

Villagio Turistico Costa Alta
80063 Piano di Sorrento.
Tel 0815 321832, Fax 0818 788368.
English spoken.
OPEN: 01/03–31/10. SIZE: 40 pitches (all with elec,
50 statics), 50 hot showers, 60 WCs.

Shop at 10 km.
PRICES: (1996) Caravan with family 69,000,
Tent with two adults 39,000. CC: none.
*Leave Napoli-Salerno motorway at Castellamare
di Stabia and go towards Penisola Sorrentina. At
the first town, Meta, follow signs on the right-
hand side to campsite.*

SOTTOMARINA 20C

Camping Miramare via Barbarigo,
30019 Sottomarina.
Tel 0414 90610. English spoken.
OPEN: 01/05–20/09. SIZE: 4 ha, 320 pitches
(all with elec), 50 hot showers, 53 WCs, 42 French
WCs, 3 CWPs.

PRICES: (1996) Caravan with family 54,000, Tent
with two adults 35,000. CC: Amex, Euro/Access.
From Venezia, south on S309 to Chioggia.

LA SPEZIA 20C

Camping River Armezzone, 19031 Ameglia.
Tel 0187 65920, Fax 0187 65183.
English spoken.
OPEN: 01/05–30/09. SIZE: 4 ha, 270 pitches
(all with elec, 100 statics), 24 hot showers,
48 WCs, 10 CWPs.

Shop at 0.7 km. Bikes and boats for hire.
PRICES: (1996) Caravan with family 48,000, Tent
with two adults 29,300. CC: Euro/Access, Visa.
*Leave the A12 motorway at Lerici/Ameglia, head
for Ameglia, 5 km. Campsite is north-west of
village.*

SPOLETO 21A

Camping Villaggio Turistico Il Girasole
Fraz Petrognano 11, 06049 Spoleto.
Tel 0743 51106, Fax 0743 51583. English spoken.
OPEN: 13/02–10/01. SIZE: 4 ha, 70 pitches (all with
elec, 10 statics), 9 hot showers, 16 WCs, 10 French
WCs, 2 CWPs.

Swimming pool is very small; 10% discount in the
restaurant.
PRICES: (1996) Caravan with family 51,000,
Tent with two adults 30,000. CC: Amex,
Euro/Access, Visa.
From Spoleto, north on S3.

SQUINZANO 21B

Camping Torre Rinalda SPA Litoranea
Salentina, 73100 Lecce.
Tel 0832 382161, Fax 0832 382165. English spoken.
OPEN: all year. SIZE: 23 ha, 1000 pitches (all with
elec), 120 hot showers, 420 WCs.

Entertainment, tennis, archery, horse-riding.
PRICES: (1996) Caravan with family 56,500, Tent
with two adults 13,500. CC: none.

TARQUINIA 21A

Camping Europa via Aurelia Km 102,
01016 Tarquinia.
Tel 0766 814010, Fax 0766 814075.
English spoken.
OPEN: 01/04–30/09. SIZE: 22 ha, 750 pitches
(700 with elec, 22 statics), 65 hot showers
(charge), 110 WCs, 8 CWPs.

PRICES: (1996) Caravan with family 75,950, Tent
with two adults 46,650. CC: none.

TAVERNELLE 20C

Camping Villaggio Turistico Tavernelle
via Val d'Enza 43, Lunigiana,
54010 Tavernelle di Licciana Nardi.
Tel 0187 425050, Fax 0187 425050.
English spoken.
OPEN: 10/05–10/09. SIZE: 10.8 ha, 115 pitches
(all with elec, 4 statics), 12 hot showers (charge),
10 WCs, 8 French WCs, 1 CWP.

Horse-riding & fishing.
PRICES: (1996) Caravan with family 41,000,
Tent with two adults 29,000. CC: none.
*In the Lunigiana Valley. Leave Parma to La
Spezia motorway at Aulla and go north-east for
18 km towards Licciana Nardi. Campsite is well
signposted.*

TERAMO 21B

Camping del Salinello contrada Piane a Mare,
64019 Tortoreto Lido.
Tel 0861 786306, Fax 0861 786451.
English spoken.
OPEN: 15/05−28/09. SIZE: 15 ha, 1000 pitches
(all with elec), 82 hot showers, 47 WCs,
188 French WCs, 2 CWPs.

Excellent sports facilities and entertainment
programme.
PRICES: Caravan with family 61,000,
Tent with two adults 42,000. CC: none.
*Campsite at end of Lungomare-Sud,
Tortoreto Lido.*

near Teramo

TERRACINA 21B

Camping Europa via Appia Km 104,500,
04019 Terracina.
Tel 0773 726523. English spoken.
OPEN: 01/05−15/09. SIZE: 3 ha, 170 pitches
(all with elec, 40 statics), 8 hot showers (charge),
45 WCs, 3 CWPs.

PRICES: (1996) Caravan with family 65,000,
Tent with two adults 45,000. CC: none.

Camping Internazionale Badino via Badino,
Km 4,800, Porto Badino, 04019 Terracina.
Tel 0773 764430. English spoken.
OPEN: 01/04−30/09. SIZE: 2 ha, 100 pitches
(all with elec), 7 hot showers (charge), 16 WCs,
1 CWP.

Shop at 0.4 km. Restaurant at 0.4 km.
PRICES: (1996) Caravan with family 56,000,
Tent with two adults 37,000. CC: none.
Porto Badino is 4 km north of Terracina.

TORBOLE 20B

Camping Bellavista Localita Linfano,
38069 Torbole.
Tel 0464 505644, Fax 0464 505166. English spoken.
OPEN: 01/04−20/10. SIZE: 2 ha, 113 pitches
(all with elec), 9 hot showers, 17 WCs, 3 CWPs.

Restaurant at 0.1 km.
PRICES: (1996) Caravan with family 44,000,
Tent with two adults 30,000. CC: Amex.
*From Trento, head south on S12 or A22. Exit on to
S240 for Torbole.*

Camping Maroadi Torbole sul Garda,
38069 Torbole.
Tel 0464 505175, Fax 0464 506291. English spoken.
OPEN: 01/04−31/10. SIZE: 3 ha, 271 pitches (all with
elec), 24 hot showers, 34 WCs, 4 CWPs.

Restaurant at 0.2 km. Windsurfing school,
mountain-bike hire.
PRICES: (1996) Caravan with family 44,000,
Tent with two adults 30,000. CC: none.
*From Trento, south on A22, exit S240 to Torbole.
1 km after Torbole (heading towards Riva del
Garda), campsite can be found on the left.*

Terme Bellavista 37010 Cassone, Verona.
Tel 045 7420244, Fax 045 7420244. English spoken.
OPEN: all year. SIZE: 3 ha, 177 pitches (all with
elec), 21 hot showers, 27 WCs, 4 CWPs.

PRICES: Caravan with family 48,000, Tent with two
adults 33,000. CC: none.

TOSCOLANO 20B

Camping Chiaro di Luna via Statale 218,
25088 Toscolano-Maderno.
Tel 0365 641179, Fax 0365 641179. English spoken.
OPEN: 01/04−30/09. SIZE: 9 ha, 60 pitches (all with
elec, 6 statics), 7 hot showers, 10 WCs, 1 CWP.

Restaurant at 1 km.
PRICES: (1996) Caravan with family 44,000,
Tent with two adults 29,500. CC: none.
From Brescia, north on S456.

TRENTO 20A/C

Camping al Castagni Loc Lobea 1, 38051 Torcegno.
Tel 0461 766129, Fax 0461 766129.
OPEN: all year. SIZE: 1 ha, 82 pitches (all with elec,
40 statics), 8 hot showers (charge), 10 WCs,
4 French WCs, 2 CWPs.

Shop at 0.3 km. Restaurant at 0.3 km. Swimming
pool 6 km.

Italy

PRICES: (1996) Caravan with family 33,500, Tent with two adults 21,500. CC: none.
From Trento, take S47 through Roncegno to Torcegno.

Camping Mario via Lungo Lago 1, 38052 Caldonazzo.
Tel 0461 723341, Fax 0461 723106. English spoken. OPEN: 15/05–15/09. SIZE: 2 ha, 128 pitches (all with elec), 10 hot showers (charge), 6 WCs, 20 French WCs, 3 CWPs. ℄

Shop at 1 km. Restaurant at 0.5 km.
PRICES: (1996) Caravan with family 42,000, Tent with two adults 28,000. CC: none.
From Trento head south on the 47 towards Padova. Turn right at Levico around the lake, to Caldonazzo.

Camping Spiaggia Lago di Molveno 38018 Molveno.
Tel 0461 586978, Fax 0461 586330. English spoken. OPEN: all year. SIZE: 3 ha, 264 pitches (all with elec, 100 statics), 28 hot showers, 32 WCs, 10 French WCs, 2 CWPs. ℄

PRICES: (1996) Caravan with family 57,000, Tent with two adults 39,000. CC: none.
From Bolzano, take A22 exit S Michele and south to Molveno, about 25 km.

Camping St Josef am Kalterer See Weinstrasse 75, 39052 Kaltern.
Tel 0471 960170. English spoken. OPEN: 15/03–05/11. SIZE: 1.4 ha, 150 pitches (all with elec, 10 statics), 15 hot showers, 21 WCs, 4 French WCs, 1 CWP.

PRICES: (1996) Caravan with family 43,600, Tent with two adults 30,100. CC: Euro/Access, Visa.
From Trento north on A22, 7 km from Ora exit.

International Camping al Sole via Maffei, 38060 Molina di Ledro.
Tel 0464 508496. English spoken. OPEN: 01/05–30/09. SIZE: 2 ha, 200 pitches (50 with elec), 12 hot showers (charge), 24 WCs, 24 French WCs, 2 CWPs. &

Situated beside Lake Ledro's finest beach.
PRICES: (1996) Caravan with family 30,800, Tent with two adults 19,400. CC: none.
9 km from Lago del Garda and 500 m from Molina de Ledro village. Well signposted.

TRIESTE   20D

Camping Imperial Aurisina Cave 55, 34011 Trieste.
Tel 0402 00459, Fax 0402 00459. English spoken. OPEN: 25/05–15/09. SIZE: 1.5 ha, 50 pitches

all with elec, 20 statics), 4 hot showers, 4 WCs, 1 CWP. ℄

Camper van service; sea:4 km. 10% LS discount.
PRICES: Caravan with family 41,000, Tent with two adults 31,000. CC: none.
From Trieste, take S14 north, leave S14 at Sistiana exit, follow signs for Aurisina.

Camping Marepineta 24019 Trieste.
Tel 040 299264, Fax 040 299265. English spoken. OPEN: 01/05–30/09. SIZE: 10.8 ha, 500 pitches (all with elec, 150 statics), 56 hot showers (charge), 75 WCs, 19 French WCs, 8 CWPs. ℄ &

Boating facilities, playground, free bus to the beach.
PRICES: (1996) Caravan with family 55,600, Tent with two adults 39,600. CC: none.
From the A4 Venezia to Trieste, exit Duino. Campsite is 1.5 km on S14.

TROPEA   21D

Camping Quattro Scogli Capo Vaticano, 88030 San Nicolo di Ricadi.
Tel 0963 663126, Fax 0963 663115. English spoken. OPEN: 01/04–31/10. SIZE: 0.8 ha, 30 pitches (all with elec, 5 statics), 8 hot showers (charge), 18 WCs, 10 French WCs, 2 CWPs. ℄ &

PRICES: (1996) Caravan with family 50,000, Tent with two adults 31,000. CC: none.
Drive north for 10 km from Tropea to Capo Vaticano. Campsite is well signposted.

VARESE   20A

Camping International Lido Lungolago, 21026 Gavirate.
Tel 0332 744707, Fax 0332 744707.
OPEN: 01/04–30/10. SIZE: 0.9 ha, 50 pitches (all with elec, 25 statics), 9 hot showers, 13 WCs, 2 CWPs. ℄

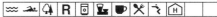

Shop at 0.5 km.
PRICES: (1996) Caravan with family 30,000, Tent with two adults 20,000. CC: none.
From Varese, 10 km west to Gavirate.

Camping Trelago via Trelago 20, 21030 Ghirla.
Tel 0332 716583, Fax 0332 719650. English spoken. OPEN: 15/04–15/09. SIZE: 3 ha, 100 pitches (all with elec, 20 statics), 10 hot showers (charge), 14 French WCs, 2 CWPs. ℄

Mini-golf, table tennis, private beach.
PRICES: (1996) Caravan with family 29,000, Tent with two adults 21,000. CC: none.
From Varese, north on S233 towards Luino.

Italy

VENEZIA (VENICE) 20C

Camping Alba d'Oro via Triestina, Ca'Noghera, 30030 Venezia. Tel 0415 415102, Fax 0415 415102. English spoken. OPEN: 01/04–30/09. SIZE: 6 ha, 80 pitches (all with elec), 8 hot showers (charge), 18 WCs, 12 French WCs, 2 CWPs. 🕭 🕭

PRICES: (1996) Caravan with family 52,000, Tent with two adults 32,000. CC: Euro/Access, Visa. *2 km from the Marco Polo airport. SS Triestina.*

Camping Carav della Serenissima via Padana 334a, 30030 Oriago, Venezia. Tel 0419 20286, Fax 0419 20286. English spoken. OPEN: 30/03–10/11. SIZE: 2 ha, 150 pitches (all with elec), 10 hot showers, 20 WCs, 4 French WCs. 🕭

Easy bus ride to Venezia. PRICES: (1996) Caravan with family 28,000, Tent with two adults 26,000. CC: Euro/Access, Visa.

Between Venezia and Padova on S11.

VERBANIA 20A

Camping Lido Toce via Per Feriolo 41, 28040 Verbania. Tel 0323 496087, Fax 0323 496220. English spoken. OPEN: 01/05–30/09. SIZE: 20 ha, 100 pitches (all with elec, 10 statics), 4 hot showers (charge), 20 WCs, 4 CWPs. 🕭

Restaurant at 1 km. PRICES: (1996) Caravan with family 48,000, Tent with two adults 30,000. CC: none. *From Stresa, take the SS33 to Feriolo. Turn right near bridge 1 km beyond crossroads.*

Village-Camping Isolino via Per Feriolo 25, 28040 Fondotoce. Tel 0323 496080, Fax 0323 496414. English spoken. OPEN: 22/03–21/09. SIZE: 12 ha, 750 pitches (all with elec, 50 statics), 58 hot showers, 130 WCs, 18 CWPs. 🕭 🕭

Ball games, water sports, entertainment. PRICES: (1996) Caravan with family 46,000, Tent with two adults 30,000. CC: none. *From Verbania, south on S34 to Fondotoce, between S34 and the Toce river.*

VIAREGGIO 20C

Bosco Verde via Kennedy 5, 55048 Torre del Lago Puccini. Tel 0584 359343, Fax 0584 341981. English spoken. OPEN: 15/04–30/09. SIZE: 5 ha, 420 pitches (all with elec, 30 statics), 30 hot showers, 70 WCs, 25 French WCs. 🕭 🕭

Shop at 0.2 km. PRICES: (1996) Caravan with family 48,000, Tent with two adults 36,000. CC: Visa. *5 km from Viareggio, 15 km from Pisa.*

Camping Europa via dei Tigli, 55048 Torre del Lago. Tel 0584 350707, Fax 0584 342592. English spoken. OPEN: 01/04–30/09. SIZE: 7 ha, 300 pitches (all with elec, 200 statics), 16 hot showers (charge), 44 WCs. 🕭 🕭

Shop at 1 km. PRICES: (1996) Caravan with family 51,000, Tent with two adults 33,000. CC: none. *From Viareggio, south on A12 towards Pisa. From Torre del Lago follow signs to campsite.*

Camping Italia via dei Tigli, 55048 Torre del Lago. Tel 0584 359828, Fax 0584 341504. English spoken. OPEN: 23/04–14/09. SIZE: 9 ha, 416 pitches (all with elec, 200 statics), 40 hot showers (charge), 75 WCs, 3 CWPs. 🕭 🕭

PRICES: (1996) Caravan with family 51,000, Tent with two adults 33,000. CC: Euro/Access. *From Viareggio, south on S1 towards Torre del Lago.*

Camping Viareggio via Comparini, ang viale dei Tigli 1, 55049 Viareggio. Tel 0584 391012, Fax 0584 395462. English spoken. OPEN: 15/04–15/09. SIZE: 2 ha, 220 pitches (all with elec, 30 statics), 12 hot showers (charge), 1 CWP. 🕭 🕭

LS discounts. PRICES: (1996) Caravan with family 38,500, Tent with two adults 27,500. CC: Euro/Access.

VICO EQUENSE 21B

Camping Seiano Spiaggia
via Murrano, CP 38, 80069 Vico Equense.
Tel 0818 028560, Fax 0818 790755. English spoken.
OPEN: 01/04–01/10. SIZE: 2 ha, 20 pitches (all with
elec), 6 hot showers (charge), 24 WCs, 10 French
WCs, 2 CWPs. ⚓ ⛱

Discounts for stays of 7 days plus.
PRICES: (1996) Caravan with family 44,700,
Tent with two adults 31,800. CC: none.
*Leave A3 at Castellammare di Stabia-Sorrento
and take highway 145; after tunnel and bridge at
Seiano turn right to Marina Aequa.*

VIESTE 21B

Camping Punta Lunga Loc Defensola,
71019 Vieste.
Tel 0884 706031, Fax 0884 706910. English spoken.
OPEN: 21/03–12/10. SIZE: 6 ha, 300 pitches
(all with elec), 25 hot showers, 48 WCs, 2 CWPs. ⚓

Watersports, entertainment.
PRICES: Caravan with family 79,500, Tent with two
adults 46,500. CC: Euro/Access, Visa.
*Campsite is right beside the beach, just north of
Vieste. Well signposted.*

Camping Touring Loc Cantano,
Santa Maria di Merino, 71019 Vieste.
Tel 0884 706275. English spoken.
OPEN: 01/05–15/09. SIZE: 4 ha, 330 pitches (all
with elec, 10 statics), 20 hot showers, 45 WCs. ⚓ ⛱

Tennis, dancing.
PRICES: Caravan with family 64,000,
Tent with two adults 41,400. CC: none.

Camping Umbramare Localita Imbarcatoio,
71019 Vieste.
Tel 0884 706174, Fax 0884 706174. English spoken.
OPEN: 01/03–30/10. SIZE: 1.2 ha, 90 pitches
(51 with elec), 10 hot showers, 2 CWPs. ⚓ ⛱

PRICES: (1996) Caravan with family 69,000,
Tent with two adults 44,000. CC: Euro/Access.
Between Vieste and Peschici.

Camping Village Castello
Lungomare E Mattei 77, 71019 Vieste.
Tel 0884 707415, Fax 0884 708912. English spoken.
OPEN: 01/03–30/10. SIZE: 2 ha, 100 pitches
(all with elec), 14 hot showers, 16 WCs. ⚓

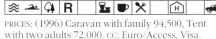

PRICES: (1996) Caravan with family 94,500, Tent
with two adults 72,000. CC: Euro/Access, Visa.
From Vieste 1 km on coast road to Mattinata.

Centro Vacanze Oriente Casella Postale 237,
71019 Vieste.
Tel 0884 707709, Fax 0884 706371. English spoken.
OPEN: 01/04–30/09. SIZE: 7 ha, 600 pitches
(all with elec), 26 hot showers, 100 WCs,
90 French WCs, 2 CWPs. ⚓ ⛱

PRICES: (1996) Caravan with family 52,000,
Tent with two adults 31,000. CC: none.
From Vieste on S159 towards Peschici.

Italy

LUXEMBOURG

Sandwiched between Belgium, Germany and France, the Grand Duchy of Luxembourg may be one of Europe's smallest states – smaller than either Lancashire or Lincolnshire – yet it has its own royal family and its own language (French and German are also official languages). It also has its own currency, the Luxembourg franc, worth the same as, and completely interchangeable with, the Belgian franc.

Luxembourg City, the capital, sits spectacularly above the Rivers Petrusse and Alzette. In the old town, the black spire of Cathédrale Notre-Dame rises high above the two rivers, and the quickest way down to the valley is by lift from the town. Beyond the Alzette, to the north of the old town, is the Centre Européen, meeting place of the European Union's Council of Ministers.

To the north of Luxembourg City, the Ardennes landscape of deep-wooded valleys spills over from the Belgian border. At Vianden, close to the German border, an 11th-century castle can be reached by cable-car from the town. Or visit the Musée historique at Diekirch for an insight into the World War II Battle of the Bulge. While for nostalgic fans of Radio Luxembourg, the tall transmitter masts at Junglinster may rate as Luxembourg's most important monument!

Emergency numbers

Police 013, Fire Brigade and Ambulance 012

Warning information

Warning triangle must be carried

Blood alcohol legal limit 80 mg

BOURSCHEID 7D

Camping Um Gritt 9164 Bourscheid-Moulin. Tel 90449, Fax 908046.
OPEN: 01/05–15/10. SIZE: 2.5 ha, 90 pitches (80 with elec, 70 statics), 11 hot showers, 19 WCs, 1 CWP.

| ~ | ✈ | ♀ | R | ⊟ | ♨ | | ✕ | | | 🚗 |

PRICES: (1996) Caravan with family 690, Tent with two adults 450. CC: none.
Well signposted in Bourscheid.

CLERVAUX 7D

Camping Officiel de Clervaux Clervaux. Tel 920042, Fax 929728. English spoken.
OPEN: 15/03–10/11. SIZE: 3 ha, 6 hot showers (charge), 20 WCs, 2 CWPs.

| ~ | ✈ | ⌂ | R | ⊟ | ♨ | | | ⤴ | ⓗ | |

Shop at 0.5 km. Restaurant at 0.5 km.
PRICES: (1996) Caravan with family 610, Tent with two adults 410. CC: none.
Follow signs in Clervaux.

DIEKIRCH 7D

Camp de la Sûre route de Gilsdorf, 9234 Diekirch. English spoken.
OPEN: 01/04–30/09. SIZE: 286 pitches (all with elec). & ⅃

| ~ | ⥬ | ⅋ | R | ⊟ | | | | | | |

Shop at 0.5 km. Restaurant at 0.3 km. Playgound; bicycles for hire.
PRICES: (1996) Caravan with family 555, Tent with two adults 360. CC: none.
From Diekirch follow directions to Gilsdorf and campsite is signposted.

Camp Op Der Sauer route de Gilsdorf, 9201 Diekirch.
Tel 808590, Fax 809623. English spoken.
OPEN: all year. SIZE: 5 ha, 270 pitches (200 with elec, 60 statics), 12 hot showers (charge), 44 WCs, 3 CWPs. & ⅃

| ~ | ⥬ | ⌂ | R | ⊟ | ♨ | ♿ | ✕ | ⓗ | |

Children's pool.
PRICES: (1996) Caravan with family 690, Tent with two adults 480. CC: Euro/Access.

Camping du Rivage Wallendorf-Pont.
Tel 86516, Fax 86516. English spoken.
OPEN: 01/04–30/09. SIZE: 1.5 ha, 70 pitches (65 with elec, 25 statics), 4 hot showers, 12 WCs, 1 CWP.

Restaurant at 0.05 km.
PRICES: Caravan with family 550,
Tent with two adults 380. CC: none.
From Diekirch, travel for 12 km towards
Echternach and follow signs to campsite.

Camping Neumuhle rue de Reisdorf,
9366 Ermsdorf.
Tel 879391. English spoken.
OPEN: all year. SIZE: 3 ha, 105 pitches (all with elec,
10 statics), 10 hot showers (charge), 12 WCs,
1 CWP.

Restaurant at 0.5 km.
PRICES: Caravan with family 720,
Tent with two adults 480. CC: none.
From Diekirch, take N14 Medernach and turn left
to Ermsdorf. Campsite is 1 km after village. Follow
signs.

ECHTERNACH 7D

Camping Bel Air Consdorf, 6211 Echternach.
Tel 79353. English spoken.
OPEN: 01/05–15/09. SIZE: 2.2 ha, 110 pitches
(80 with elec, 28 statics), 6 hot showers, 15 WCs,
1 CWP.

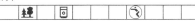

Shop at 0.3 km. Restaurant at 0.3 km.
PRICES: (1996) Caravan with family 690,
Tent with two adults 450. CC: none.
Follow signs to campsite from town centre.

Caravanning Parc Martbusch 3 Baine
Martbesch, 6552 Berdorf.
Tel 79545, Fax 799182. English spoken.
OPEN: 15/03–15/11. SIZE: 3 ha, 104 pitches
(all with elec, 56 statics), 18 hot showers, 20 WCs,
1 French WC, 1 CWP.

Shop at 1 km. Restaurant at 0.5 km.
PRICES: (1996) Caravan with family 750,
Tent with two adults 490. CC: none.
From Echternach take N10 towards Diekirch.
After 1 km turn off for Berdorf and follow signs to
campsite.

ESCH-SUR-ALZETTE 7D

Camping Gaalgebierg rue du Stade BP20,
4001 Esch-sur-Alzette.
Tel 541069, Fax 549630. English spoken.
OPEN: all year. SIZE: 3 ha, 140 pitches (all with elec,
70 statics), 10 hot showers, 17 WCs, 1 CWP.

Restaurant at 0.2 km.
PRICES: Caravan with family 590,
Tent with two adults 360. CC: Euro/Access.

2 km from the centre of Esch go towards
Rümelingen and turn right after 2 km.

ETTELBRÜCK 7D

Camping Fuusse-Kaul 2 route de Bastogne,
Heiderscheid, 9156 Ettelbrück.
Tel 89659, Fax 89707. English spoken.
OPEN: all year. SIZE: 10 ha, 300 pitches (all with
elec, 100 statics), 29 hot showers (charge),
60 WCs, 1 CWP.

Entertainment in HS.
PRICES: (1996) Caravan with family 920,
Tent with two adults 740. CC: Euro/Access, Visa.
From Ettelbrück, north-west on N15 towards
Bastogne. Follow campsite signs, 1 km from
Heiderscheid.

Camping Gritt 2 rue du Pont, 9161 Ingeldorf.
Tel 802018, Fax 809623. English spoken.
OPEN: 01/03–31/10. SIZE: 4 ha, 150 pitches
(100 with elec), 12 hot showers, 30 WCs.

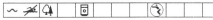

Shop at 1 km. Restaurant at 1 km.
PRICES: Caravan with family 885,
Tent with two adults 600. CC: Euro/Access.
Between Ettelbrück and Diekirch on the La Sûre
river. Follow signs to campsite.

GREVENMACHER 7D

Camping La Route du Vin
6794 Grevenmacher.
Tel 75237, Fax 758666. English spoken.
OPEN: 01/04–30/09. SIZE: 135 pitches (all with elec,
100 statics), 7 hot showers, 14 WCs.

Shop at 0.2 km. Restaurant at 0.1 km.
PRICES: (1996) Caravan with family 460,
Tent with two adults 340. CC: none.

LAROCHETTE 7D

Camping Auf Birkelt 2 rue de la Piscine,
7601 Larochette.
Tel 879040, Fax 879041. English spoken.
OPEN: 01/03–31/10. SIZE: 11 ha, 400 pitches
(all with elec), 50 hot showers, 100 WCs.

Sauna, solarium, fitness centre.
PRICES: (1996) Caravan with family 1250,
Tent with two adults 975. CC: Euro/Access, Visa.
Follow signs from town centre.

Camping Auf Kengert
7633 Larochette/Medernach.
Tel 87186, Fax 878323. English spoken.
OPEN: 07/02–08/11. SIZE: 2 ha, 186 pitches
(all with elec), 14 hot showers, 30 WCs, 1 CWP.

Luxembourg

Sauna, solarium.
PRICES: (1996) Caravan with family 1180,
Tent with two adults 780. CC: none.
Follow signs to campsite from Larochette.

LUXEMBOURG CITY 7D

ANWB Camping Mamer rue de Mersch 4,
8251 Mamer.
Tel 312349, Fax 312349. English spoken.
OPEN: all year. SIZE: 2 ha, 80 pitches (all with elec),
8 hot showers, 12 WCs.

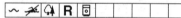

Shop at 1 km.
PRICES: (1996) Caravan with family 520,
Tent with two adults 370. CC: none.
From Luxembourg take E25 towards Arlon. Exit for Mamer, then follow signs.

Camping Bon Accueil Alzingen,
Hesperange, Luxembourg.
Tel 367069.
OPEN: 01/04–15/10. SIZE: 0.3 ha, 39 pitches
(all with elec), 4 hot showers (charge), 8 WCs,
1 CWP. ✆

Shop at 0.1 km. Restaurant at 0.1 km.
PRICES: (1996) Caravan with family 500,
Tent with two adults 280. CC: none.
Alzingen/Hesperange is just to the south-east of Luxembourg City, and campsite is well signposted.

Camping Kockelscheuer 22 rte de
Bettembourg, 1899 Kockelscheuer.
Tel 471815, Fax 405492. English spoken.
OPEN: 05/04–31/10. SIZE: 4 ha, 161 pitches
(157 with elec), 20 hot showers, 20 WCs,
2 CWPs. ♿

Restaurant at 0.1 km. Electricity extra. Sports
centre with excellent facilities nearby.
PRICES: (1996) Caravan with family 440,
Tent with two adults 340. CC: none.
Highly recommended campsite. Approx 4 km south of Luxembourg on N31 towards Bettembourg.

MERSCH 7D

Camping Krouneberg 12 rue de la Piscine,
7572 Mersch.
Tel 329756, Fax 327987. English spoken.
OPEN: 01/04–30/09. SIZE: 5.5 ha, 201 pitches (all
with elec), 18 hot showers, 34 WCs, 3 CWPs. ♿

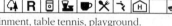

Restaurant at 1.5 km. Mini-golf, tennis, boules,
playground.
PRICES: (1996) Caravan with family 925,
Tent with two adults 705. CC: none.
Follow signs to campsite in middle of town.

STEINFORT 7D

Camping Steinfort 72 rte de Luxembourg,
8440 Steinfort.
Tel 398827, Fax 397410. English spoken.
OPEN: all year. SIZE: 4 ha, 100 pitches (70 with elec,
30 statics), 6 hot showers, 15 WCs, 1 CWP. ✆

Entertainment, table tennis, playground.
PRICES: (1996) Caravan with family 640,
Tent with two adults 400. CC: Amex, Visa.

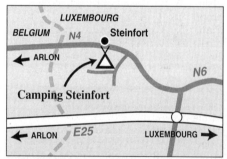

On outskirts of Steinfort; follow signs.

VIANDEN 7D

Op Dem Deich 9420 Vianden.
Tel 84375. English spoken.
OPEN: 28/03–30/09. SIZE: 200 pitches (all with
elec), 12 hot showers, 2 CWPs. ✆

Shop at 0.5 km. Restaurant at 0.5 km.
PRICES: (1996) Caravan with family 565,
Tent with two adults 390. CC: none.
Well signposted from town.

Luxembourg

NETHERLANDS

The Netherlands is one of the few countries in the world where you go *up* to the beach! About a quarter of its land mass lies *below* sea level and, over the centuries, the Dutch have worked hard on reclamation projects to create more space for an ever-growing population. To maintain the polders, as the reclaimed land is called, water is constantly pumped into the canals. Flooding has always been a danger, and the massive Oosterschelde barrier was built in the south of the country following the catastrophic floods of 1953.

One of the Dutch people's most ambitious projects was the changing of the Zuiderzee into the Ijsselmeer, separated from the Waddenzee inlet by a huge dam – the Afsluitdijk. Built across the north of the proposed lake between Den Dever and Harlingen, this impressive 30-km-long dyke carries a motorway and cycle track, with large locks at either end to allow ships to pass from the open sea into the Ijsselmeer.

If you plan to visit only one city while in the Netherlands then Amsterdam is likely to be high on the list, with its network of canals, cobbled streets and bridges, wonderful art galleries, coffee shops and busy, youthful atmosphere. But what about following the tourist board's designated route around Rotterdam, the world's largest port? – either by boat or car? Or Den Haag, or Delft, famous for its blue and white ceramic ware. Or visit Alkmaar's weekly cheese market, or the world's largest flower auction – every weekday morning, at Aalsmeer. Finally, if it's a spring holiday, don't forget the *Keukenhof* bulb gardens.

Emergency numbers
Police, Fire Brigade and Ambulance 0611

Warning information
Warning triangle must be carried

Blood Alcohol Legal Limit 50 mg

AALSMEER 13C

Camping Het Amsterdamse Bos Kleine Noorddijk 1, 1432 CC Aalsmeer.
Tel 0206 416868, Fax 0206 402378. English spoken.
OPEN: 01/04–31/10. SIZE: 6.8 ha, 500 pitches (100 with elec, 65 statics), 35 hot showers, 45 WCs, 4 CWPs. ☎ ♿

PRICES: (1996) Caravan with family 42.75, Tent with two adults 26.00. CC: none.
Take Aalsmeer exit from A9, head towards Aalsmeer and watch for signs to campsite.

Kampeenterrein, Het Amsterdamse Bos
Kleine Noorddijk 1, Post Aalsmeer, Amsterdam.
Tel 0206 416868, Fax 0206 402378.
English spoken.
OPEN: 01/04–31/10. SIZE: 6.8 ha, 500 pitches (100 with elec, 65 statics), 34 hot showers, 44 WCs, 4 CWPs. ☎ ♿

PRICES: (1996) Caravan with family 37.00, Tent with two adults 25.00. CC: none.
Motorway A9 towards Schiphol Airport. Exit Aalsmeer and follow signs to campsite.

ALKMAAR 13A

Camping Alkmaar Bergenweg 201, 1817 ML Alkmaar.
Tel 0721 16924. English spoken.
OPEN: 01/04–01/10. SIZE: 3 ha, 80 pitches (70 with elec), 8 hot showers, 18 WCs, 1 CWP. ☎

Restaurant at 0.5 km. Quiet, close to sea and city.
PRICES: (1996) Caravan with family 30.00, Tent with two adults 22.00. CC: none.
Follow N9 Alkmaar to Den Helder road and exit at Bergen. Follow signs from there.

Camping de Woudhoeve Zandweg 30, Egmond an de Hoef, 1934 BJ Alkmaar.
Tel 072 5061744, Fax 072 5065139.
English spoken.
OPEN: 01/04–31/10. SIZE: 12 ha, 400 pitches (280 with elec), 30 hot showers (charge), 60 WCs, 3 CWPs.

Shop at 2 km. Private spring water lake.
PRICES: (1996) Caravan with family 35.60, Tent with two adults 28.80. CC: none.
From Alkmaar, go towards Egmond an de Hoef (2.5 km from Egmond aan Zee).

NES

NES 13B

Camping Duinoord J v Eijckweg 4,
9163 PB Nes, Ameland.
Tel 0519 542070, Fax 0519 542146. English spoken.
OPEN: 01/04–01/11. SIZE: 17 ha, 100 pitches
(all with elec), 48 hot showers (charge), 70 WCs.

Shop at 1.5 km. Swimming pool 0.5 km.
PRICES: (1996) Caravan with family 32.00,
Tent with two adults 18.00. CC: none.
*By boat from Holwerd to the island of Ameland;
Nes is in a central position on the south coast.*

END OF NES RESORTS

AMERSFOORT 13D

King's Home Caravan Park
Birkstraat 136, 3768 HM Soest.
Tel 03346 19118, Fax 03346 10808. English spoken.
OPEN: 15/03–31/10. SIZE: 5 ha, 50 pitches (40 with
elec, 110 statics), 8 hot showers (charge), 15 WCs,
2 CWPs.

Shop at 1.5 km. Clean, quiet site.
PRICES: Caravan with family 40.00, Tent with two
adults 25.00. CC: Euro/Access, Visa.
*Amersfoort towards Soest on the N221, just past
the Hotel/Restaurant Het Witte Huis.*

AMSTERDAM 13A

Gaasper Camping Amsterdam
Loosdrechtdreef 7, 1108 AZ Amsterdam.
Tel 0206 967326, Fax 0206 969369. English spoken.
OPEN: 15/03–31/12. SIZE: 5.5 ha, 350 pitches
(125 with elec, 60 statics), 20 hot showers
(charge), 42 WCs, 3 CWPs.

Shop at 0.5 km. Fishing and boating.
PRICES: (1996) Caravan with family 39.50,
Tent with two adults 23.50. CC: none.
*Via A9 (south-east outskirts of Amsterdam) exit at
Gaasperplas and then follow camping signs.*

APELDOORN 13D

Camping de Bosgraaf
Kanaal Zuid 444, 7364 Beekbergen.
Tel 055 5051359, Fax 055 5052682. English spoken.
OPEN: 01/04–01/10. SIZE: 20 ha, 210 pitches (all with
elec), 60 hot showers (charge), 70 WCs, 5 CWPs.

PRICES: Caravan with family 41.50, Tent with two
adults 32.50. CC: Euro/Access.

*Go south from Apeldoorn on A50 for 5 km, turn
left to Beekbergen, signed from there.*

Camping de Pampel
7351 TN Hoenderloo, Apeldoorn.
Tel 0553 781760, Fax 0553 781992. English spoken.
OPEN: all year. SIZE: 14.5 ha, 165 pitches (all with
elec, 20 statics), 10 hot showers (charge), 24 WCs,
1 CWP.

Playground, boules, bike hire.
PRICES: Caravan with family 48.50,
Tent with two adults 28.00. CC: none.
Follow signs to campsite from town centre.

Camping Kerkendel
Kerkendelweg 49, 3775 KM Kootwijk.
Tel 0577 456224, Fax 05775 6545. English spoken.
OPEN: 01/04–01/11. SIZE: 8 ha, 170 pitches
(all with elec), 30 hot showers, 40 WCs, 3 CWPs.

Recently awarded 5 stars.
PRICES: unavailable. CC: Euro/Access, Visa.
*Take Kootwijk exit from A1/E30 and follow signs
to campsite.*

Harskamperdennen H v 't Hoffweg 25,
Harskamp, 3775 KB Kootwijk.
Tel 0318 456272, Fax 0318 457695. English spoken.
OPEN: 01/03–30/10. SIZE: 16 ha, 387 pitches (169 with
elec), 15 hot showers, 34 WCs, 4 CWPs.

Shop at 2.5 km. Restaurant at 6 km.
PRICES: (1996) Caravan with family 36.00,
Tent with two adults 25.00. CC: none.
*From Apeldoorn go west on A1. Turn off at
Kootwijk sign, go through the town and turn left
after approx 7 km. Campsite is then 5 km ahead
on the left.*

ARNHEM 13D

Camping Honinggraat
Lathum, 6988 BM Arnhem.
Tel 08336 32211, Fax 08336 32210. English spoken.
OPEN: all year. SIZE: 18 ha, 200 pitches (all with elec,
150 statics), 20 hot showers, 35 WCs, 2 CWPs.

PRICES: (1996) Caravan with family 40.00, Tent
with two adults 20.00. CC: none.

Camping Warnsborn
Bakenbergseweg 257, 6816 PB Arnhem.
Tel 026 4423469. English spoken.
OPEN: 01/04–01/11. SIZE: 4 ha, 75 pitches (70 with
elec, 30 statics), 7 hot showers (charge), 14 WCs,
1 CWP.

Restaurant at 0.5 km.

Netherlands

PRICES: (1996) Caravan with family 28.50, Tent with two adults 16.50. CC: none.
Follow Zoo/Openlucht museum signs; campsite is 3 km towards Oosterbeek.

ASSEN 13B

Recreation Holiday Centre Witterzomer
Witterzomer 7, 9405 VE Assen.
Tel 0592 393535, Fax 0592 393530. English spoken.
OPEN: all year. SIZE: 75 ha, 600 pitches (all with elec, 150 statics), 52 hot showers, 116 WCs, 10 CWPs. &

Pony riding.
PRICES: (1996) Caravan with family 43.00, Tent with two adults 38.00. CC: none.
Take A28 Zwolle/Groningen highway. Near Assen take the second exit (Assen/Smilde) and then follow the blue signs.

BALK 13B

Camping de Waps Fonteinwei 14, 8567 JT Oudemirdum.
Tel 0514 571437. English spoken.
OPEN: 01/04–01/11. SIZE: 6 ha, 200 pitches (160 with elec, 70 statics), 8 hot showers (charge), 16 WCs, 1 CWP. &

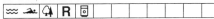

Shop at 0.5 km. Restaurant at 0.5 km. Bicycle hire.
PRICES: unavailable. CC: Euro/Access.
Oudemirdum is 7 km from Balk and well signposted.

BERGEN OP ZOOM 13C

Camping de Heide Bemmelenberg 12, 4614 PH Bergen op Zoom.
Tel 0164 235659. English spoken.
OPEN: 01/04–15/09. SIZE: 10 ha, 100 pitches (all with elec), 10 hot showers (charge), 20 WCs, 2 CWPs. & &

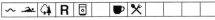

PRICES: (1996) Caravan with family 37.14, Tent with two adults 21.82. CC: none.
North of Antwerp on the N213.

BLOKZIJL 13B

Camping Tussen de Diepen 8356 VZ Blokzijl.
Tel 0527 291565, Fax 0527 291565. English spoken.
OPEN: 01/04–31/10. SIZE: 5 ha, 80 pitches (all with elec, 140 statics), 6 hot showers (charge), 20 WCs, 1 CWP. & &

Shop at 0.5 km. Boats and canoes for hire.
PRICES: (1996) Caravan with family 30.75, Tent with two adults 20.25. CC: none.

Take A6 from Amsterdam and turn off to the right at Emmeloord towards Steenwyk for Blokzijl.

BREDA 13C

Camping Liesbos Breda, Liesdreef 40.
Tel 076 5143514, Fax 076 5146555. English spoken.
OPEN: 01/04–01/10. SIZE: 7 ha, 50 pitches (40 with elec, 200 statics), 8 hot showers (charge), 14 WCs, 2 CWPs. &

Tennis, children's playground, basketball, volley ball.
PRICES: Caravan with family 30.00, Tent with two adults 18.00. CC: Euro/Access, Visa.
Campsite is west of Breda, just south of N58/A16 intersection and well signposted.

BRESKENS 13C

Camping Groede Zeeweg 1, 4503 PA Groede.
Tel 01171 1384, Fax 01171 2277. English spoken.
OPEN: 01/04–31/10. SIZE: 13 ha, 400 pitches (300 with elec, 400 statics), 39 hot showers, 44 WCs, 3 CWPs. &

PRICES: (1996) Caravan with family 39.50, Tent with two adults 28.00. CC: none.
Leave N58 before Breskens and turn left to Groede, heading towards the coast. Signposted from there.

Recreatiecentrum Pannenschurr Zeedijk 19, 4504 PP Nieuwvliet.
Tel 0117 11391, Fax 0117 11415. English spoken.
OPEN: all year. SIZE: 16 ha, 200 pitches (all with elec), 40 hot showers (charge), 30 WCs, 1 CWP. & &

Excellent facilities including covered leisure complex.
PRICES: (1996) Caravan with family 55.00, Tent with two adults 43.80. CC: Amex, Euro/Access, Visa.
From Breskens ferry take N58. Look for signpost Nieuwvlietstrand, north-west of town.

Recreatiepark Camping Schoneveld 4511 HR Breskens.
Tel 0117 383220, Fax 0117 383650. English spoken.
OPEN: all year. SIZE: 14 ha, 210 pitches (all with elec), 44 WCs, 2 CWPs. &

Bowling.
PRICES: (1996) Caravan with family 60.50, Tent with two adults 55.50. CC: Euro/Access, Visa.
Follow N58 from Brugge (in Belgium) towards coast to Breskens.

Netherlands

CALLANTSOOG 13A

Camping Callassande Groote Keeten, 1759 NX Callantsoog.
Tel 0224 581663, Fax 0224 581663. English spoken.
OPEN: 01/04–20/10. SIZE: 9 ha, 350 pitches (300 with elec), 35 hot showers, 55 WCs, 3 CWPs. ♿ ♿

≋ ⚓ 🚰 R 🔲 🍺 ☕ ✕ ⤳

PRICES: (1996) Caravan with family 50.00, Tent with two adults 35.00. CC: Euro/Access, Visa.
Callantsoog is on the coastal road towards Den Helder. The campsite is just north of Callantsoog at Groote Keeten. Signposted.

DELFT 13C

Recreatie Centrum Delftse Hout Korftlaan 5, 2616 LJ Delft.
Tel 015 2130040, Fax 015 2131293. English spoken.
OPEN: all year. SIZE: 6 ha, 200 pitches (all with elec, 40 statics), 12 hot showers, 32 WCs, 2 CWPs. ♿

≋ ⚓ 🚰 R 🔲 🍺 ☕ ✕ ⤳ (H)

PRICES: Caravan with family 43.50, Tent with two adults 33.00. CC: Euro/Access, Visa.
From Rotterdam, take 2nd exit (No 9) for Delft and follow signs to campsite.

DOMBURG 13C

Hof Domburg Schelpweg 7, 4357 RD Domburg.
Tel 0118 83210, Fax 0118 83668. English spoken.
OPEN: all year. SIZE: 14 ha, 427 pitches (all with elec), 42 hot showers, 70 WCs, 9 French WCs, 6 CWPs. ♿ ♿

≋ ⚓ ♀ R 🔲 🍺 ☕ ✕ ⤳ (H) 🦌 🚗

Good sports, health/beauty facilities. Beach 0.5 km.
PRICES: (1996) Caravan with family 67.00, Tent with two adults 48.00. CC: Amex, Euro/Access, Visa.
North-west of Middelburg, campsite is 500 m from Domburg and well signposted.

DRACHTEN 13B

Camping t'Strandheem Parkweg 2, 9865 VP Opende.
Tel 0594 659555, Fax 0594 658592. English spoken.
OPEN: 01/04–01/11. SIZE: 14 ha, 160 pitches (all with elec, 25 statics), 24 hot showers, 48 WCs, 2 CWPs. ♿ ♿

≋ ⚓ 🚰 R 🔲 🍺 ☕ ⤳ 🔘

Restaurant at 2 km. Indoor swimming pool.
PRICES: (1996) Caravan with family 35.00, Tent with two adults 21.00. CC: none.
From the A7 (Heerenveen-Groningen), take exit 31 left just after Drachten towards Surhuisterveen and Opende.

DRUTEN 13D

Camping-Park Het Groene Eiland 6629 KS Appeltern.
Tel 0487 562130, Fax 0487 561540. English spoken.
OPEN: 15/03–31/10. SIZE: 16 ha, 175 pitches (all with elec, 125 statics), 24 hot showers (charge), 24 WCs, 3 CWPs. ♿

≋ ⚓ ♀ R 🔲 🍺 ☕ ✕ 🔘

PRICES: (1996) Caravan with family 36.50, Tent with two adults 19.50. CC: none.
Going west on the A50, turn off at Druten and follow signs to Gouden Ham. Campsite is well signposted.

DWINGELOO 13B

Camping de Moraine Morainweg 20, 9417 Spier.
Tel 0593 562317, Fax 0593 562236. English spoken.
OPEN: 01/03–31/10. SIZE: 5.5 ha, 40 pitches (all with elec), 9 hot showers (charge), 13 WCs, 2 CWPs. ♿ ♿

≋ ⚓ 🚰 R 🔲 🍺 ☕ ✕ ⤳ 🔘

PRICES: Caravan with family 26.75, Tent with two adults 17.00. CC: none.
From the 371 going south-west towards Dwingeloo, campsite at Spier is well signposted.

Camping de Olde Bargen Oude Hoogeveensedijk, 7991 PD Dwingeloo.
Tel 052 1597261. English spoken.
OPEN: all year. SIZE: 2 ha, 40 pitches (all with elec, 40 statics), 4 hot showers (charge), 15 WCs, 1 CWP. ♿

🚰 R 🔲

Shop at 0.7 km. Restaurant at 0.7 km.
PRICES: (1996) Caravan with family 28.00, Tent with two adults 20.00. CC: none.

ECHT 13D

Camping Marisheem Brugweg 89, 6102 RD Echt.
Tel 0475 481458, Fax 0475 488018. English spoken.
OPEN: 01/04–30/09. SIZE: 13 ha, 270 pitches (200 with elec, 100 statics), 19 hot showers (charge), 36 WCs, 2 CWPs.

🚰 R 🔲 ⊛ ☕ ✕ ⤳ 🔘 🦌

Shop at 0.2 km.
PRICES: (1996) Caravan with family 46.40, Tent with two adults 38.10. CC: none.
From the A2 Eindhoven-Maastricht motorway, take the exit for Echt and then follow signs.

EDAM 13A

Camping Strandbad 1135 PZ Edam.
Tel 0299 371994, Fax 0299 371510. English spoken.

OPEN: 01/04–01/10. SIZE: 5 ha, 120 pitches (60 with elec), 15 hot showers (charge), 32 WCs, 2 CWPs. **(**

Shop at 0.5 km.
PRICES: (1996) Caravan with family 30.15, Tent with two adults 18.45. CC: none.
Follow the ANWB (Dutch Touring Club) signs to the campsite.

EINDHOVEN 13D

Camping Ter Spegelt
Postelseweg 88, 5521 Eersel.
Tel 0497 012016, Fax 0497 014162. English spoken.
OPEN: 01/04–29/10. SIZE: 64 ha, 320 pitches (all with elec, 380 statics), 25 hot showers, 40 WCs, 6 CWPs. **(** &

PRICES: (1996) Caravan with family 56.00, Tent with two adults 36.00. CC: none.
From Eindhoven to Eersel on motorway, exit at Eersel junction. The campsite is on south-west side of town and is well signposted.

EMMEN 13B

Recreatiepark Hunzebergen
Valtherweg 36, 7875 TB Exloo.
Tel 0591 549116, Fax 0591 549092. English spoken.
OPEN: 01/04–31/10. SIZE: 45 ha, 431 pitches (300 with elec), 40 hot showers, 60 WCs, 3 CWPs. **(** &

PRICES: (1996) Caravan with family 39.20, Tent with two adults 33.60. CC: Euro/Access, Visa.
North of Emmen on the N34.

ENKHUIZEN 13B

Camping Het Hof
Zuideruitweg 64, 1608 EX Wijdenes.
Tel 0229 501435, Fax 0229 503244. English spoken.
OPEN: 20/03–26/10. SIZE: 4 ha, 75 pitches (all with elec), 8 hot showers (charge), 16 WCs, 4 CWPs.

PRICES: (1996) Caravan with family 30.00, Tent with two adults 19.00. CC: none.
Take the old road Hoorn to Enkhuizen. By the Taveerne restaurant, turn right to Wijdenes and follow signs to the campsite.

ENSCHEDE 13D

Recreatiecentrum Klein Zandvoort 7534 PA Enschede.
Tel 053 4611372, Fax 053 4611372. English spoken.
OPEN: all year. SIZE: 10 ha, 120 pitches (all with elec, 200 statics), 14 hot showers, 36 WCs, 2 CWPs. **(**

PRICES: (1996) Caravan with family 33.00, Tent with two adults 20.00. CC: Euro/Access, Visa.
Between Enschede and Glanenbrug on the German border, signposted.

ERMELO 13B

Camping de Haeghehorst
Fazantlaan 4, 3852 AM Ermelo.
Tel 0341 553185, Fax 0341 562751. English spoken.
OPEN: all year. SIZE: 10 ha, 150 pitches (all with elec, 80 statics), 15 hot showers, 30 WCs, 4 CWPs. **(**

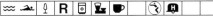

Shop at 1.5 km.
PRICES: Caravan with family 53.00. CC: none.
Off the A28 in the direction of Zwolle. Turn off to the right on the N303 to Ermelo.

GOUDA 13C

Reeuwykse Hout Oudeweg 9, 2811 NM Reeuwijk.
Tel 0182 395944. English spoken.
OPEN: 01/04–31/10. SIZE: 12 ha, 180 pitches (84 with elec, 220 statics), 12 hot showers (charge), 24 WCs, 2 CWPs. **(**

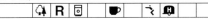

Restaurant at 1 km. Canoe, rowing and paddle boat hire, mini-golf.
PRICES: (1996) Caravan with family 29.75, Tent with two adults 17.50. CC: Euro/Access.
Close to the main road between Den Haag and Utrecht. Follow directions to Reeuwijk.

GRONINGEN 13B

Camping de Fruitberg 9755 PB Onnen, Groningen.
Tel 050 4061282, Fax 050 4061282. English spoken.
OPEN: 15/03–01/11. SIZE: 5.5 ha, 100 pitches (all with elec, 60 statics), 8 hot showers (charge), 22 WCs, 2 CWPs. **(**

Shop at 1 km.
PRICES: Caravan with family 36.00, Tent with two adults 29.00. CC: none.
From A28 going towards Assen, take Haren exit and then follow signs to campsite.

Recreatiecentrum Grunopark Hoofdweg 163, 9617 Harkstede.
Tel 050 5416371, Fax 050 5424521. English spoken.
OPEN: all year. SIZE: 4 ha, 200 pitches (all with elec, 350 statics), 42 hot showers, 56 WCs, 2 CWPs. &

PRICES: (1996) Caravan with family 32.50, Tent with two adults 19.50. CC: none.
On the east side of Groningen.

HAAKSBERGEN 13D

Camping 't Hazenbos 7481 PT Buurse.
Tel 0535 696338. English spoken.
OPEN: all year. SIZE: 6 ha, 115 pitches (all with elec,
35 statics), 7 hot showers (charge), 17 WCs,
1 CWP. ℓ

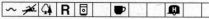

Shop at 1.5 km. Restaurant at 0.5 km.
PRICES: Caravan with family 30.00,
Tent with two adults 18.75. CC: none.
10 km from Enschede, just south of Hengelo.

Camping 't Stien'nboer Scholtenhagenweg 42,
7481 VP Haaksbergen.
Tel 053 5722610, Fax 053 5729394. English spoken.
OPEN: 15/03−15/11. SIZE: 11 ha, 125 pitches
(all with elec), 17 hot showers (charge),
3 CWPs. ঙ

Shop at 2 km.
PRICES: (1996) Caravan with family 40.70. CC: none.
*From Haaksbergen follow the ANWB (Dutch
Touring Club) signs.*

HARDERWIJK 13B

Camping Flevostrand Strandweg 1, 8256
RZ Biddinghuizen.
Tel 0320 288480, Fax 0320 288617. English spoken.
OPEN: 01/04−01/11. SIZE: 25 ha, 300 pitches
(all with elec, 250 statics), 30 hot showers,
90 WCs, 5 CWPs. ℓ

Excellent range of watersports.
PRICES: (1996) Caravan with family 46.25,
Tent with two adults 39.90. CC: none.
*From A28/E35 follow signs to
Harderwijk/Lelystad. Campsite is near the lake
Veluwenmeer and signposted.*

HARLINGEN 13B

Camping de Zeehoeve 8862 PK Harlingen.
Tel 0517 41365, Fax 0517 416971. English spoken.
OPEN: 01/04−01/10. SIZE: 8 ha, 60 pitches (all with
elec), 14 hot showers (charge), 38 WCs, 2 CWPs. ℓ

Shop at 1 km. Restaurant at 1 km.
PRICES: (1996) Caravan with family 34.00,
Tent with two adults 20.50. CC: none.

HATTEM 13B

Camping de Leemkule 8051 PW Hattem.
Tel 038 4441945, Fax 038 4446280. English spoken.
OPEN: all year. SIZE: 24 ha, 160 pitches (all with
elec, 35 statics), 14 hot showers, 28 WCs,
1 CWP. ℓ ঙ

Indoor swimming pool.
PRICES: (1996) Caravan with family 47.00, Tent
with two adults 37.00. CC: Amex, Euro/Access.
Well signposted from town.

HEERLEN 13D

Camping Colmont Colmont 2, 6367 Voerendaal.
Tel 045 7751594, Fax 045 7751594. English spoken.
OPEN: 01/04−01/11. SIZE: 4 ha, 155 pitches
(all with elec, 8 statics), 22 hot showers (charge),
2 CWPs. ℓ

Restaurant at 1 km.
PRICES: (1996) Caravan with family 22.00,
Tent with two adults 22.00. CC: Amex, Visa.
*From Heerlen head towards Maastricht on A79.
Exit at Voerendaal, follow signs through Kunrade
and on to Colmont.*

Camping de Manege
Voosterstraat 80, 6361 EW Nuth.
Tel 045 5241266, Fax 045 5241266.
English spoken.
OPEN: 01/04−01/10. SIZE: 2 ha, 50 pitches (30 with
elec), 2 hot showers (charge), 8 WCs, 1 CWP.

Shop at 0.5 km. Restaurant at 0.5 km.
PRICES: (1996) Caravan with family 30.50,
Tent with two adults 17.00. CC: none.
Close to Heerlen on the A76.

HELLEVOETSLUIS 13C

Camping 't Weergors
Zuiddijk 2, 3221 LJ Hellevoetsluis.
Tel 0188 312430, Fax 0188 311010.
English spoken.
OPEN: 01/04−01/11. SIZE: 9.7 ha, 90 pitches
(all with elec, 160 statics), 15 hot showers
(charge), 21 WCs, 2 CWPs. ℓ

Shop at 2.5 km. Restaurant at 2.5 km. Fishing.
PRICES: (1996) Caravan with family 31.00, Tent
with two adults 21.50. CC: Euro/Access.
South-west of Rotterdam.

HENGELO 13D

Camping de Molnhofte Nijhofweg 5,
7478 PX Diepenheim (Twente).
Tel 0547 51514, Fax 0547 51514. English spoken.
OPEN: 01/03−31/10. SIZE: 5 ha, 56 pitches
(all with elec, 120 statics), 10 hot showers,
25 WCs, 1 CWP. ℓ ঙ

Fishing nearby.

Netherlands

PRICES: (1996) Caravan with family 31.30, Tent with two adults 17.90. CC: none.
West from Hengelo via Delden, follow signs to Goor and Diepenheim. Campsite is well signposted.

HINDELOOPEN 13B

Camping Hindeloopen 8713 JA Hindeloopen.
Tel 0514 521452. English spoken.
OPEN: 01/04–01/11. SIZE: 16 ha, 140 pitches (92 with elec), 28 hot showers (charge), 35 WCs, 2 CWPs. &

Special pitches for camper vans. Tennis.
PRICES: (1996) Caravan with family 31.00, Tent with two adults 22.00. CC: none.
1 km south of Hindeloopen on the coast.

HOEK VAN HOLLAND 13C

Camping Hoek Van Holland
Hoek Van Holland.
Tel 0174 382550, Fax 0174 382550. English spoken.
OPEN: 01/04–01/11. SIZE: 6 ha, 60 pitches (all with elec, 120 statics), 12 hot showers, 20 WCs, 2 CWPs. & &

PRICES: (1996) Caravan with family 34.50, Tent with two adults 21.50. CC: none.
From Scheveningen take E30 south-west to campsite.

Camping Jagtveld Nieowlandsedijk 41, 2691 KV 's-Gravenzande.
Tel 0174 413479, Fax 0174 422127. English spoken.
OPEN: 01/04–01/10. SIZE: 3 ha, 120 pitches (100 with elec, 110 statics), 12 hot showers, 18 WCs, 2 CWPs. &

PRICES: (1996) Caravan with family 34.75, Tent with two adults 23.25. CC: Euro/Access.
From Rotterdam take the A20 and follow signs to the Hoek van Holland. Go straight through traffic lights near restaurant, ignoring signs to 's-Gravenzande, and head for the beach.

HOOGEZAND-SAPPEMEER 13B

Camping Meerwijck Strandweg 2, 9606 PR Kropswolde.
Tel 0598 323659, Fax 0598 321501. English spoken.
OPEN: 01/04–29/10. SIZE: 23 ha, 250 pitches (all with elec, 250 statics), 24 hot showers, 76 WCs, 6 CWPs. &

Shop at 7 km. Fishing, rowing, canoeing, tennis.
PRICES: (1996) Caravan with family 41.00, Tent with two adults 31.00. CC: none.
South of Groningen, situated on Lake Zuidlaren.

HOORN 13A

Camping Venhop
Venneweg 2, 1647 DP Berkhout.
Tel 0229 551371. English spoken.
OPEN: 01/04–31/10. SIZE: 7.5 ha, 75 pitches (60 with elec), 8 hot showers (charge), 12 WCs, 1 CWP. &

Lake 0.7 km.
PRICES: (1996) Caravan with family 27.00, Tent with two adults 21.00. CC: none.
A7 from Amsterdam towards Leeuwarden. Follow signs to Hoorn/Berkhout/Avenhorn. When leaving the highway turn left by the lights and the campsite is 1 km ahead on the right.

Camping Westerkogge
Kerkebuurt 202, 1647 MH Berkhout.
Tel 0229 51208, Fax 0229 51390. English spoken.
OPEN: 01/04–31/10. SIZE: 11 ha, 120 pitches (90 with elec, 200 statics), 20 hot showers, 29 WCs, 3 CWPs. & &

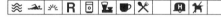

Restaurant at 4 km. Canoeing.
PRICES: (1996) Caravan with family 40.50, Tent with two adults 21.50. CC: none.
From E10/A7, take Hoorn/Berkhout exit and follow signs to the site.

KATWIJK AAN ZEE 13C

Camping de Noordduinen Campingweg 1, 2221 EW Katwijk Aan Zee.
Tel 0171 825295, Fax 0171 833977. English spoken.
OPEN: 23/03–26/10. SIZE: 11 ha, 250 pitches (all with elec, 218 statics), 29 hot showers (charge), 64 WCs, 5 CWPs. & &

PRICES: (1996) Caravan with family 43.00, Tent with two adults 27.00. CC: none.
North of Den Haag, near the coast.

Camping de Zuidduinen
Zuidduinseweg 1, 2225 JS Katwijk.
Tel 0714 014750, Fax 0714 077097. English spoken.
OPEN: 01/04–01/10. SIZE: 4 ha, 140 pitches (all with elec, 180 statics), 20 hot showers (charge), 28 WCs, 2 CWPs. & &

Swimming pool 1 km.
PRICES: Caravan with family 46.50, Tent with two adults 34.00. CC: Euro/Access, Visa.
From A44 take exit 8 on to N206 towards Katwijk. Exit Katwijk aan Zee and follow signs.

MAASTRICHT 13D

Camping de Dousberg Dousbergweg 102, 6216 GC Maastricht.
Tel 043 3432171, Fax 043 3430556. English spoken.

Netherlands

OPEN: 26/03–31/10. SIZE: 10 ha, 300 pitches (200 with elec, 20 statics), 25 hot showers (charge), 32 WCs, 3 CWPs. ⚓ ᕝ

Shop at 2 km. Tennis, children's playground. PRICES: (1996) Caravan with family 42.00, Tent with two adults 23.50. CC: Euro/Access, Visa. *From Eindhoven-Liège motorway follow signs for Hasselt and then the municipal signs for Dousberg.*

Camping Oriental 6325 Maastricht.
Tel 043 6040075. English spoken.
OPEN: 27/04–27/10. SIZE: 6 ha, 250 pitches (all with elec, 80 statics), 18 hot showers (charge), 34 WCs, 3 CWPs. ᕝ

Restaurant at 0.5 km.
PRICES: (1996) Caravan with family 44.00, Tent with two adults 33.00. CC: none.
South-east of Maastricht, towards Valkenburg. Well signposted.

MEPPEL 13B

D'Olde Lantschap Schureslaan 4, 8438 SC Wateren.
Tel 0521 387244, Fax 0521 387593. English spoken.
OPEN: 01/04–31/10. SIZE: 25 ha, 200 pitches (all with elec, 200 statics), 12 hot showers, 26 WCs, 2 CWPs. ⚓

Restaurant at 1 km.
PRICES: (1996) Caravan with family 38.15, Tent with two adults 29.15. CC: none.
Off the A32.

MIDDELBURG 13C

Camping Middelburg
Koninginnelaan 55, 4335 BB Middelburg.
Tel 0118 025395. English spoken.
OPEN: 01/04–15/10. SIZE: 2 ha, 200 pitches (60 with elec), 8 hot showers (charge), 22 WCs, 1 CWP. ⚓

Shop at 0.5 km. Restaurant at 2 km.
PRICES: (1996) Caravan with family 32.45, Tent with two adults 20.10. CC: none.
Follow directions to Middelburg and then signs to the campsite.

Duinzicht Strandweg 7, 4371 Koudekerke.
Tel 0118 51397, Fax 0118 53222. English spoken.
OPEN: 01/04–30/09. SIZE: 6 ha, 130 pitches (80 with elec, 290 statics), 15 hot showers (charge), 37 WCs, 2 CWPs. ⚓

PRICES: (1996) Caravan with family 32.60, Tent with two adults 18.90. CC: Euro/Access.

From Middelburg head north towards Koudekerke, then on towards Domburg.

Recreatiecentrum Scheldeoord
Landingsweg 1, 4435 Baarland.
Tel 0113 639900, Fax 0113 639500. English spoken.
OPEN: 01/04–30/10. SIZE: 16 ha, 215 pitches (all with elec), 30 hot showers (charge), 59 WCs, 3 CWPs. ⚓

PRICES: (1996) Caravan with family 46.00, Tent with two adults 30.00. CC: none.
From Bergen op Zoom west over causeway on A58. Exit at Gravenpolder and then go via Hoedekenskerke to the campsite.

NIJMEGEN 13D

Camping Eldorado
Witteweg 18, 6586 AE Plasmolen.
Tel 0246 961914, Fax 0246 963017. English spoken.
OPEN: 01/04–01/10. SIZE: 6 ha, 30 pitches (all with elec), 21 hot showers (charge), 42 WCs.

PRICES: (1996) Caravan with family 34.50, Tent with two adults 22.50. CC: none.
On the N271 Nijmegen to Venlo road, 10 km south of Nijmegen.

NOORDWIJK 13C

Camping Club Soleil 2204 AN Noordwijk.
Tel 02523 74225, Fax 02523 76450. English spoken.
OPEN: 01/04–01/11. SIZE: 6 ha, 140 pitches (all with elec, 120 statics), 8 hot showers, 16 WCs, 1 CWP. ᕝ

PRICES: (1996) Caravan with family 65.00, Tent with two adults 65.00. CC: none.
North of Den Haag, near the coast.

Camping de Carlton
Kraaierslaan 13, 2211 Noordwijk.
Tel 0252 372783. English spoken.
OPEN: 01/04–01/11. SIZE: 45 pitches, 8 hot showers (charge), 8 WCs, 1 CWP. ᕝ

Shop at 2 km. Restaurant at 1 km.
PRICES: (1996) Caravan with family 41.25, Tent with two adults 22.25. CC: none.
Near the sea, to the north of Den Haag.

NUNSPEET 13B

Camping Het Plashuis
Randmeerweg 8, 8071 SH Nunspeet.
Tel 03412 52406, Fax 03412 62565. English spoken.
OPEN: 04/04–30/09. SIZE: 10 ha, 170 pitches (all with elec, 300 statics), 22 hot showers (charge), 43 WCs, 2 CWPs. ⚓ ᕝ

Netherlands

Water sports.
PRICES: Caravan with family 38.00,
Tent with two adults 28.00. CC: none.
Well signposted from Nunspeet.

OEGSTGEEST 13C

Camping Koningshof
Elsgeesterweg 8, 2231 NW Rijnsburg.
Tel 0714 026051, Fax 0714 021336. English spoken.
OPEN: all year. SIZE: 8 ha, 175 pitches (all with elec,
100 statics), 25 hot showers, 35 WCs, 4 CWPs. &

PRICES: (1996) Caravan with family 43.50, Tent
with two adults 32.50. CC: Euro/Access, Visa.
*From the A44 (Den Haag to Amsterdam), exit 7 to
Oegstgeest/Rijnsburg. From Rijnsburg follow signs.*

OIRSCHOT 13D

Camping de Bocht
Oude Grintweg 69, 5688 MB Oirschot.
Tel 0499 771943, Fax 0499 77080. English spoken.
OPEN: all year. SIZE: 2 ha, 30 pitches (all with elec,
30 statics), 4 hot showers (charge), 5 WCs, 1 CWP. &

Shop at 1 km.
PRICES: (1996) Caravan with family 28.00,
Tent with two adults 18.00. CC: Euro/Access.
*On the A58 near junction 8, towards Oirschot,
follow signs to the campsite.*

Camping Latour Bloemendaal 7, 5688
GP Oirschot.
Tel 0499 575625, Fax 0499 573742. English spoken.
OPEN: 01/04–01/11. SIZE: 5 ha, 150 pitches
(all with elec, 45 statics), 9 hot showers, 28 WCs,
1 CWP. & &

Shop at 1.5 km. Indoor/outdoor tennis courts.
PRICES: (1996) Caravan with family 43.00,
Tent with two adults 29.50. CC: Euro/Access.
*From the A58 Eindhoven to Tilburg, exit at
Oirschot and then follow signs to the campsite.*

OOSTERHOUT 13C

Camping 't Haasje
Vijf Eikenweg 45, 4849 PX Dorst.
Tel 0161 411626, Fax 0161 411247. English spoken.
OPEN: 15/03–01/11. SIZE: 11 ha, 35 pitches
(all with elec, 3 statics), 18 hot showers (charge),
12 WCs, 1 CWP. &

Shop at 3 km.
PRICES: (1996) Caravan with family 36.00,
Tent with two adults 28.00. CC: none.
On the Oosterhout to Rijen road.

Camping d'n Mastendol
Oosterhoutseweg 13, 5121 RE Rijen.
Tel 0161 222664, Fax 0161 222669. English spoken.
OPEN: 01/04–31/10. SIZE: 11 ha, 60 pitches
(all with elec, 300 statics), 10 hot showers
(charge), 20 WCs, 2 CWPs. & &

Shop at 1.2 km.
PRICES: (1996) Caravan with family 34.80,
Tent with two adults 19.90. CC: none.
*On the A27 Utrecht to Breda, exit at Oosterhout-
Zuid. Follow directions to Rijen, cross the railway
and then turn right after about 500 m.*

Camping de Katjeskelder
Katjeskelder, 4904 SG Oosterhout.
Tel 3116 2453539, Fax 3116 2454090.
English spoken.
OPEN: 01/04–30/10. SIZE: 30 ha, 300 pitches
(260 with elec, 200 statics), 29 hot showers
(charge), 45 WCs, 5 CWPs. & &

Tropical pool; Internet:
http:www.Katjeskelder.NL.
PRICES: (1996) Caravan with family 50.00. CC: Visa.
*Signposted from the Oosterhout-Zuid exit on the
A27 (Utrecht to Breda road).*

OOSTKAPELLE 13C

Camping de Pekelinge
Landmetersweg 1, 4356 RE Oostkapelle.
Tel 0118 582820. English spoken.
OPEN: 01/04–01/11. SIZE: 10 ha, 335 pitches (300 with
elec), 24 hot showers, 48 WCs, 2 CWPs. & &

Shop at 1 km. Restaurant at 1 km.
PRICES: (1996) Caravan with family 43.30,
Tent with two adults 27.90. CC: none.
To the north of Middelburg.

Camping Dennenbos
Duinweg 64, 4356 GB Oostkapelle.
Tel 0118 81310, Fax 0118 83773.
English spoken.
OPEN: 01/03–30/10. SIZE: 3 ha, 150 pitches
(all with elec), 21 hot showers, 30 WCs,
2 CWPs. &

PRICES: (1996) Caravan with family 48.00, Tent
with two adults 29.50. CC: none.
*Towards the beach, the campsite is on right-hand
side and well signposted.*

Camping in de Bongerd 4356 ZG Oostkapelle.
Tel 0118 81510, Fax 0118 81510.
English spoken.
OPEN: 24/03–01/11. SIZE: 7.3 ha, 300 pitches
(all with elec, 50 statics), 44 hot showers, 58 WCs,
3 CWPs. & &

Netherlands

[≋ ⚓ 🏠 R 🍳 | 🍵 | 🏃 🏠]

Shop at 0.3 km. Restaurant at 0.3 km.
PRICES: (1996) Caravan with family 43.50,
Tent with two adults 29.00. CC: none.
*Situated to the north of Middelburg. Follow
camping signs.*

Camping Ons Buiten Aagtekerkseweg 2a,
4356 Oostkapelle.
Tel 0118 581813, Fax 0118 583771. English spoken.
OPEN: 22/03–31/10. SIZE: 7.7 ha, 349 pitches (all
with elec), 27 hot showers, 62 WCs, 3 CWPs. ⚓ ♿

[≋ ⚓ 🏠 R 🍳 🍺 🍵 ✕ 🏃 🔧 🐕]

Shop at 0.3 km. Tennis, bike hire, TV connection
on pitch.
PRICES: Caravan with family 56.50,
Tent with two adults 46.50. CC: none.
*From Middelburg go north towards Domburg. In
Oostkapelle look for camp signs.*

RENESSE   13C

Camping International
Scharendijkseweg 8, 4325 Renesse.
Tel 0111 61391, Fax 0111 62571. English spoken.
OPEN: 01/03–01/11. SIZE: 3 ha, 185 pitches (all with
elec), 14 hot showers (charge), 33 WCs, 2 CWPs. ⚓

[≋ ⚓ 🏠 | 🍳 🍺 | | | |]

Restaurant at 0.5 km.
PRICES: (1996) Caravan with family 41.25,
Tent with two adults 24.50. CC: Euro/Access.
Follow signs to campsite in Renesse.

ROLDE   13B

Diana Heide Amen 53, 9446 TE Amen-Rolde.
Tel 0592 389297, Fax 0529 389432. English spoken.
OPEN: 15/03–31/10. SIZE: 30 ha, 375 pitches
(300 with elec, 140 statics), 40 hot showers
(charge), 56 WCs, 4 CWPs. ⚓ ♿

[≋ ⚓ 🏠 R 🍳 🍺 🍵 ✕ 🏃 🔧]

Entertainment in HS; fishing.
PRICES: (1996) Caravan with family 37.50,
Tent with two adults 23.00. CC: none.
*South of Assen. From Hooghalen cross the railway
and follow signs to campsite.*

ROOSENDAAL   13C

Camping Zonneland Nispen, Roosendaal.
Tel 0165 365429. English spoken.
OPEN: 01/03–15/10. SIZE: 14 ha, 50 pitches
(all with elec, 200 statics), 4 hot showers (charge),
16 WCs, 1 CWP. ⚓

[🍺 R 🍳 🍺 🍵 | 🏃 | 🐕]

Restaurant at 3 km.
PRICES: (1996) Caravan with family 26.00,
Tent with two adults 19.50. CC: none.
South of the town towards the Belgian border.

Recreatiepark Bosbad Hoeven Oude
Antwerpsepostbaan 81B, 4741 SG Hoeven.
Tel 0165 502570, Fax 0165 504254. English spoken.
OPEN: 15/02–31/12. SIZE: 34 ha, 150 pitches
(all with elec, 750 statics), 32 hot showers
(charge), 100 WCs, 4 CWPs. ⚓ ♿

[≋ 🏊 🍺 R 🍳 🍺 🍵 ✕ 🏃 🏠 🐕]

Amusement park, flumes.
PRICES: (1996) Caravan with family 45.36,
Tent with two adults 29.50. CC: Visa.
*From A58 east towards Breda, take exit 20
towards Hoeven and then look for campsite signs.*

ROTTERDAM   13C

Stadscamping Rotterdam
Kanaalweg 84, 3041 JE Rotterdam.
Tel 010 4153440, Fax 010 4373215. English spoken.
OPEN: all year. SIZE: 4 ha, 250 pitches (60 with elec,
20 statics), 14 hot showers, 27 WCs, 2 CWPs. ♿

[🍺 | 🍳 | 🍵 ✕ | 🏠]

Shop at 1 km.
PRICES: (1996) Caravan with family 43.00, Tent
with two adults 27.00. CC: Euro/Access, Visa.

SCHOUWEN

BURGH   13C

Zeeland Camping Duinoord
Steenweg 16, 4328 RM Westenschouwen.
Tel 0111 651964, Fax 0111 653707.
English spoken.
OPEN: all year. SIZE: 5 ha, 150 pitches (all with elec),
17 hot showers (charge), 28 WCs, 1 CWP. ⚓ ♿

[≋ ⚓ 🏠 R 🍳 🍺 | | | |]

Restaurant at 0.1 km.
PRICES: (1996) Caravan with family 51.00,
Tent with two adults 36.00. CC: none.
*On N57 follow signs to Westenschouwen, which is
on west side of island.*

END OF SCHOUWEN RESORTS

SCHAGEN   13A

Camping St Maartenszee
1753 BA St Maartenszee.
Tel 02246 1401, Fax 02246 1901.
English spoken.
OPEN: 27/03–25/10. SIZE: 5 ha, 300 pitches
(200 with elec), 32 hot showers, 40 WCs,
3 CWPs. ⚓

[≋ ⚓ 🏠 R 🍳 🍺 🍵 ✕ 🌳 🏠 🐕]

PRICES: (1996) Caravan with family 48.50, Tent
with two adults 31.00. CC: none.
*From N9, going towards Den Helder, follow signs
from St Maartensvlotbrug.*

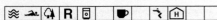

SEVENUM 13D

Camping de Schatberg
Midden Peelweg 5, 5975 MZ Sevenum.
Tel 0476 71756, Fax 0476 71772. English spoken.
OPEN: all year. SIZE: 86 ha, 600 pitches (all with
elec, 600 statics), 48 hot showers, 112 WCs,
7 CWPs. ₹ &

Fishing on site, golf course next door.
PRICES: (1996) Caravan with family 43.00,
Tent with two adults 25.00. CC: none.
*Take exit 38 for Helden from A67 Venlo-Eindhoven
road and then follow signs for De Schatberg.*

S'HERTOGENBOSCH 13D

Camping de Hooghe Heide
Werstkant 17, 5258 TC Berlicum.
Tel 073 5031522. English spoken.
OPEN: 01/04–31/10. SIZE: 5 ha, 160 pitches (120 with
elec), 8 hot showers, 20 WCs, 1 CWP. ₹ &

Children's pool.
PRICES: (1996) Caravan with family 39.00,
Tent with two adults 24.00. CC: none.
*From the motorway S'Hertogenbosch to Nijmegen,
take the Rosmalen-Berlicum exit.*

SLUIS 13C

Camping de Meidoorn 4524 LA Sluis.
Tel 0117 461662, Fax 0117 462728. English spoken.
OPEN: 22/03–20/10. SIZE: 5.5 ha, 165 pitches
(70 with elec, 87 statics), 10 hot showers (charge),
16 WCs, 1 CWP. ₹ &

Shop at 0.5 km.
PRICES: (1996) Caravan with family 36.40,
Tent with two adults 23.35. CC: none.
Follow signs from the centre of Sluis.

STEENWIJK 13B

Camping de Kom Bhltweg 25, 8346 KB De Bhlt.
Tel 0521 013736, Fax 0521 018736. English spoken.
OPEN: 01/04–01/10. SIZE: 10 ha, 100 pitches
(all with elec).

PRICES: (1996) Caravan with family 35.95,
Tent with two adults 24.75. CC: Euro/Access.
From Steenwijk follow directions to Frederiksoord.

TERSCHELLING

WEST TERSCHELLING 13B

Camping de Kooi 8882 HC Terschelling Hee.
Tel 0562 442743. English spoken.

OPEN: 14/04–15/09. SIZE: 8 ha, 70 pitches'(24 with
elec, 200 statics), 12 hot showers (charge),
26 WCs, 2 CWPs. ₹

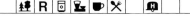

Shop at 0.4 km. Restaurant at 1.5 km.
PRICES: (1996) Caravan with family 39.75,
Tent with two adults 22.75. CC: none.
*Ferry from Harlingen to Terschelling. Hee is 5 km
from West Terschelling.*

END OF TERSCHELLIN RESORTS

TEXEL

DE KOOG 13A

Camping de Shelter
Boodtlaan 43, 1796 BD De Koog, Texel.
Tel 0222 317475, Fax 0222 317475. English spoken.
OPEN: 15/03–01/10. SIZE: 1 ha, 70 pitches (all with
elec), 8 hot showers (charge), 12 WCs, 1 CWP. ₹

Shop at 0.5 km. Restaurant at 0.5 km.
PRICES: (1996) Caravan with family 35.30,
Tent with two adults 21.05. CC: none.
*From the ferry harbour at 't Horntje follow signs to
De Koog. Campsite is signposted from the village.*

DEN HOORN 13A

Vakantiecentrum Loodsmansduin
1797 RN Den Hoorn, Texel.
Tel 02223 19203. English spoken.
OPEN: 01/04–26/10. SIZE: 38 ha, 162 pitches
(all with elec, 198 statics), 46 hot showers,
65 WCs, 12 French WCs, 9 CWPs. ₹

Shop at 1 km. Sea 2 km.
PRICES: (1996) Caravan with family 41.75,
Tent with two adults 25.25. CC: Euro/Access.
Campsite is well signposted.

END OF TEXEL RESORTS

TILBURG 13C

Camping de Reebok
Duinenweg 4, 5062 TP Oisterwijk.
Tel 013 5282309, Fax 013 5217592. English spoken.
OPEN: 01/04–01/10. SIZE: 8 ha, 70 pitches (all with
elec, 200 statics), 10 hot showers (charge),
12 WCs, 1 CWP.

Very lively site! Swimming pool 1.8 km.
PRICES: (1996) Caravan with family 38.50,
Tent with two adults 21.50. CC: none.
*Leaving Tilburg on the highway follow signs to
Oisterwijk, and then signs to the campsite.*

Netherlands

Den Bergh Bosscheweg 77, 5281 AH Boxtel.
Tel 0411 672511, Fax 0411 673260. English spoken.
OPEN: 01/04–01/10. SIZE: 2 ha, 60 pitches (45 with
elec, 20 statics), 4 hot showers (charge), 8 WCs,
1 CWP.

Restaurant at 0.1 km.
PRICES: (1996) Caravan with family 29.00,
Tent with two adults 17.00. CC: none.
*Boxtel is north-east of Tilburg and is well
signposted.*

Vakantiecentrum de Hertenwei
Wellenseind 7-9, 5094 EG Lage Mierde.
Tel 04259 1295. English spoken.
OPEN: all year. SIZE: 20 ha, 325 pitches (all with
elec, 125 statics), 27 hot showers, 55 WCs,
5 CWPs. ૯ ໐

Indoor/outdoor pools, sauna, solarium, tennis,
disco.
PRICES: (1996) Caravan with family 50.50. CC: none.
*20 km south of Tilburg on the N269, near the
Belgian border. 2 km north of Lage Mierde, in
beautiful wooded surroundings.*

URK   13B

Rekreatiepark Hazevreugd
Vormtweg 9, 8321 NC Urkerbos/Urk.
Tel 0527 681785, Fax 0527 686298. English spoken.
OPEN: 01/04–01/11. SIZE: 10 ha, 200 pitches
(150 with elec), 2 hot showers, 30 WCs, 3 CWPs. ૯

Restaurant at 1.5 km.
PRICES: (1996) Caravan with family 32.65,
Tent with two adults 18.00. CC: none.
To the left of A6 going north, on the coast.

VALKENBURG   13D

Europa-Camping 6301 Valkenburg.
Tel 0440 613097. English spoken.
OPEN: 01/04–31/10. SIZE: 10 ha, 450 pitches
(all with elec, 150 statics), 27 hot showers,
70 WCs, 4 CWPs. ໐

PRICES: (1996) Caravan with family 41.50, Tent
with two adults 34.00. CC: none.
*Coming from Maastricht, campsite is on the right
just before entering Valkenburg. Well signposted.*

VALKENSWAARD   13D

Camping de Brugse Heide Maastrichterweg
183, 5556 VB Valkenswaard.
Tel 040 2018304, Fax 040 2049312. English spoken.
OPEN: all year. SIZE: 7 ha, 235 pitches (all with
elec), 10 hot showers, 18 WCs, 1 CWP. ૯ ໐

PRICES: (1996) Caravan with family 43.00,
Tent with two adults 32.00. CC: Visa.
*From Eindhoven travel south towards
Valkenswaard. At the Mercedes garage turn left to
Achel.*

Camping de Paal
Paaldreef 14, 5571 TN Bergeyk.
Tel 0497 571977, Fax 0497 571977. English spoken.
OPEN: 01/04–01/11. SIZE: 21 ha, 375 pitches
(all with elec, 125 statics), 32 hot showers,
68 WCs, 1 CWP. ૯ ໐

PRICES: (1996) Caravan with family 60.00,
Tent with two adults 42.00. CC: none.
*Turn off the A67/E34 Eindhoven to Turnhout
road at the Eersel exit towards the town;
signposted (Bergeyk).*

VENLO   13D

Family Campingsite BreeBronne Lange Heide,
5993 RE Maasbree.
Tel 0774 652360, Fax 0774 652095. English spoken.
OPEN: 01/04–30/09. SIZE: 10 ha, 140 pitches
(all with elec, 140 statics), 9 hot showers, 20 WCs,
1 CWP. ૯ ໐

Formerly Camping de Ruige Hoek, site has been
extensively updated.
PRICES: (1996) Caravan with family 48.75,
Tent with two adults 27.50. CC: none.
*From the A67 Eindhoven-Venlo road take the
Maasbree or Sevenum exit. Follow signs for
Maasbree and you will see signs for the campsite.*

VLISSINGEN   13C

Camping de Mee-Paal
Duinweg 133, 4374 Zoutelande.
Tel 011856 1300, Fax 011856 2665. English spoken.
OPEN: 01/04–24/10. SIZE: 2 ha, 131 pitches
(all with elec), 8 hot showers, 12 WCs, 1 CWP.

Restaurant at 2 km.
PRICES: (1996) Caravan with family 59.60,
Tent with two adults 39.10. CC: none.
*Go south-east from centre of village and along
dyke to end of road.*

VROUWENPOLDER   13C

Camping Oranjezon Koningin Emmaweg 16a,
4354 KD Vrouwenpolder.
Tel 0118 591549, Fax 0118 591920. English spoken.
OPEN: 09/04–01/11. SIZE: 6 ha, 150 pitches
(140 with elec), 16 hot showers (charge), 21 WCs,
1 CWP. ໐

Netherlands (side tab)

PRICES: (1996) Caravan with family 45.00,
Tent with two adults 28.50. CC: none.
*Follow signs from the Vrouwenpolder junction on
the N255 Middelburg-Haamstede road. Campsite
is 3 km outside Vrouwenpolder, going towards
Oostkapelle.*

WASSENAAR 13C

Attractiepark and Camping Duinrell
2242 JP Duinrell.
Tel 070 5155255, Fax 070 5155371. English spoken.
OPEN: all year. SIZE: 110 ha, 1300 pitches
(1050 with elec, 80 statics), 100 hot showers,
100 WCs, 7 CWPs. ℓ &

The amusement park, including 50 attractions, is
free for campers.
PRICES: Caravan with family 80.50,
Tent with two adults 45.00. CC: none.
*From Den Haag take A44/N44 north along the
coast towards Wassenaar. Then follow ANWB
(Dutch Touring Club) signs to Duinrell.*

Camping Maaldrift
Boerderij, Maaldrift 9, 2241 BN Wassenaar.
Tel 0175 113688. English spoken.
OPEN: 01/04–01/10. SIZE: 2.5 ha, 35 pitches
(30 with elec, 60 statics), 7 hot showers (charge),
20 WCs, 1 CWP. ℓ

Shop at 2 km. Restaurant at 1 km.
PRICES: (1996) Caravan with family 28.00,
Tent with two adults 16.00. CC: none.
*A44/N44 north from Den Haag towards
Wassenaar then follow signs to Camping
Maaldrift.*

WEERT 13D

Camping Yzeren Man
Herenvennenweg 60, 6006 SW Weert.
Tel 0495 533202, Fax 0495 546812. English spoken.
OPEN: 01/04–31/10. SIZE: 10 ha, 105 pitches
(all with elec, 175 statics), 12 hot showers,
28 WCs, 2 CWPs. ℓ

Shop at 5 km. Restaurant at 2 km.
PRICES: (1996) Caravan with family 37.00,
Tent with two adults 23.50. CC: none.
*From A2 Eindhoven-Maastricht, exit Weert.
Follow campsite signs from town centre.*

WOLPHAARTSDIJK 13C

Camping De Veerhoeve
Veerweg 48, 4471 NC Wolphaartsdijk.
Tel 0113 581155, Fax 0113 581194. English spoken.
OPEN: 01/04–30/10. SIZE: 8 ha, 150 pitches
(125 with elec, 225 statics), 17 hot showers
(charge), 24 WCs, 2 CWPs. ℓ &

Restaurant at 0.1 km. Sailing and fishing nearby.
PRICES: (1996) Caravan with family 36.50,
Tent with two adults 30.00. CC: Visa.
*Campsite is well signposted approaching
Wolphaartsdijk from Goes.*

ZEIST 13C/D

Camping de Krakeling
Woudensbergseweg 17, 3707 HW Zeist.
Tel 03404 15374, Fax 03404 15374. English spoken.
OPEN: 01/04–17/10. SIZE: 16 ha, 340 pitches
(all with elec, 240 statics), 24 hot showers
(charge), 52 WCs, 5 CWPs. ℓ &

PRICES: (1996) Caravan with family 29.50, Tent
with two adults 18.00. CC: Euro/Access.
Follow signs in Zeist to campsite.

ZEVENHUIZEN 13C

Kampeerterrein Zevenhuizen
Tweemanspolder 8, 2761 ED Zevenhuizen.
Tel 0180 631654, Fax 0180 634471. English spoken.
OPEN: 01/04–01/10. SIZE: 6 ha, 60 pitches (53 with
elec), 14 hot showers, 26 WCs, 1 CWP. ℓ &

Shop at 2 km. Canoes, bikes. 2 cabins for hire.
PRICES: (1996) Caravan with family 42.50, Tent
with two adults 24.00. CC: Euro/Access, Visa.
*From Den Haag on A12 to Utrecht or from
Rotterdam on A20 to Utrecht. Turn off at
Zevenhuizen exit.*

Netherlands

NORWAY

Beyond the Arctic Circle, Norway offers seasonal extremes of either midnight sun or the winter's Northern Lights. The country has an excellent road network – covering even remotest Finnmark – and this means a Scandinavian round trip is a real possibility.

The capital, Oslo, is remarkably unmetropolitan: its houses straggle out into the forest or line the rocky coast and clear waters of the fjord. Two burial mounds south of Oslo yielded the greatest of all Viking relics, the Gokstad and Oseberg ships, now housed in a superb museum at Bydgoy, just outside the city, close to the latter-day Viking Thor Heyerdahl's *Kon Tiki* and *Ra II*. The Edvard Munch Museum betrays an angst-ridden undertone to apparently untroubled Oslo.

From Stavanger northwards, the coastline becomes a non-stop spectacle, mixing sheer-sided fjords with the more detailed world of the offshore islands. Bergen is the regular start for the Hurtigrute passenger ship, beginning an 11-day round-trip to and from Kirkenes, near the Russian frontier.

North of Trondheim, a long parade of mountains and fjords culminates in the jagged heights of the Lofoten Islands. From Narvik, north and eastwards, Norwegians overlap with indigenous Sami – or Lapps – many of whom, wearing their bright traditional costumes, still follow their reindeer herds in season. Hammerfest, in the open landscape of Finnmark, is considered the 'most northerly city in the world'. Beyond it lies the North Cape, the Pole… and, if you believe the brochures, Santa himself.

Emergency numbers

Police 112, Fire Brigade 110, Ambulance 113

Warning information

Carrying a warning triangle recommended
Blood Alcohol Legal Limit 50 mg

ÅLESUND 11A

Prinsen Strandcamping Gåseid, 6015 Ålesund. Tel 701 55204, Fax 701 54996. English spoken. OPEN: all year. SIZE: 30 ha, 100 pitches (125 with elec), 13 hot showers (charge), 14 WCs, 1 CWP.

Restaurant at 0.8 km. Sauna, bike hire.
PRICES: (1996) Caravan with family 140, Tent with two adults 120. CC: Amex, Euro/Access, Visa.
5 km east of Ålesund centre. Well signposted.

ALTA 10B

Alta River Camping 9500 Alta.
Tel 784 34353, Fax 784 36902. English spoken.
OPEN: all year. SIZE: 120 pitches (42 with elec), 7 hot showers (charge), 8 WCs, 1 CWP.

Shop at 5 km. Restaurant at 5 km.
PRICES: (1996) Caravan with family 130, Tent with two adults 80. CC: none.
Beautiful location by the river. 4 km from Alta city on the road 93 towards Kautokeino.

ÅNDALSNES 11A

Mittet Camping 6363 Mittet.
Tel 712 28483/28471. English spoken.
OPEN: 01/05–30/09. SIZE: 2 ha, 60 pitches (all with elec), 2 hot showers (charge), 5 WCs.

Shop at 0.2 km. Restaurant at 11 km.
PRICES: (1996) Caravan with family 105, Tent with two adults 80. CC: none.
Take road 64 to Afarnes then 660 to Mittet.

NAF-Camping Saltkjelsnes 6350 Eidsbygda.
Tel 712 23815/23900, Fax 712 23815.
English spoken.
OPEN: 01/05–15/09. SIZE: 1.5 ha, 60 pitches (50 with elec), 3 hot showers (charge), 7 WCs.

Shop at 2 km. Restaurant at 5 km.
PRICES: (1996) Caravan with family 120, Tent with two adults 85. CC: none.
25 km from Åndalsnes, 500 m off route 64, Åndalsnes to Molde.

ARENDAL 11A

Niddu Brygge & Camping
Vesterv. 251, 4817 Hisoy.
Tel 370 11425. English spoken.

OPEN: 01/06–30/08. SIZE: 18 ha, 100 pitches
(50 with elec), 4 hot showers (charge), 8 WCs.

Shop at 1 km.
PRICES: (1996) Caravan with family 125,
Tent with two adults 110. CC: none.
Arendal is north-east of Kristiansand on E18.
Campsite is south of the town, by the river.

BALESTRAND 11A

Sjotun Camping 5850 Balestrand.
Tel 576 91223, Fax 576 91223. English spoken.
OPEN: 01/06–30/09. SIZE: 0.7 ha, 30 pitches
(all with elec), 2 hot showers, 6 WCs.

Shop at 1 km. Restaurant at 1 km.
PRICES: (1996) Caravan with family 90,
Tent with two adults 65. CC: none.
Off the R55, 1 km from the centre of Balestrand
and near the Sogne Fjord.

Veganeset Camping Dragsvik, 5850 Balestrand.
Tel 569 1612. English spoken.
OPEN: 15/05–15/09. SIZE: 30 pitches (18 with elec),
3 hot showers (charge), 6 WCs, 1 CWP.

Shop at 5 km. Restaurant at 0.3 km.
PRICES: (1996) Caravan with family 110, Tent with
two adults 85. CC: Amex, Euro/Access, Visa.
9 km from Balestrand on the R55.

BALLANGEN 10A

Ballangen Camping 8540 Ballangen.
Tel 769 28297, Fax 769 28150. English spoken.
OPEN: all year. SIZE: 90 ha, 150 pitches (100 with
elec, 10 statics), 5 hot showers (charge), 12 WCs,
1 CWP.

Restaurant at 3 km. Tennis, boats, fishing, sauna.
PRICES: (1996) Caravan with family 120, Tent with
two adults 100. CC: Visa.
Ballangen is 40 km south of Narvik and 40 km
north of the ferry.

BERGEN 11A

Bratland Camping 5233 Haukeland.
Tel 551 01338. English spoken.
OPEN: 20/05–10/09. SIZE: 10 ha, 70 pitches (30 with
elec), 4 hot showers (charge), 8 WCs, 1 CWP.

Restaurant at 10 km.
PRICES: (1996) Caravan with family 135,
Tent with two adults 90. CC: none.
16 km from Bergen city centre on road 580,
south-east of the city.

BERKÅK 11A

Gullvag Camping Garli, 7391 Berkåk.
Tel 724 34936, Fax 724 34960.
English spoken.
OPEN: 01/05–15/09. SIZE: 14 ha, 50 pitches
(20 with elec, 40 statics), 9 hot showers (charge),
14 WCs, 1 CWP.

Restaurant at 3 km. Friendly, family site with
animals.
PRICES: (1996) Caravan with family 120,
Tent with two adults 80. CC: Visa.
E6, 70 km south of Trondheim. Campsite is beside
a small river and well signposted.

DALEN 11A

Dalen Camping Postboks 95, Buoy, 3880 Dalen.
Tel 350 77587, Fax 350 77587.
English spoken.
OPEN: 15/05–15/09. SIZE: 100 pitches (14 with elec,
100 statics), 4 hot showers, 10 WCs.

Restaurant at 0.2 km.
PRICES: (1996) Caravan with family 105,
Tent with two adults 55. CC: Visa.
About 175 m from the village square. Well
signposted.

DRAMMEN 11A

Drammen Camping
Buskerudvneien 97, 3027 Drammen.
Tel 328 21798. English spoken.
OPEN: 20/05–10/09. SIZE: 36 ha, 140 pitches
(72 with elec), 7 hot showers (charge), 21 WCs,
1 CWP.

Shop at 0.4 km. Restaurant at 4 km.
PRICES: (1996) Caravan with family 135,
Tent with two adults 105. CC: none.
On the edge of Drammen from Kongsberg
direction; follow the signs.

EGERSUND 11A

Steinsnes Camping 4370 Egersund.
Tel 514 94136, Fax 514 94136.
English spoken.
OPEN: all year. SIZE: 13 ha, 80 pitches (all with elec,
20 statics), 6 hot showers (charge), 7 WCs,
1 French WC, 1 CWP.

Shop at 0.1 km.
PRICES: (1996) Caravan with family 130,
Tent with two adults 90. CC: Visa.
From Egersund, take route 44 north towards
Stavanger for approx 3 km.

EIDFJORD   11A

Saebo Camping 5784 Ovre Eidfjord.
Tel 536 65927. English spoken.
OPEN: 01/04–31/10. SIZE: 3 ha, 100 pitches
(60 with elec, 13 statics), 7 hot showers (charge),
9 WCs, 1 CWP. ✆ &

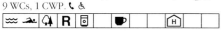

Shop at 0.4 km. Restaurant at 0.5 km. Spectacular
views.
PRICES: (1996) Caravan with family 115,
Tent with two adults 85. CC: none.
*200 m from the main road (R7) by the Eidfjord
Lake (Eidfjordvatnet). Visible and well signposted
from main road.*

ELVERUM   11A

Elverum Camping 2400 Elverum.
Tel 624 16716. English spoken.
OPEN: 01/06–30/09. SIZE: 5 ha, 200 pitches
(100 with elec), 8 hot showers, 20 WCs, 1 CWP. ✆ &

Shop at 1 km. Fishing.
PRICES: (1996) Caravan with family 145,
Tent with two adults 125. CC: Visa.
*On the main road towards Kongsvinger, 1 km
from Elverum.*

EVJE   11A

NAF-Camping Hornnes 4670 Hornnes.
Tel 379 30305. English spoken.
OPEN: 15/05–01/09. SIZE: 1.7 ha, 80 pitches (60 with
elec), 3 hot showers (charge), 5 WCs, 1 CWP. ✆

Shop at 0.4 km. Restaurant at 5 km.
PRICES: (1996) Caravan with family 105,
Tent with two adults 80. CC: none.
*From Evje, go south along route 12. Campsite is
close to Setesdal Mineral Park. Site is well
signposted.*

Odden Camping 4660 Evje.
Tel 379 30603. English spoken.
OPEN: all year. SIZE: 4 ha, 100 pitches (all with
elec), 4 hot showers (charge), 8 WCs, 1 CWP. &

Restaurant at 0.2 km. Satellite television.
PRICES: Caravan with family 130,
Tent with two adults 100. CC: none.
*500 m from the centre of Evje, by the Texaco petrol
station.*

FAGERNES   11A

Fagernes Camping A/S Tyinvegen 17,
2900 Fagernes.
Tel 613 60510, Fax 613 60751. English spoken.

OPEN: all year. SIZE: 30 ha, 200 pitches (135 with
elec), 14 hot showers (charge), 12 WCs. &

Restaurant at 0.5 km.
PRICES: (1996) Caravan with family 195, Tent with
two adults 100. CC: Euro/Access, Visa.
Well signposted from E16.

FLEKKEFJORD   11A

Camping Egenes 4400 Flekkefjord.
Tel 383 21348, Fax 383 20111. English spoken.
OPEN: 01/05–01/09. SIZE: 2.5 ha, 180 pitches
(160 with elec, 90 statics), 8 hot showers (charge),
18 WCs, 1 CWP. ✆ &

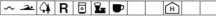

Fishing, climbing, horse-riding, canoeing.
PRICES: Caravan with family 170, Tent with two
adults 120. CC: Amex, Euro/Access, Visa.
*South of Norway, between Kristiansand and
Stavanger in Vest-Agder, 5 km east of Flekkefjord,
1.3 km from main road E18.*

GEILO   11A

Geilo Camping 3580 Geilo.
Tel 320 90733, Fax 320 91156. English spoken.
OPEN: all year. SIZE: 3.5 ha, 20 pitches (all with
elec), 8 hot showers (charge), 15 WCs.

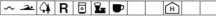

Restaurant at 0.3 km. Fishing, hunting,
mountain walks.
PRICES: (1996) Caravan with family 140,
Tent with two adults 90. CC: Euro/Access, Visa.
*300 m from Geilo town, towards Kongsberg on
R40 (8).*

GEIRANGER   11A

Geiranger Camping 6216 Geiranger.
Tel 716 3120. English spoken.
OPEN: 20/05–10/09. SIZE: 1 ha, 120 pitches (50 with
elec), 7 hot showers (charge), 13 WCs. ✆ &

Restaurant at 0.4 km.
PRICES: (1996) Caravan with family 110,
Tent with two adults 85. CC: none.
Geiranger is on the R63.

Vinje Camping 6216 Geiranger.
Tel 702 63017, Fax 702 63015. English spoken.
OPEN: 01/06–10/09. SIZE: 80 pitches (20 with elec),
4 hot showers (charge), 12 WCs.

Shop at 1 km. Restaurant at 0.5 km.
PRICES: (1996) Caravan with family 105,
Tent with two adults 80. CC: none.
Close to main road and 1.5 km east from Geiranger.

Norway

GJØVIK 11A

Camping Sveastranda Redalen, 2824 Gjøvik.
Tel 618 1529. English spoken.
OPEN: all year. SIZE: 80 ha, 300 pitches (all with elec), 15 hot showers (charge), 22 WCs, 2 CWPs. &

| ≈ | ⚓ | ♀ | R | ⊡ | 🍽 | 💧 | | | ⌂ | | |

Restaurant at 2.5 km.
PRICES: Caravan with family 140,
Tent with two adults 100. CC: Visa.
Between Lillehammer and Gjøvik on route no 4.

GOL 11A

Fossheim Hytte & Camping 3550 Gol.
Tel 320 73316, Fax 320 74112. English spoken.
OPEN: all year. SIZE: 25 ha, 50 pitches (44 with elec), 5 hot showers, 10 WCs, 2 CWPs. ₵ &

| ∿ | ⚓ | ⌂ | R | ⊡ | 💧 | | | ⌂ | | | |

Restaurant at 4 km. Fishing, cycling.
PRICES: (1996) Caravan with family 145,
Tent with two adults 120. CC: Euro/Access, Visa.
Between main road 7 and Hallingdal river, 3.5 km west of Gol.

Personbråten Camping 3550 Gol.
Tel 320 75970. English spoken.
OPEN: all year. SIZE: 55 pitches (35 with elec).

| ∿ | ⚓ | ⌂ | R | | | | | | | | |

Shop at 1.5 km. Restaurant at 1.5 km.
PRICES: (1996) Caravan with family 95,
Tent with two adults 80. CC: none.
On road 7, well signposted.

GRIMSBU 11A

Grimsbu Turistsenter Motell & Camp
2582 Grimsbu.
Tel 624 93529, Fax 624 93562. English spoken.
OPEN: all year. SIZE: 100 pitches (all with elec), 8 hot showers (charge), 12 WCs, 2 CWPs. ₵ &

| | ⌂ | R | ⊡ | 💧 | 🍽 | ✗ | | ⌂ | | | |

PRICES: Caravan with family 140, Tent with two adults 100. CC: Euro/Access, Visa.
On road 29, 30 km from Alvdal.

GRONG 10C

Harran Camping 7873 Harran, Nord Trondelag.
Tel 743 32990. English spoken.
OPEN: 01/06–01/09. SIZE: 2 ha, 50 pitches (32 with elec), 5 hot showers (charge), 8 WCs, 1 CWP. ₵ &

| ∿ | ⚓ | ♀ | R | ⊡ | 💧 | 🍽 | ✗ | | ⌂ | | |

Restaurant at 1 km.
PRICES: Caravan with family 100,
Tent with two adults 70. CC: none.
15 km north of Grong and 2 km north of the Laksakvarium (the salmon lake).

HAMMERFEST 10B

Hammerfest Turist Senter Storsvingen
Postboks 430, 9601 Hammerfest.
Tel 784 11126, Fax 784 11926. English spoken.
OPEN: 01/05–15/10. SIZE: 2.7 ha, 100 pitches (68 with elec), 10 hot showers (charge), 15 WCs, 2 CWPs. ₵ &

| ≈ | ⚓ | ⚵ | R | ⊡ | 💧 | 💧 | ✗ | | ⌂ | 🕴 | |

Mini-golf, walking, fishing trips, rowboats available.
PRICES: (1996) Caravan with family 140, Tent with two adults 110. CC: Amex, Euro/Access, Visa.
1.5 km from town centre, on the main road to Hammerfest. Campsite is on a hill overlooking the town with the best viewpoint in the area for the midnight sun.

HARSTAD 10A

Harstad Camping Nesseveien 55, 9400 Harstad.
Tel 770 73662, Fax 770 73502. English spoken.
OPEN: 01/06–01/09. SIZE: 12 ha, 100 pitches (33 with elec), 4 hot showers (charge), 7 WCs, 1 CWP. ₵ &

| ≈ | ⚓ | ⌂ | R | ⊡ | 💧 | | | ⌂ | | | |

Shop at 0.9 km. Restaurant at 5 km.
PRICES: (1996) Caravan with family 120,
Tent with two adults 95. CC: none.
5 km south from Harstad, situated by the sea 1 km east of R83.

HONNINGSVÅG 11A

Nordkapp Camping Box 361, 9750 Honningsvåg.
Tel 784 73377, Fax 784 71177. English spoken.
OPEN: 15/05–20/09. SIZE: 16 ha, 9 hot showers (charge), 10 WCs, 1 CWP. ₵ &

| ≈ | | ♀ | R | ⊡ | 💧 | 💧 | ✗ | | ⌂ | | |

Sauna. 10% discount for RAC members.
PRICES: Caravan with family 120,
Tent with two adults 80. CC: Visa.
7 km north-east of Honningsvåg.

HOVDEN 11A

Hovden Fjellstoge Caravan Camp
4695 Hovden.
Tel 379 39543, Fax 379 39818. English spoken.
OPEN: all year. SIZE: 100 pitches (all with elec).

| ∿ | ✈ | | R | ⊡ | | 💧 | ✗ | | ⌂ | | |

Shop at 3 km.
PRICES: (1996) Caravan with family 150,
Tent with two adults 100. CC: Visa.
Hovden is approx 210 km north of Kristiansand.

JOSTEDAL 11A

Gjerde Camping 5827 Jostedal.
Tel 576 83154, Fax 576 83157. English spoken.

Norway

OPEN: 20/05–01/10. SIZE: 10 ha, 25 pitches (15 with elec), 2 hot showers (charge), 5 WCs, 1 CWP. **&**

Restaurant at 0.1 km.
PRICES: (1996) Caravan with family 90, Tent with two adults 65. CC: none.
Campsite is well signposted.

KINSARVIK 11A

Harding Camping 5780 Kinsarvik.
Tel 546 3182, Fax 546 3354. English spoken.
OPEN: all year. SIZE: 18 ha, 77 pitches (61 with elec), 12 hot showers (charge), 17 WCs. **& &**

Whirlpool, sauna, solarium.
PRICES: (1996) Caravan with family 165, Tent with two adults 140. CC: Amex, Euro/Access, Visa.
Site is near national highway 13, in Kinsarvik.

Kinsarvik Camping 5780 Kinsarvik.
Tel 536 63290. English spoken.
OPEN: 01/05–30/08. SIZE: 64 pitches (all with elec, 30 statics), 2 hot showers (charge), 7 WCs. **&**

Restaurant at 0.1 km.
PRICES: (1996) Caravan with family 100, Tent with two adults 75. CC: none.
Near the national highway 13, in the centre of Kinsarvik.

KRISTIANSAND 11C

Dvergnestangen Senter Randesund, 4639 Kristiansand.
Tel 380 47155, Fax 380 43492. English spoken.
OPEN: all year. SIZE: 9 ha, 250 pitches (150 with elec, 4 statics), 14 hot showers (charge), 30 WCs, 2 CWPs. **&**

Restaurant at 12 km.
PRICES: (1996) Caravan with family 150, Tent with two adults 130. CC: Visa.
From Kristiansand town and the ferry, follow the E18 towards Oslo (east) for 6 km. Then follow signs towards Dvergnestangen (6 km).

KRISTIANSUND 10C

Atlanten Camping and Tourist Centre
Dalaveien 22, 6500 Kristiansund.
Tel 716 71104, Fax 716 71158. English spoken.
OPEN: all year. SIZE: 26 ha, 100 pitches (50 with elec), 10 hot showers, 13 WCs, 2 CWPs. **&**

Restaurant at 1.5 km.
PRICES: Caravan with family 140, Tent with two adults 80. CC: Amex, Euro/Access, Visa.
1.5 km from Kristiansund, close to main road no 1.

KROKSTRAND 11A

Krokstrand Camping
Krokstrand, 8630 Storforshei.
Tel 751 66074. English spoken.
OPEN: 20/05–20/09. SIZE: 2 ha, 50 pitches (28 with elec), 4 hot showers (charge), 6 WCs, 1 CWP. **&**

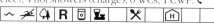

PRICES: Caravan with family 110, Tent with two adults 80. CC: none.
Near Krokstrand Bridge, campsite is 18 km south of Arctic Circle.

KVANNDAL 11A

Kvanndal Kro & Camping
5739 Kvanndal, Bergen.
Tel 562 5880, Fax 562 5855. English spoken.
OPEN: 15/05–15/09. SIZE: 40 pitches (18 with elec), 3 hot showers (charge), 6 WCs, 1 CWP. **& &**

Fishing; boat hire.
PRICES: (1996) Caravan with family 105, Tent with two adults 85. CC: Euro/Access, Visa.
10 km west of Granvin.

LILLEHAMMER 11A

Hunderfossen Camping Faberg/Lillehammer, 2638 Lillehammer.
Tel 612 77300, Fax 612 77100.
English spoken.
OPEN: all year. SIZE: 400 pitches (300 with elec), 25 hot showers (charge), 40 WCs, 2 CWPs. **& &**

12-minute train ride to Lillehammer; within walking distance to family park.
PRICES: (1996) Caravan with family 130, Tent with two adults 110. CC: Euro/Access, Visa.
Following E6, 14 km north of Lillehammer over the new bridge. The campsite is located only 5 minutes from the Olympic bob/sledge arena.

Lillehammer Camping Dampsagvegen 47, 2600 Lillehammer.
Tel 615 33333, Fax 615 33365. English spoken.
OPEN: all year. SIZE: 70 ha, 210 pitches (all with elec), 12 hot showers (charge), 12 WCs, 1 CWP. **& &**

Restaurant at 0.8 km.
PRICES: (1996) Caravan with family 150, Tent with two adults 130. CC: Euro/Access, Visa.
Lovely location on the banks of Lake Mjøsa and walking distance from Lillehammer town centre.

Stranda Camping 2823 Biristrand.
Tel 618 4672, Fax 618 4802. English spoken.
OPEN: all year. SIZE: 8 ha, 200 pitches (all with elec), 7 hot showers (charge), 18 WCs, 1 CWP.

Norway

Restaurant at 10 km.
PRICES: (1996) Caravan with family 125,
Tent with two adults 100. CC: Visa.
11 km south of Lillehammer to Biristrand on E6.

LILLESAND 11C

Tingsaker Familiecamping 4790 Lillesand.
Tel 417 0421. English spoken.
OPEN: 01/05–01/10. SIZE: 3 ha, 150 pitches
(100 with elec), 6 hot showers (charge), 19 WCs,
1 CWP. ✆ &

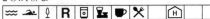

Shop at 0.5 km. Restaurant at 1 km.
PRICES: (1996) Caravan with family 130,
Tent with two adults 105. CC: Visa.
*The campsite is 0.5 km from E18, 1 km east of
Lillesand.*

LOEN 11A

Sande Camping 6878 Loen.
Tel 578 77659, Fax 578 77859.
English spoken.
OPEN: all year. SIZE: 3 ha, 60 pitches (40 with elec,
10 statics), 6 hot showers (charge), 10 WCs,
2 CWPs. &

Hotel swimming pool nearby.
PRICES: (1996) Caravan with family 145,
Tent with two adults 100. CC: Visa.
*Turn off route 60 by the Hotel Alexandra and
continue for 4.5 km towards Lodalen and
Kienndal Glacier (narrow road).*

LOFTHUS 11A

Lofthus Camping 5774 Lofthus.
Tel 536 61364, Fax 536 61500.
English spoken.
OPEN: 01/05–15/09. SIZE: 2 ha, 85 pitches (36 with
elec), 5 hot showers (charge), 10 WCs,
2 CWPs. ✆ &

Shop at 0.8 km. Restaurant at 0.8 km. Orchard site.
Fruit in season. Comfortable cabins available.
PRICES: Caravan with family 130, Tent with two
adults 94. CC: Amex, Euro/Access, Visa.
Signposted from centre of Lofthus, 1.3 km.

Lofthus Camping
at Lofthus
*Idyllic orchard between fjord,
mountain and glacier*

LOM 11A

Lom Motell & Camping Box 88, 2686 Lom.
Tel 612 11220, Fax 612 11223. English spoken.
OPEN: 01/04–30/09. SIZE: 1 ha, 100 pitches
(40 with elec), 5 hot showers (charge), 12 WCs,
1 CWP. ✆ &

PRICES: (1996) Caravan with family 140, Tent with
two adults 120. CC: Amex, Euro/Access, Visa.
Well signposted.

LUSTER 11A

Dalsoran Camping 5830 Luster.
Tel 576 85436, Fax 576 85230. English spoken.
OPEN: 01/05–15/10. SIZE: 4 hot showers (charge),
7 WCs, 1 CWP. ✆

PRICES: unavailable. CC: Euro/Access, Visa.

MERÅKER 10C

**Meråker Vandrerhjem og Brenna NAF
Camping** Brenna, 7530 Meråker.
Tel 748 10234, Fax 748 10300. English spoken.
OPEN: 01/05–15/09. SIZE: 3 ha, 90 pitches (40 with
elec), 7 hot showers (charge), 8 WCs, 1 CWP. &

Restaurant at 2 km.
PRICES: Caravan with family 90,
Tent with two adults 65. CC: none.
*From centre of Meråker go 2 km along E14,
towards Sweden. Turn left and campsite is 600 m
from main road.*

NARVIK 10A

Narvik Camping
Boks 346, Orneshaugen E6, 8500 Narvik.
Tel 769 45810, Fax 769 41420. English spoken.
OPEN: 01/01–30/12. &

PRICES: unavailable. CC: none.
1.8 km north of Narvik, by main road E6.

NESNA 10C

Nesna Camping 8700 Nesna.
Tel 750 56540, Fax 750 56697. English spoken.
OPEN: all year. SIZE: 50 ha, 100 pitches (60 with
elec), 9 hot showers (charge), 9 WCs, 2 CWPs. ✆ &

Restaurant at 0.2 km. Boat, fishing and mounatin
tours; flume, mini-golf.
PRICES: (1996) Caravan with family 130,
Tent with two adults 110. CC: Amex,
Euro/Access, Visa.
On road no.17, 65 km from Mo I Rana (E6).

NORDKJOSBOTN 10B

Bjornebo Camping 9040 Nordkjosbotn.
Tel 777 28161. English spoken.
OPEN: 01/06–01/09. SIZE: 4.5 ha, 25 pitches
(10 with elec), 3 hot showers (charge), 5 WCs. &

Shop at 0.1 km. Restaurant at 0.2 km.
PRICES: (1996) Caravan with family 100,
Tent with two adults 80. CC: none.
Junction of E69/E47 south of Tromsø.

NORHEIMSUND 11A

Mo Camping 5600 Norheimsund.
Tel 565 51727. English spoken.
OPEN: 01/06–01/09. SIZE: 4 ha, 40 pitches
(220 with elec, 24 statics), 2 hot showers (charge),
3 WCs, 1 CWP. &

Shop at 0.2 km. Restaurant at 1 km. Fishing.
PRICES: (1996) Caravan with family 86,
Tent with two adults 60. CC: none.
1 km from Norheimsund on road 7.

OLDEN 11A

Melkevoll Camping 6876 Olden.
Tel 578 73864, Fax 578 73890.
English spoken.
OPEN: 01/05–30/09. SIZE: 3 ha, 90 pitches (50 with
elec), 6 hot showers (charge), 8 WCs, 1 CWP. & &

Shop at 4 km.
PRICES: Caravan with family 80,
Tent with two adults 60. CC: none.
*From the crossroads in Olden (at Rv60) go 20 km
south towards the Briksdal Glacier. Well signposted.*

OSLO 11A

Bogstad Camp & Turistsenter
Ankerveien 117, 0757 Oslo 7.
Tel 250 7680, Fax 250 0162. English spoken.
OPEN: all year. SIZE: 180 ha, 1000 pitches (170 with
elec), 36 hot showers, 80 WCs, 3 CWPs. & &

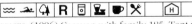

PRICES: (1996) Caravan with family 185, Tent with
two adults 125. CC: Amex, Euro/Access, Visa.
Follow signs from E6, E18, E78 or E16.

Ekeberg Camping Ekebergveien 65, 1181 Oslo.
Tel 221 98568, Fax 22 670436. English spoken.
OPEN: 01/06–31/08. SIZE: 70 ha, 24 pitches, 38 hot
showers, 53 WCs, 1 CWP. & &

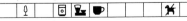

Restaurant at 0.3 km.
PRICES: (1996) Caravan with family 160,
Tent with two adults 130. CC: Euro/Access, Visa.

Oslo Fjordcamp AS Stubljan
Ljansbrukreien 1, 1250 Oslo.
Tel 2275 2055, Fax 2275 2056. English spoken.
OPEN: 15/05–15/09. SIZE: 2.8 ha, 120 pitches
(44 with elec), 6 hot showers (charge),
11 WCs, 1 CWP. &

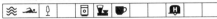

Restaurant at 1 km.
PRICES: (1996) Caravan with family 190,
Tent with two adults 110. CC: Euro/Access, Visa.

From the town centre, south on the E18.

ROTSUND 10B

Rotsundelv Camping 9077 Rotsund.
Tel 777 64124. English spoken.
OPEN: 01/06–20/08. SIZE: 10 ha, 20 pitches
(8 with elec).

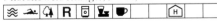

Restaurant at 20 km.
PRICES: (1996) Caravan with family 100,
Tent with two adults 70. CC: none.
*The campsite is 30 km north of Olderdalen and
1 km from the E6, near the river.*

RUNDE 11A

Goksoyr Camping 6096 Runde.
Tel 700 85905, Fax 700 85960. English spoken.
OPEN: all year. SIZE: 6 ha, 60 pitches (all with elec),
7 hot showers (charge), 9 WCs, 1 CWP. &

Restaurant at 1 km.
PRICES: (1996) Caravan with family 102,
Tent with two adults 80. CC: none.
*Runde island is a bird sanctuary; Ålesund is the
nearest large town.*

RUSSENES 10B

NAF Russenes Camping 9713 Russenes.
Tel 784 63711, Fax 784 63791. English spoken.
OPEN: 14/04–30/09. SIZE: 30 ha, 120 pitches
(100 with elec, 120 statics), 4 hot showers
(charge), 14 WCs, 1 CWP. &

Norway

[icons] Excursions to North Cape and Hammerfest.
PRICES: (1996) Caravan with family 90,
Tent with two adults 90. CC: none.
82 km east of Hammerfest and within reach of the North Cape (105 km).

RYSSTAD 11A

NAF-Camping Rysstadmo 4692 Rysstad.
Tel 379 36130, Fax 379 36345. English spoken.
OPEN: all year. SIZE: 80 pitches (40 with elec), 4 hot showers (charge), 6 WCs, 1 CWP. [icons]

[icons] Shop at 1 km. Canoeing in the river.
PRICES: (1996) Caravan with family 160, Tent with two adults 120. CC: Amex, Euro/Access, Visa.
On R39, 140 km north of Kristiansand.

SKARNES 11A

Sanngrund Camping 2100 Skarnes.
Tel 062 963631, Fax 062 963888. English spoken.
OPEN: all year. SIZE: 60 pitches (40 with elec), 4 hot showers, 6 WCs, 1 CWP. [icons]

[icons] PRICES: (1996) Caravan with family 140, Tent with two adults 50. CC: Amex, Euro/Access, Visa.
60 km from Oslo. Follow E6 to Klofta (east) then turn right and follow Rv2 to Skarnes.

SKARSVÅG 10B

Kirkeporten Camping 9763 Skarsvåg.
Tel 847 5233, Fax 847 5247. English spoken.
OPEN: 20/05–01/09. SIZE: 16 ha, 8 hot showers, 7 WCs.

[icons] PRICES: (1996) Caravan with family 170, Tent with two adults 120. CC: Amex, Euro/Access, Visa.
14 km from Nordkapp.

SOGNDAL 11A

Stedje Camping Postbox 1, 5801 Sogndal.
Tel 576 71012, Fax 576 71190. English spoken.
OPEN: 15/05–31/08. SIZE: 2 ha, 80 pitches (60 with elec), 8 hot showers (charge), 16 WCs, 1 CWP. [icon]

[icons] Shop at 0.1 km. Restaurant at 1 km.
PRICES: (1996) Caravan with family 135,
Tent with two adults 80. CC: none.
1 km from Sogndal going towards Hella.

STAVANGER 11A

Camping Mosvangen 4021 Stavanger.
Tel 515 32971, Fax 518 72055. English spoken.

OPEN: 25/05–05/09. SIZE: 200 ha, 80 pitches (30 with elec, 50 statics), 5 hot showers (charge), 16 WCs, 1 CWP.

[icons] Shop at 0.5 km. Restaurant at 0.5 km.
PRICES: Caravan with family 155, Tent with two adults 115. CC: Euro/Access, Visa.
On route 1.

Ogna Camping Varden, 4364 Sirevåg.
Tel 514 38242, Fax 514 38277. English spoken.
OPEN: 01/04–30/09. SIZE: 65 ha, 60 pitches (48 with elec), 4 hot showers (charge), 12 WCs, 2 CWPs. [icons]

[icons] Shop at 2 km. Restaurant at 2.5 km. 2 km from a salmon river.
PRICES: (1996) Caravan with family 120,
Tent with two adults 105. CC: none.
About 60 km south-west from Stavanger on Rv44 to Sirevåg and 30 km north-east from Egersund on Rv44.

STØREN 10C

Støren Camping 7090 Støren.
Tel 724 31470. English spoken.
OPEN: 01/06–31/08. SIZE: 3 ha, 120 pitches (91 with elec), 5 hot showers (charge), 8 WCs, 1 CWP. [icons]

[icons] Shop at 1 km. Restaurant at 1 km. Satellite/cable TV on hook-up.
PRICES: (1996) Caravan with family 135,
Tent with two adults 95. CC: none.
Follow signs from the motorway E6 at Støren.

STRYN 11A

Kleivenes Camping 6880 Stryn.
Tel 578 77513, Fax 578 71357. English spoken.
OPEN: 20/05–10/09. SIZE: 11 ha, 40 pitches (43 with elec), 5 hot showers (charge), 9 WCs. [icon]

[icons] Restaurant at 7 km. Salmon and trout fishing.
PRICES: (1996) Caravan with family 110, Tent with two adults 80. CC: Euro/Access, Visa.
7 km from Stryn on the R15 towards Grotli.

TROFORS 10C

Elvetun Camping 8680 Trofors.
Tel 751 81191.
OPEN: 01/06–01/09. SIZE: 16 ha, 40 pitches (12 with elec), 2 hot showers (charge), 8 WCs, 1 CWP. [icon]

[icons] Shop at 3 km. Restaurant at 3 km.

Norway

PRICES: (1996) Caravan with family 108, Tent with two adults 76. CC: none. *3 km south of Trofors.*

TROMSØ 10B

Ramfjord Camping 9027 Ramfjordbotn. Tel 776 92130, Fax 776 92260. English spoken. OPEN: all year. SIZE: 15 ha, 70 pitches (52 with elec), 4 hot showers (charge), 8 WCs, 1 CWP. ☎ ♿

Restaurant at 6 km. PRICES: (1996) Caravan with family 115, Tent with two adults 60. CC: Amex, Euro/Access, Visa. *Campsite well signposted.*

Skittenelv Camping 9022 Krokelvdalen, Tromsø. Tel 776 90026, Fax 776 90050. English spoken. OPEN: all year. SIZE: 30 ha, 100 pitches (34 with elec), 6 hot showers (charge), 11 WCs, 1 CWP. ☎ ♿

Restaurant at 25 km. Riding in summer, walking. PRICES: (1996) Caravan with family 110, Tent with two adults 90. CC: Euro/Access, Visa. *25 km north of Tromsø (road 53).*

TRONDHEIM 10C

Flak Camping 7070 Bosberg. Tel 728 43900. English spoken. OPEN: 01/05–05/09. SIZE: 2 ha, 100 pitches (24 with elec), 7 hot showers, 9 WCs, 1 CWP. ☎ ♿

Restaurant at 10 km. PRICES: (1996) Caravan with family 145, Tent with two adults 100. CC: none. *Take road 715 from Trondheim in the direction of Byneset. Site by the sea and the Flakk Ferry Lane.*

VANGSNES 11A

Solvang Camping og Motell 5865 Vangsnes. Tel 576 96620, Fax 576 96755. English spoken. OPEN: all year. SIZE: 4 ha, 50 pitches (10 with elec), 8 hot showers (charge), 9 WCs, 1 CWP. ☎

Restaurant at 10 km. PRICES: (1996) Caravan with family 95, Tent with two adults 60. CC: Visa. *The site is very near the ferry at Vangsnes.*

VASSENDEN 11A

Jolstraholmen Camping 6840 Vassenden. Tel 577 27135, Fax 577 27505. English spoken. OPEN: all year. SIZE: 5 ha, 80 pitches (all with elec), 8 hot showers (charge), 8 WCs, 1 CWP.

Trout fishing, flume.

PRICES: (1996) Caravan with family 125, Tent with two adults 80. CC: Amex, Euro/Access, Visa. *2 km from Vassenden, towards Forde. The campsite is close to the River Jolstra.*

VERDALSÖRA 10C

Stiklestad Camping 7650 Verdal. Tel 740 41294, Fax 740 41294. English spoken. OPEN: 01/06–31/08. SIZE: 28 ha, 40 pitches (all with elec, 15 statics), 3 hot showers, 11 WCs. ☎ ♿

Shop at 7 km. Restaurant at 3 km. Very quiet site; salmon fishing nearby. PRICES: (1996) Caravan with family 120, Tent with two adults 80. CC: none. *From Verdal on E6 follow signs to Stiklestad. 2 km from Stiklestad church take road 757.*

VIKERSUND 11A

Natvedt Camping Ostmodumveien, 3370 Vikersund. Tel 327 87355. English spoken. OPEN: 09/05–15/09. SIZE: 2 ha, 30 pitches (all with elec, 30 statics), 2 hot showers (charge), 6 WCs, 1 CWP.

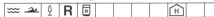

Shop at 3 km. Restaurant at 1 km. PRICES: (1996) Caravan with family 120, Tent with two adults 105. CC: none. *From Vikersund go south on route 284 for 4 km towards Sylling. Campsite is well signposted.*

VIKSDALEN 11A

Hov Hyttegrend 6836 Viksdalen. Tel 577 17937, Fax 577 17955. English spoken. OPEN: 01/05–30/09. SIZE: 25 pitches (14 with elec), 4 hot showers (charge), 7 WCs, 1 CWP. ♿

Shop at 9 km. Trout fishing. PRICES: Caravan with family 95, Tent with two adults 70. CC: none. *Street nr 13, 45 km north of Sognefjorden.*

VOSS 11A

Tvindecamping 5710 Skulestadmo. Tel 565 16919, Fax 565 16919. English spoken. OPEN: all year. SIZE: 12 ha, 20 pitches (all with elec, 40 statics), 8 hot showers (charge), 11 WCs, 1 CWP. ☎ ♿

Restaurant at 8 km. PRICES: (1996) Caravan with family 110, Tent with two adults 80. CC: Visa. *From centre of Voss, take E16 north towards Gudvangen for about 12 km. Well signposted.*

Norway

POLAND

Much of Warsaw, the capital city, was destroyed during the Second World War and what you see today is largely reconstruction. To learn more about the history and people of this remarkable country, visit the National Museum which also includes archaeological exhibits and a display of medieval altarpieces; or, at the Castle Museum, muse upon the very Canaletto paintings that inspired the new city plan. At the Historical Museum a particularly poignant exhibition tells the story of the stalwart resistance of ordinary people during the last war. Warsaw boasts many palaces, mostly open to the public but if you can't decide between them take a trip instead to Wilano and the 'Polish Versailles'.

A northern tour from the city takes you to Poznan and the holy isle of Ostrow Tumski with its many museums. On then to Gdansk, formerly Danzig, and famed for its shipyards – the Maritime Museum is housed in the 15th-century Gdansk Crane.

Emergency numbers

Police 997, Fire Brigade 998, Ambulance 999

Warning information

Warning triangle must be carried

Blood Alcohol Legal Limit 20 mg

Green card essential

JELENIA GORA 22C

Camping Stoneczna Polana
ul Rataja 9, 58 560 Jelenia Gora.
Tel 075 52566, Fax 075 52566. English spoken.
OPEN: 01/05–30/09. SIZE: 2.5 ha, 80 pitches (all with elec), 10 hot showers, 10 WCs, 1 CWP.

Shop at 0.2 km.
PRICES: Caravan with family 22.50, Tent with two adults 14.50. CC: none.
From the centre of Jelenia Gora go towards Cieplice and campsite is well signposted. (Prices in DM.)

Hotel-Camping Park ul Sudecka 42, 58 500 Jelenia Gora.
Tel 269 42, Fax 260 21. English spoken.
OPEN: all year. SIZE: 2 ha, 40 pitches (all with elec), 4 hot showers, 8 WCs. &

Shop at 0.1 km. Restaurant at 0.1 km.
PRICES: (1996) Caravan with family 38, Tent with two adults 22. CC: Amex, Euro/Access, Visa.
About 200 m from the city centre, well signposted.

KRAKOW (CRACOW) 22D

Garden Camping (No 103)
Krolowej Jadwigi 223, 30 218 Krakow.
Tel 025 2267. English spoken.
OPEN: 01/05–01/10. SIZE: 0.5 ha, 30 pitches (20 with elec, 100 statics), 4 hot showers, 7 WCs, 4 CWPs. &

Shop at 0.1 km. Restaurant at 0.5 km. Excellent bus service to town centre.
PRICES: (1996) Caravan with family 36.50, Tent with two adults 23.00. CC: none.
In the Wola Justowska district. (Prices in DM.)

OLSZTYN 22D

Camping Wagabunda ul Lesna 2, 11 730 Mikolajki.
Tel 0878 16 018, Fax 0878 16 022. English spoken.
OPEN: 01/04–31/10. SIZE: 3.5 ha, 12 hot showers (charge), 16 WCs. &

PRICES: (1996) Caravan with family 24, Tent with two adults 10. CC: Euro/Access, Visa.
Recomended campsite. Between Olsztyn and Mikolajki on R16. 1.3 km west of Mikolajki, turn right 50 m after railway viaduct.

POZNAN (POSEN) 22A

Camping Nr 111 Koszalinska 15, Poznan-Strzeszynek.
Tel 061 483129, Fax 061 334651. English spoken.
OPEN: 01/05–31/10. SIZE: 32 ha, 57 pitches (all with elec), 10 hot showers, 8 WCs, 6 French WCs, 1 CWP.

Shop at 0.1 km.
PRICES: (1996) Caravan with family 35.58, Tent with two adults 16.58. CC: none.
Campsite is 10 km north-west of the city centre, near the lake and the Poznan-Strzeszynek area. (Prices in DM.)

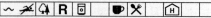

Poland

PORTUGAL

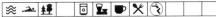

To reach Portugal by car from Great Britain, the drive through France and Spain is not for the faint-hearted. A ferry to Santander in north-western Spain reduces the ordeal. Alternatively, fly to Lisbon or Faro and hire a car.

At half past nine in the morning of 1 November 1755 a great earthquake, strong enough to be recorded as far away as Scotland, hit Lisbon. Many rushed to the foreshore for safety, to be hit by a tidal wave. Forty thousand died and the city itself was all but destroyed. Today, the centre of Lisbon is a city virtually rebuilt 200+ years ago.

From Lisbon, a trip out to Sintra will take you to the summer playground of the kings of Portugal and, earlier, of the Moors. Described by Byron in 1809 as 'having all the wildness of the Western Highlands with the verdure of the South of France'.

The Algarve is a popular beach holiday destination with a coast that is warm enough to be enjoyed out of season too. Faro, halfway along the southern coast, has an international airport and is a popular fly-drive destination.

The countryside from Faro to Lisbon is an enormous cork plantation, cork being one crop that will survive the impoverished soil. Detour to Evora and you will find a city protected by UNESCO for the wealth and variety of its buildings, from a 2nd-century Roman temple to a collection of 16th-century palaces – with the additional lure of a wonderful market every Tuesday and Saturday and a lively festival at the end of June.

Emergency numbers
Police, Fire Brigade and Ambulance 115

Warning information
Warning triangle must be carried

Green Card recommended

Blood Alcohol Legal Limit 50 mg

ALBUFEIRA   8C

Camping de Praia Armacao de Pera
8365 Armacao de Pera.
Tel 082 312260, Fax 082 315379. English spoken.
OPEN: all year. SIZE: 10 ha, 460 pitches (all with elec), 40 hot showers (charge), 96 WCs, 4 French WCs, 4 CWPs. ❤ ♿

PRICES: (1996) Caravan with family 2850, Tent with two adults 1950. CC: Amex.

ALVITO   8C

Markadia Barragem de Odivelas,
Apartado 17, 7920 Alvito.
Tel 084 76141. English spoken.
OPEN: all year. SIZE: 10 ha, 130 pitches (all with elec), 16 hot showers, 32 WCs, 1 CWP. ❤

Riding, boating, tennis, bike hire.
PRICES: (1996) Caravan with family 3930, Tent with two adults 2640. CC: none.
From Alvito, follow signs Barragem de Odivelas and Parque de Campismo.

ARGANIL   8A

Camping Orbitur Sarzedo, 3300 Arganil.
Tel 035 25706, Fax 035 25423. English spoken.
OPEN: all year. SIZE: 2 ha, 6 hot showers, 10 WCs, 1 CWP. ❤

Tennis, children's playground.
PRICES: (1996) Caravan with family 2070, Tent with two adults 1470. CC: none.
60 km from Coimbra via EN17 and EN342.

AVEIRO   8A

Camping Orbitur Sao Jacinto, 3800 Aveiro.
Tel 034 48284, Fax 034 48122. English spoken.
OPEN: 16/01–11. SIZE: 2.2 ha, 14 hot showers, 36 WCs, 1 CWP. ❤

Children's playground; up to 70% discount in LS.
PRICES: (1996) Caravan with family 3010, Tent with two adults 2120. CC: none.
On EN109 between Ovar and Sao Jacinto.

CALDAS DA RAINHA   8C

Camping Orbitur Parque D. Leonor,
2500 Caldas da Rainha.
Tel 062 832367, Fax 062 33544. English spoken.
OPEN: 16/01–15/11. SIZE: 2.4 ha, 6 hot showers, 16 WCs, 1 CWP. ❤

Shop at 0.2 km. Restaurant at 0.2 km. Children's playground; up to 70% discount in LS.
PRICES: (1996) Caravan with family 2710, Tent with two adults 1880. CC: none.
On EN114 between Caldas da Rainha and Santarém.

CAMINHA
8A

Camping Orbitur Mata do Camarido, 4910 Caminha.
Tel 058 921295, Fax 058 921473. English spoken.
OPEN: all year. SIZE: 2.1 ha, 8 hot showers, 19 WCs, 1 CWP. **℄**

≋ ⚓ 🏕 R 🔟 🍴 ☕ ✗

Tennis, children's playground; up to 70% discount in LS.
PRICES: (1996) Caravan with family 3010, Tent with two adults 2120. CC: none.
On EN13 Porto to Valença road.

CAPARICA
8C

Camping Orbitur Costa da Caparica, 2825 Monte da Caparica.
Tel 012 903894, Fax 012 900661. English spoken.
OPEN: all year. SIZE: 5.7 ha, 12 hot showers, 64 WCs, 1 CWP. **℄ ♿**

≋ ⚓ 🏕 R 🔟 🍴 ☕ ✗ [H]

Tennis, TV room, children's playground, disco in HS; up to 70% discount in LS.
PRICES: (1996) Caravan with family 2450, Tent with two adults 2410. CC: none.
Off Lisboa/Costa da Caparica motorway.

CASCAIS
8C

Camping Orbitur Mata da Crismina, Areia, Guincho, 2750 Cascais.
Tel 014 870450, Fax 014 872167. English spoken.
OPEN: all year. SIZE: 6.9 ha, 38 hot showers, 59 WCs, 1 CWP. **℄ ♿**

≋ ⚓ 🏕 R 🔟 🍴 ☕ ✗ [H]

Tennis, TV room, children's playground; up to 70% discount in LS.
PRICES: (1996) Caravan with family 3450, Tent with two adults 2410. CC: none.
On EN6 Lisboa to Cascais/Sintra.

CASTRO DAIRE
8A

Camping Orbitur 3600 Castro Daire.
Tel 032 32803. English spoken.
OPEN: 01/06–30/09. SIZE: 2 ha, 4 hot showers, 6 WCs.

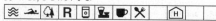

Up to 70% discount in LS

PRICES: (1996) Caravan with family 2710, Tent with two adults 1880. CC: none.
On EN2 between Viseu and Chaves.

CELORICO DA BEIRA
8A

Parque de Campismo da Ponte do Ladrao
Lageosa do Mondego, 6360 Celorico da Beira.
Tel 071 72645. English spoken.
OPEN: 01/04–01/10. SIZE: 2 ha, 50 pitches (all with elec), 8 hot showers. **℄**

~ ⚓ 🏕 R 🔟 🍴 ☕ ✗ [H]

PRICES: (1996) Caravan with family 2770, Tent with two adults 1750. CC: none.
On the new IP5, take exit 25 or 26 for Lageosa do Mondego, then head towards Acores.

COIMBRA
8A

Camp Ponte das Tres Entradas 3415 Avô.
Tel 038 57684, Fax 038 57685.
English spoken.
OPEN: all year. SIZE: 2 ha, 2 French WCs. ♿

~ ⚓ 🏕 🔟 🍴 ☕ ✗ [H]

PRICES: (1996) Caravan with family 2325, Tent with two adults 1350. CC: Euro/Access, Visa.
EN17 from Celorico Beira to Coimbra.

ELVAS
8C

Quinta de Torre das Arcas Apartado 170, Varche, 7350 Elvas.
Tel 068 625402. English spoken.
OPEN: 15/01–15/12. SIZE: 5 ha, 10 pitches (4 with elec, 2 statics), 2 hot showers, 2 WCs.

≈ ⚓ 🏕 R [H]

Shop at 1 km. Restaurant at 1 km. Farmhouse for 4/5 people available. 10% discount for RAC members.
PRICES: (1996) Caravan with family 1800, Tent with two adults 1400. CC: none.
Take the Lisboa road out of Elvas. After 3 km turn left into Varche. Take first left, fork right and follow tarred road through village. Campsite is on a farm and well signposted.

EVORA
8C

Camping Orbitur 7000 Evora.
Tel 066 25190, Fax 066 29830.
English spoken.
OPEN: all year. SIZE: 3.8 ha, 10 hot showers, 22 WCs. **℄ ♿**

Tennis, children's playground; up to 70% discount in LS.
PRICES: (1996) Caravan with family 3010, Tent with two adults 2120. CC: none.
On EN18 between Evora and Beja.

Portugal

GUARDA 8A

Camping Orbitur 6300 Guarda.
Tel 071 211406, Fax 071 221911. English spoken.
OPEN: 16/01–15/11. SIZE: 1.8 ha, 6 hot showers
(charge), 13 WCs, 1 CWP. ☕

TV room, children's playground; up to 70%
discount in LS.
PRICES: (1996) Caravan with family 3010,
Tent with two adults 2120. CC: none.
On EN18 between Guarda and Castelo Branco.

LAGOS 8C

Camping Orbitur
Valverde, Praia da Luz, 8600 Lagos.
Tel 082 789211, Fax 082 789213. English spoken.
OPEN: all year. SIZE: 9 ha, 28 hot showers,
58 WCs, 1 CWP. ☕

Tennis, TV room, children's playground; up to
70% discount in LS.
PRICES: (1996) Caravan with family 3590,
Tent with two adults 2530. CC: none.
*Praia da Luz is just to the west of Lagos, off the
N125.*

MARINHA GRANDE 8A

Camping Orbitur Sao Pedro de Muel,
2430 Marinha Grande.
Tel 044 599168, Fax 044 599148. English spoken.
OPEN: all year. SIZE: 7 ha, 31 hot showers,
46 WCs, 1 CWP. ☕ ♿

Tennis, children's playground, TV room; up to
70% discount in LS.
PRICES: (1996) Caravan with family 3010,
Tent with two adults 2120. CC: none.
West of Leiria, via Marinha Grande, off the N242.

MIRA 8A

Camping Orbitur Gald, 3080 Figueira da Foz.
Tel 033 31492, Fax 033 31231. English spoken.
OPEN: 16/01–15/11. SIZE: 6 ha, 22 hot showers,
42 WCs, 1 CWP.

Tennis, children's playground; up to
70% discount in LS.
PRICES: (1996) Caravan with family 30100,
Tent with two adults 2120. CC: none.
On EN109 between Figueira da Foz and Porto.

Camping Orbitur Praia de Mira, 3070 Mira.
Tel 031 471234, Fax 031 472047. English spoken.
OPEN: 16/01–15/11. SIZE: 3 ha, 14 hot showers,
28 WCs. ☕

TV room, children's playground; up to 70%
discount in LS.
PRICES: (1996) Caravan with family 3010,
Tent with two adults 2120. CC: none.
On EN109 between Figueira da Foz and Porto.

MONTARGIL 8C

Camping Orbitur 7425 Montargil.
Tel 042 91207, Fax 042 91220.
English spoken.
OPEN: all year. SIZE: 5.9 ha, 42 hot showers,
51 WCs, 1 CWP. ☕ ♿

Tennis, children's playgroung. Up to
70% discount in LS.
PRICES: (1996) Caravan with family 3010,
Tent with two adults 2120. CC: none.
On the EN251 between Coruche and Ponte de Sor.

NAZARE 8A

Camping Orbitur Valado, 2450 Nazaré.
Tel 062 561111, Fax 062 561137.
English spoken.
OPEN: 16/01–15/11. SIZE: 6.7 ha, 21 hot showers,
30 WCs, 1 CWP. ☕

Tennis, TV room, children's playground; up to
70% discount in LS.
PRICES: (1996) Caravan with family 3010,
Tent with two adults 2120. CC: none.
On EN8 to Nazaré.

ODEMIRA 8C

Parque de Campismo Zambujeira Zambujeira
do Mar, 7630 San Teotonio.
Tel 083 61172, Fax 083 61320.
English spoken.
OPEN: all year. SIZE: 4 ha, 16 hot showers (charge),
36 WCs, 2 CWPs.

Restaurant at 0.6 km. 30 to 60% discount from
15/10 to 30/04.
PRICES: (1996) Caravan with family 2390,
Tent with two adults 1500. CC: none.
*From Odemira, go south to San Teotonio and
then west to Zambujeira do Mar.*

Portugal

PORTALEGRE 8C

Camping Orbitur Quinta da Saude,
7300 Portalegre.
Tel 045 22848. English spoken.
OPEN: 16/01–15/11. SIZE: 2.8 ha, 6 hot showers,
6 WCs. ✆

| ♨ | R | ⬛ | ⬛ | ⬛ | | | |

Children's playground; up to 70% discount in LS.
PRICES: (1996) Caravan with family 2710,
Tent with two adults 1880. CC: none.
On EN18 between Portalegre and Estremoz.

PORTIMAO 8C

Parque de Campismo da Dourada
Alvor, Praia de Alvor, Portimao.
Tel 082 459178, Fax 082 458002.
English spoken.
OPEN: all year. SIZE: 4 ha, 200 pitches (120 with
elec, 6 statics), 14 hot showers (charge), 30 WCs,
4 CWPs. ✆

| ≋ | ⚓ | ♨ | R | ⬛ | ⬛ | ⬛ | ✗ | | ⌂ | |

Good discounts for longer stays in LS.
PRICES: (1996) Caravan with family 2950,
Tent with two adults 1850. CC: none.

Heading west from Portimao towards Lagos, Alvor is just off the EN125.

PORTO (OPORTO) 8A

Camping Orbitur Angeiras, 4460 Lavra.
Tel 029 270571, Fax 029 271178.
English spoken.
OPEN: all year. SIZE: 7 ha, 32 hot showers,
30 WCs, 1 CWP. ✆

| ≋ | ⚓ | ♨ | R | ⬛ | ⬛ | ⬛ | ✗ | | | |

Tennis, TV room, children's playground; up to
70% discount in LS.
PRICES: (1996) Caravan with family 3010,
Tent with two adults 2120. CC: none.
From Porto go towards the airport, Leca and then the campsite.

POVOA DE VARZIM 8A

Camping Rio Alto Sopete Rio Alto-Estela,
4490 Povoa de Varzim.
Tel 052 615699, Fax 052 611540. English spoken.
OPEN: all year. SIZE: 7 ha, 80 pitches (all with elec,
80 statics), 46 hot showers, 44 WCs, 3 CWPs. ✆ ♿

| ≋ | ⚓ | ⬛ | R | ⬛ | ⬛ | ⬛ | ✗ | ⬛ |

Tennis, table tennis.
PRICES: (1996) Caravan with family 3075,
Tent with two adults 1990. CC: Euro/Access, Visa.
The campsite is 13 km north of Povoa de Varzim, on the EN13.

QUARTEIRA 8C

Camping Orbitur
Barros da Fonte Santa, 8125 Quarteira.
Tel 089 302826, Fax 089 302822. English spoken.
OPEN: all year. SIZE: 9.8 ha, 45 hot showers,
74 WCs, 1 CWP. ✆ ♿

| ≋ | ⚓ | ⬛ | R | ⬛ | ⬛ | ⬛ | ✗ | | ⌂ | |

Tennis, TV room, children's playground, disco in
HS; up to 70% discount in LS.
PRICES: (1996) Caravan with family 3590,
Tent with two adults 2530. CC: none.
On EN125 between Albufeira and Faro.

VIANA DO CASTELO 8A

Camping Orbitur Cabedelo,
4900 Viana do Castelo.
Tel 058 322167, Fax 058 321946.
English spoken.
OPEN: 16/01–15/11. SIZE: 2.5 ha, 12 hot showers,
26 WCs, 1 CWP. ✆

| ≋ | ⚓ | ♨ | R | ⬛ | ⬛ | ⬛ | ✗ | | ⌂ | |

TV room, children's playground; up to 70%
discount in LS.
PRICES: (1996) Caravan with family 3010,
Tent with two adults 2120. CC: none.
On EN13 between Porto and Viana do Castelo.

VILA DO BISPO 8C

Camping Quinta dos Carricos
Praia de Salema, 8650 Vila do Bispo.
Tel 082 65201, Fax 082 65122.
English spoken.
OPEN: all year. SIZE: 15 ha, 400 pitches (200 with
elec), 25 hot showers (charge), 25 WCs,
3 CWPs. ♿

| ≋ | ⚓ | ♨ | R | ⬛ | ⬛ | ⬛ | ✗ | | ⌂ | |

Naturist park.
PRICES: (1996) Caravan with family 3440, Tent with
two adults 2400. CC: Amex, Euro/Access, Visa.
*Follow signs from Vila do Bispo. After 10 km, and
at the crossroad to Salema, is a sign to the right.
Campsite is 600 m.*

Portugal

Camping Sagres Cenno das Moitas, 8650 Vila do Bispo. Tel 082 64371, Fax 082 64445. English spoken. OPEN: 02/01–30/11. SIZE: 12 ha, 120 pitches (100 with elec). **& &**

Shop at 1 km. Children's playground, bikes for hire.
PRICES: (1996) Caravan with family 3200, Tent with two adults 2050. CC: none.
Turn left off N268 just north of Sagres. Campsite is well signposted.

VILA NOVA DE MILFONTES 8C

Camping Milfontes 7645 Vila nova de Milfontes. Tel 083 96104, Fax 083 96104. English spoken. OPEN: all year. SIZE: 6 ha, 600 pitches (540 with elec, 300 statics), 64 hot showers, 56 WCs, 1 CWP. **& &**

PRICES: (1996) Caravan with family 2625, Tent with two adults 1565. CC: Euro/Access, Visa.
On the coast, north-west of Odemira.

VILA REAL 8A

Parque de Campismo de Vila Real
Tras Montes, Vila Real. Tel 059 324724. English spoken. OPEN: 01/02–31/12. SIZE: 4 ha, 6 hot showers.

PRICES: (1996) Caravan with family 2180, Tent with two adults 1505. CC: none.

VISEU 8A

Camping Orbitur Fontelo, 3500 Viseu. Tel 032 26146, Fax 032 26120. English spoken. OPEN: 16/01–15/11. SIZE: 2.2 ha, 10 hot showers, 14 WCs, 1 CWP. **& &**

TV room, children's playground; up to 70% discount in LS.
PRICES: (1996) Caravan with family 3010, Tent with two adults 2120. CC: none.
On EN2 between Viseu and Vila Real.

Portugal

SPAIN

Browsing through the Spanish pages of a British holiday brochure, you might easily be forgiven for thinking that Spain's major, if not only attraction, is its beaches. Yet more than any other country in Europe, bar Switzerland, it is in fact a land of mountains.

The Cordillera Cantábrica mountains lie parallel to the north coast, along a line similar to that of the Pyrenees in the east. If your Spanish debut is made off the ferry at Santander, this is the mountain landscape that will shortly greet you. More mountains await those travelling to the country's epicentre at Madrid (rare among capitals for being so central); then further south lie the Sierra Morena mountains, with the Sierra Nevada lying between the old Moorish capital, Granada, and the Mediterranean.

Granada enjoys a breathtakingly beautiful situation at the foothills of the Sierra Nevada, as well as boasting one of Europe's most impressive collections of important buildings. One of these, the Alhambra Palace, recalls that Granada was for seven centuries a Moorish town (711–1491). By contrast, the cathedral at Santiago de Compostela is perhaps the most important monument to the spread of Christianity in the north.

The motorist exploring interior Spain will also happen upon the *pueblos blancos* hillside villages, close-knit communities where life goes on very much as it has done for centuries. Enjoy the hair-pin-bend exhilaration of a bus ride to market shared with the locals... and let the beaches of the Costa Brava waiting for another year.

Emergency numbers

For emergency numbers see the local directory

Warning information

Green card recommended

Bail bond recommended

Blood Alcohol Legal Limit 80 mg

ADRA 8D

Camping La Habana PO Box 129, 04770 Adra. Tel 950 522127. English spoken.
OPEN: all year. SIZE: 1.5 ha, 104 pitches (all with elec), 8 hot showers, 19 WCs, 2 CWPs.

Horse-riding nearby.
PRICES: (1996) Caravan with family 2400, Tent with two adults 1520. CC: none.
4 km east of Adra at Km 391 on the N340.

Camping Las Gaviotas 04770 Adra (Almeria). Tel 950 400660, Fax 950 400660. English spoken.
OPEN: all year. SIZE: 2 ha, 137 pitches (all with elec), 5 hot showers, 27 WCs, 1 CWP.

Children's playground.
PRICES: Caravan with family 2615, Tent with two adults 1800. CC: Euro/Access, Visa.
From Adra, go 2 km towards Malaga. Signposted.

AINSA 9A

Camping Pena Montanesa Labuerda, 22369 Ainsa.
Tel 974 500032, Fax 974 500032. English spoken.
OPEN: all year. SIZE: 9 ha, 500 pitches (all with elec, 50 statics), 34 hot showers, 44 WCs, 1 CWP.

3 swimming pools, sauna, spa. Excellent sports facilities within 2 km.
PRICES: (1996) Caravan with family 4218, Tent with two adults 2459. CC: Amex, Euro/Access, Visa.
2 km north of Ainsa on the road to Bielsa. Well signposted.

ALCOCEBER 9A

Camping Ribamar 12579 Alcoćeber.
Tel 964 414165, Fax 964 414045. English spoken.
OPEN: 22/03–28/09. SIZE: 2.2 ha, 148 pitches (120 with elec), 10 hot showers, 14 WCs, 1 CWP.

Tennis, barbecue area, separate children's pool.
PRICES: Caravan with family 3290, Tent with two adults 2025. CC: none.
From Alcoceber take road to Las Fuentes (Ribamar) and then follow signs.

ALDEANUEVA DE LA VERA 8B

Camping Yuste 10440 Aldeanueva de la Vera.
Tel 927 572522. English spoken.

OPEN: 01/04–30/09. SIZE: 3 ha, 80 pitches (all with elec), 10 hot showers, 22 WCs, 1 CWP. **℄**

PRICES: (1996) Caravan with family 2825, Tent with two adults 1700. CC: none.
On C501 at Km 44.

ALICANTE 9C

Camping Muchamiel SC Ctra Venteta 7, 03110 Muchamiel.
Tel 965 950126. English spoken.
OPEN: all year. SIZE: 1.7 ha, 105 pitches (64 with elec), 16 hot showers, 17 WCs, 1 CWP. **℄**

Restaurant at 0.2 km. Sea 5 km.
PRICES: (1996) Caravan with family 3600, Tent with two adults 2400. CC: none.
At Km 752 on N340, between San Juan and Jijona.

ALMERIA 8D/9C

Camping Los Gallardos Ctra N340, Km 525, 04280 Los Gallardos.
Tel 950 528324, Fax 950 528324. English spoken.
OPEN: all year. SIZE: 3 ha, 114 pitches (106 with elec), 10 hot showers, 12 WCs, 1 CWP. **℄**

PRICES: (1996) Caravan with family 2100, Tent with two adults 1800. CC: Euro/Access, Visa.
From Almeria, take N340 towards Murcia. Leave N340 at exit Km 525 and follow signs to campsite (500 m). Well signposted.

Camping Roquetas 04740 Roquetas de Mar.
Tel 950 343809, Fax 950 342525. English spoken.
OPEN: all year. SIZE: 8 ha, 800 pitches (all with elec), 30 hot showers, 95 WCs, 5 CWPs. **℄ &**

60% discount October to May.
PRICES: (1996) Caravan with family 2435, Tent with two adults 1600. CC: Amex, Euro/Access, Visa.
From Almeria, go on N340/E15 and take exit 429 towards Roquetas de Mar. The campsite is beside the sea beyond Aguadulce.

Camping Roquetas
near Almeria
Sand, Sea, Sun & Sangria!

La Garrofa 04002 Almeria.
Tel 950 235770. English spoken.
OPEN: all year. SIZE: 2 ha, 50 pitches (all with elec), 10 hot showers, 30 WCs, 4 CWPs.

50% price reduction in winter.
PRICES: (1996) Caravan with family 3242, Tent with two adults 1926. CC: Amex, Euro/Access, Visa.
Travelling from Malaga on N340, campsite is 4 km before arriving in Almeria, on the right. Signposted.

ALTEA 9C

Camping Cap Blanch Playa de Albir 25, 03590 Altea/Alicante.
Tel 965 845946, Fax 965 844556. English spoken.
OPEN: all year. SIZE: 4 ha, 130 pitches (all with elec, 12 statics), 20 hot showers, 48 WCs, 1 CWP. **&**

Shop at 0.1 km. Bikes for hire, organised walks, entertainment.
PRICES: (1996) Caravan with family 3900, Tent with two adults 2400. CC: Visa.
From Altea take the road to Playa de Albir and follow signs.

L'AMPOLLA 9A

Camping Sant Jordi Calle del Mar s/n, 43895 L'Ampolla.
Tel 977 460415, Fax 977 460415. English spoken.
OPEN: 01/04–12/10. SIZE: 1 ha, 95 pitches (40 with elec, 10 statics), 7 hot showers, 14 WCs. **℄ &**

Bikes for hire.
PRICES: (1996) Caravan with family 3500, Tent with two adults 2300. CC: Euro/Access, Visa.
Coming from the north, take exit 39 or 40 from motorway then N340 to L'Ampolla. Campsite is 600 m from the railway station and well signposted.

ARENYS DE MAR 9B

Camping El Carlitos N11, Km 658,550, 08350 Arenys de Mar.
Tel 937 921355, Fax 937 957342. English spoken.
OPEN: 01/05–30/09. SIZE: 5 ha, 65 pitches (all with elec, 150 statics), 19 hot showers, 24 WCs, 2 CWPs. **℄**

Water sports, fishing. Site is open weekends in LS.
PRICES: Caravan with family 3285, Tent with two adults 1980. CC: Euro/Access, Visa.
Situated on N11, at Km 658,700 between Arenys de Mar and Canet de Mar. Well signposted.

ARROS 9A

Camping Prado Verde La Bordeta Vilamos, 25551 Bossost.
Tel 937 647172, Fax 973 640456. English spoken.
OPEN: all year. SIZE: 1.5 ha, 100 pitches (90 with elec), 10 hot showers, 14 WCs, 1 French WC, 1 CWP. **℄**

Spain

PRICES: (1996) Caravan with family 2900, Tent with two adults 1800. CC: Amex, Euro/Access, Visa. *North on N230 to Bossost. Follow signs.*

Camping Verneda N230, Km 172, 25537 Pont d'Arros. Tel 973 641024, Fax 973 642400. English spoken. OPEN: 20/03–30/09. SIZE: 3 ha, 26 hot showers, 24 WCs, 2 French WCs, 2 CWPs.

PRICES: Caravan with family 3700, Tent with two adults 2200. CC: Amex, Visa. *Follow signs from Arros to campsite.*

BARCELONA 9B

El Toro Bravo 08840 Viladecans. Tel 936 373462, Fax 936 588054. English spoken. OPEN: all year. SIZE: 30 ha, 1200 pitches (800 with elec, 400 statics), 51 hot showers, 187 WCs, 5 French WCs, 4 CWPs.

Tennis, badminton. PRICES: (1996) Caravan with family 3875, Tent with two adults 2450. CC: Amex, Euro/Access, Visa. *From Barcelona, take the road towards the airport and Castelldefels. Turn left after 11 km and the campsite is 1 km ahead.*

BEGUR 9B

Camping Begur Ctra Begur-Palafrugell, Km 1,5, 17255 Begur. Tel 972 623201, Fax 972 623201. English spoken. OPEN: 01/05–05/09. SIZE: 4 ha, 197 pitches (all with elec), 16 hot showers, 24 WCs, 4 CWPs.

PRICES: (1996) Caravan with family 3100, Tent with two adults 2100. CC: Euro/Access, Visa. *On the road from Begur to Palafrugell at Km 1,5, 200 m from the crossroads to Fornells and Aigua Blava beaches. Signposted.*

Camping El Maset Playa Sa Riera, 17255 Begur. Tel 972 623023, Fax 972 623901. English spoken. OPEN: 01/04–25/09. SIZE: 1.2 ha, 14 pitches (all with elec), 14 hot showers, 14 WCs, 1 CWP.

Excellent range of water sports close by. PRICES: (1996) Caravan with family 4681, Tent with two adults 2809. CC: Euro/Access, Visa. *Site is 2 km north of Begur, 300 m from the beach.*

BENICARLO 9A

Camping Alegria del Mar Benicarlo. Tel 964 470871. English spoken. OPEN: all year. SIZE: 0.75 ha, 48 pitches (all with elec, 2 statics), 4 hot showers, 12 WCs.

Children's playground. PRICES: (1996) Caravan with family 2650, Tent with two adults 1600. CC: Euro/Access, Visa. *The campsite is 1 km north of Benicarlo, off the N340.*

BENICASIM 9A

Camping Azahar Ctra Barcelona s/n, 12560 Benicasim. Tel 964 303196. English spoken. OPEN: all year. SIZE: 4 ha, 200 pitches (all with elec), 22 hot showers, 48 WCs, 4 CWPs.

Tennis, children's playground; discounts in LS. PRICES: (1996) Caravan with family 3315, Tent with two adults 1960. CC: Amex, Euro/Access, Visa. *From A7, take exit no 45, and then N340 to Benicasim. Follow signs to campsite.*

Camping Bonterra Avda Barcelona 47, 12560 Benicasim. Tel 964 300007, Fax 964 300060. English spoken. OPEN: 03/04–30/09. SIZE: 5 ha, 400 pitches (all with elec), 56 hot showers, 67 WCs, 2 CWPs.

Good LS discounts. PRICES: (1996) Caravan with family 5115, Tent with two adults 2643. CC: Euro/Access, Visa. *From the N340 going north, turn right to Benicasim and the campsite is 1 km past the village on the left.*

BENIDORM 9C

Camping Armanello 03500 Benidorm. Tel 965 853190, Fax 965 853100. English spoken. OPEN: all year. SIZE: 18 ha, 110 pitches (all with elec, 10 statics), 20 hot showers, 20 WCs, 2 CWPs.

PRICES: (1996) Caravan with family 2800, Tent with two adults 1800. CC: Euro/Access, Visa. *On the old N330 (now Avenida de la Comunidad - Valenciana). Site is well signposted.*

Camping Benidorm Avda Rincon de Loix, 03500 Benidorm. Tel 965 860011, Fax 965 860011. English spoken. OPEN: all year. SIZE: 3 ha, 100 pitches (70 with elec), 8 hot showers, 12 WCs, 1 CWP.

Lots to do and see on site and nearby. PRICES: (1996) Caravan with family 3125, Tent with two adults 1900. CC: none. *From N332 take first exit for Benidorm and head 1.5 km towards the sea. Site is well signposted.*

BERANGA 8B

Camping Los Molinos de Bareyo 39190 Bareyo, Cantabria.

Tel 942 670569, Fax 942 630725. English spoken.
OPEN: 01/04–30/09. SIZE: 10 ha, 350 pitches
(150 with elec), 48 hot showers, 60 WCs, 8 French
WCs, 4 CWPs. ℓ

Shop at 1 km.
PRICES: Caravan with family 3375,
Tent with two adults 2000. CC: none.
*From Beranga follow signs for Somo/Pedreña/
Santander. Then follow signs for Bareyo and
campsite can be found after approx 5 km.*

BERGA   9B

Camping de Berga 08600 Berga.
Tel 38 211250, Fax 38 222388. English spoken.
OPEN: all year. SIZE: 5 ha, 200 pitches (all with elec,
50 statics), 24 hot showers, 22 WCs, 2 CWPs. ℓ க

Excellent sports facilities. Big discounts for stays
of more than 7 days.
PRICES: (1996) Caravan with family 4800, Tent with
two adults 3100. CC: Amex, Euro/Access, Visa.
*From Berga, take C1411 south to Km 75,3.
Campsite is 100 m from road. Follow signs.*

BERMEO   8B

Camping Portuondo Caserio Portuondo s/n,
48360 Mundaka.
Tel 968 76368, Fax 968 76368. English spoken.
OPEN: all year. SIZE: 1 ha, 15 pitches (all with elec,
35 statics), 16 hot showers, 19 WCs, 5 French WCs. ℓ

PRICES: (1996) Caravan with family 3627, Tent with
two adults 2247. CC: Amex, Euro/Access, Visa.
*From Bermeo take road to Mundaka. Campsite is
1 km beyond Mundaka. Follow signs.*

BLANES   9B

Camping Bella Terra
Avda Villa de Madrid s/n, 17300 Blanes.
Tel 972 331955, Fax 972 337124. English spoken.
OPEN: 01/05–30/09. SIZE: 7 ha, 25 pitches (all with
elec), 2 CWPs. ℓ க

PRICES: (1996) Caravan with family 3670, Tent with
two adults 2770. CC: Euro/Access, Visa.
Well signposted in town.

Camping El Pinar 17300 Blanes.
Tel 972 331083, Fax 972 331100. English spoken.
OPEN: 01/05–30/09. SIZE: 5 ha, 495 pitches (all with
elec, 20 statics), 26 hot showers, 26 WCs, 2 CWPs. க

Entertainment, varied activities.
PRICES: (1996) Caravan with family 3820, Tent with

two adults 2790. CC: Amex, Euro/Access, Visa.
In the village, on the beach.

Camping Roca Avda Colon, 17300 Blanes.
Tel 972 330540, Fax 972 330540. English spoken.
OPEN: 01/05–30/09. SIZE: 2 ha, 260 pitches
(230 with elec), 32 hot showers, 40 WCs, 2 CWPs. ℓ

PRICES: (1996) Caravan with family 3760, Tent with
two adults 2290. CC: none.
Well signposted from Blanes.

BROTO   9A

Camping Las Nieves 22630 Biescas.
Tel 974 485200, Fax 974 485200. English spoken.
OPEN: all year. SIZE: 4 ha, 250 pitches (all with
elec), 22 hot showers, 32 WCs, 2 CWPs. ℓ

Restaurant at 1 km.
PRICES: (1996) Caravan with family 4100,
Tent with two adults 2520. CC: Visa.
*From Broto, take the N260 to Biescas. The campsite
is 1 km from the town centre, on N260, Km 506.*

Camping Ordesa 22376 Torla.
Tel 974 486125, Fax 974 486381. English spoken.
OPEN: 28/03–01/11. SIZE: 4 ha. ℓ

PRICES: (1996) Caravan with family 3750,
Tent with two adults 2300. CC: Euro/Access, Visa.
*From Broto take the C138 to Torla. Campsite is
1 km from Torla on the road to the National Park.*

CALAFELL   9B

Bonavista San Salvador S.A. Camping Vendrell
Platja, 43880 Coma-Ruga Sant-Salvador.
Tel 977 694009, Fax 977 694106. English spoken.
OPEN: 02/04–26/09. SIZE: 7 ha, 583 pitches
(all with elec, 6 statics), 56 hot showers, 72 WCs,
4 CWPs. ℓ

PRICES: (1996) Caravan with family 3975, Tent with
two adults 2400. CC: Amex, Euro/Access, Visa.
*From A7, take exit 314 on to N340 towards
Tarragona. Turn towards Coma-Ruga and
Calafell after about 200 m. Campsite is on road
behind the beach and well signposted in Coma-
Ruga Sant-Salvador.*

Camping Vendrell Platja
at Calafell
Tree-lined site close to the beach

Spain

CALATAYUD 9A

Camping Lago Park Ctra de Alhama de Aragon, 50210 Nuevalos (Zaragoza). Tel 976 849038. English spoken. OPEN: 01/04–30/09. SIZE: 3 ha, 175 pitches (150 with elec, 150 statics), 10 hot showers, 14 WCs, 5 French WCs. ✆ &

≋ ⚓ 🏕 R ⬛ 🍺 ☕ ✗ 🏕 ⬡

Sailing, fishing, disco. Most other activities available nearby.
PRICES: (1996) Caravan with family 3900, Tent with two adults 2300. CC: none.
25 km south-west of Calatayud and 2 km north of Monasterio de Piedra. Campsite is at Km 39.15 marker and well signposted.

CALELLA DE LA COSTA 9B

Camping Botanic Bona Vista
08370 Calella de la Costa.
Tel 343 7692488, Fax 343 7695804.
English spoken.
OPEN: all year. SIZE: 3.4 ha, 160 pitches (all with elec), 20 hot showers, 20 WCs, 3 CWPs. ✆

≋ ⚓ 🏕 R ⬛ 🍺 ☕ ✗

Children's playground, fishing, water-skiing.
PRICES: Caravan with family 3155, Tent with two adults 1900. CC: Euro/Access.

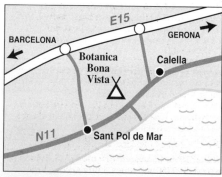

On the N11, Km 665 between Calella and Sant Pol de Mar.

Camping El Far 08370 Calella.
Tel 937 690967, Fax 937 690967.
English spoken.
OPEN: 01/04–30/09. SIZE: 2.49 ha, 50 pitches (160 with elec), 23 hot showers, 30 WCs, 3 CWPs. &

≋ ⚓ 🏕 R ⬛ 🍺 ☕ ✗ 🏕

Table tennis.
PRICES: (1996) Caravan with family 3190, Tent with two adults 1960. CC: none.
From Calella, take the N11 towards Barcelona and follow signs.

Camping La Verneda
08359 Sant Cebria de Vallalta.
Tel 376 30657/30087, Fax 376 31185.
English spoken.
OPEN: 01/04–30/09. SIZE: 1.6 ha, 150 pitches (all with elec), 16 hot showers, 22 WCs. ✆

≋ ⚓ 🏕 R ⬛ 🍺 ☕ ✗

PRICES: (1996) Caravan with family 3210, Tent with two adults 1840.
CC: Euro/Access, Visa.
From Calella de la Costa, drive south-west to Sant Pol de Mar then turn right to San Cebria de Vallalta.

CALPE 9C

Camping Ifach
Partida de Las Salinas 2B, 03710 Calpe.
Tel 965 830477. English spoken.
OPEN: 01/04–31/10. SIZE: 0.6 ha, 50 pitches (all with elec), 12 hot showers, 9 WCs, 1 CWP. ✆

≋ ⚓ 🏕 ⬛ ☕

Shop at 0.01 km. Restaurant at 0.01 km. Water sports and tennis 100 m; 20% LS discounts.
PRICES: Caravan with family 3480, Tent with two adults 2580. CC: Amex, Euro/Access, Visa.
From Calpe, take the coast road north-east to Moraira. Campsite is on the left-hand side, 100 m from the beach and close to the huge Ifach rock.

CAMBRILS 9A

Camping Joan
Pere III 1y, 43850 Cambrils.
Tel 977 364604, Fax 977 362052.
English spoken.
OPEN: 22/03–30/09. SIZE: 2 ha, 220 pitches (all with elec), 32 hot showers, 40 WCs, 3 CWPs. ✆ &

≋ ⚓ 🏕 R ⬛ 🍺 ✗ 🏕

PRICES: (1996) Caravan with family 3450, Tent with two adults 2140. CC: none.
2 km from Cambrils on road to Valencia. Entrance to campsite is near the Hotel La Dorada and well signposted.

La Torre del Sol Montroig Playa, Tarragona, 43892 Cambrils.
Tel 977 810486, Fax 977 811306.
English spoken.
OPEN: 15/03–15/10. SIZE: 24 ha, 1250 pitches (1250 statics), 150 hot showers, 165 WCs, 5 CWPs. ✆ &

≋ ⚓ 🏕 R ⬛ 🍺 ☕ ✗ 🏕 🏕 🏃

PRICES: (1996) Caravan with family 5200, Tent with two adults 4200.
CC: Amex, Visa.
Leave A7 at Cambrils exit 37. Go on N340 towards Valencia for 7 km and campsite is signposted.

Spain

CAMPRODON 9B

Camping Els Roures
17864 Sant Pau de Seguries.
Tel 972 747000, Fax 972 747109.
English spoken.
OPEN: all year. SIZE: 3.5 ha, 200 pitches (all with elec, 20 statics), 24 hot showers, 25 WCs, 1 CWP. ♥ ♿

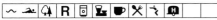

PRICES: (1996) Caravan with family 4050, Tent with two adults 2575. CC: Euro/Access, Visa.
From Barcelona take N152, turn east at Ripoll on to C151. Sant Pau is south of Camprodon on the C153.

CASTROJERIZ 8B

Camping Camino de Santiago
Casco Urbano de Castrojeriz, 09110 Castrojeriz.
Tel 947 377255/060, Fax 983 359549.
English spoken.
OPEN: 01/06–30/08. SIZE: 2.5 ha, 50 pitches (all with elec), 2 hot showers, 10 WCs, 5 French WCs, 1 CWP. ♥ ♿

Swimming pool 0.3 km.
PRICES: Caravan with family 2400, Tent with two adults 1400. CC: Visa.
Follow signs from town centre.

CASTRO URDIALES 8B

Camping Playa Arenillas 39798 Islares.
Tel 942 863152, Fax 942 863152.
English spoken.
OPEN: 01/04–30/09. SIZE: 3 ha, 200 pitches (150 with elec, 100 statics), 40 hot showers, 39 WCs, 2 CWPs. ♥

Shop at 8 km. Excellent sports/playground; good snorkelling/diving. 20% LS discount.
PRICES: Caravan with family 3600, Tent with two adults 2350. CC: Amex, Euro/Access, Visa.
8 km from Castro Urdiales towards Laredo. Exit 156 from San Sebastian to Santander motorway. (Campsite is only 20 km from Portsmouth to Santander ferry.)

CAZORLA 8D

Llanos de Arance El Tranco, Cazorla.
Tel 953 713139, Fax 953 713139. English spoken.
OPEN: 01/07–31/12. SIZE: 50 ha, 167 pitches (130 with elec), 16 hot showers (charge), 1 WC, 1 French WC, 1 CWP. ♥

PRICES: (1996) Caravan with family 1865, Tent with two adults 1195. CC: Visa.

37 km from Cazorla (Km 22) on the road to El Tranco. The campsite is in the centre of the Parque Natural de Cazorla.

CEE 8A

Camping Ruta de Finisterre
15270 Playa de Estorde.
Tel 981 746302. English spoken.
OPEN: 15/06–15/09. SIZE: 2 ha, 150 pitches (all with elec), 34 hot showers, 34 WCs. ♥ ♿

PRICES: Caravan with family 2850, Tent with two adults 1700. CC: Euro/Access, Visa.
On the main road between Corcubion and Finisterre, 50 m from beach.

CIUDAD RODRIGO 8A

Camping Sierra de Francia
Nava de Franca, 37623 El Casarito.
Tel 923 454081. English spoken.
OPEN: 01/04–30/09. SIZE: 1 ha, 100 pitches (60 with elec, 10 statics), 8 hot showers, 14 WCs, 1 CWP. ♥

PRICES: (1996) Caravan with family 3000, Tent with two adults 1770.
CC: Euro/Access, Visa.
From Ciudad Rodrigo, take C515 east to El Cabaco. Then go south towards La Alberca. Follow signs to campsite and El Casarito.

COMILLAS 8B

Camping El Helguero 39527 Ruiloba.
Tel 942 722124, Fax 942 721020.
English spoken.
OPEN: 01/04–30/09. SIZE: 6.5 ha, 240 pitches (all with elec), 32 hot showers, 26 WCs, 3 French WCs, 1 CWP. ♥ ♿

PRICES: (1996) Caravan with family 2825, Tent with two adults 1750. CC: Amex, Euro/Access, Visa.
On the road from Santillana to Comillas. Follow the signs.

Camping Playa de Cobreces Playa de Cobreces, Alfoz de Lloredo, 39320 Cobreces.
Tel 942 725120, Fax 942 725120.
English spoken.
OPEN: 15/06–15/09. SIZE: 1 ha, 10 hot showers (charge), 10 WCs. ♥ ♿

Shop at 1 km. Restaurant at 0.01 km.
PRICES: (1996) Caravan with family 3280, Tent with two adults 2150. CC: none.
Between Comillas and Santillana, on the road to Santander. Follow signs.

CONIL DE LA FRONTERA 8C

Camping Fuente del Gallo Apartado 48,
11140 Conil de la Frontera, Cadiz.
Tel 956 440137, Fax 956 442036. English spoken.
OPEN: 15/03–15/10. SIZE: 3 ha, 200 pitches
(150 with elec, 25 statics), 24 hot showers
(charge), 28 WCs, 2 CWPs. ℓ ሪ

≋ ⚓ 🛖 R ⬛ 🍴 ☕ ✗ ⚠

Tennis, bike hire.
PRICES: (1996) Caravan with family 3000, Tent with
two adults 1798. CC: Euro/Access, Visa.
*From Conil de la Frontera, take the road to
Fuente del Gallo.*

Camping Fuente del Gallo

at Conil de la Frontera

14 km of sandy beach

CORDOBA 8D

La Campina Santaella La Guijarrosa,
14547 Santaella.
Tel 957 315158, Fax 957 315158. English spoken.
OPEN: all year. SIZE: 1 ha, 35 pitches (all with elec,
6 statics), 4 hot showers, 10 WCs, 1 French WC,
2 CWPs. ℓ

⚓ R 🍴 ☕ ✗ ⚡

PRICES: (1996) Caravan with family 2695, Tent with
two adults 1575. CC: Euro/Access, Visa.
*Turn off N4 at Km 424, turn left to Santaella on
the CP8 and go for 11 km through La Victoria
and La Guijarrosa; follow camping signs from
there. Or turn off N4 at Km 441 and drive for
15 km following camping signs.*

CREVILLENTE 9C

Camping Internacional Las Palmeras
03330 Crevillente.
Tel 965 400188, Fax 965 404367. English spoken.
OPEN: all year. SIZE: 0.5 ha, 43 pitches (all with
elec, 4 statics), 12 hot showers, 12 WCs, 1 CWP. ℓ

🛖 R ⬛ 🍴 ☕ ✗ ⚡ ⚠

PRICES: (1996) Caravan with family 3100, Tent with
two adults 1900. CC: Amex, Euro/Access, Visa.
Follow signs from Crevillente.
*(a) RESORT:*Cudillero 8B

Camping Cudillero Ctra Playa de Aguilar,
33154 Cudillero.
Tel 955 90663, Fax 955 90663. English spoken.
OPEN: 01/06–25/09. SIZE: 19 ha, 49 pitches
(45 with elec, 4 statics), 17 hot showers, 19 WCs,
1 CWP. ℓ ሪ

≋ ⚓ 🛖 R ⬛ 🍴 ☕ ✗ ⚠

Table tennis, tennis, children's playground.
PRICES: Caravan with family 3200, Tent with two
adults 1825. CC: Euro/Access, Visa.
*From Cudillero, follow signs to El Pito and Playa
de Aguilar. Campsite is well signposted.*

DENIA 9C

Camping Los Llanos Playa de Vergel, 03770 Denia.
Tel 965 755188. English spoken.
OPEN: 01/04–01/09. SIZE: 2 ha. ℓ

≋ ⚓ 🛖 ⬛ 🍴 ☕ ✗ ⚡ ⚠

PRICES: (1996) Caravan with family 3275, Tent with
two adults 1750. CC: none.
*On the N332 between Valencia and Alicante at
Km 203/204 sign.*

DOS HERMANAS 8D

Camping Club de Campo 91700 Dos Hermanas.
Tel 954 723625. English spoken.
OPEN: all year. SIZE: 1 ha, 60 pitches (all with elec),
12 hot showers, 12 WCs, 3 CWPs. ℓ ሪ

🛖 R 🍴 ☕ ✗ ⚡

PRICES: Caravan with family 3110, Tent with two
adults 1900. CC: Amex, Euro/Access, Visa.
*From Sevilla, head towards Cadiz, then Dos
Hermanas and follow signs (5 km).*

ELCHE 9C

Camping Palmeral 03203 Elche.
Tel 965 422766, Fax 966 610504. English spoken.
OPEN: all year. SIZE: 18 ha, 80 pitches (all with
elec), 40 hot showers, 30 WCs, 2 CWPs. ℓ ሪ

🛖 R ⬛ 🍴 ☕ ✗ ⚡

PRICES: (1996) Caravan with family 4350, Tent with
two adults 2180. CC: none.
On the N340/A7. Signposted from Elche.

L'ESCALA 9B

Camping L'Escala Apartat de Correus 23,
17130 L'Escala.
Tel 972 770008, Fax 972 550046. English spoken.
OPEN: 22/03–28/09. SIZE: 2 ha, 219 pitches
(all with elec), 25 hot showers, 30 WCs. ℓ

≋ ⚓ 🛖 🍴 ☕ ⚠

Restaurant at 0.3 km.
PRICES: Caravan with family 3375, Tent with two
adults 2825. CC: none.
From L'Escala, follow signs to campsite.

Camping Las Dunas Apartat de Correus 23,
17130 L'Escala.
Tel 972 520400, Fax 972 550046. English spoken.
OPEN: 10/05–26/09. SIZE: 29 ha, 999 pitches (all with
elec), 192 hot showers, 186 WCs, 15 CWPs. ሪ

Windsurfing, mini-golf, tennis.
PRICES: Caravan with family 4600,
Tent with two adults 3900. CC: none.
*From L'Escala go towards San Marti d'Empuries
and follow signs to campsite.*

Camping Maite Avda Montgo 66, 17130 L'Escala.
Tel 972 770544. English spoken.
OPEN: 01/06–15/09. SIZE: 6 ha, 460 pitches (all
with elec), 36 hot showers, 36 WCs, 3 CWPs. ₺ ₫

PRICES: (1996) Caravan with family 3492, Tent with
two adults 2183. CC: none.
*Follow signposts to Playa de Riells and campsite.
The campsite is 100 m from the beach.*

Paradis Camping Caravaning 17130 L'Escala.
Tel 972 770200, Fax 972 772031. English spoken.
OPEN: 01/03–31/10. SIZE: 6 ha, 300 pitches
(all with elec, 50 statics), 36 hot showers, 40 WCs,
2 CWPs. ₺ ₫

Shop at 1.5 km.
PRICES: Caravan with family 3825,
Tent with two adults 2850. CC: Visa.
*On road to Cala Montgo. 150 m from the beach of
Montgo. Follow signs.*

ESPOT   9A

Camping Sol I Neu 25597 Espot.
Tel 973 624001. English spoken.
OPEN: 01/06–30/09. SIZE: 1.3 ha, 46 pitches (all
with elec), 9 hot showers, 11 WCs, 1 CWP. ₺ ₫

Shop at 0.5 km. Restaurant at 0.5 km.
PRICES: (1996) Caravan with family 3575,
Tent with two adults 2100. CC: Euro/Access, Visa.
*On the road to Espot, 3 km from the National
Park.*

Camping Vall d'Aneu
Ctra s/n, 25597 La Guingueta d'Aneu.
Tel 973 626390.
OPEN: 01/05–15/10. SIZE: 0.5 ha, 40 pitches
(all with elec), 4 hot showers, 9 WCs. ₺

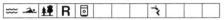

Shop at 4 km. Restaurant at 0.1 km.
PRICES: (1996) Caravan with family 3275,
Tent with two adults 1900. CC: none.
*Next to La Guingueta d'Aneu, at Km 136
on the C147.*

L'ESTARTIT   9B

Camping Castell Montgri 17258 L'Estartit.
Tel 972 758630, Fax 972 759906. English spoken.
OPEN: 10/05–12/10. SIZE: 25 ha, 880 pitches

(all with elec, 400 statics), 72 hot showers,
119 WCs, 4 CWPs. ₫

Cinema, disco, piano bar.
PRICES: (1996) Caravan with family 4665,
Tent with two adults 4100. CC: none.
*On the road from L'Estartit to Torroella de
Montgri, on the right-hand side.*

Camping L'Estartit 17258 L'Estartit.
Tel 972 751909, Fax 972 750991. English spoken.
OPEN: 01/04–30/09. SIZE: 2 ha, 80 pitches (all with
elec), 12 hot showers (charge), 22 WCs, 1 CWP. ₺

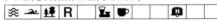

30% LS discount.
PRICES: (1996) Caravan with family 3180,
Tent with two adults 2080. CC: none.
*Follow main road into L'Estartit until you come to
the pedestrian walkway and then turn left.
Campsite is signposted.*

Camping Les Medes
Paratge Camp de l'Arbre s/n, 17258 L'Estartit.
Tel 972 758405, Fax 972 760413. English spoken.
OPEN: all year. SIZE: 2.6 ha, 194 pitches (all with
elec), 20 hot showers, 26 WCs, 2 CWPs. ₺ ₫

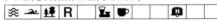

PRICES: (1996) Caravan with family 3300, Tent with
two adults 1995. CC: Amex, Euro/Access, Visa.
*On the road from Torroella de Montgri, turn right
just before L'Estartit. The campsite is 1.5 km
ahead.*

Camping Ter 17258 L'Estartit.
Tel 972 751110, Fax 972 750609.
English spoken.
OPEN: 01/04–01/10. SIZE: 3 ha, 200 pitches
(all with elec, 30 statics), 24 hot showers, 24 WCs,
1 CWP. ₺

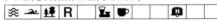

PRICES: Caravan with family 3000, Tent with two
adults 2300. CC: Amex, Euro/Access, Visa.
*On the right, L'Estartit to Torroella de Montgri
road, at Km 4,2.*

EL FERROL   8A

Camping Fontesin Meiras Valdoviño,
La Coruña, 15550 Valdoviño.
Tel 981 485028. English spoken.
OPEN: 15/06–15/09. SIZE: 0.8 ha, 60 pitches
(all with elec, 70 statics), 3 hot showers (charge),
9 WCs, 2 French WCs, 1 CWP. ₺

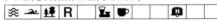

Restaurant at 0.05 km.
PRICES: (1996) Caravan with family 2100,
Tent with two adults 1400. CC: none.
*From El Ferrol, go north for 14 km towards
Valdoviño, passing through Meiras.*

FIGUERES 9B

Camping Internacional Amberes
Playa s/n, 17487 Empuriabrava.
Tel 972 450507, Fax 972 671286. English spoken.
OPEN: 15/05−30/09. SIZE: 8 ha, 600 pitches (all with elec), 70 hot showers, 70 WCs, 5 CWPs. ♨ ⛆

Mini-golf, boating, windsurfing.
PRICES: (1996) Caravan with family 3600, Tent with two adults 2700. CC: Euro/Access, Visa.
Take road from Figueres towards Roses. Go through Empuriabrava and campsite is well signposted.

Camping Mas Nou Ctra Figueres-Roses, Km 38, (Frente Empuriabrava), 17486 Castello d'Empuries.
Tel 972 454175, Fax 972 454358. English spoken.
OPEN: 22/03−30/09. SIZE: 8 ha, 450 pitches (250 with elec), 50 hot showers, 45 WCs, 1 CWP. ♨

Tennis, mini-golf; sea 3 km.
PRICES: (1996) Caravan with family 3470, Tent with two adults 2260. CC: Amex, Euro/Access, Visa.
From Figueres take the road to Roses. After Castello d'Empuries, campsite is on left-hand side.

FUENGIROLA 8D

Camping Calazul Ctra N340 Km 200, 29640 Mijas Costa.
Tel 952 493219, Fax 952 493219. English spoken.
OPEN: all year. SIZE: 360 pitches (all with elec), 20 hot showers, 30 WCs, 3 CWPs. ♨ ⛆

Sports field and children's playground.
PRICES: (1996) Caravan with family 3325, Tent with two adults 1975. CC: none.
From Fuengirola, take the N340 south for 7 km. The campsite is 300 m on the right after Cala de Mijas.

Camping Fuengirola 29640 Fuengirola.
Tel 952 474108, Fax 952 474108. English spoken.
OPEN: all year. SIZE: 226 pitches (all with elec), 18 hot showers, 22 WCs, 2 CWPs.

PRICES: (1996) Caravan with family 3600, Tent with two adults 2780. CC: none.
Heading towards Marbella, leave motorway at Fuengirola exit and follow signs to campsite from the town.

Camping Los Jarales Km 197, Mijas Costa, 29650 Mijas Costa.
Tel 952 830003, Fax 952 830003. English spoken.
OPEN: all year. SIZE: 2 ha, 174 pitches (all with elec), 18 hot showers, 18 WCs, 1 CWP. ♨ ⛆

PRICES: (1996) Caravan with family 3150, Tent with two adults 2000. CC: Euro/Access, Visa.
At Km 197 on the N340, 12 km from Fuengirola and 15 km from Marbella.

Camping Los Jarales
near Fuengirola
... And marvellous Marbella nearby

GANDIA 9C

Camping Coelius Avda del Mar s/n, 46711 Miramar.
Tel 962 819574, Fax 962 819574.
OPEN: all year. SIZE: 2 ha, 100 pitches (all with elec), 18 hot showers, 24 WCs, 10 French WCs, 2 CWPs. ♨ ⛆

Shop at 0.5 km. Entertainment in high season.
PRICES: (1996) Caravan with family 4200, Tent with two adults 2500. CC: Amex, Euro/Access, Visa.
From Gandia, go south to Bellreguart and follow signs to Miramar and the campsite.

Camping L'Aventura 46710 Playa Daimus.
Tel 962 818330, Fax 962 818330. English spoken.
OPEN: 01/03−30/09. SIZE: 2 ha, 120 pitches (all with elec, 10 statics), 20 hot showers, 14 WCs, 6 French WCs, 3 CWPs. ♨ ⛆

Disco, entertainment, mountain bikes.
PRICES: Caravan with family 4475, Tent with two adults 2490. CC: Amex, Euro/Access, Visa.
From A7, take exit 60/61 (N322) to Gandia and then follow the road to Playa Daimus (3 km).

GIJON 8B

Camping Gijon 33203 Gijon.
Tel 985 365755. English spoken.
OPEN: 01/06−30/09. SIZE: 30 pitches (all with elec), 4 hot showers, 16 WCs, 5 French WCs, 1 CWP. ♨

Shop at 1 km. Restaurant at 1 km.
PRICES: (1996) Caravan with family 2825, Tent with two adults 1625. CC: none.
1 km from town centre, at the east end of San Lorenzo beach.

GIRONA (GERONA) 9B

Camping Relax 17253 Mont-Ras.
Tel 972 301549, Fax 972 601100. English spoken.

OPEN: 31/05–31/08. SIZE: 2.6 ha, 182 pitches (all with elec, 34 statics), 18 hot showers, 26 WCs, 2 CWPs. ✆

Table tennis, boules, football.
PRICES: Caravan with family 3130, Tent with two adults 2100. CC: none.
Take the road from Girona to Palamos (Km 39) and follow signs to the campsite.

Camping Relax Naturista 17253 Mont-Ras.
Tel 972 300818, Fax 972 601100. English spoken.
OPEN: all year. SIZE: 5 ha, 308 pitches (all with elec, 28 statics), 32 hot showers, 40 WCs, 3 CWPs. ✆

Restaurant at 3 km. Naturist site. Tennis, mini-golf.
PRICES: Caravan with family 3990, Tent with two adults 2700. CC: Euro/Access, Visa.
Take the road from Girona to Palamos (Km 40) and follow signs to the campsite.

GRANADA   8D

Camping Castillo de Banos Castillo de Banos, 18750 La Mamola, Granada.
Tel 958 829528, Fax 958 829768. English spoken.
OPEN: 15/06–15/09. SIZE: 3 ha, 240 pitches (all with elec), 12 hot showers (charge), 28 WCs, 1 CWP. ✆

Entertainment, children's playground.
PRICES: Caravan with family 3010, Tent with two adults 1850. CC: Euro/Access, Visa.
On N340 at Km 360.

Camping Cubillas Albolote, 18220 Granada.
Tel 958 453328, Fax 958 453265.
English spoken.
OPEN: all year. SIZE: 5 hot showers, 2 CWPs. ✆ ふ

PRICES: (1996) Caravan with family 2650, Tent with two adults 1600. CC: Visa.
From Granada, campsite is 10 km north on the N323 at Km 117 towards Madrid-Jaen.

Camping Don Cactus Carchuna Motril, Granada.
Tel 958 623109, Fax 958 624294.
English spoken.
OPEN: all year. SIZE: 4 ha, 320 pitches (all with elec, 20 statics), 14 hot showers, 31 WCs, 2 CWPs. ✆ ふ

Cycling, basketball, football, tennis, disco and entertainment.
PRICES: Caravan with family 3140, Tent with two adults 1940. CC: Euro/Access, Visa.
At Km 343 on N340.

Camping Granada 18210 Peligros, Granada.
Tel 958 340548. English spoken.

OPEN: all year. SIZE: 2.2 ha, 70 pitches (48 with elec), 10 hot showers, 8 WCs, 1 CWP. ふ

PRICES: (1996) Caravan with family 2930, Tent with two adults 1790. CC: none.
From Granada, go north on N323 for approx 4 km then take exit 123 for Peligros. Site is well signposted.

Camping Motel Sierra Nevada Avda de Madrid 107, Granada Norte (Exit 126), 18014 Granada.
Tel 958 150062, Fax 958 150954.
English spoken.
OPEN: 01/03–31/10. SIZE: 3 ha, 250 pitches (110 with elec), 32 hot showers, 40 WCs, 2 CWPs. ✆ ふ

Shop at 0.1 km. Buses to city centre every 15 mins.
PRICES: Caravan with family 3600, Tent with two adults 2140. CC: Amex, Euro/Access, Visa.
From Granada, take road towards Madrid and then exit 126. Follow signs to campsite which is in Zone Almanjayar. Very close to the city, 100 m from bus station.

Camping Motel Sierra Nevada
at Granada!
1st Class camping – just a hop, skip and jump to the city centre

Camping Reina Isabel Ctra de La Zubia, Km 4, 18140 La Zubia, Granada.
Tel 958 590041, Fax 958 591191.
English spoken.
OPEN: all year. SIZE: 1 ha, 50 pitches (40 with elec), 8 hot showers (charge), 8 WCs, 2 CWPs. ✆

PRICES: (1996) Caravan with family 3200, Tent with two adults 2100. CC: Amex, Euro/Access, Visa.

Take exit 135 off 'Ronda Sud' (southern ring road) for La Zubia. Campsite is well signposted.

Camping Las Lomas Ctra de Guejar Sierra,
Km 6,5, 18160 Guejar Sierra.
Tel 958 484742, Fax 958 484742.
English spoken.
OPEN: all year. SIZE: 2 ha, 100 pitches (all with
elec), 12 hot showers, 12 WCs, 1 CWP. &

| | 🏕 | R | 🔢 | 🍴 | 🍵 | ✗ | 🔨 | Ⓗ | | |

PRICES: Caravan with family 3300,
Tent with two adults 2200. CC: Visa.
*In Granada follow signs to Sierra Nevada. Go
through Cenes and shortly afterwards take the
left-hand turn signposted Guejar Sierra. Follow
the mountain road and the campsite is on the
right just before entering Guejar Sierra.
SEE ADVERTISEMENT*

GRAUS 9A

Camping Bellavista Ctra Barbastro,
Embalse de Barasona,
22435 La Puebla de Castro.
Tel 974 545113. English spoken.
OPEN: all year. SIZE: 3 ha, 16 hot showers, 22 WCs. &

| ≈ | ⚓ | 🏕 | R | 🔢 | 🍴 | 🍵 | ✗ | 🔨 | ⚠ | | |

Discount for long stays.
PRICES: (1996) Caravan with family 3375, Tent with
two adults 1900. CC: Amex, Euro/Access, Visa.
*7 km south of Graus on N123. 23 km from
Barbastro. Follow signs.*

Camping Yeti Ctra Benasque s/n,
22467 Villanova (Huesca).
Tel 974 553147, Fax 974 553147.
OPEN: 01/06–30/09. SIZE: 1 ha, 70 pitches (all with
elec), 6 hot showers, 10 WCs. &

| ～ | 🏊 | 🏕 | R | 🔢 | 🍴 | | 🔨 | | |

Restaurant at 0.5 km. Quiet family campsite.
PRICES: (1996) Caravan with family 2942, Tent with
two adults 1712. CC: Euro/Access, Visa.
*From Graus go north on A139 towards Castejon
de Sos and Benasque. Campsite is well signposted
after Castejon de Sos.*

HARO 8B

Camping de Haro Avda Miranda 1,
Apartado 150, 26200 Haro.
Tel 941 312737. English spoken.
OPEN: all year. SIZE: 3 ha, 100 pitches (all with elec,
60 statics), 12 hot showers, 16 WCs, 1 CWP. & ⚑

| ～ | ⚓ | ⛲ | | 🔢 | 🍴 | 🍵 | | 🔨 | | |

Restaurant at 0.6 km.
PRICES: (1996) Caravan with family 3000,
Tent with two adults 1800. CC: none.
*Campsite is 0.6 km from the main square in Haro,
near the river.*

HERVAS 8B

El Pinajarro Km 2,7, 10700 Hervas.
Tel 927 481673, Fax 927 481673. English spoken.
OPEN: 18/03–30/09. SIZE: 2 ha, 70 pitches (60 with
elec), 18 hot showers, 20 WCs, 1 CWP. &

| | 🏕 | | 🔢 | 🍴 | 🍵 | ✗ | 🔄 | Ⓗ | | |

Mountain bikes, horse-riding, children's
entertainment.
PRICES: (1996) Caravan with family 3075,
Tent with two adults 1830. CC: Euro/Access, Visa.
Follow signs from Hervas on C513.

HOSPITAL DE ORBIGO 8B

Camping Don Suero Hospital de Orbigo,
24286 Leon.
Tel 987 361018, Fax 987 388236. English spoken.
OPEN: 01/05–30/09. SIZE: 2 ha, 200 pitches
(51 with elec), 16 hot showers, 12 WCs, 6 French
WCs, 1 CWP. &

| ～ | ⚓ | 🏕 | R | | 🍴 | 🍵 | | 🔄 | | |

Restaurant at 0.1 km.
PRICES: (1996) Caravan with family 2075. CC: none.
*Take the N120 south-west from Leon for 30 km.
The campsite is by the river in Hospital de Orbigo.*

HUELVA 8C

Camping Playa de Mazagon Moquer, Huelva,
Tel 959 376208, Fax 959 536256. English spoken.
OPEN: all year. SIZE: 670 pitches (570 with elec),

Spain

24 hot showers, 76 WCs, 28 French WCs, 2 CWPs.

PRICES: (1996) Caravan with family 3296, Tent with two adults 2033. CC: Euro/Access, Visa. *The campsite is close to Playa de Mazagan, 12 km from Palos de Frontera. Well signposted.*

HUESCA 9A

Camping San Jorge 22004 Huesca. Tel 974 227416. English spoken. OPEN: 15/04–15/10. SIZE: 0.7 ha, 35 pitches (all with elec), 6 hot showers, 10 WCs. ╚

Shop at 0.1 km. PRICES: Caravan with family 3175, Tent with two adults 1900. CC: Euro/Access, Visa. *5 mins from town centre. Follow signs for municipal swimming pool and campsite is close by.*

IBIZA

SAN ANTONIO ABAD 9D

Camping Cala Bassa Bahia de San Antonio, 07820 San Antonio Abad, Ibiza. Tel 971 344599. English spoken. OPEN: 01/05–30/10. SIZE: 1 ha, 70 pitches (all with elec, 10 statics), 10 hot showers, 8 WCs. ╚

PRICES: (1996) Caravan with family 2750, Tent with two adults. CC: Amex, Euro/Access, Visa. *From San Antonio, go towards Cala Bassa beach. Campsite is 200 m from sea.*

SAN LORENZO DE EL ESCORIAL 8B

Camping Caravaning El Escorial Ctra Guadarrama a El Escorial, Km 14,800, 28280 San Lorenzo de El Escorial. Tel 918 902412, Fax 918 961062. English spoken. OPEN: all year. SIZE: 40 ha, 400 pitches (all with elec, 800 statics), 108 hot showers, 180 WCs, 6 CWPs. ╚ ⚲

3 swimming pools; bus service to Madrid. PRICES: Caravan with family 4275, Tent with two adults 2600. CC: Euro/Access, Visa. *Highly recommended. From Madrid, take the A6 to exit 47 (Guadarrama/El Escorial). Campsite is on the left after 4 km, before reaching El Escorial.*

SANTA EULALIA DEL RIO 9D

Camping Cala Nova Playa Ctra Cala Nova, 07840 Sta Eulalia del Rio, Ibiza. Tel 971 331774. English spoken.

OPEN: 01/05–30/10. SIZE: 2 ha, 6 hot showers, 16 WCs. ╚

PRICES: (1996) Caravan with family 2600, Tent with two adults 1800. CC: Euro/Access, Visa. *From Santa Eulalia del Rio, go north-east to Es Canar and turn left towards Cala Nova beach. Campsite is 50 m from the beach and well signposted.*

Camping Vacaciones Es Cana Apartado 99, Playa Es Cana, 07840 Santa Eulalia del Rio, Ibiza. Tel 971 332117, Fax 971 339972. English spoken. OPEN: 15/05–10/10. SIZE: 2 ha, 30 pitches (all with elec, 25 statics), 20 hot showers, 20 WCs, 2 CWPs. ╚ ⚲

PRICES: (1996) Caravan with family 2500, Tent with two adults 1850. CC: Euro/Access, Visa. *From Santa Eulalia del Rio follow signs to Es Cana beach. Campsite is 300 m before the beach on the right.*

END OF IBIZA RESORTS

JACA 9A

Camping Pirineos Ctra Tarragona-San Sebastian, Km 300, 22791 Santa Cilia de Jaca. Tel 974 377351, Fax 974 377351. English spoken. OPEN: all year. SIZE: 5 ha, 250 pitches (180 with elec, 180 statics), 32 hot showers, 25 WCs, 2 CWPs. ╚ ⚲

Shop at 15 km. Pool open HS only; mini-golf; fishing, water sports and hang-gliding nearby. PRICES: (1996) Caravan with family 3705, Tent with two adults 2150. CC: Euro/Access, Visa. *17 km west of Jaca on the C134. Well signposted.*

JAVEA 9C

Camping Javea Carretera Cabo La Nao Km1, 03730 Javea. Tel 965 791070, Fax 966 460507. English spoken. OPEN: all year. SIZE: 2.5 ha, 200 pitches (180 with elec, 8 statics), 24 hot showers (charge), 28 WCs, 1 CWP. ╚

Shop at 0.7 km. PRICES: (1996) Caravan with family 3115, Tent with two adults 1740. CC: Euro/Access, Visa. *From Javea follow signs to Arenal-Playas, campsite 500 m ahead.*

LAREDO 8B

Camping Playa del Regaton El Sable No 8, 39770 Laredo. Tel 942 606011, Fax 942 606995. English spoken.

Spain

OPEN: 21/03–28/09. SIZE: 125 pitches (all with elec, 25 statics), 16 hot showers, 1 CWP. ☎ ♿

| ≋ | ⊸ | ⚐ | R | 🔥 | 🍴 | ☕ | ✕ | | | 🐕 |

Dishwashing facilities on every pitch.
PRICES: (1996) Caravan with family 3030, Tent with two adults 1930. CC: Visa.
In Laredo find the Playa Salve, and the campsite is close by, near the hospital.

LLANES   8B

Camping Palacio de Garana
33591 Nueva de Llanes.
Tel 985 410075/298, Fax 985 410075.
English spoken.
OPEN: 01/05–15/09. SIZE: 2 ha, 28 WCs. ☎

| ≋ | ⊸ | ⚐ | R | 🔥 | 🍴 | ☕ | ✕ | ⚡ | 🏠 |

Bikes for hire, boating and canoeing.
PRICES: (1996) Caravan with family 3760, Tent with two adults 2315. CC: Amex, Euro/Access, Visa.
From Llanes, go west to Nueva. Campsite is at Km 319 and well signposted.

LOGROÑO   9A

Camping Navarrete 26370 Navarrete, La Rioja.
Tel 941 440169, Fax 941 440169. English spoken.
OPEN: all year. SIZE: 3 ha, 100 pitches (all with elec, 90 statics), 20 hot showers, 26 WCs, 2 CWPs. ☎

| ⚐ | R | 🔥 | 🍴 | ☕ | ✕ | ⚡ | | | 🐕 |

Restaurant at 1 km. Tennis, mini-golf, playground.
In the heart of the pilgrims route.
PRICES: (1996) Caravan with family 3135, Tent with two adults 1940. CC: Amex, Euro/Access, Visa.
From Logroño take the N120 for 10 km, west towards Burgos. Follow signs from Navarrete.
25% discount 97

Camping Navarrete
near Logroño
In the ♥ of beautiful La Rioja

LUARCA   8A

Camping Los Cantiles 33700 Luarca.
Tel 985 640938, Fax 985 640938. English spoken.
OPEN: all year. SIZE: 2.3 ha, 100 pitches (76 with elec), 16 hot showers, 17 WCs, 4 French WCs, 1 CWP. ☎ ♿

| ≋ | ⊸ | ⚐ | R | 🔥 | 🍴 | ☕ | | | 🐕 |

Restaurant at 1 km. Swimming pool 0.3 km.
PRICES: (1996) Caravan with family 2550, Tent with two adults 1600. CC: Visa.
Well signposted from Luarca.

Camping Playa de Tauran
San Martin-Luarca, 33700 Luarca.
Tel 985 641272, Fax 985 641272. English spoken.
OPEN: 15/04–30/09. SIZE: 2 ha, 50 pitches (all with elec, 8 statics), 12 hot showers, 12 WCs, 1 CWP. ☎

| ≋ | ⊸ | 👥 | R | 🔥 | 🍴 | ☕ | ✕ | ⚡ | 🏠 |

Bike hire, games, water sports.
PRICES: (1996) Caravan with family 2775, Tent with two adults 1625. CC: none.
On the N634 at Km 508, 3 km beyond Luarca, turn right and follow signs for another 3 km.

MADRID   8B

Camping Alpha 28906 Getafe.
Tel 91 683 1659, Fax 91 683 1659. English spoken.
OPEN: all year. SIZE: 4 ha, 300 pitches (all with elec), 35 hot showers (charge), 28 WCs, 4 French WCs, 1 CWP. ☎

| | 👥 | R | 🔥 | 🍴 | ☕ | ✕ | ⚡ | 🏠 |

PRICES: Caravan with family 4259, Tent with two adults 2579. CC: Euro/Access, Visa.
From the centre of Madrid (15 minutes) take the N1V south to Ocaña, Km 12,4.

Camping Piscis 28729 Madrid.
Tel 918 432253, Fax 918 471341. English spoken.
OPEN: all year. SIZE: 20 ha, 50 pitches (all with elec), 20 hot showers (charge), 23 WCs, 4 French WCs, 3 CWPs. ☎

| | 👥 | R | 🔥 | 🍴 | ☕ | | ⚡ | ⚠ |

Restaurant at 3 km. Sports facilities including tennis; children's playground.
PRICES: (1996) Caravan with family 3375, Tent with two adults 2100. CC: Euro/Access, Visa.
Take exit 50 off the N1 towards Guadalix de la Sierra, and then first right to Navalafuente.

MARBELLA   8D

Camping La Buganvilla 29600 Marbella.
Tel 952 831973/4, Fax 952 493219.
English spoken.
OPEN: all year. SIZE: 5.3 ha, 270 pitches (all with elec), 30 hot showers, 30 WCs, 2 CWPs. ☎ ♿

| ≋ | ⊸ | 👥 | R | 🔥 | 🍴 | ☕ | ✕ | ⚡ |

Playground.
PRICES: (1996) Caravan with family 3700, Tent with two adults 2175. CC: Euro/Access.
Coming from Malaga, take N340. At Km 188.8 follow signs to campsite.

LA MARINA   9C

Camping Internacional La Marina N322, Km 76, 03194 La Marina.
Tel 965 419051, Fax 965 419110. English spoken.
OPEN: all year. SIZE: 6 ha, 371 pitches (360 with elec, 7 statics). ☎ ♿

Spain

Fitness room.
PRICES: Caravan with family 4125, Tent with two
adults 2200. CC: Euro/Access, Visa.
*On the N322 at Km 76, 2 km south of La Marina
village on the left. Follow signs.*

MAZARRON 9C

Los Madriles Ctra La Azohia Km 4,5, Isla Plana,
30868 Mazarron.
Tel 968 152151, Fax 968 152092.
English spoken.
OPEN: all year. SIZE: 5 ha, 250 pitches (all with elec,
20 statics), 40 hot showers, 44 WCs, 3 CWPs. ℓ

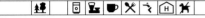
Tennis, games room.
PRICES: (1996) Caravan with family 3450,
Tent with two adults 2225. CC: none.
*East of Mazarron, take coast road towards La
Azohia. Follow signs to campsite.*

Playa de Mazarron Problado de Bolnevo,
21130 Puerto de Mazarron.
Tel 968 15 06 60, Fax 968 15 08 37.
English spoken.
OPEN: all year. SIZE: 6 ha, 400 pitches
(all with elec), 4 CWPs.

Shop at 1 km. Restaurant at 1 km. Winter and
summer activities.
PRICES: (1996) Caravan with family 3365,
Tent with two adults 1795. CC: none.
*3 km to the south of Puerto de Mazarron.
Signposted.*

MERIDA 8C

Camping Merida Km 336.6, N5, 06800 Merida.
Tel 924 303453. English spoken.
OPEN: all year. SIZE: 2.5 ha, 80 pitches (all with
elec, 80 statics), 6 hot showers, 25 WCs,
2 CWPs. ℓ

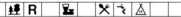
PRICES: (1996) Caravan with family 1838, Tent with
two adults 1280. CC: Amex, Euro/Access, Visa.
Well signposted on the road into Merida.

MINGLANILLA 9C

Venta de Contreras Pantano de Contreras,
Minglanilla, Cuenca.
Tel 962 186170, Fax 962 186214.
English spoken.
OPEN: all year. SIZE: 2 ha, 7 hot showers, 8 WCs,
1 CWP. ℓ

Lake and natural reserve nearby; beautiful scenery.

PRICES: Caravan with family 3000, Tent with two
adults 1600. CC: Amex, Visa.

Minglanilla is on the NIII and campsite is signposted.

MOTA DEL CUERVO 8D

Camping La Celadilla El Pedernoso, 16638 Cuenca.
Tel 967 164313, Fax 914 504899. English spoken.
OPEN: all year. SIZE: 5 ha, 10 hot showers, 22 WCs,
1 CWP. ℓ

PRICES: (1996) Caravan with family 2325, Tent with
two adults 1500. CC: Amex, Euro/Access, Visa.
*Take N301 towards Albacete, turn off at El
Pedernoso (Km 149) and campsite is 4 km ahead,
signposted.*

MOTRIL 8D

Camping Huerta Romero Paseo Maritimo,
18740 Castell de Ferro.
Tel 958 656453, Fax 958 656001. English spoken.
OPEN: all year. SIZE: 1 ha, 34 pitches (all with elec,
10 statics), 13 hot showers (charge), 19 WCs,
1 CWP. ℓ

Shop at 0.5 km.
PRICES: (1996) Caravan with family 2836,
Tent with two adults 1685. CC: none.
From Motril take the N340 east to Castell de Ferro.

MURCIA 9C

Camping Fuente Los Baños de Fortuna,
30626 Baños de Fortuna.
Tel 968 685454, Fax 968 685454. English spoken.
OPEN: 01/01–31/05 & 15/09–31/12. SIZE: 1 ha,
32 pitches (all with elec), 32 hot showers (charge),
32 WCs.

Shop at 3.5 km. Minimum 4-night stay; thermal
baths 0.2 km.
PRICES: (1996) Caravan with family 2333. CC: none.
*From Murcia head for Alicante on E15. Turn off
north to Fortuna at exit 83.*

Spain

MURILLO DE GALLEGO 9A

Camping Armalygal Ctra N240 Murillo de Gallego, 22808 Zaragoza.
Tel 974 383079, Fax 974 383011. English spoken.
OPEN: 01/04–15/10. SIZE: 8 ha, 150 pitches
(50 with elec, 5 statics), 24 hot showers, 24 WCs.

Rooms to let; good sports facilities.
PRICES: (1996) Caravan with family 3250,
Tent with two adults 1950. CC: none.
Coming from Huesca, turn right before the restaurant in Murillo, follow the lane and take first left.

NAJERA 8B

Camping El Ruedo Paseo San Julian no 24, 26300 Najera.
Tel 941 360102. English spoken.
OPEN: 01/04–01/10. SIZE: 1 ha, 30 pitches (all with elec), 11 hot showers, 16 WCs, 1 CWP.

Swimming pool 50 m.
PRICES: (1996) Caravan with family 3000,
Tent with two adults 2050. CC: none.
Follow signs from Najera.

OLIVA 9C

Camping Azul 46780 Oliva.
Tel 962 854096, Fax 962 854106. English spoken.
OPEN: all year. SIZE: 2.5 ha, 100 pitches (all with elec), 28 hot showers, 14 WCs, 1 CWP.

Shop at 1 km.
PRICES: (1996) Caravan with family 3100, Tent with two adults 2025. CC: Euro/Access, Visa.
At Km 213 post on N322 turn right towards beach and follow signs.

Camping Kiko Playa de Oliva, 46780 Oliva.
Tel 962 850905, Fax 962 854320. English spoken.
OPEN: all year. SIZE: 3 ha, 220 pitches (all with elec), 36 hot showers, 44 WCs, 2 CWPs.

PRICES: (1996) Caravan with family 4050, Tent with two adults 2300. CC: Visa.
Head towards the beach from Oliva and site is signposted after 500 m.

Euro-Camping Oliva 46780 Oliva.
Tel 962 854098, Fax 962 851753. English spoken.
OPEN: 01/03–31/10. SIZE: 5 ha, 330 pitches
(250 with elec), 45 hot showers, 82 WCs, 4 CWPs.

Bike hire, children's playground.
PRICES: (1996) Caravan with family 4400, Tent with

two adults 2800. CC: Amex, Euro/Access, Visa.
From Oliva take the N332 towards Alicante. Turn left at Km 210 and then follow the Euro-Camping signs for 1 km.

OROPESA DE MAR 9A

Camping Torre Paquita Avda Columbretes, 12594 Oropesa de Mar.
Tel 964 310006. English spoken.
OPEN: 05/04–12/10. SIZE: 1.8 ha, 107 pitches
(all with elec), 10 hot showers, 24 WCs, 1 CWP.

Children's pool, playground, tennis.
PRICES: (1996) Caravan with family 2830,
Tent with two adults 1780. CC: none.
In Oropesa de Mar, drive along main street. Campsite is not far from railway subway. Follow signposts.

PALAFRUGELL 9B

Camping Cypsela Els Rodors, 7 Playa de Pals, 17256 Pals.
Tel 972 667696, Fax 972 667300. English spoken.
OPEN: 15/05–30/09. SIZE: 20 ha, 1170 pitches (all with elec), 135 hot showers, 138 WCs, 4 CWPs.

Mini-golf, boules, squash, entertainment, tennis; sea 1.5 km.
PRICES: (1996) Caravan with family 5315,
Tent with two adults 3700. CC: none.
North from Palafrugell to Pals then follow signs for Playa de Pals. Site is well signposted.

Camping Inter-Pals 17256 Platja de Pals.
Tel 972 636179, Fax 972 667476. English spoken.
OPEN: 15/03–30/09. SIZE: 7 ha, 400 pitches
(all with elec, 40 statics), 76 hot showers, 74 WCs, 6 CWPs.

Tennis and other ball games; sea 0.3 km.
PRICES: Caravan with family 4494, Tent with two adults 3210. CC: none.
From Palafrugell go north to Pals and follow the signs to Platja de Pals and the campsite. From Girona go to La Bisbal, then Pals etc.

Camping Neptuno Els Rodors 23, 17256 Platja de Pals.
Tel 972 636731, Fax 972 636731. English spoken.
OPEN: 15/05–10/09. SIZE: 300 pitches (all with elec, 8 statics), 36 hot showers, 36 WCs, 1 CWP.

Restaurant at 0.5 km.
PRICES: (1996) Caravan with family 3325, Tent with two adults 2200. CC: Euro/Access, Visa.
North from Palafrugell to Pals, look for signs to Platja de Pals.

Spain

Camping Playa Brava 17256 Platja de Pals.
Tel 972 636894, Fax 972 636952. English spoken.
OPEN: 15/05–25/09. SIZE: 11 ha, 500 pitches
(all with elec), 52 hot showers, 74 WCs, 5 CWPs.
🌊 ⛱

≋ ⛵ 🏕 R ⊡ 🛈 🍴 ✗ ⌇ | 🍴

PRICES: (1996) Caravan with family 3990, Tent with
two adults 3470. CC: none.
*On north side of Pals turn to Playa de Pals; before
entering turn left and follow golf course for about
3 km.*

Kim's Camping Cami de la Font d'en Xeco 1,
17211 Llafranc.
Tel 972 301156, Fax 972 610894. English spoken.
OPEN: 09/04–30/09. SIZE: 5 ha, 200 pitches
(all with elec), 52 hot showers, 74 WCs, 2 CWPs. 🌊

≋ ⛵ 🏕 R ⊡ 🛈 🍴 ✗ ⌇ 🏠 🍴

PRICES: (1996) Caravan with family 3780, Tent with
two adults 3095. CC: Euro/Access, Visa.
*From Palafrugell take road to Tamariu for 1.5 km
then follow signs to Llafranc and campsite.
SEE ADVERTISEMENT.*

PALAMOS 9B

Camping Cala Gogo 17250 Platja d'Aro.
Tel 972 651564, Fax 972 650553.
English spoken.
OPEN: 30/04–25/09. SIZE: 16 ha, 300 pitches
(all with elec), 112 hot showers, 135 WCs,
20 CWPs. 🌊

≋ ⛵ 🏕 R ⊡ 🛈 🍴 ✗ ⌇ 🏠

PRICES: (1996) Caravan with family 4825, Tent with
two adults 2920. CC: none.
*South of Palamos on the C253 road in the
direction of Platja d'Aro.*

Camping Castell d'Aro Ctra S'Agaro km 1,
17249 Castell d'Aro.
Tel 972 819699. English spoken.
OPEN: 01/04–30/09. SIZE: 7 ha, 280 pitches
(all with elec, 90 statics), 20 hot showers, 22 WCs,
3 CWPs. 🌊

≋ ⛵ 🏕 R ⊡ 🛈 🍴 ✗ ⌇

PRICES: (1996) Caravan with family 2620, Tent with
two adults 2180. CC: none.
*Go south on coast road from Palamos, past
S'Agaro and towards Castell d'Aro. Campsite on
left, 1 km from road; follow signs.*

Camping Palamos Ctra La Fosca 12,
17230 Palamos.
Tel 972 314296, Fax 972 601100. English spoken.
OPEN: 22/03–30/09. SIZE: 5.5 ha, 388 pitches
(all with elec, 65 statics), 52 hot showers, 58 WCs,
2 CWPs. 🌊

≋ ⛵ 🏕 R ⊡ 🛈 🍴 ✗ ⌇ 🏠

PRICES: Caravan with family 4360, Tent with two
adults 3050. CC: Amex, Euro/Access, Visa.
Just north of Palamos on the road to La Fosca.

Camping Vilarroma Ctra del Mar s/n,
17230 Palamos.
Tel 972 314375, Fax 972 314375.
English spoken.
OPEN: 01/04–30/09. SIZE: 2 ha, 180 pitches
(all with elec, 10 statics), 23 hot showers, 18 WCs,
1 CWP. 🌊

≋ ⛵ 🏕 R ⊡ 🛈 🍴 ✗ | 🏠

PRICES: (1996) Caravan with family 3530,
Tent with two adults 2460. CC: none.
*Just south of Palamos, near petrol station and
football stadium. Signposted.*

PAMPLONA 9A

Camping Ezcaba 31194 Oricain.
Tel 948 330315, Fax 948 330315.
English spoken.
OPEN: all year. SIZE: 20 ha, 32 hot showers, 32 WCs,
1 CWP. 🌊 ⛱

〜 ⛵ 🍤 | | 🍴 🍴 ✗ ⌇ ⚠

PRICES: (1996) Caravan with family 3100,
Tent with two adults 1900. CC: Amex, Visa.
*7 km from Pamplona on the N121 to Bayonne.
Just after Oricain take a small turning to the left.*

1st CATEGORY E-17211 LLAFRANC
Tel: (34-72) 30 11 56 and 61 17 75
Fax: (34-72) 61 08 94
OPEN: Easter – 30 September

CAMPING
KiM'S
COSTA BRAVA
LLAFRANC

One of the most beautifully situated
campsites on the Costa Brava, only 350
metres from the sea, with 2 swimming
pools, children's playground, bar,
restaurant, supermarket. Just 322
pitches on a 12-acre site.

Bungalows & mobile
homes for hire.

See under Palafrugell

Spain

PEÑISCOLA 9A

Camping La Caravana Ctra de la Estacion 47, 12598 Peñiscola.
Tel 964 480824, Fax 964 216903. English spoken.
OPEN: 09/04–16/04 & 01/07–15/09. SIZE: 10 ha, 375 pitches (all with elec), 36 hot showers, 40 WCs, 20 French WCs, 4 CWPs. ⚊

Tennis, mini-golf, entertainment.
PRICES: (1996) Caravan with family 4039, Tent with two adults 2551. CC: Euro/Access, Visa.
3.5 km from Peñiscola, on road adjoining N340.

Camping Peñiscola Ctra N501 Km 29, 12598 Peñiscola.
Tel 964 473016, Fax 964 473016. English spoken.
OPEN: all year. SIZE: 20 ha. ⚊

PRICES: (1996) Caravan with family 3025, Tent with two adults 2095. CC: Visa.
Peñiscola is reached from the E15/A7 junction 43. The site is 2 km from the village.

Camping Vizmar 12598 Peñiscola.
Tel 967 473439. English spoken.
OPEN: 01/04–30/09. SIZE: 1.2 ha, 69 pitches (all with elec, 4 statics), 4 hot showers, 20 WCs, 1 CWP. ⚊

Shop at 0.5 km. Sea 0.3 km.
PRICES: (1996) Caravan with family 3100, Tent with two adults 1900. CC: Euro/Access, Visa.
Follow signs from town.

PONT DE SUERT 9A

Camping Baliera Ctra N260 Km 357,500, 25523 Bonansa.
Tel 974 554016, Fax 974 554016.
OPEN: all year. SIZE: 5 ha, 2 CWPs. ⚊ ⚊

PRICES: (1996) Caravan with family 3625, Tent with two adults 2100. CC: Euro/Access, Visa.
From Pont de Suert, drive 6 km north, then turn left on the route 144 and left again.

PORT BOU 9B

Camping Garbet Colera, 17496 Port Bou.
Tel 972 389001, Fax 972 128059.
English spoken.
OPEN: 01/04–31/10. SIZE: 90 pitches (all with elec), 9 hot showers, 18 WCs, 2 French WCs, 1 CWP. ⚊

PRICES: (1996) Caravan with family 3325, Tent with two adults 2100. CC: Euro/Access, Visa.
Coming from French border on N260, campsite is at Km 13.

Camping L'Ombra Ctra La Bisbal a Portbou 13, 17496 Llanca.
Tel 972 380 335, Fax 972 120 261. English spoken.
OPEN: all year. SIZE: 11 ha, 132 pitches (60 with elec), 10 hot showers, 26 WCs, 1 CWP. ⚊

Shop at 0.5 km. Restaurant at 0.5 km.
PRICES: Caravan with family 2700, Tent with two adults 1600. CC: Euro/Access, Visa.
From Port Bou take road to Figueres. Campsite is next to Hotel Gri-Mar in Llanca. Follow signs.

EL PUERTO DE SANTA MARIA 8C

Camping Playa Las Dunas Paseo Mto de La Puntilla s/n, Ap 21, 11500 El Puerto de Santa Maria.
Tel 956 872210, Fax 956 872210. English spoken.
OPEN: all year. SIZE: 13 ha, 140 pitches (all with elec), 17 hot showers, 30 WCs, 10 French WCs, 2 CWPs. ⚊ ⚊

Shop at 0.5 km.
PRICES: (1996) Caravan with family 3355, Tent with two adults 1985. CC: Amex, Euro/Access, Visa.
From the N4 follow the signs to the Playa de la Puntilla. Campsite well signposted.

RIBEIRA 8A

Camping Coroso Sta Eugenia de Ribeira, 15960 Ribeira.
Tel 981 838002. English spoken.
OPEN: 15/06–15/09. SIZE: 3 ha, 50 pitches (all with elec), 30 hot showers, 26 WCs. ⚊

PRICES: (1996) Caravan with family 2685, Tent with two adults 1320. CC: none.
The campsite is on the road between Ribeira and Palmeira.

RODELLAR 9A

Camping El Puente 22144 Rodellar.
Tel 974 318312, Fax 974 318312. English spoken.
OPEN: 01/04–30/09. SIZE: 3.6 ha. ⚊

PRICES: (1996) Caravan with family 2950, Tent with two adults 1750. CC: Amex, Visa.
Turn left off the Huesca to Barbastro road to Rodellar. Drive up to village and look for signs to campsite.

ROSES 9B

Camping Laguna 17486 Castello de Ampurias.
Tel 972 450553, Fax 972 450799. English spoken.
OPEN: 15/03–19/10. SIZE: 14.5 ha, 750 pitches (all with elec, 6 statics), 56 hot showers, 79 WCs, 5 CWPs. ⚊

PRICES: (1996) Caravan with family 4380, Tent with two adults 2820. CC: Euro/Access, Visa.
Going west from Roses, turn right at roundabout towards St Pere Pescador and campsite is signposted.

Camping Rodas 17480 Roses.
Tel 972 257617, Fax 972 151413. English spoken.
OPEN: 01/06–30/09. SIZE: 3.1 ha, 290 pitches (150 with elec), 34 hot showers, 36 WCs, 2 CWPs. ✆ &

Sea 0.5 km; horse-riding, water sports and tennis nearby.
PRICES: (1996) Caravan with family 3798, Tent with two adults 2407. CC: Euro/Access, Visa.
On the road going into Roses, 1 km from town centre.

SAGUNTO   9C

Camping Malvarosa de Corinto Playa Corinto, Camino Malvarrosa, 46500 Sagunto.
Tel 962 608906, Fax 962 608943. English spoken.
OPEN: all year. SIZE: 10 ha, 100 pitches (all with elec), 10 hot showers, 14 WCs, 2 CWPs. ✆

Restaurant at 0.5 km.

PRICES: (1996) Caravan with family 3050, Tent with two adults 1720. CC: none.
From N340 take exit for Almenara and go towards beach. Follow signs.

SALOU   9A

Camping La Pineda de Salou Playa de La Pineda, 43480 La Pineda.
Tel 977 370226, Fax 977 370620. English spoken.
OPEN: 01/03–30/10. SIZE: 4 ha, 336 pitches (all with elec), 26 hot showers, 30 WCs, 2 CWPs. ✆

2.5 km from Port Aventura; fishing, tennis and windsurfing nearby.
PRICES: (1996) Caravan with family 3860, Tent with two adults 2545. CC: Visa.
3 km from Salou on the Salou to Tarragona road. Campsite is 400 m from the beach.
SEE ADVERTISEMENT.

Camping Sanguli 43840 Salou.
Tel 977 381641, Fax 977 384616.
English spoken.
OPEN: 01/03–31/10. SIZE: 23 ha, 1378 pitches (1155 with elec, 112 statics), 104 hot showers, 175 WCs, 10 CWPs. ✆ &

Sports area, playground, amphitheatre.

Spain

PRICES: (1996) Caravan with family 5070, Tent with two adults 3290. CC: Euro/Access, Visa.
Take Exit 35 from the A7, and the campsite is 1 km from the centre of Salou on the coast road towards Cambrils.

La Corona Cambrils, 43840 Salou.
Tel 977 351030, Fax 977 385107. English spoken.
OPEN: 19/03–31/10. SIZE: 8 ha, 600 pitches (400 with elec, 20 statics), 24 hot showers, 60 WCs, 4 CWPs. &

| ≋ | ⚊ | ⚤ | R | ⊡ | ⅃ | ⬤ | ✕ | ⸿ | | | |

Port Aventura theme park 2 km.
PRICES: Caravan with family 2750, Tent with two adults 1960. CC: none.
Campsite is 1 km from Salou on road to Cambrils, near a petrol station. Signposted.

SAN FELIU DE GUIXOLS 9B

Camping Ridaura Ctra Girona-St-Feliu Km 25, Llagostera, 17240 Llagostera.
Tel 972 830265, Fax 972 830265.
English spoken.
OPEN: 01/06–15/09. SIZE: 4 ha, 360 pitches (all with elec), 28 hot showers, 28 WCs, 2 CWPs. ⚊

| ⌇ | ⚊ | ⚤ | R | ⊡ | ⅃ | ⬤ | ✕ | ⸿ | 🏢 | | 🛵 |

PRICES: Caravan with family 3000, Tent with two adults 2300. CC: Visa.
From San Feliu de Guixols go towards Llagostera. Campsite is at Km 25 between Llagostera and Santa Cristina d'Aro.

Camping Riembau La Platja d'Aro, 17250 S'Agaro.
Tel 72 81 71 23, Fax 72 82 52 10.
English spoken.
OPEN: 01/05–30/09. SIZE: 20 ha, 1100 pitches (all with elec, 200 statics), 184 hot showers, 167 WCs, 10 CWPs. ⚊ &

| | ⚤ | R | ⊡ | ⅃ | ⬤ | ✕ | ⸿ | | 🐕 | |

Mobile homes for hire; sea 1 km.
PRICES: (1996) Caravan with family 4329, Tent with two adults 3702. CC: none.
From San Feliu de Guixols, take the road towards La Platja d'Aro and campsite is signposted.

Camping Valldaro 17250 Playa de Aro.
Tel 972 817515, Fax 972 816662.
English spoken.
OPEN: 01/03–01/10. SIZE: 20 ha, 1224 pitches (all with elec), 140 hot showers, 8 CWPs. ⚊ &

| | ⚤ | R | ⊡ | ⅃ | ⬤ | ✕ | ⸿ | 🏠 | | |

Sports field, gymnasium, entertainment; sea 0.8 km.
PRICES: Caravan with family 4387, Tent with two adults 3745. CC: none.
North of San Feliu de Guixols, just after Castell d'Aro village on the right-hand side. Well signposted.

SAN ROQUE 8D

Camping Motel San Roque 11360 San Roque.
Tel 956 780100, Fax 956 780100. English spoken.
OPEN: all year. SIZE: 120 pitches (all with elec, 38 statics), 6 hot showers, 12 WCs, 2 French WCs, 2 CWPs. ⚊ &

| ≋ | ⚊ | ⚤ | R | ⊡ | ⅃ | ⬤ | ✕ | ⸿ | 🏠 | | |

PRICES: (1996) Caravan with family 2490, Tent with two adults 1525. CC: Amex, Euro/Access, Visa.
3 km from the centre of San Roque and 500 m from the crossing to La Linea.

SAN SEBASTIAN 9A

Camping Igueldo Paseo Padre Orkolaga, Barrio de Igueldo, 20008 San Sebastian.
Tel 943 214502, Fax 943 280411. English spoken.
OPEN: all year. SIZE: 4 ha, 100 pitches (all with elec).

| | ⚤ | | ⊡ | ⅃ | | ✕ | | | |

PRICES: (1996) Caravan with family 3100, Tent with two adults 2700. CC: none.
From San Sebastian centre follow signs to Bilbao, then Mount Igueldo (about 5 km). Signposted.

Gran Camping Zarauz
Monte Talai-Mendi s/n, 20800 Zarauz.
Tel 943 831238, Fax 943 132486. English spoken.
OPEN: all year. SIZE: 4 ha, 155 pitches (120 with elec, 120 statics), 28 hot showers, 49 WCs, 2 CWPs. ⚊ &

| ≋ | ⚊ | ⚤ | | ⊡ | ⅃ | ⬤ | ✕ | | ⚠ | |

PRICES: (1996) Caravan with family 3200, Tent with two adults 1925. CC: Amex, Euro/Access, Visa.
From San Sebastian take the N634 towards Zarauz. Turn right 400 m before Zarauz towards the beach.

SAN VINCENTE DE LA BARQUERA 8B

Camping Caravanning Playa de Oyambre
Finca Pena Gerra, 39540 San Vincente de la Barquera.
Tel 942 711461, Fax 942 711530. English spoken.
OPEN: 01/04–30/09. SIZE: 4 ha, 200 pitches (all with elec), 30 hot showers, 24 WCs, 1 CWP. ⚊

| ≋ | ⚊ | ⚤ | R | ⊡ | ⬤ | ⬤ | ✕ | ⸿ | ⚠ | |

PRICES: (1996) Caravan with family 3160, Tent with two adults 1980. CC: Amex, Euro/Access, Visa.
On N634, 3 km east of San Vincente de la Barquera, turn left towards La Revilla and Comillas, opposite the Hotel Venta Abajo. Campsite is well signposted.

SANT PERE PESCADOR 9B

Camping L'Amfora Mas Sopas, 17470 Sant Pere Pescador.
Tel 972 520540/2, Fax 972 520539. English spoken.

OPEN: 08/05–30/09. SIZE: 8 ha, 400 pitches (all with elec, 10 statics), 103 hot showers, 111 WCs, 2 CWPs. ✆ ♿

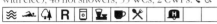

Individual shower/WC units available; entertainment, disco.
PRICES: Caravan with family 4775, Tent with two adults 3875. CC: none.
Well signposted in Sant Pere Pescador.

Camping Aquarius 17470 Sant Pere Pescador. Tel 972 520003, Fax 972 550216. English spoken. OPEN: 14/03–26/10. SIZE: 6 ha, 426 pitches (all with elec), 48 hot showers, 55 WCs, 2 CWPs. ✆ ♿

Good sports facilities; windsurfing.
PRICES: (1996) Caravan with family 4500, Tent with two adults 3000. CC: none.
Take the road to L'Escala from Sant Pere Pescador, cross the river bridge and immediately turn left to the beach. Follow signs from there.
SEE ADVERTISEMENT

Camping La Ballena Alegre 2
17470 Sant Pere Pescador.
Tel 972 520302, Fax 972 520332. English spoken.
OPEN: 01/05–30/09. SIZE: 24 ha, 1820 pitches (all with elec), 188 hot showers, 172 WCs, 6 CWPs. ♿

aquarius
c a m p i n g
17470 Sant Pere Pescador
Adjoining lovely, safe Sant Pere beach,

✱ heated toilet block
✱ windsurfer centre
✱ marvellous restaurant and beach bar
✱ take-away meals and supermarket
✱ play centre and young
   people's entertainments
✱ mountain-bike hire
✱ mini-golf

PLUS
Beautiful secluded
position

See under Sant Pere Pescador

Tennis, table tennis, disco.
PRICES: (1996) Caravan with family 4574, Tent with two adults 3879. CC: none.
From motorway, take exit 5 towards L'Escala. After 20 km turn at crossroads to St Martin D'Empuries and follow signs to the campsite.

SANTA MARINA DE VALDEON   8B

Camping El Cares
24915 Santa Marina de Valdeon.
Tel 987 742676. English spoken.
OPEN: 03/04–13/10. SIZE: 1.5 ha, 8 hot showers, 12 WCs. ✆ ♿

Mountain sports.
PRICES: (1996) Caravan with family 2650, Tent with two adults 1800. CC: none.
1 km above the village of Santa Marina De Valdeon which is on the main N621 between Potes and Riano. Campsite is signposted on the N621 and again in Santa Marina De Valdeon.

SANTANDER   8B

Camping Cabo Mayor
Avda del Faro, 39012 Santander.
Tel 942 391542. English spoken.
OPEN: 01/04–30/09. SIZE: 3 ha, 56 pitches (all with elec), 35 hot showers, 34 WCs, 1 French WC, 1 CWP. ✆

PRICES: (1996) Caravan with family 3525, Tent with two adults 2050. CC: none.
2 km from Santander on the road to Faro.

Camping Derby de Loredo 39140 Loredo.
Tel 942 504181, Fax 942 509063.
English spoken.
OPEN: 31/05–30/09. SIZE: 3 ha, 200 pitches (all with elec, 30 statics), 18 hot showers, 28 WCs. ✆

Shop at 0.2 km. Children's pool; water sports, fishing and horse-riding nearby.
PRICES: (1996) Caravan with family 2845, Tent with two adults 1770. CC: none.
From Santander go south to El Astillero then east via Pedrena and Somo to Loredo. Campsite is signposted in Loredo.

Camping Municipal Bellavista
Ctra de Faro s/n, 39012 Santander.
Tel 942 391536, Fax 942 391536. English spoken.
OPEN: all year. SIZE: 4 ha, 208 pitches (200 with elec), 30 hot showers, 72 WCs. ✆

Mini-golf, games.

PRICES: (1996) Caravan with family 3700, Tent with two adults 2250. CC: Visa.
Recommended. The campsite is situated near the lighthouse of Cabo Mayor and well signposted.

SANTA POLA 9C

Bahia de Santa Pola Valverde Bajo 10, 03130 Santa Pola.
Tel 965 411012, Fax 965 416790. English spoken.
OPEN: all year. SIZE: 5 ha, 200 pitches (all with elec), 20 hot showers, 40 WCs, 3 CWPs.

Restaurant at 0.1 km. Sea 1 km.
PRICES: (1996) Caravan with family 3150, Tent with two adults 2000. CC: Amex, Visa.
1 km from Santa Pola on the road to Elche.

SANTIAGO DE COMPOSTELA 8A

Camping As Cancelas Rua do 25 de Xullo-35, 15704 Santiago de Compostela.
Tel 981 580266, Fax 981 575553. English spoken.
OPEN: all year. SIZE: 2 ha, 150 pitches (all with elec), 36 hot showers, 38 WCs, 20 French WCs, 3 CWPs. 🌭 ⅍

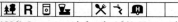

PRICES: (1996) Caravan with family 3640, Tent with two adults 1700. CC: none.
Recommended. Campsite is north of city, at Km 60 marker and down a steep hill.

SANTO DOMINGO DE CALZADA 8B

Camping Banares 26250 Santo Domingo de Calzada.
Tel 941 342804, Fax 941 340131. English spoken.
OPEN: all year. SIZE: 105 ha, 200 pitches (500 with elec, 300 statics), 40 hot showers, 76 WCs, 4 CWPs. 🌭

PRICES: (1996) Caravan with family 3625, Tent with two adults 2200. CC: Amex, Euro/Access, Visa.
From Santo Domingo go towards Logroño and campsite is 2 km on left.

SANTOÑA 8B

Camping Los Molinos Playa del Ris, 39180 Noja, Cantabria.
Tel 942 630426, Fax 942 630725. English spoken.
OPEN: 14/04–21/04 & 01/06–30/09. SIZE: 10 ha, 800 pitches, 55 hot showers (charge), 84 WCs, 4 CWPs. 🌭

Swimming pool and restaurant open July/August only.
PRICES: (1996) Caravan with family 4075, Tent with two adults 2500. CC: none.

From Santoña, go west along coast road to Noja, then head for Playa de Ris and follow signs.

Camping Playa Joyel Playa del Ris, 39180 Noja, Cantabria.
Tel 942 630081, Fax 942 631294. English spoken.
OPEN: 15/04–30/09. SIZE: 15 ha, 850 pitches (all with elec, 150 statics), 64 hot showers, 64 WCs, 9 CWPs. 🌭 ⅍

PRICES: (1996) Caravan with family 4470, Tent with two adults 3140. CC: none.
West along the coast road from Santoña or Beranga exit from E70 Santander to Bilbao road. Site is signposted.

SEGOVIA 8B

Camping Acueducto Ctra N601 Km 112, 40004 Segovia.
Tel 921 425000. English spoken.
OPEN: 01/04–30/09. SIZE: 3 ha, 200 pitches (all with elec, 2 statics), 20 hot showers, 20 WCs, 1 CWP. 🌭 ⅍

Restaurant at 0.1 km. Recreational lakeside centre 5 km.
PRICES: (1996) Caravan with family 2900, Tent with two adults 1720. CC: none.
Highly recommended. From Segovia take C601 towards La Granja. Follow signs to campsite.

SITGES 9B

Camping Sitges 08870 Sitges.
Tel 938 941080, Fax 938 949852. English spoken.
OPEN: 15/02–15/11. SIZE: 28 ha, 120 pitches (80 with elec), 14 hot showers, 16 WCs, 2 CWPs.

PRICES: (1996) Caravan with family 3650, Tent with two adults 2250. CC: Euro/Access, Visa.
Campsite is 2 km from Sitges on the C246 to Vilanova.

SOLSONA 9B

Camp/Caravan el Solsones 25280 Solsona.
Tel 973 482861, Fax 973 482861. English spoken.
OPEN: all year. SIZE: 6 ha, 300 pitches (all with elec, 150 statics), 26 hot showers, 33 WCs, 2 CWPs. 🌭 ⅍

Excellent summer and winter sporting facilities.
PRICES: (1996) Caravan with family 3520, Tent with two adults 2240. CC: Amex, Euro/Access, Visa.
2 km from the centre of Solsona.

TARIFA 8D

Camping Paloma 11380 Tarifa.
Tel 956 684203, Fax 956 681880. English spoken.

OPEN: all year. SIZE: 5 ha, 353 pitches (280 with elec), 22 hot showers, 26 WCs, 14 French WCs, 2 CWPs. ♿ &

40% discount in LS.
PRICES: Caravan with family 3500, Tent with two adults 2000. CC: Amex, Euro/Access, Visa.
At Km 74 on the N4 Cadiz to Malaga road. Follow the campsite signs from Tarifa town centre.

Camping Rio Jara 11380 Tarifa.
Tel 956 680570. English spoken.
OPEN: all year. SIZE: 3 ha, 100 pitches (all with elec), 6 hot showers, 25 WCs, 5 French WCs, 1 CWP. ♿

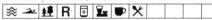

PRICES: (1996) Caravan with family 3350, Tent with two adults 1900. CC: none.
On the Cadiz motorway, 2 km from centre of Tarifa. On the left and well signposted.

Camping Tarifa Ctra N340 Km 78,87, 11380 Tarifa.
Tel 956 684778, Fax 956 684778. English spoken.
OPEN: all year. SIZE: 3 ha, 1 French WC, 2 CWPs. &

Good LS discounts for stays over 5 days.
PRICES: (1997) Caravan with family 4250, Tent with two adults 2850. CC: Amex, Euro/Access, Visa.
At Km 78,87 on N340 Tarifa-Cadiz road, near the La Cordoniz restaurant.

Torre de la Pena Ctra Cadiz, 11380 Tarifa.
Tel 956 684903, Fax 956 681898.
English spoken.
OPEN: all year. SIZE: 3 ha. ♿

Tennis, windsurfing, horse-riding, scuba-diving.
PRICES: (1996) Caravan with family 2900, Tent with two adults 1700. CC: Amex, Euro/Access, Visa.
Km 78 on the N340.

TARRAGONA 9A

Camping Marius 43892 Miami-Playa.
Tel 977 810684, Fax 977 810684.
English spoken.
OPEN: 15/04–15/10. SIZE: 4 ha, 350 pitches (all with elec), 54 hot showers, 42 WCs, 2 French WCs, 2 CWPs. ♿ &

Tennis, water sports, children's playground; bikes and television prohibited.
PRICES: (1996) Caravan with family 4000, Tent with two adults 3200. CC: Euro/Access, Visa.
Take the A7 from Tarragona, south towards Cambrils, then go towards Valencia until you reach the N340. The campsite is signposted from there.

TEULADA 9C

Camping-Caravanning Moraira Moraira, 03724 Teulada.
Tel 965 745249, Fax 965 745315. English spoken.
OPEN: all year. SIZE: 11 ha, 108 pitches (all with elec), 13 hot showers, 141 WCs, 2 CWPs. ♿ &

Big discounts in low season.
PRICES: Caravan with family 3550, Tent with two adults 2200. CC: none.
Moraira is on the coast, just a few kilometres south-east of Teulada.

TOLEDO 8D

Camping El Greco Ctra Puebla de Montalban s/n, 45004 Toledo.
Tel 925 220090, Fax 925 220090.
English spoken.
OPEN: all year. SIZE: 3 ha, 10 hot showers, 20 WCs, 1 CWP. ♿

Wonderful views; swimming pool nearby.
PRICES: (1996) Caravan with family 3691, Tent with two adults 2247. CC: Euro/Access, Visa.
Recommended. The campsite is 3 km from the centre of Toledo on the C502 towards Puebla de Montalban, at Km 190.

TORDESILLAS 8B

Camping Internacional El Astral 47100 Tordesillas.
Tel 983 770953, Fax 983 238193.
English spoken.
OPEN: 22/03–30/09. SIZE: 3 ha, 240 pitches (136 with elec, 40 statics), 16 hot showers, 20 WCs, 1 CWP. ♿

Tennis, mini-golf.
PRICES: (1996) Caravan with family 2787, Tent with two adults 1690. CC: Amex, Euro/Access, Visa.
Well signposted from the town. Follow signs to campsite or Parador Nacional.

TORREBLANCA 9A

Camping Mon Rossi 12596 Torrenostra.
Tel 964 420296, Fax 964 420296.
English spoken.
OPEN: 01/04–31/10. SIZE: 0.7 ha, 63 pitches (all with elec), 9 hot showers (charge), 12 WCs, 1 CWP. ♿

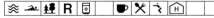

Shop at 0.3 km. Peaceful, family site.
PRICES: (1996) Tent with two adults 1800. CC: none.
Go south-east from Torreblanca, following the signs. Campsite is on the beach at Torrenostra.

Spain

TORRE-PACHECO   9C

Camping Los Alcazares Cartogonova
Mar Menor, Los Alcazares, Murcia.
Tel 968 575100, Fax 968 575225.
English spoken.
OPEN: all year. ☕ ♿

PRICES: (1996) Caravan with family 2893, Tent with
two adults 1711. CC: Visa.
*From Torre-Pacheco, east to Los Alcazares then
take N332 towards Cartagena for 2 km. (Km 21.)
Site is signposted.*

TORREVIEJA   9C

Camping Florantilles
03193 San Miguel de Salinas.
Tel 965 720456, Fax 966 723250.
English spoken.
OPEN: all year. SIZE: 6 ha, 226 pitches (all with
elec), 20 hot showers, 38 WCs, 226 CWPs. ☕

All full-service pitches; fitness centre with
qualified staff; tennis.
PRICES: (1996) Caravan with family 3350,
Tent with two adults 2200.
CC: Euro/Access, Visa.
*On the N332 Torrevieja bypass, in the direction of
Cartagena. South side of Torrevieja turn right
towards San Miguel de Salinas. Campsite is
situated approx 4 km ahead on the right.*

Camping Palm-Mar Km 36,5 Ctra Alicante-
Cartage, 03140 Guardamar del Segura.
Tel 965 728856. English spoken.
OPEN: 01/06–30/09. SIZE: 2 ha, 203 pitches
(all with elec), 26 hot showers (charge), 42 WCs,
1 CWP. ☕

PRICES: (1996) Caravan with family 3300,
Tent with two adults 2200. CC: none.
*11 km north of Torrevieja and 1 km before
reaching Guardamar del Segura. Campsite is well
signposted.*

TORROELLA DE MONTGRI   9B

Camping L'Emporda Estartit,
17258 Torroella de Montgri.
Tel 972 750649. English spoken.
OPEN: 14/06–11/09. SIZE: 7 ha, 200 pitches
(175 with elec), 16 hot showers, 12 WCs, 1 French
WC, 1 CWP. ☕

PRICES: Caravan with family 3290,
Tent with two adults 2156. CC: none.
*From Torroella de Montgri, take l'Estartit road for
4.8 km. Site is well signposted.*

TOSSA DE MAR   9B

Camping Cala Llevado Ctra Tossa a Lloret Km 3,
17320 Tossa de Mar.
Tel 972 340314, Fax 972 341187. English spoken.
OPEN: 01/05–30/09. SIZE: 13 ha, 180 pitches
(all with elec, 30 statics), 73 hot showers, 92 WCs,
6 CWPs. ☕ ♿

Water sports.
PRICES: (1996) Caravan with family 4345, Tent with
two adults 3040. CC: Amex, Euro/Access, Visa.
*3 km south of Tossa de Mar, campsite on beach,
well signposted.*
SEE ADVERTISEMENT

Camping Tossa 17320 Tossa de Mar.
Tel 972 340547, Fax 972 341531. English spoken.
OPEN: 01/04–30/09. SIZE: 10 ha, 150 pitches (all
with elec, 170 statics), 48 hot showers, 64 WCs. ☕

Shop at 3 km.
PRICES: (1996) Caravan with family 3875, Tent with
two adults 2600. CC: Amex, Euro/Access, Visa.
Site is easy to find and well signposted in Tossa.

VALDOVIÑO   8A

Camping Valdoviño Ctra de la Playa s/n,
15552 Valdoviño.
Tel 981 487076, Fax 981 486131. English spoken.
OPEN: 01/04–30/09. SIZE: 2 ha, 50 pitches (all with
elec), 16 hot showers, 10 WCs, 2 French WCs,
1 CWP. ♿

PRICES: (1996) Caravan with family 3640, Tent with
two adults 2280. CC: Amex, Visa.
*Valdoviño is on the Ferrol to Cedeira road, and
campsite is 700 m from centre of Valdoviño.
Follow camping signs.*

VALENCIA   9C

Camping Devesa Gardens Ctra El Saler Km 15,
46012 Valencia.
Tel 961 611136, Fax 961 611136.
OPEN: 01/06–30/09. SIZE: 142 pitches (all with elec,
4 statics), 8 hot showers, 24 WCs, 2 CWPs. ☕

Lovely green site.
PRICES: (1996) Caravan with family 3472, Tent with
two adults 1942. CC: Amex, Euro/Access, Visa.
*Go south from Valencia on the coast road for
approx 15 km. Site is close to beach.*

Camping Municipal El Saler 46012 Valencia.
Tel 961 830023, Fax 961 830024. English spoken.
OPEN: all year. SIZE: 10 ha, 500 pitches (450 with elec,
75 statics), 80 hot showers, 80 WCs, 8 CWPs. ☕

Spain

Restaurant at 1 km.
PRICES: (1996) Caravan with family 3365, Tent with two adults 2015. CC: Amex, Euro/Access, Visa. *10 km south of Valencia, through the village of El Saler towards the beach. Campsite entrance is to the right of La Rotonda del Paseo Maritimo.*

VALENCIA DE DON JUAN 8B

Camping Pico Verde
Valencia de Don Juan, 24200 Leon.
Tel 987 750525. English spoken.
OPEN: 15/06–13/09. SIZE: 2.7 ha, 185 pitches (190 with elec), 10 hot showers, 18 WCs, 1 CWP. **☎** **&**

Tennis, table tennis, playground.
PRICES: Caravan with family 2860, Tent with two adults 1720. CC: none.
Valencia de Don Juan is 36 km south of Leon on the N630. In Valencia de Don Juan, take the C621, Km 28,3.

VALLADOLID 8B

Camping Cubillas Ctra N620 Km 102, 47290 Cubillas Sta Maria.
Tel 983 585002, Fax 983 585016. English spoken.
OPEN: all year. SIZE: 4 ha, 150 pitches (all with

elec), 12 hot showers, 14 WCs, 2 CWPs. **☎**

PRICES: Caravan with family 2712, Tent with two adults 1712. CC: Amex, Euro/Access, Visa.
From Valladolid take N620, then exit at Km 102. Campsite signposted.

Camping El Plantio 47130 Simancas.
Tel 983 590082. English spoken.
OPEN: 15/06–20/09. SIZE: 1 ha, 50 pitches (all with elec, 50 statics), 6 hot showers, 14 WCs, 2 CWPs. **☎**

PRICES: (1996) Caravan with family 2745, Tent with two adults 1600. CC: Euro/Access, Visa.
From Valladolid go south-west on the E80 to Simancas and then follow signs.

VEGADEO 8A

Playa de Penarronda Barres-Castropol, 33794 Castropol.
Tel 985 623022. English spoken.
OPEN: 01/04–30/09. SIZE: 1.3 ha, 18 WCs, 1 CWP. **☎**

PRICES: (1996) Caravan with family 2475, Tent with two adults 1655. CC: Amex, Visa.
From Vegadeo go north to Castropol. The site is on the N634 between Castropol and Ribadeo.

Spain

VEJER DE LA FRONTERA 8C

Camping Vejer 11150 Vejer de la Frontera.
Tel 956 450098. English spoken.
OPEN: 15/06–15/09. SIZE: 1 ha, 45 pitches (36 with elec), 10 hot showers, 14 WCs, 2 French WCs, 1 CWP. 🔩

	📞	R	🗄	🍴		🏕		

Restaurant at 0.1 km.
PRICES: (1996) Caravan with family 4475,
Tent with two adults 2500. CC: none.
From Vejer go towards Algeciras for 4 km. The campsite is on the right, between two restaurants.

EL VENDRELL 9B

Camping La Plana Creixell, 43838 Vendrell.
Tel 977 662455, Fax 977 800304. English spoken.
OPEN: 01/05–30/09. SIZE: 0.72 ha, 53 pitches (all with elec), 8 hot showers, 8 WCs, 2 French WCs, 1 CWP. 🔩

≈	🏕	📞	R	🗄	🍴	📭		Ⓗ	

Restaurant at 0.3 km.
PRICES: (1996) Caravan with family 2975,
Tent with two adults 1900. CC: none.
From A2, take exit 31 to Coma-ruga (N340). Campsite is 6 km from Coma-ruga heading towards Tarragona, and 1 km after the Roman arch of Barà.

Camping Park Playa Bara Ctra N340 Km 1183, 43883 Roda de Bara.
Tel 977 802701, Fax 977 800456.
English spoken.
OPEN: 10/03–30/09. SIZE: 14 ha, 900 pitches (all with elec, 80 statics), 121 hot showers, 146 WCs, 6 CWPs. 🔩 ♿

≈	🏕	📞	R	🗄	🍴	📭	✖	🏕	Ⓗ

PRICES: (1996) Caravan with family 4930,
Tent with two adults 3280. CC: none.
From El Vendrell take A7, then exit 31 towards Tarragona over N340. After 4 km, entrance to campsite is by Roman arch.

Camping Santa Oliva Ctra Jaume Balmes 122, 43710 Santa Oliva.
Tel 977 661252. English spoken.
OPEN: all year. SIZE: 1.9 ha, 140 pitches (all with elec), 8 hot showers, 19 WCs, 1 CWP. 🔩

	📞		🗄		📭		🏕	Ⓗ	

Shop at 0.8 km. Restaurant at 0.3 km. Tennis, football, children's playground; barbecues and social evenings.
PRICES: (1996) Caravan with family 3200,
Tent with two adults 2000. CC: Amex, Euro/Access, Visa.
Towards Valls on N340, turn right to Santa Oliva/Sant Jaume dels Domenys. Right again into village. Site is well signposted

VIGO 8A

Camping Islas Cies Islas Cies,
Ria de Vigo, 36200 Vigo.
Tel 986 438358. English spoken.
OPEN: 15/06–15/09. SIZE: 3 ha, 20 hot showers, 20 WCs. 🔩

≈	🏕	📞	R		🐟	📭	✖		⚠	🐕

Tents only.
PRICES: (1996) Tent with two adults 1555.
CC: Amex, Visa.
The campsite is on the Islas Cies and is not accessible to vehicles. Boats leave from Vigo every hour between 0900 and 1900.

Camping Playa America 36350 Nigran.
Tel 986 365404, Fax 986 365404.
English spoken.
OPEN: 09/04–30/10. SIZE: 4 ha, 200 pitches (all with elec), 52 hot showers, 58 WCs. 🔩 ♿

≈	🏕	🔧		🗄	🐟	📭	✖	🏕	Ⓗ

Shop at 0.2 km. Sea 300 m.
PRICES: (1996) Caravan with family 3572,
Tent with two adults 2242. CC: Visa.
Recommended campsite. From Vigo go south for 12.9 km towards Bayona.

VILANOVA I LA GELTRU 9B

Camping Mar de Cunit Tarragona, 43881 Cunit.
Tel 977 674058, Fax 934 875282.
English spoken.
OPEN: 20/05–30/09. SIZE: 2 ha, 196 pitches (120 with elec), 10 hot showers, 16 WCs, 2 CWPs. 🔩

≈	🏕	🔧	R		🍴	📭	✖		Ⓗ

PRICES: (1996) Caravan with family 3286, Tent with two adults 2173. CC: none.
From Vilanova i La Geltru take C246 towards the beach and campsite is beside the sea.

Camping Vilanova Park Ctra Arboc, Apartado 64, 08800 Vilanova i La Geltru.
Tel 938 933402, Fax 938 935528. English spoken.
OPEN: all year. SIZE: 35 ha, 1000 pitches (all with elec, 110 statics), 64 hot showers, 103 WCs, 4 CWPs. 🔩 ♿

	📞	R	🗄	🍴	📭	✖	🏕	Ⓗ	

Tennis, disco.
PRICES: (1996) Caravan with family 4600,
Tent with two adults 3200. CC: Visa.
Follow signs in town. (10% discount for RAC members staying over 5 days).

VILLAJOYOSA 9C

Camping Hercules Ctra Nac 332, Km 141, Aptdo de Correos 42, 03570 Villajoyosa.
Tel 965 891343. English spoken.
OPEN: all year. SIZE: 6.3 ha, 457 pitches (all with elec, 46 statics), 12 hot showers, 60 WCs, 4 CWPs. 🔩

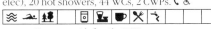

Restaurant at 1 km.
PRICES: (1996) Caravan with family 3100, Tent with two adults 1960. CC: Euro/Access, Visa.
2 km from Villajoyosa on road to Alicante.

Camping La Cala Poniente, 03500 Benidorm.
Tel 965 851461, Fax 965 851543. English spoken.
OPEN: all year. SIZE: 3 ha, 200 pitches (all with elec), 20 hot showers, 44 WCs, 2 CWPs. ℓ ⅙

PRICES: Caravan with family 3700,
Tent with two adults 2250. CC: none.
From the Alicante to Benidorm road, turn off at Poniente Beach sign and campsite is about 1 km on the right.

Camping Sertorium Ptda Torres 30 Villajoyosa, Alicante Aptdo de Correos 74, 03570 Villajoyosa.
Tel 965 891599, Fax 966 851114. English spoken.
OPEN: all year. SIZE: 6 ha, 436 pitches (all with elec, 52 statics), 33 hot showers, 56 WCs, 4 French WCs, 3 CWPs. ℓ

PRICES: Caravan with family 3741, Tent with two adults 2307. CC: Amex, Euro/Access, Visa.
Between Villajoyosa and Benidorm on the N332 Km 141. Well signposted.

VINAROZ   9A

Camping Sol de Riu Playa Partida Deveses, 12500 Vinaroz.
Tel 964 454917, Fax 964 454917. English spoken.
OPEN: all year. SIZE: 5 ha, 274 pitches (216 with elec), 26 hot showers, 36 WCs, 3 CWPs. ℓ ⅙

PRICES: (1996) Caravan with family 2730,
Tent with two adults 1790. CC: none.
On the coast, 6 km north of Vinaroz on the N340. Well signposted.

VIVEIRO   8A

Camping Viveiro 27850 Viveiro.
Tel 982 560004, Fax 982 560004.
OPEN: 01/06–30/09. SIZE: 2 ha, 70 pitches (all with elec), 28 hot showers, 24 WCs, 1 CWP. ℓ

Restaurant at 0.3 km.
PRICES: (1996) Caravan with family 2975, Tent with two adults 1700. CC: Euro/Access, Visa.
About 500 m from Viveiro, well signposted.

Spain

SWEDEN

The largest of the Scandinavian countries, sparsely populated Sweden is still half-covered in forest. It is said that God forgot to properly divide the land from the water here: off its long indented eastern coastline are some 20 000 islands, while the country as a whole boasts 100 000 lakes. Northern Sweden stretches up into the Arctic Circle, but its southern tip is on the same line of latitude as Newcastle.

Leaving England from Newcastle or Harwich, you arrive at Gothenburg, where the Göta Canal begins its journey to the Baltic. Avoid the temptation to ignore Gothenburg: a wander on foot or by boat around its old canals – as well as out to the island fortress of Nya Älvsborg – will make an excellent introduction to your Swedish holiday.

After Gothenburg, Stockholm, via a variety of alternative routes: the most direct one roughly follows the line of the 600-km-long Göta Canal; a longer, more northerly route passes through the province of Dalarna, described as the 'true heart of Sweden'.

Stockholm is known as the 'Venice of the North', and with so much to see, the Stockholm Card is recommended: available for 1, 2 or 3 days, this gives entry to 50 places of interest, bus tours, boat trips and public transport pass.

Emergency numbers

Police, Fire Brigade and Ambulance 112

Warning information

Carrying a warning triangle recommended

Blood Alcohol Legal Limit 20 mg

ÅNÄSET 10D

Lufta Camping 91534 Ånäset.
Tel 0934 20488/20215, Fax 0934 20488/20203. English spoken.
OPEN: 30/04–30/09. SIZE: 19 ha, 200 pitches (100 with elec), 10 hot showers, 13 WCs, 2 CWPs. &

Shop at 1.5 km.
PRICES: (1996) Caravan with family 130, Tent with two adults 70. CC: Euro/Access, Visa.
Halfway between Umeå and Skellefteå on the E4.

ÅRJÄNG 11A

Camping Sommarvik Fritidscenter
Sommarvik, 67200 Årjäng.
Tel 0573 12060, Fax 0573 12048. English spoken.
OPEN: all year. SIZE: 14 ha, 200 pitches (150 with elec, 30 statics), 15 hot showers (charge), 23 WCs, 2 CWPs. & &

Canoes, windsurfing, cycling, fishing, rowing boats, motorboats.
PRICES: Caravan with family 150, Tent with two adults 90. CC: Amex, Euro/Access, Visa.
On the eastern shore of Västra Silen lake in the Dasland canal lake system.

ARVIDSJAUR 10D

Camp Gileas Box 154, Jarnvagsgatan 611, 93300 Arvidsjaur.
Tel 0960 13420, Fax 0960 10615. English spoken.
OPEN: all year. SIZE: 10 ha, 40 pitches (81 with elec), 31 hot showers (charge), 31 WCs, 2 CWPs. &

Shop at 1 km. Restaurant at 1 km.
PRICES: (1996) Caravan with family 130, Tent with two adults 100. CC: Amex, Euro/Access, Visa.
Campsite is in the centre of Arvidsjaur and well signposted.

ÅSELE 10C

Åsele Camping & Stugby Norrstrand, 91060 Åsele.
Tel 0941 10904, Fax 0941 10081. English spoken.
OPEN: 01/06–31/08. SIZE: 10 ha, 200 pitches (42 with elec), 18 hot showers, 30 WCs, 1 CWP. & &

Shop at 0.5 km. Sauna; canoes for hire.

PRICES: (1996) Caravan with family 110, Tent with two adults 80. CC: Amex, Euro/Access, Visa. *Campsite is in northern outskirts of Åsele, very well signposted.*

BÅSTAD 11C

Hemmeslovs Camping 26940 Båstad.
Tel 0431 74455, Fax 0431 74653. English spoken.
OPEN: 29/04–28/08. SIZE: 3 ha, 150 pitches (100 with elec), 8 hot showers (charge), 11 WCs, 1 CWP. **C**

Restaurant at 1 km.
PRICES: Caravan with family 120,
Tent with two adults 95. CC: none.
Signposted from the 115 between the E6 and Båstad.

Torekovs Campingplats 26093 Torekov.
Tel 0431 64525, Fax 0431 64625. English spoken.
OPEN: 13/04–22/09. SIZE: 12 ha, 400 pitches (350 with elec, 100 statics), 26 hot showers, 30 WCs, 4 CWPs. **C &**

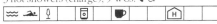

PRICES: (1996) Caravan with family 205, Tent with two adults 170. CC: Euro/Access, Visa.
A few km west of Båstad. Follow campsite signs.

BOLLNÄS 11A

Vevlingestrand Box 112, 82113 Bollnäs.
Tel 0278 12684. English spoken.
OPEN: 01/06–15/08. SIZE: 60 pitches (37 with elec), 3 hot showers (charge), 9 WCs. **C &**

Shop at 2 km. Restaurant at 3 km. Fishing, nature trail.
PRICES: (1996) Caravan with family 110,
Tent with two adults 900. CC: Visa.
3 km east of Bollnäs.

DEGERFORS 11A

Degernas Camping Degerfors kommun, 69380 Degerfors.
Tel 0586 48366, Fax 0586 48386. English spoken.
OPEN: 01/05–07/09. SIZE: 7 ha, 80 pitches (48 with elec, 8 statics), 5 hot showers, 5 WCs. **&**

Shop at 3 km. Restaurant at 3 km.
PRICES: Caravan with family 140,
Tent with two adults 110. CC: Visa.
Degernas Camping is situated immediately to the north of Degerfors along road 273 and 205 by Lake Mockeln.

EKSJÖ 11C

Eksjö Camping 57536 Eksjö.
Tel 0381 10945, Fax 0381 14096. English spoken.

OPEN: all year. SIZE: 4 ha, 117 pitches (103 with elec), 6 hot showers (charge), 12 WCs, 1 CWP.

PRICES: (1996) Caravan with family 130, Tent with two adults 110. CC: Amex, Euro/Access, Visa.
1 km east of Eksjö, well signposted.

Movanta Camping Hult, 57592 Eksjö.
Tel 0381 30028, Fax 0381 30166. English spoken.
OPEN: 15/05–01/09. SIZE: 79 pitches (70 with elec), 6 hot showers (charge), 8 WCs. **C &**

Shop at 2.5 km.
PRICES: (1996) Caravan with family 120, Tent with two adults 100. CC: Euro/Access, Visa.
From Eksjö, 10 km east on route 33. At Hult follow signs to campsite, which is about 3 km north of route 33.

ESKILSTUNA 11A

Camping Vilsta 63590 Eskilstuna.
Tel 016 136227. English spoken.
OPEN: all year. SIZE: 6 ha, 136 pitches (70 with elec, 64 statics), 25 hot showers (charge), 25 WCs, 3 CWPs. **C &**

Shop at 1 km. Restaurant at 1.5 km.
PRICES: (1996) Caravan with family 130,
Tent with two adults 80. CC: none.
South of Eskilstuna, between routes 230 and 53.

FALUN 11A

Bjursbergets Camping Box 21, 79021 Bjursas.
Tel 023 51004, Fax 023 17796. English spoken.
OPEN: 01/12–30/04 & 01/06–30/09. SIZE: 7 ha, 150 pitches (130 with elec), 10 hot showers (charge), 12 WCs, 1 CWP.

Shop at 3 km. Restaurant at 2 km.
PRICES: (1996) Caravan with family 115,
Tent with two adults 90. CC: Euro/Access, Visa.
20 km north of Falun on route 80. Well signposted.

Lugnet Camping 79183 Falun.
Tel 023 83563, Fax 023 83322. English spoken.
OPEN: all year. SIZE: 4 ha, 330 pitches (138 with elec), 12 hot showers, 16 WCs, 1 CWP. **C &**

Shop at 2 km.
PRICES: (1996) Caravan with family 130,
Tent with two adults 110. CC: none.
Follow the signs to campsite from town.

GÄLLIVARE 10D

Gällivare Campingplats 98221 Gällivare.
Tel 0970 16545, Fax 0970 14990. English spoken.

Sweden

OPEN: 03/06–04/09. SIZE: 4.3 ha, 150 pitches (40 with elec), 6 hot showers, 10 WCs. **⚡ &**

Shop at 0.3 km. Restaurant at 1 km.
PRICES: (1996) Caravan with family 135, Tent with two adults 75. CC: Amex, Euro/Access, Visa.
Just outside Gällivare on route 88 towards Jokkmokk.

GÖTEBORG (GOTHENBURG) 11C

Krono Camping Göteborg/Åby Mölndal, 43162 Göteborg.
Tel 0318 78884, Fax 0317 760240. English spoken.
OPEN: all year. SIZE: 12 ha, 538 pitches (450 with elec), 34 hot showers, 36 WCs, 4 CWPs. &

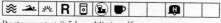

PRICES: Caravan with family 196, Tent with two adults 156. CC: Euro/Access, Visa.
Mölndal is just south of Göteborg, on the E6.

Lilleby Camping 42300 Torslanda.
Tel 031 560867, Fax 031 561605. English spoken.
OPEN: 01/05–01/09. SIZE: 3 ha, 180 pitches (100 with elec), 12 hot showers, 16 WCs, 2 CWPs. **⚡**

Restaurant at 7 km.
PRICES: (1996) Caravan with family 170, Tent with two adults 135. CC: Euro/Access, Visa.
Take road 155, Torslanda to Öckero, then follow campsite signs.

Lisebergs Camping Karralund Olbersgaten, 41655 Göteborg.
Tel 0312 52761, Fax 0312 54776. English spoken.
OPEN: all year. SIZE: 4.5 ha, 200 pitches (152 with elec), 27 hot showers, 32 WCs, 3 CWPs. **⚡ &**

Shop at 0.2 km. Children's playground; youth hostel; mini-golf and amusement park nearby.
PRICES: Caravan with family 215, Tent with two adults 170. CC: Euro/Access, Visa.
2 km north-east of Liseberg along Orgryte to Delsjon road. Signposted from E20 and E6 from south and north.

Tjornbrons Camping Centrograf ab, PO Box 22, 44074 Hjalteby.
Tel 0304 661290, Fax 0304 661942. English spoken.
OPEN: 01/05–15/09. SIZE: 3 ha, 450 pitches (250 with elec), 16 hot showers (charge), 45 WCs, 2 CWPs. **⚡ &**

Restaurant at 0.5 km. Mini-golf.
PRICES: Caravan with family 155, Tent with two adults 125. CC: Euro/Access, Visa.
From Göteborg go north on E6 for 55 km to road 160 to the big bridge at Tjornbron and the campsite is on the left.

GREBBESTAD 11A

Grebbestads Camping PL 6053, 45772 Grebbestad.
Tel 0525 61211, Fax 0525 14319. English spoken.
OPEN: all year. SIZE: 10 ha, 250 pitches (200 with elec, 250 statics), 18 hot showers (charge), 40 WCs, 2 CWPs. **⚡ &**

Shop at 1 km. Restaurant at 0.5 km.
PRICES: (1996) Caravan with family 130, Tent with two adults 105. CC: Euro/Access, Visa.
160 km north of Göteborg, directly south of Grebbestad.

HÄLLEKIS 11A

Kinnekulle Camping Strandvagen, 53394 Hällekis.
Tel 0510 44102, Fax 0510 44102.
English spoken.
OPEN: 01/05–30/09. SIZE: 8 ha, 100 pitches (50 with elec, 50 statics), 9 hot showers (charge), 15 WCs, 2 CWPs. **⚡ &**

Restaurant at 2 km. Tennis, fishing, mini-golf, pedal boats, motorboats.
PRICES: (1996) Caravan with family 130, Tent with two adults 110. CC: Euro/Access.
Go from Hällekis to Gamla Hamnen (Skyltat 4 km). Watch for signs to campsite.

HALLSTAHAMMAR 11A

Skantzö Bad Och Camping Box 507, 73427 Hallstahammar.
Tel 0220 24305, Fax 0220 24187.
English spoken.
OPEN: 15/05–30/08. SIZE: 4 ha, 160 pitches (150 with elec), 15 hot showers, 20 WCs, 1 CWP. **⚡ &**

Shop at 0.7 km. Tennis, flume, canoes.
PRICES: (1996) Caravan with family 120, Tent with two adults 90.
CC: Euro/Access, Visa.
Well signposted from Hallstahammar.

HÄRNÖSAND 11B

Snibbens Camping 87016 Ramvik.
Tel 0612 40505. English spoken.
OPEN: 23/05–01/09. SIZE: 4 ha, 70 pitches (all with elec), 6 hot showers, 8 WCs, 1 CWP. &

Shop at 1 km. Restaurant at 1 km.
PRICES: (1996) Caravan with family 125, Tent with two adults 100. CC: none.
From Härnösand, north on the E4 for 20 km to Ramvik.

Sweden (side tab)

Karlstad

HELSINGBORG 11C

Råå Vallar Camping Kustgatan, 25270 Råå.
Tel 0421 07680/1, Fax 0422 61010.
English spoken.
OPEN: all year. SIZE: 12 ha, 400 pitches (218 with
elec, 40 statics), 30 hot showers (charge), 73 WCs,
1 CWP. ℄ ⅄

Shop at 0.5 km. Sauna.
PRICES: (1996) Caravan with family 160,
Tent with two adults 105. CC: none.
From the E4, follow route 111 south to Råå.

JOKKMOKK 10D

Jokkmokks Turistcenter 96040 Jokkmokk.
Tel 0971 12370, Fax 0971 12476. English spoken.
OPEN: all year. SIZE: 7 ha, 220 pitches (160 with
elec), 14 hot showers, 13 WCs, 2 CWPs. ℄ ⅄

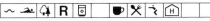

Shop at 3 km.
PRICES: (1996) Caravan with family 140,
Tent with two adults 90. CC: Euro/Access, Visa.
3 km south of Jokkmokk. Well signposted.

JÖNKÖPING 11C

Rosenlunds Camping Korallvagen 26,
55454 Jönköping.
Tel 036 122863, Fax 036 126687.
English spoken.
OPEN: all year. SIZE: 300 pitches (160 with elec),
14 hot showers (charge), 16 WCs, 2 CWPs. ⅄

PRICES: (1996) Caravan with family 145, Tent with
two adults 120. CC: Euro/Access, Visa.
*Drive towards Huskvarna and Stockholm on the
E4. Follow signs to Rosenlunds Camping and
Elmia.*

KALMAR 11C

Stenso Camping Stenso Kalmar, 39244 Kalmar.
Tel 0480 88803. English spoken.
OPEN: 01/04–29/10. SIZE: 350 ha, 16 hot showers,
35 WCs. ⅄

Swimming pool 2 km.
PRICES: (1996) Caravan with family 140, Tent with
two adults 115. CC: Amex, Euro/Access, Visa.

KAPELLSKÄR 11B

Kapellskärs Camping PL 985 Riddersholm,
76015 Graddo.
Tel 0176 44233. English spoken.
OPEN: 01/05–30/09. SIZE: 4 ha, 60 pitches (all with
elec), 9 hot showers (charge), 9 WCs, 1 CWP. ℄ ⅄

Restaurant at 1 km. Boats and sail boards for hire.
PRICES: (1996) Caravan with family 120, Tent with
two adults 60. CC: none.
*87 km north-east of Stockholm. Access from E18 to
Kapellskär.*

KARESUANDO 10B

Karesuando Campingsplats 98016 Karesuando.
Tel 0981 20139, Fax 0981 20381. English spoken.
OPEN: 01/06–15/09. SIZE: 2 ha, 24 pitches (12 with
elec), 4 hot showers, 8 WCs, 1 CWP. ℄

Shop at 3 km. Restaurant at 1.5 km.
PRICES: (1996) Caravan with family 100,
Tent with two adults 75. CC: none.
Well signposted from centre of village.

KARLSHAMN 11C

Kollevik Camping 37481 Karlshamn.
Tel 0454 81203, Fax 0454 84245. English spoken.
OPEN: 01/05–30/09. SIZE: 2 ha, 99 pitches
(76 with elec), 10 hot showers (charge), 14 WCs,
1 CWP. ℄ ⅄

PRICES: (1996) Caravan with family 145,
Tent with two adults 120. CC: none.
Situated in Karlshamn.

KARLSKRONA 11C

Dragsöbad Camping Box 205,
37124 Karlskrona.
Tel 0455 15354, Fax 0455 15354. English spoken.
OPEN: 30/04–04/09. SIZE: 7 ha, 250 pitches
(176 with elec), 10 hot showers (charge), 26 WCs,
1 CWP. ℄ ⅄

Shop at 0.5 km.
PRICES: (1996) Caravan with family 145,
Tent with two adults 120. CC: none.
*Follow signs to Dragsö. 2.5 km from the city of
Karlskrona.*

KARLSTAD 11A

Björkebo Camping Gravol 72, 68051 Stöllet.
Tel 0563 85086, Fax 0563 85111. English spoken.
OPEN: all year. SIZE: 4 ha, 100 pitches (50 with
elec), 6 hot showers (charge), 14 WCs, 2 French
WCs, 1 CWP. ℄ ⅄

Shop at 7 km. Restaurant at 10 km.
PRICES: (1996) Caravan with family 120,
Tent with two adults 100. CC: none.
115 km north of Karlstad on route 62.

Bomsta Badens Camping HB PL 8951,
65346 Karlstad.
Tel 0545 35068, Fax 0545 3575. English spoken.
OPEN: 01/05–26/09. SIZE: 9 ha, 250 pitches
(190 with elec, 110 statics), 16 hot showers
(charge), 16 WCs, 1 French WC, 1 CWP. 🚻 ♿

Shop at 4 km. Own 800 m sandy beach.
PRICES: (1996) Caravan with family 160, Tent with
two adults 110. CC: Euro/Access, Visa.
9 km west of Karlstad, near Lake Vänern.

Skutbergets Camping 65346 Karlstad.
Tel 0545 35139, Fax 0545 35170. English spoken.
OPEN: all year. SIZE: 15 ha, 350 pitches (230 with
elec, 50 statics), 18 hot showers (charge), 25 WCs,
2 CWPs. 🚻 ♿

PRICES: (1996) Caravan with family 160, Tent with
two adults 110. CC: Euro/Access, Visa.
*Skutbergets Camping is situated 7 km west of
Karlstad centre. Turn off from E18.*

KATRINEHOLM 11A

Djulo Camping 64192 Katrineholm.
Tel 0150 57242, Fax 0150 57242. English spoken.
OPEN: 01/05–30/08. SIZE: 60 pitches (all with elec,
5 statics), 11 hot showers (charge), 13 WCs,
2 CWPs. 🚻 ♿

PRICES: (1996) Caravan with family 125,
Tent with two adults 95. CC: none.
From Katrineholm, follow the E52 south for 2 km.

KIRUNA 10B

Bjorklidens Camping 98193 Bjorkliden.
Tel 0980 40040, Fax 0980 41080. English spoken.
OPEN: 01/02–31/10. SIZE: 33 pitches (79 with elec),
6 hot showers (charge), 11 WCs, 1 CWP. 🚻

Enjoy the midnight sun!
PRICES: (1996) Caravan with family 120, Tent with
two adults 60. CC: Amex, Euro/Access, Visa.
*100 km north-west of Kiruna on route 98; a
spectacularly beautiful road going through the
mountains and heading towards the Norwegian
fjords.*

LANDSKRONA 11C

Borstahusens Camping Campingvägen,
26161 Landskrona.
Tel 0418 10837, Fax 0418 22042.
English spoken.
OPEN: 03/04–08/09. SIZE: 5 ha, 450 pitches
(300 with elec, 100 statics), 20 hot showers,
48 WCs, 3 CWPs. ♿

PRICES: (1996) Caravan with family 130,
Tent with two adults 105. CC: none.
2 km north of Landskrona. Well signposted.

LEKSAND 11A

Vastanviksbadets Camping Vastanvik 180,
79392 Leksand.
Tel 0247 34201, Fax 0247 13133. English spoken.
OPEN: 23/04–28/09. SIZE: 4.5 ha, 120 pitches
(69 with elec, 1 static), 10 hot showers, 12 WCs,
10 French WCs, 1 CWP. 🚻

Fishing, boating, canoe and cycle hire.
PRICES: Caravan with family 145, Tent with two
adults 115. CC: Euro/Access, Visa.
*4 km west of Leksand towards Siljansnäs. Located
on Lake Siljan.*

LINDESBERG 11A

Kalmarslunds Camping Forwabodia,
71191 Lindesberg.
Tel 0581 52076, Fax 0581 81169. English spoken.
OPEN: all year. SIZE: 20 ha, 125 pitches (50 with
elec), 8 hot showers, 6 WCs. ♿

Shop at 5 km. Restaurant at 5 km.
PRICES: (1996) Caravan with family 110,
Tent with two adults 110. CC: none.
Follow signposts to site from Lindesberg.

LINKÖPING 11C

Glyttinge Camping Berggardsvagen,
58249 Linköping.
Tel 0131 74928, Fax 0131 75923. English spoken.
OPEN: 01/05–28/09. SIZE: 66 ha, 200 pitches
(125 with elec), 9 hot showers, 17 WCs,
28 CWPs. 🚻 ♿

Restaurant at 3 km.
PRICES: (1996) Caravan with family 170, Tent with
two adults 140. CC: Amex, Euro/Access, Visa.
Follow the signs from main road.

LJUNGBY 11C

Ljungby Campingplats 34100 Ljungby.
Tel 0372 10350, Fax 0372 12235.
English spoken.
OPEN: 30/04–30/09. SIZE: 4.5 ha.

PRICES: (1996) Caravan with family 125, Tent with
two adults 100. CC: Euro/Access, Visa.
*North of Ljungby, turn off E4 and campsite is
about 2 km.*

LUDVIKA 11A

Ludvika Camping Box 1655, 77194 Ludvika.
Tel 0240 19935. English spoken.
OPEN: 28/06–08/08. SIZE: 4 ha, 100 pitches (40 with elec), 6 hot showers (charge), 15 WCs, 3 CWPs. &

Shop at 1 km. Restaurant at 2 km.
PRICES: (1996) Caravan with family 110,
Tent with two adults 90. CC: none.
On route 60, south of Ludvika; at OK petrol station turn south towards Malingsbo and campsite is 2 km.

MARIESTAD 11A

Askeviksbadets Camping & Stugby
Askeviksbadet, 54066 Sjotorp.
Tel 0501 51409, Fax 0501 51553. English spoken.
OPEN: 26/04–31/08. SIZE: 1 ha, 60 pitches (42 with elec, 30 statics), 4 hot showers, 6 WCs, 1 CWP. ℓ

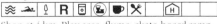

Shop at 6 km. Boats and bikes for hire.
PRICES: (1996) Caravan with family 150, Tent with two adults 120. CC: Euro/Access, Visa.
25 km north-east of Mariestad and 6 km north of Sjotorp, Gota Kanal. On the route 64.

MELLERUD 11A

Swe Camp Vita Sandars Camping
Box 14, 46421 Mellerud.
Tel 0530 12260, Fax 0530 12934. English spoken.
OPEN: all year. SIZE: 14 ha, 14 hot showers (charge), 19 WCs, 2 CWPs. ℓ &

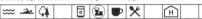

Shop at 4 km. Play area, flume, skate-board ramp.
PRICES: Caravan with family 160, Tent with two adults 130. CC: Euro/Access, Visa.
Mellerud is on route 45.

MORA 11A

Mora Camping 79200 Mora.
Tel 0250 15352, Fax 0250 12785. English spoken.
OPEN: all year. SIZE: 20 ha, 600 pitches (155 with elec), 23 hot showers, 31 WCs, 3 CWPs. ℓ &

Shop at 0.4 km.
PRICES: Caravan with family 130, Tent with two adults 100. CC: Amex, Euro/Access, Visa.
Well signposted in Mora.

NORA 11A

Trangbo Camping 71322 Nora.
Tel 0587 12361, Fax 0587 10538. English spoken.
OPEN: 05/05–01/09. SIZE: 3.75 ha, 100 pitches (40 with elec, 8 statics), 6 hot showers, 8 WCs. ℓ &

Restaurant at 1 km.
PRICES: Caravan with family 125,
Tent with two adults 100. CC: none.
Nora is approx 35 km north-west of Orebro. Site is 1 km from centre of Nora and well signposted.

Uskavi Camping Uskavi Fritidscenter, 71394 Nora.
Tel 0587 330025, Fax 0587 330370. English spoken.
OPEN: 01/05–30/09. SIZE: 14 ha, 45 pitches (24 with elec), 6 hot showers, 10 WCs. ℓ &

Shop at 5 km. Restaurant at 5 km.
PRICES: (1996) Caravan with family 125, Tent with two adults 100. CC: Euro/Access, Visa.
From Nora, drive north along the Lake of Three Seas. Follow sign to Storå for 15 km.

NORRKÖPING 11A

Kolmardens Camping 61834 Kolmarden.
Tel 0113 98250, Fax 0113 97081. English spoken.
OPEN: 22/04–08/09. SIZE: 10 ha, 450 pitches (160 with elec), 22 hot showers (charge), 40 WCs, 4 CWPs. ℓ &

PRICES: (1996) Caravan with family 145, Tent with two adults 120. CC: Euro/Access, Visa.
22 km north from Norrköping, near Braviken. Follow signs to the zoo (from the E4).

NORSJO 10D

Rannuddens Camping och Stugby 93500 Norsjo.
Tel 0918 20135, Fax 0918 20135. English spoken.
OPEN: 01/06–15/09. SIZE: 10 ha, 80 pitches (54 with elec), 7 hot showers, 9 WCs, 2 CWPs. ℓ &

Shop at 1 km. Restaurant at 6 km.
PRICES: (1996) Caravan with family 100,
Tent with two adults 55. CC: none.
Between Skellefteå and Lycksele, routes 370 and 365.

ÖLAND

BORGHOLM 11C

Krono Camping Böda Sand,
38075 Byxelkrok, Öland.
Tel 0485 22200, Fax 0485 22376. English spoken.
OPEN: 11/05–28/08. SIZE: 52 ha, 1220 pitches (850 with elec, 20 statics), 78 hot showers, 90 WCs, 6 CWPs. ℓ &

PRICES: (1996) Caravan with family 190, Tent with two adults 160. CC: Amex, Euro/Access, Visa.
From Kalmar, cross bridge to island of Öland. Go 90 km north and turn left at the third roundabout.

Sweden

ÖLAND RESORTS CONTINUED

Sandbybadets Camping
38074 Borgholm, Öland.
Tel 0485 20322, Fax 0485 20941. English spoken.
OPEN: 15/05–30/08. SIZE: 3 ha, 230 pitches
(180 with elec), 10 hot showers (charge), 20 WCs,
1 CWP. &

PRICES: (1996) Caravan with family 155, Tent with
two adults 125. CC: Amex, Euro/Access, Visa.
*45 km north of Borgholm. 1 km after the
roundabout at Hogby church.*

FÄRJESTADEN 11C

Mollstorps Camping 38690 Färjestaden, Öland.
Tel 0485 31165, Fax 0485 31086. English spoken.
OPEN: 09/04–09/10. SIZE: 15 ha, 300 pitches
(230 with elec), 14 hot showers (charge), 30 WCs,
20 CWPs. &

PRICES: (1996) Caravan with family 160, Tent with
two adults 130. CC: Amex, Euro/Access, Visa.
*Can be seen from the bridge to Öland Island.
Turn south to the right and to the right again.*

KÖPINGSVIK 11C

Klintagarden Camping Box 64,
38702 Köpingsvik, Öland.
Tel 0485 72240, Fax 0485 72047.
English spoken.
OPEN: 01/04–30/09. SIZE: 22 ha, 100 pitches
(50 with elec, 60 statics), 6 hot showers (charge),
12 WCs, 1 CWP. &

Tennis, bicycles.
PRICES: Caravan with family 160, Tent with two
adults 130. CC: Amex, Euro/Access, Visa.
Well signposted.

END OF ÖLAND RESORTS

OREBRO 11A

Gustavsviks Campingplats
70229 Orebro.
Tel 0191 96950/910, Fax 0191 96960/990.
English spoken.
OPEN: 07/05–07/09. SIZE: 11.5 ha, 720 pitches
(488 with elec, 20 statics), 30 hot showers,
32 WCs, 5 CWPs. &

PRICES: (1996) Caravan with family 215,
Tent with two adults 180.
CC: Amex, Euro/Access, Visa.
*Follow signs to Orebro and campsite from
E18/E20.*

RÄTTVIK 11A

Rättviksparken PL 2004, 79532 Rättvik.
Tel 0248 56100, Fax 0248 12660. English spoken.
OPEN: all year. SIZE: 24 ha, 300 pitches (175 with
elec), 16 hot showers (charge), 16 WCs, 1 CWP.
& &

Shop at 1 km. Camping huts also available.
PRICES: (1996) Caravan with family 140, Tent with
two adults 110. CC: Amex, Euro/Access, Visa.
Situated 1 km from Rättvik. Well signposted.

Siljanbadet Camping Strandv 1, Box 105,
79522 Rättvik.
Tel 0248 51691, Fax 0248 51689. English spoken.
OPEN: 30/04–04/10. SIZE: 6 ha, 300 pitches (225 with
elec), 24 hot showers, 29 WCs, 4 CWPs. & &

Restaurant at 1 km.
PRICES: (1996) Caravan with family 150, Tent with
two adults 120. CC: Euro/Access, Visa.
Situated on the beach near the centre of Rättvik.

SÄFFLE 11A

Duse Udde Campingplats 66180 Säffle.
Tel 0533 42000, Fax 0533 81594. English spoken.
OPEN: 09/05–11/09. SIZE: 5 ha, 300 pitches
(100 with elec), 16 hot showers (charge), 19 WCs,
2 CWPs. & &

PRICES: (1996) Caravan with family 140, Tent with
two adults 90. CC: Amex, Euro/Access, Visa.
Well signposted from Säffle.

SKELLEFTEÅ 10D

Skellefteå Camping 93141 Skellefteå.
Tel 0910 18855, Fax 0910 701890. English spoken.
OPEN: all year. SIZE: 4.5 ha, 400 pitches (277 with
elec), 20 hot showers, 40 WCs, 5 CWPs. & &

PRICES: (1996) Caravan with family 150, Tent with
two adults 100. CC: Euro/Access, Visa.
1 km north of Skellefteå on the left-hand side.

SODERHAMN 11A

Moheds Campingplats 82006 Soderala.
Tel 0270 45233, Fax 0270 45326. English spoken.
OPEN: all year. SIZE: 180 pitches (120 with elec,
60 statics), 14 hot showers, 10 WCs, 1 CWP. & &

Shop at 5 km. Youth hostel also on site.
PRICES: (1996) Caravan with family 125, Tent with
two adults 80. CC: Euro/Access, Visa.
*From Söderhamn, route 301 towards Bollnas for
12 km and then follow signs to campsite.*

Sweden

SOLLERÖN 11A

Sollerö Camping 79043 Sollerön.
Tel 0250 22255, Fax 0250 22615. English spoken.
OPEN: 15/06–15/08. SIZE: 160 pitches (80 with elec,
3 statics), 12 hot showers (charge), 16 WCs,
1 CWP.

Shop at 1.5 km.
PRICES: (1996) Caravan with family 130, Tent with
two adults 100. CC: Euro/Access, Visa.
2 km south-west from the church at Sollerön.
Follow signs to the campsite.

STOCKHOLM 11B

Angby Camping 16155 Bromma.
Tel 083 70420, Fax 083 78226. English spoken.
OPEN: all year. SIZE: 6 ha, 150 pitches (160 with
elec), 16 hot showers (charge), 21 WCs, 2 French
WCs, 2 CWPs.

Restaurant at 0.3 km. Refurbished in 1994.
PRICES: (1996) Caravan with family 155, Tent with
two adults 130. CC: none.
10 km from the centre of Stockholm. Take route
275 towards Vällingby. After 8 km, turn left
towards Drotningholm. Drive 1 km and follow the
signs.

Bredang Camping 12731 Skarholmen.
Tel 089 77071, Fax 0870 87262. English spoken.
OPEN: all year. SIZE: 12 ha, 420 pitches (140 with
elec), 22 hot showers, 34 WCs, 2 CWPs.

PRICES: (1996) Caravan with family 180, Tent with
two adults 145. CC: Euro/Access, Visa.
From the E4, exit at Bredang and follow signs to
the campsite. 5 minutes' walk from the Bredang
underground station.

STRÖMSUND 10C

Forsnäs Camping 91200 Vilhelmina.
Tel 0940 33012, Fax 0940 33068. English spoken.
OPEN: 05/05–15/09. SIZE: 1.5 ha, 25 pitches
(20 with elec).

Shop at 7 km. Restaurant at 7 km.
PRICES: Caravan with family 110,
Tent with two adults 80. CC: none.
From Stromsund take route 45 north-east to
Vilhelmina (132 km).

Strömsund Camping Box 500,
83300 Strömsund.
Tel 0670 16410, Fax 0670 16105. English spoken.
OPEN: all year. SIZE: 4 ha, 200 pitches (115 with
elec), 13 hot showers (charge), 12 WCs,
2 CWPs.

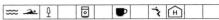

Shop at 0.2 km. Restaurant at 1.5 km.
PRICES: (1996) Caravan with family 125, Tent with
two adults 100. CC: Euro/Access, Visa.
Signposted from Strömsund.

SUNDSVALL 11A

Bergafjardens Camping 86020 Njurunda.
Tel 060 34598, Fax 060 561675. English spoken.
OPEN: 15/05–31/08. SIZE: 2 ha, 200 pitches
(180 with elec), 17 hot showers (charge), 20 WCs,
2 CWPs.

PRICES: (1996) Caravan with family 125, Tent with
two adults 75. CC: Euro/Access, Visa.
From E4 going north, turn right just before the
bridge over Ljungan in Njurundabommen.
Follow signs to the campsite and Lorudden. Well
signposted.

Flasians Camping Norrstigen 15,
85013 Sundsvall.
Tel 0605 54475, Fax 0601 24022. English spoken.
OPEN: 01/04–30/09. SIZE: 8 ha, 120 pitches
(92 with elec, 20 statics), 10 hot showers, 16 WCs,
4 French WCs, 3 CWPs.

PRICES: Caravan with family 130, Tent with two
adults 70. CC: Amex, Euro/Access.
3 km south of Sundsvall.

SYSSLEBÄCK 11A

Sysslebäcks Fiskes Camping Box 55,
68060 Sysslebäck.
Tel 0564 10514, Fax 0564 10196. English spoken.
OPEN: all year. SIZE: 4 ha, 95 pitches (65 with elec),
9 hot showers (charge), 11 WCs.

Shop at 3 km. Restaurant at 3 km.
PRICES: (1996) Caravan with family 135,
Tent with two adults 80. CC: Euro/Access, Visa.
Between route 62 and the River Klaralven in
Sysslebäck.

TORSBY 11A

Bredvikens Camping 68533 Torsby.
Tel 0560 71095. English spoken.
OPEN: 15/05–15/09. SIZE: 9 ha, 150 pitches
(116 with elec), 8 hot showers (charge), 17 WCs,
15 French WCs, 2 CWPs.

Shop at 5 km. Restaurant at 5 km.
PRICES: (1996) Caravan with family 125, Tent with
two adults 100. CC: Euro/Access, Visa.
Well signposted from Torsby.

Sweden

TRELLEBORG 11C

Dalabadets Campingplats 23132 Trelleborg.
Tel 0410 14905. English spoken.
OPEN: all year. SIZE: 250 pitches (142 with elec),
10 hot showers (charge), 23 WCs, 1 CWP. &

≋ ⚓ ♀ 🔟 🍴 💌 ✕ ⒣

PRICES: (1996) Caravan with family 135, Tent with
two adults 112. CC: Amex, Euro/Access, Visa.
The campsite is situated about 2.5 km east of
Trelleborg between the sea and route no 9.

TROLLHÄTTAN 11C

Trollhättans Camping Hjulkvarnelund
Kungsportsvägen, 46184 Trollhättan.
Tel 0520 30613. English spoken.
OPEN: 01/06–31/08. SIZE: 2 ha, 150 pitches (44 with
elec, 8 statics), 8 hot showers, 16 WCs. &

~ ⚓ ⚙ 🔟 🍴 ⒣

Restaurant at 0.7 km. Tennis; swimming pool 0.2 km.
PRICES: (1996) Caravan with family 136,
Tent with two adults 136. CC: none.
1 km north of town centre.

ULRICEHAMN 11C

Prangens Camping Box 218, 52325 Ulricehamn.
Tel 0321 10001. English spoken.
OPEN: all year. SIZE: 3 ha, 220 pitches (141 with
elec, 30 statics), 8 hot showers (charge), 14 WCs,
1 CWP. & &

≋ ⚓ ⚙ R 🔟 🍵 💌 ⒣

Restaurant at 0.2 km.
PRICES: (1996) Caravan with family 135,
Tent with two adults 105. CC: none.
Campsite is located between Lake Asunden and
route 40 (from Göteborg to Jönköping) less than
1 km north of Ulricehamn.

UMEÅ 10D

Umeå Camping & Stugby
Nydala Fritidsomrade, 90184 Umeå.
Tel 0901 61660, Fax 0901 25720. English spoken.
OPEN: all year. SIZE: 15 ha, 14 hot showers, 40 WCs,
5 CWPs. &

≋ ⚓ ♀ R 🔟 🍵 ⒣

Shop at 1 km. Restaurant at 2 km.
PRICES: (1996) Caravan with family 125, Tent with
two adults 75. CC: Amex, Euro/Access, Visa.
6 km north of Umeå on the E4.

VÄSTERVIK 11C

Lysingsbadets Campingplats 59300 Västervik.
Tel 0490 36795, Fax 0490 36175. English spoken.
OPEN: all year. SIZE: 80 ha, 1000 pitches (540 with
elec, 50 statics). &

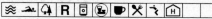

≋ ⚓ ⚙ R 🔟 🍵 💌 ✕ ⁑ ⒣

Shop at 1.5 km. Restaurant at 1 km.
PRICES: (1996) Caravan with family 205,
Tent with two adults 160. CC: Visa.
Follow signs to campsite from E22.

VÄXJÖ 11C

Evedals Camping 35233 Växjö.
Tel 0470 63034, Fax 0470 63122. English spoken.
OPEN: all year. SIZE: 3 ha, 165 pitches (122 with
elec), 6 hot showers (charge), 12 WCs, 1 CWP. ⁑ &

≋ ⚓ ⚙ R 🔟 🍵 ✕ ⒣

PRICES: Caravan with family 145, Tent with two
adults 120. CC: Amex, Euro/Access, Visa.
Signposts to campsite from Växjö.

VAXHOLM 11B

Ellboda Camping Ellboda, 18593 Vaxholm.
Tel 0854 131530, Fax 0854 135025.
English spoken.
OPEN: 15/05–15/09. SIZE: 12 ha, 100 pitches
(50 with elec), 9 hot showers, 13 WCs, 1 CWP. ⁑ &

≋ ⚓ ⚙ R 🔟 🍵 💌 ✕ ⒣

Shop at 6 km.
PRICES: (1996) Caravan with family 130, Tent with
two adults 100. CC: Euro/Access, Visa.
Ellboda is 30 km north-east of Stockholm. Turn
right off the E18 towards Vaxholm and drive for
8 km. Turn right again and campsite at Ellboda is
4 km, well signposted.

VEMDALEN 11A

Vemdals Campen 84092 Vemdalen.
Tel 0684 30200, Fax 0684 30462.
English spoken.
OPEN: all year. SIZE: 4 ha, 120 pitches (106 with
elec), 12 hot showers (charge), 18 WCs,
2 CWPs. ⁑ &

~ ⚓ ♀ R 🔟 🍴 💌 ✕ ⒣

PRICES: Caravan with family 125, Tent with two
adults 90. CC: Euro/Access, Visa.
1.5 km south-west of village.

YSTAD 11C

Sandskogens Camping Osterleden, 27160 Ystad.
Tel 0411 19270. English spoken.
OPEN: 27/04–15/09. SIZE: 8 ha, 350 pitches
(270 with elec), 16 hot showers (charge), 26 WCs,
2 CWPs. ⁑ &

≋ ⚓ ⚙ 🔟 🍵 💌 ✕ ⒣

Shop at 2 km.
PRICES: (1996) Caravan with family 140,
Tent with two adults 95. CC: Visa.
2 km east of Ystad on route 9 to Simrishamn.

SWITZERLAND

The history of Switzerland as a nation began in 1291 when representatives from the regions of Uri, Schwyz and Unterwalden met in a meadow on the edge of Lake Uri to pledge mutual assistance against the common enemy, the Austrian Emperors. Today, this confederation of cantons, the *Cantons helvétiques*, numbers 23.

Switzerland is known for its mountains, its banks, its engineering and its efficiency – this in spite of using four languages (French, German, Italian and Romansch). It is also punctuated by some very beautiful lakes.

Lake Lucerne lies at the heart of Switzerland, and the drive through the Alps from Lucerne to Lake Locarno on the Italian border is one of Switzerland's many scenic treats.

South west of Lucerne, Switzerland shares Lac Léman (often called Lake Geneva) with France. This is western Europe's largest lake, with ferry links between Geneva, Lausanne and Montreux.

To the north of Lac Léman, Lac Neuchâtel lies just below the French border parallel to the Jura mountains. Then north again and France, Germany and Switzerland meet on the Rhine at Basle, whose fine medieval city deserves a place on any itinerary.

As the Swiss and French share Lac Léman, so do the Swiss and Germans share the Bodensee, or Lake Constance, lying on the north-eastern Swiss border. The peaks here are lower but still afford mountain-railway and cable-car trips and wonderful walking.

Switzerland offers tremendous variety and makes an ideal holiday destination, no matter what the season.

Emergency numbers

For emergency numbers see the local directory

Warning information

Warning triangle must be carried

Blood alcohol legal limit 80 mg

AIGLE 18C

Camping Sémiramis 1854 Leysin.
Tel 025 341148, Fax 025 342029.
English spoken.
OPEN: all year. SIZE: 11.7 ha, 110 pitches (90 with elec, 50 statics), 9 hot showers, 14 WCs, 2 CWPs. ⌷

	⌷	R	▣	⛱	▨			⒣	

Restaurant at 0.2 km. Children's activities, tennis, skating; swimming pool 0.8 km.
PRICES: (1996) Caravan with family 48.40, Tent with two adults 30.50. CC: Amex, Euro/Access, Visa.
Leysin is just north-east of Aigle, off N11a. Site is well signposted.

ALTDORF 18B

Remo Camp Moosbad, 6460 Altdorf.
Tel 044 28541.
OPEN: all year. SIZE: 1 ha, 40 pitches (all with elec, 30 statics), 4 hot showers (charge), 6 WCs, 2 CWPs. ⌷

	⌷		▣	⛱		✕		⒣	

Walking/touring.
PRICES: (1996) Caravan with family 33, Tent with two adults 22. CC: Euro/Access.
Take the N2 Luzern to Gotthard road and exit at Altdorf. (From 23/3/96 Tel No: 041 8708541.)

AVENCHES 18A

Camping Plage Avenches 1580 Avenches.
Tel 037 751750, Fax 037 754469. English spoken.
OPEN: 01/04–30/09. SIZE: 8 ha, 700 pitches (all with elec, 500 statics), 26 hot showers, 47 WCs, 1 CWP. ⌷ ⅙

≈	⛵	⌷	R	▣	⛱	▨	✕			

PRICES: (1996) Caravan with family 42.00, Tent with two adults 27.00. CC: Euro/Access, Visa.
Drive towards Morat and turn left towards Salavaux-Plage.

BADEN 18B

Camping Sulz 5444 Küenten.
Tel 056 4964879, Fax 056 4964879.
English spoken.
OPEN: 15/03–31/10. SIZE: 2.5 ha, 20 pitches (all with elec). ⌷

~	⛵	⌷	R	▣	⛱	▨	✕	⌕		

PRICES: (1996) Caravan with family 27.00, Tent with two adults 18.00. CC: none.
Leave N1 at Baden-West and take road south towards Bremgarten for approx 12 km to Küenten. Follow signs to campsite.

BASEL (BASLE) 18A

Camping Waldhort Heideweg 16, 4153 Reinach.
Tel 061 7116429, Fax 061 3022481.
English spoken.
OPEN: 08/03–19/10. SIZE: 29 ha, 20 pitches
(all with elec, 130 statics), 12 hot showers
(charge), 20 WCs, 2 CWPs. ℓ &

Restaurant at 0.5 km. Children's playground.
PRICES: (1996) Caravan with family 31.10, Tent
with two adults 22.00. CC: Euro/Access, Visa.
*Going south from Basel on N18, take Reinach-
Nord exit after about 4 km. Campsite is well
signposted.*

BELLINZONA 18D

Camping Vera 6535 Roveredo.
Tel 092 821857, Fax 092 821898.
English spoken.
OPEN: all year. SIZE: 2.5 ha, 50 pitches (36 with
elec, 70 statics), 14 hot showers (charge), 11 WCs,
5 French WCs, 1 CWP. ℓ

Shop at 0.5 km. Tennis, canoeing.
PRICES: (1996) Caravan with family 51.50, Tent
with two adults 29.00. CC: Euro/Access, Visa.
*From Bellinzona go north-east on N13 and take
Roveredo-Calanca-Grono exit. Follow signs to site
at Roveredo.*

Parkcamping Riarena 6516 Cugnasco.
Tel 091 859 16 88, Fax 091 859 28 85.
English spoken.
OPEN: 01/04–20/10. SIZE: 3.2 ha, 170 pitches
(all with elec, 40 statics), 16 hot showers, 33 WCs,
2 CWPs. ℓ &

Playground, volley ball, barbecue; 10% discount
for stays over 10 nights.
PRICES: Caravan with family 48.50, Tent with two
adults 35.00. CC: Euro/Access, Visa.
*Exit Bellinzona south towards Locarno. Drive
10 km and at the roundabout, go towards Gudo-
Bellinzona. Follow signs to campsite at Cugnasco.*

TCS-Camping Molinazzo, 6500 Bellinzona.
Tel 091 829 1118, Fax 091 829 2355.
English spoken.
OPEN: 03/04–06/10. SIZE: 1 ha, 100 pitches
(all with elec, 20 statics), 4 hot showers, 9 WCs,
1 CWP. ℓ &

Good sports/leisure facilities on site and nearby.
PRICES: (1996) Caravan with family 40/10, Tent
with two adults 28.40. CC: Euro/Access, Visa.
*Exit N13/N2 at Bellinzona Nord exit and go
towards Bellinzona. Campsite is signposted.*

BERN (BERNE) 18A

Camping Eichholz 3084 Wabern.
Tel 031 9612602, Fax 031 9613526.
OPEN: 22/04–30/09. SIZE: 3.5 ha, 50 pitches
(all with elec), 6 hot showers (charge), 14 WCs,
1 CWP. ℓ &

Shop at 0.5 km.
PRICES: (1996) Caravan with family 33.70,
Tent with two adults 19.30. CC: none.
*Leave N1 at Bern-Ost and follow signs towards
airport. Campsite at Wabern is signposted.*

BIEL 18A

Camping Prêles 2515 Prêles.
Tel 032 3151716, Fax 032 3151716.
English spoken.
OPEN: all year. SIZE: 6 ha, 80 pitches (60 with elec),
14 hot showers (charge), 20 WCs, 3 CWPs. ℓ

Restaurant at 2 km.
PRICES: Caravan with family 35.20,
Tent with two adults 25.00. CC: none.
*Approaching from the north on N6, 3.6 km before
Biel turn right immediately after tunnel, then left
to Orvin, Lamboing and Prêles or Biel, Twann
and Prêles. Campsite is on far side of village.*

BRIG 18C

Camping Tropic 3911 Ried-Brig.
Tel 027 9232537. English spoken.
OPEN: 15/05–30/09. SIZE: 1 ha, 40 pitches (all with
elec), 2 hot showers (charge), 6 WCs. ℓ

PRICES: (1996) Caravan with family 26.00, Tent
with two adults 17.50. CC: Euro/Access.

BULLE 18C

Camping Les Sapins 1664 Epagny-Gruyères.
Tel 026 912 95 75.
OPEN: 01/05–30/09. SIZE: 2.5 ha, 30 pitches
(all with elec, 45 statics), 6 hot showers (charge),
7 WCs, 2 CWPs. ℓ &

Swimming pool 1 km.
PRICES: Caravan with family 26.00,
Tent with two adults 20.00. CC: none.
*From Bulle south on the 577 and look for the sign
for Château d'Oex, then Gruyères Molson.*

Camping-Caravaning du Lac 1643 Gumefens.
Tel 029 56162, Fax 029 52162. English spoken.
OPEN: 15/05–15/09. SIZE: 40 pitches (20 with elec,
110 statics), 5 hot showers (charge), 12 WCs,
1 CWP. ℓ

≈ ⚓ ⚲ | 🔲 🛠 🚿 ✕ | | ⊀ |

PRICES: (1996) Caravan with family 33.80,
Tent with two adults 24.90. CC: none.
8 km north of Bulle, towards Fribourg.

CHATEL-ST-DENIS 18C

TCS-Camping le Bivouac 1622 Les Paccots.
Tel 021 9487849, Fax 021 9487849. English spoken.
OPEN: all year. SIZE: 2 ha, 170 pitches (all with elec,
130 statics), 10 hot showers, 12 WCs, 1 CWP. ☏

~ ⚓ 🏠 R 🔲 🛠 🚿 ⎸ ❧ | |

Restaurant at 2 km.
PRICES: (1996) Caravan with family 34.20,
Tent with two adults 24.30. CC: none.
*From the motorway N12, take Châtel-St-Denis
exit, drive 1 km towards Les Paccots and the
campsite is on the left.*

CHUR 18B

Camping Pradafenz 7075 Churwalden.
Tel 081 382 19 21, Fax 081 382 19 21.
OPEN: 15/06–30/03. SIZE: 1.3 ha, 30 pitches (all with
elec, 120 statics), 6 hot showers, 14 WCs, 1 CWP. ☏

| | ⚲ R 🔲 | | | | | |

Shop at 0.2 km. Restaurant at 0.2 km. Swimming
pool 0.3 km.
PRICES: (1996) Caravan with family 38.30,
Tent with two adults 27.70. CC: none.
*Motorway exit Chur-Sud and head towards
Lanzerheide for 10 km to Churwalden. Campsite
next to chair-lift.*

Campingplatz Viamala AG 7430 Thusis.
Tel 081 651 24 72. English spoken.
OPEN: 01/05–30/09. SIZE: 4.5 ha, 100 pitches
(all with elec, 35 statics). ☏

~ ⚓ 🏠 R 🔲 🛠 🚿 | | |

Restaurant at 0.5 km. Swimming pool 0.3 km.
PRICES: Caravan with family 33.70,
Tent with two adults 24.80. CC: none.
Off N13, south of Chur near the river.

DISENTIS/MUSTER 18D

TCS-Camping Trun 7166 Trun.
Tel 081 943 16 66, Fax 081 943 31 49.
English spoken.
OPEN: 01/05–30/09. SIZE: 3.5 ha, 150 pitches
(50 with elec, 50 statics), 10 hot showers, 10 WCs,
1 CWP. ☏ ♿

~ ⚓ ⚲ | 🔲 🚿 🛒 ✕ | | |

Shop at 0.5 km. Tennis.
PRICES: (1996) Caravan with family 33.20,
Tent with two adults 24.80. CC: none.
*Trun is east of Disentis/Mustér on route 19.
Campsite is well signposted in Trun.*

FAIDO 18D

Camping Faido-Chiggiogna Gottardo
6799 Chiggiogna.
Tel 091 8661562, Fax 091 8662113. English spoken.
OPEN: all year. SIZE: 9 ha, 50 pitches (all with elec,
10 statics), 5 hot showers, 7 WCs, 3 French WCs,
1 CWP. ☏

~ ⚓ 🌧 R 🔲 🛠 | ✕ ❧ 🄷 | |

PRICES: Caravan with family 44.00, Tent with two
adults 25.00. CC: none.
*500 m north of Faido, off the N2. Site is well
signposted.*

FRUTIGEN 18C

Camping Frutigen 3741 Frutigen.
Tel 033 711149. English spoken.
OPEN: all year. SIZE: 1.5 ha, 70 pitches (60 with
elec, 20 statics). ☏

~ ⚓ ⚲ R 🔲 🛠 | | 🄷 | |

Shop at 0.5 km. Restaurant at 0.5 km. Children's
playground.
PRICES: (1996) Caravan with family 29.75,
Tent with two adults 21.60. CC: none.
*From Spiez on the N6 head south to Frutigen
which is at the junction of the two roads leading
to Kandersteg and Adelboden.*

Camping Ruedy-Hus 3715 Adelboden.
Tel 033 731454, Fax 033 731454. English spoken.
OPEN: 01/12–30/04 & 01/06–30/10. SIZE: 40 ha,
18 pitches (all with elec, 22 statics), 2 hot showers,
4 WCs. ☏

~ ⚓ ⚲ | | 🛠 🛒 ✕ ❧ | |

PRICES: (1996) Caravan with family 34.00,
Tent with two adults 22.00. CC: Visa.
*South-west of Frutigen. Site is well signposted in
Adelboden.*

GENEVE (GENEVA) 18C

TCS-Camping Pointe à la Bise 1222 Vésenaz.
Tel 022 7521296. English spoken.
OPEN: 03/04–27/10. SIZE: 3.2 ha, 220 pitches (100 with
elec, 80 statics), 8 hot showers, 20 WCs, 2 CWPs.

≈ ⚓ 🚻 R 🔲 🛠 🛒 ✕ | |

PRICES: (1996) Caravan with family 42.00, Tent
with two adults 29.00. CC: Euro/Access, Visa.
*Approx 5 km north of Genève on the N5 along the
eastern shore of Lac Léman. Campsite is beside the
lake and well signposted.*

GRINDELWALD 18C

Camp zum Gietscherdorf 3818 Grindelwald.
Tel 036 531429. English spoken.
OPEN: 01/05–20/10. SIZE: 10 ha, 88 pitches (all with
elec, 42 statics), 4 hot showers, 7 WCs, 1 CWP. ☏

Switzerland

| | | ϕ | | 回 | $\mathbb{L}$ | | | ⇌ | | $\maltese$ | |

Restaurant at 0.5 km.
PRICES: (1996) Caravan with family 37.50,
Tent with two adults 29.00. CC: none.
At the end of the village, near the river on the right. Signposted.

GSTAAD   18C

TCS Camping au Berceau 1837 Château d'Oex.
Tel 029 46234. English spoken.
OPEN: all year. SIZE: 1 ha, 78 pitches (all with elec, 50 statics), 4 hot showers (charge), 5 WCs, 4 CWPs. $\mathbf{C}$

| ∼ | ⚷ | ϕ | | 回 | (⚑) | | $\maltese$ ⇌ | | |

Shop at 1.5 km. Restaurant at 1.5 km.
PRICES: (1996) Caravan with family 28.80,
Tent with two adults 11.20. CC: none.
Château d'Oex is between Gstaad and Bulle, north-east of Montreux.

LES HAUDERES   18C

Camping Molignon 1984 Les Haudères.
Tel 027 283 12 40. English spoken.
OPEN: all year. SIZE: 20 ha, 135 pitches (100 with elec, 30 statics), 11 hot showers, 16 WCs, 1 CWP. $\mathbf{C}$

| ∼ | ⚷ | ⚑ | R | 回 | $\mathbb{L}$ | | $\maltese$ | | |

PRICES: (1996) Caravan with family 27.40,
Tent with two adults 19.20. CC: Visa.
From Sion, drive towards Vol d'Hérens and campsite is 2.5 km after Evolène.

INNERTKIRCHEN   18C

Camping Aareschlucht Fuhren, 3862 Innertkirchen.
Tel 033 9715332, Fax 033 9715332.
English spoken.
OPEN: all year. SIZE: 1 ha, 40 pitches (30 with elec, 12 statics), 2 hot showers (charge), 6 WCs, 1 CWP.

| ⚑ | R | 回 | $\mathbb{L}$ | | | (H) | |

Restaurant at 1 km.
PRICES: Caravan with family 29.80,
Tent with two adults 19.80. CC: none.

Camping Grund 3862 Innertkirchen.
Tel 036 714409, Fax 036 714767.
English spoken.
OPEN: all year. SIZE: 50 ha, 30 pitches (50 with elec, 20 statics), 5 hot showers, 10 WCs, 2 CWPs.

| ϕ | R | 回 | | | (H) | $\maltese$ |

Shop at 0.2 km. Restaurant at 0.2 km.
PRICES: (1996) Caravan with family 28.80,
Tent with two adults 22.80. CC: none.
Coming from Susten turn left on entering village, follow signs for 1 km.

INTERLAKEN   18C

Camping Oberai 3812 Wilderswil.
Tel 036 221335. English spoken.
OPEN: 15/03–15/10. SIZE: 60 pitches (all with elec), 4 hot showers, 7 WCs, 1 CWP.

| | ϕ | R | 回 | $\mathbb{L}$ | | | ⇌ | | |

Restaurant at 0.1 km.
PRICES: (1996) Caravan with family 31.60,
Tent with two adults 22.80. CC: none.
Just south of Interlaken following signs towards Lauterbrunnen and Grindelwald.

Camping Thalacker AG 3852 Ringgenberg.
Tel 036 221128, Fax 036 229838. English spoken.
OPEN: all year. SIZE: 80 pitches (68 with elec), 4 hot showers, 8 WCs, 2 CWPs.

| | ⚑ | | 回 | $\mathbb{L}$ | |

Restaurant at 0.25 km.
PRICES: (1996) Caravan with family 40.70,
Tent with two adults 24.50. CC: none.
East of Interlaken, on the main road towards Brienz.

Hobby Camping 3 Lehnweg 16, 3800 Unterseen.
Tel 033 8229652, Fax 033 8229657. English spoken.
OPEN: 01/04–15/10. SIZE: 1.2 ha, 85 pitches (all with elec, 25 statics), 6 hot showers (charge), 14 WCs, 3 CWPs. $\mathbf{C}$ &

| | ⚑ | R | 回 | $\mathbb{L}$ | | | |

Restaurant at 0.5 km. Large playground, barbecue; short walk to town and lake.
PRICES: (1996) Caravan with family 48.60,
Tent with two adults 37.50. CC: none.
2 km west of Interlaken and 17 km east of Thun. Follow camping sign No 3.

Jungfrau Camping Steindlerstrasse 60, 3800 Interlaken.
Tel 036 225730, Fax 036 225730. English spoken.
OPEN: 15/04–15/10. SIZE: 2 ha, 80 pitches (all with elec, 60 statics), 12 hot showers (charge), 14 WCs, 3 CWPs. $\mathbf{C}$

| | ⚑ | R | 回 | $\mathbb{L}$ | ☕ | $\maltese$ | ⇌ | (H) |

PRICES: (1996) Caravan with family 52.80, Tent with two adults 31.80. CC: Euro/Access, Visa.
On west side of Interlaken.

Jungfraublick Camping Interlaken.
Tel 036 224414, Fax 036 221619. English spoken.
OPEN: 15/04–30/09. SIZE: 1 ha, 75 pitches (all with elec), 9 hot showers (charge), 16 WCs, 1 CWP. $\mathbf{C}$ &

| | ϕ | R | 回 | (⚑) | | | ⇌ | | |

Shop at 0.8 km. Restaurant at 0.5 km.
PRICES: (1996) Caravan with family 41.00,
Tent with two adults 31.00. CC: none.
Take motorway N8 through tunnel, leave at Lanterbrunnen/Grindelwald exit. Site on left, 300 m from N8 sliproad. Well signposted.

Lazy Rancho Camping 4 3800 Interlaken.
Tel 033 822 87 16, Fax 033 823 19 20.
English spoken.
OPEN: 01/04–15/10. SIZE: 160 ha, 110 pitches
(all with elec, 45 statics), 8 hot showers (charge),
13 WCs, 4 CWPs. ℓ

Restaurant at 0.5 km. Billiards, children's
playground, TV room.
PRICES: Caravan with family 44.00,
Tent with two adults 34.00. CC: none.
*Autobahn exit Gunten/Beatenberg then follow the
signs to Lazy Rancho, campsite No 4; there is no
need to go into Interlaken itself.*

TCS-Camping Seeblick 3806 Bönigen.
English spoken.
OPEN: all year. SIZE: 116 pitches (all with elec,
12 statics), 8 hot showers, 12 WCs, 1 CWP. ℓ &

PRICES: (1996) Caravan with family 42.60, Tent
with two adults 33.20. CC: Euro/Access, Visa.
East of Interlaken on the N8.

KÜSSNACHT 18B

Camping Vitznau 6354 Vitznau.
Tel 039 71280, Fax 039 72457. English spoken.
OPEN: 01/04–06/10. SIZE: 1.8 ha, 120 pitches
(180 with elec, 60 statics), 12 hot showers
(charge), 24 WCs, 3 CWPs. ℓ

Restaurant at 0.3 km. Tennis; skiing and water
sports nearby.
PRICES: (1996) Caravan with family 45.80, Tent
with two adults 32.80. CC: Euro/Access, Visa.
*South of Küssnacht on N2b. Campsite is
signposted.*

LE LANDERON 18A

Camping des Pêches 2525 Le Landeron.
Tel 032 751 29 00, Fax 032 751 63 54.
English spoken.
OPEN: 01/04–30/09. SIZE: 1 ha, 100 pitches
(50 with elec, 330 statics), 10 hot showers
(charge), 6 WCs, 1 CWP. ℓ

PRICES: (1996) Caravan with family 32.60,
Tent with two adults 22.00.
CC: Amex, Euro/Access, Visa.
*Between Neuchâtel and Bienne. Leave N5 at Le
Landeron/La Neuveville exit then follow signs.*

LAUSANNE 18C

Camping Forel 1606 Forel.
Tel 021 781 14 64, Fax 021 781 31 26.
English spoken.

OPEN: 01/01–30/09 & 01/11–31/12. SIZE: 4 ha,
50 pitches (all with elec, 150 statics), 6 hot
showers (charge), 16 WCs, 4 CWPs. ℓ &

Fiume.
PRICES: (1996) Caravan with family 38.50,
Tent with two adults 23.00. CC: Euro/Access.
*From Lausanne, go east on the E62 for 8 km, exit
Chexbres, then north towards Moudon for 6 km
and turn left at the fuel station in Forel. Campsite
on left.*

LAUTERBRUNNEN 18C

Breithorn 3801 Stechelberg-Sandbach.
Tel 036 551225. English spoken.
OPEN: all year. SIZE: 6 hot showers, 6 WCs, 1 CWP. ℓ

Restaurant at 0.2 km.
PRICES: (1996) Caravan with family 28.50,
Tent with two adults 19.00. CC: none.
Follow signs to campsite.

LOCARNO 18D

Camping da Renato Vallemaggia,
6672 Gordevio.
Tel 091 753 13 64. English spoken.
OPEN: 01/04–20/10. SIZE: 17 ha, 104 pitches
(all with elec, 26 statics), 4 hot showers, 14 WCs.

Shop at 2 km.
PRICES: (1996) Caravan with family 43.60,
Tent with two adults 25.40. CC: none.
Follow signs to campsite from Locarno.

LUGANO 18D

Camping Palazzina 6805 Mezzovico.
Tel 091 951467. English spoken.
OPEN: all year. SIZE: 118 pitches (118 statics), 4 hot
showers, 8 WCs, 1 CWP. ℓ &

Shop at 0.1 km. Restaurant at 0.1 km. Sea 100m.
PRICES: unavailable. CC: none.

Camping La Palma 6982 Agno.
Tel 091 605 25 61, Fax 091 605 22 83.
English spoken.
OPEN: 01/04–30/10. SIZE: 2 ha, 100 pitches

Switzerland

(all with elec, 42 statics), 24 WCs, 24 French WCs, 1 CWP. **t**

Restaurant at 1 km.
PRICES: (1996) Caravan with family 31.50,
Tent with two adults 19.50. CC: none.
Motorway exit Lugano-Nord, towards Ponte-Tresa. Agno is 4 km.

Eurocampo 6982 Agno.
Tel 091 605 21 14, Fax 091 605 31 87.
English spoken.
OPEN: 01/04–31/10. SIZE: 200 pitches (all with elec, 64 statics), 18 hot showers, 42 WCs, 42 French WCs, 1 CWP. **t ら**

Shop at 0.2 km. Restaurant at 0.2 km. Swimming pool 0.3 km.
PRICES: (1996) Caravan with family 30.90,
Tent with two adults 23.40. CC: none.
From Lugano-Nord on N2, take N233 south-west towards Ponte Tresa.

Campeggio Eurocampo
at Lugano
Good base for Lakes Lugano, Maggiore & Como

MOUDON 18C

Camping du Grand Pré 1510 Moudon.
Tel 021 9051752, Fax 021 9054616. English spoken.
OPEN: 15/05–30/09. SIZE: 30 ha, 16 pitches (all with elec, 50 statics), 6 hot showers, 6 WCs, 1 CWP. **t ら**

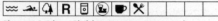

PRICES: Caravan with family 29.50, Tent with two adults 18.50. CC: none.
On Lausanne to Berne road, follow blue signs. After 25 km, exit for Moudon and follow signs.

NEUCHATEL 18A

Camping Paradis-Plage 2013 Colombier.
Tel 038 412446, Fax 038 414305. English spoken.
OPEN: 01/03–31/10. SIZE: 4 ha, 360 pitches (all with elec, 200 statics), 20 hot showers, 30 WCs, 4 CWPs. **t ら**

Shop at 0.8 km. Children's swimming pool; excellent sports facilities nearby.
PRICES: (1996) Caravan with family 34.25,
Tent with two adults 27.00. CC: none.
5 km west of Neuchâtel towards Yverdon. Campsite is beside the lake and well signposted.

ORSIERES 18C

Camping des Glaciers 1944 La Fouly.
Tel 026 831735, Fax 026 833605. English spoken.
OPEN: 20/05–30/09. SIZE: 6 ha, 150 pitches (all with elec), 27 hot showers, 27 WCs, 3 CWPs. **t**

Shop at 0.5 km. Restaurant at 0.5 km.
PRICES: (1996) Caravan with family 34.00,
Tent with two adults 23.00. CC: none.
From Orsières, go south-west to La Fouly on the road to the west of N12/E27.

ST-MORITZ 18D

Camping Plauns 7504 Pontresina-Morteratsch.
Tel 081 842 62 85, Fax 081 842 62 85.
English spoken.
OPEN: 28/05–15/10. SIZE: 250 pitches (200 with elec, 10 statics), 16 hot showers (charge), 27 WCs, 2 CWPs. **t ら**

Restaurant at 1.5 km. Children's playground.
PRICES: Caravan with family 38.00, Tent with two adults 27.00. CC: none.
From St-Moritz, north on N27 and then south-east on N29. From Pontresina follow signs to Pontresina-Morteratsch and campsite.

TCS-Camping Punt-Muragl 7503 Samedan.
Tel 041 81 8428197, Fax 041 81 8428197.
English spoken.
OPEN: 05/12–16/04 & 01/06–01/10. SIZE: 2 ha, 120 pitches (80 with elec, 30 statics), 8 hot showers, 10 WCs, 1 CWP.

Restaurant at 0.5 km.
PRICES: (1996) Caravan with family 38.80, Tent with two adults 29.20. CC: Euro/Access, Visa.
From St-Moritz, follow signs towards Pontresina for 2 km. Entrance to campsite is on main road.

SARGANS 18B

Camping am See 8877 Murg.
Tel 081 7381530, Fax 081 7382227.
OPEN: 14/04–15/10. SIZE: 25 pitches (all with elec, 22 statics), 4 hot showers (charge), 9 WCs, 1 CWP. **t**

Shop at 0.8 km. Restaurant at 0.8 km.
PRICES: (1996) Caravan with family 22.90, Tent with two adults 15.40. CC: Euro/Access.
North-west of Sargans on N3. Campsite is near the lake and well signposted.

See-Camping 8880 Walenstadt.
Tel 081 7351896, Fax 081 7351841. English spoken.
OPEN: 01/05–30/09. SIZE: 2.2 ha, 60 pitches (all with elec, 100 statics), 8 hot showers, 13 WCs, 1 CWP. **t**

Shop at 1 km. Restaurant at 1 km.
PRICES: Caravan with family 35.00,
Tent with two adults 25.00. CC: none.
North-west of Sargans on N3 at the eastern end of Walensee lake. Site is signposted.

SCHÖNENGRUND 18B

Hotel Krone 9105 Schönengrund.
Tel 071 571268, Fax 071 571161. English spoken.
OPEN: all year. SIZE: 1 ha, 10 pitches (all with elec, 70 statics), 2 hot showers (charge), 5 WCs, 1 CWP.

Shop at 0.03 km. Restaurant at 0.03 km. Playground.
PRICES: (1996) Caravan with family 23.10,
Tent with two adults 16.60. CC: none.
Drive from St-Gallen to Herisau, then Schönengrund.

SIERRE 18C

Camping Swiss Plage 3970 Salgesch.
Tel 027 55 66 08, Fax 027 41 32 15.
English spoken.
OPEN: all year. SIZE: 10 ha, 1 CWP.

PRICES: unavailable. CC: none.

Komfort-Ferienplatz Santa Monica
3942 Raron.
Tel 027 934 24 24, Fax 027 934 24 50.
English spoken.
OPEN: all year. SIZE: 4 ha, 200 pitches (all with elec, 100 statics).

Shop at 0.2 km. Restaurant at 0.2 km.
PRICES: Caravan with family 36.50,
Tent with two adults 21.50. CC: none.
East of Sierre on E62 towards Brig. Well signposted in Raron.

TCS-Camping Bella Tola 3952 Susten.
Tel 027 4731491, Fax 027 4733641.
English spoken.
OPEN: 15/05–29/09. SIZE: 3.6 ha, 208 pitches (all with elec, 51 statics).

Games room.
PRICES: Caravan with family 61.00, Tent with two adults 45.00. CC: Amex, Euro/Access, Visa.
Susten is east of Sierre on the N9. Site is signposted from the main road in Susten, 2 km up the hill, going south.

TCS-Camping Bois de Finges 3960 Sierre.
Tel 027 550284. English spoken.
OPEN: 01/05–29/09. SIZE: 2 ha, 90 pitches (62 with elec, 10 statics), 6 hot showers, 9 WCs, 2 CWPs.

Restaurant at 1 km.
PRICES: (1996) Caravan with family 37.60, Tent with two adults 27.20. CC: Euro/Access, Visa.
From Sion drive through Sierre, cross the river and the campsite is on the left.

SILVAPLANA 18D

Camping Silvaplana 7513 Silvaplana.
Tel 081 828 84 92. English spoken.
OPEN: 20/05–20/10. SIZE: 100 pitches (all with elec, 150 statics).

PRICES: (1996) Caravan with family 41, Tent with two adults 28. CC: none.
South-west of St-Moritz.

SION 18C

Camping Evolène 1983 Evolène.
Tel 027 831144, Fax 027 833255. English spoken.
OPEN: all year. SIZE: 1 ha, 50 pitches (all with elec), 6 hot showers, 6 WCs, 6 French WCs, 1 CWP.

Shop at 0.3 km. Mountain-bike hire.
PRICES: (1996) Caravan with family 26.90, Tent with two adults 17.20. CC: Euro/Access, Visa.
From Sion take road south to Evolène. Drive through the village and campsite is 300 m on right.

Camping Sedunum Bois d'Aproz, 1950 Sion.
Tel 027 346 42 68, Fax 027 346 42 57.
English spoken.
OPEN: 01/04–30/10. SIZE: 3 ha, 80 pitches (60 with elec, 80 statics), 8 hot showers, 16 WCs, 1 CWP.

Restaurant at 1 km. Table tennis, boules.
PRICES: (1996) Caravan with family 23.00, Tent with two adults 13.00. CC: none.
Exit motorway Couthey or Sion-Ouest then follow 'Les Isles'. On the right before the Rhône.

Camping Sedunum

near Sion

Relax, right on the Rhône

Camping Grand Paradis Nax, 1961 Sion.
Tel 027 311730, Fax 027 311730. English spoken.
OPEN: 01/04–01/10. SIZE: 2 ha, 70 pitches (50 with elec, 20 statics), 4 hot showers, 12 WCs.

Shop at 0.5 km.

Switzerland

PRICES: (1996) Caravan with family 21.80, Tent with two adults 14.70. CC: none.
8 km from Sion via Bramois. Well signposted.

TCS-Camping Botza 1963 Vétroz.
Tel 027 346 19 40, Fax 027 346 25 35. English spoken.
OPEN: all year. SIZE: 3 ha, 156 pitches (all with elec, 69 statics), 24 hot showers (charge), 40 WCs, 3 CWPs. ▪ &

Tennis, volley ball, table tennis.
PRICES: (1996) Caravan with family 36.70, Tent with two adults 26.90. CC: Euro/Access.
West of Sion on N9.

SPIEZ 18C

Camping Panorama 3703 Aeschi.
Tel 033 654 43 77, Fax 033 223 36 65. English spoken.
OPEN: 15/05–20/10. ▪

Shop at 2 km. Restaurant at 2 km. Playground; 10% discount in LS.
PRICES: (1996) Caravan with family 35.30, Tent with two adults 24.90. CC: none.
From Spiez, follow the signs to Aeschi.

SPLÜGEN 18D

Camping auf dem Sand 7435 Splügen.
Tel 081 6641476, Fax 081 6509031. English spoken.
OPEN: all year. SIZE: 1 ha, 40 pitches (all with elec, 60 statics), 8 hot showers, 10 WCs, 2 CWPs.

Restaurant at 0.5 km. Children's playground.
PRICES: (1996) Caravan with family 50.20, Tent with two adults 27.20. CC: none.
From the N13 motorway turn off at Splügen and follow the signs.

STEIN 18B

Camping Wagenhausen 8260 Wagenhausen.
Tel 052 741 42 71, Fax 052 741 41 57. English spoken.
OPEN: 01/04–31/10. SIZE: 4.5 ha, 50 pitches (all with elec, 240 statics), 8 hot showers (charge), 18 WCs, 2 CWPs. ▪ &

PRICES: Caravan with family 39.00, Tent with two adults 25.00. CC: none.
3 km from Stein-am-Rhein on the Kreuzlingen to Schaffhausen road.

SURSEE 18A

Camping Sursee 6216 Mauensee.
Tel 041 9211161. English spoken.
OPEN: 01/04–30/09. SIZE: 2 ha, 60 pitches (all with elec, 80 statics), 2 hot showers, 8 WCs, 1 CWP.

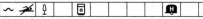

Restaurant at 1 km.
PRICES: (1996) Caravan with family 22.00, Tent with two adults 15.00. CC: none.
Leave Basel/Luzern motorway at Sursee exit. Right at first crossroads, straight over at second, right towards Basel at third crossroads, then 600 m on left.

SUSTEN 18C

Camping Gemmi 3952 Agarn.
Tel 027 473 11 54, Fax 027 473 42 54. English spoken.
OPEN: 25/04–15/10. SIZE: 1 ha, 70 pitches (all with elec, 3 statics), 6 hot showers, 8 WCs, 1 CWP. ▪

Restaurant at 1 km.
PRICES: (1996) Caravan with family 42.00, Tent with two adults 26.00. CC: Euro/Access, Visa.
2 km east of Susten, just off the main road. Campsite is well signposted.

ZERMATT 18C

Camping Alphubel 3929 Täsch.
Tel 028 673635, Fax 028 664667. English spoken.
OPEN: 01/05–15/10. SIZE: 0.7 ha, 100 pitches (35 with elec), 8 hot showers, 8 WCs, 1 CWP.

Shop at 0.2 km. Restaurant at 0.1 km.
PRICES: (1996) Caravan with family 27.50, Tent with two adults 19.00. CC: none.
Beside the River Mattervisp, approx 8 km north of Zermatt.

ZÜRICH 18B

Camping Seebucht Seestrasse 559, 8038 Zürich-Wollishofen.
Tel 014 821612, Fax 014 821660. English spoken.
OPEN: 01/05–30/09. SIZE: 2.5 ha, 200 pitches (60 with elec, 20 statics). ▪ &

PRICES: (1996) Caravan with family 30.00, Tent with two adults 25.00. CC: none.
South of Zürich, near the lake and well signposted.

ZURZACH 18B

Campingplatz Oberfeld 5330 Zurzach-Oberfeld.
Tel 056 2492575, Fax 056 2492579. English spoken.
OPEN: 01/04–31/10. SIZE: 2 ha, 20 pitches, 10 hot showers (charge), 16 WCs, 2 CWPs. ▪

PRICES: (1996) Caravan with family 29.50, Tent with two adults 16.30. CC: none.
Well signposted in Zurzach

Switzerland

TURKEY

Turkey is partly in Europe and partly in Asia, one of the few countries in the world that spans a continental division. The Bosporus, which is part of the waterway leading from the Mediterranean to the Black Sea, marks this division and astride it lies Istanbul, the largest city in Turkey.

On the European side are the great tourist attractions of Aya Sofya and the Topkapi Palace. Take the lift up the Galata Tower for a view over the domes and minarets of this exciting city. A boat trip at twilight along the Bosporus is a wonderful way to appreciate this most eastern of European cities.

For quiet beach-based holiday, choose from resorts on the Black Sea, the Aegean Sea and, in the south, on the Mediterranean.

The Aegean coast is becoming more developed with each year that passes. Not much remains of the ancient city of Troy but further south, Ephesus, home to the Temple of Diana, was one of the Seven Wonders of the World, and still impresses. It is classed as one of Asia Minor's three great wonders; the limestone terraces at Pamukkale is another, and the third is the rock dwellings in the Göreme valley, near Kayseri, central Turkey. These are carved out of amazing pyramids of rock and, although some are just simple houses, many are churches with wonderful wall paintings.

Ankara, the country's capital, was selected to be the seat of government for modern Turkey in 1928.

Emergency numbers
Police 155, Fire Brigade 110, Ambulance 112

Warning information
Fire Extinguisher essential

First aid kit compulsory

2 Warning Triangles must be carried

Blood Alcohol Legal Limit 50 mg

AKCAKOCA 24B

Hamburg Camping
Degirmenagzi Mevkii, 14700 Akcakoca.
Tel 374 6112991, Fax 374 6114448. English spoken.
OPEN: all year. SIZE: 1 ha, 130 pitches (30 with elec, 15 statics), 4 hot showers, 6 WCs, 4 French WCs, 1 CWP. &

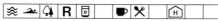

Shop at 0.5 km.
PRICES: (1996) Caravan with family 12.00, Tent with two adults 8.00. CC: none.
From the centre of the city, 2 km west then turn right before bridge over river. Sign to campsite after 300 m. (Prices in DM.)

Tezel Camping
Istanbul cad no 10, 14700 Akcakoca.
Tel 374 6114115, Fax 374 6114115. English spoken.
OPEN: 31/03–01/12. SIZE: 40 pitches (30 with elec), 6 hot showers, 8 WCs, 4 French WCs. &

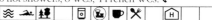

Shop at 0.01 km. Own beach; beautiful countryside.
PRICES: (1996) Caravan with family 21.00, Tent with two adults 14.00. CC: none.
Akcakoca is between Ankara and Istanbul and the campsite is about 600 m west of the town. (Prices in DM.)

ANTALYA 24D

Erman Holiday Camp Beldibi, 07983 Antalya.
Tel 242 8248196, Fax 242 8248231. English spoken.
OPEN: all year. SIZE: 6 ha, 208 pitches (all with elec), 25 hot showers, 33 WCs, 12 French WCs, 1 CWP. &

Canoes and boats for hire.
PRICES: (1996) Caravan with family 25.00, Tent with two adults 18.00. CC: Euro/Access.
Going from Antalya towards Kemer, pass through two tunnels. After the second, turn left to Beldibi and carry on for about 1.5 km. Look to the left for the campsite, which is near the sea. (Prices in DM.)

AYVALIK 24B

Ada Camping Alibey Adasi, 10400 Ayvalik.
Tel 266 3271211, Fax 266 3272065. English spoken.
OPEN: 01/04–30/10. SIZE: 100 pitches (50 with elec), 6 hot showers, 12 WCs, 6 French WCs, 1 CWP.

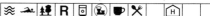

Shop at 3 km.

PRICES: (1996) Caravan with family 29.00, Tent with two adults 18.00. CC: none.
North of Ayvalik cross over the dam and bridge to the island. The site is 2 km from town, down a gravel track. (Prices in DM.)

BODRUM 24D

Camping Zetas 48400 Gümbet.
Tel 252 3162231, Fax 252 3165741. English spoken.
OPEN: 01/03–31/12. SIZE: 150 pitches (all with elec, 50 statics), 16 hot showers, 16 WCs, 3 CWPs.

| ≋ | ⚓ | 👫 | R | | | 🛢 | ⛽ | ✕ | | | |

Water sports, children's playground.
PRICES: (1996) Caravan with family 8.50, Tent with two adults 5.50. CC: none.
Gümbet is 5 km from Bodrum and campsite is well signposted. (Prices in UK£.)

BURHANIYE 24B

EGE Camp Pelitkoy, 10730 Burhaniye.
Tel 266 4251006. English spoken.
OPEN: 01/04–30/09. SIZE: 30 pitches (all with elec, 30 statics), 2 hot showers, 6 WCs.

| ≋ | ⚓ | 🛗 | | | | ✕ | | ⓗ | |

Shop at 1 km. Site shop planned for 1996.
PRICES: (1996) Caravan with family 20.00. CC: none.
Burhaniye is on the E87 Canakkale to Izmir road. (Prices in DM.)

BURSA 24B

NUR Camping Yeni Yalova Yolu 8 Km, 16365 Bursa.
Tel 24 54 7453, Fax 24 54 8503.
English spoken.
OPEN: all year. SIZE: 220 pitches (all with elec), 4 hot showers, 6 French WCs.

| | | ⚲ | R | 🛢 | | | | 🏠 | |

Shop at 0.5 km. Restaurant at 0.5 km.
PRICES: Caravan with family 16, Tent with two adults 12. CC: none.
Bursa is on the E90, near the north-west coast. The campsite is 8 km from Bursa. (Prices in DM.)

CORUM 24B

Asikoglu 19310 Bogazkale.
Tel 0364 4522004, Fax 0364 4522171.
English spoken.
OPEN: 10/03–31/12. SIZE: 90 pitches (80 statics), 12 hot showers, 10 WCs.

| | 🛗 | R | 🛢 | 🛁 | | ✕ | | | |

Shop at 0.1 km.
PRICES: (1996) Caravan with family 15, Tent with two adults 10. CC: none.
Bogazkale is to the south of Corum. (Prices in DMs.)

ECEABAT 24B

Kum Motel and Camping Canakkale, 17900 Eceabat.
Tel 286 8141466/55, Fax 286 8141917.
English spoken.
OPEN: 01/04–30/10. SIZE: 5 hot showers, 7 WCs, 7 French WCs.

| ≋ | ⚓ | 🛗 | R | 🛢 | 🛁 | ⛽ | ✕ | | ⓗ | |

Shop at 15 km.
PRICES: Caravan with family 90,000, Tent with two adults 85,000. CC: none.
On the coast south-west of Istanbul. In the National Park.

EDIRNE 24B

Fifi Touristik Camping 22030 Edirne.
Tel 284 2357908, Fax 284 2129888.
English spoken.
OPEN: 01/04–31/10. SIZE: 15 ha, 100 pitches (50 with elec), 10 hot showers, 10 WCs, 10 French WCs, 1 CWP.

| | | 🛗 | R | | 🛁 | ⛽ | ✕ | ≺ | ⓗ | |

PRICES: (1996) Caravan with family 16.00, Tent with two adults 12.00. CC: Euro/Access, Visa.
On route 100/E80, approx 6 km south-east of town near the turn-off to Kirklareli. (Prices in US$.)

EDREMIT 24B

Altin Camp 10700 Burhaniye.
Tel 266 4222432, Fax 266 4223333.
English spoken.
OPEN: all year. SIZE: 5 ha, 200 pitches (all with elec), 20 hot showers, 25 WCs, 15 French WCs, 1 CWP.

| ≋ | ⚓ | 🛗 | R | | 🛁 | ⛽ | ✕ | | ⓗ | |

Tennis, volley ball, horse-riding.
PRICES: (1996) Caravan with family 31.00, Tent with two adults 20.50. CC: none.
8 km south of Edremit turn off at Burhaniye (route 550/E87) towards Oren. The campsite is signposted and is about 3 km ahead. (Prices in DM.)

ERDEK 24B

Camping ANT 10500 Erdek.
Tel 266 8557044. English spoken.
OPEN: 15/05–01/10. SIZE: 2 ha, 80 pitches (65 with elec), 5 hot showers, 11 WCs, 3 French WCs, 1 CWP.

| ≋ | ⚓ | 🛗 | R | | | | | | | |

PRICES: Caravan with family 19.00, Tent with two adults 13.00. CC: none.
Well signposted, 7 km from Erdek and close to the Hotel Pinar. (Prices in DMs).

Turkey

FETHIYE 24D

Deniz camping 48340 Oludeniz.
Tel 615 66012, Fax 615 66008. English spoken.
OPEN: 01/03–30/10. SIZE: 4 ha, 20 pitches
(all with elec), 10 hot showers, 12 WCs, 2 French
WCs, 1 CWP.

Perfect situation for walking holiday, daily
excursions.
PRICES: (1996) Caravan with family 7.00, Tent with
two adults 5.00. CC: Euro/Access, Visa.
*From Fethiye, take the road for Oludeniz, 12 km
south. The road is very steep in places. Turn left
on reaching beach and campsite is signposted
150 m. (Prices in UK£.)*

GÜMÜLDÜR 24D

Mocamp Denizati Denizati,
35480 Gümüldür-Izmir.
Tel 232 7931019, Fax 232 7931692. English spoken.
OPEN: 15/05–15/09. SIZE: 9 ha, 400 pitches (all with
elec), 12 hot showers, 24 WCs, 24 French WCs.

10% discount to RAC members.
PRICES: (1996) Caravan with family 28,
Tent with two adults 20. CC: Visa.
*Between Gümüldür and Ozdere, 6 km from the
beach. (Prices in DM.)*

ISTANBUL 24B

Ataköy Mocamp Istanbul.
Tel 212 5596014, Fax 212 5606505. English spoken.
OPEN: all year. SIZE: 12 ha, 500 pitches (250 with
elec, 250 statics), 42 hot showers, 80 WCs,
10 French WCs.

Recommended campsite.
PRICES: (1996) Caravan with family 1.3M,
Tent with two adults 950,000. CC: Amex.
*1 km from E5, 3 km from the airport and 10 km
from town centre*

IZMIR 24D

Oba Holiday Site Mithat Pasa cad no 25,
35310 Guzelbahce.
Tel 232 2342015, Fax 232 2342231. English spoken.
OPEN: all year. SIZE: 35 ha, 160 pitches (all with
elec, 20 statics), 4 hot showers (charge), 12 WCs,
6 French WCs, 2 CWPs.

Sports facilities nearby.
PRICES: (1996) Caravan with family 250,000,
Tent with two adults 170,000. CC: Amex,
Euro/Access, Visa.

*The site is 20 km from Izmir on the Cesme road.
Follow the coastal road towards the town of
Cesme.*

KÖYCEGIZ 24D

**Int Anatolia 1 Camping & Caravaning -
Köycegiz** PO Box 7, 48800 Köycegiz.
Tel 252 2622752. English spoken.
OPEN: all year. SIZE: 5 ha, 60 pitches (all with elec,
10 statics), 8 hot showers, 8 WCs, 8 French WCs,
2 CWPs.

Boat tours, water sports, treking.
PRICES: Caravan with family 25.75,
Tent with two adults 16.00. CC: none.
*Campsite is signposted from the main Mugla to
Fethiye road. (Prices in DM.)*

KUSADASI 24D

Yat Camping Ataturk Blvd no 76,
09400 Kusadasi.
Tel 256 6141333, Fax 256 6145569. English spoken.
OPEN: all year. SIZE: 2 ha, 150 pitches (all with
elec), 18 hot showers, 22 WCs, 4 French WCs.

PRICES: Caravan with family 7.00, Tent with two
adults 5.00. CC: none.
*On the northern edge of town, opposite the
harbour. (Prices in UK£.)*

SILE 24B

Camping Akkaya 1 Sile.
Tel 0216 7277010, Fax 0216 7277223.
English spoken.
OPEN: 01/05–01/09.

Shop at 10 km. Restaurant at 10 km.
PRICES: (1996) Caravan with family 35.00,
Tent with two adults 25.00. CC: none.
*The site is on the north coast, 50 km from
Istanbul. (Prices in DMs).*

Fener Camping-Motel 81800 Sile.
Tel 711 2824. English spoken.
OPEN: 01/05–30/09. SIZE: 0.6 ha, 10 pitches
(all with elec, 40 statics), 6 hot showers, 6 WCs,
4 French WCs, 1 CWP.

Shop at 0.5 km. Restaurant at 0.5 km.
PRICES: (1996) Caravan with family 430,000,
Tent with two adults 290,000. CC: none.
The campsite is 500 m from Sile. Follow signs.

Turkey

KEY TO MAPS

LEGEND

• Tonnerre	town with one campsite
• Alençon	town with more than one campsite
▬▬▬	motorway
▬▬▬	main road
▪▪▪▪▪▪▪	international border
··············	regional border

Cartography by RAC Publishing

ENGLAND

English   Channel

Barfleur
Cherbourg
les Pieux
Quettehou
Ste Mere
Barneville-Carteret
Eglise
Arromanches-les-Bains
La Haye-du-Puits
Carentan
Trévières
Bayeux
Lessay
Agon-Coutainville
Coutances

Perros-Guirec
Pleubian
Tregastel-Plage
Trelevern
Ploubazlanec
Trébeurden
Paimpol
Granville
Roscoff
Lannion
Tréguier
Plouézec
Plouguerneau
Plougasnou
la Roche-Derrien
Carantec
Plouezoch
Pontrieux
Etables-sur-Mer
St Cast-le-Guildo
Cancale
Le Mont-St Michel
Brécey
Avranches
Lannilis
N12
Binic
Erquy
St Malo
Pontaubault
Morlaix
Dinard
Ducey
Le-Conquet
Plougastel-Daoulas
St Brieuc
Plêneuf-Val-André
N176
Dinan
Dol-de-Bretagne
N176
Camaret-sur-Mer
Crozon
le Faou
Huelgoat
Combourg
Fougères
Ceauce
Telgruc-sur-Mer
Châteaulin
Carhaix-Plouguer
Rostrenen
N12
Douarnenez
N165
Mur-de-Bretagne
Tinténiac
D175
Ernée
Quimper
Elliant
le Faouët
Merdrignac
N12
Plozevet
Fouesnant
Josselin-Guegon
Rennes
Bénodet
la Fôret-Fouesnant
N24
Guichen
Laval
Pont-l'Abbé
Concarneau
Quimperlé
Ploërmel
N137
Guilvinec
Nevez
Moëlan-sur-Mer
Baud
Craon
Pont-Aven
Guidel Plages
Le Pouldu
Lorient
Auray
Rochefort-en-Terre
Pouancé
Isle-de-Groix
Etel
Crach
Vannes
Redon
Chateaubriant
Plouharnel
Arradon
Muzillac
Nozay
Carnac
Quiberon
Penestin
Blain
Nort-sur-Erdre
Angers
la Trinite sur-Mer
Pontchâteau
la Turballe
Guérande
Ancenis
le Croisic
la Baule
A11
Nantes
Beaulieu-sur-Layon
la Plaine-sur-Mer
St Brevin-les-Pins
N160
Atlantic   Ocean
Pornic
Mortagne-sur-Sèvre
N149
Notre Dame de-Monts
Challans
A83
Les Herbiers
St Jean-de-Monts
Aizenay
St Gilles-Croix-de-Vie
St Hilaire-de-Riez
N160
Bretignolles-s-Mer
la Mothe-Archard
Olonne-sur-Mer
les Sables-d'Olonne
Talmont St Hilaire
N148

0   50   100 km

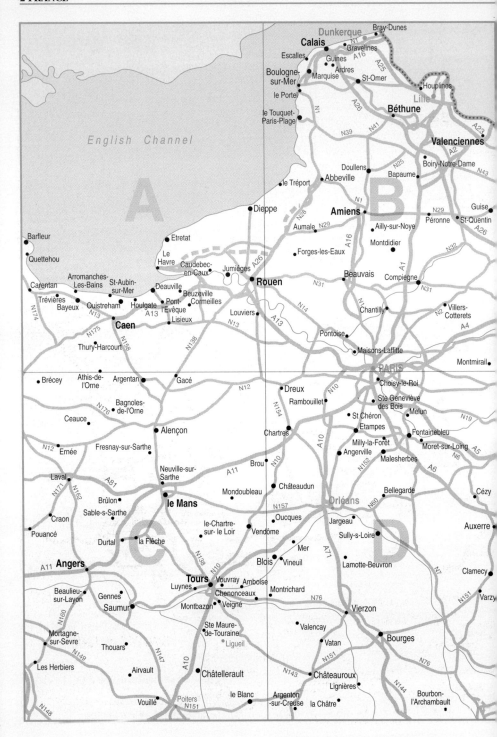

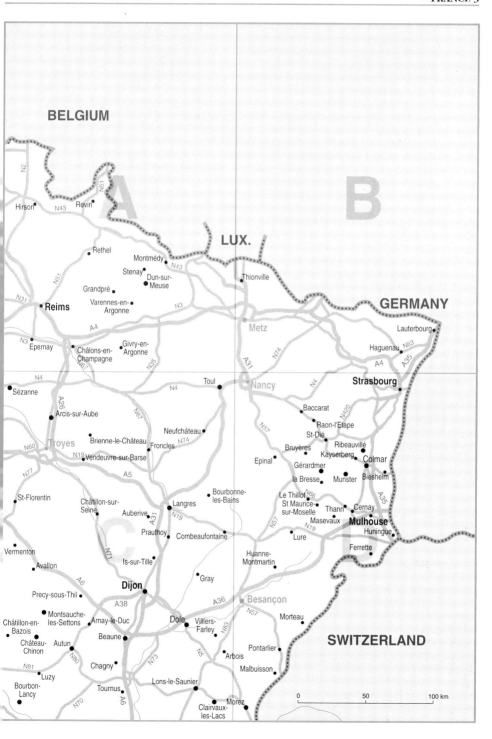

BELGIUM

N2

N51

Hirson N43 Revin

A

B

LUX.

Rethel

Montmédy

N43

Stenay Dun-sur-
N51 Meuse Thionville

Grandpré

N31 Varennes-en-
Reims Argonne N3

A4 GERMANY

Metz Lauterbourg

N3 Epernay Givry-en-
Châlons-en- Argonne N74 Haguenau N63
Champagne N35 A4 A35

N57

N4 Toul N4
N4 Nancy Strasbourg
Sézanne
A26 Baccarat N420

Arcis-sur-Aube N67 Raon-l'Etape
Neufchâteau St-Dié
N57 Ribeauvillé
Troyes Brienne-le-Château Froncles N74 Bruyères Kaysersberg Colmar
N60 N19 Epinal
N19 Vendeuvre-sur-Barse Gérardmer
A5 la Bresse Munster Biesheim

Bourbonne- Le Thillot N66 A35
St-Florentin Châtillon-sur- Langres les-Bains St Maurice- Thann Cernay
N177 Seine Auberive N19 sur-Moselle Masevaux Mulhouse
A31 N57 N19 Huningue
Prauthoy Combeaufontaine Lure Ferrette

Vermenton Huanne-
N71 Is-sur-Tille Montmartin
Avallon
A6 Gray
Precy-sous-Thil Dijon
A38 A36 Besançon
Montsauche- N57 Morteau
Châtillon-en- les-Settons Arnay-le-Duc Dole Villiers-
Bazois Farley N83
Château- Autun Beaune N5 Pontarlier SWITZERLAND
Chinon Arbois
N81 N60 Chagny N73 Malbuisson
Luzy
Bourbon- Tournus Lons-le-Saunier
Lancy N70 A6
Morez
Clairvaux-
les-Lacs

0 50 100 km

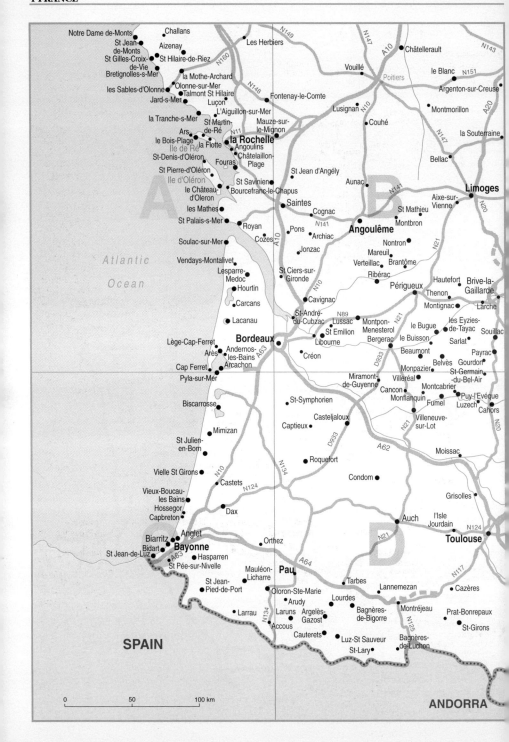

Notre Dame de-Monts
Challans
St Jean-de-Monts
Aizenay
Les Herbiers
Châtellerault
N149
N147
A10
N143
St Gilles-Croix-de-Vie
St Hilaire-de-Riez
N160
Bretignolles-s-Mer
la Mothe-Archard
Vouillé
Poitiers
le Blanc
N151
Olonne-sur-Mer
les Sables-d'Olonne
Talmont St Hilaire
N148
Argenton-sur-Creuse
A20
Jard-s-Mer
Luçon
Fontenay-le-Comte
Lusignan
N10
Montmorillon
la Tranche-s-Mer
St Martin-de-Ré
L'Aiguillon-sur-Mer
Mauze-sur-le-Mignon
Couhé
la Souterraine
N147
Ars
N11
la Flotte
la Rochelle
Angoulins
le Bois-Plage
Île de Ré
St-Denis-d'Oléron
Fouras
Châtelaillon-Plage
Bellac
St Pierre-d'Oléron
Île d'Oléron
St Savinien
St Jean d'Angély
Aunac
Limoges
le Château-d'Oleron
Bourcefranc-le-Chapus
N141
Aixe-sur-Vienne
N20
les Mathes
Saintes
Cognac
St Mathieu
St Palais-s-Mer
Royan
Pons
N141
Angoulême
Montbron
Soulac-sur-Mer
Cozes
A10
Archiac
Nontron
N21
Vendays-Montalivet
Jonzac
Mareuil
Verteillac
Brantôme
Lesparre-Medoc
St Ciers-sur-Gironde
Ribérac
Hautefort
Brive-la-Gaillarde
Hourtin
N10
Périgueux
Thenon
Carcans
Cavignac
Montignac
Larche
Lacanau
St-André-du-Cubzac
Lussac
N89
Montpon-Menesterol
N21
le Bugue
les Eyzies-de-Tayac
Souillac
St Emilion
Bergerac
le Buisson
Sarlat
Lège-Cap-Ferret
Bordeaux
Libourne
Beaumont
Payrac
Andernos-les-Bains
A63
Créon
Belvès
Gourdon
Arès
Monpazier
St-Germain-du-Bel-Air
Cap Ferret
Arcachon
Miramont-de-Guyenne
Villeréal
Montcabrier
Puy-l'Evêque
Pyla-sur-Mer
Cancon
Monflanquin
Fumel
Luzech
Cahors
Biscarrosse
St-Symphorien
Casteljaloux
Villeneuve-sur-Lot
N21
N20
Mimizan
Captieux
D933
Moissac
St Julien-en-Born
Roquefort
A62
Vielle St Girons
N10
N134
Condom
Grisolles
Castets
N124
Vieux-Boucau-les Bains
Hossegor
Dax
Auch
l'Isle Jourdain
N124
Capbreton
Anglet
Toulouse
Biarritz
Bayonne
Orthez
N21
N117
Bidart
St Jean-de-Luz
A63
Hasparren
Pau
A64
St Pée-sur-Nivelle
Mauléon-Licharre
Tarbes
Lannemezan
Cazères
St Jean-Pied-de-Port
Oloron-Ste-Marie
Lourdes
Arudy
N125
Larrau
N134
Laruns
Argelès-Gazost
Bagnères-de-Bigorre
Montréjeau
Prat-Bonrepaux
Accous
St-Girons
Cauterets
Luz-St Sauveur
Bagnères-de-Luchon
SPAIN
St-Lary

Atlantic Ocean

0   50   100 km

ANDORRA

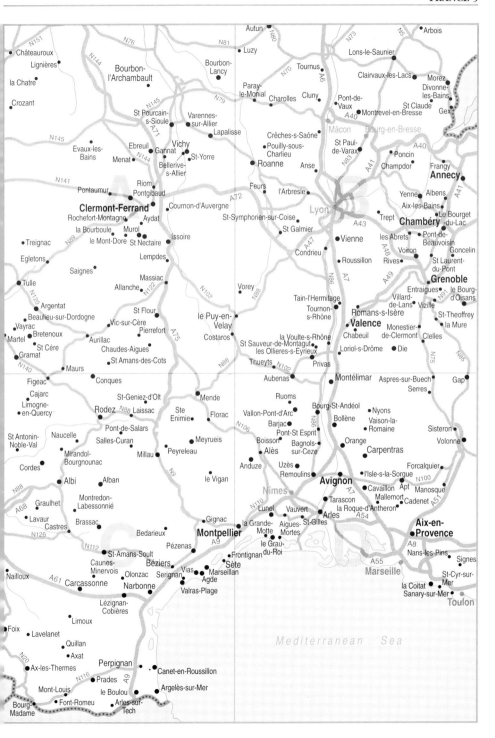

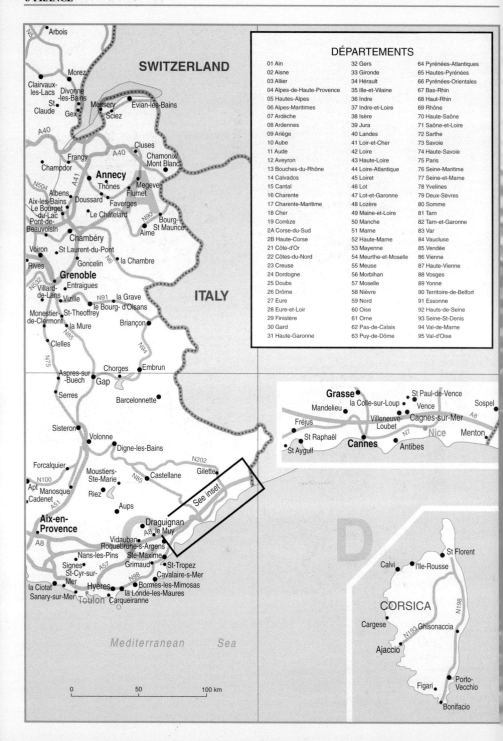

DÉPARTEMENTS

01 Ain	32 Gers	64 Pyrénées-Atlantiques
02 Aisne	33 Gironde	65 Hautes-Pyrénées
03 Allier	34 Hérault	66 Pyrénées-Orientales
04 Alpes-de-Haute-Provence	35 Ille-et-Vilaine	67 Bas-Rhin
05 Hautes-Alpes	36 Indre	68 Haut-Rhin
06 Alpes-Maritimes	37 Indre-et-Loire	69 Rhône
07 Ardèche	38 Isère	70 Haute-Saône
08 Ardennes	39 Jura	71 Saône-et-Loire
09 Ariège	40 Landes	72 Sarthe
10 Aube	41 Loir-et-Cher	73 Savoie
11 Aude	42 Loire	74 Haute-Savoie
12 Aveyron	43 Haute-Loire	75 Paris
13 Bouches-du-Rhône	44 Loire-Atlantique	76 Seine-Maritime
14 Calvados	45 Loiret	77 Seine-et-Marne
15 Cantal	46 Lot	78 Yvelines
16 Charente	47 Lot-et-Garonne	79 Deux-Sèvres
17 Charente-Maritime	48 Lozère	80 Somme
18 Cher	49 Maine-et-Loire	81 Tarn
19 Corrèze	50 Manche	82 Tarn-et-Garonne
2A Corse-du-Sud	51 Marne	83 Var
2B Haute-Corse	52 Haute-Marne	84 Vaucluse
21 Côte-d'Or	53 Mayenne	85 Vendée
22 Côtes-du-Nord	54 Meurthe-et-Moselle	86 Vienne
23 Creuse	55 Meuse	87 Haute-Vienne
24 Dordogne	56 Morbihan	88 Vosges
25 Doubs	57 Moselle	89 Yonne
26 Drôme	58 Nièvre	90 Territoire-de-Belfort
27 Eure	59 Nord	91 Essonne
28 Eure-et-Loir	60 Oise	92 Hauts-de-Seine
29 Finistère	61 Orne	93 Seine-St-Denis
30 Gard	62 Pas-de-Calais	94 Val-de-Marne
31 Haute-Garonne	63 Puy-de-Dôme	95 Val-d'Oise

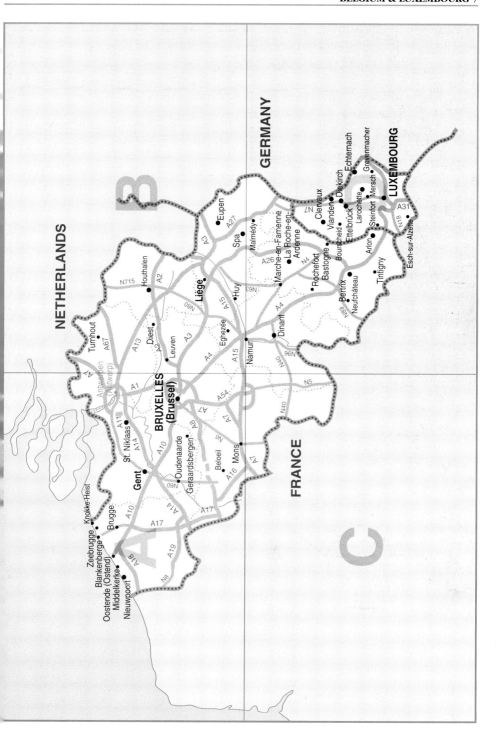

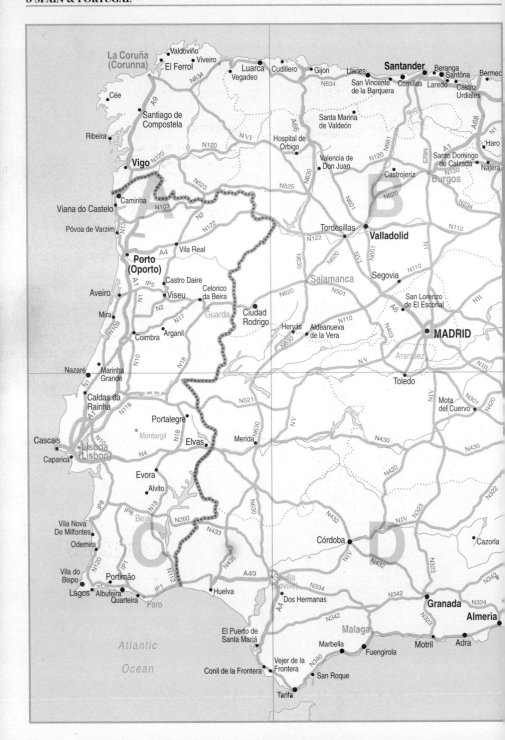

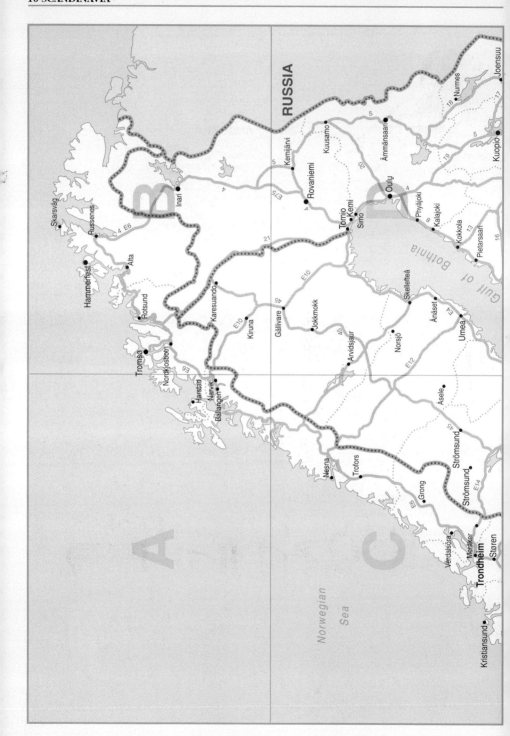

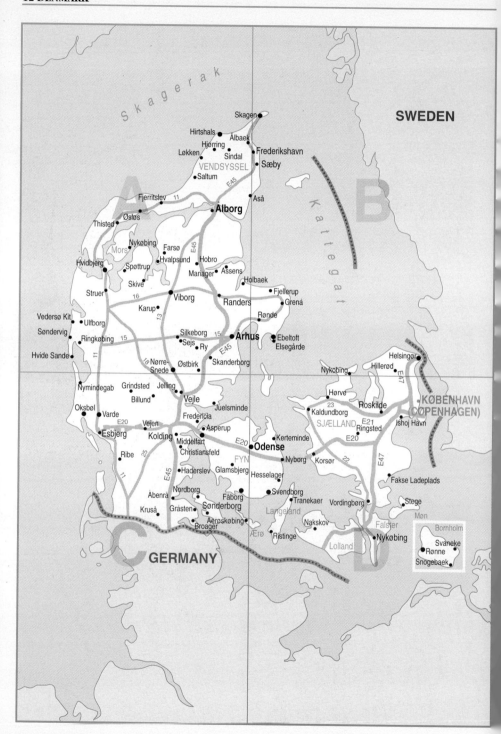

SWEDEN

Skagerak

Skagen
Hirtshals
Albaek
Hjørring
Løkken Sindal Frederikshavn
VENDSYSSEL Sæby
Saltum
E45
Fjerritslev 11 Aså
Øsløs
Thisted **Alborg**
Nykøbing Farsø
Mors E45
Hvidbjerg Spøttrup Hvalpsund Hobro
Mariager Assens
Struer Skive Holbaek
16 Viborg Fjellerup
Karup Randers Grenå
Vedersø Kit 13 Rønde
Ulforg
Søndervig Silkeborg 15 **Arhus** Ebeltoft
Ringkøbing 15 Sejs Ry Elsegårde
Hvide Sande Nørre- Østbirk Skanderborg
Snede E45

Kattegat

Nymindegab Grindsted Jelling Nykøbing Helsingør
Billund Vejle Hillerød E47
Oksbøl Varde Juelsminde Hørve
Vejen Frederica Kaldundborg 23 Roskilde **KØBENHAVN**
Esbjerg Kolding Asperup E20 Ringsted (COPENHAGEN)
E20 Middelfart SJÆLLAND E21 Ishøj Havn
Ribe 25 Christiansfeld Kerteminde E20
E45 Haderslev **Odense** Nyborg Korsør 22
Åbenrå Nordborg Glamsbjerg Hesselager E47 Fakse Ladeplads
Kruså Gråsten Sønderborg Fåborg Svendborg
Broager Ærøskøbing Langeland Tranekaer Vordingborg Stege
Ærø Ristinge Nakskov Falster Møn
Lolland Nykøbing Bornholm
Svaneke
Rønne
Snogebaek

GERMANY

A B C D

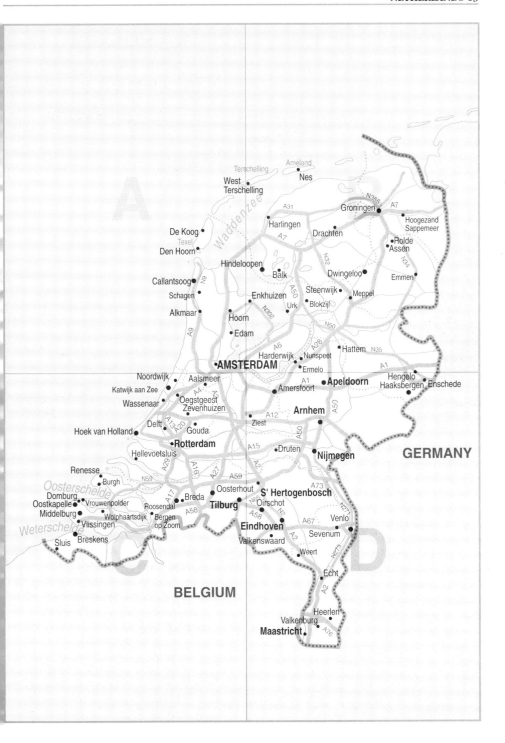

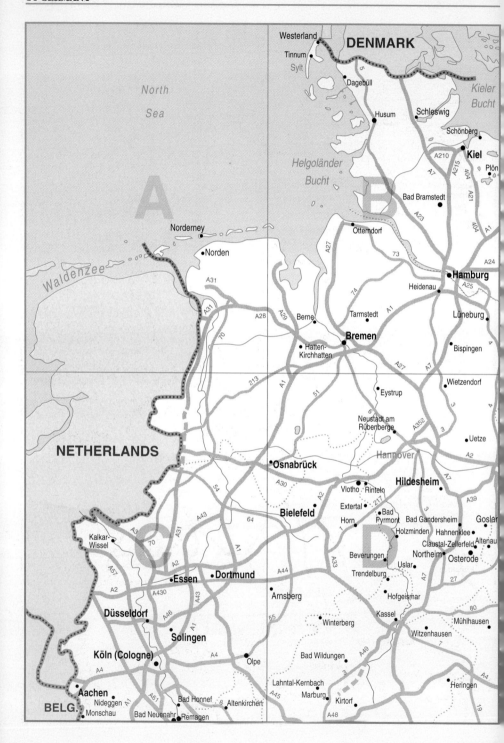

GERMANY 15

Femer Bœlt

Landkirchen
Fehmarnsund
Fehmarn
Burg
Wulfen
Oldenburg
Eutin
Dahme
Neustadt im
Holstein
Travemünde
Wismar
Lübeck

Mecklenburger
Bucht

Bad
Doberan
Rostock

Baltic

Sea

Lohmen
Vollrathsrühe

Bleckede
Rechlin
Warnitz

POLAND

Potsdam
BERLIN
Rangsdorf
Storkow

Helmstedt
Niewisch

Braunlage
Elbingerode

Weiswasser

Leipzig
Meissen

Naumburg
Weissensee
Altenburg
Jena
Waltershausen
Kranichfeld
Chemnitz
Altenberg

Dresden

CZECH REPUBLIC

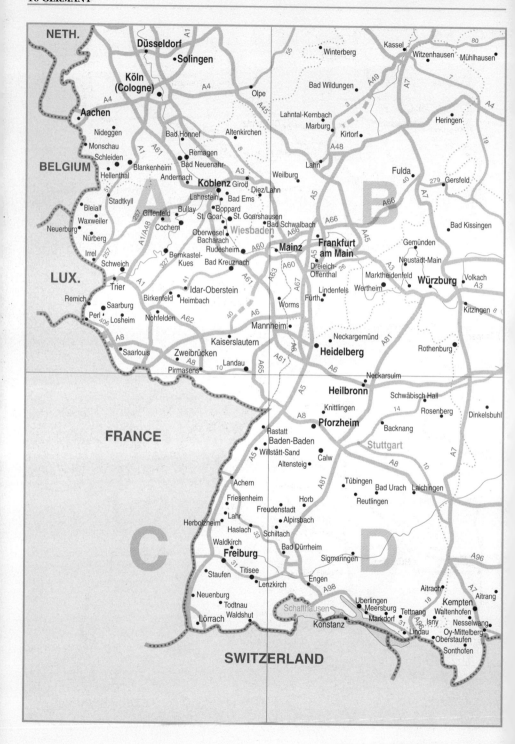

NETH.

Düsseldorf
•Solingen

Köln
(Cologne)

Aachen

Nideggen
Monschau
Schleiden

BELGIUM
Hellenthal

Bad Honnef
Altenkirchen
Remagen
Blankenheim Bad Neuenahr-
Andernach

Olpe

Lahntal-Kernbach
Marburg Kirtorf

A48

Weilburg

Koblenz Girod
Lahnstein Diez/Lahn
Bad Ems

Winterberg Kassel Witzenhausen Mühlhausen

Bad Wildungen

Heringen

Fulda
Gersfeld

Lahn

279

Bleialf Stadtkyll
Waxweiler
Neuerburg
Nürberg
Irrel

Gillenfeld Bullay Boppard
Cochem St. Goar St. Goarshausen
Oberwesel Bad Schwalbach
Bacharach Wiesbaden
Rudesheim
Bernkastel- Bad Kreuznach
Kues

A66
Bad Kissingen

Frankfurt
am Main

Mainz

Neustadt-Main

Gemünden

Schweich

LUX.

Trier
Remich
Saarburg
Perl
Losheim
Saarlouis

Birkenfeld
Heimbach
Nohfelden

Idar-Oberstein

Zweibrücken
Pirmasens
Landau

Dreieich-
Offenthal
Marktheidenfeld Wertheim
Lindenfels
Worms
Fürth

Mannheim

Kaiserslautern

Würzburg
Volkach

Kitzingen

Neckargemünd

Heidelberg

Rothenburg

FRANCE

Neckarsulm

Heilbronn

Schwäbisch Hall

Knittlingen
Rosenberg Dinkelsbuhl

Pforzheim
Backnang

Rastatt
Baden-Baden
Willstätt-Sand
Altensteig

Calw

Stuttgart

Achern
Friesenheim
Lahr
Herbolzheim
Haslach
Waldkirch

Horb
Freudenstadt
Alpirsbach
Schiltach

Tübingen
Bad Urach Laichingen
Reutlingen

Freiburg
Staufen
Titisee
Neuenburg
Todtnau
Lörrach Waldshut

Lenzkirch

Bad Dürrheim
Sigmaringen
Engen

Aitrach
Aitrang
Kempten
Überlingen
Schaffhausen
Meersburg Tettnang Waltenhofen
Markdorf
Konstanz
Lindau
Isny
Nesselwang
Oy-Mittelberg
Oberstaufen
Sonthofen

SWITZERLAND

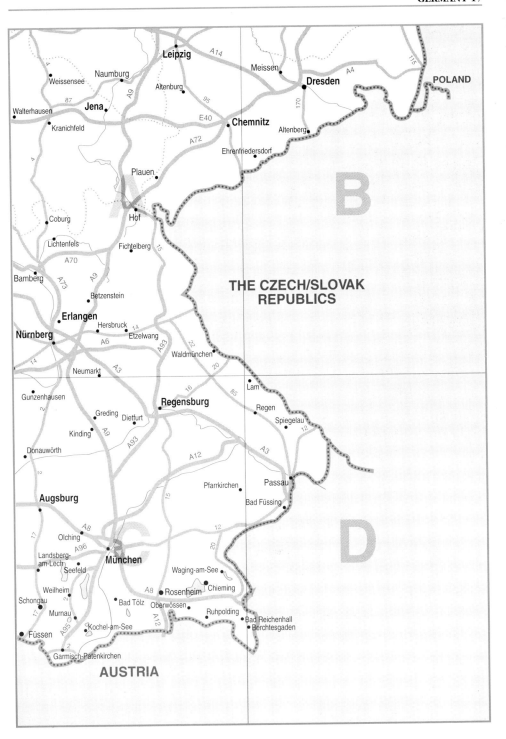

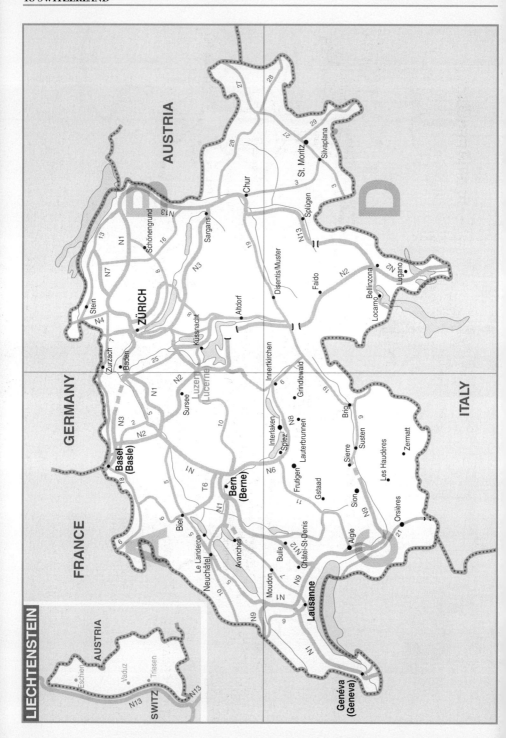

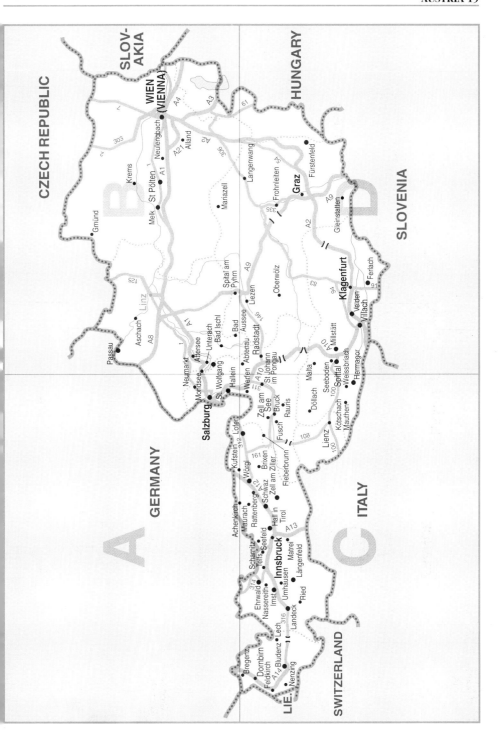

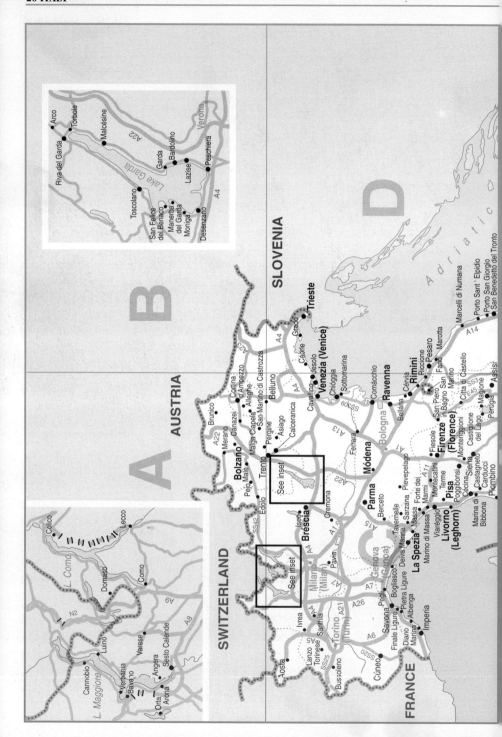

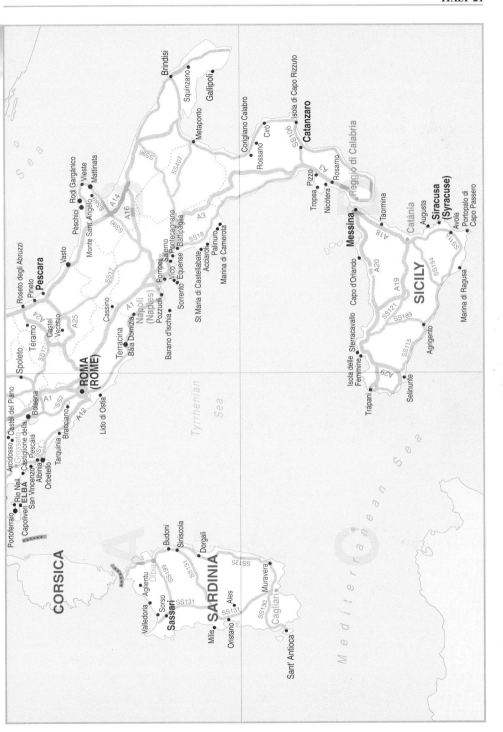

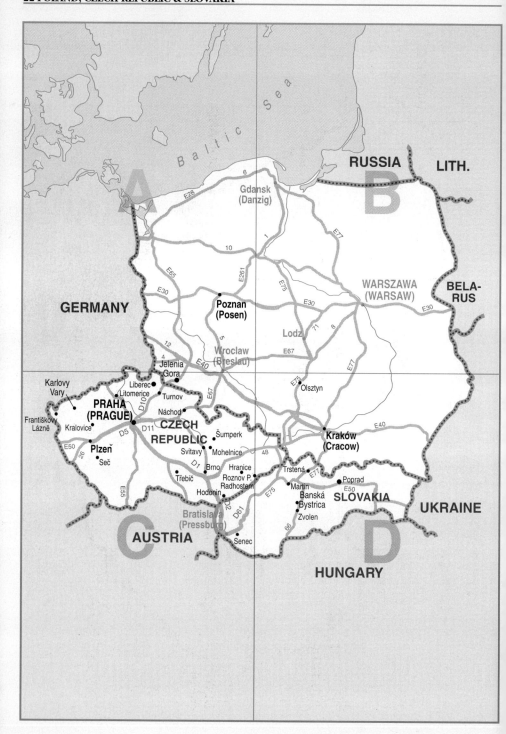

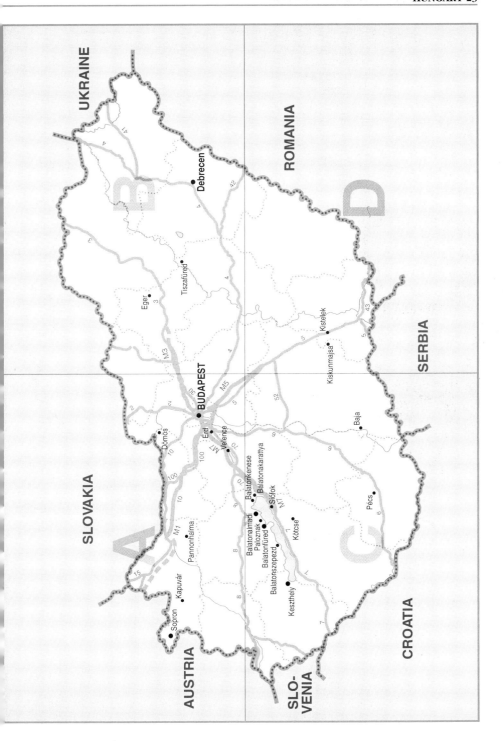

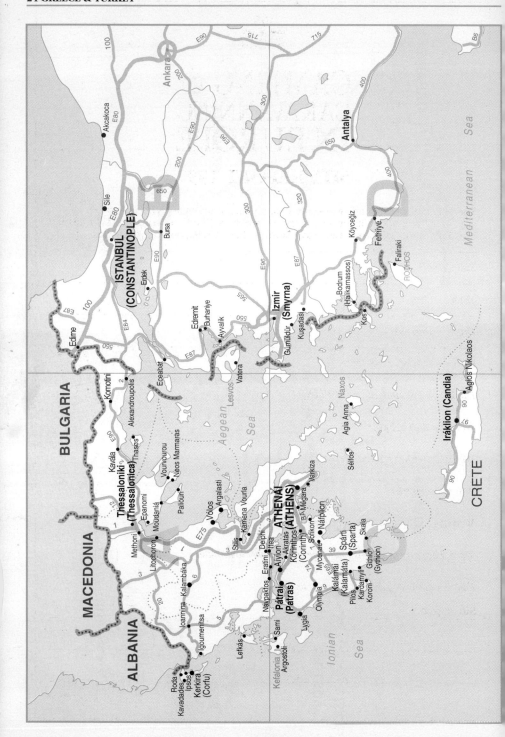

CAMPING &
CARAVANNING
IN EUROPE

SITE REPORT 1997

The publisher of this guide welcomes your comments about any sites visited that appear in this guide. Whatever your experience, good, indifferent or poor, do write to RAC Publishing, PO Box 8, Harleston, Norfolk IP20 0EZ, expressing your views.

Site name

Town

Dates of your stay

Please tick appropriate box   Yes   No

Did any of the site staff speak English?   ☐   ☐

Were the staff helpful?   ☐   ☐

Were the washing facilities clean?   ☐   ☐

Was the site quiet?   ☐   ☐

Were the parking areas adequate?   ☐   ☐

Were there any problems towing your caravan to the site?   ☐   ☐

Did this guide accurately describe the site as it is now?   ☐   ☐

Site report

continued

Site report *continued*

_____

_____

_____

_____

_____

_____

_____

_____

_____

_____

_____

_____

_____

_____

_____

_____

_____

Name

Address

CAMPING &
CARAVANNING
IN EUROPE

SITE REPORT 1997

The publisher of this guide welcomes your comments about any sites visited that appear in this guide. Whatever your experience, good, indifferent or poor, do write to RAC Publishing, PO Box 8, Harleston, Norfolk IP20 0EZ, expressing your views.

Site name

Town

Dates of your stay

Please tick appropriate box   Yes   No

Did any of the site staff speak English?   ☐   ☐

Were the staff helpful?   ☐   ☐

Were the washing facilities clean?   ☐   ☐

Was the site quiet?   ☐   ☐

Were the parking areas adequate?   ☐   ☐

Were there any problems towing your caravan to the site?   ☐   ☐

Did this guide accurately describe the site as it is now?   ☐   ☐

Site report

continued

Site report *continued*

_____

_____

_____

_____

_____

_____

_____

_____

_____

_____

_____

_____

_____

_____

_____

_____

_____

_____

Name

Address

RAC

CAMPING &
CARAVANNING
IN EUROPE

SITE REPORT 1997

The publisher of this guide welcomes your comments about any sites visited that appear in this guide. Whatever your experience, good, indifferent or poor, do write to RAC Publishing, PO Box 8, Harleston, Norfolk IP20 0EZ, expressing your views.

Site name

Town

Dates of your stay

Please tick appropriate box	Yes	No
Did any of the site staff speak English?	☐	☐
Were the staff helpful?	☐	☐
Were the washing facilities clean?	☐	☐
Was the site quiet?	☐	☐
Were the parking areas adequate?	☐	☐
Were there any problems towing your caravan to the site?	☐	☐
Did this guide accurately describe the site as it is now?	☐	☐

Site report

continued

Site report *continued*

KIRCHZARTEN

HINTERZARTEN

B 31

Name

Address